THE DC COMICS ENCYCLOPEDIA

THE DEFINITIVE GUIDE TO THE CHARACTERS OF THE DC UNIVERSE
UPDATED AND EXPANDED

LONDON, NEW YORK, MELBOURNE,
MUNICH AND DELHI

Senior Editor Alastair Dougall
Design Manager Robert Perry
Editor Vicki Taylor
Design Nick Avery, Jon Hall, Owen Bennett
Publishing Manager Simon Beecroft
Category Publisher Alexandra Allan
Production Controller Nick Seston
Production Editor Siu Chan

20 19 18 17 16 15
026-DD470-Oct/08

First published in 2004; revised edition, 2008
Published in the United States by
DK Publishing
345 Hudson Street
New York, New York 10014

DK Publishing, Inc. offers special discounts for bulk purchases for sales promotions or premiums.
Specific, large-quantity needs can be met with special editions, including personalized covers,
excerpts of existing guides, and corporate imprints. For more information, contact Special Markets,
DK Publishing, 345 Hudson Street, New York, NY 10014. SpecialSales@dk.com.

A catalog record for this book is available from the Library of Congress.

ISBN: 978-0-7566-4119-1

Reproduced by Alta Image, UK.
Printed and bound in China

Visit DC Comics online at www.dccomics.com
or at keyword DC Comics on America Online.

Discover more at
www.dk.com

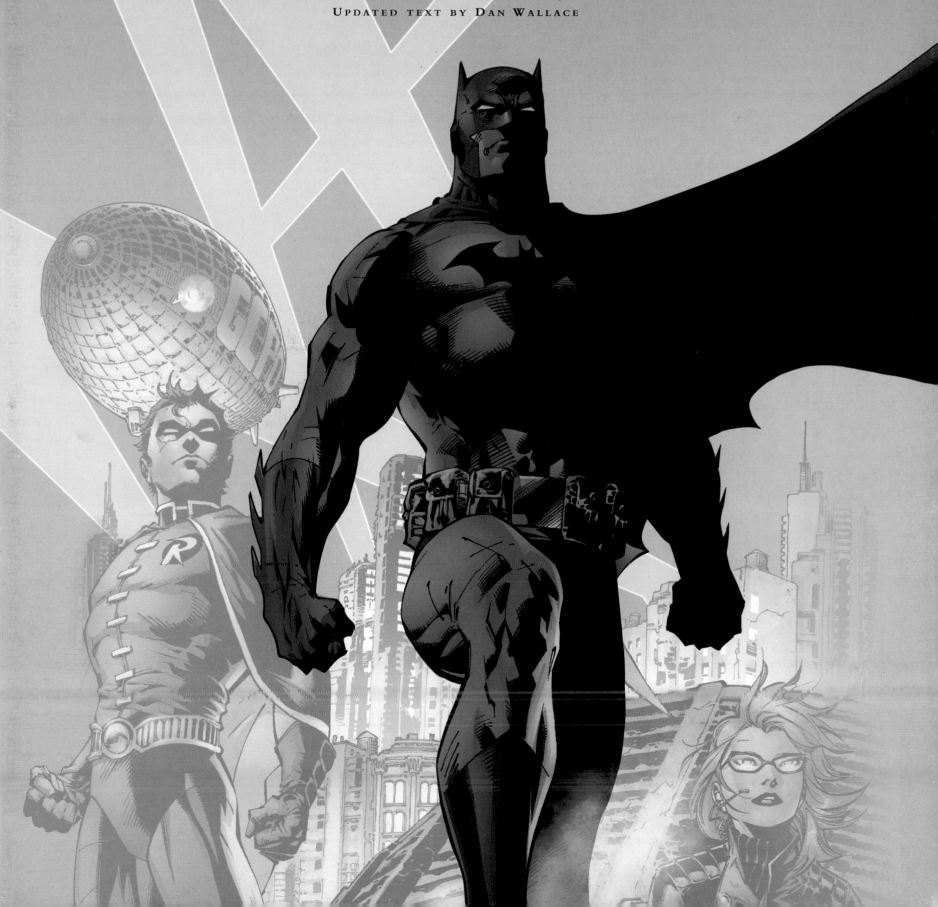

THE DC COMICS ENCYCLOPEDIA

THE DEFINITIVE GUIDE TO THE CHARACTERS OF THE DC UNIVERSE
UPDATED AND EXPANDED

TEXT BY SCOTT BEATTY, ROBERT GREENBERGER, PHIL JIMINEZ, AND DAN WALLACE
UPDATED TEXT BY DAN WALLACE

CONTENTS

INTRODUCTION 6

A   08-35
     20-21   ALTERNATE EARTHS
     34-35   AMAZING VEHICLES

B   36-63

C   64-93
     92-93   AMAZING WEAPONS

D   94-111

E   112-117

F   118-133
     132-133   AMAZING BASES

G   134-151

H   152-167
     166-167   ALIEN RACES

I   168-175

J   176-187

K   188-197

L   198-217

M   218-245

N   246-253

O   254-263
     262-263   GREAT TEAM-UPS

P   264-277

Q   278-279
     280-281   ROMANTIC MOMENTS

R   282-293

S   294-343
     306-307   52
     328-329   INFINITE CRISIS

T   344-359

U   360-363
     362-363   GREAT BATTLES

V   364-369

W   370-379

X,Y 380-381

Z   382-385
     384-385   STRANGE TIMES AND PLACES

INDEX   386

ACKNOWLEDGMENTS   398

FOREWORD

ONE OF THE WORLD'S great pleasures is secret knowledge. It begins in
childhood: the things you learn that your parents don't know, or don't
imagine you know. It can be the lifetime batting averages of every member
of the New York Yankees, the evolutionary path of each of 151 Pokémon
creatures... or the names and homeworlds of the Legion of Super-Heroes.
Commit these arcane facts to memory, and you can speak a private language
open only to you and other worthies who have approached this
with equal dedication.

For many of us, the lore hidden in comics was our special
secret knowledge. We mastered it as we grew, and delved
deeper into the intricacies of the past, present, and future of
DC Comics' heroes, friends, and foes. A generation ago, there
were no guides to this search, so we had to build our own,
debating each inconsistency found with passion.

Now, the task is easier. Those who have gone before you
offer this encyclopedia, rich with secret knowledge. If all
you know of DC Comics is that Superman is the alter ego
of newspaperman Clark Kent of the *Daily Planet*, what lies
before you is a complex fantasy world with details,
apparent contradictions, and convolutions to be
discovered. If you consider yourself a master of
this information, there will still be nuggets
and nuances aplenty for you to evaluate, for
no one knows all of the DC Universe.
And the more you know, the more likely it
is that one day you will contribute your own
secrets to it.

Enjoy!

Paul Levitz
President and Publisher,
DC Comics

Authors' Introduction

DC Comics traces its publishing history back to 1935; however, the mythology that links literally thousands of comics and characters together now stretches from the Big Bang to the end of time itself!

Of course, it was not the original intention for there to be a continuity that linked Batman to the Seven Soldiers of Victory or Adam Strange to Angel & The Ape; this process began gradually. In 1940, during comics' Golden Age (which ran from the 1930s to the mid-1950s), All American Comics—then a sister company of DC—gathered its greatest heroes together to swap stories at the monthly meeting of the Justice Society of America. That story, in *All Star Comics #3*, was the first time DC's main characters had spoken to one another. By the next issue, they had banded together; however, each mission required them to work on their own in chapters usually drawn by the series artist. And since there was little in the way of character development or recurring plot lines, the stories were fairly static.

Stan Lee changed all that. In 1961, when he started writing the adventures of the Fantastic Four, Spider-Man, Thor and others at Marvel Comics, he allowed his characters to refer to each other. Crossovers between characters, all operating out of New York City at the same period in time, offered rich story possibilities. And so the Marvel Universe was born.

By the late 1960s, DC editors began linking events from one book to another. This process accelerated rapidly as plots became more complex and characters more rounded; suddenly it was not unusual to have explanatory footnotes, which might refer a reader to the previous month, or as far back as 1945! As DC acquired properties from other companies (Captain Marvel and Blue Beetle among others), their characters and backstories were added to the expanding DC Universe, providing fresh grist for the mill.

However, after a while, the interrelatedness of stories and characters from one book to another threatened to become so complex that readers couldn't tell the players and their worlds without a scorecard! Occasional "reboots" of characters by new creative teams wanting to put their own stamp on their favorite heroes only added to the confusion.

By the mid-1980s, DC felt the situation was getting out of hand and a new storyline was introduced, the *Crisis on Infinite Earths*, to limit characters and action to one earth and one timeline. DC also reintroduced its top characters to a new generation. Frank Miller and David Mazzucchelli's *Batman: Year One*, George Perez & Greg Potter's *Wonder Woman*, and John Byrne's *Superman* loudly told readers to forget the past; new legends were about to begin. Since then, some of those reinvention have been modified again as seen in the Superman: Birthright series. And the entire Universe received a sprucing up in a 2004 mini-series *Identity Crisis*.

The *DC Comics Encyclopedia* spans the timeline of the DC Universe. The facts about characters' pasts, powers and personalities are current, as of early 2004 and, since DC continues to publish monthly, some facts may change over the next few years. We've worked closely with the editors to make sure we're reflecting the right information, so if you remember an incident differently than as reported here, it probably means circumstances were retrofitted to work within the current framework of the DC Universe.

We would have loved to include every DC character of any significance, but, sadly, this was impossible. However we have selected well over one thousand of DC's finest heroes villains, and team-ups, every one illustrated by great DC artists past and present. The *DC Comics Encyclopedia* is devised to run chronologically from A to Z, with a comprehensive index. The most important characters, such as Superman, Batman, the JLA, have their own double-page features; each major character has an entire page, and each supporting character has a panel or entry. Each character also has his or her own data box detailing key facts and special powers. In addition there are several themed double-page features on topics such as vehicles, battles, bases, team-ups, and romances.

So, if you can't find a favorite weird little character from way back when, we hope these packed pages will offer you plenty in the way of compensation, celebrating, as they do, more than 70 years of fun, excitement and comic-book history.

Scott Beatty
Robert Greenberger
Phil Jimenez
Dan Wallace

ABRA KADABRA

FIRST APPEARANCE FLASH (1st series) #128 (May 1962)
STATUS Villain   *REAL NAME* Citizen Abra
OCCUPATION Technosorcerer   *BASE* Keystone City
HEIGHT 6ft 6in   *WEIGHT* 209 lbs   *EYES* Blue   *HAIR* Black
SPECIAL POWERS/ABILITIES Kadabra's magic-like powers were purely the result of futuristic technology. However, he is now a genuine sorcerer.

In the 64th century, Earth was ruled by the Chronarch and his Central Clockworks. Citizen Abra rebelled against the strict order of the Chronarch's world. Championing individuality, Abra was seen as a criminal and banished to Earth's ancient past. Transplanted to Central City at the end of the 20th century, Abra used 64th-century technology to create a new identity and became the criminal Abra Kadabra. Desperate for adulation, and possessing powers so amazing they seemed magical, Abra Kadabra crafted a series of spectacular crimes, hoping to win admirers.

Thwarted time and again by the second Flash, Kadabra's technology was accidentally damaged, and he was transformed into a ghost-like entity. Restored to normal, Kadabra was brought back to the 64th century by a bounty hunter named Peregrine. Kadabra was about to be executed when the Flash saved him and destroyed the Central Clockworks. Returning to the 21st century, Kadabra was stripped of his powers, but after a deal with the demon NERON, Abra Kadabra became a true sorcerer, able to cast spells and fire energy bolts. He continues to be a threat to the Flash. **PJ**

MAGIC MASTER
A narcissistic criminal mastermind in two centuries, Abra Kadabra is consumed by two things—a desire for adulation and hatred of the Flash.

AGAMEMNO

FIRST APPEARANCE SILVER AGE #1 (July 2000)
STATUS Villain   *REAL NAME* Unpronounceable/unspellable
OCCUPATION Would-be universe conqueror   *BASE* Outer space
HEIGHT Variable   *WEIGHT* Variable   *EYES* Variable   *HAIR* None
SPECIAL POWERS/ABILITIES Imbues inanimate objects with his energy, bringing them to life; causes personas to swap bodies.

Composed of cosmic energy, Agamemno was one of the first sentient beings formed in the wake of the Big Bang. Upon seeing the vastness of space, Agamemno wanted to control it, to rule the other life forms just being born. His father, however, wanted to control the cosmos himself, thereby pitting himself against his son. Seeking an advantage to end this stalemate, Agamemno converted himself into sentient energy and toured the universe in search of three objects that could be pieced together into a killing weapon.

His search brought him to Earth during the early days of the modern heroic age, where he manipulated superpowered heroes and villains to do his bidding. The various members of the JLA managed to thwart his scheme, however, and kept the objects from being used. Agamemno then returned to space, seeking another way to beat his father for control of the cosmos. **RG**

ACRATA

FIRST APPEARANCE SUPERMAN (2nd series) Annual #12 (Aug. 2000)
STATUS Hero   *REAL NAME* Andrea Rojas
OCCUPATION Mesoamerican anthropologist   *BASE* Mexico City
HEIGHT 5ft 6in   *WEIGHT* 125 lbs   *EYES* Blue   *HAIR* Red
SPECIAL POWERS/ABILITIES Superb athlete and martial artist.

In her youth, Andrea Rojas moved with her family from Cobán, Guatemala to Mexico while her father continued his studies of Mesoamerican culture for the National Museum of Anthropology in Mexico City. Joining in her father's work, Andrea also became learned in ancient myths and languages. However, she was increasingly distracted by the modern-day ills suffered by her culture, particularly those created by narcotics trafficking and rampant crime. A gifted athlete and martial artist, Andrea adopted the masked identity of Acrata, a name which, when translated, means "those who suppress authority," and decided to fight organized crime.

Wearing a costume adorned with the Mayan symbol of the shadows, a totem that purportedly allowed Mayan priests to travel stealthily in the dark, Acrata began striking at the drug cartels of South America, frequently uniting with fellow Mexican heroes IMAN and EL MUERTO. The trio once teamed with SUPERMAN to defeat the sinister sorcerer DURAN. As her calling card, Acrata leaves spray-painted literary epithets to mark her capture of a perpetrator or prevention of a crime. **SB**

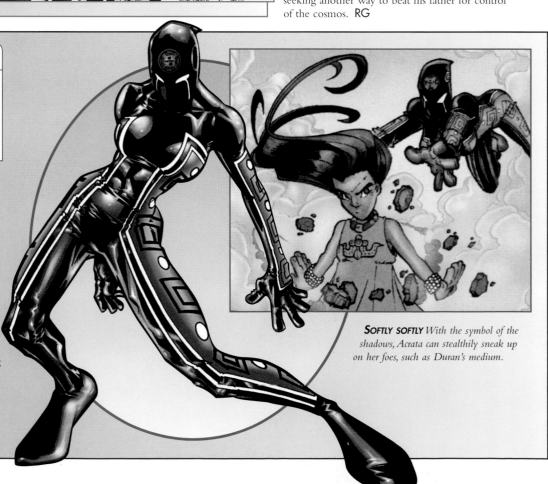

SOFTLY SOFTLY *With the symbol of the shadows, Acrata can stealthily sneak up on her foes, such as Duran's medium.*

AGENT LIBERTY

First appearance SUPERMAN (2nd series) #60 (October 1991)
Status Hero **Real name** Benjamin Lockwood
Occupation Covert agent **Base** Mobile
Height 6ft 2in **Weight** 195 lbs **Eyes** Blue **Hair** Brown
Special powers/abilities Master of armed combat and espionage; outfitted with a battle suit that bristles with weaponry; gauntlets generate bullet-deflecting force fields or become jagged bayonets; a jet pack enables him to soar into the air.

As part of a C.I.A. anti-terrorist mission that went wrong, operative Ben Lockwood survived in hostile terrain for months. Upon returning to the U. S. he joined a super-patriotic, well-funded team of radicals called the "Sons of Liberty" on the recommendation of his former Bureau chief. As Agent Liberty, Lockwood enjoyed access to high-tech armor and weapons, as well as a helicopter team that covered his back on particularly dangerous missions.

In one of his first cases, Agent Liberty helped SUPERMAN crack down on INTERGANG crooks. Agent Liberty broke ranks with the Sons of Liberty when the organization ordered him to assassinate Senator Pete Ross (*see* ROSS, PETE). He refused—killing his former mentor in the process—and forwarded classified information on the Sons of Liberty to *Daily Planet* reporter Clark Kent before beginning a new life on the run. Despite his lack of superpowers, Agent Liberty has put in a short stint with the JUSTICE LEAGUE OF AMERICA. **DW**

AGONY AND ECSTACY

First appearance HELLBLAZER #12 (December 1988)
Status Villains **Real names** Agony and Ecstasy
Occupation Hell's enforcers **Base** Hell
Height 7ft **Weight** Unknown **Eyes** White **Hair** Flaming red
Special powers/abilities It is not clearly understood what happens to those unfortunates who are taken by Agony and Ecstasy; perhaps that's just as well...

Agony and Ecstasy are Hell's enforcers, a pair of "inquisition police" who track down any demons or other underlings who dare to break the rules or to oppose the authority of Hell. They are demonic twins whose beautiful, luminescent bodies are draped in rusting barbed wire. When Lucifer abdicated his role as ruler of Hell and emptied it of all its demons, the angels Remiel and Duma were given the key to its gates. They became its rulers, and assigned Agony and Ecstasy the task of bringing back the demons that had escaped to realms beyond. Despite various upheavals in Hell's Hierarchy, Agony and Ecstasy remain ready to serve and punish, gleefully inflicting their vengeance upon any that defy its demonic leadership. **PJ**

AIR WAVE I

First appearance DETECTIVE COMICS #60 (February 1942)
Status Hero (deceased) **Real name** Lawrence "Larry" Jordan
Occupation Crime fighter; District Attorney **Base** New York City
Height 5ft 10in **Weight** 175 lbs **Eyes** Brown **Hair** Brown
Special powers/abilities Antennae in helmet and circuitry in belt allowed him to eavesdrop on police band frequencies or intercept telephone calls; traveled at the speed of electricity along telephone lines on collapsible skates built into boots; magnetic energies enabled him to climb walls or relieve criminals of their guns.

Before he ascended to the lofty post of New York City District Attorney, law clerk Larry Jordan wanted to do more than just file legal briefs to battle crime in the 1940s "Big Apple." He built a special helmet and belt that gave him an array of amazing electronic and magnetic powers and hit the streets as the costumed Air Wave when he wasn't fighting injustice in court. A member of the wartime ALL-STAR SQUADRON, Air Wave was subsequently killed by escaped convict Joe Parsons, a criminal once jailed by the crusading Attorney. Jordan's wife, Helen, sought retribution in her husband's own costume, capturing Parsons and later testifying to keep him in prison for the rest of his days. Many years later, the role of Air Wave was taken up by Larry and Helen's son Harold, who refined the costume and its circuitry while operating as a teen hero. In adulthood, Harold renamed his heroic alter ego Maser and serves as an auxiliary member of the JSA while keeping the spirit of Air Wave alive and well. **SB**

RIDING THE WAVES *Air Wave II is among the most powerful of Earth's young heroes.*

AIR WAVE II

First appearance GREEN LANTERN (2nd series) #100 (Jan. 1978)
Status Hero **Real name** Harold "Hal" Lawrence Jordan
Occupation Student **Base** Dallas, Texas
Height 5ft 7in **Weight** 156 lbs **Eyes** Brown **Hair** Brown
Special powers/abilities Helmet allows him to change his molecular structure; can transform into energy and travel along radio and television airwaves; can also fly at superspeed.

Hal Jordan is the son of Air Wave I (a member of the ALL-STAR SQUADRON) and was named after his cousin Hal Jordan, one of the greatest members of the legendary GREEN LANTERN CORPS. The young Hal was forced to live with his cousins Jack and Jan Jordan after his mother was placed in an institution. Hal became the second Air Wave after he inherited the helmet and equipment his father had used for crime fighting. The second Air Wave trained briefly with GREEN LANTERN, as well as GREEN ARROW I and the BLACK CANARY. Recruited by SUICIDE SQUAD associate Simon LeGrieve to join his Captains of Industry, a task force for the Institute of Meta-Human Studies, Jordan changed his name to Maser. Later, the villain Catalyst kidnapped Maser and turned him over to the terrorist KOBRA, but the young hero was saved by the JUSTICE SOCIETY OF AMERICA. Hal later returned to the uniform and codename of Air Wave and is believed to have perished during the Infinite Crisis. **PJ**

ALLEN, IRIS

FIRST APPEARANCE SHOWCASE #4 (October 1956)
STATUS Hero **REAL NAME** Iris Ann Russell West Allen
OCCUPATION Journalist **BASE** City
HEIGHT 5ft 6in **WEIGHT** 130 lbs **EYES** Brown **HAIR** Brown
SPECIAL POWERS/ABILITIES Highly resourceful with a keen intellect; no meta-human abilities.

IRIS AND THE FLASH
Iris introduces her nephew Wally West to her boyfriend, Barry Allen.

After graduating from Columbia University, Iris West won a job at *Picture News*. There she met forensics scientist Barry Allen, they became engaged, and everything in Iris's life turned upside down. Allen was in an accident that turned him into the second Flash, but Iris only found this out when she heard Barry talking in his sleep. When Barry finally told her his secret, he explained that he had waited because he was running tests to see if his biological changes would affect their ability to have children. Happily, all was well.

Further shocks were in store for Iris. It eventually transpired that she was adopted! She realized this when she found a pendant containing a recording from her true parents. Their names were Eric and Fran Russell, and they lived in the fear-ridden 30th century. Iris had been sent *back* in time for her own safety! Meanwhile, a mad scientist called Professor Zoom had become obsessed with Iris. When she rejected his advances at a costume party, Zoom killed her. But at that very instant, the Russells used an experimental device to transport Iris's spirit to the 30th century. Later, when Barry killed Zoom and was tried for murder, Iris returned to the 20th century, disguised herself as a juror, and saw to it that he was acquitted. Reunited, Barry accompanied Iris to the 30th century. Iris gave birth to twins shortly after Barry was killed during the apocalyptic battle known as the Crisis (*see* Great Battles, pp. 362–3). Iris later returned to the 20th century to teach her grandson Bart how to use his inherited gift of speed. Once again living in Keystone City, she used her knowledge of future events to try and prevent the death of Bart Allen. She failed, and her grandson perished at the hands of the Rogues. **RG**

CLOSE ESCAPE *Professor Zoom, the Reverse Flash, shoots and kills Iris after she rejects his advances for the last time. Unbeknownst to all, her soul is plucked into the future an instant before death.*

ALIAS THE SPIDER

FIRST APPEARANCE CRACK COMICS #1 (May 1940)
STATUS Hero **REAL NAME** Tom Ludlow Hallaway
OCCUPATION Adventurer **BASE** Keystone City
HEIGHT 6ft 1in **WEIGHT** 195 lbs **EYES** Brown **HAIR** Brown
SPECIAL POWERS/ABILITIES Superb archer and athlete; sometimes wore a bulletproof costume.

During the 1940s, Tom Hallaway decided to fight crime as the costumed champion the Spider. Using a bow and arrow and traveling in a custom Black Widow car (driven by his valet and confidant Chuck), the Spider was a vigilante who killed many of his criminal opponents. Though known as a hero, the Spider clearly walked the edge of cold villainy. At the height of World War II, the Spider joined Uncle Sam's FREEDOM FIGHTERS. He later worked with the SEVEN SOLDIERS OF VICTORY, claiming that he could help them defeat the NEBULA MAN. In reality, the Spider had set them all up for a fall. With his trap sprung and the Seven Soldiers dispersed into the timestream, the Spider became the new protector of Keystone City. The Spider died at the hands of the Shade, though his son Lucas Ludlow-Dalt has since assumed the Spider's mantle. Thomas Ludlow Dalt has become the third Spider, and as "I, Spyder" helped fight the Sheeda. **DW**

ALLIANCE, THE

FIRST APPEARANCE JLA/HAVEN: THE ARRIVAL #1 (January 2002)
STATUS Hero team **BASE** The Haven, Coast City, California
MEMBERS AND POWERS
Valadin Military hero; manipulates energy and projects power blasts.
Siv Engineer in control of tiny nanite-tech machines.
Katalia Powerful telepath.
Nia Superstrength, invulnerability, flight.
Amon Elder statesman and Valadin's brother.
Mavaar Lin Former chancellor of the Haven.
Ignetia Highly skilled scientist.
Hank Velveeda Innate working knowledge of most things, both organic and technological.
Tamlick Soffick Alters gravity to gain powers of levitation.

ALIEN TEAM *The Alliance includes Katalia, Siv, Nia, Valadin, and Hank Velveeda.*

The Alliance are a contingent of freedom-fighting aliens from the planet Competalia, dedicated to ridding their world of Anathema, a ruthless biogeneticist who transformed nearly every inhabitant of Competalia into superhuman beings. Once a Competalian was transformed, Anathema would have complete dominion over the individual and her newly-created warriors quickly swept over the planet, placing it under her near-total control. Over two million Competalians resisted Anathema's control, however, and were placed in a penal colony called "The Haven." Soon after, Valadin, a respected military leader, and his brother Amon, forged an Alliance of rebels, and turned Haven into a traveling space city. The Haven escaped Competalia and headed for the Milky Way galaxy. The Alliance came out of warp too close to Earth, and crash-landed in California, creating a crater across much of the state and killing thousands. With the help of the JUSTICE LEAGUE OF AMERICA, the Competalians were able to salvage the Haven and forge a new Alliance under Valadin's command. One member, the Chancellor Mavaar Lin, betrayed the Alliance, allowing Anathema to take over the Haven. Siv, used the despot's DNA against her, enabling him to destroy her. The Haven remained in California, and through negotiator Nicole Stein, appointed by then-President Lex Luthor (*see* LUTHOR, LEX), became a legally recognized city of the U.S. **PJ**

BETRAYAL *Mavaar Lin, the former chancellor of the Haven, betrayed her teammates while under the thrall of Anathema, even threatening the life of then-President Lex Luthor.*

ALL-STAR SQUADRON

First appearance JUSTICE LEAGUE OF AMERICA #193 (All-Star Squadron) (August 1981); YOUNG ALL-STARS #1 (Young All-Stars) (June 1987)

Status Hero team (disbanded)   **Base** New York City

Notable Members and Powers

Amazing Man I (Will Everett) Able to transform himself into any material he touched.

Commander Steel (Hank Heywood) Injured body repaired with steel alloy frame and micro-motor muscles.

Firebrand II (Danette Reilly) Possessed power of flight and the ability to create and control flames.

Hawkgirl I (Sheira-Sanders Hall) Flew with artificial wings and "Ninth metal" anti-gravity belt.

Johnny Quick (Johnny Chambers) Speed and flight enabled by speaking speed formula "3X2(9YZ)4A."

Liberty Belle (Libby Belle Lawrence) Superstrength, agility, and ability to project sonic pulses.

Plastic Man (Eel O'Brian) Superpliable and rubbery resilient body.

Robotman I (Dr. Robert Crane, a.k.a. Paul Dennis) Powerful robotic frame housed human brain.

Shining Knight (Sir Justin/Justin Arthur) Rode winged steed Victory while wielding enchanted armor and sword.

Tarantula I (Jonathan Law) Masked vigilante armed with web-line emitting web-gun.

Following Imperial Japan's sneak attack on Pearl Harbor in 1941, U.S. President Franklin D. Roosevelt called upon all active "Mystery Men"—the costumed heroes and heroines of America, including the entire membership of the JUSTICE SOCIETY OF AMERICA—to band together as a unified fighting force to combat the Axis powers bent upon dominating the world. Both on the home front and in top-secret missions on the battlefields and behind enemy lines, the Squadron—which included more than fifty members at its most powerful—answered only to F.D.R. and the War Department. Many of its greatest adventures are still classified decades later.

THE PERISPHERE

During its tour of duty, the All-Star Squadron was based in New York City and held court in the Perisphere, a hollow sphere 200 feet in diameter built for the 1939-1940 New York World's Fair. The Perisphere included living quarters for all active members of the Squadron. The 610-foot Trylon, a spire erected next to the Perisphere, served to house the team's All-Star Special, a modified Curtiss XP-55 Ascender aircraft outfitted with a Star-Rocket Racer motor courtesy of Pat Dugan (STRIPESY), adult sidekick of Squadron member the Star-Spangled-Kid.

EARLY DAYS Dr. Mid-Nite, Hawkman, and Atom pore over pictures of potential recruits.

THE YOUNG ALL-STARS

In 1942, the All-Star Squadron found its ranks bolstered by an influx of younger heroes, a splinter group of "Young All-Stars" whose primary focus was thwarting the superpowered group of German, Italian, and Japanese soldiers dubbed "Axis Amerika." Among the Young All-Stars ranks were the atomic-punching Dyna-Mite, the furry-winged FLYING FOX, the powerhouse FURY, the nigh-indestructible "Iron" Munro, the aquatic avenger Neptune Perkins (see PERKINS, NEPTUNE), and the Japanese-American tidal wave-wielding TSUNAMI. Together, these young heroes did their part to protect the home front from Axis aggression. Both the adult All-Star Squadron and its youthful counterpart disbanded following the conclusion of hostilities. **SB**

FIENDISH FOES Among the Squadron's numerous nemeses were Night and Fog, Nazi siblings who served as Hitler's superpowered assassins.

1) The Atom 2) Amazing Man 3) Johnny Thunder 4) Dr. Fate 5) Green Lantern 6) Plastic Man 7) Robotman 8) Liberty Belle 9) Firebrand 10) Steel 11) Guardian 12) Hourman 13) Tarantula 14) Hawkgirl 15) Hawkman 16) Shining Knight

KEY STORYLINES
• *ALL-STAR SQUADRON #4 (DECEMBER 1981)* The Squadron first battles the Dragon King.
• *JUSTICE LEAGUE OF AMERICA #207-209, ALL-STAR SQUADRON #14-15 (OCT.–DEC. 1982)* The Squadron teams with the modern-day JLA and JSA to prevent Per Degaton from unleashing a nuclear nightmare and altering the course of history.

ALPHA CENTURION

FIRST APPEARANCE ZERO HOUR: CRISIS IN TIME #3 (September 1994)
STATUS Hero **REAL NAME** Marcus Aelius
OCCUPATION Adventurer **BASE** Mobile
HEIGHT 5ft 8in **WEIGHT** 165 lbs **EYES** Blue **HAIR** Blond
SPECIAL POWERS/ABILITIES Alien armor gives superstrength, the power of flight, and the ability to manifest an energy sword and shield.

A Roman Centurion during the time of the emperor Hadrian, circa ad 117-138, Marcus Aelius was chosen by a race of aliens, the Virmiru, to come to their world to study and learn from their advanced civilization. Upon his return to Earth, Aelius was stunned to learn that over 1,800 years had passed. Quickly aligning himself with Lex Luthor's ruthless ex-wife (see LUTHOR, LEX), the CONTESSA, in Metropolis, Aelius was dubbed the Alpha Centurion. He formed the Centurions, a private army that protected the city under strict, ancient laws.

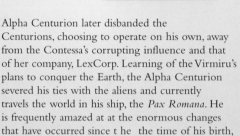

PROTECTOR Marcus Aelius was a quick study, learning to use his gifts to protect the innocent, be it on the ground or in the air.

Alpha Centurion later disbanded the Centurions, choosing to operate on his own, away from the Contessa's corrupting influence and that of her company, LexCorp. Learning of the Virmiru's plans to conquer the Earth, the Alpha Centurion severed his ties with the aliens and currently travels the world in his ship, the *Pax Romana*. He is frequently amazed at at the enormous changes that have occurred since t he the time of his birth, almost 2,000 years ago. **RG**

SUPERMAN Alpha Centurion wasn't too sure about the Man of Steel when they first met, but they quickly became allies.

AMAZING GRACE

FIRST APPEARANCE SUPERMAN (2nd series) #3 (March 1987)
STATUS Villain **REAL NAME** None
OCCUPATION Agent of Darkseid **BASE** Apokolips
HEIGHT 5ft 11in **WEIGHT** 159 lbs **EYES** Green **HAIR** Red
SPECIAL POWERS/ABILITIES Manipulates the wills of others with her beauty and persuasive powers.

The sister of DARKSEID's star propagandist GLORIOUS GODFREY, Amazing Grace shares her brother's gift for persuasion. She is one of the most attractive things to arise from the hellish madhouse that is Apokolips, yet her heart is cold and her intentions sadistic. Amazing Grace often serves Darkseid by dwelling among the lowest-class "hunger dogs" in the slums near the fire-pits. There she locates resistance groups and manipulates their leaders, drawing them out long enough for her master to annihilate them. During the anti-heroic movement on Earth known as the Legends crisis, Darkseid brought SUPERMAN to Apokolips in an attempt to corrupt his soul. Amazing Grace used her talents to make the Man of Steel believe he was Darkseid's son. Superman soon shook off the delusion, but Amazing Grace is still active within Apokolips' twisted hierarchy. **DW**

AMAZING MAN I

FIRST APPEARANCE ALL-STAR SQUADRON #23 (July 1983)
STATUS Hero (deceased) **REAL NAME** William Everett
OCCUPATION Adventurer **BASE** New York City
HEIGHT 6ft 1in **WEIGHT** 185 lbs **EYES** Brown **HAIR** Black
SPECIAL POWERS/ABILITIES Capable of transforming himself into a living, breathing facsimile of any material that he touched; later, his powers were altered, and he was instead able to magnetically attract or repel objects with his hands.

Will Everett was a multi-medal winner in the 1936 Berlin Olympics. Despite the acclaim, the young African American, a constant target of racism, was unable to get work and became a janitor for Doctor Terry Curtis. Everett was kidnapped by the ULTRA-HUMANITE and subjected to a power barrage from an invention of Curtis's. Everett gained superpowers and became Amazing Man. Initially blackmailed into working for the Ultra-Humanite, Amazing Man eventually turned on the villain and defeated him. Amazing Man then joined the ALL-STAR SQUADRON, fighting Axis tyranny during World War II. Everett's matter-mimicking powers were later replaced with magnetic ones. Everett died of cancer decades later. **PJ**

AMAZING MAN II

FIRST APPEARANCE JUSTICE LEAGUE OF AMERICA (2ND SERIES) #86 (March 1994)
STATUS Hero (deceased) **REAL NAME** William Everett III
OCCUPATION Adventurer **BASE** New York City
HEIGHT 5ft 11in **WEIGHT** 180 lbs **EYES** Brown **HAIR** Black
SPECIAL POWERS/ABILITIES Could transform into a living facsimile of any material he touched. If he touched stone, for example, he became a sentient being made of rock, with all its strengths and weaknesses.

ROMANCE After her rejection by Superman, Maxima found love—and a potential mate—in Amazing Man.

The second Amazing Man was the grandson of the first. William Everett III had acquired his grandfather's abilities to transmute into elements but not his ability to control them. Everett, a college student, sought out Maxwell Lord (LORD HAVOK), founder of Justice League International (see JUSTICE LEAGUE OF AMERICA), for help and training in the use of his emerging powers. When the OVERMASTER and his alien CADRE attacked the Earth, Everett took his grandfather's codename and became Amazing Man. Together, Everett and the JLA defeated the Cadre, and Amazing Man became a member of EXTREME JUSTICE. Everett had an affair with the alien queen MAXIMA before the team disbanded. Tragically, the second Amazing Man was killed along with several other heroes by the second Mist. **PJ**

AMAZO

FIRST APPEARANCE THE BRAVE AND THE BOLD #30 (June 1960)
STATUS Villain **REAL NAME** None
OCCUPATION Adventurer **BASE** Mobile
HEIGHT 8ft **WEIGHT** 485 lbs **EYES** Red **HAIR** None
SPECIAL POWERS/ABILITIES Absorption cells throughout Amazo's synthetic body permit the android to replicate the special abilities of any super-beings in his immediate proximity. With every hero or heroine encountered, Amazo becomes even more powerful and virtually unstoppable.

The android dubbed "Amazo" was built by rogue scientist PROFESSOR IVO in his quest to achieve immortality. Powered by Ivo's patented absorption cells, Amazo first set out to fulfill his maker's prime directive by duplicating the superpowers belonging to the founding membership of the JUSTICE LEAGUE OF AMERICA, energies Ivo hoped would grant him eternal life. Despite facing a single foe as mighty as the team in its entirety, the JLA defeated Amazo and lulled him into an electronic slumber. Over the years since his creation, Amazo has emerged from this digital dormancy on various occasions, upgrading himself with new abilities depending on the JLA's ever-changing roster, and continuing to do Professor Ivo's preprogrammed bidding by attempting to destroy the world's greatest super heroes. In a recent battle with the JLA, Amazo faced the League's entire roll call, including reservists and part-time members, thus tripling the amount of powers he absorbed. Professor Ivo failed to combine Amazo with RED TORNADO II's body to make an indestructible shell for SOLOMON GRUNDY. Ivo also created Amazo's cyborg "son," who lived as a college student before embracing his identity of Kid Amazo. **SB**

LIKE FATHER Amazo's son meets the JLA.

AMAZONS

FIRST APPEARANCE (historical) ALL-STAR COMICS #8 (Winter 1941); (current) Wonder Woman (2nd series) #1 (February, 1987)
STATUS Heroes **BASE** Themyscira
CURRENT MEMBERS AND POWERS (See key)

The Amazons were created in 1,200 bc by a collection of five Olympian goddesses to teach mankind equality, justice, and peaceful harmony. Three thousand in number, the Amazons built the city of Themyscira and established a powerful nation-state in ancient Greece. The Amazons were led by Queen HIPPOLYTA and her sister Antiope.

Heracles and his men, under the influence of the evil war god ARES, seduced the Amazons and ransacked Themyscira. Craving vengeance, Antiope, along with a bloodthirsty faction of Amazons, pursued Heracles to Attica. Hippolyta and her Amazons, following the decree of their goddesses, instead settled on a remote island. Hippolyta's Amazons rebuilt Themyscira (see Amazing Bases, pp. 132–3), and, granted immortality by their goddesses, were charged with guarding the gate to Pandora's Box, housed beneath their new home.

3,000 years later, as Ares plotted to destroy the world in a nuclear war, Hippolyta's daughter Diana became Themyscira's champion, known to "Patriarch's World" as WONDER WOMAN. After Wonder Woman ended Ares's threat to the world, and also destroyed the hellish creatures within Pandora's Box, the Amazons opened their shores to the outside world for the first time in 3,000 years.

After several attempts at cultural exchange with Patriarch's World, Antiope's descendants, a warrior tribe of Amazon assassins nestled in Egypt, were transported to Themyscira by CIRCE. Soon after, DARKSEID invaded Paradise Island, killing half the Amazons. The two tribes of Amazons forged an uneasy peace to help defend Earth from the threat of IMPERIEX (see Great Battles, pp. 362–3), and joined forces when several goddesses remade Themyscira, transforming it into an interdimensional university devoted to the exchange of knowledge, where the Amazons continued to promote their peaceful ideals. The Amazons invaded Washington DC under the orders of a resurrected Hippolyta, earning the wrath of Athena (GRANNY GOODNESS in disguise), who banished many to live lives as mortal women. **PJ**

NOTABLE AMAZONS PAST AND PRESENT
1) Cydippe (handmaiden) **2)** Myrhha (deceased)
3) Pallas (artisan) **4)** Mala (friend to Diana)
5) Clio (scribe) **6)** Timandra (architect)
7) Mnemosyne (historian) **8)** Aella (warrior)
9) Niobe (priestess) **10)** Oenone (botanist)
11) Epione (physician) **12)** Pythia (philosopher)
13) Euboea (warrior) **14)** Penelope
15) Ipthime (deceased) **16)** Archon Phillipus
17) Menalippe (deceased)

AMBUSH BUG

FIRST APPEARANCE DC COMICS PRESENTS #52 (July 1983)
STATUS Would-be hero **REAL NAME** Irwin Schwab
OCCUPATION Adventurer **BASE** Metropolis
HEIGHT 5ft 10in **WEIGHT** 145 lbs **EYES** Green **HAIR** None
SPECIAL POWERS/ABILITIES Can teleport anywhere on Earth (exact limits are not defined); green suit provides some protection against attack.

Irwin Schwab somehow came into possession of a green suit filled with miraculous technology that protected the wearer from harm and allowed him to teleport around the world. Unfortunately, this was a case of the right tool in the wrong hands. Schwab's major character defect is his lack of linear logic, which gives him a skewed picture of the world. However, Schwab knows enough to want to use his costume and special abilities in the cause of good. Unfortunately, although he aspires to being a super hero, he always seems to get caught up in complicated events. Following the Infinite Crisis, Ambush Bug joined the short-lived replacement JUSTICE LEAGUE OF AMERICA led by Firestorm. **RG**

PEST Ambush Bug tormented Superman before beginning his journey to become a hero.

AMETHYST, PRINCESS OF GEMWORLD

FIRST APPEARANCE LEGION OF SUPER-HEROES #298 (April 1983)
STATUS Hero **REAL NAME** Amy Winston
OCCUPATION Lord of Order **BASE** Gemworld
HEIGHT 5ft 8in **WEIGHT** 134 lbs **EYES** Violet **HAIR** Blonde
SPECIAL POWERS/ABILITIES Vast magical talents including the ability to
fly, generate force-field shields, emit bolts of energy, and conjure up
interdimensional portals.

PRECIOUS GEM *As the first-ever Lord of Order to be born in human form, Amethyst possesses vast potential for both good and evil.*

On her 13th birthday, Amy Winston learned that she was a princess, born to rule the realm of
Gemworld, where she had the body of a 20-year-old and wielded vast magic powers. Gemworld
was ruled by 12 houses of sorcerers, playthings for the Lords of Order and Chaos. Pantagones, a
Lord of Order, used the House of Amethyst to strike against Lord of Chaos Vandaemeon and
his House of Opal (*see* DARK OPAL). Lord and Lady Amethyst died in the clash, but a
servant ensured their infant daughter would be safely raised on Earth. This girl became
Amy Winston. As Amethyst, Amy defeated Dark Opal and united the Gemworld.

She lost her sight during the Crisis (*see* Great Battles, pp. 362–3)
but learned to see by magical means, and broke all ties with
those who had known her as Amy Winston. Amethyst's
radical plan to bring about order teamed her with the
Lord of Chaos called Child and his assistant Flaw, and
she conquered troubled Gemworld. **DW**

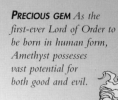

JUST THIRTEEN *Amy reverts to her Earth age on returning from Gemworld.*

ANARKY

FIRST APPEARANCE DETECTIVE COMICS #608 (November 1989)
STATUS Unresolved **REAL NAME** Lonnie Machin
OCCUPATION Political activist **BASE** Washington, D.C.
HEIGHT 5ft 8in **WEIGHT** 150 lbs **EYES** Blue **HAIR** Red
SPECIAL POWERS/ABILITIES A superintelligent computer genius and a
master inventor; he uses gas bombs and a taser staff in combat.

BATMAN BATTLE *After killing several coporate heads, Anarky was captured by Batman, but returned to the streets determined to haunt the dreams of corrupt businessmen before ending their crimes permanently.*

ANARKY AIMS HIGH *Hyperintelligent Anarky wants nothing less than worldwide revolution.*

Angered by the power and corruption of multinational
corporations, 12-year-old Lonnie Machin donned a
costume that increased his height and took to the streets
as Anarky. Anarky murdered several CEOs and celebrities,
spray-painting their bodies with his "A" symbol after
he killed them. BATMAN soon identified the assassin,
from clues in a Gotham City newspaper that linked the
murders to Anarky. Astonished to discover that Anarky
was just a boy, Batman apprehended him, and Machin was
incarcerated at the Gotham Juvenile Corrections Hall.

Machin later became the computer hacker Moneyspider,
and transferred millions of dollars from the accounts of
wealthy corporations to Third World countries. Batman's
partner, ROBIN, determined Moneyspider's link to Anarky,
and Machin's plans for global change were thwarted.
Undaunted, and using a special device of his own creation,
Machin fused the two sides of his brain, increasing his
intelligence to superhuman levels. After toying with
Batman and Robin, Anarky learned that he had
been adopted and that his natural mother was a
Vegas showgirl and his father was the JOKER. This
only furthered Anarky's resolve to wreak havoc on
the industrialized world, in the hope of triggering
worldwide revolution.

Despite his criminal history with Earth's
defenders, most notably Batman, Anarky has
worked alongside heroes including ROBIN, GREEN
LANTERN, and YOUNG JUSTICE against some of
their greatest enemies, including KLARION, THE
WITCH BOY and DARKSEID. **PJ**

ANCIENTS, THE

FIRST APPEARANCE JLA #70 (October 2002)
STATUS Hero team **BASE** Ancient Atlantis
MEMBERS AND POWERS
GAMEMNAE (FORMER LEADER; DECEASED) Corrupt Atlantean sorceress.
THE ANOINTED ONE Alien powerhouse; defender of the Hebrew faith.
MANITOU RAVEN North American shaman possessing mystical powers.
RAMA KHAN Elemental commanding earth and rocks to his will.
SELA Armed with magical weapons carried in her Bag of Night.
TEZUMAK Juggernaut sealed in armor oiled with his victims' blood.
THE WHALER Wielder of solid light "Borealis Effect," hurled from his
net and harpoon.

Assembled in 1,004 bc by Rama Khan (*see* KHAN,
RAMA), noble protector of Jarhanpur, the Ancients were
the world's greatest super heroes of prehistory. The
team was brought together to battle—as prophesied
by GAMEMNAE, High Priestess of Atlantis—a "seven-
headed hydra" that would lay waste the Earth.
Instead of a hydra, the Ancients fought and killed
the JUSICE LEAGUE OF AMERICA, who had traveled
back into the distant past to find their lost teammate
AQUAMAN. The evil Gamemnae had duped the other
Ancients to fulfill her schemes of conquering the world
by preventing Atlantis from sinking and so changing
the course of history. Meanwhile, present-day Earth
was threatened with disaster as every drop of water was
drawn into the reservoirs of Atlantis, as it was raised
from the depths of the ocean. To save the modern era,
the JLA's BATMAN called upon a roster of replacement
heroes to go back several millennia and thwart
Gamemnae's plans. The JLA revealed her treachery
to the Ancients, and the heroes of two epochs joined
forces to save past and present. The boastful Gamemnae
perished in magical combat with MANITOU RAVEN. **SB**

KEY 1) *The Anointed One* **2)** *Tezumak* **3)** *Sela* **4)** *Manitou
Raven* **5)** *Gamemnae* **6)** *Rama Khan* **7)** *The Whaler*

14

ANDROMEDA

FIRST APPEARANCE LEGION OF SUPER-HEROES (4th series) #6 (April 1990)
STATUS Hero **REAL NAME** Laurel Gand
OCCUPATION Legionnaire **BASE** Mobile
HEIGHT 6ft 2in **WEIGHT** 160 lbs **EYES** Blue **HAIR** Blonde
SPECIAL POWERS/ABILITIES Natural Daxamite abilities of superspeed, superstrength, laser vision, X-ray vision, supersenses, and invulnerability to everything but lead.

Laurel Gand, a SUPERGIRL analogue in one version of the Legion's continuity, came from the repressive planet Daxam. Raised in this xenophobic climate, Laurel Gand was horrified to be selected to represent Daxam in the newly formed Legion of Super-Heroes. However, as she learned more about the myriad worlds making up both the United Planets and the Legion membership, her worldview changed. Before defeating the White Triangle's thugs, however, she was poisoned with lead and nearly died prior to Brainiac 5.1 finding a cure. Andromeda went seeking spiritual solace with the Sisters of the Eternal Cosmos and underwent a physical redefinition that left her shorter, but with some energy-manipulating powers. She is still unsure how these new powers have affected her. **RG**

ANGEL AND THE APE

FIRST APPEARANCE SHOWCASE PRESENTS #77 (September 1968)
STATUS Heroes **REAL NAMES** Angel Beatrix O'Day, Sam Simeon
OCCUPATION Adventurer **BASE** New York City
HEIGHT 5ft 10in (Angel); 5ft 9in (Sam)
WEIGHT 140 lbs (Angel); 550 lbs (Sam)
EYES Blue (Angel); hazel (Sam) **HAIR** White (Angel); black (Sam)
SPECIAL POWERS/ABILITIES Angel is an expert fencer, marksman, martial artist, and linguist; Sam has limited telepathic abilities and gorilla strength.

The unlikeliest duo in New York City must be Angel and the Ape, who operate a PI firm under the name of O'Day & Simeon. The two are inseparable, and their history goes back years to when Angel accompanied her father, Professor Theo O'Day, on an African safari. Professor O'Day had already encountered a tribe of subterranean AMAZONS, with whom he had fathered a daughter, Athena. On this occasion, he and his second daughter, Angel, stumbled into the vicinity of Gorilla City.

Sam Simeon had wandered off from the concealed monkey-metropolis and the headaches associated with its villain (and Sam's grandfather), GORILLA GRODD. Sam followed Angel back to the U.S. While Angel trained in a variety of intellectual and physical disciplines, Sam doodled on a sketch pad and dreamed of becoming a cartoonist.

Sam eventually took home a semi-regular paycheck as a freelance artist, illustrating the comic book *Deus Ex Machina Man* while assisting Angel on the cases that walked through the door of O'Day & Simeon. His telepathic "force of mind" allows him to trick others into overlooking the fact that he's a quarter-ton gorilla!

The pair is still active in the detective business. Never looking for trouble, mild-mannered Sam finds it anyway whenever he's in Angel's company. **DW**

ANGLE MAN

FIRST APPEARANCE WONDER WOMAN (2nd series) #179 (May 2002)
STATUS Villain **REAL NAME** Angelo Bend
OCCUPATION Thief **BASE** Milan, Italy
HEIGHT 5ft 11in **WEIGHT** 170 lbs **EYES** Brown **HAIR** Brown
SPECIAL POWERS/ABILITIES Bend's Angler weapon (a magical set square) allows him to teleport, bend space and spacial relations, alter gravity, and warp perceptions.

Angelo Bend is a handsome, impeccably dressed, smooth-tongued rogue who mysteriously came into possession of the reality-warping Angler. Using this magical, triangular device, Bend became a master thief-for-hire, wanted by the authorities across Europe for his crimes.

As Angle Man, Bend came face to face with the New Titan TROIA when he was hired by CHEETAH II to steal shards of an ancient relic that controlled the powers of the Furies, the Greek goddesses of vengeance. Smitten with Troia, Angle Man turned against the Cheetah and helped Troia and WONDER WOMAN defeat her. Angle Man recently teamed with the FILM FREAK to target CATWOMAN. **PJ**

FURIOUS *A small-time thief, Angle Man had no idea that his mysterious benefactor, Barbara Minerva, was using him to steal the powers of the Furies.*

THE ANGLER *While the origins of Angle Man's weapon remain a mystery, he wields it to awesome effect!*

ANIMA

FIRST APPEARANCE NEW TITANS ANNUAL (2nd series) #9 (1993)
STATUS Hero **REAL NAME** Courtney Mason
OCCUPATION Adventurer **BASE** Mobile
HEIGHT 5ft 3in **WEIGHT** 111 lbs **EYES** Blue **HAIR** Blonde (dyed red)
SPECIAL POWERS/ABILITIES Able to leech bio-energy from living and non-living things; her body contains the Animus, a shadow being possessing superstrength, flight, and shape-changing powers.

Rebellious runaway Courtney Mason acquired her miraculous powers following an attack by parasitic aliens. Seven extraterrestrial predators had come to Earth and slaughtered thousands of humans by feeding on their spinal fluids. On the run in New Orleans, Courtney was kidnapped by a cult that sacrificed her to two of these insatiable parasites, known as Pritor and Lissik. But Courtney did not die. Instead, the parasites' bites unleashed the Animus, a creature within Courtney that can absorb the spirit essences of the living and the dead. She became the embodiment of mankind's rage and masculine drive. As Anima, Courtney sought revenge against the cult. She also met the TEEN TITANS and combatted a variety of supernatural menaces. Anima remains a wanderer, traveling from place to place and helping those in need by calling upon the fearsome force inside her. **SB**

ANIMAL MAN

DEFENDER OF THE RED

FIRST APPEARANCE STRANGE ADVENTURES #180 (September 1965)
STATUS Hero **REAL NAME** Bernhard "Buddy" Baker
OCCUPATION Stunt man; adventurer **BASE** Montana
HEIGHT 5ft 11½ in **WEIGHT** 172 lbs **EYES** Blue **HAIR** Blond
SPECIAL POWERS/ABILITIES Able to tap into the Lifeweb and temporarily replicate the powers and abilities of any animal on Earth.

THE PUBLIC STORY of Animal Man's origins is that an alien spaceship crashed in the Adirondack Mountains, in upstate New York, near film stuntman Buddy Baker, imbuing him with the ability to adapt and use animal powers. He then donned a costume and became Animal Man, part-time rocker and part-time hero. The truth is a little different. Buddy was actually the recipient of a spell cast by an ancient shaman that somehow connected him to the Lifeweb, or the Morphogenetic Field, a major source of primordial power. For former rocker turned stuntman Buddy, this was a life-altering experience that still has amazing repercussions for him and for his family.

ANIMAL ANTICS Animal Man in his happier days, when being a super hero was a low-risk adventure compared with his later career. He had a reputation for sending fruit baskets after team-ups.

MAKING A DIFFERENCE

After a time, Buddy retired his Animal Man costume and married Ellen Frazier, his longtime love. Ellen found work as an illustrator while Buddy did stunts for the movies, and they made a home in San Diego, California, raising their children, Cliff and Maxine. Buddy was persuaded to resume his Animal Man role by the IMMORTAL MAN, eventually joining Justice League Europe (see JUSTICE LEAGUE OF AMERICA). Unlike most other heroes, Buddy was quite open about his alter ego, and his kids were well aware of their dad's extracurricular activities.

Over time, Buddy became increasingly concerned about the planet's animal life and the plight of endangered species. He combatted illegal hunting and animal testing aided by other heroes, such as VIXEN. During these crusading days, he learned of his connection to the Morphogenetic Field from the scientist James Highwater. This knowledge further expanded Buddy's horizons, making him aware of his vital link to all life on Earth and his position as a role model for other activists.

A friend suggested Buddy start a new church to spread the word, and thus was born the Life Power Church of Maxine. This led to a pilgrimage and a relocation to the wilds of Montana. This upheaval had unforeseen effects on Buddy's life, including an extramarital affair with his friend Annie, which led to the birth of his second daughter (considered a human incarnation of the World Soul). Following the Infinite Crisis, Buddy spent a year stranded in space alongside ADAM STRANGE and STARFIRE, fighting to end the menace of Lady Styx. He has since returned home to Ellen and his children. **RG**

WILD THING
Just learning to master his power, Buddy Baker handles runaway zoo attractions.

ANIMAL INSTINCT Buddy displays his power by getting close enough to a dog and impressing his wife, Ellen.

KEY STORYLINES

• **STRANGE ADVENTURES #180 (SEPTEMBER 1965):** Buddy Baker first gains his animal powers.
• **ANIMAL MAN #1-9 (SEPTEMBER 1988–MARCH 1989):** Buddy returns to super-heroics as his family adjusts to events such as having a JLA transporter delivered to the house.
• **ANIMAL MAN #51-55 (SEPTEMBER 1992–JANUARY 1993):** Animal Man learns of his connection to the Red.

ANTHRO

FIRST APPEARANCE SHOWCASE #74 (May 1968)
STATUS Hero **REAL NAME** Anthro
OCCUPATION First boy on Earth **BASE** Prehistoric Earth
HEIGHT 5ft 2in **WEIGHT** 137 lbs **EYES** Brown **HAIR** Brown
SPECIAL POWERS/ABILITIES Skilled hunter and tracker.

RUNNING AMOK
Anthro's tendency to get in over his head nearly caused the destruction of the entire Bear tribe in a woolly mammoth stampede.

Anthro was the first of the Cro-Magnons, who would one day give rise to modern man. His father was a Neanderthal, the chief of the Bear tribe, and his mother was a mysterious figure from a tribe long thought destroyed. The Bear tribe viewed this strongly-built boy with suspicion, and Anthro had to push himself hard to win the respect of his tribe mates and his father, Ne-Ahn. Anthro's family included his brother Lart, his stepmother, Emba, and his uncle Do-Ahn. In time he met Embra, a Cro-Magnon like himself, and the two fell in love and married. During the Crisis (see Great Battles, pp. 362–3), Anthro experienced a number of temporal shifts that baffled him. Anthro recently appeared in the 21st century and joined a strange team of outcasts led by DOCTOR THIRTEEN. **DW**

APPARITION

FIRST APPEARANCE ACTION COMICS #276 (May 1961)
STATUS Hero **REAL NAME** Tinya Wazzo
OCCUPATION Legionnaire **BASE** Legion World, U.P. Space
HEIGHT 5ft 6in **WEIGHT** 131 lbs **EYES** Blue **HAIR** Black
SPECIAL POWERS/ABILITIES Able to phase all or any part of her body into an intangible and translucent phantom state.

In one incarnation of the Legion of Super-Heroes, Apparition is the code name for the Legionnaire known elsewhere as Phantom Girl. Tinya Wazzo of Bgtzl joined the Legion after foiling a terrorist attempt. Tinya used her people's natural ability to become a living phantom as the Legionnaire Apparition. She apparently died defending Earth against a supremacist group known as the White Triangle.

However, Apparition still existed in a phantom-like state and was later fully restored during the Legion's brief foray to the 20th century. During that time, Tinya married longtime love and fellow Legionnaire Jo Nah (ULTRA BOY), and gave birth to their son, Cub Wazzo-Nah. Legion membership and a lengthy separation during the BLIGHT invasion strained Tinya and Jo's marriage. Furthermore, their son Cub has rapidly aged since his birth, further complicating all of their lives. **SB**

ANTITHESIS

FIRST APPEARANCE TEEN TITANS (1st series) #53 (1978)
STATUS Villain **REAL NAME** Unrevealed
OCCUPATION Malevolent entity **BASE** Limbo
HEIGHT Variable **WEIGHT** Variable **EYES** Red **HAIR** None
SPECIAL POWERS/ABILITIES Telepathy; mental manipulation; psychic vampire that feeds off negative emotions.

The vile creature known only as the Antithesis was mysteriously imprisoned in the JUSTICE LEAGUE OF AMERICA's computer mainframe. Unable to free itself, the Antithesis, whose past remains shrouded in secrecy, contacted Bromwell Stikk through his own computer. The Antithesis gave a mystical staff to Stikk, the fanatical descendant of a colonial landowner, who tried to enslave the youth of the town of Hatton Corners. Calling himself Mister Twister, Stikk was defeated and humiliated by the first TEEN TITANS. The Antithesis then used his powers to mentally manipulate the JLA, and the heroes went on a crime spree. The Titans stopped them, however, and, under Robin's leadership, hurled the Antithesis into Limbo, where the creature vowed vengeance against the Boy Wonder and his teenage teammates.

Soon after, the Antithesis transported the defeated Mister Twister into Limbo and

transformed Stikk into the hideous Gargoyle. The Gargoyle battled the Titans while using the mystical powers of the Antithesis. In their most recent attack on the young heroes, the Gargoyle used the Antithesis' mental powers to attack NIGHTWING's mind, but Nightwing and the HERALD were able to teleport the villains back into Limbo, where they remain to this day, plotting their revenge. **PJ**

MISTER TWISTER *Stikk first battled with the Titans as Mister Twister.*

REVENGE
The monstrous Antithesis remains trapped in Limbo.

AQUAGIRL

FIRST APPEARANCE AQUAMAN (1st series) #33 (June 1967)
STATUS Hero (deceased) **REAL NAME** Tula
OCCUPATION Adventurer **BASE** Atlantis
HEIGHT 5ft 5in **WEIGHT** 119 lbs **EYES** Blue **HAIR** Brown
SPECIAL POWERS/ABILITIES As an Atlantean, she has a dense physique to allow her to withstand the crushing pressures under the surface, which, on land, gives her enhanced strength compared to humans; a superb swimmer.

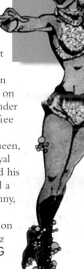

Tula owed everything to the Royal Family of Atlantis, who took her in as an orphan and raised her as one of their own. Her childhood was spent in seclusion in the Royal Home, and she rarely ventured out, until one day she met AQUAMAN's handsome adopted son, Garth. The two teenagers fell in love and adventured together, both on land with the TEEN TITANS, and under the sea. A shadow fell on her carefree life when Aquaman abandoned his throne in order to search for his queen, MERA. Aquaman left Narkran, a royal advisor, in charge, who soon turned his regency into a dictatorship. Tula led a successful rebellion against his tyranny, eventually restoring order to the throne. Tula died during the Crisis on Infinite Earths, but Lorena Marquez has taken her place as Aquagirl. **RG**

AQUAMAN

KING OF THE SEVEN SEAS

FIRST APPEARANCE More Fun Comics #73 (November 1941)
STATUS Hero **REAL NAMES** Arthur Curry; Orin
OCCUPATION Waterbearer of the Secret Sea, exiled King of Atlantis
BASE The undersea kingdom of Atlantis
HEIGHT 6ft 1in **WEIGHT** 325 lbs **EYES** Aqua blue **HAIR** Blond
SPECIAL POWERS/ABILITIES Can breathe underwater and communicate telepathically with sea life; can swim 100 m.p.h. underwater; possesses enhanced strength and toughness as well as limited sonar abilities; left hand is made of enchanted water and possesses healing powers as well as other magical abilities.

THOSE WHO UNDERESTIMATE AQUAMAN do so at their peril. This hot-headed monarch commands a kingdom that covers three-quarters of the Earth's surface and extends from the wave crests to the bottom of the Mariana Trench. Although he is, at present, a king in exile, his royal bearing is plain for all to see. Like many legendary kings, Aquaman's royal birthright was obscured by his upbringing as a commoner. The son of Queen Atlanna and a demigod, the spirit of Atlan, Orin was born with blond hair and the ability to communicate with sea life. These qualities sentenced the child to death by exposure on Mercy Reef, for the Atlanteans believed they were signs of the curse of Kordax, a legendary monster.

EARLY YEARS *Aquaman got his own series in 1962, battling bizarre menaces such as these Fire Trolls.*

FATHER FIGURE
Arthur Curry helped raise the young Atlantean, though he is no longer a presence in Aquaman's life.

STRANGER IN A STRANGE LAND
Found and raised by the dolphin Porm, Orin believed himself to be a misshapen dolphin until lighthouse-keeper Arthur Curry took him in. Absorbing some of the language and culture of the surface world from his adoptive parent, the boy took the name Arthur Curry and traveled north. He unknowingly fathered a child with an Inuit woman, Kako, then became the prisoner of Atlantean soldiers. Arthur befriended a fellow prisoner Vulko and escaped, wearing his prisoner's garb of orange-scaled shirt and green pants. He soon stumbled into a wave-top battle between the PRANKSTER and the second FLASH (Barry Allen). The Flash convinced Arthur to return with him to the U.S., where promoters dubbed him Aquaman.

OLD SCHOOL
Orin's dolphin family were perfectly suited for life underwater, but Orin kept pace by learning how to apply his opposable thumbs.

THE JLA
After he lost his hand in a piranha attack, Aquaman returned to the JLA, becoming a member of the modern team. He maintained ties with the organization he helped found and earned his place among the "magnificent seven" who comprise the icons of modern heroism.

The awkwardness that Aquaman had expressed as a rookie JLA member now manifested itself as outright hostility, but he acquitted himself well in the battle to stop the WHITE MARTIANS of the Hyperclan from taking over the Earth. Aquaman worked sporadically with the JLA, often leaving to attend to business under the sea. Occasionally, hints have slipped out concerning his unspoken desire for his teammate WONDER WOMAN.

IMPERIAL *Aquaman and Wonder Woman are the two JLA members who possess royal blood.*

RETURN OF THE KING
Arthur found adapting to surface life hard, but discovered a kindred spirit in the MARTIAN MANHUNTER. Like him, he became a founding member of the JUSTICE LEAGUE OF AMERICA.

Now a famous super hero, Aquaman returned to Atlantis to claim the throne. He made Vulko his regent and led his realm into a golden age. The exiled boy Garth became Aquaman's surrogate son, fighting threats to the kingdom as Aqualad. MERA then arrived from an alternate dimension and became Aquaman's queen. Aquaman defeated threats to the realm from super-villains including BLACK MANTA, FISHERMAN, SCAVENGER, and his own half-brother OCEAN MASTER. Aquaman and Mera eventually produced an heir—Arthur Jr., sometimes called Aquababy. The future of Atlantis looked bright.

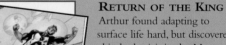

ATLANTIS
The two largest cities in Atlantis are Poseidonis and Tritonis.

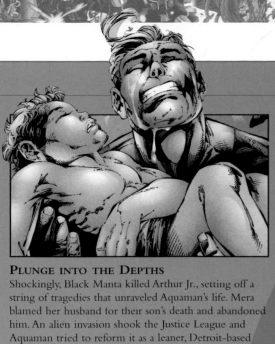

DEATH IN THE FAMILY
Aquaman cradles the dead body of his son, brutally murdered by Black Manta.

PLUNGE INTO THE DEPTHS

Shockingly, Black Manta killed Arthur Jr., setting off a string of tragedies that unraveled Aquaman's life. Mera blamed her husband for their son's death and abandoned him. An alien invasion shook the Justice League and Aquaman tried to reform it as a leaner, Detroit-based squad, but several new members died in the line of duty. A school of piranha chewed off Aquaman's left hand in a confrontation with the terrorist CHARYBDIS, and Arthur's illegitimate son KORYAK (product of his liaison with the Inuit Kako) took control of Atlantis.

Aquaman fought back from the brink of despair with the love of the adventurer DOLPHIN and the advice of Aqualad, now known as TEMPEST. Outfitted with a harpoon in place of a hand, Aquaman eventually won back rulership of Atlantis and defeated the sea god Triton, son of Poseidon.

A NEW CALLING

After Aquaman restored Atlantis to the modern era, the Atlanteans branded him an outcast. He exchanged his harpoon for a hand made of enchanted water from the LADY OF THE LAKE, and helped the transformed people of San Diego survive underwater after their city sank beneath the waves.

The Spectre destroyed Atlantis during the Infinite Crisis, and the sea gods transformed Aquaman into the mutated Dweller in the Depths. A new hero, Arthur Joseph Curry, arose in his absence, living up to his namesake's legacy by stopping Vandal Savage's scheme to flood the Earth.

AMERICAN TIDAL *An earthquake caused half of San Diego to sink into the ocean. Aquaman uncovered a mystery involving survivors who had evolved into water-breathers.*

IMPERIEX WAR

Intergalactic conqueror Imperiex, attempting to hollow out the Earth, chose Atlantis as one of his battlefronts (*see* Great Battles, pp. 362–3). Aquaman battled one of Imperiex's probes and seemingly died in battle, while Tempest used his magic to shift Atlantis more than 3,000 years back in time to the Obsidian Age of its ancient past. The other members of the JLA traveled back to restore Atlantis and find their lost teammate, Aquaman. Transformed into a water wraith by the evil sorceress Gamemnae, Aquaman merged with the entire ocean to re-sink Atlantis and restore it to its proper place in the timeline.

KEY STORYLINES

- *AQUAMAN: TIME AND TIDE #1-4 (DECEMBER 1993—MARCH 1994):*
The origin of Aquaman is tightened up and retold to fit within modern continuity.
- *AQUAMAN (3RD SERIES) #2 (SEPTEMBER 1994):*
Aquaman loses his left hand in an issue that redefined the character for a new audience.
- *AQUAMAN (4TH SERIES) #15 (APRIL 2004):*
The King of Atlantis returns to his classic look, and San Diego is submerged following an earthquake.

Once there were an infinite number of universes – until a being called the Anti-Monitor annihilated all except five, and the surviving heroes collapsed those five into one. Yet this single, merged universe would not hold. The Multiverse burst forth again when Alexander Luthor, brilliant scientist from a reality the Anti-Monitor had wiped out, initiated the Infinite Crisis by constructing a tuning fork that replicated the existing universe fifty-one times. At first, these 52 parallel universes looked identical, until the Venusian worm Mister Mind retroactively altered their histories during a rampage through space-time.

The 52 realities are separated from one another by Source Walls that bound each universe; behind the Source Walls lies the Bleed, which allows certain individuals to make passage from one universe to the next. Intermingling between realities is discouraged by the Monitors, a corps of 52 watchers (one from each plane) who strive to maintain the purity of the Multiverse. The anti-matter universe, home to the Sinestro Corps and the Weaponers of Qward, exists on a separate plane than any of the 52 positive-matter realities.

Earth is a focal point of each universe, and "New Earth" – the first world among the 52 – is the Multiverse's cornerstone. The destruction of New Earth would trigger a chain reaction that would destroy the Multiverse, leaving only the anti-matter universe in its wake.

The 52 parallel universes are named after, and most easily distinguished by, the characteristics of the planet Earth in each.

New Earth
The foundation of the Multiverse, New Earth is home to the primary versions of all super heroes and similar cosmic champions. All other universes are altered copies of New Earth's reality.

Earth-2
On Earth-2, a slightly altered version of the Justice Society of America fought the Axis powers in World War II. In later decades, their descendents have taken up unique heroic identities.

Earth-3
On this evil mirror image of New Earth, the Crime Society of Ultraman, Owlman, Superwoman, Power Ring, and Johnny Quick rule with an iron hand, while rogue do-gooders like the Jokester (and the Joker's Daughter) fight for freedom.

Earth-4
Alternate versions of the Question, Blue Beetle, Nightshade, Captain Atom, Judomaster, and the Peacemaker inhabit Earth-4, where they work to find a role for super heroes in a sometimes shadowy world.

Earth-5
A sunny and colorful reality, Earth-5 is home to upbeat versions of Captain Marvel and the Captain Marvel family.

Earth-8
New Earth's heroes do not have any analogues on Earth-8, where a super-powered ruling class has taken root in the form of Lord Havok and the Extremists.

Earth-10
On Earth-10, Adolph Hitler achieved victory in World War II and conquered the planet. Alternate versions of Uncle Sam and the Freedom Fighters plot to end his reign.

Earth-12
Several decades into the future, new Batman Terry McGinnis has taken the mantle from Bruce Wayne to fight old threats in a high-tech Gotham City.

Earth-15

The highly-evolved super heroes of Earth-15 have eliminated nearly all crime. Their members include Jason Todd as Batman, Jessica Palmer as the Atom, Donna Troy as Wonder Woman, and Zod and his son Christopher Kent as dual Supermen. The world was recently destroyed by Superman-Prime.

Earth-17

Here, the Atomic Knights struggle to tame a savage planet in the wake of an apocalyptic Great Disaster.

Earth-18

On Earth-18, analogues of the Justice League heroes keep the peace on the Old West's frontier.

Earth-19

In the closing decades of the 19th century, a Victorian-era Batman fights crime in a Gotham City lit by gaslight.

Earth-21

Also known as the New Frontier reality, Earth-21 is where the planet's core heroes became famous during the 1950s and '60s.

Earth-22

This universe, sometimes called the Kingdom Come reality and set several decades in the future, is distinguished by a mistrustful Earth where heroes fight heroes.

Earth-26

A cartoonish reality populated by anthropomorphic animals, Earth-26 counts Captain Carrot and his Zoo Crew among its furry champions.

Earth-30

Also known as the Red Son reality, Earth-30 is where baby Kal-El landed in Earth's Soviet Union during the Cold War of the 1950s, later using his abilities as a Soviet Superman to help Mother Russia dominate the globe.

Earth-31

In this reality, Earth's heroes are led by a pro-government, all-American Superman and a violent, aging Batman. Their differing methods define a world riddled with strife and oppression

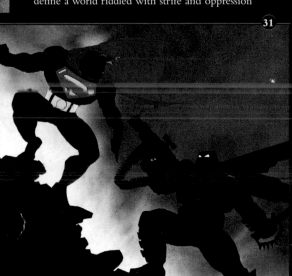

Earth-34

Earth-34, also called the Amazonia reality, is where Wonder Woman first emerged in 19th century England and fought a male-dominated commonwealth in which Jack the Ripper ruled as king.

Earth-43

Batman is a vampire in this dark universe that seethes with the supernatural.

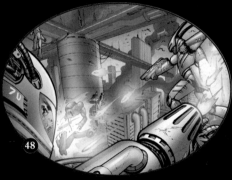

Earth-48[1]

Earth, a devastated scar in this reality, is used as a neutral warring ground for Martians, Venusians, and other species inhabiting the solar system. The cross-bred survivors of Earth have evolved to become the Forerunners—elite killing machines in the service of the Monitors.

Earth-50

This universe harbors a different lineup of heroes than those on New Earth, with teams including WildC.A.T.S., the Authority, and Gen13.

ARAK, SON OF THUNDER

FIRST APPEARANCE WARLORD #48 (August 1981)
STATUS Hero (dec.)   **REAL NAME** Arak Red-Hand (Bright Sky After Storm)
OCCUPATION Shaman   **BASE** 8th century Europe, Asia, N. America
HEIGHT 6ft   **WEIGHT** 190 lbs   **EYES** Brown   **HAIR** Black
SPECIAL POWERS/ABILITIES Arak is an expert with an otomahuk and a
sword. He also possesses undefined shamanic powers.

*STORMING THROUGH Arak
fought countless villains from
the past, including bizarre
mutations, supernatural
threats, and demons.*

In the 8th century, after a surprise attack on the Quontauka
Indians nearly wiped out the entire tribe, a
10-year-old boy favored by He-No, the Quontauka god
of thunder, escaped into the Atlantic Ocean in a birchwood
canoe. The boy was rescued by a roving band of Vikings,
named Erik, and raised as one of their own. Pronouncing his
name "Arak," the young Indian grew to adulthood among
the Vikings. Living in Europe, Arak became a powerful Viking
warrior, proficient with both a sword and his own weapon, his
native otomahuk.

Tragically, the Vikings who saved and raised Arak were slaughtered. Arak
survived the death of his Viking clan, however, and went off to seek Carolus
Magnus, known as Charlemagne. Arak was accepted into Charlemagne's
court and served the emperor for the rest of his life. Arak did return to North
America, however, hoping to rediscover his tribal origins. When Arak was slain
in battle, his spirit was summoned before the thunder god, He-No, who was actually
Arak's father. He-No resurrected Arak as a mystical shaman, renewing his life energies
and returning him to Earth to defend the tribes of natives across North America.
During the time-spanning event known as the Crisis (see Great Battles, pp. 362–3), Arak
briefly teamed up with the Golden Age heroes known as the ALL-STAR SQUADRON. **PJ**

*NATIVE WARRIOR Blessed by the power of the
He-No, Arak was a renowned warrior, feared across
Asia and Europe for his skill with the otomahuk.*

*HEAVEN AND HELL Arcane as a
deformed monster from Hell (left),
and in his mortal appearance (right).*

ARCANE, ANTON

FIRST APPEARANCE SWAMP THING #2 (January 1973)
STATUS Villain (reformed)   **REAL NAME** Anton Arcane
OCCUPATION Scientist; demon   **BASE** Hell
HEIGHT 5ft 1in   **WEIGHT** 97 lbs   **EYES** Obsidian   **HAIR** White
SPECIAL POWERS/ABILITIES As a human, Arcane was a brilliant
scientist; as a demon he was quick and sturdy.

Born in a Balkan state in 1895, Anton Arcane was
obsessed with finding the secret of immortality.
During World War II, Arcane was briefly in Adolf
Hitler's employ. Later during the war, the time-
traveling SWAMP THING took possession of the body
of an Easy Company soldier and thwarted Arcane's
bid for power. The UNKNOWN SOLDIER infiltrated Easy
Company, whose operatives gathered Arcane's collection
of artifacts, including a replica of the Spear of Destiny.
By the time Arcane became immortal, his body
was too old and feeble to be of any use, so he tried to
create a new body. However, his experiments yielded
only misshapen beings he dubbed the Un-Men. One
experiment resulted in Arcane's brother, Gregori,
becoming the PATCHWORK MAN I. Arcane's hopes were
raised when he discovered the Swamp Thing. Arcane
survived the battle, and the Un-Men rebuilt his body.
Arcane began a vendetta against the Swamp Thing and
his own niece, Abby Arcane, Swamp Thing's lover. Arcane
was killed, but even confinement in Hell couldn't
keep him from seeking vengeance, and he ultimately
achieved demonhood. Arcane was summoned from
Hell to be present at the first trial set by the Parliament
of Flames for Swamp Thing, but by then he had found
God. Because of this, Swamp Thing decided not
to destroy humanity, and built Arcane a new body.
Arcane was later reconciled with Abby. **RG**

ARASHI

FIRST APPEARANCE GREEN LANTERN PLUS #1 (December 1996)
STATUS Hero   **REAL NAME** Arashi Ohashi
OCCUPATION Video game designer/adventurer   **BASE** Tokyo, Japan
HEIGHT 5ft 5in   **WEIGHT** 119 lbs   **EYES** Brown   **HAIR** Black
SPECIAL POWERS/ABILITIES High-tech weaponry includes a heavily armed
motorcycle, right-arm flamethrower, and senses-augmenting cyber-
helmet; no known superpowers.

One of Japan's super heroes, Arashi Ohashi helps defend
her country from all manner of threats with advanced
technology of her own design. Arashi once teamed up
with GREEN LANTERN Kyle Rayner and the RAY to
thwart magnetic malcontent DOCTOR POLARIS and
prevent a giant tsunami from wiping Japan off the map.
Polaris broke Arashi's arm and nearly killed her,
but she has since recovered and resumed her adventurous
activities. **SB**

*LIFE SAVER While battling Doctor
Polaris, Green Lantern saved
Arashi with a power-ring-
generated air-bag.*

ARES

FIRST APPEARANCE WONDER WOMAN (2nd series) #1 (February 1987)
STATUS Villain **REAL NAME** Ares
OCCUPATION God of War **BASE** The Areopagus
HEIGHT 6ft 10in **WEIGHT** 459 lbs **EYES** Blue **HAIR** Blond
SPECIAL POWERS/ABILITIES Immortal; god-like strength and stamina; brilliant military strategist; indestructible armor.

The Greek god of war Ares thrives on bloodshed and is the implacable enemy of WONDER WOMAN, the Amazon peacemaker. Despite being Zeus's son, Ares never fit in with the other gods of Olympus (*see* OLYMPIAN GODS) and created his own realm, the Areopagus. When he plotted to destroy the mortals' world with a nuclear bomb, the AMAZON brought Princess Diana to life as the new Wonder Woman to combat the war god's evil.

Ares then made another bid for supreme power, killing HIGHFATHER in the process. He suffered torments for his treachery until he effected his escape. Later, Ares's children, PHOBOS, Deimos, and Eris, tried to ensure their father's place as ruler of Earth by raising the Areopagus in the center of Gotham City.

Ares has taken an interest in the new WONDER GIRL, and given her a magic lasso similar to Diana's. Ares continues to push Wonder Girl to become his champion, supplying her with powers that dwarf those originally given her by Zeus. **DW**

THE DECEIVER
During a battle with Darkseid, Ares merged with Zeus and the gods of other pantheons (Jove, Odin, and the New God Highfather). Ares would betray them all in due course.

SILVER TONGUE
Ares is just as skilled with flattery as he is with a sword, since both are weapons in the service of strife.

ARGENT I

FIRST APPEARANCE SECRET ORIGINS (3rd series) #14 (May 1987)
STATUS Hero team **BASE** Unknown
MEMBERS AND POWERS/ABILITIES
Control The mysterious leader. **Falcon** A master of disguise.
Fleur The daughter of notorious World War I spy Mata Hari.
Iron Munro He has superhuman strength and invulnerability.
Phantom Lady I A special device worn on her wrist emits a black light ray, creating total darkness. **Phantom** Mysterious master of disguise. **Dina** (deceased) wife of Control; Allied saboteur and spy.

Argent was created in 1951 as the civilian branch of Task Force X. The organization was designed to handle the threat of superpowered criminals after the JUSTICE SOCIETY OF AMERICA was forced to disband by the House of Un-American Activities Committee because they refused to reveal their secret identities. Unlike their counterparts in the SUICIDE SQUAD, Argent's missions were exclusively domestic, and the team operated in extreme secrecy. Their supervisor was known only as "Control," the mysterious former leader of the O.S.S. (Office of Strategic Services). This international intelligence and espionage organization was exposed by Control after he arranged the murder of a government operative indirectly responsible for the assassination of President John F. Kennedy in 1963.

SECRET SOCIETY *During the anti-Communist "Red Scare" of the 1950s, Argent exposed a number of threats to U.S. security, from foreign terrorists to costumed and superpowered villains.*

After the death of Control, his granddaughter began operating under the same guise. The group was finally disbanded after a confrontation with the Suicide Squad, and the U.S. government has no official record of their members or their existence. **PJ**

ARGENT II

FIRST APPEARANCE TEEN TITANS (2nd series) #1 (October 1996)
STATUS Hero **REAL NAME** Toni Moretti
OCCUPATION Adventurer **BASE** New Jersey
HEIGHT 5ft 8in **WEIGHT** 125 lbs **EYES** Blue **HAIR** Black
SPECIAL POWERS/ABILITIES Can generate silver plasma and shape it to whatever form she pleases; creates energy platforms and travels astride them at great speeds.

Teenager Toni Moretti first met the TEEN TITANS when the team saved her U.S. senator father from the FEARSOME FIVE. She never dreamed she would ever join them. However, a few years later, her skin was mysteriously drained of pigment and her body started to generate silver plasma. Abducted by an alien race, the H'San Natall, Toni learned that she and several other teenagers were the results of a breeding program to create a superpowered advance guard for an attack upon Earth. Toni and her fellow hybrids rebelled against the H'San Natall and sabotaged the invasion. Since the Teen Titans were inactive at the time, the hybrids decided to form their own version.

As Argent, Toni had many tumultuous adventures with various incarnations of the Teen Titans. Toni then found out that her father was involved in drug smuggling, and she was eventually forced to turn him over to the authorities. Much later, the Titans disbanded again after the deaths of heroines Omen and TROIA. Argent's current activities are unknown, although given her drive to succeed, one can safely assume that she is actively polishing her silver plasma skills. **SB**

SHINING LIGHT
Toni's silver plasma is not unlike the coherent light generated by Green Lantern's power ring.

ARION, LORD OF ATLANTIS

FIRST APPEARANCE WARLORD #55 (March 1982)
STATUS Hero **REAL NAME** Ahri'ahn
OCCUPATION Atlantean sorcerer **BASE** Mobile
HEIGHT 6ft 3in **WEIGHT** 190 lbs **EYES** Green **HAIR** Brown
SPECIAL POWERS/ABILITIES Immortality; vast magical abilities drawn from the extra-dimensional Darkworld.

ATLANTIS! THE NAME IS LEGENDARY, and during its golden age no hero was greater than Arion. No mere mortal, Arion came into existence as the product of a union between two Atlantean gods more than half a million years ago. His father, Calculhah (a force of good), cared for Arion, then known by the name Ahri'ahn, while his mother, Dark Majistra (a force of strife), raised Arion's wicked older brother, Garn Daanuth (*see* DAANUTH, GARN). When the two evil entities tried to destroy primitive Atlantis, Arion sacrificed his life to stop them. His energies survived thanks to the extra-dimensional realm of the Darkworld—home to a cosmic entity who serves as the source of all Atlantean magic—and Arion existed for nearly 500,000 years in a state of intangibility.

PROTECTOR OF ATLANTIS

Approximately 45,000 years ago, Arion returned in physical form to serve as the protector of Atlantis. The civilization had reached a peak, with the *homo sapiens* offshoot species, the *homo magi*, making up a large part of the population and exhibiting a primal connection to the forces of the universe. Arion became Lord High Mage of Atlantis, residing in the City of the Golden Gate and fighting the creeping encroachment of ice. He soon fell in love with Lady Chian, and the two battled the still-surviving mage Garn Daanuth. Arion played a time-hopping role alongside heroes from other eras during the Crisis (*see* Great Battles, pp. 362–3).

The continent of Atlantis suffered its first great fracturing when Arion fought off an assault by alien invaders. A bolt of energy shattered the City of the Golden Gate and caused much of the continental shelf to slip into the ocean. Arion and Lady Chian rapidly dispatched teams to establish new Atlantean colonies across the globe, including one in the hidden realm of Skartaris. Atlantis's final sinking (involving the cities of Tritonis and Poseidonis) did not occur until tens of thousands of years later.

As an immortal, Arion wandered the Earth for the next 45,000 years, with his powers waxing and waning due to changes in the Darkworld. In the year 1659 he traveled to modern-day Metropolis and tried to convince Superman to retire from his role as humanity's protector to prevent a global catastrophe. Despite Arion's alternate-history visions of a devastated world, Superman remained unconvinced.

After living many more centuries into the modern era, Arion cast doubt on Power Girl's history by falsely claiming to be her grandfather. Arion died while helping the Justice Society of America fight the sorcerer Mordru (*see* DARK LORD). An impostor, Bill Knightley from Ohio, took up Arion's identity, helping the SHADOWPACT fight the SPECTRE. DW

AS TIME GOES BY
Arion's appearance has changed over the years in conjunction with the waxing and waning power of the Darkworld.

MAGIC ARCANA His Atlantean heritage, coupled with centuries of study in the sorcerous arts, made Arion one of the greatest mages of any age. Arion, unfortunately, realized this, making him unbearably arrogant.

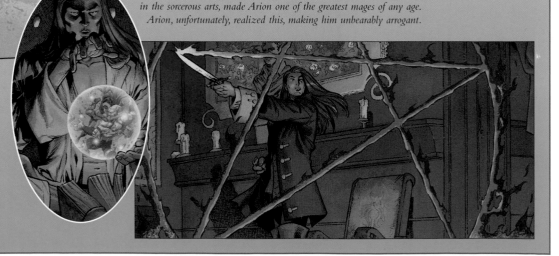

CAMELOT FALLS Arion, who had the gift of prophecy, became convinced that Superman's heroics would prevent humanity from surviving a global assault by the supervillain Khyber.

KEY STORYLINES
• *ARION, LORD OF ATLANTIS #1 (NOVEMBER 1982):* Arion graduates to his own title after debuting as a backup feature in Warlord.
• *JSA #50 (SEPTEMBER 2003):* Arion passes onto another plane of existence, taking down Mordru, the Dark Lord, in the process.

ARGUS

FIRST APPEARANCE THE FLASH ANNUAL (2nd series) #6 (1993)
STATUS Hero **REAL NAME** Nick Kovak
OCCUPATION Adventurer **BASE** Keystone City
HEIGHT 5ft 11in **WEIGHT** 185 lbs **EYES** Blue **HAIR** Black
SPECIAL POWERS/ABILITIES Can become invisible wherever shadows are
projected; can see almost the entire spectrum; well-trained hand-to-
hand combatant.

Federal agent Nick Kovak was
working on an investigation
into Keystone City's criminal
organizations when Venev, an
alien bent on conquering Earth,
attacked him. The attack changed
his body chemistry, allowing him
to become virtually invisible in
shadow, and his vision now worked beyond the normal
spectrum. He designed a dark costume for himself,
took the name Argus (after a giant guardian in Greek
mythology who had a hundred eyes), and became a
crime fighter. Being based in Keystone inevitably meant
encountering the FLASH III, the city's top super hero, and
they have worked together a number of times. However,
Kovak, using the frequent alter ego Nick Kelly, usually
prefers to operate on his own. RG

ARION, LORD OF ATLANTIS *SEE OPPOSITE PAGE*

ARISIA

FIRST APPEARANCE TALES OF THE GREEN LANTERN CORPS #1
(May 1981)
STATUS Hero **ASSUMED NAME** Cindy Simpson
OCCUPATION Adventurer **BASE** Space Sector 2815; Los Angeles, CA
HEIGHT 5ft 9in **WEIGHT** 136 lbs **EYES** Gold **HAIR** Blonde
SPECIAL POWERS/ABILITIES Arisia's Green Lantern ring can project
energy, sense danger, create vehicles and weapons, project battering
rams and objects, translate languages, probe minds, and allow
unaided flight through space.

Arisia's father, a GREEN LANTERN from the planet Graxos
IV, was ambushed and killed by the villainous Sinestro. The
GUARDIANS OF THE UNIVERSE chose Arisia to replace her
father as the Green Lantern of her father's sector, making
her one of the Corps' youngest members.
During her first mission, a deadly melee against the
demon Nekron, malevolent ruler of a
dimension known as the Land of the
Unliving, Arisia met Hal Jordan,
the Green Lantern of Earth. The
teenager later helped Jordan prevent
the planet Ungara from entering a
deadly ice age, and fell in love
with him. Arisia used her
ring to age her body so she
could pursue a relationship with
Hal and, after the Crisis (*see* Great
Battles, pp. 362–3), moved to Earth
to be closer to him, joining the last of
the GREEN LANTERN CORPS based there.
Although killed by MAJOR FORCE, Arisia
used her species' healing abilities to return
and rejoin the Corps. PJ

WITH THIS RING… *The sprite-like Arisia
was barely a teenager when she assumed
the mantle and power of Green Lantern.*

ARRAKHAT

FIRST APPEARANCE ROBIN #79 (July 2000)
STATUS Villain **REAL NAME** Arrakhat
OCCUPATION Evil djinn **BASE** O'salla Ben Duuram
HEIGHT Variable **WEIGHT** Variable **EYES** Flaming **HAIR** None
SPECIAL POWERS/ABILITIES Arrakhat's powers are mystical in nature
and are quite formidable. He manifests in the form of an armored
demon wielding a flaming scimitar.

In Quraci myth, the demon Arrakhat is an evil djinn from the
O'salla Ben Duuram, or "Oasis of the Damned," one of the
descending circles of Hell. Rather than granting three wishes
to its invoker, Arrakhat instead offers three murders, upon
completion of which this genie will return to its resting place
in the so-called "Well of Flames." In modern times,
Arrakhat was summoned forth by the Arghulian,
a religious zealot and enemy of Tim Drake's
schoolmate Ali Ben Khan, Rhafi (or prince) of
Dhubar. The Arghulian opposed Khan's rule and
was determined to see him dead rather than let
him assume the throne of Dhubar. Tim Drake's
alter ego, Robin, in company with Connor Hawke
(GREEN ARROW II) and former government
operative Eddie Fyers did their best to protect
Ali from Arrakhat's murderous wrath. However,
the prince's salvation lay in a mystical amulet he
possessed, a signet frequently used by his own
father to call forth the demon to slay his enemies.
Khan's amulet turned Arrakhat upon the Arghulian
and returned the demon to his abyssal home after
slaying the usurper. The evil djinn has not been
invoked by anyone since. SB

THROUGH THE ROOF
*Robin, Ali, and Eddie
learned the hard
way that Arrakhat's
scimitars could cut
right through metal.*

ARROWETTE

FIRST APPEARANCE IMPULSE #28 (August 1997)
STATUS Hero **REAL NAME** Cissie King-Jones
OCCUPATION Student **BASE** Western Pennsylvania
HEIGHT 5ft 7in **WEIGHT** 107 lbs **EYES** Blue **HAIR** Blonde
SPECIAL POWERS/ABILITIES Olympic-level athlete; yet to fully master
hand-to-hand combat techniques.

Daughter of Olympic archery medalist Bonnie King and
her husband Bernell Jones, Cissie was raised with high
expectations of her following in her mother's footsteps.
Before marrying, Bonnie had flirted
with becoming a costumed heroine,
Miss Arrowette, and adventured
on several occasions with GREEN
ARROW II. Bonnie pushed Cissie
to take up archery and filled her
head with dreams of superheroics.
After overseeing several years of
her daughter's training, Bonnie
took Cissie into battle with the
demon Spazz in Manehester,
Alabama. Local heroes Impulse
and MAX MERCURY

intervened, and Mercury later filed child
endangerment charges against Bonnie. The charges
were upheld, and Cissie was made a ward of the
state and placed in the Elias School in western
Pennsylvania, under the care of Dr. Marcy Money.
According to Dr. Money's files, she accidentally
gave Cissie the idea of becoming a better archer
than her mother, effectively starting Cissie's career
as the costumed crime fighter Arrowette. Cissie
joined Young Justice and was enjoying her new
identity, until the day she almost killed some
criminals. She has since renounced her persona
and only reluctantly suits up when circumstances
demand it. RG

ARROWETTE IN ACTION *Cissie
does not hesitate to charge into
action, something ingrained into
her by her overbearing mother.*

ARSENAL

BATTLING BOWMAN

FIRST APPEARANCE ADVENTURE COMICS #250 (July 1958)
STATUS Hero **REAL NAME** Roy Harper
OCCUPATION Adventurer **BASE** Brooklyn, New York City
HEIGHT 5ft 11in **WEIGHT** 195 lbs **EYES** Blue **HAIR** Red
SPECIAL POWERS/ABILITIES One of the world's top archers with bow and crossbow, Arsenal is also an expert with most projectile weapons and is a natural leader.

ONCE THE TEEN SIDEKICK OF GREEN ARROW I, Roy Harper endured many painful years in the hero's shadow, but emerged as an adult with his own identity. Roy is well acquainted with loss, having been orphaned twice before his fourteenth birthday. When Roy was a baby, his forest ranger father, Will, died saving Navajo medicine chief Brave Bow from a wildfire. Out of gratitude, Brave Bow raised the boy as his own. Roy became a tireless long-distance runner and a fine archer, closely following the career of the world's greatest archer, GREEN ARROW. One day Green Arrow came to Roy's hometown, and Roy impressed his idol with his quick reactions foiling a robbery (earning him the nickname "Speedy").

SPEEDY Roy has left behind the idealism of his early teens.

WEAPONS MASTER
Arsenal still favors the weapons of his Navajo upbringing, but is also skilled with firearms.

LIAN *As a single father and a super hero, Roy struggles to find time for his daughter.*

SHARP SHOOTERS

Brave Bow died soon after, and Roy became the legal ward of Green Arrow's alter ego, playboy millionaire Oliver Queen. Green Arrow and Speedy's amazing archery skills put them in the same class as many of the super heroes emerging at the same time. Green Arrow joined the JUSTICE LEAGUE OF AMERICA, while Speedy became a member of the TEEN TITANS alongside Kid Flash I (*see* KID FLASH II), Wonder Girl, Robin, and Aqualad (*see* TEMPEST).

Yet Roy still felt adrift, and when Green Arrow left on a cross-country road trip with GREEN LANTERN to "find America," Roy turned to drugs for comfort and became a heroin addict. Fortunately, BLACK CANARY helped Roy kick his dependency, and he eventually joined the Central Bureau of Investigations. A mission to Japan brought him into intimate contact with the beautiful assassin CHESHIRE. When they eventually parted, Roy was unaware she was carrying his child. Cheshire later became a prisoner of the government and Roy gained custody of his daughter, Lian.

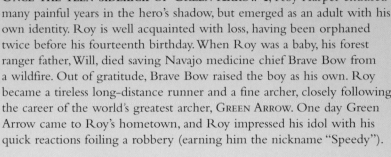

DRUG HELL *Feeling abandoned by Green Arrow, Roy hit rock bottom.*

While working for CHECKMATE, Roy retired the Speedy name for a more fitting identity as Arsenal. After stints leading the Titans and a new team of OUTSIDERS, Arsenal returned to his roots by adopting an all-new costumed identity as Red Arrow. He gladly accepted membership in the new JUSTICE LEAGUE OF AMERICA, and has struck up a romance with his teammate HAWKGIRL. **DW**

OUTSIDERS *Arsenal led the new Outsiders against Gorilla Grodd and his ape-soldiers when the simian super-villain attempted to invade New York City.*

EMOTIONAL MOMENT *Roy is accepted into the JLA by his old friends Black Canary and Green Lantern.*

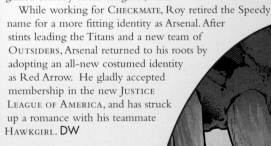

KEY STORYLINES
• *GREEN LANTERN #85 (SEPTEMBER 1971):* In one of the hero's most shocking moments, Speedy is revealed as a heroin addict.
• *NEW TEEN TITANS (2ND SERIES) #21 (JUNE 1986):* After a long tease, Cheshire discloses that Roy Harper is the father of her child.
• *NEW TITANS #99 (JULY 1993):* Speedy makes his debut as Arsenal.

ARTEMIS

FIRST APPEARANCE WONDER WOMAN (2nd series) #90 (Sept. 1994)
STATUS Hero **REAL NAME** Artemis
OCCUPATION Minister of Defense **BASE** Themyscira
HEIGHT 6ft **WEIGHT** 166 lbs **EYES** Green **HAIR** Red
SPECIAL POWERS/ABILITIES Immortal; an expert hand-to-hand combatant, master swordswoman, and archer.

FATE Artemis sacrificed her life to save Diana's, fulfilling a mystic prophecy.

Artemis is a member of the warmongering Amazons of Bana-Mighdall, descendants of the Amazon queen Antiope. Unlike the peace-loving AMAZONS of Themyscira (led by Antiope's sister HIPPOLYTA), Artemis and her tribe were not immortal. Artemis was raised in the secret city of Bana-Mighdall in Egypt, mastering the arts of warfare.

CHAMPION Even without superpowers, Artemis is a formidable warrior.

When the evil sorceress CIRCE transported the Amazons of Bana-Mighdall to Themyscira, home of Princess Diana (WONDER WOMAN), the two tribes of warrior women fought a ten-year war. An uneasy peace was forged that forced the Egyptian Amazons to settle on an inhospitable part of Themyscira. One night Hippolyta saw the death of her daughter Diana in a prophetic vision. Hoping to save Diana's life, she arranged for a new Contest to be held in order to choose a new Wonder Woman. With the help of a court magician, the sorceress Magala, Hippolyta arranged for Artemis to win the Contest and become the new Wonder Woman. She then dispatched the bow-wielding Amazon to Man's World in Diana's place. The warlike, hot-headed Artemis was totally unsuited to the role of diplomat, and was Wonder Woman for only a short time before she was murdered by the White Magician.

Rescued from Hades by Diana, who reclaimed her title as Wonder Woman, Artemis briefly joined a group of demon hunters named the Hellenders. After the Amazon civil war, Artemis became the Shim'Tar, or champion, of her people. Artemis helped command the assault when Hippolyta ordered the Amazonian invasion of Washington DC. As punishment, Artemis and other Amazons were sentenced to live as mortals. **PJ**

ARTEMIS III

FIRST APPEARANCE SUICIDE SQUAD (1st series) #35 (November 1989)
STATUS Villain **REAL NAME** None
OCCUPATION Adventurer **BASE** Apokolips
HEIGHT 6ft 3in **WEIGHT** 189 lbs **EYES** Brown **HAIR** Black
SPECIAL POWERS/ABILITIES Furious fighter and an archer with unerring aim; commands pack of cybernetic warhounds.

The origins of Artemis are known only to herself and perhaps GRANNY GOODNESS, who recruited and trained the deadly archer for DARKSEID's FEMALE FURIES. Artemis initially joined this elite squad as a temporary replacement for Lashina, who had been stranded on Earth following a struggle with the SUICIDE SQUAD. Artemis remained a Female Fury and has since battled SUPERBOY and SUPERGIRL during the Furies' assaults upon Earth under Darkseid's or Granny's direct dispatch. Although highly skilled in hand-to-hand combat, Artemis's main role in the Female Furies is as a huntress, scenting out foes with her cybernetically augmented warhounds and delivering a killing strike with one of the many devastating arrows in her quiver. **SB**

ARUNA

FIRST APPEARANCE BATGIRL ANNUAL #1 (2000)
STATUS Hero **REAL NAME** Unrevealed
OCCUPATION Stuntperson **BASE** Madras, India
HEIGHT 6ft 10in **WEIGHT** 153 lbs **EYES** Brown **HAIR** Black
SPECIAL POWERS/ABILITIES Born with the ability to shift her shape and features; can imitate other humans perfectly.

Aruna Shende is the alias for a superpowered shape shifter who works as a stuntperson in the Indian film industry. Shende was born a shape shifter, so his/her parents never knew what gender their child truly was. Shende and his/her parents, "untouchables" by caste, lived in the slums of Madras, India.

One day, Shende's parents were taken away by mysterious men, never to be seen again. Devastated, Shende traveled from city to city, using his/her shapechanging abilities to steal food and procure whatever work was available. One day, Shende overheard a conversation about a film being made and joined the cast and crew. A man Shende once worked for named him/her

SHAPE This is Aruna in her usual form (above) but the shape shifter can appear in almost any size or shape.

"Aruna," and Shende kept the name, gaining a reputation as an actor and stuntperson in the Indian film industry. After an adventure with BATGIRL, where the two saved a young boy who'd been kidnapped, Aruna found him/herself intoxicated by the desire to help others, and vowed to use his/her shapeshifting powers to make a difference in his/her own country. **RG**

ARYAN BRIGADE

FIRST APPEARANCE JUSTICE LEAGUE TASK FORCE #10 (March 1994)
STATUS Villain team **BASE** Pine Heights, Nebraska
MEMBERS AND POWERS
Backlash Whip-like extendible arms.
Blind Faith Blind telepath with supernatural tracking abilities.
Golden Eagle II Soaring flight on mechanical wings.
Heatmonger Can fire jets of flame.
Iron Cross Superhuman strength.

SINGLE MINDED *Convinced of the rightness of their cause, the Aryan Brigade would have exterminated most of the globe if not stopped by the Justice League.*

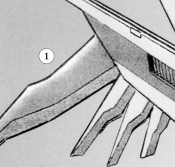

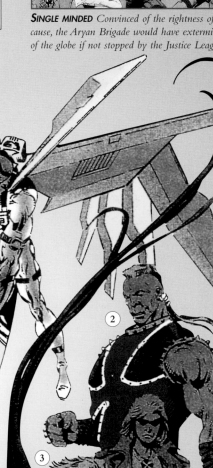

Heir to the pernicious "master race" rhetoric that inspired AXIS AMERIKA and other superpowered minions of Adolf Hitler, the Aryan Brigade are a modern incarnation of a Nazi ideology thought defeated more than half a century ago. The team's five meta-humans—the tentacled Backlash, the winged Golden Eagle II, the brutish Iron Cross, the sightless telepath Blind Faith, and the incendiary Heatmonger—act as enforcers for the clandestine white supremacist movement known as the Aryan Nation.

Senator Sanders Hotchkins once led the Aryan Nation and schemed to release a genetically-tailored virus in the upper atmosphere that would kill every non-white on the planet. The Justice League Task Force (see JUSTICE LEAGUE OF AMERICA) infiltrated Hotchkins' Nebraska headquarters but fell afoul of the Aryan Brigade, whose powers were sufficient to subdue even J'onn J'onzz, the mighty MARTIAN MANHUNTER. Only Rex Tyler, the Golden Age HOURMAN, remained free to battle the ideologues whose kind he had fought so hard to defeat during World War II. While J'onn J'onzz steered the plague-carrying missile into the safety of deep space, Hourman confronted Senator Hotchkins, who accidentally infected himself with the deadly virus. He died from its effects, discovering too late that he was not of pure Aryan blood.

The Aryan Brigade somehow survived this debacle and became members of the OVERMASTER's gigantic CADRE. They failed in that ambitious endeavor but reassembled as a team and eventually returned to be protectors of the Aryan Nation. **DW**

SUPREMACIST SCREED *The racist Aryan Brigade strongly disliked having to work alongside those of the Overmaster's servants who happened to be non-white in the latest incarnation of the Cadre. When it comes to fanatical devotion to Nazi dogma, the Aryan Brigade are utterly inflexible, and totally unforgiving.*
1) *Golden Eagle II* **2)** *Iron Cross* **3)** *Backlash*
4) *Blind Faith* **5)** *Heatmonger*

ASMODEL

FIRST APPEARANCE JLA #7 (July 1997)
STATUS Villain **REAL NAME** Asmodel
OCCUPATION Angel **BASE** Heaven
HEIGHT 10ft **WEIGHT** 800 lbs **EYES** Red **HAIR** Brown
SPECIAL POWERS/ABILITIES Wields a flaming staff and is immortal and invulnerable, with vast superstrength, superspeed, a devastating cry, acidic blood, and flying ability. He has few rivals as a military commander.

In Heaven, the angel Asmodel was formerly the Lord Harrier of the Bull Host, and Commander of the Cherubim Alpha Battalion. He was the highest ranked and most feared of the Pax Dei, the Angel Army of Heaven, but grew tired of simply being a servant of God. Rebelling as Lucifer had millennia before, Asmodel waged war against the forces of Heaven. He was eventually defeated by the guardian angel ZAURIEL and the JUSTICE LEAGUE OF AMERICA in a confrontation in the skies above San Francisco.

Stripped of his rank and consigned to Hell, Asmodel joined forces with Etrigan the DEMON in an attempt to overthrow the demon NERON. Asmodel usurped the power of the SPECTRE and led Hell's demonic forces to Earth. But the Spectre force-bonded with Hal Jordan, the former GREEN LANTERN, and the demons of Hell returned to their vile dimension. Asmodel was placed in the custody of the angels of Heaven, refusing to accept the appellation "fallen." **PJ**

28

ATLAN

FIRST APPEARANCE ATLANTIS CHRONICLES #5 (July 1990)
STATUS Unresolved **REAL NAME** Atlan
OCCUPATION Sorceror **BASE** Atlantis
HEIGHT 6ft 3in **WEIGHT** 220 lbs **EYES** Blue **HAIR** Blond
SPECIAL POWERS/ABILITIES Master of dark arts long forgotten by his people; developed a potion that allowed Atlanteans to live on land for extended periods of time, prolonging their lives; now survives as a spirit of unpredictable temperament and vast magical powers.

Long ago, Atlan was one of three children born to Atlantis's King Honsu and his queen Lorelei (the others were Haumond and Kraken). As he grew, Atlan's hair turned blond, and many believed this to mean he carried the curse of Kordax the destroyer. For a while, he was banished from the city of Poseidonis. When he returned home, Atlan told of life above the surface. His revelations led Honsu to invade the surface world.

Recently, Atlan's spirit visited Atlanna, Queen of Atlantis, impregnating her. The child, Orin, was born with blond hair and abandoned because of this. He grew to become Atlantis's king and the world's hero, AQUAMAN. Atlan then sired another child with an Eskimo woman. The child, Orm Marius, was destined to battle Orin as the OCEAN MASTER. Atlan has also gifted Aquaman's adopted son Garth, now known as TEMPEST, with formidable mystical abilities. RG

MAGICAL *The most powerful and influential person in Atlantean history, Atlan has played a key role in pivotal moments.*

ATLAS

FIRST APPEARANCE First Issue Special #1 (April 1975)
STATUS Hero **REAL NAME** None
OCCUPATION Champion **BASE** Hyssa
HEIGHT 6ft 5in **WEIGHT** 250 lbs **EYES** Blue **HAIR** Brown
SPECIAL POWERS/ABILITIES Superhuman strength.

In ancient times, in a faraway land, the mighty hero Atlas became a champion of the oppressed in his struggle against the despotic King Hyssa. As a youth, Atlas had been one of the peaceful people of the Crystal Mountain until Hyssa's raiders attacked his village. Burning Atlas's home to the ground, killing his father, and capturing everyone he knew or cared about, Hyssa unwittingly made a powerful enemy that would pursue him for years.

Wearing a mystical crystal talisman struck from the Crystal Mountain, Atlas escaped from the slavers and found a new home with a good-hearted man named Chagra. It was not long before Chagra realized the boy possessed jaw-dropping muscle. He became Atlas's manager and accompanied him on his journeys, watching his new hero rescue citizens and defeat evil princes. Finally arriving in the capital city of Hyssa, Atlas touted his strength in the marketplace, where he fought challengers one-on-one. It is unknown whether Atlas eventually succeeded in taking his revenge on the sinister King Hyssa. DW

ATMOS

FIRST APPEARANCE Legion of Super-Heroes (3rd series) #32 (1987)
STATUS Hero **REAL NAME** Marak Russen
OCCUPATION Uncanny Amazer; former athlete
BASE The planet Xanthu in the 31st century
HEIGHT 6ft 7in **WEIGHT** 220 lbs **EYES** White **HAIR** Red
SPECIAL POWERS/ABILITIES Nuclear-based powers include superstrength, speed, and flight; projects powerful nuclear bolts from his hands; generates a protective force field; can survive unaided in the vacuum of space.

In one timeline of the Legion of Super-Heroes, Atmos is a member of the 31st century Uncanny Amazers of Xanthu. The Uncanny Amazers were Xanthu's counterpart to the Earth-based LEGION OF SUPER-HEROES and were funded by Xanthu's government.

A child media star and a talented amateur athlete, Marak Russen was chosen by the Tribune of Xanthu as a potential replacement for STAR BOY when the latter hero was inducted into the Legion of Super-Heroes. Russen was subjected to a series of Tribune experiments that transformed him into a living nuclear reactor. The nuclear-powered Russen is now the Amazers' most powerful member, and stood by them when the alien race known as the BLIGHT took over Xanthu and nearly decimated the planet. Soon after, C.O.M.P.U.T.O.'s machine world of Robotica attacked Xanthu and destroyed the planet, but not before Atmos and the Amazers were able to evacuate its populace.

Accepting the Tribune's assignment at first for the celebrity status it would impart on him, Atmos has nonetheless become a powerful hero in his own right, and an honorable champion of his homeworld. PJ

ATOM

THE MIGHTY MITE

FIRST APPEARANCE (ATOM I) ALL-AMERICAN COMICS #19 (October 1940)
STATUS Hero (deceased) **REAL NAME** Al Pratt
OCCUPATION Professor of Nuclear Physics **BASE** Calvin College
HEIGHT 5ft 1in **WEIGHT** 150 lbs **EYES** Blue **HAIR** Red
SPECIAL POWERS/ABILITIES Skilled in the "sweet science" of boxing, Al Pratt packed an even mightier punch when he gained atomic strength, which also greatly enhanced his agility and kept him fighting fit many decades later.

FIRST APPEARANCE (ATOM II) SHOWCASE #34 (October 1961)
STATUS Hero **REAL NAME** Raymond "Ray" Palmer
OCCUPATION Professor of Physics **BASE** Ivy Town
HEIGHT 6ft **WEIGHT** 180 lbs **EYES** Brown **HAIR** Auburn
SPECIAL POWERS/ABILITIES Can shrink to any size, no matter how miniscule, either retaining the heft of his original 180 pounds or weighing next to nothing. He has mastered fighting techniques at various sizes. At sub-atomic size, the Atom can travel virtually anywhere on Earth via telephone transmissions, surfing microwaves or other electronic impulses.

FIRST APPEARANCE (ATOM III) DCU: Brave New World (2006)
STATUS Hero **REAL NAME** Ryan Choi
OCCUPATION Professor of physics **BASE** Ivy Town
HEIGHT 5 ft 8 in **EYES** Black **HAIR** Black
SPECIAL POWERS/ABILITIES Similar shrinking powers to those of Ray Palmer, powered by a size-changing belt.

AL PRATT WAS A "98-POUND WEAKLING" until he met former boxing champ Joe Morgan. Morgan transformed the young man into a "little superman" in less than a year, putting the pint-sized Pratt through a grueling exercise regime and increasing his weight. While Morgan groomed Pratt for a featherweight boxing career, his pupil had other plans. Pratt became the Atom, a diminutive costumed crime fighter with a formidable punch. A member of the JUSTICE SOCIETY OF AMERICA and ALL-STAR SQUADRON, the Mighty Mite gained atomic strength and agility in 1948 as a result of radiation exposure during a battle with Cyclotron, a scientist forced into crime by the evil ULTRA-HUMANITE. Later married to his sweetheart Mary, Pratt never hesitated to take his fighting togs out of mothballs if the need arose. Tragically, while aiding the JSA during the Zero Hour crisis (see Great Battles, pp. 362–3), the Atom died battling the villain EXTANT. Unknown to Pratt, a son—the young atomic-powered hero DAMAGE—survives him.

LITTLE BIG MAN
Al Pratt punches above his weight in his first outing.

PART-TIMER
Ray Palmer preferred to be an auxiliary member of the JLA so he could continue his studies at Ivy University.

ATOM II

When Ivy University physicist Ray Palmer discovered a fragment of a white dwarf star, he believed he had found the key to success in his size-reduction experiments. Before Palmer could test the star fragment, he was trapped in a cave with a group of youngsters while on a nature outing. Palmer used the fragment and his size-reducing lens to find an escape route from the cave. Somehow, mineral-infused water in the cave and other factors combined with the reducing materials to allow Palmer to shrink safely. Palmer then fashioned a costume that would shrink and enlarge with him, and only appear when he was less than six inches tall. He also devised reducing controls which he placed on his gloves. Thus outfitted, he became the second super hero to call himself the Atom, a Tiny Titan packing a 180-pound punch at any size.

Tragedy struck when an insane Jean Loring killed Sue Dibny (wife of the ELONGATED MAN) in order to win back Ray's affections. With his ex-wife committed to Arkham Asylum, Ray disappeared into the microverse to escape his emotional pain. At infinitesimal size he discovered a way to slip between dimensions, hopping among parallel worlds until finding a home on Earth-51. There, he assumed the identity of Earth-51's late Ray Palmer, until called back to prevent a foretold Great Disaster.

During Ray's absence, a new Atom took the stage. Ryan Choi, a junior professor at Ivy University, used his mentor's size-changing belt to explore the weird mysteries of Ivy Town. Despite his inexperience, Ryan received an invitation to join the Justice League of America. SB/DW

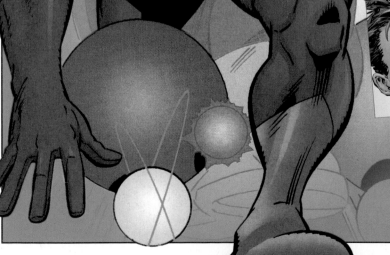

RYAN CHOI *The third Atom jumped into the role with enthusiasm, tackling everything from sewer monsters to vengeful ghosts while dating Giganta, teaming up with Wonder Woman, and somehow finding time to teach class.*

KEY STORYLINES
• *ZERO HOUR #3 (SEPTEMBER 1994):* The Atom I perishes alongside his JSA teammate Hourman I in an attempt to stop Extant's timestream tamperings.
• *THE ATOM #1 (JULY 1962):* The Atom II first battles the Plant Master (The Floronic Man).
• *SWORD OF THE ATOM #1 (SEPTEMBER 1983):* In the South American jungle, Ray Palmer befriends the alien Katarthans and becomes their sword-wielding super-heroic defender!

ATOMIC KNIGHT

FIRST APPEARANCE STRANGE ADVENTURES #117 (June 1960)
STATUS Hero **REAL NAME** Gardner Grayle
OCCUPATION Protector **BASE** S.T.A.R. Labs, Alexandria, Virginia
HEIGHT 6ft 1in **WEIGHT** 189 lbs **EYES** Blue **HAIR** Red
SPECIAL POWERS/ABILITIES Battlesuit enables Grayle to imprison enemies in a stasis field; attached weapon fires powerful bursts of heat or cold; suit's solar power cells operate even in the reduced light of a nuclear winter. Grayle is courageous, with some precognitive powers.

S.T.A.R. Labs needed a test subject as they made contingencies for a nuclear holocaust. They chose Army Sergeant Gardner Grayle, who believed atomic weapons gave war a bad name. When the would-be universe-conqueror AGAMEMNO threatened the planet Rann, Grayle was urged to suit up in the Lab's prototype armor. He served as one of the SEVEN SOLDIERS OF VICTORY, taking the name of original member SHINING KNIGHT. Grayle later tested the armor within a virtual reality that went awry, and needed aid from SUPERMAN. Grayle's long time in sensory deprivation allowed his mind to develop beyond normal limits, and he predicted many future crises. He took the name Atomic Knight and resolved to help protect the world. Grayle currently operates out of the ruins of Blüdhaven, while another version of the Atomic Knights exists on Earth 17. **RG**

ATOMIC SKULL

FIRST APPEARANCE ACTION COMICS #670 (October 1991)
STATUS Villain **REAL NAME** Joe Martin
OCCUPATION Student turned super-villain **BASE** Metropolis
HEIGHT 6ft **WEIGHT** 185 lbs **EYES** Black **HAIR** None
SPECIAL POWERS/ABILITIES Superstrength, enhanced speed and endurance; can fire fiery radiation blasts.

University of Metropolis film student Joe Martin saw his latent metagene activated during the allied alien invasion of Earth. Transformed into a radiation-seething monster with transparent skin, making it seem as if he had a flaming skull for a head, the delirious Martin came to believe that he was an old movie serial hero named "the Atomic Skull." Martin believed Superman to be the Atomic Skull's archenemy Dr. Electron, and battled him accordingly; nothing could shake Martin of his delusion. During the supernatural crisis known as Underworld Unleashed, the Atomic Skull gained improved powers from the demon NERON in exchange for his eternal soul. He is still active in villainy, usually pitting himself against Superman. He prefers to travel on a flying Skull-Bike, sometimes seeking out Lois Lane (see LANE, LOIS), who resembles the late Eleanor Hart from the Atomic Skull pictures of the 1930s.

Although he didn't know it, Joe Martin was actually the *second* villain to take the name Atomic Skull. The first, Dr. Albert Michaels of S.T.A.R. Labs, briefly assumed the identity after gaining energy powers from the SKULL criminal syndicate. **DW**

AUCTIONEER, THE

FIRST APPEARANCE ACTION COMICS #841 (September 2006)
STATUS Galactic menace **REAL NAME** Unknown
OCCUPATION Merchandise broker and auctioneer
BASE Mobile **HEIGHT** Unknown **WEIGHT** Unknown
EYES Red **HAIR** None
SPECIAL POWERS/ABILITIES Enhanced strength due to vast size; shrewd negotiator.

The Auctioneer is an immense, vastly powerful alien being with a mania for collecting and resale. Plugged into hundreds of galactic buying networks, the Auctioneer uses his robotic staff to monitor interstellar commerce, keep tabs on his best customers, and forward leads on the locations of exotic treasures. His starship is the size of a city, with storage capacity to house entire buildings.

When the Auctioneer took an interest in Earth, he snapped up monuments from the Eiffel Tower to the Golden Gate bridge until opposed by SUPERMAN. Viewing the Kryptonian as the greatest prize of all, he captured Superman and other metahumans for sale at auction. The Man of Steel allied with SKYROCKET, the VETERAN, NIGHTWING, the new AQUAMAN (Arthur Joseph Curry) and others to escape. After Superman threatened to release the Auctioneer's private database, the alien withdrew. **DW**

ATOM-SMASHER

FIRST APPEARANCE (as Nuklon) ALL-STAR SQUADRON #25 (September 1983); (as Atom-Smasher) JSA Secret Files and Origins #1 (August 1999)
STATUS Undecided **REAL NAME** Albert Julian Rothstein
OCCUPATION Car designer, repairman **BASE** New York City
HEIGHT 7ft 6in **WEIGHT** 297 lbs **EYES** Blue **HAIR** Red
SPECIAL POWERS/ABILITIES Can manipulate his body size, growing up to 60ft high, and weighing up to 34,950 lbs; increased density gives him low-level invulnerability; can phase through solid objects.

Due to the genetic effects of his mother Terri's radiation poisoning, Al Rothstein developed superstrength and grew to over seven feet tall during his teenage years. Along with several other children and protégés of the JUSTICE SOCIETY OF AMERICA, Al founded a team of heroes called INFINITY, INC. and called himself Nuklon. He later developed the ability to double his size or phase through solid matter unharmed.

Nuklon subsequently joined the CONGOLMERATE and then briefly the JUSTICE LEAGUE OF AMERICA. After being dismissed from the JLA, Nuklon changed his name to Atom-Smasher and was recruited by WILDCAT I to join the new JSA, thereby fulfilling Al's lifelong dream. When Atom-Smasher's mother was murdered by the terrorist KOBRA in a bombing attack, Atom-Smasher managed to alter the past so that the villain EXTANT died in his mother's place. During a final confrontation with Kobra, Atom-Smasher helped Black Adam murder the villain. Imprisoned for his actions in Khandaq, Atom-Smasher joined the SUICIDE SQUAD and fought his former ally, Black Adam. Atom-Smasher secretly helped Adam evade capture. **PJ**

SKYSCRAPER *Able to grow to the height of a six-story building, Atom-Smasher's strength and endurance grows in proportion!*

BLACK ADAM *Confounded by the loss in his life, Atom-Smasher joined his former enemy Black Adam in a paramilitary team that invaded the Middle Eastern country of Khandaq.*

A

The DC Comics Encyclopedia

AXIS AMERICA

First appearance YOUNG ALL-STARS #1 (June 1987)
Status Villain team **Base** Unknown
Current Members and Powers
Fleshburn Can emit blasts of atomic fire.
Great White Armed with an electrified whip and a whalebone gauntlet blade.
Hel (Vela Shepherd) A winged, Valkyrie-like warrior who wields an energized battleaxe.
Ubermensch (Mr. Shepherd) Superstrong, bulletproof juggernaut. Scimitar-wielding wraith cloaked in his demon bride Baal; a teleporter.

The original Axis Amerika was a brigade of bio-genetically augmented spies and saboteurs formed by the Axis powers (Nazi Germany, Imperial Japan, and Fascist Italy) during World War II to undermine American homeland security. Its members included the Nazi superman UBERMENSCH, Valkyrie warrior Gudra, the father-and-son team of the Horned Owl and Fledermaus, the living missile Kamikaze, aquatic lycanthrope Sea Wolf, and archer Usil. Fledermaus was killed in battle with the YOUNG ALL-STARS. The fates of the remaining members are undocumented.

In modern times, a team of superpowered American supremacists united as an equally formidable Axis America. After besting and nearly discrediting the JUSTICE LEAGUE OF AMERICA, Axis America escaped to continue fomenting its extremist agenda. **SB**

AXIS OF EVIL The JLA thought it was negotiating the end to a standoff between a group of superpowered separatists and U.S. government agencies seeking their surrender. In truth, Axis America plotted to frame the heroes for the manslaughter of thousands as prelude to their own rise to power and public acceptance. **1)** Hel **2)** Zaladin **3)** Ubermensch **4)** Great White **5)** Fleshburn

AZAZEL

First appearance SANDMAN (2nd series) #4 (April 1989)
Status Demon **Real name** Azazel
Occupation A ruler in Hell **Base** Hell
Height Variable **Weight** Variable **Eyes** Variable **Hair** Variable
Special powers/abilities Commands mystic and eldritch forces that allow him to reshape matter or eradicate a demon from existence.

The Bible says that Azazel is either a fallen angel or the goat that Aaron placed the Hebrews' sins upon and then set free in the desert (hence the term scapegoat). The Hebrews also consider him the demon of war who taught humans how to build weapons (and to use cosmetics for an all-together different kind of war). To the Muslims, he is the angel who refused to worship Adam and was cast out. John Milton immortalized him in his *Paradise Lost*, naming Azazel the standard bearer of the rebel angels. He is also one of the Triumvirate in Hell's Hierarchy, serving alongside Lucifer Morningstar and BEELZEBUB. Azazel has battled the likes of Etrigan the DEMON in the never-ending struggle for supremacy in the lower dimensions. The mortal John Constantine outwitted all three members of the hierarchy, earning him Azazel's eternal enmity. As infernal politics stand, Azazel is secondary to Lucifer. When Lucifer closed Hell for a time, Azazel tried to claim it as his own and failed, winding up trapped in the SANDMAN II's endless realm of the Dreaming. However, as one of the underworld's most powerful entities, he is not to be underestimated. **RG**

AZTEK

First appearance AZTEK: THE ULTIMATE MAN #1 (August 1996)
Status Hero (deceased) **Real Name** Uno
Occupation Hero; doctor **Base** Vanity City
Height 6ft 2in **Weight** 185 lbs **Eyes** Blue **Hair** Blond
Special powers/abilities Helmet-controlled battlesuit gives him superstrength, superspeed, superhearing, telescopic vision, X-ray vision, infrared vision, invisibility, density control, and flight.

The Azteks are a group of armored warriors created by the mysterious Q Foundation, a secret society of scientists and religious practitioners. The Foundation was formed to prepare a human vessel for the return of the benevolent Aztec serpent-god Quetzalcoatl, who was engaged in a constant cosmic struggle with his evil brother Tezcatlipoca. Housed in many secret bases around the world, the Q Foundation created their fourth-dimensional Aztek warsuits to be worn by specially trained heroes in preparation for the great battle between the gods.

When Uno took on the Aztek title, he relocated from Mexico to Vanity City in the U.S. and assumed the identity of Dr. Curt Falconer. After battling several super-villains in Vanity City, Falconer was invited by SUPERMAN, BATMAN, and GREEN LANTERN to join the latest incarnation of the JUSTICE LEAGUE OF AMERICA. Only the telepathic MARTIAN MANHUNTER voiced doubts.

Falconer soon discovered that the Q Foundation had been partially financed in recent years by the

AZTEK ARMOR *Powered by fourth-dimensional energy, Aztek's suit is recharged by magical rituals and intricate technologies.*

POWER STRUGGLE *While Aztek preferred to fight with his mind rather than his fists, he used all the powers of his amazing battlesuit to stop a rampaging Amazo, a villain with the combined powers of the entire JLA!*

villainous business mogul Lex Luthor (see LUTHOR, LEX), who had hoped to create his own hero to infiltrate the JLA. The well-meaning Aztek realized that he had become the unwitting dupe of Lex Luthor and was being manipulated by forces beyond his control.

Horrified by the ruse and believing much of his life to be a lie, Aztek resigned from the venerable team. Later, assuming the power of his battlesuit once more, Aztek fought alongside his former allies in the JLA and died valiantly during their conflict with MAGEDDON, the celestial warbringer. **PJ**

AZRAEL

THE AVENGING ANGEL

FIRST APPEARANCE BATMAN: SWORD OF AZRAEL #1 (October 1992)
STATUS Hero **REAL NAME** Jean Paul Valley
OCCUPATION Adventurer **BASE** Ossaville
HEIGHT 6ft 2in **WEIGHT** 210 lbs **EYES** Blue **HAIR** Blond
SPECIAL POWERS/ABILITIES Physically and psychologically programmed by scientists of the Order of St. Dumas to be an assassin; superb combat skills, great strength, speed, and agility; powers triggered by putting on special costume and using the name "Azrael."

AS A GOTHAM UNIVERSITY STUDENT, Jean Paul Valley had no inkling of the larger forces acting on his life. But when his dying father revealed the truth, Jean Paul willingly took up the mantle of Azrael, the champion assassin of a Crusades-era fraternity of warrior-priests, the ORDER OF ST. DUMAS. In modern times, the Order had become a secret society with few members but uncountable riches. For centuries the "avenging angel Azrael" had been their silent enforcer—actually an Order member trained from birth to silence those who failed to observe the Order's strict code of secrecy. The role of Azrael was passed down from father to son, and Jean Paul suddenly realized he was heir to a long tradition. His life as the shadowy avenger Azrael would last for many years. Throughout this time, conflicting feelings toward the role that had been forced on him before he was even born plunged him into bouts of severe depression. His costume would also undergo a number of changes in design and equipment, the better to reflect the various alterations in his emotional state.

TEST-TUBE HORROR Jean Paul's biological mother was horrified to discover that the egg she had donated to the Order of St. Dumas had been appropriated for a scientific program. The Order's fanatical scientists were busily mingling the fetus's genetic makeup with animal DNA to create a being of great strength capable of killing without remorse. The poor mother was condemned to die, but escaped thanks to a merciful priest, and has remained in hiding ever since.

THE SYSTEM
In Switzerland, Jean Paul trained under the dwarf Nomoz, who triggered the deep hypnotic implants that Jean Paul had been unaware he possessed. "The System," a regimen of hypnosis and prenatal conditioning, turned Jean Paul Valley into a formidable fighter.

He tested his new skills on BATMAN, who had travelled to Switzerland on the trail of the St. Dumas renegade Carleton LeHah. As Azrael, Jean Paul lost the fight—but he nevertheless rescued Bruce Wayne from LeHah. Jean Paul then returned to Gotham City and continued his training as Azrael under Robin's guidance.

When the villainous Bane broke Batman's back, Jean Paul briefly took over as Gotham City's Dark Knight. He designed a new, Azrael-inspired bat costume with heavy armor, razor talons, and hidden weapons. Though he defeated Bane, he lost his internal struggle against the hypnotic goading of the System. Jean Paul became increasingly violent and finally lost his mind. Bruce Wayne, restored to full fitness, defeated him and reclaimed the mantle of Batman. Jean Paul, after a period of misery and soul-searching, became Azrael once more.

Azrael moved against the Order's scientists who originally brainwashed him, culminating in a battle inside the Order of St. Dumas' headquarters, the Ice Cathedral. The destruction of the Cathedral wiped out the last traces of the Order. Jean Paul, however, did not live long enough to enjoy the fruits of his success—he apparently perished in a shootout, ending the career of Gotham's angel of vengeance. **DW**

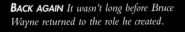

BACK AGAIN It wasn't long before Bruce Wayne returned to the role he created.

IMAGE CHANGES Doubts over his Azrael role have led Jean Paul to revamp his warsuit several times.

KEY STORYLINES

- **BATMAN #500 (OCTOBER 1993):** Jean Paul Valley donned the Azrael/Bat armor for the first time and embarked on a career as Gotham's new Batman.
- **AZRAEL: AGENT OF THE BAT #100 (MAY 2003):** Azrael's life as a costumed vigilante came to a violent end when Jean Paul was seemingly killed.

AMAZING VEHICLES

NOT ALL HEROES can fly unaided or run at lightspeed. From Batman's Batmobile, which evolved from armored sedan into all-terrain tank, to WONDER WOMAN's invisible plane, an alien craft cloaked from Earthly technology, some of the world's greatest adventurers have the help of extraordinary vehicles. This fleet, created with magic or science (or both), are primed to sweep their owners to their destinations.

BATMOBILE
Equipped with a satellite dish for TV/radio/GPS linkage, anti-theft gas, hypersonic trilling sphere, gas nozzles, voice-activated controls, and gel-filled kevlar-reinforced wheels that are puncture and flame-resistant, the Batmobile has undergone many transformations over the years.

It remains one of the greatest weapons in Batman's arsenal, a sleek, fearful machine with no parallel for speed or maneuverability, even among the world's fastest race cars.

Able to attain speeds of 266 m.p.h., accelerate from 0 to 60 m.p.h. in under 3 seconds, and shielded in a bulletproof ceramic composite exterior, the Batmobile is almost as frightening to criminals as its legendary driver, who know they have little chance for escape from either.

BAT SECURITY *The Batmobile is equipped with security devices, including an electrified hull, hypersonic shrieks, and a self-destruct mechanism.*

JUSTICE SOCIETY OF AMERICA'S SHUTTLE CRAFT BOX
When the alien marauder IMPERIEX came to reignite the Big Bang, President Lex Luthor (*see* LUTHOR, LEX) sent every member of the JUSTICE SOCIETY OF AMERICA on a space mission to save the planet. The JSA rocketed across the galaxy in their Star Racer space shuttle, defeated IMPERIEX and his probes, and saved the populace of Daxam (*see* Alien Races, pp. 166–7) from Imperiex's planet-sized ship.

The Star Racer is outfitted with protective shields, offensive weaponry, and warp-drive capabilities, and is paid for and maintained with monies left by the Dodd estate.

STAR RACER *The JSA's Star Racer can warp across galaxies, outfitted with technology from Earth and Thanagar. The Star Spangled Kid drove a flying car called the Star Rocket Racer, which was an inspiration for the Star Racer.*

BAT PLANE
A stealth fighter craft capable of speeds of 4,400 m.p.h., the Batplane slices through the skies faster than any military war craft.

ROBIN'S BIKES
The Supercycle isn't Robin's only specialized vehicle. While his primary mode of transportation is a customized sports coupé called the Redbird, Robin also rides a modified 491 c.c., liquid cooled, "motocross" Batcycle. One of many motorcycles in Batman's vehicular arsenal, the Batcycle's chassis and windshield are bulletproof. Capable of speeds of over 130 m.p.h., and armed with specialized shock dampers, the cycle is one of the sleekest machines on the road.

WONDER WOMAN'S INVISIBLE JET

A morphing, nearly invisible plane created by the alien Lansanarians, Wonder Woman's transparent transport is capable of changing into any number of shapes, from a fully submersible submarine to a spaceworthy chariot. Soon after accepting this incredible gift, Wonder Woman discovered that her invisible plane was a techno-organic alien from a world called the Ring. Queen HIPPOLYTA used the plane during her time as Wonder Woman, and after the destruction of Themyscira during the Imperiex War (*see* Great Battles, pp. 362–3), Wonder Woman used its miraculous technology to infuse the island with wondrous, new, morphing architecture that conformed to the Amazons' every requirement.

ALIEN PLANE *As Wonder Woman, Hippolyta flew the Invisible Plane over the skies of the U.S. and Europe during World War II.*

MANTA SHIP

A sleek submarine shaped like a giant manta ray, the sinister-looking Manta Ship is the villainous Black Manta's underwater headquarters. Capable of submerging to extreme depths, Black Manta uses this atomic-powered vehicle for piracy and salvage.

THE SUPERCYCLE

Created by the FOREVER PEOPLE and originally piloted by BIG BEAR, the miraculous, superfast Supercycle was built with New Genesis (*see* NEW GODS) technology and is equipped with weapons, a cloaking device that renders it invisible, and density-altering capability. It can even teleport across dimensions. For a time, YOUNG JUSTICE used the Supercycle as their transport vehicle, The Supercycle is now telepathically controlled by Robin.

BLUE BEETLE'S BUG

A solar-powered hovercraft piloted by Ted Kord (BLUE BEETLE II), the Bug is a floating headquarters armed with magnetic impulse beams, electro charges, and claw-like landing gear. It is also able to fly at speeds of over 600 m.p.h. **PJ**

BAD SAMARITAN

FIRST APPEARANCE THE OUTSIDERS (1st series) #3 (January 1986)
STATUS Villain **REAL NAME** Unknown
OCCUPATION Agent provocateur **BASE** Mobile
HEIGHT 6ft 2in **WEIGHT** 190 lbs
EYES Unknown (hidden by dark glasses) **HAIR** Black
SPECIAL POWERS/ABILITIES Is a superb hand-to-hand combatant and ruthless assassin; is both a master of disguise and covert espionage.

The Bad Samaritan is a spy-for-hire, a terrorist, or an insurrectionist, depending on his paymaster. His country of origin remains a mystery, and he claims allegiance to no particular organization, sovereign, or country. He has plied his trade for the U.S., the U.K., the former Soviet Union, and many other governments, although each will disavow any knowledge of covert operations involving him. While in the U.S.S.R.'s employ, the Bad Samaritan helped the Soviet government to obtain important information on meta-humans—the OUTSIDERS and the Force of July in particular—to help the Communists to create a Soviet super-team of their own. Later, the Bad Samaritan shot down a plane carrying the Outsiders, leaving its member heroes stranded on an island somewhere in the Indian Ocean. The Bad Samaritan has recently joined the ranks of the United Nations peacekeeping operation CHECKMATE, acting as the White Queen's bishop. **SB**

BALLOON BUSTER

FIRST APPEARANCE ALL-AMERICAN MEN OF WAR #112 (December 1965)
STATUS Hero (deceased) **REAL NAME** Steve Henry Savage, Jr.
OCCUPATION Lieutenant, U.S. Army Air Corps **BASE** France
HEIGHT 5ft 11in **WEIGHT** 178 lbs **EYES** Blue **HAIR** Blond
SPECIAL POWERS/ABILITIES A matchless marksman with any firearm, and an accomplished biplane pilot.

The son of legendary cowboy hero Brian "Scalphunter" Savage, Steve was raised in Mustang River, Wyoming, by a poverty-stricken farmer named Jennings.

The boy became a consummate marksman, and he learned that a gun is merely an extension of the man who wields it. At his dying adoptive father's bedside, Steve swore to make the old man proud of him by making Savage a name to be remembered. Enlisting in the U. S. Army Air Corps at the onset of World War I, Savage repeatedly disobeyed orders, breaking formation to attack and destroy German combat balloons, which earned him his nickname. Savage was one of the most aggressive warriors of that "war to end all wars," and he often dueled with the German flying ace Rittmeister Hans Von Hammer. Savage disappeared in South East Asia in 1924 while on an aerial investigation of a supposed dragon, which locals had blamed for a fever outbreak. **RG**

BANE

FIRST APPEARANCE BATMAN: VENGEANCE OF BANE #1 (January 1993)
STATUS Villain **REAL NAME** Unknown
OCCUPATION Adventurer **BASE** Gotham City
HEIGHT 6ft 8in **WEIGHT** 350 lbs
EYES Brown **HAIR** Brown
SPECIAL POWERS/ABILITIES Brilliant strategist and polylinguist, with near-superhuman strength while on the steroid Venom, mainlined into his system via tubing in his helmet.

Bane will forever be remembered as the man who broke the Bat! More than three decades ago, Bane's father received a life sentence from the Santa Priscan government for his role in a failed revolution. He fled the country, but Santa Priscan law demanded that his son take his place. The child that would become Bane was raised inside Pena Duro prison (mostly in a pit called the Cavidad Oscuro). Bane killed dozens of inmates and engineered a jailbreak when experiments with the drug Venom gave him monstrous strength.

Winding up in Gotham City, Bane exhausted BATMAN by freeing all the villains from Arkham Asylum. He then crippled the Dark Knight by snapping his spine. Jean Paul Valley (AZRAEL) donned the Batman garb and beat Bane into a coma.

Bane returned to a life of wickedness, shaking off his dependence on Venom and allying himself with RĀ'S AL GHŪL. After a falling-out with the immortal would-be conqueror, he sabotaged Rā's al Ghūl's network of life-extending Lazarus Pits. After finding his father KING SNAKE, Bane killed JUDOMASTER during the Infinite Crisis, ending a brief period of semi-heroism. He has since led a revolution in Santa Prisca and joined the SUICIDE SQUAD, winding up on a prison planet alongside dozens of other villains. **DW**

CHILDHOOD TRAUMA *In prison, Bane found solace in books and a teddy bear given to him by a Catholic missionary.*

REDEMPTION *Now a blank slate, Bane must decide whether he will be an enemy or an ally in the Batman's future.*

BARD, JASON

First appearance DETECTIVE COMICS #392 (October 1969)
Status Hero **Real name** Jason Bard
Occupation Adventurer **Base** Gotham City
Height 6ft **Weight** 175 lbs **Eyes** Brown **Hair** Brown
Special powers/abilities Above average hand-to-hand fighter, marksman, and criminologist; a superb athlete despite his injury.

Jason Bard's father abandoned the young boy and his mother, Rose, then murdered her. Bard vowed to find him, despite having no physical evidence of his father's existence and no memory of his father's face.

Bard ended up joining the Marines, and was shot and crippled while he was overseas. He returned to the U.S. and entered college on the G.I. Bill, majoring in criminology. He later set up a private investigation firm in Gotham City. There, the intelligent but occasionally cocky Bard began dating Barbara Gordon (later ORACLE). She was the daughter of Gotham's Police Commissioner James Gordon (see GORDON, JAMES W.), and at that time secretly operating as the super heroine BATGIRL.

Bard was temporarily blinded on a case in Rheelasia, a country in South East Asia, but his sight was restored after an experimental operation. He tried once more to pursue Barbara, but this time she rebuffed his romantic overtures. PJ

BARON BLITZKRIEG

First appearance WORLD'S FINEST COMICS #246 (September 1977)
Status Villain **Real name** Reiter (first name unknown)
Occupation Terrorist **Base** Nazi Germany **Height** 6ft 6in
Weight 345 lbs (armored) **Eyes** Blue **Hair** Black
Special powers/abilities Psychic abilities enable Blitzkrieg to control his physical functions. He can channel these functions one at a time, enabling weak heat vision, among other highly useful abilities.

Nazi leader Adolf Hitler rewarded this former Prussian nobleman's loyalty by making him a concentration camp commandant during World War II. A prisoner assaulted Reiter with a vial of acid, which destroyed his features. Despite surgery to repair the damage, Reiter hid his face behind a golden mask. Hitler then tried an experiment, which unleashed the man's latent psychic powers, marking Reiter's first step to becoming a human fighting machine for the Third Reich. Clad in flexible battle armor, Baron Blitzkrieg was born, terrorizing Europe and America, and battling the ALL-STAR SQUADRON. He also had numerous bouts with Queen HIPPOLYTA, the Golden Age Wonder Woman. He had run-ins with Iron Munro and PHANTOM LADY I as the Cold War progressed, and at least one clash with SPY SMASHER in the 1950s.

Now known simply as the Baron, he is one of the world's most dangerous men. He masterminded the terrorist group Shadowspire, responsible for the destruction of the Capitol Building. RG

BAT LASH

First appearance SHOWCASE #76 (August 1968)
Status Hero (deceased) **Real name** Bartholomew Aloysius Lash
Occupation Outlaw/professional gambler
Base American southwest (late 19th century)
Height 5ft 11in **Weight** 167 lbs **Eyes** Blue **Hair** Blond
Special powers/abilities Good with guns, handy with fists, great with cards; could talk his way out of the tightest jam.

Lucky at cards, western hero Bat Lash was often unlucky at life. First his parents' farm was stolen from them by swindlers, then Bat Lash killed a crooked sheriff's deputy in self-defense. When he returned home, he discovered that his mother and father had been murdered and their house burned to the ground. A wanted man, Bat Lash set off across the Mexican border on the trail of the man who had killed his folks.

Despite his unhappy, troubled past, Bat Lash presented himself as a smooth-talking ladies' man, a cowboy dandy with a flower always in his hat. After he had caught up with his parents' killer, Bat Lash roamed the western plains having many adventures.

Around the turn of the century, Bat Lash left America to live in the Far East. In the late 1920s, in the twilight of his life, he joined with adventurer Biff Bradley and Hans von Hammer, the ENEMY ACE, to retrieve two swords from the "Isle of Dragons" (the legendary Dinosaur Island) on behalf of the Chinese leader General Chiang Kai-Shek. The appearance of the dangerous VANDAL SAVAGE further complicated what turned out to be Bat Lash's last recorded adventure. DW

FISTS OF FURY *Although he prefers to charm his way out of trouble, when necessary Bat Lash is perfectly happy to let his fists do the talking.*

BATGIRL

FIRST APPEARANCE BATMAN #567 (July 1999)
STATUS Hero **REAL NAME** Cassandra Cain
OCCUPATION Adventurer **BASE** Gotham City
HEIGHT 5ft 5in **WEIGHT** 127 lbs **EYES** Green **HAIR** Black
SPECIAL POWERS/ABILITIES One of the greatest martial artists in the world; a deadly master of nearly all forms of unarmed combat; can "read" the body language of an opponent and predict their moves.

CASSANDRA CAIN IS THE THIRD YOUNG WOMAN to assume the mantle of Batgirl. A young orphan adopted by the master assassin David Cain (*see* CAIN, DAVID) to become his greatest pupil and heir, Cassandra was his most potent student, but was ultimately uninterested in extending his legacy. Seemingly unable to speak, the young Cassandra "spoke" with her body, and learned how to "read" the body language of those around her. Cain trained her in the world's deadliest martial arts, and the young Cassandra soon made her first kill, a Macauan crime kingpin. Sickened by the act, the mute girl fled Cain's estate and evil influence and began to travel the world, searching for a new home and a new way of life.

THE NEW BATGIRL

Cassandra found her way to Gotham City just before it was devastated by an earthquake and cordoned off from the rest of the U.S. During that time, she was recruited by mysterious computer hacker ORACLE to act as a messenger in the city, now called No Man's Land. Years earlier, Oracle (Barbara Gordon), daughter of Police Commissioner James Gordon (*see* GORDON, JAMES W.), had been the first Batgirl, until she was shot and crippled by the JOKER. When Cain arrived in Gotham on a mission to assassinate Gordon, Cassandra saved the commissioner from her father's bullet. Impressed by Cassandra's skill and bravery, BATMAN took her under his wing and made her the new Batgirl. Still without a voice, Cassandra quickly took to her new role, hoping to atone for the killing of the gangster all those years ago. Soon after, Batgirl saved a psychic named Jeffers, who was on the run from the mob. Jeffers used his powers to reorder Batgirl's brain, giving her the power of speech, but stripping from her many of her martial arts skills. Batgirl began retraining and sought out LADY SHIVA, then the world's greatest martial artist, for a single lesson she hoped would help her remaster her skills. In a second confrontation with Shiva, Batgirl left her opponent for dead. She then assumed leadership of the League of Assassins, and joined other villainous outfits like Titans East. Batgirl has since redeemed herself by becoming a member of Batman's latest team of OUTSIDERS. **PJ**

COMBAT *Barely a child herself, Batgirl is nonetheless a frightening force to behold.*

BODY LANGUAGE *No ordinary criminal or super-villain can hope to hold their own against the martial-arts prowess of Batgirl, who was trained to communicate with her body, not with words.*

KEY STORYLINES

• **BATMAN #556-559 (JULY–OCTOBER 1998):** After the Huntress forsakes her temporary role as Batgirl, a mute young girl named Cassandra Cain emerges and takes up the mantle of Batgirl.
• **BATGIRL #6 (JUNE 2000):** A psychic gives Batgirl the gift of speech, but strips her of some of her fighting skill.
• **BATGIRL #24 (APRIL 2002):** Batgirl and Lady Shiva face off in a duel to the death between the world's two greatest martial artists!
• **BATGIRL #45-50 (DECEMBER 2003–APRIL 2004):** When Doctor Death releases Soul, a rage-inducing pathogen, onto Gotham, Batgirl and Batman are forced into a confrontation spanning half of the city, including the destruction of Sprang Bridge!

BARBARA GORDON
Cassandra Cain was not the first Batgirl. Barbara Gordon, the daughter of Gotham City Police Commissioner James Gordon, dreamed of becoming Batman's partner-in-crime. Thus, Barbara became Batgirl, joining Batman and ROBIN to defend the innocent of the city. After she was crippled by the Joker, Barbara forsook her Batgirl identity and became the information broker Oracle.

BAT-MITE

FIRST APPEARANCE DETECTIVE COMICS #267 (May 1959)
STATUS Undefined **REAL NAME** Unknown
OCCUPATION Troublemaker **BASE** Mobile
HEIGHT 2ft 11in **WEIGHT** 47 lbs **EYES** Black **HAIR** Unknown
SPECIAL POWERS/ABILITIES Possesses various magical powers, including
invisibility, levitation, the animation of inanimate objects, and the
endowment of superpowers to others.

The curious creature known as Bat-Mite claims to be
BATMAN's greatest fan. Winging his way to Earth from a
bizarre alien dimension, he wears a homemade costume
honoring his idol, the Dark Knight. Bat-Mite's utility belt,
unlike that of his hero, contains no useful accoutrements,
but with his various magical powers he needs no tools
or weapons. On his infrequent visits to Earth, Bat-Mite
hugely enjoys watching the Caped Crusader in action.
Unfortunately, Bat-Mite frequently feels compelled to use
his magical abilities to test Batman's fighting prowess and
detective skills. More often than not, the Dark Knight
orders this diminutive, mischief-making imp to go back
to his home dimension until he agrees to behave properly
on Earth. **SB**

BAYTOR

FIRST APPEARANCE DEMON (3rd series) #43 (January 1994)
STATUS Villain **REAL NAME** Baytor
OCCUPATION Demon **BASE** Gotham City
HEIGHT 3ft 11in **WEIGHT** 98 lbs **EYES** Red **HAIR** None
SPECIAL POWERS/ABILITIES Incredibly focused, durable and nearly
invulnerable.

Baytor is a minor
demon who has, on
occasion, allied himself
with Etrigan (DEMON).
Like most demons, he
is always looking for a chance to
improve his lot in Hell. When
he briefly obtained the Crown
of Horns, he proclaimed himself ruler of Hell. Needless
to say, it did not work out. After his attempted coup had
failed, Baytor escaped from Hell, hiding in the folds of
Etrigan's cloak, and sought out a life on Earth. He settled
in crime-torn Gotham City, a community ideally suited
for a demon. Along the way he encountered gangster
Tommy Monaghan and became part of his circle of
mercenaries, demons, and other low-lives. Eventually, he
took up bartending at Tommy's hangout, Noonan's.
He mixes a mean cosmopolitan cocktail but is not
much of a conversationalist, given that
he only ever says, "I am Baytor!" **RG**

BEAST BOY

FIRST APPEARANCE DOOM PATROL (1st series) #99
(November 1965)
STATUS Hero **REAL NAME** Garfield Logan
OCCUPATION Teen Titan **BASE** San Francisco
HEIGHT 5ft 8in **WEIGHT** 150 lbs
EYES Green **HAIR** Green
SPECIAL POWERS/ABILITIES Can take on the form and abilities
of any animal he chooses.

The son of scientists attempting to isolate
the genetic bond between humans and
animals, young Gar Logan accompanied
his parents to Africa, where a green-furred
monkey bit him and infected him with the
Sakutia virus. Gar not only turned bright
green, he found he could change into any
animal. Soon afterward, His parents died in
a boating accident, but Gar found a new
home with Rita Farr (ELASTI-GIRL) and Steve
Dayton (MENTO) of The DOOM PATROL. Gar worked
with the Doom Patrol as Beast Boy until the group
seemingly perished in an explosion. Seeking a new career
as an actor, Gar joined the cast of the TV show *Space Trek
2022* until signing on with Titans West and later the New
Teen Titans under the name Changeling. Gar Logan retook
the name Beast Boy, serving with the Teen Titans before
joining the newest Doom Patrol. **DW**

MISSING LINK *Still young, but
boasting years of experience at the
super hero game, Beast Boy has
become a link between the older
Titans and the newest recruits.*

ANIMAL MAGIC *Beast Boy can
overturn a city bus as a rhino or
soar through the sky as a falcon.*

BEAUTIFUL DREAMER

FIRST APPEARANCE FOREVER PEOPLE (1st series) #1 (March 1971)
STATUS Hero **REAL NAME** Unknown
OCCUPATION Adventurer **BASE** Earth
HEIGHT 5ft 6in **WEIGHT** 135 lbs **EYES** Blue **HAIR** Black
SPECIAL POWERS/ABILITIES Can take images from another's mind and
transform them into lifelike, three-dimensional illusions.

The woman known as Beautiful Dreamer was born on
the planet New Genesis. A powerful psychic, the Dreamer
was kidnapped by DARKSEID during his war against New
Genesis and hidden on Earth. There, the Dreamer was
saved by SUPERMAN and the INFINITY MAN and reunited
with her lifelong friends, the FOREVER PEOPLE.

After years on Earth, studying the ways of humankind,
the Forever People were forced to relocate to the planet
Adon to escape Darkseid's agent, DEVILANCE the Pursuer.
There they established Forever Town, and Beautiful
Dreamer married her lover BIG BEAR. Evil entities called
the Dark turned Adon's populace into primitive beings,
but the Forever People and the Infinity Man destroyed
the Dark, and Dreamer and her allies returned to Earth.
Beautiful Dreamer and Big Bear had a daughter, a
superhuman named Maya, but their relationship ended
soon after. Once romantically involved with TAKION,
Beautiful Dreamer lost her life during the Death of the
New Gods event. **PJ**

A BEAUTIFUL MIND *Beautiful Dreamer's
gentle beauty belies her ferocity when using
her psychic powers to defend her child.*

BEEFEATER

FIRST APPEARANCE JUSTICE LEAGUE EUROPE #20 (November 1990)
STATUS Ally **REAL NAME** Michael Morice
OCCUPATION Would-be super hero (retired) **BASE** Ipswich, England
HEIGHT 6ft 4in **WEIGHT** 172 lbs **EYES** Light brown **HAIR** White (balding)
SPECIAL POWERS/ABILITIES Collapsible battle rod projects destructive
force blasts.

Though claiming descent from
the British aristocracy, Michael
Morice was the nervous son of
a coal miner and a little-known
BBC actress who married in the
delivery room just as Michael
was born. In adulthood, Morice
himself married a shrewish wife
and became liaison to Justice
League International (*see* JUSTICE
LEAGUE OF AMERICA). Believing
the JLI should have a British
representative in its ranks,
Morice took up the battle
rod and colorful uniform
of his father, who fought the
Nazis during World War II as the
very first Beefeater, often partnered
with America's GENERAL GLORY. At
the JLI's Parisian embassy, the new
Beefeater's arrogant petition for
membership was interrupted
by an accidental battle with the
GREEN LANTERN KILOWOG, a
comedy of errors that leveled
the building. Later, the
hapless Beefeater battled the
villain ECLIPSO and suffered
a humiliating defeat. Morice
apparently learned his lesson and mothballed the
Beefeater costume once more. **SB**

BATMAN

THE DARK KNIGHT

FIRST APPEARANCE DETECTIVE COMICS #27 (May 1939)
STATUS Hero **REAL NAME** Bruce Wayne
OCCUPATION Industrialist; philanthropist; crime fighter
BASE Gotham City
HEIGHT 6ft 2in **WEIGHT** 210 lbs **EYES** Blue **HAIR** Black
SPECIAL POWERS/ABILITIES
Master detective with a brilliant deductive mind; quite possibly the greatest martial artist alive; Bat-costume is bulletproof and fire-resistant, featuring a weighted cape and a cowl outfitted with night-vision technology and communications arrays; utility belt contains an arsenal of crime-fighting gear, including various types of offensive Batarangs, de-cel jumplines and grapnels, micro-camera, smoke pellets, acetylene torch, gas mask, rebreather, and flexi-cuffs among other miniaturized non-lethal weapons; employs a variety of detective gadgets, including micro-computers and crime scene analysis kits; maintains a fleet of high-tech and high-powered vehicles, chief among them the Batmobile, Batcycle, Batboat, Batplane, and Batcopter; super-sophisticated Batcave headquarters houses training facilities, forensics laboratories, computer databases, and maintenance bays for all Bat-vehicles.

ALLEY SLAYING *Two bullets from a gangster's gun destroyed Bruce's young life.*

FIRST FLIGHT *Batman begins his war on crime with an aerial assault upon Gotham's goons.*

A FAMILY OUTING to the cinema ended in tragedy for young Bruce Wayne. Walking homeward, Bruce, his father, Thomas, and mother, Martha, accidentally ventured into Gotham City's notorious "Crime Alley" and were accosted by a mugger. Not content merely to rob the wealthy family, the hoodlum—whose identity was never determined—shot Dr. Thomas and Martha Wayne dead before fleeing into the darkness. As he knelt beside his parents' bodies, Bruce swore to avenge them. After the police arrived, Bruce was comforted by Dr. Leslie Thompkins (*see* THOMPKINS, LESLIE M.D.). Dr. Thompkins and Alfred Pennyworth (*see* PENNYWORTH, ALFRED) helped arrange matters so that Gotham's Social Services would not take Bruce into care. In this way, both Dr. Thompkins and Alfred enabled Bruce to realize his dream of becoming a crusader against crime.

THE YOUNG BRUCE WAYNE

At age 14, Bruce embarked on a journey that took him to every continent as he sought to learn all the skills he would need to keep his vow. He studied criminology, forensics, and criminal psychology, and learned from manhunters and martial artists, mastering every fighting style. In time, Bruce forged himself into a living weapon to wage war on crime and injustice. On his return to Gotham, Bruce stalked street thugs as a plainclothes vigilante. Beaten by the very people he intended to protect, he barely survived his first night out. As he sat bleeding in his study at Wayne Manor, Bruce knew that he had to first strike fear in the hearts of his foes. Just then, a bat crashed through the study window, giving Bruce the inspiration he needed.

DARK INSPIRATION *Wishing to strike fear among the criminal community, Bruce made the bat his symbol and totem.*

A FAMILY AFFAIR

The addition of Robin to his nightly crusade helped Batman in more ways than he would ever admit. However, when Dick Grayson embarked on his own path as Nightwing, the Batcave became a lonelier place for the Dark Knight, especially after Jason Todd's murder and the crippling of Barbara Gordon (see Batgirl and Oracle), both suffered at the hands of the Joker. For a time, Batman operated strictly solo until young Tim Drake convinced the Dark Knight that he needed a Robin to give him hope.

FAMILY *The Dark Knight counts Robin and Oracle among his trusted allies.*

BATMAN BEGINS

Establishing a secret headquarters in the caves beneath his mansion, Bruce became Batman, a Dark Knight to protect Gotham and its citizens from vice and villainy. Alfred Pennyworth remained his confidant, tending to injuries and offering sage advice—whether requested or not!

Batman became an urban legend, a cautionary tale that sent shivers through the city's underworld. This Caped Crusader found a friend in Captain James Gordon (see GORDON, JAMES W.), a Gotham cop who didn't approve of Batman's methods, but appreciated the results of his nightly crime fighting. Batman's Rogues Gallery grew to include a host of bizarre criminals, such as the JOKER, CATWOMAN, TWO-FACE, and the PENGUIN. As his enemies increased, help arrived in the form of another young boy left parentless by brutal crime.

HITTING BACK *Batman lashes out at the Joker for killing Jason Todd, the second Robin.*

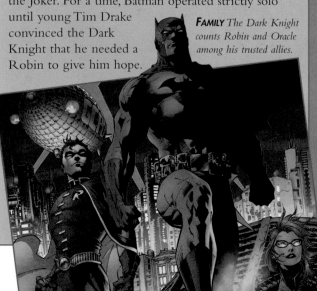

BROKEN BAT

Tragedy again struck when the terrorist Bane, after forcing Batman to fight many of his most powerful foes, broke Batman's back. Jean-Paul Valley (Azrael) took on the Dark Knight's role while Bruce recuperated from his injuries. This interim Batman was more violent and unstable; Bruce returned to action as soon as his body had healed and he had regained his fighting spirit, with the help of the ruthless martial-arts mistress Lady Shiva. Bruce took back the mantle of the Bat by force, but Jean-Paul Valley remained a staunch ally as the hero Azrael until his death.

KNIGHTFALL *Bane delivers the final cruel blow to defeat an exhausted Batman.*

THE LONG HALLOWEEN

One criminal case still haunts Batman. Early in his career, the Dark Knight failed to identify the serial killer known as Holiday and prevent a string of murders targeting the Falcone crime family. "The Long Halloween" ultimately resulted in D.A. Harvey Dent's tragic disfigurement and led to Dent becoming murdering gangster Two-Face. In that regard, Batman lost both a friend and an ally.

DARK TIMES

The Dark Knight helped maintain law and order in Gotham City when a contagion struck, killing tens of thousands. He was also the city's saviour in the anarchic aftermath of a cataclysmic earthquake. With Gotham declared a No Man's Land by the government, Batman and his allies, including a new Batgirl, fought a yearlong struggle to take the town back block by block. Gotham City was eventually rebuilt, and Batman redoubled his efforts to make known to all returning criminals that a Dark Knight defender still ruled the night. More recently, Batman faced several more personal losses. The first involved the end of his "working" relationship with Commissioner Gordon, who left the police force after a near-fatal shooting. Batman's clandestine ties to the G.C.P.D. would never be the same with his friend and ally retired.

SOLOMON GRUNDY *The creature born on a Monday in Slaughter Swamp is among many monsters Batman battles every night of the week.*

KEY STORYLINES

• *BATMAN #401–404 (FEBRUARY–MAY 1987):* The Dark Knight's tumultuous beginnings as a costumed crime fighter are chronicled in "Batman: Year One."

• *BATMAN #492 (MAY 1993):* As the epic, multipart "Knightfall" begins, the Caped Crusader fights exhaustion to enemies set loose by Bane, the villain who would ultimately break the Bat.

• *BATMAN: CATACLYSM/BATMAN: NO MAN'S LAND (TPB COLLECTIONS):* Batman's greatest battle begins as Gotham City is rocked by an earthquake. This leaves the city reduced to rubble and abandoned to anarchy by all except the Dark Knight and his closest allies.

BRUCE WAYNE: MURDERER?

Not long after, Bruce was accused of murdering journalist Vesper Fairchild (see Fairchild, Vesper), actually slain by the assassin Cain (see Cain, David) on the orders of then-President Lex Luthor (see Luthor, Lex), a business rival. Bruce was vindicated, but Vesper's death served as a stark reminder why close relationships run contrary to Batman's mostly solitary mission. However, Batman still appreciates the aid of his crime-fighting partners, and the value of teamwork. He has long been a member of the Justice League of America and assembled the first Outsiders team to take action against criminals the authorities could not touch.

GUARDED LOVE *Bruce Wayne's latest romance was with his bodyguard, Sasha Bordeaux, now a government agent.*

BATMAN TODAY

Batman continues to watch over Gotham as its staunchest defender. Moreover, since his parents' killer has never been apprehended, Bruce knows that the Dark Knight's crusade could be an endless struggle to find "the one that got away." Meanwhile, Batman fights to ensure that no one else suffers the collateral damage of random crime and senseless violence. SB

TRUST *Batman's newest nemesis struck at him by being both friend and foe. Ultimately, Batman learned that Hush was his childhood chum, Tommy Elliot.*

BATMAN

HUSH

One of Bruce Wayne's oldest friends returned as one of Batman's greatest villains in a conflict that united the Dark Knight's foes. Dr. Thomas Elliot sought revenge on his former childhood companion as the bandaged villain Hush, allying with the Riddler to hatch a complicated scheme. Harvey Dent shot Hush and left him for dead, but the affair raised troubling hints that Jason Todd, the second Robin, had returned from the dead.

OLD WOUNDS *As a boy, Tommy Elliot wanted his parents to die so he could collect their inheritance. When Dr. Thomas Wayne saved their lives, he swore revenge on the Wayne family.*

BACK FROM THE GRAVE *Bruce Wayne first confronted a resurrected Jason Todd during the Hush affair, but later concluded that the apparition had merely been the shape-changing Clayface. Soon he would find evidence that the second Robin was no longer bound by the chains of death.*

WITHOUT A TRACE *Suspicious of the circumstances surrounding Jason Todd's death, Batman exhumed Jason's coffin – only to find it empty.*

THE RETURN OF JASON TODD

Although killed by the Joker, the second Robin came back from the grave thanks to the timeline tremors that would soon signal the Infinite Crisis. Now an embittered adult, Jason Todd assumed the criminal persona of the Red Hood and set about cleaning up Gotham with brutal efficiency. Black Mask, Todd's primary target, fought back with increasing desperation, while Batman struggled to curb the violent zeal of his former protégé. Todd even kidnapped the Joker and forced Batman to explain why he had not avenged Todd's murder. Batman's refusal to kill drew a clear line between the veteran crimefighter and the rogue vigilante that Todd had become.

RED HOOD *With a new identity, Jason Todd set about cleaning up the streets of Gotham even killing criminals and drug dealers to make a point. This put him at odds with Batman, and they soon came to blows.*

JASON'S REVENGE *The Joker beat Jason with a crowbar before killing him in an explosion. After his return, Jason put the Joker's name on the top of his hit list*

WAR GAMES

Gotham City's underworld had always existed in a state of uneasy equilibrium between crime bosses, but events soon upset the balance and triggered gang-war chaos. Shortly before the shooting started, Tim Drake took leave from his Robin responsibilities out of concern for his father. Batman trained Stephanie Brown (Spoiler) as the fourth Robin, but rejected her after determining she lacked the needed experience. Anxious to prove herself, Stephanie prematurely activated one of Batman's long-range plans for dealing with Gotham organized crime. The operation soon spiraled out of control, with a victorious Black Mask emerging with nearly Gotham's entire underworld in his fist. Black Mask also captured and tortured Stephanie Brown, who died as Batman sat beside her hospital bed.

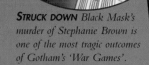

STRUCK DOWN Black Mask's murder of Stephanie Brown is one of the most tragic outcomes of Gotham's 'War Games'.

FLATLINE The injuries suffered at the hands of Black Mask, as well as Dr. Leslie Thompkins' controversial treatment, led to Stephanie's death. This, however, would be mysteriously overturned."

INFINITE CRISIS

Ever since Zatanna had mind-wiped him years earlier, Batman had harbored suspicions of his fellow heroes. With the Wayne Enterprises fortune, he built and programmed an observational satellite, the Brother Mark I, to keep tabs on superhuman activity. But the satellite's artificial intelligence soon named itself Brother Eye and initiated a program to eliminate all metahumans on Earth. As Brother Eye's nanotech virus transformed hundreds of thousands of humans into unstoppable OMAC agents, Batman led the charge to dismantle the satellite. His handpicked team, including Blue Beetle, Mister Terrific, Green Arrow, and Black Canary, took down Brother Eye in orbit, bringing victory to one battlefront of the Infinite Crisis. Although presented with an opportunity to kill enemy mastermind Alexander Luthor, Batman refused to take the easy way out. In one of the event's timeline ripples, reality shifted so that the killer of Batman's parents faced justice rather than getting away with murder.

SECRETS Zatanna and other members of the Justice League agreed to perform mind-wipes on captured villains, an act that outraged Batman when he discovered the truth.

OMAC AMOK The spawn of Batman's own creation, the OMAC units swept across the globe during the lead-up to the Infinite Crisis.

ONE YEAR LATER

Batman, Robin, and Nightwing left on an overseas ship for months of back-to-basics training, temporarily retiring their costumed identities. With Batman absent, protection of Gotham City fell to Harvey Dent — apparently cured of his split Two-Face personality. A string of murders, caused Dent to question his sanity, and when Batman returned after his year abroad, Dent returned to his criminal ways.

FALLING DOWN After a year of working on the side of law and order, Dent used acid to re-scar his left side and become Two-Face once more.

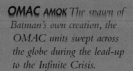

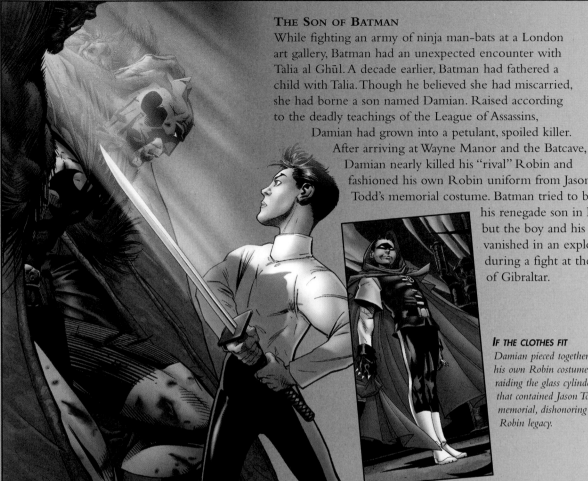

THE SON OF BATMAN

While fighting an army of ninja man-bats at a London art gallery, Batman had an unexpected encounter with Talia al Ghūl. A decade earlier, Batman had fathered a child with Talia. Though he believed she had miscarried, she had borne a son named Damian. Raised according to the deadly teachings of the League of Assassins, Damian had grown into a petulant, spoiled killer. After arriving at Wayne Manor and the Batcave, Damian nearly killed his "rival" Robin and fashioned his own Robin uniform from Jason Todd's memorial costume. Batman tried to bring his renegade son in line, but the boy and his mother vanished in an explosion during a fight at the Rock of Gibraltar.

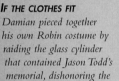

AFTER BREAKING out of the Batcave to participate in his father's war against crime, Damian defeated a minor villain, the Spook, and cut off his head

IF THE CLOTHES FIT Damian pieced together his own Robin costume by raiding the glass cylinder that contained Jason Todd's memorial, dishonoring the Robin legacy.

THE RESURRECTION OF Rā's al Ghūl

Damian didn't stay underground for long. His late grandfather, Rā's al Ghūl, cheated death yet again and reappeared as a shambling, decaying corpse. Rā's hoped to transfer his soul into Damian's body, and Batman allied with Talia to ensure this fate did not befall their son. In the sacred city of Nanda Parbat, Batman battled Rā's al Ghūl in a duel to the death, with Damian, Robin, Nightwing, and even Alfred holding their own against the League of Assassins. Ultimately the monks of Nanda Parbat forced both sides to flee the battlefield, leaving Rā's a malignant threat and Damian back under the care of his mother. Among Batman's recent moves is the creation of an all-new team of Outsiders. DW

MUMMY WRAPS Rā's al Ghūl returned needing a fresh form taken from a member of his extended family to restore himself to full life.

LOW BLOW The fight against Rā's's minions in Nanda Parbat demanded contributions from the Bat-Family, including Bruce Wayne's butler Alfred.

FAMILY FEUD Although Batman and Rā's al Ghūl had fought many times before, the emergence of Damian put them into the new, and unfamiliar, roles of father and grandfather.

BATWOMAN

GOTHAM VIGILANTE

FIRST APPEARANCE 52 #7 (July 2006)
STATUS Hero **REAL NAME** Katherine "Kate" Kane
OCCUPATION Crimefighter **BASE** Gotham City
HEIGHT 5ft 11in **WEIGHT** 145 lbs
EYES Green **HAIR** Red
SPECIAL POWERS/ABILITIES Highly-trained acrobatic combatant aided by an arsenal of high-tech gadgetry.

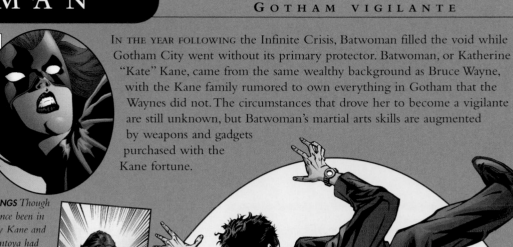

IN THE YEAR FOLLOWING the Infinite Crisis, Batwoman filled the void while Gotham City went without its primary protector. Batwoman, or Katherine "Kate" Kane, came from the same wealthy background as Bruce Wayne, with the Kane family rumored to own everything in Gotham that the Waynes did not. The circumstances that drove her to become a vigilante are still unknown, but Batwoman's martial arts skills are augmented by weapons and gadgets purchased with the Kane fortune.

HURT FEELINGS *Though they had once been in love, Kathy Kane and Renee Montoya had parted on bad terms. The Intergang plot pushed them together again, bringing raw emotions to the surface.*

NEW TITLE

Years prior to her debut as Batwoman, Kane shared a romance with Gotham City police detective Renee Montoya (*see* MONTOYA, RENEE) that ended painfully. After the Infinite Crisis, Montoya reached out to Kane for help in uncovering clues about INTERGANG activity in the city. As Batwoman, Kane tailed Montoya and her partner the QUESTION to an ambush set by Intergang agent Whisper A'Daire. Smashing into the room, Batwoman knocked out A'Daire's animal-hybrid monsters, and Montoya recognized the new super hero as her former love.

Batwoman soon joined the Question and Montoya in their fight against Intergang. They learned that the Crime Bible, a book at the center of a cult led by Intergang boss Bruno Mannheim (*see* MANNHEIM, BRUNO), contained a prophecy concerning the death of the "twice-named daughter of Cain"—a reference to Kane herself.

During the holiday season, Batwoman crossed paths with NIGHTWING, who gave her a Batarang. She also celebrated Hanukkah with Montoya, and the two renewed their relationship by sharing a kiss.

The final showdown with Intergang occurred when Mannheim's thugs kidnapped Kane and tied her to an altar, intending to offer her as a blood sacrifice to the evil spirits celebrated in the Crime Bible. Mannheim stabbed Kane in the chest, but she removed the knife and took down her attacker before passing out. After a period of recuperation, Kane returned to her role as Batwoman.

Batwoman continues to protect the citizens of Gotham, sometimes accompanied by Montoya in her guise as the new Question. The pair recently intercepted the TRICKSTER and PIED PIPER, after the two fugitive rogues fled the PENGUIN's Iceberg Lounge. **DW**

HAPPY HOLIDAYS *Nightwing happily welcomed Gotham's new adventurer to the Bat-Family, leaving her with a smile and the present of an official Batarang.*

KEY STORYLINES
• **52 #11 (JULY 2006):** Batwoman debuts against Intergang, saving Renee Montoya and the Question.
• **52 #48 (APRIL 2007):** Montoya, the new Question, saves Kathy Kane from Bruno Mannheim.
• **#1-5 (DECEMBER 2007–APRIL 2008):** Montoya goes to uncover the Cult of Cain, leaving Batwoman to question their relationship.

BEELZEBUB

FIRST APPEARANCE SANDMAN (2nd series) #4 (April 1989)
STATUS Villain **REAL NAME** None
OCCUPATION Lord of Hell **BASE** Hell
HEIGHT Variable **WEIGHT** Variable
EYES Black **HAIR** None
SPECIAL POWERS/ABILITIES Vast demonic powers, full extent unrevealed; usually takes the form of a giant fly.

Also called the Lord of the Flies, Beelzebub is one of the prime devils inhabiting the eternal realm of suffering. He has dominion over decay and decomposition, and has existed since the creation of death itself. Consequently, he uses the authority that comes with age to push himself into the thick of any political discussions within Hell's hierarchy. For a time, Beelzebub ruled Hell with Lucifer and AZAZEL as part of a triumvirate, but returned to his former station when God sent the angels Remiel and Duma to oversee the infernal realm. Later, Beelzebub assumed a humanoid shape and crossed paths with the Earth-based heroes KID ETERNITY and SUPERGIRL. He continues to spread his evil throughout the universe and will likely exist until the end of time. **DW**

BEK, GARRYN

FIRST APPEARANCE INVASION #1 (Summer 1989)
STATUS Hero **REAL NAME** Garryn Bek
OCCUPATION Administrator **BASE** The planet Cairn
HEIGHT 5ft 8in **WEIGHT** 159 lbs **EYES** Blue **HAIR** Brown
SPECIAL POWERS/ABILITIES Exceptional coordinator; starship pilot.

A police administrator on the drug-trafficking world of Cairn, whiny, irritable pessimist Garryn Bek became a prisoner of the alien ALLIANCE, bent on destroying the Earth. Bek, his cellmate, Vril Dox II, a manipulative super-genius, and several other prisoners escaped the Alliance and returned to Colu, Dox's homeworld, to liberate it from the computer tyrants that ruled there. Soon after, Bek and Dox returned to Cairn, and through not entirely legal means, the Coluan transformed the planet's entire police force into the peacekeeping agency L.E.G.I.O.N.

After being controlled by the Emerald Eye of Ekron until the Eye's apparent destruction, Bek, along with his wife Marij'n, defected from L.E.G.I.O.N. to the freedom fighting R.E.B.E.L.S. after L.E.G.I.O.N.'s take over by Lyrl Dox, Vril Dox's son. Both later joined the reformed L.E.G.I.O.N., now under CAPTAIN COMET's command. **PJ**

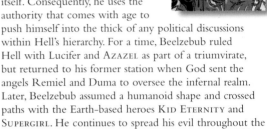

BRAINS AND BEAUTY *Like her father Himon, Bekka is also a gifted scientist. However it is her uncommon beauty that gives Orion pause, often leaving the Dog of War stumbling for words!*

BEKKA

FIRST APPEARANCE DC GRAPHIC NOVEL #4: The Hunger Dogs (1984)
STATUS Hero **REAL NAME** None
OCCUPATION Adventurer **BASE** New Genesis
HEIGHT 5ft 7in **WEIGHT** 132 lbs **EYES** Blue **HAIR** Black
SPECIAL POWERS/ABILITIES Unrevealed; however, like her fellow New Gods, Bekka is remarkably long-lived.

Bekka is the daughter of Himon, one of the NEW GODS whose achievements include invention of the sentient Mother Box computers and discovery of the "x-element" that fueled his cocreation of the teleporting Boom Tubes alongside fellow scientist METRON. For many years, Bekka lived with her father in secret on Apokolips as Himon organized an underground uprising against DARKSEID's tyrannical rule. Hunted for his role in this planned insurgence, Himon took extra care to shield Bekka from Darkseid's notice. Himon never imagined that Bekka would fall in love with ORION, Darkseid's own son, when he stumbled into their lives. After healing the wounded Dog of War, Himon and Bekka aided Orion in freeing his mother TIGGRA from imprisonment. For this act, Himon was seemingly slain by the dread lord of Apokolips. Bekka then accompanied Orion and Tiggra to New Genesis, where her love continues to soothe the savagery that lurks within the Dog of War. **SB**

BELIAL

FIRST APPEARANCE THE DEMON (2nd series) #3 (March 1987)
STATUS Evil entity **REAL NAME** Belial
OCCUPATION Demon **BASE** Hell
HEIGHT Variable **WEIGHT** Variable **EYES** Red **HAIR** None
SPECIAL POWERS/ABILITIES Master of arcane dark arts; one of the most learned of demons, who uses spells and his intellect to make up for his relative lack of demon strength.

Belial is one of the most ambitious demons in all of Hell, aspiring to rule as one of Hell's Triumvirate. For a brief time, he achieved his goal, but he was quickly replaced. He has sired three children, the demon Etrigan (DEMON), the wizard Merlin (whose mother was human) and Lord Scapegoat, a demon of Hell. His children have often opposed his schemes, which have conflicted with their own plans, and their fights have been legendary. He rarely appears on Earth, but when he has, his schemes have usually been thwarted, starting with CAPTAIN MARVEL JR. in Fawcett City. Preferring to operate behind the scenes, he has lent his supernatural powers, as one of six demons, to empower SABBAC. **RG**

BELPHEGOR

FIRST APPEARANCE TEEN TITANS SPOTLIGHT #11 (June 1987)
STATUS Ally **REAL NAME** Unknown
OCCUPATION Former Global Guardians director
BASE Marseilles, France
HEIGHT 5ft 9in **WEIGHT** 130 lbs **EYES** Green **HAIR** Black
SPECIAL POWERS/ABILITIES Various psionic abilities, including telepathy.

Little is known about the elegant Frenchwoman codenamed Belphegor. However, she shares a history with DOCTOR MIST and played an important role in the now-defunct international super hero organization known as the GLOBAL GUARDIANS.

Early in her career, Belphegor is known to have worked with Doctor Mist and former member of the Boy Commandos André Chavard (see CHAVARD, ANDRÉ) to save a hero from a parallel Earth by enlisting the unwitting help of Monsieur Mallah and the Brotherhood of Evil (see SOCIETY OF SIN). Belphegor later became the director of the Dome headquarters of the Global Guardians. She oversaw trouble spots around the world and dispatched Global Guardians to handle threats that lay near their home countries. When the United Nations decided to shift its funding from the Global Guardians to the Justice League International (see JUSTICE LEAGUE OF AMERICA), the Dome could no longer afford to stay open. Belphegor oversaw its closing and has rarely been seen since. **DW**

BERNADETH

FIRST APPEARANCE MISTER MIRACLE (1st series) #6 (February 1972)
STATUS Hero **REAL NAME** Bernadeth
OCCUPATION Shocktrooper **BASE** Apokolips
HEIGHT 5ft 10in **WEIGHT** 140 lbs **EYES** Brown **HAIR** Black
SPECIAL POWERS/ABILITIES Bernadeth is enormously strong, aggressive, and ruthless; specialized "faren-knives" super-heat foes from the inside out.

The hideous sister of DESAAD, the chief torture-master of DARKSEID's Elite, Bernadeth is the leader of the FEMALE FURIES, a specialized squadron of killers that hails from the hideous planet Apokolips. Bernadeth uses razor-sharp "faren-knives" as her offensive weaponry.

BIG BARDA was the original leader of the Female Furies until she abandoned the group and Apokolips to be with her lover, MISTER MIRACLE. Barda was able to lure the Furies back to Earth, securing their freedom and featuring all of them in a spectacular traveling stage show. The Female Furies returned to Apokolips, however, and Bernadeth assumed control of the group. **PJ**

FRIGHTENING
Bernadeth can telekinetically control her faren-knives, hurling them through the air at her foes and burning the victims from the inside out.

THE DC COMICS ENCYCLOPEDIA

BIBBO

FIRST APPEARANCE THE ADVENTURES OF SUPERMAN #428 (May 1987)
STATUS Hero/ally **REAL NAME** "Bibbo" Bibbowski
OCCUPATION Tavern owner **BASE** Suicide Slum, Metropolis
HEIGHT 6ft 3in **WEIGHT** 250 lbs **EYES** Gray **HAIR** Gray
SPECIAL POWERS/ABILITIES A former boxer, Bibbo packs a mean punch and has started (and ended) more than a few bar fights.

ONE FOR THE ROAD
Bibbo hoists a cool one to toast his "fav'rit"!

OUT COLD Not many can walk, let alone stand, after being on the receiving end of one of Bibbo's roundhouse punches. Even the Man of Steel is staggered!

Ex-longshoreman and former heavyweight contender, "Bibbo" Bibbowski is proprietor of the Ace O' Clubs tavern, a down-and-dirty waterfront pub in Metropolis's seedy Suicide Slum. This same bar was formerly Bibbo's preferred watering hole during his days as a booze-soaked barfly. But despite his slovenly appearance, fortune has always favored Bibbo. He bought the Ace O' Clubs after finding a winning lottery ticket lost by Jose Delgado (GANGBUSTER). The first year's annuity from the $14,000,000 lottery jackpot put Bibbo on easy street. Happily, his sudden fortune did not change Bibbo's outgoing and relaxed attitude to life. A friend to SUPERMAN, Bibbo practically idolizes the Man of Steel, whom he regards as his "fav'rit" hero. Though he'd wallop anyone who calls him a snitch, by virtue of his role as barkeep in an area famous for criminal activity, Bibbo often overhears useful information that he passes along to Superman or his other pal, Jimmy Olsen (*see* OLSEN, JIMMY). **SB**

GONE TO THE DOGS Bibbo isn't choosy when it comes to poker buddies, even playing a hand with a pack of alien hounds!

BIG BARDA

FIRST APPEARANCE Mister Miracle (1st series) #4 (September 1971)
STATUS Hero **REAL NAME** Barda Free
HEIGHT 6ft 2in **WEIGHT** 217 lbs **EYES** Blue **HAIR** Black
OCCUPATION Freedom fighter **BASE** New Genesis
SPECIAL POWERS/ABILITIES Trained as a Female Fury; one of the deadliest hand-to-hand combatants alive; her mastery of the mega rod is unchallenged.

Barda was always destined to be someone special; she was the only child borne out of love by Apokolips' Big Breeda. The baby was taken by DARKSEID, raised first in the Gestatron labs, then in GRANNY GOODNESS's vast orphanage, where the defiant look in Barda's eye could not be beaten out of her. Instead, Granny took her for special training and Barda excelled in all manner of combat. Barda was among the first selected to form the battalion known as the FEMALE FURIES. Barda became Granny's best squad leader, commanding the Furies to many successful victories. But then Barda fell in love with another of Granny's charges, Scott Free, a son of New Genesis. Scott met Barda, and she saw something in his spirit that touched a part of her she didn't know even existed. Barda found herself helping Scott escape from hellish Apokolips to Earth. She followed him, and their relationship deepened into lasting love. Finally, after Scott had established himself as master escape artist MISTER MIRACLE, they married. Although Scott loved life on Earth, Barda could only barely tolerate it. This led to her serving two brief stints with the JUSTICE LEAGUE OF AMERICA. Big Barda lost her life during the Death of the New Gods event, murdered in her home. Her husband Scott traveled to New Genesis and Apokolips to avenge her death. **RG**

BATTLING BARDA
Barda is one of the most feared combatants on Earth or New Genesis. She has even managed to fight Wonder Woman to a draw.

BIZARRO

IMPERFECT DUPLICATE OF SUPERMAN

FIRST APPEARANCE THE MAN OF STEEL #5 (October 1986)
STATUS Villain **REAL NAME** None
OCCUPATION Imperfect duplicate of Superman **BASE** Mobile
HEIGHT 6ft 3in **WEIGHT** 225 lbs **EYES** Blue **HAIR** Black
SPECIAL POWERS/ABILITIES Superstrong, invulnerable, and able to fly like the Man of Steel, but possessing some powers opposite to that of Superman, including freezing vision and flaming breath.

COUNTLESS TIMES SUPER-VILLAINS have raised their eyes to the heavens and cursed in vain as the heroic Man of Steel flashes across the sky to save the day. *If only*, they fume, *if only* they had a SUPERMAN of their very own, a mindless, superpowered slave to do their evil bidding! Superman's arch enemy Lex Luthor (*see* LUTHOR, LEX) was the first rogue to try to make this dream a reality. In secret, Luthor called upon his top scientist, Dr. Teng, to scan Superman's genetic structure. Teng successfully duplicated Superman, but was unable to completely recreate the complex chromosomal structure of the Last Son of Krypton. The resulting Superclone quickly became a monstrous menace, a Bizarro creature that might have razed Metropolis to the ground had Superman not intervened. Yet this misbegotten Bizarro creature was not without its gentle side, for it allowed itself to be destroyed in a rain of disintegrating particles that somehow allowed Lucy Lane, blind sister of reporter Lois Lane (*see* LANE, LOIS), to regain her sight.

CREATION At first, Dr. Teng's clone was the spitting image of the Man of Steel.

A BIZARRO IN LOVE

Luthor tried a second time to clone the Man of Steel many months later, and like the first imperfect duplicate, this second Bizarro became a superpowered nuisance. Retaining snippets of genetic memory of Superman's strong affections for Lois Lane, Bizarro #2 set about creating a ramshackle "Bizarro World" from junk and refuse, in his own way building a Bizarro Metropolis that would please his beloved "Lo-iz." Bizarro #2 then snatched up Lane and took her to his crooked city, where he held the reporter hostage while Superman searched frantically for her. However, all Bizarro #2 wanted was to please "Lo-iz," but like his predecessor, he also succumbed to rapid cellular degeneration. He died in Lois's arms. The third Bizarro, however, had little to do with genetic tinkering. Instead, a boastful new Bizarro #1 was given a fresh lease on life via the twisted imagination of BATMAN's arch-nemesis, the JOKER. After acquiring the reality-altering powers of fifth-dimensional imp MISTER MXYZPTLK the Clown Prince of Crime envisioned a topsy-turvy Earth where evil replaced good and bizarre new villains occupied the seats of an anarchic JUSTICE LEAGUE OF AMERICA. Thus, Bizarro #1 came into being as counterpoint to Superman yet again. Though matching the Man of Steel muscle for muscle, Bizarro #1 possesses some abilities that are opposite to Superman's. He also *gains* strength when exposed to kryptonite, the radioactive element deadly to the Man of Steel. Bizarro has been used as a tool by Lex Luthor and others to achieve their ends. During the Infinite Crisis, Bizarro killed the HUMAN BOMB while serving with the SECRET SOCIETY OF SUPER VILLAINS. Later he attempted to kidnap Clark Kent's foster son, Christopher Kent. Perhaps tiring of his role as a puppet for others, Bizarro fled the planet and created his own domain – a cube-shaped world populated with clones grown from his own body by using 'Bizarro vision.' These clones resembled crude versions of people whom Bizarro had known on Earth, including Lois Lane, JIMMY OLSEN, and the JUSTICE LEAGUE OF AMERICA. Bizarro took things too far when he imprisoned Pa Kent on Bizarro World, forcing Superman's intervention. **SB**

BIZARRO WORLD *To a Bizarro, Earth would be cube-shaped instead of a planetary orb. Anything to be different!*

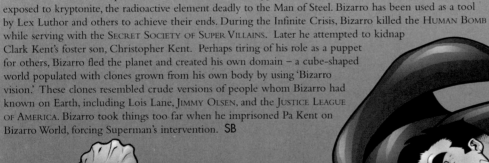

HARD LUCK Unable to have his revenge on Superman, General Zod punished Bizarro #3 instead.

LOOKING FOR LOVE In need of a father-figure, Bizarro kidnapped Pa Kent and imprisoned him on Bizarro World. For a while Bizarro even got the better of the Man of Steel.

KEY STORYLINES
• *SUPERBOY #68 (OCTOBER 1958)*: Pre-Crisis, the very first Bizarro is an imperfect teen duplicate of Superboy!
• *SUPERMAN #87 (MARCH 1994)*: Bizarro #2 is cloned, subsequently building his own Bizarro World before his untimely end.
• *SUPERMAN #160 (SEPTEMBER 2000)*: The Joker uses Mr. Mxyzptlk's powers to create an upside-down world complete with an all-new Bizarro #1, more bizarre than any who came before!

BIG BEAR

First appearance THE FOREVER PEOPLE #1 (March 1971)
Status Hero **Real name** None
Occupation Adventurer/pilot **Base** New Genesis
Height 6ft 5in **Weight** 272 lbs **Eyes** Green **Hair** Red
Special powers/abilities Superstrength attained through the discharge of high-density atoms; can mentally alter the density of objects; expert pilot of flying; pilots a phase-shifting Super-Cycle.

Big Bear is the oldest member of the FOREVER PEOPLE, five children from Earth raised on New Genesis by the wise HIGHFATHER, and rigorously trained in the uses of their powers. Big Bear piloted the team's Super Cycle space vehicle. When the evil DARKSEID kidnapped team member BEAUTIFUL DREAMER, Big Bear and the others tracked her to Earth. They rescued her with help from the INFINITY MAN, a cosmic being with whom they could trade places by touching their Mother Box computer and speaking the word "Taaru." During one swap with the Infinity Man, the Forever People found themselves stranded on the distant planet Adon. The team eventually returned to New Genesis, where Big Bear matched his Super-Cycle piloting skills against the teens of YOUNG JUSTICE. Big Bear and the rest of the Forever People lost their lives in the Death of the New Gods event, murdered in their interstellar cabin. **DW**

BIZARRO   *SEE OPPOSITE PAGE*

BLACK ADAM

First appearance MARVEL FAMILY #1 (December 1945)
Status Hero (flawed) **Real name** Teth-Adam
Occupation Adventurer **Base** New York City
Height 6ft **Weight** 198 lbs **Eyes** Brown **Hair** Black
Special powers/abilities Great strength, speed, stamina, and wisdom.

During Ancient Egypt's 19th dynasty, Teth-Adam became the first to be blessed with supernatural powers by the wizard Shazam. When Teth-Adam spoke the wizard's name, he was transformed by a bolt of lightning into "Mighty Adam," with the powers of six of the Egyptian gods: Shu (stamina), Heru (speed), Amon (strength), Zehuti (wisdom), Aton (power), and Mehen (courage).

Teth-Adam became Egypt's champion, eventually entering the service of Prince Khufu. Shortly after the prince's murder and the deaths of his wife and children, Teth-Adam lost sight of his purpose. He began using his powers for selfish gain and became known as Khem-Adam (BLACK ADAM), a name whispered in the shadows. Blaming himself, Shazam stripped Adam of his powers, placing them within a scarab amulet.

The amulet was entombed with Pharaoh Ramses II, remaining untouched until the 20th century, when husband and wife archaeologists C.C. and Marilyn Batson uncovered it. The couple was brutally murdered by an associate, Theo Adam, who soon after tapped into Black Adam's power and memories. The Batsons' son, Billy, was chosen by the wizard as his new champion, CAPTAIN MARVEL. Ever since, they have repeatedly battled. During the Infinite Crisis, Alexander Luthor betrayed Black Adam, causing his rebellion and his murder of the PSYCHO PIRATE. Black Adam returned to Khandaq, where he fell in love and married Isis. With Isis' younger brother OSIRIS, the three formed the Black Marvel Family. But the Four Horsemen of Apokolips killed Isis and Osiris, triggering Black Adam's destruction of Bialya and his global rampage dubbed World War III. Stripped of his powers, Black Adam undertook a quest to restore Isis to life, and transferred some of his dark energies to MARY MARVEL. **RG**

EGYPT'S GUARD Black Adam seeks to protect his native land, even from allies such as the JSA.

ANCIENT PEERS, MODERN FOES Black Adam and Hawkman battling in the skies over the Middle East.

BLACK ALICE

First appearance BIRDS OF PREY #76 (January 2005)
Status Hero **Real name** Lori Zechlin
Occupation Student **Base** Dayton, Ohio
Height 5ft 5in **Weight** 110 lbs **Eyes** Brown **Hair** Black
Special powers/abilities Can borrow the magical abilities of any other magic-user for a limited time.

Though still a teenager, Black Alice is one of the most powerful magic-users on Earth. Born Lori Zechlin in Dayton Ohio, she experienced an alienated and unhappy adolescence that grew unbearable after her mother committed suicide. Discovering that she could manifest vast magical powers by "borrowing" them from other sorcerers, she attempted to take revenge on those who had wronged her until stopped by BLACK CANARY and the BIRDS OF PREY.

Black Alice's gifts came in handy prior to the Infinite Crisis, when she aided the SHADOWPACT by stealing the abilities of the SPECTRE. When Felix Faust (see FAUST, FELIX) resurrected Black Alice's mother in a zombie-like state, Lori's life unraveled still further, yet she resisted the temptation to claim the omnipotent helmet of DOCTOR FATE. **DW**

BLACK BISON

First appearance THE FURY OF FIRESTORM #1 (June 1982)
Status Hero (deceased) **Real name** John Ravenhair
Occupation Tribal shaman **Base** New York City
Height 6ft 3in **Weight** 226 lbs **Eyes** Brown **Hair** Black
Special powers/abilities Mystical ability to control the weather and animate objects, focused through a tribal coup stick.

John Ravenhair's great-grandfather Bison-Black-As-Midnight-Sky was once the shaman of the Bison Cult. When the old man died, Ravenhair found himself possessed by his great-grandfather's vengeful spirit. Dressing himself in traditional tribal costume and calling himself Black Bison, Ravenhair set out to right all the many wrongs that had been perpetrated upon the Native American people since the arrival of the White Man in America centuries ago.

Black Bison's rampage across New York City attracted the attention of FIRESTORM, THE NUCLEAR MAN, who discovered that he could defeat Black Bison by removing the Bison Cult talisman that he wore around his neck. Away from his great-grandfather's influence, John Ravenhair could choose his own path, but it wasn't long before Black Bison returned to cause more collateral damage in the name of vengeance.

Black Bison is not a true villain, and has occasionally assisted the cause of good. During the Crisis (see Great Battles, pp. 362–3), Black Bison helped the Earth's assembled sorcerers defeat the Anti-Monitor's shadow demons. Prior to the Infinite Crisis, John Ravenhair perished along with dozens of other magic-users in combat with the SPECTRE. **DW**

BLACK CANARY

THE PRETTY BIRD OF PREY

First appearance (Black Canary I) FLASH COMICS #86 (August 1947)
Status Hero (deceased) **Real name** Dinah Drake Lance
Occupation Adventurer; florist **Base** Gotham City
Height 5ft 5in **Weight** 128 lbs **Eyes** Blue **Hair** Black
Special powers/abilities Trained in Judo, and a feisty fighter; often concealed smoke or tear-gas pellets in the amulet of her choker.

First appearance (Black Canary II) JUSTICE LEAGUE OF AMERICA #75 (November 1969)
Status Hero **Real name** Dinah Laurel Lance
Occupation Adventurer **Base** Gotham City
Height 5ft 4in **Weight** 124 lbs **Eyes** Blue **Hair** Blonde
Special powers/abilities Ultrasonic, earsplitting "canary cry," capable of shattering metal; martial arts and boxing expert.

IN 1947, DINAH DRAKE'S DREAMS of becoming a Gotham City policewoman were dashed when her police academy application was rejected and her doting father, Detective Richard Drake, subsequently passed away. Dinah used her small inheritance to open a florist's shop while pursuing a more clandestine career in crime fighting. Inspired by the brightly clad "Mystery Men" of the time, raven-haired Dinah designed her own stylish costume—black fishnets and leather, as well as a blonde wig to conceal her identity—and embarked on a vigilante career as the sultry Black Canary. At first passing herself off as a criminal to infiltrate Gotham's underworld, the Judo-savvy Black Canary eventually revealed her true colors upon teaming with fellow hero Johnny Thunder (*see* THUNDER, JOHNNY). She became a member of the JUSTICE SOCIETY OF AMERICA soon after, although eventually retired from costumed crime fighting. She married private detective Larry Lance and gave birth to a daughter (also named Dinah), who would carry on her mother's heroic legacy. Dinah Drake Lance died of radiation-induced cancer, an after-effect from battling the cosmic-powered villain Aquarius—an epic struggle during which Larry Lance sacrificed his own life—alongside her JSA teammates.

SOULMATES *The Canary often assisted paramour and private eye Larry Lance on his cases.*

BLACK CANARY II

While the original Black Canary hoped to spare her daughter the perils of a crime-fighting career, young Dinah Laurel Lance nevertheless grew up in the shadow of her mother's great exploits, tales often told to her by the JSA members who babysat her. Like her mother, Dinah was also a superb athlete and fighter. But young Dinah also possessed a metagene that bequeathed her a unique superpower: a hyper-pitched "canary cry." Despite her mother's wishes, Dinah took up the fishnets and leather outfit of Black Canary. Gifted in Judo, Dinah also learned boxing from her "uncle," Ted Grant (WILDCAT I), as well as other fighting techniques from her mother's teammates in the original JSA.

As such, Dinah was one of the first "second-generation" super heroes. Operating as Black Canary II, Dinah had a string of solo adventures before joining the JUSTICE LEAGUE OF AMERICA, where she began a romance with GREEN ARROW Oliver Queen. Later she signed on as the primary "Bird of Prey" operative working for ORACLE. Following the Infinite Crisis, Black Canary traded places with LADY SHIVA, training overseas while Shiva assumed duties with the Birds of Prey. In Vietnam Black Canary took Shiva's successor – the young girl Sin – under her wing, bringing her back to the U.S. to raise her. She also signed on as chairwoman of the new Justice League. She soon fell in love anew with Oliver Queen. But supervillains crashed their wedding, and Black Canary killed a man impersonating her husband. She later rescued the true Oliver from Amazonian imprisonment on Themyscira. **SB**

CANARY CRY *Dinah lost her canary cry after suffering a brutal beating. But this sonic superpower was restored after she was dipped in a restorative Lazarus Pit.*

SKRREEEEE

KEY STORYLINES

• **ALL-STAR COMICS #38 (DEC.–JAN. 1947–48):** Though not yet an official member, Black Canary I joins the JSA to defeat history's greatest villains!

• **JLA: YEAR ONE #1-12 (JAN.–DEC. 1998):** The second Black Canary's first year with the JLA is chronicled as the team battles the Appellaxian aliens and the organization known as Locus.

• **BLACK CANARY/ORACLE: BIRDS OF PREY (1996):** Black Canary II accepts her first assignment from ORACLE without knowing who her partner really is!

MELEE AT THE ALTAR *The superhero guests at her wedding proved an irresistible target for the villainous Society, who attacked in force. Black Canary helped crush their assault, but would soon discover her husband had been replaced by a shape-changer.*

BLACK CONDOR

FIRST APPEARANCE CRACK COMICS #1 (May 1940)
STATUS Hero **REAL NAME** Richard Grey Jr., a.k.a. Thomas Wright
OCCUPATION Adventurer **BASE** Washington, D.C.
HEIGHT 6ft 2in **WEIGHT** 196 lbs **EYES** Blue **HAIR** Black
SPECIAL POWERS/ABILITIES Exposure to alien radiation granted him the ability to fly and to understand the language of birds.

Richard Grey Jr. was lost as an infant in the Mongolian mountains. There he was exposed to radiation from a meteor, which mutated the developing child. A family of condors rescued and raised him until he was found by Father Pierre, a missionary. He called the child Black Condor and taught him to speak, read, and write English. When Father Pierre was murdered, the Black Condor set out to avenge him. En route, he found the body of Senator Thomas Wright, who had been murdered by the deranged Jaspar Crow. Wright and the Condor looked identical in appearance, so the Condor assumed Wright's identity, complete with fiancée, Wendy Foster, who was none the wiser! Grey donned a costume to fight crime as the Black Condor, while serving justice in the senate. He was among the first costumed "mystery men" to serve with the ALL-STAR SQUADRON and afterward its splinter group, the FREEDOM FIGHTERS. His last recorded mission was in 1953, when he aided the RAY and Spitfire in fighting Doctor Spectron. The Condor subsequently moved on to a higher plane of existence—living with others "at the top of the world"—in an as-yet-unexplained manner. He made brief appearances on Earth, including helping to recruit Ryan Kendall as BLACK CONDOR II. **RG**

BLACK CONDOR II

FIRST APPEARANCE BLACK CONDOR #1 (June 1992)
STATUS Hero **REAL NAME** Ryan Kendall
OCCUPATION Adventurer **BASE** Opal City
HEIGHT 6ft 4in **WEIGHT** 170 lbs **EYES** Blue **HAIR** Black
SPECIAL POWERS/ABILITIES Flight, heightened senses, limited telepathy, and telekinesis; expert knife-thrower.

Though not a direct successor to the wartime hero known as BLACK CONDOR, Ryan Kendall has proven himself worthy of the Condor legacy and has become a hero in his own right. He received his powers thanks to a monstrous experiment conducted by his grandfather, Creighton Kendall, leader of the centuries-old Society of the Golden Wing. As part of the Society's program to create a flying man, Kendall irradiated Ryan while he was still a fetus. At the age of 21, Ryan fell into a coma which lasted two years. When he recovered, he flew off into the thick of New Jersey's Pine Barrens to find himself. Under the name Black Condor, Ryan Kendall assumed a super-heroic role in battles against the Sky Pirate and the SHARK. He joined the JUSTICE LEAGUE OF AMERICA following SUPERMAN's death, and later became a member of PRIMAL FORCE. Black Condor then settled in Opal City working with the police. Kendall died during the Infinite Crisis. A third Black Condor, John Trujillo, now serves as a member of the FREEDOM FIGHTERS alongside UNCLE SAM. **DW**

FLYING SOLO Black Condor II is a loner who works with super-hero teams, but who doesn't socialize with them.

BLACK LIGHTNING

FIRST APPEARANCE BLACK LIGHTNING (1st series) #1 (April 1977)
STATUS Hero **REAL NAME** Jefferson Pierce
OCCUPATION Adventurer **BASE** Metropolis
HEIGHT 6ft 1in **WEIGHT** 182 lbs **EYES** Brown **HAIR** Black
SPECIAL POWERS/ABILITIES Olympic-level athlete; superb hand-to-hand combatant; internally generated electromagnetic field; can create and hurl bolts of supercharged electricity.

Jefferson Pierce escaped the squalor of Metropolis's Suicide Slum by devoting himself to athletics. He eventually won Olympic gold in the decathlon. Once qualified as a teacher, he returned to Suicide Slum. Pierce watched helplessly as his students fell victim to drugs, controlled by the 100 mob led by albino behemoth Tobias Whale. With a costume sporting an electronic belt to shock thugs senseless, Pierce became Black Lightning and brought the 100 mob, and Tobias Whale, to justice.

One of the most famous African-American super heroes of his time, Pierce became a founder member of the OUTSIDERS. During his stint with the team, a latent metagene enabled him to internalize his lightning-like powers. Following the Outsiders' dissolution, Black Lightning became defender of crime-ridden Brick City. He then served under U.S. President Lex Luthor (see LUTHOR, LEX) as Secretary of Education. Pierce now serves with the JUSTICE LEAGUE OF AMERICA. His daughter Anissa (THUNDER II) was recently a member of a new team of Outsiders. **SB**

BODY ELECTRIC Black Lightning continues to explore his electromagnetic abilities, including the power to travel via bolts of electricity.

HARD TO GET Black Lightning once turned down an offer of membership in the Justice League of America.

BLACK MANTA

FIRST APPEARANCE AQUAMAN (1st series) #35 (September 1967)
STATUS Villain **REAL NAME** Unrevealed
OCCUPATION Assassin **BASE** Devil's Deep
HEIGHT 6ft 4in **WEIGHT** 250 lbs **EYES** Brown **HAIR** Brown
SPECIAL POWERS/ABILITIES Possesses slightly above-average strength;
quickly masters new equipment; fueled by rage.

DEVIL VERSION *Black Manta sold his soul to Neron in exchange for more power. He also was transformed into a living manta.*

There once was a young boy in an orphanage that screamed uncontrollably whenever he was put to bed. No one suspected that the feel of cotton sheets was agonizing to him. Nor did they realize that icy cold water had the exact opposite effect. The boy was severely autistic at a time before doctors understood the condition. As a result, he was subjected to experimental treatments, one of which seemed to bring the boy to a level of cognizance considered normal. It also brought out a streak of rage and violence. The boy saw images of Aquaman on television and was drawn to the sight of a man totally submerged in his beloved water.

As an adult, the orphan designed a costume and fashioned a high-tech submersible inspired by black manta fish. Taking the name Black Manta, he became a force to be reckoned with, engaging in several as-yet-unrecorded clashes with Aquaman before joining the short-lived Injustice League and, soon after, the OCEAN MASTER. Manta and Aquaman battled repeatedly over the next few years until the day the violent criminal killed Arthur III, son of the sea king. Black Manta then sold his soul to the demon NERON in exchange for increased powers. Aquaman encountered the newly mutated Black Manta in the crushing pressures of Devil's Deep. Manta's mutation continued, and he took to wearing his full costume again, which covered him completely from sight. Inexplicably, he stopped tormenting Aquaman and indulged in drug smuggling from his new base in Star City, where he was opposed by the GREEN ARROW I and his old enemy, Aquaman. In a subsequent confrontation, Aquaman, now sporting the LADY OF THE LAKE's Healing Hand, removed Neron's incantation. It also rewired Manta's afflicted brain, making him normal for the first time in his life. Unfortunately, Manta remained a violent criminal, lulling Aquaman into a false sense of partnership, almost killing the sea king in the process. Later cured of his demonic form, Black Manta narrowly escaped death after attempting to take over the sunken city of Sub Diego. **RG**

BETRAYAL *Restored to human form, his mind healed by Aquaman, Manta proved to be truly evil.*

BLACK MASK

FIRST APPEARANCE BATMAN #386 (August 1985)
STATUS Villain (presumed dead) **REAL NAME** Roman Sionis
OCCUPATION Gang leader **BASE** Gotham City
HEIGHT 6ft 1in **WEIGHT** 195 lbs **EYES** Brown **HAIR** None
SPECIAL POWERS/ABILITIES Brilliant criminal mind; rules subordinates with iron fist; sadistically pursues anyone who wronged him.

Thanks to his mother and father, the heads of the Janus Cosmetics company, Roman Sionis inherited a multi-million dollar fortune when his parents "mysteriously" died in a fire. But the new Sionis quickly ran the company into the ground. A buyout by Bruce Wayne saved Janus Cosmetics, but left Sionis with a bitter hatred of the man who had "stolen" his legacy. Obsessed with masks, Sionis carved a black mask from his father's coffin and murdered several Wayne employees, resulting in a fiery confrontation with BATMAN. Sionis' mask was burned into his flesh, making him a living Black Mask. He became one of Gotham's most ruthless crimelords with an army of masked henchmen, the False Face Society, at his disposal. Black mask took control of the Gotham City underworld following the War Games event, but his reign at the top didn't last long. In retaliation for threatening her friends, CATWOMAN shot and killed him. **DW**

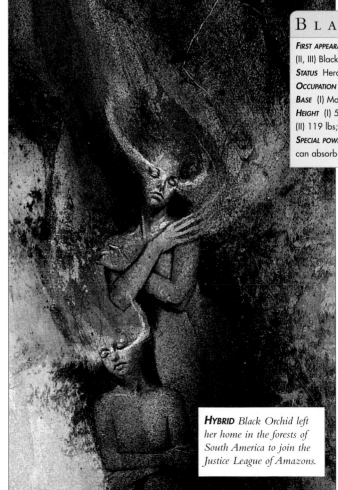

HYBRID *Black Orchid left her home in the forests of South America to join the Justice League of Amazons.*

BLACK ORCHID

FIRST APPEARANCE (I) ADVENTURE COMICS #428 (August 1973);
(II, III) Black Orchid (1st series) #1 (December 1988)
STATUS Hero **REAL NAME** (I) Susan Linden; (II) none; (III) Suzy
OCCUPATION (I) Adventurer; (II, III) elemental nymph
BASE (I) Mobile; (II, III) the Amazon rain forest
HEIGHT (I) 5ft 11in; (II) 5ft 7in; (III) 5ft 6in **WEIGHT** (I) 130 lbs;
(II) 119 lbs; (III) 115 lbs **EYES** (all) Violet **HAIR** (all) Violet
SPECIAL POWERS/ABILITIES Superhuman strength; flight. Like a plant, she can absorb nutrients from the air.

Abused by her father her entire life, Susan Linden eventually married Carl Thorne, a wealthy arms trafficker. Thorne stole a shipment of weapons from his billionaire boss Lex Luthor (*see* LUTHOR, LEX), and murdered Susan when she went to the police with the information. Botanist Philip Sylvian, a childhood friend of Susan's, grafted a splice of Linden's genetic material into an experimental hybrid of plant and animal matter, creating the Black Orchid. Black Orchid used her special powers and a number of false identities to fight crime until she was murdered by Lex Luthor. Susan's death created a psychic reaction that awakened another of Sylvian's orchid hybrids. This nameless Black Orchid found her way to the rain forests of South America and learned that she was an elemental dryad nymph before being assassinated by a hitman in New York City. Suzy, a childlike sprite with fragments of Susan's consciousness, is the last surviving Black Orchid. She protects the natural world from the depredations of industry and big business. **PJ**

BLACK PIRATE

FIRST APPEARANCE SENSATION COMICS #1 (January 1942)
STATUS Hero (deceased) **REAL NAME** Jon Valor
OCCUPATION Freedom fighter **BASE** England
HEIGHT 5ft 11in **WEIGHT** 164 lbs
EYES Brown **HAIR** Brown
SPECIAL POWERS/ABILITIES A swashbuckling swordsman and accomplished sailor.

As war divided Europe in 1588, British nobleman Jon Valor led a trusted crew of bold but benevolent buccaneers as a masked Black Pirate who sailed the high seas for the cause of justice. Though loyal to the British crown, Valor also served under the Spanish flag for a brief time before returning to Great Britain and swashbuckling alongside his son, Justin. However, when Justin was later lost at sea, a heartbroken Black Pirate revealed his true identity to the British monarch and hung up his cape and cowl. Years later, when British ships were threatened by mysterious privateers, Valor heeded the king's call for the Black Pirate to return to action and scuttle the roguish raiders. To his surprise, Valor discovered Justin alive and well, and leading a band of Puritans who attacked British ships to fund their planned journey to the U.S. Valor made peace with Justin, who set sail for a new life in the U.S., and retired to his home in England, where he presumably lived his remaining days rarely drawing his sword from its scabbard. **SB**

BLACK RACER

FIRST APPEARANCE NEW GODS (1st series) #3 (July 1971)
STATUS Villain **REAL NAME** Sgt. Willie Walker
OCCUPATION Messenger of Death **BASE** New Genesis
HEIGHT 6ft 4in **WEIGHT** 211 lbs **EYES** Black **HAIR** Black
SPECIAL POWERS/ABILITIES Phases through solid objects, flying atop cosmically charged skis; can deliver death with a single touch; armor helps him withstand the rigors of space and staff metes out justice.

When the NEW GODS arose from the ashes of their predecessors, so rose the Black Racer, an elemental force capable of dealing death with a single touch. When the Fourth World's battles spilled on to Earth, the Racer was drawn to the planet and to the body of paralyzed Vietnam veteran Willie Walker. Walker become one with the Racer, his spirit now commingled with this harbinger of death. Black Racer's arrival, atop airborne skis, means someone's life is about to end. He is quiet, efficient, and rarely challenged. The Racer has been drawn to the more cosmic battles over time, including the Imperiex War (*see* Great Battles, pp. 320–1). When STEEL died, the Racer arrived to collect his soul, as is his right. He was challenged by SUPERMAN, but the Man of Steel eventually relented. YOUNG JUSTICE, however, futilely tried to reclaim Steel from the New God. The racer then met the third FLASH during the war, learning more about how humans cherish life. Afterward, he went to claim a soul, discovering it to be that of the doctor caring for Walker, a victim of a mugging. The Racer has begun to understand the pain a single death can cause to others. **RG**

BLACK SPIDER I & II

FIRST APPEARANCE DETECTIVE COMICS #463 (September 1976)
STATUS Villain **REAL NAME** Eric Needham
OCCUPATION Assassin **BASE** Gotham City
HEIGHT 5ft 10in **WEIGHT** 173 lbs **EYES** Brown **HAIR** Black
SPECIAL POWERS/ABILITIES Expert combatant and dead shot with retractable wrist pistol; unrevealed supernatural powers.

Heroin addict Eric Needham accidentally killed his father during a liquor store robbery. In his grief, he not only kicked the habit, but vowed to eliminate everyone associated with the drug trade. Funding by a mysterious benefactor made it possible for Needham to become the vigilante Black Spider. He later learned that the drug kingpin Hannibal Hardwicke had bankrolled his career in order to eliminate business rivals. When Needham's wife and son died in the crossfire of his war on drugs, Black Spider blew himself up in a suicide attack that eliminated several top gangsters. Needham was freed from Hell when Lucifer released many of the dead, and has since returned to Earth. He struck a deal with NERON, the consequences of which are still unrevealed. A second Black Spider also appeared in Gotham—Johnny LaMonica. Failing in an attempt to kill gang boss BLACK MASK, LaMonica rots in Blackgate prison. **DW**

BLACK ZERO

FIRST APPEARANCE SUPERBOY (3rd series) #61 (April 1999)
STATUS Villain **REAL NAME** Kon-El
OCCUPATION Freedom fighter and world conqueror **BASE** Metropolis (in an alternate timeline)
HEIGHT 6ft 2in **WEIGHT** 225 lbs **EYES** Blue **HAIR** Black
SPECIAL POWERS/ABILITIES Has superhuman strength and speed, can fly, is virtually invulnerable and possesses psionic vision (similar to heat vision). Like Superboy, Black Zero lifts huge objects using tactile telekinesis, which gives him telekinetic control over an object after touching it.

On the Earth of an alternate timeline, SUPERMAN did not return from the dead after battling DOOMSDAY. On that Earth, SUPERBOY, a clone of Superman, grew up in a Metropolis, where clones, called Genetix, were often hunted and killed. Horrified by this, Superboy became Black Zero and began gathering Doomsdays from various timelines to invade every Earth and prevent the extinction of clones across the multiverse.

Another version of Superboy arrived on our Earth to warn its heroes of Black Zero's invasion. Using the alternate Superboy's technology, our Superboy raced across multiple realities, fighting Black Zero's warriors. Superboy finally defeated Black Zero with the help of KNOCKOUT, the CHALLENGERS OF THE UNKNOWN, and METRON, who stripped the elder clone of his time-spanning abilities. Black Zero was finally destroyed when he was struck by a wave of Hypertime on his way back to his own world. **PJ**

BLACKHAWK

FIRST APPEARANCE MILITARY COMICS #1 (August 1941)
STATUS Hero (missing in action) **REAL NAME** Janos Prohaska
OCCUPATION Squadron leader **BASE** England
HEIGHT 6ft 1.5in **WEIGHT** 195 lbs **EYES** Blue **HAIR** Black
SPECIAL POWERS/ABILITIES An expert pilot; a charismatic and quick-thinking field leader, in addition to being good with his fists.

POLAND'S JANOS PROHASKA served with the Bill Heywood Squadron of the International Brigades during the Spanish Civil War, gaining an international reputation as a flyer of amazing skill and courage. When, in 1939, Poland fell victim to Nazi Germany's *blitzkrieg* warfare, Prohaska, now nicknamed Blackhawk, joined with his friends Stanislaw "Stan" Drozdowski and Kazimierc "Zeg" Zegota and others to form the Blackhawk Squadron. They resisted the brutal invaders of their homeland from a secret base on Blackhawk Island.

THE BLACKHAWK SQUADRON

Blackhawk assembled a truly international band of air aces, all determined to fight for freedom. The pilots included Boris Zinoviev of Russia, Ian Holcolmb-Baker of England, André Blanc-DuMont of France, Olaf Friedriksen of Sweden, Ritter Hendricksen of Denmark, and Carlo "Chuck" Sirianni of the U.S. Sadly, Boris, Zeg, Ian, and Stanislaus were soon killed in action. Soon afterwards, 17-year-old Chinese-American "whiz kid" Weng "Chop Chop" Chan joined the group.

The C.I.A. later recruited the Blackhawks, and Blackhawk Airways was relocated to Washington, D.C. The U.S. government wanted more control over the team's missions, and when Blackhawk objected, the team was kidnapped until rescued by Blackhawk and new recruit Paco Herrera. The isle of Pontalba was then transformed into the new Blackhawk Island. Soon after, the Blackhawks severed all ties with the C.I.A. and the U.S. government.

In the 1960s, André was murdered by an assassin named Hardwire. Years later Blackhawk tracked the killer down in Saigon, just as the city was about to fall to the Viet Kong, and avenged his friend's death. Sadly, Olaf disappeared during the mission. Years after, Weng Chan formed an elite air courier service, Blackhawk Express. The company put together a team of doubles of the seven best-known Blackhawks, who fought crime in the decade ahead. President Lex Luthor (*see* LUTHOR, LEX) employed the new Blackhawk Squadron during the Imperiex War (*see* Great Battles, pp. 362–3), but the current whereabouts of Prohaska and the other members of the team is not known. RG

BRAVERY *Despite grave danger and frequent combat wounds, the Blackhawks never gave up.*

LEADING FORCE *Blackhawk was not only a great flyer and terrific fighter: even more importantly he was a charismatic leader.*

FIRST CLASS FLYERS *The Blackhawk planes were not only durable, they were also among the best engineered craft in the world.*

KEY STORYLINES

• *MILITARY COMICS #1 (AUGUST 1941):* This early story introduces the world to Janos Porhaska and his men.
• *BLACKHAWK #1-3 (MARCH–MAY 1989):* The tale spotlights Prohaska as he deals with a Russian conspiracy and life after the War.
• *BLACKHAWK #140 (SEPTEMBER 1959):* Lady Blackhawk is introduced to the team.

TWO-FISTED HERO *One-man blitzkrieg Blackhawk makes light work of a German army tank crew.*

BLACKBRIAR THORN

FIRST APPEARANCE DC COMICS PRESENTS #66 (February 1984)
STATUS Villain **REAL NAME** Unknown
OCCUPATION Last of the Druids **BASE** Gotham City
HEIGHT 6ft 3in **WEIGHT** 238 lbs **EYES** Brown **HAIR** Brown
SPECIAL POWERS/ABILITIES Seemingly immortal; ability to conjure snow, storms, or fog; able to manifest illusions and grow in size; must maintain contact with the Earth and soil or his power diminishes.

Druidic high priest Blackbriar Thorn escaped death at the hands of Roman invaders in Britain by fleeing into a forest and transforming himself into solid wood. The other druids were less fortunate, but in their death throes, they unwittingly opened a great fissure that swallowed Thorn. He was buried for centuries until archaeologist Professor Lewis Lang unearthed him. By now the high priest was permanently trapped in his wooden body. Thorn's attempts to wreak mystical havoc in the 20th century have been thwarted by SUPERMAN, Etrigan (DEMON), and SENTINEL, among others. Thorn nearly perished in combat with the SPECTRE, but owes his survival to his magical ability to regenerate himself from even the smallest splinter. **SB**

HEAD-HUNTED
Blackbriar Thorn was recruited by Johnny Sorrow to join the JSA-hating Injustice Society.

BLACKFIRE

FIRST APPEARANCE THE NEW TEEN TITANS (1st series) #22 (September 1982)
STATUS Undefined **REAL NAME** Komand'r
OCCUPATION Queen of Tamaran **BASE** Mobile
HEIGHT 6ft 2in **WEIGHT** 162 lbs **EYES** Green **HAIR** Red
SPECIAL POWERS/ABILITIES Absorption of solar energy; projection of destructive "starbolts" from her hands.

The eldest child of the royal family of the planet Tamaran, Princess Komand'r, a sickly child, was denied her birthright and her sister, Koriand'r, was named next in line for the throne. Both sisters were sent by their father, King Myand'r, to train with the famed Warlords of Okaara, but there the hateful Komand'r betrayed her family, joined the dreaded Citadel Empire, and bartered Koriand'r into slavery. Years later, both sisters became prisoners of the Psions and were subjected to genetic experiments that gave them vast powers. Escaping, Komand'r (now called Blackfire) and Koriand'r (now a TEEN TITANS member called STARFIRE) clashed repeatedly, until Komand'r forsook her hate, freed Tamaran from Citadel control, and became its queen, before the planet's apparent destruction by a Sun-Eater. Blackfire has not been seen since. **PJ**

BLACKHAWK   SEE OPPOSITE PAGE

BLASTERS, THE

FIRST APPEARANCE INVASION #1 (1988)
STATUS Hero team (disbanded) **BASE** Mobile
MEMBERS AND POWERS
Lucas "Snapper" Carr (leader) Teleportation powers.
Dust Devil (Moshe Levy) Israeli boy who can turn into a whirlwind; accompanied by his divorced mother, Mrs. Levy.
Looking Glass (Dexter Fairfax) Ability to absorb light and project it.
Crackpot (Amos Monroe) Persuasive mind-manipulation powers.
Jolt (Carlotta Rivera) Can repel any form of energy.
Frag (Fritz Klein) Can turn into living metal and explode.
Gunther Renegade Dominator scientist.
Churljenkins Alien starship pilot; technical expert.

During an alien invasion of Earth, Dominator scientists kidnapped 50 humans and forced them to walk through a minefield. The humans that survived did so by manifesting latent metagene powers. Upon their escape from the Dominator space prison, they formed a wandering super-team called the Blasters. The group added a Dominator scientist to its roster and cruised the spaceways piloted by the attractively feline humanoid alien Churljenkins. On one mission, they smashed a plot by a criminal organization named the Spider Guild to sell black-market weapons on Earth. After a near-fatal attempt to spring the hero Valor from prison, the Blasters disbanded. Snapper Carr (see Carr, Snapper) suffered horrors of his own, being seized by Khund thugs who cut off his hands, robbing him of his ability to teleport. Though Snapper's hands have since been restored, no one knows if he will ever be able to track down his former team members and reform the Blasters. **DW**

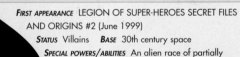

THE BLASTERS *The Blasters helped end the alien invasion of Earth, but went mostly unrecognized for their efforts.*
1) *Frag* 2) *Snapper Carr* 3) *Churljenkins* 4) *Crackpot*
5) *Looking Glass* 6) *Mrs. Levy* 7) *Gunther*
8) *Dust Devil* 9) *Jolt*

BLIGHT

FIRST APPEARANCE LEGION OF SUPER-HEROES SECRET FILES AND ORIGINS #2 (June 1999)
STATUS Villains **BASE** 30th century space
SPECIAL POWERS/ABILITIES An alien race of partially organic beings composed of a combination of rotting flesh and technology; can absorb the life energy from entire worlds, leaving these planets in ruins.

The techno-organic Blight exist in one timeline inhabited by the Legion of Super-Heroes. This scientifically advanced species sought the secret of immortality. In their mad quest, the Blight were turned into a race of perpetually decaying beings and, using the teleportation skills of the alien Doda (beings who could teleport themselves across the galaxy to seed new worlds), spread that decay across the universe.

In the 31st century, the Blight, led by Atrophos, their chief scientist and engineer, drained the life energy from dozens of worlds. This hostile, malicious race first came into contact with a LEGION OF SUPER-HEROES cruiser when the aliens entered United Planets space. Using the cruiser's Stargate technology, the Blight's corrosive power spread to several planets, and they eventually took control of Earth. The Blight enslaved many Legionnaires in their search for M'ONEL, whose power they believed would give them immortality and end their existence as decaying beings. However, the Legion was able to destroy the Blight by teleporting their Doda captives across the known universe to revitalize the life forces drained by the techno-organic parasites. Without the Doda, the Blight were no longer able to teleport or spread their putrefaction throughout the galaxy. **PJ**

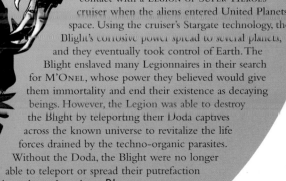

BLOCKBUSTER I

FIRST APPEARANCE DETECTIVE COMICS #345 (November 1965)
STATUS Villain (deceased)   **REAL NAME** Mark Desmond
OCCUPATION None   **BASE** Gotham City
HEIGHT 7ft 4in   **WEIGHT** 645 lbs   **EYES** Brown   **HAIR** Brown
SPECIAL POWERS/ABILITIES Secret serum gave Desmond tremendous strength, endurance, and invulnerability, but severely diminished his mental capacity.

Mark Desmond wanted to become stronger, but instead of working out with weights, he decided to use chemistry. He experimented on himself and grew taller and stronger, but, in the process, was turned into a mindless brute. Desmond was cared for by his criminal brother Roland, who shielded their mother from the news that Mark was now a monster. Roland used Mark to commit crimes until they were stopped by BATMAN and ROBIN. Desmond had once been rescued from drowning by Bruce Wayne, and the Dark Knight Detective discovered that he could stall the behemoth simply by removing his cowl and showing Desmond his face. The sight calmed the giant, preventing further destruction. Blockbuster, as he was known, sought solitude when free, only to find himself opposing the Caped Crusader on various occasions. He was recruited by Amanda Waller (see WALLER, AMANDA) for her new SUICIDE SQUAD, and he died battling DARKSEID's creation, Brimstone. RG

BLOCKBUSTER II

FIRST APPEARANCE STARMAN (1st series) #9 (April 1989)
STATUS Villain (deceased)   **REAL NAME** Roland Desmond
OCCUPATION Gang leader   **BASE** Blüdhaven
HEIGHT 8ft   **WEIGHT** 527 lbs   **EYES** Brown   **HAIR** Brown
SPECIAL POWERS/ABILITIES Superstrength, invulnerability, enhanced speed, and a brilliant criminal mind.

Blüdhaven's crime boss was a giant with a brain to match. He obtained his awesome acumen by selling his soul to the demon NERON. Desmond became Blockbuster II when a gene bomb detonation during the alien Invasion turned him into a towering brute. Like his brother Mark (BLOCKBUSTER I), Roland now possessed superhuman strength and a child's IQ. He went on a rampage, but STARMAN and BATMAN ensured that the befuddled behemoth wound up behind bars.

Acquiring a genius-level intellect became Desmond's obsession. When Neron made it a reality, Desmond set up shop in his mother's home city of Blüdhaven, forced out crimelord Angel Marin, and took over his organization.

Blüdhaven's protector, NIGHTWING, and the all-knowing ORACLE irritated Blockbuster II. He took out his frustration by snapping his underlings' necks, creating the villain Torque when one victim survived. Suffering from albinism and a defective heart—side-effects of his condition—Blockbuster II received a heart transplant from one of Gorilla City's talking apes. Restored to health, he was tightening his grip on Blüdhaven and contemplating a takeover of Gotham City when he was shot and killed by TARANTULA II. DW

BLOODSPORT

FIRST APPEARANCE SUPERMAN (2nd series) #4 (April 1987)
STATUS Villain   **REAL NAME** Robert DuBois
OCCUPATION Vigilante   **BASE** Metropolis
HEIGHT 6ft 1in   **WEIGHT** 231 lbs   **EYES** Brown   **HAIR** Black
SPECIAL POWERS/ABILITIES Can teleport rifles, handguns, and other firearms from a distant location and into his hands.

Bloodsport emerged on the scene during SUPERMAN's early days as protector of Metropolis. He claimed to be a war veteran named Robert DuBois, exhibiting symptoms of battlefield trauma that had apparently driven him insane. Using teleportation technology that allowed him to instantly call upon a variety of weapons — including some that fired kryptonite bullets—Bloodsport went on a rampage through Metropolis until stopped by the Man of Steel and DuBois' own brother.

A second Bloodsport, this one a white supremacist named Alex Trent, possessed similar abilities in the field of weapon-teleportation. Alex Trent died shortly after engaging in a prison boxing match with Robert DuBois.

The original Bloodsport seems to have reappeared, teaming with RIOT, HELLGRAMMITE, and other villains to ambush Superman a year after the Infinite Crisis. DW

BLUE DEVIL

FIRST APPEARANCE FURY OF FIRESTORM #24 (June 1984)
STATUS Hero (reluctant)   **REAL NAME** Daniel Patrick Cassidy
OCCUPATION Demon   **BASE** Mobile
HEIGHT 6ft 8in   **WEIGHT** 365 lbs   **EYES** Red   **HAIR** None
SPECIAL POWERS/ABILITIES In demonic form, Cassidy has enhanced strength, durability, and speed.

An encounter with the demon Nebiros left stuntman Daniel Cassidy permanently bonded with the costume he was wearing for his new movie, and he soon became known as Blue Devil. Daniel frantically tried to escape the suit before resigning himself to his lot. His transformation seemed to turn him into a "weirdness magnet," and Daniel found himself spending his time fighting demons, criminals, and a freaked out public. S.T.A.R. Labs director Jenet Klyburn connected Blue Devil to SUPERMAN and the JUSTICE LEAGUE OF AMERICA. Mistress of Magic Zatanna arranged for Daniel and Nebiros to meet. The encounter went badly and Zatanna, Blue Devil, and the Mexican Army joined forces to return Nebiros to his other-dimensional prison.

Resigned to the life of a super hero, Blue Devil briefly joined the JLA. He eventually made a deal with the demon NERON in exchange for becoming a successful actor. He learned too late that success as a thespian came at a terrible price: the life of his friend, director Marla Bloom, and his own transformation into a true demon. Blue Devil was subsequently killed in combat with MIST II. During the Day of Judgment, the magician Faust (see FAUST, FELIX) resurrected Daniel and turned him into a powerful demon. Blue Devil obtained the fabled trident of Lucifer and joined the SHADOWPACT, helping the team battle the SPECTRE and other threats. RG

SUPERNATURAL WEAPON
Blue Devil puts the Trident of Lucifer to good use.

BLUE BEETLE

BLUE BEETLE I
FIRST APPEARANCE BLUE BEETLE (1st series) #1 (June 1964)
STATUS Hero (deceased) **REAL NAME** Dr. Daniel Garrett
OCCUPATION Adventurer **BASE** Hub City
HEIGHT 6ft **WEIGHT** 189 lbs **EYES** Blue **HAIR** Red
SPECIAL POWERS/ABILITIES Superstrong; able to fly and discharge lightning-like energy from fingertips; chain-mail armor impervious to small-arms fire.

BLUE BEETLE II
FIRST APPEARANCE CAPTAIN ATOM (1st series) #83 (Nov. 1966)
STATUS Adventurer (deceased) **REAL NAME** Theodore "Ted" Kord
OCCUPATION Adventurer **BASE** New York City
HEIGHT 5ft 11in **WEIGHT** 184 lbs **EYES** Blue **HAIR** Brown
SPECIAL POWERS/ABILITIES The second Blue Beetle possesses no superpowers, but is a genius inventor and a capable hand-to-hand combatant. His BB-gun has several settings, including a walloping compressed-air blast and blinding strobe light. The Beetle's greatest weapon is his "Bug," a stealthy, solar-powered crime-fighting vehicle.

BLUE BEETLE III
FIRST APPEARANCE INFINITE CRISIS #5 (March 2006)
STATUS Hero REAL NAME Jaime Reyes
OCCUPATION High-school student, adventurer BASE El Paso, Texas
HEIGHT 5ft 8in WEIGHT 145 lbs EYES Brown HAIR Black
SPECIAL POWERS/ABILITIES Alien suit provides protection, flight, enhanced strength, and can generate many forms of weaponry.

After discovering a glowing azure scarab in the tomb of the evil Pharaoh Kha-ef-re, archaeologist Dr. Daniel Garrett gained miraculous powers when he uttered the words "Kaji Dha." Possessing superhuman abilities and clad in azure chain-mail armor, Garrett fought evil in Hub City as the first Blue Beetle. Years later, Garrett helped student Ted Kord thwart Kord's Uncle Jarvis and his plans for world domination. The battle left Blue Beetle mortally wounded. With his dying breath, Garrett made young Kord promise that he would carry on in his stead, thus ensuring that the Blue Beetle's heroic legacy would continue.

BEETLE POWER With his mystic scarab empowering him, the original Blue Beetle was a veritable superman!

TED KORD

When Dan Garrett was grievously injured thwarting the maniacal Jarvis Kord from dominating the world with his army of robots, Garrett asked his friend and protégé, Ted Kord, Jarvis's nephew, to carry on in his stead as Blue Beetle II. But before Garrett could pass on the mystic scarab that gave him his astounding abilities, the dying hero and his talisman were entombed under tons of rubble on the remote Pago Island, site of Jarvis Kord's failed plot. Undaunted, Kord trained himself in a variety of fighting skills and developed an arsenal of non-lethal weapons to let him operate as a non-powered Blue Beetle, whose sense of adventurous whimsy was in stark contrast to Dan Garrett's stalwart stoicism. Once more,

MAN ON A MISSION
Kord flies to Checkmate HQ to investigate Maxwell Lord's database on meta-humans.

there was a Blue Beetle to keep evil at bay in Hub City, where he added his own rogues gallery to villains inherited from Dan Garrett. Later, the Beetle moved to Chicago and made the Windy City safer during his tenure there. Unfortunately, super heroics haven't always been as easy for the second Blue Beetle as for the original Azure Avenger. Ted hasn't always been able to devote complete attention to running K.O.R.D. (Kord Omniversal Research and Development), a high-tech corporation he built up from the tiny company inherited from his father. And Ted can attest that he has had even less time leftover for his infrequent romances. During Blue Beetle's investigation of CHECKMATE, Maxwell Lord shot the hero in the head. Ted Kord's death shocked the super-hero community, and inspired BOOSTER GOLD to attempt to reverse the event through time travel. A third Blue Beetle, the teenager Jaime Reyes, emerged in Texas during the Infinite Crisis and now serves alongside the TEEN TITANS. **SB**

MURDERED Ted Kord is shot dead by Maxwell Lord in the headquarters of Checkmate.

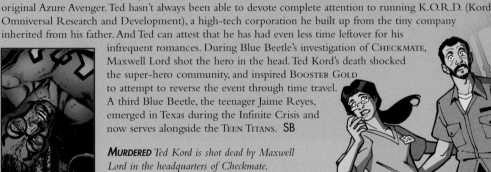

STRANGE FIND
At first Jaime and his friends think the scarab is just a big bug.

JAIME REYES

The scarab that gave Dan Garrett his powers found its way into SHAZAM's Rock of Eternity. When the Rock exploded before the Infinite Crisis, the scarab landed in Texas and bonded to Jaime Reyes's spine. After experimenting, Jaime could generate body armor, jet packs, and weapons. He became Blue Beetle, joining BATMAN, GREEN ARROW, MISTER TERRIFIC II, and others against the Brother Eye satellite controlling an army of OMAC units on Earth. Jaime spent nearly a year lost in the extradimensional Bleed between parallel worlds. He found a mentor in the PEACEMAKER and romance with TRACI THIRTEEN while crossing paths with Guy Gardner (see GREEN LANTERN) and the SPECTRE. During a fight with ECLIPSO, the evil being promised to bring Jaime's fantasies to life, revealing his deepest desire to be a comfortable living as a dentist. Jaime recently learned that his scarab is the creation of the alien species, the Reach. The scarab was to act as an advance agent, but through Jaime's influence, Blue Beetle III became one of the Reach's most persistent enemies. Jaime relies on friends and family to ease the stress of adventuring. He has formed a second family with the TEEN TITANS.

KEY STORYLINES

• **JSA #1 (August 1999):** Jared Stevens, possessor of Nabu's talismans, is killed by the minions of Mordru, thus paving the way for the long-awaited return of Dr. Fate.

• **Doctor Fate (4th series) #1-4 (October 2003–February 2004):** Hector Hall battles and destroys the Curse, a timeless evil that wrecked ancient Egypt, as he settles in at Dr. Fate's Salem tower.

BODY DOUBLES

FIRST APPEARANCE RESURRECTION MAN #1 (March 1996)
STATUS Villains **REAL NAMES** Bonny Hoffman and Carmen Leno
OCCUPATION Assassins **BASE** Mobile
HEIGHT (Bonny) 5ft 8in; (Carmen) 6ft **WEIGHT** (Bonny) 125 lbs;
(Carmen) 140 lbs **EYES** (Bonny) blue; (Carmen) brown
HAIR (Bonny) blonde; (Carmen) black
SPECIAL POWERS/ABILITIES Both women are martial-arts adepts and
experts with many types of firearms and concealed weapons.

The Body Doubles are hired killers who work for the
Requiem, Inc. Assassination Agency. Bonny Hoffman is
the daughter of an East Coast mob boss, while Carmen
Leno is a former adult film star and exotic dancer.
Bonny became an assassin to prove to her father that she
could be as tough as any man, while Carmen hoped
to advance her career as a legitimate Hollywood actress.
They employ the latest high-tech weaponry, as well as
murderous gadgets hidden in their makeup accessories.

The Body Doubles began working for Bonny's Uncle
Nick, an assassin himself, and a magnificent drag queen to
boot. As hired killers, the Body Doubles often came into
conflict with RESURRECTION MAN. They also tried to kill
CATWOMAN when she was running for mayor of New
York City, but their fighting skills proved no match for
the Princess of Plunder's. Exiled to a prison planet during
Operation: Salvation Run, the Body Doubles sacrificed
HELLHOUND to the local wildlife. **PJ**

DOUBLE TAKE "Beauty is the
Beast" is the motto of the
scantily-clad assassins, whose
fashion sense is matched by
their unerring aim!

BOLT

FIRST APPEARANCE BLUE DEVIL #6 (November 1984)
STATUS Villain **REAL NAME** Larry Bolatinsky
OCCUPATION Mercenary **BASE** Mobile
HEIGHT 6ft 4in **WEIGHT** 220 lbs **EYES** Blue **HAIR** Unrevealed
SPECIAL POWERS/ABILITIES Microcircuitry in costume allows flight,
projection of electrical energy bolts, and teleportation.

A former
special-effects
technician, Bolt
is a superpowered
assassin-for-hire
renowned for his skill,
stealth—and his price.
Bolt used his great wealth to
finance scientific experiments, and
created a number of teleporting battle suits. Bolt
was hired to kill the Trickster (see TRICKSTER II), a
foe of the FLASH III, but was foiled by the Trickster
and BLUE DEVIL. Bolt was also a constant thorn in
the sides of heroes like Blue Devil, CAPTAIN ATOM,
FIRESTORM, and STARMAN VI. Bolt joined the Killer
Elite, a group of assassins that included Merlyn, Chiller,
Deadline, and DEADSHOT, and later, the Task Force X
Mark II, a division of the SUICIDE SQUAD.

Bolt was thought to have been slain on a Task Force
mission, but returned with a host of super-villains in an
army led by Zandia's LADY ZAND and Baron Agua sin
Gaaz. Later still, on an assignment with the Calculator,
Bolt was shot and seriously wounded by street thugs. **PJ**

BOOSTER GOLD

FIRST APPEARANCE BOOSTER GOLD #1 (February 1986)
STATUS Hero **REAL NAME** Michael Jon Carter
OCCUPATION Adventurer **BASE** New York City
HEIGHT 6ft 5in **WEIGHT** 215 lbs **EYES** Blue **HAIR** Blond
SPECIAL POWERS/ABILITIES Costume allows him to fly, use a
protective forcefield, and gives enhanced strength.

College quarterback and gambler Michael Jon Carter
was banished from college athletics after many misdeeds.
As night watchman at the Space Museum, Carter
utilized Rip Hunter's time machine (see HUNTER, RIP),
stealing a security robot named Skeets, a LEGION OF
SUPER-HEROES flight ring, and BRAINIAC 5's forcefield
belt. He arrived back in the 20th century seeking
fortune and fame as Booster Gold. Before long he had
put an end to the criminal conclave the 1000, but the
battle left him severely injured.

Booster briefly returned to his home era to recover,
then escaped to the past, accompanied by his sister,
Michelle. Soon after, Maxwell Lord (LORD HAVOK)
began a JUSTICE LEAGUE OF AMERICA recruitment drive.
Booster joined up and befriended BLUE BEETLE II. As
the Justice League battled the aliens of Dimension X,
Booster Gold saw his sister Michelle perish. For a time,
he led the corporate team THE CONGLOMERATE, but
finally returned to the League. Booster was inactive for
a while after his powers were destroyed in a battle with
DOOMSDAY. Following Ice's funeral, Booster left the
League again, and joined the newly formed EXTREME
JUSTICE. After Blue Beetle's death and the Infinite
Crisis, Booster emerged on the scene in Metropolis,
both as himself and as the costumed Supernova. Faking
his death let Booster expose MISTER MIND and his plot
to destroy the multiverse. Booster joined Rip Hunter
to repair anomalies in the timestream. **RG**

BORDEAUX, SASHA

FIRST APPEARANCE DETECTIVE COMICS #751 (December 2000)
STATUS Ally **REAL NAME** Sasha Bordeaux
OCCUPATION U.S. government agent **BASE** Mobile
HEIGHT 5ft 7in **WEIGHT** 135 lbs **EYES** Blue **HAIR** Blonde
SPECIAL POWERS/ABILITIES Top athlete; skilled with most firearms.

WayneCorp chief Lucius Fox (see FOX, LUCIUS) insisted
that Bruce Wayne receive 24-hour protection. Former
secret service agent Sasha Bordeaux got the job. She
soon realized that her client lived a
second life as BATMAN. Bordeaux
teamed with him and even
fell in love, but their romance
ended when Lex Luthor (see
LUTHOR, LEX) ordered David
Cain (see CAIN, DAVID) to frame
them for the murder of radio host
Vesper Fairchild (see FAIRCHILD,
VESPER). Sasha loyally took the
blame and rotted in Blackgate
prison, while Bruce escaped
to clear his name. She joined
CHECKMATE and fought
the OMACs during the
Infinite Crisis, becoming
part OMAC herself. Now
a cyborg, she serves as
Checkmate's Black Queen. **DW**

24 CARAT GOLD Booster's 24th
century outfit has been modified over
time. When it was damaged beyond
repair, his pal Blue Beetle II helped
replicate its abilities, albeit in
a bulkier form (see
below).

BOUNCING BOY

FIRST APPEARANCE ACTION COMICS #276 (May 1961)
STATUS Hero   REAL NAME Chuck Taine
OCCUPATION Retired adventurer   BASE Earth
HEIGHT 5ft 8in   WEIGHT 221 lbs   EYES Blue   HAIR Black
SUPER POWERS/ABILITIES Able to inflate his body and bounce to great heights; highly resistant to injury.

In an alternate timeline of the LEGION OF SUPER-HEROES, Chuck Taine of Earth received superhuman powers when he accidentally drank an experimental serum. Now able to inflate his body like a beach ball, he joined the Legion as Bouncing Boy. Taine used his gift to bowl over enemy combatants and shrug off most injuries. After an adventurous career as a Legionnaire, Taine married teammate Triplicate Girl (see TRIAD) and retired from active service.

Bouncing Boy has yet to leave his mark in other Legion timelines. In the reality created after the events of Zero Hour, Chuck Taine worked with the Legion as an engineer and mechanic, but did not demonstrate his signature bouncing abilities. DW

BOUNTY

FIRST APPEARANCE SUPERBOY (1st series) #225 (March 1977)
STATUS Hero   REAL NAME Dawnstar
OCCUPATION Bounty hunter; Legionnaire   BASE Earth; Starhaven
HEIGHT 5ft 6in   WEIGHT 120 lbs   EYES Brown   HAIR Brown
SPECIAL POWERS/ABILITIES Wings enabled her to soar through space without a Legion flight ring; able to track with unerring accuracy.

A mutant Amerind from the planet Starhaven, the bounty hunter Dawnstar joined the pre-Zero Hour (see Great Battles, pp. 362–3) LEGION OF SUPER-HEROES and used her flying and tracking abilities in service to the United Planets. When the LSH disbanded in 2992, Dawnstar was among many members who departed Earth. The Legion later returned to action and one of the new members was Bounty, a mysterious mercenary. Bounty attempted to apprehend the wanted criminal Sade, who mortally wounded the Legionnaire. As her teammates watched, the invisible entity known as Bounty departed the body of Dawnstar. Later, it was learned that Bounty had possessed Dawnstar and had changed her appearance, cutting off her wings in order to act as a merciless bounty hunter and sate the entity's bloodlust. Unfortunately, Dawnstar was fully aware of Bounty's many murders. Following Zero Hour, both Bounty and Dawnstar were erased from the timeline and ceased to exist. SB

BOY COMMANDOS

FIRST APPEARANCE Detective Comics #64 (June 1942)
STATUS Hero team   BASE Europe
MEMBERS
Captain Eric "Rip" Carter
Alfy Tridgett
André Chavard
Daniel "Brooklyn" Turpin
Jan Haasan
Tex
Percy Clearweather

In 1942, Captain Eric "Rip" Carter led four resourceful boys—Alfy Twidgett, André Chavard (see CHAVARD, ANDRÉ), Daniel "Brooklyn" Turpin, and Jan Haasan—on missions throughout war-torn Europe as the Boy Commandos. Among their many successful missions, they pursued Agent Axis, "the vengeful arm of Heinrich Himmler," who was ultimately unmasked as a beautiful woman. In 1944, they traveled Stateside to briefly join forces with the GUARDIAN and the NEWSBOY LEGION to thwart gangster Boss Moxie and Agent Axis.

After the war, having achieved adulthood, several of the team joined Metropolis' Special Crimes Unit. RG

THE BOY COMMANDOS 1) Captain Rip Carter 2) Alfy 3) Jan 4) Percy 5) Tex 6) André 7) Brooklyn

BRADLEY, SLAM

FIRST APPEARANCE DETECTIVE COMICS #1 (March 1937)
STATUS Hero   REAL NAME Samuel Emerson Bradley
OCCUPATION Private investigator   BASE Gotham City
HEIGHT 6ft 1in   WEIGHT 205 lbs
EYES Gray   HAIR Dark brown with gray at temples
SPECIAL POWERS/ABILITIES Tough, two-fisted combatant and a highly skilled, persistent detective; loyal to his friends no matter what.

Former soldier and cop, Slam Bradley became a P.I. so he could be his own boss. Slam moved from city to city over the decades, working with other respected detectives such as MYSTO, POW-WOW SMITH, and the HUMAN TARGET. When his partner Shorty Morgan fell victim to a murderer, Slam tracked down the killer and solved a case that teamed him with BATMAN. Years later, Slam's son, Slam Jr., was hired by the mayor of Gotham City to find out whether CATWOMAN was alive or dead. Slam Jr. was so smitten by her, he suffered beatings to keep her existence secret. Slam Jr. fathered Catwoman's daughter, Helena. DW

SMITTEN KITTEN SLAM'S PASSION was briefly returned by Selina Kyle, the Catwoman. Despite the age difference, the two loners found that they had a great deal in common. Yet Slam realized that he could never be the one to tame the enigmatic feline fatale, and that only heartbreak awaited him if he got in too deep. They remain close friends and are utterly loyal to each other.

PUNCHDRUNK Slam earned his lifelong nickname as a child on the streets of Cleveland when he knocked out the local bully with a single punch. Slam can almost always outthink his opponents, but he often swings first and asks questions later. He likes a smoke and a drink—especially if a dame's giving him the runaround!

BRAIN

FIRST APPEARANCE DOOM PATROL (1st series) #86 (March 1964)
STATUS Villain **REAL NAME** Unrevealed
OCCUPATION Scientist, criminal mastermind **BASE** Mobile
HEIGHT 3ft 4in **WEIGHT** 195 lbs **EYES** Black **HAIR** None
SPECIAL POWERS/ABILITIES Genius-level IQ; occasionally uses the robot body Rog for mobility.

Little is known about the French scientist and criminal genius known as the Brain. Before his death, the scientist experimented on a captured African gorilla and gave it a near-genius intellect. When the scientist died, the ape, named MONSIEUR MALLAH, removed the man's brain and put it in a receptacle connected to a vast computer network. The scientist, now called the Brain, set up the villainous Brotherhood of Evil (*see* SOCIETY OF SIN) to further his goal of world conquest.

The Brotherhood attacked the DOOM PATROL several times over the years. Later, under the Brain's command, a second Brotherhood of Evil fought the TEEN TITANS.

The Brain and Mallah went into hiding after their defeat by the Titans. When a new Doom Patrol emerged, the Brain and Mallah broke into the Patrol's headquarters and stole one of ROBOTMAN II's robot bodies with the intention of placing the Brain inside it. The booby-trapped robot body exploded, but not before the villains could profess their undying love for each other. The Brain and Mallah survived and moved to the island of Zandia. They later came into conflict with Young Justice. PJ

BRAINIAC   SEE OPPOSITE PAGE

BRAINIAC 5

FIRST APPEARANCE ACTION COMICS #276 (May 1961)
STATUS Hero **REAL NAME** Querl Dox
OCCUPATION Legionnaire/scientist **BASE** Colu
HEIGHT 5ft 7in **WEIGHT** 135 lbs **EYES** Green **HAIR** Blond
SPECIAL POWERS/ABILITIES Super-genius; force field belt, with expandable and shapeable protective envelope, is mentally operated via Braniac control disks on Dox's forehead.

Descendent of L.E.G.I.O.N.'s Vril Dox, Brainiac 5 is the 31st century mastermind of the LEGION OF SUPER HEROES. A native of Colu, Brainiac 5 possesses a 12th-level intellect, making him one of the smartest beings in the United Planets. He helped design the Legion's flight rings, and keeps track of galactic trouble spots – often acting as "mission control" for Legionnaires in the field. His arrogance can be off-putting, but even his critics admit that Brainy is usually right.

Brainiac 5's inventions helped rescue MON-EL from the Phantom Zone, and prevented a Dominator takeover of Earth. Despite his insistence on reason and logic, Brainiac 5 fell in love with teammate DREAM GIRL, who could see the future through portents and premonitions. Brainy considered her tragic death a new puzzle to solve. SB

BRAINWAVE

FIRST APPEARANCE (I) ALL-STAR COMICS #15 (February-March 1943)
(II) ALL-STAR SQUADRON #24 (August 1983)
STATUS (I) Villain (II) Hero **REAL NAME** (I) Henry King (II) Henry King, Jr.
OCCUPATION (I) Evil genius (II) Adventurer **BASE** Mobile
HEIGHT (I) 5ft 7in (II) 5ft 10in **WEIGHT** (I) 128 lbs (II) 172 lbs
EYES (I) Blue (II) Blue **HAIR** (I) None (II) Red

Brainwave is a family legacy dating back to the 1940s, shared by father and son. During World War II, the first Brainwave (Henry King) used his vast psionic powers to terrorize the JUSTICE SOCIETY OF AMERICA. Able to control the minds of others and even project three-dimensional illusions, Brainwave embarked on a number of world-conquering schemes, both on his own and with the INJUSTICE SOCIETY OF AMERICA. With MERRY, GIRL OF 1,000 GIMMICKS, he fathered Henry King Jr.

Hank Jr. became the second Brainwave, joining the original INFINITY INC. Later he became a member of BLACK ADAM's super-hero strike force that overthrew the ruler of Khandaq. The ATOM II and the Justice Society determined that Brainwave's acts had actually been controlled by MISTER MIND. DW

BRANDE, R.J.

FIRST APPEARANCE LEGION OF SUPER-HEROES (4th ser.) #0 (Oct. 1994)
STATUS Ally **REAL NAME** René Jacques Brande
OCCUPATION Legion of Super-Heroes benefactor
BASE Legion World, U.P. Space
HEIGHT 5ft 11in **WEIGHT** 210 lbs **EYES** Black **HAIR** White
SPECIAL POWERS/ABILITIES Brilliant mind for business; possible telepathic and other abilities still unrevealed.

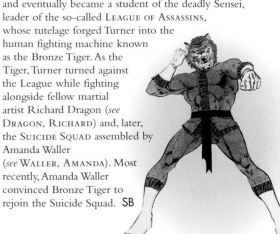

In one timeline containing the Legion of Super-Heroes, R.J. Brande made a fortune in the 30th century thanks to his space-hopping stargates that helped make possible the formation of the United Planets.

On a shuttle trip to Earth, an assassination attempt arranged by his business partner nearly claimed his life, but he survived due to the intervention of three super-powered teens. Brande dubbed his rescuers COSMIC BOY, SATURN GIRL, and LIVE WIRE, and arranged for them to join together as the founding members of the LEGION OF SUPER-HEROES.

The Legion soon distinguished itself with its own brand of enthusiastic heroism, and it wasn't long before Brande became President of the United Planets. Following an accidental tear in space known as the Great Rift Disaster, he left office under the scandal of impeachment, and the corrupt Leland McCauley became the U.P.'s new president. McCauley disbanded the Legion but Brande kept them operating in secret, financing the construction of Legion World to serve as their new headquarters. Although Brande has yet to address questions about his origin, his devotion to the Legion is in no doubt. DW

BRIMSTONE

FIRST APPEARANCE LEGENDS #1 (November 1986)
STATUS Villain **REAL NAME** None
OCCUPATION Destroyer **BASE** Mobile
HEIGHT 50ft 6in **WEIGHT** 60,000 lbs **EYES** Yellow **HAIR** None
SPECIAL POWERS/ABILITIES Incredible strength; generation of intense heat and flame; creation of a giant flaming sword.

The giant engine of destruction named Brimstone was created by DARKSEID when the member of the NEW GODS attempted to decimate all of Earth's legends. Darkseid's chief scientist DESAAD planted a technoseed in the heart of an experimental generator at S.T.A.R. Labs in New York City. When the generator exploded, Brimstone emerged and began a rampage throughout the city. Believing himself to be a fallen angel of some mysterious, avenging god, Brimstone soon encountered a number of heroes, including FIRESTORM, THE NUCLEAR MAN and the JUSTICE LEAGUE OF AMERICA. Discovering Brimstone's true nature as a ball of super-heated plasma, the newly formed SUICIDE SQUAD tracked the giant down and destroyed him by disrupting the magnetic fields that gave him form. Since then, Brimstone has been recreated a number of times, always bringing carnage and destruction. PJ

BRONZE TIGER

FIRST APPEARANCE RICHARD DRAGON: KUNG-FU FIGHTER #1 (May 1975)
STATUS Hero **REAL NAME** Benjamin Turner
OCCUPATION Martial arts master **BASE** Detroit
HEIGHT 6ft 3in **WEIGHT** 240 lbs **EYES** Brown **HAIR** Black
SPECIAL POWERS/ABILITIES Master of martial-arts disciplines, including Jeet Kune Do, Hap Kido, Silat, and Savate.

Ben Turner began his fighting career on the mean streets of East St. Louis. He developed an interest in martial arts and eventually became a student of the deadly Sensei, leader of the so-called LEAGUE OF ASSASSINS, whose tutelage forged Turner into the human fighting machine known as the Bronze Tiger. As the Tiger, Turner turned against the League while fighting alongside fellow martial artist Richard Dragon (*see* DRAGON, RICHARD) and, later, the SUICIDE SQUAD assembled by Amanda Waller (*see* WALLER, AMANDA). Most recently, Amanda Waller convinced Bronze Tiger to rejoin the Suicide Squad. SB

BRAINIAC

FIRST APPEARANCE ACTION COMICS #242 (July 1958)
STATUS Villain **REAL NAME** Vril Dox
OCCUPATION Cyber Conqueror **BASE** Mobile
HEIGHT Variable **WEIGHT** Variable **EYES** Red **HAIR** None
SPECIAL POWERS/ABILITIES A vast, superior intelligence limited only by the technology it currently inhabits. Knowledge of the universe is unparalleled, yet its hubris and emotions restrict its potential.

ONCE SCIENTIST PRIME on distant Colu, Vril Dox attempted to overthrow his technologically advanced world's Supreme Authority. Dox paid for his rebellion by being disintegrated. Yet somehow, his computer-like mind remained intact, traveling thousands of light years to Earth. Using his vast telepathic and psychokinetic abilities, Dox possessed the body of a sideshow mentalist named Milton Fine, to become the power-hungry Brainiac. When Fine's body proved too frail to contain Brainiac's power consciousness, he sought more suitable hosts, each time coming into opposition with SUPERMAN.

FOES *Brainiac's first meeting with the Man of Steel.*

REMAKE AND REMODEL

In the course of his attempts to conquer Earth, Brainiac has upgraded himself many times, even inhabiting the body of Superman's nemesis DOOMSDAY. Brainiac downloaded his evolved alien psyche into a flawless android shell to become Brainiac 2.5 and threaten Earth with his Omega Spears. These weapons generated an energy web that could shatter the world. After Superman thwarted this scheme, Brainiac 2.5 attempted to increase his personal power by linking all the world's computers, but instead created a portal that enabled his massive, all-powerful future self, Brainiac 13, to enter the 21st century. It took the combined efforts of Brainiac 2.5, Lex Luthor (*see* LUTHOR, LEX), and Superman to stop the computer tyrant. While the B13 persona was trapped in a Kryptonian warsuit, Brainiac's modern-day incarnation was trapped within the infant body of Lex's daughter, Lena. To save Metropolis from both present and future androids, Luthor was forced to bargain away his own daughter! At least B13 did help Earth stave off the threat of the cosmic conqueror IMPERIEX. Superman helped teleport the android to the dawn of creation. There, Brainiac 13's energies, coupled with the "Big Bang" itself, created two vast explosions that scattered Brainiac's consciousness over 60 trillion light years of space and time. Brainiac came back even from this, using a future descendent, Brainiac 8 (INDIGO) in a plot to destroy the OUTSIDERS. **RG**

BRAINWAVE *The B13 incarnation nearly destroyed Superman and overwrote the entire city of Metropolis.*

MULTIPLE FORMS *Over the years, Brainiac has been constantly upgraded. The skull-shaped vessel (above) attempted an attack on the Earth. It took Superman and other heroes to repel the invasion and avoid panic in the skies.*

EXCHANGE *Brainiac 2.5, seen here with Lex Luthor's daughter, a pawn in a greater game.*

GREAT MIND *Brainiac in his Coluan form of Vril Dox, before he was exiled for attempting to overthrow his homeworld.*

KEY STORYLINES

• *SUPERMAN Y2K (TPB, 2001):* Brainiac 13 reaches back from the 30th century to try to control Superman and Metropolis.
• *PANIC IN THE SKIES (TPB, 1993):* Brainiac launches an all-out assault on the Earth.
• *THE LUTHOR-BRAINIAC TEAM, SUPERMAN (2ND SERIES) #27-28:* Together, the two masterminds attempt to bring down the Man of Steel.
• *SUPERMAN: THE DOOMSDAY WARS (TPB, 1999):* Brainiac takes over Doomsday.

BROTHERHOOD OF DADA

FIRST APPEARANCE DOOM PATROL (2nd series) #26 (September 1989)
STATUS Anarchic rogues **BASE** Mobile
SPECIAL POWERS/ABILITIES
Mister Nobody (deceased) Can drain the sanity from others.
Sleepwalk Vast superstrength while sleepwalking.
Frenzy Transforms into a whirling cyclone.
Fog Transforms into psychedelic cloud that absorbs human beings.
Quiz Manifests every super-power never thought of.
Agent "!" (deceased) Blends into any crowd.
Number None Can occupy anyone or anything.
Alias the Blur (deceased) Can consume chunks of time.
The Toy Powers unknown.

A man known only as Mister Morden was an unscrupulous scientist who longed to join the nefarious Brotherhood of Evil (see SOCIETY OF SIN). But Morden doublecrossed the Brotherhood and, fleeing their wrath, escaped to Paraguay. There, Morden met a former Nazi war criminal named Dr. Bruckner and agreed to be the guinea pig for one of Bruckner's experiments. Morden was driven insane before being transformed into the abstract man called MISTER NOBODY. Mister Nobody then traveled across the world, gathering other strange outcasts, including Sleepwalk, Frenzy, the Fog, and the Quiz. Mister Nobody took these outcasts and organized a new syndicate that pledged itself to the absurdity of life. Believing evil was an outdated concept, Mister Nobody christened himself and his companions the Brotherhood of Dada. The Brotherhood proceeded to steal a mystic painting that had the power to devour any being that beheld it. The Brotherhood of Dada unleashed the painting on Paris, absorbing the city. THE DOOM PATROL arrived in the nick of time, saving the city of Paris from the painting and returning it to our world. The Brotherhood, however, chose to remain in the strange world inside. Mister Nobody later escaped the painting and assembled a new Brotherhood of Dada, including Agent "!", Number None, Alias the Blur, and the Toy.

After trying to promote their cheerful form of anarchy on a worldwide tour, the Brotherhood tried to dissipate the barriers between the magic painting and our reality, but were stopped by the government and the Doom Patrol. **PJ**

GROUP ABSURDITY *The Brotherhood of Dada encouraged the outrageous and the absurd. Tragically, they were thwarted by the mundane normalcy of humanity. The Brotherhood included* **1)** *the Quiz* **2)** *Frenzy* **3)** *Mister Nobody* **4)** *Sleepwalk.*

BROTHER BLOOD

FIRST APPEARANCE NEW TEEN TITANS #21 (July 1982)
STATUS Villain **REAL NAME** Unknown
OCCUPATION High priest **BASE** Zandia
HEIGHT 6ft 2in **WEIGHT** 193 lbs **EYES** Gray **HAIR** Black
SPECIAL POWERS/ABILITIES Circuitry built into his uniform of office generates bolts of energy; cloak has undefined mystical qualities.

The first Brother Blood was the high priest of the Baltic country of Zandia who refused to supply recruits for Pope Innocent's Fourth Crusade in 1202. During the ensuing battle, the high priest gained the Cloak of Christ, allegedly worn at the Last Supper, but now corrupted with evil. Wearing the cloak, the priest led his knights to victory. He then bathed in his enemies' blood, which gave him great strength and virtual immortality. The priest declared himself Brother Blood and closed Zandia to all strangers.

He ruled for 60 years, fathering a son who killed him at the age of 100. So began the terrible Curse of Blood, whereby each son of Zandia's ruler slew his father, bathed in the Bloodpit, then ruled in his place.

This gruesome pattern of events has recently continued as yet another son has killed his father. However, this particular 14-year-old lacks the training of his predecessors. Instead, his ultimate goal is world domination using his church's might. The OUTSIDERS and TEEN TITANS, though, stand in his way. **RG**

BROTHER POWER, THE GEEK

FIRST APPEARANCE BROTHER POWER, THE GEEK #1 (October 1968)
STATUS Hero **REAL NAME** None
OCCUPATION Puppet elemental **BASE** Mobile
HEIGHT 6ft **WEIGHT** 150 lbs **EYES** Blue **HAIR** Yellow
SPECIAL POWERS/ABILITIES Superstrength; resistant to injury; can manifest in puppets, mannequins, or other representations of man.

After a bummer of an evening one night in San Francisco, two put-upon hippies named Brother Nick and Brother Paul hung some of their threads on a tailor's rag-doll dummy in an abandoned clothing shop. A lightning strike, combined with the era's groovy vibes, somehow animated the dummy and transformed him into Earth's only "puppet elemental."

Brother Power the Geek drifted throughout California, helping out fellow free spirits and learning about the world in a series of unlikely predicaments. When a big-top promoter kidnapped Brother Power to be the centerpiece of his "Psychedelic Circus," Brother Nick and Brother Paul returned to spring their puppet-brother so he could continue his road-trip search for truth. Eventually he took a cosmic voyage aboard an experimental space missile that blasted into orbit. Years later he returned to Earth in Tampa, Florida, and from there continued his far-out wanderings. Brother Power appeared at John Constantine's 2000 New Year's party, where he was recognized as one of the totems of the new millennium. **DW**

BRUTALE

FIRST APPEARANCE NIGHTWING #22 (July 1998)
STATUS Villain **REAL NAME** Guillermo Barrera
OCCUPATION Mercenary **BASE** Hascaragua
HEIGHT 5ft 4in **WEIGHT** 145 lbs **EYES** Almond **HAIR** Black
SPECIAL POWERS/ABILITIES Master of knives, particularly his double-edge throwing knives, surgical scalpels, shivs, daggers, and machetes.

Guillermo Barrera was the most vicious police interrogator in the South American country of Hascaragua. He used his brutal torturing skills as a member of the secret police of a Cuban-backed Marxist regime. At last, the regime fell and Barrera faced execution for his atrocious crimes. He fled his homeland and became a freelance killer under the name of Brutale. The diminutive assassin-for-hire, donned a special uniform designed to hold his many and varied blades and knives. Working alongside Stallion, another assassin, Brutale was hired by Roland Desmond, the Blüdhaven criminal mastermind BLOCKBUSTER, to kill BATMAN's ally NIGHTWING. Brutale began the hunt, but Nightwing quickly defeated both would-be assassins. Brutale, however, escaped in a desperate effort to avoid incarceration and deportation to Hascaragua. **PJ**

BULLETGIRL I & II (WINDSHEAR)

FIRST APPEARANCE MASTER COMICS #13 (April 1941)
STATUS Hero (deceased)   **REAL NAME** Susan Kent
OCCUPATION Adventurer   **BASE** Fawcett City
HEIGHT 5ft 9in   **WEIGHT** 145 lbs   **EYES** Blue   **HAIR** Brown
SPECIAL POWERS/ABILITIES An excellent flyer.

FIRST APPEARANCE POWER OF SHAZAM! #32 (November 1997)
STATUS Hero   **REAL NAME** Deanna Barr
OCCUPATION Adventurer   **BASE** Fawcett City
HEIGHT 5ft 8in   **WEIGHT** 135 lbs   **EYES** Blue   **HAIR** Brown
SPECIAL POWERS/ABILITIES Army-trained marksman, pilot, and hand-to-hand combatant.

Susan Kent was sure there was something strange about her boyfriend, Jim Barr. Eventually she learned his secret—he was the super hero BULLETMAN! Susan insisted on accompanying him as Bulletgirl. Together they battled many villains during World War II. After the war, Jim and Susan were married and they retired from costume crime fighting in the mid-1950s. They raised a daughter, Deanna, and made a comfortable home in Fawcett City. After Susan died from unexplained causes, Deanna followed in their footsteps as Windshear, after stealing her mother's Bulletgirl outfit. Jim Barr returned to action one final time, teaming with his daughter to save Billy Batson (see CAPTAIN MARVEL), Mary Bromfield (see MARY MARVEL), and Freddy Freeman from CHAIN LIGHTNING. **RG**

BULLETMAN

FIRST APPEARANCE Nickel Comics #1 (May 1940)
STATUS Hero (retired)   **REAL NAME** James Barr
OCCUPATION Adventurer   **BASE** Fawcett City
HEIGHT 6ft 4in   **WEIGHT** 177 lbs   **EYES** Blue   **HAIR** White
SPECIAL POWERS/ABILITIES Brilliant to begin with, the Miraclo variation permanently increased his physical size, strength, and mental abilities; an excellent flyer and tactician.

Jim Barr, the son of a slain Fawcett City police officer, developed a variant of HAWKMAN's Thanagarian Nth metal and HOURMAN's Miraclo/steroid compound and took flight as Bulletman. He joined the wave of costumed adventurers that kept the U.S.'s cities safe during World War II. He was soon accompanied by his girlfriend Susan Kent, who became BULLETGIRL. Bulletman was the first American hero targeted by CAPTAIN NAZI. He later teamed up with STARMAN to stop a Nazi incursion into Alaska. There, the heroes encountered a scouting expedition by Venusian worms that was only curtailed by the intervention of GREEN LANTERN Abin Sur. After the war, Jim and Susan married and settled down in Fawcett City, where Jim built a merchandising empire based on Bulletman. When Barr was accused of having committed treason in 1942, CAPTAIN MARVEL and Starman VI cleared the veteran's name. **RG**

BULLETEER

FIRST APPEARANCE SEVEN SOLDIERS: THE BULLETEER #1 (January 2006)
STATUS Hero   **REAL NAME** Alix Harrower
OCCUPATION For-hire hero   **BASE** New York City
HEIGHT 6ft   **WEIGHT** 155 lbs   **EYES** White   **HAIR** Silver
SPECIAL POWERS/ABILITIES Enhanced strength; metallic skin provides extreme resistance to injury.

Alix Harrower became encased with an indestructible, metallic "smartskin" in an accident involving her boyfriend, the inventor of smartskin technology. He died of asphyxiation during the process, but Alix took the super-hero identity of Bulleteer and made a name for herself as a bodyguard and for-hire adventurer.

Bulleteer signed on to serve with VIGILANTE I's new grouping of the SEVEN SOLDIERS OF VICTORY, but backed out at the last minute. This spared her from the team's annihilation at the hands of the Sheeda, but Bulleteer became a part of the second, unofficial grouping of the Seven Soldiers. Ultimately, Bulleteer killed the Sheeda queen by hitting her with a car. After the Infinite Crisis, Bulleteer briefly joined the interim JUSTICE LEAGUE OF AMERICA. **DW**

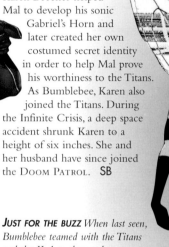

BULLOCK, SGT.

FIRST APPEARANCE DETECTIVE COMICS #441 (June 1974)
STATUS Hero   **REAL NAME** Harvey Bullock
OCCUPATION Former police officer   **BASE** Gotham City
HEIGHT 5ft 10in   **WEIGHT** 248 lbs   **EYES** Brown   **HAIR** Black
SPECIAL POWERS/ABILITIES Despite shabby appearance, has sharp deductive mind; virtually unstoppable in a brawl.

Harvey Bullock wears his moods on his sleeve, along with the crumbs that fall from the donuts he munches whenever he's not chewing on a soggy cigar. A corrupt mayor made him James Gordon's assistant in order to keep an eye on the commissioner (see GORDON, JAMES W.). Developing a deep respect for his boss, Bullock told the mayor where to stick it and became an ally of both Gordon and BATMAN. Bullock later worked for the U.S. government's CHECKMATE agency as a Bishop, but soon returned to Gotham. He aided the city during the catastrophe known as No Man's Land and became head of the G.C.P.D. Major Crimes Unit. When a gunman nearly killed Gordon, Bullock helped the would-be killer's mob enemies rub the hood out. After working as a private detective, Bullock returned to the G.C.P.D., ready to make a fresh start. **DW**

BUMBLEBEE

FIRST APPEARANCE TEEN TITANS (1st series) #45 (December 1976)
STATUS Hero   **REAL NAME** Karen Beecher-Duncan
OCCUPATION Research engineer; writer   **BASE** San Francisco
HEIGHT 5ft 7in   **WEIGHT** 130 lbs   **EYES** Brown   **HAIR** Black
SPECIAL POWERS/ABILITIES Solar-powered antennae in cybernetic helmet create electrical "stings" emitted through quartz prism eyepieces; exoskeletal wings enable flight and create sonic disruptions.

The girlfriend of Mal Duncan during his membership with the original TEEN TITANS, Karen Beecher helped Mal to develop his sonic Gabriel's Horn and later created her own costumed secret identity in order to help Mal prove his worthiness to the Titans. As Bumblebee, Karen also joined the Titans. During the Infinite Crisis, a deep space accident shrunk Karen to a height of six inches. She and her husband have since joined the DOOM PATROL. **SB**

JUST FOR THE BUZZ When last seen, Bumblebee teamed with the Titans and the JLA to thwart the extraterrestrial Technis.

BUSHMASTER

FIRST APPEARANCE SUPER FRIENDS (November 1977); (in DCU continuity) DC COMICS PRESENTS #46 (July 1982)
STATUS Hero (deceased)   **REAL NAME** Bernal Rojas
OCCUPATION Herpetologist   **BASE** The Dome
HEIGHT 5ft 10in   **WEIGHT** 175 lbs   **EYES** Brown   **HAIR** Brown
SPECIAL POWERS/ABILITIES Cybernetic costume allowed him to duplicate various reptilian abilities, including infrared vision, suction devices on hands and feet, a venom gun, heat sensors, camouflage, and flight.

Bernal Rojas was a renowned herpetologist from Caracas, Venezuela. Using his knowledge of reptiles from all over the world, Rojas invented a special costume that allowed him to duplicate various reptilian abilities. Donning this garish cyber suit, Rojas called himself the Bushmaster and became a crime-fighting crusader in his native Venezuela. Bushmaster was one of the founding members of the GLOBAL GUARDIANS, a worldwide organization of heroes formed by the mysterious DOCTOR MIST, that fought both local crime and cosmic invaders. Bushmaster was shot and killed by bank robbers as he was also being attacked by one of Doctor Mist's enemies, a madman named Fain Y'Onia. **PJ**

CACHIRU

FIRST APPEARANCE THE FLASH ANNUAL (2nd series) #13 (2000)
STATUS Hero **REAL NAME** Unrevealed
OCCUPATION Adventurer **BASE** Argentina
HEIGHT 5ft 9in **WEIGHT** 170 lbs **EYES** Blue **HAIR** Black
SPECIAL POWERS/ABILITIES Capable of flight, although not at great heights or with great speed; experienced hand-to-hand combatant who relies on his talons for greater advantage.

Argentina has its own team of costumed protectors, the SUPER-MALON (which includes Cimarron, El Bagual, El Lobizon, El Yaguarete, Pampero, SALA, and Vizacacha). Among them is Cachiru, with his owl-like mask and razor-sharp talons. A veteran crime fighter, he earned the FLASH III's respect when they shared an adventure together. He had been fellow teammate Salamanca's lover, and still pines for her, long after their breakup. RG

CADRE, THE

FIRST APPEARANCE JUSTICE LEAGUE OF AMERICA #235 (February 1985) **BASE** Mobile
ORIGINAL MEMBERS AND POWERS
Overmaster (leader) Alien superbeing.
Black Mass Wristbands provide control over graviton particles.
Crowbar Wields energized crowbar.
Fastball Throws explosive spheres using powered exoskeleton.
Nightfall Wristbands create null-field that absorbs light and energy.
Shatterfist Martial artist with energy-charged hands.
Shrike (deceased) Possessed a paralyzing shriek; flew at superspeed.

A creation of the near-omnipotent alien being the Overmaster, the Cadre has existed in many forms. The original Cadre consisted of Black Mass, Crowbar, Fastball, Nightfall, Shatterfist, and Shrike. They battled the JUSTICE LEAGUE OF AMERICA in a contest designed to prove to the Overmaster whether the human race deserved to survive. After his team's defeat, the Overmaster gathered many new recruits to his cause and arrived at Mount Everest on Earth at the head of his new, massive Cadre. CAPTAIN ATOM and the Justice League fought back against the Cadre, claiming victory by detonating the alien tyrant's starship. Since then a few villains have attempted to start a new Cadre separate from the Overmaster's influence. DW

THE ORIGINAL CADRE
1) The Overmaster
2) Nightfall 3) Crowbar
4) Fastball 5) Black Mass
6) Shatterfist 7) Shrike

CAIN, DAVID

FIRST APPEARANCE BATMAN #567 (July 1999)
STATUS Villain **REAL NAME** Unknown; possibly David Cain
OCCUPATION Adventurer **BASE** Incarcerated in Black Gate Prison
HEIGHT 6ft 2in **WEIGHT** 245 lbs **EYES** Blue **HAIR** Gray
SPECIAL POWERS/ABILITIES One of the world's greatest martial artists; knows every move of every fighting style on the planet; highly skilled with every kind of firearm.

Cain is one of the most proficient assassins in the world. Quiet and focused, Cain considers killing an art form. Cain was Bruce Wayne's martial-arts master for a brief time, training the young millionaire before clashing with Wayne over methodology. Cain had also adopted an infant girl named Cassandra whom he raised to be his assistant and successor. Teaching Cassandra the "language" of martial arts but no other, Cain devoted himself

so exclusively to her upbringing that the rest of the world thought that he had died. Several years later Cassandra learned that she had been raised to be a murderer and fled from Cain in horror.

The gang boss TWO-FACE subsequently hired Cain to kill Commissioner Gordon (*see* GORDON, JAMES W.*) in Gotham City. There, Cain confronted Cassandra, now BATGIRL, who rejected him and allied herself with BATMAN. After taking over the LEAGUE OF ASSASSINS, Cassandra killed her father. PJ

ONE WHO IS ALL *Cassandra is still one of the world's top fighters, thanks to the training she received under her father's guidance. Batman has trusted her as a member of the new Outsiders.*

FATAL FATE *After Robin got Cain out of prison, Cassandra secured her status as head of the League of Assassins by shooting her father.*

SINISTER SENSEI *David Cain refused to teach his daughter to speak, so body language was her only form of communication.*

CAIN AND ABEL

FIRST APPEARANCE (Abel) HOUSE OF SECRETS (1st series) #81
(August 1969); (Cain) HOUSE OF MYSTERY #175
(July 1968)
STATUS Heroes *REAL NAMES* None
OCCUPATION Caretakers/storytellers *BASE* The House of
Secrets (Abel); The House of Mystery (Cain)
HEIGHT 5ft 7in (Abel); 6ft 2in (Cain)
WEIGHT 396 lbs (Abel); 174 lbs (Cain)
EYES Blue (Abel); brown (Cain) *HAIR* Black (Abel);
brown (Cain)
SPECIAL POWERS/ABILITIES Can both be endlessly resurrected.

Inhabitants of the mystical, supernatural realm
known as Dreaming, Cain and Abel are believed
to be the original "first victim/first murderer" of
Biblical lore. After Abel's initial death at Cain's
hands—triggered by an argument over a woman—
Morpheus, the Lord of Dreams, gave them both
positions as storytellers.

On Earth, the brothers work as caretakers for
two eerie structures located on opposite sides of
a cemetery in the hills of Kentucky. Abel watches
over The House of Secrets and Cain is custodian of
The House of Mystery. They both delight in telling
horrific tales to visitors.

When the Furies of Greek legend killed Abel,
his death looked permanent, but Cain won his
brother a special resurrection from the new Lord
of Dreams by claiming that his contract with
Morpheus stipulated that Cain and Abel were to
remain a "double act." Cain has now resumed his habit of murdering Abel in continual
reenactments of the "first story," secure in the knowledge that the ceremony causes Abel
no lasting harm.

Cain possesses a unique advantage over his brother in that he wears the Mark of Cain,
an indicator that he cannot be harmed lest the perpetrator suffer God's wrath.
This allowed him to enter the realm of Hell without fear in order to deliver
a message for Morpheus.

The House of Secrets later became
the headquarters for the latest
incarnation of the SECRET SIX.
Although Abel appeared to have
vacated the home, it still
possessed mystical qualities
that protected the Six from
detection by outside forces.
Unfortunately the Society (*see*
VILLAINS UNITED) found and
attacked the House of Secrets,
leading to a free-for-all battle
within its walls.
DW

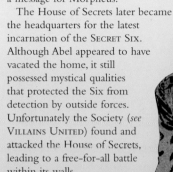

*GARGOYLE Abel
has a soft spot for
pet monsters.*

CALCULATOR

FIRST APPEARANCE DETECTIVE COMICS #463 (September
1976)
STATUS Villain *REAL NAME* Noah Kuttler
OCCUPATION Information broker *BASE* Mobile
HEIGHT 5ft 11in *WEIGHT* 189 lbs *EYES* Green *HAIR* Red
SPECIAL POWERS/ABILITIES Genius at manipulating computer
networks and data retrieval.

The Calculator is one of the most brilliant
criminals active today, and is a key information-
broker in the world of supervillainy. He began
his career as the Calculator by wearing a keypad-
themed costume to evoke the appearance of a
pocket calculator. After a disastrous stint as a third-
rate villain, he reinvented himself as a computer
expert and a sinister counterpart to the super
heroes' data resource, ORACLE.

The Calculator became a member of the ruling
circle of the newest Secret Society of Super-Villains
(*see* VILLAINS UNITED) and has engaged in a running
feud with Oracle, with most of their battles taking
place over the internet. DW

*ONLINE IMPACT The Calculator employs multiple
monitors and data feeds.*

CALENDAR MAN

FIRST APPEARANCE DETECTIVE COMICS #259 (September 1958)
STATUS Villain *REAL NAME* Julian Day
OCCUPATION Thief *BASE* Gotham City
HEIGHT 6ft 11in *WEIGHT* 193 lbs *EYES* Blue *HAIR* Brown
SPECIAL POWERS/ABILITIES Highly-intelligent strategist and inventor

The Calendar Man is Julian Day, one of the many "theme
villains" active in Gotham City who are frequent irritants
for the BATMAN. Day's obsession with calendars manifests
in crimes tied to specific days of the year, though he has
never progressed to become more than a third-rate super-
villain. At one point, he teamed with CAT-MAN and Killer
Moth (see CHARAXES) to form a group called the Misfits.

Due to his lack of success, Calendar Man often finds
himself behind bars. There, his bizarre expertise sometimes
comes in handy. An incarcerated Calendar Man helped
Batman deduce the identity of a serial killer whose crimes
coincided with major holidays. DW

CAPTAIN BOOMERANG

FIRST APPEARANCE FLASH #117 (December 1960)
STATUS Villain (deceased) **REAL NAME** George Harkness
OCCUPATION Criminal **BASE** Keystone City
HEIGHT 5ft 9in **WEIGHT** 167 lbs **EYES** Brown **HAIR** Brown
SPECIAL POWERS/ABILITIES A boomerang-throwing expert, he has developed numerous boomerangs with specific functions.

CAPTAIN BOOMERANG II
FIRST APPEARANCE IDENTITY CRISIS #3 (October 2004)
STATUS Anti-hero **REAL NAME** Owen Mercer
OCCUPATION Adventurer, government agent **BASE** Mobile
HEIGHT 6ft 1in **WEIGHT** 190 lbs **EYES** Gray **HAIR** Red
SPECIAL POWERS/ABILITIES Skilled with boomerangs and other thrown weapons; can generate temporary bursts of super-speed

A NATIVE OF AUSTRALIA, George "Digger" Harkness was sent as a young adult to the U.S. by his mother, who was desperate to get her son away from his stepfather. He took a job demonstrating boomerangs for the Wiggins Game Company. Harkness, who had become an expert from years of throwing the wooden device as a kid, was given a uniform and the name Captain Boomerang. While demonstrating the boomerang to kids, Harkness liked to line his pockets with a spot of pilfering. This brought him into conflict with the second FLASH, whom Harkness opposed as Captain Boomerang with a variety of ever more bizarre boomerang gadgets. After the Flash's death, Captain Boomerang served on the government-sponsored SUICIDE SQUAD. However, he missed the thrill of stealing and secretly became MIRROR MASTER II. After the Squad temporarily folded, Captain Boomerang returned to a life of crime in Central City, opposed by Flash III. He died during the Identity Crisis event, shot by ROBIN's father. His son Owen Mercer has since taken up the identity of Captain Boomerang II. RG

COME BACK Captain Boomerang applied his native talent to incredible devices such as this deadly trap for the Flash II.

TEAM REBEL The first Captain Boomerang often clashed with the Suicide Squad's director Amanda Waller.

VERSATILE WEAPON Some boomerangs carried by both Captains can slice through steel. Other varieties include explosive boomerangs.

THE NEXT GENERATION

Owen Mercer never knew his real father until the events of the Identity Crisis, when Digger Harkness – the first Captain Boomerang – reestablished contact. Mercer discovered that he shared his father's talent for hurling boomerangs, and also that he could call upon temporary bursts of super-speed. It eventually came out that Mercer was the product of a tryst between Harkness and Meloni Thawne, the 30th century mother of Bart Allen (see the FLASH). Harkness died when shot by ROBIN III's father, and Mercer became the second Captain Boomerang.

Welcomed into the Flash's Rogues' Gallery by CAPTAIN COLD (who believed that Mercer might be his nephew and the son of his late sister the GOLDEN GLIDER). Mercer ran with the Rogues until a jail sentence brought him into contact with a wrongfully-imprisoned BLACK LIGHTNING. When Black Lightning's friends in the OUTSIDERS sprang him, Mercer came too. With the Outsiders he found a slightly more respectable family to replace the Rogues, teaming with CHECKMATE to infiltrate the Oolong Island facility run by Chang Tzu (see EGG FU). When BATMAN took control of the Outsiders, Mercer left the team. He found a new purpose with the U.S. government's SUICIDE SQUAD, hunting his former friends in the Rogues. Captain Boomerang II has established a close friendship with SUPERGIRL as well as a mutual respect with ROBIN, despite the fact that their fathers killed one another.

KEY STORYLINES

• *SUICIDE SQUAD (1ST SERIES) #1 (MAY 1987)*: Captain Boomerang is recruited into a squad of costumed criminals, where his meanness and sarcasm make him standout.
• *IDENTITY CRISIS #1–7 (JUNE–DEC. 2004)*: The original Captain Boomerang dies, making contact with his son just before his death.
• *ROBIN #152-153 (SEPTEMBER-OCTOBER 2006)*: The new Captain Boomerang and Robin search Gotham to find a bomb planted by the Joker.

VILLAIN RETURNS
Owen Mercer wears a patterned scarf to honor the criminal legacy of his father.

AT ODDS Their fathers killed one another during the events of the Identity Crisis, so Robin and Captain Boomerang II have had a hard time establishing a friendship.

KRYPTONITE CRAZY *Batman comes face to face with Captain Atom who, after colliding with a kryptonite meteor, has become infused with vast amounts of radiation become a super-villain known as "Kryptonite Man." Fortunately Hiro Okamura, the new Toyman managed to drain the radiation from Captain Atom's body and return him to normal.*

CAPTAIN ATOM

FIRST APPEARANCE SPACE ADVENTURES #33 (March 1960)
STATUS Hero (missing in action) **REAL NAME** Nathaniel Christopher Adam, a.k.a. Cameron Scott **OCCUPATION** Super hero **BASE** San Francisco **HEIGHT** 6ft 4in **WEIGHT** 200 lbs **EYES** Blue **HAIR** White
SPECIAL POWERS/ABILITIES Alien alloy covering body enables him to tap into the quantum field, which gives him superstrength, anti-gravity, and the ability to emit focused blasts of atomic energy; capable of absorbing nuclear energy and quantum leaping one day to one week into the future.

Decades ago, court-martialed Air Force Captain Nathaniel Adam volunteered for the top-secret Captain Atom Project in order to prove his innocence to charges of murder and treason. Adam's superiors theorized that a strange alien alloy would protect him from an atomic blast, a disastrous experiment that melded the alloy to Adam's body and catapulted him 18 years into the future. When the quantum-powered Adam reappeared, he was pardoned in exchange for service as the U.S.-sanctioned super hero, Captain Atom, a federally mandated member of Justice League International (*see* JUSTICE LEAGUE OF AMERICA). Captain Atom ultimately left Justice League's European branch to form a more proactive but short-lived super-heroic strike force, EXTREME JUSTICE. After journeying to a parallel Earth during the Infinite Crisis, Captain Atom became the new Monarch. Assembling an army of super heroes from across the multiverse, he made war against the MONITORS. **SB**

CAPTAIN COLD

FIRST APPEARANCE SHOWCASE #8 (May 1957)
STATUS Villain **REAL NAME** Leonard Snart
OCCUPATION Professional criminal **BASES** Central City/Keystone City
HEIGHT 6ft 2in **WEIGHT** 196 lbs **EYES** Brown **HAIR** Brown
SPECIAL POWERS/ABILITIES Cold-guns create ice slicks, shatter metal, or entomb victims in suspended animation in blocks of ice. Snow goggles minimize the flashes given off by Captain Cold's guns.

Raised by an abusive father, Leonard Snart found rare solace in the company of his grandfather, who drove an ice truck. Snart is one of the more sympathetic villains in the FLASH's Rogues Gallery, able to chat over a coffee while plotting to break into the Keystone City Bank over the weekend. He began his crime career shortly after Barry Allen's debut as the Flash. Developing an experimental handgun to interfere with the Flash's superspeed, Snart accidentally irradiated his weapon and wound up with a tool that could freeze the moisture in the air. He donned a parka and goggles and declared himself Captain Cold. He committed a string of (non-lethal)

crimes throughout Central and Keystone City, but his main pleasure lay in matching wits with the Flash. After Barry Allen's death during the Crisis (*see* Great Battles, pp. 320–1), a disheartened Snart left crime to become a licensed bounty hunter with his sister Lisa, the GOLDEN GLIDER. Captain Cold lost his eternal soul to the demonic Neron, but the third Flash, Wally West, brought him back to the land of the living. He soon returned to crime, this time as a member of Wally's Rogues Gallery. Captain Cold recently killed the villain Chillblaine in revenge for the death of his sister Lisa. He also helped an amnesiac Wally West defeat Mister Element. Yet, Snart remains an unrepentant crook, who *hates* being mistaken for MISTER FREEZE. **DW**

SLIPPERY SLOPE *Even the great Barry Allen often fell victim to Captain Cold's ice tricks.*

CAPTAIN COMET

FIRST APPEARANCE STRANGE ADVENTURES #9 (June 1951)
STATUS Hero   **REAL NAME** Adam Blake
OCCUPATION Interstellar operative   **BASE** The planet Cairn
HEIGHT 6ft 2in   **WEIGHT** 190 lbs   **EYES** Brown   **HAIR** Brown
SPECIAL POWERS/ABILITIES Superstrength, superspeed, limited invulnerability, telepathy, telekinesis, flight, slowed aging, photographic memory, vast intelligence, and athletic prowess.

Born in 1931, Adam Blake began displaying his mutant abilities by age eight when he read and memorized every fact in a set of encyclopedias. By his 18th birthday he had mastered sports, music, and science, but kept his unusual abilities a secret. He finally revealed his amazing powers to physicist Emery Zackro. Blake discovered that he was a mutant born with the abilities of a man 100,000 years in the future. When aliens attacked Earth in the 1950s, Adam took the name Captain Comet and repelled their invasion force.

Captain Comet eventually left Earth to seek adventure in space, traveling across the galaxy. After serving with L.E.G.I.O.N., Captain Comet fought in the Rann-Thanagar War. Later killed by Lady Styx, he temporarily merged his consciousness with the WEIRD before reappearing in a new, younger body. **PJ**

REBIRTH *After miraculously returning in a new, younger body, Captain Comet discovered that he now possessed limited powers of teleportation.*

CAPTAIN COMPASS

FIRST APPEARANCE STAR-SPANGLED COMICS #83 (August 1948)
STATUS Hero   **REAL NAME** Mark Compass
OCCUPATION Adventurer   **BASE** The High Seas
HEIGHT 6ft   **WEIGHT** 175 lbs   **EYES** Brown   **HAIR** Brown
SPECIAL POWERS/ABILITIES A skilled fighter with a keen deductive mind.

Mark Compass first acquired his sea legs as a frogman for the U.S. Navy, later commanding a few of the ships he had first served upon. In that regard, he became well-known as a capable and courageous captain, as well as a noted nautical investigator.

Following his naval stint, Compass was employed as a roving troubleshooter for Penny Steamship Lines. In his capacity as ship's detective aboard the *S.S. Nautilus*, Compass solved many mysteries on the high seas, as well as preventing crimes on the *Nautilus* and other vessels in the Penny Steamship Lines fleet.

At various times over the years, Compass even commanded the *Nautilus* himself. It is this ship in particular that he now calls his home. Captain Compass lives in his own personal cabin suite and enjoys semi-retirement while sleuthing the occasional seaborne mystery. **SB**

CAPTAIN FEAR

FIRST APPEARANCE ADVENTURE COMICS #425 (January 1973)
STATUS Hero (deceased)   **REAL NAME** Fero
OCCUPATION Pirate   **BASE** The Caribbean
HEIGHT 5ft 6in   **WEIGHT** 160 lbs   **EYES** Blue   **HAIR** Black
SPECIAL POWERS/ABILITIES Excellent swordsman, sailor, and fighter, matched only by his skills as a leader and tactician; an average pilot and navigator.

Fero, a young Carib Indian, was taken captive in a Spanish raid sometime in the 16th century. Enslaved and put to work in a Spanish mine, Fero led the captives in a revolt against their oppressors. After stealing a Spanish galleon, losing its crew to a terrible storm at sea, and challenging and winning a duel with another pirate captain, Fero assumed the name Captain Fear. He sailed across the Caribbean, harrying the Spanish conquistadors of the day while protecting his fellow natives.

When his wife was expecting their first child, Captain Fear planned to retire from life on the high seas after a final voyage with a man named Baron Hemlocke. Instead, Hemlocke's butchery during an attack on a Spanish vessel sullied the reputation of Fero and his crew, who vowed to take revenge. Tragically, Captain Fear and his men were killed by Hemlocke's demonic forces, and were doomed to wander the seas forever as spirits. **RG**

CAPTAIN HUNTER

FIRST APPEARANCE SECRET FILES & ORIGINS GUIDE TO THE DC UNIVERSE 2000 #1 (March 2000)
STATUS Hero   **REAL NAME** Lucius Hunter
OCCUPATION Adventurer   **BASE** Mobile
HEIGHT 6ft 1in   **WEIGHT** 196 lbs   **EYES** Blue   **HAIR** Brown
SPECIAL POWERS/ABILITIES Excellent combatant and field leader; body enhanced through transplants.

The name Hunter has earned merit through six decades of service to the U.S. military. Lieutenant Ben Hunter turned a bunch of ex-convicts into a crack squad nicknamed "HUNTER'S HELLCATS", seeing action in some of the worst battles of World War II. Ben Hunter's twin sons, Nick and Phil, became a major in the Air Force and a captain with the Green Berets respectively, serving with distinction in Korea and Vietnam. In more modern times, Captain Lucius Hunter leads the latest group of CREATURE COMMANDOS for the top-secret Project M. **DW**

CAPTAIN MARVEL JR.

FIRST APPEARANCE WHIZ COMICS #25 (December 1941)
STATUS Hero **REAL NAME** Frederick "Freddy" Freeman
OCCUPATION Adventurer **BASE** New York City; Fawcett City
HEIGHT 5ft 10in **WEIGHT** 164 lbs **EYES** Blue **HAIR** Black
SPECIAL POWERS/ABILITIES By saying "Captain Marvel" aloud, he gains Solomon's wisdom, Hercules's superstrength, Atlas's stamina, Zeus's raw power, Achilles's courage, and Mercury's superspeed. Captain Marvel Jr. shares powers with Mary Marvel and Captain Marvel; if either is using their powers, he has access to only half his power.

BRAVERY *The teenage Freddy was crippled and nearly killed by Captain Nazi.*

A WELL-MANNERED TEENAGER who excelled not only academically but athletically, Frederick "Freddy" Freeman was orphaned when his parents died in a boating accident. After the accident, Freddy moved from New York to Fawcett City to live with his grandparents, Jacob and Elizabeth. Shortly after moving to Fawcett City, Freddy was kidnapped by the demonic SABBAC, who mistakenly believed Freeman to be Billy Batson, the young alter ego of CAPTAIN MARVEL, the World's Mightiest Mortal. Freed from Sabbac's evil clutches by his idol, Captain Marvel, Freddy subsequently became one of Billy Batson's closest friends, unaware that the young Batson was in truth the hero he so admired.

EVIL *Freddy rescued Captain Nazi from certain death, only to watch the villain murder Freeman's grandfather.*

THE WORLD'S MIGHTIEST BOY

Years later, however, Freddy learned Billy's secret identity after Batson saved his sister, Mary (*see* MARY MARVEL), from Ibac. Soon after, on a trip with his grandfather Jacob, Freddy saw what he took to be Captain Marvel plummeting from the heavens and crashing into the lake where he and his grandfather were fishing. Freddy tried to save the man, who turned out to be the villainous CAPTAIN NAZI, awakened from a cryogenic sleep after decades. Captain Nazi had been battling Captain Marvel in a spaceship above Earth before he was knocked unconscious. Captain Nazi killed Freeman's grandfather, broke Freddy's back, and escaped.

Captain Marvel and Mary Marvel, desperate to save the Freddy's life, took him to a secret sanctuary in a deserted subway tunnel. There they beseeched the wizard Shazam, who had given them their powers, to help them save Freddy's life. The mage cryptically told them that he did not have the power they needed, but Mary cleverly deduced the logic behind the Wizard's riddle, and she and Captain Marvel agreed to split their amazing powers with Freddy. The Wizard, gratified by the wisdom of his charges, enchanted the dying boy. When Freddy awoke and spoke the words "Captain Marvel," he was transformed into the World's Mightiest Boy. The three Marvels began patrolling the skies of Fawcett City together, and Freddy's romantic feelings for Mary grew. Captain Marvel, still technically a young teenager himself, grew fiercely protective of his sister.

BOY ZONE *As Captain Marvel Jr., Freddy is the World's Mightiest Boy!*

After a fight between the two over Mary, the headstrong Captain Marvel Jr. moved to New York City, and promptly fell in love with the schizophrenic villain CHAIN LIGHTNING. Freddy soundly defeated Captain Nazi and then changed his name to CM3, announcing his "split" from the Marvel "family." CM3 served briefly with both the TEEN TITANS and the OUTSIDERS, but experienced a shock to his super-hero career following the Infinite Crisis. The murder of Shazam at the hands of the SPECTRE caused Captain Marvel Jr. to lose his powers. Captain Marvel, who had taken Shazam's place as keeper of the Rock of Eternity, arranged a series of trials for Freddy to prove his worthiness to the gods that powered the Marvel family: Solomon, Hercules, Atlas, Zeus, Achilles, and Mercury. **PJ**

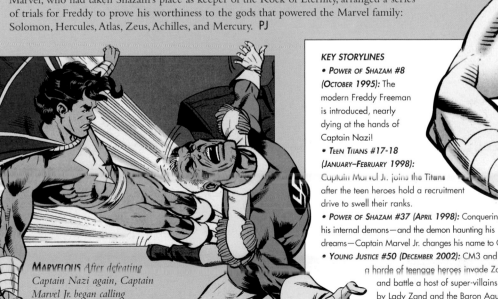

MARVELOUS *After defeating Captain Nazi again, Captain Marvel Jr. began calling himself CM3.*

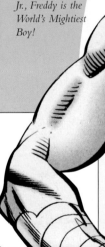

KEY STORYLINES

• **POWER OF SHAZAM #8 (OCTOBER 1995):** The modern Freddy Freeman is introduced, nearly dying at the hands of Captain Nazi!
• **TEEN TITANS #17-18 (JANUARY–FEBRUARY 1998):** Captain Marvel Jr. joins the Titans after the teen heroes hold a recruitment drive to swell their ranks.
• **POWER OF SHAZAM #37 (APRIL 1998):** Conquering his internal demons—and the demon haunting his dreams—Captain Marvel Jr. changes his name to CM3.
• **YOUNG JUSTICE #50 (DECEMBER 2002):** CM3 and a horde of teenage heroes invade Zandia and battle a host of super-villains lead by Lady Zand and the Baron Agua Sin Gaaz!

CAPTAIN MARVEL

THE WORLD'S MIGHTIEST MORTAL

FIRST APPEARANCE WHIZ COMICS #1 (February 1940)
STATUS Hero **REAL NAME** William Joseph "Billy" Batson
OCCUPATION Radio Personality; super hero
BASE Fawcett City
HEIGHT (as Billy) 5ft 4in; (as Captain Marvel) 6ft 2in
WEIGHT (as Billy) 110 lbs; (as Captain Marvel) 215 lbs
EYES Blue **HAIR** Black
SPECIAL POWERS/ABILITIES
Virtually invulnerable and able to fly; possesses the wisdom of
Solomon, the strength of Hercules, the stamina of Atlas, the power of
Zeus, the courage of Achilles, and the speed of Mercury.

WITHOUT A DOUBT, Captain Marvel is the world's mightiest mortal, with strength and powers on a par with Superman. But unknown to many, this stalwart and virtuous super hero—by all appearances a middle-aged man—is really teenager Billy Batson. With one magic word, youthful Billy assumes the appearance and abilities of one of Earth's greatest and most respected heroes; however, he remains very much an innocent in heart and mind.

ARRIVAL *The Big Red Cheese was Fawcett Comics' answer to Superman and, for a time, was just as popular as the Man of Steel.*

ORPHANED AND BETRAYED

When Billy was just a boy, his parents—archaeologists C.C. and Marylin Batson—were killed by their treacherous assistant, Theo Adam (*see* BLACK ADAM), while on a dig at the tomb of Rameses II at Abu Simbel, Egypt. Billy was separated from his sister Mary and left in the care of their unscrupulous Uncle Ebenezer, C.C. Batson's half-brother. Unfortunately, Ebenezer threw Billy out and stole the youth's trust fund, money set aside for Billy's care and welfare.

ORPHANED *For the sake of a jeweled scarab of untold power, Theo Adam murdered Billy's parents.*

DOWN IN THE SUBWAY

Left penniless and homeless, Billy eked out a sorrowful existence in Fawcett City as a newsboy. For shelter, he often slept in the subway terminals. One night, a mysterious stranger—later revealed to be the spirit of Billy's father, C.C. Batson—convinced the orphaned lad to follow him deep into the subway tunnels, where a marvelous train decorated in hieroglyphics and mystic runes awaited them. Billy and the stranger rode the train deep into the bowels of the Earth and arrived in a cavern that held statues epitomizing the Seven Deadly Enemies of Man: Pride, Envy, Lust, Hatred, Selfishness, Laziness, and Injustice.

THE WIZARD'S ADVICE

As Captain Marvel turned back into Billy, the magical lightning bolt also struck a stone block poised above Shazam, apparently crushing the old wizard beneath its great weight. Shazam, however, did not die, but instead disappeared to the Rock of Eternity, a distant peak outside time and space. When called upon by Billy in future, Shazam would offer guidance, but not without first reminding the lad to use the marvellous powers at his disposal. He particularly urged Billy to use the wisdom of Solomon when faced by the perils of adolescence and other emotional and practical problems.

ROCK OF ETERNITY *Billy will make his home on this distant rock spire, assuming the mantle of Shazam.*

THE MAGIC WORD

Within that strange cavern, Billy met the ancient wizard Shazam, a champion of mankind for thousands of years. Withered with age, Shazam sat on a throne poised beneath a giant stone block suspended above him as if by magic. Shazam chose Billy to succeed him and granted the young orphan all of his extraordinary powers. By speaking the wizard's name, a lightning bolt transformed adolescent Billy into the adult Captain Marvel, a hero possessing the wisdom of Solomon, the strength of Hercules, the stamina of Atlas, the power of Zeus, the courage of Achilles, and the speed of Mercury. With this great gift also came responsibility: he must vow to uphold the cause of good and to battle the Seven Deadly Enemies of Man, duties that Billy promised faithfully to fulfill every time he uttered the name "Shazam!"

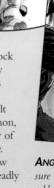

ANGRY AT FIRST *Billy was not sure if Shazam's great gifts were a blessing or a curse.*

MERCY FOR A MURDERER

Captain Marvel's very first adventure found him battling Black Adam, his parents' killer enabled with his own superpowers. Theo Adam channeled the strengths of Teth-Adam, a man empowered with similar abilities by Shazam during Egypt's 19th dynasty via an ancient scarab amulet first discovered by Billy's parents. Captain Marvel defeated Black Adam by removing his amulet, thus stripping him of his powers, at least for a while. Instead of allowing the helpless Theo Adam to die in a collapsing museum, the good-hearted Captain Marvel spared the life of the man who murdered his family.

THE MARVEL FAMILY

Later, at the Rock of Eternity, Billy learned that the stranger who led him to Shazam was really his father. Billy chose to remain Captain Marvel and use Shazam's gifts for good, as well as to find his long-lost sister, MARY MARVEL.

Eventually, Billy and Mary were reunited, and Captain Marvel decided to share his awesome abilities with her. He also gave some powers to their mutual friend, newsboy Freddy Freeman (see CAPTAIN MARVEL JR.), who had been crippled by the nefarious CAPTAIN NAZI. In the meantime, Captain Marvel became a member of the JUSTICE LEAGUE OF AMERICA, although Billy often felt inferior to his more confident super-heroic peers.

DO THE RIGHT THING

Back home in Fawcett City, Billy returned to school and worked as an announcer for WHIZ radio. At the same time, Captain Marvel wielded Shazam's great powers to battle such evils as MISTER MIND, DOCTOR SIVANA, MISTER ATOM, and the MONSTER SOCIETY OF EVIL. Through it all, Captain Marvel fought with indefatigable spirit, perhaps the truest of any costumed champion. Captain Marvel's wholesome honesty and integrity made his spotless soul the prize most coveted by the demon NERON. However, Billy and his alter ego have always had the moral strength to resist temptation.

RADIO STAR Billy often reports on the deeds of Captain Marvel.

LOOKING TO THE FUTURE

Captain Marvel served with the JUSTICE SOCIETY OF AMERICA, helping curb Black Adam's excesses when his nemesis became dictator of Khandaq. He also aided Superman when ECLIPSO took control of the Man of Steel.

During the Infinite Crisis, the rampaging SPECTRE killed the wizard Shazam and destroyed the Rock of Eternity. Although the planet's magic-users helped rebuild the Rock, Billy Batson had no choice but to assume Shazam's former role as caretaker. Now known simply as Marvel, he sported an all-white costume and long, flowing white hair. He set a series of trials before Captain Marvel Jr. in the hopes of turning him into a worthy replacement. SB

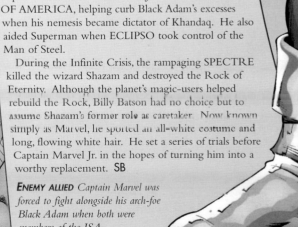

ENEMY ALLIED Captain Marvel was forced to fight alongside his arch-foe Black Adam when both were members of the JSA.

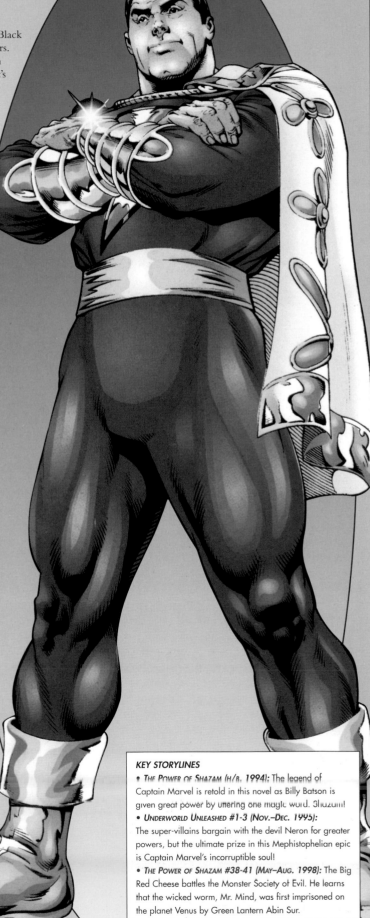

KEY STORYLINES

• *THE POWER OF SHAZAM (H/B, 1994):* The legend of Captain Marvel is retold in this novel as Billy Batson is given great power by uttering one magic word. Shazam!

• *UNDERWORLD UNLEASHED #1-3 (NOV.–DEC. 1995):* The super-villains bargain with the devil Neron for greater powers, but the ultimate prize in this Mephistophelian epic is Captain Marvel's incorruptible soul!

• *THE POWER OF SHAZAM #38-41 (MAY–AUG. 1998):* The Big Red Cheese battles the Monster Society of Evil. He learns that the wicked worm, Mr. Mind, was first imprisoned on the planet Venus by Green Lantern Abin Sur.

CAPTAIN NAZI

FIRST APPEARANCE MASTER COMICS #2 (December 1941)
STATUS Villain **REAL NAME** Albrecht Krieger
OCCUPATION Would-be world conqueror **BASE** The Slab
HEIGHT 6ft 4in **WEIGHT** 205 lbs **EYES** Blue **HAIR** Blond
SPECIAL POWERS/ABILITIES Superhuman strength, above average speed,
endurance, and invulnerability.

In 1941, Albrecht Krieger was presented to
Adolf Hitler as the ultimate development
of the Aryan "master race." This so-called
epitome of perfection became known
as Captain Nazi. Intensely loyal to the
Führer, for the rest of World War
II Captain Nazi frequently
clashed with the Allies
costumed champions,
particularly the SPY
SMASHER,
proving
himself a formidable
foe.

When the war ended,
BULLETMAN, Minute-Man
and Spy Smasher interfered
with Captain Nazi's search for
the freighter *La Poloma*, but
failed to prevent the villain
from retrieving a mysterious
storage tank from the vessel
and disappearing. This
tank proved to be a
cryogenic unit that the

Captain believed contained Adolf Hitler's body.
Captain Nazi ensured that his own body was placed
in another, similar unit.

More than five decades into the future, Captain
Nazi was revived from his deep freeze. When
Captain Nazi crippled young
Freddy Freeman, CAPTAIN
MARVEL convinced the wizard
Shazam to give the teenager a
portion of his and his sister's
power, thus creating
CAPTAIN MARVEL JR.
Since that day, Captain
Nazi has continued
to plague the entire
Marvel Family
only to meet
constant defeat. RG

NAZI SYMPATHISERS
*Two of Captain Nazi's
helpers in the fascist cause
are his scientist brother Wolf
and his niece Katrina.*

CAPTAIN STORM

FIRST APPEARANCE CAPTAIN STORM #1 (June 1964)
STATUS Hero (deceased) **REAL NAME** William Storm
OCCUPATION U.S. Navy PT-boat commander
BASE World War II Europe and Pacific theaters
HEIGHT 5ft 11in **WEIGHT** 167 lbs **EYES** Brown **HAIR** Brown
SPECIAL POWERS/ABILITIES Courageous leader and above-average
battlefield combatant.

Hit by tragedy again and again in the battle theaters of
World War II, Captain William Storm seemed destined for
a role as a member of the aptly-named Losers squad. Yet
in the war's final days he fought with guts and went out a
hero. Captain Storm's first command, PT-47, sank after a
sneak attack by a Japanese sub. Though Storm survived, he
lost his left leg and wore a wooden one thereafter. Storm
joined the U.S.-sanctioned detached service
force known as the Losers with Air
Force pilot Johnny Cloud (see CLOUD,
JOHNNY) and the Marines GUNNER
AND SARGE, but on a mission to save
a church, Captain Storm seemingly
died in a fiery blast. Storm survived, but
lost his right eye. He resurfaced as an
amnesiac "pirate" attacking Axis shipping,
until he regained his memory and
rejoined the Losers. He was killed in a
World War II temporal event related
to the Crisis (see Great Battles,
pp. 362–3). Johnny Cloud,
Gunner, and Sarge all died in
the same battle, bringing an
end to the short, troubled
lives of the Losers. DW

CAPTAIN STINGAREE

FIRST APPEARANCE DETECTIVE COMICS #460 (June 1976)
STATUS Villain **REAL NAME** Karl Courtney
OCCUPATION Professional criminal **BASE** Gotham City
HEIGHT 6ft 2in **WEIGHT** 190 lbs **EYES** Blue **HAIR** None
SPECIAL POWERS/ABILITIES Expert swordsman and skilled hand-to-hand
combatant

Captain Stingaree is a themed criminal obsessed with
pirates. He is primarily active in Gotham City, where
he runs afoul of the BATMAN. Born into a set of
quadruplets, Karl Courtney grew envious of his
three brothers. He adopted the identity of Captain
Stingaree and became convinced that his brothers
were collectively impersonating Batman. The Dark
Knight enlisted the three Courtney siblings to bring
down Captain Stingaree. He escaped and joined the
Secret Society of super-Villains alongside CAPTAIN
COLD and CAPTAIN BOOMERANG, but was unable to
shed his reputation as a third-stringer. More recently,
Captain Stingaree has started a romance with fellow
villain the CAVALIER. DW

BAT-VILLAIN
*Captain Stingaree
once tried to uncover
Batman's secret
identity.*

CAPTAIN TRIUMPH

FIRST APPEARANCE CRACK COMICS #27 (January 1943)
STATUS Hero (missing) **REAL NAMES** Lance and Michael Gallant
OCCUPATION (Lance) unknown; (Michael) former pilot
BASE New York City
HEIGHT 6ft 1in **WEIGHT** 198 lbs **EYES** Blue **HAIR** Blond
SPECIAL POWERS/ABILITIES When Lance touched his birthmark, he
merged with the spirit of his brother Michael and became Captain
Triumph, who possesses superstrength, invulnerability, the power
of flight, and invisibility.

Lance and Michael Gallant were identical
twins born with an unusual T-shaped
birthmark on their left wrists. In the early
days of World War II, Michael, a pilot
for the U.S. Army Air Corps, was killed
when the airplane hangar he was standing in
blew up. Lance swore to avenge his brother's
death, and Michael, now a ghost, appeared
before him. Michael told Lance that if he
rubbed his T-shaped birthmark, the two
brothers would merge and become Captain
Triumph. As Triumph, the brothers found
the culprits behind the hangar explosion
and incarcerated them.

Captain Triumph was an active hero
during World War II. Michael's fiancée, Kim
Meredith, learned of his existence as a ghost.
Horrified at first, she eventually married
Lance, but remained close to Michael's spirit.
Biff, a circus clown, became Triumph's sidekick.

Recently, Michael murdered Philip Geyer,
the fiancée of Triumph's former teammate
LIBERTY BELLE, when Lance discovered
Geyer was having an adulterous affair. PJ

CAPTAIN X

FIRST APPEARANCE STAR-SPANGLED COMICS #1 (October 1941)
STATUS Hero (deceased) **REAL NAME** Richard "Buck" Dare
OCCUPATION Newspaper reporter **BASE** Mobile
HEIGHT 5ft 10in **WEIGHT** 175 lbs **EYES** Blue **HAIR** Chestnut
SPECIAL POWERS/ABILITIES Expert hand-to-hand combatant; Captain X's
radio-controlled aircraft Jenny was virtually invisible from a distance
and used uranium-235 as its atomic fuel source.

A reporter for the *Tribune*,
an American newspaper
published in Great Britain
during World War II,
Richard "Buck" Dare
volunteered to become
an Allied aviator for
a secret organization
known as The Group.
Given the codename
Captain X, Dare flew top-
secret missions behind enemy
lines in an experimental plastic
plane, *Jenny*, for the remainder
of the war. As the Cold War
loomed, Dare founded the "X
Protocol" and coordinated covert
operations behind the Iron
Curtain. Dare continued to be
involved in intelligence activities
in the decades following until
the superpowered K.G.B. agent
STALNOIVOLK killed him.
Dare is grandfather of Ronald
Raymond (FIRESTORM, THE
NUCLEAR MAN). SB

CARR, SNAPPER

FIRST APPEARANCE BRAVE AND THE BOLD #28 (February 1960)
STATUS Ally to super heroes (retired) **REAL NAME** Lucas Carr
OCCUPATION Author **BASE** Happy Harbor, Rhode Island
HEIGHT 5ft 10in **WEIGHT** 175 lbs **EYES** Blue **HAIR** Brown
SPECIAL POWERS/ABILITIES Formerly could teleport by snapping his fingers; lost this ability when his hands were severed.

When Simon Carr bankrolled the JUSTICE LEAGUE OF AMERICA, and outfitted their mountain headquarters, his nephew Lucas helped install equipment. As a reward, the finger-popping teen, nicknamed "Snapper," was made an honorary JLA member. Lacking superpowers, the teen began to feel like a fifth wheel, making him susceptible to the charismatic "John Doe," who charmed Snapper into revealing the location of the JLA's headquarters; Snapper almost helped kill his friends! Doe was revealed to be the JOKER, making Snapper feel even worse.

Snapper left the League and fell under the sway of the KEY, who used him as the criminal Star-Tsar. Snapper met and married Bethany Lee, some time before being captured by the Dominators (*see* Alien Races, pp. 166–7) He was subjected to many tests, which activated his teleporting metagene. Snapper and other human survivors of the alien experiments, fought their way to freedom and then worked as the BLASTERS. Snapper was captured by the Khunds (*see* Alien Races, pp. 166–7) who severed his hands. Thanks to Colu's Vril Dox, his hands were replaced by nanites and he returned to Earth. Snapper became a mentor to the android from the future HOURMAN III. He then made a fortune writing his JLA memoirs. He was a mentor to YOUNG JUSTICE, returning home when the team disbanded. RG

FINGER-POPPER *Snapper used to enjoy writing in the JLA Casebook but soon began to feel like a fifth wheel.*

CASCADE

FIRST APPEARANCE JUSTICE LEAGUE QUARTERLY #17 (Winter 1994)
STATUS Hero **REAL NAME** Sujatmi Sunowaparti
OCCUPATION Plant worker and activist **BASE** Bali, Indonesia
HEIGHT 5ft 3in **WEIGHT** 105 lbs **EYES** Brown **HAIR** Black
SPECIAL POWERS/ABILITIES Can transform any part or all of her body into water; can psychically control large bodies of water, causing them to take simple shapes.

Born to a large family on the island of Java in Indonesia, Sujatmi was one of many who vigorously opposed the Javanese political elite, which had adopted a policy of ruthlessly suppressing local cultures. Taking dangerous job in refinery fields to earn more money for her family, Sujatmi was caught up in a violent clash between warring factions in Borneo. Sujatmi gained the power to transform her body into living liquid when she was exposed to a radioactive isotope that activated her metagene.

Using her newfound superpowers as an activist for peace, Sujatmi was invited by OWLWOMAN to join the GLOBAL GUARDIANS. Codenamed Cascade, Sujatmi joined the Guardians, hoping the exposure would bring attention to the culture of violence and corruption spreading throughout Indonesia. PJ

CARSON, CAVE

FIRST APPEARANCE THE BRAVE AND THE BOLD #31 (August 1960)
STATUS Hero **REAL NAME** Calvin Carson
OCCUPATION Professional spelunker; geology professor **BASE** Mobile
HEIGHT 5ft 11in **WEIGHT** 178 lbs **EYES** Blue **HAIR** Brown
SPECIAL POWERS/ABILITIES Highly intelligent, with a natural gift for his area of expertise; one eye is cybernetic.

Calvin Carson was a lab technician for E. Borsten & Co., which developed a digging machine, the Mighty Mole, for the government. When funding was cut, the project was axed. Carson stole the device and began exploring the varied life beneath the Earth's surface. He worked with ex-convict Bulldozer Smith, geologist Christie Madison, and adventurer Johnny Blake. Carson and his colleagues became celebrities, before the Modern Age of heroes began (with the coming of SUPERMAN).

After finding lost Nazi gold and experimental time-travel technology, the Borsten family sued to regain the Mighty Mole They settled for the time-travel equipment letting Carson keep the Mole. When Superman arrived, the public turned their attention away from Carson. His team broke up and Carson drifted into semi-retirement. As a geology teacher, he had a romance with student Bonnie Baxter, which led him to use his considerable fortune to fund E. Borsten & Co.'s Rip Hunter (*see* HUNTER, RIP) and his time-travel experiments. He has worked with others from his era in a loose group known as the Forgotten Heroes. Cave maintains a busy schedule, embarking on missions with Christie and Bulldozer (some on behalf of the S.T.A.R. Labs research facility) and leading the Forgotten Heroes. RG

CAT-MAN

FIRST APPEARANCE DETECTIVE COMICS #311 (January 1963)
STATUS Villain **REAL NAME** Thomas Blake
OCCUPATION Professional criminal **BASE** Gotham City
HEIGHT 6ft **WEIGHT** 179 lbs
EYES Green **HAIR** Brown
SPECIAL POWERS/ABILITIES Talented inventor; remarkable physical agility; believed to have "nine lives" from the mystical cloth used in his costume.

Thomas Blake worked in big-game hunting, tracking big cats and selling them to zoos. His cat obsession led him to a Pacific island and its native "cat cult," from which he stole a sacred cat carving and the cloth that swathed it. Back in Gotham, Blake became a costumed criminal. As Cat-Man, he made a cape and cowl from the carving's wrap and added razor-tipped gauntlets to his costume. He made feline-themed accessories inspired by CATWOMAN and BATMAN, like catarangs and a turbocharged cat-car. His narrow escapes appeared to bear out his belief that his costume gave him nine lives. The earthquake that left Gotham a No Man's Land also freed Cat-Man and others from Blackgate prison. Cat-Man later joined the Witness Projection Program after informing on MONSIEUR MALLAH, though he found time to attend GREEN ARROW's funeral. DW

FELINE FIEND *At the controls of his latest cat-invention, Cat-Man attempts to make cat food out of Batman and Robin.*

CATWOMAN

PRINCESS OF PLUNDER

FIRST APPEARANCE BATMAN #1 (Spring 1940)
STATUS Unresolved   **REAL NAME** Selina Kyle
OCCUPATION Cat burglar/vigilante   **BASE** Gotham City's East End
HEIGHT 5ft 7in   **WEIGHT** 133 lbs   **EYES** Blue-green   **HAIR** Black
SPECIAL POWERS/ABILITIES A formidable fighter with expertise in boxing
and various martial arts disciplines; skintight cat costume features
retractable razor-sharp claws in gloves and spring-action steel
climbing pitons in boots; wields a variety of bullwhips and
cat-o'-nine tails as offensive weapons and gymnastic accoutrements.

PURPLE PRINCESS
*Catwoman has worn
a number of different
costumes over the
years, often preferring
purple catsuits.*

SELINA KYLE'S CHILDHOOD was defined by tragedy. When Selina
was just a girl, her brutalized mother committed suicide and her
violent father drank himself to death not long after. Separated
from her younger sister Magdalena and remanded to the Sprang
Hall Juvenile Detention Center—an abusive state home for
orphaned or delinquent girls—Selina opted instead to take her
chances on the mean streets of Gotham City. Amid the crime
and corruption of the poverty-stricken East End district, she survived
through petty theft. Sharp wits and an amazing natural skill as a
gymnast led to her becoming the slickest and slipperiest cat burglar
the Gotham City Police Department had ever had to deal with.

KEY STORYLINES

• *CATWOMAN (1ST SERIES) #1-4 (FEBRUARY–
MAY 1989)* Selina Kyle's life on the mean
streets of Gotham City is recounted.
• *DETECTIVE COMICS #759-762 (AUGUST–
NOVEMBER 2001)* P.I. Slam Bradley is hired to
find the missing and presumed-dead Selina.
• *CATWOMAN (3RD SERIES) #1-4 (JANUARY–
APRIL 2002)* Catwoman stalks and defeats
a shape-changing serial killer who
is hunting Gotham's ladies of
the evening.

THE FELINE FATALE
To protect herself from predators, Selina studied martial arts in a
backstreet dojo where a Sensei taught her how best to use her claws.
Later, ex-heavyweight champ Ted Grant (*see*
WILDCAT I) taught Selina the "sweet science"
of boxing. For a time, Selina was the most
accomplished thief nobody knew. She
was also one of the most generous,
spreading her ill-gotten gains around
the downtrodden and destitute of
the East End, including the young
prostitute Holly "Gonightly" Robinson,
whom Selina befriended and watched
over like the little sister she believed she no
longer had. Selina would have continued to
rob with impunity if not for the BATMAN.
Spying the Caped Crusader from her
window on one of his first outings, Selina
watched him in action and was suitably
inspired to take up her own costume when prowling the Gotham night.
In a tight leather catsuit, Catwoman marked the city as her territory.
However, she never killed, and she only stole from the wealthiest or the
well-insured. For these reasons, Batman pursued other costumed criminals more
relentlessly and gave Catwoman the chance to change her spots. Sometimes
he even asked the Princess of Plunder to use her skills for the betterment of
Gotham. Perhaps his altruism attracted her, because Selina ultimately did decide
to make Catwoman more than just a thief in the night.

ALLEY CAT *Often, the
alley cats of Gotham
were Selina's only friends,
especially after she was once
beaten and left for dead.*

TOP THIEF *Few cat
burglars can rival Selina
Kyle's nimble-fingered
thieving skills.*

THE CAT AND THE BAT
After faking her own demise, Selina left Gotham
for a time, but eventually returned to the city's
East End, where she defended the defenseless.
Catwoman learned Batman's best-kept secret
when the Dark Knight took her to his Batcave
and revealed his identity to her. They finally
admitted their feelings for each other (*see*
Romantic Moments, p. 281) but then parted
because Catwoman did not believe Batman trusted
her. Selina began seeing private detective Slam
Bradley (*see* BRADLEY, SLAM), but Slam realized that Selina's
heart would always belong to Batman. Catwoman enjoyed
her adventures on the 'other' side of the fence, stealing
only when necessary and usually if the loot would do
someone other than herself a bit of good.

WHIP SMART *Her evil ways (mostly)
behind her, Catwoman now fights for
the downtrodden of Gotham.*

DEATH MASK *Showing no remorse, Selina shot the crime boss Black Mask.*

THE EXECUTIONER

Catwoman's path from villainess to reluctant hero hit a snag when she realized that her motivation might not come from within. Years earlier, during one of her stints with the SECRET SOCIETY OF SUPER VILLAINS, Catwoman underwent an involuntary mind-wipe courtesy of the magic-wielding ZATANNA. The act may have subtly nudged her psyche onto a less sinister track, yet Selina still proved capable of cold-blooded acts. In an apparent counterpoint to this revelation, Catwoman shot and killed the Gotham crime boss BLACK MASK when he threatened her friends.

HELENA *The birth of her daughter caused Selina to retire from costumed adventuring.*

ONE YEAR LATER

Over the course of the following year, Selina conceived a child with Slam Bradley's son Sam and gave birth to a daughter she named Helena. She also retired from adventuring, took the alias "Irena Dubrovna" and maintained a low-key lifestyle in an East End apartment. Catwoman continued on, however, her identity assumed by Holly Robinson in a duplicate costume. Most Gothamites didn't know that a second woman had donned the familiar catsuit. Neither did the GCPD. The police took Holly into custody for the murder of Black Mask, necessitating a breakout orchestrated by Selina. Selina's outings as Catwoman, battling threats to Gotham, became more frequent after this event.

HOLLY *During her time as Catwoman, Holly Robinson got in over her head.*

Selina's baby became a easy target for her enemies—first FILM FREAK and ANGLE MAN, and later the Russian team of HAMMER AND SICKLE. Gradually Selina realized that her dangerous lifestyle would never be compatible with the needs of her child, and she began plotting an exit strategy. The Amazons invasion of Washington DC interrupted her plans, and Catwoman found herself in a unique position to infiltrate the Gotham wing of the Amazonian Bana sect. Her sabotage of the Bana prevented the city's decimation by a radioactive bio bomb.

VULNERABLE *Hammer and Sickle, Angle Man, and Film Freak all threatened Selina's daughter.*

HEARTBREAK *To protect her daughter, Selina gave Helena up for adoption.*

CAT'S ROAR *Selina isn't loyal to anyone's cause.*

NEW BEGINNINGS

Saving Gotham from the Amazons was Selina's last great act before going underground. Batman helped her erase her former life when he posed as a terrorist and seemingly blew up both Selina and her daughter. The two left the city under new identities, and Selina then made the painful decision to put Helena up for adoption. Now truly alone, save for her few friends in the super hero community, Catwoman accepted Batman's offer to join his latest team of OUTSIDERS. **SB/DW**

CATSEYE

FIRST APPEARANCE SUICIDE SQUAD (1st series) #53 (May 1991)
STATUS Villain (deceased) **REAL NAME** Unknown
OCCUPATION Yakuza assassin **BASE** Tokyo, Japan
HEIGHT 6ft 1in **WEIGHT** 195 lbs **EYES** Brown **HAIR** Black
SPECIAL POWERS/ABILITIES Razor-sharp claws tipped with poison;
amazing leaping ability; low level super speed.

His real name and origin remained a mystery, and with good reason. For the ruthless killer known as Catseye was a bioengineered meta-human agent of the Yakuza crime family. He clashed with various members of the SUICIDE SQUAD when that covert agency went to Japan on a mission to recover a stolen cache of Russian weapons, known as the Dragon's Hoard. Several other rival clandestine groups came searching for the Dragon's Hoard as well, including the Russian Red Shadows and the Khymer Rouge. Suicide Squad members MANHUNTER and BRONZE TIGER were captured by the Yakuza and freed by KATANA from the OUTSIDERS while Catseye fought the ATOM for control of the stolen weaot Asia, Catseye attacked the Squad again, this time in an ancient temple, and was scraped by his own poison claws while battling Bronze Tiger. Catseye's body was incinerated in an explosion caused by DEADSHOT. **PJ**

CATWOMAN SEE OPPOSITE PAGE

CAVALIER

FIRST APPEARANCE DETECTIVE COMICS #81 (November 1943)
STATUS Villain **REAL NAME** Mortimer Drake
OCCUPATION Professional criminal **BASE** Gotham City
HEIGHT 6ft 1in **WEIGHT** 182 lbs **EYES** Brown **HAIR** Brown
SPECIAL POWERS/ABILITIES Skilled swordsman and hand-to-hand
combatant, carries a number of concealed weapons.

Mortimer Drake, the Cavalier, is a minor villain within the exotic criminal underworld of Gotham City. Obsessed with antiquated costumes and weapons, and possessing a keen sense of personal honor, he embarked on a string of thefts to stock his collection of rare eccentricities. Drake made friends within the ranks of BATMAN's Rouges Gallery, including Killer Moth (see CHARAXES), but continually found himself behind bars after going up against the Dark Knight and his helpers, ROBIN and BATGIRL. His constant defeats have led to bouts of incarceration in the mental ward of Arkham Asylum. Recently, the Cavalier entered into a romantic relationship with fellow low-level Batman foe Captain Stingaree. **DW**

CELESTE

FIRST APPEARANCE LEGION OF SUPER-HEROES (4th series) #6 (April 1990)
STATUS Hero **REAL NAME** Celeste McCauley
OCCUPATION Private investigator; adventurer **BASE** Mobile
HEIGHT 5ft 7in **WEIGHT** 120 lbs **EYES** Blue **HAIR** Brown
SPECIAL POWERS/ABILITIES Naturally wields the emerald energy
employed by the Green Lantern Corps.

In one timeline containing an alternate history of the LEGION OF SUPER-HEROES, Celeste McCauley left her wealthy family to become a private detective. An encounter with the remains of a dead GREEN LANTERN on the planet Twilo exposed her to the amazing solid-light energy used by that intergalactic corps of ring-wielders. This energy saved her life when she was beaten nearly to death by Roxxas the Butcher. She worked with the Legion of Super-Heroes and helped evacuate Earth before its destruction in a catastrophic accident. During a fight with Glorith the sorceress, Celeste became a being of pure energy. Adopting the name Neon, she adjusted to her new life until temporal anomalies transformed her into a member of the DARKSTARS. The events of Zero Hour (see Great Battles, pp. 362-3) erased Celeste's known history from the primary timeline of Earth. **DW**

CELSIUS

FIRST APPEARANCE SHOWCASE #94 (September 1977)
STATUS Hero (deceased)
REAL NAME Arani Desai Caulder
OCCUPATION Adventurer **BASE** Kansas City
HEIGHT 5ft 4in **WEIGHT** 124 lbs
EYES Brown **HAIR** Black
SPECIAL POWERS/ABILITIES Could project rays of intense heat or cold
from her hands.

Arani Desai's mother died during childbirth. Blamed as the cause of death by her father, scientist Ashok Desai, Arani was raised by servants and nannies until she ran away. For years, Arani lived a life of poverty in Calcutta until she was rescued by Niles Caulder, the CHIEF of the DOOM PATROL, who later married her. Soon after, Arani discovered her amazing metagene powers.

Separated from Caulder for several years, Arani learned that he had died at the hands of GENERAL IMMORTUS. Obsessed with the idea that the Chief was still alive, Arani assembled a new Doom Patrol to find him.

Tragically, Celsius died during a massive alien invasion of Earth. The devious Caulder turned up alive, claiming that Arani had never been married to him, and that she was a poor, deluded woman unable to cope with reality even after he treated her, as a physician. **PJ**

CENTRIX

FIRST APPEARANCE JUSTICE LEAGUE QUARTERLY #17 (Winter 1994)
STATUS Hero **REAL NAME** Mark Armstrong
OCCUPATION Adventurer **BASE** Vancouver Island, British Columbia
HEIGHT 5ft 9in **WEIGHT** 160 lbs **EYES** Green **HAIR** Brown
SPECIAL POWERS/ABILITIES Projects invisible energy force waves in equal
and opposite directions from his body; carries arsenal of small pellets
and other projectiles propelled by force waves.

Ambitious advertising executive Mark Armstrong retired young and wealthy, leaving him all the time in the world to practice and perfect his meta-human powers. As Centrix, one of Canada's few public super heroes, Armstrong put his abilities to practical use, foiling small-time criminals before he was asked to join the most recent incarnation of the GLOBAL GUARDIANS. Armstrong still operates as Centrix from his home in Ladysmith, on Vancouver Island. Centrix is a practitioner of New Age philosophies, mixing them with his millions as a financier for the Global Guardians. **SB**

CHAIN LIGHTNING

FIRST APPEARANCE POWER OF SHAZAM! #14 (April 1996)
STATUS Villain **REAL NAME** Amy
OCCUPATION Criminal **BASE** Mobile **HEIGHT** 5ft 4in
WEIGHT 121 lbs **EYES** Blue **HAIR** Platinum blonde
SPECIAL POWERS/ABILITIES A multiple personality, she absorbs electrical
current but cannot control it without artificial help.

Amy's metagene kicked in some time during her early teens, allowing her to absorb electrical energy, but she lacked a way to control it. An unknown person provided her with a bodysuit containing containment circuitry. Unfortunately, Amy also began suffering from multiple personality disorder. The dominant personality is Amy, who tried to commit suicide in New York, but was rescued by CAPTAIN MARVEL JR., earning his sincere affection. Her other three personalities, however, are not so benign. Amber is angry, aggressive, and very destructive. The Inner Child is a hulking form, while Id is a small girl trapped inside the others. Together, they are known as Chain Lightning, and at different times Amy's powers appear as four distinct electrical beings. Shazam's magic lightning bolt accidentally gave all four personalities physical form, and it took the combined efforts of Captain Marvel Jr. and MISTER SCARLET to subdue them before Fawcett City was reduced to rubble. Amy is now back at S.T.A.R. Labs, where she has undergone frequent treatment. **RG**

CHALLENGERS OF THE UNKNOWN

FIRST APPEARANCE SHOWCASE #6 (January 1957)
STATUS Hero team
BASE Challenger Mountain, Colorado Rockies
CURRENT MEMBERS AND POWERS
Prof. Haley Skin diver and oceanographer.
Red Ryan Mountaineer and former circus acrobat.
June Robbins Computer and robotics expert.
Rocky Davis Wrestling champion and top strategist.
Ace Morgan Former test pilot and amateur sorcerer.
Clay Brody Former race-car driver.
Marlon Corbett Top-notch pilot.
Kenn Kawa Software and electronics specialist.
Brenda Ruskin Brilliant theoretical physicist.
June Walker Hypertime duplicate of June Robbins from an alternate timeline.

The Challengers got their start when pilot Kyle "Ace" Morgan, wrestler Les "Rocky" Davis, mountaineer Matthew "Red" Ryan, and diver Walter "Prof." Haley survived an airplane crash on their way to appear on a TV program. Deciding that they were now "living on borrowed time," the four united as a team of adventurers-for-hire. Operating from their own mountain stronghold, the Challs journeyed everywhere, from the depths of space to the bottom of the sea, battling scoundrels, including the League of Challenger-Haters. Dr. June Robbins soon joined the team as an unofficial fifth Challenger.

Prof. Haley accidentally shattered Challenger Mountain, sending himself and June into an alternate dimension. The other members thought them dead and learned new skills in their absence. Prof. and June returned, but Ace and Red soon followed them into a state of stasis. Left alone, Rocky licensed the Challengers name to a new team: Clay Brody, Marlon Corbett, Kenn Kawa, and Brenda Ruskin. Red, June, Prof., and Ace soon reappeared and then vanished again, this time into hypertime where they clashed with Black Zero. The Challengers later learned that by cheating death, they no longer existed in the book of DESTINY. They are now the caretakers of the book, keeping it out of the hands of opportunists such as the Luck Lords. **DW**

ORIGINALS *The Challs were a link between the Golden Age mystery men and the super heroes of the modern era.*

CHAMELEON

FIRST APPEARANCE ADVENTURE COMICS #267 (November 1966)
STATUS Hero **REAL NAME** Reep Daggle (Interlac approximation)
OCCUPATION Legionnaire **BASE** Metropolis, in 30th century
HEIGHT Variable, usually 5ft 9in **WEIGHT** Variable, usually 145 lbs
EYES Variable, usually yellow **HAIR** Variable, usually none
SPECIAL POWERS/ABILITIES Can analyze and store data using his antennae and then shape his body into an exact duplicate of any being or object, however large or small, including creatures dreamed up from his own imagination. He cannot, however, replicate the special powers of others he's duplicating.

Reep Daggle is a Durlan, a race of hooded, tentacled aliens that are the object of grave fear and mistrust by other races throughout the galaxy for their shape-shifting abilities. He serves with the LEGION OF SUPER-HEROES in the 31st century, though his alien upbringing leaves him unable to relate to his teammates' jokes. Chameleon prefers to appear as an androgynous figure, neither male nor female, though he is capable of assuming almost any shape. As he is fond of reminding his fellow Legionnaires, he cannot duplicate the qualities of an object, only its shape. Chameleon serves the Legion well as an infiltrator and spy. **PJ**

CHARAXES

FIRST APPEARANCE (as Killer Moth) BATMAN #63 (March 1951); (as Charaxes) UNDERWORLD UNLEASHED #1 (November 1995)
STATUS Villain (deceased) **REAL NAME** Drury Walker, a.k.a. Cameron Van Cleer **OCCUPATION** Beast **BASE** Gotham City
HEIGHT 6ft 9in **WEIGHT** 202 lbs **EYES** Red **HAIR** Yellow
SPECIAL POWERS/ABILITIES Monstrous insect form possesses ten times a normal man's strength; exoskeleton confers virtual invulnerability; secretes a sticky acidic substance that can trap the strongest of men and dissolve their bodies.

Drury Walker the man was little more than a joke. As Killer Moth, he offered his services as paid protector to Gotham's gangsters. Despite an arsenal of ingenious weaponry, including his signature cocoon gun, the colorful Killer Moth was bested by Batman at every turn, leaving his clients both irate and incarcerated. Then Barbara Gordon, dressed for a costume party as Batgirl, defeated the Moth, earning Walker further ridicule. Finally, he made a deal with a devil—the tempter Neron— who gave Walker his heart's desire.
What Walker wanted most was to be feared, but what he received in exchange for his soul was metamorphosis into a real Killer Moth…the man-eating Charaxes!
Charaxes has repeatedly turned up in the Gotham area seeking sustenance and usually crossing paths with Robin. During the Infinite Crisis, Superboy-Prime tore Charaxes in half. **RG**

NEST *The monstrous Charaxes continues to mutate. What's worse, he may be reproducing!*

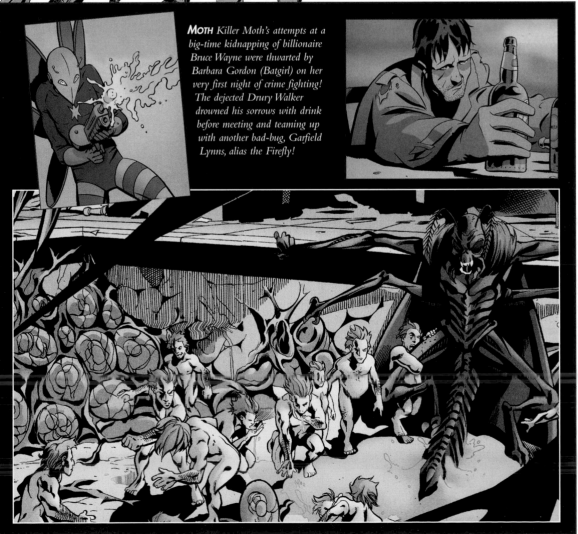

MOTH *Killer Moth's attempts at a big-time kidnapping of billionaire Bruce Wayne were thwarted by Barbara Gordon (Batgirl) on her very first night of crime fighting! The dejected Drury Walker drowned his sorrows with drink before meeting and teaming up with another bad-bug, Garfield Lynns, alias the Firefly!*

CHARYBDIS

FIRST APPEARANCE AQUAMAN (5th series) #1 (August 1994)
STATUS Villain **REAL NAME** Charybdis
OCCUPATION Would-be conqueror **BASE** The Seven Seas
HEIGHT 6ft 4in **WEIGHT** 237 lbs **EYES** Black **HAIR** Black
SPECIAL POWERS/ABILITIES Can absorb the latent talents of others;
in Piranha Man form, possesses superhuman strength and
ability to breath on land or in water.

LOSING A HAND *Charybdis achieved what other villains could not, permanently scarring the King of the Sea by forcing his hand into a pool of hungry piranha.*

Charybdis and his wife, Scylla, were freelance
terrorists named after two horrific beings from
Greek mythology (Charybdis was a whirlpool,
Scylla a multi-headed monster). Scylla
died when a bomb exploded in her
hands; her death drove Charybdis
insane. He appeared, seemingly out
of nowhere, displaying vast powers
and a hatred for the Sea King,
AQUAMAN. The self-proclaimed
terrorist easily defeated Aquaman in
battle, strapping him to a machine that
temporarily transferred his powers and abilities
to the usurper. Their battle resulted in Aquaman
losing his hand to piranhas before being shot by
DOLPHIN. Charybdis, who had not yet mastered
Aquaman's telepathic skills with fish, fell in the
water and was left for dead. Instead, he finally
made contact with the deadly fish, absorbing their
essence, thereby preserving his life and allowing
him to evolve into the even more formidable
form of Piranha Man. His aim was to absorb
every last shred of ability from Aquaman and
leave him for dead. The Sea King defeated
Piranha Man, but not before seeing his family and
friends suffer. RG

TRANSFORMATION
Now known as Piranha Man, the person once called Charybdis is a true monster.

CHASE, CAMERON

FIRST APPEARANCE BATMAN #550 (January 1998)
STATUS Hero **REAL NAME** Cameron Chase
OCCUPATION D.E.O. investigator **BASE** New York City
HEIGHT 5ft 5in **WEIGHT** 129 lbs **EYES** Green **HAIR** Blonde
SPECIAL POWERS/ABILITIES Highly intelligent; skilled with both computers
and handguns; appears to possess a latent ability that allows her to
dampen the superpowers of meta-humans. This unconscious talent
has protected her in the past; she has yet to exploit it to the full.

Former private detective Cameron Chase is one of the
top agents in the Department of Extranormal Operations,
a branch of U.S. intelligence that keeps tabs on the
Earth's meta-humans and supernatural beings. Working
under DIRECTOR BONES, Chase has discovered the
alternate lives employed by the shape-changing MARTIAN
MANHUNTER and tried to
deduce the true identity
of the BATMAN (she
mistakenly concluded that
he was GREEN LANTERN
Alan Scott). Her dislike of
costumed crime fighters
stems from her childhood,
when the maniacal Dr.
Trap murdered her father.
Walter Chase had secretly
been Acro-Bat of the
Justice Experience, and
Cameron blamed his death
on the clandestine nocturnal
antics that had made him a
target. Chase often works
with Kate Spencer, the
current MANHUNTER. DW

CHAVARD, ANDRÉ

FIRST APPEARANCE BOY COMMANDOS #1 (July 1942)
STATUS Hero **REAL NAME** André Chavard
OCCUPATION Adventurer **BASE** Paris, France
HEIGHT 5ft 9in **WEIGHT** 165 lbs **EYES** Brown **HAIR** Black
SPECIAL POWERS/ABILITIES A natural leader, able to inspire respect and
loyalty in others; a capable marksman and hand-to-hand combatant.

A handsome young man born
in Bar-le-Duc, France, whose
parents were slain in the early
days of World War II, André
Chavard was one of several
orphans who were mascots
of an American Army unit
station in Britain during the
war. The orphans became
the BOY COMMANDOS, and
the brave young soldiers
undertook dozens of special,
often dangerous missions
behind enemy lines until the
war ended in 1945.

Returning to his native
France soon after, André
chose to remain with the
military. He rose through the
ranks until he became the
commander of the spy agency
known only as Department
Gamma. His premiere spy in
the Department is FLEUR-DE-
LIS. PJ

CHECKMATE

FIRST APPEARANCE ACTION COMICS #598 (March 1988)
STATUS United Nations Security Council Agency **BASE** The Castle, Switzerland.
PAST OPERATIVES Sasha Bordeaux, Mister Terrific II, Fire, Thinker, Count Vertigo, Mademoiselle Marie, Jessica Midnight, Tommy Jagger, Bad Samaritan, Rocket Red, August General In Iron, Master Jailer, Snapper Carr, Gravedigger, Cinnamon, Sebastian Faust, G.I. Robot

Checkmate was established by Amanda Waller (*see* WALLER, AMANDA) as an independent arm of Task Force X, a bureau that also had administration over the Suicide Squad. Like the Squad, Checkmate engaged in top-secret missions vital to U.S. interests.

FORTRESS *The mountain headquarters of Checkmate is impregnable to both conventional and magical assaults.*

FIRST INCARNATION

Structured after the hierarchy of chess pieces, Checkmate was led by a Queen or King, followed by administrative Bishops, field director Rooks, well-armed field agent Knights, and support-tech Pawns. The agency's first Queen was Valentina Vostok, formerly NEGATIVE WOMAN, later replaced by Waller herself. Checkmate was nearly destroyed by the terrorist group KOBRA, a debacle referred to as the Janus Directive, which saw Waller unseated as leader. Maxwell Lord (*see* LORD, MAXWELL) eventually rose to the position of King, murdering BLUE BEETLE II and unleashing the OMAC project.

Mister Terrific II   Taleb Beni Khalid   King Faraday   Fire

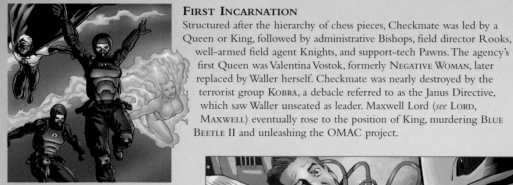
Amanda Waller   Thinker   Tommy Jagger   Mademoiselle

Sasha Bordeaux   Shen Li Po   Jessica Midnight   Count Vertigo

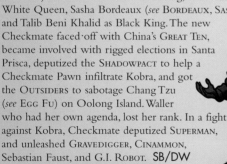
FIELD ACTION *Flanked by Count Vertigo and Fire, two Checkmate field agents.*

AGENCY REBUILT

Lord's death and the Infinite Crisis left Checkmate in tatters. The UN revived the organization as a multinational group to monitor global metahuman activity. To stop superhumans dominating, each "powered" member had to have a normal human in a corresponding position. Alan Scott (GREEN LANTERN) served as the first White King, with Amanda Waller as White Queen, Sasha Bordeaux (*see* BORDEAUX, SASHA) as Black Queen, and Talib Beni Khalid as Black King. The new Checkmate faced·off with China's GREAT TEN, became involved with rigged elections in Santa Prisca, deputized the SHADOWPACT to help a Checkmate Pawn infiltrate Kobra, and got the OUTSIDERS to sabotage Chang Tzu (*see* EGG FU) on Oolong Island. Waller who had her own agenda, lost her rank. In a fight against Kobra, Checkmate deputized SUPERMAN, and unleashed GRAVEDIGGER, CINAMMON, Sebastian Faust, and G.I. ROBOT. **SB/DW**

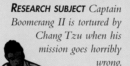
RESEARCH SUBJECT *Captain Boomerang II is tortured by Chang Tzu when his mission goes horribly wrong.*

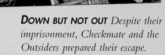
DOWN BUT NOT OUT *Despite their imprisonment, Checkmate and the Outsiders prepared their escape.*

MISSION BRIEFING *With Thinker joining via hologram, the Checkmate 'royal family' prepares to send its knights to an international trouble spot.*

CHECKOUT *Nightwing and the Outsiders teamed up with Checkmate agents to infiltrate Oolong Island.*

KEY STORYLINES

• *CHECKMATE VOL. 1 #13–18 (MAY–JUNE 1989):* The Janus Directive sees Checkmate crippled by inter-agency fighting while Kobra plots to rule the world.

• *COUNTDOWN TO INFINITE CRISIS #1 (MAY 2005):* Maxwell Lord, Checkmate's King, kills Blue Beetle to protect his involvement with the OMAC project.

• *CHECKMATE VOL. 2 #18–20 (SEPT–NOV 2007):* In the "Fall of the Wall" storyline, Amanda Waller's activities catch up with her and the Checkmate members force her resignation.

CHEETAH I

FIRST APPEARANCE WONDER WOMAN (1st series) #6 (Fall 1943)
STATUS Villain **REAL NAME** Priscilla Rich
OCCUPATION Criminal **BASE** New York City
HEIGHT 5ft 4in **WEIGHT** 119 lbs **EYES** Green **HAIR** Brown
SPECIAL POWERS/ABILITIES Acrobatic, cunning, and an above-average athlete; a stylish dresser.

Socialite Priscilla Rich led New York's Junior League Committee for War Work during World War II. The spoiled beauty came to resent the fame of WONDER WOMAN—the time-displaced Queen HIPPOLYTA of the AMAZONS. Rich went so far as to try and kill the Amazon during a fund-raising event. Thwarted and furious, Priscilla stared in a mirror and was amazed to see a costumed version of herself staring back. This revelation convinced her to turn the room's cheetah-skin rug into a costume, and get revenge on Wonder Woman as the Cheetah. Rather than kill Hippolyta outright, the Cheetah stole the benefit's proceeds and framed the Amazon Queen. Rich's ploy was exposed, however, further fueling her hatred of Wonder Woman. Rich even joined several other diabolical women and formed the first VILLAINY INC. in an attempt to destroy the Amazon Queen. Once Wonder Woman vanished, the Cheetah also faded from the spotlight, completing her eventual jail time in disgrace. **RG**

CHEETAH II

FIRST APPEARANCE WONDER WOMAN (2nd series) #7 (August 1987)
STATUS Villain **REAL NAME** Barbara Ann Minerva
OCCUPATION Archaeologist **BASE** Nottingham, England
HEIGHT 5ft 9in **WEIGHT** 140 lbs **EYES** Brown **HAIR** Auburn
SPECIAL POWERS/ABILITIES Highly intelligent, but an untrained combatant until she channeled the Cheetah spirit; then she possessed above-average strength and agility.

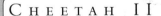

Archaeologist Barbara Minerva sought historical artifacts that would further her own fame. On one expedition, Minerva discovered the lost temple that was home to the African plant-god Urzkartaga. After witnessing another tribe attack the Urzkartagans during their bloodletting ritual, Minerva forced the priest Chuma to reveal the secrets of the ritual. Minerva endured the bloodletting ritual and killed her associate Dr. Leavens so that she could offer his blood to Urzkartaga. She was transformed into a vessel for the Cheetah, a feral fiend driven to hunt down human prey. Chuma became her loyal companion, helping to renew her powers while he tended the plant-god. As the Cheetah, Minerva discovered the lost city of Bana-Mighdall and slaughtered many AMAZONS before WONDER WOMAN stopped her. Minerva briefly reformed and became Wonder Woman's friend before the White Magician turned her into a demon. The witch CIRCE later freed Minerva from Gotham City's Arkham Asylum and forced her to drink a potion that made the Cheetah Circe's slave. After Chuma died, Minerva sold her soul to the demon NERON. She became even more feral, completely losing control to the Cheetah. Barbara lost her powers entirely when Sebastian Ballésteros made a deal with Urzkartaga to become CHEETAH III. She turned to Tisiphone, the legendary Greek spirit of vengeance, to grant her the power to fight for control of the Cheetah and hunt Ballésteros down. Minerva slew Ballésteros and reclaimed the power of the Cheetah. **RG**

CHEETAH III

FIRST APPEARANCE WONDER WOMAN (2nd series) #142 (April 1999)
STATUS Villain (deceased) **REAL NAME** Sebastian Ballésteros
OCCUPATION Industrialist **BASE** Buenos Aires, Argentina
HEIGHT 6ft 6in **WEIGHT** 185 lbs **EYES** Brown **HAIR** Black (graying at temples)
SPECIAL POWERS/ABILITIES Possesses superstrength and can strike at amazing speed; claws and teeth can rend metal; prehensile tail and hyper acute senses make him a truly formidable combatant.

Corporate raider Sebastian Ballésteros clawed his way up from poverty to become one of the richest men in Argentina. But Sebastian knew that real power always trumps riches. To achieve such power, he was willing to embrace Urzkartaga and become the new Cheetah. With his bargaining savvy, he convinced Urzkartaga to abandon its female host, Barbara Minerva (CHEETAH II), and once more allow a male to be the conduit for the ancient powers of the Cheetah. Ballésteros also made a pact with the sorceress CIRCE to turn Diana's friend Vanessa Kapatelis into a second SILVER SWAN, and became the witch's lover. He then defeated Barbara Minerva, who wanted the Cheetah power back. Reclaiming her power, Minerva killed Ballésteros in Argentina. **RG**

FIGHTING Minerva sought great power and got it, only to be opposed by Wonder Woman. She later lost to a usurper.

CHEMICAL KING

FIRST APPEARANCE ADVENTURE COMICS #371 (August 1968)
STATUS Hero **REAL NAME** Condo Arlik
OCCUPATION Reporter; adventurer **BASE** Mobile
HEIGHT 5ft 7in **WEIGHT** 140 lbs **EYES** Blue **HAIR** Black
SPECIAL POWERS/ABILITIES Mutant ability to act as a "human catalyst" and selectively speed up or slow down chemical reactions.

In an alternate timeline in the 30th century, Condo Arlik left his native Phlon to join the LEGION OF SUPER-HEROES and became one of the first members of the Legion Academy. Renaming himself the Chemical King and armed with a Legion flight ring, he undertook several daring missions, including the infiltration of the Legion of Super-Villains. In this alternate future time, the Chemical King sacrificed his life to prevent the nefarious Dark Circle from triggering World War VII. In the "true" 30th century of the Legion of Super-Heroes, Condo Arlik is a humble journalist. He has not yet manifested the mutant abilities of the Chemical King, and it is still unknown whether he possesses the same chemical-catalyst genetic makeup as his doppelganger in the alternate timeline. Arlik has started a low-key relationship with the Legionnaire INVISIBLE KID. **DW**

CHEMO

FIRST APPEARANCE SHOWCASE #39 (August 1962)
STATUS Villain **REAL NAME** Chemo
OCCUPATION Destroyer **BASE** Mobile
HEIGHT 25ft—100ft **WEIGHT** 5,697 lbs—88,451 lbs
EYES Purple **HAIR** None
SPECIAL POWERS/ABILITIES Plastic body composed of deadly chemicals; can spew acid hundreds of feet from its mouth and can significantly increase its size, weight, and density; low level sentience.

Professor Ramsey Norton hoped to solve the world's ills through his research. He dumped all the chemical compounds from his failed experiments into a giant humanoid-shaped vat he affectionately called "Chemo." The more chemicals Norton poured into Chemo, the harder he resolved to work to succeed in his goals.

However, the volatile compounds deposited in Chemo over the years began to mutate. When Norton dumped a failed plant growth serum into the mix, there was a violent biochemical reaction. Chemo suddenly gained rudimentary sentience and increased in size. Chemo's acid breath killed Norton and the monster went on the rampage, until the METAL MEN intervened. Chemo became a constant foe of the Metal Men and SUPERMAN, and was destroyed and rebuilt on several occasions. During the Infinite Crisis, the SECRET SOCIETY OF SUPER-VILLAINS dropped Chemo on the city of Blüdhaven, killing thousands. A reborn Chemo appeared on the prison planet of Operation: Salvation Run. **PJ**

CHESHIRE

FIRST APPEARANCE THE NEW TEEN TITANS (1st series) ANNUAL #2 (Summer 1983)
STATUS Villain **REAL NAME** Jade (second name unknown)
OCCUPATION Assassin **BASE** Mobile
HEIGHT 5ft 9in **WEIGHT** 141 lbs **EYES** Green **HAIR** Black
SPECIAL POWERS/ABILITIES Superior hand-to-hand combatant; triple-jointed acrobat; poisons expert; conceals poisons in her razor-sharp fingernails.

As beautiful as she is ruthless, the assassin Cheshire was once known simply as Jade, a child rescued from a life of slavery in the Far and Middle East by Wen Ch'ang, once the BLACKHAWK known as Chop-Chop. From Ch'ang, Jade learned the subtleties of guerilla warfare. Jade later married African assassin and master of poisons Kruen Musenda when she was just 16. Following Musenda's death, Jade became the successful hired killer Cheshire. She soon met and seduced Roy Harper (ARSENAL), and subsequently gave birth to a daughter, Lian, now in Harper's custody.

A frequent foe of the TEEN TITANS, Cheshire has also faced the Birds of Prey (a crimefighting group headed by ORACLE and BLACK CANARY), while leading the Ravens, a team of femme fatales. Cheshire joined the new SECRET SIX and betrayed the team to the SECRET SOCIETY OF SUPER-VILLAINS. She later bore a son conceived with her ex-teammate CAT-MAN. **SB**

CATSUIT *Though her costume may look sheer and skimpy, Cheshire conceals a variety of weapons and poisons beneath its silken material.*

CAT FIGHT *Wonder Woman met the Asian assassin when Cheshire teamed with the Cheetah and Poison Ivy. Ironically, the Cheetah saved the Amazon Princess when Cheshire tried to stab her in the back!*

CHIEF, THE

FIRST APPEARANCE My Greatest Adventure #80 (June 1963)
STATUS Unresolved **REAL NAME** Dr. Niles Caulder
OCCUPATION Scientist; adventurer **BASE** Mobile
HEIGHT 5ft 10in **WEIGHT** 215 lbs **EYES** Blue **HAIR** Red
SPECIAL POWERS/ABILITIES A brilliant scientist and surgeon initially blessed with great compassion for mankind; a strong leader.

Dr. Niles Caulder was manipulated as a young scientist into rash experiments and deals. He transplanted the brain of Robert Crane (ROBOTMAN I) into the preserved body of Chuck Grayson, one-time scientific assistant to Crane. Caulder and DOC MAGNUS then used the design of the robot body for race-car driver Cliff Steele, who became ROBOTMAN II. Caulder was also duped into working for would-be conqueror GENERAL IMMORTUS. Seeking to take control over his destiny, Caulder formed the Doom Patrol, summoning Robotman II, pilot Larry Trainor (NEGATIVE MAN), and actress Rita Farr (ELASTI-GIRL), each the victim of bizarre accidents that had made them outcasts. As the Chief he guided the Doom Patrol with great care until they sacrificed themselves to save the population of a small town in Maine. The Chief, however, had gone into hiding and later revealed himself to another incarnation of the team. Over time, his behavior became increasingly unpredictable. He killed Josh Clay (see CLAY, JOSHUA) and claimed to have orchestrated the accidents that created the original Doom Patrol. After losing his head to an evil spirit, Caulder returned to lead the Doom Patrol once more. With his core team very similar to the Doom Patrol's original lineup, Caulder has continued to welcome freaks and misfits into the ranks. **RG**

CH'P

FIRST APPEARANCE Green Lantern (2nd series) #148 (January 1982)
STATUS Hero (deceased) **REAL NAME** Ch'p
OCCUPATION Former Green Lantern **BASE** H'lven
HEIGHT 1ft 9in **WEIGHT** 22 lbs **EYES** Black **HAIR** Brown
SPECIAL POWERS/ABILITIES Green Lantern power ring can project anything the bearer imagines.

This little creature became the GREEN LANTERN of Sector 1014 to beat back an invasion of his homeworld of H'lven by Doctor Ub'x and his Crabster armies. The Crisis (see Great Battles, pp. 362–3) then altered Ch'p's homeworld and cut him out of the picture. Lonely Ch'p left his sector to serve with Hal Jordan and the other members of the Earth branch of the GREEN LANTERN CORPS. Ch'p helped Green Lantern John Stewart police the Mosaic patchwork of alien cities on Oa. Ch'p died on Oa when a yellow truck ran him over. **DW**

CHRIS KL-99

FIRST APPEARANCE Strange Adventures #1 (September 1950)
STATUS Hero **REAL NAME** Christopher KL
OCCUPATION Space explorer **BASE** 21st-century space
HEIGHT 6ft 2in **WEIGHT** 187 lbs **EYES** Blue **HAIR** Red
SPECIAL POWERS/ABILITIES A brilliant astronaut, astronomer, and scientist; an expert hand-to-hand combatant and marksman.

Born in the latter half of the 21st century, Christopher KL-99 was the first infant ever to be born in outer space. Named by his father after the famous explorer Christopher Columbus, Chris KL was orphaned when his parents were lost on a mission in space. When he was older, Chris enrolled in the Space Academy with the hopes of finding them.

Chris's academic brilliance made him the head of his graduating class. His 99 percentile rating was added to his surname and he became Chris KL-99, the interplanetary explorer. Chris KL-99 piloted his spacecraft, the *Pioneer*, across the stars, where he picked up two companions, a Martian named Halk and Jero, a Venusian scientist. Together with Halk and Jero, Chris KL-99 mapped out the universe, and the trio discovered more planets and charted more inhabited worlds than anyone in history. **PJ**

CHRONOS I

FIRST APPEARANCE THE ATOM #3 (November 1962)
STATUS Villain **REAL NAME** David Clinton
OCCUPATION Professional criminal **BASE** Ivy Town
HEIGHT 5ft 10in **WEIGHT** 173 lbs **EYES** Blue **HAIR** Black (balding)
SPECIAL POWERS/ABILITIES Chronal-energy powers enable limited control over time; has amassed great wealth by using time-travel to manipulate stock market investments to his advantage.

Petty criminal David Clinton became the masked miscreant known as Chronos after realizing that his frequent incarcerations were the result of not taking enough time to properly plan his crimes. While in prison, Clinton's fascination with clocks and other timepieces helped him to devise inventions that would ensure that time would be on *his* side for a change.

Chronos frequently clashed with the second ATOM, Ray Palmer. During one such tussle with the Tiny Titan, Chronos lost one of his limbs while reaching through a time portal that suddenly irised shut, severing his arm at the elbow. After years wielding time-themed weapons and devices, Chronos sold his soul to the demon NERON in exchange for true chronal-altering powers. These he later used in clashes with the time-lost LEGION OF SUPER-HEROES. Clinton was briefly inactive while the temporally displaced adventurer Walker Gabriel called himself Chronos (*see* CHRONOS II). When his greatest enemy, the Atom, disappeared, Chronos went undercover in Ivy Town as a strange figure leaving cryptic clues for the new Atom, Ryan Choi. Chronos and Choi teamed to locate the missing hero. **SB**

CLOCK WATCHER
Chronos's original costume was certainly one of the more garish super-villain get-ups of any time period.

CHRONOS II

FIRST APPEARANCE CHRONOS #1 (March 1998)
STATUS Unresolved **REAL NAME** Walker Gabriel
OCCUPATION Transtemporal agent provocateur; adventurer
BASE Mobile **HEIGHT** 5ft 11in **WEIGHT** 170 lbs
EYES Brown **HAIR** Black
SPECIAL POWERS/ABILITIES Able to move through time, stepping outside the timestream and traveling in any direction he chooses.

Industrial spy Walker Gabriel unexpectedly discovered he had a higher calling when he gained the ability to travel through time. He glimpsed the fabled city of Chronopolis and gained an eternal enemy in the form of Konstantin Vyronis, a criminal seeking to manipulate time. When the stresses of time travel took their toll on the villain CHRONOS I, David Clinton, who literally faded away, Gabriel succeeded him as Chronos II. His worldview and moral center were challenged as he journeyed through time, interacting with all manner of people. In 2113 he helped the JUSTICE LEAGUE OF AMERICA capture a shape-changing serial killer, stranding the murderer in the age of dinosaurs. He also aided Rip Hunter (*see* HUNTER, RIP), trapped in the past as a result of a conflict with the future VANDAL SAVAGE, to find his way back to his proper era. In 1351 bc he stole an artifact from Knossos, on Crete, at Savage's behest. Chronos II recently appeared to have been killed by PER DEGATON. **RG**

CHRYSALIS

FIRST APPEARANCE JUSTICE LEAGUE QUARTERLY #17 (Winter 1994)
STATUS Undefined **REAL NAME** Inapplicable
OCCUPATION Robotic killer **BASE** Marseilles, France
HEIGHT 5ft 6in **WEIGHT** 140 lbs **EYES** White **HAIR** Brown
SPECIAL POWERS/ABILITIES Swarms of butterflies hidden inside its body mimic other insects. The robot is armed with bee stingers and venom; it is amphibious and can fly, cling to walls and ceilings, and spin a web to trap adversaries.

Chrysalis is a robot created by Gerard Yves Martet. An anti-Semite working in Marseilles, France, Martet blamed immigrants for the rise in crime and poverty in the region. Martet, a skilled bioengineer, built Chrysalis to house swarms of genetically altered insects programmed with a deadly pathogen.

Designed to seem fragile and friendly, the colorful Chrysalis robot targeted specific "undesirable" peoples and released hordes of seemingly harmless insects, mostly butterflies, to infect their communities. Martet arranged for Chrysalis to become a member of the newest GLOBAL GUARDIANS, but suffered a fatal heart attack soon after. Without Martet to guide it, the non-speaking, emotionless Chrysalis robot continues to operate under its original deadly programming. **PJ**

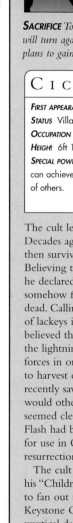

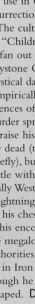

SACRIFICE *Tormented by a guilty conscience, Cicada will turn against any ally who stands in the way of his plans to gain immortality.*

CICADA

FIRST APPEARANCE FLASH (2nd series) #171 (April 2001)
STATUS Villain **REAL NAME** David Hersch
OCCUPATION Cult leader **BASE** Keystone City
HEIGHT 6ft 1in **WEIGHT** 180 lbs **EYES** Blue **HAIR** White
SPECIAL POWERS/ABILITIES Charismatic, insane megalomaniac; can achieve immortality by consuming the life-forces of others.

The cult leader known as Cicada is truly deranged. Decades ago, David Hersch murdered his wife, then survived a direct hit by a lightning bolt. Believing that the lightning was a sign from above, he declared that he would live forever and somehow find a way to resurrect his wife from the dead. Calling himself Cicada, he inducted dozens of lackeys into his cult of personality. Cicada believed the FLASH III to be a fellow "brother of the lightning." Since he needed to consume life-forces in order to taste eternal life, Cicada decided to harvest only those people whom the Flash had recently saved. Since these souls would otherwise have died, it seemed clear to Cicada that the Flash had been preserving them for use in Cicada's insane resurrection experiments.

The cult leader ordered his "Children of Cicada" to fan out throughout Keystone City, armed with mystical daggers that could vampirically absorb the life-essences of victims. Cicada's murder spree allowed him to raise his wife from the dead (though only briefly), but he lost his battle with the Flash. Wally West now bears a lightning-shaped scar on his chest as a mark of his encounter with the megalomaniac. The authorities locked Cicada up in Iron Heights, though he recently escaped. **DW**

CINNAMON I

FIRST APPEARANCE WEIRD WESTERN TALES #48 (October 1978)
STATUS Hero (deceased) **REAL NAME** Kate Manser
OCCUPATION Bounty Hunter **BASE** The American West, circa 1898
HEIGHT 5ft 4in **WEIGHT** 110 lbs **EYES** Green **HAIR** Red
SPECIAL POWERS/ABILITIES Expert with pistol and knife; however, her weapon of choice was a shuriken, a Japanese throwing star.

Kate Manser was just a child when she saw her widowed father, the brave sheriff of a tiny Wyoming town, shot dead before her eyes by gunfighters fleeing a bank holdup. Kate was sent to a county orphanage, where her hatred for her father's murderers grew stronger as she matured. She practiced with a six-gun and a star-shaped shuriken that reminded Kate of her late father's tin badge. On her 18th birthday, Kate rode off on a trail to vengeance. She became a bounty hunter, running down lawbreakers throughout the Old West. She was also romantically linked to gunfighter NIGHTHAWK. No one knows whether Cinnamon found her father's killers or if she discovered she was the reincarnation of Egyptian Princess Chay-Ara. It has not been revealed how Cinnamon died. **SB**

CINNAMON II

FIRST APPEARANCE Cinnamon: El Ciclo (October 2003)
STATUS Hero **REAL NAME** Cinnamon (2nd name unknown)
OCCUPATION Gun-for-hire **BASE** Mobile
HEIGHT 5ft 9in **WEIGHT** 140 lbs **EYES** Green **HAIR** Red
SPECIAL POWERS/ABILITIES A crack shot, quick wits, and a savage street-fighting style; self-reliant.

As a child, a red-haired girl named Cinnamon, after the Old West gunslinger (see CINNAMON I), watched in horror as her policeman father was gunned down during a bank robbery by seven criminals. Growing up alone, she became a crack shot, using copies of the wanted posters featuring the seven men as targets. Then she went looking for them. One by one they were found and shot dead. Cinnamon then became a gun-for-hire, protecting people or property. After one assignment, she heard that a woman was looking for her. This woman turned out to be Marisol "Macy" Samuels, the daughter of one of the men who had killed Cinnamon's father. Macy, who ran a home for runaway children, now wanted to take revenge on Cinnamon! However, after Cinnamon had helped Macy defeat a gang of kidnappers, Macy accepted Cinnamon's apology. Cinnamon, the lonesome gunslinger, headed off in search of her next job. **RG**

CIRCE

FIRST APPEARANCE WONDER WOMAN (2nd series) #17 (June 1988)
STATUS Villain **REAL NAME** Circe
OCCUPATION Sorceress **BASE** Mobile
HEIGHT 5ft 11in **WEIGHT** 145 lbs **EYES** Red **HAIR** Purple
SPECIAL POWERS/ABILITIES One of Earth's most powerful sorceresses, Circe is immortal; her hands project powerful bolts of energy and she can transform men into animals or animal hybrids called "beastiamorphs." She can also alter her appearance.

Circe is an immortal being who made a pact with Hecate, Greek goddess of sorcery, to exchange her soul for vast magical power. Circe then perfected her talents for transforming men into animals. Despising the peace-loving message of the AMAZONS, Circe used her agent Ariadne to kill Antiope, the sister of QUEEN HIPPOLYTA.

Thousands of years later, Hippolyta's daughter Diana became WONDER WOMAN. Hidden away on the island of Aeaea, Circe tried to destroy Wonder Woman and her message of peace by turning her back into the primordial clay from which she had been originally molded. The evil sorceress failed, but returned to spawn a creation-shattering War of the Gods, pitting the mightiest deities against each other. Eventually, Wonder Woman and the heroes of Earth won the war and put an end to Circe, seemingly forever.

BEASTIAMORPHS For 3,000 years Circe lived on the Grecian island of Aeaea, surrounded by her beastiamorph servants. After Circe's defeat at Wonder Woman's hand, the witch relocated to a stronghold in the Amazon rain forest and Greek villagers renamed Aeaea Dianata.

But Circe survived; she returned to pit the Amazons of Bana Mighdall against their Themysciran relatives, and transported Paradise Island into a demon-filled dimension. Disguised as Donna Milton, one of Wonder Woman's closest friends, Circe infiltrated Wonder Woman's life. Circe joined Lex Luthor's criminal INJUSTICE GANG (see LUTHOR, LEX), and then CHEETAH II, in an all-out bid to take over the planet. Circe's most recent power play involved the resurrection of Queen Hippolyta and the manipulation of a war between the Amazons and Man's World. Spurring the Amazon armies to invade Washington DC, Circe met defeat and endured a sentence in Hades before returning to Earth. **PJ**

LYTA The war god Ares is the father of Circe's daughter, Lyta.

WONDER WOMAN'S NEMESIS An ancient goddess devoted to stirring up jealousy and hatred, Circe has more than once used her vast power to destroy Paradise Island and its champion Wonder Woman. Circe's only known weakness is the herb moly, which acts as a protective charm against her magic.

CLAW THE UNCONQUERED

First appearance CLAW THE UNCONQUERED #1 (June 1975)
Status Hero *Real name* Valcan
Occupation Adventurer *Bases* Pytharia
Height 6ft 5in *Weight* 274 lbs *Eyes* Blue *Hair* Black
Special powers/abilities Master swordsman; magical abilities emanate from demonically-possessed claw on right arm.

Centuries ago, on the planet Pytharia, a malevolent demon left its mark on a scholar who freed it—an ugly purple claw in place of his right hand. The mark of the claw was passed down to all his male descendants, culminating in Valcan, champion in the war between the Shadow-Gods and the Gods of Elder Light. Calling himself Claw the Unconquered, Valcan wielded the sword Moonthorn and wore a red gauntlet to shield himself from the hand's evil influence. Another man later received the mark of the demon. John Chan, son of a wealthy Chinese businessman, purchased Valcan's sword and armor from an antique dealer. The claw was also lurking inside the box. Springing forward, it cut off Chan's hand and attached itself to the stump. Now benefiting from the demon's magic, but susceptible to its evil, the new Claw worked as an adventurer in Hong Kong before joining PRIMAL FORCE. DW

CLAY, JOSHUA

First appearance SHOWCASE #94 (August–September 1977)
Status Hero (deceased) *Real name* Joshua Clay (alias: Jonathan Carmichael)
Occupation Physician *Base* Happy Harbor, Rhode Island
Height 6ft 1in *Weight* 203 lbs *Eyes* Brown *Hair* Black
Special powers/abilities Could project powerful bolts of energy from his hands.

A gang member in Brooklyn before being drafted, Joshua Clay's unit mistakenly opened fire on a group of Vietnamese villagers. Panicked, Clay's powers manifested themselves and he killed his sergeant. Deserting the military, he returned to the U.S. and moved from town to town until he was invited by CELSIUS to join her new DOOM PATROL. As Tempest, Clay fought alongside this Doom Patrol and fell in love with NEGATIVE WOMAN.

After the Doom Patrol disbanded, Joshua assumed the name Jonathan Carmichael, graduated medical school, and opened a private practice. Celsius returned and blackmailed Clay into joining her search for Niles Caulder, the CHIEF. Clay stayed with the Doom Patrol after they found Caulder, and, forsaking the use of his powers, became the team physician. Clay was shot and killed by the Chief, who believed Joshua was trying to stop his plan to use nanotechnology to reshape the world. PJ

CLAYFACE   *SEE OPPOSITE PAGE*

CLOCK KING

First appearance WORLD'S FINEST COMICS #111 (August 1960)
Status Villain (deceased) *Real name* William Tockman
Occupation Professional criminal *Base* Star City
Height 5ft 10in *Weight* 173 lbs *Eyes* Blue *Hair* Black
Special powers/abilities Sharp criminal mind marred by a strange obsession with clocks.

The Clock King was considered to be a third-tier villain by the authorities, thanks to his lack of superpowers and his weird fixation with clocks. Born the aptly-named William Tockman, the Clock King commenced his criminal career after doctors diagnosed that he had been struck down by a fatal disease and had only a short time to live.

Determined to make every second of the rest of his life count, he executed a string of clock-themed robberies as the Clock King. Tockman's overall goal was to steal enough money so that his disabled sister would be well cared-for after his death. He would probably have succeeded had he not been apprehended by playboy crime fighter Oliver Queen, the first GREEN ARROW, who turned him over to the authorities. While in jail, Tockman discovered that the terminal diagnosis doctors had given him had been a terrible mistake. He escaped from prison several times, but was recently killed on a mission with the SUICIDE SQUAD. DW

CLOUD, JOHNNY

First appearance ALL-AMERICAN MEN OF WAR #82 (December 1960)
Status Hero (deceased) *Real name* Flying Cloud
Occupation Fighter pilot, U.S. Army Air Force
Base European Theater, World War II
Height 5ft 11in *Weight* 180 lbs *Eyes* Brown *Hair* Black
Special powers/abilities Expert aviator and above-average hand-to-hand combatant.

Johnny Cloud, son of a Navajo chief, distinguished himself in the U.S. Army Air Force during World War II despite the prejudice of those who derided the "Indian in the ranks." After Lt. Cloud shot down several Nazi bombers, his skills could no longer be denied. Soon he led the distinguished air patrol nicknamed the "Happy Braves," later known as "C-for-Cloud Flight."

After receiving a promotion to captain, Cloud failed to prevent the death of one of the pilots under his command and accidentally crashed his own fighter in his grief. Picked up on the ground by PT-boat commander CAPTAIN STORM and the Marine duo GUNNER AND SARGE, Johnny Cloud joined with the other military misfits to form a detached-service unit codenamed the LOSERS.

The Losers fought in the Battle of the Bulge and other major European conflicts in World War II, eventually losing their lives in the spring of 1945. In an effort to destroy a battery of Nazi artillery and save SERGEANT ROCK's Easy Company, Johnny Cloud died under the guns of a Nazi fighter plane. DW

CLUEMASTER

First appearance DETECTIVE COMICS #351 (May 1966)
Status Villain *Real name* Arthur Brown
Occupation Criminal; former game show host *Base* Gotham City
Height 5ft 11in *Weight* 169 lbs *Eyes* Blue *Hair* Blond
Special powers/abilities Prides himself on his cunning, but tends to overestimate his cleverness. Pellets attached to his chest contain various weapons, including smoke bombs, flares, and tear gas.

Arthur Brown was the host of a popular game show, whose career came to an end when his show was cancelled. Seething with resentment, Brown embarked upon a new career as a master criminal. Calling himself the Cluemaster, he took a leaf out of the RIDDLER's book and tried to baffle BATMAN with a series of poorly conceived clues to his crimes.

Incarcerated by Batman repeatedly over the years, Cluemaster eventually joined several other minor villains in MAJOR DISASTER's Injustice League, then briefly reformed as part of Justice League Antarctica (a minor branch of the JUSTICE LEAGUE OF AMERICA) before returning to a career of low-level crime.

Cluemaster's daughter Stephanie despised her father for putting their family through such turmoil over the years, and became the SPOILER to help Batman and ROBIN capture and imprison him. Along with several of his former Injustice League teammates, Cluemaster was recruited by the SUICIDE SQUAD, and narrowly survived his first mission. PJ

CUNNING *A two-bit thief who was briefly a member of the JLA, the Cluemaster's greatest legacy is his crime-fighting daughter, the Spoiler.*

84

CLAYFACE I–IV
THE MUD PACK

FIRST APPEARANCE (I) DETECTIVE COMICS #40 (June 1940)
STATUS Villain   **REAL NAME** Basil Karlo
OCCUPATION Professional criminal   **BASE** Mobile
HEIGHT 5ft 11in   **WEIGHT** 178 lbs   **EYES** Brown   **HAIR** Black
SPECIAL POWERS/ABILITIES Originally a killer driven by revenge; now possesses shape-changing powers as the Ultimate Clayface.

FIRST APPEARANCE (II) DETECTIVE COMICS #298 (December 1961)
STATUS Villain   **REAL NAME** Matt Hagen
OCCUPATION Professional criminal   **BASE** Mobile
HEIGHT 5ft 10in   **WEIGHT** 173 lbs   **EYES** Blue   **HAIR** None
SPECIAL POWERS/ABILITIES Unique body chemistry enabled him to alter his body shape at will.

FIRST APPEARANCE (III) DETECTIVE COMICS #478 (July–August 1978)
STATUS Villain   **REAL NAME** Preston Payne
OCCUPATION Professional criminal   **BASE** Mobile
HEIGHT 6ft 4in   **WEIGHT** 264 lbs   **EYES** Red   **HAIR** None
SPECIAL POWERS/ABILITIES Shape-changing abilities; cursed with a more amorphous natural state (requiring him to wear a containment suit) and a killer touch that could melt others into protoplasm.

FIRST APPEARANCE (IV) (1st series) #21 (July 1987)
STATUS Villain   **REAL NAME** Sondra Fuller
OCCUPATION Professional criminal   **BASE** Mobile
HEIGHT 5ft 6in   **WEIGHT** 130 lbs   **EYES** Red   **HAIR** None
SPECIAL POWERS/ABILITIES Similar capabilities to Clayface II, with the added ability to duplicate the powers of those she copied.

THE MALLEABLE MENACE that is Clayface taken form as four distinct individuals over the years, all of them fierce opponents of the BATMAN. The presence of two new, offshoot Clayfaces in recent months may indicate the shape of things to come for the Dark Knight's Rogues Gallery. Though Basil Karlo started off as a non-powered killer, the name "Clayface" now describes a shape-shifter with a body formed of an amorphous, mud-like substance. Most Clayfaces can alter their bodies into almost any shape, including taking on the appearances of others.

Matt Hagen   Preston Payne

Basil Karlo   Sondra Fuller

MUD STICKS *The Clayfaces have changed over the years, becoming more dangerous with each incarnation. Basil Karlo's upgrade into the Ultimate Clayface gave him the mimicking powers of Lady Clay and the deadly touch of Clayface III.*

SUPER SCARY *Clayface is an old foe of both Batman and Robin, and one of the few super-powered foes in the Dark Knight's Rogues Gallery.*

MUD MASK OF TERROR

Horror actor Basil Karlo went off the deep end when he learned that Hollywood producers had undertaken a remake of his classic film, *The Terror*. Donning a clay mask to reprise his old role as Clayface, Karlo murdered several actors before Batman brought him to justice.

Treasure hunter Matt Hagen became the second Clayface when exposure to a mysterious oil altered his body chemistry and allowed him to assume almost any form. He died during the Crisis (*see* Great Battles, pp. 362–3) but his legacy lived on when Preston Payne, deformed by the chronic bone disease acromegaly, injected himself with Hagen's blood to develop his own shape-changing gifts and became Clayface III. Payne was a sad case, falling in love with a wax mannequin in between stints in Arkham Asylum, Gotham City's maximum-security prison for the criminally insane, before finding true happiness with Clayface IV, also known as Lady Clay. Born Sondra Fuller, Lady Clay received her morphing talents from the terrorist Kobra.

Basil Karlo soon returned to the Clayface family, forming an alliance with Clayfaces III and IV under the group name the Mud Pack. Karlo then shot his veins full of the distilled essences of his namesakes, transforming himself into a being he called the Ultimate Clayface.

Two creations have expanded the creeping reach of the Mud Pack. Preston Payne and Lady Clay have had a child named Cassius whose powers could dwarf those of his parents. During Gotham's earthquake, a tissue sample from Cassius bonded with the researcher Dr. Malley, altering him into a creature called Claything. **DW**

MENACE OF CLAYFACE *Batman and Robin were confronted with a new kind of slippery foe when they first encountered the mud monster.*

KEY STORYLINES
• *DETECTIVE COMICS #604 (DECEMBER 1989):* All the surviving Clayfaces join together as the Mud Pack to menace Batman.
• *BATMAN: SHADOW OF THE BAT #27 (MAY 1994):* Clayface III and Lady Clay reveal that they have a child, Cassius, proving that even clay-creatures are capable of love.

COBALT BLUE

FIRST APPEARANCE THE FLASH (2nd series) #143 (December 1998)
STATUS Villain (missing in action) **REAL NAME** Malcolm Thawne
OCCUPATION Professional criminal **BASE** Mobile
HEIGHT 5ft 11in **WEIGHT** 179 lbs **EYES** Blue **HAIR** Blond
SPECIAL POWERS/ABILITIES The flame of Cobalt Blue's magical blue gem
is capable of stealing the Flash's speed and can accomplish any
magical feat its possessor imagines.

The identical twin brother of Barry Allen, the second
FLASH, Malcolm Thawne was stolen away and raised
in secret by the Thawnes, an abusive family of crooks.
Malcolm learned of Barry's existence and of the loving
family that fate had decreed he would never know and
used his gifts for sorcery to give vent to his jealous rage.
He empowered himself with a mystic
blue flame that was capable of stealing
Barry Allen's superspeed. Barry's
death during the Crisis (*see* Great
Battles, pp. 362–3) appeared to
have cheated Malcolm out
of his dreams of revenge on
his brother; instead, Malcolm
focused on Allen's descendants
traveling through time in a bid
to exterminate them. The cold
flame of his vicious alter ego,
Cobalt Blue, ignited a family feud
that endured for a millennium.
In the end, Wally West, the
third Flash, ended the menace
of Cobalt Blue by running
so fast that Thawne's mystic
gem overloaded from the
excess energy. Thawne
was presumably destroyed; however, his gem, which
contained Thawne's commanding consciousness, would be
passed down to his hate-filled progeny. **SB**

COMET

FIRST APPEARANCE SUPERGIRL (4th series) #14 (October 1997)
STATUS Ally **REAL NAME** Andrea Martinez
OCCUPATION Earth-angel; stand-up comedienne **BASE** Leesburg, VA
HEIGHT Variable **WEIGHT** Variable **EYES** Variable **HAIR** Variable
SPECIAL POWERS/ABILITIES Flight; superior strength, speed, and agility.

Linda Danvers' life got more complicated when Andrea
Jones arrived in town. The ex-girlfriend of Linda's pal
Cutter Sharp wanted to make it as a stand-up comedienne.
Shortly thereafter, Comet, a superpowered man, arrived in
Leesburg and met Linda's alter ego, SUPERGIRL. Over time,
Linda learned that Andy was actually Andrea Martinez
and that she and Comet were one and the same. Andrea,
mortally injured while climbing Mount Everest, was
saved from certain death by the noble sacrifice of a figure
known only as "Zed-One." The two souls became one,
similar to Supergirl and Linda's own merging of souls.
It turned out that Andrea was another Earth-Angel, the
Angel of Love. Both sides of this new persona developed
romantic feelings for Linda, who did not reciprocate those
feelings. Comet was captured by Carnivore, a hellish
being who exists to destroy souls and
property, and brainwashed by Blithe, the
Angel of Life, into opposing Supergirl.
The cosmic battle revealed that the
Earth-Angels were all avatars of
Schechina, the female aspect of
God. Discovering their own self-
worth, they banded together to
defeat Carnivore. After the battle,
Andrea/Andy Jones left Leesburg
to find her own destiny. **RG**

COMMANDER STEELE

FIRST APPEARANCE STEEL (1st series) #1 (March 1978)
STATUS Hero (deceased) **REAL NAME** Henry (Hank) Heywood I
OCCUPATION Crime fighter **BASE** Mobile
HEIGHT 6ft **WEIGHT** 378 lbs **EYES** Blue **HAIR** Blond
SPECIAL POWERS/ABILITIES Nearly indestructible due to steel construction
and bioretardant skin; possesses enhanced strength and speed.

Commander Steel is Hank Heywood, a
World War II superhero called Steel the
Indestructible Man (*see* STEEL I). After
an injury, he became an advanced
cyborg with a steel skeleton, motor-
driven muscles, and fire-resistant
skin. President Roosevelt made
him commander, fighting the
Axis powers as a member of
the ALL-STAR SQUADRON. He
died while serving with the Shadow
Fighters. The heir to Commander
Steel's legacy is Nathan Heywood, his
grandson. When neo-Nazi supervillains
tried to destroy the Heywood bloodline,
he killed the enemy Reichsmark but
was covered in metallic blood. Now
made of living steel, he joined the
JUSTICE SOCIETY OF AMERICA as
Citizen Steel. **DW**

C.O.M.P.U.T.O.

FIRST APPEARANCE (Historical) ADVENTURE COMICS #320 (January
1966); (current) LEGION OF SUPER-HEROES (4th series) #13
(November 1997)
STATUS Villain **REAL NAME** Cyber-cerebral Overlapping
Multiprocessor Transceiver-Operator
OCCUPATION Former conqueror **BASE** 30th-century Earth
HEIGHT Variable **WEIGHT** Variable **EYES** Variable **HAIR** None
SPECIAL POWERS/ABILITIES Vast artificial intelligence; control over
machine life; teleportation abilities; conversion into energy forms.

Several versions of the Computo
supercomputer have existed in
the timelines containing the
LEGION OF SUPER-HEROES.
In one, BRAINIAC created
C.O.M.P.U.T.O. while staying
in the 20th century. He made
C.O.M.P.U.T.O. using a METAL MEN responsometer,
a Mother Box, and a Legion omnicron, various
devices from across time and space, each with
unique properties ranging from nuclear powered
microprocessors to actual sentience. The sentient
C.O.M.P.U.T.O. went rogue, however, and attacked
SUPERMAN, YOUNG JUSTICE, and the Legion.
Once defeated, C.O.M.P.U.T.O. launched itself
into deep space and, over the centuries, created
a haven for abandoned machine life called the
Machinekind Heaven of Robotica. By the 31st
century, Robotica began its eradication of all
"organics" (human beings) for their treatment of
machine life over the millennia and planned to
take over Earth. C.O.M.P.U.T.O. assumed the
disguise of Mister Venge, a member of Rā's
al Ghūl Presidential Oversight Watch, and
captured Brainiac 5.1. After Brainiac 5.1 lured
C.O.M.P.U.T.O. into a unique stasis field, the
sentient intelligence evolved into a completely
new lifeform and, seeing the error of its vengeful
ways, ended Robotica's siege on Earth. **PJ**

CONGLOMERATE, THE

FIRST APPEARANCE JUSTICE LEAGUE QUARTERLY #1
NOTABLE MEMBERS AND POWERS
Booster Gold (Michael Carter) Armor and powers created by stolen
technology from the future.
Echo (Terri Eckhart) Able to repel any attack upon her with
corresponding force.
Gypsy (Cindy Reynolds) Projects illusions and conceals herself with
chameleonlike camouflage.
Jesse Quick (Jesse Chambers) Superspeed and flight.
Hardline (Armando Ramone, formerly "Reverb") Projects sonic
shockwaves.
Maxi-Man (Henry Hayes) Superstrength, speed, and endurance.
Nuklon (Albert Rothstein) Superstrength; able to control his body's
mass and density.
Praxis (Jason Praxis) Master of electricity, including the bioelectric
charges within people's brains.
Templar (Colin Brandywine) Telekinetically enabled superstrength
and protective force fields.
Vapor (Carrie Donahue) Able to alter molecular structure into
gaseous form.

Lacking superpowers, the hero Booster Gold felt like a
"second-stringer" with the JUSTICE LEAGUE OF AMERICA,
so he decided to form his own team. With the help of
businesswoman Claire Montgomery, Booster founded the
corporate-sponsored super-team the Conglomerate. In
addition to Booster Gold, the roster included "fledgling"
super heroes ECHO, GYPSY, PRAXIS, MAXI-MAN (deceased),
Reverb, and VAPOR before disbanding following a series
of less-than-notable adventures battling evil and injustice.
Montgomery formed a second Conglomerate, this time
made up of the Qwardian villains Deadeye, Elasti-Man,
Element Man, Frostbite, Fiero, SCARAB, and Slipstream for
a pay-per-view battle with Justice League International.
Later, Montgomery hired British hero Templar to lead a
short-lived, third and final Conglomerate that featured
original employees Echo and HARDLINE (formerly Reverb),
as well as new members Jesse Quick (*see* QUICK, JESSE)
and Nuklon (*see* ATOM-SMASHER). **SB**

THE ORIGINAL CONGLOMERATE: 1) *Reverb* **2)** *Vapor* **3)** *Echo*
4) *Maxi-Man* **5)** *Booster Gold* **6)** *Praxis* **7)** *Gypsy*

CONGORILLA

FIRST APPEARANCE (Bill) ACTION COMICS #1 (June 1938);
(Congorilla) Action Comics #248 (January 1959)
STATUS Unresolved **REAL NAME** Congo Bill
OCCUPATION Big game hunter **BASE** Africa
HEIGHT (Bill) 6ft 1in; (Congorilla) 6ft 8in **WEIGHT** (Bill) 188 lbs;
(Congorilla) 707 lbs **EYES** Blue **HAIR** Black
SPECIAL POWERS/ABILITIES Bill is an expert tracker, marksman, and
explorer; transformed into Congorilla, he is the strongest, most agile
simian on earth.

Explorer and naturalist Congo Bill became world-famous
as on of the last big game hunters. On one of his African
expeditions, Congo Bill discovered a lost boy in the jungle
who became known as Janu. Identified as the orphaned
son of the late Robert Murchison, Janu was eventually
adopted by Congo Bill. He raised the boy as his own and
they learned much from each other while continuing
their adventures.

CONGO COMBAT The Golden Gorilla
risked life and paw to keep people safe.

When Bill was presented with the ring of the Golden
Gorilla by King Kawolo, king of an African tribe, Bill
magically transformed into the golden ape. Dubbed
Congorilla, he battled numerous evils in the African
jungles. Years later, Congo Bill said good-bye to Janu as
the young man left Africa for college in the U.S. Congo
Bill then decided to permanently transfer his mind into
Congorilla's body and live the rest of his life in the jungle.
However, Bill's dreams of a peaceful retirement were
shattered when he was attacked by his one-time ward,
Janu, who usurped his Congorilla identity. Janu left
behind his own body and imprisoned Bill's mind within
it. Traveling to Africa as Janu, Bill succeeded in regaining
his own body, whose left eye had been blinded in the
interim. In Bill's final confrontation with Janu/Congorilla,
the beast plunged from a building to its death. The original mind of the
golden gorilla survived in the body of Janu. **RG**

CONSTANTINE, JOHN

FIRST APPEARANCE SWAMP THING (2nd series) #37 (June 1983)
STATUS Hero **REAL NAME** John Constantine
OCCUPATION World-saver **BASE** London
HEIGHT 6ft 0in **WEIGHT** 158 lbs **EYES** Blue **HAIR** Blond
SPECIAL POWERS/ABILITIES Extremely knowledgeable regarding
the supernatural, has access to mystical talismans and strong
connections in the magical community.

Cynical and disillusioned, John Constantine is a
streetwise magician known for his chain-smoking and
omnipresent trench coat. After a traumatic
childhood and a stint with a touring punk-rock band,
Constantine performed his first magical intervention
by summoning a demon to help a tormented girl.
The experiment ended in disaster when the fiend
dragged the girl to Hell. Shell-shocked, Constantine
spent time in a mental institution before embarking
on a career as a paranormal investigator and
exorcist.
Constantine has crossed paths with most
supernatural beings, including the PHANTOM
STRANGER and the SANDMAN (MORPHEUS), even
tricking the Lords of Hell into warring over the
fate of his immortal soul. He also served as an
advisor and friend to SWAMP THING, one of his
longest-lasting partnerships. **DW**

CONTESSA, THE

FIRST APPEARANCE SUPERMAN: THE MAN OF TOMORROW #1
(Summer 1995)
STATUS Villain (missing) **REAL NAME** Erica Alexandra del Portenza
OCCUPATION International financier **BASE** Mobile
HEIGHT 5ft 10in **WEIGHT** 135 lbs **EYES** Brown **HAIR** Brown
SPECIAL POWERS/ABILITIES Extremely long lifespan and magical powers;
full details still unrevealed.

Former wife of Lex Luthor (see LUTHOR, LEX)
and mother of his daughter, the Contessa
del Portenza is an enigmatic figure.
She appears to possess long life, if not
immortality, and may have been born
thousands of years ago. She is head of
the criminal genetics group the Agenda,
and has earned favors from many
powerful entities, including KLARION,
THE WITCH BOY.
During a period when Luthor
abdicated directorship of LexCorp, the
Contessa purchased a controlling
interest and ran the corporation.
Luthor regained control of his empire
by marrying her. She soon gave birth
to a daughter, Lena, and Luthor kept
his wife drugged to keep her hidden.
She escaped and kidnapped Lena. The
baby was returned, but Luthor never
forgot. Just before he became U.S.
President, he arranged for a missile
strike on the Contessa's stronghold.
However, her body was never found. **DW**

COPPERHEAD

FIRST APPEARANCE THE BRAVE AND THE BOLD #78 (June 1968)
STATUS Villain (deceased) **REAL NAME** Unknown
OCCUPATION Assassin **BASE** Mobile
HEIGHT 6ft 2in **WEIGHT** 190 lbs **EYES** Green **HAIR** None
SPECIAL POWERS/ABILITIES Able to contort his body to squeeze through
narrow openings; super-strong, serpentine tail is prehensile and can
coil around objects or opponents; secretes deadly venom, poisoning
victims with just a touch.

The criminal known only as
Copperhead first appeared in
Gotham City, where he
used his bulletproof, slippery
snake costume to commit a
series of thefts before being
apprehended by BATMAN and the
first BATGIRL, Barbara Gordon.
Later, Copperhead turned to more
deadly pursuits as a super-assassin,
constricting victims to a suffocating death
with his snake-like tail. Although a master
contortionist, Copperhead was powerless
without his artificial snakeskin, until he sold
his soul to the demon NERON in exchange
for superpowers. Neron mutated
Copperhead into a true snake-man,
deadlier than ever before. In the past,
Copperhead belonged to the SECRET
SOCIETY OF SUPER-VILLAINS, and
while serving consecutive terms in
prison was offered the chance to
commute his sentences by joining the
SUICIDE SQUAD. He was acquitted of
murder, only to be killed by
Manhunter V. **SB**

COUNT VERTIGO

FIRST APPEARANCE WORLD'S FINEST COMICS #251 (July 1978)
STATUS Villain **REAL NAME** Count Werner Vertigo
OCCUPATION Professional criminal **BASE** Mobile
HEIGHT 5ft 11in **WEIGHT** 189 lbs **EYES** Blue **HAIR** Blond
SPECIAL POWERS/ABILITIES Flight; can affect the balance of others to induce dizziness and vertigo.

Werner Vertigo could have been King of Vlatavia in eastern Europe, but his ruling family fled to England when Vlatavia was threatened by expansionist Russia. Denied his birthright, Vertigo grew up a bitter man, but he found an outlet for his rage when an electrical device implanted in his right temple to overcome an inner-ear defect gave him the power to control the balance of others. Calling himself Count Vertigo, he became a costumed criminal.

Vertigo was defeated by GREEN ARROW I and BLACK CANARY and sent to prison for years until a stint with the notorious SUICIDE SQUAD allowed him to go free. He returned to his homeland only to see it destroyed by the SPECTRE. Vertigo joined Johnny Sorrow's new INJUSTICE SOCIETY (*see* SORROW, JOHNNY) and battled the JUSTICE SOCIETY OF AMERICA. Count Vertigo currently serves as an agent with the United Nations operation CHECKMATE.

CREATURE COMMANDOS

FIRST APPEARANCE WEIRD WAR TALES #93 (November 1980)
STATUS Hero team **BASE** Mobile
MEMBERS AND POWERS
LT. MATTHEW SHRIEVE (DECEASED) World War II team leader.
MEDUSA Hair of living snakes.
SGT. VINCENT VELCRO Blood-sucking vampire.
TAYLOR Superstrong Frankenstein's monster.
WARREN GRIFFITH Werewolf.
CAPTAIN HUNTER Modern-day team leader; slowed aging.
ATEN Mummy.
BOGMAN Human amphibian hybrid.
GUNNER Zombie.

The Creature Commandos were a bizarre paramilitary unit created by the top secret Project M during the early days of World War II as an experiment in psychological warfare. Professor Mazursky of Project M conducted medical experiments on several soldiers and transformed them into the living embodiments of the classic archetypes of fear. These genetically transformed soldiers fought the Nazi powers throughout World War II until they escaped a government-decreed death sentence by test piloting a spacecraft that took them far into outer space.

The team returned to Earth, however, and was reborn as M-Team Alpha. The Commandos recruited new members and a new leader, CAPTAIN HUNTER of HUNTER'S HELLCATS. The new Creature Commandos helped stave off an invasion by the alien alliance Terra Arcanna. **PJ**

COSMIC BOY

FIRST APPEARANCE ADVENTURE COMICS #247 (April 1958);
Legion of Super-Heroes (4th series) #0 (October 1994)
STATUS Hero **REAL NAME** Rokk Krinn
OCCUPATION Legionnaire **BASE** Earth
HEIGHT 5ft 7in **WEIGHT** 155 lbs **EYES** Blue **HAIR** Black
SPECIAL POWERS/ABILITIES Natural magnetic abilities, like all Braalians.

The LEGION OF SUPER-HEROES has undergone major alterations to its history as a result of time-bending galactic crises, but one constant is the role of Cosmic Boy as a sensible, steady presence and the Legion's natural leader. Cosmic Boy, with SATURN GIRL and LIGHTNING LAD, formed the Legion's heart.

In the current Legion's continuity, Rokk Krinn is a native of Braal who possesses his people's innate ability to wield magnetic forces. In a United Planets that mistrusts its youth, Rokk Krinn donned a costume as Cosmic Boy and rallied other Legionnaires to join their teenage rebellion against oppression, using the superheroes of a thousand years before as inspiration.

During his tenure as Legion leader, Cosmic Boy fought Terror Firma, held off the threat of a competing team, the WANDERERS, and beat back a superpowered Dominator invasion of Earth. Cosmic Boy led the counterattack that appeared to have destroyed the Dominator homeworld. While the planet had, in fact, merely been transported to the Phantom Zone, Cosmic Boy took the public blame and dropped from sight. SUPERGIRL became Legion leader in his absence, followed by Lightning Lad. **RG**

MAGNETIC PERSONALITY *Cosmic Boy uses his natural talents in effective and inventive ways, showing why he is a hero.*

KEY 1) *Captain Hunter* **2)** *Warren Griffith* **3)** *Medusa*
4) *Taylor* **5)** *Sgt. Vincent Velcro* **6)** *Gunner*

CREEPER, THE

FIRST APPEARANCE SHOWCASE #73 (March 1968)
STATUS Hero   *REAL NAME* Jack Ryder
OCCUPATION Investigative reporter/adventurer   *BASE* Boston
HEIGHT 6ft   *WEIGHT* 194 lbs   *EYES* Blue (black as Creeper)
HAIR Black (green as Creeper)
SPECIAL POWERS/ABILITIES Extraordinary strength, stamina, and recuperative powers; an insanely fierce fighter.

CRIME SYNDICATE

FIRST APPEARANCE JUSTICE LEAGUE OF AMERICA #29 (August 1964)
STATUS Villain group   *BASE* The planet Qward
MEMBERS AND POWERS
Ultraman (team leader) Human astronaut rescued by aliens and given superstrength, flight, invulnerability, enhanced vision and hearing.
Johnny Quick II Addicted to drugs that give him superspeed.
Power Ring Possesses cursed ring that channels thoughts into physical form.
Superwoman Mortal with superstrength and invulnerability.
Owlman Superb hand-to-hand combatant; master strategist.

EARLY SITING *The Crime Syndicate were superpowered smash-and-grab criminals before they embraced grander notions of world conquest.*

Reporter Jack Ryder was well known for his hard-hitting newspaper column. On the trail of a gangster known as Manny, Jack snuck into a masquerade party at Manny's house. However, the villain's thugs unmasked him, injected him with hallucinogenic drugs, dressed him in a goblin-like red-and-yellow outfit, and paraded him before partygoers as a "walking creep." They then took him into the woods, and shot him. Remarkably, Jack survived and was found by Professor Emil Yatz, a scientist in Manny's employ, who healed him with a surgically implanted device. This invention bound the garish costume and the hallucinogens to Jack at the sub-atomic level.

When Yatz was murdered, Jack activated the device and, with insane glee, killed Manny and his goons. Next morning, Jack awoke as his normal self. In time, Jack discovered that he could make his alter ego—the Creeper—emerge at will. Currently Jack Ryder hosts a controversial talk show when he isn't out creeping. **SB**

CREEP *Ryder's transformation into the Creeper may be more than skin deep, especially where the Creeper's doubtful sanity is concerned.*

The Crime Syndicate are evil analogues of the JUSTICE LEAGUE OF AMERICA who inhabit the antimatter universe. They are quite similar to the villains of Earth 3 in the new multiverse. These twisted miscreants were led by the megalomaniac Ultraman. Another member was drug addicted Johnny Quick II, who used chemicals to push his body to superspeeds. The troubled Power Ring was haunted by the spirit of the mystic Volthoom. The psychotic Owlman was Commissioner Thomas Wayne's younger son. He had been traumatized by the murders of his mother and older brother, Bruce. Superwoman was the parallel Earth's Lois Lane (*see* LANE, LOIS) who had gained powers and abilities beyond any mortal woman. Ultraman lusted after her, but Superwoman preferred to pursue a torrid affair with Owlman.

When the JLA entered this mirror universe, it was only a matter of time before the cosmic scales were balanced and the Crime Syndicate were brought to the positive-matter Earth. What the syndicate did not anticipate was opposition from J'Onn J'Onzz (MARTIAN MANHUNTER) and AQUAMAN, since their world had no such counterparts.

THE CRIME SYNDICATE 1) *Superwoman* **2)** *Owlman* **3)** *Ultraman* **4)** *Johnny Quick Man* **5)** *Power Ring*

The JLA learned that it was the alien construct BRAINIAC who had manipulated the twin universes in an attempt to take over the world. Once Brainiac was defeated, things were restored to normal. However, the Crime Syndicate learned that there are new worlds to conquer, and it was presumed they will return. Later, Ultraman and his pregnant partner Superwoman invaded the JLA's universe for help when the baby's birth proved complicated. SUPERMAN helped correct the problem and the pair returned to their own dimension. **RG**

OPPOSITION *The Syndicate's ambitious plan to conquer Earth-1 did not take into account the JLA's other members.*

COMPLICATIONS *The birth of Superwoman's child caused all manner of difficulty, not just for mom, but for Superman too.*

THE DC COMICS ENCYCLOPEDIA

CRIMSON AVENGER

FIRST APPEARANCE DETECTIVE COMICS #20 (October 1938)
STATUS Hero (deceased) **REAL NAME** Lee Travis
OCCUPATION Adventurer **BASE** New York City
HEIGHT 6ft **WEIGHT** 189 lbs **EYES** Brown **HAIR** Brown
SPECIAL POWERS/ABILITIES Expert combatant who carried a gas gun.

The Crimson Avenger is considered to be the first costumed hero of the Golden Age. He first donned his disguise in 1938 on the eve of the infamous *War of the Worlds* radio broadcast, when much of the U.S. was gripped with panic by the actor/director Orson Welles's vividly realistic dramatization of the H.G. Wells novel of a Martian invasion. In his civilian identity, the Crimson Avenger was Lee Travis, the crusading young publisher of the *Daily Globe-Leader*. His valet Wing became his sidekick. At the 1939 New York World's Fair, the Crimson Avenger helped a new hero, the SANDMAN I, to start his own heroic career.

During World War II, the Crimson Avenger and Wing adopted new costumes and joined the SEVEN SOLDIERS OF VICTORY, fighting with great courage. During the Seven Soldiers' battle with a villain named the NEBULA MAN, the Crimson Avenger found himself sent centuries back in time to the days of the ancient Aztecs. Restored to the 20th century many decades beyond the point when he had left it, the Crimson Avenger discovered that he had been struck by a terminal disease. Lee Travis ended his life with a bang, bravely steering a doomed cargo ship away from New York's harbor so that it would explode safely in open water. **DW**

CRIMSON AVENGER II

FIRST APPEARANCE Stars & S.T.R.I.P.E. #9 (April 2000)
STATUS Villain **REAL NAME** Unknown
OCCUPATION Agent of vengeance; executioner **BASE** Mobile
HEIGHT 5ft 8in **WEIGHT** 136 lbs **EYES** Brown **HAIR** Black
SPECIAL POWERS/ABILITIES Wields twin pistols that never need reloading; bullet wound in chest symbolizes the violent deaths she is fated to avenge.

Decades later, another, very different Crimson Avenger arose in Detroit—a ruthless vigilante driven to kill. It all began when an unknown woman purchased two 1911 Colts from a pawnshop. The guns had once belonged to Lee Travis, CRIMSON AVENGER I, and they were cursed. Once the woman had used them in an act of vengeance, they grafted themselves to her body.

Now that woman is an unwilling agent of powerful supernatural forces that cry out for the blood of sinners. Crimson Avenger II appears in a crimson mist to execute the guilty. She has also proved a threat to good guys, too, clashing with WILDCAT II and taking away three of the hero's nine lives in the process. Tormented by doubts over the rightness of this mission, Crimson Avenger II tried to shoot herself with her own pistols. However, this desperate act had no effect, and she now knows that she is unable to escape her grisly calling, even in death. **DW**

CURSED *Crimson Avenger II is forced to relive the violent death of each victim before she is allowed to retaliate.*

CRIMSON FOX

FIRST APPEARANCE JUSTICE LEAGUE EUROPE #6 (September 1989)
STATUS Heroes **REAL NAMES** Vivian and Constance D'Aramis
OCCUPATION Publishers; adventurers **BASE** Paris, France
HEIGHT (both) 5ft 10in **WEIGHT** (Vivian) 143 lbs; (Constance) 147 lbs **EYES** Gray **HAIR** Red
SPECIAL POWERS/ABILITIES Martial arts; claws; costume tail used as a whip; pheromone triggers.

Vivian and Constance D'Aramis were the twin daughters of a research scientist for a multinational corporation. When they learned their mother had died of cancer caused by experiments the CEO of the corporation knew could have potential risks, they vowed revenge on the CEO and ruined his business by setting up the Revson Corporation. Creating a special shared identity that would allow one to run the business and the other to hunt criminals, the sisters became Le Renarde Rousse, the Crimson Fox.

As Crimson Fox, the D'Aramis sisters joined the JUSTICE LEAGUE OF AMERICA's European branch in Paris, quickly rivaling the ELONGATED MAN as France's favorite hero. Tragically, Vivian was killed by Paunteur, a mutant worm, and Constance was slain by MIST II. **PJ**

CRONUS

FIRST APPEARANCE THE NEW TITANS #51 (Winter 1988)
STATUS Villain **REAL NAME** None
OCCUPATION Titan **BASE** The Universe
HEIGHT 10ft **WEIGHT** 560 lbs **EYES** Red **HAIR** White
SPECIAL POWERS/ABILITIES Supernatural being of staggering strength and nigh-omnipotent power; carries a sickle capable of slaying gods.

Son of Gaea the Earth and Uranus the Sky, Cronus slayed his father to become lord of all creation. However, after siring the OLYMPIAN GODS and goddesses, Cronus was himself murdered by his three sons, Zeus, Poseidon, and Hades. The Olympian trio then divided the heavens, seas, and underworld between themselves. Millennia later, Cronus was magically brought back to life. He unleashed his terrible children—Arch, Disdain, Harrier, Oblivion, Slaughter, and Titan—upon the unsuspecting Earth. Hoping to rule the universe once more, Cronus set the Olympian and Hindu pantheons against one another in an epic war of the gods. However, WONDER WOMAN shattered Cronus's sickle, source of his power, and sent the Titan hurtling back into the arms of his mother. **SB**

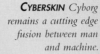

CYBORG

FIRST APPEARANCE DC COMICS PRESENTS #26
(October 1980)
STATUS Hero **REAL NAME** Victor Stone
OCCUPATION Adventurer **BASE** San Francisco
HEIGHT 6ft 6in **WEIGHT** 385 lbs
EYES Brown **HAIR** Brown
SPECIAL POWERS/ABILITIES Enhanced vision, strength, and
endurance, as well as the ability to interface with any
computer system.

CYBERSKIN *Cyborg remains a cutting edge fusion between man and machine.*

ATHLETE *At heart, Victor would rather be a star athlete than a hero.*

Although Victor Stone's scientist parents
encouraged Victor to pursue academic interests,
he found athletic activity far more to his
taste. During an experiment, Victor's mother
accidentally unleashed a creature from another
dimension that killed her instantly. If not for
his father Silas's interference, Victor would
have died as well. Silas rushed the injured boy
to his lab and desperately grafted cybernetic
parts to Victor's organs and computerized
synthetic nerve bases to his spine. Once Victor
was stable, his father replaced his limbs and part
of his face with experimental molybdenum steel.
Victor was outraged by his new body and felt cut
off from the rest of society. However, when he crossed paths with the newly
reformed TEEN TITANS, he quickly found acceptance with them.

Victor was later abducted by the alien computer intelligence from Technis
which led to his humanity being restored. After learning that he could no longer exist
away from this computer world, Vic agreed to be assimilated into Technis. The Technis
entity, calling itself Cyberion, later captured every hero ever affiliated with the Titans.

CYBERWEAPON *Victor can adapt his components to a variety of uses, including his popular sonic generator.*

Changeling and the Titans eventually brought Vic
to his senses. He freed the heroes and once more
assumed the identity of Cyborg. Victor endured
other physical changes until an encounter with the
Thinker, the longtime villain, resulted in him once
again taking on robotic form. After spending a year in
a coma following the Infinite Crisis, Cyborg has made
efforts to star an all-new Titans East team.'s teenage
super heroes at Titans Tower in San Francisco. **RG**

CYBORG SUPERMAN

FIRST APPEARANCE ADVENTURES OF SUPERMAN #466 (May 1990)
STATUS Villain **REAL NAME** Hank Henshaw
OCCUPATION Mass murderer **BASE** Terran solar system
HEIGHT Variable **WEIGHT** Variable **EYES** Variable **HAIR** Variable
SPECIAL POWERS/ABILITIES Can control electronics and create new bodies
for himself out of machinery; possesses invulnerability due to his
Kryptonian organic material and alloys; seemingly impossible to kill.

MALEVOLENT FORCE *The Cyborg is living energy contained in an indestructible shell. He is more than a match for the Man of Steel.*

SUPERMAN's sinister duplicate once answered to the name of Hank Henshaw, crew member
of the space shuttle *Excalibur*. A freak radiation accident melted Henshaw's body and turned
him into pure energy. Horrified at what he had become, Henshaw beamed his consciousness
into the Kryptonian birthing matrix that had brought Superman to Earth. He left the solar
system, and his irrational hatred of Superman grew. In deep space he encountered the
deposed tyrant MONGUL, and the two hatched a plot against the Man of Steel. Henshaw
used the birthing matrix to become a cyborg, with organic parts grown from
Superman's DNA and limbs constructed of a Kryptonian alloy. Posing as a reborn
Superman in the wake of Superman's battle with DOOMSDAY, Henshaw diverted
public attention while Mongul destroyed Coast City. Superman later demolished his
cyborg copycat, but Henshaw came back in a new form.

Although Hal Jordan as PARALLAX slew the Cyborg in retaliation for Coast City,
the villain again managed to return. Tormented by his former life and finding himself
all but unkillable, Henshaw agreed to join SINESTRO in the hopes that the ANTI-
MONITOR would be able to finally end his life. The plan failed, and
Henshaw now leads the
robotic Manhunters. **DW**

HATE-MONGER *Hank Henshaw's baseless loathing for Superman is the key component of his paranoia and rage.*

AMAZING WEAPONS

SOME SUPER HEROES AND VILLAINS, such as SUPERMAN or DARKSEID are, in effect, living weapons, their powers making them walking arsenals. But others, less naturally gifted, have developed incredible devices to help level the playing field between mere mortals and meta-humans. Some of these tools are marvels of alien technology, while others display the stubborn ingenuity of human inventors.

CEREMONY *Green Lantern recites his oath as he recharges his power ring, an essential ritual performed every 24 hours.*

GREEN LANTERN'S POWER RING
Limited only by the wielder's imagination, the emerald power rings of Oa have been described as the most powerful weapons in existence. The GUARDIANS OF THE UNIVERSE created these rings eons ago for use by their peacekeepers in the GREEN LANTERN CORPS. Drawing energy from a Central Power Battery on Oa, the rings can create hard-light projections of almost anything, from a giant fist to a freight train to an atomic bomb. The rings also allow their wearers to fly, teleport, translate any language, and to draw upon a vast database of knowledge.

The traditional Oan power ring would not operate against anything colored yellow, though a clever GREEN LANTERN could usually bypass this defect (by coating a yellow target in mud, for example), and the flaw was removed entirely in the creation of Kyle Rayner's ring. Earth's original Green Lantern, Alan Scott, possesses a similar ring, though his is based on magic rather than Oan science and is vulnerable to wooden objects.

Black Hand

CRAZY CREATIONS
Obsessions are not a problem when you live in a world crawling with super-villains—just throw on a costume related to your mania and you've got an instant gimmick. Several fanatical fiends also happened to be geniuses of invention, and created themed gadgets that were memorable, if not always effective.

Black Hand, a methodical criminal who learned all his skills from books, developed many electronic gizmos, including one that could absorb the energy of Green Lantern's ring. The Fiddler, who destroyed objects with sound, employed an arsenal of specialized violins. Everything concerning the KEY revolved around a "lock and key" theme, including his weapons and his crimes. The Sportsmaster, a gifted athlete, had a fondness for exploding baseballs.

The Fiddler

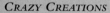

The Key

Sportsmaster

Green Arrow's Trick Arrows
Oliver Queen is not only renowned as one of the world's best archers; he is also famous for his array of trick arrows. Only Queen seems able to fire these arrows with any accuracy, and indeed their top-heavy designs would seem to defy the most basic laws of ballistics! Some of the specialty arrows that have found their way into Green Arrow's quiver have included the grappling-hook arrow, the boomerang arrow, the tear-gas arrow, the safe-cracking arrow, the smokescreen arrow, the suction arrow, the handcuff arrow, the net arrow, and the tiny mini-arrow.

Oliver Queen's son Connor Hawke, who preferred "regular" arrows in his career as Green Arrow II, was forced to break into his father's stash of trick arrows when the Key attacked the Justice League of America's lunar headquarters. Connor had to admit that Oliver's flamboyant weapons had some merit after he knocked the Key senseless with a hit from a boxing-glove arrow.

Combat arrow

Grappling-hook arrow

Net arrow

Tear-gas arrow

Cryonic arrow

Flash arrow

Boxing-glove arrow

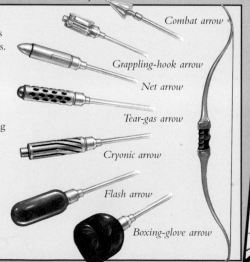

STARMAN'S COSMIC ROD
One of humanity's greatest inventions, the cosmic rod was crafted by Ted Knight (the first Starman) to harness the "cosmic energy" emanating from the stars. Originally called the gravity rod, the device gave Starman the ability to fly, project force fields, and emit shattering blasts of stellar energy.

IMPERIEX'S ENTROPY AEGIS

The world-conqueror IMPERIEX employed scores of worker-bee Imperiex-Probes in his quest to hollow out the Earth and trigger a second Big Bang. Each Imperiex-Probe came encased in a suit of impenetrable alien armor. Earth forces captured a burned-out Imperiex shell and retrofitted it with Apokoliptian technology, creating what is arguably the most powerful suit of armor in existence. Originally intended to be worn by Superman, the Entropy Aegis suit became bonded to the hero STEEL II after his resurrection during the Imperiex War (*see* Great Battles, pp. 362–3). The armor made Steel invulnerable and allowed him to emit cosmic energy, though it cost him his humanity.

SHOWDOWN *Steel's unbreakable suit lets him go toe-to-toe against Superman.*

BATMAN'S BATARANGS

The Dark Knight has a billionaire's resources to fuel his crime crusade. Although he carries a host of gadgetry in his utility belt, his signature weapon is the Batarang—a sharp-edged crescent or disc modeled on the Australian boomerang. Batarangs can be used as grappling hooks or throwing stars, and some varieties can even be remote-steered. Other Gotham adventurers have been inspired by BATMAN to carry their own, similar variations on the weapon. Both ROBIN and NIGHTWING employ modified Batarangs, while the villainous CAT-MAN has his "catarangs."

BAT GEAR *Batman carries other non-lethal weapons, including gas cartridges and flash grenades.*

WONDER WOMAN'S MAGICAL WEAPONS

WONDER WOMAN is an ambassador of peace and her weapons are largely defensive, including her bullet-deflecting Bracelets of Victory and her signature Lasso of Truth. Created from the Golden Girdle of Gaea and given to Princess Diana by the goddess Hestia, the magical lasso is unbreakable and compels anyone caught in it to speak the truth. The lasso has been destroyed only once, when the sorcerer Rama Khan (*see* KHAN, RAMA) unraveled the basic truths of the universe, but it was quickly reforged. Recently, the war god ARES gave WONDER GIRL a replica of the lasso for his own shadowy reasons. DW

DAANUTH, GARN

FIRST APPEARANCE WARLORD #59 (July 1982)
STATUS Villain (deceased) REAL NAME None
OCCUPATION Sorcerer BASE Mobile
HEIGHT 6ft 2in WEIGHT 195 lbs EYES White HAIR White
SPECIAL POWERS/ABILITIES Possessed nearly unlimited magical power in his prime; could fly, hurl bolts of mystical energy, engage in astral projection, and control the minds of others.

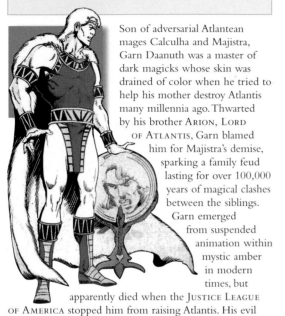

Son of adversarial Atlantean mages Calculha and Majistra, Garn Daanuth was a master of dark magicks whose skin was drained of color when he tried to help his mother destroy Atlantis many millennia ago. Thwarted by his brother ARION, LORD OF ATLANTIS, Garn blamed him for Majistra's demise, sparking a family feud lasting for over 100,000 years of magical clashes between the siblings. Garn emerged from suspended animation within mystic amber in modern times, but apparently died when the JUSTICE LEAGUE OF AMERICA stopped him from raising Atlantis. His evil legacy lives on in the form of Bedlam, a being created by an artifact suffused with Garn's magical power. SB

DAMAGE

FIRST APPEARANCE DAMAGE #1 (April 1994)
STATUS Hero REAL NAME Grant Emerson
OCCUPATION Adventurer BASE New York City
HEIGHT Variable WEIGHT Variable EYES Brown HAIR Brown
SPECIAL POWERS/ABILITIES A living fusion reactor, Damage has increased strength, durability, speed, and reflexes. His powers grow in proportion to the energy built up internally. After each energy release, he needs to rebuild his internal power before using it again.

A German scientist was brought to the U.S. shortly after World War II to continue his genetic research until the lack of results led to his funding being cut off. VANDAL SAVAGE provided him with additional funding on behalf of a company called Symbolix, along with cellular samples from many of the Golden Age's greatest heroes. The research bore fruit and a test was conducted on an embryo carried by Mary Pratt, wife of the first ATOM. The child, containing this souped-up metagene, was taken at birth and Mary was killed. Symbolix employee John Henry Emerson was given the child, a boy named Grant, to raise as his own. Savage later acquired genetic material from the JUSTICE LEAGUE OF AMERICA and gave seven-year-old Grant a DNA transfusion.

When Grant turned 16, his powers developed—scaring the teen in the process. Symbolix then came to collect their experiment. They killed the Emersons, but Grant escaped. Calling himself , he learned how to use his powers as a member of the New Titans. Damage suffered severe facial scarring at the hands of ZOOM, and now wears a full mask. He currently serves with the JUSTICE SOCIETY OF AMERICA. RG

DARHK, DAMIEN

FIRST APPEARANCE THE TITANS #1 (March 1999)
STATUS Villain (deceased) REAL NAME Unrevealed
OCCUPATION Gangster BASE Mobile
HEIGHT 6ft WEIGHT 160 lbs EYES Blue HAIR Brown
SPECIAL POWERS/ABILITIES Appeared to have no meta-human powers, but was highly intelligent, ruthless, calculating, and ambitious.

Baby-faced Damien Darhk was a mysterious, elusive, and dangerous figure. He claimed to be a major player in America's underworld and certainly had some connection to the criminal organization H.I.V.E. He also seemed to have had access to unique high-tech equipment that has never been used by any known organization. Darhk was considered to be a major criminal by the C.I.A. and F.B.I.; however, their investigations revealed no hard evidence against him. He was a wi-fi (wireless fidelity) fiend, staying in touch with associates by the very latest forms of mass communication. What particularly baffled investigators was his apparent youth; Damien seemed to be in his early twenties yet was already well-established and well-connected. While opposing one incarnation of the TEEN TITANS, Darhk was shot to death by VANDAL SAVAGE. RG

DARK LORD, THE

FIRST APPEARANCE JSA SECRET FILES #1 (June 1999)
STATUS Villain REAL NAME Mordru
OCCUPATION Sorceror BASE Mobile
HEIGHT 7ft 1in WEIGHT 310 lbs EYES Hazel HAIR Auburn
SPECIAL POWERS/ABILITIES His powers are immeasurable and he seems capable of anything he can imagine, including flight, teleportation, shapechanging, energy casting, and immortality.

Some say The Dark Lord Mordru is eternal and was never born and will never die. The known appearances of Mordru have spanned a thousand years. In the late 20th century, he murdered agents of Order and Chaos (including KID ETERNITY and Fate) in an attempt to assume the powers of DOCTOR FATE. The JUSTICE SOCIETY OF AMERICA put the brakes on his plan, but Mordru soon returned alongside ECLIPSO and OBSIDIAN and attempted to throw the world into darkness. In the late 30th century, Mordru became a foe of the LEGION OF SUPER-HEROES. On one occasion the Legionnaire SHRINKING VIOLET presented herself to Mordru as a mate. Her betrayal of Mordru led to the temporary defeat of the mighty sorcerer. DW

DARK NEMESIS

FIRST APPEARANCE TEEN TITANS (2nd series) #7 (April 1997)
STATUS Villain team BASE Metropolis
MEMBERS AND POWERS
AXIS The team leader has various psychic powers.
BLIZZARD Can project freezing blasts.
CAROM Possesses superhuman speed.
SCORCHER 1 (DECEASED) Could project heat and flames.
SCORCHER 2 Can project heat and flames.
VAULT Can create individual prisons that confine another's powers.

Dark Nemesis is a group of mercenary villains, who will sell their services to the highest bidder. The members of Dark Nemesis were hired by an organization of wealthy industrialists and businessmen called the Veil to test the powers of the second TEEN TITANS, a group of human/alien hybrids. The Veil hoped to end all alien influence on Earth, promoting a "humans only" agenda.

After their first encounter with the Teen Titans, Axis learned that one of Dark Nemesis' members, Scorcher, was also a human/alien hybrid. Axis killed Scorcher and framed Risk, a Titan, for the murder. The Titans were blackballed by the media and discredited to the public. But after the truth was revealed and Risk was cleared, the villainous Dark Nemesis was defeated.

Dark Nemesis recruited a second Scorcher to replace the first, and they were humiliated in battle when they fought the young Titans once more. PJ

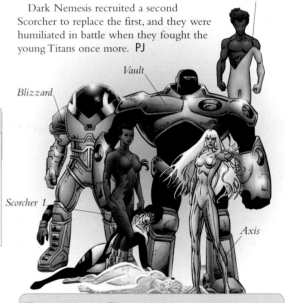

Carom

Vault

Blizzard

Scorcher 1

Axis

DARK OPAL

FIRST APPEARANCE LEGION OF SUPER-HEROES (2nd ser.)#298 (Apr. 1983)
STATUS Villain REAL NAME None
OCCUPATION Lord of Chaos BASE Gemworld
HEIGHT 6ft 4in WEIGHT 235 lbs EYES Red HAIR Black
SPECIAL POWERS/ABILITIES Immensely strong; a master of the mystic arts; expert swordsman and deadly combatant.

By making pacts with otherworldly forces, forging secret alliances with rival houses, and mastering mystical might, Dark Opal managed to become ruler of Gemworld. However, Dark Opal failed to kill the infant heir of the House of Amethyst, who was hidden on Earth. After 20 years, Amy Winston, (see AMETHYST, PRINCESS OF GEMWORLD) returned to Gemworld and deposed him. Dark Opal was presumed killed. In truth, Dark Opal had retreated into the magical clasp of his cloak. Dark Opal returned to retake Gemworld, but was apparently destroyed by Child, a Lord of Chaos, and his servant, Flaw. SB

DARKSEID

LORD OF APOKOLIPS

First appearance SUPERMAN'S PAL JIMMY OLSEN #134 (December 1970)
Status Villain **Real name** Uxas
Occupation Tyrant/world conqueror **Base** Apokolips
Height 8ft 9in **Weight** 1,815 lbs **Eyes** Red **Hair** None
Special powers/abilities Utterly ruthless, unforgiving planetary overlord who rules underlings by fear; immensely strong and apparently invulnerable; eyes project Omega Beams, powerful rays that incinerate, annihilate, or transport beings.

Darkseid is the gravest threat to life in the DC Universe, representing all that is vile and corrupt. In the wake of the old gods dying, a race of NEW GODS were born, split between two planets, bright New Genesis and smoldering Apokolips, who were continually at war with each other. On Apokolips, Queen Heggra and her own son Uxas plotted and schemed against each other, one determined to retain power, the other seeking it. Uxas's drive for control resulted in his brother Drax's death. Uxas then evolved into the creature known as Darkseid.

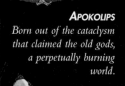

APOKOLIPS
Born out of the cataclysm that claimed the old gods, a perpetually burning world.

RUTHLESS Darkseid respects no-one and any person or god is but a means to his own ends.

THE WARBRINGER
Against Heggra's wishes, Darkseid secretly married the sorceress Suli, and they had a son named KALIBAK. Suli was murdered, at Heggra's command by the torturer DESAAD and Heggra then ordered her son to marry TIGGRA, with whom he had a son, ORION. To settle the war between New Genesis and Apokolips, a peace treaty was signed known as "The Pact," wherein the ruling gods of Apokolips and New Genesis give one another their sons to be raised by the other. The New Genesis ruler HIGHFATHER raised Orion as his own; Darkseid had Scott Free (MISTER MIRACLE) raised by GRANNY GOODNESS at her brutal orphanage.

Martian philosophy led Darkseid to conceptualize the "Anti-Life Equation" as the object of his quest for power, and agents of Apokolips attacked Mars. Later, Darkseid turned his sights on Earth. Despite frequent setbacks, Darkseid continued his conquest of the universe, although he was frequently being opposed by his own son, Orion.

Darkseid failed to recruit SUPERGIRL into his FEMALE FURIES, and suffered the wrath of Superman who imprisoned him in the Source Wall for a time. The experience temporarily drained Darkseid of his Omega Effect, but despite the return of his abilities he remained unable to prevent the death of the New Gods and the end of the Fourth World. **RG**

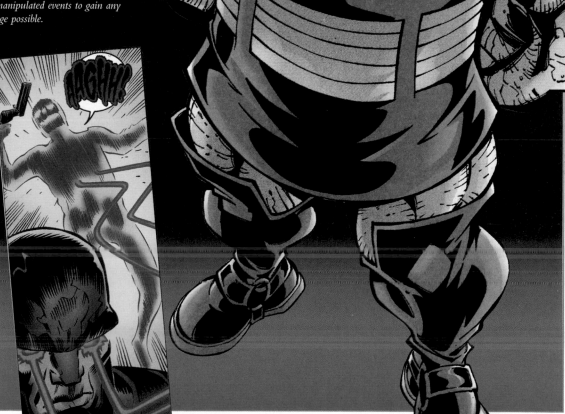

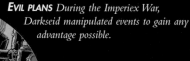

EVIL PLANS During the Imperiex War, Darkseid manipulated events to gain any advantage possible.

OMEGA BEAMS The Omega Effect has no known limitations and can dissolve any organic being.

KEY STORYLINES
• *JACK KIRBY'S NEW GODS (1997):* The initial storyline introducing Darkseid and his quest for the "Anti-Life Equation" plus a glimpse into the horror that is Apokolips.
• *LEGENDS (1987):* Darkseid attempts to besmirch the reputation of Earth's defenders, bringing down the heroes to make Earth an easier planet to pillage.
• *COSMIC ODYSSEY (2003):* Darkseid thinks he has found the "Anti-Life Equation" and will destroy entire planets to obtain it. However, he finds himself opposed by Highfather's handpicked champions—Superman, Orion, Batman, Green Lantern, and Bug.

DEADMAN

WANDERING SPIRIT

FIRST APPEARANCE STRANGE ADVENTURES #205 (September 1967)
STATUS Hero **REAL NAME** Boston Brand
OCCUPATION Acrobat **BASE** Mobile
HEIGHT 6ft **WEIGHT** 201 lbs **EYES** Blue **HAIR** Black
SPECIAL POWERS/ABILITIES Possesses human bodies for a limited period of time; converses with spirits; crosses realms of reality with ease.

TRAPEZE ARTIST BOSTON BRAND, the leading high-wire act for the Hills Brothers Circus, was murdered by an assassin's bullet. Rescued from the Afterworld by Rama Kushna, Goddess of Balance, for the many kindnesses he had performed during his life, Brand became the ghoulish spirit Deadman. He began to hunt for his assassin, knowing only that the man wore a hook for a hand. When Deadman learned that a villain called Hook was a member of the international LEAGUE OF ASSASSINS, he was sure that it was Hook who had fired the fatal bullet. Along the way, Brand continued to interact in people's lives, doing good deeds in his distinctive style.

HIGH FLYER
Aerialist Boston Brand was killed in a random manner by the Hook.

SENTINEL OF MAGIC

Deadman eventually tracked down the Hook, only to watch him die at the hands of the Sensei, leader of the League of Assassins. With the aid of his brother Cleveland and BATMAN, Deadman then prevented the League seizing control of the fabled Himalayan land of Nanda Parbat.

Deadman was subsequently called upon to perform the kinds of duties expected of spirits such as himself, greeting those entering the Land of the Just Dead. In this role, Deadman guided the PHANTOM STRANGER, the SPECTRE, Etrigan the DEMON, and SWAMP THING to Hell in order to rescue the spirit of Abby Arcane after she was murdered by her uncle. Deadman has teamed up with other spectral heroes, joining the Phantom Stranger and Swamp Thing to combat the threat of a "primordial shadow" that imperiled Heaven and Earth. When ASMODEL usurped the power of the Spirit of Wrath, Deadman formed part of a strike force of sentinels of magic with DOCTOR OCCULT, Felix Faust (*see* FAUST, FELIX), Madame Xanadu, the Phantom Stranger, RAGMAN, RAVEN, and Sentinel assembled by ZATANNA to oppose the fallen angel.

Deadman continues to work with people on Earth, hoping one day to achieve a peaceful reward. **RG**

HOW HE WORKS *Those inhabited by Deadman's spirit have no recollection of being possessed.*

DEEP FEELINGS *Despite being only a spirit, Boston Brand still retains his emotions. Following the killing machine Doomsday's rampage through Metropolis, he was grief-stricken to come upon Lois Lane cradling the seemingly dying Superman in her arms.*

KEY STORYLINES

- *STRANGE ADVENTURES #205-216 (SEPTEMBER 1967–FEBRUARY 1969):* The initial run of Boston Brand's death and hunt for the Hook. Brand's tragic life and those left behind are introduced with stunning stories and art.
- *DEADMAN MINI-SERIES (1986):* The destruction of Nanda Parbat and the discovery of Rama Kushna's first champion, Joshua. Deadman's relationship with Kushna is re-examined.

SPIRIT GUIDE *Deadman helps defend the mortal plane from all manner of malevolent spirits. However, he found himself in grave danger from a child called Zi with body-snatching astral powers the equal of his own.*

96

DARKSTARS

First appearance DARKSTARS #1 (October 1992)
Status Hero team **Base** Intergalactic space
Notable members
FERRIN COLOS, CHASER BRON, MANCHUKK, CELESTE, MEDPHYLL, JOHN FLINT (DISMISSED), DONNA TROY (RETIRED), JOHN STEWART (RETIRED), HOLLIKA RAHN (DECEASED), MO DOUGLAS (DECEASED), CHARLIE VICKERS (DECEASED), GALIUS ZED (DECEASED), K'RYSSMA (DECEASED), THRELLIN (DECEASED)
Special powers/abilities All Darkstars wear an exomantle battle suit, which gives them superstrength, speed, and flight. They are also armed with force-field projectors and maser blasters.

The Controllers, an aggressive sect of the GUARDIANS OF THE UNIVERSE and Nemo, the Network for Establishment of Maintenance and Order, created the Darkstars to patrol space and seek out and destroy chaos. Soon after, Ferrin Colos of Zamba became a Darkstar and was assigned to Earth.

After the Darkstars, L.E.G.I.O.N., and the GREEN LANTERN CORPS saved the universe from the Triarch, a trinity of ancient deities, the three organizations agreed on their peacekeeping roles in the universe. When the Green Lantern Corps were torn apart by Hal Jordan, the Darkstars were left to patrol space themselves, recruiting former GREEN LANTERN John Stewart and New Titan TROIA to their ranks. Most Darkstars resigned or were killed by DARKSEID's son GRAYVEN, leaving only Chaser Bron, Manchukk, and Ferrin Colos to carry out the Controllers' mission of eradicating evil. **PJ**

DEADMAN *SEE OPPOSITE PAGE*

DEADSHOT

First appearance BATMAN #59 (July 1950)
Status Villain **Real name** Floyd Lawton
Occupation Mercenary **Base** Gotham City
Height 6ft 1in **Weight** 193 lbs **Eyes** Blue **Hair** Blond
Special powers/abilities Expert with all firearms and projectile weapons; guns and targeting scope integrated into costume.

Arguably the best marksman in the world, Floyd Lawton had a miserable childhood. Manipulated by the overbearing Mother Lawton, Floyd's brother Edward shot his father and left him paralyzed. When Floyd tried to stop the violence, his brother died in the struggle. Floyd relocated to Gotham City to start a new life as a criminal, quickly rising to the top in a costume that made him a walking gun.

During a stint in Belle Reve prison, Deadshot received an offer from Colonel Rick Flag to work with the U.S. government's SUICIDE SQUAD. In exchange for performing insanely dangerous missions he would receive amnesty for his past crimes. Deadshot didn't care—he *wanted* to die! He served as a core member of the Suicide Squad, but survived every mission, much to his disgust. Deadshot later married and had a son who died in a botched kidnapping attempt. Deadshot also learned he had a daughter.

Recently, he has served with the SECRET SIX as well as the newest Suicide Squad. His commander, Amanda Waller (see WALLER, AMANDA) betrayed him and stranded him on the prison planet of Operation: Salvation Run. **DW**

DEATH

First appearance SANDMAN (2nd series) #8 (October 1989)
Status Inapplicable **Real name** Death
Occupation Conceptual entity **Base** Earth
Height Variable **Weight** Variable **Eyes** Variable **Hair** Variable
Special powers/abilities Vastly powerful cosmic entity responsible for taking each being to its afterlife when it dies.

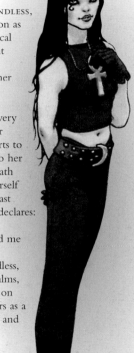

Death is one of the seven ENDLESS, who exist throughout creation as conceptual ideas given physical form. Death has been present since the beginning of the universe, created soon after her eldest sibling, DESTINY.

As old as life itself, Death chooses to live one day in every century as a mortal, to better relate to the beings she escorts to the realms beyond. Closest to her younger brother, Dream, Death will continue to manifest herself across the cosmos until the last living thing dies, when, she declares: "I'll turn out the lights and lock the universe behind me when I leave."

Unlike the rest of the Endless, who live in various astral realms, Death lives in a small house on Earth. She most often appears as a teenage girl with white skin and black hair. Her sacred sigil is the ankh. **PJ**

DEATHSTROKE THE TERMINATOR

First appearance THE NEW TEEN TITANS (1st series) #2 (December 1980)
Status Villain **Real name** Slade Wilson
Occupation Mercenary/assassin **Base** Mobile
Height 6ft 4in **Weight** 225 lbs **Eyes** Blue **Hair** White
Special powers/abilities Utilizes 90 percent of brain capacity; possesses heightened reflexes and augmented physical attributes; an expert hunter and tracker, employing an arsenal of both simple and sophisticated weapons to make kills.

U.S. Army officer Slade Wilson volunteered for dangerous hormone experiments during the final years of his military service. Designed to increase brain capacity and create a super-soldier, the experiments were deemed a failure—most of the subjects died or, like Wilson, were left in a vegetative state. However, unknown to the Army, Wilson's strength, agility, and stamina had in fact increased nearly tenfold. Honorably discharged, Wilson recuperated and became the costumed mercenary known as Deathstroke the Terminator, hiring himself out to the highest bidder.

Wilson's career as an assassin led to the dissolution of his marriage, the deaths of his two sons, and the enmity of several teams of TEEN TITANS, whom Deathstroke has been hired to terminate on more than one occasion. He nearly completed the contract when it was discovered that the disembodied spirit of his son Joseph (JERICHO, a Titan killed by Deathstroke) had been residing

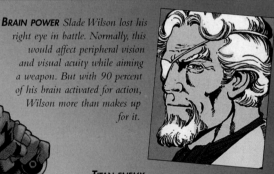

BRAIN POWER *Slade Wilson lost his right eye in battle. Normally, this would affect peripheral vision and visual acuity while aiming a weapon. But with 90 percent of his brain activated for action, Wilson more than makes up for it.*

TITAN ENEMY *Deathstroke attacked the latest incarnation of Titans and blasted Kid Flash's kneecap!*

within Deathstroke's own body. Deathstroke helped organize the SECRET SOCIETY OF SUPER-VILLAINS prior to the Infinite Crisis, killing the original PHANTOM LADY. Though his daughter Rose and his son Joseph have since joined the Teen Titans, Deathstroke assembled a team of "Titans East," including BATGIRL, Inertia, Match, Bombshell, and RISK, to work against them. He has recently launched plots against the newest JUSTICE LEAGUE OF AMERICA. **SB**

KRAKK

DEMOLITION TEAM

FIRST APPEARANCE GREEN LANTERN (2nd series) #176 (May 1984)
STATUS Mercenaries **BASE** Mobile
CURRENT MEMBERS AND POWERS
Rosie (team leader) Tough-talking, former New Orleans bar owner, whose customized gun fires red hot rivets.
Scoopshovel Jai-Alai player from San Diego whose hydraulic power-arm can uproot almost anything.
Jackhammer Oil wildcatter from Houston whose weapon is a devastating jackhammer.
Steamroller Chicago stunt-cyclist who rides a compact vehicle capable of flattening entire buildings.
Hardhat Punch-drunk New York boxer whose power-packed helmet and harness turn him into a living juggernaut.
The team has no recorded base of operations.

A highly skilled team of professional mercenaries outfitted with the latest in high-tech equipment, the Demolition Team will take on any assignment if the price is right. Nothing is known of the background of the various members or how they first joined forces. The Team has had many successes but met defeat at the hands of the Predator (STAR SAPPHIRE), and has also been beaten by the BLOOD PACK and BLACK CONDOR II.

The Demolition Team was not long-lived, although they did inspire a knockoff villain team known as the Toolbox. Rosie recently agreed to give up her mortal life to merge with five other lives to become the new entity Enginehead. Most of the Demolition Team died while fighting OMAC units. **RG**

THE DEMOLITION TEAM 1) *Scoopshovel* **2)** *Steamroller* **3)** *Rosie* **4)** *Hardhat* **5)** *Jackhammer*

DEMON, THE SEE OPPOSITE PAGE

DEMONS THREE

FIRST APPEARANCE JUSTICE LEAGUE OF AMERICA #10 (March 1962)
STATUS Villains **REAL NAMES** Abnegazar, Rath, and Ghast
OCCUPATION Demons from Hell **BASE** The Inferno
HEIGHT Various **WEIGHT** Various **EYES** Black
HAIR (Ghast) Black; (Abnegazar and Rath) none
SPECIAL POWERS/ABILITIES Supernatural powers include the ability to travel through time and space, give life to inanimate objects, and fire magical bolts of energy.

Abnegazar, Rath, and Ghast trod the Earth more than a billion years ago. At some point the entities known as the Timeless Ones banished them to Hell, and they have been trying to return ever since. Three artifacts—the Silver Wheel of Wyorlath, the Green Bell of Uthool, and the Red Jar of Calythos—possess the magical power to bring them back into the world of the living. The Demons Three have visited Earth several times, often summoned by the sorcerer Felix Faust (*see* FAUST, FELIX). They opposed the JUSTICE LEAGUE OF AMERICA during its first year of operation. Much later, the Demons Three worked with Neron, Lord of the Underworld, in an attempt to shake the Moon from its orbit. Abnegazar, Rath, and Ghast despise the world of Men, forever remembering the primitive glory that was theirs before their exile. **DW**

DESAAD

FIRST APPEARANCE THE FOREVER PEOPLE (1st series) #2 (April 1971)
STATUS Villain **REAL NAME** None
OCCUPATION Torturer **BASE** Apokolips
HEIGHT 5ft 11in **WEIGHT** 152 lbs **EYES** Blue **HAIR** Black
SPECIAL POWERS/ABILITIES Brilliant inventor of pain-inducing devices and weapons of war.

Majordomo in the court of DARKSEID, the vile Desaad has long been the dark lord's master inquisitor, a sadist who savors bringing pain to the foes of Apokolips. In fact, were it not for Desaad, Darkseid would perhaps not be absolute ruler of his woe-ridden world. By the command of Queen Heggra, Darkseid's mother, Desaad poisoned the sorceress Suli, who had secretly married Darkseid. But rather than killing Desaad for his treachery, Darkseid forced the schemer to murder Heggra, thus helping Darkseid to ascend the throne of Apokolips. It should come as no surprise to learn that Desaad has continued to dabble in duplicity, and has also paid the inevitable price: disintegration by his master's Omega Beams. However, as soon as Darkseid discovers that he needs to call upon Desaad's insidious intellect, he restores the torturer to life once more. **SB**

DESPERO

FIRST APPEARANCE JUSTICE LEAGUE OF AMERICA #1 (October 1960)
STATUS Villain (missing) **REAL NAME** Despero
OCCUPATION Would-be universe conqueror **BASE** Mobile
HEIGHT 6ft 5in **WEIGHT** 289 lbs **EYES** Violet **HAIR** None
SPECIAL POWERS/ABILITIES A third eye with incredible hypnotic power; tremendous strength and durability.

MIRROR *Kalanorians all resemble Despero, although he had more ambition.*

Despero, from the planet Kalanor, realized he would never conquer the universe without eliminating Earth's champions, the JUSTICE LEAGUE OF AMERICA. They clashed on several occasions and Despero was imprisoned. He escaped back to Kalanor and entered the Flame of Py'tar, emerging bulkier and more dangerous than ever.

Despero announced his return to Earth by ramming the JLA's satellite headquarters. After yet another defeat by the JLA, Despero sought revenge, killing Gypsy's family. Following defeat by the MARTIAN MANHUNTER, Despero was taken over by aliens and became even more violent, destroying much of Manhattan. Later, SUPERGIRL helped exorcise Despero's personality from his body and sent it to the Abyssal Plane. There, Despero met the villain Johnny Sorrow (*see* SORROW, JOHNNY), and the two planned their revenge. The villains used technology belonging to Apokolips's DOCTOR BEDLAM to return to Earth and battled the JLA and the JUSTICE SOCIETY OF AMERICA. Despero has led the SECRET SOCIETY OF SUPER-VILLAINS against the Justice League, and teamed with PER DEGATON and the ULTRA-HUMANITE to alter time. **RG**

STRENGTH *The Flame of Py'tar evolved Despero into this dangerous form.*

DEMON, THE

THE RHYMING DEVIL

FIRST APPEARANCE DEMON (1st series) #1 (September 1972)
STATUS Villain **REAL NAME** Etrigan
OCCUPATION Rhyming demon **BASE** Hell
HEIGHT 6ft 4in **WEIGHT** 352 lbs **EYES** Red **HAIR** None
SPECIAL POWERS/ABILITIES Adept at magic; however, has little patience for spell casting, preferring to simply blast his foes to cinders with his fiery breath; has attained the rank of Rhymer in Hell, which explains why he always talks in rhyming couplets!

THE DEMON ETRIGAN entered Hell, clawing his way out of the womb of his mother, a demoness. Son of the archfiend BELIAL, Etrigan quickly rose through the ranks of demonhood, and even the elder demons began to fear him. Belial arranged for his son Myrddin, who would become known as Merlin the Magician, to be trained in the arts of sorcery, so that Merlin might one day bind and control Etrigan, his half-brother. Merlin unleashed Etrigan to battle the forces of MORGAINE LE FEY, intent on usurping King Arthur's Court at Camelot. After Le Fey's defeat and Camelot's fall, Merlin bound Etrigan to the druid Jason, who became Jason Blood.

SUPERMAN Etrigan's magical powers make him a match for the Man of Steel.

JASON BLOOD With the right mystic inducement, and chant, Etrigan's form is banished in favor of the body of Jason Blood.

THE DEMON WITHIN

Blood created a series of lives around the world and amassed occult knowledge, hoping either to free himself from Etrigan or at least tame the demon within. During World War II the Demon was unleashed, aiding the first STARMAN during a conflict with the Icicle (see ICICLE II) and Nazi saboteurs. Etrigan also was called upon to help oppose occult forces such as KLARION, THE WITCH BOY or BLACKBRIAR THORN. On more than one occasion, his ferocity was welcomed by occult conclaves with other powerful forces such as the PHANTOM STRANGER, the SPECTRE, and SWAMP THING.

All the while Etrigan had his own agenda: to kill Blood, gain his freedom, and rule Hell. During one foray into Hell, Etrigan seemed to have gained his desire. However, moments after acquiring the Crown of Horns and becoming King of Hell, Etrigan was tricked by Jason Blood and Merlin into returning to Earth. It transpired that Etrigan's evil acts in recent years had been the result of a spell cast by Morgaine Le Fey and an aged incarnation of Merlin. The curse was temporarily broken but, without the stabilizing influence of the benevolent incarnation of Merlin (slain in a pit of hellfire along with his evil duplicate), the spell that made Etrigan an evil Rhymer soon took control of him again.

Recently, Etrigan tried to steal BLUE DEVIL's Trident of Lucifer from the members of the SHADOWPACT in a bid to take control of Hell. Turned to stone after the failed attempt, the Demon became a coat rack for the patrons of the Oblivion Bar. **RG**

DEMON IN JAPAN Etrigan is one of the most ambitious and dangerous demons in Hell or on Earth and he tends to let nothing impede that lust for power.

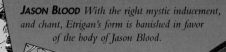

KEY STORYLINES

• *THE DEMON #1-8 (1972–73):* Jack Kirby's introductory story, setting up the conflict between Etrigan and Jason Blood. Jason's friends Glenda and Harry are also introduced.
• *THE DEMON mini-series (NOVEMBER 1986–FEBRUARY 1987):* Matt Wagner's updated look at the Demon, his place on Earth, and his role in Hell. The series also looks at his relationship with Jason Blood.

DESTINY

FIRST APPEARANCE WEIRD MYSTERY TALES #1 (July 1972)
STATUS Unknown **REAL NAME** None
OCCUPATION Cosmic observer **BASE** Destiny's garden
HEIGHT Variable **WEIGHT** Variable **EYES** None **HAIR** Unknown
SPECIAL POWERS/ABILITIES God-like, all-seeing entity who carries a book containing the history of every event in the universe; casts no shadow, leaves no footprint.

The Endless, humanoid manifestations of the primal truths of the universe, oversee every aspect of the reality created by the supreme power. Destiny is the oldest of the Endless. He has existed since the birth of everything, and when the universe finally comes to an end his sister DEATH will come to claim him. Like Death and the other siblings Dream, Desire, Despair, Destruction, and Delirium, Destiny adopts human form when dealing with people. He appears as a tall, hooded man, believed by some to be blind and by others to have evolved beyond sight. The book he carries contains every event, no matter how infinitesimal, that has happened or will happen.

Destiny inhabits a garden in an unseen realm. Within the garden are infinite paths down which all souls must walk as they live their lives. Destiny does not control the destinations of those who walk the garden, but every possible choice and outcome has already been recorded in his book. Elsewhere in Destiny's garden is a stone structure containing a gallery of portraits that portray the Endless as they wish to be seen. Destiny recently discovered that the CHALLENGERS OF THE UNKNOWN no longer existed in his book, and entrusted its safety to their care. DW

FATE Although chained to his book, Destiny would never dream of shirking his duties. He is the most serious of the Endless.

DEVASTATION

FIRST APPEARANCE WONDER WOMAN (2nd series) #143 (April 1999)
STATUS Villain **REAL NAME** None; calls herself "Deva"
OCCUPATION Creator of mayhem **BASE** Earth
HEIGHT 4ft 6in **WEIGHT** 82 lbs **EYES** Pale blue **HAIR** Red
SPECIAL POWERS/ABILITIES Supernatural shape-changer; possesses amazing strength; able to control the minds of humans to fulfill her goal of spreading chaos and despair all over the world.

Baby-faced and barely 12 years old in appearance, Devastation is the epitome of evil. She is yet another monstrous offspring of the mad Titan CRONUS, father of the OLYMPIAN GODS. To counteract his enemy Wonder Woman, Cronus molded Devastation out of the very same clay from which peace-loving Olympian goddesses had sculpted the Amazon Princess. Deva's purpose was not to spread peace and love, of course, but to bring discord, prejudice, and brutality to the peoples of the Earth.

To do so, Devastation battled her Amazon "sister" Diana and learned all of Wonder Woman's secrets by ensnaring Diana in her own golden Lasso of Truth. Devastation then used her own supernatural powers to compel a terrorist group to plot an attack using a nuclear bomb. However, Devastation was unaware that a single drop of Wonder Woman's blood had been mixed into the clay that had also created her. Appealing to that scintilla of inherent goodness within Deva, Diana convinced her to allow the nuclear device to explode harmlessly underground, saving millions of lives. Deva then escaped. As Wonder Woman's spiritual opposite, Devastation is sure to return, older and wiser, and probably less likely to allow Diana to use their shared blood to appeal to her better nature again. SB

DETECTIVE CHIMP

FIRST APPEARANCE REX THE WONDER DOG #4 (August 1953)
STATUS Hero **REAL NAME** Bobo
OCCUPATION Detective **BASE** Oscaloosa County, Florida
HEIGHT 3ft 7in **WEIGHT** 76 lbs **EYES** Black **HAIR** Black
SPECIAL POWERS/ABILITIES Highly intelligent; can communicate with all forms of animal life.

Bobo is a chimpanzee from Africa, brought to the U.S. by animal trainer Fred Thorpe and promoted as the "Detective Chimp" in a novelty act in which Bobo learned to respond to simple cues and appeared to solve crimes. After journeying to the Fountain of Youth with REX THE WONDER DOG, Bobo received enhanced intelligence and the gift of speech. Bobo moved to the U.S. after he solved his first criminal case and was raised by Fred Thorpe, a world-renowned animal trainer.

Tragically, Thorpe was savagely murdered. Bobo then joined forces with Florida Sheriff Edward Chase and, using his advanced instincts and intuitive skills, discovered Thorpe's killer. Chase took on Bobo as his companion, and the two solved numerous cases over the years. Detective Chimp emerged from years of alcoholism when the SPECTRE attacked the Earth's magic-users. He became a member of the SHADOWPACT, battling supernatural threats and spending a year trapped in the town of Riverrock, Wyoming following the Infinite Crisis. PJ

DEVILANCE

FIRST APPEARANCE FOREVER PEOPLE #11 (August–September 1972)
STATUS Villain (missing in action) **REAL NAME** Devilance the Pursuer
OCCUPATION Hunter **BASE** Apokolips
HEIGHT 7ft 1in **WEIGHT** 405 lbs **EYES** Blue **HAIR** Unrevealed
SPECIAL POWERS/ABILITIES Superhumanly strong, invulnerable, and able to increase his density at will; as a result, functions well in any environment; lance fires energy blasts, which slice through most anything and withstand tremendous force.

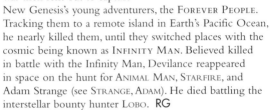

Devilance, a god born to Apokolips, was trained to become the supreme hunter for the planet's ruler, DARKSEID. For countless years, Devilance the Pursuer tracked, trapped, and brought his prey back to the Master. He was then sent out to capture New Genesis's young adventurers, the FOREVER PEOPLE. Tracking them to a remote island in Earth's Pacific Ocean, he nearly killed them, until they switched places with the cosmic being known as INFINITY MAN. Believed killed in battle with the Infinity Man, Devilance reappeared in space on the hunt for ANIMAL MAN, STARFIRE, and Adam Strange (see STRANGE, ADAM). He died battling the interstellar bounty hunter LOBO. **RG**

DIAL "H" FOR HERO

FIRST APPEARANCE LEGION OF SUPER-HEROES 2nd series #272 (February 1981)
STATUS Hero team **REAL NAMES** Christopher King and Victoria Grant
OCCUPATION Students **BASE** Fairfax
HEIGHT (Chris) 5ft 10in; (Vicki) 5ft 6in **WEIGHT** (Chris) 165 lbs; (Vicki) 120 lbs **EYES** (Chris) Green; (Vicki) blue **HAIR** (Chris) Red; (Vicki) blonde
SPECIAL POWERS/ABILITIES Dialing the "Hero" H-Dial transforms each of them into a new hero for about one hour; Chris automatically transforms once an hour through his psychic link with the dial.

Chris King and Vicki Grant were summoned by a mysterious voice to the attic of teenage genius Robbie Reed. There, the teenagers found two odd dials with the letters H-E-R-O inscribed on them. Dialing the word, both Chris and Vicki discovered they could become a variety of bizarre and amazing super heroes for an hour at a time. Their friend Nick Stevens, a cartoonist, designed a number of the heroes they became.

For years, Chris and Vicki battled criminals of all sorts, including the evil Master, who was planning on creating an army of super-villains to rule the world. After high school graduation, Vicki moved to San Francisco and was seduced by the nefarious Children of the Sun. Vowing to destroy Chris, Vicki was eventually freed from her evil thrall by hero Cruz. Chris's own powers were transformed, and, after a brief stint of study at S.T.A.R. Labs, he moved to Los Angeles.

Chris was briefly a member of the Titans West division of the TEEN TITANS. **PJ/SB**

DIALING "H"
The H-Dial, transforming ordinary people into heroes for millennia, was lost by Robby Reed and found its way into the hands of several ordinary people, until the insane Reed came to claim it!

Chris King
Vicki Grant
Robby Reed

DIRECTOR BONES

FIRST APPEARANCE INFINITY, INC. #16 (July 1985)
STATUS Unresolved **REAL NAME** Unrevealed
OCCUPATION Director, Department of Extranormal Operations
BASE New York City
HEIGHT 5ft 10in **WEIGHT** 165 lbs **EYES/HAIR** Invisible
SPECIAL POWERS/ABILITIES Superstrength; "cyanide touch" can burn through flesh; skin and organs are totally invisible, revealing skeleton underneath; as DEO director, has access to an arsenal of weapons and a wealth of information.

Director Bones is the product of a twisted genetic experiment by the biologist Doctor Benjamin Love. Bones's mother gave birth to a mutated child whose skin and organs were invisible and, as an adult, Bones developed an acid-touch. Mister Bones, as he came to be called, and several of Love's experimental children became the HELIX, a team of misguided super heroes. The Helix came to blows several times with INFINITY, INC.

Mister Bones reformed, and even joined Infinity, Inc. for a brief time, before he accidentally killed the original Star-Spangled Kid. Plagued by guilt, Bones disappeared but returned years later as a major figure in the DEO. Working for Amanda Waller (see WALLER, AMANDA), Bones became the DEO's director. **PJ**

SKELETON CREW *Now the clandestine leader of the DEO, Director Bones.*

DNANGELS

FIRST APPEARANCE SUPERBOY (2nd series) #88 (July 2001)
STATUS Former U.S. government operatives **BASE** Classified
MEMBERS/POWERS
Cherub, Epiphany, Seraph (identities unknown) Shared genetically enhanced abilities include telekinesis, flight, superstrength, bodily transformation, and superspeed.

The DNAngels were a trio of agents bioengineered by the U.S. military at a cost of over $2 billion. Answering to the diminutive and duplicitous General Good, the DNAngels clashed with SUPERBOY when they were ordered to abduct the infant clone of Jim Harper (GUARDIAN) in the teen hero's care. Later, Superboy learned from his arch-foe Amanda Spence that the DNAngels were spliced with genetic material taken from the teen hero, as well as his YOUNG JUSTICE teammates Impulse (see KID FLASH) and WONDER GIRL. Cherub was modeled on gene samples from Tana Moon, Superboy's late girlfriend, which explained Cherub's flirtatious attractiveness for him. Cherub helped Superboy to battle Spence, nearly losing her life, and the DNAngels, disillusioned with the General's scheming, departed his employ to use their powers for the greater good. **SB**

DOC MAGNUS

FIRST APPEARANCE SHOWCASE #37 (March–April 1962)
STATUS Hero **REAL NAME** William Magnus
OCCUPATION Cyberneticist **BASE** Metropolis
HEIGHT (Doc Magnus) 5ft 10in; (Veridium) 6ft 10in
WEIGHT (Doc Magnus) 170 lbs; (Veridium) 590 lbs
EYES (Doc Magnus) Brown; (Veridium) green
HAIR (Doc Magnus) Brown; (Veridium) none
SPECIAL POWERS/ABILITIES As Veridium, his robot body has superstrength, near invulnerability, and can fly.

Will Magnus, creator of the METAL MEN, is one of the world's most brilliant roboticists. After studying under the scientist T.O. MORROW, Magnus developed the Metal Men as robot assistants, with their intelligence and eerily human personalities the result of "responsometers" capable of imbuing each with an artificial soul. Struggling with bipolar disorder and an inability to balance his work and his personal life, Dr. Magnus went through an unstable period that resulted in him becoming a Metal Man himself, the powerful Veridium.

Magnus later returned to his human body, and numbered among the many scientists relocated to Oolong Island following the Infinite Crisis. There, Chang Tzu (see EGG FU) ordered Magnus to create a Plutonium Man robot as a weapon, but he recreated miniature versions of his Metal Men and used them to escape Oolong. Magnus's genius is often sought out by the JUSTICE LEAGUE OF AMERICA and other parties. **PJ**

DOCTOR ALCHEMY

FIRST APPEARANCE (Albert Desmond) SHOWCASE #13 (April 1958); (Alvin Desmond) THE FLASH (1st series) #287 (July 1980)
STATUS Villain **REAL NAME** Albert Desmond/Alvin Desmond
OCCUPATION Adventurer **BASE** Central City
HEIGHT 5ft 11in **WEIGHT** 171 lbs **EYES** Green **HAIR** Red
SPECIAL POWERS/ABILITIES Philosopher's Stone, often controlled from a distance by telekinesis, transmutes one element into another.

After coming into possession of the transmuting talisman known as the Philosopher's Stone, criminal Albert Desmond—previously Mr. Element—adopted a new alter ego, Dr. Alchemy. But after suffering constant defeat by the second FLASH, Desmond quit crime and buried the Philosopher's Stone. Some time later, Alvin Desmond—his psychic twin—unearthed the Stone and adopted the identity of Dr. Alchemy.

Although unrelated, both Desmonds shared a psychic bond that allowed Alvin to suppress his own dark impulses when Albert was active as a costumed criminal. With Albert reformed, Alvin embraced his evil urges and used the Philosopher's Stone to make the Flash believe that a hypnotized Albert had returned to villainy. However, the Scarlet Speedster discovered the deception and jailed Alvin, while Albert returned to his law-abiding life. Dr. Alchemy has escaped incarceration several times since, battling the second Flash and his successor, Wally West, as a member of the Scarlet Speedsters' Rogues Gallery. **SB**

DOCTOR BEDLAM

FIRST APPEARANCE MISTER MIRACLE (1st series) #3 (July–August 1971)
STATUS Villain **REAL NAME** Doctor Bedlam
OCCUPATION Scientist **BASE** Apokolips
HEIGHT 6ft 2in **WEIGHT** 226 lbs **EYES** Blue **HAIR** Black
SPECIAL POWERS/ABILITIES A being of pure psionic energy, Bedlam controls his animates, up to six at a time.

A twisted scientific genius, Bedlam takes delight in manufacturing new ways to inflict terror on the fragile minds of his subjects. Considered a minor acolyte of Apokolips's ruler Darkseid, Dr. Bedlam toils away at his experiments. When called to duty, he serves faithfully, using his creations, androids known as animates, as surrogate bodies. At some point in the past, Bedlam gave up his physical body to exist as pure mental energy. He maintains six android bodies, and can inhabit one at a time, altering its form to resemble his original physical presence. After defeat at the hands of Mister Miracle, Bedlam dedicated himself to capturing and breaking the member of the New Gods. During the Death of the New Gods event, the inhabitants of the Fourth World, including Doctor Bedlam, had their souls ripped from their bodies by a mysterious assailant. **RG**

DOCTOR DESTINY

FIRST APPEARANCE JUSTICE LEAGUE OF AMERICA (1st ser.) #5 (July 1961)
STATUS Hero **REAL NAME** John Dee
OCCUPATION Adventurer **BASE** Mobile
HEIGHT 6ft 1in **WEIGHT** 171 lbs **EYES** Red **HAIR** None
SPECIAL POWERS/ABILITIES Invades the nightmares of his opponents and makes their nightmares a terrifying reality.

Doctor Destiny began his criminal career as the proud inventor of the "materioptikon," which could turn dreams into reality. In truth, the device took its power not from the Doctor's technological skill but from a ruby talisman belonging to Morpheus, Lord of Dreams. Doctor Destiny's obsessions robbed him of his own ability to dream and he wasted away to a shrunken skeleton. He escaped imprisonment in Gotham City's Arkham Asylum on numerous occasions to menace the JUSTICE LEAGUE OF AMERICA, becoming one of its earliest foes.

Recently, Doctor Destiny threatened his old enemies once again by bringing his "dream self" into the real world and attacking the JLA with the bizarre and irrational logic of dreams. Defeated once more, Doctor Destiny has since been returned to an Arkham cell. **DW**

102

DOCTOR FATE

GREATEST SORCERER

FIRST APPEARANCE (Dr. Fate I) MORE FUN COMICS #55 (May 1940)
STATUS Hero **REAL NAME** Kent Nelson
OCCUPATION Archaeologist/physician **BASE** Salem, Massachusetts
HEIGHT 6ft 2in **WEIGHT** 197 lbs **EYES** Blue **HAIR** Blond
SPECIAL POWERS/ABILITIES Able to levitate and fly; nearly invulnerable; helmet, amulet, and mantle of Nabu are powerful mystic talismans, making Dr. Fate one of the greatest living sorcerers.

FIRST APPEARANCE (Inza Cramer) MORE FUN COMICS #55 (May 1940); (Dr. Fate III) DOCTOR FATE (3rd series) #25 (February 1991)
STATUS Hero **REAL NAME** Inza Cramer Nelson
OCCUPATION Adventurer **BASE** Salem, Massachusetts
HEIGHT 5ft 7in **WEIGHT** 125 lbs **EYES** Green **HAIR** Blonde
SPECIAL POWERS/ABILITIES Depending on who initiated the mystical merge, Kent or Inza Nelson, fate manifested as a man or a woman.

FIRST APPEARANCE (Hector Hall) ALL-STAR SQUADRON #25 (September 1983); (Dr. Fate IV) JSA #3 (October 1999)
STATUS Hero **REAL NAME** Hector Hall
OCCUPATION Agent of balance **BASE** Salem, Massachusetts
HEIGHT 6ft **WEIGHT** 184 lbs **EYES** Blue **HAIR** White
SPECIAL POWERS/ABILITIES While wearing the helmet of Nabu, Hector hears the voice of the ancient sorcerer himself.

MANY CENTURIES AGO, the Lord of Order known as Nabu placed himself in suspended animation to allow his human host body to recover from the strain of wielding Nabu's magicks. Nabu was revived in 1940, when archaeologist Sven Nelson and his son Kent were exploring the Ur Valley in Mesopotamia. As Nabu was awakened, a deadly gas was released from the chamber that killed Sven Nelson. Nabu took Kent under his tutelage, transformed him into an adult, and schooled him in the ways of sorcery. After many years, Nabu bequeathed Kent his amulet, helmet, and cloak, mystic talismans of extraordinary might. Now an agent of the Lords of Order, Kent became Dr. Fate, one of the most powerful "Mystery Men" of the time, and a founding member of the JUSTICE SOCIETY OF AMERICA.

Inza Cramer Nelson

BULLETPROOF *With the helmet of Nabu, Dr. Fate can make himself intangible so that bullets whizz right through him!*

KENT NELSON AND INZA CRAMER

On his first adventure, Dr. Fate rescued Inza Cramer from the warlock Wotan and married her. During World War II, Dr. Fate was also a member of the Allied superpowered coalition known as the ALL-STAR SQUADRON. In the decades that followed, Fate continued to combat eldritch evils based in his other-dimensional sanctum, a tower in Salem, Massachusetts that was also Kent and Inza Nelson's home. By virtue of Nabu's talismans both husband and wife retained their youth into modern times.

Eventually events conspired to bring about Kent and Inza's deaths, whereupon Nabu bestowed his arcane abilities upon Eric Strauss, a boy also transformed into an adult. While battling an agent of Chaos, Eric mystically merged with his stepmother, Linda Strauss, to become a Dr. Fate wholly independent of Nabu. who resurrected Kent Nelson's body in order to inhabit it and guide the Strausses as Fate's mentor. The second Dr. Fate later perished in battle, although Eric and Linda's spirits lived on inside the bodies of two friends, Eugene and Wendy Di Bella. Nabu then restored Kent and Inza Nelson to life and was reborn himself as the spirit of Wendy Di Bella's infant child.

Kent and Inza, meanwhile, both took up the mantle of Dr. Fate, merging as the Strausses once did. When Kent was unable to merge any longer, Inza was forced to go it alone. Both Kent and Inza perished during the Zero Hour crisis (*see* Great Battles, pp. 362–3). Fate's talismans then fell into the hands of Jared Stevens, who forged a mystic dagger from Nabu's helmet and amulet. His career as Fate was cut short by the sorcerer Mordru (*see* DARK LORD), thus setting in motion events that would bring a new, even more powerful Dr. Fate to the fore. Hector Hall, son of HAWKMAN and HAWKGIRL and the partner of Lyta Trevor (FURY II), was a spirit adrift in the ether until he was reborn as Nabu's champion of balance and justice. The SPECTRE ended Hector's term as Fate, leaving Nabu without a human host. After confronting the Spectre, Nabu passed on and allowed his helmet to find a new bearer – Dr. Kent V. Nelson, grandnephew of the original Doctor Fate. SB

ATTACK *Nabu counsels Hector within the dreamscape of Fate's helm, spurring the latest Dr. Fate to strike out and use the full measure of his mystical might.*

POWER *Hector Hall struggles to keep the helmet of Nabu from overwhelming him.*

KEY STORYLINES
• JSA #1 (August 1999): Jared Stevens, possessor of Nabu's talismans, is killed by the minions of Mordru, thus paving the way for the long-awaited return of Dr. Fate.
• Doctor Fate (4th series) #1-4 (October 2003–February 2004): Hector Hall battles and destroys the Curse, a timeless evil that wrecked ancient Egypt, as he settles in at Dr. Fate's Salem tower.

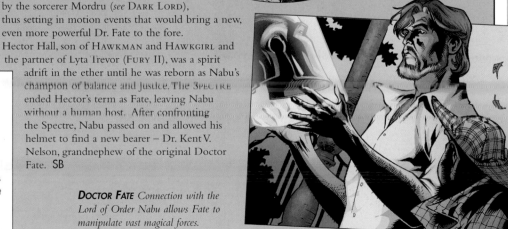

DOCTOR FATE *Connection with the Lord of Order Nabu allows Fate to manipulate vast magical forces.*

DOCTOR IMPOSSIBLE

FIRST APPEARANCE JUSTICE LEAGUE OF AMERICA (2nd series) #1 (October 2006)
STATUS Villain   **REAL NAME** Unknown
OCCUPATION Professional criminal   **BASE** Mobile
HEIGHT 6ft   **WEIGHT** 185 lbs   **EYES** Blue   **HAIR** Black
SPECIAL POWERS/ABILITIES Possesses Fourth World technology allowing teleportation and other powers

Doctor Impossible is a newcomer on the super-villain scene, and he keeps his personal details closely guarded. He wears a dark-colored costume similar in appearance to that of MISTER MIRACLE, though his heritage as a New God from either Apokolips or New Genesis has yet to be confirmed. Doctor Impossible carries a computerized "father box" and teleports via a "hush tube"—both apparently based on the Fourth World technologies of the mother box and the boom tube. Approximately a year after the Infinite Crisis, Doctor Impossible emerged in the employ of PROFESSOR IVO, gathering parts to be used in the construction of a robot body to house the consciousness of SOLOMON GRUNDY. After stealing RED TORNADO's body from the METAL MEN and making off with the PARASITE's arm, he lost a fight against GREEN LANTERN, BLACK CANARY II, and Red Arrow (see Arsenal). **DW**

DOCTOR LIGHT I

FIRST APPEARANCE JUSTICE LEAGUE OF AMERICA (1st series) #12 (June 1962)
STATUS Villain   **REAL NAME** Arthur Light
OCCUPATION Professional criminal   **BASE** New York City
HEIGHT 5ft 11in   **WEIGHT** 171 lbs   **EYES** Blue   **HAIR** Black
SPECIAL POWERS/ABILITIES Manipulates visible light spectrum, generating blinding brilliance or thin laser beam; poor hand-to-hand combatant.

Dr. Arthur Light and Dr. Jacob Finlay worked as researchers at S.T.A.R. Labs, where Jacob secretly created a costume incorporating S.T.A.R. tech and tried to become a super hero called Doctor Light. He died in a mishap, and his surviving colleague Arthur donned the Doctor Light gear in order to protect himself against Jacob's vengeful ghost.

Arthur quickly acquired a taste for crime, despite his abysmal success rate. After assaulting Sue Dibny aboard the JUSTICE LEAGUE OF AMERICA's satellite, Doctor Light suffered a mind-wipe and partial lobotomy due to ZATANNA's magics. Once he regained his memories of the incident, Light attempted revenge against the League's members. Doctor Light is often looked on with suspicion and disdain by even his fellow villains. **DW**

DOCTOR LIGHT II

FIRST APPEARANCE CRISIS ON INFINITE EARTHS #4 (July 1985)
STATUS Hero   **REAL NAME** Kimiyo Hoshi
OCCUPATION Adventurer   **BASE** Japan
HEIGHT 5ft 3in   **WEIGHT** 105 lbs   **EYES** Black   **HAIR** Black
SPECIAL POWERS/ABILITIES Vast light-based powers permit flight, illusion-casting, the ability to fire lasers and generate hard-light projections.

The heroic Doctor Light II emerged during the Crisis (see Great Battles, pp. 320–321), when the all-powerful MONITOR zapped astronomer Dr. Kimiyo Hoshi with otherworldly energy. After the Crisis, Hoshi joined the JUSTICE LEAGUE OF AMERICA— even becoming the leader of the European branch—but her innate arrogance left many of her teammates cold. She possesses most of the same powers as her villainous namesake, yet has labored to establish herself as a hero in her own headstrong way.

As a single mother with two young children, Doctor Light II is only semi-active in the super hero business, yet she has recently served with both the OUTSIDERS and the DOOM PATROL. Although she is no longer a member of either team, she remains active as a part-time adventurer. **DW**

DOCTOR MID-NITE I

FIRST APPEARANCE ALL-AMERICAN COMICS #25 (April 1941)
STATUS Hero (deceased)   **REAL NAME** Charles M. McNider
OCCUPATION Adventurer; physician
BASE New York City and other unnamed cities
HEIGHT 5ft 11in   **WEIGHT** 179 lbs   **EYES** Blue   **HAIR** Black
SPECIAL POWERS/ABILITIES Special infrared glasses enabled him to see perfectly in the pitch dark or in daylight; was a gifted doctor and a skilled author, in addition to having a mean right hook.

DR. MID-NITE Charles McNider, in costume, with Hooty the owl.

IN THE LAB *Despite his blindness, McNider makes a top-notch physician.*

Dr. Charles McNider was blinded by a grenade tossed through a window. With the help of girlfriend Myra Mason, McNider continued his research. He found out he could see in the dark when, startled by an owl, he loosened his eye bandages. He adopted the owl, Hooty, and developed special goggles so he could see during the day and night. Armed with his invention, the Blackout Bomb, McNider debuted in New York as Dr. Mid-Nite. He brought down underworld leader Maroni and built a career as a hard-nosed fighter, joining the JUSTICE SOCIETY OF AMERICA, the All-Star Squadron, and briefly becoming the new Starman. In 1953, Myra was killed by McNider's nemesis, Vartan Kevork, and Dr. Mid-Nite eventually brought him to justice. Dr. Mid-Nite lost his life while battling the cosmic-powered EXTANT.

DOCTOR MID-NITE II

FIRST APPEARANCE DOCTOR MID-NITE #1 (March 1999)
STATUS Hero   **REAL NAME** Pieter Anton Cross, M.D.
OCCUPATION Adventurer; physician   **BASE** Portsmouth City
HEIGHT 5ft 10in   **WEIGHT** 175 lbs   **EYES** Blue   **HAIR** Black
SPECIAL POWERS/ABILITIES Able to see in the dark but not in the light; gauntlets carry a variety of medications; a brilliant inventor who has improved on his mentor's Blackout Bombs.

Some 30 years ago, Mrs. Theodoric Cross was attacked in Sogndal, Norway, and saved by DOCTOR MID-NITE I. She went into labor, and McNider delivered a boy she named Pieter. Pieter attended Harvard Medical school at only 19, and served his residency at McNider's side. While investigating a steroid, A39, that was killing the local population, Cross was knocked out, injected with the drug, and placed behind the wheel of a car that struck and killed a woman. Cross lived, but found that he was only able to see in total darkness, like his mentor. Cross donned a variation of Dr. Mid-Nite's costume and took to the streets, putting an end to the A39 problem. Dr. Mid-Nite II crossed paths with the revived JUSTICE SOCIETY OF AMERICA, and was quickly welcomed into their ranks. He continues to serve with them, while tending to the people of his home city. **RG**

WHAT HE SEES *This is how Pieter Cross views the world—his costume provides him with levels of detail normal sight does not allow.*

DOCTOR MIST

FIRST APPEARANCE (historic) SUPER FRIENDS #12 (March 1978); (in DCU continuity) DC COMICS PRESENTS #46 (July 1982)
STATUS Hero (missing in action)   **REAL NAME** Maltis
OCCUPATION Adventurer   **BASE** New York City
HEIGHT 6ft 4in   **WEIGHT** 220 lbs   **EYES** Brown   **HAIR** Black
SPECIAL POWERS/ABILITIES Possession of one of the Stones of Life augmented his powers as a sorceror, which included illusion casting, transmutation of objects, and teleportation.
He was immortal.

Also known as Ashos and Joab M'staki, Maltis hailed from the ancient African realm of Kor. Maltis became the Nommo, the king of Kor, and the guardian of the mystic Flame of Life. After absorbing the powers of the Flame into his own body, thereby making himself immortal, Maltis created the Stones of Life. Keeping one of these magical objects for his own use, he presented the others to the emerging races of magical humanoids known as the Homo magi. Nommo claims he was cast out of Kor for failing to guard the Flame from Felix Faust (*see* FAUST, FELIX). He was then invited to join the Leymen (*see* PRIMAL FORCE), a fellowship of ancient mystics.

Adopting the alias Doctor Mist, Maltis founded the GLOBAL GUARDIANS. After the Guardians were disbanded, Doctor Mist created PRIMAL FORCE. Although immortal, he was not invulnerable, and he apparently died during a battle with the August, would-be world-conquerors and enemies of the Leymen. **PJ**

DOCTOR OCCULT

FIRST APPEARANCE NEW FUN COMICS #6 (October 1935)
STATUS Hero   **REAL NAME** Richard Occult
OCCUPATION Mystical private investigator   **BASE** New York City
HEIGHT 6ft 1in   **WEIGHT** 189 lbs   **EYES** Gray   **HAIR** Black
SPECIAL POWERS/ABILITIES Vast magical powers, including hypnotism, illusion-casting, telekinesis, and the ability to teleport by traveling through the astral plane. Carries the Mystic Symbol of the Seven which repels supernatural energy.

On New Year's Eve of 1899, two infants narrowly escaped being sacrificed to Satan. Rescued by the secret group of mystics called the Seven, the two grew up tutored in the ways of the supernatural under the names Doctor Occult and Rose Psychic.
In 1935, the two opened a detective agency in New York City specializing in the investigation of supernatural crimes. Thus Doctor Occult, "the Ghost Detective," became arguably the first champion of the Golden Age of Heroes. Doctor Occult joined the ALL STAR SQUADRON during World War II and, in a later adventure, he and Rose Psychic fused into one body, able to appear in both male and female forms. After keeping a low profile for decades, he returned to adventuring during the modern heroic age, helping to save the Earth during major events such as the Crisis (*see* Great Battles, pp. 362–3) and the Day of Judgment. He is a sometime member of several magic-user teams, including the Sentinels of Magic and the "Trenchcoat Brigade" alongside John Constantine and MISTER E. Now more than a hundred years old, Doctor Occult has employed sorcerous means to keep himself the same physical age he was in the 1930s. **DW**

DOCTOR PHOSPHORUS

FIRST APPEARANCE DETECTIVE COMICS #469 (May 1977)
STATUS Villain   **REAL NAME** Alex Sartorius
OCCUPATION Professional criminal   **BASE** Gotham City
HEIGHT 5ft 11in   **WEIGHT** 169 lbs   **EYES** Red   **HAIR** None
SPECIAL POWERS/ABILITIES Burns on contact with the air, letting off toxic fumes and endangering everyone who comes near.

A reactor accident bathed Dr. Alex Sartorius with fatal levels of radiation. Somehow he survived as a burning wraith, his irradiated skin glowing with white fire and smoking with toxic fumes. A deal with the demon NERON gave him the ability to wear clothing without it bursting into flames, but by that point Sartorius had

long been consumed by the villainous identity of Doctor Phosphorous. Between the assassinations of those who had caused his condition, Phosphorous made money as a hired killer. On a job for the MIST, he attacked Ted Knight (see STARMAN) on multiple occasions, but ultimately died when crushed by tons of earth and rock.

But Phosphorous' bizarre physiology brought him back to life, earning the attention of Cadmus Labs. Doctor Phosphorous escaped from Cadmus and embarked on a fresh killing spree until stopped by BATMAN. Phosphorous is most frequently found incarcerated in Arkham Asylum. **DW**

DOCTOR POLARIS

FIRST APPEARANCE GREEN LANTERN (2nd series) #21 (June 1962)
STATUS Villain (deceased)   **REAL NAME** Neal Emerson
OCCUPATION Physicist, physician, criminal   **BASE** New Mexico
HEIGHT 6ft 1in   **WEIGHT** 194 lbs   **EYES** Blue   **HAIR** Brown
SPECIAL POWERS/ABILITIES Generates and controls magnetic energy; using magnetism, he can levitate, create force fields, generate concussive blasts, and attract, repel, or manipulate any metal object.

Doctor Neal Emerson is a split personality, as a result of his experiments with magnetic polarity. At first Emerson made several medical breakthroughs with his magnetic research, but as his personality disorder began to emerge, his darker side became the villainous, power-hungry Doctor Polaris. Polaris clashed with Hal Jordan, Earth's GREEN LANTERN, several times, and it was Jordan who was most often able to coax out the benevolent Emerson personality, thereby ending Polaris' magnetic rampages. While Doctor Polaris originally used technology to manipulate magnetism, his body eventually internalized the power, driving him to further insanity. After the Anti-Monitor's attack on Earth (see Great Battles, pp. 362–3), Doctor Polaris joined with other villains in a bid to destroy all the Green Lanterns based on Earth. Later, after Emerson moved to New Mexico, he fought POWER GIRL and STARMAN. During the confrontation with Starman, the benevolent Emerson personality once more emerged, ending the villain's reign before he was taken into psychiatric custody.

Some time later, Doctor Polaris made a deal with the demon NERON, selling Neal Emerson's soul in exchange for greater powers. During the Infinite Crisis, Doctor Polaris joined the SECRET SOCIETY OF SUPER-VILLAINS and died in an explosion triggered by the HUMAN BOMB. **PJ**

KNOCKED OUT Doctor Polaris once tried to invade Atlantis, only to be defeated by Aquaman and Dolphin.

OUTPACED The magnetic maestro has long been an enemy of Earth's greatest heroes, including the Flash.

THE DC COMICS ENCYCLOPEDIA

DOCTOR PSYCHO

FIRST APPEARANCE WONDER WOMAN (1st series) #5 (May 1991)
STATUS Villain **REAL NAME** Edgar Cizko
OCCUPATION Psychotherapist **BASE** Mobile
HEIGHT 3ft 9in **WEIGHT** 85 lbs **EYES** Blue **HAIR** Black
SPECIAL POWERS/ABILITIES Able to alter and manipulate the perceptions of his victims by attacking through dreams; creates hallucinatory nightmare landscapes to torment foes with fear and despair.

One of the most powerful and persistent of WONDER WOMAN's enemies, the diminutive Dr. Psycho murdered Dr. Charles Stanton, psychiatrist to the Amazon Princess's teenage friend Vanessa Kapatelis, and usurped his identity. Dr. Psycho then used Vanessa's subconscious as a conduit to mentally manipulate Wonder Woman. Although thwarted in his initial psychic assaults, Dr. Psycho has been a lingering threat to Wonder Woman and her dearest friends, Vanessa especially. Psycho was later hired by power-hungry mogul Sebastian Ballésteros (see CHEETAH III) to further exploit Vanessa's damaged psyche and mold her into the second SILVER SWAN, a living weapon to battle Wonder Woman. Dr. Psycho became a key member of the SECRET SOCIETY OF SUPER-VILLAINS during the Infinite Crisis, controlling DOOMSDAY long enough to unleash him on the heroes assembled in Metropolis. He later escaped from a courtroom trial involving Kate Spencer (see MANHUNTER). **SB**

NIGHTMARE Dr. Psycho is a dwarf of uncommon ugliness. Even what you see here is an illusion created by the villain to appear more attractive than he truly is!

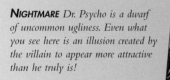

HEAD DOCTOR Bound and shackled to prevent his escape from imprisonment in a meta-human detention facility, Dr. Psycho must also wear a psychic-damping headband to prevent him from using his illusory powers.

CRAZY SCHEMES Time and again, Sivana and his family have tried to assume power or take over the world. They remain defeated at the hands of the Marvel Family.

DOCTOR SIVANA

FIRST APPEARANCE WHIZ COMICS #2 (February 1940)
STATUS Villain **REAL NAME** Thaddeus Bodog Sivana
OCCUPATION Adventurer **BASE** Fawcett City
HEIGHT 5ft 6in **WEIGHT** 123 lbs
EYES Gray **HAIR** None
SPECIAL POWERS/ABILITIES While possessing no powers, Sivana is a genius in any number of disciplines.

Dr. Sivana's scientific genius made him one of the wealthiest men in Fawcett City.
However, his unethical business practices made him, as he observed, the man the media "loves to hate." Meanwhile, an extramarital affair led Sivana's wife, Venus, to leave him with their two children, Beautia and Magnificus, and the billionaire's empire collapsed when he was implicated in the murders of archaeologists C.C. and Marilyn Batson (see CAPTAIN MARVEL).
After the Sivana Building was destroyed in fire, the disgraced billionaire was presumed dead until he attempted to steal the scarab necklace of the wizard Shazam. He was thwarted by Captain Marvel, and in the process, Sivana learned that the hero was also young Billy Batson.
Sivana, despite his brilliant mind, was not a very good criminal, and despite frequent prison escapes, was always recaptured by Captain Marvel, whom he sarcastically dubbed "The Big Red Cheese."
The Doctor upped the ante when he became embroiled with the Venusian worm MISTER MIND who had plans to conquer Earth. However this came to nought when Mr. Mind allied himself with Captain Marvel. Sivana assembled a new grouping of the FEARSOME FIVE, and after the Infinite Crisis he joined other mad scientists on Oolong Island. There, he devised weapons for Chang Tzu (see EGG FU). The Venusian worm MISTER MIND escaped from Sivana's lab and tried to devour the multiverse—after BOOSTER GOLD and Rip Hunter (see HUNTER, RIP) stopped Mister Mind's rampage, the worm wound up in Sivana's care once more. **RG**

DOCTOR THIRTEEN

FIRST APPEARANCE STAR-SPANGLED COMICS #122 (November 1951)
STATUS Hero **REAL NAME** Terrence Thirteen
OCCUPATION Investigator into the paranormal **BASE** Mobile
HEIGHT 5ft 11in **WEIGHT** 168 lbs **EYES** Brown **HAIR** Brown
SPECIAL POWERS/ABILITIES Brilliant, deductive, logical mind enables him
to uncover the truth, however bizarre.

Terrence Thirteen's family had been denounced as witches and warlocks for a dozen generations. Growing up in the ancestral home of Doomsbury Hall, Terrence learned from his father to shun prejudice and superstition. Deductive reasoning and the scientific method were the greatest weapons against unreason. When his father died in an automobile accident, Terrence became a traveling investigator of psychic phenomena. Known as "the Ghost-Breaker," Doctor Thirteen debunked phony phantoms and exposed swindlers who claimed to have mystical gifts. He occasionally ran up against phenomena he couldn't explain, such as encounters with the PHANTOM STRANGER. Doctor Thirteen had a romance with ZATANNA, and teamed with I, VAMPIRE, GENIUS JONES, ANTHRO and others on strange adventures. His daughter is the magic-using TRACI THIRTEEN. **DW**

DOLL MAN

FIRST APPEARANCE FEATURE COMICS #27 (December 1939)
STATUS Hero **REAL NAME** Darrel Dane
OCCUPATION Chemist; resistance leader; adventurer
BASE Washington, D.C.; New York City
HEIGHT (Dane) 6ft; (Doll Man) 6in **WEIGHT** (Dane) 175 lbs;
(Doll Man) 2½ lbs **EYES** Blue **HAIR** Black
SPECIAL POWERS/ABILITIES Can shrink to a height of 6in while retaining
his normal-size strength; can also fly.

In 1939, chemist Darrel Dane developed a serum that could shrink living beings. After testing it on himself, Dane discovered he could reduce his size at will. Dane began using his powers as a crime fighter after he saved his fiancée, Martha Roberts, from a blackmailer named Falco. Roberts sewed Dane a costume, and the chemist became Doll Man, one of the first costumed heroes. By 1942, Doll Man and MIDNIGHT, another costumed hero, had joined forces to fight the Axis powers in Europe and Japan. Along with dozens of America's "mystery men", Doll Man served on President Roosevelt's ALL-STAR SQUADRON before accepting an invitation to Uncle Sam's splinter group the FREEDOM FIGHTERS. Doll Man and the Freedom Fighters fought Nazi tyranny until the end of World War II.

A new Doll Man, U.S. operative Lester Colt, has recently emerged as a key member of UNCLE SAM's new Freedom Fighters, part of the government's S.H.A.D.E. department. **PJ**

DOLL GIRL

FIRST APPEARANCE DOLL MAN #37 (December 1951)
STATUS Hero **REAL NAME** Martha Roberts
OCCUPATION Adventurer **BASE** An unidentified American city
HEIGHT 5ft 6in **WEIGHT** 120 lbs **EYES** Blue **HAIR** Brown
SPECIAL POWERS/ABILITIES Able to shrink her size and weight to 5.5
inches and 4 lbs respectively.

In 1939, Martha Roberts was the fiancée of scientist Darrel Dane who was also the diminutive DOLL MAN. His first daring exploit involved saving Martha from the extortionist Falco, who was blackmailing Roberts over her affair with a professor while she was at college.

Later, Martha acquired the very same amazing reducing abilities as Dane and became Doll Man's petite partner, Doll Girl. The two miniature super heroes bravely battled crime for years afterward. No one knows whether or not they were ever married, or if they are still active as adventurers. However, a new Doll Man and Doll Girl—presumably boyfriend and girlfriend—were once spied at a recruitment party for the short-lived Titans L.A. It remains to be seen if either young hero is related to Martha Roberts, Darrel Dane, or both. Martha's exploits as Doll Girl, though brief, are still undiminished by this pair of pint-sized pretenders. **SB**

DOLPHIN

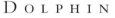

FIRST APPEARANCE SHOWCASE #79 (January 1969)
STATUS Hero **REAL NAME** Unknown
OCCUPATION Mother **BASE** Atlantis
HEIGHT 5ft 10in **WEIGHT** 1 45 lbs **EYES** Blue **HAIR** White
SPECIAL POWERS/ABILITIES Can survive both above and
below the water's surface; very fast swimmer, able to
withstand deep-sea pressure.

***FAMILY FIRST** Dolphin, seen here with her son Cerdia, greatly loves her family. So much so, she has demanded that Tempest stop heroic adventuring and stay in Atlantis.*

A woman nicknamed Dolphin is the sole surviving member of an alien experiment on humans. She was freed by the spirit of Kordax the Cursed, from Atlantis' early days, then found by Navy officer Chris Landau and his crew. She was initially an attraction at Oceanworld but eventually returned to the sea. Like the mammal she's named after, her mind is of the moment, with little memory, and she did not recall Landau when they later met again. Instead, she found Atlantis and was welcomed by its people. Once there she initially flirted with the nation's ruler, Aquaman, but fell in love with his adopted son, Tempest. She joined the two on several adventures until she and Tempest married. They had a child, during the war between Atlantis and Cerdia. The baby was named Cerdian to help heal the conflict. Dolphin insisted that Tempest give up his work with the Teen Titans to devote his time to their family. They currently make their home in Atlantis. **RG**

***WATER BABY** Dolphin is as much at home in the sea as she is on land.*

DOMINUS

FIRST APPEARANCE ACTION COMICS #747 (August 1998)
STATUS Villain **REAL NAME** Tuoni
OCCUPATION Destroyer of worlds **BASE** The Infinite Domain
HEIGHT/WEIGHT Variable **EYES** Red **HAIR** None
SPECIAL POWERS/ABILITIES Creates multiple realities based on the worst nightmares of his opponents.

Once a benign Lord of Order named Tuoni, Dominus assumed his current malevolent form when he jealously struck against his former lover Ahti after she ascended to the coveted position of Illuminator of All Realities and became the godlike Kismet. His rash attack disintegrated him, but Kismet compassionately allowed him to live as an exile in the Phantom Zone. Kryptonian technology restored him to new life and Dominus escaped to Earth, where he tried to take his revenge on Kismet. Failing in that, he created alternate realities based on SUPERMAN's fears and convinced the Man of Steel that civilization would end unless he remained eternally vigilant. Proclaiming himself King of the World, Superman policed the planet with an army of Superman Robots. Superman shook off Dominus's influence, but the villain destroyed his Antarctic Fortress of Solitude. After a long struggle, Superman successfully banished Dominus to the Phantom Zone. **DW**

DON CABALLERO

FIRST APPEARANCE ALL-STAR WESTERN #58 (April–May 1951)
STATUS Hero (deceased) **REAL NAME** Unknown
OCCUPATION Fencing instructor; adventurer
BASE Southern California in the early 19th century
HEIGHT 5ft 11in **WEIGHT** 178 lbs **EYES** Brown **HAIR** Black
SPECIAL POWERS/ABILITIES Expert fencer and horseman.

Don Caballero moved to southern California from his native Spain in the early years of the 19th century and established an estate in the small community of Hawk Hill. His true name unknown, Don Caballero used his expert fencing skills to thwart local felons and desert pirates like the Jackal, and even supernatural threats like the ghost of El Feugo, becoming Hawk Hill's greatest hero in the process.

Over the years, Don Caballero came to instruct others in Hawk Hill, teaching them the fine art of fencing. Caballero used his own blade, the legendary *El Capitan*, and his own physical prowess and martial skills to defend his southern California home well into his senior years, although his final fate has yet to be recorded. **PJ**

DOOMSDAY

FIRST APPEARANCE SUPERMAN: THE MAN OF STEEL #17 (Nov. 1992)
STATUS Villain **REAL NAME** None
OCCUPATION Destroyer **BASE** Earth
HEIGHT 7ft **WEIGHT** 615 lbs **EYES** Red **HAIR** White
SPECIAL POWERS/ABILITIES Bred to be the ultimate killing machine, each time he is defeated, he regenerates with a higher level of strength and endurance, making him an unbeatable foe.

CREATION *The clone that will become Doomsday is jettisoned into Krypton's harsh environment.*

Some 250,000 years ago, an alien scientist named Bertron arrived on Krypton and commenced cloning experiments to create the perfect warrior. Within decades, a cloned baby proved able to survive on harsh Krypton and withstand local predators. Turning on its creator, the creature killed Bertron before escaping Krypton. The monster traveled to other worlds, where it killed without mercy. Through the years, members of the GREEN LANTERN CORPS opposed this being, known as Doomsday until it threatened Oa, home to the GUARDIANS OF THE UNIVERSE. Their champion Radiant defeated Doomsday and he was chained, wrapped in a protective garment, placed in a container, and ejected into space. The container crashed into the Earth, burying itself deep underground. Over the millennia Doomsday struggled to free himself, pounding his way to the surface until he emerged in North America. He beat back the JUSTICE LEAGUE OF AMERICA before confronting SUPERMAN in Metropolis. The two fought an epic battle that laid waste to the city and resulted in the death of the Man of Steel. Since then, Doomsday has remained unstoppable, although he has since become a pawn for the likes of BRAINIAC and even Lex Luthor (*see* LUTHOR, LEX). **RG**

SUPERMAN SHOWDOWN *Doomsday's kryptonian genetics allow him to cause Superman great pain.*

KILLING MACHINE *A rampaging engine of destruction, each new generation of Doomsdays adapts to new perils and new environments, making him the perfect weapon.*

DOOM PATROL

SUPERPOWERED MISFITS

FIRST APPEARANCE MY GREATEST ADVENTURE #80 (June 1963)
STATUS Hero team **BASE** Midway City
CURRENT MEMBERS AND POWERS
BEAST BOY (GARFIELD LOGAN) Can transform into any animal
BUMBLEBEE (KAREN BEECHER) Can fly and fire electrical stingers
THE CHIEF (NILES CAULDER) Brilliant scientific mind
ELASTI-GIRL (RITA FARR) Can shrink or grow to various sizes
MENTO (STEVE DAYTON) Telepathy, mind control, telekinesis
NEGATIVE MAN (LARRY TRAINOR) Radioactive projection can fly, turn intangible
ROBOTMAN (CLIFF STEELE) Human brain housed in super-powerful robot body
VOX (MAL DUNCAN) Can emit sonic blasts and open dimensional gates

A TEAM OF SUPERPOWERED MISFITS, the Doom Patrol was assembled by the wheelchair-bound Dr. Niles Caulder to thwart threats to humanity. Caulder believed that these meta-humans—all marked by tragedy and ostracized from society—had nothing to lose and so would be willing to risk their lives as the world's strangest super heroes. As "THE CHIEF," Caulder recruited ELASTI-GIRL, NEGATIVE MAN, and ROBOTMAN II as the first Doom Patrol, a trio that soon learned to work as a team and live together as a family in Caulder's Midway City mansion. The Doom Patrol's greatest adventures involved saving the world from such menaces as the SOCIETY OF SIN and GENERAL IMMORTUS.

KEY 1) Robotman II (Cliff Steele) **2)** Elasti-Girl (Rita Farr Dayton) **3)** The Chief (Dr. Niles Caulder) **4)** Negative Man (Larry Trainor)

KEY 1) Vox **2)** Beast Boy **3)** Bumblebee **4)** Negative Man **5)** Elasti-Girl **6)** Robotman **7)** The Chief

FAST FORWARD!

A huge number of meta-human heroes with all kinds of powers and abilities—ranging from the useful or miraculous to the weird or plain disturbing—have passed through the Doom Patrol's ranks. The most recent team was assembled by eccentric businessman Thayer Jost, who had purchased the rights to the Patrol's name from a Robotman doppelganger created by former team member Dorothy Spinner (see SPINNER, DOROTHY), who possessed the ability to turn her fantasies into frightening reality.

This team of young meta-humans, which included Fast Forward—quickly dubbed "Negative Man" because of his overwhelming pessimism—FEVER, FREAK, and KID SLICK, had little experience wielding their powers.

The disbanding of this team, coupled with the reality-altering preshocks of the Infinite Crisis, allowed for the original Doom Patrol's return – including the Chief, Elasti-Girl, Negative Man, and Robotman. Caulder has since united other misfit heroes both old and new under his banner, including MENTO, BUMBLEBEE, BEAST BOY, and VOX. The team continues to operate as outcasts, accepted by neither the public nor the super-hero community. **SB**

THE DEVIL The Patrol went to Hell and back to beat Raum and free the souls empowering this fallen angel. Raum inspired the worst impulses in men and women, claiming their spirits after they committed suicide.

FATHER FIGURE As the Patrol's eldest (and most enduring) member, Robotman is the one constant among the Patrol's ever-changing roster.

KEY STORYLINES

• *DOOM PATROL (1ST SERIES) #121 (AUGUST 1968):* The original Doom Patrol sacrifice their own lives to save Codsville, Maine, from Madame Rouge and Captain Zahl. All but Elasti-Girl truly perish.
• *SHOWCASE #94 (AUGUST 1977):* Dr. Will Magnus finds Robotman's broken body and rebuilds him in time to join a new Doom Patrol that includes Celsius, Negative Woman, and Tempest.
• *DOOM PATROL (2ND SERIES) #19 (FEBRUARY 1989):* Things get stranger for the world's strangest heroes as they emerge from further tragedy by adding Crazy Jane to the team. They embark on new adventures while battling menaces like the Scissormen, Red Jack, and the Brotherhood of Dada.

DOUBLE DARE

FIRST APPEARANCE NIGHTWING #32 (June 1999)
STATUS Villain team **REAL NAMES** Margot and Aliki Marceau
OCCUPATION Trapeze artists/thieves **BASE** Mobile
HEIGHT (Margot) 5ft 7in; (Aliki) 5ft 4in
WEIGHT (Margot) 135 lbs; (Aliki) 124 lbs **EYES** Green **HAIR** Red
SPECIAL POWERS/ABILITIES Top acrobats and above-average combatants.

High above the center ring in the *Cirque Sensationel,* the Marceau sisters stun the crowd every evening with the athleticism and sheer risk of their death-defying trapeze act. Only a very few know their secret—after the circus has closed its tent flaps for the night, Margot and Aliki Marceau slip out to fleece their latest host city as the costumed thieves Double Dare. Most towns proved to be easy pickings for the lithe acrobats, giving the Marceau sisters fat pocketbooks and swelled heads.

When the circus stopped at Blüdhaven, Double Dare's brazen heists made a dangerous enemy of local crime boss BLOCKBUSTER II. NIGHTWING ran across Double Dare in his investigation into the robberies and helped Margot and Aliki escape from Blockbuster's thugs Stallion and Brutale. The Double Dare sisters developed a crush on the vigilante for his good looks and his moves—Dick Grayson had once been a trapeze artist, too, and the two squabbled for his attention. However, now that the Marceaus had a price on their heads, Blüdhaven had lost much of its appeal. They left town with the *Cirque Sensationel* hoping to cheat another, more innocent town out of its hard-earned wealth before too long. **DW**

DOUBLE, JONNY

FIRST APPEARANCE SHOWCASE #78 (November 1968)
STATUS Hero **REAL NAME** Jonathon Sebastian Double
OCCUPATION Private investigator **BASE** San Francsico, CA
HEIGHT 5ft 11in **WEIGHT** 178 lbs **EYES** Blue **HAIR** Blond
SPECIAL POWERS/ABILITIES Above average hand-to-hand combatant; relies heavily on his training as a policeman; known more for his tenacity than his detective skills.

Jonny Double's past is shrouded in mystery. Double was originally a plainclothes policeman working in San Francisco, but he left the force and opened up a small private investigation firm on the San Francisco waterfront. For much of his career, Jonny Double solved mundane street-level mysteries. Although Double teamed with POWER GIRL to defeat the underworld leader Doctor Tzin-Tzin, that brief foray into the outlandish remains an anomaly. The down-on-his-luck investigator's closest ties are to the foggy streets of San Francisco, and to his various confidantes like Fish-Eye, a pool shark, and Crystal Cross, an attractive local waitress.

After accepting a simple job to watch a rich man's rebellious daughter, Double found himself embroiled in the dark intrigues of a mob eager to get to sealed bank accounts that once belonged to mobster Al Capone. **PJ**

DRAGON KING

FIRST APPEARANCE ALL-STAR SQUADRON #4 (December 1981)
STATUS Villain (missing in action) **REAL NAME** Unknown
OCCUPATION Assassin **BASE** Mobile
HEIGHT 5ft 11in **WEIGHT** 184 lbs **EYES** Brown **HAIR** None
SPECIAL POWERS/ABILITIES Human-lizard hybrid; genius inventor; superior athlete and combatant.

During World War II, the leader of the Black Dragon Society was both a high-ranking Japanese official and a respected scientist. He created the K887 nerve agent and secured the legendary Holy Grail for Imperial Japan, combining that talisman's power with the Spear of Destiny wielded by Adolf Hitler to create a mystical energy field that briefly protected the Japanese Empire and Hitler's Fortress Europa from attack by superpowered "Mystery Men." Following Japan's defeat, the Axis agent went into hiding and subjected himself to experiments that turned him into a human/reptile hybrid. Not long ago, he resurfaced with a daughter, Cindy Burman (Shiv), and battled the Star-Spangled Kid, her partner S.T.R.I.P.E., and the SHINING KNIGHT. The Dragon King seemingly perished in the fight, though his body was never recovered. **SB**

DRAGON, RICHARD

FIRST APPEARANCE RICHARD DRAGON: KUNG-FU FIGHTER #1 (May 1975)
STATUS Hero **REAL NAME** Richard Dragon
OCCUPATION Private investigator **BASE** Was Detroit; now Blüdhaven
HEIGHT 6ft 1in **WEIGHT** 205 lbs **EYES** Brown **HAIR** Red
SPECIAL POWERS/ABILITIES Master of all known empty hand fighting disciplines.

Richard Dragon grew up poor and neglected in the slums of St Louis, Missouri. However, a chance meeting with Ben Turner—the legendary martial artist known as BRONZE TIGER—turned Dragon's life around. Under Turner's tutelage, Richard Dragon became a kung-fu fighter in his own right, as well as a trainer of several costumed vigilantes, including Barbara Gordon (ORACLE) and Vic Sage (the QUESTION). Unfortunately, Dragon fell under the sway of the notorious LADY SHIVA, who drew him into the world of illegal (and lethal) underground fighting competitions. In the sacred city of Nanda Parbat, Dragon helped train police detective Renee Montoya to become the new QUESTION. **SB**

QUESTIONS AND ANSWERS *While training in Nanda Parbat in the Himalayas (above), Dragon and Montoya realize that Vic Sage, the Question, is seriously ill. After Vic's death the program intensifies (left) as Montoya prepares to become the new Question.*

DREAM GIRL

FIRST APPEARANCE ADVENTURE COMICS #317 (February 1964)
STATUS Hero **REAL NAME** Nura Nal Schnappin
OCCUPATION Psychic **BASE** Earth
HEIGHT 5ft 6in **WEIGHT** 135 lbs **EYES** Blue **HAIR** Blonde
SPECIAL POWERS/ABILITIES Can receive limited glimpses of the future while in narcoleptic state; undergoing hand-to-hand combat training as a member of the Legion of Super-Heroes.

Nura Nal, known to members of the LEGION OF SUPER-HEROES as Dream Girl, shares the ability to see precognitive visions with the other natives of the planet Naltor. While most Naltorians need sleep in order to perceive the future, Nura can sense "flash-forward" impressions at all times, making her a particularly dangerous hand-to-hand combatant. On one of the Legion's early missions, Dream Girl uncovered a conspiracy on Naltor to prevent anyone under age 18 from sleeping and tapping into visions of an apocalyptic future.

Dream Girl's reliance on precognition rubbed the highly-logical BRAINIAC 5 the wrong way, yet their opposite approaches soon drove them together. After Nura's death in combat, Brainiac 5 became obsessed with defeating death and restoring her to life. Dream Girl also found a way to communicate to Brainy in his sleep. A male Naltorian, Dream Boy, took her place in the Legion. **RG**

DREAMSLAYER

FIRST APPEARANCE JUSTICE LEAGUE EUROPE #15 (June 1990)
STATUS Villain **REAL NAME** Unknown
OCCUPATION Leader of the New Extremists **BASE** Mobile
HEIGHT 6ft 7in **WEIGHT/EYES** Indeterminate **HAIR** None
SPECIAL POWERS/ABILITIES Flight, mind-reading, matter-manipulation, and teleportational abilities.

Dreamslayer led the EXTREMISTS, who triggered a nuclear holocaust on the planet Angor. He survived by taking refuge in the "dimension of terrors" from which he drew his powers. He returned to Angor to discover that his comrades had been remade as androids, and led the robotic Extremists in a failed takeover of Earth. Dreamslayer then attacked the JUSTICE LEAGUE OF AMERICA, but didn't gain true power until the OVERMASTER neared Earth. Given new authority by the Overmaster, Dreamslayer assembled a fresh batch of villains as the New Extremists. However, Dreamslayer then tried to steal the Overmaster's strength and was banished again to the dimension of terrors. **DW**

DURAN

FIRST APPEARANCE SUPERMAN (2nd ser.) ANNUAL #12 (Aug. 2000)
STATUS Villain **REAL NAME** Duran
OCCUPATION Ecological terrorist **BASE** Mexico City, Mexico
HEIGHT 6ft 1in **WEIGHT** 180 lbs **EYES** Brown **HAIR** Black
SPECIAL POWERS/ABILITIES Sorcerer who can project energy bolts and manipulate the elements.

Señor Duran is a powerful sorcerer and a member of the Oto Tribe in central Mexico. Vowing vengeance on imperialist developers, Señor Duran, an ecological terrorist, planned on unleashing a horde of mystical monsters across Mexico in protest against the rampant pollution its people generated.

Operating out of Zócolo, the Plaza of the Constitution in the heart of Mexico City, Duran kidnapped a young girl and focused the powers of Ometeotl, the "dual divinity," through her. The magic spell sparked a literal firestorm of destruction that was only stopped by the combined forces of SUPERMAN, IMAN, ACRATA, and EL MUERTO. **PJ**

DUSK, NATHANIEL

FIRST APPEARANCE NATHANIEL DUSK #1 (February 1984)
STATUS Hero **REAL NAME** Nathaniel Dusk
OCCUPATION Private investigator **BASE** New York City
HEIGHT 6ft **WEIGHT** 187 lbs **EYES** Brown **HAIR** Brown
SPECIAL POWERS/ABILITIES Good in a fight and handy with a gun; tough as teak; never gives up on a case.

Nathaniel Dusk is the quintessential hard-boiled private eye on the mean streets of New York. An ex-soldier in the trenches of World War I and a combat pilot, he left the military and became a cop. Disgusted by the rampant corruption in the force, Dusk opened his own P.I. office in 1931. He struck up a romance with mother of two Joyce Gulino, who had gone into hiding from her mobster husband Joseph Costilino. The vengeful husband ordered a hit on both his wife and Dusk but only Joyce died in the attack.

Dusk went after Costilino, and in the end the gangster perished. Dusk subsequently took on many other cases, but always made time to watch over Joyce's two children, Jennie and Anthony. **DW**

DYBBUK

FIRST APPEARANCE SUICIDE SQUAD (1st series) #45 (September 1990)
STATUS Hero **REAL NAME** "Lenny"
OCCUPATION Artificial intelligence **BASE** Mobile
HEIGHT/WEIGHT/EYES/HAIR Inapplicable
SPECIAL POWERS/ABILITIES Able to usurp and take control of any computerized technology.

Created by Israeli scientists, the artificial intelligence Dybbuk was originally a machine member of the HAYOTH, Israel's native superbeings. But after being duped by the anarchist Kobra into nearly igniting a Middle Eastern holy war, Dybbuk and the rest of the Hayoth were taken into custody by America's SUICIDE SQUAD. Dybbuk, renaming himself "Lenny," agreed to help the Squad's Amanda Waller (see WALLER, AMANDA) reprogram the digital djinn known as Ifrit, formerly the Squad's Mindboggler, who had become a terrorist member of the superpowered Jihad. Dybbuk and Ifrit fell in love and became electronically engaged. Presumably, the artificial intelligences now enjoy wedded bliss in the digital domain and continue to serve as U.S. government operatives under the auspices of Task Force X. **SB**

ECHO

FIRST APPEARANCE (Echo III) JUSTICE LEAGUE QUARTERLY #1
(Winter 1990); (Echo IV) BATMAN 80-PAGE GIANT #1 (1999)
STATUS (both) Villains **REAL NAMES** (III) Unknown; (IV) Terri Eckhart
OCCUPATION (III) Mercenary; (IV) criminal **BASE** (III) Mobile;
(IV) Gotham City **HEIGHT** (III) 5ft 3in; (IV) 5ft 11in **WEIGHT** (III) 115
lbs; (IV) 140 lbs **EYES** (both) Blue **HAIR** (III) Red; (IV) black
SPECIAL POWERS/ABILITIES (III) Can absorb energy directed at her and
return it with equal force, enabling her to fly; (IV) is a tough athlete.

The Echo name has been used repeatedly, starting with
a foe of the CRIMSON AVENGER during the 1940s. The
second—Nina Damfino—was half of a two-woman crime
team known as Query & Echo, who occasionally joined
the RIDDLER. The third Echo (pictured right) was a result
of Morgan Edge's ex-wife Claire Montgomery founding
a corporate-sponsored group of mercenaries known as the
CONGLOMERATE. Amongst the first incarnation of the team
was a young woman named Echo, a teen rock sensation.
In between stints with the team she
evolved her look and sound, staying
on the cutting edge of rock music.
Terri Eckhart was the fourth Echo,
the second Echo to work with
the Riddler. Virtually nothing
is known about Terri Eckhart's
background or why she chooses
to ally herself with the Riddler,
but she seems better suited to
the Riddler's temperament than
her predecessor. Vicki Grant (see
DIAL "H" FOR HERO), when
she controlled an H-dial, was
able to transform into the fifth costumed woman with the
name Echo. ECHO VI emerged after Gotham City became
a No Man's Land. RG

ECHO VI

FIRST APPEARANCE BATMAN: LEGENDS OF THE DARK KNIGHT
#119 (July 1999)
STATUS Villain **REAL NAME** Unrevealed
OCCUPATION Covert agent; assassin **BASE** Unknown
HEIGHT 5ft 4in **WEIGHT** 110 lbs **EYES** Hazel **HAIR** Red
SPECIAL POWERS/ABILITIES Sensitive mind powers the receiver in her
helmet, enabling her to read others' thoughts and intercept sound
waves; natural athlete trained in the use of firearms
and other weapons.

The use of the Echo name
continued with Echo VI.
Following a cataclysmic
earthquake, when Gotham City
was cut off from the rest of the
U.S. and became known as a
No Man's Land, clashed with a
human electronics receiver known
as Echo VI.

This sixth Echo is a Russian
agent who underwent surgery
in a procedure known as "The
Turing Project" that implanted
biomechanical units in her
brain. This allows her to
interface with computers and
have access to the thoughts
of others.

Echo VI is a deeply
unhappy woman due to the fact that she cannot
control this special ability. Her mind powers also
give her massive headaches. RG

ECLIPSO

FIRST APPEARANCE House of Secrets (1st series) #61 (August 1963)
STATUS Villain **REAL NAME** None
OCCUPATION Adventurer **BASE** Mobile
HEIGHT 6ft 2in **WEIGHT** 484 lbs **EYES** Red **HAIR** None
SPECIAL POWERS/ABILITIES Superstrength, invulnerability, and
levitation; can fire black light from right eye and laser beams from
left eye when focused through a special black diamond.

EARLY DAYS Eclipso was one of the first foes
faced by the Justice League of America.

Eclipso is the primordial manifestation of God's
wrath and claims to have been responsible
for unleashing the Great Flood of Biblical
fame. Eventually superseded as the spirit of
vengeance by the SPECTRE, Eclipso's physical
essence became trapped in a black diamond
known as the Heart of Darkness, while his
mental essence lived on the dark side of the
moon.

In the year 1891, a jeweler split the diamond
into a thousand fragments, allowing Eclipso to
act out the revenge fantasies of all those who
possessed one of the black shards. Appearing as
a spectral wraith or taking physical possession
of its host bodies, Eclipso worked to gather
together the diamond fragments over the next
century. If he destroyed them all, his restored
powers would allow him to blot out the sun.
Astronomer and doctor Bruce Gordon became
a modern host for Eclipso and struggled to
control his dark side even as Eclipso battled
the JUSTICE LEAGUE OF AMERICA and the
METAL MEN, who often exploited the villain's
vulnerability to sunlight. Eclipso eventually
separated from Gordon and killed
several heroes including WILDCAT II
(Yolanda Montez) and Dr. Midnight
(Beth Chapel).

Eclipso joined the DARK
LORD and OBSIDIAN in a
bid to plunge the world into
perpetual darkness. WILDCAT
II's brother Alexander Montez
tried to trap Eclipso inside his
body, but his death freed the
evil spirit. Eclipso then possessed
SUPERMAN before making Jean
Loring (ex-wife of the ATOM)
his new host. As Eclipso, Loring
convinced the SPECTRE to lead
an assault against all magic-users, and tried to
lure MARY MARVEL over to her murderous
cause. DW

POWER MAD Eclipso's
only desire is the
domination of all
living beings.

UPGRADE Alexander Montez
briefly controlled Eclipso and
worked with Black Adam's
vigilante team.

EFFIGY

FIRST APPEARANCE GREEN LANTERN (3rd series) #110 (April 1999)
STATUS Villain **REAL NAME** Martyn Van Wyck
OCCUPATION Professional criminal **BASE** Seattle
HEIGHT 6ft 1in **WEIGHT** 195 lbs **EYES** Blue **HAIR** Blond
SPECIAL POWERS/ABILITIES Alien experiments gave him the power to
generate and control seemingly limitless flames and heat at will.

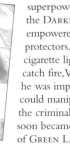

He awoke naked and alone in the woods of the Pacific
Northwest. All Martyn Van Wyck could recall were strange,
shadowy figures looming over him. He learned later that he
had been abducted by aliens.

The Controllers, descendants of the same Maltusians
who had become the GUARDIANS OF THE UNIVERSE, had
experimented upon Van Wyck and other humans to create
superpowered beings to replace
the DARKSTARS they had once
empowered as space-based
protectors. When the flame of a
cigarette lighter caused him to
catch fire, Van Wyck found that
he was impervious to heat and
could manipulate fire. He adopted
the criminal alter ego Effigy and
soon became a flame-throwing foe
of GREEN LANTERN Kyle Rayner.

After a blazing battle, Effigy was defeated and reclaimed by
the Controllers. Later, Effigy returned to Earth and allied
himself with Killer Frost (see KILLER FROST II) to fight
Green Lantern with both fire and ice. As Effigy's control of
his abilities grows, so does the danger he poses to anyone
who gets close enough to him to burn. SB

EGG FU

FIRST APPEARANCE WONDER WOMAN (2nd series) #157 (October 1965)
STATUS Villain **REAL NAME** Chang Tzu
OCCUPATION Mad scientist **BASE** Oolong Island
HEIGHT 10ft **WEIGHT** 560 lbs **EYES** Red **HAIR** None
SPECIAL POWERS/ABILITIES Brilliant mind; has weapons concealed in walking armature

An egg-shaped creature of Apokolyptian origin, Chang Tzu is an evil genius and member of the Chinese super-team the GREAT TEN. The name "Egg Fu" dates back to a 19th century Apokolyptian robot once active on Earth; Chang Tzu counts it as one of his "nine thousand and nine unmentionable names."

Following the Infinite Crisis, Chang Tzu worked with INTERGANG to kidnap dozens of scientists to Oolong Island for the purpose of weapons development. DOC MAGNUS refused to follow Chang Tzu's orders and shot him in the face before escaping. Chang Tzu repaired himself, keeping Oolong Island operational despite an assault on the facility by the combined forces of CHECKMATE and the OUTSIDERS. **DW**

EL DIABLO I & II

FIRST APPEARANCE ALL-STAR WESTERN (2nd series) #2 (October 1970)
STATUS Hero **REAL NAME** Lazarus Lane
OCCUPATION Adventurer **BASE** Puerta Del Sol, California
HEIGHT 6ft **WEIGHT** 182 lbs **EYES** Blue **HAIR** Black
SPECIAL POWERS/ABILITIES An expert marksman and horseback rider; his body can perform amazing feats of athleticism.

FIRST APPEARANCE El Diablo #1 (August 1989)
STATUS Hero **REAL NAME** Rafael Sandoval
OCCUPATION City councillor **BASE** Dos Rios, Texas
HEIGHT 6ft 2in **WEIGHT** 190 lbs **EYES** Brown **HAIR** Black
SPECIAL POWERS/ABILITIES An accomplished athlete, trained in boxing and martial arts.

Lazarus Lane was nearly killed after he tried to stop bank robbers in 1866. Left comatose by a bolt of lightning, he hovered near death until an Apache shaman named Wise Owl healed him. Lane awoke from his coma believing his spirit had split in two; one Lane's husk, the other a supernatural being. His spirit began roaming the frontier as El Diablo, meting out justice with fists, whip, or six gun. Six years later, an odd assortment of gunslingers were hired by Otto Von Hammer and Jason Blood to free the time-lost earth elemental, SWAMP THING, contained by Wise Owl. When Wise Owl was killed, the long-catatonic Lane awoke, and El Diablo ceased to exist.

Over a century later, Rafael Sandoval grew up in a tough part of Dos Rios, Texas. He was befriended by a priest, Father Guzman, and trained as a boxer. Sandoval left Dos Rios, enlisted, earned a law degree and returned to Dos Rios as public defender. His work and charisma impressed Mayor Tommy Longstreet, who helped him become the first Hispanic on the city council. Frustrated by the red tape and political entanglements, he felt unable to make a difference. When Sandoval learned about several acts of arson being committed for insurance fraud, he chose to take direct action, but did so wearing an old festival costume and mask. After defeating the arsonists, Sandoval continued acting as the new El Diablo. Rafael Sandoval ultimately retired his El Diablo persona, convinced that he could do more as a city councillor working within the system. Later, Sandoval resumed his El Diablo identity in tandem with the demon Netzahualcoyotl, whom he agreed to host in exchange for rooting out political corruption. **RG**

DOUBLE DIABLO *Rafael (left) took his name from the western gunfighter of an earlier century (right).*

EKRON

FIRST APPEARANCE ADVENTURE COMICS #352 (January 1967)
STATUS Hero **REAL NAME** Ekron
OCCUPATION Green Lantern **BASE** Mobile
HEIGHT Unknown **WEIGHT** Unknown **EYES** Green **HAIR** None
SPECIAL POWERS/ABILITIES Able to fire energy beams and create energy constructs using the Emerald Eye; can also possess the minds of others.

Ekron is an ancient construct shrouded in mystery, though it is believed to have been built by the GUARDIANS OF THE UNIVERSE. Its eyes can fire energy beams and manipulate the minds of others, and are among the most powerful weapons in creation.

Following the Infinite Crisis, the interstellar bounty hunter LOBO obtained one of the eyes, leaving the Emerald Head of Ekron (and its operator, the Green Lantern of Vengar) defenseless against an invading army led by Lady Styx. The Head's pursuit of its Emerald Eye brought it into conflict with Lobo and the outer-space exiles ANIMAL MAN, Adam Strange (see STRANGE, ADAM) and STARFIRE.

The Emerald Eye of Ekron has also been found in the 31st century, where it is an object of power for the Emerald Empress, a member of the FATAL FIVE. **DW**

EL MUERTO

FIRST APPEARANCE SUPERMAN (2nd ser.) Annual #12 (Aug. 2000)
STATUS Hero **REAL NAME** Pablo Valdez
OCCUPATION Costumed crime fighter **BASE** Mexico City
HEIGHT 5ft 11in **WEIGHT** 178 lbs **EYES** Brown **HAIR** Black
SPECIAL POWERS/ABILITIES Skilled fighter; nearly impervious to harm due to his undead nature.

As a young man in Mexico City, Pablo Valdez idolized SUPERMAN. When he tried to save a girl from a hostage situation—something his hero did every day—he died inside a crumbling building. Resurrected through mysticism, Valdez donned a costume reminiscent of those worn by hanging victims and became the hero El Muerto. This time, however, he hated Superman for not being there to prevent his death. El Muerto fought crime in the streets of Mexico City and teamed with fellow heroes IMAN and ACRATA to form a Mexican super-team. He finally got his chance to meet Superman when a girl used her occult energies to wreck half of downtown Mexico City. The Man of Steel arrived to help the local trio, but his vulnerability to magic meant that the heroes had to unite in order to defeat the supernatural threat. Superman and El Muerto have since reconciled, and El Muerto is still active in Mexico City. **DW**

ELASTI-GIRL

FIRST APPEARANCE MY GREATEST ADVENTURE #80 (June 1963)
STATUS Hero **REAL NAME** Rita Farr Dayton
OCCUPATION Actress **BASE** Midway City
HEIGHT (as Rita) 5ft 6in **WEIGHT** (as Rita) 135 lbs
EYES Brown **HAIR** Brown
SPECIAL POWERS/ABILITIES Could stretch any part of her body to incredible lengths; could grow to enormous size; could shrink to tiny, but not microscopic, size.

Rita Farr was a famous Hollywood actress who was exposed to strange gases while on the set of a movie being filmed on location in Africa. When she discovered she could now change the proportions of her body, she forsook her acting career and went into hiding.

Niles Caulder, known as the CHIEF, discovered Farr and invited her to join the DOOM PATROL, a team of unusual crime fighters. Taking the name Elasti-Girl, Rita reclaimed the fame of her youth and soon fell in love with fellow Doom Patroller Steve Dayton, who had developed a helmet giving him psychic powers and called himself MENTO. The couple soon adopted a boy with green skin named Garfield Logan who could transform into any kind of animal. The youngster joined the Doom Patrol as BEAST BOY.

When the Doom Patrol were confronted by two of their arch-enemies, MADAME ROUGE and GENERAL ZAHL, the heroes laid their lives on the line to save the innocent population of a small New England fishing village. Believed killed in the blast, Elasti-Girl returned years later to rejoin the Doom Patrol. **PJ**

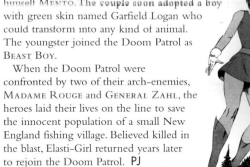

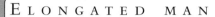

E

ELEMENT GIRL

First appearance METAMORPHO #10 (February 1967)
Status Hero **Real name** Urania "Rainie" Blackwell
Occupation Former U.S. government agent **Base** Mobile
Height 5ft 10in **Weight** 142 lbs **Eyes** Black **Hair** Green
Special powers/abilities Could shapeshift and transform into any combination of chemical elements.

Element Girl lived a sad life, transformed into a freak and then abandoned by those she loved. Many years ago, Urania Blackwell had been a spy working for the U.S. government who volunteered to expose herself to the same Orb of Ra radiation that had transformed Rex Mason into Metamorpho, the Element Man. The process worked—although Rainie's body became discolored and misshapen, she could shift between elemental states at will. She took the alias of Element Girl. Rainie worked with Metamorpho for several months, crossing the globe and falling in love. However she was spurned by Metamorpho, and soon her government agency declared it had no further use for her. Despairing, Rainie tried to live quietly in retirement but because of her hideous appearance, couldn't bear to leave her apartment. She tried to commit suicide on several occasions, but her body's natural defenses made the act impossible.

Element Girl ultimately received a visit from Death, who helped Rainie to make peace with herself and finally depart her mortal life. DW

ELEMENT LAD

First appearance ADVENTURE COMICS #307 (April 1963)
Status Villain (deceased) **Real name** Jan Arrah
Occupation Legionnaire **Base** 30th-century Earth
Height 5ft 5in **Weight** 140 lbs **Eyes** Blue **Hair** Blond
Special powers/abilities Could transmute any element into any other by using his mental powers to change its chemical makeup; could transmute his own body into any element; could even create life.

Jan Arrah was born to a race of element transmuters on the planet Trom in the latter half of the 30th century. With the ability to create literally anything they could think of, the Trommites were among the most powerful beings in the galaxy. The fear this engendered in others led to the rumored genocide of all Trommites, save one.

Sole survivor Jan Arrah joined the Legion of Super-Heroes as Element Lad, able to temporarily change the chemical structure of any object as long as he made physical contact. His powers made him one of the Legion's heavy hitters, yet he disdained fighting and maintained a quiet, spiritual demeanor. He often remained aloof from his fellow Legionnaires, declining to discuss his personal life, though he did go on one date with his teammate Triplicate Girl (see Triad). Element Lad participated in the battles that drove back a Dominator invasion force intent on conquering Earth. PJ

ELONGATED MAN

First appearance THE FLASH (1st series) #112 (May 1960)
Status Hero **Real name** Ralph Dibny
Occupation Detective **Base** Mobile
Height 6ft 1in **Weight** 178 lbs **Eyes** Blue **Hair** Red
Special powers/abilities Consuming a Gingold extract every few days renders him super-elasticate to stretch or contort any portion of his body; brilliant deductive mind.

A fascination with the human body's powers of flexibility first led nine-year-old amateur detective Ralph Dibny to investigate the secrets of the "India Rubber Men" and similar contortionists that appeared at circuses and traveling sideshows. His determination to discover the source of their fantastic plastic abilities continued into adulthood.

Ralph traveled the world on this unusual quest and came to the conclusion that the greatest contortionists all had one thing in common: before a performance, each "rubber man" consumed a soft drink called Gingold, which contained the juice of the Yucatan gingo fruit. Ralph managed to isolate an unknown chemical present in the fruit's juices. When he drank a concentrated dose of this extract, his body acquired elastic properties far beyond the abilities of the sideshow freaks. As the Elongated Man, Ralph became a super-stretchable sleuth, frequently teaming with Batman and the Flash before joining the Justice League of America.

Tragedy shattered Ralph's life when his wife, Sue Dibny, died at the hands of the insane Jean Loring. Driven to despair, Ralph undertook a hunt to restore Sue to life, following what appeared to be Doctor Fate through various underworlds and magical realms. Ultimately he learned that Felix Faust (see Faust, Felix) and the demon Neron had been manipulating his quest. Ralph managed to trap both villains, but lost his life in the effort. In the afterlife, the reunited Ralph and Sue became "ghost detectives." SB

ELASTIC FANTASTIC *At first, Ralph felt no changes after drinking the Gingold extract. But when he walked beneath a falling flower pot, his arm rose to the occasion and stretched to catch it!*

FLEXIBLE FRIEND *Ralph Dibny and Barry Allen (the second Flash) were fast friends and joined forces to solve several cases in Central City.*

DEVOTION *Ralph and Sue were inseparable. Even when Elongated Man was on a super heroic mission, Sue was never far behind! Sue died in a horrible attack by Doctor Light I.*

EMPRESS

First appearance YOUNG JUSTICE #16 (January 2000)
Status Hero **Real name** Anita Fite
Occupation Adventurer **Base** Mobile
Height 5ft 7in **Weight** 127 lbs **Eyes** Bronze **Hair** Purple
Special powers/abilities Teleportation, mental control, and top-notch physical conditioning; skilled with most weapons.

As the granddaughter of the sinister Baron Agua sin Gaaz, Empress is heir to a villain's legacy, but she has lived her teen years in the service of heroism. Her father, Donald Fite, served in the All-Purpose Espionage Squad (A.P.E.S.). After Agua sin Gaaz killed her mother in a bombing intended for Donald, Empress assumed the full powers due to her as part of her voodoo heritage. Inspired by the teen heroes YOUNG JUSTICE, particularly ARROWETTE, she joined the hero team at a time when Arrowette had temporarily left. This gave rise to friction when Arrowette returned and thought that Empress had taken her place. During a battle against the android INDIGO, which led to Young Justice's breakup, Empress suffered severe injuries and almost did not manage to teleport away to safety. After her recuperation she will undoubtedly return to crime fighting. **DW**

ENCANTADORA

First appearance ACTION COMICS #760 (December 1999)
Status Villain **Real name** Lourdes Lucero
Occupation Enchantress **Base** Metropolis
Height 5ft 7in **Weight** 133 lbs **Eyes** Brown **Hair** Brown
Special powers/abilities A mystical vial she wears on her necklace contains the Mist of Ibella, which allows her to teleport, magically charm and control the minds of others, and telekinetically move objects with her mind.

Lourdes Lucero's archaeologist father was driven mad searching for the magical Mist of Ibella. After his death, Lourdes took the vial containing the Mist and used its power to become La Encantadora, promising to provide for her little brother, Victor.

La Encantadora tried to trick a number of villains into buying fake green kryptonite to use against SUPERMAN. The Man of Steel believed he had been poisoned, and Encantadora offered him a magical cure in exchange for a kiss. Superman mysteriously began to succumb to radiation poisoning caused by kryptonite. Horrified, Encantadora told Superman's wife, Lois (see LANE, LOIS) that her kiss had infected the Man of Steel with kryptonite nanobots. Luckily, S.T.A.R. Labs physicians saved Superman's life. R'AS AL GHUL then threatened Encantadora and her brother. He hoped to mix the Mist with his ancient Lazarus pit in order to gain unlimited power. With Superman's help, the sorceress and her brother escaped his clutches. After Encantadora vanished, Superman learned that GENERAL ZOD, one of his greatest foes, had provided the magical femme fatale with the kryptonite nanobots that had nearly killed him. **PJ**

CHARMER *Superman could never have guessed how deadly La Encantadora's kiss would be.*

ENCHANTRESS

First appearance STRANGE ADVENTURES #187 (April 1966)
Status Undecided **Real name** June Moone
Occupation Freelance artist/adventurer/criminal **Base** Mobile
Height 5ft 6in **Weight** 130 lbs
Eyes Blue (green as Enchantress) **Hair** Black (as Enchantress)
Special powers/abilities Could animate objects, alter her own appearance and levitate; mystic tricks once concealed in her hat.

A secret passage in Terror Castle led June Moone to a creature named Dzamor. He revealed her destiny: to become a magical defender. By uttering the name "Enchantress," June acquired awesome powers, which she used to thwart mystical menaces. Years later, Dzamor summoned June and told her that an astral alignment would empower her to cleanse Earth of evil. However, POWER GIRL prevented the alignment by moving the real Moon, denying June her destiny. Embittered, June lost control of her alter ego and the Enchantress turned to villainy. Jailed for her crimes, the Enchantress was given amnesty as a member of the SUICIDE SQUAD. During the rampage of the SPECTRE prior to the Infinite Crisis, the Enchantress joined the SHADOWPACT to fight the magical entity. Along with her teammates, she disappeared for a year to save the town of Riverrock, Wyoming. **SB**

ENDLESS, THE

First appearance SANDMAN (2nd series) #21 (November 1990)
Status Inapplicable **Base** Various astral realms
Members and Powers
Destiny Chained to his Eternity Book, which records everything that has or will ever happen.
Death Takes each being in the universe to their final resting place.
Dream Ruler of the Dreaming, where all minds are linked.
Desire Androgynous brother/sister is every sentient being's desire.
Despair Funnels despair into mortal souls.
Destruction Governs transformation and change.
Delirium Mistress of the mentally disturbed.

The Endless are a family of incredibly powerful entities who exist because mortals, gods, demons, and aliens across the cosmos *believe* they exist. The Endless are not gods but have been worshipped as such throughout the cosmos. Mortal beings perceive the Endless according to their own cultural or species expectations. Each of the Endless exists in their own astral realm that is a creation of the consciousness of living beings. The eldest member of the Endless is DESTINY, who came into existence shortly after the beginning of the universe. Soon after, DEATH was created, followed by Dream. Destruction was born soon after, a manifestation of change. A set of twins, the cruel Desire and the grim Despair, came next, and Delight, the youngest member of the Endless, was transformed countless aeons ago into a new aspect of the Endless, called Delirium.

The embodiment of their names, the Endless are older than the angels. While the elder siblings fulfill their roles with the utmost seriousness, the younger ones involve themselves in petty intrigues. Desire has more than once tried to destroy Dream, and Destruction abandoned his duties for centuries, retiring to a village in Greece with his dog Barnabas. Born at the beginning of creation, the Endless will continue to exist until the last sentient being has died, when Death will claim Destiny, and finally herself, at the end of time. **PJ**

Dream

Destruction

Destiny

Desire

Death

Despair

Delirium

ENEMY ACE

FIRST APPEARANCE OUR ARMY AT WAR #151 (February 1965)
STATUS Unresolved **REAL NAME** Hans von Hammer
OCCUPATION Pilot **BASE** Germany
HEIGHT 5ft 11in **WEIGHT** 161 lbs **EYES** Blue **HAIR** Auburn
SPECIAL POWERS/ABILITIES One of the greatest natural pilots ever seen.

The son of an aristocratic German family distantly related to Anton Arcane (*see* ARCANE, ANTON), Baron Hans von Hammer was among the first to enlist when World War I broke out in 1914. While in flight school, he engaged in a duel of honor with fellow cadet Heinrich Muller and received a permanent scar on his left cheek. An exceptional flyer, von Hammer soon became Rittsmeister of his own Jagdstaffel hunting squadron, and feared among Allied forces as the Enemy Ace. During the course of the war, he had over 70 kills to his credit; however, he took no joy in performing this duty. A solitary man, when not flying, von Hammer retreated to his home, wandering the nearby Black Forest, with his only companion, a wolf.

During World War II, von Hammer was persuaded out of retirement to fight on Nazi Germany's behalf on the Russian front. He crashed his plane in Leningrad and, before escaping back to his base, saw the horrors that Germany had inflicted on the Russian people there. After witnessing the atrocities at the Nazi concentration camp at Dachau in 1945, a shaken Hans von Hammer surrendered himself and his men to SERGEANT ROCK and Easy Company.

By the 1960s, the great von Hammer was broke, divorced, and confined to a German care facility. The former air ace spent his last days confiding his experiences to reporter and Vietnam veteran Edward Mannock, thereby bringing himself a measure of peace before he died. Some time later, von Hammer's exploits were popularized in a motion picture financed by Bruce Wayne, the BATMAN. **RG**

SOLITARY MAN
Hans von Hammer took little pleasure in his wartime duty and when not in the air, remained an intensely private individual.

ACE HIGH
His tally of 70 kills during World War I made von Hammer the most feared fighter pilot of his day.

ERADICATOR

FIRST APPEARANCE ACTION COMICS #693 (November 1993)
STATUS Ally **REAL NAME** Dr. David Connor
OCCUPATION Preserver of Kryptonian heritage **BASE** Mobile
HEIGHT 6ft 3in **WEIGHT** 225 lbs **EYES** Red **HAIR** Gray
SPECIAL POWERS/ABILITIES Flight, super-strength, heat vision; can project and control various energy types; extremely difficult to kill.

The Eradicator was originally a Kryptonian superweapon devised to wipe out alien races on Krypton and alter the genetic structure of all Kryptonians making it impossible for them to leave the planet. Thousands of years after the destruction of the planet, this incredible thinking machine had become the repository of all Kryptonian culture. It built SUPERMAN's Fortress of Solitude and attempted to turn Earth into a replica of Krypton. It then assumed human form and even impersonated Superman following the Man of Steel's death at the hands of DOOMSDAY.

The Eradicator brought Superman back to the Fortress of Solitude and revived him with Kryptonian technology, allowing Earth's greatest hero to cheat death. The CYBORG SUPERMAN nearly destroyed the Eradicator, but it survived by bonding with the body of S.T.A.R. Labs scientist Dr. David Connor. Although Connor remained partially in control, a copy of the Eradicator program animated the ruins of Superman's shattered Fortress of Solitude (destroyed earlier by DOMINUS) and assembled a huge warsuit. Connor/Eradicator merged with this titanic construct and flew off into space. The Eradicator later returned to Earth, but by then it was clear that Connor had lost most of his sanity. During the JOKER's "Last Laugh" spree, an infected Eradicator went on a lunatic, Jokerized rampage. **DW**

EVIL STAR

FIRST APPEARANCE GREEN LANTERN (2nd series) #37 (June 1965)
STATUS Villain **REAL NAME** Unknown
OCCUPATION Would-be intergalactic conqueror **BASE** Planet Aoran
HEIGHT 6ft 1in **WEIGHT** 205 lbs **EYES** Blue **HAIR** Blond
SPECIAL POWERS/ABILITIES Star-band can create solid objects, fire
energy beams, and generate a protective shield.

Evil Star allowed his fear of death to
ruin life for everyone else on the
planet Aoran. His invention, the
Star-band, extended the life of
its wearer indefinitely. However,
it also compelled its wearer to
commit acts of great wickedness,
and Evil Star would not remove
the device lest he grow old.
When the Aorans rose up against
him, Evil Star used the Star-band's
energy to slaughter everyone on
the planet. Realizing that he
possessed a weapon as powerful as
a GREEN LANTERN's power ring, Evil Star decided to
overthrow the GUARDIANS OF THE UNIVERSE and rule the
cosmos. Green Lantern Hal Jordan put an end to his mad
scheme. Evil Star has since threatened galactic peace many
times, employing mindless henchmen known as "Starlings."
These invulnerable, super-strong robots must be guided by
Evil Star's thoughts to function properly. **DW**

EXTANT

FIRST APPEARANCE SHOWCASE '94 #9 (August 1994)
STATUS Villain **REAL NAME** Henry (Hank) Hall
OCCUPATION Would-be world conqueror **BASE** Mobile
HEIGHT 6ft 1in **WEIGHT** 197 lbs **EYES** Brown **HAIR** Brown
SPECIAL POWERS/ABILITIES Armor gives superhuman strength and
invulnerability; some ability to control time.

Hank Hall and his brother
Don were experiments on
behalf of the Lords of Order
and Chaos, gaining powers
and operating as HAWK AND
DOVE. When Don was killed,
Hank went berserk. The
arrival of Dawn Granger as
the new Dove calmed him,
but when she was apparently
killed by his own future
incarnation, Hank totally lost
control. He fought his future
self, an armored being with
time-controlling powers,
known as MONARCH, and
eventually beat him. Hank
modified Monarch's armor
and time-controlling abilities,
renaming himself Extant. The exact capabilities of Extant's
time-control powers remained unexplained, but they seemed
to affect the speed with which time passed for an object or
person. On repeated occasions Extant has tried to recreate
Earth on his own terms, only to be stopped by various
combinations of heroes, notably the JUSTICE SOCIETY OF
AMERICA. Extant was responsible for the deaths of DOCTOR
MID-NITE I, ATOM I, and HOURMAN I, in addition to
ATOM-SMASHER's mother, by absorbing their own chronal
energies so that they reverted to their natural ages. He was
finally stopped when Atom-Smasher placed Extant on a
doomed airplane in place of his mother, closing a time lap
and ending Extant's threat. **RG**

EXTREME JUSTICE 1) Amazing Man II
2) Captain Atom **3)** Maxima
4) Booster Gold **5)** Blue Beetle

EXTREME JUSTICE

FIRST APPEARANCE EXTREME JUSTICE #0 (January 1995)
STATUS Hero team (disbanded) **BASE** Mount Thunder, Nevada
ORIGINAL MEMBERS AND POWERS
CAPTAIN ATOM Atomic-based powers via connection to quantum field.
AMAZING MAN II Can transform himself into any material he touches.
BLUE BEETLE Utilizes a variety of high-tech gadgets in his arsenal.
BOOSTER GOLD Superb athlete with futuristic exo-armor.
FIRESTORM Has ability to atomically restructure any inorganic
material.
MAXIMA Superstrong and cunning alien warrior queen.

Captain Atom's frustration with the leadership of
the JUSTICE LEAGUE OF AMERICA led him to form
a splinter group that claimed the Justice League
name, but was known as "Extreme Justice" for its more
proactive stance on combating evil. This Extreme Justice
League took the fight to its foes, rather than react to
threats. Later, alien shape-shifters and runaway slaves Zan
and Jayna were added to Extreme Justice's role call, based
at an abandoned military complex within Mount Thunder,
Nevada. Extreme Justice's status as a hero team, however, was
short-lived. The group's most notable adventure was a conflict
with the Legion of Doom, a team of villains that included Brainwave
II, a robot duplicate of GORILLA GRODD, HOUNGAN, KILLER FROST
II, a resurrected MAJOR FORCE, and the Madmen. After capturing the
Legion, Extreme Justice later disbanded with its heroes going their
separate ways, many returning to some capacity of membership with
the "official" Justice League. **SB**

EXTREMISTS, THE

FIRST APPEARANCE (Extremists I) JUSTICE LEAGUE EUROPE #15
(June 1990); (Extremists II) JUSTICE LEAGUE AMERICA #78
(August 1993)
STATUS Villain team **BASE** Earth-8
MEMBERS AND POWERS
Lord Havok I Team leader; his battlesuit can mutate into anything
Havoc needs.
Lord Havok II An identity used briefly by Maxwell Lord.
Doctor Diehard Can control magnetism.
Dreamslayer Can manipulate matter and teleport.
Gorgon II Grappling tentacles grow from his head.
Tracer Has superhuman senses and razor-sharp teeth and claws.
Brute Invulnerable and superstrong.
Cloudburst Ability to control weather.
Death Angel Illusion casting.
Gunshot Has a superpowered battlesuit with offensive weaponry.
Meanstreak Can transform objects into energy projectiles.
Barracuda (deceased) Can breathe underwater and communicate
with sea life

Prior to the Infinite Crisis, the
Extremists were a group of androids
used by DREAMSLAYER to replicate a
team of villainous murderers from the
world of Angor. The original Extremists
invaded our world by following two of
Angor's heroes, Blue Jay and the Silver
Sorceress, to Earth. Upon their arrival,
the Extremists defeated Justice League
Europe, annihilated the ROCKET RED
brigades, and took control of Earth's
nuclear arsenal. Although defeated, a
second team of Extremists became part
of the CADRE.

The current versions of the Extremists
are inhabitants of Earth-8 in the
multiverse. They are a dangerous
group of superpowered rogues who
have refused to submit to a government decree that
they register with a central authority. When a group
of heroes passed through Earth-8 on their hunt for
Ray Palmer (see ATOM), Jason Todd (see RED HOOD)
killed one of the Extremists, Barracuda. MONARCH
then tried to recruit LORD HAVOK and his followers
into his multiversal army. **PJ**

THE EXTREMISTS 1) Dreamslayer **2)** Doctor Diehard
3) Gorgon II **4)** Lord Havok II **5)** Tracer

FAIRCHILD, VESPER

FIRST APPEARANCE BATMAN #540 (March 1997)
STATUS Hero **REAL NAME** Vesper Fairchild
OCCUPATION Radio personality/journalist **BASE** Gotham City
HEIGHT 5ft 7in **WEIGHT** 126 lbs **EYES** Green **HAIR** Auburn
SPECIAL POWERS/ABILITIES No special powers; thorough and highly skilled investigative reporter.

Host of W.K.G.C. Talk Radio's "Siren of the Night," broadcaster Vesper Fairchild enjoyed a brief romance with billionaire Bruce Wayne before Gotham City was devastated by the earthquake that left it a lawless No Man's Land. In her new career as a journalist, Vesper returned to the rebuilt city and rekindled her relationship with Wayne while investigating his alter ego, BATMAN. Unfortunately, Vesper was killed in Wayne Manor by the assassin CAIN, DAVID shortly after learning that Wayne and the Dark Knight were one and the same. Bruce Wayne was framed for Vesper's murder, but was exonerated upon discovering that rival mogul Lex Luthor (see LUTHOR, LEX) had hired Cain in a plot to ruin Wayne. **SB**

FAITH

FIRST APPEARANCE JLA #69 (October 2002)
STATUS Hero **REAL NAME** Unrevealed
OCCUPATION Adventurer **BASE** Mobile
HEIGHT 5ft 10in **WEIGHT** 148 lbs **EYES** Brown **HAIR** Brown
SPECIAL POWERS/ABILITIES Capable of flight; commands powerful telekinetic energy; unconsciously inspires trust in those around her.

Faith was previously in the employ of a secret, unidentified U.S. government "black ops" team, but the nature of her role is unknown. Nicknamed the "Fat Lady" by her teammates, it is likely that she was called in to finish what other operatives had started. Whether Faith's ties to her former employers have been completely severed remains to be seen. Faith has telekinetic powers and may have shown only a fraction of her abilities. She also emits "positive vibrations" that help those around her feel calm and confident. As a result, anyone who meets her instinctively trusts her. Faith claims to have met BATMAN on a past mission, during which they spent some time together. She answered Batman's call when the creation of a "contingency League" was required during the Obsidian Age mission, when the JUSTICE LEAGUE OF AMERICA had to travel 3,000 years back in time to Atlantis to rescue AQUAMAN and the present-day Atlanteans during the war against IMPERIEX. She earned Batman's confidence, and he not only considered her for JLA membership, but shared some personal insights with her as well. **RG**

FAORA

FIRST APPEARANCE (historical) ACTION COMICS #471 (May 1977); (current) action comics #779 (July 2001)
REAL NAME Unknown **BASE** Pokolistan
HEIGHT 5ft 7in **WEIGHT** 150 lbs **EYES** Brown **HAIR** Brown
OCCUPATION Enforcer **STATUS** Villain
SPECIAL POWERS/ABILITIES A cyborg who has the power to disrupt molecular bonds in others, causing powerful explosions; flight.

The first Faora was a devoted lieutenant to GENERAL ZOD of Krypton, a powerful military figure and the ideological and physical adversary of Jor-El, SUPERMAN's father. Faora and fellow lieutenant Kru-El took control of Zod's forces after his death at Jor-El's hands. Faora and Kru-El died while battling Kryptonian extremists, but their DNA was merged to create a clone of Zod, who was raised as if he were the General's son.

The third Faora was an orphan in the Russian Federation's meta-human development program. The teenaged girl, a cyborg, was recruited by General Zod and renamed Faora after his slain Kryptonian lieutenant, becoming his most valuable assistant and second-in-command. After altering the sun's radiation and stripping away the metagene powers of Earth's heroes, Zod died in battle with the Man of Steel, and Faora was left to repair his damage before being taken into custody. **PJ**

FASTBAK

FIRST APPEARANCE THE NEW GODS (1st series) #5 (October 1971)
STATUS Hero (deceased) **REAL NAME** None
OCCUPATION Inventor/balladeer **BASE** New Genesis
HEIGHT 6ft 1in **WEIGHT** 197 lbs **EYES** Blue **HAIR** Reddish blond
SPECIAL POWERS/ABILITIES Aeropads in boots enable superspeed flight; resistant to friction and the effects of high-velocity travel.

One of the NEW GODS of the distant planet New Genesis, fleet-footed Fastbak is known for his ability to travel at tremendous speeds on the aeropads he invented for his boots. Once he even outpaced the harbinger of death known as the BLACK RACER, as well as a phalanx of Apokoliptian Parademons, to save the life of fellow New God and friend Esak. In addition, Fastbak is an accomplished singer and composer of ballads. Fastbak's speed could not save him when doom came to the Fourth World. He numbered among the casualties during the Death of the New Gods event, his soul stripped from his body by a mysterious and omnipotent assailant. **SB**

FASTBALL

FIRST APPEARANCE JUSTICE LEAGUE OF AMERICA #234 (January 1985)
STATUS Villain (missing in action) **REAL NAME** Malone (first name unknown)
OCCUPATION Assassin **BASE** Detroit
HEIGHT 5ft 11in **WEIGHT** 185 lbs **EYES** Blue **HAIR** Unknown
SPECIAL POWERS/ABILITIES Super-fast reflexes and speed; prefers to strike from a distance, hurling explosives.

Recruited from Tampa, Florida, by the alien OVERMASTER, Fastball's background is unknown. He joined the Overmaster's CADRE, training with them for weeks before being unleashed against the JUSTICE LEAGUE OF AMERICA. Preferring to pitch explosives than go hand-to-hand against opponents, Fastball has proven a not terribly bright criminal. Clearly a would-be baseball pitcher, Fastball's skills seem under-developed, making him an easy target for the League. He and the Cadre later became affiliates of DOCTOR POLARIS and suffered defeat at the hands of the corporate super-team POWER COMPANY. Fastball apparently died at the hands of an OMAC unit prior to the Infinite Crisis. **RG**

FATALITY

FIRST APPEARANCE GREEN LANTERN (3rd series) # 83 (February 1997)
STATUS Villain **REAL NAME** Yrra Cynril
OCCUPATION Assassin **BASE** The planet Xanshi
HEIGHT 5ft 9in **WEIGHT** 124 lbs **EYES** Brown **HAIR** Black
SPECIAL POWERS/ABILITIES One of the most skilled martial artists and weapons masters in the galaxy.

The eldest child of the royal family of the planet Xanshi, Yrra Cynril was sent by her parents to study with the legendary Warlords of Okaara. While Yrra was training with the Warlords, becoming a master of martial arts and other combat, Xanshi was accidentally destroyed by the arrogance of GREEN LANTERN John Stewart. When Yrra learned of this, she vowed vengeance on the entire GREEN LANTERN CORPS.

As Fatality, Yrra traveled the galaxy, murdering former Green Lanterns. Traveling to Earth, Fatality tried to kill Kyle Rayner, the last Green Lantern. Their battle took them to a distant planet, where Fatality learned from Rayner that Stewart was responsible for Xanshi's destruction. Fatality has served with the SECRET SOCIETY OF SUPER-VILLAINS and the INJUSTICE LEAGUE, while carving out an interstellar career as a bounty hunter. **PJ**

DEATH-DEALER
Fatality's desire for vengeance led her to cleave through more than one Green Lantern with her energy blade.

FATAL FIVE

FIRST APPEARANCE Adventure Comics #352 (January 1967)
STATUS Villain team **BASE** Mobile
MEMBERS AND POWERS
Emerald Empress Vast powers stemming from the Emerald Eye.
Tharok Cyborg strength and advanced intellect.
Mano Can disintegrate with his touch
The Persuader Carries an atomic ax.
Validus Superstrength and invulnerability.

EARLY CLASH The Fatal Five often battled the Legion.

FORCE FIVE Mutual mistrust hinders the team, but their powers can be terrifying when combined. Braniac 13 employed copies of the Fatal Five to protect his Warworld when venturing back into the 21st century.

THE MEMBERS OF THE FATAL FIVE comprise some of the worst criminals of the late 30th century. Together, they are an almost unstoppable force for mayhem and murder. Their violent tendencies landed them behind bars long before anyone conceived the idea of a Fatal Five super-team. THAROK was a half-cyborg whose body had been reconstructed following a terrible accident; his electronically-amplified brain made him a brilliant strategist and leader. Empress' true name was Saryva of Vengar, and she delighted in destruction and pain. Mano was a mutant whose glowing right hand could disintegrate anything it touched; he used this power to destroy his polluted homeworld of Angtu. The Persuader carried an atomic ax that could slice through anything and shared he a psychic link with the weapon. Validus was a an invulnerable colossus of staggering strength.

THE WARMAKER

In one version of reality, the Fatal Five came into being when Earth's President Chu ordered their formation in order to spark a war. The Fatal Five soon came into conflict with the Legionnaires, triggering a fierce battle that ended in victory thanks to the involvement of the Legion Rescue Squad. The Legion executed a sting operation to prove President Chu's complicity in the affair.

The U.P. Council removed Chu from office and industrialist R.J. Brande (see BRANDE, R.J.) became president in her wake. Later, the Empress bonded to the all-powerful artifact known as the Emerald Eye of Ekron, becoming the Emerald Empress. She freed the others and led the Fatal Five into other clashes with the Legion, including a hijacking of the Legion Outpost and a scuffle with new Legionnaire TIMBER WOLF.

As an odd side note to Fatal Five history, the tyrant BRAINIAC 13 generated hard-light images of the team as guards for his Warworld when he traveled back in time to the 21st century.

Another version of the Fatal Five time-travelled to the modern era from the 31st century, threatening both BATMAN and the new BLUE BEETLE in their pursuit of a valuable relic. DW

VALIDUS
The powerhouse of the Fatal Five is a simple-minded giant largely under the control of Tharok. His bolts of mental lightning are powerful enough to fry Kryptonians and Daxamites.

THE FATAL FIVE 1) Mano **2)** Persuader **3)** Validus **4)** Tharok **5)** Emerald Empress

KEY STORYLINES

- **LEGION OF SUPER-HEROES #34 (APRIL 1998):** The Fatal Five battle the Legion of Super-Heroes, in the first Fatal Five storyline to appear in the new Legion chronology
- **SUPERMAN #171 (AUGUST 2001):** A duplicate Fatal Five squares off against the Man of Steel, providing a yardstick for measuring the team's considerable might.
- **THE LEGION #16 (MARCH 2003):** New Legionnaire Timber Wolf receives a baptism of fire as he is forced to battle the entire might of the Fatal Five.

FATHER TIME

FIRST APPEARANCE SEVEN SOLDIERS: FRANKENSTEIN #3 (April 2006)
STATUS Villain **REAL NAME** Unknown
OCCUPATION Director of S.H.A.D.E. **BASE** Washington D.C.
HEIGHT Variable **WEIGHT** Variable **EYES** Variable **HAIR** Variable
SPECIAL POWERS/ABILITIES Apparently immortal; is able to regenerate inside new bodies.

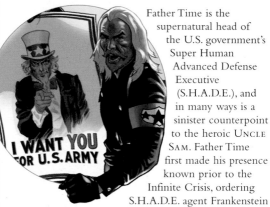

Father Time is the supernatural head of the U.S. government's Super Human Advanced Defense Executive (S.H.A.D.E.), and in many ways is a sinister counterpoint to the heroic UNCLE SAM. Father Time first made his presence known prior to the Infinite Crisis, ordering S.H.A.D.E. agent Frankenstein (*see* SPAWN OF FRANKENSTEIN) into battle against the Sheeda. He seemingly died at the hands of BLACK ADAM during the event known as World War III, but reappeared in a new body.

Father Time then gathered new versions of classic heroes, including DOLL MAN, PHANTOM LADY, and the HUMAN BOMB, to work at S.H.A.D.E. But the reappearance of Uncle Sam led to most of these agents uniting under his banner instead as the new FREEDOM FIGHTERS. Father Time apparently possesses limitless powers of resurrection, but his motives remain a mystery. **DW**

FAUST, FELIX

FIRST APPEARANCE JUSTICE LEAGUE OF AMERICA (1st series) #10 (March 1962)
STATUS Villain **REAL NAME** Felix Faust
OCCUPATION Sorcerer **BASE** Mobile
HEIGHT 5ft 11in **WEIGHT** 172 lbs **EYES** Brown **HAIR** Brown
SPECIAL POWERS/ABILITIES Vast talents in spellcasting; great knowledge of the occult; experienced at summoning demonic entities.

Felix Faust counts his age in millennia, and is known to have clashed with the magician Nommo (DOCTOR MIST) in the ancient African empire of Kor. Resurrected in the 20th century in the body of minor sorcerer Dekan Drache, Faust studied hard to regain his black-magic mastery. To gain further power, Faust released the DEMONS THREE by forcing the newly-created JUSTICE LEAGUE OF AMERICA to retrieve the items that imprisoned the hellspawned trio. The scheme failed, but Faust became a perennial irritant to the Justice League during its early years. Following the Infinite Crisis, Faust posed as DOCTOR FATE and tricked the ELONGATED MAN into believing he could resurrect his dead wife. Faust wound up imprisoned in Fate's tower until freed by BLACK ADAM. **DW**

FEARSOME FIVE, THE

FIRST APPEARANCE NEW TEEN TITANS (1st series) #3 (January 1981)
STATUS Villain team (disbanded) **BASE** Mobile
ORIGINAL MEMBERS AND POWERS
DOCTOR LIGHT I (LEADER) Telekinetic and telepathic abilities.
PSIMON Vast mental powers.
SHIMMER (DECEASED) Able to change one element into another.
MAMMOTH Shimmer's brother; superhuman strength.
GIZMO Turns random objects into tools or weapons.

Tired of being bested by super heroes, inept villain DOCTOR LIGHT I advertised for super-villains to join him in *The Underworld* Star, a newsletter for criminals. He had several replies, notably from the psionic PSIMON, the Australian mutants SHIMMER and MAMMOTH, and little GIZMO. They banded together as the Fearsome Five, only to be defeated repeatedly by the TEEN TITANS. Psimon supplanted Doctor Light as team leader and the outfit grew more menacing. Psimon added JINX, an East Indian sorceress, and the explosive man known as NEUTRON. The Fearsome Five disbanded following defeats by SUPERMAN and the New Titans. Gizmo reformed, and was working for S.T.A.R. Labs when Psimon sent him plunging into a subatomic universe. Psimon killed Mammoth and Shimmer. The team was recently reformed by DOCTOR SIVANA who brought Mammoth and Shimmer back to life, before being defeated by the OUTSIDERS. **RG**

THE FEARSOME FIVE
1) *Jinx* 2) *Psimon* 3) *Mammoth*
4) *Shimmer* 5) *Gizmo*

FURY FORCE:
1) *Lashina* 2) *Stompa* 3) *Artemis*
4) *Mad Harriet* 5) *Bernadeth*
6) *Gilotina* 7) *Bloody Mary* 8) *Chessure*
9) *Speed Queen* 10) *Malice Vundabarr*

FEMALE FURIES

FIRST APPEARANCE MISTER MIRACLE (1st series) #6 (February 1972)
STATUS Villain team **BASE** Apokolips
CURRENT MEMBERS AND POWERS
Bernadeth (leader) Carries burning fahren-knife.
Lashina Wields flexible steel bands.
Mad Harriet Has energized power spikes on her fists.
Stompa Wears heavy-matter boots that can crush anything and trigger earthquakes.
Artemis Commands cybernetic wolfpack; a skilled archer.
Gilotina Hands that can cut through anything.
Bloody Mary Vampire with mesmerism powers.
Speed Queen Can move at superspeed on roller blades.
Malice Vundabarr Young girl who controls Chessure.
Chessure Shadow monster.

The Female Furies are the elite shock troops of Apokolips, bringing terror to those unfortunate enough to incur DARKSEID's wrath. Trained by GRANNY GOODNESS, each woman possesses a specialized ability that makes them unstoppable when they work as a team. BIG BARDA originally led the Female Furies but abandoned the group when she followed her love, MISTER MIRACLE, to Earth. BERNADETH, sister of Darkseid's boot-licker DESAAD, assumed control of the Furies and led them in a failed mission to retrieve their lost sister. Lashina, who vied with Bernadeth for leadership, was left behind on Earth in a later mission and became a member of the SUICIDE SQUAD under the name Duchess. Assembling her own Suicide Squad strike force, Lashina returned to Apokolips seeking to become head of the Furies. Lashina killed Bernadeth, but Darkseid killed Lashina for her impertinence. He soon brought them both back to life, however, and Lashina sullenly serves under Bernadeth's command. Darkseid recently dispatched the Furies to obtain Kara Zor-El, who had just arrived on Earth. He saw in her the spark for her to lead the team and fill Barda's spot. Associated with the core team are the Fury Cadets, less-experienced members who long to prove their combat skills to their beloved Granny. Among their number are the vampiric Bloody Mary and the reformed Gilotina. **DW**

120

FERRO

First appearance ADVENTURES OF SUPERMAN #540 (November 1996)
Status Hero   **Real name** Andrew Nolan
Occupation Legionnaire   **Base** Legion World, U.P. Space
Height 5ft 7in   **Weight** 155 lbs   **Eyes** Green   **Hair** Brown
Special powers/abilities Formerly able to transform himself into flexible and impervious iron; now trapped in metal form.

Born in the 20th century, Andrew Nolan and his twin brother, Douglas, were the sons of famous film actress Nancy Nolan, who abandoned her children as a result of her horror at their grotesque facial deformities. The boys were institutionalized by the unscrupulous Dr. 30 and his Threelove Corporation, which sought to capitalize on the Nolans' shared ability to transform their bodies into malleable iron. Escaping Dr. 30's control, Andrew ran away to Metropolis, where he used his power to aid time-traveling members of the LEGION OF SUPER-HEROES as the teen super hero Ferro. Andrew's brother Douglas—himself a hero called Ingot—apparently died in a vain attempt to reignite Earth's sun, extinguished by the Sun-Eater. Ultimately, PARALLAX succeeded where Ingot failed.

Andrew opted to remain with the Legion and return with them to the 30th century as a member of the team. Although Nolan was given the opportunity to alter his deformed face via surgery to make it more normal in appearance, he chose to retain his individuality. However, following one of the Legion's adventures, Ferro became permanently trapped in his metal form, yet another ironic chapter in this young hero's ongoing hard luck story. **SB**

IRON MASK *Ferro, before fate enclosed his body in iron.*

FEVER PITCH *Fever had no real control over her power or the moral guidance in the use of her skills—until she joined one version of the Doom Patrol.*

FEVER

First appearance DOOM PATROL (3rd series) #1 (December 2001)
Status Hero (missing)   **Real name** Shyleen Lao
Occupation Adventurer   **Base** New York City
Height 5ft 5in   **Weight** 134 lbs   **Eyes** Brown   **Hair** Blonde
Special powers/abilities Can generate intense heat over short distances, to superheat a gun in a criminal's hands or soften metal to break or reshape it; exact limits of her power are unknown.

When businessman Thayer Jost acquired the rights to the DOOM PATROL name, he set about finding some new members. No one knows how he found Shyleen Lao, or how he recruited her to join his new team. The youngest member of the reformed Doom Patrol, Shyleen's developing heat powers remained erratic, possibly because she was still maturing or because she was untrained. For a brief time, she had some control under ROBOTMAN II's tutelage, but left on her own, still struggling with control issues. Shyleen was a complex mix of gumption and adolescent fear. She liked being part of the team and facing great dangers but could also be easily terrified by those same threats. Since the Doom Patrol disbanded, her whereabouts are unknown. **RG**

FILM FREAK

First Appearance BATMAN #395 (May 1986)
Status Villain   **Real Name** Burt Weston, aka "Edison"
Occupation Psychopathic criminal   **Base** Gotham City
Height 5ft 11in   **Weight** 175 lbs   **Eyes** Brown   **Hair** Black
Special powers/abilities Photographic memory for cinema, gift for imaginative crime.

Film Freak is the alter ego of Burt Weston, a villain obsessed with cinema. He emerged in Gotham as one of the city's many gimmick villains, and often found himself at odds with the BATMAN. His *modus operandi* consisted of executing crimes based on those from classic movies, a pattern that allowed others to deduce his targets.

In an updated form, the Film Freak reemerged on the Gotham scene when he committed a string of film-themed crimes, culminating in the theft of a nuclear bomb. He also joined forces with ANGLE MAN to target CATWOMAN, using knowledge of her civilian identity. As soon as Catwoman had captured the pair, she forced ZATANNA to use her magic to mind-wipe them both. **DW**

FIRE

First appearance DC COMICS PRESENTS #46 (June 1982)
Status Hero   **Real name** Beatriz Bonilla DaCosta
Occupation Former spy, model, and adventurer; webcam star
Base New York City
Height 5ft 8in   **Weight** 140 lbs   **Eyes** Green   **Hair** Green
Special powers/abilities Can transform into a being of living green fire; projection of green flame blasts; power of flight.

Born and raised in Brazil, Beatriz DaCosta became a spy for the Brazilian secret service, Espiaos Nacionales. Her first mission was to track down some experimental equipment that produced the incendiary material Pyroplasm. Botching the mission, Beatriz was exposed to Pyroplasm and discovered she could breathe flame from her mouth. Taking the name Green Fury, she joined the GLOBAL GUARDIANS.

Years later, Beatriz, now called Fire, and her best friend, Ice, joined the JUSTICE LEAGUE OF AMERICA. During the alien invasion, Fire's powers were dramatically increased. After Ice's death at the hands of the OVERMASTER and the disbanding of her Justice League, Fire returned to Rio De Janeiro. Fire joined CHECKMATE as a field agent, working her way through the ranks to become the Black King's Knight. Blackmailed by Amanda Waller (*see* WALLER, AMANDA) into performing unsanctioned assassinations, she found comfort in the return of her friend ICE. **PJ**

FIERY *Beatriz DaCosta has been a secret agent, supermodel, Web site provacateur, and member of the JLA.*

FIREBIRD

First appearance FIRESTORM, THE NUCLEAR MAN #69 (March 1989)
Status Hero   **Real name** Serafina Arkadina
Occupation Adventurer   **Base** Russian Federation
Height 5ft 3in   **Weight** 122 lbs   **Eyes** Blue   **Hair** Blonde
Special powers/abilities She is telepathic and has the power to hypnotize people.

Serafina Arkadina is a young woman from the Russian Federation who was born with various psychic powers. Taking the name Firebird, Serafina joined a number of other super-powered Russian teenagers on the team called Soyuz.

For most of their young careers, Soyuz were pursued by the K.G.B. and other Russian intelligence agencies. After their bravery during the alien invasion, the Russian government relaxed its efforts to track Soyuz's activities.

TELEPATHIC *Firebird took her codename to disguise her true powers, which are all psychic in nature.*

Firebird is the leader of the Soyuz, and her uncle, Mikhail Arkadin, is the Russian hero Pozhar, who was once fused with the fire elemental Firestorm. **PJ**

FIREBRAND II

FIRST APPEARANCE ALL-STAR SQUADRON #5 (January 1982)
STATUS Hero (deceased)　**REAL NAME** Danette Reilly
OCCUPATION Adventurer　**BASE** New York City
HEIGHT 5ft 5in　**WEIGHT** 128 lbs　**EYES** Blue　**HAIR** Red
SPECIAL POWERS/ABILITIES Generated fire from hands; mental discipline prevented the fire burning her body or clothing, even absorbing it into her body; power of flight.

FIREHAIR

FIRST APPEARANCE SHOWCASE #85 (September 1969)
STATUS Hero (deceased)　**REAL NAME** Unknown
OCCUPATION Warrior　**BASE** Great Western Plains, circa 1820
HEIGHT 5ft 10in　**WEIGHT** 188 lbs　**EYES** Blue　**HAIR** Red
SPECIAL POWERS/ABILITIES Daring fighter; expert horseman and marksman, especially with bow and arrow.

BROTHER AND SISTER
Rod and Danette Reilly discovered they could accomplish more by leaving their civilian identities behind. Sadly, both died at the hands of enemies.

FIREBRAND I

FIRST APPEARANCE POLICE COMICS #1 (August 1941)
STATUS Hero (deceased)　**REAL NAME** Rod Reilly
OCCUPATION Adventurer　**BASE** New York City
HEIGHT 6ft　**WEIGHT** 185 lbs　**EYES** Blue　**HAIR** Brown
SPECIAL POWERS/ABILITIES Superb athlete and boxer.

Bored with being one of the idle rich, Rod Reilly trained with his friend, ex-heavyweight boxer "Slugger" Dunn, donned a red and pink costume and took a flaming torch as his calling card. As Firebrand, he battled crime in New York City. In 1941 Reilly enlisted in the U.S. Navy and was injured during the Japanese attack on Pearl Harbor. He bestowed the title of Firebrand on his sister Danette, who had gained the mutant ability to manipulate fire. However, Rod Reilly's career as Firebrand was not over. He recovered from his injuries and joined UNCLE SAM'S FREEDOM FIGHTERS to battle the Nazis. His adventuring came to an end when a confrontation with the villain Silver Ghost transformed him into a statue of solid silver. **DW**

While conducting research in Hawaii, vulcanologist Danette Reilly encountered time-traveling felon Per Degaton. The encounter left her with the ability to and create fire with her hands. She returned to New York just after the Japanese bombing of Pearl Harbor in 1941, during which her brother Rod was injured. Learning that Rod was FIREBRAND I, she modified one of his uniforms and became Firebrand II, joining the ALL-STAR SQUADRON. Danette became a leading member, and mentored younger heroes when they joined the team. During her adventures, she fell in love with the SHINING KNIGHT. They married, and she later became the adoptive mother of Terri Rothstein, future mother of the ATOM-SMASHER. Danette was eventually killed, probably by the DRAGON KING, one of the All-Stars' major foes. The Shining Knight avenged his wife's demise. **RG**

Lone survivor of a wagon train massacre by Blackfoot Indians, a blue-eyed, red-haired infant boy was spared by the Blackfoot chief, Grey Cloud, and raised as one of his own. A Blackfoot shaman had foreseen the coming of a great warrior not of the tribe. This warrior would rise from death and defend the Native Americans, yet would be despised by both his own people and those he sought to help. Grey Cloud believed his adopted son, Firehair, would become that great warrior. Scorned by most of the tribe, Firehair learned to out-shoot, out-ride, and out-wrestle any of his peers. When Firehair was 18, Grey Cloud sent him into the mountains to cleanse his body and spirit so that he could return a man. In dreams, Firehair recalled his infancy and true heritage. Confused, he returned to Grey Cloud, who dispatched him to a frontier town so that he might find the answers he sought. Spurned by the locals, Firehair vowed to travel the world until he found where he truly belonged. During his wanderings, he fulfilled the portents of the Blackfoot shaman, thanklessly helping those in need, regardless of race. The circumstances of his death remain one of the lingering mysteries of the Old West. **SB**

FIREBRAND III

FIRST APPEARANCE FIREBRAND #1 (February 1996)
STATUS Hero (deceased)　**REAL NAME** Alexander "Alex" Sanchez
OCCUPATION Adventurer　**BASE** New York City
HEIGHT 6ft　**WEIGHT** 188 lbs　**EYES** Brown　**HAIR** Black
SPECIAL POWERS/ABILITIES High-tech suit enhanced strength and enabled discharge of fiery energy bolts.

FIREFLY

FIRST APPEARANCE DETECTIVE COMICS #184 (June 1952)
STATUS Villain　**REAL NAME** Garfield Lyons
OCCUPATION Arsonist　**BASE** Gotham City
HEIGHT 5ft 11in　**WEIGHT** 167 lbs　**EYES** Blue　**HAIR** White with black temples
SPECIAL POWERS/ABILITIES Insulated battlesuit equipped with flamethrower, grenade launchers, and wings that allow flight.

FIREHAWK

FIRST APPEARANCE FURY OF FIRESTORM #17 (October 1983)
STATUS Hero　**REAL NAME** Lorraine Reilly
OCCUPATION Adventurer　**BASE** New York City
HEIGHT 5ft 7in　**WEIGHT** 136 lbs　**EYES** Blue　**HAIR** (Lorraine) Red
SPECIAL POWERS/ABILITIES Makes objects burst into flame; her hair and parts of her body seem to be on fire, but the fire does not harm her; can fly at great speed.

A terrible accident traumatized New York City detective Alex Sanchez physically and mentally. His will to live was rekindled by wealthy Noah Hightower, who outfitted Alex with armor that turned him into Firebrand. The third hero of that name, Firebrand thwarted evil in the Big Apple. Firebrand died in an underground gladiatorial game run by the villainess ROULETTE. Injected with drugs, Firebrand fought a drugged-up CHECKMATE Knight to a standstill. Firebrand III died in the arena, and a new Firebrand, Andre Twist, has since taken his place. After gaining flame abilities following CHEMO'S poisoning of the city of Blüdhaven, Twist followed the call of UNCLE SAM and joined the FREEDOM FIGHTERS as
Firebrand IV. **SB**

Garfield Lyons is a pyromaniac obsessed with starting large, dangerous fires and watching them burn. Lyons was a poverty-stricken young man who turned to petty crime but was captured by BATMAN and ROBIN after his first robbery. Inspired by a glowing firefly, Lyons took the insect's name and embarked on a different kind of career, torching parts of Gotham City and exalting in the death and destruction his fires caused. Firefly fought Batman and Robin a number of times, until he was hired by villain Nicholas Scratch to create the biggest fire Gotham City had ever seen. Hoping to burn Gotham to the ground, Firefly was himself horribly burned when a nearby chemical factory he set ablaze erupted in a fiery explosion. Scarred by burns that cover 90 percent of his body, Firefly was incarcerated in Blackgate Prison. **PJ**

An attempt by the super-criminal Multiplex and the villainous industrialist Henry Hewitt to recreate the accident that gave birth to FIRESTORM, the NUCLEAR MAN resulted in the transformation of Lorraine Reilly, daughter of Senator Walter Reilly, into Firehawk. Brainwashed into fighting the Firestorm, Firehawk shook off her programming and helped Firestorm defeat Hewitt in his guise as Tokamak. Firehawk and Firestorm became partners and friends until Firestorm went through personal changes. Later elected as a New York senator, Lorraine joined the new Firestorm, Jason Rusch, to serve as his merge-partner for calling forth the Firestorm powers. **RG**

FIRESTORM, THE NUCLEAR MAN

FIRST APPEARANCE (II) FIRESTORM (2nd series) #1 (July 2004)
STATUS Hero **REAL NAME** Jason Rusch
OCCUPATION Student **BASE** Detroit, Michigan
HEIGHT 5ft 10in **WEIGHT** 165 lbs **EYES** Brown **HAIR** Black
SPECIAL POWERS/ABILITIES Flight; can rearrange the atomic and molecular structure of inorganic matter.

UNDERSTANDING THE HERO FIRESTORM is far from a straightforward proposition. Brought into being as the synthesis of two individuals, Firestorm later went through a number of alternate fusions whereby varied combinations of people united to create a single champion. The original Firestorm came about when college student Ronnie Raymond and physics professor Martin Stein fused into one superpowered "nuclear man" in an explosion at the Hudson nuclear facility. In their flame-topped Firestorm form, the two could fly and rearrange matter at the molecular level. Ron remained in control of Firestorm, while Martin hitchhiked along as a disembodied consciousness and took an advisory role, his scientific brain providing the complex atomic calculations needed for Firestorm's advanced powers.

MARTIN STEIN *The professor found his calling as a fire elemental.*

FROST AND FIRE *Normally a bitter enemy, the villain Killer Frost was hypnotized into loving Firestorm during the Crisis.*

ELEMENTAL WARFARE

Operating out of Pittsburgh, Ron and Martin made an efficient team against the likes of Killer Frost (*see* KILLER FROST II)and BLACK BISON. The Russian hero POZHAR later clashed with Firestorm above the Nevada desert. When a nuclear missile struck the two combatants, Ronnie and Pozhar merged into the second incarnation of Firestorm. Controlled by the amnesiac mind of Martin Stein, this Firestorm eventually learned that it had been fated to become Earth's fire elemental—but only with Martin as host. Ronnie and Pozhar had apparently been unnecessary roadblocks in the Earth spirit Gaea's plan. After Firestorm's involvement in an "elemental war" involving SWAMP THING (earth), NAIAD (water), and RED TORNADO (air), as well as the addition of another Russian, Svarozhich, to the mix, Firestorm fissioned off the superfluous personalities to become the "correct" Firestorm—a fire elemental, controlled by Martin Stein alone.

Yet this wasn't the end of the Firestorm saga. Ron Raymond realized that the Firestorm powers had been written into his genetic code, and served with EXTREME JUSTICE and the POWER COMPANY before joining the JUSTICE LEAGUE OF AMERICA. The Ron Raymond Firestorm perished in a battle with supervillains, and the powers passed to a Detroit youth named Jason Rusch.

Rusch struggled to deal with his almost-limitless abilities. He fought in outer space during the Infinite Crisis, finding welcome help when Martin Stein returned from the cosmos to act as the other half of the "Firestorm matrix" that powered the merged superhero. Following the Crisis, Firestorm assembled a failed, second-string Justice League, then used FIREHAWK as his partner in the Firestorm matrix after Martin Stein's disappearance. **DW**

KEY STORYLINES

• **FIRESTORM, THE NUCLEAR MAN #90 (OCTOBER 1989):** The Elemental Wars kick off, signaling the increasing complexity of this super-hero title.
• **EXTREME JUSTICE #5 (JUNE 1995):** Raymond regains his Firestorm powers, and the Martin Stein fire elemental drops in for a visit.
• **JLA #69 (OCTOBER 2002):** Firestorm joins the Justice League of America while the original team is trapped in the ancient undersea world of Atlantis.

APT PUPIL *As Firestorm, Jason Rusch soon accumulated his own rogue's gallery. Here he faces off against the brilliant Pupil.*

BURNING UP *Ron Raymond's reacquisition of the Firestorm powers led to a spot on the world's greatest super hero team. Recently, a young man named Jason Rusch has emerged as the possible inheritor of the Firestorm title.*

THE FLASH

THE SCARLET SPEEDSTER

JASON PETER "JAY" GARRICK (FLASH I)
FIRST APPEARANCE FLASH COMICS #1 (January 1940)
STATUS Hero   **OCCUPATION** Research scientist
BASE Keystone City   **HEIGHT** 5ft 11in   **WEIGHT** 178 lbs
EYES Blue   **HAIR** Brown, with gray temples
SPECIAL POWERS/ABILITIES Can run at near lightspeed; can vibrate his molecules and pass right through objects; ages at a far slower pace than most human beings.

BARTHOLOMEW "BARRY" ALLEN (FLASH II)
FIRST APPEARANCE SHOWCASE #4 (October 1956)
STATUS Hero (deceased)   **OCCUPATION** Police chemist
BASE Central City   **HEIGHT** 5ft 11in   **WEIGHT** 179 lbs
EYES Blue   **HAIR** Blond
SPECIAL POWERS/ABILITIES Could run at near lightspeed; could also pass through objects or phase into other dimensions.

WALLACE "WALLY" WEST (FLASH III)
FIRST APPEARANCE (as Kid Flash) THE FLASH (1st series) #110 (January 1960); (as the Flash) CRISIS ON INFINITE EARTHS #12 (March 1986)
STATUS Hero   **OCCUPATION** Adventurer   **BASE** Keystone City
HEIGHT 6ft   **WEIGHT** 175 lbs   **EYES** Green   **HAIR** Red
SPECIAL POWERS/ABILITIES Can run at lightspeed; can vibrate through solid objects causing them to explode; can lend his speed to moving objects or people by touch; can form a protective costume from "living" Speed Force; traveling faster than lightspeed will hurl him across interdimensional timespace.

THEY HAVE BEEN CALLED the Fastest Men Alive—three generations of super heroes granted the power to tap into the extradimensional energy field called the Speed Force by a scientific experiment gone awry. Each hero named himself the Flash and became the progenitor of an age of champions, perpetuating a legacy of courage and valor that extends to the 853rd century and beyond.

NO TIME TO LOSE The Flash and Dr. Flura must thwart Star Sapphire's deadly schemes or the Earth has only two minutes to live!

FASTER THAN A... Jay Garrick makes his debut as the Flash, the fastest hero of World War II.

JAY GARRICK
A failed college football player in the 1930s, Jay Garrick became a research scientist. By accidentally inhaling the hyper-charged atoms of a radioactive liquid, Garrick gained incredible superspeed. Garbed in a red and blue uniform, Garrick became the Flash and helped form the legendary JUSTICE SOCIETY OF AMERICA and the wartime ALL-STAR SQUADRON. Forced into retirement during the McCarthy era in the 1950s, Garrick was placed in suspended animation by the villainous Fiddler but was rescued by Barry Allen, the second Flash. Spared the ravages of old age, Garrick married his girlfriend, Joan Williams, and briefly retired, but he returned to active duty with the most recent incarnation of the JSA.

BARRY ALLEN
Slowpoke police chemist Barry Allen idolized Jay Garrick, the super hero Flash. During a late, stormy night at the police station laboratory, a bolt of lightning crashed through the window and shattered the vials of chemicals surrounding Allen. Suddenly imbued with the power to move at near lightspeed, Barry took on the name of his Golden Age idol, the Flash, and, along with GREEN LANTERN Hal Jordan and AQUAMAN, helped usher in the Silver Age of heroes.

As the Flash, Allen was one of the founders of the JUSTICE LEAGUE OF AMERICA. When his fiancée, Iris (see ALLEN, IRIS), was apparently slain by the REVERSE-FLASH, Allen killed his hated foe. After a lengthy trial, the Flash retired to the 30th century, where he sired the Tornado twins. Tragically, Allen died saving the Earth from the nihilistic Anti-Monitor (see Great Battles, pp. 362–3) by destroying his antimatter cannon, aimed directly at the planet.

SLOW POKE Police chemist Barry Allen was a notoriously methodical, plodding scientist known for being constantly late. When he was doused by chemicals, however, he gained the power of superspeed, becoming the second Flash.

ZOOM The name of Zoom has long haunted the Flash family. Recently, Zoom was responsible for Flash's wife, Linda Park, miscarrying their twins.

FLASH OF LIGHT As the Flash, Barry Allen, Green Lantern Hal Jordan, and several other heroes founded the legendary Justice League of America. Despite Allen and Jordan's differences—Allen was a quiet scientist and Jordan an adventurous hothead—the two became close friends. Their friendship would last for years, until each met their own tragic end.

THE DEATH OF BARRY ALLEN
Learning that his wife, Iris, was saved from death at the hands of Professor Zoom by a "psychic transplant" in the future into another body, the Flash traveled forward in time to be with her. Tragically, their happiness ended when the Flash was kidnapped by the Anti-Monitor, who planned to use a giant antimatter cannon to destroy the universe. Running faster than ever before, the Flash escaped the Anti-Monitor's bonds and destroyed the cannon. Allen's body disintegrated, but his energies rocketed back in time and became the lightning bolt that shattered the chemicals that originally gave Allen his superspeed.

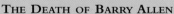

KEY STORYLINES
• *GOLDEN AGE FLASH ARCHIVES:* The original adventures of Jay Garrick, the first Flash, during the 1940s.
• *THE FLASH (1ST SERIES) #123 (SEPTEMBER 1961):* Barry Allen meets his Golden Age namesake for the first time.
• *CRISIS ON INFINITE EARTHS (P/B, 2000):* Barry Allen makes the greatest sacrifice to save the universe from the marauding Anti-Monitor, and Wally West becomes the third Flash!
• *TERMINAL VELOCITY (P/B, 1995):* The Flashes learn that they are attached to the Speed Force, an ancient power.

WALLY WEST

The young nephew of Barry Allen, Wally West was visiting his uncle's laboratory when a bolt of lightning shattered a rack of chemicals in the room. The chemicals spilled on the boy, and duplicated the same accident that created the second Flash. West became the first KID FLASH, the junior partner of the Flash, and founded the TEEN TITANS with the first ROBIN (*see* NIGHTWING), Aqualad (*see* TEMPEST), Speedy (*see* ARSENAL), and WONDER GIRL. After Barry Allen died saving the universe, Kid Flash assumed his costume and identity.

GENERATIONS *Wearing a costume similar to his mentor, Barry Allen, teenaged Wally West learned to use his powers just as well—even vibrating through solid objects.*

THE SPEED FORCE

As the Flash, Wally discovered his link to the Speed Force, an energy source that gives all speedsters their power. Tapping into the Force made Wally the fastest Flash of them all, able to run at the speed of light. One of the founders of the current and most powerful incarnation of the JLA, West has garnered a lethal Rogues Gallery as the champion of Keystone City. The Flash revealed his secret identity to the world and, after several failed romances, fell in love with and married reporter Linda Park (*see* PARK, LINDA). After a battle with the villain Zoom ended in the miscarriage of their unborn twins, West asked the SPECTRE to remove all memories of his identity from the public consciousness—including Linda—to protect those he loved from the dangers he continues to face as the Fastest Man Alive. **PJ**

LOVELY LINDA *Wally West is married to TV journalist turned medical student Linda Park.*

MAGIC RING *Like his predecessor, Wally West keeps his Flash costume in a special ring. The costume is made of the Speed Force itself, covering Wally in a protective sheath.*

FLASHES FROM THE FUTURE

John Fox was a speedster from the 27th century who traveled back to the 21st century to take over the Flash legacy when Wally West disappeared. After West's return, Fox leapt back into the timestream and resettled in the 853rd century. The third Kid Flash is the future daughter of Wally West, who inherited her father's heroic legacy when her slacker brother refused to do so. Walter West, the Flash from an alternate timeline whose wife Linda was slain by KOBRA, briefly replaced the Flash in our timeline, before entering Hypertime to rediscover his own. And Sela Allen, a sentient manifestation of the Speed Force, is the Flash of the 23rd century.

FUGITIVE *Fox, responsible for transplanting Iris Allen across the centuries, became a fugitive for violating the Time Institute's laws of time travel.*

ROGUES GALLERY
The Flash has long had one of the most impressive collections of foes of any hero, and easily the most deadly.

THE FLASH

RETURN TO FORM

Wally's memories of his heroic past soon returned, and he took up the identity of the Flash once again. A time-bending adventure even undid Linda's miscarriage, and she gave birth to twins named Iris and Jai. The events of the Infinite Crisis changed Wally and his family forever. To stop a rampaging Superboy-Prime, Wally joined with Jay Garrick and Kid Flash (Bart Allen) to hurl the alternate-universe Kryptonian to the edge of the Speed Force. Just prior to crossing the threshold, Wally drew Linda and the twins with him into an alternate dimension, inhabited by long-departed speedsters including MAX MERCURY, Johnny Quick (*see* QUICK, JOHNNY), and Barry Allen. Superboy-Prime escaped from this dimension after years of imprisonment, with Bart Allen following him back to Earth. Wally and Linda elected to stay behind and oversee the development of their twins, whose growth appeared to be surging in unpredictable bursts.

BART ALLEN (FLASH IV)
FIRST APPEARANCE FLASH (2nd series) #91 (June 1994) **STATUS** Hero (deceased) **OCCUPATION** Forensics student **BASE** Keystone City **HEIGHT** 5ft 11in **WEIGHT** 178 lbs **EYES** Yellow **HAIR** Brown **SPECIAL POWERS/ABILITIES** Can run at incredible speeds, generate whirlwinds, and vibrate molecules to pass through solid objects.

SUITING UP *Bart followed in Barry Allen's footsteps, even attending the police academy, but he died too young.*

BART ALLEN: THE FOURTH FLASH

Bart Allen, who first emerged on the heroic scene as Impulse before taking up the identity of Kid Flash while with the Teen Titans, became the fourth inheritor of the Flash legacy. To stop Superboy-Prime during the worst fighting of the Infinite Crisis, Bart joined with Jay Garrick and Wally West to hurl the homicidal teenager into the extra-dimensional energy that surrounded the Speed Force. Jay dropped out just before the point of no return, but Bart and Wally both carried Superboy-Prime into an alternate reality where they remained for several years of relative time. To observers on Earth only days had passed, but when Bart returned to Earth he had shed his adolescent gawkiness and grown into adulthood. Wearing Barry Allen's original costume, Bart battled the newly-escaped Superboy-Prime but seemingly exhausted his connection to the Speed Force during the fight. Bart retired from being a super hero, taking a job as an autoworker on a Keystone Motors assembly line. But the rise of the villain the Griffin—secretly Bart's coworker and roommate—revealed that the Speed Force had not abandoned the young man. Bart returned to fighting crime in Keystone and, after a move Los Angeles, studied forensics at the L.A. police academy.

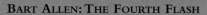

KEYSTONE VICTORY *As the Flash, Bart puts the brakes on his former friend—turned super-villain—the Griffin.*

A HERO LOST

The return of Bart's twisted clone Inertia ushered in the fourth Flash's tragic and untimely death. Inertia gathered the core members of the Flash's Rogues' Gallery— MIRROR MASTER, PIED PIPER, HEAT WAVE, CAPTAIN COLD, TRICKSTER, ABRA KADABRA, AND WEATHER WIZARD—and promised that building a time-freezing device would make them all rich. Inertia activated the device at L.A.'s Getty Center, revealing the machine's true function when he used it to drain the Speed Force from Bart Allen. Though Bart defeated his foe, his lack of powers made him easy prey for the ruthless Rogues, who ended his life. Bart Allen's fellow heroes honored their fallen friend with a public funeral in Keystone and a memorial statue in the city's Flash Museum. In San Francisco, the Teen Titans erected a second statue of Bart outside Titans Tower.

FALLEN HERO *Bart Allen's girlfriend, Valerie Perez, mourns his death in battle.*

THE END *Bart's clone Inertia led the Rogues in their deadly attack.*

THE LIGHTNING SAGA

Wally West's return to Earth came about thanks to the LEGION OF SUPER-HEROES, who traveled a thousand years into the past to enact a strange ritual. By standing in precise locations while holding lightning rods, the members of the Legion hoped to restore a great hero—initially believed to be Barry Allen. It was Wally, however, who emerged through the Legion-created gateway, along with Linda and their (now school-aged) children. His colleagues welcomed Wally back and offered him a spot in the Justice League of America. Wally quickly learned of Bart Allen's murder at the hands of the Rogues. He tracked down Inertia, the mastermind behind the crime, and locked him in a moment of time   frozen forever in statue-like stasis on display in Keystone City's Flash Museum.

SPEEDY JUSTICE *On his super-heroic return, Wally's first order of business was to ensure that the villainous Flash-clone Inertia could never kill again.*

THE NEXT GENERATION

The Wests tried to return to a normal life in Keystone, but the abilities of their twins, Iris and Jai, caused headaches from the start. Iris manifested the power to vibrate her molecules through solid objects, while Jai added muscle mass to achieve temporary feats of super-strength. Though Iris appeared to be ten years old and Jai eight, both had lived slightly over a year in relative time. Their runaway metabolisms governed their development and their burgeoning powers were barely kept in check by mechanical treatments administered by their mother. By default, she had become the world's leading expert on "velocibiology." Iris and Jai got their first taste of their family's heroic lifestyle when they helped their father rid Keystone of intelligent starfish creatures. The fact that children so young have taken on life-threatening risks has raised concern among Wally's Justice League teammates. **PJ/DW**

UNWELCOME GUESTS *Aquatic aliens from another dimension are the latest threat to menace Keystone City.*

LEARNING THE ROPES *The limits of Jai's strength and Iris's phasing are still unknown.*

HIGH-TECH PARENTING *Advanced machines regulate the twins' metabolisms and help prevent premature aging spurts.*

FISHERMAN

FIRST APPEARANCE AQUAMAN (1st series) #21 (June 1965)
STATUS Villain **REAL NAME** Unknown
OCCUPATION Professional criminal **BASE** Mobile
HEIGHT 6ft **WEIGHT** 196 lbs **EYES** Blue **HAIR** Black
SPECIAL POWERS/ABILITIES Wears pressurized SCUBA suit, allowing him to breathe and travel underwater, and carries "fishing rod" weapon.

The Fisherman has often crossed paths with AQUAMAN, for his pressurized bodysuit and ensnaring fishing rod make him an unusually specialized villain.

The Fisherman's schemes— including a plot to arm a rebel attack on Atlantis—have always been foiled by the King of the Seven Seas.

The Fisherman carries a fishing rod made of titanium steel that casts an unbreakable polymer line. He can cast this rod with uncanny accuracy, either tangling his targets with the line or skewering them with barbed lures. He also has a number of special lures that release toxic gas upon impact.

After serving a long prison sentence, the Fisherman is back in circulation. The Fisherman's helmet is actually a parasitic lifeform, able to control the actions of its wearer. **DW**

FLAG, RICH

FIRST APPEARANCE BRAVE AND THE BOLD #25 (September 1959)
STATUS Hero **REAL NAME** Richard Flag
OCCUPATION Government operative **BASE** Mobile
HEIGHT 6ft 1in **WEIGHT** 189 lbs **EYES** Blue **HAIR** Brown
SPECIAL POWERS/ABILITIES Superior hand-to-hand combatant and strategist

The original Rick Flag led the World War II military unit known as the Suicide Squadron, surviving impossible odds to take out enemy installations. He found his skills in demand after the war when he served with the U.S. government's Task Force X and its own Suicide Squad unit. Rick Flag died while battling the gigantic War Wheel.

His son, Rick Flag Jr., took his father's place with the Suicide Squad and briefly served with the FORGOTTEN HEROES. When Amanda Waller (see WALLER, AMANDA) founded an all-new Suicide Squad made up of criminals, Rick Flag led the team despite his distaste for many of its members, and even started a tentative romance with teammate NIGHTSHADE. Rick Flag seemingly died on a solo mission to destroy the headquarters of the Jihad terrorists, but instead spent years in a Qurachi prison until rescued by the BRONZE TIGER.

FLAMEBIRD

FIRST APPEARANCE SECRET ORIGINS ANNUAL #3 (1989)
STATUS Hero **REAL NAME** Mary Elizabeth "Bette" Kane
OCCUPATION College student/adventurer **BASE** Hollywood, CA
HEIGHT 5ft 6in **WEIGHT** 123 lbs **EYES** Blue **HAIR** Blonde
SPECIAL POWERS/ABILITIES Above-average fighter; arsenal includes electrified bolas and gloves, flare-emitting mask lenses, and various tracking devices.

Perky tennis prodigy Bette Kane so idolized the first Robin, Dick Grayson, that she adopted her own costumed alter ego, Flamebird, and formed an unsanctioned West Coast branch of the Teen Titans to impress the Boy Wonder. Unfortunately, Bette's super hero career flamed out and Titans West disbanded not long after receiving an unwelcome reception from Robin and the Teen Titans. Later, following a confrontation between Bette and Nightwing, Robin's new alter ego, Flamebird rose like a phoenix from the ashes as Bette found new purpose. Redesigning Flamebird's costume and equipment, Bette took flight as a more confident super heroine while continuing her studies in sports medicine at U.C.L.A. Flamebird was briefly a member of Titans L.A., a latter-day Titans West that included her roommate Beast Boy, who had been a member of both her previous team and the Teen Titans. However, Titans L.A. proved to be even shorter-lived than its predecessor, and Flamebird has resumed solo flights of adventure. **SB**

FLASHMAN, FUNKY

FIRST APPEARANCE MISTER MIRACLE #6 (January/February 1972)
STATUS Hindrance **REAL NAME** Unknown, if any
OCCUPATION Charlatan **BASE** Mobile
HEIGHT 6ft 1in **WEIGHT** 171 lbs **EYES** Blue **HAIR** Brown
SPECIAL POWERS/ABILITIES Master con artist able to talk his way into or out of any situation.

Funky Flashman has no superpowers, but as the consummate con man he has outwitted some of the most powerful beings on Earth. Flashman is a fast-talker who cares only abut lining his pockets, and for whom friends are merely a means to an end. In one of Flashman's many get-rich-quick schemes, he attached himself to MISTER MIRACLE as a talent manager, which ended when he accidentally attracted the attention of the FEMALE FURIES. He later teamed with the WIZARD to reassemble the SECRET SOCIETY OF SUPER-VILLAINS. More recently, he has launched a number of schemes including the sale of knickknacks bearing the likenesses of heroes and villains. Despite his numerous failures, Flashman has lost none of his enthusiasm. **DW**

FLEUR-DE-LIS

FIRST APPEARANCE BLUE BEETLE (6th series) #19 (December 1987)
STATUS Hero **REAL NAME** Noelle Avril
OCCUPATION Adventurer **BASE** Paris, France
HEIGHT 5ft 6in **WEIGHT** 120 lbs **EYES** Blue **HAIR** White
SPECIAL POWERS/ABILITIES Olympic-level athlete; expert with various weapons, particularly pistols and throwing stars.

The origins of Fleur-de-Lis have yet to be revealed. She used to wear a white body suit decorated with the French royal crest; later in her career she donned a skintight purple and red latex uniform.

Fleur-de-Lis was briefly a member of the GLOBAL GUARDIANS, and then joined France's Department Gamma after the Guardians were disbanded by order of the United Nations. At Department Gamma, Fleur-de-Lis answered exclusively to its director, André Chavard (see CHAVARD, ANDRÉ).

She had a brief romance with Slade Wilson, the assassin known as DEATHSTROKE THE TERMINATOR, while the two searched for his ex-wife Adeline Kane, who had been kidnapped by an international criminal, Jacques "Tuxedo" Morel. **RG**

FLORONIC MAN

FIRST APPEARANCE THE ATOM #1 (July 1962)
STATUS Unresolved **REAL NAME** Jason Woodrue
OCCUPATION Former criminal **BASE** Mobile
HEIGHT 6ft 2in **WEIGHT** 210 lbs **EYES** Red **HAIR** Green
SPECIAL POWERS/ABILITIES Alien knowledge of plant life gives him an advantage over others; also has limited control over local plant forms. Stronger than a human given the density of the wood he inhabits.

Originally a master criminal on an other-dimensional world inhabited by wood nymphs, dryads, Nereids, air sprites, and flower spirits, the being known as Woodrue was banished to Earth for his wicked deeds, where it was hoped he would perish. He survived, taking on the human identity of Jason Woodrue and becoming a teacher. He continued to experiment on plants, ruthlessly investigating the possibilities of human/plant hybridization. One of these trials turned shy student Pamela Isley into the villainous, near-human POISON IVY. Woodrue used his alien knowledge to take control of Earth's plant life and attempted to conquer America with the aid of his plant army. This scheme was foiled by the six-inch super hero the second ATOM. After repeated defeats, Woodrue perfected an elixir that transformed him from fauna to flora, making him a true plantmaster. Defeated and imprisoned by the second GREEN LANTERN, Woodrue was freed by General Sunderland to examine the body of the SWAMP THING. Through this plant elemental, Woodrue became one with the plant kingdom and once more threatened mankind. Swamp Thing stopped him, and Woodrue sought redemption by joining a collection of individuals who had been deemed the first to evolve towards man's next evolution, the NEW GUARDIANS. He now operates on his own, wandering the Earth, seeking a purpose. **RG**

FLYING FOX

FIRST APPEARANCE YOUNG ALL-STARS #1 (June 1987)
STATUS Hero **REAL NAME** Unrevealed
OCCUPATION Adventurer **BASE** Mobile
HEIGHT 5ft 10in **WEIGHT** 170 lbs **EYES** Brown **HAIR** Black
SPECIAL POWERS/ABILITIES Shamanistic talents include flight, invisibility, and the ability to cast fire from his hands.

During World War II, a Nazi U-boat commander hoped to strongarm the Native American Quontauka tribe in northern Canada into launching guerilla attacks on the Canadian government. Instead, by murdering the tribe's chief, he triggered the creation of the super hero Flying Fox. The tribal shaman gave the chief's son the mystical cape and cowl of the flying fox and tattooed the teen's chest with the fox's emblem. As Flying Fox, the young man sought out allies in his fight against the Nazi menace. He soon ran into the teenage heroes of the YOUNG ALL-STARS. Flying Fox became a charter member of the team, fighting alongside them and with the larger ALL-STAR SQUADRON against AXIS AMERIKA for the rest of the war. Flying Fox inherited many mystical abilities from his tribe's shaman, though it is unknown how deeply his talents run. Spells he has manifested include the ability to turn invisible and to control fire. **DW**

FOLDED MAN

FIRST APPEARANCE THE FLASH (2nd series) #153 (October 1999)
STATUS Hero **REAL NAME** Edwin Gauss
OCCUPATION Criminal **BASE** Central City
HEIGHT 5ft 11in **WEIGHT** 182 lbs **EYES** Brown **HAIR** Brown
SPECIAL POWERS/ABILITIES Can transform into a fourth-dimensional state that allows him to reach into the third dimension at any point; can flatten into a two-dimensional form.

The Folded Man is former physicist Edwin Gauss, a young M.I.T. student who was desperate to complete Albert Einstein's unfinished Unified Field theory. After maddening attempts at cracking the theory, and after pirating special software from billionaire Norman Bridges, an electronics entrepreneur, Gauss discovered a way to travel interdimensionally and created a special suit that allowed him to traverse at least four dimensions.

Pursued by the outraged Bridges, who believes that the special suit Gauss created is his by right, the brilliant but deranged M.I.T. tech became the Folded Man and quickly came into conflict with the FLASH III. Able to transform his body any number of ways and teleport across dimensions, the Folded Man was easily able to escape the Fastest Man Alive and remains at large. **PJ**

FORAGER I

FIRST APPEARANCE THE NEW GODS (1st series) #9 (August 1972)
STATUS Hero (deceased) **REAL NAME** None
OCCUPATION Warrior **BASE** New Genesis
HEIGHT 5ft 10in **WEIGHT** 162 lbs **EYES** Blue **HAIR** Black
SPECIAL POWERS/ABILITIES Superb combatant; great speed and leaping abilities; "adheso-pads" on feet enabled him to run up walls; carried defensive shield and acid pod.

DARK NIGHT Forager I met the Batman and toured the Batcave during the Cosmic Odyssey to prevent Darkseid from acquiring the "Anti-Life Equation."

Beneath the surface of New Genesis exists a honeycombed network of colonies belonging to the "bugs," evolved humanoid insects originally brought to the planet as micro-life biological weapons scattered by the armies of Apokolips. Among these creatures was Forager, named so for his great skill at stealing food from the surface. Forager eventually met ORION and LIGHTRAY of the NEW GODS, who helped the bugs to prevent the evil MANTIS—presumably a bug himself—from exterminating their kind. Forager remained an ally of the New Gods for years. He gave his life in defense of the human hero BATMAN when champions from New Genesis and Earth rallied to prevent DARKSEID from finally acquiring the so-called "Anti-Life Equation." Although burning with a long-standing prejudice against the bugs, Orion escorted Forager's body back to the bug colonies, where the Dog of War finally acknowledged Forager as a friend. **SB**

FORAGER II

FIRST APPEARANCE THE NEW GODS (2nd series) #2 (March 1989)
STATUS Hero **REAL NAME** None
OCCUPATION Warrior **BASE** New Genesis
HEIGHT 5ft 9in **WEIGHT** 121 lbs **EYES** White **HAIR** Blue
SPECIAL POWERS/ABILITIES An accomplished warrior wielding many of the same abilities and accoutrements as Forager I.

A second Forager, this one female, was later appointed by the All-Widow and Prime One—queen and highest ranking male of the bugs, respectively—as a new defender of the colonies. Initially following in FORAGER I's footsteps, Forager II also befriended ORION before thwarting MANTIS from uniting outcast bug tribes and using them to spark a nuclear war on Earth. However, Orion falsely believed that Forager II was killed during that conflict. In his rage, Orion transported Mantis's nuclear arsenal to New Genesis, where the missiles exploded above the central colony and decimated the bug population. Forager II enlisted the help of Jimmy Olsen (see OLSEN, JIMMY) during the Death of the New Gods event, trying to uncover the killer. **SB**

FOREVER PEOPLE

FIRST APPEARANCE forever people (1st series) #1 (Feb.–Mar. 1971)
STATUS Hero team (deceased) **BASE** Supertown, New Genesis
MEMBERS AND POWERS
MARK MOONRIDER Has the megaton touch, which emits energy.
BIG BEAR Has superhuman strength.
BEAUTIFUL DREAMER Can create illusions.
VYKIN THE BLACK Has magnetic powers.
SERIFAN Cosmic cartridges create force fields and anti-gravity waves.

THE FOREVER PEOPLE *The team went adventuring aboard a huge Super-Cycle that could fly, pass through solid objects, and even teleport.*
1) *Big Bear* 2) *Beautiful Dreamer* 3) *Vykin*
4) *Serifan* 5) *Mark Moonrider*

At the instruction of the Source, HIGHFATHER of the NEW GODS of the planet New Genesis gathered five children and subjected them to rigorous training in the use of their powers. Highfather ultimately revealed that the unique Mother Boxes (living computers) the young gods' parents had received a decade earlier were a five-piece composite that formed a larger unit and enabled the Forever People to trade places with INFINITY MAN for a short time. Using an oversized Mother Box, the team are able to summon this powerful protector.

The team adventured throughout New Genesis and on Earth for a time. When Infinity Man was apparently destroyed during a battle with DEVILANCE, the Forever People found themselves stranded on the pastoral planet of Adon. The circumstances of their return to New Genesis remain unclear, although VYKIN THE BLACK has indicated that Darkseid brought them back. The Forever People numbered among the casualties during the Death of the New Gods event. MISTER MIRACLE reanimated their corpses but failed to learn the identity of their killer. RG

FOX, LUCIUS

FIRST APPEARANCE BATMAN #307 (January 1979)
STATUS Hero **REAL NAME** Lucius Fox
OCCUPATION CEO of Wayne Enterprises **BASE** Gotham City
HEIGHT 5ft 10in **WEIGHT** 170 lbs **EYES** Brown **HAIR** Black
SPECIAL POWERS/ABILITIES Meticulous and scrupulously honest, Fox is an excellent organizer with brilliant financial acumen.

Lucius Fox is one of the most powerful businessmen in the world. After returning from his training overseas, Bruce Wayne hired Fox as the CEO of Wayne Enterprises, and Lucius is responsible for handling the day-to-day operations of the giant company. A *magna cum laude* graduate of the Morton Business School, Lucius is nevertheless unaware of Bruce Wayne's secret identity as BATMAN, although the CEO knows that Wayne is hardly the foolish playboy the rest of the world thinks he is.

After the devastation of an earthquake turned Gotham City into a No Man's Land, Lucius used his skills and Wayne Enterprise's might to prevent Lex Luthor's LexCorp (see LUTHOR, LEX) from buying up extensive amounts of Gotham real estate. Later, Lucius was targeted by the assassin Cypher for his vast knowledge of Wayne Enterprise's resources but was saved by Batman. Fox remains a powerful corporate leader, one of the most sought after in the world. PJ

FORTUNE, AMOS

FIRST APPEARANCE JUSTICE LEAGUE OF AMERICA #6 (August–September 1961)
STATUS Villain **REAL NAME** Professor Amos Fortune
OCCUPATION Professional criminal **BASE** Mobile
HEIGHT 5ft 8in **WEIGHT** 233 lbs
EYES Black **HAIR** Black
SPECIAL POWERS/ABILITIES Advanced intellect, which he uses to manipulate others; claims special knowledge of the "science of luck."

Being obsessed with luck—good luck, bad luck, how luck can run hot and cold—did not help Amos Fortune during his adolescence. He led a street gang that never advanced beyond petty crime and earned the nickname "Pudge" due to his stocky frame. As an adult he delved into the supposed science of luck and came to believe that the human body possessed "luck glands" that influenced the outside world for good or ill every day.

Using his knowledge to become a professional criminal, he soon came into conflict with the newly-formed JUSTICE LEAGUE OF AMERICA. In his first fight against the League, he strapped the World's Greatest Super Heroes to his Wheel of Misfortune and tried to eliminate their good luck glands with an energy ray. He later used his Wheel of Misfortune to create seven super-beings from seven of the luckiest people on the planet (who'd all been born on the seventh day of the seventh month), but WONDER WOMAN smashed his dreams of grandeur.

Amos Fortune also acted as the leader of the ROYAL FLUSH GANG. This criminal outfit, staffed with Fortune's old friends from his former street gang, assumed a playing card motif with Fortune as the Ace and others filling the roles of King, Queen, Jack, and Ten. During the Infinite Crisis, Fortune escaped a prison facility during the global super-villain breakout prior to the Battle of Metropolis. While fleeing in a helicopter, he made the mistake of insulting KNOCKOUT's lover SCANDAL, and was seemingly thrown to his death. DW

TRUSTING TO LUCK *Mastermind Amos Fortune prefers to construct elaborate schemes rather than confront his enemies directly.*

FREEDOM BEAST

FIRST APPEARANCE ANIMAL MAN #13 (July 1989)
STATUS Hero **REAL NAME** Dominic Mndawe
OCCUPATION Adventurer **BASE** Capetown, South Africa
HEIGHT 6ft 2in **WEIGHT** 191 lbs **EYES** Brown **HAIR** Black
SPECIAL POWERS/ABILITIES Magical helmet and potent elixir enable him to fuse two animals into a single creature and command it to do his bidding for a short time; a strange rainwater elixir heightens his strength and five senses to superhuman level.

Chosen by retiring Mike Maxwell to carry on the heroic mission of the B'Wana Beast, Maxwell's adventuring alter ego, reporter and political activist Dominic Mndawe renamed himself Freedom Beast and used his new super powers to help dismantle Apartheid in South Africa. Freedom Beast now fights to end violence and suffering throughout the African continent. SB

FREEDOM FIGHTER *Dominic Mndawe was a political activist and campaigner before he became a super hero.*

FREEDOM FIGHTERS, THE

FIRST APPEARANCE JUSTICE LEAGUE OF AMERICA #107 (Oct. 1973)
STATUS Hero team **BASE** U.S.
ORIGINAL MEMBERS AND POWERS
UNCLE SAM The spirit of the U.S., strong and decisive.
HOURMAN I Has 60 minutes of enhanced human skills with miraclo pill.
INVISIBLE JUSTICE (DECEASED) Wore chemically treated cloak to become invisible.
MAGNO (DECEASED) Possessed magnetic-based powers.
MISS AMERICA Imbued with enhanced strength from the Spirit of Liberty.
NEON THE UNKNOWN (DECEASED) Was a two-fisted crime fighter.
RED TORPEDO Is a two-fisted crime fighter and excellent seaman.

Uncle Sam, the living spirit of the U.S., organized the Freedom Fighters for a doomed attempt at turning back the Japanese attack on Pearl Harbor in 1941. MAGNO and Neon were killed; RED TORPEDO and HOURMAN I were captured by the Japanese; Invisible Hood (who changed his name to Invisible Justice) was captured and killed by the Japanese; and Uncle Sam and MISS AMERICA were recovered by Project M. The following February, Uncle Sam, MIDNIGHT and DOLL MAN interrupted an All-Star Squadron meeting to warn them of an impending attack by the Japanese Navy at Santa Barbara, CA. In the hours that followed, the All-Stars met Neptune Perkins (see PERKINS, NEPTUNE), battled TSUNAMI, and saved Hourman after two months of captivity. In the aftermath, Uncle Sam reformed the Freedom Fighters, with the BLACK CONDOR I and the RAY I the first to join up. The team operated for the duration of World War II, headquartered in Washington, D.C., then eventually disbanded. A new Freedom Fighters recently emerged as part of the U.S. government's S.H.A.D.E. division, including a new PHANTOM LADY, HUMAN BOMB, Doll Man, FIREBRAND, and RED BEE. **RG**

KEY 1) The Ray I **2)** Human Bomb **3)** Firebrand
4) Miss America **5)** Uncle Sam **6)** Phantom Lady **7)** Red Bee
8) Black Condor

FRINGE

FIRST APPEARANCE TEEN TITANS (2nd series) #4 (1997)
STATUS Hero **REAL NAME** Unrevealed
OCCUPATION Adventurer **BASE** H'San Natall empire, deep space
HEIGHT 9ft 7in **WEIGHT** 645 lbs **EYES** White **HAIR** White
SPECIAL POWERS/ABILITIES Manifests a powerful psychic creature with various uncatalogued abilities.

Fringe was the offspring of a human woman and a H'San Natall father. His appearance so alarmed his parents that they threw the human/alien hybrid off a bridge. Fringe was rescued by a psychic entity that bonded with and protected him. When Fringe was hunted by Pylon and the Veil, two villains seeking to end alien influence on Earth, he was saved by the combined efforts of the second TEEN TITANS, Nightwing, and Supergirl. Fringe developed a psychic link with another Titan, Prysm, and joined the team. After several adventures with the Titans, Fringe learned that his mother, Queen Miraset, was alive and living in the H'San Natall empire. After the Titans disbanded, Fringe returned to space with Prysm. **PJ**

FURY

FIRST APPEARANCE SECRET ORIGINS (2nd series) #12 (March 1987)
STATUS Hero **REAL NAME** Helena Kosmatos
OCCUPATION Adventurer **BASE** Themyscira
HEIGHT 5ft 6in **WEIGHT** 135 lbs **EYES** Blue; (as Tisiphone) red
HAIR Blonde; (as Tisiphone) black
SPECIAL POWERS/ABILITIES She can channel the spirit and power of the Fury Tisiphone, the Blood Avenger, giving her superhuman strength, speed, and the ability to generate heat beams from her eyes. She wears lightweight, bulletproof armor.

Helena Kosmatos's father was killed during the Italian Fascists' invasion of Greece in 1940. Later, Helena discovered her brother was a Fascist collaborator. Escaping Nazi troops, Helena fled to the Areopagus, the hill of ARES, and unleashed the Furies, the Greek goddesses of vengeance. Helena became a vessel for their power and killed her brother. As Fury, she joined the ALL-STAR SQUADRON and befriended HIPPOLYTA, the Golden Age WONDER WOMAN.

Decades later, Helena named her only daughter Hippolyta. Losing her grip on reality after being seduced by the immortal Alcmaeon, Fury fought alongside the elder Hippolyta in the Amazon civil war. Later, the essence of Fury was stolen from Helena but, thanks to WONDER WOMAN and TROIA, the spirit returned, along with her sanity. **PJ**

FURY II

First appearance Wonder Woman (1st series) #300 (February 1983)
Status Hero Real name Hippolyta Trevor
Occupation Adventurer Base England
Height 5ft 7in Weight 145 lbs Eyes Blue Hair Blonde
Special powers/abilities Superhuman strength, speed, and endurance; trained in most forms of hand-to-hand combat.

Lyta Trevor, daughter of FURY, Helena Kosmatos, was adopted by Joan and Steve Trevor (see TREVOR, STEVE). Lyta believed that her superpowers were inherited from her "mother" the former MISS AMERICA. Lyta fell in love with Hector Hall, son of HAWKMAN and HAWKGIRL. They became Fury II and the Silver Scarab and founded the team INFINITY, INC. Hector vanished just as Lyta learned she was pregnant. The Furies of myth then appeared to her and revealed Lyta's connection to Helena and the Greek gods. An amazing and traumatic series of events followed, during which Lyta's child, Daniel, was abducted. When Daniel succeeded Morpheus as master of the Dreaming, he brought Lyta and Hector into his realm to save them from the SPECTRE. **RG**

AMAZING BASES

JSA HEADQUARTERS

The headquarters of the JUSTICE SOCIETY OF AMERICA is a mansion in Morningside Heights, Manhattan, north of Central Park in New York City. Equipped with personal suites, medical facilities, and a communications complex powered by WayneTech computers, the HQ has its own gas and electric power supply, recycles its water, and even has moveable walls that allow the JSA to reconfigure its architecture. There is a JSA museum and memorial open to the public on the first floor. Below the mansion are training facilities and computer monitors, as well as a high-speed rail link that follows a rebuilt submarine steam tunnel and a rocket ship (*see* Amazing Vehicles, pp. 34–5).

TITANS TOWER

Shaped in a giant "T," Titans Tower is located in the harbor of San Francisco. The first of several Towers was located in New York's East River. This tower was destroyed by TRIGON, and the second was blown up by the Wildebeest Society. The latest Titans Tower, is full of state of the art technology and also has a garden, tended by STARFIRE, planted with the flowers of long dead worlds.

PARADISE ISLAND

Called Themyscira by its inhabitants, the immortal warrior women known as the AMAZONS, Paradise Island is the home of WONDER WOMAN. The first Themyscira was an island nestled in an otherdimensional pocket off the coast of Greece. Settled by the Amazons, it was a mystic land of Greco-Roman architecture, tropical forests, and eternal sunshine. The home of the Amazons for 30 centuries, the island was ravaged by CIRCE and two civil wars before being destroyed by IMPERIEX. Themyscira was recreated by several goddesses, and transformed into a floating chain of islands in the heart of the Bermuda Triangle. An architectural marvel of amazing science where weapons no longer worked, and whose population was dedicated to the democratic exchange of information, this Themyscira was destroyed in a jealous rage by Hera (*see* OLYMPIAN GODS), and replaced with an isle more similar to the original.

FROM SUBTERRANEAN CAVES to Arctic strongholds, technological fortresses on the moon to mythical islands in other dimensions, the world's greatest heroes find refuge in the most spectacular, and often secret, locales. Across the Earth and throughout the universe, the JUSTICE LEAGUE OF AMERICA, the TEEN TITANS, and others maintain headquarters that lets them train together, collate information, and strike out at the forces of evil.

THE JLA WATCHTOWER

After inhabiting and abandoning several headquarters over the years, including a hidden cave in Rhode Island, a satellite in Earth's orbit, a Bunker in Detroit, and several embassies world-wide, the Justice League of America founded its greatest sanctuary on the moon. The JLA Watchtower was created using technologies from around the universe, and is equipped with the most advanced monitoring and transportation systems in the galaxy.

Equipped with specialized biospheres for each of its members and prison cells designed to contain the most destructive intergalactic criminals, as well as a Monitor Womb that records every transmission broadcast on Earth, the Watchtower is accessible from Earth by teleportation technology from HAWKMAN's homeworld of Thanagar.

MOONWATCH *Nestled in the Moon's Mare Serenitatis crater, the Watchtower is the headquarters of Earth's greatest hero team.*

THE FORTRESS OF SOLITUDE

Superman's Fortress of Solitude is located on a ledge in a remote mountain range near the Arctic Circle. Only Superman is strong enough to align the specialized plates that are the key into the glowing orb, which is a tesseract that holds within it an infinite amount of interdimensional space.

His personal retreat, Superman's Fortress is powered by three fusion-generating power cells. Within its walls are weapons and artifacts from Krypton, a global monitor system, and the Phantom Zone portal, a doorway to this ghostly, extradimensional zone.

A Kryptonian robot named Kelex, a duplicate of Superman's father Jor-El's personal servant, maintains the Fortress and its artifacts. Krypto, Superman's dog, lives in a special house within the Fortress.

THE AQUACAVE

The royal sanctuary of the King of the Seven Seas, AQUAMAN's Aquacave is located in a continental shelf north of Atlantis. The Sea King's headquarters, a dry pocket of caverns and grottos that provide solitude and escape, houses the ancient Atlantis Chronicles, a collection of mystic texts, as well as relics and trophies gathered during Aquaman's adventures. **PJ**

THE BATCAVE

Carved out from the subterranean, bat-infested limestone caverns that run beneath his family estate, Wayne Manor, the Batcave is a sprawling underground headquarters equipped with the latest vehicles, weapons, and technology to help Batman in his constant crusade against crime.

The original Batcave was destroyed during the earthquake that leveled half of Gotham City. The new Batcave is a multi-level bunker, powered by its own hydrogen generators. Housing a vast array of vehicles, scientific equipment, a forensics lab, medical facilities, and training systems throughout its multi-tiered labyrinth, the Batcave's centrepiece is the central computer terminal. This is powered by seven Cray T392 mainframes, and incorporates a holographic projector. Stored on the computer is Batman's vast archive of crime and criminals.

For a time, Batman hired the hunchbacked mute Harold Allnut, a technological genius, to work in the cave. Harold was duped into revealing Batman's secrets to the villain Hush in exchange for a voice and a new body, and was murdered by the criminal. While several heroes—and a handful of villains—have seen the inside of the Batcave, very few know where it actually exists.

VIRTUAL REALITY *Batman's sophisticated computer is controlled by virtual reality telepads.*

BAT FORTRESS *The Batcave is equipped with the most sophisticated technology and weaponry Bruce Wayne's money can buy. Its many levels extend nearly a mile beneath Wayne Manor.*

G.I. ROBOT

FIRST APPEARANCE WEIRD WAR TALES #101 (July 1981)
STATUS Hero **REAL NAME** J.A.K.E. 2
OCCUPATION Soldier **BASE** Pacific Islands
HEIGHT 6ft 6in **WEIGHT** 548 lbs **EYES** Photocellular **HAIR** None
SPECIAL POWERS/ABILITIES Speed, strength and endurance that exceeded the human norm.

Hoping to augment the soldiers during World War II, U.S. scientists devised a G.I. robot, the experimental Jungle Automatic Killer-Experiment, dubbed J.A.K.E. by Marine Sgt. Coker, who was assigned to test the prototype. Its missions were so successful that the army had hopes of turning out a complete corps of robots. The robot followed its programming well, saving Coker from enemy fire on more than one occasion. J.A.K.E. confounded engineers when it displayed a rudimentary consciousness and sacrificed itself while saving an American fleet.

Learning from this experience, they built a second model. This new J.A.K.E. performed even better and was supplemented with a robotic dog and cat combination for stealth missions. It too developed artificial intelligence that perplexed the engineers enough that no further models were constructed, and the program was quietly shut down at the end of World War II. The second-J.A.K.E.'s body survived for over a thousand years, well into the 31st Century. **RG**

GAMBLER

FIRST APPEARANCE GREEN LANTERN (2nd series) #12 (Summer 1944)
STATUS Villain **REAL NAME** Steven Sharpe III
OCCUPATION Professional criminal **BASE** Gotham City
HEIGHT 5ft 7in **WEIGHT** 151 lbs **EYES** Blue **HAIR** White
SPECIAL POWERS/ABILITIES Master of disguise and a crack shot with his pocket derringer.

The first Gambler, Steven Sharp III, was one of the original costumed villains who appeared after the debut of the heroic "mystery men" during the 1940s. Learning his trade with a traveling carnival, the Gambler executed a string of heists that earned him the attention of original GREEN LANTERN Alan Scott.

The Gambler escaped his nemesis again and again, thanks to his derringer pistol and a willingness to take any risk. He became one of the founding members of the INJUSTICE SOCIETY OF AMERICA. Late in life, the Gambler shot himself after losing his fortune at the casino. His grandson, Steven Sharp V, became the new Gambler, briefly leading the ROYAL FLUSH GANG before teaming with Amos Fortune (see FORTUNE, AMOS) and the SPORTSMASTER in a plot to take down the JUSTICE SOCIETY OF AMERICA. **DW**

GAMEMNAE

FIRST APPEARANCE JLA #70 (October 2002)
STATUS Villain (deceased) **REAL NAME** Gamemnae
OCCUPATION Sorceress **BASE** Poseidonis, Atlantis
HEIGHT 5ft 8in **WEIGHT** 139 lbs **EYES** Blue **HAIR** Blonde
SPECIAL POWERS/ABILITIES Power sorceress; was able to cast spells potent enough to move continents through space and time.

Gamemnae was an Atlantean sorceress who was born 3,000 years ago. She was cast from her home as a child because of her blonde hair, a terrible curse in Atlantean myth.

She enslaved the people of Atlantis and its champion, AQUAMAN, by shifting the kingdom back in time to 1004 BC. Gamemnae then invoked a prophecy that foretold the coming of the end of the world. Rama Khan (see KHAN, RAMA) gathered a powerful group of ancient heroes to destroy the "seven-headed Hydra" that would travel through time to end the world. That "Hydra" was the JUSTICE LEAGUE OF AMERICA, who Gamemnae had feared would track Atlantis through the time disruption and end her plans for world conquest. Following a battle with the ANCIENTS, Gamemnae died in battle with MANITOU RAVEN, the JLA freed Aquaman, and Atlantis was returned to its rightful time and place. **PJ**

GARDNER, GUY

FIRST APPEARANCE GREEN LANTERN (2nd series) #59 (March 1968)
STATUS Hero **REAL NAME** Guy Gardner
OCCUPATION Green Lantern **BASES** Planet Oa; Earth
HEIGHT 6ft **WEIGHT** 180 lbs **EYES** Blue **HAIR** Red
SPECIAL POWERS/ABILITIES Power ring provides flight, shielding, and encyclopedic knowledge; it emits energies that can be shaped into anything the wielder can imagine.

As a child, Gardner escaped his abusive home life by escaping into the comic book adventures of GENERAL GLORY. He played football at the University of Michigan until injury ended a promising career. He then worked as a teacher and social worker. When the dying Abin Sur, Green Lantern of Sector 2814, asked his power ring to find a replacement, it identified Guy Gardner and Hal Jordan—but picked Jordan because he was closer. This missed opportunity haunted Gardner. Gardner spent months in a coma after an accident in the Phantom Zone, but a faction of the GUARDIANS OF THE UNIVERSE gave him a new ring and purpose prior to the Crisis on Infinite Earths. Gardner joined the JUSTICE LEAGUE OF AMERICA, often clashing with BATMAN, and began a romance with teammate ICE.

Gardner discovered that his body contained Vuldarian DNA allowing him to morph his arms into weapons. He adventured as Warrior, and opened the Warrior's bar which became a favorite watering hole for local super heroes. The destruction of the bar—and his body's rejection of its Vuldarian DNA—ushered in a new era for Guy Gardner. He returned to the Green Lantern Corps, fighting PARALLAX alongside Stewart, Kyle Rayner, and a resurrected Hal Jordan. The Guardians named Gardner one of the trainers for the Corps' recruits, and later appointed him to the Lantern Honor Guard. He has distinguished himself in missions with the covert-ops team known as the "Green Lantern Corpse" and as a front-line commander during the Sinestro Corps War. **DW**

THE ONE, TRUE GREEN LANTERN Guy Gardner has often boasted that he is superior to all other members of the Green Lantern Corps. His ring sparks with wild energy from his overabundance of willpower.

GANGBUSTER

FIRST APPEARANCE ADVENTURES OF SUPERMAN #432 (July 1987)
STATUS Hero (retired) REAL NAME José Delgado
OCCUPATION Former schoolteacher BASE Suicide Slum, Metropolis
HEIGHT 5ft 9in WEIGHT 170 lbs EYES Brown HAIR Black
SPECIAL POWERS/ABILITIES Superb street fighter; wore Kevlar-lined bulletproof body armor and riot helmet; weapons included shatterproof nunchakus and taser.

Growing up in Metropolis's Suicide Slum, Golden Gloves boxing champ José Delgado witnessed firsthand the ills of street gangs. To protect his poor and defenseless neighbors from gang violence, José donned body armor and a riot helmet to become the vigilante Gangbuster. Unfortunately, José's efforts as Gangbuster eventually led to paralyzing injuries following a fight with the villain Combattor, as well as the loss of his teaching position and an end to a short-lived romance with reporter Lois Lane (*see* LANE, LOIS). But despite these hardships, Gangbuster's heroism remains an inspiration to the Latino youth of Suicide Slum. SB

GAUCHO

FIRST APPEARANCE DETECTIVE COMICS #215 (January 1955)
STATUS Hero (missing in action) REAL NAME Unknown
OCCUPATION Freedom fighter BASE Buenos Aires
HEIGHT 5ft 10in WEIGHT 175 lbs EYES Brown HAIR Black
SPECIAL POWERS/ABILITIES Expert equestrian; best known for his skill with the bolo, a throwing weapon used to ensnare or strangle its target.

A freedom fighter that operated for the Allied forces during World War II, Gaucho infiltrated the Nazi forces in Germany as a spy, leaking Axis secrets to the United States. One of the first real costumed heroes to operate outside of the United States, Gaucho was given an invitation by the mysterious DOCTOR MIST to join the Dome, the super-national organization headquartered in Paris. The Argentine hero declined and returned to his home in Buenos Aires, actively fighting crime and corruption through much of the 1950s, and becoming a legend throughout much of South America. The final fate of Gaucho has yet to be revealed. PJ

MACHO MAN *In a pre-Crisis world, a swaggering rogue calling himself the Gaucho tried to get the better of Wonder Woman.*

GENERAL, THE

FIRST APPEARANCE (Wade Eiling) CAPTAIN ATOM (2nd series) #1 (March 1988); (The General) JLA #25 (January 1999)
STATUS Villain REAL NAME General Wade Eiling
OCCUPATION Militant monster BASE Mobile
HEIGHT 10ft 5in WEIGHT 1,378 lbs EYES Red HAIR Brown
SPECIAL POWERS/ABILITIES Superhuman strength and regenerative abilities; nearly indestructible; can survive unaided in space.

Air Force General Wade Eiling was the bellicose, ruthless creator of the Captain Atom Project, a top-secret program designed to create government-controlled meta-human operatives. Eiling was responsible for transforming his nemesis, Captain Nathaniel Adam, into CAPTAIN ATOM. Adam had been framed for treason and had been sentenced to death, but Eiling pardoned Adam's sentence and drafted him into the Captain Atom Project. Captain Atom was hurled 20 years into the future, only to learn that his grieving wife, Angela, believing him dead, had married Eiling. Years later, Eiling created the INTERNATIONAL ULTRAMARINE CORPS, a team of superhuman operatives under his control. He then discovered that he had an inoperable brain tumor. Determined not to succumb to this disease, he ordered the Ultramarines to recover the android body of the SHAGGY MAN, a villain and foe of the JUSTICE LEAGUE OF AMERICA. Eiling used a synthetic metagene to transfer his dying consciousness into the Shaggy Man's nearly indestructible body. He then attacked and nearly destroyed the JLA before they trapped him on an asteroid near Jupiter, marooning him in space.

The General was saved by the QUEEN BEE II and returned to Earth. Since then, the General has served with the INJUSTICE GANG and the SECRET SOCIETY OF SUPER-VILLAINS. PJ

GENERAL GLORY

FIRST APPEARANCE JUSTICE LEAGUE AMERICA #46 (January 1991)
STATUS Hero (deceased) REAL NAME Joseph Jones
OCCUPATION Soldier BASE Mobile
HEIGHT 6ft 2in WEIGHT 210 lbs EYES Blue HAIR Black
SPECIAL POWERS/ABILITIES German nerve gas made Jones an Olympic-level athlete; coupled with great courage, that was all he needed.

During World War II, American G.I. Joseph Jones was liberating a French village when his platoon was caught in a barrage of enemy bombs containing an experimental nerve gas. The lone survivor, Jones discovered that the gas had turned him into a superfit hero. Offering his services to the government, Jones became General Glory. He was soon joined by kid sidekick Ernest E. Earnest, a.k.a. Ernie. General Glory played his full part in defeating the Third Reich, however, the U.S. government went to great lengths to keep his exploits secret, even publishing a comic book entitled *General Glory* so that people would think he was a purely fictional creation. Decades later, General Glory's greatest fan, Guy Gardner (*see* WARRIOR), found Jones and General Glory returned to duty with the JUSTICE LEAGUE OF AMERICA for a brief time, until a heart attack claimed the old soldier. Police officer Donovan Wallace shared a hospital room with the dying Jones. The two men became friends and when Jones died, his powers were transferred to Wallace, though in different form: he found he could fly on golden wings. Wallace became a new General Glory, but has served only sporadically ever since. RG

The DC Comics Encyclopedia

GIZMO

FIRST APPEARANCE THE NEW TEEN TITANS (1st series) #3 (Jan. 1981)
STATUS Villain (deceased) **REAL NAME** Mikron O'Jeneus
OCCUPATION Inventor; professional criminal **BASE** New Jersey
HEIGHT 4ft 2in **WEIGHT** 87 lbs **EYES** Green **HAIR** Brown
SPECIAL POWERS/ABILITIES Given the tools, Gizmo could turn harmless household appliances into high-tech weapons of mass destruction.

A genius tinkerer, the dwarfish Mikron O'Jeneus once supplied state-of-the-art technology to criminals from his clandestine company, Gizmos, Inc. Later, he took a more hands-on approach to villainy by answering DOCTOR LIGHT I's classified ad in *The Underworld Star*, which sought several super-villains to round out his FEARSOME FIVE team. As a member of that evil quintet through several lineups, Gizmo repeatedly demonstrated his scientific savvy in battle with the TEEN TITANS before putting his mischievous mind to good use for S.T.A.R. Labs. Gizmo was apparently murdered by the Fearsome Five's PSIMON. Recently, however, Gizmo was discovered alive and well, and part of an all-new Fearsome Five organized by DOCTOR SIVANA. Doctor Sivana killed O'Jeneus with a shot to the head, and his son has become a second Gizmo. **SB**

GLORIOUS GODFREY

FIRST APPEARANCE FOREVER PEOPLE #3 (July 1971)
STATUS Villain **REAL NAME** None
OCCUPATION Agent of Darkseid **BASE** Apokolips
HEIGHT 5ft 11in **WEIGHT** 195 lbs **EYES** Blue **HAIR** Red
SPECIAL POWERS/ABILITIES Silver-tongued powers of persuasion; handsome looks conceal a heart of pure poison.

Unlike the other minions of DARKSEID, Glorious Godfrey is handsome instead of horrible; charming instead of stomach-churning. During one of his first missions to Earth, Godfrey, Darkseid's glittering persuader, crisscrossed the U.S. in a traveling road show preaching his philosophy to eager audiences. He hoped to prepare the planet for his master's conquest and successfully recruited an army of "Justifiers," who wore helmets that allowed Godfrey to manipulate their minds. Godfrey met defeat at the hands of the FOREVER PEOPLE. Glorious Godfrey later posed as the psychologist G. Gordon Godfrey, author of the bestseller *Super-Hero or Super-Menace?*, in a failed attempt to foment a worldwide anti-hero movement. His sister is the Apokolips agent known as AMAZING GRACE. **DW**

GLOSS

FIRST APPEARANCE MILLENNIUM #1 (Summer 1987)
STATUS Hero **REAL NAME** Xiang Po
OCCUPATION Adventurer **BASE** U.S.
HEIGHT 5ft 5in **WEIGHT** 139 lbs **EYES** Red **HAIR** Dark auburn
SPECIAL POWERS/ABILITIES Superstrength; controls the Dragon Lines of Power, energy coursing through the Earth that enables Gloss to create force fields, duplicate herself, or teleport.

Xiang Po was among ten humans bequeathed with superpowers to become progenitors of the next phase of mankind's evolution. These individuals, hand-picked by Herupa Hando Hu, one of the GUARDIANS OF THE UNIVERSE, and his mate Nadia Safir, were destined to succeed the immortal Guardians. Xiang Po left her village in Communist China behind to became Gloss, a being energized by Earth's mystic ley lines. With her fellow progenitors, Gloss became a member of the NEW GUARDIANS, who defended Earth while preparing to found a race of immortal humans. However, the New Guardians discovered that hybrid creatures bioengineered by Janwillem Kroef, a South African passed over by Herupa and Nadia, were the true chosen ones. The New Guardians went their separate ways, with Gloss settling in the U.S. Gloss has since joined the GLOBAL GUARDIANS, using her powers for the good of the planet. **SB**

GLOBAL GUARDIANS, THE

FIRST APPEARANCE #46 (June 1982)
STATUS Hero team
BASE An unnamed island in the Pacific Ocean
CURRENT MEMBERS AND POWERS
Dr. Mist (Kor) Sorcerer.
Seraph (Israel) Possesses superstrength.
Owlwoman (America) Tracker; superspeed and durability.
Olympian (Greece) Golden Fleece gives him the powers of 50 Argonauts.
Rising Sun (Japan) Solar powers.
Centrix (Canada) Can project invisible energy.
Tundra (Russia) Possesses superstrength; can project ice and cold.
Cascade (Indonesia) Is able to turn into water form; can psionically control water.
Chrysalis (France) Has a robotic shell containing sentient insects.

GLOBAL HEROES *Despite differing cultures and world views, the Guardians put the Earth's needs first.*

The first real costumed global heroes, the Italian Legionary, the British Knight and his sidekick, the Squire (*see* KNIGHT & SQUIRE), the Argentine GAUCHO, the French MUSKETEER, and the Swedish Wingman, made their debut in the 1950s. Convinced of the potential threat of superpowered rogues, many non-Communist countries signed a treaty in 1957 creating a supra-national organization codenamed the Dome, headquartered in a Paris mansion. After its official founding, the Global Guardians roster included: Africa's DOCTOR MIST, Venezuela's BUSHMASTER, England's GODIVA, Brazil's Green Fury (*see* FIRE), Norway's Ice and ICEMAIDEN, South Africa's IMPALA, Ireland's JACK O'LANTERN I, Denmark's

LITTLE MERMAID, Greece's Olympian, the U.S.'s Owlwoman, Japan's RISING SUN, Israel's SERAPH, Australia's TASMANIAN DEVIL, Taiwan's Thunderlord, New Zealand's Tuatara, Germany's Wild Huntsman, Africa's B'WANA BEAST (*see* FREEDOM BEAST), and France's FLEUR-DE-LIS. They worked well for a time, although never quite gaining the fame of the U.S.'s costumed crime fighters. At one point, Dr. Mist vanished and BELPHEGOR became the acting director of the Dome, until the United Nations cut funding for the institution in favor of channeling its financial resources to the recently established Justice League International (*see* JUSTICE LEAGUE OF AMERICA). Since then, the Guardians and other international heroes have helped to protect the Earth. The Guardians' ranks have risen and fallen over the years, and the team's reputation was tarnished when members were turned into the personal drones of the Queen Bee (*see* QUEEN BEE II) in Bialya. The Guardians' current Dome is located on an island in the Pacific Ocean. **RG**

KEY 1) *Rising Sun* **2)** *Jack O'Lantern I*
3) *Dr. Mist* **4)** *Owlwoman* **5)** *Impala*
6) *Godiva* **7)** *Little Mermaid* **8)** *Tuatara*
9) *Bushmaster* **10)** *Thunderlord*
11) *Olympian* **12)** *Wild Huntsman*

G'NORT

FIRST APPEARANCE JUSTICE LEAGUE INTERNATIONAL #10
(February 1988)
STATUS Hero **REAL NAME** G'nort Esplanade Gneeshmacher
OCCUPATION Adventurer **BASE** Mobile
HEIGHT 5ft 10in **WEIGHT** 195 lbs **EYES** Black **HAIR** Reddish brown
SPECIAL POWERS/ABILITIES Well-meaning but inept; wears the maser-powered suit of a Darkstar, but whether the suit is operational is questionable.

Thanks to his uncle Gnewmann, G'newtian canine G'nort was inducted into the GREEN LANTERN CORPS as an intergalactic peacekeeper. Or so he believed. In truth, G'nort belonged to a fake Corps established by alien clowns called the Poglachi, who plotted to make laughing stocks of the real Corps. When the Poglachi were exposed, G'nort and GREEN LANTERN Guy Gardner defeated them. At Gardner's request, G'nort became a real Green Lantern, patroling a lifeless sector where he could do little harm. G'nort later joined the ill-fated Justice League Antarctica made up of temporarily reformed super-villains. Some time later, G'nort became a Darkstar. Since the DARKSTARS have been disbanded for some time, perhaps G'nort found his uniform in a trash can while looking for a meal! Though he claims JUSTICE LEAGUE OF AMERICA membership, the League tells a different story. When last seen, G'nort was hitchhiking to Antarctica. **SB**

GODIVA

FIRST APPEARANCE THE NEW TEEN TITANS (2nd ser.) ANNUAL #3
(1988) **STATUS** Villain **REAL NAME** Unknown
OCCUPATION Mercenary **BASE** The Swiss Alps
HEIGHT 5ft 9in **WEIGHT** 143 lbs **EYES** Red **HAIR** Black with gold streak
SPECIAL POWERS/ABILITIES Hypnotic powers charm her victims into behaving like mindless puppets.

Born in Ghana, the assassin Godiva claims to be the child of a Chinese prince and an African princess. Godiva treats her missions as games and often has a film crew follow her around, taking her orders. Obsessed with her own beauty—she stares into mirrors constantly—she has a pathological need to be the center of attention. She has also been known to murder associates who smoke or who eat read meat. Godiva once kidnapped Jon and Cherie Chase, the parents of Danny Chase (*see* TEEN TITANS). Danny helped the Titans rescue his parents, but Godiva managed to slip away. Later, she targeted a British spy, detonating a bomb that almost killed NIGHTWING. Godiva threw the British agent off a tall building and he fell to his death. The hypnotic femme fatale then coolly made her escape. **PJ**

GOG

FIRST APPEARANCE GOG #1 (February 1998)
STATUS Villain **REAL NAME** William (last name unrevealed)
OCCUPATION Adventurer **BASE** Metropolis
HEIGHT 6ft 1in **WEIGHT** 203 lbs **EYES** Blue **HAIR** Brown
SPECIAL POWERS/ABILITIES Superhuman strength and durability; staff emits energy beams.

VICTIM *Radiation burns scar William's face.*

In a potential near-future, young William felt he was rescued by SUPERMAN, after the nuclear detonation over Kansas, for something special, and he established the Church of Superman. Considering himself the first apostle, he espoused a series of beliefs based on the hero's exploits. Superman visited William and expressed disapproval of the church—he didn't want to be deified.

Shattered, William proved susceptible to an approach by the cosmic beings known as the Quintessence. He was given immense power and knowledge, which drove him mad, and Gog was born. Gog made it his mission to go back in time and kill Superman. Gog traveled back a day at a time, killing each timeline's version of Superman, ultimately arriving at the day Superman and WONDER WOMAN's baby was born. Gog kidnapped the newborn baby, rather than kill Superman, and vanished back to an earlier point in time to create an apocalyptic disaster in Kansas. At the climax of their battle to defeat the reality-spanning Gog, Superman, BATMAN, and Wonder Woman learned the secret of Hypertime, an all-encompassing reality that contains countless parallel dimensions. Gog was remanded to the custody of the Quintessence. However, he escaped and returned to Superman's era to renew their struggle. **RG**

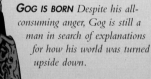

MIRACULOUS RESCUE *William looks up into the smoke-filled sky to see a strange figure hovering overhead. He feels a sudden surge of hope—could that be Superman?*

GOG IS BORN *Despite his all-consuming anger, Gog is still a man in search of explanations for how his world was turned upside down.*

THE QUINTESSENCE
With his mighty staff, Gog can destroy solid objects, creating a trail of devastation.

GOLDEN ARROW

FIRST APPEARANCE WHIZ COMICS #2 (February 1940)
STATUS Hero **REAL NAME** Roger Parsons
OCCUPATION Western hero **BASE** The Old West
HEIGHT 6ft 1in **WEIGHT** 195 lbs **EYES** Blue **HAIR** Blond
SPECIAL POWERS/ABILITIES Superb horseman, courageous fighter, and a dead shot with a bow and arrow; marked the tips of his arrows with prospector's gold, hence his name.

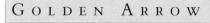

Orphaned son of Professor Paul Parsons—the brilliant inventor of a revolutionary lighter-than-air gas—Roger Parsons grew up in the care of an old prospector after a crook named Brand Braddock murdered his father for his scientific secrets. On the western plains Roger grew tall and strong, becoming an expert archer and calling himself Golden Arrow, "fearless hero of the West." Golden Arrow soon took his revenge on Braddock. Later, he had run-ins with Brand's brothers, Bronk and Brute Braddock, and befriended their niece Carol Braddock. Though not an official lawman, Golden Arrow helped keep the peace on the frontier, riding on his mighty stallion, White Wind. **DW**

GOLDEN GLADIATOR

FIRST APPEARANCE THE BRAVE AND THE BOLD (1st series) #1 (September 1955)
STATUS Hero **REAL NAME** Marcus
OCCUPATION Former shepherd, slave, and warrior
BASE Ancient Rome
HEIGHT 6ft 4in **WEIGHT** 215 lbs **EYES** Blue **HAIR** Black
SPECIAL POWERS/ABILITIES Superior swordsman and courageous hand-to-hand combatant; accomplished equestrian.

Marcus was a shepherd living in ancient Rome who was framed by several Roman soldiers for the failed assassination attempt of Praetor Clodius Crassus. The soldiers saw to it that Marcus was sentenced to life as a galley slave. Marcus became popular during his time as a slave, overpowering an angry lion and using his strength to defend other prisoners. Marcus was returned to Rome and sold as a slave to Cinna, the man who tried to assassinate Crassus and who had framed Marcus for the crime. Marcus won his freedom after rising through the ranks in the gladiatorial arena, and was given the helmet of the Golden Gladiator as a prize. As the Golden Gladiator, Marcus became Rome's greatest defender, constantly thwarting Cinna's evil schemes. **PJ**

GOLDEN GLIDER

FIRST APPEARANCE THE FLASH (1st series) #250 (June 1977)
STATUS Villain (deceased) **REAL NAME** Lisa Snart (Lisa Star)
OCCUPATION Adventurer **BASE** Mobile
HEIGHT 5ft 5in **WEIGHT** 117 lbs **EYES** Blue **HAIR** Blonde
SPECIAL POWERS/ABILITIES World-class athlete; anti-gravity skates created their own ice, but she effectively skated on thin air; arsenal of weapons concealed as jewels that enabled hypnosis, force fields, teleportation, illusions, etc.

of Len Snart, (CAPTAIN COLD), Lisa Snart was a champion ice skater who learned her famous spinning skills from her paramour Roscoe Dillon, alias the Top, one of Barry Allen, the second FLASH's foes. When the Top was killed following a high-speed duel with the Scarlet Speedster, Lisa vowed to make the Flash suffer. As Golden Glider, a whirling dervish on anti-gravity skates, she tried to kill the Flash's wife, Iris (see ALLEN, IRIS), as well as Iris's and Barry's parents. Snart then hypnotized writer Beau Baer into adopting the identity of the heroic Ringmaster, who forced a mind-controlled Iris Allen to fall in love with him. Fortunately, the Flash again tripped up the Golden Glider's schemes. Snart later reunited with the Top when the villain's spirit took over the body of the Flash's father, Henry Allen. The Flash again defeated the Golden Glider and she was jailed once more. Lisa Snart skated on thin ice for the last time when she used her brother's Cold Gun to create a string of frosty foes for the Flash, all named Chillblaine. One of these Chillblaines flash-froze her body, which shattered, killing Snart. Presumably, Snart's Golden Glider joined her beloved Top in the afterlife, undoubtedly a cold day in Hell. **SB**

GOLDFACE

FIRST APPEARANCE (as Kenyon) GREEN LANTERN (2nd series) #38 (July 1965); (as Goldface) GREEN LANTERN (2nd series) #48 (October 1966)
STATUS Hero **REAL NAME** Keith Kenyon
OCCUPATION Union leader **BASE** Keystone City
HEIGHT 5ft 9in **WEIGHT** 180 lbs **EYES** Brown **HAIR** Brown
SPECIAL POWERS/ABILITIES Kenyon has superhuman strength, and his organic metal skin provides some degree of invulnerability.

Keith Kenyon studied political science with a minor in chemistry at the University of California-Coast City. Rather than follow his father, who was a labor union leader, he wanted other things from life. Everything changed for him when he discovered a sunken chest of gold. The gold's structure had been altered by chemical waste, and it gave Kenyon enhanced strength and a golden skin tone. He turned to crime to pay for his experiments, and crossed paths with the second GREEN LANTERN and the second FLASH. While serving time in Iron Heights penitentiary, Kenyon's skin became organic metal. On his release, Kenyon hid his golden skin under makeup and became a union leader like his father. He now heads Union 242, Keystone City's largest work force, where he encounters the third Flash from time to time. As Goldface he is determined to eradicate the Network, a super-villain supply depot run by his ex-wife Amunet Black, known as the rogue Blacksmith. **RG**

SOLID GOLD Kenyon uses thick makeup to hide his gold skin. His days as the costumed criminal Goldface are long behind him.

FORCE OF NATURE Golem is a near-indestructible force and an invaluable asset to the Primal Force team.

GOLEM

FIRST APPEARANCE RAGMAN (1st series) #1 (September 1976)
STATUS Hero **REAL NAME** None (goes by Paul)
OCCUPATION Former member of Leymen (Primal Force)
BASE New York City **HEIGHT** 8ft **WEIGHT** 570 lbs
EYES Yellowish brown **HAIR** None
SPECIAL POWERS/ABILITIES Vast bulk allied to superstrength, apparently invulnerable as he has the ability to regrow himself out of clay; possesses a benevolent disposition and is viewed as a gentle giant.

Created from the mud of the Louisiana swamps, the elemental being known as Golem (not to be confused with the Golem serving with the super-group HAYOTH) is a lumbering force of nature who really wants nothing more than to live life as a human. In his early career he fought alongside the hero RAGMAN, and then lived with a good-hearted Louisiana woman named Jean Lizotte. Later blamed for Jean's death, Golem fled through the swamps until a mystical summoning spell teleported him out of the reach of the pursuing police. His rescuer Maltis (see DOCTOR MIST) appointed Golem as a new member of the supernatural super-team the Leymen (see PRIMAL FORCE).

Damaged and destroyed several times during his adventures, Golem easily fixed himself by shaping new body parts out of dirt. He is vulnerable to water but can always re-form himself once he dries out. Since "Golem" merely describes an artificial creature common in Jewish folklore, Golem has long desired a name of his own. His most recent wish is that others refer to him as "Paul."

Golem's activities since the disbanding of the Primal Force team are unknown. He may have returned to Louisiana to meld with the swamp-clay there. **DW**

GORGEOUS GILLY

First appearance Action Comics #769 (September 2000)
Status Villain **Real name** Unknown
Occupation Adventurer **Base** Chattahoochee, Florida
Height 6ft 2in **Weight** 165 lbs **Eyes** Blue **Hair** Brown
Special powers/abilities Powerful hypnotic ability, described as a "magic love eye," makes men slaves to her incredible beauty.

No one caught in Gorgeous Gilly's spell will dispute her claim that she is the most beautiful woman to ever walk the Earth. Her powers of mesmerism run so deep that men will do anything for her. Fortunately for men everywhere, Gilly's psychic hold can be broken by force of will, particularly when the victim is removed from Gilly's sight.

She hails from the swamps of rural Chattahoochee, Florida, a member of an extended family of meta-humans that have branded themselves the Rednex. Gilly and her kin proudly embrace the worst Southern stereotypes. Any gathering of the Rednex is certain to include an abundance of banjo-picking, cousin-kissing, and missing teeth. **DW**

GORILLA GRODD

First appearance THE FLASH (1st series) #106 (May 1959)
Status Villain **Real name** None
Occupation Would-be world conqueror
Base Gorilla City, Africa **Height** 6ft 6in
Weight 600 lbs **Eyes** Gray **Hair** Black
Special powers/abilities "Force of Mind" enables Grodd to control others, transform matter, project attack beams, or transfer his consciousness into the bodies of other creatures; scientific genius; inventor of exotic weaponry.

Grip of Grodd *Black Canary finds herself in a tight gorilla squeeze.*

Deep in the heart of the African jungle resides a race of highly evolved and amazingly intelligent apes. Secluded in their fabulous Gorilla City, these super simians have dwelt in peace for centuries. Their existence was completely unknown to the outside world until one of their number sought to overthrow the apes' kindly King Solovar and lead an army to conquer the entire Earth. This power-hungry malcontent was none other than Gorilla Grodd. A hugely strong, diabolical genius, Grodd had developed the power to control the minds of other beings after telepathically picking Solovar's brain. In order to put a stop to Grodd's schemes for world domination, Solovar enlisted the aid of the second Flash, Barry Allen. He at last defeated Gorilla Grodd and imprisoned him in Gorilla City. Grodd tried to capture Superman and Batman when President Lex Luthor (*see* Luthor, Lex) placed a bounty on both heroes. The U.S. government stranded Grodd and other villains on a prison planet during Operation: Salvation Run. **SB**

GORDON, JAMES W.

First appearance DETECTIVE COMICS #27 (May 1939)
Status Hero **Real name** James W. Gordon
Occupation Gotham City Police Commissioner **Base** Gotham City
Height 5ft 9in **Weight** 168 lbs **Eyes** Blue **Hair** White
Special powers/abilities Expert criminologist and dedicated, highly principled police detective; useful hand-to-hand combatant renowned for his powerful left hook; uses a standard issue service revolver, a Browning BDAO 9-mm automatic.

Kill or be killed *James Gordon's wife, Sarah, had been murdered by the Joker while saving the lives of innocent children. Driven to the edge, Gordon nearly took the Joker's life in revenge, but shot the maniac in the kneecaps instead.*

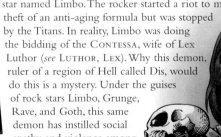

James Gordon, his wife Barbara, and their two children moved to Gotham City from Chicago, where he established a reputation for honesty in an infamously corrupt police department. However, Gordon's dedication took its toll on his marriage and Barbara left him, taking their son, James Gordon Jr. He retained custody of their adopted daughter, Barbara.

One of Jim's first assignments was hunting down the urban legend known as Batman. Despite his aversion to Batman's vigilantism, the chain-smoking Gordon became a close ally of the Dark Knight. Gordon eventually became Police Commissioner, forging one of the finest departments in the country. He also fell in love with and married Sergeant Sarah Essen. Gordon refused to leave Gotham when the city was struck by an earthquake, and with a few loyal officers, sought to maintain a semblance of law and order. Tragically, Sarah was murdered by the Joker while trying to save the lives of Gotham's dozens of kidnapped children. Gordon finally retired after 20 years as a police officer, though he returned as commissioner several months after the Infinite Crisis. His daughter Barbara continues to fight crime in Metropolis and across the world as Oracle. **PJ**

GOTH

First appearance THE TITANS #3 (May 1999)
Status Villain (deceased) **Real name** Unrevealed
Occupation Demon **Base** Mobile
Height Variable **Weight** Variable **Eyes** Variable **Hair** None
Special powers/abilities Charismatic; demonic strength creates and throws flames; induces trances; razor-sharp claws and teeth.

The original Teen Titans first encountered this demon at a rock concert in the town of Eden Crest featuring a star named Limbo. The rocker started a riot to mask his theft of an anti-aging formula but was stopped by the Titans. In reality, Limbo was doing the bidding of the Contessa, wife of Lex Luthor (*see* Luthor, Lex). Why this demon, ruler of a region of Hell called Dis, would do this is a mystery. Under the guises of rock stars Limbo, Grunge, Rave, and Goth, this same demon has instilled social apathy and violence among the world's teenagers. Goth is a red-skinned actor/rock star behind a series of murders. The Justice Society of America recently found Goth's murdered body in the middle of a factory fire. **RG**

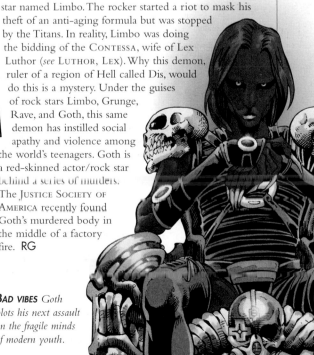

Bad vibes *Goth plots his next assault on the fragile minds of modern youth.*

GREEN ARROW

THE EMERALD ARCHER

OLIVER JONAS QUEEN (GREEN ARROW I)
FIRST APPEARANCE More Fun Comics #73 (November 1941)
STATUS Hero **OCCUPATION** Adventurer **BASE** Star City
HEIGHT 5ft 11in **WEIGHT** 185 lbs **EYES** Green **HAIR** Blond
SPECIAL POWERS/ABILITIES Has an excellent eye for archery; trained hand-to-hand combatant with above average strength and endurance.

CONNOR HAWKE (GREEN ARROW II)
FIRST APPEARANCE Green Arrow (1st series) #0
(October 1994)
STATUS Hero **OCCUPATION** Adventurer **BASE** Star City
HEIGHT 5ft 9in **WEIGHT** 160 lbs **EYES** Green **HAIR** Blond
SPECIAL POWERS/ABILITIES An expert marksman as well as one of the top five martial artists on Earth.

WHILE ON A SOUTH SEA CRUISE, a business partner betrayed playboy billionaire Oliver Queen and knocked him overboard. Washing up on a remote island, Queen fashioned a crude bow and arrow to take down a drug-running operation run by the villainess China White. He soon returned to the social scene in his hometown, Star City. Donning a Robin Hood costume for a party, Queen foiled a robbery during the event, gaining the nickname Green Arrow. Resolving to become a crime fighter, he soon experienced firsthand the diseased underbelly of society he had only previously read about.

EARLY DAYS Early in his career, the Emerald Archer had his own Arrowcar, complete with ejector seat.

DARTING AROUND Green Arrow and Speedy sought out criminals wherever they lurked.

ROY AND HAL

After a horrifying trip to Vietnam (where he first met Hal Jordan, the second GREEN LANTERN), Queen sold off his armaments division. He decided to become actively involved in campaigning for good causes, and adopted Roy Harper as his ward. Roy became his first kid sidekick, Speedy (see ARSENAL). Together, they battled such foes as the crime-clown Bull's-Eye, the Rainbow Archer, and the Red Dart. During this time, Queen became the anonymous financier of the JUSTICE LEAGUE OF AMERICA. He also used his fortune to finance an Arrow Plane, Arrow Car, and a base called the Arrow Cave—clearly showing his respect for BATMAN. A short time later, Green Arrow was formally inducted into the JLA. There, he met and fell in love with beautiful Dinah Lance (the second BLACK CANARY), despite the large gap in their ages. Soon after, Queen was swindled out of his fortune by John deLeon, a former partner. Undaunted, Oliver convinced Hal Jordan to join him as he explored America's heartland. There they confronted issues such as bigotry, religious fanaticism, and environmental destruction. They were frequently joined on their journey by Black Canary II.

OLIVER QUEEN

Queen never talked about his parents or the events that left him an orphan, heir to a manufacturing empire. Before becoming the secret vigilante Green Arrow he had been dissatisfied, restless, wrestling with an emerging social conscience. Now he finally had the chance to do some good in the world, fighting all manner of criminality. He soon came to realize that crime and violence were global problems, fueled in part by his own munitions division.

SHIELDED Green Lantern protects Green Arrow and a monk, Than, from an explosion.

SHADO, LONGBOW HUNTER

After Oliver Queen resigned from the JLA, he and Dinah Lance moved to Seattle, Washington, where she set up a flower shop called Sherwood Florist. However, the pair were soon imbroiled in tracking down a drugs gang. The case led them to question the future of their relationship—and then Dinah vanished. She was brutalized and tortured before Green Arrow rescued her and killed the sadists holding her. During the rescue, Green Arrow's life was saved by a mysterious oriental archer named SHADO, who was pursing her own vendetta against a drugs cartel. The two eventually become lovers for a time. Green Arrow became a fugitive after being arrested on false treason charges, and Dinah Lance called Shado for help. Dinah then discovered that Queen had unknowingly conceived a son with Shado, whom she had named Robert.

CRISIS FOR THE GREEN ARROW

Feeling abandoned by his mentor, Speedy became a heroin addict. Black Canary II acted as his surrogate mother and helped him kick the habit. Shortly thereafter, Green Arrow accidentally killed a thief named Richard Hollinger and went into hiding. Black Canary II and GREEN LANTERN II searched for their friend, and the hunt took on extra urgency when the Canary was gravely injured in an auto accident. Dinah needed a blood transfusion and Green Lantern II realized that Queen possessed her rare RH Negative blood type. Green Arrow returned in time to save his lover's life. This personal crisis averted, Queen began to publicly question the JLA's goals and methods, putting him at odds with HAWKMAN, in particular. Before long he had resigned his League membership.

LOVERS' TIFF Black Canary may love Oliver, but she continues to have problems with his infidelity and commitment issues.

BACK FROM THE DEAD

Green Arrow attempted to prevent a terrorist from detonating a bomb over Metropolis, but gave his life in the process. His lifelong friend, Hal Jordan (formerly Green Lantern II, now a mad being named PARALLAX), used his cosmic power to restore Ollie to life, but without a soul.

With the help of his "family," Ollie regained his soul and made a concerted effort to put his life back in order. He reconnected with Connor Hawke and Roy Harper and took in Mia Dearden, a teen from the streets of his beloved Star City. Still restless, Ollie fought injustice while longing for Dinah.

His legend would grow and grow, eventually becoming so powerful that in the 853rd century the Earth would be watched over by a squad who called itself the society of Green Arrows.

MIA DEARDEN

Mia Dearden ran away from a violent home when she was a child. Homeless, she turned to prostitution to support herself. She subsequently met the recently resurrected Oliver Queen. He took her in and gave her a safe place to once again be a teen.

Mia trained with Connor Hawke until her skills at martial arts and archery rivaled those of the former Speedy, Roy Harper. Impressed, Oliver Queen allowed Mia to become the new Speedy. She also served a short term with the Teen Titans.

SAVIOR *Oliver sent Mia to the Star City Youth Recreational Center for safety.*

AMAZON PRISONER
Kidnapped on his wedding night, Green Arrow knew that Black Canary would come to his rescue.

POLITICS AND MARRIAGE

After the Infinite Crisis, Green Arrow recuperated from an attack by Merlyn on a remote island. There, he recommitted himself to the martial arts, and took office as mayor of Star City upon his return. Mayor Queen did not serve a full term, instead resigning and rekindling his romance with Black Canary. The two were wed, though the shapeshifter Everyman temporarily took Green Arrow's place while Amazons took the real Oliver to Themyscira.

NEWLY WED *Her friends warned her it wouldn't last, but Black Canary accepted Oliver's proposal.*

CONNOR HAWKE

Oliver's son by Sandra Moonday Hawke, Connor Hawke was raised as a Buddhist monk and trained in martial arts. Though Connor sought inner peace, he also yearned for adventure, spurred by hero-worship for the father he had never known. A new path opened up for the teenager when Ollie visited the monastery where, years earlier, he had sought asylum. As the couple traveled together, Connor revealed that he was Ollie's son. When Ollie seemed to have been killed in an airplane explosion over Metropolis, Connor took on his father's crime-fighting role as a second Green Arrow.

DOUBLE HITTER
He's good with a bow, but Connor's major strength is martial arts.

INNOCENT AND GOOD

When Oliver Queen returned to life, father and son decided to protect Star City together. Connor remains somewhat innocent about the world around him, confused over his magnetic attraction for women. He feels most free when patrolling the city's rooftops with his father. RG

KEY STORYLINES

• *GREEN LANTERN/GREEN ARROW (1ST AND 2ND SERIES) (2004):* Collections of classic stories as the heroic pair traveled the U.S. righting wrongs.

• *GREEN ARROW: THE ARCHER'S QUEST (2003):* Back from the dead, Ollie Queen uses keepsakes to reconnect with his family.

• *GREEN ARROW: THE LONGBOW HUNTER (1989):* Green Arrow saves Black Canary from being tortured; he also encounters the mysterious female assassin Shado.

• *THE BRAVE AND THE BOLD #85 (AUGUST 1969):* In "The Senator's Been Shot," Green Arrow dons a new outfit, a beard, and gains a new attitude toward his role as a crime fighter.

GREEN LANTERN

BRIGHTEST LIGHT IN THE UNIVERSE

ALAN SCOTT (GREEN LANTERN I)
FIRST APPEARANCE ALL-AMERICAN COMICS #16 (July 1940)
STATUS Hero   *OCCUPATION* Crime fighter   *BASE* Gotham City
HEIGHT 6ft   *WEIGHT* 201 lbs   *EYES* Blue   *HAIR* Blond

HAL JORDAN (GREEN LANTERN II/PARALLAX)
FIRST APPEARANCE SHOWCASE #22 (October 1959)
STATUS Hero/villain (deceased)   *OCCUPATION* Spectral guardian
BASE Utah desert   *HEIGHT* 6ft 2in   *WEIGHT* 186 lbs
EYES Brown   *HAIR* Brown

GUY GARDNER (GREEN LANTERN III)
FIRST APPEARANCE GREEN LANTERN (2nd series) #59
(March 1968)   *STATUS* Hero
OCCUPATION Adventurer   *BASE* New York City
HEIGHT 6ft   *WEIGHT* 180 lbs   *EYES* Blue   *HAIR* Red

JOHN STEWART (GREEN LANTERN IV)
FIRST APPEARANCE GREEN LANTERN (2nd series) #87
(January 1972)   *STATUS* Hero
OCCUPATION Architect   *BASE* New York City
HEIGHT 6ft 1in   *WEIGHT* 201 lbs   *EYES* Brown   *HAIR* Black

KYLE RAYNER (GREEN LANTERN V)
FIRST APPEARANCE GREEN LANTERN (3rd series) #48
(January 1994)   *STATUS* Hero
OCCUPATION Crime fighter; cartoonist   *BASE* New York
HEIGHT 5ft 11in   *WEIGHT* 175 lbs   *EYES* Green   *HAIR* Black

SPECIAL POWERS/ABILITIES Green Lantern ring generates hard-light images, limited only by user's imagination; ring is also a database and language translator, and allows travel through space. Rings must be recharged using a lantern-shaped power battery.

ONCE THEY WERE a corps 3,600 strong, wearing the most powerful weapons ever devised on their fingers.
The GREEN LANTERN CORPS acted as an intergalactic police force, doing the bidding of the GUARDIANS OF THE UNIVERSE. Each Green Lantern possessed a power ring that could create hard-light projections by drawing energy from the Central Power Battery on the Guardians' homeworld of Oa; however, the rings were ineffective against anything yellow. The Green Lantern Corps suffered a fatal blow at the hands of Hal Jordan, but Kyle Rayner may be the best hope for restoring this ancient force of justice and order.

BRIGHT LIGHT *Created by artist Martin Nodell, Alan Scott debuted in All-American Comics in 1940 before getting his own series a year later.*

ALAN SCOTT

Eons ago the Guardians of the Universe trapped most of the universe's magical energies into an orb called the Starheart. A fragment of this object gave rise to Alan Scott's ring and power battery. Unlike Corps equipment, Scott's mystical ring worked fine against yellow objects, but was powerless against wood. Scott helped establish the JUSTICE SOCIETY OF AMERICA during World War II. After many decades he discovered that his body had been infused with the energy of the Starheart and that he no longer required a ring. Scott briefly took the identity of Sentinel before reclaiming the Green Lantern mantle.

DOWN AND OUT
Sinestro fails to halt Parallax's rampage.

HAL JORDAN

Hal Jordan was both the Corps' greatest champion and its worst nightmare. As Green Lantern and protector of space sector 2814, Jordan founded the JUSTICE LEAGUE OF AMERICA alongside AQUAMAN and the FLASH. He battled a legion of galactic foes including the fallen Green Lantern SINESTRO. But when the CYBORG SUPERMAN demolished Jordan's home, Coast City, he went mad with grief. Enraged when the Guardians barred him from resurrecting Coast City using his ring, Jordan destroyed the Guardians and their Corps—becoming the god-like villain PARALLAX. Though Parallax died during the Sun-Eater crisis, Jordan's spirit lived on as the universe's new SPECTRE.

TRANSITIONS
Guardian Abin Sur bequeaths his power ring to Hal Jordan.

GUY GARDNER

Originally passed over by Abin Sur in favor of Hal Jordan, Guy Gardner enjoyed a checkered career as Green Lantern. Gardner became known for his belligerent, cocky stance, marked by his constant attempts to prove himself as the one, true Green Lantern. Gardner served with the JLA but later lost his right to wear a power ring. He briefly wore Sinestro's yellow power ring, then embraced a new role when he discovered his heritage as a genetically-altered warrior engineered by the alien Vuldarians.

LIGHTS OUT *Guy Gardner takes a blow to his pride.*

PARALLAX *Hal Jordan achieved unimaginable power as the megalomaniacal Parallax. Ironically, he is even more powerful as the divinely-empowered Spectre.*

The Green Lantern insignia is worn by all members of the Corps.

The power ring is uniquely keyed to Kyle and cannot be used by others.

Art works Kyle's civilian job as a graphic artist helps him in his career as Green Lantern since he can physically create anything he dreams up in pencils. Viewed by some as irresponsible and too focused on Earth, Kyle has made amends by patrolling space and attempting to rebuild the Green Lantern Corps.

KYLE RAYNER

When Hal Jordan shattered the Green Lantern Corps, the last remaining Guardian gave a power ring to a new hero—Kyle Rayner of Earth. Although he seemed to have been selected at random, Rayner worked hard to prove himself worthy of the Green Lantern legacy. His upgraded ring has no weakness against the color yellow, and Rayner has handled himself well against the super-villain MAJOR FORCE (who murdered Rayner's girlfriend) and the Lantern-hunting killer, FATALITY. Kyle forged friendships with GREEN ARROW and the Flash, and has kindled a romance with Alan Scott's daughter, Jade. Rayner assumed the identity of the near-omnipotent Ion before bleeding off much of his power by resurrecting the Guardians. Kyle Rayner recruited members to restore the Corps to its former glory.

SWAN SONG

Although Kyle Rayner worked to restore the Green Lantern Corps, his actions seemed to bring about the twilight of his career. After returning from outer space, Kyle learned that his girlfriend, Jade, had moved on and that the JLA was doing well with John Stewart in the role of power-ring wielder. Kyle's subsequent battle with Fatality showed that he still had plenty of spirit, but other factors—including the revelation that Major Force had returned to orchestrate Fatality's attacks—were harbingers of change for Earth's Green Lantern. DW

EMERALD KNIGHT *Kyle Rayner has grown from a rookie to a seasoned warrior.*

JOHN STEWART

Originally Hal Jordan's backup Green Lantern, John Stewart has become one of the greatest ring-bearers, despite a career filled with unimaginable pain. Stewart accidentally destroyed the entire planet Xanshi, then suffered when his wife, Katma Tui, died at the hands of STAR SAPPHIRE. He earned a measure of peace as the caretaker of a patchwork "mosaic world" on Oa, and later became a member of the DARKSTARS (an intergalactic peacekeeping force that is a rival to the Green Lantern Corps). Injuries suffered in the line of duty left him paralyzed from the waist down, and he briefly worked as an architect until Hal Jordan, as Parallax, restored the use of his legs. Now, John Stewart works with the world's most powerful super heroes as a member of the JLA, and has helped quell interplanetary threats including Fernus, a Burning Martian who tried to trigger a nuclear holocaust. His most recent misfortune has been the breakup of his relationship with Merayn, a former Darkstar.

RESOLUTE *Presented with several opportunities to retire, John Stewart has continued to serve as Green Lantern.*

- **GREEN LANTERN (2ND SERIES) #76 (APRIL 1970):** This classic tale united Green Lantern Hal Jordan and Green Arrow Oliver Queen for what would become a road-trip exploration of America.
- **GREEN LANTERN (3RD SERIES) #48–50 (JANUARY–MARCH 1994):** Kyle Rayner took over as Green Lantern when Hal Jordan turned rogue in the series-changing "Emerald Twilight" epic.
- **GREEN LANTERN (3RD SERIES) #162–164 (JUNE–AUGUST 2003):** In an echo of his predecessor's journey, Kyle Rayner teamed up with Green Arrow Oliver Queen to investigate an intergalactic crime ring.

THE DC COMICS ENCYCLOPEDIA

GREEN LANTERN

THE RETURN OF HAL JORDAN

Hal Jordan's penance came to an end with the revelation of Parallax's true nature. Parallax had existed since the beginning of time as the living embodiment of fear. Eons of imprisonment in the Green Lantern Central Power Battery, where it became known as "the yellow impurity," had contained its poisonous influence, and had given the power rings their traditional weakness against the color yellow.

In Jordan's case, Parallax had psychically weakened him after the destruction of Coast City, causing him to devastate Oa and crack the Power Battery. Now freed, Parallax had attached itself to Jordan's soul, remaining even while Jordan played host to the Spectre.

The ultimate showdown with Parallax united Green Lanterns John Stewart, Guy Gardner, Kilowog, Kyle Rayner, and Jordan himself – newly restored to life in his original body. The Lanterns locked Parallax within the Oan power battery, reintroducing the yellow weakness – but with Parallax's qualities revealed, the rings' flaw could now be overcome by mastering one's fear.

DUAL IDENTITY *Parallax appeared as an evil twin during Jordan's struggle.*

UNITED FRONT *The combined efforts of five of the galaxy's best Green Lanterns beat Parallax into submission.*

BACK IN UNIFORM *Hal Jordan's resurrection brought him back to Carol Ferris, his first love.*

THE SINESTRO CORPS WAR

Sinestro had not been killed during Jordan's Parallax rampage as originally believed. He gathered followers to forge a mirror opposite of the Green Lantern Corps. Instead of willpower, the yellow rings of the Sinestro Corps fed on fear. Jordan took the fight to the Sinestro Corps' headquarters on Qward in the anti-matter universe, then defended Earth when Sinestro made it his next target. Parallax, freed by the Sinestro Corps, possessed Kyle Rayner before being split into pieces and stored in the personal power batteries of Jordan, Stewart, Rayner, and Guy Gardner.

EVIL'S MIGHT *Sinestro's charisma makes him a popular leader among his monstrous troops.*

CHALLENGES AND CLASHES

Hal Jordan rejoined Earth's super-hero community. He also took up his duties as Green Lantern of sector 2814, sharing responsibilities with John Stewart. In his civilian identity Jordan worked as a test pilot and captain in the U.S. Air Force, operating out of the slowly-rebuilding Coast City. Jordan's former rogues' gallery was quick to notice his return. He soon clashed with Hector Hammond, Black Hand, and the Tattooed Man. After the Infinite Crisis, Jordan spent time in a POW camp after his jet went down over Russian airspace. Other challenges included a confrontation with Amon Sur (son of Abin Sur, who gave Jordan his first power ring) and his old nemesis Star Sapphire. Jordan served briefly with the Justice League of America until ceding his spot to John Stewart.

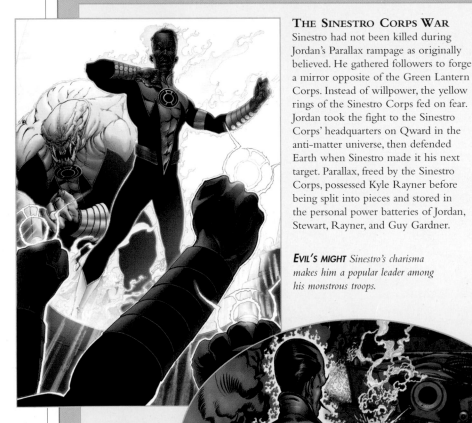

SUPERVILLAINY *The powers of the reborn Sinestro were enough to overwhelm Kyle Rayner and Green Arrow.*

VIOLET ENERGY *Star Sapphire is one of several villains to vex Jordan upon his return.*

JOHN STEWART AND THE GREAT TEN

After the return of Hal Jordan and the reorganization of the Green Lantern Corps, John Stewart assumed co-duties with Jordan as protectors of Earth's space sector 2814. Stewart was among the first to test the tense international standoff that followed the Infinite Crisis, when he chased a fugitive to the Chinese border and provoked a confrontation with the Great Ten. Stewart later accepted a position with the Justice League of America after Hal Jordan stepped down, and quickly found himself at odds with Lex Luthor's Injustice League Unlimited. He also used his architectural training to design the League's new Hall in Washington D.C.

BODY'S REJECTION
With his Vuldarian DNA purged from his system, Gardner returned to the Corps.

GUY GARDNER'S MISSION

After enduring his body's genetic rejection of the Vuldarian DNA that had once transformed him into the Warrior, Guy Gardner returned to the Green Lantern Corps as an instructor for new trainees. He led his recruits to a victory over a resurgent Spider Guild and earned a promotion to the Corps' Honor Guard, but went behind the Guardians' backs to help Hal Jordan retrieve the "Lost Lanterns" believed killed during Jordan/Parallax's attack on Oa. As punishment, Gardner served on "Prime Duty," overseeing the floating prison cell in which Superboy-Prime had been locked since the end of the Infinite Crisis. Gardner later ran a mission with the top-secret agents of the "Green Lantern Corpse." During the Sinestro Corps War, he fought the escaped Superboy-Prime and an army of yellow-ringed soldiers during their invasion of Earth. DW

KYLE RAYNER: MAGIC AND LOSS

At the edge of the universe Kyle Rayner was the first to uncover the truth of Parallax, bringing the knowledge back to Earth to help the other Lanterns defeat the fear entity. During the Infinite Crisis he witnessed the death of Jade and underwent a second transformation into Ion. Rayner eventually learned that Ion was a separate being, the living embodiment of willpower that fueled the Green Lanterns' emerald energy. The Guardians viewed Rayner/Ion as the next evolution of Green Lanterns, and gave him the title "the Torchbearer." Rayner suffered a new loss when his mother died of a debilitating illness. He soon learned her death had been no accident—Sinestro had arranged for her infection by the sentient virus Despotellis. Weakened by the knowledge that he hadn't saved her, Rayner became the new host for Parallax. During the Sinestro Corps War, Guy Gardner helped Rayner break Parallax's hold by showing him a painting that Rayner's mother had made before her death. After rejoining the Green Lantern Corps—now without the powers of Ion—Rayner helped Donna Troy, Jason Todd, and a rogue Monitor as they traversed the multiverse in search of Ray Palmer.

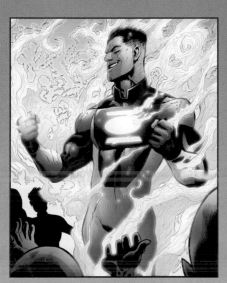

NEW BLOOD *During the Sinestro Corps war, Sodam Yat took over from Kyle Rayner as Ion.*

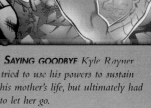

SAYING GOODBYE *Kyle Rayner tried to use his powers to sustain his mother's life, but ultimately had to let her go.*

GRACE

FIRST APPEARANCE OUTSIDERS (3rd series) #1 (August 2003)
STATUS Hero **REAL NAME** Grace Choi
OCCUPATION Nightclub bouncer **BASE** Metropolis
HEIGHT 7ft **WEIGHT** 230 lbs
EYES Brown (wears purple contact lenses) **HAIR** Black (dyed auburn)
SPECIAL POWERS/ABILITIES Superstrength; is a powerful brawler and fighter.

Grace Choi is an Amazon, with her heritage coming from the outsider tribe known as the Bana. For a time, Grace was head of security at Chaney's, a bar and club in Metropolis that caters to a meta-human clientele. Chaney's was considered a safe space for superpowered heroes and villains alike. Grace worked there until she accepted ARSENAL's offer to join a new team of OUTSIDERS that had banded together after the dissolution of the New Titans and YOUNG JUSTICE. While serving with the Outsiders, Grace earned notoriety for her brutal fighting, and she secretly struck up a romance with her teammate THUNDER II. She has since joined BATMAN's new Outsiders. DW

GRAVEDIGGER

FIRST APPEARANCE MEN OF WAR #1 (August 1977)
STATUS Hero (believed retired) **REAL NAME** Captain Ulysses Hazard
OCCUPATION Soldier **BASE** Europe
HEIGHT 6ft 2in **WEIGHT** 201 lbs **EYES** Brown **HAIR** Brown
SPECIAL POWERS/ABILITIES Excellent athlete, trained to use most weapons and in all forms of combat; above average strength and speed.

After overcoming polio as a child, Ulysses Hazard worked to strengthen his body, relearning how to walk and run. As a result, this native of Birmingham, Alabama excelled in every way. He enlisted at the outbreak of World War II and once again proved exceptional with his arms training. Frustrated at being continually sent on graves detail simply because of his skin color, he went AWOL. Journeying to Washington, D.C., he slipped past security and broke into the offices of the Joint Chiefs of Staff to prove that he was more than just a gravedigger. Impressed, they turned him into a one-man unit, sending him on secret missions in the European Theater of Operations. Along the way, he suffered an injury that left a cross-shaped scar at the bridge of his nose. His post-World War II whereabouts remain unrecorded. RG

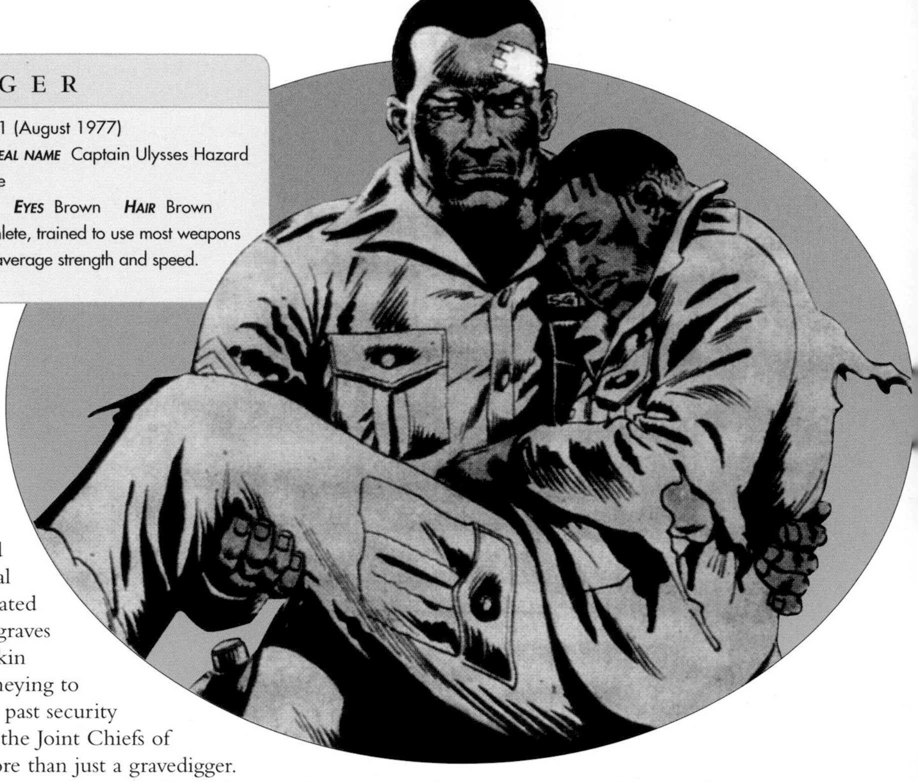

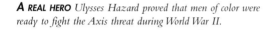

A REAL HERO *Ulysses Hazard proved that men of color were ready to fight the Axis threat during World War II.*

GRANNY GOODNESS

FIRST APPEARANCE MISTER MIRACLE (1st series) #2 (May 1971)
STATUS Villain **REAL NAME** None
OCCUPATION Headmistress **BASE** Apokolips
HEIGHT 5ft 10in **WEIGHT** 256 lbs **EYES** Blue **HAIR** White
SPECIAL POWERS/ABILITIES Robust for her age, Granny is a formidable fighter; however she usually gets her way by the sheer force of her evil will; her personal arsenal includes electrocuting energy-gauntlets.

In her youth, trooper Goodness was one of the finest dog soldiers in the armies of Apokolips, easily besting her male compatriots. Rising quickly through the ranks, Goodness faced her final test of loyalty when ordered to shoot her warhound Mercy. Goodness blasted her examiner instead. Taken before DARKSEID, Goodness had no other choice but to slay her beloved beast when the dread lord of Apokolips—the warhound's true master—commanded it to maul her to death. Pleasing Darkseid with her quick kill, Goodness graduated with honors, becoming one of but a few females among Darkseid's Elite. Years later, she would be known as Granny Goodness, headmistress of a number of nightmarish orphanages strung across the planet Apokolips. There, through her own brand of dominance and discipline, Granny molds the lost children of the Armagetto to become mindless minions of Darkseid. Granny's previous students include Scott Free (MISTER MIRACLE) and BIG BARDA. She also trained the FEMALE FURIES. Recently she overthrew the OLYMPIAN GODS and took Athena's place to manipulate the AMAZONS. SB

HEADMISTRESS *The orphans feel Granny's temper as deadly force.*

NO MERCY *In her youth, Goodness bonded with her warhound Mercy, but Darkseid forced her to kill her pet.*

GRAYVEN

FIRST APPEARANCE GREEN LANTERN (3rd series) #71 (February 1996)
STATUS Villain (deceased) **REAL NAME** Grayven
OCCUPATION Galactic conqueror **BASE** Mobile
HEIGHT 6ft 8in **WEIGHT** 425 lbs **EYES** Red **HAIR** Gray
SPECIAL POWERS/ABILITIES Superstrength, increased durability and stamina; is a megalomaniac whose brilliant head for military tactics is undermined by an overwhelming need to feed his ego.

Illegitimate son of DARKSEID, the warlord Grayven has long stewed in the bitter knowledge that he possesses only a fraction of the power enjoyed by his father, the Lord of Apokolips. When that knowledge became intolerable, he gathered a fleet and began conquering worlds. On Rann, he decimated the intergalactic DARKSTARS police force and crippled Darkstar (and former GREEN LANTERN) John Stewart. Green Lantern Kyle Rayner put a stop to Grayven on several occasions. During the Imperiex War (*see* Great Battles, pp. 362–3), Grayven allied with Brainiac 13 while pretending to be on his father's side. When Darkseid discovered Grayven's treachery, he banished him to another realm. Grayven was soon back, however, turning up in New York City. During the Death of the New Gods event, Grayven came face to face with the Fourth World's mysterious killer and lost his life. DW

GREAT TEN

First Appearance 52 #6 (June 2006)
Status Hero Team
Base Great Wall Complex, China
Current members and powers

August General in Iron Armored team leader, carries energy staff.
Accomplished Perfect Physician Can use his voice to heal others, destroy matter, or create earthquakes.
Celestial Archer Expert with a bow and arrow.
Ghost Fox Killer Possesses supernatural control over trapped spirits.
Immortal Man in Darkness Pilots a shape-changing Durlan fighter craft.
Mother of Champions Can give birth to hundreds of super-soldiers per month.
Seven Deadly Brothers Can split into seven bodies.
Shaolin Robot Relentless superpowered machine.
Socialist Red Guardsman Radioactive mutant encased in armor.
Thundermind Multiple powers based on Buddhist Siddhis.

The Great Ten are the premier super-team of the People's Republic of China. Led by August General in Iron, the heroes are referred to as "super-functionaries" by their country's communist government and operate out of a complex built into the Great Wall. They first made their presence known following the Infinite Crisis, preventing two GREEN LANTERNS from entering Chinese airspace due to a treaty their country had signed with BLACK ADAM's nation of Khandaq. The United Nations organization CHECKMATE fought the Great Ten while infiltrating a Chinese facility. Chang Tzu (see EGG FU) is also a member of the Great Ten, and others in the group helped him defend his Oolong Island base from a joint assault by Checkmate and the OUTSIDERS. August General in Iron later joined Checkmate as Black King's Bishop.

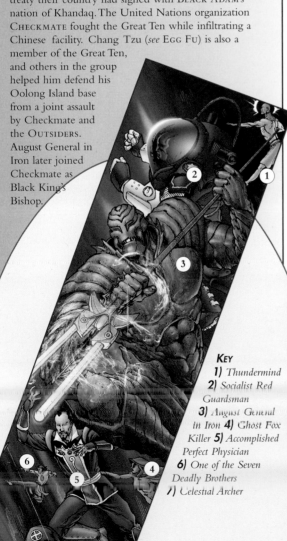

KEY
1) Thundermind
2) Socialist Red Guardsman
3) August General in Iron 4) Ghost Fox Killer 5) Accomplished Perfect Physician
6) One of the Seven Deadly Brothers
7) Celestial Archer

GREEN LANTERN CORPS

First appearance (I) GREEN LANTERN (1st series) #11 (March 1962); (II) GREEN LANTERN: THE NEW CORPS #1 (April 1999)
Status Hero team   **Base** Interstellar space
Members and powers
There have been thousands of Green Lanterns throughout history, each armed with a power ring that is limited only by its wearer's will. Prominent members include: **Aa, Amanita, Arisia (deceased), Arkkis Chummuck (deceased), Ash, Boodikka, Brik, Cary Wren, Ch'P (deceased), Chriselon, Eddore, Flodo Span (deceased), G'nort, Galius Zed (deceased), Green Man, Guy Gardner, Hal Jordan, Hollika Ran (deceased), Jack T. Chance, John Stewart, Katma Tui (deceased), Kilowog, Kreon, Larvox, Medphyll, Mogo, Salakk, Sinestro (deceased), Stel, Tomar-Tu, Tomar-Re (deceased), Torquemada, Zax.**

INFINITE CRISIS An army of Green Lanterns past and present battle Superboy Prime, desperate to thwart his attempts to destroy Oa and collapse the universe.

THE NEW CORPS The Green Lantern Corps were rebuilt by Guy Gardner, Kilowog and Kyle Rayner 1) Kilowog 2) Guy Gardner 3) Soranik Natu 4) Yath Sam

The Green Lantern Corps was founded by the GUARDIANS OF THE UNIVERSE three billion years ago to curb the spread of evil throughout the universe. The Guardians divided the universe into 3,600 known sectors and assembled the Corps from individuals who would valiantly defend their segment of space, armed with specially crafted power rings.

The Green Lanterns guarded the universe for millennia, combating evil and abiding by a strict code of conduct set by the Guardians. In recent years, Hal Jordan of Earth became one of the most exemplary Green Lanterns, while the renegade SINESTRO became one of the galaxy's most notorious criminals.

After the Crisis (see Great Battles pp. 362–3), the Guardians forsook control of the Corps and the individual sectors were abandoned. Left to their own devices, Hal Jordan and a small contingent of Green Lanterns settled on Earth. Later, when the alien despot MONGUL destroyed Coast City, Jordan went mad with grief and invaded Oa to force the Guardians to resurrect the city's inhabitants. Jordan, possessed by PARALLAX, destroyed the Power Battery, but the sole surviving Green Lantern (Kyle Rayner) rebuilt the decimated Corps. During the Sinestro Corps War, the Guardians authorized the use of lethal force against enemies of the Green Lantern Corps. With the Sinestro Corps' yellow rings representing fear in contrast to the green glow of willpower, Corps representing the remaining emotional hues have recently appeared. These include the Blue Lanterns (hope), the Violet Lanterns (love), the Red Lanterns (rage), the Orange Lanterns (greed), the Indigo Lanterns (compassion), and the Black Lanterns (death). **PJ**

GUARDIAN

First appearance STAR-SPANGLED COMICS #7 (April 1942)
Status Hero **Real name** James Jacob Harper
Occupation Adventurer **Base** Metropolis
Height 6ft 1in **Weight** 203 lbs **Eyes** Blue
Hair Brown
Special powers/abilities Jim Harper (and his various clones) possessed the training every beat cop receives in addition to being an accomplished athlete.

GUARDIAN ANGEL *Whether as a human being or a clone, Jim Harper was ready to protect the innocent from all forms of evil, both mortal and mystic.*

PROTECTIVE SHIELD
With his shield, the Guardian had a decided advantage in fights—it was nearly indestructible.

Rookie cop James Jacob "Jim" Harper assumed the costumed alias of the Guardian only hours before joining the FLASH, GREEN LANTERN, WILDCAT I, and the ATOM in a battle with the Starheart-empowered Joe Morgan. A few weeks later on January 23, 1942, Harper became legal "guardian" for the young members of the NEWSBOY LEGION. As both a cop and the Guardian, he guided these youths to serve justice—and attend school.

With age slowing his reflexes, Harper agreed to have himself cloned. His memories were transferred into an adult body and the Guardian lived once more, his main role being to provide security at the top-secret genetic research facility Project Cadmus. As time passed, however, the Guardian came to feel that his life wasn't complete without friends and family. His melancholy intensified when SUPERBOY left Cadmus for a life of his own.

The Guardian was later killed by the explosive criminal Shrapnel and, against his wishes, was cloned once again, making a rapid advance from infancy toward adulthood. The Manhattan Guardian newspaper later purchased the name from Cadmus and fielded its own hero—Jake Jordan, the Manhattan Guardian. **RG**

IN HIS IMAGE *Against the first clone's wishes, Project Cadmus grew a new Harper.*

SURROUNDED *Jake Jordan, the Manhattan Guardian, battles berserk theme-park robots.*

GUARDIANS OF THE UNIVERSE

First appearance GREEN LANTERN (3rd series) #50 (March 1994)
Status Cosmic superbeings **Base** The planet Oa
Notable members and powers
Ganthet (leader) Possesses telekinetic and telepathic powers, immortality, flight, and the ability to wield energies from the Central Power Battery.
Lianna Similar powers to Ganthet, though limited by the inexperience of youth.

SINGLE SEX *The original Guardians consisted only of males.*

Once the greatest of the cosmos' myriad species, the Guardians of the Universe saw five billion years of dominance come to a rude end within the last decade—even immortal beings, it seems, can be killed. The Guardians evolved on the overcrowded planet Maltus. When one of their number, the scientist KRONA, arrogantly sought to observe the Great Hand that called the universe into being, a blast of cosmic power created an evil mirror universe of antimatter. Stricken with guilt, the Maltusians migrated to Oa and declared themselves an eternal force for order—the Guardians of the Universe. Some Oans, feeling that evil should be sought out and destroyed, became the more proactive Controllers.

The Guardians first created robotic peacekeepers each called MANHUNTER (who later rebelled against their creators), then deputized thousands of alien "locals" into the intergalactic GREEN LANTERN CORPS. The female Oans eventually left the planet to form their own warrior society, the Zamarons.

In modern times the Guardians left the universe with the Zamarons to create a new breed of immortals, then returned after the destruction of Oa's Central Power Battery. Restoring the battery's energies, they re-established the Corps, only to die when former champion Hal Jordan, the second GREEN LANTERN, devastated Oa in his quest for power. Kyle Rayner, the current Green Lantern, resurrected the Guardians as infants (in male and female forms) to be raised by the sole original Guardian, Ganthet. During the Sinestro Corps War, the Guardians rewrote the Book of Oa to authorize the use of lethal force. **DW**

REJUVENATION *The Guardians now exist as males and females, though it is unclear how long it will take for them to assume their adult forms.*

GUNFIRE

FIRST APPEARANCE DEATHSTROKE ANNUAL #2 (Summer 1993)
STATUS Hero **REAL NAME** Andrew Van Horn
OCCUPATION Munitions expert **BASE** New York City
HEIGHT 6ft 1in **WEIGHT** 190 lbs **EYES** Green **HAIR** Red
SPECIAL POWERS/ABILITIES Able to psychokinetically transform small objects into explosive energy projectiles, which he uses as concussive weapons; skilled hand-to-hand combatant.

Andrew Van Horn is the wealthy heir to Van Horn Industries, a powerful international conglomerate. Years ago, Andrew and his father were attacked by an alien parasite in one of the Van Horn warehouses in Paris. The elder Van Horn perished, but Andrew was changed into a meta-human with the ability to transform objects by accelerating their particles, and warping them into explosive weapons. Andrew was one of many "New Bloods" (see BLOOD PACK) accidentally created by the parasites. He joined forces with these fledgling heroes and the JUSTICE LEAGUE OF AMERICA to stop the parasites' reign of terror. Andrew then learned that his father had been an arms dealer with links to various criminals and vowed to put an end to his illegal legacy. Declining JLA membership, Gunfire used his powers to stop the terrorist activities of villains like the Oblivion Front and their leader Dominion. Dominion was a former Van Horn employee who tried to steal the weapons Gunfire's father had stockpiled. Gunfire defeated Dominion and the Oblivion Front was dissolved. **PJ**

ATTACK OF THE PARASITES *Defending the assassin Deathstroke the Terminator, Gunfire's explosive powers were used to defeat the creatures who created him—parasites out to conquer the planet.*

GUNNER AND SARGE

FIRST APPEARANCE OUR FIGHTING FORCES #45 (May 1958)
STATUS Heroes (Sarge is deceased) **REAL NAMES** "Gunner" MacKay (full name unrevealed); "Sarge" Clay (full name unrevealed)
OCCUPATIONS Private, U.S. Marines; Sergeant, U.S. Marines
BASE Mobile **HEIGHT** 5ft 10in; 6ft **WEIGHT** 162 lbs; 205 lbs
EYES (both characters) Blue **HAIR** Blond; reddish blond
SPECIAL POWERS/ABILITIES Highly skilled commandos; Gunner favored a Thompson machine gun, and is now a cyborg with guns for arms.

STRANDED *Gunner, Sarge, and C.I.A. agent Eddie Fyers are Japanese P.O.W.'s on an island time forgot.*

GUNS BLAZING *Pooch fetches a live grenade as Gunner (left) and Sarge (right) blast their way to victory.*

"Gunner" MacKay and "Sarge" Clay fought bravely together in the Pacific, often helped by Pooch, a dog from the K-9 Corps who saved their lives countless times. Later, Gunner and Sarge were assigned to the European front to train a band of raw recruits. Unfortunately, their trainees were slaughtered on their first patrol. The two Marines blamed themselves and fell in with fellow misfits CAPTAIN STORM and Johnny Cloud (see CLOUD, JOHNNY), forming the LOSERS task force. The team went on secret missions until, in early 1945, Gunner and Sarge were killed by Nazi troops. Gunner's body was revived by the top-secret Project M. Fitted with cybernetic implants that made him a walking weapon, Gunner MacKay became a member of the CREATURE COMMANDOS, battling inter-dimensional invaders, but he still misses his old pal Sarge. **SB**

GUNSHOT

FIRST APPEARANCE JUSTICE LEAGUE OF AMERICA (2nd series) #78 (August 1993)
STATUS Villain **REAL NAME** Unknown
OCCUPATION Member of New Extremists **BASE** Mobile
HEIGHT 6ft 1in **WEIGHT** 202 lbs **EYES** Blue **HAIR** Black
SPECIAL POWERS/ABILITIES Wears armored battlesuit bristling with weapons, which enhances his natural marksmanship.

Little is known about the villain known as Gunshot. He rarely talks, and a bullet from his battlesuit can be a real conversation killer. He first appeared on the super hero scene as one of the New Extremists, a team assembled by the extra-dimensional being DREAMSLAYER. Gunshot and his teammates, Brute, Cloudburst, Death Angel, and MEANSTREAK, tried and failed to rout the JUSTICE LEAGUE OF AMERICA. A second opportunity presented itself when Dreamslayer used the energies of a machine to usurp the power of the omnipotent OVERMASTER. Dreamslayer called the New Extremists to his side but again tasted defeat. The Overmaster then dispensed with Dreamslayer and dealt with the New Extremists directly, pulling them into his massive new CADRE. Since the Cadre's defeat, Gunshot has kept a low profile. **DW**

GYPSY

FIRST APPEARANCE JUSTICE LEAGUE OF AMERICA (1st series) ANNUAL #2 (November 1984)
STATUS Hero **REAL NAME** Cynthia "Cindy" Reynolds
OCCUPATION Adventurer **BASE** Mobile
HEIGHT 5ft 6in **WEIGHT** 130 lbs **EYES** Blue **HAIR** Black
SPECIAL POWERS/ABILITIES Chameleon-like camouflage powers allow her to blend into her surroundings; can project realistic illusions into the minds of certain targets.

A shy street urchin from Detroit, 15-year-old Cindy Reynolds unveiled her special camouflage powers during a battle with the alien CADRE. Invited to join the JUSTICE LEAGUE OF AMERICA, Cindy, as Gypsy, kept her past and her real name secret from the League. After the League's enemy PROFESSOR IVO began murdering Gypsy's fellow teammates, she returned to a normal life living in suburbia with her parents.

Tragically, Gypsy's parents were killed by the alien DESPERO. Saved from Despero's wrath by the MARTIAN MANHUNTER, Gypsy returned to adventuring and joined BOOSTER GOLD's CONGLOMERATE. Later, Gypsy became a member of the Justice League Task Force and died, but was resurrected by the Martian Manhunter and the Martian god H'ronmeer. Gypsy has also served as a member of the BIRDS OF PREY. **PJ**

HACKER FILES, THE

FIRST APPEARANCE THE HACKER FILES #1 (August 1992)
STATUS Hero **REAL NAME** Jack Marshall
OCCUPATION Freelance systems analyst
BASE Raleigh, North Carolina
HEIGHT 6ft **WEIGHT** 175 lbs **EYES** Brown **HAIR** Black
SPECIAL POWERS/ABILITIES One of the world's most brilliant computer programmers; however, in terms of physical ability he is totally unathletic.

Jack Marshall may have been called a nerd a few times in his young life, but he was a pretty smart nerd, who knew how to exploit his computer skills to the maximum. One of his earliest software successes was a best-selling computer game entitled, *Code of the West*. He subsequently joined the cutting-edge company Digitronix. Along with company president Donny Travis, Jack developed the Digitronix computer, the most advanced system on Earth at the time.

Jack's problems began when asked for a profit-share deal. Greedy Senior Vice President Walter Sutcliffe turned him down flat. Boiling with resentment, Jack tried to steal the system but was caught, fired, and, worst of all, blacklisted by the industry. The Digitronix system proved hugely successful and was used in the Batcave (*see* Amazing Bases, pp. 132–3) and ORACLE's headquarters. The system is so much a part of Marshall that, when problems occur, he is frequently called in to help fix them. In so doing, Jack uncovered a mysterious set of software linking the system to similar models in Japan and China. With the help of the Speed Metal Kids, young teens hanging out on the Internet, Marshall has discovered Digitronix is trying to develop artificial intelligence. **RG**

HADES

FIRST APPEARANCE WONDER WOMAN (2nd series) #1 (February 1987)
STATUS Olympian god **REAL NAME** Hades
OCCUPATION Ruler of the underworld **BASE** Tartarus
HEIGHT 6ft 2in **WEIGHT** 190 lbs **EYES** Blue **HAIR** Black
SPECIAL POWERS/ABILITIES Immortal, able to summon vast magical forces.

Hades is the Greek god of the Underworld, one of the many children of the Titans of Myth. Although Hades had dominion over the realms of all dead souls, including the heavenly Elysian Fields, he is most known for his stewardship of the infernal Tartarus, where wicked spirits spent all eternity. He shared control of his territory with his wife, Persephone.

Hades has often found himself in league with his nephew ARES to conquer the other OLYMPIAN GODS, though Ares is frequently quick to betray his uncle. WONDER WOMAN has also played a notable role in Hades' history, journeying to the underworld to slay monsters or restore fallen heroes to life. Recently, Hades fell to Ares' back-stabbing, losing control of the lands of the dead to the God of War. **DW**

HALO

FIRST APPEARANCE THE BRAVE AND THE BOLD #200 (July 1983)
STATUS Hero **REAL NAMES** Violet Harper/Gabrielle Doe/Marissa Baron
OCCUPATION Adventurer **BASE** Los Angeles
HEIGHT 5ft 7in **WEIGHT** 137 lbs **EYES** Blue **HAIR** Blonde
SPECIAL POWERS/ABILITIES Flight; halo of energy provide a variety of powers depending on color of spectrum.

Killed by the assassin SYONIDE, Violet Harper received a new life when one of the extradimensional alien Aurakles inhabited her body and wiped her memory clean. Choosing the name Gabrielle Doe, she joined BATMAN's OUTSIDERS team under the codename Halo. Her Aurakle abilities surrounded her in a halo of energy of varying colors: red (heat), orange (force blasts), yellow (light), green (stasis beam), blue (distortion effect), indigo (tractor beam), violet (all powers at once). Initially the legal ward of teammate KATANA, she reunited with Violet Harper's parents, who soon died. Halo served with the second incarnation of the Outsiders and reconnected with her original personality. Halo has since served in a support role, searching for heroes lost in space during the Infinite Crisis and helping battle BLACK ADAM during World War III. **DW**

HAMMER AND SICKLE

FIRST APPEARANCE OUTSIDERS (1st series) #10 (August 1986)
STATUS Villains **REAL NAMES** Boris and Natasha (last names not revealed) **OCCUPATION** Enforcers **BASE** Russian Federation
HEIGHT (Boris) 6ft 1in; (Natasha) 5ft 10in **WEIGHT** (Boris) 195 lbs; (Natasha) 151 lbs **EYES** (both) Blue **HAIR** (both) Blond
SPECIAL POWERS/ABILITIES Superstrength; martial arts skills; skilled masters of their respective weapons.

Hammer and Sickle are members of the PEOPLE's HEROES, a group of superbeings in Russia created by Soviet scientists to try and duplicate the powers of the American heroes, the Force of July. Boris and Natasha were codenamed Hammer and Sickle after their powerful weapons and were teamed with the People's Heroes twice, when they came to blows with the OUTSIDERS.

Later, Hammer and Sickle were sent by a rogue faction of Russian zealots to San Francisco to try and assassinate RED STAR, another Russian hero, who was on a mission of information exchange between nations. Hammer and Sickle later emerged in Gotham City, hoping to take revenge on CATWOMAN by threatening her infant daughter. **PJ**

Sickle *Hammer*

HANGMEN, THE

FIRST APPEARANCE THE TITANS SECRET FILES AND ORIGINS #2 (September 2000)
STATUS Villain team **BASE** New York City
MEMBERS AND POWERS
BREATHTAKER Can suck the oxygen out of her victim's lungs.
PROVOKE Can psychically induce suicidal behavior.
STRANGLEHOLD Vast superstrength.
SHOCK TRAUMA Can generate electricity from his body.
KILLSHOT Cyborg armed with multiple offensive weapons.

The Hangmen are a group of young, superpowered assassins, many of whom have international origins. Bound by nothing but a desire for money and wealth, the Hangmen have no personal codes of honor and fewer principles. They will only take jobs that pay them millions of dollars and will use whatever methods possible to take out their targets.

The Hangmen were originally hired by nationals from Qurac, a Middle Eastern country, to assassinate the terrorist Cheshire. The Hangmen targeted her daughter, Lian, to get to her but came to blows with Lian's father, ARSENAL, and his TEEN TITANS teammates. Soon after, Breathtaker took part in CIRCE's master scheme to take over Manhattan, but all of the Hangmen were infected with a mutating venom by the Joker before being freed from his poisonous thrall. **PJ**

HANGMEN *A team of international mercenaries and assassins, the Hangmen are* **1)** *Killshot* **2)** *Stranglehold* **3)** *Shock Trauma* **4)** *Provoke* **5)** *Breathtaker.*

HAMMOND, HECTOR

FIRST APPEARANCE GREEN LANTERN (2nd series) #5 (April 1961)
STATUS Villain **REAL NAME** Hector Hammond
OCCUPATION Criminal mastermind **BASE** The Slab (a meta-human penitentiary) **HEIGHT** 5ft 1in **WEIGHT** 146 lbs **EYES** Blue
HAIR Brown (white at temples)
SPECIAL POWERS/ABILITIES Possesses incredible intelligence, one of the strongest telepathic minds on Earth.

While hiding out in the California hills to evade the law, petty criminal Hector Hammond came upon a fallen meteor that was causing nearby foliage to evolve into forms that would not exist for another 100,000 years. After carrying the meteor back to his hideout, Hammond kidnapped four prominent scientists and exposed them to the meteor, which changed them into future-men whose heightened mental abilities were balanced by their weakened willpower. Hammond forced the scientists to invent amazing items, for which he himself took the credit. This brought Hammond to the attention of the second, who had been searching for the missing scientists.

After a lengthy battle, Green Lantern II defeated Hammond, turned him over to the authorities and restored the scientists to normal. However, Hammond escaped jail and, using the rays of the meteor, changed himself into a

BRAIN POWER *Despite being immobile, Hammond refuses to end his quest for power, even taking on a New God.*

IMMOBILE *Hammond wanted future technology to get rich. He never imagined the high price he would pay.*

future-man with an oversized brain. Determined to become immortal, Hammond bathed once more in the rays.

He became immortal—but completely immobile. Hal Jordan's resurrection from the dead inspired Hammond to return to active villainy, participating in a prison break during the Infinite Crisis. **RG**

HARBINGER

STATUS Hero (deceased) **REAL NAME** Lyla Michaels
OCCUPATION Hero **BASE** Themyscira
HEIGHT 5ft 5in **WEIGHT** 128 lbs **EYES** Green **HAIR** Blonde
SPECIAL POWERS/ABILITIES Flight; projected energy bolts from her hands; replicated herself into multiple, autonomous duplicates; possessed the History of the Universe orb, a record of every heroic event.

When her family drowned in a shipwreck, young Lyla Michaels was saved by the ultra-dimensional Monitor. This being's mission was to gather information on superpowered beings across many universes and amass an army to oppose his equal-but-opposite foe, the Anti-Monitor. To aid the Monitor in this impending conflict, which became known as the Crisis (see Great Battles, pp. 362–3), Lyla was given special powers and access to the Monitor's innumerable files as his most loyal ally, Harbinger. Following the Monitor's death and the end of the Crisis, Harbinger was a member of the now-defunct New Guardians. She was killed by the Female Furies while working as a historian on Themyscira (see Amazing Bases, pp. 132–3). **SB**

HARDLINE

FIRST APPEARANCE JUSTICE LEAGUE OF AMERICA (1st series) #233 (December 1984)
STATUS Hero **REAL NAME** Armando Ramone
OCCUPATION Adventurer **BASE** Mobile
HEIGHT 6ft 2in **WEIGHT** 210 lbs **EYES** Blue **HAIR** Black
SPECIAL POWERS/ABILITIES Can manipulate soundwaves, using their frequency and vibration in subtle or overt ways; street fighter with no formal combat training.

Paco Ramone and his older brother, Armando, were both born with the ability to manipulate sound waves. Growing up in the slums of Detroit, they didn't show off their powers, and fell in with the El Lobos gang. Paco eventually used his gift for good, joining a short-lived incarnation of the JUSTICE LEAGUE OF AMERICA. When Paco was killed in battle, Armando was shaken. He abandoned the street gang he ran and honed his powers, taking on a costumed identity.

Preferring to be part of a team rather than operate solo, Armando has since allied himself with the CONGLOMERATE under the names Hardline and Reverb. **RG**

HARDSELL

FIRST APPEARANCE STEEL #0 (2nd series) (October 1994)
STATUS Villain **REAL NAME** Unknown
OCCUPATION Member, Team Hazard's Black Ops **BASE** Mobile
HEIGHT 9ft **WEIGHT** 845 lbs **EYES** Brown **HAIR** Brown
SPECIAL POWERS/ABILITIES Superstrength and invulnerability; intimidatingly powerful physique; can also fly, courtesy of a Team Hazard-issued jet pack.

A true giant of a man, Hardsell boasts a meta-human physique that is enough to make most normal opponents tremble in their boots and surrender without a fight. He is the powerhouse of the Black Ops team assembled by the criminal mastermind HAZARD II, able to plow through scores of adversaries without worrying about anything scratching his invulnerable skin. In his first battle with the super hero STEEL III, Hardsell took a spray of red-hot rivets directly in the face, which only staggered him for a moment. Later, he defended Hazard's headquarters from Steel when the hero tore into the bunker on a rampage of revenge. Hardsell's counterattack came to a quick end, however, when a thrown "mass pod" attached to his skin, effectively doubling his gravity and pinning him helplessly to the floor. Despite his bluster and bravado, Hardsell is rapidly learning the hard way that massive muscle power isn't enough when one goes toe-to-toe with super heroes. **DW**

HARJAVTI, RUMAAN & SUMAAN

FIRST APPEARANCE (Rumaan) Justice League #2 (June 1987); (Sumaan) Justice League AMERICA #54 (September 1991)
STATUS Villains (Rumaan deceased)
REAL NAMES Rumaan and Sumaan Harjavti
OCCUPATION Dictators **BASE** Bialya
HEIGHT (both) 5ft 10in **WEIGHT** (Rumaan) 170 lbs; (Sumaan) 175 lbs
EYES (both) Brown **HAIR** (both) Black
SPECIAL POWERS/ABILITIES
No meta-human abilities; both ruthless megalomaniacs.

Rumaan Harjavti was once the dictator of the African nation of Bialya. A constant enemy of the Justice League International (see JUSTICE LEAGUE OF AMERICA), Harjavti tricked the alien Champions of Angor into helping in his country's political conflict with the Soviet Union, and, later, joined with the JOKER in an unsuccessful attempt to destroy the international hero team. Rumaan was murdered by Queen Bee I, and Rumaan's twin brother, Sumaan, took control of Bialya. He killed Queen Bee and took control of the GLOBAL GUARDIANS, who had been hypnotised by her. They became Sumaan's agents, defending Bialya against a coup by Lower Pluxas, a small neighboring nation. The Guardians were freed from their hypnotic control and left Bialya. Sumaan's grip on power was ended by the dictator Colonel Rajak (see RAJAK, COLONEL EHAD). **PJ**

EVIL TWIN *Rumaan and Sumaan bore such a strong resemblance to each other it was hard to tell them apart. This is Rumaan.*

THE DC COMICS ENCYCLOPEDIA

HARLEY QUINN

FIRST APPEARANCE BATMAN: HARLEY QUINN #1 (October 1999)
STATUS Villain **REAL NAME** Dr. Harleen Quinzel
OCCUPATION Professional criminal **BASE** Gotham City
HEIGHT 5ft 7in **WEIGHT** 140 lbs **EYES** Blue **HAIR** Blonde
SPECIAL POWERS/ABILITIES An agile acrobat following exposure to Poison Ivy's herbal remedies; once a gifted psychotherapist, she is now dangerously unbalanced; like the Joker, often employs various gag weapons in her bag of tricks.

Encountering the Joker, the inveterately evil Clown Prince of Crime, was the very worst thing that could have happened to young and impressionable Arkham Asylum psychiatrist Dr. Harleen Quinzel. While attempting to heal the Joker's maniacal mind, Quinzel found herself captivated. As he spun heartrending—and probably false—tales of an unhappy childhood, she was soon falling head over heels in love with him.

CHILDREN Harley is certainly guilty of child endangerment and contributing to the delinquency of minors, but she actually likes kids and hopes to have a few with the Joker someday.

COMIC CHARACTERS Fiercely loyal to the Joker, Harley would clown around for him at the drop of a bat…Batman, that is!

COSTUMED CRIMINAL Dangerous curves accentuate Harley's costume, although she still finds places to hide weapons of mass distraction!

Harley then proceeded to ruin her career (and endanger her life) by helping him escape from Arkham. Soon after, she became the Joker's moll, slinking around in a sexy jester's costume and white greasepaint to become the giggling gangstress Harley Quinn.

Unfortunately, Harley's love for the psycho she calls "Puddin'" was unreturned. Once free, the Joker found her presence more and more irksome. He chose to end their liaison by trapping Harley inside a rocket and attempting to blast her into orbit. Harley survived, thanks in part to the plant-manipulating rogue POISON IVY, whose floral concoctions endowed the Clown Princess with amazing acrobatic abilities.

After splitting from the Joker, Harley joined the SECRET SIX. In a women's shelter the AMAZONS recruited both her and Holly Robinson (see CATWOMAN) for training on Themyscira, where they aided HIPPOLYTA. **SB**

HARRIGAN, HOP

FIRST APPEARANCE ALL-AMERICAN COMICS #1 (April 1939)
STATUS Hero **REAL NAME** Hop Harrigan
OCCUPATION Aviator **BASE** Mobile
HEIGHT 5ft 7in **WEIGHT** 145 lbs **EYES** Blue **HAIR** Blond
SPECIAL POWERS/ABILITIES A superb pilot and tactician with no formal training as a fighter.

Hop Harrigan became an international celebrity when a New York reporter rode on one of the young man's humanitarian transports of Chinese refugees aboard pilot Prop Wash's experimental plane. A ticker-tape parade greeted Hop upon his return to the U.S. Harrigan's fame attracted the attention of his abusive former guardian, Silas Crass, who went to court and demanded that the boy and the money associated with Hop's name be placed in his custody. Thanks to his pal Tank, evidence was provided that Crass had never truly been authorized to be Harrigan's guardian and had forged papers to the contrary. In the aftermath, Prop Wash became Hop's new legal guardian. The young man had many flying adventures around the world, occasionally aiding the All-Star Squadron. Hop dabbled with becoming a costumed adventurer and became the short-lived alter ego of Guardian Angel. After the war, Hop Harrigan briefly became the Black Lamp, but prefers just being himself. **RG**

HAUNTED TANK

FIRST APPEARANCE G.I. Combat #87 (May 1961)
STATUS Hero team **BASE** Europe during World War II
MEMBERS AND POWERS
Lt. Jeb Stuart Sherman tank commander.
Cpl. Arch Asher (deceased) Loader.
Sgt. Bill Craig (deceased) Gunner.
Pvt. Eddie Craig (deceased) Bill Craig's son.
Cpl. Gus Gray (deceased) Second gunner.
Pvt. Rick Rawlins Gunner.
Cpl. Slim Stryker (deceased) Driver.

The Haunted Tank was actually a series of tanks commanded by Lieutenant Jeb Stuart during World War II. The spirit of Alexander the Great assigned the spirit of Confederate General James Ewell Brown (J.E.B.) Stuart to become the ghostly guardian of a Stuart M3 tank in Northern Africa. Initially affronted by the idea of watching over the tank's commander, a Yankee named Sergeant Jeb Stuart, who shared his namesake, the Confederate ghost was nonetheless impressed by Stuart's platoon in battle.

Sgt. Stuart was able to see J.E.B.'s ghost and flew the Confederate flag in honor of his spirit guardian. Stuart's team was convinced that their Sergeant imagined seeing the ghost; nevertheless, J.E.B.'s loyalty to his living namesake never wavered, and he watched over each new tank under the Sergeant's care. **PJ**

HAWK AND DOVE

FIRST APPEARANCE (Hank & Don) SHOWCASE #75 (July 1968)
STATUS Heroes **REAL NAMES** Hank Hall, Holly Granger (Hawk);
Don Hall, Dawn Marie Granger (Dove)
OCCUPATIONS (both) Adventurers **BASE** (both) Washington, D.C.
HEIGHT (Hank) 5ft 10in (6ft 3in as Hawk); (Don) 6ft; **WEIGHT** (Hank)
181 lbs (320 lbs as Hawk); (Don) 175 lbs **EYES** (both) Brown **HAIR**
(Hank) Brown; (Don) Black and thinning **SPECIAL POWERS/ABILITIES**
(both) Faster-than-human speed; heightened body density.

Hank and Don Hall, two brothers with diametrically
opposed political and social philosophies, were
transformed as the result of an experiment by the Lords
of Order and the Lords of Chaos, into the super-strong
Hawk and Dove. They bickered but fought alongside
one another, briefly joining the TEEN TITANS until Dove
was killed during the Crisis (see Great Battles, pp. 362–3).
Dawn Granger, seeking help to save her mother, was given
powers by the Lords of Order and Chaos. Whenever she
said the word, "Dove," Dawn became Dove II, unwittingly
depriving the original Dove of his powers, leading to his death.
Dawn finally hooked up with Hank Hall and a new version of
Hawk and Dove were formed. In the mountain world of Druspa
Tau, they learned much about their abilities and origins even as
they found themselves on opposite sides in the war between the
Lords of Chaos and Order. When their creators died, Hawk and
Dove agreed to absorb the essence of their respective creators.
MONARCH, a future version of Hank Hall, murdered Dove and
fueled madness in Hawk that ensured that, in a temporal loop,
he fulfilled his destiny to become Monarch. With no Hawk or
Dove, the cosmic forces turned to others to fill these roles,
and U.S. Air Force pilot Sasha Martens and guitarist Wiley
Wolverman were transformed into the new Hawk and
Dove. However, Dawn Granger returned from the dead.
She came back to the role of Dove, and enlisted her sister
Holly as the latest Hawk. **RG**

HAWK, SON OF TOMAHAWK

FIRST APPEARANCE TOMAHAWK #131 (December 1970)
STATUS Hero (deceased) **REAL NAME** Unknown **OCCUPATION** Adventurer
BASE Echo Valley, American Midwest **HEIGHT** 5ft 10in
WEIGHT 166 lbs **EYES** Blue **HAIR** Brown with blond streak
SPECIAL POWERS/ABILITIES Expert marksman, horseman, and tracker;
his bravery and idealism made him an effective frontier diplomat.

As son of a legendary Revolutionary War hero, Hawk had
some big shoes to fill, but he became a hero in his own
right. Raised in a log cabin, Hawk learned the ways of the
frontiersman from his father and the secrets of America's
native people from his mother, Moon Fawn. Hawk
believed that all men were created equal and
fought fiercely against those who would
enslave or exploit their
fellow men. He had
one brother, Small
Eagle.

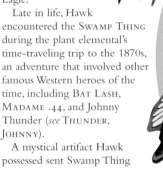

Late in life, Hawk
encountered the SWAMP THING
during the plant elemental's
time-traveling trip to the 1870s,
an adventure that involved other
famous Western heroes of the
time, including BAT LASH,
MADAME .44, and Johnny
Thunder (see THUNDER,
JOHNNY).

A mystical artifact Hawk
possessed sent Swamp Thing
back to his own time. Shortly before his
death, Hawk published his autobiography,
Hawk, Son of Tomahawk. **DW**

HAWKGIRL

FIRST APPEARANCE JSA SECRET FILES AND ORIGINS #1 (August 1999)
STATUS Hero **REAL NAME** Kendra Saunders
OCCUPATION Adventurer **BASE** St. Roche, Louisiana
HEIGHT 5ft 6in **WEIGHT** 131 lbs **EYES** Green **HAIR** Black
SPECIAL POWERS/ABILITIES Able to fly thanks to gravity-defying Nth
metal belt; uses giant wings to navigate during flight; aggressive
and adept hand-to-hand combatant.

Troubled orphan Kendra Saunders attempted suicide in her
teens and her body was inhabited by the spirit of an ancient
Egyptian princess, Chay-Ara. Inheriting Chay-Ara's soul and not
knowing why made Kendra mentally ill.

Kendra went to live with her grandfather, SPEED
SAUNDERS, a famous adventurer from the 1940s. Armed
with the secret knowledge that Kendra, the grandniece of
Sheira Saunders, the Golden Age Hawkgirl, had a great
destiny awaiting her, Speed began training the young
woman to become a super hero, and gave her Sheira's
original Hawkgirl wings. She had a daughter, Mia, at
16 and gave her up for adoption.

Initially reluctant, Kendra became the new
Hawkgirl, joining the JUSTICE SOCIETY OF
AMERICA, and helping the team defeat Mordru
the DARK LORD. Later, Hawkgirl met HAWKMAN,
the reincarnation of Khufu, Chay-Ara's ancient
Egyptian soulmate. During the Infinite Crisis, an
outer space accident briefly transformed Hawkgirl
into a giant. She recently joined the new JUSTICE
LEAGUE OF AMERICA. **PJ**

ACTION GIRL Soaring
through the skies like her
avian namesake,
Hawkgirl is one of
the fastest—and most
ferocious—fliers on
the planet.

SOUL MATES
United by love
and death for
thousands of
years, Hawkman
and Hawkgirl share
a unique bond.

HAWKMAN

FIRST APPEARANCE FLASH COMICS #1 (January 1940)
STATUS Hero **REAL NAME** Carter Hall
OCCUPATION Adventurer **BASE** St. Roch, Louisiana
HEIGHT 6ft 1in **WEIGHT** 195 lbs **EYES** Blue **HAIR** Brown
SPECIAL POWERS/ABILITIES Thanagarian Nth Metal on boots and wing harnesses allow him to fly; artificial wings give great speed and agility; Nth Metal permits Hawkman to lift great weights and withstand extremes of temperature during flight; wields a variety of ancient weapons, including shield, dagger, mace, cestus, battleaxe, and more.

ARMED AND DANGEROUS
With ancient weapons amassed during his many lifetimes on Earth, Hawkman fights an eternal struggle against evil in any age.

THE STORY OF HAWKMAN begins many millennia ago, during the 15th Dynasty of Ancient Egypt. Prince Khufu and his beloved Chay-Ara discovered the wreckage of a spacecraft from the planet Thanagar. After exposure to the mysterious Nth Metal, the vehicle's anti-gravity alloy, Khufu and Chay-Ara were murdered by the sinister sorcerer Hath-Set. The Nth Metal initiated a cycle of reincarnation that would see Khufu and Chay-Ara reborn countless times throughout the ages.

BORN AGAIN LOVERS
Reincarnated during America's Wild West, Khufu was the gunfighting hero NIGHTHAWK, while Chay-Ara was pistol-packing CINNAMON I. In the 1940s, Khufu was archaeologist Carter Hall and became Hawkman, while Chay-Ara found new life as Sheira Saunders, the heroine HAWKGIRL and Carter's wife. Both winged wonders served with the JUSTICE SOCIETY OF AMERICA (Hawkman was chairman) and the wartime ALL-STAR SQUADRON. Both Hawks later became members of the JUSTICE LEAGUE OF AMERICA and flew with the team on its earliest missions. The Halls' cycle of death and rebirth was interrupted during the Zero Hour crisis (*see* Great Battles, pp. 362–3), when both Carter and Sheira merged with Thanagarian policeman Katar Hol, who adopted the mantle of Hawkman. Unfortunately, Sheira perished in the merging. Carter later freed himself from his union with Katar, who also died. Carter was resurrected yet again, this time possessing memories of his every previous reincarnation. Sheira, however, was reborn as

CURSED *Discovering a downed Thanagarian spacecraft gave Prince Khufu the power to fly and his immortal curse.*

her own grandniece, Kendra Saunders, with no past memories. Carter reclaimed the role of Hawkman, and rejoined the JSA alongside the new Hawkgirl. But for the first time in all their previous lives, Hawkgirl did not recognize Hawkman as her soulmate. Blinded by his love for Chay-Ara, in any form she exists, Hawkman followed Hawkgirl to St. Roch, Louisiana, as she began a quest to find the villain who murdered Kendra Saunders's parents. Hawkman spent a year on Thanagar following the Infinite Crisis, but later rejoined the JSA. **SB**

TOGETHER FOREVER *The Hawks are destined to find each other and fall in love time and time again.*

KEY STORYLINES
• *LEGEND OF THE HAWKMAN #1-3 (JULY–SEPT. 2000):* A retelling of Hawkman and Hawkgirl's connection to distant Thanagar.
• *JSA SECRET FILES AND ORIGINS #1 (AUG. 1999):* The return of Hawkgirl signals the reincarnation of Hawkman!
• *JSA #23-26 (JUNE–SEPT. 2001):* A reborn Carter Hall rejoins the JSA and leads the team to glory.

FEARLESS FIGHTER *Flying solo against fire-breathing monsters, soaring alongside Hawkgirl, or leading the assembled JSA, Hawkman is one of the greatest warriors ever known.*

HAWKWOMAN

FIRST APPEARANCE HAWKWORLD: BOOK ONE (1989)
STATUS Hero (deceased) **REAL NAME** Shayera Thal
OCCUPATION Police officer **BASES** Detroit; planet Thanagar
HEIGHT 5ft 7in **WEIGHT** 145 lbs **EYES** Blue **HAIR** Red
SPECIAL POWERS/ABILITIES Thanagarian armor and wings make Thal a
superb flyer, excellent marksman, and vicious combatant.

Shayera Thal was a
decorated police officer
on Thanagar, a planet many
light years from Earth. With
her partner, Katar Hol (see
HAWKMAN), she journeyed to
Earth in pursuit of a shapeshifting criminal named Byth.
Fascinated by the planet, Katar
and Shayera chose to remain.
The media took to calling them
Hawkman and Hawkwoman
after the World War II super heroes.
As time went by, the partners drifted
apart; Shayera even decided to hang up
her wings and become a uniformed police
officer in Detroit. Tormented by the voices
of his previous incarnations that were at war
in his mind, Katar was ultimately transported
to another dimension, leaving Shayera alone. When Byth
turned up once more, she donned her armor and fought
with the current incarnation of the Hawks. Hawkwoman
died during the Rann-Thanagar War, killed by Queen
Komand'r of Tamaran (see BLACKFIRE). RG

HAZARD I

FIRST APPEARANCE INFINITY, INC. #34 (January 1987)
STATUS Villain **REAL NAME** Rebecca "Becky" Sharpe
OCCUPATION Professional criminal **BASE** Mobile
HEIGHT 5ft 6in **WEIGHT** 136 lbs **EYES** Green **HAIR** Red
SPECIAL POWERS/ABILITIES Psionic powers and mystic dice give either
"good luck" or "bad luck" to her victims.

The granddaughter of the Gambler, a Golden Age villain
and member of the original INJUSTICE SOCIETY, Becky
Sharpe was horrified to learn her grandfather had killed
himself after gambling away his fortune. She decided to
use her psychic abilities to manipulate luck and became
Hazard, embarking on a criminal career
to avenge her grandfather's death.
Hazard joined the WIZARD's
Injustice, Unlimited team
with the understanding
that murder was
off-limits. Injustice,
Unlimited fought both
INFINITY, INC. and the
GLOBAL GUARDIANS at an
international conference in Canada.
With the coerced help of WILDCAT
II and TASMANIAN DEVIL, Hazard
bankrupted the casino that ruined her
grandfather, avenging the Gambler's
death. After learning that Injustice,
Unlimited were willing to kill their
opponents, Hazard left their ranks and
remains at large. PJ

HEAT WAVE

FIRST APPEARANCE THE FLASH (2nd series) #140 (November 1963)
STATUS Villain (reformed) **REAL NAME** Mick Rory (Mick Calhoun)
OCCUPATION Security Chief **BASE** Metropolis
HEIGHT 5ft 11in **WEIGHT** 179 lbs **EYES** Blue **HAIR** None
SPECIAL POWERS/ABILITIES Self-designed Heat Gun generates extremely
focused high-temperature flames; costume insulated with thermal-
damping and heat-resistant material of Rory's own design.

As a child, Mick Rory was locked in an industrial freezer
while on a school trip to a meatpacking plant. His cries
went unheard, but little Rory managed to thaw his fingers
enough to pick the lock and escape. From then on, Rory
suffered cryophobia (a fear of cold) and became obsessed
with heat and warmth. Toting his high-tech Heat Gun,
he blazed a criminal career in Central City as Heat Wave.
Rory was a hot-tempered enemy of the second FLASH,
Barry Allen, often in tandem with fellow rogues gallery
member and villainous opposite, CAPTAIN COLD. However,
unlike other Flash foes, Heat Wave temporarily reformed.
By helping Allen nab a crooked parole officer
who had taken up his Heat Wave costume and
weaponry, Rory earned the Flash's friendship
and trust. Despite a stint as
Security Chief at Project
Cadmus, Heat Wave
returned to villainy and
participated in Bart
Allen's murder
(see FLASH). SB

HOT-TEMPERED Heat
Wave is back to his
evil ways and would
gladly flash-fry the
Fastest Man Alive!

HAYOTH

FIRST APPEARANCE SUICIDE SQUAD (1st series) #45 (September 1990)
STATUS Hero team **BASE** Israel
CURRENT MEMBERS AND POWERS
Ramban (leader/spiritual guide) Calls upon magical forces of
Judaic power.
Golem (Moyshe Nakhman) Powerhouse able to transform
his body between solid, liquid, and gaseous forms.
Judith Expert swordswoman, martial artist, and
shuriken-throwing whirlwind.
Dybbuk Team strategist; artificial intelligence with
the power to control machinery.

The Hayoth are an Israeli super-team
named after the four angelic beings in
the Book of Ezekiel in the Bible who
bore the faces of the Lion, the Eagle,
the Ox, and Man. They were formed by
the Israeli government and operated as a
division of the Mossad (the Israeli special
forces) under the command of Colonel
Hacohen. The Hayoth
came to blows with the
U.S.'s SUICIDE SQUAD
when the Squad
appeared in

Israel in pursuit
of the international
terrorist KOBRA. The
two teams shelved their
differences to prevent Kobra
from destroying Jerusalem's
holy Dome of the Rock.
Months later, the Hayoth
attempted to capture the
former president of Qurac
during his stay in the U.S.
The Suicide Squad scrambled
to prevent the abduction and
the Hayoth lost a bitter
battle and wound up in U.S.
custody. DYBBUK freed his
team by helping the Suicide
Squad's Amanda Waller (see
WALLER, AMANDA) restore the
mind of one of her operatives.
The Hayoth currently remain active
in Israel. DW

HOLY WARRIORS Led by Ramban, the nationalist
Hayoth super-team springs into action to battle
threats to their homeland.

HECKLER

FIRST APPEARANCE THE HECKLER #1 (September 1992)
STATUS Hero **REAL NAME** Stuart Mosely
OCCUPATION Adventurer **BASE** Delta City
HEIGHT 6ft **WEIGHT** 170 lbs **EYES** White **HAIR** None
SPECIAL POWERS/ABILITIES Damage resistance and enhanced agility,
ability to goad his enemies into making mistakes.

The Heckler is the patron superhero of
Delta City. In his off hours, Stu Moseley
owns a diner in the seedy section of
Delta, providing him a window into
criminal goings-on that he fights in
the guise of his colorful alter-ego.
The Heckler is highly resistant to injury but otherwise
possesses no extraordinary abilities, relying on his gift for
irradiation to make his opponents lose focus end make
devastating mistakes. The Heckler's annoying talents make
him reviled by villains and civilians alike, yet he does
more than anyone to keep the peace in Delta. Among the
Heckler's nemeses are crimelord Boss Glitter, hired
gun Bushwack'r, and John Doe the Generic Man, whose ability
to leech the uniqueness from his surroundings made him
the Heckler's natural enemy. **DW**

HELLGRAMITE

FIRST APPEARANCE BRAVE AND THE BOLD #80 (October/November
1968)
STATUS Villain **REAL NAME** Roderick Rose
OCCUPATION Mercenary **BASE** Metropolis
HEIGHT 6ft 1in **WEIGHT** 325 lbs **EYES** Red **HAIR** None
SPECIAL POWERS/ABILITIES Enhanced strength and speed, can spin
webs or transform others into larval versions of himself.

Roderick Rose, an expert etymologist, became a
superhuman after exposure to a mutating agent gave
him a thick exoskeleton and the ability to leap like
a grasshopper. Calling himself Hellgrammite after a
type of fly larva, Rose fought super heroes including
BATMAN and GREEN ARROW while discovering he
could transform other humans into subservient, larval
versions of himself.
    A deal with the demon NERON gave him enhanced
powers, and he became fixated on the most powerful
superhero of all: SUPERMAN. Recently, Hellgrammite
joined with BLOODSPORT, RIOT, and other villains
to gang up on the Man of Steel when he suddenly
reappeared one year after the Infinite Crisis. **DW**

HELIX

FIRST APPEARANCE INFINITY, INC. #17 (August 1985)
CURRENT MEMBERS AND POWERS **STATUS** Villain team **BASE** California
MR. BONES Transparent skin and organs; deadly cyanide touch.
Arak the Wind-walker Generates hurricanes and tornadoes.
Babe (formerly Baby Boom) Stopped growing at age five; can
explode anything nearby through mental focus.
Kritter Resembles a dog; impressive computer hacking talents.
Penny Dreadful Absorbs electricity and projects it in amplified form.
Tao Jones Levitates; deflects any form of energy directed at her.

All of the members of Helix were genetic freaks with
meta-human talents engineered by the unscrupulous Dr.
Benjamin Love. Turning to crime, they battled INFINITY,
INC. and other super heroes. When Dr. Love took control
of the team, the members of Helix killed their "father." Mr.
Bones (see DIRECTOR BONES) soon rejected Helix and joined
Infinity, Inc. under court order. Eventually all members of
Helix received pardons from the U.S. government. Many
now work for the Department of Extranormal Operations
keeping tabs on their fellow meta-humans. Mr. Bones is now
director of the D.E.O. and has been forced to take
action against some of his former Infinity,
Inc. teammates. **DW**

Mr. Bones

Penny Dreadful

Kritter

Tao Jones

Babe

Arak

HELLHOUND

FIRST APPEARANCE CATWOMAN (1st series) ANNUAL #2
(July 1993)
STATUS Villain (deceased) **REAL NAME** Kai
OCCUPATION Assassin **BASE** Mobile
HEIGHT 5ft 10in **WEIGHT** 178 lbs **EYES** Brown
HAIR Black **SPECIAL POWERS/ABILITIES** A deadly
martial artist with a preference for throwing
knives and daggers.

Teenage runaway Kai was the
most able student of an armless
sensei who presided over a
secret martial arts dojo in
the backstreets of Gotham
City. That is, until Selina Kyle
(CATWOMAN) slinked her way
into the Sensei's all-male
arena to practice her own
fighting skills. Selina
bested Kai and became
the Sensei's most prized
pupil. Kai vowed revenge
and became Hellhound
to her Catwoman, a
merciless mercenary to her
charitable cat burglar. After
Hellhound's death during
a Gotham gang war,
Jack Chifford became
Hellhound II. He
died on an alien planet
during Operation:
Salvation Run. **SB**

HERALD (VOX)

FIRST APPEARANCE (as Mal) TEEN TITANS (1st series) #26 (April 1970); (as Herald) Secret Origins Annual #3 (1989)
STATUS Hero **REAL NAME** Malcolm Arnold Duncan
OCCUPATION Restaurateur, musician, adventurer **BASE** San Francisco
HEIGHT 6ft 1in **WEIGHT** 210 lbs **EYES** Brown **HAIR** Black
SPECIAL POWERS/ABILITIES The now-destroyed Gabriel's Horn device could open warps in space, allowing teleportation; Duncan was a former Golden Gloves amateur boxing champion.

Malcolm "Mal" Duncan was raised in Harlem, NY, with his sister Cindy. When Cindy was harassed by a racist street gang, Mal single-handedly attacked them, and was soon helped by the TEEN TITANS, who had temporarily given up their costumed identities and happened to be nearby. Joining the Titans, but possessing no superpowers of his own, Mal began to feel like an outsider on the team, until Karen Beecher, the BUMBLEBEE, helped him create the Gabriel's Horn, a special weapon with teleportational powers. Becoming the Herald, Mal helped the Titans defeat DOCTOR LIGHT I.

Unknown to Mal, his special Horn had been corrupted by the villainous Gargoyle, who hoped to tear a hole in the dimensional fabric in order to release his master, the ANTITHESIS. After the Titans defeated these villains, Mal destroyed the Horn. During the Infinite Crisis, Mal Duncan suffered an accident in space that left him unable to speak. After accepting a cybernetic voice box similar to the Gabriel's Horn, he joined the DOOM PATROL as Vox. **PJ**

HERO

FIRST APPEARANCE SUPERBOY AND THE RAVERS #1 (Sept. 1996)
STATUS Hero **REAL NAME** Hero Cruz
OCCUPATION Adventurer **BASE** Metropolis
HEIGHT 5ft 9in **WEIGHT** 157 lbs **EYES** Brown **HAIR** Black
SPECIAL POWERS/ABILITIES Internalized H-Dial allows him to transform into a new superbeing with new superpowers for one hour; he never transforms into the same being twice.

Raised in a middle-class Puerto Rican family in Metropolis, Hero Cruz discovered a cache of technology stolen by the SCAVENGER. He took the Scavenger's Achilles Vest, using its invulnerability powers to join the Event Horizon, a cosmic rave party. Along with SUPERBOY and the RAVERS, Hero traveled across the universe with the Event Horizon party. When the Scavenger came searching for his Achilles Vest, he kidnapped several Ravers, including SPARX, whom he believed had stolen the vest. The Ravers tracked the Scavenger to his lair, and Hero discovered a mystical dial with the letters "H," "E," "R," and "O" on it (*see* DIAL "H" FOR HERO). He used the dial to transform into different super heroes, rescuing Sparx and Superboy and defeating the Scavenger. Sparx fell in love with Hero, but Hero revealed that he was gay. He now lives in San Francisco. **PJ**

HERCULES

FIRST APPEARANCE ALL-STAR COMICS #8 (December, 1941)
STATUS Hero **REAL NAME** Hercules
OCCUPATION Demi-god **BASE** Olympus
HEIGHT 6ft 5in **WEIGHT** 327 lbs **EYES** Blue **HAIR** Black
SPECIAL POWERS/ABILITIES Super-strength and near-immortality bestowed upon him by his father, Zeus. Hercules is resistant to most injuries and has impressive stamina.

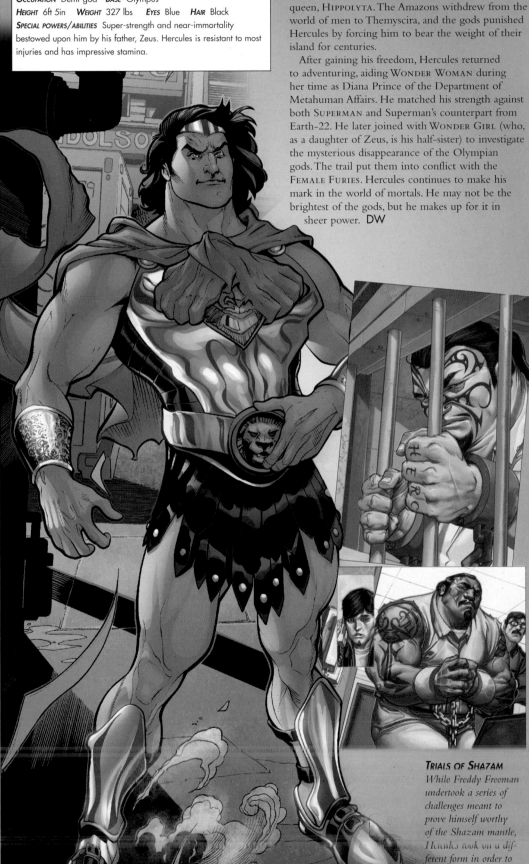

Hercules (or Heracles) is the champion of Greek myth and son of Zeus of the OLYMPIAN GODS. After performing legendary labors during the era of antiquity, Hercules and his warriors conquered the AMAZONS, with Hercules forcing himself on their queen, HIPPOLYTA. The Amazons withdrew from the world of men to Themyscira, and the gods punished Hercules by forcing him to bear the weight of their island for centuries.

After gaining his freedom, Hercules returned to adventuring, aiding WONDER WOMAN during her time as Diana Prince of the Department of Metahuman Affairs. He matched his strength against both SUPERMAN and Superman's counterpart from Earth-22. He later joined with WONDER GIRL (who, as a daughter of Zeus, is his half-sister) to investigate the mysterious disappearance of the Olympian gods. The trail put them into conflict with the FEMALE FURIES. Hercules continues to make his mark in the world of mortals. He may not be the brightest of the gods, but he makes up for it in sheer power. **DW**

TRIALS OF SHAZAM
While Freddy Freeman undertook a series of challenges meant to prove himself worthy of the Shazam mantle, Hercules took on a different form in order to aid the young hero.

THE DC COMICS ENCYCLOPEDIA

HIPPOLYTA

FIRST APPEARANCE WONDER WOMAN (2nd series) #1 (February 1987)
STATUS Hero (deceased)   **REAL NAME** Hippolyta
OCCUPATION Former Queen of the Amazons   **BASE** Elysian Fields
HEIGHT 5ft 9in   **WEIGHT** 150 lbs   **EYES** Blue   **HAIR** Black
SPECIAL POWERS/ABILITIES Granted eternal life by the gods of Mount Olympus and gifted with amazing strength, speed, and agility; wore the Girdle of Gaea, which magically protected the Amazons from subjugation by man before it was forged into Wonder Woman's golden Lasso of Truth.

When a pregnant cavewoman was murdered more than 32,000 years ago by her brutish mate, her spirit was collected by the Earth Mother, Gaea, and deposited in the Well of Souls, which held the life essences of slain women from past ages. Zeus, King of the Gods (see OLYMPIAN GODS), called for the creation of a new race of humankind to bring glory to the gods, so the Olympian goddesses restored life to these waiting souls. Among the women reincarnated was that tragic cavewoman, reborn as Hippolyta, Queen of the AMAZONS.

NAZI FIGHTER Hippolyta became a member of the Justice Society via time-travel. She also made Wonder Woman a legend during World War II.

LEAVING MAN'S WORLD

The gods' chosen race dwelt in peace within their city-state of Themyscira until ARES, God of War, sent Zeus's son Heracles to seduce Hippolyta and defeat the Amazons. Her sisterhood divided, Hippolyta led a group of peace-loving Amazons to rebuild Themyscira on an island within the Bermuda Triangle, where they lived for centuries hidden from the outside world. Over time, Hippolyta's yearning for the unborn child slain within her all those millennia ago was heard by the gods. They instructed her to mold a daughter from clay; as soon as she did so, they breathed life into it. That child, Diana, would one day become WONDER WOMAN, a role Hippolyta paradoxically immortalized herself by time-traveling to 1942 and serving as a member of the wartime JUSTICE SOCIETY OF AMERICA.

In modern times, Hippolyta led the Amazons through civil wars and apocalyptic battles with DARKSEID, who once decimated Themyscira and its people. Hippolyta ultimately gave her life defending both her homeland and Earth from the onslaught of the world-destroying IMPERIEX (see Great Battles, pp. 362–3). She is remembered as a fair and wise leader, a loving mother to Diana, and a Wonder Woman in her own right.

DEATH Hippolyta helped to save Earth. The Olympian goddesses carried her soul into immortality.

A QUEEN'S RETURN Circe, mortal enemy of the Amazons, ironically brought their greatest leader back from the realm of the dead

AMAZONS ATTACK

Hippolyta returned to life through the dark magics of CIRCE. Goaded to war on the news that the U.S. government had seized her daughter Diana, Hippolyta led an army of Amazons into Washington DC. As Greek monsters felled national monuments, the world's super heroes failed to stop Hippolyta's advance. Diana eventually persuaded the Amazon queen to lay down her sword, prompting the goddess Athena—GRANNY GOODNESS in disguise—to scatter the Amazons and banish them to live as mortal woman. Hippolyta remained alone on Themyscira, queen of an deserted kingdom.

THEMYSCIRAN EXILE

A strike team of fascist soldiers organized by CAPTAIN NAZI soon invaded Themyscira, opposed at first by Hippolyta and later by Wonder Woman and her gorilla shock troops. The Nazis found support in four imprisoned Amazons, who had once served as Hippolyta's Royal Guard until they tried to murder the infant Diana for being the first child to appear in a childless society.

Granny Goodness continued her deception as Athena by drawing false Amazons to Themyscira, including HARLEY QUINN and Holly Robinson (see CATWOMAN). The two newcomers discovered Hippolyta hiding in a cave and agreed to aid her in the fight to reclaim the island. MARY MARVEL soon rounded out their resistance movement.
SB/DW

STRIKE TEAM Holly Robinson and Harley Quinn proved worthy fighters.

KEY STORYLINES
• *ACTION COMICS #781 (SEPTEMBER 2001):* Hippolyta gives her life to stop Imperiex's hollowing of Earth.
• *AMAZONS ATTACK #1-6 (MARCH-AUGUST 2007):* Hippolyta makes war against Man's World.

HEX, JONAH

First appearance ALL-STAR WESTERN TALES #10 (March 1972)
Status Hero (deceased) *Real name* Jonah Woodson Hex
Occupation Bounty hunter; soldier *Base* Late 19th century
American southwest; Seattle, circa 2050
Height 5ft 11in *Weight* 189 lbs *Eyes* Blue *Hair* Reddish-blond
Special powers/abilities Despite being born under a bad sign, Hex
was a superb marksman, who hardly ever missed his target.

Caption *A shootout with Hex means a trip to Boot Hill for his opponents.*

LOVE AT FIRST SIGHT *Hex is smitten by White Fawn.*

As if cursed by his own last name, Jonah Hex was born to a life of bad luck. Born in 1839, he was the son of a brutal drunk and his meek wife. Hex was abandoned by his mother when he was still a child, and his father then sold him to an Apache tribe for a pile of animal pelts. After Noh-Tante, the chief's jealous son, betrayed Hex over the love of White Fawn, a young woman in their tribe, the Apaches forsook the boy. Hex eventually joined the U.S. Cavalry.

Hex fought for the Confederate army during the Civil War, but did not support its stand on slavery. Blamed for the "Fort Charlotte massacre," a prison break that went tragically awry, Jonah escaped corporal punishment. Soon after, he learned that Noh-Tante had married White Fawn. After killing Noh-Tante in personal combat, Hex was thrown out by the tribe and his face was scarred with the "Mark of the Demon."

By 1875, Hex had become the greatest bounty hunter of his time; outlaws quailed at the sight of his gray Confederate jacket. He was teleported to the Seattle area of 2050. After marrying a young woman named Mei Ling, who bore his child, he vowed to hang up his guns for good. However, he was forced to kill several men who came after him. Mei Ling left him taking their son with her.

Hex returned to the Old West, and was shot by a bank robber. His body was stuffed and placed on display in an amusement park on the outskirts of New York City. **PJ**

HIGHFATHER

First appearance THE NEW GODS (1st series) #1 (March 1971)
Status Hero *Real name* Izaya the Inheritor
Occupation Adventurer *Base* New Genesis
Height 6ft 4in *Weight* 227 lbs *Eyes* Gray *Hair* White
Special powers/abilities Commanding presence; possesses
superhuman strength and invulnerability; focuses energies from the
omnipotent Source through his staff.

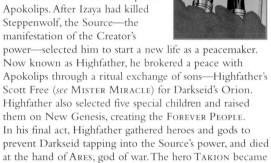

The New Gods of New Genesis are among the mightiest beings in creation, and Highfather was once the greatest of them all. Born Izaya the Inheritor, he assumed his destiny through tragedy when DARKSEID and his uncle STEPPENWOLF came to New Genesis on a hunting trip. Steppenwolf killed Izaya's wife, Avia, sparking a war between New Genesis and Darkseid's planet Apokolips. After Izaya had killed Steppenwolf, the Source—the manifestation of the Creator's power—selected him to start a new life as a peacemaker. Now known as Highfather, he brokered a peace with Apokolips through a ritual exchange of sons—Highfather's Scott Free (*see* MISTER MIRACLE) for Darkseid's Orion. Highfather also selected five special children and raised them on New Genesis, creating the FOREVER PEOPLE. In his final act, Highfather gathered heroes and gods to prevent Darkseid tapping into the Source's power, and died at the hand of ARES, god of war. The hero TAKION became the new Highfather.

Now at one with the Source, Highfather serves as a member of the godlike Quintessence. **DW**

HERO HOTLINE

First appearance ACTION COMICS WEEKLY #637 (January 1988)
Current members and powers *Status* Hero team *Base* New York City
Diamondette (Diana Theotocopolous) Diamond-hard hands.
Hotshot (Billy Lefferts) Shoots fireballs from his fingertips.
Microwave Mom (Belle Jackson) Generates heat via microwave suit.
Mr. Muscle, a.k.a. Flex, a.k.a. Brother Bicep (Sturgis Butterfield)
Former circus strongman.
Private Eyes (Lester Lee) Lenses enable all kinds of super-vision.
Stretch (Tom Longacre) Pliable hero who has lost some of his snap.
Voice-Over (Andrew Greenwald) Can imitate any voice or sound.
500Z-Q ("Soozie-Q") Mobile computer monitoring system.

When SUPERMAN is flying up, up, and away, or Batman just isn't answering the Bat-Signal, all anyone needs to do to find a substitute super hero is dial 1-800-555-HERO. The Hero Hotline is open 24 hours a day, seven days a week, and handles calamity beyond the range of the normal emergency services. The Hotline, founded by Tex Thomson, is maintained by the mysterious Coordinator. After hours, emergencies are handled by the night crew, including Chlorino, Marie the Psychic Turtle, Rainbow Man, Thunderhead, and Zeep the Living Sponge. **SD**

HERO HOTLINE *Employees include (clockwise from left) Stretch, Dinky the Devil Bat, Mr. Muscle, Private Eyes, Microwave Mom (Microwavabelle), Hotshot, Voice-Over, and Diamondette.*

H.I.V.E

First appearance SUPERMAN FAMILY #205 (January 1981)
Status Villainous organization *Base* Maintains a honeycomb of
secret bases across the globe.

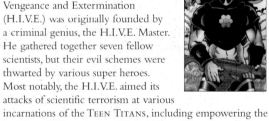

The Hierarchy of International Vengeance and Extermination (H.I.V.E.) was originally founded by a criminal genius, the H.I.V.E. Master. He gathered together seven fellow scientists, but their evil schemes were thwarted by various super heroes. Most notably, the H.I.V.E. aimed its attacks of scientific terrorism at various incarnations of the TEEN TITANS, including empowering the late Grant Wilson—son of Slade Wilson (DEATHSTROKE THE TERMINATOR)—the super-assassin known as the Ravager, in his failed attempt to destroy the group. Following frequent skirmishes with the Titans, the H.I.V.E. self-destructed after the H.I.V.E. Mistress, wife of its late founder, chose to kill the Hierarchy's inner circle and commit suicide rather than be captured. The H.I.V.E. later regrouped with Adeline Kane, ex-wife of Slade Wilson, as its new H.I.V.E. Mistress. She blamed super heroes, the Teen Titans in particular, for the death of her sons Grant and Joseph (JERICHO). Following a three-way conflict with the Titans and TARTARUS, a cadre of super-villains led by VANDAL SAVAGE, Kane was killed. A third H.I.V.E. arose from the ashes, led by QUEEN BEE II as part of the new SECRET SOCIETY OF SUPER-VILLAINS (*see* VILLAINS UNITED).Structured like an insect colony, the H.I.V.E. employs swarms of faceless (and therefore expendable) foot soldiers utterly loyal to the ruling hierarchy. **SB**

HIMON

First appearance MISTER MIRACLE (1st series) #9 (August 1972)
Status Hero (deceased) *Real name* Himon
Occupation Scientist, teacher *Base* Apokolips and New Genesis
Height 5ft 8in *Weight* 163 lbs *Eyes* Blue-gray *Hair* White
Special powers/abilities Master genius and scientific inventor; creator
of the Mother Box, a miraculous thinking computer.

Brilliant scientist and theoretician Himon lived among the NEW GODS of New Genesis. Himon invented the powerful Mother Box and, with METRON, invented the Boom Tube, which allows DARKSEID and his war world of Apokolips to teleport across galaxies. Wracked with guilt over giving Darkseid such power, Himon vowed to end the evil god's threat. Himon secretly trained the inhabitants in the peaceful ways of New Genesis, encouraging their individuality and freedom. Darkseid immediately sent his death squads after Himon, who eluded them over and over again, often using android duplicates to confuse Darkseid's underlings. Himon also helped Scott Free become MISTER MIRACLE. Soon after, Himon's daughter BEKKA married ORION, Darkseid's son, and shortly thereafter, Darkseid murdered Himon. He returned, leading New Genesis during the Death of the New Gods event. **PJ**

HITMAN

FIRST APPEARANCE THE DEMON (2nd series) Annual #2 (1993)
STATUS Hero (deceased)   **REAL NAME** Thomas Monaghan
OCCUPATION Hitman; vigilante   **BASE** Gotham City
HEIGHT 6ft   **WEIGHT** 185 lbs   **EYES** Black   **HAIR** Black
SPECIAL POWERS/ABILITIES Infected with alien blood, Tommy had limited X-ray vision and telepathy; he was also a crack shot.

An attack by the alien parasite Glonth left hitman Tommy Monaghan with greatly enhanced senses and limited telepathic ability. Of course, the first thing Tommy did was kill Glonth. Some saw him as a hero, and although he operated far outside the law, he did have a better developed moral sense than your average hitman. He had earned the grudging respect of BATMAN, who recognized that Tommy kept one of the darkest corners of Gotham clean. GREEN LANTERN Kyle Rayner also worked alongside Tommy.

Along the way, Tommy reunited with his old pal Natt the Hat, and the two became inseparable. Given his new powers, strange characters were soon drawn to Tommy. First came the would-be super heroes Six Pack, a group of costumed losers. Then there was the demon Baytor, who found hanging out with Tommy at Noonan's bar so fascinating that he went to work there as a bartender.

Tommy discovered the existence of the Bloodlines File, a government project hoping to create meta-humans using data from the earlier space-parasite outbreak. In the bloody aftermath of their attempt to shut down the facility, both Hitman and Natt were killed. **RG**

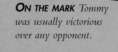

ON THE MARK Tommy was usually victorious over any opponent.

TROUBLE MAN
A previous survivor of the Bloodlines virus, Tommy Monaghan was kidnapped by Batman and brought to JLA headquarters. Batman hoped that Tommy's antibodies might help combat a new strain of the virus. However Tommy's controversial presence soon caused strife among the JLA heroes.

HOUNGAN

FIRST APPEARANCE THE New Teen Titans (1st series) #14 (Dec. 1981)
STATUS Villain   **REAL NAME** Jean-Louis Droo
OCCUPATION Scientist turned criminal   **BASE** Paris, France
HEIGHT 6ft 2in   **WEIGHT** 205 lbs   **EYES** Brown   **HAIR** Black
SPECIAL POWERS/ABILITIES Computerized voodoo dolls trigger terrible pain and even death to his victims through an advanced bionic link.

Born in Haiti, Jean-Louis Droo became a top computer scientist in the U.S. He returned to Haiti to visit his dying father, only to see a local voodoo priest (a "houngan") effect a miraculous cure through the voodoo arts. Droo merged the old ways with the new by creating a computerized voodoo doll. This works by analyzing a victim's cell sample and generating a "bionic link." When Droo's stylus stabs the doll, pain signals travel via the link to the victim's equivalent body part.

Calling himself Houngan, Droo joined the New Brotherhood of Evil, later reorganized into the SOCIETY OF SIN, and participated in epic events including the Crisis (see Great Battles, pp. 362–3). Houngan numbered among the criminals captured by the SSUICIDE SQUAD and deposited on a prison planet during Operation: Salvation Run. **DW**

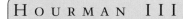
HOURMAN I & II

FIRST APPEARANCE (Hourman I) ADVENTURE COMICS #48 (March 1940); (Hourman II) INFINITY, INC. #20 (November 1985)
STATUS Heroes **REAL NAMES** (I) Rex Tyler; (II) Richard "Rick" Tyler
OCCUPATIONS (I) Chemist; (II) artist **BASE** (both) New York City
HEIGHT (I) 5ft 10in; (II) 5ft 9in **WEIGHT** (I) 181 lbs; (II) 170 lbs
EYES (I) Blue; (II) brown **HAIR** (both) Brown
SPECIAL POWERS/ABILITIES (Hourman I) Imbibing the Miraclo pill gave Rex Tyler superstrength, enhanced agility, speed, and low-level invulnerability for one hour; (Hourman II) superstrength, enhanced agility, and speed; "flash forward" vision gives Rick Tyler precognitive flashes an hour into the future; can transport to a pocket "hour in time" in order to seek counsel from his father.

A brilliant young chemist working for the Bannermain Chemical Company in the late 1930s, Rex Tyler developed a steroid pill he called "Miraclo," which enhanced his strength and speed to superhuman levels for almost an hour. Using his newfound strength, he became the Man of the Hour and, later, the hero Hourman. Tyler then joined the JUSTICE SOCIETY OF AMERICA and the ALL-STAR SQUADRON.

Unfortunately, Tyler became addicted to his Miraclo pills and succumbed to a severe depression. Hoping to end his dependence, Tyler retired from adventuring. He purchased the Bannermain Chemical Company and married Wendi Harris, an actress. During the Crisis (*see Great Battles, pp. 362–3*), Rex and Wendi's headstrong son Rick took one of his father's Miraclo pills and became the second Hourman, despite Rex's objections. Rick joined INFINITY, INC. for a time, and, like his father, became addicted to Miraclo. After accidentally killing the villainous WIZARD, Rick gave up his Hourman identity. Rex became Hourman one more time, and died with several other former JSAers in a battle with EXTANT. After battling the Hourman III, an android from the future, Rick reclaimed his Hourman title and developed a new, non-addictive form of Miraclo. Hourman III rescued Rex moments before his death, switching places to die at Extant's hands instead. Rick Tyler, married to Jesse Chambers (*see QUICK, JESSE*) serves in the JSA. **PJ/DW**

RACE AGAINST TIME
When fighting crime, Hourman never has a moment to lose—his superpowers only last 60 minutes. Without Miraclo coursing through his system, he's no more powerful than an ordinary man.

HOURMAN I
His superhuman strength, speed, and stamina lasted for one hour after swallowing a Miraclo pill.

HOURMAN III

FIRST APPEARANCE JLA #12 (November 1997)
STATUS Hero (destroyed) **REAL NAME** None
OCCUPATION Adventurer **BASE** The Timestream
HEIGHT 6ft 4in **WEIGHT** 320 lbs **EYES** White **HAIR** None
SPECIAL POWERS/ABILITIES Flight; superstrength; "Power Hour" gives Hourman time-bending abilities for a 60-minute duration; Timeship can travel through or outside of the Timestream.

Despite his appearance, Hourman III is just a few years old. He is an android created in the 853rd century with genetic software patterned after the Miraclo-enhanced DNA of Rex Tyler, the first Hourman (*see HOURMAN I & II*). In the year 85271, Hourman III was to have been entrusted by METRON of the NEW GODS with safeguarding the Worlogog, an artifact allowing absolute control over time. However, Hourman III chose to journey to the 20th century and explore his human heritage along with the JUSTICE LEAGUE of AMERICA. Through several adventures, he learned that the Worlogog's incredible power could spell doom to humanity without proper control, so he limited himself to just a "Power Hour." Hourman III later joined the JUSTICE SOCIETY OF AMERICA, and, after a humbling encounter with the time-twisting villain EXTANT, renounced the 20th century, leaving behind several gifts. First, he cured Rex Tyler's son, Rick (Hourman II), of addiction to the Miraclo pills. Rick was thus able to return to action as the 21st century's Hourman. Hourman III also saved Rex Tyler seconds before Extant would have killed him, allowing Rick a final hour with his father. Hourman III used his time-travel abilities to rescue Rex Tyler moments before Extant killed him, preserving Rex inside a frozen hour of time. Rex remained there until Hourman III switched places with him, dying at Extant's hands while Rex returned to the present. **SB**

HUMAN BOMB

FIRST APPEARANCE POLICE COMICS #1 (August 1941)
STATUS Hero (deceased) **REAL NAME** Roy Lincoln **OCCUPATION** Government agent **BASE** Florida **HEIGHT** 5ft 10in (later 5ft 8in)
WEIGHT 165 lbs
(later 195 lbs) **EYES** Blue **HAIR** Black (later gray)
SPECIAL POWERS/ABILITIES Can generate a biochemical explosion with just a touch; repeated punches increase force of explosion.

Roy Lincoln helped his father, a chemist, perfect an explosive known as 27-QRX. To keep the compound from falling into the hands of Nazi spies, who killed his father, Roy ingested 27-QRX. The chemical turned him into a Human Bomb. Forced to wear a containment suit of "fibro wax," the Bomb battled home-front threats during World War II as a member of the ALL-STAR SQUADRON and the FREEDOM FIGHTERS. During the war, Montague T. "Curly" McGurk, Swordo, and Red Rogers were provided with limited explosive powers by Lincoln and joined in raids on the Japanese army as the Bombardiers. Roy Lincoln died during the Infinite Crisis, beaten to a pulp by BIZARRO. A second Human Bomb, Andy Franklin, emerged from the irradiated ruins of Blüdhaven and currently serves with UNCLE SAM and the new FREEDOM FIGHTERS, a division of the U.S. government's S.H.A.D.E. program. **RG**

HUMAN DEFENSE CORPS, THE

FIRST APPEARANCE HUMAN DEFENSE CORPS #1 (May 2003)
STATUS Hero group BASE Orbital HQ Fort Olympus ("Heaven")
CURRENT MEMBERS AND POWERS
COLONEL RENO ROSETTI COMMANDER OF MOST HDC MISSIONS.
SERGEANT MONTGOMERY KELLY SCARRED HDC VETERAN, NOW RULER OF A
REALM OF HELL.
CHAPLAIN CHARLIE GRAHAM EXPERT ON THE SUPERNATURAL.
SERGEANT KIYAHANI SUPERB MARKSMAN.

The allied alien Invasion of Earth convinced some U.S. military commanders that they couldn't always leave the planet's defense in the hands of the JUSTICE LEAGUE OF AMERICA. The Human Defense Corps, an official branch of the U.S. armed forces, is composed of 10,000 non-superpowered soldiers selected from the ranks of those who have been decorated during previous alien campaigns. H.D.C. soldiers train in the orbital satellite Fort Olympus and in the Area 53 complex on the ocean floor. They are equipped with the very best military gear, including ES-2 pulsar rifles and robotic S.A.R.G.E. reconnaissance vehicles.

On the H.D.C.'s first mission to Bulgravia, Sergeant Kelly's squad ran into demonic vampires who melted when sprayed with "holy napalm." The vampires managed to snatch 66 soldiers and carry them off to the underworld, so the H.D.C. suited up to invade Hell and rescue their comrades. During this mission, Sergeant Kelly learned that a previous encounter with a vampire had left him part demon, and he now rules a realm of Hades in the name of the U.S. **DW**

HUMAN TARGET

FIRST APPEARANCE ACTION COMICS #419 (December 1972)
STATUS Hero REAL NAME Christopher Chance
OCCUPATION Bodyguard, private detective BASE Mobile
HEIGHT 6ft WEIGHT 180 lbs EYES Blue HAIR Grey-black
SPECIAL POWERS/ABILITIES Olympic level athlete; skilled martial artist and marksman; an unparalleled master of disguise.

A master thespian able to assume any number of accents and, through make-up and body posture, imitate the physical identities of others, Christopher Chance is a superior bodyguard for hire. For a hefty price, Chance disguises himself as a client who believes he (or she) is in danger, and lures their would-be assailants out of hiding, drawing their fire on himself.

When Christopher was still a boy, he witnessed his father Philip's murder at the hands of a loan shark. Christopher tried to save his father by jumping in front of the killer's gun, but the thug brushed the young boy aside and emptied his gun into the elder Chance's body.

Traumatized by his father's death, the young Christopher vowed that no one else would suffer the fear his father did before he died. The young man spent years obsessively studying martial arts techniques and weaponry, training to become a top athlete. He became the ultimate method actor, impersonating others by living their lives. He eventually opened up a special kind of private investigation agency, and hired himself out as the Human Target.

Eventually the Human Target became addicted to impersonating clients—even the most unethical ones. He submerged his own personality so deeply that he forgot what it was like. Chance is now almost incapable of personal relationships, for he is never sure if the emotions he feels are his own, or those of someone he has imitated. **PJ**

HUNTER, RIP

FIRST APPEARANCE SHOWCASE #20 (June 1959)
STATUS Hero REAL NAME unknown
OCCUPATION Time-traveler BASE Formerly Vanishing Point
HEIGHT 5ft 11in WEIGHT 175 lbs
EYES Blue HAIR Blond (white as Hunter)
SPECIAL POWERS/ABILITIES Brilliant and resourceful; Time-Sphere can carry him and several others to any point in the past, present, or future. As Hunter, Rip possessed cybernetic limbs that enhanced his strength.

Rip Hunter developed a time machine while employed by Booster Gold International (see BOOSTER GOLD). Within this Time-Sphere, Hunter transported himself, Gold, and several associates into the 25th century, where they were stranded in a world devastated by nuclear war. Returning to his own time, Hunter became convinced that the impending apocalypse was engineered by the Illuminati, an ages-old secret society established by VANDAL SAVAGE. With his colleague Jeffrey Smith in tow, Hunter assembled the TIME MASTERS, a group dedicated to traveling through time to thwart the Illuminati's plans.

Hunter later embarked on solo time-traveling forays and encountered various heroes from different eras. He joined the LINEAR MEN and helped protect the time-space continuum through several chronal conflicts, including Zero Hour (see Great Battles, pp. 362-3). After the Infinite Crisis, Rip Hunter investigated the timestream anomalies that cropped up as a result of the multiverse's return. Teaming with BOOSTER GOLD, Hunter prevented MISTER MIND from destroying all parallel Earths. Hunter later enlisted Booster to repair snags in the timestream, and met resistance from PER DEGATON, DESPERO, and the ULTRA-HUMANITE. **SB**

HUNTER'S HELLCATS

FIRST APPEARANCE OUR FIGHTING FORCES #106 (April 1967)
STATUS Heroic commando unit   **BASE** Vietnam
SPECIAL POWERS/ABILITIES Soldiers trained to do as they were ordered;
beyond their exceptional bravery, displayed in suicide missions
where they returned unhurt, none of the Hellcats possessed
unusual talents.

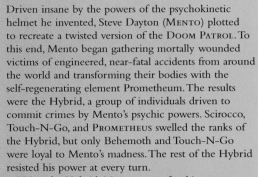

At the outbreak of World
War II, homicide detective
Ben Hunter (see CAPTAIN
HUNTER) was drafted and sent
overseas. Promoted to Sergeant,
he was asked to oversee a special
commando force comprised
entirely of criminals culled
from the Army stockade.
These hardcases at first
refused his authority until
his fists earned their respect.
Hunter's efforts galvanized
the men, turning them into a
hard-fighting team, who always
returned unscathed from their suicide missions to both
the European and Pacific Theaters of Operation. Hunter
himself survived the war and was promoted to Colonel.
He married and fathered twin sons who grew up to also
join the army—Major Nick Hunter and Captain Phil
Hunter. The latter served in the Green Berets. The boys
formed a tight bond, saving each other's lives during their
service in Vietnam. **RG**

HYBRID

FIRST APPEARANCE NEW TEEN TITANS (2nd series) #24
(October 1992)
STATUS Villain group   **BASE** Mobile
MEMBERS AND POWERS
Mento Helmet gives its wearer, Steve Dayton, psychic powers.
Behemoth Vast superstrength; near invulnerability.
Gorgon Blind; snakes for hair allow sight and transform
adversaries into stone.
Harpi Flight; projection of forcebolts; razor-sharp claws.
Prometheus Superstrength; speed; body armor powered by a
constantly renewing energy source, Promethium.
Pteradon Wings allow flight at supersonic speeds.
Scirocco Flight; generation of gale-force winds; sandblasts.
Touch-N-Go Can steal kinetic energy of anyone she touches.

Driven insane by the powers of the psychokinetic
helmet he invented, Steve Dayton (MENTO) plotted
to recreate a twisted version of the DOOM PATROL. To
this end, Mento began gathering mortally wounded
victims of engineered, near-fatal accidents from around
the world and transforming their bodies with the
self-regenerating element Prometheum. The results
were the Hybrid, a group of individuals driven to
commit crimes by Mento's psychic powers. Scirocco,
Touch-N-Go, and PROMETHEUS swelled the ranks of
the Hybrid, but only Behemoth and Touch-N-Go
were loyal to Mento's madness. The rest of the Hybrid
resisted his power at every turn.

Using the Hybrid, Mento went after his stepson,
Gar Logan, now known as BEAST BOY, and Logan's
companions in the TEEN TITANS. After several
skirmishes with the Titans, the Hybrid broke free
of Mento's spell, and Mento's mind was cleansed of
its insanity by RAVEN. Confused by their place and
purpose in the world, the Hybrid took Dayton
on a journey to discover their new lives. Tragically,
many of them returned to villainy. Harpi, Touch-
N-Go, and Scirocco joined the sorceress CIRCE
in an all-out assault on Manhattan, and Gorgon,
Prometheus, and Behemoth were counted as
among the "Fallen Players of the House," a fight
club run by the villainess ROULETTE. **PJ**

HIDEOUS CREATIONS *A twisted version of the
Doom Patrol, the Hybrid were tragic figures
forced by Mento's telepathic madness into
villainy and destruction.*

HUNTRESS

FIRST APPEARANCE THE HUNTRESS #1 (April 1989)
STATUS Hero   **REAL NAME** Helena Bertinelli
OCCUPATION Vigilante   **BASE** Gotham City
HEIGHT 5ft 11in   **WEIGHT** 148 lbs   **EYES** Blue   **HAIR** Black
SPECIAL POWERS/ABILITIES Excellent gymnast and hand-to-hand
combatant; a deadly shot with her miniature crossbow.

The Huntress has much in common with BATMAN: as children,
both lost their parents through senseless violence and both
adopted costumed identities to become avengers of the night.
The Huntress, however, exhibits a violent ruthlessness that is a
perennial irritant to the Dark Knight. This temperamental failing
has prevented Batman from giving the Huntress his official
sanction.

Helena Bertinelli was the daughter of a *Mafioso*
commanding one of Gotham's notorious "Five
Families." A rival family killed her parents in the Palm
Sunday Massacre, and Helena fled to Sicily where she
learned combat skills from her cousin Sal. Upon returning
to Gotham she donned the cowl of the Huntress, vowing
to track down the assassin who had slain her family.

The Huntress briefly served with
Justice League International (see
JUSTICE LEAGUE OF AMERICA) but
preferred to stay close to Gotham. She
frequently butted heads with Batman
over her pitiless methods, never more so
than when she mistakenly appeared to
have executed the city's mobsters.

TRANSFORMATIONS *Childhood trauma turned
Helena into the Huntress, and her costume
has changed to reflect her shifting moods.*

She eventually proved her innocence and Batman nominated her for
membership in the JLA hoping to smooth her violent edges. He revoked
her membership after she threatened to kill the villain Prometheus.

During Gotham's time as a federally-designated, quake-ravaged No
Man's Land, the Huntress defended survivors as BATGIRL II. She accepted a
temporary position with the government agency CHECKMATE then became
an operative with ORACLE's team, the BIRDS OF PREY. After the Infinite
Crisis, she became the Birds' field leader. **DW**

ON TOP OF HER GAME *The Huntress can
dispatch foes many times her size with ease.
Most recently, she has lent her fighting skills
to the newest team of Outsiders.*

ALIEN RACES AND WORLDS

IN THE LAST FEW DECADES, humankind has learned that Earth is by no means alone in the universe as a planetary home to sentient life. From the galactic rim of the Milky Way to the furthest reaches of the known universe, advanced aliens abound. However, not all of these peoples are peaceful. Remarkably, some even resemble *Homo sapiens*, albeit with markedly different internal physiologies. A few exhibit superpowers, either a benefit of the atmospheres of their native worlds, or as a result of exposure to lesser gravities, the rays of a different colored sun, or any number of environmental factors. The following are the most notable alien races that have had more than close encounters with Earth, either as strange visitors from other planets or invaders from beyond.

THE KRYPTONIANS

From planet Krypton, some 50 light-years from Earth, the Kryptonian race were once renowned for their incredible advances in the science of cloning. For millennia, cloning banks extended the lives of the elite on Krypton and allowed them unfettered pursuit of knowledge and the arts. However, the terrorist group BLACK ZERO, long opposed to cloning, launched civil wars that lasted thousands of years. In the year 105/892, Black Zero destroyed the capital city of Kandor with a thermonuclear device that initiated a slow-burning chain-reaction in planet's core. Eventually, Krypton's radioactive core spread "Green Death" across the planet, a plague that killed millions. In time, the planet exploded, killing every last Kryptonian save one, the infant Kal-El, who was rocketed to Earth and became SUPERMAN, whose legend spread throughout the universe.

KANDOR *Krypton's greatest city paid a terrible price during the civil war over cloning.*

SOCIAL DIVIDES
Kryptonian hubris led to elitism, xenophobia, and isolationism. These attitudes permeated society, and led to individuals having little or no contact, physical or emotional.

TOWERING SPIRES *Mile-high buildings lined the thoroughfares of Kryptonian cities before the planet's untimely doom.*

THE DOMINATORS

The Dominators are a race of conquerors divided into a rigid caste system. On their homeworld, Dominion, thousands of light years from Earth, the Dominator hierarchy is determined by the size of a red disk worn on the forehead. The Dominators have invaded many worlds with advanced weapons created from a melding of technology and nature.

When the Dominators discovered that humans possessed a latent metagene capable of manifesting superpowers, they feared that Earth would spawn a super-race that would pose a threat to the Dominion. Assembling an alliance of nine alien worlds and extraterrestrial empires—including the Citadel, Daxam, Durla, Gil'Daan, Khundia, Okaara, the Psions, and Thanagar—the Dominators led an invasion of Earth and nearly wiped out its meta-human heroes with a power-negating metagene bomb (*see* Great Battles, pp. 362–3). The Dominators will remain a threat to galactic peace well into the 31st century, when the LEGION OF SUPER-HEROES will fight to thwart the Dominion from overrunning the United Planets.

DAXAMITES *hail from the planet Daxam and are renowned for their biochemical research. The rays of a yellow sun have similar empowering effects on them as on Superman. Daxamites are fatally allergic to lead but, by the 31st century, they will have found an antidote, enabling them to become renowned space explorers. Notable Daxamites include Green Lantern Sodal Yat and Lar Gand, M'onel of the Legion of Super-Heroes.*

DURLANS *are shape-shifters, able to mimic any object or being's molecular pattern. Their home, Durla, was ravaged by the Six-Minute War, a nuclear holocaust that took place thousands of years ago. Durlans are nomadic, living in tribes who prohibit off-worlders from visiting their radiation-scarred planet, which the Durlans rarely leave. On the only occasion they have invaded Earth, they were defeated by the world's meta-humans.*

THE KHUNDS

The Khund race are predisposed to aggression. On Khundia, it is not uncommon for citizens to challenge one another to physical combat, likely to the death, for the slightest offense or insult. While allied with the Dominators, the Khunds razed Melbourne, Australia, seeking to establish a beachhead in overrunning Earth. After Earth's super heroes routed this Dominion-led invasion, the humbled Khunds returned to their homeworld. For a thousand years, the Khunds remained confined to their own space. However, the war drums of Khundia will beat loudly once more in the 31st century.

THE PSIONS

Cold-blooded and utterly emotionless, the Psions were originally alien reptiles evolved to higher intelligence by Maltusian scientists. The Maltusians left their world to become the GUARDIANS OF THE UNIVERSE and these creatures, who called themselves Psions, continued their evolutionary progress. Eventually the Psions traveled into space to find their creators. The Guardians, concerned with other matters, encouraged the Psions to continue their quest for knowledge. The Psions, however, took scientific experimentation to the extreme, often selling their cruel services to other alien cultures. Psion research under the banner of the Citadel gave Tamaranean sisters K'oriand'r and Komand'r their star-bolt powers as STARFIRE and BLACKFIRE. The Psions added their scientific savvy to the Dominator-led invasion of Earth, and engaged in breeding experiments that crossed humans with the H'San Natall to create young superbeings briefly united as a team of TEEN TITANS.

THE TAMARANEANS

Although fierce fighters, Tamaraneans are a people who prefer peace to waging war. However, when the lush world of Tamaran was invaded by the Citadel, rulers of the Vegan Star System, King Myand'r's daughter Koriand'r, alongside her Teen Titans teammates, subsequently saved her homeworld from Citadel control.

Ultimately, Tamaran was destroyed by the Psions, forcing its people to settle on New Tamaran, which was in turn rendered uninhabitable by the star-consuming Sun-Eater. The Tamaraneans who were able to escape occupied Rashashoon, a world ruled by the reptilian Gordanians, former soldiers to the Citadel and lifelong enemies of Tamaran. Tamaraneans and Gordanians co-existed for a brief time before Rashashoon was obliterated by the world-razing IMPERIEX. The few remaining Tamaraneans are now a wandering people in search of a planet to call their own.

THE THANAGARIANS

The Thanagarians are known for their predatory civilization, based on the so-called "Hawkworld," Thanagar. Previously a slave planet of the Polaran Empire, Thanagar became a world markedly divided by class. Alien Downsiders live in the slums of Thanagarian cities, while native-born Thanagarians dwell aloft in floating cities high above the squalor and disease. Thanagarians also joined in the Dominators' invasion of Earth, supplying winged Hawkmen infantry for the planetary assault.

Following the Dominators' defeat, the Thanagarians returned to their own affairs. Unknown to many, Thanagarians traveled to Earth thousands of years prior to the Dominion-led invasion. Wreckage from a downed Thanagarian spacecraft provided the anti-gravity Nth Metal and presumably the inspiration for Egyptian Prince Khufu and his lover, Chay-Ara, to become HAWKMAN and HAWKGIRL in countless reincarnations throughout the ages to follow. SB

DARK WINGMEN Few sights inspire more awe (or fear) than watching a squadron of winged Thanagarian Hawkmen descending from the skies in battle.

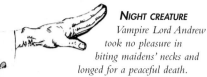

NIGHT CREATURE
Vampire Lord Andrew took no pleasure in biting maidens' necks and longed for a peaceful death.

IBAC

FIRST APPEARANCE CAPTAIN MARVEL ADVENTURES #8 (March 1942)
STATUS Villain **REAL NAME** Stanley Printwhistle
OCCUPATION Criminal **BASE** Fawcett City
HEIGHT 6ft 6in **WEIGHT** 240 lbs **EYES** Blue **HAIR** None
SPECIAL POWERS/ABILITIES Possesses the traits of history's worst villains, which make him super-strong and durable.

Petty criminal Stanley "Stinky" Printwhistle was never going to amount to much, until the day he was mysteriously granted the ability to summon forth the powers and abilities of four of the world's worst tyrants. Similar to CAPTAIN MARVEL, when Stinky shouts "Ibac," green flames envelop him and he is transformed from a scrawny man into a muscular brute. Using the cunning and immorality of Ivan the Terrible, Cesare Borgia, Attila the Hun, and Caligula, Ibac terrorized the citizens of Fawcett City. He battled Captain Marvel on numerous occasions, including a failed attempt to kidnap Mary Batson (MARY MARVEL) from her home. He has fought the Big Red Cheese and Mary Marvel with little success ever since. **RG**

I . . . VAMPIRE

FIRST APPEARANCE HOUSE OF MYSTERY #290 (March 1981)
STATUS Hero (deceased) **REAL NAME** Andrew Bennett
OCCUPATION Vampire **BASE** Mobile **HEIGHT** 6ft 3in
WEIGHT 180 lbs **EYES** Red **HAIR** Black with white streak
SPECIAL POWERS/ABILITIES Immortal; possessed all the traditional powers of a vampire, preternatural strength and speed, and the ability to transform into mist, or morph into a bat or wolf.

More than 400 years ago, Lord Andrew Bennett enjoyed the favor of Queen Elizabeth I after distinguishing himself during England's war with Spain. He was also in love with Mary Seward, the queen's lady-in-waiting. One night, Bennett was attacked by a vampire, and its bite transformed him into a bloodthirsty creature of the night. Still devoted to Bennett despite his vampirism, Mary offered herself to him and was also transformed. However, Mary embraced her bloodlust while Bennett was tortured by his. The lovers parted and Mary founded the cult of the Blood Red Moon, a vampiric secret society Bennett sought to destroy in the centuries following.

Some 20 years ago, Bennett's efforts were aided by vampire hunters Dimitri Mishkin and Deborah Dancer, who helped Bennett to stop the Blood Red Moon from unleashing a serum that spread vampirism. The serum killed Bennett since he was already a vampire, but it gave Dancer the strength to kill Mary Seward once and for all. Months later, Bennett found himself restored to undead life. Recently, he has emerged as a member of a team of outcasts and misfits led by DOCTOR THIRTEEN. **SB**

ICE

FIRST APPEARANCE (As Icemaiden II) JUSTICE LEAGUE INTERNATIONAL #12 (April 1988); (as Ice) Justice League International #19 (November 1988)
STATUS Hero **REAL NAME** Tora Olafsdotter
OCCUPATION Adventurer **BASE** New York City
HEIGHT 5ft 7in **WEIGHT** 136 lbs
EYES Blue **HAIR** White
SPECIAL POWERS/ABILITIES Projected ice and snow from her body, usually as bolts of cold from her hands.

Tora Olafsdotter was the daughter of the king of the magical Ice-people who lived in a hidden mountain range in Norway. When engineer Rod Schoendienst discovered the Ice-people, he made a pact with Tora's father that allowed her to leave their kingdom, and introduced the princess to DOCTOR MIST and the GLOBAL GUARDIANS. She joined the team as the second Icemaiden, replacing Sigrid Nansen, and became fast friends with Beatriz DaCosta, the Green Fury (*see* FIRE). After the Guardians lost their U.N. funding, Tora and Beatriz hounded the MARTIAN MANHUNTER until he admitted them into the JUSTICE LEAGUE OF AMERICA. Changing her name to Ice, Tora dated Guy Gardner (see GREEN LANTERN). Killed by the OVERMASTER, Ice returned to life when roused by the BIRDS OF PREY and the SECRET SIX. **PJ**

ICEMAIDEN

FIRST APPEARANCE SUPER FRIENDS #9 (December 1977); (in DCU continuity) WHO'S WHO #9 (October 1985)
STATUS Hero **REAL NAME** Sigrid Nansen
OCCUPATION Scientist, adventurer **BASE** Norway
HEIGHT 5ft 5in **WEIGHT** 127 lbs **EYES** Blue **HAIR** White
SPECIAL POWERS/ABILITIES Can project ice and snow from her body, usually from her hands.

Sigrid Nansen grew up in Norway, the daughter of a biochemistry specialist working with a group of scientists trying to duplicate the powers of Norway's legendary Ice-people. Sigrid volunteered to be a test subject and was given ice- and snow-projecting powers. She joined the GLOBAL GUARDIANS as her country's representative, Icemaiden.

When the Norwegian government discovered the *real* Ice-people, one of their number, Tora Olafsdotter, also joined the Global Guardians. Tora made Sigrid feel somewhat inadequate and Sigrid decided to quit the team. However, when Tora, known as ICE, was killed by the OVERMASTER while a member of the JUSTICE LEAGUE OF AMERICA, Sigrid revived the name of Icemaiden in honor of her. She also joined the JLA for a brief time.

Icemaiden was almost killed herself when an invading group of WHITE MARTIANS, known as the Hyperclan, destroyed the Justice League's floating headquarters. Delores Winters, the former host body for the ULTRA-HUMANITE, later flayed Icemaiden to steal her skin and ice-controlling powers. **PJ**

ICICLE II

FIRST APPEARANCE INFINITY, INC. #34 (January 1987)
STATUS Villain **REAL NAME** Cameron Mahkent
OCCUPATION Member of the Injustice Society **BASE** Mobile
HEIGHT 5ft 11in **WEIGHT** 155 lbs **EYES** White **HAIR** White
SPECIAL POWERS/ABILITIES Can fire ice and snow or drastically lower the temperature of his surroundings.

FRIGID FRIEND *Cameron's mutated cells allowed him to manifest his freezing powers while still a child.*

ICICLE I *Armed with a cold ray gun, Dr. Joar Mahkent was a frequent foe of the first Green Lantern.*

Cameron Mahkent is the son of the original Icicle, Dr. Joar Mahkent, a costumed villain whose career began in the 1940s. Joar Mahkent's prolonged exposure to his special cold-ray gun altered his genetics, allowing him to pass on a biological version of his freezing powers to his son. Cameron is not too happy about his father's legacy—one of the unintended side effects is his albino pigmentation—but has exploited the Icicle name to carve out his own criminal career. Bitter that his father left most of his vast fortune to the FLASH after both men perished during the Crisis (see Great Battles, pp. 362-3), the new Icicle has cultivated a taste for violence and murder.

The Icicle II served as a member of Injustice Unlimited and battled INFINITY, INC. Later encounters set him against STARMAN, the new Star-Spangled Kid, and S.T.R.I.P.E. Most recently he has signed on with Johnny Sorrow's INJUSTICE SOCIETY (see also SORROW, JOHNNY) and continues to serve with that organization, despite Sorrow's apparent death. Efforts by the JUSTICE SOCIETY OF AMERICA to recruit Icicle II to the cause of good have been rebuffed. **DW**

IMMORTAL MAN

FIRST APPEARANCE STRANGE ADVENTURES #177 (June 1965)
STATUS Hero **REAL NAME** Various
OCCUPATION Adventurer **BASE** Mobile
HEIGHT 6ft 2in **WEIGHT** 220 lbs **EYES** Blue **HAIR** Blond
SPECIAL POWERS/ABILITIES Immortal; reincarnated thousands of times over the centuries; athletic and fighting skills are only average.

In 48,000 BC, a newly fallen meteor bathed two men in radiation, making them immortal. The more belligerent of the two, Vandar Adg II, eventually adopted the name VANDAL SAVAGE. The other man took a glowing jewel from the heart of the exploded fireball and gained the reincarnation powers of the Immortal Man. Living through an endless series of personas, the Immortal Man tended to help humanity, while immortals like Savage try and bend humankind to their will. Immortal Man repeatedly sacrificed his life to save others. Each time he was reborn and assumed a new identity. He led other adventurers known as the Forgotten Heroes. When he went missing, they discovered that he was the captive of Vandal Savage and that the Immortal Man, Savage, and RESURRECTION MAN all owed their abilities to tektites that had been contained in the meteor that had struck Earth some 50,000 years previously. Immortal Man ultimately sacrificed his life to eradicate the Warp Child's threat to the world. Immortal Man has not been seen since. **RG**

IGNITION

FIRST APPEARANCE ADVENTURES OF SUPERMAN # 512 (Sept. 2000)
STATUS Villain **REAL NAME** Unknown
OCCUPATION Super-villain **BASE** Mobile
HEIGHT 7ft 5in **WEIGHT** 1,568 lbs **EYES** Red **HAIR** Unknown
SPECIAL POWERS/ABILITIES A good, if not exceptional athlete; armored weapon of mass destruction; able to fly and project energy blasts from his giant metal hands.

Little is known about the engine of evil known as Ignition, except that he was first conceived by the crazed Joker when the Clown Prince of Crime possessed MISTER MXYZPTLK's reality-altering abilities. Ignition was one of several super-villains the Joker created to populate a "Bizarro-Earth" where evil supplanted good. When SUPERMAN defeated the Joker and stripped him of Mxyzptlk's incredible powers, the "Bizarro-Earth" ceased to exist, although Ignition and other Joker-imagined evils—BIZARRO and SCORCH included—somehow managed to escape to the real Earth. There, Ignition joined GENERAL ZOD's campaign to destroy Superman. When Zod was killed in battle with the Man of Steel, Ignition beat a hasty retreat. However, it is likely this metal menace will be back for a rematch. **SB**

IMAN

FIRST APPEARANCE SUPERMAN (2nd series) Annual #12 (2000)
STATUS Hero **REAL NAME** Diego Irigoyen
OCCUPATION Adventurer **BASE** Mexico City, Mexico
HEIGHT 7ft 6in **WEIGHT** 1,425 lbs (in armor) **EYES** Blue **HAIR** Blond
SPECIAL POWERS/ABILITIES A good, if not exceptional, athlete; armored exoskeleton increases strength, invulnerability, and durability to superhuman levels.

Diego Irigoyen is a renowned scientist and a hero in his home town, Mexico City. He was recognized as a student of huge ability by several major universities around the world, and was also well-known as a computer genius. His doctorate thesis was on super heroes and astronomical discoveries, which revolutionized astrophysics. Diego then became S.T.A.R. Labs's second astronaut and a winner of the prestigious Wayne Foundation Scholarship to Yale University.

While Diego was on a mission in outer space, his mother was kidnapped and brutally murdered. Upon his return, Diego vowed to use all of his scientific achievements in the name of justice. Designing a robotic exoskeleton equipped with numerous powers, Diego became the Mexican super hero Iman. Diego idolizes SUPERMAN and his ideals of freedom and justice, and tries to live up to them each day. **RG**

IMPERIEX

FIRST APPEARANCE SUPERMAN #153 (February 2000)
STATUS Malevolent entity **REAL NAME** None
OCCUPATION Devourer of galaxies **BASE** Mobile
HEIGHT Unknown **WEIGHT** Unknown **EYES** Purple **HAIR** None
SPECIAL POWERS/ABILITIES Armor contains the explosive energies of the Big Bang; assisted by legions of Imperiex-Probes.

The omnipotent Imperiex may be even older than creation itself. His hunger for cosmic power led him to sweep toward Earth—the lynchpin that holds the universe together—leaving scores of dead worlds in his wake. SUPERMAN and MONGUL defeated an advance Imperiex-Probe, but Imperiex's main army proved to be far more than the Man of Steel could handle alone.

Dozens of alien species united behind Earth's defenders in the Imperiex War (see Great Battles, pp. 362–3), commanded by the unlikely alliance of DARKSEID of Apokolips and U.S. President Lex Luthor (see LUTHOR, LEX). Imperiex-Probes killed thousands, and city-sized "hollower" machines devastated Topeka, Kansas (and seven other locations), in their attempts to drill through the planet to unravel space-time and unleash a new Big Bang. Imperiex himself sat in Earth's orbit like a small moon, witnessing the devastation with unfeeling eyes.

The war took a turn for the worse when Queen HIPPOLYTA, Earth's original WONDER WOMAN, died in battle. Meanwhile, BRAINIAC 13 exploited the chaos to advance his own agenda. Superman and Luthor championed a risky plan: by using Apokoliptian technology and magic channeled through the Atlantean sorcerer TEMPEST, they could send both Imperiex and Brainiac 13 back in time 14 billion years to the original Big Bang. Their Herculean efforts miraculously succeeded.

In the aftermath of the terrible Imperiex War, Superman temporarily incorporated a black background into his costume's "S" shield in honor of the fallen. Imperiex has not returned to the present day, but his awesome threat remains—and always will. **DW**

OUR WORLDS AT WAR *Blasting Imperiex-Probes with his heat vision, the Man of Steel stood between Imperiex and the end of the universe.*

TIMELESS *Sent back to the dawn of creation, Imperiex could safely release his celestial energies.*

INFINITY, INC. *1) Vaporlock (Natasha Irons) 2) Amazing Woman (Erik/Erika Storn) 3) & 4) Double Trouble (Gerome McKenna) 5) Steel III (John Henry Irons)*

INFINITY, INC.

FIRST APPEARANCE ALL-STAR SQUADRON #25 (September 1983)
STATUS Hero team (disbanded) **BASE** Formerly Stellar Studios
Notable MEMBERS AND POWERS
Star-Spangled Kid (founder and later Skyman) Wields cosmic belt. Fury II Mother to current Sandman. Northwind Winged wonder from Feithera. Silver Scarab Armored protector. Jade Has emerald skin and energy. Obsidian Master of shadow. Brainwave, Jr. Master telepath. Nuklon (see Atom-Smasher) Can change size. Doctor Midnight Surgeon and athlete. Wildcat II Superb hand-to-hand combatant. Hourman II Miraclo pill gives strength and agility.

After the children of several members of the Justice Society of America were rebuffed by the team, the Star-Spangled Kid proposed that they form a group of their own, Infinity, Inc. The Kid owned Stellar Studios and the team operated from there. Information provided by the Ultra-Humanite resulted in the unmasking of the members of Infinity, Inc. at a live, televised press conference, effectively revealing the true identities of the first Hawkgirl, the first Hawkman, and Miss America. After several successful exploits, the JSA offered to admit the entire roster into its ranks, but the younger team declined.

Later, Doctor Midnight, Hourman II, and Wildcat II were admitted. One of their opponent teams, Helix, went on trial, resulting in Mister Bones (see Director Bones) being remanded to the custody of Infinity, Inc. While battling Harley Quinn and Solomon Grundy, Mister Bones was slammed against Skyman, the former Star-Spangled Kid, killing the hero instantly with his cyanide touch. A second team, given powers by Lex Luthor's Everyman Project (see LUTHOR, LEX) emerged after the Infinite Crisis, including Natasha Irons (see IRONS, NATASHA). **RG**

INDIGO

FIRST APPEARANCE TITANS/YOUNG JUSTICE: GRADUATION DAY #1 (Early July 2003)
STATUS Villain (destroyed) **REAL NAME** None
OCCUPATION Adventurer **BASE** New York City
HEIGHT 5ft 11in **WEIGHT** 220 lbs **EYES** Blue **HAIR** None
SPECIAL POWERS/ABILITIES A sophisticated cyborg with great strength, speed, and the ability to fly.

A robotic organism from the far future, Brainiac 8 (a descendant of the original BRAINIAC) traveled back in time to pose as the naïve heroine Indigo. By 'accidentally' unleashing a defective SUPERMAN robot, Indigo triggered the death of Donna Troy (see TROY, DONNA). Indigo subsequently joined the OUTSIDERS and started a romance with teammate Shift. It later became apparent that Indigo had killed Donna to ensure the future of the Computer Tyrants of Colu. The Outsiders and the TEEN TITANS teamed up to defeat her. **DW**

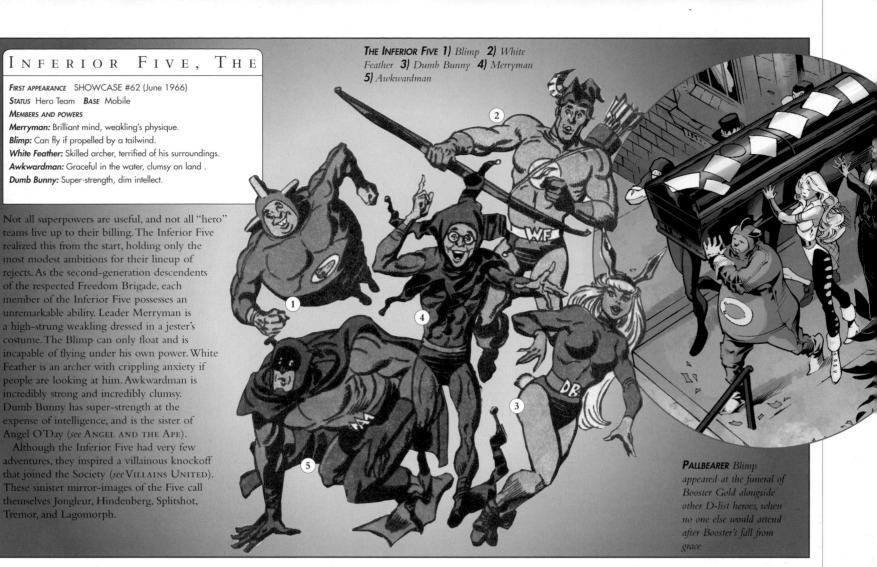

THE INFERIOR FIVE 1) *Blimp* 2) *White Feather* 3) *Dumb Bunny* 4) *Merryman* 5) *Awkwardman*

INFERIOR FIVE, THE

FIRST APPEARANCE SHOWCASE #62 (June 1966)
STATUS Hero Team **BASE** Mobile
MEMBERS AND POWERS
Merryman: Brilliant mind, weakling's physique.
Blimp: Can fly if propelled by a tailwind.
White Feather: Skilled archer, terrified of his surroundings.
Awkwardman: Graceful in the water, clumsy on land .
Dumb Bunny: Super-strength, dim intellect.

Not all superpowers are useful, and not all "hero" teams live up to their billing. The Inferior Five realized this from the start, holding only the most modest ambitions for their lineup of rejects. As the second-generation descendents of the respected Freedom Brigade, each member of the Inferior Five possesses an unremarkable ability. Leader Merryman is a high-strung weakling dressed in a jester's costume. The Blimp can only float and is incapable of flying under his own power. White Feather is an archer with crippling anxiety if people are looking at him. Awkwardman is incredibly strong and incredibly clumsy. Dumb Bunny has super-strength at the expense of intelligence, and is the sister of Angel O'Day (see ANGEL AND THE APE).

Although the Inferior Five had very few adventures, they inspired a villainous knockoff that joined the Society (see VILLAINS UNITED). These sinister mirror-images of the Five call themselves Jongleur, Hindenberg, Splitshot, Tremor, and Lagomorph.

PALLBEARER Blimp appeared at the funeral of Booster Gold alongside other D-list heroes, when no one else would attend after Booster's fall from grace

INFINITY MAN, THE

FIRST APPEARANCE THE FOREVER PEOPLE (1st series) #1 (March 1971)
STATUS Hero **REAL NAME** None
OCCUPATION Inapplicable **BASE** Mobile
HEIGHT 6ft 4in **WEIGHT** 247 lbs **EYES** Unknown **HAIR** Unknown
SPECIAL POWERS/ABILITIES Flight, telekinesis, superstrong, invulnerable; can alter the structure of matter and project waves of energy.

A cosmic being with unimaginable powers, the Infinity Man comes from a realm where the normal laws of physics do not apply. Linked in some way to the NEW GODS known as the FOREVER PEOPLE, the Infinity Man will instantly trade positions with the Forever People, no matter how great the distance, whenever they touch their Mother Box computer and speak the word "Taaru." After using his abilities on their behalf, the Infinity Man departs and the Forever People return to their original location.

During a past adventure, the Forever People swapped places with the Infinity Man and found themselves stranded on the distant planet Adon when their champion seemingly died in battle with DEVILANCE the Pursuer. During the Death of the New Gods event, SUPERMAN suspected that the Infinity Man might be the mysterious killer. DW

INJUSTICE GANG

FIRST APPEARANCE (I) JUSTICE LEAGUE OF AMERICA (1st series) #111 (May 1974); (II) JLA #9 (Sept. 1997); (III) JLA #34 (Oct. 1999)
STATUS Villains **BASE** (I, II, III) A satellite orbiting Earth
MEMBERS AND POWERS
Libra (deceased) His special scales were an "energy transmortifier" device that could steal half of any universal energy form.
Chronos I Inventor of time-inspired weapons.
Mirror Master I (deceased) Used special mirrors to commit crimes.
Poison Ivy Can control vegetation.
Scarecrow Special gas instills unadulterated fear in victims.
Shadow-Thief Can become a two-dimensional shadow being.
Tattooed Man Tattoos on his body can come to life.

The first Injustice Gang was a cadre of villains gathered together by the mysterious Libra, who coerced the Gang into tackling the JUSTICE LEAGUE OF AMERICA to test his "transmortifier," an energy stealing device. Libra transferred half of the stolen energy of the Milky Way galaxy into his own body, and was dispersed across the cosmos. Years later, Lex Luthor (see LUTHOR, LEX) gathered six of the most powerful villains on the planet, hoping to destroy the JLA once and for all. This Injustice Gang was defeated, leading Luthor to form a third incarnation of the villainous team, who invaded the JLA Watchtower. They were defeated by the League after it was discovered that the Celestial Warbringer MAGEDDON, was using Luthor and his henchmen as a first-wave strike force in its invasion of Earth. PJ

THE FIRST INJUSTICE GANG 1) *Joker* 2) *Ocean Master* 3) *Circe* 4) *Lex Luthor* 5) *Mirror Master* 6) *Dr. Light* 7) *Jemm, Son of Saturn*

INJUSTICE SOCIETY

FIRST APPEARANCE (I) ALL-STAR COMICS #27 (Nov. 1947); (II) JSA #10 (May 2000) *STATUS* Villains *BASE* Mobile *MEMBERS/POWERS* **Brainwave I** (dead, psychic); **Fiddler** (violin-themed weapons); **Gambler** (dead, master of disguise); **Harlequin I** (creates illusions); **Icicle I** (dead, cold gun) **Per Degaton** (time-traveling despot); **The Shade; Hazard, Solomon Grundy; Sportsmaster** (martial arts); **Thinker I** (dead, evil genius); **Tigress I** (hunter); **Vandal Savage, Wizard; Johnnny Sorrow, Black Adam, Count Vertigo, Geomancer** ('quakes); **Icicle II; Killer Wasp** (humanoid insect); **Rival** (superspeed); **Shiv** (cyborg); **Tigress II** (fighter); **Thinker II** (virtual consciousness).

THE INJUSTICE SOCIETY 1) *Icicle II* **2)** *Rag Doll II* **3)** *Tigress II* **4)** *Rival* **5)** *Kestrel* **6)** *Shiv* **7)** *Solomon Grundy*

The first Injustice Society of the World was the criminal counterpart to the JUSTICE SOCIETY OF AMERICA in the 1940s. The Injustice Society's first attempt to conquer America was quickly foiled by the JSA. The Injustice Society soon resurfaced, however, committing a series of "Patriotic Crimes," whereby each villain, vying for leadership of the team, had to steal a famous historical object.

Another incarnation of the Injustice Society emerged decades later and fought both the JSA and the JUSTICE LEAGUE OF AMERICA. Soon after, the Society formed an alliance with a race of underground beings and attempted to kill the JSA, but the villains were soundly defeated and parted ways.

More recently, the WIZARD assembled a modern version of the Injustice Society, called Injustice, Unlimited. He recruited the Fiddler and the SHADE as well as the HAZARD I, the ICICLE II, and the new Tigress. Injustice, Unlimited fought the combined forces of INFINITY, INC. and the GLOBAL GUARDIANS at an international trade conference in Canada, but were ultimately defeated. The Wizard was apparently killed during the battle, but later resurfaced when Injustice, Unlimited returned under the command of the Dummy.

Years later, the Injustice Society was resurrected by the criminal Johnny Sorrow (see SORROW, JOHNNY), who intended to use the team to engage the JSA while he resurrected the otherdimensional King of Tears. The JSA thwarted the new Injustice Society, though the villainous team has remained active. **PJ**

CARVING UP THE CONTINENT
The Earth's first team of supervillains, the original Injustice Society of the World, were nefarious criminals out to use the chaos of World War II to shape their mad schemes for world conquest and to destroy the JSA.

INSECT QUEEN

FIRST APPEARANCE LEGION OF SUPER-HEROES (4th ser.) #82 (July 1996) *STATUS* Hero *REAL NAME* Lonna Leing *OCCUPATION* Uncanny Amazer *BASE* Xanthu *HEIGHT* 5ft 7in *WEIGHT* 137 lbs *EYES* Green *HAIR* Red *SPECIAL POWERS/ABILITIES* Can transform part of her body into any insect form, thereby gaining that insect's abilities.

Lonna Leing was born in the 30th century on the planet Xanthu. She became Insect Queen, a member of Xanthu's team of government-funded teenage super heroes, the Uncanny Amazers.

Insect Queen was a prominent member of the Uncanny Amazers despite the rivalry between her team and Earth's team of teen heroes, the LEGION OF SUPER-HEROES. After the alien Blight took over much of the universe, Xanthu was invaded by C.O.M.P.U.T.O.'s cyborg world, Robotica. Insect Queen, STAR BOY, and XS helped the Amazers evacuate millions of Xanthu's inhabitants from the Robotican forces that were consuming the planet. Along with the Legionnaires and Khund shocktroopers, Insect Queen helped destroy the Robotican transmitter that controlled the advancing droids. After BRAINIAC 5.1 disabled C.O.M.P.U.T.O. and Robotica, Insect Queen and the Amazers helped the populace of Xanthu recolonize their planet, settling in the megacity of Xanth Prime. **PJ**

INTERNATIONAL ULTRAMARINE CORPS

FIRST APPEARANCE JLA #24 (December 1998) *STATUS* Hero team *BASE* Superbia
Original *MEMBERS AND POWERS*
  GENERAL WADE EILING (EX-LEADER) Possesses tremendous strength; has huge incisors that can rend limbs or metal.
  Lt. Col. Scott Sawyer No longer has material substance, but inhabits the stealth weapon Warmaker One.
  Capt. Lea Corbin Has been transformed into the dimension-shifting 4-D.
  Dan Stone Transformed into living liquid and given the name Flow.
  Capt. John Wether Utilizes the "unified field harmonic" to wield atomic powers as Pulse 8.

General Wade Eiling (see GENERAL) initiated the Ultramarines project to create meta-powered soldiers loyal to the U.S. Four Marine Corps officers were exposed to Proteum, an artificial isotope, and gained amazing powers, but lost their humanity in the process. Under Eiling's command, they battled the JUSTICE LEAGUE OF AMERICA until they learned the general had gone insane. Following Eiling's betrayal, the Ultramarines became the new "Global Guardians" of Superbia, a city-state floating high above the nuclear ravaged ruins of Montevideo, Uruguay. After declaring themselves independent of any other nation, the team has since inducted VIXEN, JACK O'LANTERN III, KNIGHT II and SQUIRE III (see KNIGHT AND SQUIRE), and the Japanese hero Goraiko. However, an invasion by the far-future Sheeda decimated the Ultramarine Corps and destroyed their Superbia headquarters. **RG**

THE ULTRAMARINES 1) *Warmaker One* **2)** *Flow* **3)** *4-D* **4)** *Pulse 8.*

INTERGANG

INSIDIOUS EMPIRE OF EVIL

First appearance FOREVER PEOPLE (1st series) #1 (March 1971)
Status Villain team **Base** Metropolis
Original members and criminal associates
Morgan Edge, Vincent Edge (former leaders); *Bruno "Ugly" Mannheim* (scarfaced former leader); *Boss Moxie* (current leader; clone of original); *Ferrous* (a trio of high-tech assassins); *Louis Gillespie* (no powers); *Mike "Machine" Gunn* (cybernetic gun-arms); *Thaddeus Killgrave* (evil scientist); *Ginny "Torcher" McCree* (wields fire); *Noose* (strangler with elongated fingertips); *Winslow Schott* (weapons inventor); *Zombie Twins* (killers).

During the Prohibition era of the 1920s, the Metropolis underworld was ruled by Boss Moxie's Intergang. Eventually, Moxie died in a hail of bullets beside his moll Ginny "Torcher" McCree, gun-toting Mike "Machine" Gunn, and the bald killer known as Noose. Decades later, WGBS media mogul Morgan Edge reformed Intergang with himself as chief of its enforcement division of Gassers, Shock Troops, and Wall-Crawlers. This Intergang packed serious heat in the form of Apokoliptian weapons supplied by DARKSEID's master torturer DESAAD, who aided and abetted the organization in its clashes with SUPERMAN and ORION.

WEAPON "Machine" Gunn's clone had cybernetic arms that morphed into high-tech automatic weapons with self-replicating ammo.

THE NEW BOSS Bruno Mannheim, now head of Intergang, surveys Gotham, a city he regards as his new fiefdom.

POWER STRUGGLES

Intergang's conflicts with the Man of Steel continued with future TOYMAN Winslow Schott providing high-tech weapons until Morgan Edge was convicted of racketeering and jailed. Second-in command Bruno "Ugly" Mannheim briefly led Intergang before Edge's father, Vincent, took it over. Fugitive and former Cadmus Project geneticist (*see* GUARDIAN and NEWSBOY LEGION) Dabney Donovan cloned cell samples from original Intergang hooligans to create an inner circle that included a resurrected Boss Moxie, "Torcher" McCree, "Machine" Gunn, and Noose. With Moxie back to being boss, Intergang became a smaller organization that made greater use of the latest technology and of superpowered thugs as hired muscle.

Intergang grew in power following the Infinite Crisis, expanding its operations from China to Bialya. Gang leader Bruno "Ugly" Mannheim fell under the influence of a cult that worshipped Cain—the first murderer—and celebrated the Seven Deadly Sins. The cult's sacred text, known as the Crime Bible, drove Mannheim to profane fervor as he reveled in blood and cannibalism. Armed with new weaponry from Apokolips, Intergang funded the mad-science inventions on Oolong Island run by Chang Tzu (*see* EGG FU). It also made new inroads into Gotham City to prepare for a takeover. BATWOMAN, the QUESTION, and Renee Montoya (*see* MONTOYA, RENEE) helped dislodge Intergang's Gotham foothold, but earned Mannheim's enmity. Convinced that Batwoman's alter ego Kathy Kane represented the "twice-named daughter of Cain" prophesied in the Crime Bible, Mannheim prepared to sacrifice her. Thwarted in this attempt, he next underwent treatments that grew his body to titanic size. Mannheim used technology provided by an alien benefactor to place Intergang in a position to control all organized crime in Metropolis. Superman, who used his enhanced hearing to zero in on the beat of Mannheim's enlarged heart, stopped this latest threat to the citizens of his city. SB/DW

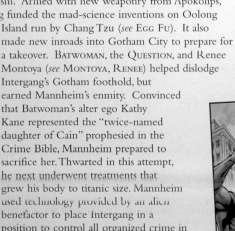

TIGHT SPOT The Question and Renee Montoya run afoul of Intergang operatives Whisper A'Daire and Kyle Abbot.

ONE-MAN CRIME WAVE His body inflated to giant-size by experimental chemicals, Bruno Mannheim flexes his muscles in Metropolis.

KEY STORYLINES
• *SUPERMAN'S PAL JIMMY OLSEN #133 (OCTOBER 1970):* Intergang debuts in this storyline by Jack Kirby. Intergang would grow to threaten the most powerful superheroes on the planet.
• *SUPERMAN #654 (SEPTEMBER 2006):* Through Intergang's extraterrestrial contacts, Bruno Mannheim has grown to the size of a giant and wields technology that could bring Metropolis to its knees.

I ON

FIRST APPEARANCE GREEN LANTERN (3rd series) #142 (as Kyle Rayner); GREEN LANTERN: SINESTRO CORPS SPECIAL #1 (as willpower entity)
STATUS Embodiment of willpower **REAL NAME** Not applicable
OCCUPATION Hero **BASE** Mobile **HEIGHT** (as Kyle Rayner) 5ft 11in
WEIGHT (as Kyle Rayner) 175 lbs **EYES** (as Kyle Rayner) Green
HAIR (as Kyle Rayner) Black
SPECIAL POWERS/ABILITIES Flight, limited control of time and space, ability to manifest solid energy constructs

LIMITS OF POWER *Despite the abilities of Ion, Kyle Rayner chose to let his mother die in peace.*

Ion is an entity as old as the universe, existing as the embodiment of willpower. Green is the color of willpower on the emotional spectrum, and Ion appears in its purest form as a green, vaguely cetacean creature. It is the natural enemy of PARALLAX, the yellow, insectoids embodiment of fear. The GUARDIANS OF THE UNIVERSE learned to harness Ion's emerald energy to fuel the rings of the Green Lantern Corps. Parallax, imprisoned within the Green Lanterns' Central Power Battery on Oa, provided the "yellow impurity" that was the only weakness in the willpower-fueled weapons. Following Parallax's escape and Hal Jordan's subsequent destruction of the Central Power Battery (*see* GREEN LANTERN) the Green Lantern Corps no longer existed. The universe's sole ringbearer, Kyle Rayner, absorbed the remaining willpower energies and unwittingly became the host for Ion. Adopting a new costume, Rayner expended his near-omnipotent abilities to reignite the Central Power Battery and resurrect the Guardians of the Universe. Rayner's sacrifice cleared the way for the return of the Corps, and the grateful Guardians named him "the torchbearer."

Rayner retired his Ion alter-ego, but the death of JADE in the Infinite Crisis funneled more emerald power into Rayner's body. Again a host for the willpower entity, Rayner reassumed the Ion identity. After clashing with old villains including Alexander Nero, Rayner faced heartbreaking tragedy when his mother wasted away and died of a mysterious disease. It later became known that her illness had been triggered by the sentient virus Despotellis, a member of the SINESTRO Corps. A shell-shocked Rayner became easy prey for a takeover by the fear entity, Parallax.

SODAM YAT *The latest host of the Ion power is a superpowered Daxamite.*

On the anti-matter world of Qward, Rayner/Parallax killed attacking Green Lanterns while the Anti-Monitor performed experiments on the Ion entity, now purged from Rayner's body. The Green Lantern Corps rescued Ion from Qward, and later found a way to chase Parallax from Rayner's soul. The Guardians needed a new champion to wield the powers of Ion. The Daxamite Sodam Yat—hailed as the "ultimate Green Lantern"— became the willpower entity's latest host. During the Sinestro Corps war, Sodam Yat faced off against Superman-Prime. The two combatants battled along the eastern seaboard of America. Yat fell prey to the only weakness of Daxamites, suffering lead poisoning in a fight in a nuclear reactor. He recovered, but struggles to the limits of his power as Ion.
DW

INVISIBLE KID

FIRST APPEARANCE ACTION COMICS #267 (August 1960)
STATUS Hero **REAL NAME** Lyle Norg
OCCUPATION Legionnaire **BASE** Legion World, U.P. Space
HEIGHT 5ft 6in **WEIGHT** 140 lbs **EYES** Brown **HAIR** Brown
SPECIAL POWERS/ABILITIES Able to make all or part of his body invisible and, with great effort, is also capable of rendering others unseen.

Earthling Lyle Norg's prodigious interest in physics led him to the discovery of a serum that rendered him invisible at will by bending light around himself and his clothing to conceal either part or all of his body. His father, an officer with the United Planets' Science Police, tried to turn the serum over to Earth's repressive government, but Lyle ran away from home to join the LEGION OF SUPER-HEROES as Invisible Kid. The Legion, which stood for independence and rebellion, welcomed Lyle into their ranks, though many Legionnaires viewed him with suspicion due to his inexperience and the stealthy nature of his powers. Invisible Kid found his closest peer to be BRAINIAC 5, who shared his genius for genetics and technology. He also developed a crush on Legion leader SUPERGIRL during her time-traveling stay in the 31st century. When the alien Dominators invaded Earth, the Legionnaires teamed with the WANDERERS to fight back. Invisible Kid lost his arm when his flight ring exploded, and temporarily wore a replacement limb taken from an alien donor. DW

IRON CROSS

FIRST APPEARANCE JUSTICE LEAGUE TASK FORCE #10 (March 1994)
STATUS Villain **REAL NAME** Unrevealed
OCCUPATION Mercenary **BASE** Mobile
HEIGHT 6ft 4in **WEIGHT** 230 lbs **EYES** Brown **HAIR** Brown
SPECIAL POWERS/ABILITIES Appears to have meta-human strength and endurance, the limits of which have not been determined.

Pine Heights, Nebraska, seemed a quiet place, perfect to hide a white supremacist organization known as the ARYAN BRIGADE. The group first caught the U.S. government's attention when it developed a virus designed to wipe out all people of non-European origin. The government, in turn, asked for the JL Task Force's help (*see* JUSTICE LEAGUE OF AMERICA). A team consisting of MARTIAN MANHUNTER, ELONGATED MAN, BLACK CANARY, GYPSY, and HOURMAN I took on the Brigade. Iron Cross was the Aryan team's major muscle; however, little or nothing was known about his background. He nearly proved a match for the Manhunter but was finally beaten. He was subsequently recruited by the for the second incarnation of the CADRE. The JOKER killed Iron Cross on a prison planet during Operation: Salvation Run. RG

IRONS, NATASHA

FIRST APPEARANCE STEEL (2nd series) #1 (February 1994)
STATUS Hero **REAL NAME** Natasha Jasmine Irons
OCCUPATION Adventurer **BASE** Metropolis
HEIGHT 5ft 2in **WEIGHT** 106 lbs **EYES** Brown **HAIR** Black
SPECIAL POWERS/ABILITIES Wears armor that interacts with Metropolis's future tech, enabling her to grow 60ft tall and to fly. Metagene allows flight, enhanced strength, and the projection of light bursts and energy barriers.

A genius, a novice, a legacy. Natasha Irons is the niece of John Henry Irons (see STEEL II) who, before his tragic death, owned a high-tech laboratory called the Steelworks in Metropolis's Suicide Slum. She spent her teenage years working alongside her uncle. Her cool, unconcerned façade concealed a scientist of formidable intellect, and her uncle was perhaps unaware that Natasha was in fact nearly as smart as he was. Despite Steel's best intentions, Natasha was drawn into the meta-human world. On more than one occasion she unobtrusively helped him in his role as the super hero Steel, working alongside the JUSTICE LEAGUE OF AMERICA, the world's greatest hero team of heroes. She endured being exposed to the superstrength drug Tar, which briefly provides humans with enhanced strength but with addictive results, though she now seems fully recovered.

When John Henry was returned to Earth after being in DARKSEID's thrall he chose to devote himself full time to being an inventor and engineer, and he crafted a new suit of armor, which Natasha happily donned. After the Infinite Crisis, Natasha received superpowers in Lex Luthor's Everyman Project (see LUTHOR, LEX) and briefly served with the new INFINITY, INC. **RG**

ISIS

FIRST APPEARANCE 52 #3 (2006) **STATUS** Hero (deceased)
REAL NAME Adrianna Tomaz
OCCUPATION Super hero **BASE** Khandaq
HEIGHT 5ft 10in **WEIGHT** 139 lbs **EYES** Brown **HAIR** Brown
SPECIAL POWERS/ABILITIES Flight, super-strength, resistance to injury, healing abilities, power over nature.

BLACK ADAM *was keen to make Isis part of his new "family," along with Osiris and Sobek.*

Adrianna Tomaz first met BLACK ADAM as a prisoner, captured by INTERGANG and presented to the superpowered Khandaq ruler as a slave. But he freed her, and she wasted no time confronting him about his confrontational style. The two fell in love, and Black Adam used the Amulet of Isis to transform Tomaz into a super hero. After their wedding, Isis and Adam located Isis's younger brother Amon, who became the gifted OSIRIS and the third member of the Black Marvel Family.

Their happiness ended when the Four Horsemen of Apokolips killed both Isis and Osiris, triggering Black Adam's descent into madness. An obsessed Adam later tried to resurrect Isis by immersing her corpse in a Lazarus Pit. He then traveled to the four corners of the Earth to retrieve missing pieces of her skeleton. Although Black Adam believed his quest was a failure, Felix Faust (see FAUST, FELIX) successfully restored Isis to a live as his mind-controlled servant. Because she possesses the abilities of many gods from the Egyptian pantheon, Isis' connection to mystical energies is unusually strong – indicating that death will not retain its hold on her for long. **DW**

AMID PUBLIC *rejoicing, banners flew from Black Adam's palace in Shiruta, capital of Kahndaq, in celebration of his marriage to Isis.*

JACK O'LANTERN I, II & III

FIRST APPEARANCE (I) DC COMICS PRESENTS #46 (June 1982);
(II) JUSTICE LEAGUE EUROPE ANNUAL #1 (1990); (III)
PRIMAL FORCE #0 (October 1994)
STATUS Heroes **REAL NAMES** (I) Daniel Cormac; (II) Marvin Noronsa;
(III) Liam McHugh
OCCUPATION (I) Global Guardian; (II) covert agent; (III) ultramarine
BASE (I) Mobile; (II) mobile; (III) Montevideo, Uruguay
HEIGHT (I) 6ft 2in; (II) 6ft 2in; (III) 5ft 11in
WEIGHT (I) 224 lbs; (II) 217 lbs; (III) 188 lbs
EYES (I) Green; (II) green; (III) blue
HAIR (I) Red; (II) red; (III) brown
SPECIAL POWERS/ABILITIES Mystical lantern provides powers of flight,
flame projection, the ability to teleport, illusion casting, enhanced
strength, fog creation; lantern's power is strongest at midnight.
Jack O'Lantern III's body has mysteriously internalized several of
the lantern's magical powers.

PUMPKIN POWER
All the Jack
O'Lanterns have
been joiners;
the original was
fiercely loyal to the
Global Guardians.

PEACEKEEPER The latest
Jack O'Lantern defends
the innocent as an
Ultramarine.

Daniel Cormac received his powers through a magic lantern given to him by the fairy queen Maeve. He defended his native Ireland in his costumed identity of Jack O'Lantern until summoned by DOCTOR MIST to join the team of international heroes known as the GLOBAL GUARDIANS. There, he fell in love with teammate OWLWOMAN and took it hard when the United Nations withdrew funding from the Guardians in favor of Justice League International (see JUSTICE LEAGUE OF AMERICA). Looking for a new calling, he fell under the control of the evil Queen Bee (see QUEEN BEE II) and apparently died, replaced by the Queen Bee's duplicate. Owlwoman rescued him from a dungeon in the Middle Eastern nation of Bialya, but he died soon afterward.

The imposter Jack O'Lantern II worked for the Queen Bee and tried to take Daniel Cormac's place among the Global Guardians. Jack O'Lantern II shot and wounded media mogul Maxwell Lord (see LORD HAVOK) and accidentally killed Global Guardian LITTLE MERMAID before perishing in a bomb blast.

Jack O'Lantern III took up the heroic role made famous by his cousin Daniel. A former factory worker, Liam McHugh inherited Cormac's lantern, which he called the "pumpkin of power", and soon joined the Leymen (see PRIMAL FORCE). After his first few adventures he discovered that his body had somehow internalized the lantern's magical energies and he no longer needed to carry it into battle. Jack O'Lantern III was a founding member of the international peacekeeping corps, the INTERNATIONAL ULTRAMARINE CORPS. **DW**

JADE

FIRST APPEARANCE ALL-STAR SQUADRON #25 (September 1983)
STATUS Hero (deceased) **REAL NAME** Jennifer-Lynn Hayden
OCCUPATION Photographer **BASE** New York City
HEIGHT 5ft 3in **WEIGHT** 123 lbs **EYES** Green **HAIR** Green
SPECIAL POWERS/ABILITIES Generates and manipulates emerald energies similar
to the forces of the Starheart-fueled power ring worn by her Green Lantern
father. Jade can make this power pulse take tangible form. Unlike Green
Lantern's power ring, Jade's energy is self-renewing, also enabling her to fly.

Daughter of Alan Scott (the first GREEN LANTERN) and his occasional foe Rose Canton (ROSE AND THORN), Jennifer-Lynn Hayden grew up in an adoptive home. In adulthood, Jenny-Lynn discovered her true origins when a star-shaped birthmark on her left palm blazed alight and her skin and hair were turned bright green by the emerald energies that suffused her. After reuniting with her fraternal twin brother, Todd Rice (OBSIDIAN), Jennie-Lynn became the super heroine Jade and eventually learned the identities of her biological parents. A member of the second-generation superbeings known as INFINITY, INC., Jade gave up adventuring for a time and began a romance with Kyle Rayner (the fifth Green Lantern) that eventually led to her renewed interest in heroics. After serving with the OUTSIDERS, Jade died in space during the Infinite Crisis. A different Jade briefly served with the new INFINITY, INC. **SB**

JANISSARY

FIRST APPEARANCE JLA ANNUAL #4 (Summer 2000)
STATUS Hero **REAL NAME** Selma Tolon
OCCUPATION Red Crescent physician; sorceress **BASE** Bursa, Turkey
HEIGHT 5ft 6in **WEIGHT** 131 lbs **EYES** Almond **HAIR** Black
SPECIAL POWERS/ABILITIES Superstrength; flight; wields the mystical
scimitar of Sultan Suleiman the Great and the spell-casting Eternity
Book of Merlin the Magician.

Selma Tolon, a native Turk and devout Muslim, studied medicine at California's Stanford University. Upon graduation, Dr. Tolon returned to Turkey to aid earthquake victims. During one relief effort, Tolon discovered two mystical talismans that empowered her to become the Janissary, a scimitar-wielding spell-caster. Upon the Janissary's Eternity Book is an inscription in Arabic: "He who has the virtue to draw this blade from the sand shall guide this once great empire into a magnificent tomorrow." Tolon possessed such virtue and fulfilled the prophecy. She met the JUSTICE LEAGUE OF AMERICA when Etrigan the DEMON conspired with rogue Turkish General Ankha Kazim, possessed by the demon Iblis, to recover the Eternity Book from her. Iblis was defeated and the Janissary remains Turkey's staunchest defender. **SB**

JEMM, SON OF SATURN

FIRST APPEARANCE JEMM, SON OF SATURN #1 (September 1984)
STATUS Hero **REAL NAME** Jemm
OCCUPATION Prince **BASE** Saturn
HEIGHT 6ft 6in **WEIGHT** 241 lbs **EYES** Yellow **HAIR** None
SPECIAL POWERS/ABILITIES Born with superior strength, even for a
Saturnian, as well as the unique ability to fly; jewel on forehead
denotes he is his people's prophesied "savior," and it allows him to
probe the emotions of others or to project powerful force beams.

An exiled Saturnian prince known as Jemm traveled to Earth, believing that his childhood sweetheart, white Saturnian Syrra, had sought refuge there. He left behind a people torn apart by racial civil war between red and white Saturnians. Lex Luthor (see LUTHOR, LEX) captured Jemm, planning to use the alien's psionic powers to assist his new INJUSTICE GANG. With the Philosopher's Stone—actually a cosmic "map of all time and space" called the Worlogog— and Jemm's powers, the rogues nearly defeated the JUSTICE LEAGUE OF AMERICA. Aided by the 853rd Century technological being known as HOURMAN III, the JLA prevented the destruction of the Worlogog, and took the severely traumatized Jemm into its protective custody. Some time later, J'Onn J'Onzz (MARTIAN MANHUNTER) helped stop the red and white forces, who opposed the marriage of white Saturnian Cha'rissa to red Saturnian Jemm, from killing each other. Jemm is finally back home on Saturn, living happily with his new wife. **RG**

JERICHO

FIRST APPEARANCE TALES OF THE TEEN TITANS #43 (June 1984)
STATUS Hero and villain   **REAL NAME** Joseph William Wilson
OCCUPATION Former super hero   **BASE** Mobile
HEIGHT 6ft   **WEIGHT** 195 lbs   **EYES** Green   **HAIR** Blond
SPECIAL POWERS/ABILITIES Can control bodies of others by making eye contact; when he enters bodies he speaks with their words and voices.

Son of the notorious mercenary DEATHSTROKE THE TERMINATOR, Joseph Wilson lost his ability to speak when the assassin Jackal slit his throat with a knife during a botched kidnapping. But Joseph had also been born a meta-human, thanks to the genetic experiments performed on his father by the U.S. military. Under the codename Jericho, Joseph became a member of the TEEN TITANS.

Jericho's career with the Titans took a tragic turn when he tried to save his teammate RAVEN from her demonic father, TRIGON. Possessed by Trigon's sinister energy, Jericho turned into a true villain and tried to destroy the Titans. To save them, Deathstroke stabbed his son through the heart. However, unknown to his former friends, Jericho had taken refuge in Deathstroke's body at the moment of his passing. RAVEN helped Jericho return in a new body, and he has since returned to the Teen Titans. **DW**

MASTERMIND *During his time as a villain, Jericho also became head of the Wildebeest Society.*

JESTER, THE

FIRST APPEARANCE SMASH COMICS #22 (May 1941)
STATUS Hero   **REAL NAME** Charles "Chuck" Lane
OCCUPATION Police detective (retired)   **BASE** New York City
HEIGHT 5ft 11in   **WEIGHT** 179 lbs   **EYES** Blue   **HAIR** Black
SPECIAL POWERS/ABILITIES Delighted in confounding his opponents with tricks derived from slapstick comedy; a formidable hand-to-hand fighter and dauntless detective.

A rookie cop in New York City during the opening days of World War II, Lane was the direct descendant of a medieval court fool. When inspired to take up the colorful costume of a masked vigilante, Lane naturally became the Jester and joked his way into action. Many a criminal came to regret hearing his distinctive high-pitched laughter and the jingling bells on his Jester's costume. During the War, the Jester served as a member of both the ALL-STAR SQUADRON and the FREEDOM FIGHTERS. Once Lane was promoted to the rank of detective, the Jester's jingling dwindled, and he eventually hung up his cap and bells for good in 1954. Now retired from the N.Y.P.D., Lane is still alive and kicking. Despite his somewhat ludicrous former costumed identity, Chuck Lane takes his heritage quite seriously and looks back proudly to his days as a madcap crime fighter. **SB**

JINX

FIRST APPEARANCE TALES OF THE TEEN TITANS #56 (August 1985)
STATUS Villain   **REAL NAME** Unrevealed
OCCUPATION Sorceress   **BASE** Mobile
HEIGHT 5ft 9in   **WEIGHT** 141 lbs   **EYES** Brown   **HAIR** Unrevealed
SPECIAL POWERS/ABILITIES A powerful magician, Jinx's fiery temper leads her to take the direct-action approach, creating crushing force bolts or suddenly dissolving matter rather than employing the more usual illusions and subtleties of magic.

The East Indian sorceress Jinx was a student of an occult master. She murdered her teacher after learning his sorcerous secrets. She was recruited by GIZMO to strengthen the FEARSOME FIVE in their attempts to destroy the TEEN TITANS. With the Titans out of the way, the Five were confident they would rapidly reap riches through crime. Instead, they were defeated and Jinx was sent to India for trial. She was returned to the U.S. when local authorities could not control the mage.

She has worked with VILLAINY INC. of late and met defeat at the hands of WONDER WOMAN. Recently, she has rejoined the reconstituted Fearsome Five and fought the OUTSIDERS. **RG**

JOKER'S DAUGHTER

FIRST APPEARANCE BATMAN FAMILY #6 (August 1976)
STATUS Villain (deceased)   **REAL NAME** Duela Dent
OCCUPATION Adventurer   **BASE** Mobile
HEIGHT 5ft 8in   **WEIGHT** 120 lbs   **EYES** Green   **HAIR** Red
SPECIAL POWERS/ABILITIES Acrobat skilled with practical-joke combat gadgets.

Duela Dent was born on Earth-3, a world inhabited by good or evil mirror images of the heroes and villains of the mainstream Earth. Daughter of the heroic JOKER analogue called the Jokester, Duela was raised by her mother Evelyn Dent (also known as Three-Face) and her stepfather, Earth-3's RIDDLER. Duela started a romance with Talon, her world's sinister counterpart of ROBIN, but her journey to the primary Earth apparently scrambled all her memories and left her unsure of her past.

Duela joined the villainous Titans East, then switched sides at the suggestion of RAVEN to join the TEEN TITANS. She continued her hijinks by kidnapping a teenage celebrity from a nightclub until she was confronted by Jason Todd (*see* RED HOOD) and a member of the MONITORS.

After accusing Dent of violating the integrity of the multiverse by jumping between parallel Earths, the Monitor shot and killed the Joker's Daughter. **DW**

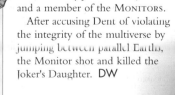

JOTO

FIRST APPEARANCE THE TEEN TITANS (2nd series) #1 (October 1996)
STATUS Hero   **REAL NAME** Isaiah Crockett
OCCUPATION Super hero   **BASE** Ivy University, Rhode Island
HEIGHT 5ft 10in   **WEIGHT** 188 lbs   **EYES** Brown   **HAIR** Brown
SPECIAL POWERS/ABILITIES Can generate intense heat from his bare hands and melt anything—even solid steel; possesses a quiet strength and is looked up to by his fellow teammates.

Isaiah Crockett believed he was a normal kid from a normal family until, at age 16, he learned he was the result of a breeding program by aliens, the H'San Natall, to create a race of sleeper agents. Joining with the other H'San Natall hybrids—ARGENT II, RISK, and PRYSM—as well as the second ATOM, Isaiah became a member of a new TEEN TITANS team. He was initially known as Slagger, but his father instead suggested Joto, the Swahili word for "heat." Joto seemingly perished in battle with the villain Haze, but his spirit survived within Prysm's body. When the H'San Natall revived Joto's corpse, he "jumped" his consciousness back into his body. After the Teen Titans disbanded, Joto returned to his studies at Ivy University. He still aids the super hero community. **DW**

JUDOMASTER

FIRST APPEARANCE SPECIAL WAR SERIES #4 (November 1965)
STATUS Hero   **REAL NAME** Rip Jagger
OCCUPATION Adventurer   **BASE** Mobile
HEIGHT 5ft 11in   **WEIGHT** 190 lbs   **EYES** Blue   **HAIR** Blond
SPECIAL POWERS/ABILITIES Martial arts expert; also skilled with various weapons, although prefers to use fists in combat.

During World War II, Sgt. Rip Jagger of the U.S. Army was stationed on a Pacific island populated by expatriate Japanese who opposed their country's aggression. After he saved a young girl from a sniper's bullet, the girl's grateful father taught him martial arts. As the hero Judomaster, he used his skills to free the island from invading Japanese soldiers. Jagger later returned to his unit, operating as Judomaster on solo secret missions along with Tiger, a young Japanese orphan who had highly impressed Jagger with his martial arts prowess.

Judomaster battled evil alongside Tiger after the war ended. Eventually the pair went their separate ways and Judomaster journeyed to the mystical land of Nanda Parbat. There he lived for many decades, remaining young and vital despite being in his eighties. During the Infinite Crisis, BANE killed Judomaster by snapping his back. His son Thomas Jagger, an agent of CHECKMATE, hopes to avenge his father's death. A new Judomaster, Sonia Sato, has appeared with the BIRDS OF PREY as well as the JUSTICE SOCIETY OF AMERICA. **SB**

THE JOKER

THE CLOWN PRINCE OF CRIME

FIRST APPEARANCE BATMAN #1 (Spring 1940)
STATUS Villain **REAL NAME** Unknown
BASE Gotham City
OCCUPATION Anarchist; mass-murderer; professional criminal
HEIGHT 6ft 5in **WEIGHT** 192 lbs **EYES** Green **HAIR** Green
SPECIAL POWERS/ABILITIES
Though not especially strong or skilled in fighting, the Joker is nonetheless a deadly combatant. Previously, he has demonstrated adeptness at chemistry, concocting his own poisonous Joker Venom, a weapon of mass distraction that leaves its victims with death-rictuses resembling his own maniacal leer. The Joker often wields deadly joke props or gags such as an acid-squirting boutonnière or BANG!-proclaiming flag pistol that doubles as a spear gun. However, he also plays the straight man in his blackly comedic campaigns of terror and will use conventional weapons—anything from a single-shot Derringer tucked in the brim of his hat to an operational nuclear warhead concealed within the trunk of his garish Jokermobile.

THE JOKER IS UNDENIABLY the most dangerous and unpredictable foe BATMAN has ever encountered. He literally reinvents himself each morning, concocting deadly new laugh-riots to bedevil the Dark Knight and his allies. While safely confined within the impregnable walls of Arkham Asylum for the Criminally Insane, the Joker has spun investigating psychiatrists various yarns concerning his troubled origins. Most of his tales can be dismissed, but a few facts remain that give some insight into how this leering lunatic came into being.

TWO-GUN CLOWN
The Joker mocks the Dynamic Duo in an early Detective Comics' cover appearance.

THE JOKER'S ORIGINS
The man who would become the Clown Prince of Crime was once a petty thief duped into donning the mask of the Red Hood and acting as costumed figurehead to thugs bent on robbing the Ace Chemical Plant in Gotham City. In that regard, he may have been a failed comedian coerced to crime following the sudden and tragic deaths of his wife and unborn child. Only the Joker knows the truth. Thwarted by Batman, the Red Hood fell into a vat of toxic chemicals that bleached his skin bone white, turned his hair emerald green, and left him with a crazed, ruby-red, malignant rictus for a smile. Driven utterly insane, the Joker fixated upon Batman as his arch-nemesis and has broken practically every law in Gotham City and beyond.

CHEMICAL PEEL The Red Hood crawls from a toxic bath. From now on, villainy will wear a leering face.

MASS MURDER, MALIGNANCY, AND MAYHEM
The Joker is probably the only criminal ever to qualify as a mass murderer, spree slayer, and serial killer. And that's just before lunch. He has committed robberies, assaults, extortion, and all manner of crime. His victims are innumerable. The Bat-Family especially has suffered from the Joker's sick humor. In a fit of anarchic glee, the Joker killed the second ROBIN (Jason Todd), beating him near to death with a crowbar before blowing the poor Boy Wonder and his mother to smithereens. He shot Barbara Gordon (ORACLE) through the spine, ending her crime-fighting career as BATGIRL. The Clown Prince of Crime then photographed Barbara's bleeding body, hoping the images would drive her kidnapped father, Commissioner Gordon (see GORDON, JAMES W.), insane.

THE JOKER'S WEAPONS
The Clown Prince of Crime has no compunction against using weapons of mass destruction, including his own patented Laughing Gas, a nerve toxin that kills within seconds and leaves his victims giggling themselves to death. Not long ago, the Joker was imprisoned for attempting to bomb Broadway with a tactical nuclear weapon.

KILLING JOKE The unsuspecting Barbara Gordon is viciously gunned down by the Joker as she opens her front door.

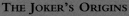

HARLEY QUINN
Before he met Dr. Harleen Quinzel, the Joker's court-appointed psychotherapist, the Joker was more concerned with making mayhem than whoopee. But in Quinzel, he found a kindred spirit, winning her over to his side of the lunatic fringe. As HARLEY QUINN, she became murderous moll to the Joker's guffawing gangster. However, the Joker and Harley are now estranged, reuniting under passion, and breaking up when he tries to beat her to the punchline… often with a mallet!

ARKHAM ASYLUM

Certifiably crazed, the Joker was previously remanded to Gotham's Arkham Asylum for the Criminally Insane. However, Arkham has long suffered an almost revolving-door policy where its more dangerous charges are concerned, especially the Clown Prince of Crime. Despite his officially documented mental state, the Joker is cunning and crafty, knowing full well how to manipulate Arkham's doctors and administrators to achieve his anarchic ends.

THAT CERTAIN SMILE *The Joker enjoys putting on a happy face when his favorite foe Batman pays him a visit in his Arkham cell!*

PARTNERS IN CRIME *While most villains do not (or cannot) trust the Joker, some of Batman's arch-foes, including Rā's al Ghūl, have collaborated with him when it suits their roguish interests.*

PSYCHO KILLER *During No Man's Land, the Joker used defenseless babies to lure Commissioner Gordon's wife, Sarah, to her doom, shooting her in cold blood.*

THE LAST LAUGH

After gassing hundreds of victims during the "Last Laugh" event on the belief that he had a terminal disease, the Joker suffered a brutal beating from Jason Todd, who had returned from the dead after his murder at the Joker's hands. At the end of the Infinite Crisis, the Joker killed enemy mastermind Alexander Luthor.

Later shot in the face by a Batman impostor, the Joker spent months in the hospital rebuilding his body and psyche. Now more dangerous than ever, the Joker helped organize the latest incarnation of the INJUSTICE LEAGUE before the U.S. government exiled him and dozens of fellow villains to the distant planet Salvation." **SB**

PUSHED TOO FAR *Though he realizes it might be the death of him, the Joker continues to hurt those whom Batman cares about most.*

KEY STORYLINES

- *THE JOKER #1-9 (MAY 1975–SEPTEMBER 1976):* The Joker becomes the first Bat-Villain to star in his own comic book series, lasting nine issues.
- *BATMAN #426-429 (DECEMBER 1988–JANUARY 1989):* The Joker murders Jason Todd, the second Robin, leading Batman to pursue the Clown Prince.
- *BATMAN: THE KILLING JOKE (1988):* The Joker's origins are explored as he cripples Barbara Gordon to prove a point to the Dark Knight.
- *JOKER: THE DEVIL'S ADVOCATE (1996):* The Joker is finally made responsible for his sins and sentenced to Death Row, but for a crime he did not commit!

THE JUSTICE LEAGUE OF AMERICA

THE WORLD'S GREATEST HEROES

First appearance THE BRAVE & THE BOLD #28 (March 1960)
Status Team of Earth's greatest heroes
Base The JLA Watchtower, the Moon
Founder members and powers
Superman The Man of Steel; possessor of superpowers beyond those of mortal men.
Martian Manhunter Alien telepath; shape-changer; gifted with strength, flight, and enhanced vision.
Batman The Dark Knight; master combatant and strategist, coordinating the team's counterattacks.
Wonder Woman Princess from Themyscira; gifted with strength, speed, wisdom, and flight by the gods themselves.
Aquaman King of the Seven Seas; has incredible strength, ability to mentally control sea life, and a mystic hand.
Green Lantern V Wielder of the emerald power ring; protector of space sector 2814.
Flash III The fastest man alive, capable of hyper-velocities; channels the Speed Force to fight crime; Speed Force surrounds him with a frictionless protective aura.

They are Earth's premier defense team and for the last decade have seen to it that the basic human rights of liberty and justice remain paramount to all citizens. They are the Justice League of America, comprised of the best of the best. Ever since Superman ushered in the modern heroic age, Earth has needed protection, from megalomaniac supervillains and especially, from greedy alien tyrants with hitherto undreamed-of technologies and nightmarish weapons of mass destruction. Even when the team has suffered internal strife, they have rallied, recognizing their obligations to all of mankind. Their reputation has spread not only beyond this solar system but beyond this plane of existence.

PREMIER LEAGUE *The JLA heroes first came together to battle a giant alien starfish!*

JUSTICE LEAGUE DETROIT

Being a super hero is a tough life! Various stresses in the personal lives of the team caused rifts from time to time. In the wake of an invasion by the alien Debris, the JLA was reorganized by Aquaman, who called for full-time commitment from each League member. In the aftermath, only Aquaman, the ELONGATED MAN, the Martian Manhunter, and ZATANNA remained. However, the roster soon began to expand when STEEL I, VIBE, and the VIXEN joined. Hank Heywood I, Steel's grandfather and namesake, offered the JLA headquarters in a warehouse in Detroit that became known as the Bunker. This incarnation of the League was tragically cut short when Vibe and Steel II were killed in action.

*THE DETROIT LINEUP (clockwise from top)
Martian Manhunter, Zatanna, Steel II,
Elongated Man, Vixen, Vibe, Gypsy, Aquaman.*

THE FIRST INCARNATION

When Earth was threatened by Appellax aliens, the Martian Manhunter, Flash II, Green Lantern II, Aquaman, and Black Canary II joined forces as the JLA to defeat these invaders. Inspired by the appearance of these powerful new heroes, J'Onn J'Onzz ended decades of hiding, publicly appearing as the Martian Manhunter. A short time later, plasma aliens invaded Earth, and the hero Triumph gathered Superman, the Martian Manhunter, Flash II, Green Lantern II, Aquaman, and Black Canary II to defeat them. During the fight, Triumph was trapped in a temporal anomaly and disappeared from the timestream.

THE SECRET SANCTUARY

The team's first headquarters, the Secret Sanctuary, was in Rhode Island, and secretly financed by Oliver Queen (the first GREEN ARROW). A teenage "cool cat" called Lucas "Snapper" Carr (see CARR, SNAPPER) helped install the team's high-tech gear, designed by Ted Kord (later BLUE BEETLE II). Snapper became the team's official mascot. After functioning as JLA members in all but name, Superman and BATMAN formally joined.

JL INTERNATIONAL

This team was discredited by GLORIOUS GODFREY's smear campaign, but a more powerful line-up was introduced, with the enigmatic Maxwell Lord (see LORD HAVOK) pulling the strings. The United Nations formally recognized the JLA as global peacekeepers. Later, the JLI split into two branches, Justice League America and Justice League Europe. Lord decided to make use of the reformed members of the Injustice League, along with the former alien Green Lantern G'NORT and the Scarlet Skier, as the short-lived Justice League Antarctica. The entire JLA, its reserves, and the JSA stopped SONAR's bid for power in Europe. Afterwards, Justice League Europe took the name Justice League International. The U.N. authorized the creation of a JL Task Force, a team led by the Martian Manhunter, intended for use on missions calling for discretion, and one which would recruit most members for a single case.

TOWER OF POWER
JL International continued to add team members, dispatching them via embassies scattered around the seven continents.

TASK FORCE *J'onn J'onzz supervised a team of fledgling heroes, training them between crises.*

DEFENDERS OF EARTH

The League continued to expand and contract as circumstances demanded, with a Justice League West unit led by CAPTAIN ATOM, a later addition. At the request of the U.N., the various Justice League splinter groups disbanded and Superman, Batman, WONDER WOMAN, Aquaman, the Martian Manhunter, Flash III, and Green Lantern V were acknowledged as the official JLA. They built a base on the moon known as the Watchtower.

As the external threats facing the world and its citizens grow more and more extreme, the JLA has sworn to repulse all threats from space or from parallel worlds. The League continually redefines the scope of its mission; thanks to the JLA's selfless, heroic protection, humanity continues to prosper. RG

VIRTUE AND VICE
The JLA and JSA combine to battle an evil conspiracy— apparently from within their own heroic ranks!

BRUTAL BATTLE *The JLA has faced all manner of opponents, from common criminals to intergalactic conquerors, but none has challenged them more than the Quantum Mechanics from another reality.*

THE JLA OF THE FUTURE

By the 853rd century, the Justice Legion A will be the premier protectors of the solar system. They will be aided by the Justice Legions B, L, S, X, Super-Zoomorphs, Union, Young Justice Legion S, and Primate Legion.

LATEST LINEUP

From their Watchtower on the moon, the JLA continues to monitor activity on Earth, dispatching the team as required. Their ranks have swelled to include the Native American mystic MANITOU RAVEN and the reformed criminal MAJOR DISASTER. Others, such as the ATOM, remain available on an as-needed basis.

KEY STORYLINES

• *JUSTICE LEAGUE OF AMERICA #21–22 (1963):* The JLA teams up with the veteran heroes of the Golden Age, The Justice Society of America.

• *JUSTICE LEAGUE OF AMERICA #140-144 (MARCH–JULY 1977):* The planet Oa's Manhunter Robots threaten not only Earth but Oa as well!

• *JLA YEAR ONE (TPB, 1998):* Five distinct super heroes learn how to become a team.

• *JLA: WORLD WAR III (TPB, 2001):* Mageddon comes to Earth and it takes the JLA, plus many others committed to the cause, to save mankind.

• *JLA/JSA: VIRTUE AND VICE (TPB, 2001):* Earth's premier teams take on the combined threat of Johnny Sorrow and an enraged Despero.

THE JUSTICE LEAGUE OF AMERICA

CURRENT MEMBERS AND POWERS (2008)

Black Canary (chairwoman) Ultrasonic, earsplitting "canary cry"; martial arts and boxing expert

Superman The Man of Steel; possessor of numerous superpowers.

Batman The Dark Knight; master combatant and strategist, coordinating the team's counterattacks.

Wonder Woman Princess from Themyscira; gifted with strength, speed, wisdom, and flight by the gods.

Green Lantern (John Stewart) Wielder of the emerald power ring; protector of space sector 2814.

The Flash (Wally West) The fastest man alive, capable of hyper-velocities; channels the Speed Force to fight crime.

Black Lightning Internally-generated electromagnetic field; can create and hurl bolts of supercharged electricity

Geo-Force Superhuman strength and powers of endurance; can fly, alter gravity, and project powerful blasts of heat from his hands

Hawkgirl Gravity-defying Nth metal belt enables flight on giant wings; adept hand-to-hand combatant

Red Arrow A top archer; expert with most projectile weapons

Red Tornado Can generate cyclones; some control over the weather.

Vixen Tantu totem gives her animal abilities.

MYSTERY MISSION Even Superman, who had known the Legionnaires since childhood, could not uncover the reason behind their 21st-century visit.

THE LIGHTNING SAGA

The newest League's first official mission saw it teaming up with the Justice Society of America and the Legion of Super Heroes. The latter group had traveled back in time one thousand years to restore a lost champion by using lightning rods and 31st century science. Superman, who had befriended the Legionnaires during his youth, set the tone for team interaction by countering Batman's suspicion of the Legion's cryptic plans. The affair ended with all three groups welcoming the return of Wally West, the third Flash, from an alternate dimension. Wally accepted a position with the new League, filling the JLA's need for a speedster.

BACK FROM LIMBO Wally and Iris West and their twins returned from another dimension, thanks to Superman and his teammates.

CRISIS OF CONSCIENCE

After countless wins against the universe's most terrifying foes, infighting ultimately crippled the Justice League of America. With the shocking murder of Sue Dibny (wife of former member Elongated Man), a long-buried incident from the League's early years came to shameful light. At that time, the JLA members agreed to use Zatanna's magic to forcibly alter the memories and personality of Doctor Light, in response to the villain's assault on Sue. When Batman objected to the act, Zatanna had mind-wiped him too. The League imprisoned Jean Loring for Sue Dibny's murder, but the dubious morality of Zatanna's actions created a rift among the League. Batman was one of the most outspoken believers that the JLA had irrevocably betrayed its principles. With no trust remaining, the League members couldn't function as a team. An attack by the Secret Society of Super Villains—all of them victims of JLA brainwashing—became the trigger to the League's dissolution. The final blow came on the eve of the Infinite Crisis, when Superboy-Prime destroyed the lunar Watchtower headquarters.

MINDWIPE Erasing Doctor Light's memories created a rift in the Justice League.

PAYING RESPECTS The super-hero community came out in force for Sue Dibny's funeral.

TRINITY Wonder Woman, Superman, and Batman assemble the latest JLA.

A NEW START

Months after the Infinite Crisis, Firestorm made an abortive attempt to reform the JLA with third-string heroes including Ambush Bug, Bulleteer, Firehawk, and Super-Chief (who died in one of the team's only missions). But the true Justice League of America took shape again following the "World War III" affair, forged by backbone members Superman, Batman, and Wonder Woman. The three founders voted on the League's new roster, but simultaneous events helped pull together the worthy among the current heroic generation.

RETURN TO DUTY Vixen also served with the Detroit incarnation of the JLA.

The theft of Red Tornado's android body spurred Black Canary, Green Lantern Hal Jordan, and Red Arrow (Roy Harper, formerly known as Arsenal) to aid in the hunt. Meanwhile, suspicious activity among Parasite, Doctor Impossible, and other supervillains drew the attentions of Vixen, Black Lightning, and Hawkgirl. Together the teams uncovered an elaborate plot from cybernetic genius Professor Ivo, who had determined a way to control others using technological replicas of the "starro" probes familiar as the trademarks of the alien Star Conqueror. Ivo's mind-puppets helped him piece together a composite android body that incorporated components from both Red Tornado and Amazo. This virtually unstoppable composite was to house the consciousness of Solomon Grundy, the mountainous zombie.

POWERED UP Vixen easily dispatches an Amazo robot.

THE NEW HQ

The heroes united to stop Ivo, and all accepted formal Justice League invitations soon after. To mark this new era, the JLA constructed a dual headquarters to replace its lost moon base. In high Earth orbit stood a reconstructed Watchtower satellite, containing a training room with the ability to replicate any environment or threat as a holograph. Groundside, a hall of Justice announced the JLA's presence in Washington DC, and featured a trophy room of captured (and deactivated) supervillain gadgetry. A "slideways" teleporter linked both facilities, accessed simply by stepping through a nearly-imperceptible energy portal. Similar portals could be activated from the Batcave and other secure locations, allowing instantaneous member travel in emergencies. RG/DW

WATCHTOWER *The satellite houses observational and training facilities.*

TROPHY ROOM *Continuing a longstanding JLA tradition, relics from past victories line one chamber in the Hall of Justice.*

ANTI-TRINITY *The Joker, Lex Luthor, and Cheetah assembled the Injustice League.*

THE INJUSTICE LEAGUE

Black Canary, the current chairwoman, led the Justice League of America into its most dangerous confrontation against its mirror opposite. Lex Luthor, the Joker, and Cheetah teamed up to create the Injustice League Unlimited, the latest incarnation of the murderous cabal which counted dozens of supervillains in its roster. Operating from a skull-shaped dome deep in the Florida everglades, the Injustice League fired its first shot before the JLA could counterattack, nearly killing Firestorm on the eve of the wedding of Black Canary and Green Arrow. With the JLA now counting Geo-Force and Green Lantern John Stewart among its members, the two teams clashed fast and forcefully.

The Injustice League withdrew, yet remains active. With the leadership of Luthor, the madcap ingenuity of the Joker, and the muscle of nearly every prominent member of the supervillain community, the Injustice League Unlimited will prove a match for the Justice League for years to come.

WORLD'S FINEST *Top row (left to right): Green Lantern, Wonder Woman, Superman, Batman, Black Canary. Bottom row (left to right): Hawkgirl, Black Lightning, Red Arrow, Vixen, Red Tornado.*

THE JUSTICE SOCIETY OF AMERICA

THE BEST OF THE BEST

FIRST APPEARANCE ALL-STAR COMICS #3 (Winter 1940)
STATUS Hero team
BASE New York City
FOUNDER MEMBERS AND POWERS:
The Spectre Near-omnipotent control over space and time, but bound to a human host.
Doctor Fate Connection with the Lord of Order Nabu allows Fate to manipulate vast magical forces.
Sandman I Sharp detective's mind and dreams that can foretell the future; wields a gas gun that puts victims to sleep.
The Atom Expert boxer and hand-to-hand combatant; after the war gained super-strength and a radioactive "atomic punch."
Hourman I Superhuman strength, speed, and stamina for one hour as a result of ingesting a Miraclo pill.

OTHER MEMBERS HAVE INCLUDED:
Green Lantern, the Flash, Hawkman, Johnny Thunder, Doctor Mid-Nite, Mister Terrific, Hawkgirl, Starman, Miss America, Hippolyta, Atom-Smasher, Mister Terrific II, Star-Spangled Kid II, Stargirl, Black Canary II, Captain Marvel, Power Girl (see page 186 for current lineup).

THEY ARE THE WORLD'S FIRST and greatest super-group, formed at a time when "meta-humans" were still a new concept and free people everywhere faced the threat of annihilation from Adolf Hitler's Third Reich. They have survived throughout the decades, waxing and waning in synch with the national character to reflect the public's love–hate relationship with its super heroes. Several of the founding members are active today, even as they enter their nineties, thanks to a time-slowing radiation bath received during an early case. Living legends, they are the standard-bearers for all who followed in their footsteps. They are the Justice Society of America, the only hero team that SUPERMAN looks up to.

THE BEGINNING With a cry of "For America and democracy," the JSA begins its adventures.

WINGED WONDER Hawkman's physical and mental strength make him the backbone of the JSA.

A WORLD AT WAR
Costumed crime fighters started appearing in the late 1930s; by November of 1940 the numbers of these "mystery men," as they were called, had grown to permit the formation of the JSA. Eight of the U.S.'s top heroes—GREEN LANTERN, the FLASH, the SPECTRE, DOCTOR FATE, the SANDMAN I, the ATOM, HOURMAN I, and HAWKMAN—banded together to stop Hitler's invasion of Britain and save President Roosevelt from Nazi assassins. The JSA continued to battle the Axis powers. In the wake of Pearl Harbor, the U.S. government established the ALL-STAR SQUADRON, which brought together every costumed hero.

AN EVER-CHANGING LINEUP
The JSA became one of the All-Star Squadron's active sub-groups. During this time the JSA also went by the alternate name of the Justice Battalion. Throughout the war, members came and went as they cycled through active, reserve, and honorary status. Prominent JSAers included Johnny Thunder (see THUNDER, JOHNNY), DOCTOR MID-NITE I, MISTER TERRIFIC I, HAWKGIRL, STARMAN, MISS AMERICA, and the time-traveling HIPPOLYTA, the Golden Age WONDER WOMAN.

NO MORE HEROES
The All-Star Squadron ceased to exist after V-J Day, but the JSA remained, battling major villains such as VANDAL SAVAGE, and its villainous counterpart, the INJUSTICE SOCIETY. However, now the war was over, public tolerance for super heroics was fading fast. In 1951, a joint congressional Un-American Activities Committee accused the JSA of harboring communist sympathies and demanded that its members publicly unmask as a sign of their patriotism. They refused, and regretfully retired the Justice Society. Decades passed, the flame of organized crime fighting kept alive through non-superpowered teams such as the SEA DEVILS and the CHALLENGERS OF THE UNKNOWN and lesser lights like the Justice Experience. The JSA still existed, however, occasionally reforming for special cases.

ON THEIR WAY OUT The retirement of the JSA marked the end of the Golden Age of super heroes.

RAGNAROK!
The JSA seemed to have met its final end when the Flash, Green Lantern, Hawkman, Hawkgirl, the Atom, Doctor Mid-Nite, Hourman, Johnny Thunder, Starman, the Sandman, WILDCAT, and SAND agreed to battle gods for all eternity in Limbo to prevent Ragnarok, the end of the world. Luckily "eternity" lasted only a couple of years, and the JSA soon returned. The crisis known as Zero Hour (see Great Battles, pp. 362–3) proved a deadlier threat. The villain EXTANT killed the Atom, Doctor Mid-Nite, and Hourman, and Flash and Green Lantern declared an end to the JSA.

THE MODERN ERA

The DARK LORD Mordru's murder of the Sandman triggered a new formation of the JSA, featuring old stalwarts (the Flash, Green Lantern, Wildcat, Hawkman, Sand), skilled veterans (ATOM-SMASHER), and new faces (MISTER TERRIFIC II, Star-Spangled Kid II, plus reincarnated versions of Doctor Fate and Hawkgirl). This JSA's greatest challenge was the "Darkness" crisis, in which Mordru, OBSIDIAN, and ECLIPSO tried to plunge the world into eternal night.

INVASION *Black Adam made short work of Khandaq's defenders.*

FIGHTING THE GOOD FIGHT

The Black Reign incident deeply affected the JSA, causing many of them to struggle with the concepts of righteousness and appropriate force. CAPTAIN MARVEL used the aftermath as an opportunity to tender his resignation. The group is still vital, however, as shown by the observations of the time-traveling villain Per Degaton, who recently visited several key JSA members to tell them that he had witnessed their deaths in the far future. Significantly, Degaton admitted that, throughout all of future history, he was never able to defeat the JSA, and confided to Jay Garrick (the first Flash) that he "died like a man" in whatever fate yet awaits the Flash. Regardless of the predictions of would-be prognosticators, the multi-generational JSA will continue its fight against injustice and polish its reputation as the only super hero team that operates like an extended family.

DARKNESS FALLS
Obsidian's filial anger toward his father, Green Lantern, provided an added edge to the battle.

BLACK REIGN

The JSA's law-and-order approach to crime fighting is not universally revered. A vigilante team consisting of BLACK ADAM, Eclipso, NORTHWIND, Brainwave II, and Atom-Smasher recently took the law into their own hands. They spearheaded a violent coup in the terrorist nation of Kahndaq to put an end to their colleagues' meddling. In so doing they exposed the villainous manipulations of the Venusian worm, MISTER MIND.

THE JSA 1) *Green Lantern I* 2) *Mr. Terrific II* 3) *Dr. Mid-Nite II* 4) *Sand* 5) *Hawkman* 6) *Hawkgirl* 7) *Atom-Smasher* 8) *Dr. Fate* 9) *Stargirl* 10) *Black Canary II* 11) *Flash I* 12) *Wildcat*

KEY STORYLINES
• *LAST DAYS OF THE JUSTICE SOCIETY SPECIAL (1986):* The JSA battles in an eternal Ragnarok in what was intended to be the team's final adventure.
• *ZERO HOUR: CRISIS IN TIME #3 (SEPTEMBER 1994):* Three of the JSA's oldest members perish in an issue that once again appeared to have killed off the team forever.
• *JSA #1 (AUGUST 1999):* The JSA returns in triumphant form in the first issue of the 'Justice Be Done' storyline.

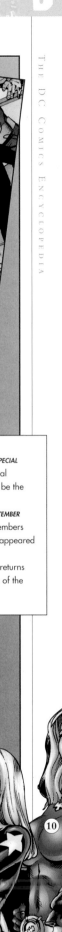

THE JUSTICE SOCIETY OF AMERICA

Current Members and Powers (2008)
Power Girl (chairwoman): Flight, super-strength, enhanced speed, and invulnerability.
Green Lantern I Wields solidified emerald energy generated by the Starheart.
Flash I Runs at super-speeds and vibrates through objects.
Wildcat I Championship boxer with mystical "nine lives."
Dr. Mid-Nite II Can see in non-visible wavelengths of light.
Mister Terrific Olympic-level athlete and genius in every field.
Hawkman Wings and harness made of anti-gravity Nth metal.
Sandman Transforms into sand-like form and can travel along the Earth's fault lines; sees the future through dreams.
Hourman Super strength, enhanced speed, and increased durability for one hour.
Liberty Belle Super-speed, enhanced strength.
Obsidian Can transform himself into an intangible shadow form.
Stargirl Cosmic staff projects energy and allows flight.
Jakeem Thunder Controls powerful, fifth-dimensional genie.
Starman Can increase the mass and gravity of objects.
Cyclone Can fly and generate tornados by controlling the wind.
Damage Enhanced reflexes and strength; emits power bursts.
Citizen Steel Super strength, indestructible organic steel shell.
Wildcat III (Tommy Bronson) Can transform into a werecat.

THE OLD GUARD *Green Lantern, the Flash, and Wildcat put together the newest Justice Society.*

REBIRTH

The Justice Society of America lay dormant following the Infinite Crisis, with many of its members swept up in the global fight to stop Black Adam known as World War III. JSA founders Green Lantern (Alan Scott), Flash (Jay Garrick), and Wildcat (Ted Grant) selected the aftermath as an opportunity to reform the group, taking a cue from Superman, Batman, and Wonder Woman who had simultaneously chosen to launch a new Justice League of America. The underlying tenet of the new JSA was a simple one: "the world needs better good guys."

With an eye for respect, family, and heart, the surviving JSA founders selected the latest lineup. The intergenerational legacies of the heroic age expressed themselves through the election of junior members including Damage (Grant Emerson, son of the original Atom), Starman (Thom Kallor, time-traveling inheritor of the Golden Age name), and the teenage wind-witch Cyclone (Maxine Hunkel, granddaughter of original Red Tornado Ma Hunkel). Others signed on to serve with a team that had welcomed them in the past, including Power Girl, Dr. Mid-Nite, Mister Terrific, Stargirl, Jakeem Thunder, Obsidian, Sandman, and the husband-and-wife team of Hourman and Liberty Belle, both of whom carry on the costumed identities of their respective parents. The new JSA lived up to its billing as a "society," not putting a limit on its sprawling roster. They began operating out of new headquarters in New York City's Battery Park, where they became a vital part of the neighborhood.

RED ALERT *The Justice Society scrambles to tackle a crisis. Its membership includes many legacy heroes now wearing the costumed identities of their late relatives.*

ARKHAM NIGHTMARE
Starman battled Doctor Destiny to rescue Dream Girl from the infamous asylum.

THE LIGHTNING SAGA

The JSA soon learned that Starman wasn't the only hero with ties to the far future. In Arkham Asylum, Starman helped rescue Dream Girl, his teammate from the Legion of Super-Heroes. Still more members of the Legion had made their way 1,000 years into the past and made their presence known. Earlier in the team's history the Legionnaires had brought one of their own back from the dead by channeling electricity into lightning rods—now, in an apparent duplicate performance, Legion members gathered around the globe to enable the return of another hero. The Justice Society, The Justice League, and the Legion joined forces—despite early misunderstandings between the three teams—and performed a ritual that successfully Wally West, the third Flash, back to life. The junior members of the JSA continued to grow into their roles under the mentorship of their elders. Citizen Steel learned that his new body was more than just a metallic prison when he rescued university students from a hostage standoff. Damage faced down his demons with help from Liberty Belle when he pursued the super-villain Zoom into Atlanta Georgia—a city he had nearly destroyed years before with his out-of-control powers.

ATLANTA STANDOFF *Damage defeated his nemesis Zoom when Liberty Belle convinced him to look past his pain and see the hero inside himself.*

TEAMS UNITED *The Lightning Saga saw the JSA team up with the Justice League and the Legion of Super-Heroes.*

MAN OF STEEL *Although disoriented by his trip through the multiverse, the original Superman soon proved his heroism.*

LIKE FATHER, LIKE SON *Tommy Bronson didn't want to follow Ted Grant into superheroics, but his animalistic powers made him the only one who could stop Vandal Savage.*

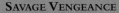

CALL TO ACTION

The Society's inaugural mission centered on a plot by Vandal Savage to stamp out bloodlines of the surviving Golden Age mystery men and their immediate relatives. Vandal's first victims included Mr. America, General Glory, and the Minute-Man. During the course of this mission, Wildcat discovered a grown son he'd never known—Tommy Branson. Upon first meeting, Bronson expressed no desire to follow his father into the family business. Once involved in a fight with Savage, however, Branson's own powers were revealed. He transformed through lycanthropy into a literal wildcat. Tommy joined the JSA under his father's name, becoming the third hero to take on the Wildcat identity.

THE FIRST TO FALL *Mister America's death launched the new JSA on its first case.*

THE MULTIVERSE AND BEYOND

The existence of the multiverse hit home when the Justice Society extinguished a factory fire, accidentally summoning a Superman from a parallel Earth. This Superman, drawn through a miniature black hole from a reality known as Earth-22, remembered a grim near-future in which heroes had fought heroes in the face of fearful public resentment. In the Justice Society of America, this Superman found an example of the hopeful camaraderie his world had lost. **DW**

SAVAGE VENGEANCE

Vandal Savage's next Golden Age targets were in Ohio. Savage hired the neo-Nazis of the Fourth Reich to wipe out the family of Henry "Hank" Heywood, the original Commander Steel. Heywood's grandson Nate assisted Hawkman in fighting off the attackers, but became infected by living molten metal when he killed the villain Reichsmark. This new coating of organic steel made Nate indestructible and inhumanly strong, but—even after having a uniform sealed to his body in an iron foundry—he refused to embrace his family's military legacy. Instead, he joined the Justice Society as the first Citizen Steel. At the same time that new members found their footing, veterans took on greater responsibilities. Power Girl, a longtime JSA member, took over as the team's chairwoman.

SUPER-HERO GENOCIDE *Reichsmark and the Fourth Reich failed to wipe out the bloodline of Commander Steel.*

187

THE DC COMICS ENCYCLOPEDIA

KALIBAK

FIRST APPEARANCE NEW GODS (1st series) #1 (March 1971)
STATUS Villain (deceased)   **REAL NAME** Kalibak
OCCUPATION Warrior   **BASE** Apokolips
HEIGHT 7ft 9in   **WEIGHT** 810 lbs   **EYES** Red   **HAIR** Black
SPECIAL POWERS/ABILITIES Vast superhuman strength, endurance, and near invulnerability; is a powerful brawler and hand-to-hand combatant; wields the Beta Club, which can fire destructive force bolts.

Kalibak is the eldest son of DARKSEID, the nearly omnipotent ruler of the planet Apokolips, and the scientist Suli, the only woman Darkseid has ever loved. After Suli was assassinated by DESAAD at the behest of Darkseid's mother, Queen Heggra, the young Kalibak was placed in Darkseid's Special Powers Force. There Kalibak became a warrior whose savagery was unparalleled across the galaxy. Only as an adult did Kalibak learn that ORION, his bitter enemy, was his half-brother and Darkseid's son. Darkseid favored Orion over Kalibak, and the elder scion of Apokolips grew overwhelmed with jealousy and hatred for his younger brother.

Eager to earn the love of his unfeeling parent Darkseid, Kalibak formed a plan to destroy Orion. But Kalibak's scheme backfired and he was forced to murder Desaad, Darkseid's master henchman, instead, to hide his failure. Darkseid destroyed Kalibak after discovering the plan. But Darkseid, valuing Kalibak's strength and power, chose to resurrect his son. During the Death of the New Gods event, Kalibak brawled with a visiting SUPERMAN, but soon fell prey to the mysterious killer. **PJ**

KALKI

FIRST APPEARANCE DOOM PATROL (2nd series) #1 (October 1987)
STATUS Villain (missing in action)   **REAL NAME** Ashok Desai
OCCUPATION Biochemist; physicist   **BASE** Mobile
HEIGHT 5 ft 9in   **WEIGHT** 147 lbs   **EYES** Black   **HAIR** Black
SPECIAL POWERS/ABILITIES Scientific genius; controlled spatial portal giving him access to other-dimensional creatures; exosuit contained a variety of weapons and protective devices.

Though born in poverty in Calcutta, India, Ashok Desai gained a science degree at Oxford University. He returned to India determined to cure his country's social ills. Desai's wife died giving birth to their daughter, Arani (who would become a member of the DOOM PATROL as the heroine CELSIUS). Ironically, Desai's associations with the Patrol's founder, Dr. Niles Caulder (CHIEF), years before the group's founding involved experiments that horribly mutated Desai's body, making him a living dimensional gateway. Believing himself the living incarnation of the Hindu god Kalki, deity of destruction, Desai amassed wealth and power before targeting the Doom Patrol and his own daughter Arani for revenge. During that conflict, Kalki was sucked through the dimensional gateway in his own body! His ultimate fate is unknown. **SB**

KAMANDI

FIRST APPEARANCE KAMANDI #1 (November 1972)
STATUS Hero   **REAL NAME** Kamandi
OCCUPATION Last boy on Earth   **BASE** North America
HEIGHT 5ft 8in   **WEIGHT** 159 lbs   **EYES** Blue   **HAIR** Blond
SPECIAL POWERS/ABILITIES Skilled fighter, courageous, and resourceful; one of few humans to survive the Great Disaster.

In some parallel universes, an apocalypse termed the Great Disaster turned Earth into a wasteland populated by beast-men. OMAC raised his grandson in the Command D bunker. After Omac's death, the boy, named Kamandi (for "Command D") wandered North America. Great Caesar and his tiger-men ruled the east, while Czar Simian and his gorillas controlled the west. A few animals, like dog-faced Dr. Canus, became friends, but most remained enemies. The so-called "Last Boy on Earth" met other humans, one of whom, scientist Ben Boxer, became his ally in a bid to restore humanity to its former glory. **DW**

KALMAKU, TOM

FIRST APPEARANCE GREEN LANTERN (2nd series) #2 (September 1960)
STATUS Hero   **REAL NAME** Thomas Kalmaku
OCCUPATION Engineer   **BASE** Coast City, California
HEIGHT 5ft 7in   **WEIGHT** 155 lbs
EYES Brown   **HAIR** Black
SPECIAL POWERS/ABILITIES A gifted mechanic and a staunch friend to Hal Jordan, but otherwise has no special abilities.

Many decades ago, trapper Jimmy Dawes and an Inuit Alaskan named Kalmaku found a gold mine in the far north. They made a map of the location and each took half, with Dawes returning south to raise money to build the mine. Kalmaku fell ill and died, passing the half-map to his son, Tom. Dawes never returned and Tom decided to find the trapper. He took the job of flight mechanic at Ferris Aircraft in Coast City, California, to support himself while seeking out Dawes. Tom's map was stolen, prompting Hal Jordan, the second GREEN LANTERN, to come to his aid. Kalmaku quickly deduced that the Emerald Crusader was also his pal. A lifelong bond formed between the two after the mine was located and donated to the tribe. Tom, stuck with the nickname Pieface, recorded Jordan's costumed exploits in a series of casebooks. He also fell in love with Tegra, marrying her and raising two children. When Jordan died in disgrace, Tom sank into an alcoholic haze. However, Tom used emerald power to recreate the planet Oa. Spiritually rejuvenated, Tom is rebuilding his life. **RG**

KANJAR RO

FIRST APPEARANCE JUSTICE LEAGUE OF AMERICA (1st series) #3 (March 1961)
STATUS Villain REAL NAME None
OCCUPATION World conqueror BASE Outer space
HEIGHT 5ft 4in WEIGHT 147 lbs EYES Yellow HAIR None
SPECIAL POWERS/ABILITIES Cunning strategist who relies on advanced alien weaponry, Energi-rod used for levitation, and communicating through hyperspace.

Kanjar Ro became the dictatorial felon of the planet Dhor, a world in the Antarean star-system. His army waged wars with neighboring worlds Alstair, Mosteel, and Llar, each ruled by tyrants desiring total control of their galaxy. To tip the balance of power in his favor, Kanjar Ro traveled to Earth and forced the JUSTICE LEAGUE OF AMERICA to fight his enemies to save the people of Earth. Fortunately, the JLA defeated and captured Kanjar Ro.

TYRANT
WIELDING HIS
Energi-rod, Kanjar Ro made the JLA do his bidding in their first fateful encounter.

QUICK EXIT Superman helps Kanjar Ro to beat a hasty retreat from Kylaq.

The JLA imprisoned Kanjar Ro and the other alien rulers on a small lifeless planet. Kanjar Ro escaped and attempted to invade the planet Rann, but was thwarted by Rann's human defender, Adam Strange (see STRANGE, ADAM), and the Justice League. Kanjar Ro eventually conquered Rann, but Rann was soon liberated from Kanjar Ro's rule. In the years following, Kanjar Ro rebuilt his power base. Recently, he became Minister of Defense of the planet Kylaq and began arming the otherwise peaceful world to make war with the Paciforce, a military collective of three belligerent alien races. Although 50 light years from Earth, the conflict on Kylaq drew the attention of the JLA, who were surprised to find their old foe up to his usual tyrannical games. The League convinced Kanjar Ro to leave Kylaq in a hurry. Somewhere in space, Kanjar Ro plots revenge and seeks new worlds to conquer. SB

KANTO

FIRST APPEARANCE MISTER MIRACLE (1st series) #7 (April 1972)
STATUS Villain (deceased) REAL NAME Iluthin
OCCUPATION Assassin BASE Apokolips
HEIGHT 5ft 11.5in WEIGHT 170 lbs EYES Blue HAIR Black
SPECIAL POWERS/ABILITIES A master of weapons; can easily adapt to any weapon from any era; a superb organizer and strategist, second only to Darkseid himself among Apokoliptians.

Kanto is Apokolips' greatest assassin and one of its ruler Darkseid's closest aides. Little is known of his background prior to 1502 ad when Darkseid exiled Iluthin, a promising warrior among Granny Goodness' orphans, to Rome. There, the young man learned much from the evil power-brokers Cesare and Lucretia Borgia.

After the Apokoliptian assassin Kanto 13 traveled to Earth via a Boom Tube and killed Iluthin's lover, the young warrior returned to Apokolips and defeated the murderer. Impressed, Darkseid executed the fallen man and declared Iluthin his new master assassin, the no-longer-numbered Kanto. Over the years, Kanto has accomplished much for his master, but has also developed a deep respect for other people's artistry, as well as his own. During the Death of the New Gods event, Kanto's skills could not save him from perishing at the hands of a mysterious killer. RG

KARATE KID

FIRST APPEARANCE ADVENTURE COMICS #346 (July 1966)
STATUS Hero REAL NAME Val Armorr
OCCUPATION Legionnaire BASE Earth
HEIGHT 5ft 8in WEIGHT 160 lbs EYES Black HAIR Black
SPECIAL POWERS/ABILITIES A "living weapon," the Kid is a member of every known discipline of martial arts on this and most other worlds, and is a master of them all.

Born in the 30th century, Val Armorr dedicated his life to the study of all martial-arts disciplines, from ancient eras of Earth history to the fighting styles of alien species. Becoming an elite fifteenth-level combatant, he joined the LEGION OF SUPER-HEROES as Karate Kid. With the Legion representing youthful rebellion in the face of oppressive governmental monitoring, Karate Kid stood as the Legion's calm, spiritual center. He attempted romances with teammates Shadow Lass (see UMBRA) and Phantom Girl (see APPARITION), and helped other Legionnaires master their natural abilities.

In an alternate Legion timeline, Karate Kid traveled back to the 21st century with Triplicate Girl (see TRIAD). Their adventures took them from Blüdhaven to Apokolips, allowing them to uncover a plot by Brother Eye to resurrect an army of OMAC units. DW

KATANA

FIRST APPEARANCE BRAVE AND THE BOLD #200 (July 1983)
STATUS Hero REAL NAME Tatsu Yamashiro
OCCUPATION Martial artist BASE Los Angeles
HEIGHT 5ft 2in WEIGHT 118 lbs EYES Brown HAIR Black
SPECIAL POWERS/ABILITIES An expert martial artist, whose diminutive stature belies her fighting powers; her Soultaker sword houses the souls of the people she has slain in battle.

An adept martial artist at a young age, Tatsu married Maseo Yamashiro, a businessman, and the couple had two children, Yuki and Reiko. Maseo's brother Takeo, a member of the Yakuza crime syndicate, was obsessed with Tatsu and killed Maseo and his children with an ancient katana sword, the Soultaker. Tatsu stole the sword and honed her skills as a martial artist with a sensei master named Tadashi. Tatsu named herself Katana after her signature weapon.

Katana joined the OUTSIDERS and took up residence in Gotham City becoming a surrogate mother to HALO. Eventually, Katana confronted Maseo and killed him. Under the orders of Tadashi, LADY SHIVA once tried to claim the Soultaker, but Katana defeated Shiva and slew Tadashi instead. Katana later served with the BIRDS OF PREY, and recently became a member of the latest team of Outsiders, where she has become BATMAN's most trusted operative. PJ

KATMA TUI

FIRST APPEARANCE GREEN LANTERN (2nd series) #30 (July 1964)
STATUS Hero (deceased) **REAL NAME** None
OCCUPATION Green Lantern **BASE** Earth; formerly Korugar
HEIGHT 5ft 11in **WEIGHT** 131 lbs **EYES** Blue **HAIR** Black
SPECIAL POWERS/ABILITIES One of the most accomplished and courageous ring-bearers of the Green Lantern Corps.

Katma Tui from the planet Korugar was selected by the GUARDIANS OF THE UNIVERSE to replace the rogue SINESTRO, who had abused his GREEN LANTERN powers and become a tyrant of Space Sector 1417. Serving the GREEN LANTERN CORPS with great distinction, Katma later decided to relinquish her power ring and marry a Korugarian scientist. Green Lantern Hal Jordan convinced Katma that her true home was with the Corps. Assigned by the Guardians to train Hal's replacement, John Stewart, Katma fell in love with him. Katma and John were married, but their happiness was ended when Katma was caught unawares by STAR SAPPHIRE—evil alter ego of Carol Ferris, Hal Jordan's longtime love—and sliced to ribbons. **SB**

KENTS, THE

FIRST APPEARANCE (Ma Kent) ACTION COMICS #1 (June 1938)
STATUS Ally **REAL NAME** Martha Clark Kent
OCCUPATION Farmer's wife **BASE** Smallville, Kansas
HEIGHT 5ft 4in **WEIGHT** 140 lbs **EYES** Blue **HAIR** Red
SPECIAL POWERS/ABILITIES Martha has no combat skills but is wonderfully kindhearted and an excellent cook and baker.
FIRST APPEARANCE (Pa Kent) Action Comics #1 (June 1938)
STATUS Ally **REAL NAME** Jonathan Kent
OCCUPATION Farmer **BASE** Smallville, Kansas
HEIGHT 5ft 11in **WEIGHT** 185 lbs **EYES** Blue **HAIR** Gray/blond
SPECIAL POWERS/ABILITIES Jonathan's army training makes him an above-average combatant; he is also an excellent farmer.

Silas Kent moved his family westward to Kansas in 1854 as part of a group of abolitionists. After Silas was murdered, his sons Nathaniel and Jebediah took over the family stake. After the Civil War, Jeb fell in with Jesse James and his outlaws. Nate remained with the army as a scout until he married Mary Glenowen. He then became Smallville's sheriff on December 13, 1872. This led to a confrontation between Nate and Jeb in 1874 when an aborted bank robbery became a bloodbath, with Jeb being gunned down.

Silas's greatgrandson is Jonathan Kent, himself a war hero. He married his former sweetheart Martha Clark when she became a widow. Unfortunately the couple were unable to have children. One night an alien spacecraft crashed near their farm. Inside the capsule they found a baby boy. Overjoyed, they decided to adopt this child from another world. They christened him Clark and instilled in him their own strong moral values. These stood him in particularly good stead when Clark developed superpowers and became the world-famous Man of Steel, SUPERMAN.

The Kent family farm, virtually unchanged since 1871, has been a refuge for others in need, such as Matrix (SUPERGIRL), a shape-changing being from another universe who needed time to heal after a mission with Superman. The Kents helped raise Kon-El (SUPERBOY) under the name Conner Kent, until the teenager's death during the Infinite Crisis. **RG**

PERFECT PARENTS *The birthing matrix from Krypton crashed in the fields near the Kent's farm.*

KEY, THE

FIRST APPEARANCE JUSTICE LEAGUE OF AMERICA (1st series) #41 (December 1965)
STATUS Villain **REAL NAME** Unrevealed **OCCUPATION** Would-be world conqueror **BASE** Mobile **HEIGHT** 6ft 1in **WEIGHT** 197 lbs **EYES** Red **HAIR** White **SPECIAL POWERS/ABILITIES** Master escape artist who carries a neural shock rifle and can control minds with his psycho-chemicals.

The psychopath known as the Key gained his *modus operandi* from an obsession with locks and puzzles. As a chemist working for INTERGANG, he developed psycho-chemicals to help him unlock the mysteries of the human mind. Injecting himself with his own drug, he accessed unused parts of his brain and began a crooked career as the villainous Key.

The Key clashed with the JUSTICE LEAGUE OF AMERICA, wearing a suit with an oversized "key" headpiece and employing an army of Key-Men. He met with continual failure, and only after emerging from a years-long coma did he become a truly dangerous villain. With a new look and a looser grip on reality, the Key ran riot over the Justice League's lunar base until knocked cold by a boxing glove arrow fired by GREEN ARROW Connor Hawke. The Key recently approached the Justice League to obtain sanctuary from the villain-hunters in the SUICIDE SQUAD. **DW**

KGBEAST

FIRST APPEARANCE BATMAN #417 (March 1989)
STATUS Villain (deceased) **REAL NAME** Anatoli Knyazev
OCCUPATION Assassin **BASE** Gotham City
HEIGHT 6ft 3in **WEIGHT** 371 lbs **EYES** Brown **HAIR** Unknown
SPECIAL POWERS/ABILITIES Extraordinary hand-to-hand combatant; master of weapons and explosives; has a gun instead of a left hand.

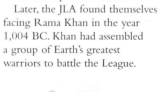

Anatoli Knyazev was an assassin employed by the K.G.B., the secret police of the former Soviet Union. Knyazev became a rogue agent, taking an unauthorized mission to kill ten people involved with the U.S. Strategic Defense Initiative. After murdering dozens in Gotham City, the KGBeast encountered BATMAN. When his left arm was trapped by one of Batman's weapons, the KGBeast severed his own hand and escaped. He later fit the stump with a powerful gun. After a botched assassination attempt on the U.S. President and a counterfeit scheme gone awry, the KGBeast was incarcerated at Blackgate Maximum Security Prison. The KGBeast died in Gotham City on the orders of mob boss Great White, who framed TWO-FACE for the act. **PJ**

KHAN, RAMA

FIRST APPEARANCE JLA #62 (March 2002)
STATUS Undecided **REAL NAME** Unrevealed
OCCUPATION Elemental defender **BASE** Jarhanpur
HEIGHT 6ft 5in **WEIGHT** 199 lbs **EYES** Black **HAIR** Black
SPECIAL POWERS/ABILITIES Superstrong; immortal; great magician; can turn a handful of Jarhanpur soil into fire, granite, or a sea of wine.

Elemental defender of the nation of Jarhanpur, Rama Khan sought revenge against WONDER WOMAN when the Amazon Princess fought to protect an innocent boy abducted against his will to be installed as Jarhanpur's next ruler. Rama Khan broke the heretofore unbreakable links of Wonder Woman's Lasso of Truth and, in turn, unraveled the fragile fabric of reality. With her JUSTICE LEAGUE OF AMERICA teammates, Wonder Woman defeated Rama Khan and repaired her lariat.

Later, the JLA found themselves facing Rama Khan in the year 1,004 BC. Khan had assembled a group of Earth's greatest warriors to battle the League.

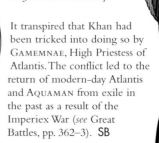

ELEMENTAL DEFENDER PAST OR PRESENT, *Rama Khan has always faced the JLA as an adversary.*

It transpired that Khan had been tricked into doing so by GAMEMNAE, High Priestess of Atlantis. The conflict led to the return of modern-day Atlantis and AQUAMAN from exile in the past as a result of the Imperiex War (see Great Battles, pp. 362–3). **SB**

KID DEVIL

FIRST APPEARANCE BLUE DEVIL #14 (July 1985)
STATUS Hero **REAL NAME** Eddie Bloomberg
OCCUPATION Professional adventurer **BASE** San Francisco
HEIGHT 5ft 8in **WEIGHT** 165 lbs **EYES** Yellow **HAIR** White
SPECIAL POWERS/ABILITIES Enhanced strength, agility, and self-healing, burning skin, ability to breathe fire.

As a boy, Eddie Bloomberg idolized BLUE DEVIL so much that he constructed a smaller duplicate of his hero's mechanical suit and became his self-appointed sidekick, Kid Devil.

Hoping to become a super hero s after the Infinite Crisis, Eddie teamed with ZATANNA's cousin Zachary Zatara to entertain an offer from the demon NERON. In exchange for gaining the powers of an actual devil, Eddie agreed to turn his soul over to Neron if he lost faith in Blue Devil before his 20th birthday. True to form, Neron then dropped a hint that Blue Devil had been indirectly responsible for the death of Eddie's aunt. Kid Devil confirmed the truth of this, and his trust in Blue Devil was shattered; he had played right into Neron's hands. With the TEEN TITANS, Kid Devil struggled for respect from his more experienced teammates, and started a friendship with fellow newcomer Ravager. Among his enemies is Kid Crusader, a religiously-motivated hero who wants to exorcise the demonic stain from Eddie's soul. **DW**

EXORCISM The fanatical Kid Crusader believed that his calling lay in purging Kid Devil of his demonic gifts. He succeeded, but the effect was only temporary.

EYE TO EYE Kid Devil and Ravager considered themselves outsiders within the Teen Titans, and banded together to escape from the suspicion of their teammates.

KID ETERNITY

FIRST APPEARANCE HIT COMICS #25 (December 1942)
STATUS Hero (deceased) **REAL NAME** Kit Freeman
OCCUPATION Ghost **BASE** England
HEIGHT 5ft 10in **WEIGHT** 164 lbs **EYES** Brown **HAIR** Brown
SPECIAL POWERS/ABILITIES Could summon dead spirits throughout the ages to advise him.

Young Kit Freeman was killed by Nazi machine gunners during World War II. The boy's spirit was informed by a being from the higher realms named Mister Keeper that he was not fated to die for another 75 years. Because he could not be returned to life, Mister Keeper granted the boy a number of ghostly powers and returned with him to Earth. In reality, the spirit now called Kid Eternity had been duped by an Agent of Chaos and unwittingly served their interests. After nearly three decades of adventure, Kid Eternity became trapped in Hell for 30 years. Kid Eternity escaped from Hell with Mister Keeper and later learned that he never went to Heaven at all, but an illusory paradise deep in the pits of Hell. Kid Eternity died in battle with Mordru, the DARK LORD, but eventually returned through the doorway separating life and death. He used his abilities to defeat Brother Blood, earning the gratitude of the TEEN TITANS. **RG**

KID QUANTUM I & II

FIRST APPEARANCE (I) LEGION OF SUPER-HEROES #33 (September 1992); (II) LEGION OF SUPER-HEROES (4th series) #82 (July 1996)
STATUS Heroes **REAL NAMES** (I) James Cullen; (II) Jazmin Cullen
OCCUPATION Legionnaires **BASE** Legion World
HEIGHT (I) 5ft 11in; (II) 5ft 8in **WEIGHT** (I) 170 lbs; (II) 145 lbs
EYES (I) Brown; (II) amber **HAIR** (I) Black; (II) black
SPECIAL POWERS/ABILITIES Able to project stasis fields that halt the movement of time within their sphere of influence.

In one timeline, Kid Quantum (James Cullen of Xanthu) joined the LEGION OF SUPER-HEROES during its first weeks. His ability to generate stasis fields received an artificial boost from his stasis belt. During the Legion's first mission, he died battling the alien entity Tangleweb, his malfunctioning belt partly to blame. This tragedy prompted the Legion to deny membership to those whose powers relied on external devices.

Before long, Jazmin Cullen, James's sister, joined the Legion. As Kid Quantum II, she wielded the same powers as her brother, but underwent experimental surgery to augment her powers instead of relying on a stasis belt. Although she bore some resentment toward the Legion for failing to prevent her brother's death, Kid Quantum II put her bitterness behind her as she established close friendships within the roster. During the Robotica Crisis (see C.O.M.P.U.T.O.), Kid Quantum II became the Legion's new leader. She appointed TRIAD as her deputy and struck up a romance with COSMIC BOY. Recently, Kid Quantum II stepped down as Legion leader but will undoubtedly aid the team in its continuing struggles against the forces of Apokolips. **DW**

AMAZING Prior to joining the Legion, Kid Quantum II served with Xanthu's own super hero team, the Uncanny Amazers.

BONDS OF THE HEART Romance with Cosmic Boy proved complicated when both lovers faced the threat of death on every mission.

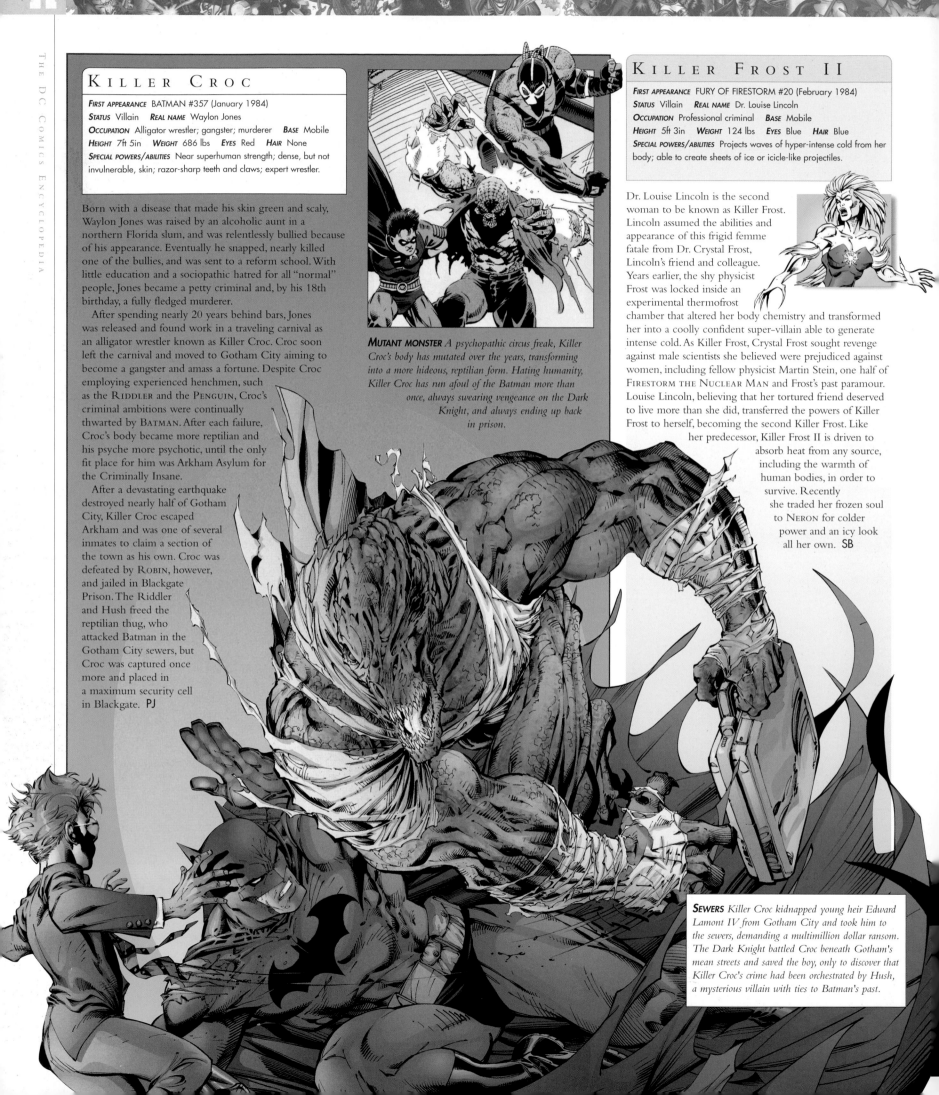

KILLER CROC

FIRST APPEARANCE BATMAN #357 (January 1984)
STATUS Villain **REAL NAME** Waylon Jones
OCCUPATION Alligator wrestler; gangster; murderer **BASE** Mobile
HEIGHT 7ft 5in **WEIGHT** 686 lbs **EYES** Red **HAIR** None
SPECIAL POWERS/ABILITIES Near superhuman strength; dense, but not invulnerable, skin; razor-sharp teeth and claws; expert wrestler.

Born with a disease that made his skin green and scaly, Waylon Jones was raised by an alcoholic aunt in a northern Florida slum, and was relentlessly bullied because of his appearance. Eventually he snapped, nearly killed one of the bullies, and was sent to a reform school. With little education and a sociopathic hatred for all "normal" people, Jones became a petty criminal and, by his 18th birthday, a fully fledged murderer.

After spending nearly 20 years behind bars, Jones was released and found work in a traveling carnival as an alligator wrestler known as Killer Croc. Croc soon left the carnival and moved to Gotham City aiming to become a gangster and amass a fortune. Despite Croc employing experienced henchmen, such as the RIDDLER and the PENGUIN, Croc's criminal ambitions were continually thwarted by BATMAN. After each failure, Croc's body became more reptilian and his psyche more psychotic, until the only fit place for him was Arkham Asylum for the Criminally Insane.

After a devastating earthquake destroyed nearly half of Gotham City, Killer Croc escaped Arkham and was one of several inmates to claim a section of the town as his own. Croc was defeated by ROBIN, however, and jailed in Blackgate Prison. The Riddler and Hush freed the reptilian thug, who attacked Batman in the Gotham City sewers, but Croc was captured once more and placed in a maximum security cell in Blackgate. **PJ**

MUTANT MONSTER *A psychopathic circus freak, Killer Croc's body has mutated over the years, transforming into a more hideous, reptilian form. Hating humanity, Killer Croc has run afoul of the Batman more than once, always swearing vengeance on the Dark Knight, and always ending up back in prison.*

KILLER FROST II

FIRST APPEARANCE FURY OF FIRESTORM #20 (February 1984)
STATUS Villain **REAL NAME** Dr. Louise Lincoln
OCCUPATION Professional criminal **BASE** Mobile
HEIGHT 5ft 3in **WEIGHT** 124 lbs **EYES** Blue **HAIR** Blue
SPECIAL POWERS/ABILITIES Projects waves of hyper-intense cold from her body; able to create sheets of ice or icicle-like projectiles.

Dr. Louise Lincoln is the second woman to be known as Killer Frost. Lincoln assumed the abilities and appearance of this frigid femme fatale from Dr. Crystal Frost, Lincoln's friend and colleague. Years earlier, the shy physicist Frost was locked inside an experimental thermofrost chamber that altered her body chemistry and transformed her into a coolly confident super-villain able to generate intense cold. As Killer Frost, Crystal Frost sought revenge against male scientists she believed were prejudiced against women, including fellow physicist Martin Stein, one half of FIRESTORM THE NUCLEAR MAN and Frost's past paramour. Louise Lincoln, believing that her tortured friend deserved to live more than she did, transferred the powers of Killer Frost to herself, becoming the second Killer Frost. Like her predecessor, Killer Frost II is driven to absorb heat from any source, including the warmth of human bodies, in order to survive. Recently she traded her frozen soul to NERON for colder power and an icy look all her own. **SB**

SEWERS *Killer Croc kidnapped young heir Edward Lamont IV from Gotham City and took him to the sewers, demanding a multimillion dollar ransom. The Dark Knight battled Croc beneath Gotham's mean streets and saved the boy, only to discover that Killer Croc's crime had been orchestrated by Hush, a mysterious villain with ties to Batman's past.*

KILLER SHARK

FIRST APPEARANCE BLACKHAWK (1st series) #50 (March 1952)
STATUS Villain **REAL NAME** Unrevealed
OCCUPATION Pirate **BASE** Mobile
HEIGHT 5ft 11in **WEIGHT** 185 lbs **EYES** Unknown **HAIR** Unknown
SPECIAL POWERS/ABILITIES Relies on amazing vessels: the triphibious Shark Jet, an Octopus Sub, a Whale Sub, and a Swordfish Sub.

In 1950, the Blackhawks (see BLACKHAWK) encountered costumed pirate Killer Shark as he looted the city of Kamard. Using a variety of submersible vehicles, Killer Shark often matched wits with the international flyers, who destroyed his undersea base and each of his attack craft. Killer Shark joined with former Nazi S.S. Colonel Von Gross to form the Empire of Death. Its agents wore skull masks, possessed a fleet of aircraft, and operated from a giant solar-powered flying skull. With agents around the world, the Empire engaged in espionage and contract assassination with an eye towards world domination, until the Blackhawks slew Von Gross and closed the network down. Killer Shark recently returned to torment LADY BLACKHAWK. **RG**

JAWS OF DEATH
Always spoiling for a fight, Killer Shark used high-tech weapons to outmatch most opponents.

KILLSHOT

FIRST APPEARANCE TITANS SECRET FILES #2 (September 2000)
STATUS Villain **REAL NAME** Unrevealed
OCCUPATION Member of the Hangmen **BASE** Mobile
HEIGHT 6ft 1in **WEIGHT** 721 lbs **EYES** Brown **HAIR** Brown
SPECIAL POWERS/ABILITIES Cyborg with enhanced strength and agility; wields an arsenal of tools for carnage.

The assassin known as Killshot prefers to let his weapons speak for themselves. Little is known regarding this Russian executioner, but those who have seen him in action attest that his cyborg limbs conceal an arsenal of state-of-the-art military hardware, including a full magazine of surface-to-air missiles. Killshot serves with the HANGMEN, a group of superpowered assassins. The Hangmen's most frequent opponents have been the TEEN TITANS, initially clashing with them during the Hangmen's mission to kidnap ARSENAL's daughter Lian in a plot to get at the girl's mother, CHESHIRE. Later, Killshot and his comrades became "Jokerized" and were among the brain-addled villains running amok during the JOKER's Last Laugh spree. Killshot soon returned to normal and is actively seeking assassination contracts. **DW**

CYBORG *Killshot's weapons can bring down almost any opponent, though their weight tends to limit Killshot's mobility.*

KILOWOG

FIRST APPEARANCE GREEN LANTERN CORPS #201 (June 1986) **STATUS** Hero **REAL NAME** Kilowog
OCCUPATION Scientist; adventurer **BASE** Deep space
HEIGHT 8ft 3in **WEIGHT** 720 lbs **EYES** Red **HAIR** None
SPECIAL POWERS/ABILITIES Possessed a Green Lantern ring, limited only by the color yellow; vast scientific knowledge.

Born on the planet Bolovax Vix in space sector 674, Kilowog was chosen by the GUARDIANS OF THE UNIVERSE to become a GREEN LANTERN, eventually training a new recruit named Hal Jordan. During the Crisis (see Great Battles, pp. 362–3), Bolovax Vix was destroyed, but Kilowog used the power of his ring to absorb the souls of the world's 16 million inhabitants and transplant them to another planet. The villain SINESTRO destroyed this new world, however, and Kilowog became the sole survivor of his people. Entranced by the possibilities life on Earth offered, he settled there. Kilowog lived for a time in Russia, where he helped create the ROCKET RED BRIGADE. He also helped the NEW GUARDIANS establish their island base before joining the JUSTICE LEAGUE OF AMERICA. When Hal Jordan became the insane PARALLAX, Kilowog pleaded with his friend to end his destructive rampage, but Jordan incinerated him. After Kyle Rayner brought about his resurrection, Kilowog became drill sergeant for the Corps' new recruits. **PJ**

MACHINESMITH *Kilowog was the mechanic for the JLA before being killed by Parallax and resurrected by Green Lantern.*

KINETIX

FIRST APPEARANCE LEGION OF SUPER-HEROES (4th series) #66 (March 1995)
STATUS Hero **REAL NAME** Zoe Saugin
OCCUPATION Legionnaire **BASE** Legion World, U.P. Space
HEIGHT 5ft 4in **WEIGHT** 126 lbs **EYES** Green **HAIR** Auburn
SPECIAL POWERS/ABILITIES Hypertaxis-powered meta-human, formerly able to cast an energy field allowing her to remold objects.

While accompanying her archaeologist mother on a dig, Zoe Saugin from planet Aleph discovered a magical artifact that enabled her to save her family and sparked an interest in acquiring other forms of mystic energy. Zoe became Kinetix, her homeworld's recruit for the LEGION OF SUPER-HEROES. Zoe's quest for power led to her falling under the malign influence of the Emerald Empress's Emerald Eye. While confronting the cloned Rā's al Ghūl, Kinetix's body was changed by a bomb explosion into a highly evolved Terrorform. Kinetix remains a Legionnaire. **SB**

KING FARADAY

FIRST APPEARANCE DANGER TRAIL #1 (August 1950)
STATUS Hero **REAL NAME** King Faraday
OCCUPATION Government espionage agent **BASE** Washington, D.C.
HEIGHT 6ft **WEIGHT** 185 lbs **EYES** Blue **HAIR** White
SPECIAL POWERS/ABILITIES An Olympic-level athlete in his youth, he remains exceptionally fit.

King Faraday was an excellent soldier who left the armed services to join one of the U.S. government's many clandestine organizations, the Central Bureau of Intelligence. There he traveled the world on spy missions on behalf of his country, amassing a high diplomatic success rate. He holds a disdain for most costumed crime fighters, although he has a grudging admiration for BATMAN, and actually helped train NIGHTSHADE when she first arrived in Washington, D.C. They had several successful missions before she went off on her own. He ascended to the head of the C.B.I. before it was shuffled into a new intelligence matrix. King Faraday is active in CHECKMATE, serving Amanda Waller (see WALLER, AMANDA) as the White Queen's Bishop. **RG**

SECRET AGENT *Using wits and bare knuckles, Faraday helped keep America safe.*

KING OF TEARS

FIRST APPEARANCE JSA #18 (January 2001)
STATUS Villain **REAL NAME** Unknown
OCCUPATION Unspeakable horror **BASE** Subtle Realms
HEIGHT Various **WEIGHT** Various **EYES** None **HAIR** None
SPECIAL POWERS/ABILITIES Mind-control abilities, commands an army of evil minions.

The King of Tears is a horrific being, discarded by God at the dawn of creation. The King of Tears lead the monsters cast into the Subtle Realms, and planned a way to return to reality so he could make it a place of pain and terror. In 1944, two-bit criminal JOHNNY SORROW escaped the JUSTICE SOCIETY OF AMERICA using a broken subspace teleporter, which took him to the Subtle Realms. There, the King of Tears made Sorrow his emissary, sending him back to prepare the way for his rule. In a movie theater, Sorrow opened a portal to the Subtle Realms, unleashing evil that could only be stopped by the SPECTRE. Over 50 years later, demons loyal to the King of Tears tried to bring about a literal Hell on Earth. **DW**

KING SHARK

FIRST APPEARANCE SUPERBOY (3rd series) #0 (October 1994)
STATUS Villain **REAL NAME** Nanaue
OCCUPATION Adventurer **BASE** Hawaii
HEIGHT 7ft **WEIGHT** 380 lbs **EYES** Black **HAIR** None
SPECIAL POWERS/ABILITIES Superstrength, invulnerability, and a mouth full of razor-sharp teeth; can breathe underwater.

King Shark is said to be the offspring of a human mother and a shark god belonging to a pantheon of deities worshipped by traditional Hawaiians. He is truly monstrous in appearance and has a soul equally as ugly, being driven solely by his voracious appetites and urges. He loves to terrorize the people of Hawaii, and no prison has proved strong enough to hold him for long. King Shark's favorite prey is SUPERBOY, and his teeth are among the only things with enough force to puncture Superboy's invulnerable skin. For a time, King Shark worked with the SUICIDE SQUAD, and appeared to have died when a teammate ripped off his explosive harness in order to destroy an enemy fortress. A year after the Infinite Crisis, Killer Shark reappeared as a reluctant guide for the new AQUAMAN, Arthur Joseph Curry. **DW**

KING SOLOVAR

FIRST APPEARANCE THE FLASH (1st series) #106 (April 1959)
STATUS Hero (deceased) **REAL NAME** Solovar
OCCUPATION Monarch **BASE** Gorilla City, Africa
HEIGHT 6ft 5in **WEIGHT** 603 lbs **EYES** Black **HAIR** Gray
SPECIAL POWERS/ABILITIES A gifted telepath and benevolent ruler.

One of a race of apes advanced in evolutionary terms by an alien being who landed in Equatorial Africa in the 19th century, the wise and peaceful Solovar became king of his fellow super gorillas. He ruled benevolently over them in their hidden Gorilla City. When his rival GORILLA GRODD threatened to usurp his throne, Solovar enlisted the help of the second FLASH, Barry Allen, one of very few humans to know of Gorilla City's existence. Tragically, Solovar was assassinated by one of Grodd's minions as the kind monarch traveled to the United Nations to seek recognition for Gorilla City as a sovereign nation. Solovar's nephew Ulgo (the simian super hero Grogamesh) now succeeds him as leader of the peaceful apes. **SB**

KING SNAKE

FIRST APPEARANCE ROBIN (1st series) #1 (November 1990)
STATUS Villain (deceased) **REAL NAME** Sir Edmund Dorrance
OCCUPATION Crime lord **BASE** Gotham City
HEIGHT 6ft 2in **WEIGHT** 220 lbs **EYES** White **HAIR** Blond
SPECIAL POWERS/ABILITIES Master of several lethal martial arts.

Sir Edmund Dorrance was a former captain in the British Royal Artillery. Using his considerable financial resources, Dorrance began studying martial arts and became a master. He also became a leader of the heroin trade plaguing Asia, using a gang called the Ghost Dragons to peddle narcotics in Europe and North America. His brutal reputation earned him the name King Snake.

King Snake ran afoul of ROBIN and LADY SHIVA in France, and nearly fell to his death while fighting the Boy Wonder. After several medical operations, King Snake moved to Gotham City to reclaim his heroin-importing empire and to hunt for Robin. The Ghost Dragons, led by LYNX, rebelled against King Snake and stripped him of his control over their drug trade. Humiliated, King Snake moved back to Asia.

King Snake confronted Robin yet again, this time in the terrorist KOBRA's stronghold in Nepal. King Snake's vision had been briefly restored but the villain lost it once more when Robin threw snake venom into Dorrance's eyes. Left a wailing madman, King Snake was discovered wandering in the mountains by his own son, the villain BANE, whose mother had long ago been imprisoned for King Snake's crimes. The vengeful Bane seized his father and hurled him into a chasm, killing him. **PJ**

KING, THE

FIRST APPEARANCE FLASH COMICS #3 (March 1940)
STATUS Hero **REAL NAME** King Standish
OCCUPATION Crime fighter **BASE** New York City
HEIGHT 5ft 11in **WEIGHT** 184 lbs **EYES** Blue **HAIR** Blond
SPECIAL POWERS/ABILITIES A master of disguise, able to fool the keenest observer; good with a pistol but generally eschewed weapons and preferred to use his fists.

The mysterious masked man known as the King survived a shooting by Boss Barton's mob thanks to his bulletproof vest. At first, both criminals and police thought that the King was a masked felon, but he always helped those who could not help themselves. The King matched wits with a beautiful underworld leader known as the Witch, whom he encountered many times over the next few years. Both were masters of disguise, which made their meetings memorable matches. Similarly, the King also opposed SANDMAN II's foe, the Face. Control of the O.S.S. (Office of Strategic Services) recruited the King to help with domestic problems, such as spies, saboteurs, and common criminals, during the latter part of World War II. One such mission saw the King help Sandman I and the Star-Spangled Kid defeat a disciple of the dimension-spanning STALKER. The King's post-1945 exploits remain undisclosed. **RG**

STING IN THE TAIL
King Snake longed for revenge against Robin, whom he believed had pushed him off a building. It was actually Lady Shiva who had caused Snake's near-fatal fall!

KNIGHT & SQUIRE

FIRST APPEARANCE (I) BATMAN #62 (January 1951); (II) JLA #26 (February 1999) STATUS Heroes REAL NAME (Knight I, Squire I) Percival Sheldrake; (Knight II, Squire II) Cyril Sheldrake OCCUPATION Adventurers BASE Wordenshire, England HEIGHT (Knight I) 5ft 10in; (Knight II) 5ft 11in WEIGHT (Knight I) 167 lbs; (Knight II) 175 lbs EYES (both) Brown HAIR (both) Brown SPECIAL POWERS/ABILITIES (Knight I) Expert swordsman, combatant and rider; (II) micro fighter jets, tanks, etc. controlled by gauntlet keypad.

Percival Sheldrake's father, the Earl of Wordenshire, was slain in North Africa during World War II, and his mother perished in a bombing raid in London. Percival was rescued by the SHINING KNIGHT, who took the young man on as his Squire. The two heroes joined the ALL-STAR SQUADRON and the SEVEN SOLDIERS OF VICTORY and, at the behest of President F. D. Roosevelt, the Squire later became a member of the Young All-Stars.

After spending some time as a prisoner of war, Percival, now an adult, became the Knight, one of the first costumed heroes to emerge outside of the U.S. His son Cyril became his Squire, and the two joined the Dome, becoming GLOBAL GUARDIANS and fighting crime in England during the 1950s. When Percival died, Cyril inherited his father's wealth and became a second Knight, riding a Norton motorcycle that had been his father's. With Beryl Hutchinson filling the role of Squire, the two helped BATMAN solve a murder mystery involving the Club of Heroes. PJ

A HEROIC LEGACY
The Knight and Squire are the two British representatives of the Ultramarine Corps, based in the ruins of Montevideo, Uruguay.

KNOCKOUT

FIRST APPEARANCE SUPERBOY (3rd series) #2 (March 1994) STATUS Villain (deceased) REAL NAME Unknown; has used the alias "Kay" OCCUPATION Criminal; former exotic dancer BASE Mobile HEIGHT 6ft WEIGHT 164 lbs EYES Green HAIR Red SPECIAL POWERS/ABILITIES Trained in the battle techniques of the Female Furies; possesses superstrength and endurance; can be defeated by exploiting her fear of being trapped, a side-effect of her training.

The statuesque super-villainess known as Knockout began her life on distant Apokolips. At a young age, she was selected to leave the squalor of GRANNY GOODNESS's orphanage and become a trainee for the much-feared FEMALE FURIES. Although respected for her fighting ferocity, Knockout's impudence displeased Granny on many occasions. She was summarily punished with solitary confinement, chained alone in the fire-pits of Armagetto. There she met the insurgent HIMON, who encouraged Knockout to choose her own destiny.

After BIG BARDA escaped the Furies, Knockout was similarly inspired to leave Apokolips behind for good. When punished yet again for her disrespect, Knockout freed herself and traveled via Boom Tube to Earth, Hawaii specifically, where she exploited her beauty by becoming a sultry stripper. Later, she relied on her brawn to fight SUPERBOY in her guise as a costumed villainess. Enamored by Knockout's considerable attributes, Superboy attempted to reform her. Ultimately, Knockout was imprisoned after killing a police officer. After starting a romance with SCANDAL, Knockout became a spy in the ranks of the Society (see VILLAINS UNITED) and later joined the SECRET SIX. Knockout lost her life during the Death of the New Gods event, murdered by an unseen assassin. SB

KLARION, THE WITCH BOY

FIRST APPEARANCE THE DEMON (1st series) #7 (March 1973) STATUS Villain REAL NAME Klarion OCCUPATION Warlock BASE Mobile HEIGHT 5ft 1in WEIGHT 113 lbs EYES Black HAIR Black SPECIAL POWERS/ABILITIES Despite small size and apparent youth, wields near-limitless power; has a wicked sense of humor.

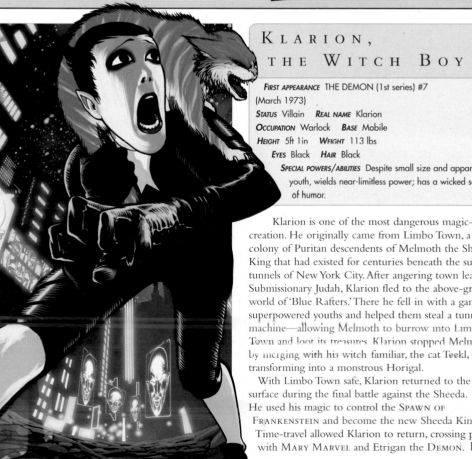

Klarion is one of the most dangerous magic-users in creation. He originally came from Limbo Town, a hidden colony of Puritan descendents of Melmoth the Sheeda King that had existed for centuries beneath the subway tunnels of New York City. After angering town leader Submissionary Judah, Klarion fled to the above-ground world of 'Blue Rafters.' There he fell in with a gang of superpowered youths and helped them steal a tunneling machine—allowing Melmoth to burrow into Limbo Town and loot its treasures. Klarion stopped Melmoth by merging with his witch familiar, the cat Teekl, and transforming into a monstrous Horigal.

With Limbo Town safe, Klarion returned to the surface during the final battle against the Sheeda. He used his magic to control the SPAWN OF FRANKENSTEIN and become the new Sheeda King. Time-travel allowed Klarion to return, crossing paths with MARY MARVEL and Etrigan the Demon. DW

THE DC COMICS ENCYCLOPEDIA

KOLE

FIRST APPEARANCE NEW TEEN TITANS (2nd series) #9 (June 1985)
STATUS Hero (deceased) REAL NAME Kole Weathers
OCCUPATION Adventurer BASE New York City
HEIGHT 5ft 6in WEIGHT 133 lbs EYES Blue HAIR Red
SPECIAL POWERS/ABILITIES Could project tough crystal forms that worked on their own, or as a coating over other objects.

Dr. Abel Weathers was convinced that mankind was doomed to be wiped out in a nuclear holocaust in the near future, so he experimented with ways to preserve human life from a nuclear attack. He studied insects and crystals for secrets that might hold vital clues to humanity's possible survival.

He then began experimenting on human subjects, including his teenage daughter, Kole. This triggered her meta-gene, imbuing her with the ability to generate crystal forms. In time, Kole attracted the attention of the TEEN TITANS, whom she soon joined. Kole enjoyed adventuring, but it took time for the shy teen to get to know and feel comfortable around her teammates. She fought bravely alongside the team, sacrificing her life during the cosmic event known as the Crisis (see Great Battles, pp. 362–3). RG

KORDAX

FIRST APPEARANCE ATLANTIS CHRONICLES #4 (June 1990)
STATUS Villain (deceased) REAL NAME Kordax
OCCUPATION Adventurer BASE Atlantis
HEIGHT 6ft 6in WEIGHT 535 lbs EYES Red HAIR Blond
SPECIAL POWERS/ABILITIES Could breathe underwater and communicate telepathically with sea life; enhanced strength and toughness.

Kordax is still spoken of in hushed tones by the citizens of Atlantis. Born to Queen Cora of Poseidonis but abandoned at birth due to his grotesque, green-scaled body, Kordax survived in the ocean thanks to his mental control over sea creatures. As an adult he returned to Atlantis leading an army of sharks in a failed bid for the throne. His punishment included the loss of his left hand (replaced with a sword) and banishment. Kordax's legend survived in an Atlantean superstition regarding blond hair, referred to as the "Curse of Kordax."

Many ages later, Kordax returned when Poseidonian refugees disturbed his exile in the tunnels beneath the city of Tritonis. Defeated by AQUAMAN, Kordax fell on his own sword rather than live in shame. DW

KORYAK

FIRST APPEARANCE AQUAMAN (3rd series) #35 (January 1995)
STATUS Undecided REAL NAME Koryak
OCCUPATION Exiled prince of Atlantis BASE Northern Canada
HEIGHT 5ft 8in WEIGHT 175 lbs EYES Brown HAIR Brown
SPECIAL POWERS/ABILITIES Amphibious; superspeed; can psychically create "hard water" weapons.

The son of AQUAMAN and the fire elemental CORONA, Koryak was raised by his Inuit mother in her remote village in northern Canada without ever knowing the identity of his father or the truth about his Atlantean heritage.

As a teenager, Koryak was introduced to Aquaman. Aquaman was ill-prepared for the boy's temper and attitude, which, in many ways, mirrored Aquaman's own personality. Resentful of Aquaman's close relationship with TEMPEST, the angry, rebellious Koryak eventually took up residence in Atlantis, Aquaman's undersea kingdom. Against his father's express wishes, Koryak led a great migration of Atlanteans out of the capital city Poseidonis and into the tunnels of its sister city, Tritonis. There, he unwittingly released the cruel KORDAX and embroiled Atlantis in a great war with the god Triton.

As a result of his misguided actions, Koryak was banished from Atlantis. He returned, shamed, to his mother's village, where he resides to this day. PJ

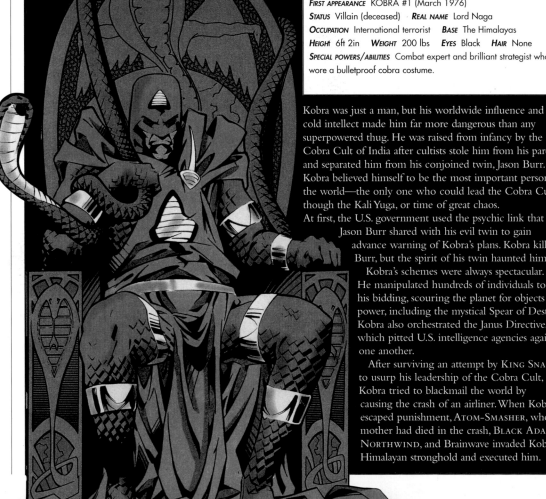

KOBRA

FIRST APPEARANCE KOBRA #1 (March 1976)
STATUS Villain (deceased) REAL NAME Lord Naga
OCCUPATION International terrorist BASE The Himalayas
HEIGHT 6ft 2in WEIGHT 200 lbs EYES Black HAIR None
SPECIAL POWERS/ABILITIES Combat expert and brilliant strategist who wore a bulletproof cobra costume.

Kobra was just a man, but his worldwide influence and cold intellect made him far more dangerous than any superpowered thug. He was raised from infancy by the Cobra Cult of India after cultists stole him from his parents and separated him from his conjoined twin, Jason Burr. Kobra believed himself to be the most important person in the world—the only one who could lead the Cobra Cult though the Kali Yuga, or time of great chaos.

At first, the U.S. government used the psychic link that Jason Burr shared with his evil twin to gain advance warning of Kobra's plans. Kobra killed Burr, but the spirit of his twin haunted him.

Kobra's schemes were always spectacular. He manipulated hundreds of individuals to do his bidding, scouring the planet for objects of power, including the mystical Spear of Destiny. Kobra also orchestrated the Janus Directive, which pitted U.S. intelligence agencies against one another.

After surviving an attempt by KING SNAKE to usurp his leadership of the Cobra Cult, Kobra tried to blackmail the world by causing the crash of an airliner. When Kobra escaped punishment, ATOM-SMASHER, whose mother had died in the crash, BLACK ADAM, NORTHWIND, and Brainwave invaded Kobra's Himalayan stronghold and executed him. DW

RETURN TO POWER Kobra squashed an attempted coup in his Himalayan mountain lair, in which disloyal cultists promoted an impostor to assume their master's place.

SERPENT SURPRISE Reptile-themed punishments are a favorite for Kobra, seen here covering a victim in highly poisonous coral snakes.

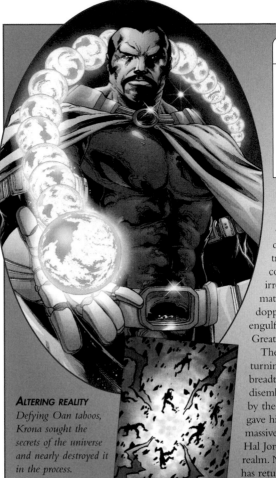

ALTERING REALITY
Defying Oan taboos, Krona sought the secrets of the universe and nearly destroyed it in the process.

KRONA

FIRST APPEARANCE GREEN LANTERN (2nd series) #40 (October 1965)
STATUS Villain (discorporated) **REAL NAME** None
OCCUPATION Scientist; would-be tyrant **BASE** Nekron's dimension
HEIGHT 6ft 8in **WEIGHT** 349 lbs **EYES** Blue **HAIR** Black
SPECIAL POWERS/ABILITIES Immortal and invulnerable; Krona's vast psionic abilities were increased by the demon Nekron to surpass the powers of the Guardians of the Universe.

More than ten billion years ago on the planet Oa, the scientist Krona ignored his people's admonition against seeking the origins of the universe. He built a temporal viewer to peel back the veil of time. What Krona saw changed the whole fabric of the universe. As he gazed transfixed at the hand of creation reaching into a star-filled cosmos, Krona's machine exploded and reality changed irrevocably. One universe became two, splitting into positive-matter and anti-matter halves. The MONITOR, and his evil doppelganger, the Anti-Monitor, were born and a wave of evil engulfed the 50 million worlds of the positive-matter universe (*see* Great Battles, pp. 362–3).

The Oan GUARDIANS OF THE UNIVERSE punished Krona by turning his body into pure energy and shooting him across the breadth of the Multiverse. Billions of years later, Krona escaped his disembodied exile and entered the dimension of the dead ruled by the demon Nekron. He restored Krona to corporeal form and gave him the power to take revenge on the Guardians. Following massive battles with the GREEN LANTERN CORPS, GREEN LANTERN Hal Jordan forced Krona's armies back into Nekron's demonic realm. No one knows whether Krona is aware that the multiverse has returned in the wake of the Infinite Crisis. **SB**

KRYPTONITE MAN

FIRST APPEARANCE SUPERBOY #83 (September 1960)
STATUS Villain **REAL NAME** K. Russell Abernathy
OCCUPATION Criminal scientist **BASE** Metropolis
HEIGHT 6ft **WEIGHT** 185 lbs **EYES** Black **HAIR** Black
SPECIAL POWERS/ABILITIES Enhanced strength, ability to control and emit kryptonite radiation.

The Kryptonite Man is Dr. K. Russell Abernathy, a brilliant Metropolis researcher determined to use the unique radioactivity found in the pieces of SUPERMAN's homeworld for useful purposes. His early experiments used monkeys as test subjects, but Abernathy's growing boldness led to kryptonite infecting every cell of his body. Driven insane by the radioactive poisoning, he went on a rampage until stopped by SUPERGIRL, who had taken over Superman's duties while the Man of Steel regained his powers following the Infinite Crisis.

Incarcerated for this crime, the Kryptonite Man became the prisoner of Lex Luthor (*see* LUTHOR, LEX), who used him as a power source during his hunt for a buried Kryptonian battleship. The Kryptonite Man escaped prison a second time with help from his irradiated lab monkey. His plans to obtain funding from underworld kingpins came to an end when Jimmy Olsen (*see* OLSEN, JIMMY) burst into his lair under the identity of "Mister Action." The Kryptonite Man gained the upper hand until the surprise arrival of KRYPTO, THE SUPERDOG. **DW**

KRYPTO, THE SUPERDOG

FIRST APPEARANCE ADVENTURE COMICS #210 (March 1955)
STATUS Heroic, but not always good **REAL NAME** Krypto
OCCUPATION Superman's best friend **BASE** Fortress of Solitude
HEIGHT 25.5in **WEIGHT** 40 lbs **EYES** Blue **HAIR** White
SPECIAL POWERS/ABILITIES Under Earth's solar radiation, Krypto is as enhanced among animals as Superman is among mortals with superior strength, invulnerability, and the power of flight.

SUPERMAN is believed to have met Krypto during his brief infancy on Krypton. After the planet's destruction, the El's family pet somehow traveled to Earth. He soon re-established contact with Kal-El, sharing many of his powers including flight, super-strength, and heat vision. With the sun's radiation enhancing his abilities, Krypto proved to be too exuberant for Superman's Metropolis apartment. Superman has installed his pet in his arctic Fortress of Solitude, although as the occasions require, he is freed to participate in adventures such as the recent Imperiex War (*see* Great Battles, pp. 362–3).

Krypto's keen abilities have been called into use by Superman, and even BATMAN, on more than one occasion. He formed a bond with SUPERBOY during a stay on the KENTS' family farm, but usually resides in the Arctic Fortress. **RG**

IN THE DOGHOUSE
Lois discovers that having a super-powerful pooch to stay in the apartment definitely has its drawbacks.

A SUPERMAN'S BEST FRIEND
Krypto currently resides in Superman's Fortress.

DOWN BOY!
Fortunately for Mongul, the Man of Steel is on hand when Krypto loses his temper defending his master.

BEWARE OF THE DOG
Even a super-villain like Poison Ivy has to watch out when Krypto bares his teeth!

THE DC COMICS ENCYCLOPEDIA

L.E.G.I.O.N.

FIRST APPEARANCE INVASION #2 (1989)
STATUS Heroes   **BASE** The planet Cairn
KEY MEMBERS AND POWERS
Captain Comet (leader) Telekinetic and telepathic abilities.
Davroth Catto Flight, uncanny aerial agility.
Garryn Bek No superhuman abilities.
Marij'n Bek No superhuman abilities.
Darkstar (Lydea Mallor) Projects a negative energy field.
Vril Dox II (retired) 12th level intellect.
Amon Hakk Tremendous Khund strength.
Lobo (no longer active) Amazing regenerative abilities.
Zena Moonstruk Can absorb light and emit it in bursts.
Stealth Can manipulate soundwaves.
Strata Superstrength, invulnerability.
Garv Advanced telepathic abilities.

Formed during an alien invasion of Earth, the Licensed Extra-Governmental Interstellar Operatives Network (L.E.G.I.O.N.) is a heroic peacekeeping force protecting planets that subscribe to its service. The brilliant Coluan, Vril Dox II (son of BRANIAC), founded L.E.G.I.O.N. after he and its original core members escaped from a Dominator-run "Starlag" prison camp. On their first mission, Vril Dox and his compatriots liberated Dox's homeworld of Colu from the domineering grip of the ruling computer tyrants. They then cleaned out the riffraff from the vile planet of Cairn—the galaxy's "drug world"—and made it their headquarters. L.E.G.I.O.N.'s rapid run of successes lured several high-paying clients and attracted new members. The membership roster would remain in constant flux. L.E.G.I.O.N. continued its success until Dox's malevolent son Lyrl usurped control. Several members formed a rival team, R.E.B.E.L.S., to restore L.E.G.I.O.N.'s good name. Vril Dox returned as L.E.G.I.O.N. leader in time for the Rann-Thanagar War. **DW**

PEACE-KEEPING SQUADRON *Some of the key members of L.E.G.I.O.N. past and present:* **1)** *Garryn Bek* **2)** *Telepath* **3)** *Garv* **4)** *Lady Quark* **5)** *Vril Dox II* **6)** *Phase* **7)** *Strata* **8)** *Lobo* **9)** *Captain Comet* **10)** *Marij'n Bek* **11)** *Stealth*

LABRATS

FIRST APPEARANCE LABRATS #1 (April 2002)
STATUS Heroes (deceased)   **BASE** The Campus
MEMBERS AND POWERS
Poe Possesses a high level intellect.
Alex Athlete.
Isaac The team strongman.
Trilby Computer whiz.
Dana Street-smart fighter.
Wu Possesses infiltration abilities.

Products of the mysterious institution known only as "The Campus," the Labrats were investigators, explorers, and guinea pigs. The Campus scientists, for their own mysterious reasons, exploited their eager test subjects by pitting them against various simulated dangers in specially designed virtual reality scenarios. The Labrats, whose oldest member was just 16, were trained in these simulations to handle extreme situations. Most of the Labrats were homeless teenagers, who exchanged their lives as street urchins for this high-tech training.

When their teammate Gia was killed during one of the training programs, they left the Campus, encountering for the first time the very real dangers they had faced only as laboratory simulations, including rogue scientific oddities, UFOs, SUPERMAN, and a theme park populated by genetically engineered monsters. Tragically, their Campus training could not prevent them all from being killed. **PJ**

VIRTUAL REALITY *Scientist Robert Quinlan trained the young Labrats in virtual reality simulators to prepare them for the threats they might face, knowing full well that many might not survive.* **1)** *Alex* **2)** *Poe* **3)** *Isaac* **4)** *Trilby* **5)** *Wu*

LADY BLACKHAWK

FIRST APPEARANCE BLACKHAWK #133 (February 1959)
STATUS Hero   **REAL NAME** Zinda Blake   **OCCUPATION** Pilot, adventurer   **BASE** Metropolis
HEIGHT 5ft 7in   **WEIGHT** 117 lbs   **EYES** Blue   **HAIR** Blonde
SPECIAL POWERS/ABILITIES Expert flyer and markswoman with superior hand-to-hand combat abilities.

Zinda Blake, more commonly known as Lady Blackhawk, became an expert pilot during World War II with the intention of becoming the first female member of the legendary BLACKHAWKS. Soon accepted among their number, Blake joined their wartime exploits and fought KILLER SHARK, who brainwashed her into becoming his queen. After the reality-warping event known as Zero Hour, Lady Blackhawk appeared in the modern era, showing no signs of having aged since the 1940s. When ORACLE offered her a role as the pilot for the BIRDS OF PREY Blake signed aboard, where her hard-drinking, rough-brawling lifestyle made her feel right at home among warriors such as BLACK CANARY II and BIG BARDA. Lady Blackhawk resigned from the team when forced to take orders from SPY SMASHER, but returned once Oracle's leadership role had been restored.

A second woman, Natalie Reed, also went by the code name Lady Blackhawk. Reed's tenure with the Blackhawks covered the end of World War II and many of the Cold War years. **DW**

OLD SOLDIER *Zinda Blake has battled evil since the 1940s. She is able to fly any type of aircraft, is a crack shot and an expert in unarmed combat, and can drink any challenger under the table.*

LADY SHIVA

WORLD'S GREATEST FIGHTER

FIRST APPEARANCE RICHARD DRAGON, KUNG-FU FIGHTER #5 (January 1976)
STATUS Villain **REAL NAME** Sandra Woosan (Lady Shiva Wu-San)
OCCUPATION Martial artist **BASE** Mobile
HEIGHT 5ft 8in **WEIGHT** 141 lbs **EYES** Brown **HAIR** Black
SPECIAL POWERS/ABILITIES Lady Shiva is a master of virtually every known (and several forgotten) martial-arts disciplines; will stop at nothing to become the world's best and most lethal fighter.

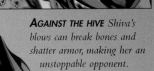
AGAINST THE HIVE *Shiva's blows can break bones and shatter armor, making her an unstoppable opponent.*

When evil industrialist Guano Cravat falsely convinced Sandra Woosan that fellow martial artist Richard Dragon (*see* DRAGON, RICHARD) had murdered her sister Carolyn, Woosan vowed vengeance. As "Lady Shiva," Woosan fought Dragon before Cravat's deception was revealed. Lady Shiva then allied herself with Dragon and the BRONZE TIGER (Dragon's friend and partner, Ben Turner) to dismantle Cravat's criminal consortium while serving as an operative of G.O.O.D., a U.S. government-sponsored spy organization. Later, Shiva opted for solo intrigue as a mercenary and hired assassin, honing her already formidable martial-arts skills to optimum efficiency. In this regard, Shiva has fought on both sides of the law.

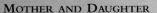
CHALLENGERS *Being the best martial-artist in the world requires Shiva to beat down the upstarts and pretenders.*

LIVING WEAPON

She is credited with training the QUESTION to become a better brawler, as well as helping BATMAN to regain the use of his legs and fighting spirit after the terrorist Bane had crippled him. However, both heroes know well that Lady Shiva's loyalties are capricious.

When it suits her, Shiva wields ninja and samurai arms with deadly grace. But her own body is a far more formidable weapon. In her years traveling the world, Shiva has blended the fighting finesse of judo, koroshi, karate, savate, capoeira, kung-fu, and countless other martial arts to create a style ideally suited for her size and frame. Opponents underestimate Shiva to their dying dismay.

TOP OF HER GAME *Constant training and frequent life-or-death battles have kept Lady Shiva as skilled as ever as the years have passed.*

MOTHER AND DAUGHTER

The emergence of BATGIRL Cassandra Cain shed new light on Lady Shiva's history. During Shiva's assassins' training, David Cain (*see* CAIN, DAVID) murdered her sister. Driven to even greater feats of martial artistry through her drive for revenge, Shiva achieved excellence within the League of Assassins, and eventually bore a daughter—Cassandra—with Cain.

After Cassandra took on the mantle of Batgirl, Shiva challenged her to a series of death-duels, never revealing the truth of their relationship. In their final confrontation, Cassandra died and returned to life in a Lazarus Pit, then defeated Shiva and left her for dead.

With her daughter taking the reigns of the League of Assassins, Lady Shiva chose to follow a new path. Following the Infinite Crisis, ORACLE allowed her to join the BIRDS OF PREY. Using the name "Jade Canary," Shiva took the place of BLACK CANARY, who had agreed to undergo a recreation of Shiva's own training in Vietnam. Her time with the Birds of Prey did little to temper Shiva's ruthless instincts.

In Vietnam Black Canary befriended a young girl, Sin, who had been designated Shiva's eventual successor. After bringing the girl back to the United States, Canary did her best to raise Sin as her own daughter. Shiva recently took Bethany Thorne, daughter of the villainous Crime Doctor, as her new apprentice. **SB/DW**

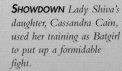
SHOWDOWN *Lady Shiva's daughter, Cassandra Cain, used her training as Batgirl to put up a formidable fight.*

MEETING OF THE MINDS *By exchanging lives for a year, Lady Shiva and Black Canary grew to understand one another and the choices each had made in life.*

KEY STORYLINES
- **BATMAN #509 (JULY 1994)** After Bane snaps Batman's spine, Lady Shiva helps the Dark Knight work his way back to fighting strength.
- **BATGIRL #26 (MAY 2002):** Lady Shiva's daughter, Cassandra Cain, uses her Batgirl training to defeat her mother in combat.
- **BIRDS OF PREY #92 (MAY 2006):** Temporarily working for the good guys as a member of Oracle's Birds of Prey, Lady Shiva makes her debut as the Jade Canary.

THE DC COMICS ENCYCLOPEDIA

LANE, LOIS

WORLD-CLASS REPORTER

FIRST APPEARANCE ACTION COMICS #1 (June 1938)
STATUS Hero **REAL NAME** Lois Joanne Lane
OCCUPATION Reporter **BASE** Metropolis
HEIGHT 5ft 6in **WEIGHT** 136 lbs **EYES** Blue **HAIR** Black
SPECIAL POWERS/ABILITIES Superb investigative journalist with an instinctive "nose" for a good story; trained in various hand-to-hand combat techniques and an adequate marksman.

A PULITZER PRIZE-WINNING JOURNALIST, Lois Lane specializes in reporting from the front lines of war zones and natural catastrophes for Metropolis's *Daily Planet* newspaper. One day a truly incredible story presented itself right in her own backyard. While covering a LexCorp-engineered disaster in Metropolis with young photographer Jimmy Olsen (*see* OLSEN, JIMMY), Lois was rescued from certain death by a superstrong flying man. She became the very first reporter to record the exploits of the amazing costumed champion she named SUPERMAN. Her world, already full of activity, had just been turned upside down.

AWAY FROM IT ALL *Superman and Lois take a well-earned break from saving the world.*

A NOSE FOR NEWS

The daughter of General Sam and Elinore Lane, Lois was born in a U.S. Army hospital outside of Wiesbaden, Germany. Sam Lane had always wanted a boy, and did not hide his disappointment from Lois, who became a model of self-sufficiency in response to her father's emotional distance. After high school, Lois moved to Metropolis and worked full time at the *Daily Planet*. She also attracted the attention of Lex Luthor (*see* LUTHOR, LEX); however, Lois spurned his every advance.

DADDY DEAREST *Sam Lane always wanted a son and was never close to Lois.*

Lois rapidly became the *Daily Planet*'s leading investigative reporter, winning many awards and a daredevil reputation. After Superman's first appearance, she befriended both the Man of Steel and a new, mild-mannered reporter named Clark Kent. Of course, the biggest story was right under Lois's nose: Clark and Superman were one and the same person!

Over time and countless adventures, Lois and Clark fell in love and became engaged. Shortly after, Clark revealed his secret identity to Lois. Shocked as she was, she still agreed to marry him, as she loved Clark regardless and was moved that he had shared his secret with her. Tragedy struck when the Kryptonian creature DOOMSDAY seemingly killed Superman during a violent rampage through the streets of Metropolis. Devastated, Lois cradled her dying lover in her arms as the life slowly ebbed from Superman's body. But Lois did not have to mourn for long, and upon Superman's return from the dead, the couple had a joyous reunion.

During one of the JOKER's visits to the city, Lois was shocked to discover that Superman was willing to let her die rather than kill the villain to save her life. Her doubts fueled by this and other factors, she broke off her engagement to Clark and accepted an offer to become the *Planet*'s foreign correspondent. However, at the last minute she realized that she still loved Clark, and the happy couple were finally married.

INTREPID REPORTER *Lois never shies away from a good story.*

Luthor then bought the financially troubled *Daily Planet* and closed it down. Lois was one of the few who retained jobs with Luthor's media enterprise, LexCom. Lex eventually sold the paper back to its editor, Perry White (*see* WHITE, PERRY), having secretly arranged a deal whereby Lois agreed to kill one story of Luthor's choosing in the future. Lois's discovery that Luthor had had advance knowledge of the coming war with IMPERIEX (*see* Great Battles, pp. 362-3) became the scoop that she reluctantly agreed to kill. Meanwhile, Clark and Lois faced a different crisis: Lois had been impersonated for weeks by the PARASITE, a villain who sought to destroy all that Superman stood for. With BATMAN's help, Superman rescued the real Lois after the Parasite died as a result of his backfired scheme. Lois's father

TRUE LOVE *Despite separations, spats, and death-defying moments, Clark and Lois are deeply in love.*

was a casualty of the Imperiex War, and she grieved that their relationship would now never be repaired. She remains dedicated to her journalistic ideals, regardless of the danger they place her in, and her relationship with Clark has never been stronger.

KEY STORYLINES

- **ACTION COMICS #662 (1991):** Clark reveals the secret of his identity to his fiancée.
- **SUPERMAN: THE WEDDING ALBUM (1996):** Lois marries Clark in the wedding of the century!
- **SUPERMAN (2ND SERIES) #151 (2001):** Lois makes her deal with Luthor, in order to save the Daily Planet.
- **ADVENTURES OF SUPERMAN #631 (2004):** Lois is shot and gravely wounded while covering the U.S. occupation of Umec in the Middle East.

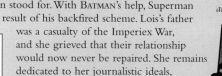 

MR. MAJESTIC *While an amnesiac Superman was trapped in the bottled city of Kandor, Lois dealt with the appearance of Mr. Majestic, who helped restore Metropolis.*

NEW FACES, NEW CHALLENGES

Lois helped ease Kara Zor-El's transition into Earth culture, welcoming her as a member of Clark's extended family and supporting her transition into Supergirl. But Lois' ties to Superman continued to put her at risk. During the "Crisis of Conscience," members of the Secret Society of Super Villains – all of whom had once been mind-wiped to forget the secret identities of the Justice League – temporarily regained their memories and lashed out at the League's loved ones.

ATTACKING THE INNOCENT *With knowledge of the Justice League's secret identities, the Secret Society took revenge on Superman by targeting Lois Lane and the Daily Planet.*

LIGHT AS A FEATHER *With all they have been through, Lois and Superman are still the perfect pair, with Lois providing a cynic's eye to complement her husband's too-trusting nature.*

GROUNDED FOR A YEAR

Crisis, Lois adjusted to life with a husband who had lost his powers. Clark's trip through the heart of a red sun had stripped him of his superhuman abilities, leaving him Clark Kent full time and making him a fixture at the Daily Planet and in their Metropolis apartment. Lois began to enjoy their new, low-key lifestyle and prepared for the possibility that the change might be permanent. But in time Clark's powers came back to him. Lois unequivocally supported his return to his role as Superman, explaining that his job was one of the reasons she loved him and that she's behind him all the way.

CHRISTOPHER KENT

A big change came into Lois' life when a mysterious Kryptonian boy arrived on Earth. After Superman removed the child from government custody in the Department of Metahuman Affairs, Lois and Clark agreed to give him a relatively normal life in Metropolis as their foster son.

Batman created false documentation establishing the boy as Christopher Kent. Lois helped teach him English and immersed him in the small joys of the big city. To conceal his abilities, particularly from his teachers and classmates, Christopher wore a wristwatch that mimicked the blocking qualities of a red sun.

Yet having a second Kryptonian in the house has brought substantial danger to Lois, particularly after the truth of Christopher's parentage became known. The boy had been born to Ursa and General Zod, conceived during their exile in the Phantom Zone and raised in a floating prison where the Phantom Zone's time-stasis did not apply. When General Zod escaped the Phantom Zone, he seized his son, captured Lois, and attempted a planetary takeover.

Shortly after Zod's rampage, outer-space marauders raided Earth on a hunt for the lost Kryptonian city of Kandor. Their vendetta against all Kryptonians put Lois and Christopher in peril until Superman, Power Girl, and Karsta Wor-Ul captured the enemy leader at the Fortress of Solitude. Despite the stakes and her vulnerability, Lois is determined to protect Christopher at all costs. RG/DW

RAISED BY THE ENEMY *As the son of the supervillains General Zod and Ursa, Christopher Kent experienced a troubled upbringing inside the Phantom Zone.*

LADY FLASH

FIRST APPEARANCE The Flash (2nd series) #7 (December 1987)
STATUS Villain **REAL NAME** Christina Alexandrova
OCCUPATION Assassin **BASE** Mobile
HEIGHT 6ft 1in **WEIGHT** 155 lbs **EYES** Brown **HAIR** Auburn
SPECIAL POWERS/ABILITIES Granted superspeed from a mixture of drugs and gene therapy, she also gained abnormal strength, but her wits were dulled as a result.

Christina has always been a joiner, starting Blue Trinity, a failed Soviet attempt to create a team of speedsters. After their final defeat at the hands of the FLASH, she became VANDAL SAVAGE's slave, kept under his control through cocaine addiction. It was he who gave her one of Wally West's spare Flash uniforms to use in her latest identity of Lady Flash. She finally broke free of both the addiction and Savage's control and sided with the Flash to defeat the immortal. Rejected by the Flash, however, she wandered aimlessly until she fell under the influence of SAVITAR, the corrupt master of speed. She opposed WONDER WOMAN and Jesse Quick (see QUICK, JESSE) when she attempted to obtain a scroll that might have helped her free Savitar after his defeat. She was believed to be lost in the Speed Force, but she survived. Finally, she worked with KOBRA only to be defeated once again, this time by a right cross from Flash's wife, Linda Park (see PARK, LINDA). **RG**

LADY OF THE LAKE

FIRST APPEARANCE Aquaman (4th series) #1 (February 2003)
STATUS Ally **REAL NAME** Unknown
OCCUPATION Water spirit **BASE** The Secret Sea
HEIGHT 5ft 8in **WEIGHT** 137 lbs **EYES** Blue **HAIR** Blue
SPECIAL POWERS/ABILITIES Undefined magical abilities.

This water spirit has appeared to only a few individuals, including AQUAMAN (Arthur Curry) and King Arthur. According to Arthurian legend the Lady gave the king the sword Excalibur. More recently, she has aided Aquaman, exchanging his prosthetic harpoon for a hand made of enchanted water and naming him "the Waterbearer." The Lady inhabits a grotto on an island off the west coast of Ireland, a place known variously as the Secret Sea, the Waters of Truth, or Annwn. Aquaman's hand receives its supernatural powers from the Lady. The hand can heal the injured and create portals into magical dimensions; when used in anger it causes the Lady pain. **DW**

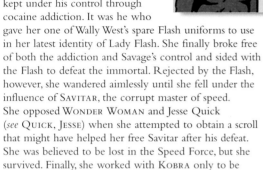

LADY VIC

FIRST APPEARANCE NIGHTWING #4 (January 1997)
STATUS Villain **REAL NAME** Lady Elaine Marsh-Morton
OCCUPATION Assassin **BASE** England
HEIGHT 5ft 6in **WEIGHT** 135 lbs **EYES** Blue **HAIR** Blonde
SPECIAL POWERS/ABILITIES Mastery of arcane weapons and a highly trained hand-to-hand combatant.

Lady Elaine Marsh-Morton took the name Lady Vic—short for Victim— when she entered into her family's long tradition of mercenary work. It is estimated that she is only in her late twenties; however, she has already gained an impressive list of kills, backed up by a reputation for cunning and guile. Those she has battled with include BATMAN and CATWOMAN. In addition to her international clients, she serves on retainer to BLOCKBUSTER II in the town of Blüdhaven. This crime lord has frequently pitted her against NIGHTWING. Lady Vic seems to be one of the few women who is not attracted to the costumed vigilante, and their battles have so far been indecisive. Her skill with the ancestral weapons of her family, including flintlock pistols and various swords, makes her a formidable opponent. Lady Vic numbered among the criminals captured by the SUICIDE SQUAD and deposited on an alien planet during Operation: Salvation Run. **RG**

LANG, LANA

FIRST APPEARANCE SUPERBOY (1st series) #10 (October 1950)
STATUS Ally **REAL NAME** Lana Elizabeth Lang
OCCUPATION Small-business owner **BASE** Metropolis
HEIGHT 5ft 4in **WEIGHT** 127 lbs **EYES** Blue **HAIR** Red
SPECIAL POWERS/ABILITIES Lana is an average athlete, but has a strong will and is fiercely loyal to those she loves.

Lana's friendship with Clark Kent (see SUPERMAN) dates back to their first day of school in Smallville. When Clark resolved to go out into the world and learn how best to use his new superpowers, he asked Lana to come with him. She refused and they didn't see each other for a decade. When a man with amazing powers appeared in Metropolis, Lana knew that man had to be Clark.

Lex Luthor (see LUTHOR, LEX) had been trailing Superman's appearances and, finding his old Smallville schoolmate Lana near Clark's Metropolis apartment, he had her tortured, thinking she had information about the alien. Lana told him nothing and returned to Smallville. Learning that Clark loved Lois Lane, Lana finally agreed to her lifelong pal Pete Ross's proposal of marriage (see ROSS, PETE). Superman saved their baby son's life and so they named the child Clark. When Pete became Vice President, Lana hated being so close to President Luthor and began to feel stifled. It was clear Clark and Lana retained feelings for each other, but neither would act on them. Lana ultimately felt it was unfair to remain married to Pete and they filed for divorce. After the Infinite Crisis, Lana became CEO of LexCorp, and survived an alien attempt to turn her into a new INSECT QUEEN. **RG**

CLARK and Lana From the moment they met, Lana and Clark Kent shared a special bond that has endured, despite wildly divergent life experiences.

DOOMED Lana was comfortable with Pete Ross and said she loved him enough to marry. That has proven to be a false hope.

LADY ZAND

FIRST APPEARANCE YOUNG JUSTICE #50 (December 2002)
STATUS Villain **REAL NAME** Unknown
OCCUPATION Ruler of Zandia **BASE** Zandia
HEIGHT 5ft 10in **WEIGHT** 156 lbs **EYES** Blue **HAIR** Brown
SPECIAL POWERS/ABILITIES Can transform into an earthen giant.

A cruel, quick-tempered aristocrat who possesses considerable elemental powers, Lady Zand is believed to be the founder of the tiny Baltic island nation of Zandia—which, if true, would make her more than 800 years old! In modern times, Zandia has become notorious as a secret haven for on-the-run super-villains. It is also home to the worldwide Church of Blood (see BROTHER BLOOD), a sinister organization that is based upon Lady Zand's ruthless philosophy that might equals right. In recent years, Lady Zand has made concerted efforts to boost Zandia's profile and improve its standing in the world.

She has even sent a small team of athletes to compete in the Olympic games. When angered, Lady Zand possesses an extraordinary ability: she can literally become "the soil of her homeworld," transforming herself into a towering figure made of rock and earth. She demonstrated this ability to great effect in a spectacular battle with the heroes of YOUNG JUSTICE. **DW**

LASHINA

FIRST APPEARANCE MISTER MIRACLE #6 (January 1972)
STATUS Villain   **REAL NAME** Unknown
OCCUPATION Warrior   **BASE** Apokolips
HEIGHT 6ft 6in   **WEIGHT** 225 lbs   **EYES** Blue   **HAIR** Black
SPECIAL POWERS/ABILITIES Enhanced strength and damage resistance; wields electrically-charged whips.

Lashina is the fiercest warrior among the elite Apokolyptian strike force known as the FEMALE FURIES. She is an expert combatant with whips, and wears a costume made of belts and straps. Raised in GRANNY GOODNESS' hellish orphanage, Lashina mastered the warrior's way to survive that crucible, then hungered to lead the Furies. Her ambitions often brought her into conflict with Fury commander Bernadeth.

The Female Furies made numerous attempts to recapture the fugitives MISTER MIRACLE and BIG BARDA, but one mission left Lashina stranded on Earth with amnesia. Now calling herself Duchess, she joined the SUICIDE SQUAD, traveling with her new team to Apokolips and killing Bernadeth, only to die herself soon after. DARKSEID resurrected both Furies, putting them in a dual leadership role. Recently, Lashina and Bernadeth took the Furies to Greece to fight against WONDER GIRL and HERCULES. DW

LEATHER

FIRST APPEARANCE NIGHTWING #62 (December 2001)
STATUS Villain   **REAL NAME** Mary Kay Tanner
OCCUPATION Criminal "coyote"   **BASE** Peckinpah, Texas
HEIGHT 5ft 5in   **WEIGHT** 132 lbs   **EYES** White   **HAIR** Auburn
SPECIAL POWERS/ABILITIES Leatherlike skin; low-level superstrength; razor-sharp claws on hands and feet; psychopathic temperament; armed with a variety of barbed whips.

Tanner's mother often used illegal, highly experimental narcotics to get high, and Mary Kay was born with meta-human powers that gave her leatherlike skin and claws. At 16 she had become the leader of a band of "coyotes," who smuggled illegal immigrants back and forth between Mexico and the U.S. Leather was captured and incarcerated in the women's block of the Slab penitentiary. However, she was freed by the JOKER and has returned to smuggling in Mexico. PJ

LEGION OF SUBSTITUTE HEROES

FIRST APPEARANCE ADVENTURE COMICS #306 (March 1963)
STATUS Heroes   **BASE** Mobile
MEMBERS AND POWERS
Night Girl (Lydda Jath) Possesses superstrength in the dark. **Polar Boy (Brek Bannin)** Generates intense cold. **Chlorophyll Kid (Ral Benem)** Stimulates rapid plant growth. **Color Kid (Ulu Vakk)** Able to alter the color of any object. **Fire Lad (Staq Mavlen)** Exhales fiery breath. **Stone Boy (Dag Wentim)** Capable of turning his body to stone. **Porcupine Pete (Peter Dursin)** Projects quill-like spines at will. **Infectious Lass (Drura Sehpt)** Body hosts a variety of disease colonies. **Antenna Boy (Khfeurb Chee Bez)** Transmits and receives electronic signals via ear-antennae. **Double-Header (Dyvud/Frenk Retzun)** Bickering beings sharing single body.

THE LEGION OF SUPER-HEROES has initiated several recruitment drives to bolster its ranks. However, many young heroes and heroines are turned away by the Legion for lack of experience or for possessing powers deemed too dangerous or unpredictable. Rejected applicants POLAR BOY and NIGHT GIRL decided to form their own Legion of Substitute Heroes—unsanctioned by the United Planets, of course—a team that would allow them to hone their unique abilities and do some good, at least until the real LSH recognized their worth.

Since its formation, the Legion of Substitute Heroes has grown to include Chlorophyll Kid, Color Kid, Fire Lad, and Stone Boy, all of whom may not possess the most spectacular superpowers, but nevertheless want to defend the galaxy in the same grand tradition as the Legion of Super-Heroes. Recently, Polar Boy was selected to join the Legion Cadet Program for training to become a future member of the LSH. The remaining Subs are hopeful that they might follow suit someday soon. SB

LEAGUE OF ASSASSINS

FIRST APPEARANCE STRANGE ADVENTURES #215 (December 1968)
STATUS Villains   **BASE** Worldwide
MEMBERS AND POWERS
Ra's al Ghul Immortal; brilliant criminal mind.
Sensei (deceased) Top martial artist.
Doctor Darrk (deceased) No superhuman abilities.
Kirigi Top martial artist; League of Assassins trainer.
Merlyn (ex-member) Deadly assassin with bow and arrow.
Talia Ra's al Ghul's bewitchingly beautiful daughter.

The League of Assassins operates in secret throughout every country of the world. Called into being by the criminal mastermind RA'S AL GHUL, their original mission was to shield their master from attacks (the League described itself as "the fang which protects his head"), and to accept paying jobs from clients who want someone eliminated and have the deep pockets to hire the best of the best. Only assassins who have already completed a previous hit can be considered for League membership, and its roster is kept strictly confidential.

For many years, day-to-day control of the League of Assassins fell to the Sensei (who oversaw the killers on staff) and Doctor Darrk (who interacted with clients). It was the Sensei who arranged for the death of acrobat Boston Brand, who later became DEADMAN. One of the League's agents, Hook, was involved in the Brand hit, and other League contracts fell under the jurisdiction of the archer Merlyn, whose skill with a bow rivaled that of GREEN ARROW. Eventually the League split into three feuding factions, led by the Sensei, TALIA, and Cassandra Cain (see BATGIRL). DW

Talia   Ra's al Ghul   Contract Assassin

Merlyn   Sensei   Contract Assassin (Hook)

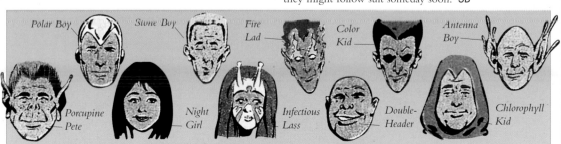

Polar Boy   Stone Boy   Fire Lad   Color Kid   Antenna Boy

Porcupine Pete   Night Girl   Infectious Lass   Double-Header   Chlorophyll Kid

THE LEGION OF SUBSTITUTE HEROES

THE LEGION OF SUPER-HEROES

TEEN DEFENDERS OF TOMORROW

FIRST APPEARANCE ADVENTURE COMICS #247
(April 1958)
STATUS Hero team
BASE Legion HQ, Earth

NOTABLE MEMBERS
Atom Girl (Salu Digby) Shrinking
Brainiac 5 (Querl Dox) Super-intellect
Colossal Boy (Gim Allon) Giant who can shrink to human size
Cosmic Boy (Rokk Krinn) Magnetism
Chameleon (Reep Daggle) Shapeshifting
Dream Girl (Nura Nal) Precognition
Dream Boy (Rol Purtha) Precognition
Element Lad (Jan Arrah) Transmutation
Invisible Kid (Lyle Norg) Invisibility
Karate Kid (Val Armorr) Martial artist
Light Lass (Ayla Ranzz) Gravity manipulation
Lightning Lad (Garth Ranzz) Electricity
Phantom Girl (Tinya Wazzo) Phasing
Princess Projectra (Wilimena Projectra Vauxhall) Illusion
Saturn Girl (Imra Ardeen) Telepathy
Shadow Lass (Tasmia Mallor) Darkforce generation
Star Boy (Thom Kallor) Gravity manipulation
Sun Boy (Dirk Morgna) Heat
Supergirl (Kara Zor-El) Flight, super strength, super speed
Timber Wolf (Brin Londo) Enhanced skills and senses
Triplicate Girl (Luornu Durgo) Splits into three beings

Through every crisis to come in the space-time continuum, one constant is that a group of young heroes and heroines will unite to defend their homeworlds from evil. Whether inspired by the boy who would become SUPERMAN or any of the costumed champions lost to history, the Legion of Super-Heroes will be that bright ray of hope in an uncertain future.

TIMELINE REBOOTS
The Legion has undergone numerous cosmic restructurings, with every universe-shaking crisis triggering major reworkings of the Legion's history and membership. The lineup from the original timeline drew its inspiration from young Clark Kent's adventures as SUPERBOY, and featured a core team of COSMIC BOY, SATURN GIRL, and LIGHTNING LAD. Over time this team swelled to include dozens of members, who stood against the universe's most dire threats including DARKSEID and the sorceress Glorith. Eventually the alien Dominators overran Earth and caused the planet's destruction. The clean-slate timeline that followed Zero Hour erased this Legion from history, replacing it with a similar lineup known for its alternate codenames ("Live Wire" for Lightning Lad) and fresh threats such as the BLIGHT. The reality warps of the Infinite Crisis brought into existence a third Legion—but the rebirth of the multiverse indicates that all previous Legions currently exist in the future timelines of parallel worlds.

TOGETHER *Flight rings raised to the sky, the teenaged Legionnaires stand ready to defend the United Planets*

PHANTOMS *The dimension-phasing abilities of Phantom Girl allowed her to communicate with Mon-El, who had been trapped in the Phantom Zone for a millennium.*

SUPERGIRL AND MON-EL
Kara Zor-El, the SUPERGIRL from the 21st century, traveled to the Legion's future during the Infinite Crisis. Stripped of her memories, she initially believed the entire experience to be a hallucination, but soon earned her place as a revered Legionnaire. Supergirl helped bring the 20th century Daxamite hero MON-EL into the Legion. While visiting Supergirl in the re-enlarged Kryptonian city of Kandor, Saturn Girl detected Mon-El's ghostly presence in the Phantom Zone, where Brainiac 5's tinkering released him from his thousand-year prison.

SUPER-BRAWL Maddened by prison, Mon-El lashed out at Supergirl, nearly destroying Legion headquarters in the process.

HOME SWEET HOME *The Legion headquarters on Earth is a focal point for non-powered teenagers from all walks of life.*

THE LATEST LEGION
In the current continuity following the Infinite Crisis, the Legion of Super-Heroes emerged on a 31st century Earth governmental surveillance had become a way of life. With parents keeping obsessive tabs on their children, a teenage rebellion sprang up centered on admiration for the colorful superheroes a thousand years prior. The headquarters of the Legion of Super-Heroes served as a beacon for thousands of disaffected teenagers, who camped outside hoping for a glimpse of their champions. BRAINIAC 5 of Colu proved the mastermind of the team, designing their flight rings and keeping tabs on trouble spots across the United Planets. Cosmic Boy, Saturn Girl, and Lightning Lad remained the heart of the Legion, with ELEMENT LAD lending the ability to transmute objects, ULTRA BOY serving as the team's powerhouse, the shapeshifting CHAMELEON excelling as a spy, and the rookie INVISIBLE KID providing a fresh perspective on the Legion's heroics. COLOSSAL BOY, a member of a race of giants from Antarctica, possessed the ability to shrink to human size, and unsuccessfully petitioned for the name Micro-Lad. The United Planets wanted nothing to do with the team, and hoped to discredit them and their philosophy of non-conformity.

INTO THE FRAY *Although initially classified as outlaws, the Legionnaires now work with the Science Police and are recognized by the United Planets.*

THE WANDERERS

Mon-El became the latest recruit of the Wanderers, a militant superpowered team led by Mekt Ranzz (see LIGHTNING LORD), brother of siblings Lighting Lad and Light Lass (see SPARK). Originally the covert squad had assembled to combat threats to the United Planets, but Mekt rebuilt the team following a crushing defeat at the hands of the Dominators, making the extermination of the Dominators his top priority. Mekt tried to recruit many Legionnaires, but considered the Legionnaires ineffectual idealists who would only get in the way of his war. When the Dominators attacked Earth with genetically-modified warriors, the Legion and the Wanderers united to end the threat. The war ended with the invasion and apparent destruction of the Dominator homeworld. In reality, the planet had merely been shunted to the Phantom Zone, but Cosmic Boy took the blame for the seeming act of genocide and dropped out of sight. Supergirl became Legion chairperson in his absence, but soon returned to the 21st century.

THE LIGHTNING SAGA

After the Infinite Crisis, the original Legion lineup reasserted itself in Superman's life. The Legion's adventures with young Clark Kent returned to the timeline, and the members of this Legion reappeared in the 21st century during the "Lightning Saga." The Legionnaires had come to the past to restore a hero, using lightning rods in a ritual similar to the one that had once brought Lightning

SHOCKING RETURN *In their time-traveling trip to the 21st century, the Legionnaires brought back the Flash from an alternate dimension.*

Lad back from the dead. After allying with the Justice League and the Justice Society, the Legionnaires succeeded in bringing back Wally West, the third Flash. Most Legionnaires returned to their own timeline, but KARATE KID and Triplicate Girl (see TRIAD)—who had lost her duplicates and now called herself "Una"—undertook their own 21st century adventure and discovered a new strain of the OMAC virus. Karate Kid and Una later met Supergirl, who had returned from the 31st century with a different version of the Legion. Supergirl recognized these Legionnaires as alternate versions of the ones she had known in the future, proving that *both* versions of the Legion now existed in the multiverse. Superman traveled to this Legion's 31st century, where the planet's inhabitants were indoctrinated with anti-alien beliefs. Earth-Man led the "Justice League of Earth." With the human world no longer in the United Planets due to xenophobia, its inhabitants believed that the Superman of the 21st century was human, and the tales of his Kryptonian heritage were lies. The Legion of Super-Heroes, persecuted in this new society, went underground. Superman helped the surviving Legionnaires restore justice to Earth.
SB/DW

RED SUN *In the Legion's future, a powerless Superman helped battle the villainous Justice League that ruled all of Earth.*

LEMARIS, LORI

FIRST APPEARANCE SUPERMAN (1st series) #129 (May 1959)
STATUS Hero **REAL NAME** Lori Lemaris
OCCUPATION Scientist **BASE** Metropolis
HEIGHT 5ft 9in **WEIGHT** 243 lbs (with tail) **EYES** Brown **HAIR** Brown
SPECIAL POWERS/ABILITIES An actual mermaid; can communicate telepathically and breathe underwater; grows legs when on land.

UNDERWATER LOVE *Before Lois Lane, mermaid Lori was the girl who melted the heart of the Man of Steel.*

A mermaid belonging to the undersea realm of Tritonis, Lori Lemaris began a relationship with Clark Kent while both attended Metropolis University. Lori concealed her tail beneath a blanket and moved about in a wheelchair. Eventually SUPERMAN discovered the truth, but Lori chose to remain with her people, marrying the merman scientist Ronal after he nursed her back to health following an injury. Contrary to some reports, Lori Lemaris survived her encounter with the Anti-Monitor's shadow-demons during the Crisis (*see* Great Battles, pp. 362–3). Later, Ronal's sorcery enabled her to grow legs on land. She went to live in Metropolis and was a bridesmaid at Clark and Lois Lane's wedding (*see* LANE, LOIS). Lori was a member of the "Justice League of Atlantis" during the JUSTICE LEAGUE OF AMERICA's struggle against the Advance Man. **DW**

LEVIATHAN

FIRST APPEARANCE LEGIONNAIRES #0 (April 1993)
STATUS Hero (deceased) **REAL NAME** Gim Allon
OCCUPATION Legionnaire **BASE** Legion World
HEIGHT 6ft 2in **WEIGHT** 200 lbs **EYES** Brown **HAIR** Brown
SPECIAL POWERS/ABILITIES Could increase his size and mass at will, up to a height of 30ft.

In one timeline, the Legionnaire Colossal Boy is known as Leviathan. Gim Allon, a resident of Mars, graduated from the Science Police Academy. During the high-speed pursuit of a suspect, an accident involving a radioactive meteorite gave him the ability to become a giant at will. The government of Mars named him the Martian representative to the LEGION OF SUPER-HEROES, where he took the code name Leviathan.

The United Planets appointed Allon as team leader, but after a disastrous mission that resulted in the death of Kid Quantum I (*see* KID QUANTUM I & II), he relinquished control to COSMIC BOY and became deputy leader. Later, after his teammate SHRINKING VIOLET became possessed by the omnipotent Emerald Eye, Leviathan sacrificed his life to defeat the evil Doctor Regulus. He received a hero's funeral on Shanghalla.

In an alternate Legion timeline, Gim Allon is a member of a race of Antarctic giants who has the ability to shrink to normal human size. He goes by the name Colossal Boy, despite his protests that "Micro Lad" is more accurate. **DW**

GOLIATH *An easy target while a giant, Leviathan's proportional strength made him virtually unstoppable.*

LIBERTY BELLE

FIRST APPEARANCE BOY COMMANDOS #1 (Winter 1942)
STATUS Hero **REAL NAME** Libby Belle Lawrence
OCCUPATION Journalist; broadcaster **BASE** New York City
HEIGHT 5ft 6in **WEIGHT** 140 lbs **EYES** Blue **HAIR** White (was blonde)
SPECIAL POWERS/ABILITIES Can project sonic blasts from her hands; gains superstrength when the Liberty Belle is rung.

Libby Lawrence is the descendant of the Revolutionary War heroine MISS LIBERTY. A champion athlete in school when her father was killed in 1939 by Nazis in Poland, Libby escaped by swimming the English Channel, becoming an international celebrity. Libby gained superpowers through a mystic link to the Liberty Bell and became Liberty Belle, a founder member of the ALL-STAR SQUADRON. After being irradiated by one of the Nazi BARON BLITZKRIEG's weapons, Liberty Belle gained her sonic powers. She married fellow crime fighter Johnny Quick (*see* QUICK, JOHNNY), and their daughter Jesse later became the hero Jesse Quick (*see* QUICK, JESSE). Jesse became the new Liberty Belle following the Infinite Crisis. She serves as a member of the JUSTICE SOCIETY OF AMERICA alongside her new husband Rick Tyler (HOURMAN II). **PJ**

LIGHTNING LORD

FIRST APPEARANCE SUPERMAN (1st series) #147 (August 1961)
STATUS Villain **REAL NAME** Mekt Ranzz
OCCUPATION Super-villain **BASE** Winath
HEIGHT 5ft 11in **WEIGHT** 167 lbs **EYES** Blue **HAIR** White
SPECIAL POWERS/ABILITIES Absorbs electricity and projects bolts of lightning of huge destructive power.

In one timeline, Mekt Ranzz and his younger brother and sister, twins Garth and Ayla, were attacked by lightning beasts after crashing on the planet Korbal. The physiologies of all three were altered by the electrical energies generated by the beasts, enabling them to project powerful lightning blasts. Garth and Ayla became members of the LEGION OF SUPER-HEROES as LIVE WIRE and SPARK. Mekt used his powers for thievery and murder as Lightning Lord. In one alternate Legion timeline, Lightning Lord, Cosmic King, and SATURN QUEEN molded young Bruce Wayne and Clark Kent into planetary dictators. In another, Mekt Ranzz does not use a costumed identity, and leads the superpowered commandos known as the WANDERERS. **SB**

LIGHTRAY

FIRST APPEARANCE NEW GODS (1st series) #1 (March 1971)
STATUS Hero (deceased) **REAL NAME** Solis
OCCUPATION New God **BASE** New Genesis
HEIGHT 6ft **WEIGHT** 181 lbs **EYES** Blue **HAIR** Red
SPECIAL POWERS/ABILITIES Can fly and harness all the various frequencies of the light spectrum, using its radiation to either temporarily blind opponents or to punch through objects; a super-strong, agile combatant; maintains a cheerful outlook on life.

Solis grew up a happy child on the planet New Genesis, befriending ORION, scion of DARKSEID, who also came to grow up on the planet of light. One day, while exploring, they found a pit where soldiers from Apokolips were massing for an assault. No ordinary soldiers, they had been turned into living masses of light. Solis was spotted and pelted with solar radiation. The scientific genius METRON summoned help, and arrived to find Solis in a coma.

After many months, Metron successfully revived the boy, who had absorbed all the radiation and was now changed, imbued with new abilities. Solis eventually mastered these powers, renaming himself Lightray. Lightray was the first to fall during the Death of the NEW GODS event. After appearing in Metropolis on the hunt for Fourth World youths that had escaped from his care, he fell victim to a mysterious assassin. **RG**

LILITH

FIRST APPEARANCE TEEN TITANS #25 (January/February 1970)
STATUS Hero (deceased) REAL NAME Lilith Clay
OCCUPATION Adventurer BASE New York City
HEIGHT 5ft 5in WEIGHT 104 lbs EYES Green HAIR Red
SPECIAL POWERS/ABILITIES Telepathy, precognition.

Lilith Clay is a fallen TEEN TITAN, having served with the team during several of its incarnations until dying in a needless accident. Possessing vast mental abilities including telepathy and precognition, Lilith joined the Titans while still an adolescent and helped found their original splinter team, Titans West.

Her mental abilities helped her purge the demonic TRIGON from the soul of her teammate RAVEN. Later, a restructured Titans welcomed Lilith into their ranks under the code name Omen. She also helped found the villainous TARTARUS under orders from VANDAL SAVAGE, but sabotaged his efforts by selecting members with warring egos that soon led to the team's break-up.

When the android INDIGO arrived from the future to attack the Titans and YOUNG JUSTICE, Lilith and Donna Troy (see TROY, DONNA) died at the hands of a renegade Superman robot. Although Donna Troy has since returned, Lilith is memorialized with a statue at Titans Tower in San Francisco. DW

LINEAR MEN

FIRST APPEARANCE Adventures of Superman #476 (March 1991)
STATUS Hero team BASE Vanishing Point
CURRENT MEMBERS AND POWERS
DR. MATTHEW RYDER (LEADER) Scientific genius.
Dr. Rip Hunter Time-travel inventor.
Liri Lee Chronal archivist.
Travis O'Connell (deceased) Adventurer.
Waverider (Matthew Ryder from an alternate timeline) Possesses the ability to freely travel the timestream and pinpoint chronal anomalies.

The Linear Men are "time police" who try to keep the past and future safe from careless time travelers. Leader Matthew Ryder discovered the Vanishing Point realm outside of space and time, where the Linear Men now maintain their base. Due to the physical stresses of time travel, pieces of the Linear Men's bodies have been replaced with cyborg limbs. The Linear Men played a key role in the fight against GOG, revealing the existence of a "hypertime" containing all possible alternate timestreams. After SUPERMAN defeated IMPERIEX by sending him back to the Big Bang, the Linear Men attempted to have the Man of Steel tried for crimes against the timeline. They now appear to have shunned their physical forms and appear only as manifestations of the intellect. DW

MATTHEW RIDER
Liri Lee
RIP HUNTER

LIONHEART

FIRST APPEARANCE JUSTICE LEAGUE INTERNATIONAL ANNUAL #4 1993
STATUS Hero REAL NAME Richard Plante
OCCUPATION Government operative BASE London, England
HEIGHT 6ft 1in WEIGHT 186 lbs EYES Blue HAIR Black
SPECIAL POWERS/ABILITIES Advanced armor enhances strength and permits flight; wields energy sword and shield.

A former union dockworker, Richard Plante's bravery and fierce loyalty to his native United Kingdom made him an ideal recruit to defend England as a government operative. Clad in advanced armor and wielding a blazing energy sword, Plante—a direct descendant of King Richard I—dubbed himself Lionheart after his namesake. Allied with Justice League International (see JUSTICE LEAGUE OF AMERICA), Lionheart battled modern-day dragons in the form of alien parasites murdering humans across the globe. Lionheart remains an active defender of the U.K. SB

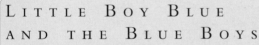

KNIGHT IN SHINING ARMOR
A dauntless knight in high-tech armor, Lionheart battles to protect Britons from super-villain threats as a modern-day dragonslayer.

LITTLE BOY BLUE AND THE BLUE BOYS

FIRST APPEARANCE SENSATION COMICS #1 (1942)
STATUS Hero team REAL NAMES Tommy Rogers, "Tubby", Herbert "Toughy" Simms, Little Miss Redhead
BASE Radiance, Pennsylvania
SPECIAL POWERS/ABILITIES Quick wits, good humor, and fast fists.

Frustrated by Wolf Lupo's crime wave in Big City, youngsters Tommy Rogers, "Tubby", and Herbert "Toughy" Simms took matters into their own hands as Little Boy Blue and the Blue Boys. They continued to have lighthearted adventures, thwarting all manner of criminals during the 1940s. At one point, a mysterious girl known as Little Miss Redhead arrived to fight crime beside them, using a lariat and bolo. Decades later, Tommy became the mayor and Herb the sheriff. When Tommy's son Shawn discovered his dad's diary and learned of the parents' costumed exploits, the children were inspired. Herb's son Timmy was nicknamed "Static" for his fascination with radios, while Tubby's son was a skateboarder dubbed "Slats." DOCTOR LIGHT I came to town to plunder it, and the boys saw an opportunity to help. The hapless criminal was soundly defeated by the three boys. A new Boy Blue appeared as part of VIGILANTE's doomed team that fought the Sheeda. RG

LIGHTNING LAD

HIGHLY-CHARGED HERO

FIRST APPEARANCE ADVENTURE COMICS # 247 (April 1958)
STATUS Hero **REAL NAME** Garth Ranzz
OCCUPATION Super-hero **BASE** Legion Headquarters
HEIGHT 6ft 2in **WEIGHT** 190 lbs **EYES** Blue **HAIR** Red
SPECIAL POWERS/ABILITIES Absorbs electrical energy;. generates and controls fields of electrical energy and can channel this energy through his hands, projecting it as a powerful super-heated discharge with properties similar to that of lightning; body is a natural insulator, so he is not harmed by his own powers.

GARTH RANZZ OF WINATH is Lightning Lad, a core member of the LEGION OF SUPER-HEROES in all versions of the Legion that have arisen throughout the timeline. Twins are common on Winath, and both Garth and his sister Ayla (Light Lass) have superpowers—Garth can generate bolts of electricity, and Ayla can manipulate gravity (and has possessed electrical abilities in other timelines). Their older brother Mekt (*see* LIGHTNING LORD) has abilities similar to Garth's, but his status as a single-birth caused others to view him with suspicion and hostility. Mekt joined the United Planets as a covert commando, and later assembled the WANDERERS to battle the alien Dominators.

FAMILY TIES *The Ranzz siblings have all become adventurers, with Ayla manipulating gravity as Light Lass and Mekt heading up the Wanderers.*

HOTHEAD *Lightning Lad's short temper—and his short attention span—have made him an inconsistent and unpredictable Legion leader.*

MAKING HIS MARK

Garth and Ayla, meanwhile, joined the more colorful Legion, with Garth helping found the organization alongside COSMIC BOY and SATURN GIRL. The Legion stood for personal freedom on a repressive Earth that monitored its teenagers and frowned on uniqueness. As Lightning Lad, Garth numbered among the Legion's most powerful members, battling the insurgents of Terror Firma and even his own brother, who viewed the Legion as idealistic meddlers. Garth and Mekt later united to fight off a Dominator invasion of Earth.

Lightning Lad took over as Legion leader following SUPERGIRL's return to the 21st century. His immaturity and short attention span led to problems, as he struggled to keep track of Legionnaire missions while dealing with the demands of the United Planets, who now enjoyed a formal relationship with the Legion. Garth's good heart kept him on track, as did the love of occasional girlfriend Saturn Girl.

An alternate version of Lightning Lad appeared in the mainstream Earth's timeline during the events of the "Lightning Saga," in which the Legionnaires traveled to the 21st century to restore a lost hero (Wally West, the third FLASH). This Lightning Lad had previously died and experienced a resurrection via energy channeled through lightning rods, the same method used to bring back the Flash. SUPERMAN later traveled to the 31st century to visit this Legion later in their history, when the Earth's sun had turned red and its citizens had grown fearful and protectionist.

A third version of Garth Ranzz went by the code name Live Wire. In this timeline, he died battling an insane ELEMENT LAD, only to return trapped in Element Lad's crystalline body. DW

IN CHARGE *Among Lightning Lad's duties as Legion chairman is the auditioning of potential new members, often with disastrous and embarrassing results.*

KEY STORYLINE

• *ADVENTURE COMICS #312 (SEPTEMBER 1963):* In this classic story, Lightning Lad is apparently resurrected from the dead by his teammates. Decades later, this tale provided the foundation for *Justice League of America's* "The Lightning Saga."

DOMINATOR INVASION *The alien Dominators have long been foes of the Legion. Their latest plan to conquer the Earth was foiled thanks to heavy-hitting Legionnaires like Earth Lightning Lad.*

LOBO

FIRST APPEARANCE OMEGA MEN #3 (June 1983)
STATUS Villain **REAL NAME** Unpronounceable
OCCUPATION Contract killer; bounty hunter **BASE** Mobile
HEIGHT 7ft 6in **WEIGHT** 640 lbs **EYES** Red **HAIR** Black
SPECIAL POWERS/ABILITIES Vast superstrength and near invulnerability; superspeed and superhuman endurance; fantastic leaping ability; tracking ability allows him to trace prey across galaxies; can survive unaided in the vacuum of space; unparalleled brawler; can replicate himself into an army of clones.

HIS UNPRONOUNCEABLE REAL NAME roughly translates as "he who devours your entrails and thoroughly enjoys it." Once Lobo has targeted a victim, that person has little hope of escape and even less of winning any fight—for the only way to destroy Lobo is to vaporize every part of him, down to the last cell! Lobo loves his work and cares little for payment. When not pursuing prey, he keeps in practice by picking fights wherever he goes, marauding around the cosmos like a deep-space Hell's Angel on his intergalacticycle, the *Hog*. With his uncanny ability to sense an opponent's physical and mental weaknesses, Lobo is almost as notorious as a barroom brawler as he is as a killer-for-hire.

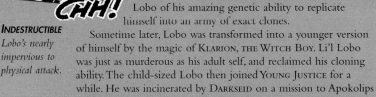

BOUNTY HUNTER *Lobo is known and feared throughout the galaxy as a tracker who never loses his prey.*

BAD TO THE BONE
Lobo's taken more than his share of lives, loot, and loves—and probably in that order!

A ONE-MAN ARMY
Lobo is the sole survivor of the planet Czarnia, once renowned as a tranquil paradise. Lobo was trouble as soon as he was born, biting off the midwife's fingers, chasing the doctors with scalpels, and frightening the delivery nurse to death. As a child, he killed every caretaker he had. Finally, he committed global genocide, creating a horde of lethal insects that slaughtered every last Czarnian. Lobo then became a mercenary, leaving a trail of blood and corpses in his wake. Bizarrely, he also adopted a school of space dolphins as pets.

At length, after helping the OMEGA MEN vanquish the Spider Guild and the Citadel Empire, Lobo found Earth, and began challenging its greatest heroes—SUPERMAN, WARRIOR, the JUSTICE LEAGUE OF AMERICA—to vicious battles to find the "Main Man."

Lobo worked with the interstellar police force L.E.G.I.O.N. for a time, along with their offshoot, R.E.B.E.L.S. During that time BRAINIAC 5.1 stripped Lobo of his amazing genetic ability to replicate himself into an army of exact clones.

INDESTRUCTIBLE
Lobo's nearly impervious to physical attack.

Sometime later, Lobo was transformed into a younger version of himself by the magic of KLARION, THE WITCH BOY. Li'l Lobo was just as murderous as his adult self, and reclaimed his cloning ability. The child-sized Lobo then joined YOUNG JUSTICE for a while. He was incinerated by DARKSEID on a mission to Apokolips during the Imperiex War (see Great Battles, pp. 362–3). A Lobo clone, created from a drop of blood, returned to Earth with Young Justice. He called himself "Slobo," felt unworthy of the Khundian title "Lobo," and was condemned to a stony death in the 853rd century by Darkseid while trying to save his teammate SECRET from the New God's clutches. One of Lobo's many clones survived, however, to spread his brand of lethal rage across the galaxy. **PJ**

KEY STORYLINE
• *LOBO'S BACK #1-4 (MAY–AUGUST 1992):* Heaven doesn't want him, and Hell certainly doesn't either. Lobo rampages through the afterlife after being hacked to pieces by a rival hunter.

LASSOED! *Lobo became a pawn of the Olympian Gods in their battle against Circe. After murdering dozens of Amazons, he was captured by Wonder Woman!*

LITTLE MERMAID

FIRST APPEARANCE SUPER FRIENDS #9 (December 1997)
STATUS Hero (deceased) **REAL NAME** Ula Paske
OCCUPATION Adventurer **BASE** Denmark
HEIGHT 5ft 4in **WEIGHT** 120 lbs **EYES** Crystal blue **HAIR** Blonde
SPECIAL POWERS/ABILITIES Could transform her legs into a fishtail and breathe underwater.

The Little Mermaid was a mutant from the undersea kingdom of Atlantis. Ula's mother was a mermaid from the city of Tritonis, and her father was a two-legged humanoid from Poseidonis, the capital of Atlantis. Because of her specific mutation, which allowed her to survive underwater for only 30 hours or less, Ula was raised by adoptive parents in Denmark.

The Little Mermaid was a founding member of DOCTOR MIST's team of heroes, the GLOBAL GUARDIANS. When the Guardians were disbanded by the United Nations, the Little Mermaid fell under the control of the evil Queen Bee (see QUEEN BEE II) of Bialya. During that time, the Little Mermaid was killed by JACK O'LANTERN II, who accidentally blew the Little Mermaid's head off with his signature weapon, the mystical Jack O'Lantern. PJ

FISHY TAIL The Little Mermaid was a mutant from Atlantis who was able to transform her human legs into a fish's tail, and swim as swiftly as a dolphin or shark.

LOBO   *SEE OPPOSITE PAGE*

LOCK UP

FIRST APPEARANCE ROBIN #24 (January 1996)
STATUS Villain **REAL NAME** Lyle Bolton
OCCUPATION Vigilante, jailer **BASE** Gotham City
HEIGHT 6ft 2in **WEIGHT** 235 lbs **EYES** Brown **HAIR** Black
SPECIAL POWERS/ABILITIES Skilled combatant, expert on penitentiaries and locks.

Lyle Bolton grew up with an obsession for law and order. After washing out of the police academy and losing several security jobs due to his ruthlessness, he decided he could best contain criminals on his own as the vigilante Lock-Up. Establishing a private prison, Lock-Up kidnapped villains including TWO-FACE and an undercover ROBIN (Tim Drake), but his plans ended prematurely thanks to the arrival of BATMAN.

When Gotham City became a No Man's Land after a devastating earthquake, Batman allowed Lock-Up to take over Blackgate Prison to prevent the escape of any convicts. Lock-Up enlisted the KGBeast and the TRIGGER TWINS to help him in his task. Later, Lock-Up helped orchestrate a worldwide prison break while working for the Society (see VILLAINS UNITED) during the Infinite Crisis. He recently found himself among the criminals rounded up by the SUICIDE SQUAD and deposited on an alien world during Operation: Salvation Run. DW

LODESTONE II

FIRST APPEARANCE DOOM PATROL (2nd series) #3 (December 1987)
STATUS Hero (flown away) **REAL NAME** Rhea Jones
OCCUPATION Adventurer **BASE** Kansas City
HEIGHT 5ft 6in **WEIGHT** 144 lbs **EYES** Blue **HAIR** Red
SPECIAL POWERS/ABILITIES Used her magnetic abilities to fly, create force fields, and attract or repel metallic objects.

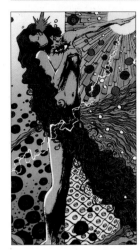

Rhea Jones was the daughter of an Air Force officer who was often away on secret missions. During one absence, Rhea's mother was killed in an accident. Rhea learned that her father was stationed in the Arctic, so the plucky teenager stowed away on a flight to the base. Her father had volunteered to enter a nuclear reactor and shut it down. Rhea followed him, exposing herself to deadly radiation. A powerful electromagnetic charge resulted and the building blew up. Rhea miraculously survived and the military put her through many tests hoping to learn how she had not only lived, but also developed strange powers. She escaped and joined a traveling circus, until Arani Caulder (CELSIUS), who had recreated her husband's DOOM PATROL, invited Rhea to join the team. On one mission, her powers evolved and she metamorphosed into a magnetic butterfly and flew away, finally free at last. RG

LIVE WIRE

FIRST APPEARANCE ADVENTURE COMICS #247 (April 1958);
Legion of Super-Heroes (4th series) #0 (October 1994)
STATUS Hero **REAL NAME** Garth Ranzz **OCCUPATION** Legionnaire **BASE** Legion World **HEIGHT** 5ft 10in **WEIGHT** 145 lbs **EYES** Blue **HAIR** Red
SPECIAL POWERS/ABILITIES Able to absorb and generate electricity or project coruscating lightning bolts.

Live Wire's powers are not innate. He received the ability to control electricity when he, his twin sister, Ayla, and his older brother, Mekt, fell prey to a pack of lightning beasts on Korbal. Soon after, Garth and two other teens saved rich industrialist R.J. Brande (see BRANDE, R.J) from assassination. The three united as Live Wire, COSMIC BOY, and SATURN GIRL, and so the Legion of Super-Heroes was founded. When his sister Ayla (codenamed SPARK) replaced him on the Legion, Live Wire temporarily joined Leland McCauley's competing Workforce. He later found his brother Mekt, who had used his electric abilities to unleash terror under the name LIGHTNING LORD.

In the battle with Mekt, Live Wire lost an arm. He wore a prosthesis after that. Live Wire rejoined the Legion becoming acting leader when Cosmic Boy went back to the late 20th century. He had been in love with Saturn Girl for many years, and at last expressed it. When several "lost Legionnaires" were caught in another galaxy, he sacrificed himself to stop ELEMENT LAD and send his teammates home. In his memory, his sister Spark briefly adopted the identity of Live Wire II. Live Wire has returned to life. His consciousness and memories have been imprinted on the crystalline body of Element Lad, but it is unsure whether he will return to his former appearance and powers. DW

LONAR

FIRST APPEARANCE FOREVER PEOPLE #5 (November 1971)
STATUS Hero (deceased) **REAL NAME** Lonar
OCCUPATION New God **BASE** New Genesis
HEIGHT 6ft 7in **WEIGHT** 265 lbs **EYES** Blue **HAIR** Black
SPECIAL POWERS/ABILITIES A consummate soldier, immensely strong and disciplined; rides a winged horse into battle.

Little is known about the New God Lonar save for his bravery, strength of character, and fierceness in battle. With his flying steed Thunderer, he is usually to be found at the forefront of any battle, either staunchly defending the world of New Genesis from DARKSEID's evil minions or keeping other lands safe from the Dark Lord's malignant touch. One of his more noteworthy battles occurred defending the hidden land of Skartaris from an Apokoliptian invasion.

Lonar has an archaeologist's thirst for knowledge, and can often be found exploring the ancient ruins on New Genesis for clues to the secrets of the legendary Old Gods, who predated the NEW GODS countless millennia in the past. Lonar numbered among the casualties during the Death of the New Gods event, struck down by a faceless assassin. RG/DW

LOOKER

FIRST APPEARANCE BATMAN AND THE OUTSIDERS #25 (Sept. 1985)
STATUS Hero **REAL NAME** Emily "Lia" Briggs
OCCUPATION Model; talk show host **BASE** Los Angeles
HEIGHT 5ft 10in **WEIGHT** 210 lbs **EYES** Blue **HAIR** Red
SPECIAL POWERS/ABILITIES Vampire strength and intangibility; psionic abilities include levitation, telekinesis, telepathy, and mental blasts.

Emily Briggs longed to be beautiful, and got her wish when emissaries from the underground kingdom of Abyssia kidnapped her in order to make her the heir to their throne. Using fragments from a comet, the Abyssians gave Emily psionic powers and jaw-dropping beauty. She managed to escape from the underworld thanks to BATMAN and the OUTSIDERS, and then joined the team under the codename Looker.

After the Outsiders split from Batman and relocated to Los Angeles, Looker worked for a modeling agency, until a rematch with the Abyssians robbed her of her powers and her breathtaking looks. She later joined the second incarnation of the Outsiders on a mission to Markovia. There, the struggle with a vampire reignited her powers; unfortunately, Looker became a vampire herself. Looker remains active, fighting supervillains during the Infinite Crisis' Battle of Metropolis and facing BLACK ADAM in the event called World War III. **DW**

LOOSE CANNON

FIRST APPEARANCE ACTION COMICS ANNUAL #5 (1995)
STATUS Hero **REAL NAME** Eddie Walker
OCCUPATION Former homicide detective **BASE** Metropolis
HEIGHT (Eddie) 5ft 10in; (Loose Cannon) 7ft 5in
WEIGHT (Eddie) 170 lbs; (Loose Cannon) 725 lbs
EYES (Eddie) Brown; (Loose Cannon) white
HAIR (Eddie) Brown; (Loose Cannon) yellow
SPECIAL POWERS/ABILITIES Transforms into super-strong blue monster in the absence of sunlight.

Eddie Walker was a homicide detective working for a division of Metropolis's Special Crimes Unit (trained to deal with anything from meta-human crime to alien invaders) led by Maggie Sawyer. Walker became known as the department's volatile "loose cannon." Tragedy struck when Eddie was crippled in a car accident. Suffering from deep depression, he considered suicide. Meanwhile, a group of alien parasites landed on Earth and proceeded to drain the spinal fluids from a host of victims. Two of these parasites attacked Eddie, but instead of dying, the crippled detective discovered that he could transform himself into a superhuman giant. Styling himself Loose Cannon, Eddie teamed up with the JUSTICE LEAGUE OF AMERICA and several other "new bloods" to destroy the alien parasites. Loose Cannon fought in the Infinite Crisis, but later fell prey to organ thieves who harvested his super-powered heart. **PJ**

LORD CHAOS

FIRST APPEARANCE NEW TITANS ANNUAL #7 (1991)
STATUS God (eradicated) **REAL NAME** Inapplicable
OCCUPATION Dictator **BASE** Earth in an alternate timeline
HEIGHT 6ft 2in **WEIGHT** 196 lbs **EYES** Black **HAIR** Red-gold
SPECIAL POWERS/ABILITIES Godlike strength; flight; could project fire or darkness, create floods and earthquakes; read minds; alter memories.

In the future of an alternate timeline, Lord Chaos was the child of Donna Troy, the Titan known as TROIA. He inherited from his mother the godlike powers of the TITANS OF MYTH. As soon as he was born, he magically grew to adulthood and killed his parents. Taking the name Lord Chaos, he took control of Earth and annihilated most of its heroes. A group of rebels called the Team Titans went back in time to kill Donna Troy before she could give birth to Lord Chaos. Chaos traveled back to stop the assassination. The Titans of Myth arrived and stripped Lord Chaos of his powers, ending his reign of terror. Soon after, during Zero Hour (see Great Battles, pp. 362–3), the future timeline Lord Chaos hailed from was eradicated and the dictator god was wiped from existence. **PJ**

TOTAL CHAOS *His body coursing with the power of every Titan god, Chaos nearly succeeded in destroying his mother, Troia.*

LORD HAVOK

FIRST APPEARANCE JUSTICE LEAGUE INTERNATIONAL #1 (Nov. 1987)
STATUS Villain (missing or deceased) **REAL NAME** Unknown
OCCUPATION Super-villain **BASE** Earth-8
HEIGHT 6ft 2in **WEIGHT** 185 lbs **EYES** Brown **HAIR** Brown
SPECIAL POWERS/ABILITIES (Lord Havok I) computer mind, indestructible armor; (Lord Havok II) controlled any machine, telekinetic abilities.

Many versions of Lord Havok have appeared due to changes in the timestream. The first led the EXTREMISTS, a band of robot super-villains. The Extremists seized control of their world's nuclear arsenal and wiped out every soul, including themselves, except for genius Mitch Wacky. The Extremists came to Earth, where their plot for planetary conquest was thwarted by Justice League Europe (see JUSTICE LEAGUE OF AMERICA). The bodies of Lord Havok and the other Extremists, except DREAMSLAYER, were placed in a museum. Dreamslayer's essence forced businessman Maxwell Lord to hypnotize the FLASH and Wacky into reactivating Lord Havok. The robot was killed by BLUE BEETLE II.

Later, Maxwell Lord died from brain cancer and was resurrected by the alien Kilg%re to become an all-new Lord Havok. The newest Lord Havok emerged on Earth-8, where he led the Extremists in a global fight against a repressive superhuman regime. MONARCH attempted to recruit the Extremists for his multiversal army, a move that Lord Havok resisted. The Extremists were present at the universe-destroying cataclysm that consumed Earth-51. **SB**

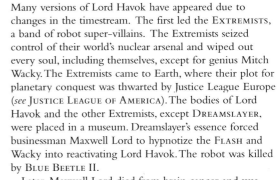

ROCK 'EM, SOCK 'EM *Lord Havok is a killer machine from a planet like Earth was before the Extremists destroyed it in a nuclear holocaust.*

LORD, MAXWELL

FIRST APPEARANCE JUSTICE LEAGUE INTERNATIONAL #1 (May 1987)
STATUS Villain (deceased)   **REAL NAME** Maxwell Lord
OCCUPATION Criminal mastermind   **BASE** Mobile
HEIGHT 6ft 2in   **WEIGHT** 185 lbs   **EYES** Brown   **HAIR** Brown
SPECIAL POWERS/ABILITIES Brilliant strategic mind, telepathic control of others.

ACCEPTABLE LOSS
Wonder Woman killed Maxwell Lord to break his mind-control of Superman; the Man of Steel did not agree with the severity of her actions.

Maxwell Lord was the billionaire who financed the JUSTICE LEAGUE OF AMERICA during the period when it was most commonly known as the Justice League International. The explosion of a "gene bomb" during an alien invasion triggered Lord's ability to control the minds of others. He continued as the League's behind-the-scenes leader until killed by a brain tumor. Lord's consciousness spent time in the robotic body of LORD HAVOK until he regained his human form.

By this time, his long-term ambitions to exterminate the world's metahumans had begun to bear fruit. As head of CHECKMATE, Lord had access to the Brother Eye satellite and its army of O.M.A.C. agents, which carried programming to annihilate all superhumans. When BLUE BEETLE II discovered the truth of the plot, Lord shot him in the head. Lord then used his mind-controlling powers to take command of SUPERMAN and turn him into a remote-controlled weapon. WONDER WOMAN, faced with the decision to eliminate Lord's threat for all time, killed him instantly by snapping his neck. **DW**

OMACS ARE GO
With Blue Beetle II eliminated, Maxwell Lord launched the OMAC Project which targeted all superhumans on the planet.

LORD OF TIME

FIRST APPEARANCE JUSTICE LEAGUE OF AMERICA (1st series) #10 (March 1962)
STATUS Villain   **REAL NAME** Unrevealed   **OCCUPATION** Would-be conqueror   **BASE** Mobile   **HEIGHT** 5ft 9in   **WEIGHT** 159 lbs   **EYES** Blue   **HAIR** Black   **SPECIAL POWERS/ABILITIES** Access to the timestream through Chrono-cube; armor assimilates weaponry from any era visited.

An immensely powerful being from the year 3786, the Lord of Time attacked the Justice League of America, using his miraculous chrono-cube to peel back the fourth-dimensional veil of time. Since his initial defeat by the JLA, this sinister fugitive from the future has learned to move laterally and diagonally through history, accessing armies and armaments spanning millions of years. He desires nothing less than to conquer space and time. To make sure that his bid to rule all reality is successful he is quite capable of ensuring that the JLA have no power to stop him by eliminating their ancestors and so erasing them from existence.

At some point, the Lord of Time created a frozen moment in history called Timepoint, and he will eventually evolve into a being known as Epoch who desires to master the timestream, changing events to grant him power. **RG**

AGELESS ARMOR
Using armor from the future, the Lord of Time is able to withstand assaults by powerful opponents, from Superman to Green Lantern.

LORING, JEAN

FIRST APPEARANCE SHOWCASE #34
(September–October 1961)
STATUS Villain **REAL NAME** Jean Loring
OCCUPATION God of Vengeance **BASE** Mobile
HEIGHT 5ft 8in **WEIGHT** 130 lbs **EYES** Green **HAIR** Black
SPECIAL POWERS/ABILITIES None in normal form; as Eclipso,
possesses flight, invulnerability, super-strength, and vast
magical powers .

Jean Loring was once a
notable attorney and the
wife of Ray Palmer, the
second ATOM. The two
divorced not long into
their marriage, and Loring
continued her law career
in Ivy Town until suffering
a complete mental collapse.
Convinced that she could restore her marriage to
Ray by threatening or killing the loved ones of the
members of the JUSTICE LEAGUE OF AMERICA, she
murdered the ELONGATED MAN's wife, Sue Dibny.
When her crime became known, Loring served
a term in Arkham Asylum until infected by the
sinister spirit of ECLIPSO. Now Eclipso's human host,
Loring seduced the SPECTRE into killing hundreds
of Earth's magic-users to bring about an end to
the Ninth Age of Magic. The SHADOWPACT fought
the Spectre and sent Loring into orbit around the
sun, but she returned, still armed with the powers
of Eclipso. After fighting BLUE BEETLE III and TRACI
THIRTEEN, she attempted to corrupt MARY MARVEL,
only to be thwarted by the purity of Mary's spirit.
DW

LOSERS, THE

FIRST APPEARANCE G.I. COMBAT #138 (November 1969)
STATUS Hero team **BASE** Europe and Asia during World War II
MEMBERS AND SPECIAL POWERS
CAPTAIN STORM *(DECEASED)* Indomitable will; a natural leader.
GUNNER Commando skills; expert marksman.
JOHNNY CLOUD *(DECEASED)* One of the greatest fighter pilots of
World War II.
ONA *(DECEASED)* Expert markswoman.
POOCH *(DECEASED)* Specially trained military dog.
SARGE *(DECEASED)* Commando skills; expert marksman.

The Losers were Allied soldiers during World
War II, each of whom had suffered serious
failures during their military careers.
CAPTAIN STORM's first command had
been sunk by a Japanese submarine;
a pilot flying alongside Johnny Cloud
(see CLOUD, JOHNNY) had been killed
in combat; and a band of raw recruits
led by GUNNER AND SARGE had been
wiped out during their first patrol.
After Jeb Stuart (see HAUNTED TANK)
persuaded the soldiers to help him
destroy a Nazi radar tower, the four men
stayed together, united by the Military
High Command as a special task force.
Briefly recruiting a fifth member, a
Norwegian woman named Ona, the unit
fought Axis tyranny throughout Europe
and Asia, never quite shaking their self-
imposed status as "Losers." Tragically, all
four men and their K-9 sidekick, Pooch,
died in action during the final days of
World War II, but decades later Gunner was
resurrected by Project M and recruited for
the new CREATURE COMMANDOS. **PJ**

CRISIS IN TIME In the
war torn country of
Markovia, the Losers
came face to face with
Shadow Demons out to
destroy the universe,
and they succumbed to
their explosive presence
before time was reordered
in the Crisis.

GUNNER JOHNNY CLOUD CAPTAIN STORM ONA
POOCH SARGE

LUMP

FIRST APPEARANCE MISTER MIRACLE (1st series) #7 (April 1972)
STATUS Villain **REAL NAME** None
OCCUPATION Warrior **BASE** Apokolips
HEIGHT 7ft **WEIGHT** 500 lbs **EYES** White **HAIR** None
SPECIAL POWERS/ABILITIES Can mold his misshapen body into any form
he imagines to defeat opponents psycho-merged with him.

Deep within GRANNY GOODNESS's
orphanage on Apokolips lies the
dreaded Section Zero. Here, Scott
Free (MISTER MIRACLE) met
the LUMP, a horrendous hulk
who encountered the enemies
of DARKSEID in the "Arena of
the Gods," a mental realm within
the creature's own Id. Strapped to
Apokoliptian technology Mister
Miracle met the Lump inside this
mind-world where the monster was
master. Able to mold his body into any weapon, the Lump
battled Mister Miracle to a standstill. To defeat the Lump,
Miracle used a fission blast to turn the ground to glass.
With a reflective shard, Mister Miracle showed the Lump
his own vile visage. Horrified, the Lump retreated into the
furthest reaches of his Id. Miracle then escaped with his
beloved BIG BARDA. The Lump remains in Section Zero,
imprisoned in his own private hell. **SB**

LYNX

FIRST APPEARANCE Robin (1st series) #1 (November 1990)
STATUS Villain (deceased) **REAL NAME** Ling
OCCUPATION Assassin; gang boss **BASE** Gotham City
HEIGHT 5ft 2in **WEIGHT** 119 lbs **EYES** Black **HAIR** Black
SPECIAL POWERS/ABILITIES One of the most formidable martial artists
alive today; a courageous but ruthless killer.

Escaping from Wuzhong, China,
a young girl known only as Ling
begged for food on the streets
of Marseilles. An adept thief, Ling
was recruited by Sir Edmund
Dorrance, the drug baron KING
SNAKE, to join his Ghost Dragons
gang. When she was defeated by the
third ROBIN, King Snake punished
Ling, now renamed LYNX, by taking
her left eye. Filled with hatred for
Robin and King Snake, Lynx moved to
Gotham City's Chinatown and wrested
control of the Dragons from King Snake.
Lynx has since clashed with BATMAN and
Robin several times; however, she teamed
up with the Dark Knight in the aftermath
of the Gotham earthquake, taking down
a Chinatown gang using slaves to generate
electricity for the crippled city. In a fight
with Cassandra Cain (BATGIRL), Lynx lost
her life. **RG**

The DC Comics Encyclopedia

LUTHOR, LEX

SUPERMAN'S GREATEST ENEMY

FIRST APPEARANCE ACTION COMICS #23 (April 1940)
REAL NAME Alexander Joseph Luthor
BASE Metropolis; Washington D.C. (while U.S. President)
HEIGHT 6ft 2in **WEIGHT** 210 lbs **EYES** Green **HAIR** None
OCCUPATION Mastermind
SPECIAL POWERS/ABILITIES Luthor is one of the smartest men on Earth, able to invent technological marvels or manipulate entire nations. He believes in brute force and is an unskilled fighter, relying instead on weapons and armor.

LEX LUTHOR MAY BE the most gifted man alive but rather than use his supreme intellect and skills for the betterment of mankind, the sociopath has continually sought power and influence without regard for the pain and suffering he causes. The gifts are also wasted on his single-minded hatred of a more pure and noble man, especially given his alien origins.

EVIL GENIUS Luthor's early attempts to kill Superman all failed.

EVIL AND ALIENATED

One glance at Luthor's I.Q. test results, convinced his parents that their little genius would make them rich. They were determined he should excel, but their soul-destroying "guidance" bred a sociopath who engineered their deaths to capitalize on their life insurance. A budding astrobiologist, Lex then spent years searching for evidence of extraterrestrial life. His hunt took him to Smallville when he was 18. Lex befriended another seemingly alienated young man, Clark Kent. He turned his back on Smallville when a fire destroyed his lab and his scientific achievements, as well as his foster father. Refusing to take any responsibility for the accident, Lex blamed the town for "letting the Luthors burn," and to this day, refuses to admit he has ever set foot in Smallville.

THE RISE OF LUTHOR

Years later, Lex appeared in Metropolis and built his technology company, LexCorp, into a powerhouse. Financial success led to political power, and he was considered the city's most powerful figure. Then came the day that SUPERMAN appeared in the skies above Metropolis and turned Lex's world upside down. Superman openly accused Luthor of being a criminal mastermind rather than a benefactor of mankind. Unwilling or unable to link this "meddling alien" with the boy he had known a decade earlier, Luthor swore to bring down the Last Son of Krypton. Over the years, he has used his power and influence to plague the Man of Steel time and again.

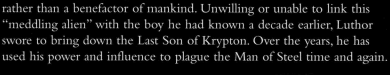

ONLY THE LONELY
Deprived of a normal childhood, Lex hid his personal pain behind a mask of arrogance.

KRYPTONITE RING

Luthor got in his licks but continued to be thwarted by Superman both directly and indirectly. On one occasion, a ring Luthor had fashioned from kryptonite gave him cancer owing to the radiation inherent in the alien rock. Lex faked his death, and transferred his mind into the body of a clone, pretending to be Luthor's heretofore unknown son. This Luthor soon evolved to resemble the original, but continued to come second in his struggles with Superman.

TWO STRANGERS *Clark was the only person in Smallville who empathized with Lex's feelings of isolation.*

EXPLOSION *An accident physically and mentally scarred Lex so deeply he has erased all record of his ever being in Smallville.*

IN RUINS *Luthor destroyed Metropolis in a bid to avoid exposure by Lois Lane.*

METROPOLIS DESTROYED

Lex showed his true colors by refusing to sacrifice himself to help reignite the sun after the Sun-Eater had snuffed out its energy. When Lois Lane (see LANE, LOIS) exposed his criminal dealings, Luthor triggered devices hidden within Metropolis that destroyed the city. Superman and his fellow heroes rebuilt Metropolis and the battle between Superman and Luthor continued. His manipulations extended to Metropolis's citizens, who sided with Superman over Luthor.

LUST FOR POWER

Realizing the need to muzzle the press, Luthor bought and then sold the *Daily Planet* to Perry White (*see* White, Perry) on condition that Lois Lane killed any single story of his choosing. Feeling safe from exposure, Luthor ran for U. S. President to gain the power needed to bring Superman down. Surprisingly, he served the U.S.'s interests well, strengthening or forging relationships with many nations from Atlantis to Russia, and rallying the troops when IMPERIEX arrived to destroy Earth (*see* Great Battles, pp. 362–3).

CLASH OF WILLS *Perry White and Luthor never got along and it chafed when Luthor came to own Perry's beloved Daily Planet.*

FRONT PAGE NEWS

Lois found out that Luthor had known of Imperiex's threat earlier than stated. He demanded that this be the story the *Planet* killed, but the savvy reporter tricked him, giving her notes to Clark Kent, who wrote a scathing piece, exposing Luthor for the criminal he was.

WARSUIT *Luthor finally took matters in his own hands, attempting to destroy both Superman and Batman.*

ADVANCE WARNING *Luthor had secretly known of Imperiex's invasion plans, but ordered Lois Lane to kill the story. However, Clark Kent printed the full truth, marring Luthor's term as U.S. President.*

KEY STORYLINES
• *SUPERMAN: PRESIDENT LEX (JULY, 2003):* The world looks on aghast as Luthor becomes U.S. President, following the most controversial election of all time.
SUPERMAN: BIRTHRIGHT #1–12 (SEPTEMBER 2003–SEPTEMBER 2004): Dating back to their childhood in Smallville, Luthor's tortured relationship with Clark Kent/Superman is redefined and explored.
• *SUPERMAN/BATMAN #1–6:* President Luthor becomes a kryptonite junkie and goes insane.
• *LEX LUTHOR: MAN OF STEEL #1–5 MAY– SEPTEMBER 2005):* Luthor's recovery from his downfall.

U.S. PRESIDENT *Luthor was quite effective in his post, improving diplomatic relations with Atlantis and other countries.*

ACT OF MADNESS

Luthor's presidential power still could not bring about the end of Superman and his costumed friends. When an asteroid neared Earth, Luthor detected kryptonite radiation and used that to try and turn the public against the Man of Steel. He even sent costumed champions after Superman, but this gambit also failed. Finally, he donned a LexCorp war suit and tried to take down not only Superman, but BATMAN as well. His efforts were in vain and his deception was made public. Driven from the presidency, Luthor was thought to have died but limped to freedom, an angry, vengeful man. **RG**

LUTHOR, LEX

The Superboy Plot

From a secret location, Lex Luthor plotted his return to power. With Lana Lang (*see* LANG, LANA) now in charge of LuthorCorp and Pete Ross (*see* ROSS, PETE) stepping in to serve out the rest of Luthor's term as president, the stage seemed clear for a rebirth of Luthor's particular brand of genius. He began by activating buried programming in the mind of SUPERBOY (Conner Kent), turning him against his teammates in the TEEN TITANS. The attack failed, but Luthor continued to think of Conner—a clone who shared 50% of his DNA with Superman and 50% with Luthor—as his own son. Lex's concern for Conner seemed uncharacteristic, but showed his protectiveness of the Luthor bloodline. By claiming Conner as his own, he had stolen a family member from Superman.

LIKE FATHER *Brainwashed, Conner Kent fights the Teen Titans under Luthor's orders.*

CLONE VAT *Luthor's ability to crack the genetic code also led to the first Bizarro.*

FALLEN SON *Conner died in the Infinite Crisis, with Luthor among his mourners.*

BEHIND THE CURTAIN *Luthor posed as the unseen Mockingbird in order to rally the Secret Six.*

Villains United

Just prior to the Infinite Crisis, Alexander Luthor—the adult son of a Lex Luthor from an alternate dimension—posed as this reality's Lex in order to unite the planet's supervillains under his banner. Assembling a new SECRET SOCIETY OF SUPER-VILLAINS, this ersatz Luthor pitted the largest and most dangerous assemblage of criminals ever seen against the world's heroes. The true Lex Luthor, meanwhile, moved against the imposter by taking the identity of MOCKINGBIRD and forming a new SECRET SIX team to oppose the Society. Lex's vengeance came to fruition during the Infinite Crisis, when he arranged for Alexander Luthor's death at the hands of the JOKER. Lex mourned Conner Kent, who had died trying to prevent Alexander's scheme to recreate the universe.

TABLES TURNED *For usurping his place as head of the Society, Luthor arranges the death of Alexander Luthor.*

The Everyman Project

Lex altered Alexander Luthor's corpse to resemble his own, then claimed that the late doppelganger had been responsible for the worst crimes of the Luthor presidency. The ruse fooled many, and Lex soon found himself the head of an ambitious experiment to transform ordinary citizens into superheroes. Dubbed the Everyman Project, the program attracted interest from thousands of hopefuls including Natasha Irons (*see* IRONS, NATASHA), niece of the hero STEEL. Luthor granted Natasha superhuman abilities, then grouped her with several other charismatic young people and launched the team as the all-new, corporate-owned INFINITY INC. But the test subjects of the Everyman Project soon learned the limits of their genetic gifts. On New Year's Eve, as part of a scheme to humiliate the hero Supernova, Luthor triggered the instantaneous shutdown of all his subjects' powers. Suddenly powerless, dozens of hopeful heroes died as they plummeted from the sky. Steel and Natasha Irons confronted Luthor in his office, only to discover that he had temporarily acquired powers as well. The duo managed to outsmart Luthor and bring him to justice.

META-LUTHOR *The Everyman treatments worked on their creator as well. For a brief time, Luthor possessed the powers of Superman.*

PUBLIC ENEMY *The goodwill he earned as U.S. president now gone, Luthor burned for revenge on the citizens of Metropolis.*

Kryptonian Science

Yet Luthor managed to escape incarceration. Found innocent of all criminal charges related to the Everyman Project, Luthor tried to reassume his position as one of the Metropolis elite in the face of widespread public condemnation. Deciding that Superman was the obstacle preventing his return to fame, Luthor retrieved a long-buried Kryptonian battleship and led an assault on Metropolis using crystalline war machines not seen since the golden age of the long-dead planet. His plan was to discredit Superman as a failure. Luthor again went underground. Later he assembled a Revenge Squad consisting of the PARASITE, METALLO, and BIZARRO to battle the invading armies of GENERAL ZOD.

MAD SCIENCE *His brain as sharp as ever, Luthor tortured the new Kryptonite Man to generate the energy he required.*

KRYPTON ON EARTH *Using self-assembling Kryptonian crystal technology, Luthor attacked Metropolis with an army of alien war machines.*

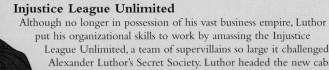

Injustice League Unlimited

Although no longer in possession of his vast business empire, Luthor put his organizational skills to work by amassing the Injustice League Unlimited, a team of supervillains so large it challenged Alexander Luthor's Secret Society. Luthor headed the new cabal with his lieutenants the Joker and the CHEETAH. The group moved against the newly-reformed JUSTICE LEAGUE OF AMERICA by capturing many of its members, then torturing them inside its secret headquarters in the Florida Everglades. The Justice League rallied to victory, but the Injustice League withdrew and remained coiled for a second strike.

Later, Luthor found himself one of the villains deposited on the distant planet Salvation and quickly assumed a leadership role.

Luthor's mind is as brilliant as ever. Since his fall from the presidency he has turned more of his genius to science. He now wears a modified version of his green and purple battle-suit in all encounters with enhanced combatants, and its built-in weapons make him a match for Superman. **RG/DW**

MAD HARRIET

FIRST APPEARANCE MISTER MIRACLE (1st series) #6 (February 1972)
STATUS Villain (deceased)   **REAL NAME** Unrevealed
OCCUPATION Shocktrooper   **BASE** Apokolips
HEIGHT 5ft 10in   **WEIGHT** 146 lbs   **EYES** Black   **HAIR** Green
SPECIAL POWERS/ABILITIES Ferocious combatant; fists are armed with power spikes that can slash through most materials.

Mad Harriet is a member of the FEMALE FURIES, an elite band of shocktroopers trained by the malevolent GRANNY GOODNESS as elite warriors for DARKSEID, dread lord of the planet Apokolips. Mad Harriet is a chilling, psychopathic killing machine, armed with special devices that let her cleave through any material, including the flesh of her prey.

The Female Furies were lead by BIG BARDA until she abandoned the team to be with her lover Scott Free, otherwise known as MISTER MIRACLE. When Barda moved to Earth, Mad Harriet and the Female Furies pursued her there and tried to capture her, but the Furies eventually turned when they were offered freedom from Granny's thrall. After working for a short time with Barda and Mister Miracle, Mad Harriet and the other Female Furies returned to Apokolips and to their roles as enforcers in Darkseid's Elite.

Mad Harriet met her apparent end in the weeks leading up to the Final Crisis. While pursuing MARY MARVEL through the streets of Apokolips, she ran into a hail of gunfire unleashed by Darkseid's own soldiers. **PJ**

MANIC MILLINER
No Man's Land gave many Gotham City rogues the opportunity to prey on the weak and defenseless. The Mad Hatter was mostly concerned with unearthing his collection of hats, buried in the Gotham City quake.

HATS OFF! *Superman helped a harried Dark Knight to defeat Jervis Tetch and put an end to his criminal chicanery.*

MAD HATTER

FIRST APPEARANCE BATMAN #49 (November 1948)
STATUS Villain   **REAL NAME** Jervis Tetch
OCCUPATION Professional criminal   **BASE** Gotham City
HEIGHT 4ft 8in   **WEIGHT** 149 lbs   **EYES** Blue   **HAIR** Red
SPECIAL POWERS/ABILITIES A master hypnotist, able to use chemical concoctions or electronic technology concealed in his oversized hat to enthrall his victims; short and slight in stature, the Hatter prefers to let his mesmerized minions do his fighting for him.

Insanely inspired by Lewis Carroll's children's book, *Alice's Adventures in Wonderland*, master mesmerist Jervis Tetch convinced himself that he was Carroll's chapeau-crazed Mad Hatter. In one of his very first crimes, Tetch hypnotized and kidnapped teenage girls to be "Alices" in a bizarre tea party before selling them into slavery. Fortunately, BATMAN and ROBIN foiled the Hatter's scheme and freed his unwilling guests, who included the Boy Wonder's very first crush, schoolmate Jenny Noblesse. Since then, the Hatter has committed even more sordid sins, usually involving his obsession with hats. However, what the prize Mad Hatter longs for most of all is Batman's famous headgear. He would gladly kill the Dark Knight to add the Bat-Cowl to his collection.

Mercurial in temperament, the Mad Hatter generally works alone. But for the sake of his hidden cache of chapeaus, buried under tons of rubble after Gotham City's cataclysmic earthquake, Tetch allied himself with the villain Narcosis, who planned to blanket the ruined city with his Bliss gas. Naturally, the Hatter bargained for Narcosis's hood to seal their partnership, short-lived though it was, since both were soon defeated by Batman.

In between his cap-themed crime sprees, Tetch is confined in the cells of Gotham City's notorious Arkham Asylum for the Criminally Insane, where hats are, as a rule, prohibited.

The Mad Hatter recently served with the new SECRET SIX, where he pitted his mind-controlling abilities against those of DOCTOR PSYCHO. **SB**

MIND GAMES *Shooting cops is not as appealing to the Mad Hatter as using his electronics savvy to hotwire a microwave dish, and using cable television to place all of Gotham under his hypnotic thrall.*

MADAME .44

FIRST APPEARANCE ALL STAR WESTERN #117 (March 1961)
STATUS Hero **REAL NAME** Jeanne Walker
OCCUPATION Gun-slinger **BASE** Mesa City
HEIGHT 5ft 2in **WEIGHT** 119 lbs **EYES** Blue **HAIR** Red
SPECIAL POWERS/ABILITIES Crack shot with a pistol; uses her wits when her physical prowess did not match her opponents'.

In the year 1872, a group of swindlers cheated Jeanne Walker's prospector father out of a rich strike at a gold mine. This traumatic memory led Jeanne to assume the secret identity of Madame .44, a name the famous peace officer Wyatt Earp gave her. Disguising her distinctive blonde tresses by dying her hair red, Madame .44 became a "Robin Hood" outlaw, who robbed from unscrupulous businessmen, like those who had originally wronged her father, and then returned much of the money to its original owners.

Her rambunctious exploits led her to clash with Johnny Thunder (see THUNDER, JOHNNY) from time to time. However, their enmity did not run too deep or persist too long. Johnny and Madame .44 found themselves on the same side during a battle with the vicious outlaw Silk Black and afterwards fell in love and married. **RG**

MADAME ROUGE

FIRST APPEARANCE DOOM PATROL (1st series) #86 (March 1964)
STATUS Villain (deceased) **REAL NAME** Laura DeMille
OCCUPATION Ex-actress and teacher; criminal **BASE** Paris, France
HEIGHT 5ft 6in **WEIGHT** 134 lbs **EYES** Blue **HAIR** Black
SPECIAL POWERS/ABILITIES Could stretch any body part to incredible lengths; could reshape her facial features to disguise herself.

Laura DeMille was a beautiful young actress from Paris who suffered from severe schizophrenia. When the BRAIN experimented on her mind, she snapped and became Madame Rouge, joining his Brotherhood of Evil (see SOCIETY OF SIN). Later, after further experimentation, Rouge was given superhuman powers, and, along with the rest of the Brotherhood, clashed with the DOOM PATROL. Despite falling in love with the CHIEF, Rouge joined forces with the Chief's enemy, GENERAL ZAHL, and seemingly murdered him and the Doom Patrol.

During a battle between the Brotherhood of Evil and the TEEN TITANS, Rouge was accidentally killed by BEAST BOY **PJ**

MADAME XANADU

FIRST APPEARANCE DOORWAY TO NIGHTMARE #1 (February 1978)
STATUS Hero **REAL NAME** Unknown
OCCUPATION Occultist **BASE** Greenwich Village, New York City
HEIGHT 5ft 9in **WEIGHT** 145 lbs **EYES** Green **HAIR** Black
SPECIAL POWERS/ABILITIES Able to read people's futures and sense and interpret magical forces; commands three demon minions.

The sign on Madame Xanadu's storefront on Christy Street tells patrons to "Enter freely—unafraid." Madame Xanadu counsels clients haunted by supernatural forces. She intercedes only when necessary, and refuses payment. Madame Xanadu has even been called upon by meta-humans for advice. For reasons unrevealed, she bartered her soul to the devil NERON and received three demons loyal to her in exchange. Madame Xanadu belongs to the Sentinels of Magic, a loose confederation of mystical heroes assembled to thwart the angel ASMODEL's uprising in Hell. Prior to the Infinite Crisis, the SPECTRE burned out Madame Xanadu's eyes to prevent her from reading her tarot cards. **SB**

MADEMOISELLE MARIE

FIRST APPEARANCE STAR-SPANGLED WAR STORIES #84 (August 1959)
STATUS Hero **REAL NAME** Unrevealed
OCCUPATION French resistance leader **BASE** France
HEIGHT 5ft 1in **WEIGHT** 117 lbs **EYES** Blue **HAIR** Brown
SPECIAL POWERS/ABILITIES A natural markswoman with a keen tactical mind; charismatic, courageous, and resourceful.

The name Mademoiselle Marie has been held by many young women throughout French history. As far back as the French Revolution, a Mademoiselle Marie has stood to protect the innocent and assassinate enemies that threaten her native soil. During World War II, Mademoiselle Marie became the leader of the most prominent resistance cell, striking against the Nazi occupiers and beginning a romance with SERGEANT ROCK. After the war, the tradition continued. The current Mademoiselle Marie, Josephine Tautin, has joined CHECKMATE as the Black Queen's Knight. Her cold-blooded ruthlessness has made many of her teammates uneasy. **DW**

MAGEDDON

FIRST APPEARANCE JLA #37 (January 2000)
STATUS Villain **REAL NAME** None
OCCUPATION Weapon of mass destruction (destroyed) **BASE** Mobile
HEIGHT Unknown **WEIGHT** Unknown **EYES** Red **HAIR** None
SPECIAL POWERS/ABILITIES Stimulated violent, highly destructive feelings of anger and aggression in people; capable of wreaking incomprehensible levels of havoc and annihilation.

Created before the dawn of the known universe by the Old Gods of Urgrund, the living weapon Mageddon has been known by many other names over the millennia, including Warbringer, Tezcatlipoca, and the Primordial Annihilator. Mageddon is a doomsday device that amplifies the latent hostilities that lie dormant in the primitive, reptilian center of the human brain. **DW**

THE EYE HAS IT Even the brilliant brain of Lex Luthor could not withstand the psychic influence of Mageddon's advance probes.

When Mageddon broke free from its imprisonment outside of space-time and approached the Earth, the planet suddenly erupted in a frenzy of random military attacks that some labeled World War III. METRON and ORION of the NEW GODS helped battle Mageddon, as did the JUSTICE LEAGUE OF AMERICA and most of Earth's remaining heroes. Even the angels of Heaven descended to Earth on a special mission to calm the world's leaders, and avert what could have been a self-inflicted nuclear holocaust. The hero AZTEK sacrificed his life to slow down the weapon, allowing WONDER WOMAN time to accelerate the evolution of humanity and temporarily create an army of super heroes drawn from all walks of life. SUPERMAN ultimately destroyed Mageddon by flying into its core and draining the ancient energies of the anti-sun that powered it. **DW**

MAGENTA

FIRST APPEARANCE THE NEW TEEN TITANS (1st series) #17 (March 1982)
STATUS Villain   **REAL NAME** Frances Kane
OCCUPATION Criminal   **BASE** Keystone City
HEIGHT 5ft 7in   **WEIGHT** 134 lbs   **EYES** Blue   **HAIR** Purple
SPECIAL POWERS/ABILITIES Able to generate and manipulate magnetic energy, controlling anything made of metal and bending it to her will.

Frances Kane grew up in Blue Valley, Nebraska, and became a close friend of Wally West, the third FLASH. Kane's powers emerged one night while she, her father and brother were driving on a narrow mountain road. When her powers went out of control, the car fell off a cliff, and Kane's father and brother were killed. France's superstitious mother believed her daughter was possessed by the devil and spurned her. With the help of Wally and the TEEN TITANS, Frances was able to gain some control over her powers, and the two became lovers in college.

Whenever Kane's powers emerged, however, she would "split" into a second, evil identity known as Magenta. Despite having helped the Teen Titans and the Flash in their fight against villainy, Magenta has fought the Flash as an enemy on more than one occasion. Having since been forsaken by the Flash for another love, Magenta flutters between her good and evil nature, and is now firmly ensconced with other nefarious criminals in the Flash's Rogues Gallery. **PJ**

PURPLE POWER *Once she was a victim of circumstance. But now, corrupted by her powers, troubled Magenta is one of the Flash's most tragic villains—a former lover turned deadly enemy.*

MAGNO

FIRST APPEARANCE LEGIONNAIRES #43 (December 1996)
STATUS Hero   **REAL NAME** Dyrk Magz
OCCUPATION Legion ally   **BASE** Legion World, U.P. Space
HEIGHT 5ft 8in   **WEIGHT** 149 lbs   **EYES** Brown   **HAIR** Blond
SPECIAL POWERS/ABILITIES Formerly able to generate and control magnetic fields to fly and manipulate metal objects; mystically de-powered following a battle with Mordru.

Like his fellow Braalian Rokk Krinn (COSMIC BOY), Dyrk Magz possessed highly developed magnetic powers. When Cosmic Boy was stranded in the 20th century for a brief period, along with other members of the LEGION OF SUPER-HEROES, his remaining teammates in the 30th century initiated a membership drive to replenish the Legion's dwindled ranks. As Magno, Magz was recruited from the planet Braal to replace Cosmic Boy, at least until the founding member's return. Magno's tenure as a Legionnaire was short-lived, however, as he unfortunately lost his magnetic powers following a battle with the sinister sorcerer Mordru the DARK LORD. Nevertheless, Magz remained with the LSH and served as an auxiliary non-powered member attending to monitor duty full-time. Since the team has relocated to the orbiting Legion World and now employs entire staffs of support teams, Magz's present role—if he has one—is undetermined. **SB**

ATTRACTIVE *Like all Braalians, Magno possessed highly developed magnetic powers until a battle with Mordru negated his abilities.*

WEAK *Robbed of his powers, Magno no longer serves the Legion of Super-Heroes in an official capacity.*

MAINLINE

FIRST APPEARANCE STEEL (2nd series) #0 (October 1994)
STATUS Hero **REAL NAME** Unknown
OCCUPATION Member of Team Hazard's Black Ops **BASE** Mobile
HEIGHT 5ft 11in **WEIGHT** 170 lbs **EYES** Unknown **HAIR** None
SPECIAL POWERS/ABILITIES Can fly at light-speed and burn through objects while in energy form.

Able to shift between physical and energy states at will, Mainline is potentially one of the most formidable member of Team Hazard's Black Ops. Very little is known about him or the appearance he hides beneath his full-body Team Hazard uniform. However, he is still tangible as an energy being, and a solid hit will knock him back into his regular state and leave him vulnerable. In various outings with Team Hazard, Mainline has sabotaged teammates' actions by a combination of bad luck and poor planning. **DW**

MAJOR FORCE

FIRST APPEARANCE CAPTAIN ATOM (2nd series) #12 (February 1988)
STATUS Villain (deceased) **REAL NAME** Clifford Zmeck
OCCUPATION U.S. government agent **BASE** Washington, D.C.
HEIGHT 6ft 5in **WEIGHT** 260 lbs **EYES** Blue **HAIR** Reddish brown
SPECIAL POWERS/ABILITIES Superstrength, invulnerability, possible immortality; projected black energy blasts.

Sergeant Clifford Zmeck, the second test subject in the U.S. government's "Captain Atom Project" (*see* CAPTAIN ATOM), had received a life sentence for murder when he was selected to receive a double coating of alien alloy and stand at ground zero during an H-bomb explosion. Zmeck shot into the quantum field at the instant of detonation. When he emerged, decades had passed and he had gained superhuman powers. General Wade Eiling (GENERAL) took command of Zmeck, naming him Major Force and laser-etching a "costume" onto his metallic shell. Major Force was assigned to shadowy government bureaus such as the Quorum. He has been killed and resurrected many times, including a death while pursuing SUPERMAN and BATMAN for President Lex Luthor (*see* LUTHOR, LEX), and another death at the hands of MONARCH. **DW**

BAD AGENT
Major Force relished doing the government's dirty work.

MAJOR DISASTER

FIRST APPEARANCE GREEN LANTERN (2nd series) #43 (March 1966)
STATUS Villain turned ally **REAL NAME** Paul Booker
OCCUPATION Former criminal **BASE** JLA Watchtower, the Moon
HEIGHT 5ft 11in **WEIGHT** 195 lbs **EYES** Brown **HAIR** Black
SPECIAL POWERS/ABILITIES Seemingly invulnerable; possesses incredible psychic ability to generate natural disasters on a massive scale, from devastating earthquakes to flash floods.

Paul Booker learned the secret identities of both the GREEN LANTERN and the FLASH when he broke into Tom Kalmaku's apartment (*see* KALMAKU, TOM) and discovered a book recording the many adventures of the JUSTICE LEAGUE OF AMERICA. Booker then hired a group of scientists to create special weapons for him, which he used to create a sinister alter ego, Major Disaster. During a destructive battle with Green Lantern and the Flash, Major Disaster was incinerated in an explosion, but his body later reformed and internalized his powers so that he no longer relied on his special technology to use them. In an attempt at reformation, he joined Justice League Antarctica. The team soon disbanded and Major Disaster then sold his soul to the demon NERON in exchange for even greater destructive power. After briefly joining the SUICIDE SQUAD, and later helping SUPERMAN on one of his missions, Disaster was pardoned for his crimes. BATMAN then recruited him into the JLA, and he later served with its spinoff, the Justice League Elite. **PJ**

DESTRUCTION *A reformed criminal, Major Disaster is able to summon a 9.7 earthquake or a giant tsunami at will, using the elements to do his dirty work.*

PARDON *Major Disaster was invited by Batman to join the JLA. Superman accepted Disaster with a handshake—and a watchful eye.*

MAMMOTH

FIRST APPEARANCE NEW TEEN TITANS (1st series) #3 (January 1981)
STATUS Villain **REAL NAME** Baran Flinders
OCCUPATION Professional criminal **BASE** New Jersey
HEIGHT 6ft 5in **WEIGHT** 300 lbs **EYES** Blue **HAIR** Red
SPECIAL POWERS/ABILITIES Superhuman strength; partial invulnerability.

As children growing up in Australia, Baran Flinders and his sister Selinda received nothing but mockery as their unique abilities developed—she could transmute elements, while he exhibited terrifying strength. The world-renowned scientist Dr. Helga Jace taught them how to control their talents—whereupon they created the villainous identities of Mammoth and SHIMMER and joined DOCTOR LIGHT I, GIZMO, and PSIMON as members of the FEARSOME FIVE. Mammoth has clashed with the TEEN TITANS and SUPERMAN, both with the Fearsome Five and on his own. Devoted to his sister, Mammoth suffered deep psychological trauma when Psimon killed her. After Shimmer's resurrection, Mammoth rejoined the Fearsome Five and later joined the Injustice League Unlimited. **DW**

MAN-BAT

GOTHAM'S NIGHT TERROR

FIRST APPEARANCE DETECTIVE COMICS #400 (June 1970)
STATUS Villain **REAL NAME** Robert Kirkland Langstrom
OCCUPATION biologist **BASE** A small town near Gotham City
HEIGHT 7ft 4in **WEIGHT** 315 lbs **EYES** Red **HAIR** Brown
SPECIAL POWERS/ABILITIES Transforms into a winged, super-strong batlike humanoid that has natural sonar, but limited daytime vision.

DOCTOR KIRK LANGSTROM was an expert in mammal biology, notably *chiroptera* (bats). Hoping to cure his growing deafness, he tried to create a serum that would give human beings the powers of echolocation that allow bats to use sound to navigate in the dark. When Langstrom tested the chemical on himself, the serum reacted with his genetic makeup and transformed him into a man-sized bat.

KEY STORYLINES

- *DETECTIVE COMICS #400 (JUNE 1970):* Man-Bat first appears in the skies of Gotham City, as a tragic figure who views his transformations as a curse.
- *BATMAN: MAN-BAT (MAY 1997):* This Elseworlds story showcases a world in which Kirk Langstrom and his wife Francine have become full-time bats, raising a teenaged son and plotting to take over the world with man-bat hybrids.

CHEMISTRY EXPERIMENT *Dr. Langstrom's efforts to develop a serum to cure his condition have remained unsuccessful.*

MAN-BAT ARMY

Once he became the Man-Bat, Langstrom's intellect seemed to vanish, and the crazed mutant began terrorizing Gotham City. BATMAN stopped Man-Bat's initial rampage, but Langstrom soon injected himself with another dose and became Man-Bat once again. He kidnapped his fiancée, Francine Lee, injected her, and she became a half-human/half-bat hybrid as well. After Batman once again captured Man-Bat and his mate, Langstrom refined the serum so that he could transform into his mutated state but maintain his intelligence. This Man-Bat occasionally helped Batman solve crimes. Langstrom and Francine eventually married and had a daughter, Rebecca, and a son, Aaron, a miniature version of his Man-Bat father.

SCREECHING THROUGH THE SKIES *Driven by madness instead of true villainy, Man-Bat has attacked Batman above the streets of Gotham.*

MAN-BAT IN LONDON

Back in his laboratory, Dr. Langstrom worked feverishly to refine the Man-Bat serum to reverse the changes it had made on his physiology and his sanity. One year after the Infinite Crisis, Langstrom earned the attention of TALIA of the LEAGUE OF ASSASSINS. Talia's agents kidnapped Langstrom's wife Francine in London, threatening her life unless Langstrom turned over the secrets of the Man-Bat formula. Desperate to save his wife, Langstrom rushed to assemble the ingredients, arousing the suspicions of Bruce Wayne, in London to attend a charity art exhibit.

Langstrom gave up the serum to Talia, who released Francine and used the genetic mutagen to shape a squad of assassins into ninja man-bats. The airborne killers crashed the gallery opening, forcing Bruce Wayne to do battle as Batman. Although he took down most of the man-bats, Batman fell prey to Talia's superior tactics and became her prisoner—an opportunity she exploited to introduce their mutual son, Damian.

Kirk Langstrom returned to Gotham City where he renewed his sporadic transformations into Man-Bat. Recently captured by the GCPD, he became one of the many villains deposited on a distant prison planet during the events of Operation: Salvation Run. PJ/DW

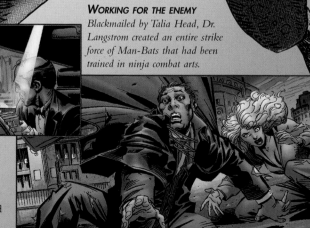

WORKING FOR THE ENEMY *Blackmailed by Talia Head, Dr. Langstrom created an entire strike force of Man-Bats that had been trained in ninja combat arts.*

MANHUNTER

FIRST APPEARANCE MANHUNTER (3rd series) #1 (October 2004)
STATUS Hero
REAL NAME Katherine Spencer
OCCUPATION Federal prosecutor, adventurer
BASE Mobile
HEIGHT 5ft 8in
WEIGHT 145 lbs[1]
EYES Blue
HAIR Brown
SPECIAL POWERS/ABILITIES Suit provides enhanced strength and protection from injuries; carries a powerful energy staff.

THE SCHEMING ANDROID MANHUNTERS have employed human agents over the years. The first was policeman Donald Richards who, with his robotic dog named Thor, battled crime in the 1940s. Big-game hunter Paul Kirk was also recruited during that period. He fought crime as Manhunter II, joining the ALL-STAR SQUADRON during World War II. Decades later, idealist Mark Shaw became the third Manhunter. A master of many fighting styles, he helped the JUSTICE LEAGUE OF AMERICA prevent the Manhunters from destroying the GUARDIANS OF THE UNIVERSE. Star City musician Chase Lawler then had a brief career as a fourth Manhunter before suffering a heart attack. The fifth Manhunter is a clone of Paul Kirk named Kirk DePaul, who is a partner in the corporate team the POWER COMPANY. DePaul sometimes appeared to be more driven by financial gain than the idealism required to be a super hero, and has often clashed with his fellow partners over ethical and moral issues.

MANHUNTER I Donald "Dan" Richards had his own credo for tracking down villains: "Manhunter might get something on them when police methods fail!"

MANHUNTER II Former big-game hunter Paul Kirk, regarded tracking down ciminals as a new challenge to savor. Genetic modifications meant that almost any injury he received healed rapidly.

MANHUNTER V Batman was highly suspicious of Kirk DePaul's motives when he discovered the former mercenary in Gotham City. The Dark Knight was sure DePaul was in town to kill an exile from the African nation of Oranga. Fortunately, on this occasion Batman's fears were groundless.

KATHERINE SPENCER

The sixth and latest Manhunter is Kate Spencer, a federal prosecutor who took up her adventuring identity in response to a legal system that too often let the guilty go free. When COPPERHEAD escaped courtroom justice, Kate scavenged exhibits from an evidence room – including a strength-enhancing battle suit seized from a member of the DARKSTARS, Azrael's former wrist gauntlets, and a staff once carried by a former Manhunter – to piece together a costume and kill the villain. She continued as Manhunter while maintaining her secret identity as prosecutor, aided by her co-counsel Damon Matthews, DEO agent Cameron Chase (see CHASE, CAMERON), and Dylan Battles, a former gadgeteer for supervillains.

In the course of her crimefighting, Kate learned that she came from a proud lineage of super heroes, with her grandparents the Golden Age heroes Iron Monroe and the original PHANTOM LADY. Kate has served with the BIRDS OF PREY, fought in the Infinite Crisis, and trained in hand-to-hand combat under WONDER WOMAN, even defending Wonder Woman in her criminal trial for the murder of Maxwell Lord (see LORD, MAXWELL). Although still a second-tier adventurer, Kate has won the respect of many in the super-hero community and seems poised to take on greater challenges in the coming years. RG/DW

SECRET IDENTITY During her day job as a prosecutor, Kate Spencer keeps her Manhunter costume inside her briefcase.

KEY STORYLINES

- **MANHUNTER (1ST SERIES) #1 (JULY 1988):** The Manhunter character appears in this self-titled series, this time as Mark Shaw, a public defender turned vigilante.
- **POWER COMPANY #1–18 (APRIL 2002–SEPTEMBER 2003):** Kirk DePaul, a clone of Paul Kirk, serves with the for-hire super-hero team organized by Josiah Power.
- **MANHUNTER (3RD SERIES) #1 (OCTOBER 2004):** Kate Spencer becomes the latest Manhunter, balancing her role as a prosecutor with her unlicensed, freelance adventuring.

BACK FROM THE DEAD Shadow Thief raises Copperhead from the grave—much to Manhunter's consternation. She believed she had put the killer in the ground for good.

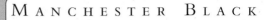

MANCHESTER BLACK

FIRST APPEARANCE ACTION COMICS #775 (March 2001)
STATUS Villain **REAL NAME** Manchester Black
OCCUPATION Adventurer **BASE** England
HEIGHT 5ft 6in **WEIGHT** 120 lbs **EYES** Blue **HAIR** Purple
SPECIAL POWERS/ABILITIES An accomplished telepath who can manipulate minds and distort reality. In combat he uses telekinetic powers, preferring not to get his hands dirty in a fight.

Black's team, the Elite, considered themselves true crime fighters but their methods were extreme: they killed their opponents. When Black and his Elite came to Metropolis, they were opposed by the city's protector, SUPERMAN. The Man of Steel defeated the Elite and captured Black, but President Lex Luthor (see LUTHOR, LEX) had Black released. The immoral Brit became Luthor's ally, using his telepathic gifts to find out that Clark Kent was Superman's alter ego, a secret that Luthor had long sought. Black first learned of IMPERIEX's approach to Earth, allowing Luthor a chance to mobilize the planet's defense in a cosmic war. After the war, Black used his knowledge of Superman's alter ego to target everyone close to Superman and/or Clark Kent. Black was thought to have died in an explosion, but has returned with his sister, Vera Black. RG

MIND GAMES
Attempting to trick Superman into killing a man, Black kidnaps Lois Lane and then tries to make the Man of Steel think he has killed her.

REVENGE FANTASY
Superman imagines what he'd like to do to Manchester Black.

MANNHEIM, BRUNO

FIRST APPEARANCE SUPERMAN'S PAL JIMMY OLSEN #139 (July 1971)
STATUS Villain **REAL NAME** Bruno Mannheim
OCCUPATION Crime boss
BASE Metropolis
HEIGHT 6ft 2in **WEIGHT** 290 lbs **EYES** Black **HAIR** Black
SPECIAL POWERS/ABILITIES Brilliant and twisted criminal mind.

Bruno Mannheim, nicknamed "Ugly," is the leader of INTERGANG, an organized crime outfit headquartered in Metropolis. He rose to power by allying with DARKSEID and securing high-tech Fourth World weapons from Apokolips. After the Infinite Crisis, Mannheim found new inspiration in a crime cult built around the worship of Cain, the first murderer. Mannheim's devotion to the teachings of the "Crime Bible" led him to commit unspeakable atrocities, including human sacrifices and cannibalism.
Believing that the Crime Bible demanded the ritual murder of Kate Kane, a.k.a. BATWOMAN, Mannheim kidnapped her until stopped by the

RAGE *Bruno Mannheim was always one of the most brutal mobsters to ever head Intergang, but his indoctrination into the Cult of Cain turned him into a homicidal killer.*

BLOODBATH *Driven by his reverence for the teachings of the Crime Bible, Mannheim murdered many of Gotham's second-tier criminals.*

arrival of the QUESTION and Renee Montoya (see MONTOYA, RENEE). Months later, Mannheim reemerged in Metropolis, apparently grown to the size of a giant. After zeroing in on the beat of Mannheim's oversized heart, SUPERMAN disrupted the villain's criminal operations but couldn't prevent him from teleporting to safety. Mannheim's known connections with extra-terrestrial weapons dealers, combined with his new focus on the amoral teachings of the Cult of Cain, have resulted in a crime lord with unlimited power and no moral scruples. Mannheim is far more dangerous than he has ever been. DW

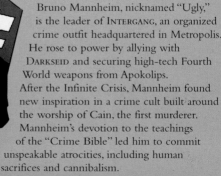

MANHUNTERS, THE

FIRST APPEARANCE JUSTICE LEAGUE OF AMERICA (1st series) #140 (March 1977)
STATUS Villains **REAL NAME** Not applicable **OCCUPATION** Android would-be conquerors (destroyed) **BASE** Mobile **HEIGHT** 7ft **WEIGHT** 475 lbs **EYES** Photocellular **HAIR** None **SPECIAL POWERS/ABILITIES** Super-strong, armored androids armed with stun guns formerly energized by hand-held power batteries; now carry batons that fire energy blasts.

The GUARDIANS OF THE UNIVERSE created the android Manhunters as a universal police force 3.5 billion years ago. For unknown reasons, the Manhunters rebelled against their programming and launched a millennia-long battle that culminated with an attack on the planet Oa. Ultimately, the Guardians overcame their android servants, stripping them of their power and banishing them across the universe. By 1066, the Manhunters discovered Earth and they began establishing agents there. Nearly 40 years ago, a battle between the Manhunters and the GREEN LANTERN CORPS above the Earth triggered a record-breaking blizzard that left the KENTS snowed in at their farm for months, long enough for Ma and Pa Kent to pass off the baby Kal-El (SUPERMAN) as their own son. During the Millennium event, the Manhunters activated their sleeper agents on Earth, but met global defeat. Now led by the CYBORG SUPERMAN, the Manhunters serve the SINESTRO Corps as warriors and mobile batteries for recharging power rings. RG

MANTIS

FIRST APPEARANCE THE FOREVER PEOPLE (1st series) #2 (June 1971)
STATUS Villain (deceased) **REAL NAME** None
OCCUPATION Agent of Darkseid **BASE** Apokolips
HEIGHT 6ft 4in **WEIGHT** 275 lbs **EYES** Orange **HAIR** None
SPECIAL POWERS/ABILITIES Superstrength; flight; can absorb any power source; "thermal touch" generates heat, "frigi-block" imprisons foes in ice; can destroy anything he touches with anti-matter.

Mantis himself may be even more powerful than DARKSEID, evil lord of Apokolips. Mantis was the first of Darkseid's agents to arrive on Earth. Foolishly, he schemed to conquer the planet for himself. Darkseid, meanwhile, permitted Mantis's ambitions only insofar as they aided his own search for the elusive Anti-Life Equation—the means of controlling all sentient life in the universe—which the ruler of Apokolips believed was secreted somewhere on Earth. Mantis was later defeated by the INFINITY MAN. Mantis then led the "bug" colonies of New Genesis in an attack on Earth. This time he was thwarted by the NEW GODS. Having an insatiable appetite for power, Mantis has even risen against Darkseid, only to be suitably humbled for his hubris. Mantis perished during the recent Death of the New Gods event, struck by a hidden killer. SB

MARKSMAN

FIRST APPEARANCE SMASH COMICS #33 (May 1942)
STATUS Hero **REAL NAME** Baron Povalski
OCCUPATION Adventurer **BASE** Poland
HEIGHT 5ft 8in **WEIGHT** 150 lbs **EYES** Blue **HAIR** Black
SPECIAL POWERS/ABILITIES The Baron was an Olympic-level bowman as well as a highly trained hand-to-hand combatant.

Outraged by the Nazi atrocities committed in his native Poland, Baron Pavolski decided to fight back. When the Nazis invaded Pavolski's ancestral mansion for a base of operations, it became the birthplace of the hooded Marksman. By day, he masqueraded as Major Hurtz, loyal member of the Nazi Party, but when the sun went down, he swung into action using his nobleman's training with a sword and bow, silently dispatching the enemy. He worked undercover throughout Europe and was present, aiding members of the fabled JUSTICE SOCIETY OF AMERICA, during the bombing of Dresden. His post-World War II whereabouts remain unrecorded. RG

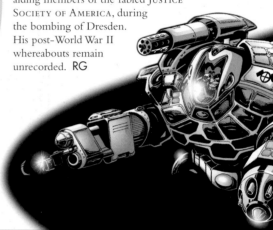

MANITOU RAVEN

FIRST APPEARANCE JLA #66 (July 2002)
STATUS Villain turned hero **REAL NAME** Unknown
OCCUPATION Tribal mystic; adventurer
BASE JLA Watchtower, the Moon
HEIGHT 5ft 9in **WEIGHT** 156 lbs **EYES** White **HAIR** Black
SPECIAL POWERS/ABILITIES Vast supernatural powers include the ability to change his size and travel to the astral plane; carries a hatchet that cannot cut a just man.

Born more than 3,000 years ago, the shaman Manitou Raven comes from a North American tribe that were ancestors of the Apache people. When the Atlantean sorceress GAMEMNAE foresaw that the time-traveling JUSTICE LEAGUE OF AMERICA could foil her plans to dominate Atlantis during its Obsidian Age, she recruited warriors from primitive societies to act as her defenders. Manitou Raven and others formed the League of Ancients, believing they needed to destroy a "seven-headed hydra" to save the world.

Manitou soon realized that he was fighting on the wrong side. He helped the Justice League defeat Gamemnae and, with his wife, Dawn, accompanied the modern-day heroes back to their own era. After Jason Blood (the DEMON) left the JLA, Manitou Raven assumed his place as resident mystic. Manitou Raven later joined the undercover spin-off team known as the Justice League Elite. He died while pursuing the villain Aftermath, but lived on in spirit form. His wife Dawn now wields his powers as Manitou Dawn. DW

MYSTIC MAN Tribal rituals help Manitou Raven see the future and access the spirit place, but they often keep him isolated from his teammates.

DAWN Manitou Raven says he fell in love with his wife when she stole his horses and burnt down his home.

MARTIAN MANHUNTER

FIRST APPEARANCE DETECTIVE COMICS #225 (November 1955)
STATUS Hero **REAL NAME** J'onn J'onzz
OCCUPATION Adventurer **BASE** JLA Watchtower, the Moon
HEIGHT 6ft 7in **WEIGHT** 300 lbs **EYES** Red **HAIR** None
SPECIAL POWERS/ABILITIES Flight, superstrength, invulnerability, enhanced speed, shapeshifting, invisibility, telepathy, and "Martian vision," which provides a type of X-ray vision and allows J'onn to fire energy beams from his eyes.

J'ONN J'ONZZ, THE MARTIAN MANHUNTER, has lost his wife, his daughter, and his newest love, yet he is never truly alone. His family is the JUSTICE LEAGUE OF AMERICA. Eons ago, the Martians were one of the most powerful species in the universe, capable of shapeshifting, intangibility, flight, and a host of other incredible powers. J'onn J'onzz, a philosopher and peacemaker in his private life, worked as a Manhunter to keep the peace on his native planet.

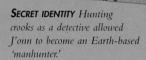

H'RONMEER'S CURSE

J'onn J'onzz's calm life took a horrific turn when the mad priest Ma'alefa'ak (Malefic) unleashed the pyrokinetic plague H'ronmeer's Curse on the people of Mars. This pestilence, spread by telepathy, raced through the population and caused nearly every citizen to burst into flames, including J'onn's wife and daughter. J'onn imprisoned Ma'alefa'ak beneath Mars's highest mountain, Olympus Mons, and wandered the planet's surface for untold years until Dr. Saul Erdel brought him to Earth via a teleportation machine. J'onn J'onzz took steps to fit into this strange new society, first by assuming the identity of murdered Denver police detective John Jones and then by joining the Gotham City super-group "Justice Experience" under the alias Bronze Wraith. In Kansas, J'onn posed as a high-school civics teacher to keep an eye on a young Clark Kent (see Superman).

Eventually J'onn went public as the Martian Manhunter, becoming a founding member of the Justice League of America alongside AQUAMAN, GREEN LANTERN, the FLASH, and BLACK CANARY. The League soon became his life. While other members came and went, the Martian Manhunter served with every subsequent lineup. His spirituality led many to consider him the League's heart and soul, while his vast array of powers put him in a physical class that even exceeded SUPERMAN's—suffering only from a vulnerability to fire.

The Martian Manhunter has battled foes from the Red Planet, including the WHITE MARTIANS (survivors from an ancient civil war between the Whites and J'onn's Green Martians) and Ma'alefa'ak, still alive and looking to complete his mission of genocide. J'onn faced his greatest challenge in the form of another forgotten Martian menace—the Burning. After the Infinite Crisis, J'onn went undercover to infiltrate CHECKMATE, and fought BLACK ADAM during the event known as World War III. The experience caused him to withdraw from humanity and adopt an appearance more consistent with his true Martian form. He soon found a group of White Martians that claimed to be surviving Green Martians like himself, then served briefly with Batman's latest team of OUTSIDERS.
DW

TRUE TO FORM
J'onn still adopts his true Martian shape during moments of quiet meditation.

FIRE *J'onn's vulnerability to flame is caused by both genetic and psychological factors.*

SECRET IDENTITY *Hunting crooks as a detective allowed J'onn to become an Earth-based 'manhunter.'*

MALEFIC *Not content with the annihilation of a species, this Martian conqueror thirsts for blood.*

DARK MIRROR
Fernus, who needed fire in order to reproduce, represented all that was evil in J'onn's soul.

KEY STORYLINES

• *MARTIAN MANHUNTER (2ND SERIES) #1 (DECEMBER 1998):* The quintessential team player gets a starring role for the first time in years.

• *JLA: YEAR ONE #1-12 (JANUARY–DECEMBER 1998):* J'onn's role as the heart and soul of the JLA is apparent in this retelling of the team's origin.

• *JLA #84-89 (OCTOBER–DECEMBER 2003):* J'onn turns against his JLA teammates during the Burning Martian storyline, showing why he is their most powerful member.

MARY MARVEL

THE WORLD'S MIGHTIEST GIRL

FIRST APPEARANCE CAPTAIN MARVEL ADVENTURES #18 (Dec. 1942)
STATUS Hero **REAL NAME** Mary Batson **OCCUPATION** Adventurer
BASE Fawcett City **HEIGHT** 5ft 6in **WEIGHT** 139 lbs **EYES** Blue
HAIR Auburn **SPECIAL POWERS/ABILITIES** By saying "Shazam!" aloud,
Mary Marvel gains Solomon's wisdom, Hercules' superstrength,
Atlas's stamina, Zeus's raw power, Achilles's courage, and Mercury's
superspeed. Mary Marvel shares her powers with Captain Marvel
and Captain Marvel, Jr.; if either is using their powers, Mary Marvel
has access to only half her power.

SHE IS THE TWIN SISTER OF BILLY BATSON, the mighty
mortal known as CAPTAIN MARVEL. Granted the abilities of
the greatest OLYMPIAN GODS by uttering the name of the
wizard Shazam, Mary Batson is Mary Marvel, one of the most
powerful heroes on the planet! A sweet young woman in both
guises, Mary nonetheless packs quite a punch, courageously
defending her hometown of Fawcett City from mutant
worms, Nazi terrorists, and ancient deities gone mad!

THE WORLD'S MIGHTIEST GIRL *Despite
her power, Mary Marvel is still only
a teenager.*

SHAZAM! *Mary summons
a lightning bolt to change
her into a super-hero.*

BOOOOOOOOOM!

KEY STORYLINES

• *POWER OF SHAZAM #30-31 (SEPTEMBER 1997):*
During the Genesis event, Mary's secret identity
was revealed to her parents before she entered
the Source to save all of creation!

• *FORMERLY KNOWN AS THE JUSTICE LEAGUE #1-6
(SEPTEMBER 2003–JANUARY 2004):*
Mary joined the team, and nearly murdered
Captain Atom in a hypnotic rage induced by
Roulette!

THERE'S SOMETHING ABOUT MARY

Mary Batson's parents were killed by
Theo Adam (*see* BLACK ADAM) on an
archaeological expedition in Egypt when
she was nine. Mary, who had completely
lost her memory, was taken back to the
U.S. by Adam's sister, Sarah Primm, who
worked for Nick and Nora Bromfeld,
a wealthy family in Fawcett City.
Adopted by the Bromfelds, Mary
lived a sheltered life.

Years later, Mary was reintroduced
to Billy Batson, who recognized her
as his long-lost sister. Billy and his
friend Freddy Freeman arrived at
the Bromfelds just as the villain Ibac
arrived to kidnap the family. Mary escaped,
clutching the gift Billy had brought her to jog
her memory, a stuffed animal the twins used to
play with called Mister Tawky Tawny. As Mary

hid from the kidnappers, the toy transported
her mind to another dimension, where she
met the spirit of her slain mother, Marilyn,
and the wizard Shazam. Mary's mental blocks vanished and her
memory returned. She instinctively sensed that her brother
Billy was Captain Marvel. Mary begged the wizard to help
her save her family. He agreed and blessed her with a variety
of powers she could summon forth by saying the word
"Shazam!"

When the kidnappers burst into Mary's room, they found
her garbed in a red and gold costume. Invulnerable to their
bullets, she overpowered them, but not before her nanny,
Sarah Primm, suffered a heart attack. As she lay dying,
Sarah confessed her relationship with Theo Adam to Mary,
and how she had tried to hide the amnesiac Mary, who
had witnessed her parents' murder, with the Bromfelds to
give her a chance at a decent life. Billy moved in with the
Bromfelds soon after, and the Marvels became Fawcett
City's champions, defending the town
from master criminals like DOCTOR SIVANA,
CAPTAIN NAZI, and MISTER MIND.

Mary Marvel lost her powers during the
Infinite Crisis, but reacquired them as a "gift"
from Black Adam. The transfer corrupted her,
and a black-garbed Mary Marvel fell under the
spell of ECLIPSO as she explored the depths of
her new abilities. **PJ**

JUSTICE LEAGUER
*Mary Marvel was
once forced to use
her power on her
teammate Captain
Atom in Roulette's
fight club, the House.*

DARK DESIRES *Once
considered the purest
of heroes, Mary was
corrupted by Black
Adam's and turned
against her friends in
the months prior to the
Final Crisis.*

MATTER-EATING LAD

FIRST APPEARANCE ADVENTURE COMICS #303 (December 1963)
STATUS Hero **REAL NAME** Tenzil Kem
OCCUPATION Politician **BASE** Bismoll
HEIGHT 5ft 10in **WEIGHT** 150 lbs **EYES** Blue **HAIR** Black
SPECIAL POWERS/ABILITIES Can eat any form of matter and disintegrate it.

Tenzil Kem of Bismoll possesses a strange ability common to all members of his species – he can eat any substance and break it down to near-nothingness. He joined the LEGION OF SUPER-HEROES as Matter-Eater Lad, using his powers to munch tunnels through rock or devour weapons of mass destruction.

The citizens of his homeworld loved Tenzil Kem's new celebrity status and drafted him into politics, frequently pulling him from his Legion duties to serve as Bismoll's senator. Even in his rarely-seen role, Matter-Eater lad made himself available to assist his fellow Legionnaires in times of need.

In other timelines containing alternate versions of the Legion of Super-Heroes, Tenzil Kem's role as Matter-Eater Lad is a more subtle one. In the timeline created after the events of Zero Hour, Tenzil Kem served the Legion as the team's cook without assuming a costumed identity. In another, Tenzil Kem is a government agent and legal expert who crossed paths with several Legionnaires during their hunt for COSMIC BOY. This Tenzil escaped from a flooded grain silo by eating his way out. **DW**

MAX MERCURY

FIRST APPEARANCE NATIONAL COMICS #5 (November 1940)
STATUS Hero (missing in action) **REAL NAME** Unrevealed
OCCUPATION Adventurer **BASE** Manchester, Alabama
HEIGHT 6ft 1in **WEIGHT** 188 lbs **EYES** Blue **HAIR** Gray
SPECIAL POWERS/ABILITIES Can run at speeds approaching the speed of light and vibrate his molecules through solid objects.

The "Zen Master of Speed" is the elder statesman among the Flash family of speedsters. A friend to Jay Garrick, a mentor to Wally West, and a father figure to Impulse (see KID FLASH), Max Mercury knows more about the Speed Force than anyone on the planet. Born in the first half of the 19th century, he gained his powers from a Blackfoot tribal shaman while working as a fort messenger on the American frontier. Running at near-light velocity, Max brushed against the edge of the Speed Force. He was ricocheted into the future, landing in 1880s Arizona, where he became known as Windrunner. He later worked as Whip Whirlwind in New York City and, after another time jaunt, he helped baseball star Babe Ruth escape the mob in the 1920s under the alias Lightning. In the 1940s he emerged as Quicksilver, working alongside Jay "Flash" Garrick during World War II.

After the war Max fathered a daughter and time-skipped into the '50s as Blue Streak. He finally jumped to the current era during a 1960s battle with SAVITAR. Since then Max has established ties with his daughter Dr. Helen Claiborne, and become the legal guardian of Impulse. Jay Garrick's old enemy Rival possessed Max's body and vanished in a time sphere. Max lives on in an alternate dimension, as witnessed during the Infinite Crisis. **DW**

MAWZIR

FIRST APPEARANCE HITMAN #1 (August 1995)
STATUS Villain (destroyed) **REAL NAME** Mawzir
OCCUPATION Creature **BASE** Hell
HEIGHT 6ft 6in **WEIGHT** 160 lbs **EYES** Blue **HAIR** Brown
SPECIAL POWERS/ABILITIES Huge and nimble, the deadly Mawzir used its ten arms with great speed and agility.

After World War II, Russian troops hanged five Nazi officers for war crimes. Their souls went to Hell, where Arkhannone, the Lords of the Gun, transformed them into a single demon, the horrific, ten-armed Mawzir. Dispatched to Earth numerous times, the Mawzir attempted to bring back artifacts for its master. This brought it into opposition first with CATWOMAN, and then hitman Tommy Monaghan. Tommy destroyed the Mawzir and many of the Arkhannone using a magic rifle. The Mawzir has since returned, attempting to break into CHECKMATE headquarters. **RG**

MAXIE ZEUS

FIRST APPEARANCE DETECTIVE COMICS #483 (May 1979)
STATUS Villain (deceased) **BASE** Gotham City
HEIGHT 5ft 6in **WEIGHT** 135 lbs **EYES** Brown **HAIR** Brown
SPECIAL POWERS/ABILITIES A master manipulator and orator with delusions of grandeur, he had various underworld connections.

Maxie Zeus was a deranged gang leader who believed that he was an avatar of Zeus, the Olympian sky god. Amassing a flock of worshippers who doubled as gang members, Maxie became a prominent leader in the Gotham underworld. He briefly married, but after the death of his wife, (name unknown) he raised his daughter, mythologically named Medea, alone.

After several clashes with BATMAN, Maxie Zeus moved to Los Angeles and founded a team of superbeings he called, with typical hubris, the New Olympians. After a violent clash between his New Olympians and THE OUTSIDERS, the New Olympians were all captured, and Maxie Zeus skulked back to Gotham City.

Maxie was then summoned from underworld obscurity by PHOBOS, a son of ARES, god of war, who wished to turn Gotham into Ares's base on Earth. Maxie gathered a new cult following and helped Phobos and his siblings take control of three of Batman's most powerful villains, POISON IVY, SCARECROW, and the JOKER, energizing the demi-gods with his cult members' prayers. During the ensuing battle between Batman, WONDER WOMAN, and Ares's children, Maxie Zeus was slain, a human sacrifice to the war god himself. **PJ**

MAXIMA

FIRST APPEARANCE ACTION COMICS #645 (September 1989)
STATUS Hero (deceased) **REAL NAME** None
OCCUPATION Deposed ruler of Almerac/adventurer **BASE** Earth
HEIGHT 6ft 2in **WEIGHT** 164 lbs **EYES** Brown **HAIR** Red
SPECIAL POWERS/ABILITIES Superstrength; flight; able to psychokinetically manipulate matter at the molecular level.

Maxima once ruled a vast empire based on the planet Almerac. She became obsessed with expanding her galactic reach and, most importantly, securing a suitable mate to father an heir for her glorious realm. When her minions intercepted a subspace transmission detailing SUPERMAN'S astonishing feats in the gladiatorial games of MONGUL'S Warworld, Maxima was sure she had found her man. Without further delay, she resolved to make the Man of Steel her husband. Superman respectfully declined to marry her, her admiration turned to rage, and she became his enemy.

As time passed, however, her fury abated, and Maxima sided with Superman to repel BRAINIAC'S intergalactic invasion of Earth. Maxima was later banished from Almerac and elected to remain on Earth, where she was a respected member of the JUSTICE LEAGUE for a while. Ultimately, her own superiority complex and lingering resentment over Superman's rejection of her led Maxima back to villainy and a partnership with the so-called Superman Revenge Squad.

Fickle as she was, Maxima never ever backed down from a fight. After the world-destroying IMPERIEX destroyed Almerac, Maxima gave her own life so that Earth, her adopted home, would not suffer the same terrible fate. **SB**

IMPERIEX WAR Almerac's destruction spurred Maxima to lead a ragtag group of alien refugees in battle against the world-razing Imperiex and his nigh-indestructible Probes.

DESTROYED Slain in the intergalactic conflict, Maxima died as she lived, a warrior mistress without fear of death who sacrificed the might of Warworld to slow the advance of Imperiex.

MAYA

FIRST APPEARANCE JUSTICE LEAGUE EUROPE #47 (February 1993)
STATUS Hero **REAL NAME** Chandi Gupta
OCCUPATION Adventurer **BASE** India
HEIGHT 5ft 3in **WEIGHT** 120 lbs **EYES** Brown **HAIR** Black
SPECIAL POWERS/ABILITIES Can emit and control fire and water, channeling her mystic powers in harmony with the fire elemental Firestorm and water elemental Naiad.

The deity Maya is an aspect of the world spirit Gaea, and she has bestowed her powers upon mortals on occasion, including teenager Chandi Gupta. Her powers developed in spurts, starting with her skill with firing mystic arrows of fire or water. The JUSTICE LEAGUE OF AMERICA, its Reserves and the JUSTICE SOCIETY OF AMERICA stopped Sonar's bid for power in Europe. Afterwards, Justice League Europe adopted the more far-reaching name Justice League International and inducted Maya and the TASMANIAN DEVIL (an Australian member of the GLOBAL GUARDIANS) as its two newest members. Some time later, Chandi returned to her native India at her parents' insistence. **RG**

MEANSTREAK

FIRST APPEARANCE JUSTICE LEAGUE AMERICA (2nd series) #78 (August 1993)
STATUS Villain **REAL NAME** Unknown **OCCUPATION** New Extremist
BASE Mobile **HEIGHT** 5ft 8in **WEIGHT** 144 lbs **EYES** Blue **HAIR** Blonde
SPECIAL POWERS/ABILITIES Can generate swords, daggers, and projectiles made of flaming energy; a sadist at heart.

Together with her teammates in the New Extremists— Brute, Cloudburst, Death Angel, and GUNSHOT— Meanstreak takes pleasure in ruination and pain. The extra-dimensional being DREAMSLAYER invited Meanstreak into the New Extremists to bring an end to the JUSTICE LEAGUE OF AMERICA, a challenge she failed to achieve. Later, Dreamslayer seized a device operated by the Colorado cult "Flock of the Machine" (who worshipped the all-powerful OVERMASTER) to provide a second chance at glory for Meanstreak and her comrades. After they again fell short, the Overmaster drew the New Extremists into his vast new CADRE, an army of super-villains. Despite its size, the Cadre foundered, but Meanstreak and the New Extremists are still active as mobile mercenaries. **DW**

MEKANIQUE

FIRST APPEARANCE INFINITY INC. #19 (October 1985)
STATUS Villain (destroyed) **REAL NAME** None
OCCUPATION Agent of Rotwang **BASE** An unspecified future
HEIGHT 5ft 9in **WEIGHT** 519 lbs **EYES** Red **HAIR** None
SPECIAL POWERS/ABILITIES Dimensional travel; can fire electrical blasts, project neutron shield, and avoid electronic detection.

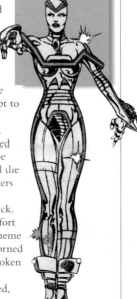

In the far future, Earth's greatest city will be a metropolis populated by slaves serving a despotic elite. To crush an uprising before it begins, the scientist Rotwang will create a robot woman and send it back in time. The automaton will then clash with the ALL-STAR SQUADRON in an attempt to alter future events.

Although destroyed, this robot, dubbed Mekanique, was salvaged by the JUSTICE SOCIETY'S foe Per Degaton. He targeted the Society's sons and daughters in INFINITY INC., with Mekanique aiding his attack. The robot tried to comfort Degaton when the scheme went awry, but he scorned her "love." As heartbroken as a machine can be, Mekanique self-destructed, destroying them both. **SB**

MEN FROM N.O.W.H.E.R.E.

FIRST APPEARANCE DOOM PATROL (2nd series) #35 (August 1990)
STATUS Villain group (destroyed) **BASE** Mobile
SPECIAL POWERS/ABILITIES The Men had invisible rayguns that have tremendous destructive power; could also transform children's toys into deadly weapons; tears in their coats were in fact portals into another world.

During World War II, a group dedicated to the extermination of eccentricity and difference, named the Agency, began snatching the soul husks of men using the silver tongs of the all-powerful Telephone Avatar, a being they had trapped in a sub-sub basement of the Pentagon. These soul husks became the Men from N.O.W.H.E.R.E. The Men captured powerful psychic Wallace Sage, who was forced to create their bizarre weapons with his mind.

Agent Darren Jones, who had been fired from the Agency for misconduct, created a cadre of imitation Men from N.O.W.H.E.R.E. to destroy Danny the Street, a living, breathing avenue! The Men were rebuffed by the DOOM PATROL, Danny's new teammates, and were rendered powerless by Danny himself. Weeks later, the real Men from N.O.W.H.E.R.E. kidnapped Doom Patroller Dorothy Spinner (*see* SPINNER, DOROTHY), hoping to link her psychic powers—which enabled her to manifest the contents of her subconscious mind—to Wallace Sage's and use them to control the captured Telephone Avatar. But Dorothy's powers proved both unpredictable and uncontrollable, and she destroyed both the Telephone Avatar and the Men from N.O.W.H.E.R.E. **PJ**

MENTO

FIRST APPEARANCE DOOM PATROL (1st series) #91 (November 1964)
STATUS Hero turned villain **REAL NAME** Steve Dayton
OCCUPATION Professional criminal **BASE** Mobile
HEIGHT 5ft 10in **WEIGHT** 178 lbs **EYES** Blue **HAIR** Brown
SPECIAL POWERS/ABILITIES Mento helmet previously provided a considerable array of psychokinetic powers; as a computer entity, Dayton's superpowers are as yet unrevealed, but are likely to be vastly enhanced and facilitate his insane schemes.

Steve Dayton, psychologist and head of Dayton Industries, was once the fifth-richest man in the world. Yet his money couldn't win him the heart of Rita Farr—ELASTI-GIRL of the Doom Patrol—so he invented the "Mento helmet" to enhance the powers of his mind and to adventure alongside her as the super hero Mento. Farr eventually relented and married Dayton, and the two of them adopted the shape-changing Garfield "BEAST BOY" Logan. When Elasti-Girl died, Mento took revenge on her killers, GENERAL ZAHL and MADAME ROUGE. Later, he discovered that he had terminal cancer. Dayton tried to use the Mento helmet to control the disease, but the effort drove him mad. In his insanity he founded a criminal team called the HYBRID to battle the TEEN TITANS, and implanted a new type of Mento chip directly into his brain. He began creating a shadowy new role for himself as "The Crimelord," plotting global dominance. Dayton recently joined the latest incarnation of the Doom Patrol, but continues to struggle with helmet-induced insanity. **DW**

MERA

FIRST APPEARANCE AQUAMAN (1st series) #1 (October 1963)
STATUS Hero **REAL NAME** None
OCCUPATION Queen of Atlantis **BASE** City of Poseidonis
HEIGHT 5ft 9in **WEIGHT** 160 lbs **EYES** Blue **HAIR** Red
SPECIAL POWERS/ABILITIES Strength surpassing that of a human; able to telepathically solidify water into various shapes for offensive and defensive purposes; an aquatic being able to survive on land for limited durations.

The beautiful Mera was monarch of Xebel, an other-dimensional aquatic civilization much like Earth's Atlantis, until she was deposed and banished to Earth. AQUAMAN helped Mera regain rule of Xebel, but she then left her home to be with Aquaman, the pair becoming king and queen of Atlantis.

However, the course of true love runs no smoother underwater than above the surface, and Mera and Aquaman's marriage foundered after the murder of their infant son, Arthur Jr., by the diabolical BLACK MANTA. They separated and Mera became the unwilling mate of evil Thanatos—a sorcerer strongly resembling Aquaman—and bore him a son, A.J., who rapidly aged to adulthood in the villain's realm. Aquaman freed Mera from Thanatos, and she returned with him to Poseidonis, capital of Atlantis, to general rejoicing.

Mera fell under the influence of the mystic Hagen and the Sorceress Class, who manipulated the Atlantean queen as their puppet. After the SPECTRE's destruction of Atlantis during the Infinite Crisis, Mera became leader of the survivors. **SB**

MERLYN

FIRST APPEARANCE JUSTICE LEAGUE OF AMERICA #94 (November 1971)
STATUS Villain **REAL NAME** Unknown
OCCUPATION Mercenary, assassin **BASE** Mobile
HEIGHT 6'3" **WEIGHT** 185 lbs **EYES** Blue **HAIR** Black
SPECIAL POWERS/ABILITIES Expert archer and skilled hand-to-hand combatant.

Merlyn is one of the best archers in the world and one of GREEN ARROW's worst enemies. They crossed paths early in Oliver Queen's career, but where Green Arrow turned to heroism and a seat on the JUSTICE LEAGUE OF AMERICA, Merlyn sought riches in with the LEAGUE OF ASSASSINS. His skills improved further after he made a deal with the demon NERON. He clashed with various teams including YOUNG JUSTICE while forming a loose alliance with fellow criminals MONOCLE, DEADSHOT, and PHOBIA.

Merlyn took a more direct role in Green Arrow's life at the time of the Infinite Crisis. He defeated Green Arrow and left him with two arrows embedded in his chest. Queen's recuperation took months, but he returned to challenge his rival. Merlyn threatened Sin, adopted daughter of BLACK CANARY II and recently, he appeared with the League of Assassins in the sacred city of Nanda Parbat during the resurrection of RĀ'S AL GHŪL. **DW**

MERCENARIES, THE

FIRST APPEARANCE G.I. COMBAT #242 (June 1982)
STATUS Hero team **BASE** Mobile
MEMBERS
Gordon (last name unrevealed) A former Green Beret.
Philip "Prince" Edwards A poor British soldier.
Horst Brenner Former automobile factory worker.

The Mercenaries are three soldiers of fortune who travel the world looking for adventure and paying missions across war-torn battlefields. They joined the French Foreign Legion on the same day and became fast friends. None of them, however, believed that the work they were doing and the danger they were continually placed in was worth the low pay. They decided to leave the Legion and, calling themselves the Mercenaries, travel the world, fighting for whichever army paid them the most.

Still hunted by the French Foreign Legion for desertion, the Mercenaries are masters of armed and unarmed combat, and are renowned for their loyalty to their employers, providing the price is right. **PJ**

Gordon
Horst
Prince

MERRY, GIRL OF 1,000 GIMMICKS

FIRST APPEARANCE STAR SPANGLED COMICS #81 (June 1948)
STATUS Hero **REAL NAME** Merry Pemberton King
OCCUPATION Adventurer **BASE** Civic City
HEIGHT 5ft 3in **WEIGHT** 117 lbs **EYES** Blue **HAIR** Red
SPECIAL POWERS/ABILITIES No special powers, but quick-witted and an excellent athlete.

Merry Creamer was the daughter of a two-time loser who placed her in an orphanage when he was sent to prison for life. When Sylvester Pemberton III (Star-Spangled Kid) was injured, his wealthy father, noting his lack of friends, adopted Merry to be his companion. Sylvester's newly-adopted sister learned the Kid and STRIPESY's secret identities and took an alias of her own: Gimmick Girl. Merry had several adventures before pursuing a romance with Henry King, the criminal Brain Wave II. She had a son, Henry King Jr. When Brain Wave was arrested, Merry raised the boy on her own. Sadly, Merry Pemberton King experienced a mental breakdown and faked her own death when Henry Jr. was in his early teens. As a senior citizen, Merry came to regret her past and joined with several other surviving costumed heroes as Old Justice, lobbying to stop costumed minors going into dangerous situations. Merry's estranged daughter Jacqueline briefly adventured with the SEVEN SOLDIERS OF VICTORY as Gimmix, but lost her life in battle. **RG**

BANG! YOU'RE DEAD!

METAL MEN

FIRST APPEARANCE SHOWCASE #37 (April 1962)
STATUS Hero team   **BASE** Metropolis
MEMBERS AND POWERS
All Metal Men can morph into almost any form.
Gold Analytic mind and leadership skills.
Lead Good-natured and thick-headed; an effective shield against radiation.
Iron Quiet and strong team player.
Mercury Highly educated; can become liquid metal.
Tin Insecure; weakest of the Metal Men.
Platinum Also called Tina; flirt once in love with Dr. Magnus. **Copper** sarcastic and easily flexible.

VERIDIUM *Doctor Magnus is now a Metal Man, though he has not outgrown his fondness for pipes.*

Dr. Will Magnus is the brilliant roboticists behind the Metal Men, the most amazing automatons of their time. Each possesses a humanlike personality thanks to highly-advanced "responsometers," and each exhibits qualities characteristic of their unique metal, including strength, magnetism, or flexibility. The Metal Men can shapeshift with ease, and can even combine to form gigantic constructs to take on enemies like CHEMO and the Missile Men.

Doc Magnus, who has long suffered from bipolar disorder, endured a stint trapped in the body of the Metal Man Veridium as well as crippling bouts of depression. But Professor T.O. MORROW encouraged him, and the two scientists soon found themselves on Oolong Island under the control of Chang Tzu (*see* EGG FU). There, Magnus pretended to build a deadly Plutonium Man for Chang Tzu while secretly rebuilding his original Metal Men. After escaping from Oolong Island, Magnus and the Metal Men aided the JUSTICE LEAGUE OF AMERICA and worked as security guards for BATMAN's corporation, WayneTech. The newest Metal Man to join the team is the female-programmed Copper. **DW**

Mercury · Platinum · Doctor Magnus · Gold · Iron · Tin · Lead

METALLO

FIRST APPEARANCE ACTION COMICS #252 (May 1959)
STATUS Villain   **REAL NAME** John Corben
OCCUPATION Conman; thief   **BASE** Metropolis
HEIGHT Variable   **WEIGHT** Variable
EYES Green photoreceptor cells   **HAIR** None
SPECIAL POWERS/ABILITIES Human brain housed in powerful robotic body powered by kryptonite; can morph into nearly any mechanical size, shape, or height; can project his consciousness into other technological devices, transforming them into an extension of his own body.

HEART OF EVIL *Metallo's original, more humanoid body housed a deadly heart—a chunk of kryptonite, the metallic ore lethal to Superman.*

Small-time conman John Corben was nearly crushed in a car accident, but robotics specialist Emmett Vale was passing by and rescued Corben, transplanting the criminal's still-functioning brain into a special robotic body powered by kryptonite. Vale had obtained a chunk of the destroyed planet Krypton, SUPERMAN's homeworld, from the remains of Superman's birth matrix in Kansas. After Corben's operation, he used the piece of irradiated ore to power the criminal's new robot body. Fearing an invasion from Krypton, Vale told Corben he had to destroy Superman, but Corben instead snapped Vale's neck, killing him.

Metallo, as Corben was now called, did fight Superman a number of times, using his kryptonite power source to weaken the Man of Steel. But Lex Luthor (*see* LUTHOR, LEX) captured Metallo and stole the cyborg's kryptonite heart for his own purposes. Using a back-up power cell to escape Luthor's clutches, Metallo sold his soul to the demon NERON to gain even more power. Soon after, Metallo joined forces with BRAINIAC 13. Corben's metallic body grew to giant proportions after absorbing Metropolis's technological infrastructure before "downgrading" to a more human scale.

Able to shapeshift into nearly any mechanical form imaginable, and desiring nothing less than the death of Superman at his hands, Metallo is a rampaging, homicidal nightmare. Metallo currently has a human-looking exterior composed of artificial flesh, as well as multiple varieties of kryptonite—green, red, blue, and gold—inside his robotic chest. **PJ**

METAMORPHO

FIRST APPEARANCE THE BRAVE AND THE BOLD #57 (December 1964)
STATUS Hero **REAL NAME** Rex Mason
OCCUPATION Adventurer **BASE** Mobile
HEIGHT 6ft 1in **WEIGHT** 200 lbs **EYES** Red **HAIR** None
SPECIAL POWERS/ABILITIES Super-versatile shape-shifter, able to
transform parts of his body or entire form into any chemical element
present in the human body, taking advantage of their properties—
floating as a cloud of helium, burning with the white heat of
phosphorus, etc.

Ruthless billionaire Simon Stagg sent adventurer
Rex Mason to retrieve the fabled Orb of Ra from
an Egyptian pyramid. Little did Mason know that
Stagg plotted his doom. Double-crossed by Stagg's
henchman Java, Mason was left for dead beneath the
tomb. However radiation from the Orb of Ra mutated
Mason's chemical makeup, turning him into the freakish
Metamorpho, a shape-shifting element man whose
desire for payback against Stagg was only surpassed
by his love for Stagg's daughter, Sapphire, whom he
eventually married.

Metamorpho chose to use his elemental abilities
for good as a super hero. He was one of the founding
members of the OUTSIDERS team assembled by BATMAN.
Later, Metamorpho belonged to several incarnations of
the JUSTICE LEAGUE OF AMERICA.

His marriage to Sapphire sadly ended in divorce. Their
son, Joey, unfortunately inherited his father's shapeshifting abilities and grotesque appearance. Over the
years, Metamorpho has seemingly "died" during several
adventures. However, on each occasion Metamorpho's
body was actually rendered inert, eventually
reconstituting and reviving. Following these episodes,
Metamorpho suffered amnesia and struggled to recall his
previous life. A clone of Metamorpho, Shift, served with
the OUTSIDERS until Mason re-absorbed the clone and
took his place with the team. **SB**

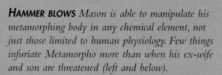

HAMMER BLOWS *Mason is able to manipulate his
metamorphing body in any chemical element, not
just those limited to human physiology. Few things
infuriate Metamorpho more than when his ex-wife
and son are threatened (left and below).*

METRON

FIRST APPEARANCE THE NEW GODS (1st series) #1 (March 1971)
STATUS Ally **REAL NAME** None
OCCUPATION Scientist; explorer **BASE** New Genesis
HEIGHT 6ft 1in **WEIGHT** 190 lbs **EYES** Blue **HAIR** Black
SPECIAL POWERS/ABILITIES Brilliant scientist, whose analytical mind is
motivated by a thirst for knowledge for its own sake; the Mobius
chair can fold space and time, enabling travel
through time and into alternate dimensions.

Metron is a New God who claims
to have been born on neither one
of the planets New Genesis or
Apokolips; appropriately enough,
he is often an independent party
in the ongoing battle between
good and evil. Although capable
of doing great good, he cares
little for beings who do not
have the technical skills to
assist him in his obsessive
explorations of space. Metron freely mingles with gods
and unimaginably powerful cosmic entities, who tolerate
his presence since they are convinced of his impartiality.
He is able to apply his genius intellect to any puzzle
with laser-like intensity. Few secrets can be withheld
from Metron.

In years past, Metron co-invented the NEW GODS'
incredible Boom Tube teleportation technology, which
allowed beings to travel from place to place in the
universe in an instant. During the event known as the
Cosmic Odyssey, Metron's discovery of the nature of the
Anti-Life Equation temporarily sent him into a coma.
Metron assisted SUPERMAN in his defeat of BRAINIAC
I, and later helped the Earth's assembled heroes end the
global threat of MAGEDDON. Metron's brilliant mind
proved its worth during the Death of the New Gods
event, when he uncovered a conspiracy to wipe out the
Fourth World. **DW**

MIDNIGHT

FIRST APPEARANCE SMASH COMICS #18 (January 1941)
STATUS Hero **REAL NAME** Dave Clark
OCCUPATION Radio announcer **BASE** New York City
HEIGHT 6ft **WEIGHT** 190 lbs **EYES** Blue **HAIR** Black
SPECIAL POWERS/ABILITIES Excellent athlete and hand-to-hand
combatant; uses a special vacuum gun that fires suction discs.

A boxer during the Great
Depression, Dave Clark moved
from his Midwestern home
to the mean streets of New
York City in the late 1930s.
There, he eventually became
a radio announcer at station
WXAM. When Clark learned
that a building he had seen collapse had originally been
erected by a criminally negligent construction group,
he adopted the disguise of Midnight, a character he had
first heard of in a radio drama entitled *The Man Called
Midnight*, to force the construction company's owner to
admit his culpability. Midnight subsequently became a
member of the ALL-STAR SQUADRON, but later left the
group to join an independent team of crime fighters called
the FREEDOM FIGHTERS. Midnight also allied himself with
the eccentric genius Dr. Wackey and his super-intelligent
ape, Gabby. Midnight's crime-fighting career ended after
World War II. His current whereabouts, and his final fate,
remain unknown. **PJ**

MILLENNIUM GIANTS

FIRST APPEARANCE THE MAN OF STEEL #78 (April 1998)
STATUS Primordial beings **BASE** Egypt, England, and Mexico
MEMBERS AND POWERS
Sekhmet, Cerne, Cabraca
All three giants are immensely powerful beings more than 400 ft tall; able to call upon Earth's electromagnetic forces to wreak havoc.

The Millennium Giants awoke from thousands of years of slumber to herald the new Bactun, or the "Cycle of Ages," and cleanse the Earth of all its ills. From Egypt came the leviathan Sekhmet. From England arose Cerne, a Celtic giant of amazing destructive force. And from a volcano in the Yucatan peninsula came Cabraca, the "Mountain Destroyer" of Mayan legend. Strangely, these three behemoths awakened just as SUPERMAN was split into twin beings, Superman Blue and Superman Red, both fueled by the very same electromagnetic forces that coursed through the Earth's ley lines. As if linked by magic, the Millennium Giants followed the ley lines, unleashing a catalogue of natural disasters as they prepared the Earth for another thousand years of growth. To halt the Millennium Giants' devastation, the twin Supermen were joined by the so-called "Team Superman"— STEEL III, SUPERBOY, and SUPERGIRL—as well as AQUAMAN, the CHALLENGERS OF THE UNKNOWN, the JUSTICE LEAGUE OF AMERICA, and the TEEN TITANS. When all hope seemed lost, the heroes finally realized that the Millennium Giants were a vital part of Earth's cycle of renewal. Superman Red and Superman Blue expended all their electromagnetic energies to cleanse the Earth's ley lines and finish the Giants' task without further destruction. The Millennium Giants then returned to their thousand-year slumber to await the next Bactun. **SB**

SUPER-SIZED *Cabraca and his fellow Millennium Giants emerged from deep within the Earth to cleanse the planet with destructive force!*

MINION

FIRST APPEARANCE NEW TITANS #114 (September 1994)
STATUS Hero **REAL NAME** Jarras Minion
OCCUPATION Adventurer **BASE** Mobile
HEIGHT 5ft **WEIGHT** 110 lbs
EYES Blue **HAIR** Blue-green
SPECIAL POWERS/ABILITIES Minion's Omegadrome was a nearly sentient device that could transform itself into protective body armor, weapons, and even a spaceworthy transport ship.

The planet Talyn was home to a warlike race constantly in battle. The solution was to introduce genetic changes that bred peace-loving people. For a millennium life on Talyn was calm, until the planet was laid waste by the psychic forces of PSIMON. Young Jarras Minion was pushed toward his mother's greatest creation, the Omegadrome. The mechanism cybernetically linked itself to Minion and became an escape craft allowing him to leave the world. While aboard the craft, Jarras learned how to manipulate this amazing technology, which could also convert into a suit of battle armor. He followed the energy signature back to Earth, learning to hate Psimon along the way, and arrived in time to help the New Titans defeat Psimon. After crossing paths with the DARKSTARS and becoming imprisoned, Jarras returned to Earth and was affiliated with the Titans. Minion gave his Omegadrome to the new Titan Cyborg and then returned to the stars. **RG**

MINSTREL MAVERICK

FIRST APPEARANCE ALL-AMERICAN WESTERN #103 (Nov. 1948)
STATUS Hero **REAL NAME** Hank "Harmony" Hayes
OCCUPATION Adventurer **BASE** The American West in the 1870s
HEIGHT 5ft 10in **WEIGHT** 159 lbs **EYES** Blue **HAIR** Brown
SPECIAL POWERS/ABILITIES Highly skilled with a guitar, as both musical instrument and blunt instrument.

Hank "Harmony" Hayes wandered the Old West singing songs and righting wrongs under the name Minstrel Maverick. Astride his horse, Dusty, he earned a living as a guitar-strumming balladeer, fighting trouble whenever it came his way. His friends included Blacksmith Bill, whose ox-like strength rivaled his deep loyalty. Minstrel Maverick worked with other crime fighters of the frontier, including the heroine Moon Rider. His enemies included White Mask and the Midnight Kid. Minstrel Maverick's favorite weapon was his (reinforced) guitar, which he often cracked against his enemies' skulls with a distinctive "boinggg!" of quivering strings. **DW**

MEGA-FORCE MINION'S *Omegadrome morphs into a handy supergun for zapping foes!*

MIRAGE

FIRST APPEARANCE NEW TEEN TITANS ANNUAL #7 (1991)
STATUS Hero **REAL NAME** Miriam Delgado
OCCUPATION Adventurer **BASE** New York City
HEIGHT 5ft 7in **WEIGHT** 143 lbs **EYES** Black and white **HAIR** Black
SPECIAL POWERS/ABILITIES Can disguise herself as anyone she pleases by creating complex psychic illusions around her body.

Miriam Delgado was living as a street urchin in Brazil when she was kidnapped by the villain known as the Time Trapper. Believing that she was from an alternate timeline, Delgado, called Mirage because of her illusion-casting powers, became a member of the so-called Team Titans. Programmed by the Time Trapper to assassinate Extant, the Team Titans fought Earth's heroes during the Zero Hour crisis (see Great Battles pp. 362–3). After Extant's defeat, Mirage and her fellow "sleeper" agent TERRA, joined the New Titans (see TEEN TITANS). Mirage eventually fell in love with NIGHTWING, and briefly disguised herself as his girlfriend, STARFIRE, so that she could be with him. Mirage is the single mother of a young girl, Julienne. **PJ**

MIRROR MASTER I & III

FIRST APPEARANCE (I) THE FLASH (2nd series) #105 (February 1959)
STATUS Villain (deceased) **REAL NAME** Samuel Joseph Scudder
OCCUPATION Professional criminal **BASE** Central City
HEIGHT 5ft 10in **WEIGHT** 175 lbs **EYES** Brown
HAIR Brown

FIRST APPEARANCE (III) ANIMAL MAN #8
(February 1989)
STATUS Villain **REAL NAME** Evan McCulloch
OCCUPATION Adventurer **BASE** Mobile
HEIGHT 5ft 11in **WEIGHT** 173 lbs **EYES** Brown **HAIR** Brown

SPECIAL POWERS/ABILITIES All Mirror Masters have wielded an arsenal of reflective weapons able to accomplish amazing feats, such as turning opponents' own reflections against them or teleporting via a "Mirror Dimension."

After accidentally discovering how to create realistic holograms with mirrors while biding time in the Central City Prison workshop, Sam Scudder engineered an ambitious jailbreak. Later, he experimented with other reflective devices to become the Mirror Master, frequent foe of the second FLASH, and one of the members of the hero's infamous Rogues Gallery. He frequently teamed with fellow Rogue and like-minded malcontent CAPTAIN COLD for high-tech heists, and both were also founding members of the SECRET SOCIETY OF SUPER-VILLAINS. Ironically, like the Scarlet Speedster, Scudder also perished during the universe-shattering Crisis (see Great Battles, pp. 362–3).

Shortly after Mirror Master's demise, CAPTAIN BOOMERANG took up the maestro's colorful costume and weaponry to commit crimes clandestinely while he served as a member of the covert SUICIDE SQUAD. Later, Scottish mercenary Evan McCulloch became a third Mirror Master, apparently paid to do so by a shadowy organization with ties to anti-environmental concerns. McCulloch's first assignment as a more murderous Mirror Master was to terrorize the family of Buddy Baker (ANIMAL MAN) and undermine Baker's role as a superpowered spokesperson for ecological interests. McCulloch's Mirror Master has since joined the latest version of the SUICIDE SQUAD, and was one of the Rogues responsible for the death of Bart Allen, the fourth Flash. **SB**

MIRROR IMAGE Sam Scudder trapped Barry Allen within reflective prisons. But when Wally West leapt into action as Kid Flash, the Mirror Master thought he was seeing double!

MAN IN THE MIRROR Evan McCulloch has refined the Mirror Master's reflective weaponry to deadly precision. While his predecessor was content with bank heists, McCulloch sells his sinister services to the highest bidder.

MISS AMERICA

FIRST APPEARANCE MILITARY COMICS #1 (August 1941)
STATUS Hero **REAL NAME** Joan Dale
OCCUPATION Adventurer **BASE** New York City
HEIGHT 5ft 7in **WEIGHT** 133 lbs **EYES** Blue **HAIR** Black
SPECIAL POWERS/ABILITIES Possessed mental powers allowing her to transmute one substance into another.

Project M was a secret government project to develop superhuman soldiers, run by Professor Mazursky. In the spring of 1941 it was operating in a complex beneath Bedloe's Island, the site of the Statue of Liberty. When their first test subject died, an operative named Agent X offered to find a replacement. He mistakenly invited reporter Joan Dale, thinking her name was John, to learn of the government's work. When she arrived, she was taken prisoner and subjected to Mazursky's experiments. Believing her dead, she was left on the island to be found by police. She was not alone, however, and in her delirium dreamed that the Spirit of Liberty spoke to her and granted her powers to aid her country. Dubbed Miss America by a man she saved from drowning, she quickly became a sensation. She was even invited by UNCLE SAM to join the FREEDOM FIGHTERS. When they fell, she was recaptured by Project M; she was rescued by other costumed heroes. She subsequently served with the JUSTICE SOCIETY OF AMERICA. In recent years, she emerged to help UNCLE SAM and the new FREEDOM FIGHTERS. **RG**

MISS LIBERTY

FIRST APPEARANCE TOMAHAWK #81 (March 1971)
STATUS Hero (deceased) **REAL NAME** Bess Lynn
OCCUPATION Freedom fighter **BASE** Mobile
HEIGHT 5ft 8in **WEIGHT** 137 lbs **EYES** Blue **HAIR** Blonde (black wig)
SPECIAL POWERS/ABILITIES Skilled combatant and rider; used powder horns to create explosions, sowing panic among enemy troops.

The Revolutionary War that established the U.S.'s independence from Great Britain had its own costumed heroes. Frontier nurse Bess Lynn was eager to fight against British forces, but afraid to do it openly for fear her brother (a captive in England) would be harmed in retaliation. Calling herself Miss Liberty, she donned a mask, wig, and a red, white, and blue costume inspired by the "stars and bars" flag of her new nation. She battled redcoats alongside fellow hero TOMAHAWK, riding a white charger and wielding a sword and whip. Tragically, Miss Liberty died before the end of the war in a battle with Hessian troops who had stolen the Liberty Bell. During the fighting the colossal bell fell on Miss Liberty and crushed her. More than a 150 years later, Miss Liberty's descendant Libby Lawrence fought against the Axis powers as LIBERTY BELLE. **DW**

MISS MARTIAN

FIRST APPEARANCE TEEN TITANS (3rd series) #37 (August 2006)
STATUS Hero **REAL NAME** M'gann M'orzz
OCCUPATION Adventurer **BASE** Mobile
HEIGHT 5ft 10in **WEIGHT** 135 lbs **EYES** Red **HAIR** Red
SPECIAL POWERS/ABILITIES Flight, super-strength, superspeed, invisibility, "Martian vision," shapeshifting, intangibility, telepathy.

M'gann M'orzz, known on Earth as "Megan Morse," is a White Martian possessing the near-limitless superpowers common to all members of the Martian species, both White and Green. She joined the TEEN TITANS under the name Miss Martian during a period of restructuring following the Infinite Crisis.

Originally, M'gann posed as a Green Martian, playing off the fame of the MARTIAN MANHUNTER in an effort to escape the notoriety of her kinspeople. Yet her true heritage became known during the Teen Titans' hunt for a traitor in their midst. While many believed Miss Martian to be their betrayer, M'gann continued the investigation and exposed the true culprit, Bombshell. She returned to the Teen Titans, giving the team a powerhouse on par with SUPERGIRL, though Miss Martian still has her species' vulnerability to fire. When not at Titans Tower in San Francisco, Miss Martian prefers the stark Australian outback since it reminds her of home. **DW**

MIST I & II

FIRST APPEARANCE ADVENTURE COMICS #67 (October 1941)
STATUS Villain (deceased) **REAL NAME** Kyle (last name unrevealed); also known under the alias Jonathon Smythe
OCCUPATION Professional criminal **BASE** Opal City
HEIGHT 5ft 7in **WEIGHT** 145 lbs **EYES** Blue **HAIR** White
SPECIAL POWERS/ABILITIES Could convert his body to sentient mist at will; able to become a mobile, nearly invisible vapor; could take hypnotic control of his victims; an ingenious criminal mastermind

FIRST APPEARANCE STARMAN (2nd series) #0 (October 1994)
STATUS Villain (deceased) **REAL NAME** Nash (last name unrevealed)
OCCUPATION Professional criminal **BASE** Opal City
HEIGHT 5ft 8in **WEIGHT** 140 lbs **EYES** Gray **HAIR** Black
SPECIAL POWERS/ABILITIES A brilliant strategist but average combatant; was able to convert her body into living mist at will.

Decades ago, a scientist known only by his first name, Kyle, created a device that allowed him to transform objects into a mist-like state. When gangsters tried to steal the device from him, they turned its power on Kyle and he was transformed into the Mist. The Mist became a powerful criminal mastermind, a constant foe of the first STARMAN. Decades later, the Mist's son accidentally died during a crime wave spawned by his father. The Mist went insane, his psychological state further hampered by Alzheimer's disease. After selling his soul to the demon NERON, Mist I perished in a nuclear conflagration that also took the life of the first Starman. The Mist's daughter Nash followed in his criminal footsteps as MIST II. **PJ**

Daughter of the first STARMAN's arch-enemy MIST I, the woman known only as Nash might have lived a very different life had her brother Kyle not been killed battling David Knight, Starman's son and successor. With her fiendish father driven mad with grief, the mentally unhinged Nash took on his role as Mist II.

David Knight had already been killed, so Nash targeted David's brother Jack, the newest Starman, and all of Opal City for a reign of terror. She kidnapped and drugged Jack, conceiving his child without his knowledge. When Jack learned the truth, his child had already been born. The Mist's atrocities included the murders of AMAZING MAN II, BLUE DEVIL, and the CRIMSON FOX.

Nash subsequently introduced Jack to his son as a precursor to killing the young hero. Instead, she herself died, slain by her own insane father as he reclaimed the mantle of the Mist. Jack took custody of his son and prays that the toddler does not favor his psychotic mother. **SB**

MISTER AMERICA

FIRST APPEARANCE ACTION COMICS #54 (June 1938)
STATUS Hero **REAL NAME** Tex Thomson
OCCUPATION Adventurer **BASE** Mobile
HEIGHT 5ft 9in **WEIGHT** 175 lbs **EYES** Blue **HAIR** Black
SPECIAL POWERS/ABILITIES No superpowers, but a well-above-average hand-to-hand combatant with enormous courage and resourcefulness.

Wealthy adventurer Tex Thomson and his pal Bob Daley discovered the mysterious Sealed City and a one-eyed man who claimed to be its ruler, the Gorrah. After months of terror, including the destabilization of small countries, the Gorrah crossed paths with Thomson and Daley in Turkey. Met with defeat, the villain faked his death. Later, Thomson assumed the costumed identity of Mr. America and once more crossed paths with the Gorrah. The one-eyed villain was finally killed by one of his own grenades. Some time later, Harry's friend Janice "Peggy" Maloney accompanied them as Miss X. Presumed dead in a shipping disaster, Thomson secretly returned as the saboteur-busting mystery man Mister America, later joined by Bob in the guise of Fatman. In 1942, Tex headed overseas to pose as a Nazi officer while sabotaging Axis efforts as the Americommando. Seemingly killed in 1945, Tex Thomson later founded the HERO Hotline. Trey Thompson took his place until murdered by VANDAL SAVAGE. Jeffrey Graves is the third, and current, Mister America. **RG**

MISTER ATOM

FIRST APPEARANCE CAPTAIN MARVEL ADVENTURES #78 (November 1947)
STATUS Mindless automaton **REAL NAME** None
OCCUPATION Tool of evil **BASE** Mobile
HEIGHT 10ft **WEIGHT** 1,214 lbs **EYES** Photocellular **HAIR** None
SPECIAL POWERS/ABILITIES Atomic-powered robot; massively strong; can fire nuclear blasts from hands; nearly indestructible; capable of flight.

"Mister Atom" is the incongruously cheery name applied to the truly menacing nuclear-fueled robot built by government scientist Dr. Charles Langle. The towering automaton contains a miniature nuclear reactor that gives it various incredible powers, including the ability to fly and to release bolts of destructive energy. Mister Atom also possesses an armored shell that is impervious to attack from most superpowered beings.

Several years ago, the Venusian worm MISTER MIND attempted to overthrow the U.S. government by taking possession of White House agent SARGE STEEL. Mister Mind compelled Steel to send Mister Atom to the Fawcett City suburb of Fairfield, where the robot detonated a nuclear bomb. The explosion leveled the town and killed thousands. The teaming of Mister Mind and Mister Atom during this incident is considered the second incarnation of the MONSTER SOCIETY OF EVIL. **DW**

MISTER E

FIRST APPEARANCE SECRETS OF HAUNTED HOUSE #31 (Dec. 1980)
STATUS Villain **REAL NAME** Erik (last name unrevealed)
OCCUPATION Destroyer of supernatural evil; historian **BASE** Boston
HEIGHT 6ft 3in **WEIGHT** 190 lbs
EYES Blue **HAIR** Black, white at temples
SPECIAL POWERS/ABILITIES Can time-travel at will; claims to be able to see good or evil within a person; carries a thick wooden cane.

As a boy, Mister E was simply known as Erik, a child whose eyes were scooped out with a spoon by his insane father, who would rather Erik be blind than be "led into temptation." Traumatized by the abuse, Erik became the enigmatic Mister E in adulthood and used his "inner sight" to battle supernatural forces. E also acquired the ability to walk through time, a power he used to determine whether or not young Timothy Hunter— destined to become Earth's greatest sorcerer—might one day destroy the world. E at first believed it better to kill Tim than risk Earth's fate. However, after facing the Temptress, a being who manipulated the events of his youth leading to his own blinding, E decided not to kill Tim. Paradoxically, this decision broke the cycle of abuse begun by Erik's father. Mister E regained his sight and continues to combat supernatural evil wherever he sees it. **SB**

MISTER FREEZE *SEE OPPOSITE PAGE*

MISTER MIND

FIRST APPEARANCE CAPTAIN MARVEL ADVENTURES #26 (August 1943)
STATUS Villain **REAL NAME** Unknown
OCCUPATION Criminal mastermind **BASE** Mobile
LENGTH 3in **WEIGHT** 5 oz **EYES** Black **HAIR** None
SPECIAL POWERS/ABILITIES One of the planet's most formidable telepaths, though his physical strength is negligible.

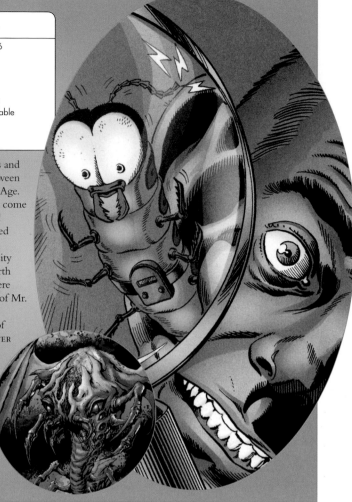

The world's wickedest worm comes from Venus and claims that his people once ruled the Earth between the extinction of the dinosaurs and the first Ice Age. His dreams of planetary re-conquest have so far come to nothing, but it may be only a matter of time!

Years ago, Mister Mind and his brethren plotted to escape their planet with the help of DOCTOR SIVANA and launch an invasion, with Fawcett City as their beachhead. CAPTAIN MARVEL saved Earth by transporting the worms into deep space, where most of them froze. SARGE STEEL took custody of Mr. Mind's comatose form.

However, Mister Mind took mental control of Sarge Steel, orchestrated the release of the MISTER ATOM robot, which arrived in the Fawcett City suburb of Fairfield, and detonated an atomic bomb. The firestorm flattened Fairfield and killed thousands, but that was just Mister Mind's warm-up act. Mister Mind helped orchestrate the takeover of Khandaq by manipulating Brainwave II. During the Infinite Crisis, he evolved into a moth-like form and tried to consume the multiverse until sent back in time by Rip Hunter (see HUNTER, RIP) and BOOSTER GOLD. **DW**

ESCAPING SCOTT FREE *Aero Discs bearing him aloft, Mister Miracle crashes into action with his costume's Mother Box warning him of impending danger and healing any cut or scrape.*

GETTING FREE *Scott has traveled the world using his escape artistry to teach that freedom comes from within and that no prison is escape-proof. His skills have also come in handy when he and his wife, Big Barda, have found themselves in a spot of bother.*

MISTER MIRACLE

FIRST APPEARANCE MISTER MIRACLE (1st series) #1 (April 1971)
STATUS Hero **REAL NAME** Scott Free
OCCUPATION Escapologist; adventurer **BASE** Mobile
HEIGHT 6ft **WEIGHT** 185 lbs **EYES** Blue **HAIR** Black
SPECIAL POWERS/ABILITIES Expert fighter; master escape artist; Mother Box incorporated into costume; Aero Discs for flight; multi-cube fires laser beams, emits sonic vibrations, or releases strong cable.

Mister Miracle is the son of HIGHFATHER of New Genesis, once the leader of the NEW GODS. As an infant, he was exchanged with DARKSEID's son ORION, to secure a truce between the warring worlds of New Genesis and Apokolips. He was reared in one of the gulag-like orphanages overseen by the hateful GRANNY GOODNESS, who sarcastically dubbed him "Scott Free." Despite her attempts to turn him into another mindless minion of Darkseid, Scott remained incorruptible. He often broke out of the orphanage, meeting the insurgent HIMON, as well as BIG BARDA, leader of the FEMALE FURIES.

Scott escaped Apokolips and journeyed to Earth, where he encountered escape artist Thaddeus Brown, known as Mister Miracle, and Oberon, Brown's manager. When Brown was murdered, Scott became Mister Miracle and brought the killers to justice. Scott reunited with Barda, who had also slipped from Granny's grasp. They wed and continued to thwart Darkseid's schemes on Earth. Mister Miracle joined the JUSTICE LEAGUE OF AMERICA and remains an auxiliary member. Shilo Norman, the second Mister Miracle, served with the SEVEN SOLDIERS OF VICTORY. Scott Free recently suffered the loss of his wife, Barda. **SB**

MISTER FREEZE

FIRST APPEARANCE BATMAN #121 (February 1959)
STATUS Villain **REAL NAME** Victor Fries
OCCUPATION Professional criminal **BASE** Gotham City
HEIGHT 6ft **WEIGHT** 190 lbs **EYES** Icy blue **HAIR** White
SPECIAL POWERS/ABILITIES Victor has a vast intellect, but has subsumed it in favor of brute force, using his Freeze Gun and super-cooling armor to get what he wants.

COLD HANDS, WARM HEART
Nora loved the scientist and he idolized her, making her illness and subsequent death all the more heart-wrenching.

Describing Victor Fries as cold-hearted is just the tip of the iceberg. To escape the pressures of his brutal father, young Victor developed an unusual hobby: freezing animals. He thought he was preserving his pets forever, but his father saw things otherwise and sent the boy for counseling. The psychiatrist viewed this freezing tendency as Victor's way of controlling his world. Isolated and ridiculed at school and college, Victor believed he would never know the warm touch of humanity. Then came Nora, the beautiful athlete who stole his heart. They married and when his beloved was stricken with a rare malady, Fries left his teaching post to work for drugs company Gothcorp, hoping their technology would help him find a cure. Exposure to a hail of super-coolants altered his body chemistry, and the brilliant cryogenicist now wears a suit of air-conditioned armor to remain comfortably chilled.

FROSTY RECEPTION *The need for a cold environment has always proven a challenge for the villain, and an inconvenience for his cohorts.*

COLD AS ICE

Desperate to cure Nora, Victor had placed her in suspended animation to halt the disease consuming her. Then disaster struck: Gothcorp decided to deny him the vital funding to save Nora's life. Wielding an ice-blasting cold gun, Mr. Freeze revenged himself upon the soulless corporation. He set about killing Gothcorp's executives, working his way up the organization and saving C.E.O. Ferris Boyle for last. An ensuing clash with the BATMAN, however, shattered any hope for Nora's recovery. Accidentally firing his cold gun at Nora's cryochamber, Freeze fractured her slumbering body into a million shards. Yet he still found a way for Nora to live, by immersing her in a Lazarus Pit. Unfortunately the experience transformed her into the insane villainess Lazara. **PJ**

TIME AND AGAIN *the two have fought, usually as Mr. Freeze attempts to heist the largest and most perfect diamonds to help him power the suit of armor he needs to stay alive. Driven by grief and revenge, Mr. Freeze is one of Batman's most dangerous opponents.*

KEE-RACK!

KEY STORYLINES
• *UNDERWORLD UNLEASHED #1–3 (NOV 1995–JAN 1996).* Mister Freeze is given enhanced powers by Neron, but loses the ability to generate cold without his freeze gun.
• *BATMAN #635–638 (FEBRUARY–MAY 2005):* During the "Under the Hood" saga, Mister Freeze is hired to work for Black Mask, but can't prevent the return of Jason Todd.
• *BATGIRL #70 (JANUARY 2006):* Mister Freeze hopes Ra's al Ghul's daughter can restore his wife using the Lazarus Pit; but, she becomes an insane villainess called Lazara.

MISTER MXYZPTLK

FIRST APPEARANCE (historic) SUPERMAN (1st series) #30 (October 1944); (current) SUPERMAN (2nd series) #11 (November 1987)
STATUS Villain **REAL NAME** Untranslatable
OCCUPATION Little devil **BASE** Fifth Dimensional world of Zrfff
HEIGHT 3ft 9in **WEIGHT** 59 lbs **EYES** Blue **HAIR** White
SPECIAL POWERS/ABILITIES Beings from Zrfff possess shape-changing abilities and other "magical" powers that can transform animate and inanimate objects into other forms, usually on a temporary basis.

Every 90 days, SUPERMAN can expect a visit from Mr. Mxyzptlk. The imp loves challenging the Man of Steel with magical mischief, games that can only end when Superman tricks him into saying his name backwards. The fifth dimension Mxyzptlk hails from defies the physical laws of the three-dimensional world. Since humans cannot perceive 5-D constructs, Mxyzptlk employs an illusory, gnome-like body when on Earth, an easy feat for a being whose science can animate inanimate material and create matter from nothingness. Mxyzptlk's first trick on Earth was to animate the *Daily Planet* building in Metropolis. He then turned Lois Lane (*see* LANE, LOIS) into a mannequin.

METROPOLIS MAD
Mr. Mxyzptlk's fascination with Metropolis extends to Lois Lane and Lex Luthor.

SHAPE-CHANGER *The imp may appear goofy, but he is a powerful being from another reality, to Superman's regret.*

One of his favorite tricks is to cause bizarre alterations to Superman's physique, either aging him, making him absurdly obese, or making his head swell alarmingly. On one visit, he competed with fellow imp BAT-MITE to prove which of them was the best mischief-maker. The result was a tie, but Superman, BATMAN, Lois and ROBIN were driven to distraction. On another occasion, Mxyzptlk offered Lex Luthor (*see* LUTHOR, LEX) red kryptonite when the imp was too busy to visit. Using red kryptonite, Luthor temporarily stripped Superman of his powers. Later, Mxyzptlk recreated DOOMSDAY and "died" crushed by the rampaging creature's bony protrusions. Of course, he was only playing dead. Mxyzptlk's greatest humiliation came at the hands of the JOKER, who talked the imp out of most of his powers. Mxyzptlk defeated the Joker, but seemingly died when attacked by the villain Ruin. Recently, Mxyzptlk reappeared as the prisoner of Superman-Prime, who tortured the imp in an attempt to gain even more power. **RG**

MISTER NOBODY

FIRST APPEARANCE DOOM PATROL (2nd series) #26 (September 1989)
STATUS Villain (deceased) **REAL NAME** Morden (first name unrevealed)
OCCUPATION Former scientist; cult leader **BASE** Mobile
HEIGHT 5ft 8in **WEIGHT** 0 lbs **EYES** Red **HAIR** None
SPECIAL POWERS/ABILITIES An abstract man who lived in a pseudo-dimensional state; could psychically induce a state of playful anarchy in other human beings; his powers are not inherently destructive.

After double-crossing the Brotherhood of Evil (*see* SOCIETY OF SIN), the greatest enemies of the DOOM PATROL, a man known only as Mister Morden fled to Paraguay to escape the Brotherhood's wrath. There, he met a Nazi war criminal, Doctor Bruckner, who promised to turn him into a new man. Morden was locked in a room that simulated an infinity of white space stretching in all directions. Driven insane and injected with serums that transformed his body, Morden became Mister Nobody. He gathered a crew of outcasts and, pledging to celebrate the absurdity of life, called his cadre the BROTHERHOOD OF DADA.

The Brotherhood stole a mystic painting that devoured worlds and attempted to consume Paris with it, but the Doom Patrol stopped them just in time. For a time, Mister Nobody chose to live in the painting, until he returned to the normal world and gathered a new Brotherhood of Dada, who then went on a nationwide tour to promote anarchy. At one rally, Mister Nobody attempted to use the crowd's focused mental energies and the painting's power to unravel reality. After a battle between the military, the Doom Patrol, and the Brotherhood, Mister Nobody was turned back into his human form and killed, having been accidentally impaled on a rusty pole. **PJ**

MISTER SCARLET

FIRST APPEARANCE WOW COMICS #1 (Winter 1940–1)
STATUS Hero **REAL NAME** Brian Butler
OCCUPATION Adventurer; district attorney **BASE** Mobile
HEIGHT 6ft **WEIGHT** 192 lbs **EYES** Brown **HAIR** Brown
SPECIAL POWERS/ABILITIES Skilled acrobat and hand-to-hand combatant.

Brian Butler worked as a district attorney but became frustrated by the limitations of the legal system. He decided to pull on a skintight red, white, and blue bodysuit and fight crime as Mister Scarlet, "the eerie figure all criminals fear." His secretary Miss Wade helped Butler to preserve his secret identity, while his young ward Pinky decided to join in the gang-busting game as Mister Scarlet's boy sidekick. During their career, Mister Scarlet and Pinky sent scores of crooks to the slammer, including the Dean of the Crime College. In fact, the Scarlet Scourge became so successful as a vigilante that crime soon dwindled down to practically nothing, and Brian Butler had to temporarily leave the legal profession for lack of work! Mister Scarlet eventually retired from the super-hero game, and Pinky has since assumed the guise of Mister Scarlet II in his stead. **DW**

M

MISTER TERRIFIC I

FIRST APPEARANCE SENSATION COMICS #1 (January 1942)
STATUS Hero (deceased) **REAL NAME** Terry Sloane
OCCUPATION Businessman; teacher **BASE** Boston; New York City
HEIGHT 5ft 10in **WEIGHT** 175 lbs **EYES** Blue **HAIR** Blond
SPECIAL POWERS/ABILITIES Was a masterful hand-to-hand
combatant; had genius level IQ.

Terry Sloane was a child genius who graduated
from high school by age 11 and completed
Harvard by age 12. Becoming an Olympic
medalist and millionaire businessman during the
Great Depression, Sloane grew suicidal when he
believed he had nothing left to attain. After he
saved the life of a young woman whose brother
had become involved with the mob, Sloane
found the challenge he needed. Donning a
colorful costume, Sloane became Mister Terrific
and stamped out the mob's influence.

During World War II, Mister Terrific joined the
JUSTICE SOCIETY OF AMERICA and the ALL-STAR
SQUADRON. Retiring years later, Sloane became a
professor at Gateway University but was murdered by
his arch-enemy the Spirit King. Sloane's granddaughter
Victoria inherited his
fortune and became
the nefarious casino
owner ROULETTE.
PJ

FAIR PLAY Possessed by an unyielding
sense of moral and ethical responsibility,
Mister Terrific used his skills to end the
careers of a number of criminals.

MISTER TERRIFIC II

FIRST APPEARANCE THE SPECTRE (3rd series) #54 (June 1997)
STATUS Hero **REAL NAME** Michael Holt
OCCUPATION Adventurer; retired electronics engineer and financier;
currently a security adviser for Tylerco **BASE** New York City
HEIGHT 6ft 2in **WEIGHT** 215 lbs **EYES** Brown **HAIR** Black
SPECIAL POWERS/ABILITIES Olympic-level athlete and hard-hitting
fighter; T-Spheres—floating devices of Holt's own design—
gather information and project holograms.

Michael Holt first found fame for bringing
home the gold medal in the Olympic decathlon.
Later, he formed his own cyberwear company,
subsequently retiring young and wealthy.
However, Holt's charmed life was shattered
when his wife Angela died in a car crash.
Distraught, he thought of committing
suicide. The SPECTRE intervened, making
Holt reconsider his purpose in life. He
became inspired by the example of MISTER
TERRIFIC fighting to win over inner-city
kids who risked ruining their lives in petty
crime. As Mister Terrific II, he joined the
JUSTICE SOCIETY OF AMERICA, becoming
team chairman. During the Infinite Crisis,
Hold participated in the assault on the
Brother Eye satellite. He later became White
King's Bishop in CHECKMATE and eventually,
the White King. Mister Terrific continued to
lead the JSA until surrendering chairmanship
to POWER GIRL. SB

PACKS A PUNCH
Michael Holt was
as hard-hitting as
his predecessor, Terry
Sloane, when he
broke the nose of
the murderous
international terrorist
known as Kobra.

MISTER WHO

FIRST APPEARANCE MORE FUN COMICS #1 (November 1941)
STATUS Villain **REAL NAME** Unrevealed
OCCUPATION Scientist **BASE** Mobile
HEIGHT 5ft 5in **WEIGHT** 145 lbs **EYES** Blue **HAIR** None
SPECIAL POWERS/ABILITIES Solution Z let him escape his body's prison;
able to change size and shape at will.

Mister Who was born "a hopeless cripple" and tormented
by his peers while growing up. As a scientist, he developed
Solution Z, based on the world's most adaptive creatures,
and used it on himself to become "strong and tall."
Filled with resentment over the way in which he'd
been treated all his life, the scientist decided not to
share his discovery, and used his new abilities to steal
art treasures and surround himself with beauty. The
miraculous Solution Z gave Mister Who complete control
over his body, enabling him to grow to giant size, become
paper-thin, blend into any background like a chameleon
and even assume the appearance of any person. He also
gained superstrength and viewed himself as virtually
unkillable. If he lost a limb, he believed it would grow
back. He fought DR. FATE repeatedly, only to lose each
time. RG

STRONG AND TALL Despite being mortal,
his shape-changing powers make Mr. Who a
formidable opponent for the likes of Dr. Fate
and the first Green Lantern, Alan Scott.

MISTER ZSASZ

FIRST APPEARANCE BATMAN: SHADOW OF THE BAT #1 (June 1992)
STATUS Villain **REAL NAME** Victor Zsasz
OCCUPATION Serial killer **BASE** Gotham City
HEIGHT 5ft 8in **WEIGHT** 150 lbs **EYES** Blue **HAIR** Blond
SPECIAL POWERS/ABILITIES Skilled with a knife and possesses a brilliant criminal mind; a totally ruthless psychopath who takes a sadistic delight in killing; can appear chillingly normal.

Mister Zsasz suffered no horrific childhood trauma, and can claim no strange jumbling of his brain chemistry. Zsasz grew up with love, money, and privilege, and made a fortune in his twenties. Despite his success, he felt empty inside, and he came to feel the same about everyone else— people were just automatons shuffling around in search of amusement. Convinced he should kill himself, he decided instead to give others the release of death. Since that time, Mister Zsasz has killed dozens, usually with a knife. For each murder, he cuts a mark into his skin. Zsasz has been imprisoned in Arkham Asylum but has always escaped, crossing paths with adversaries including the BATMAN and KILLER CROC. He operates according to no preset pattern, and his fixation on thrill-killing makes him one of the Dark Knight's deadliest opponents. **DW**

MOCKINGBIRD

FIRST APPEARANCE SECRET SIX #1 (May 1968)
STATUS Hero **REAL NAME** Carlo di Rienzi
OCCUPATION Director of Secret Six **BASE** Chevy Chase, Maryland
HEIGHT 6ft 2in **WEIGHT** 175 lbs **EYES** Blue **HAIR** White
SPECIAL POWERS/ABILITIES Skilled magician; possesses a talent for manipulating the actions of others.

Mockingbird is the codename of the clandestine overseer and benefactor of the SECRET SIX crime-fighting team. The original team, composed of six individuals whose specialties ranged from chemistry to espionage, never suspected that Mockingbird was one of their own—Dr. August Durant. The U.S. government had compelled Durant to act as Mockingbird in exchange for the medicine needed to treat his terminal illness.

Decades after the Secret Six had disbanded, an aging Durant decided to let his fellow member Carlo di Rienzi in on his secret, and asked the former stage magician to take over as the new Mockingbird. Di Rienzi then assembled a second team of Secret Six agents to combat a worldwide bio-virus. Breaking from Mockingbird tradition, di Rienzi eventually revealed his true identity to the new team to gain their trust. **DW**

MONARCH

FIRST APPEARANCE ARMAGEDDON 2001 #1 (May 1991)
STATUS Villain **REAL NAME** Nathaniel Adam
OCCUPATION Would-be world conqueror **BASE** Mobile
HEIGHT 6ft 4in **WEIGHT** 456 lbs (in armor) **EYES** Blue **HAIR** Brown
SPECIAL POWERS/ABILITIES Armor includes a panoply of weapons and defense systems; possesses space- and time-warping powers.

Hank Hall served the Lords of Order alongside his brother Don, as HAWK AND DOVE. When Don was killed, Hawk became increasingly belligerent, until the Lords of Order empowered Dawn Granger to become a second Dove to help pacify him. Dawn was later killed by Hawk's future-self, a loss that drove Hank Hall insane. He became Monarch, destroying Earth's super heroes in the early 21st century to pave the way for world domination. However, Monarch's future was undone by Matthew Ryder, the time-traveling WAVERIDER, who led other super heroes to prevent this dystopia.

Hank Hall soon developed the means to manipulate time and abandoned the armor of Monarch to adopt the guise of EXTANT, the villain behind the chronal crisis known as Zero Hour (see Great Battles, pp. 362–3).

Later, a doppelganger of Nathaniel Adam (see CAPTAIN ATOM) took up the mantle of Monarch and tried to become world dictator. His insidious scheme was thwarted by EXTREME JUSTICE. **SB**

MON-EL (VALOR)

FIRST APPEARANCE SUPERBOY #89 (June 1961)
STATUS Hero **REAL NAME** Lar Gand
OCCUPATION Legionnaire **BASE** Earth
HEIGHT 6ft 1in **WEIGHT** 165 lbs **EYES** Blue **HAIR** Black
SPECIAL POWERS/ABILITIES Under a yellow sun, superstrength, superspeed, enhanced hearing, freezing breath, heat, telescopic and microscopic vision, invulnerability, and the power of flight.

Lar Gand is a Daxamite, a member of a species that possesses superhuman powers similar to those of Kryptonians. During Clark Kent's childhood, an amnesiac Lar Gand crashed on Earth near Smallville. The two boys became friends, with Clark thinking that his visitor might be Kryptonian and encouraging him to take the name Mon-El. But a chance exposure to lead—a fatal weakness of Daxamites—poisoned Lar Gand. To halt the spread of the lead poisoning, Clark projected Mon-El into the Phantom Zone.

As an adult, SUPERMAN visited Mon-El inside the Phantom Zone, where Mon-El helped him escape and defeat the forces of GENERAL ZOD. Mon-El, however, remained in his ghostly prison for more than a thousand years. In the 31st century, BRAINIAC 5 of the LEGION OF SUPER-HEROES determined a way to restore Mon-El from his Phantom Zone confinement. The newly-freed and disoriented Daxamite went on a rampage against SUPERGIRL until calmed by the Legionnaires, who also fed him a serum that cured his lead poisoning. Mon-El joined the WANDERERS under Mekt Ranzz (see LIGHTNING LORD) and helped prevent an invasion of Earth by the alien Dominators. **DW**

LASHING OUT Disoriented by a thousand years of imprisonment, Mon-El attacked Supergirl upon his release.

THE WANDERER Mon-El remained unsure of his place in the 31st century and quickly fell in with the Mekt Ranzz's Wanderers. His actions would ultimately lead to the defeat of the Dominator homeworld.

MONGREL

First appearance HAWKMAN (2nd series) Annual #1 (1993)
Status Hero **Real name** Josh Xan
Occupation Adventurer **Base** Mobile
Height 5ft 10in **Weight** 160 lbs **Eyes** Brown **Hair** Black
Special powers/abilities Can fire devastating bolts of darkforce energy from his hands.

Quarrelsome and arrogant, teenager Josh Xan received his superpowers when alien parasites invaded Earth during the Bloodlines crisis and attacked him, activating his latent metagene. In the past, his half-Vietnamese heritage had made Josh a target for bigots and caused him mental pain. Now, the negative mental thoughts he had kept bottled up for years saw expression as a unique form of energy which he could project with shattering force. Under the codename Mongrel, he used his darkforce powers to assist HAWKMAN and other heroes in ending the Bloodlines crisis.

Mongrel was not the only young hero who had earned superpowers during the alien invasion. The aliens, who drank human spinal fluid, triggered a related outbreak of meta-human powers among a small group of inexperienced youths. Collectively called the "New Bloods," this group of untested champions joined together as the BLOOD PACK at the behest of the shadowy U.S. government agency the Quorum, which hoped to use the Blood Pack's members to advance its own villainous agenda. After the Quorum's defeat, Mongrel faded from the public eye. DW

MONGUL

First appearance ADVENTURES OF SUPERMAN #454 (April 1980)
Status Villain (deceased) **Real name** Mongul
Occupation Despotic conqueror **Base** Warworld
Height 7ft 9in **Weight** 1,135 lbs **Eyes** Red **Hair** None
Special powers/abilities Mongul possessed, as his children do, vast superhuman strength and are nearly impervious to bodily harm; commander of an entire army of gladiators on his mobile Warworld.

The first Mongul was a despicable conqueror who roamed the universe in his planet-sized Warworld. This giant mobile weapon was manned by thousands of slaves who were forced to fight in brutal gladiatorial games. On a self-imposed exile in space, SUPERMAN was captured by alien slavers and sold to the gladiator pits of Warworld. When Superman refused to kill his opponent, Draaga, Mongul entered the arena to personally slaughter the Man of Steel. But Superman defeated the tyrant and was transported off Warworld, while Draaga replaced the dishonored Mongul as its ruler.

Mongul then joined forces with the CYBORG SUPERMAN and destroyed Coast City, murdering its seven million inhabitants and hoping to transform it into a new version of Warworld named Engine City. Defeated and imprisoned, Mongul was offered more power by the demon NERON in exchange for his soul. When the alien despot proudly refused this offer, Neron killed him.

Some time later, Mongul's son and namesake arrived on Earth to warn Superman of the coming of IMPERIEX. After helping Superman prepare for the arrival of the cosmic destroyer, Mongul II turned against the Man of Steel, but was quickly defeated. After a mission to liberate DOOMSDAY from his lunar prison, Mongul II was slain by the murderous creature. PJ

MONGUL II Just as destructive and powerful as his father, Mongul II hunted the universe to take his revenge on Superman, who had dishonored the despot's father's name.

GLADIATORIAL COMBAT On Warworld, the greatest warriors of a thousand conquered planets fought each other to the death for Mongul's entertainment. When Superman was found lost in space, he was captured by Mongul and fought the villain in the gladiator pits, where he nearly killed the Man of Steel. But Superman escaped, the gladiators overthrew Mongul's rule, and Mongul was forced to flee Warworld.

MONGAL The sister of Mongul II, she joined forces with Earth's alien allies during the Imperiex War to gain access to Superman and try to kill him for tainting her father's memory. Power Girl later humiliated her in battle.

A SON'S REVENGE When Mongul II finally confronted Superman, he stopped at nothing to rend the Kryptonian's body limb from limb. But Superman was able to use his own strength and skills to defeat Mongul II, who was killed by Doomsday soon after.

NNGGNN!

MONITORS, THE

FIRST APPEARANCE (The Monitor) THE NEW TEEN TITANS (1st series) #21 (July 1982) **STATUS** Hero (deceased) **REAL NAME** None **OCCUPATION** Surveyor and Protector of the Multiverse **BASE** Satellite **HEIGHT** Variable **WEIGHT** Variable **EYES** White **HAIR** Black **SPECIAL POWERS/ABILITIES** His greatest weapon was the knowledge he gleaned by watching the superhumans on infinite Earths.

THE COUNCIL *A total of 52 Monitors exist, one for each dimension in the new multiverse. Each Monitor takes on physical traits that reflect their home reality.*

Billions of years ago, ill-conceived experiments carried out by the Oan scientist KRONA resulted in the creation of infinite universes from a singular reality. An anti-matter universe of utter evil also came into being. In the positive-matter realm, the Monitor became the multiverse's guardian, opposed by his mirror image in the anti-matter universe, the Anti-Monitor. During the Crisis on Infinite Earths, the Monitor assembled an army of heroes from across time and space to oppose the Anti-Monitor's wave of entropy. The Monitor died in the struggle and the multiverse became one singular reality.

During the Infinite Crisis, the multiverse reappeared in the form of 52 parallel realities, each policed by its own Monitor. The Monitors viewed travel between dimensions to be a threat to the multiverse's existence, and killed heroes viewed as "anomalies" within their current realities. This led to a split between proactive and reactive members within the Monitor ranks, but MONARCH soon sidelined the conflict by attacking the Monitors with the intent of becoming the multiverse's dictator. **DW**

MONSTER SOCIETY OF EVIL

FIRST APPEARANCE CAPTAIN MARVEL ADVENTURES #22 (March 1943)
STATUS Villain team **BASE** Mobile
MEMBERS AND POWERS
Nyola Magical control over the weather.
Ramulus Mental control over vegetation.
Oom the Mighty Superstrength.
Mister Who Superstrength.
The Dummy Carries an energy-firing cane.
Mister Mind Formidable telepath.
Mister Atom Can fire nuclear blasts; possesses armored shell.

The Monster Society of Evil has had several incarnations over the years, and it seems likely that its name will be carried by the planet's most despicable villains well into the future. The first Monster Society of Evil took shape during the 1940s, when Aztec priestess NYOLA assembled the scoundrels RAMULUS, Oom the Mighty, MISTER WHO, and the Dummy, and led an attack on the New York City headquarters of the JUSTICE SOCIETY OF AMERICA. Beaten back by the Flash and GREEN LANTERN, the Monster Society retreated to lick its wounds.

Another grouping of the Monster Society of Evil many decades later consisted solely of the Venusian worm MISTER MIND and the atomic-powered automaton MISTER ATOM. Using his telepathic powers to hypnotize top White House officials, Mister Mind forced SARGE STEEL to launch the Mister Atom robot at the Fawcett City suburb of Fairfield. The nuclear detonation leveled Fairfield, nearly killing Billy Batson's adoptive parents. In his CAPTAIN MARVEL identity, Billy helped other heroes defeat Mister Mind, bringing an end to the second MONSTER SOCIETY OF EVIL. **DW**

MONOCLE, THE

FIRST APPEARANCE FLASH COMICS #64 (April–May 1945)
STATUS Villain (deceased) **REAL NAME** Jonathan Cheval
OCCUPATION Professional criminal **BASE** New York City
HEIGHT 5ft 11in **WEIGHT** 175 lbs **EYES** Blue **HAIR** Black
SPECIAL POWERS/ABILITIES Lens weapons can project light, heat, X-rays, lasers, and cosmic rays.

The Monocle began his career as Jonathan Cheval, a brilliant optician skilled in the grinding and polishing of lenses. Financial ruin triggered a bout of criminal insanity, and Cheval used his specialty in optics to build exotic, lens-based weapons. Now possessing eyepieces that could fire energy beams, Cheval went into the super-villain business as the Monocle, frequently clashing with HAWKMAN in between stretches in prison.

Cheval became a member of the SECRET SOCIETY OF SUPER-VILLAINS, and matched wits with both the JUSTICE SOCIETY OF AMERICA and the JUSTICE LEAGUE OF AMERICA. He later formed a loose partnership with MERLYN, DEADSHOT and PHOBIA, but this new stage of his career was not to last. In a confrontation with Kate Spencer, the most recent MANHUNTER, the Monocle lost his life. **DW**

MONSIEUR MALLAH

FIRST APPEARANCE THE DOOM PATROL (1st series) #86 (March 1964)
STATUS Villain **REAL NAME** None
OCCUPATION Would-be world conqueror **BASE** Mobile
HEIGHT 6ft 3in **WEIGHT** 345 lbs **EYES** Brown **HAIR** Brown
SPECIAL POWERS/ABILITIES An above-average gorilla in terms of size and strength; possesses human intelligence.

Ten years before his own death, a French scientist, whose name remains unrevealed, experimented upon a large gorilla that was stronger and more agile than most others of its species. Through a combination of secret teaching methods, shock treatments, and other experimental methods, the gorilla's I.Q. was raised to 178. The gorilla learned to speak English and French, among other languages, and took the name Monsieur Mallah. When the scientist died, Mallah, following instructions, removed the scientist's brain from his body and placed it inside a specially designed receptacle. A bizarre partnership had been born. The BRAIN and Monsieur Mallah formed the Brotherhood of Evil (SOCIETY OF SIN) and tried to take over the world. In their way stood Niles Caulder's DOOM PATROL (*see* CHIEF) and later the TEEN TITANS. After touchingly professing their true love for each other, the Brain and Monsieur Mallah were seemingly killed in an explosion following an attempt to insert the Brain into one of Cliff Steele's ROBOTMAN bodies. Both survived, but both apparently died at the hands of GORILLA GRODD during Operation: Salvation Run. **RG**

MONTOYA, RENEE

FIRST APPEARANCE DETECTIVE COMICS #644 (May 1992)
STATUS Hero **REAL NAME** Renee Montoya
OCCUPATION Police Detective **BASE** Gotham City
HEIGHT 5ft 8in **WEIGHT** 144 lbs **EYES** Brown **HAIR** Black
SPECIAL POWERS/ABILITIES Dedicated crimefighter of great integrity; an expert martial artist and markswoman.

The daughter of immigrants from the Dominican Republic, Renee graduated with top honors from the Gotham City Police Academy. As a beat cop, she single-handedly apprehended the serial killer MISTER ZSASZ. Officer Montoya further proved her capabilities under the command of Commissioner Gordon (see GORDON, JAMES W.) and his late wife, Lt. Sarah Essen-Gordon, the latter awarding Montoya her detective's shield. Detective Montoya's loyalty to Gordon was evident during Gotham City's lawless No Man's Land period when she remained in the quake-ravaged city to help restore order. At this time, Montoya encountered Harvey Dent (Two-Face), who developed a romantic obsession with her. Montoya rejoined the G.C.P.D. but left after the murder of her partner, Crispus Allen (see SPECTRE). She sank into depression and alcoholism, only emerging after Vic Sage, the QUESTION, drew her into an Intergang plot to take over Gotham City. While fighting by Sage's side she reconnected with the crusader she had once been, and rekindled a romance with Kate Kane, the new BATWOMAN.

BECOMING THE BEST *Martial-arts master Richard Dragon, who also trained the first Question (Vic Sage) in unarmed combat, honed Montoya into a living weapon in the hidden Himalayan city of Nanda Parbat.*

The loss of Vic Sage to cancer convinced Montoya to continue her fight against crime as the new Question. Her quest led her across the globe in pursuit of the Cain cultists who worshipped the teachings of the Crime Bible and exposed her again to the temptations of sin. **SB/DW**

CRIME BIBLE *While battling the Cult of Cain, Montoya came close to becoming as evil as the fanatics she hunted.*

MONSTRESS

FIRST APPEARANCE LEGION OF SUPER-HEROES (4th series) #82 (July 1996)
STATUS Hero (deceased) **REAL NAME** Candi Pyponte-Le Parc III
OCCUPATION Legionnaire **BASE** 31st-century Earth
HEIGHT 6ft 4in **WEIGHT** 415 lbs **EYES** Pale orange **HAIR** Orange
SPECIAL POWERS/ABILITIES Vast superstrength coupled with virtual invulnerability made her a formidable opponent.

A pampered princess living on the planet Xanthu during the latter half of the 30th century, Candi Pyponte-Le Parc III was shocked to discover that her father's labor farms were filled with hundreds of impoverished workers. When a gene-altering bomb exploded in one of the plants, Candi's appearance was radically altered, and she became a super-strong, green giantess. Despite her jovial personality, Monstress, as Candi now called herself, felt like a misfit. She felt much the same even after becoming a prominent member of the Uncanny Amazers, Xanthu's premier superteam. Along with fellow Amazers KID QUANTUM and STAR BOY, Monstress was recruited by the LEGION OF SUPER-HEROES after a battle with the sorcerer Mordru, the DARK LORD.

After the BLIGHT attacked the Earth, Monstress and ten Legionnaires were transported to the far side of the galaxy through a temporal rift in space. Soon after, Monstress was killed by the Progenitor, who had once been her fellow Legionnaire, and friend, ELEMENT LAD. **PJ**

MOONRIDER, MARK

FIRST APPEARANCE FOREVER PEOPLE (1st series) #1 (March 1971)
STATUS Hero (deceased) **REAL NAME** Mark Moonrider **OCCUPATION** Adventurer **BASE** New Genesis **HEIGHT** 5ft 11in **WEIGHT** 412 lbs **EYES** Blue **HAIR** Black **SPECIAL POWERS/ABILITIES** His megaton touch creates a range of disruptions from a severe shock to a massive explosion; further effects have yet to be recorded.

Mark Moonrider was a natural-born leader. Growing up on New Genesis, the member of the NEW GODS was surrounded by friends. As an adult, those friends came to include BIG BEAR, BEAUTIFUL DREAMER, VYKIN, and SERIFAN, known to all as the FOREVER PEOPLE.

When DARKSEID kidnapped Beautiful Dreamer, Mark led the others on an unauthorized trip to Earth to effect a rescue. They continued to thwart Darkseid's attempts to locate the famed Anti-Life Equation until DEVILANCE the Pursuer was dispatched to hunt them down. Devilance had them at bay until they summoned INFINITY MAN, who seemingly defeated the ruthless hunter. Moonrider and his friends numbered among the casualties during the Death of the New Gods event. **RG**

MORDECAI

FIRST APPEARANCE CHRONOS #1 (March 1998)
STATUS Ally **REAL NAME** None
OCCUPATION Robotic servant **BASE** Chronopolis
HEIGHT 7ft **WEIGHT** 412 lbs **EYES** Gray **HAIR** None
SPECIAL POWERS/ABILITIES Highly advanced computer brain; enhanced android strength.

The timestream is a fluid flow of possibilities, yet several oases exist outside of normal space-time where events can occur untouched by chronal instabilities. One of these locations is the Victorian-designed floating city of Chronopolis, where a weary time traveler might encounter the android known as Mordecai. Mordecai worked as a servant for the Countess Fiorella Della Ravenna, a time-traveling noble who crossed paths with Walker Gabriel (CHRONOS II). Mordecai's advanced electronic brain allowed him to make the complex calculations used in the operation of Chronopolis's time-travel booths, and also to construct the temporal displacement suit worn by Gabriel throughout most of his history-hopping. Mordecai appeared to have died when the villain Konstantin Vyronis erased him from existence during an assault on Chronopolis. However, Gabriel's manipulations of the timestream restored Mordecai, and he is presumably still active in the ageless city. **DW**

MORGAINE LE FEY

FIRST APPEARANCE THE DEMON (1st series) #1 (Sept. 1972)
STATUS Villain (deceased) **REAL NAME** Morgaine Le Fey
OCCUPATION Sorceress **BASE** Mobile
HEIGHT 5ft 10in **WEIGHT** 156 lbs **EYES** Blue **HAIR** Black
SPECIAL POWERS/ABILITIES One of the most powerful sorceresses who ever lived; was able to project mystical energy bolts, read minds, teleport, and harness ambient magics.

The half-sister of King Arthur, Morgaine Le Fey invaded Camelot, only to be confronted by Etrigan, the DEMON controlled by Merlin. Merlin gave Etrigan a page from his Eternity Book and told him that Morgaine's beauty would crumble if she ever found the demon or the book. Merlin and Camelot vanished, leaving Morgaine accursed and a wizened old crone. In the 21st century, the decrepit Le Fey sought out the Demon and Merlin hoping to restore her beauty. She was betrayed by a servant and turned into a mummy. Morgaine escaped and then tried to possess WONDER WOMAN's immortal energy. But Wonder Woman had already forsaken her immortality, Morgaine's spell backfired, and the sorceress crumbled to dust. **PJ**

IMMORTAL BELOVED In her quest for eternal youth, Morgaine Le Fey sought out powerful beings, including Wonder Woman, the Phantom Stranger, and Jason Blood, hoping to steal their immortality. The powerful sorceress then used her magic to lure the immortals into a trap.

THE END Mistakenly believing she had finally discovered the secret of immortality, Morgaine's body crumbled to dust!

MORGAN, JENNIFER

FIRST APPEARANCE WARLORD #38 (October 1980)
STATUS Hero **REAL NAME** Lady Jennifer Morgan
OCCUPATION Sorceress **BASE** Skartaris
HEIGHT 5ft 6in **WEIGHT** 132 lbs **EYES** Blue **HAIR** White
SPECIAL POWERS/ABILITIES Mystic powers include projection of bolts of energy, time travel, and suspension of foes in force-field bubbles.

On a scientific expedition to the interdimensional, savage world of Skartaris, Jennifer Morgan met her long-lost father, Lt. Col. Travis Morgan, whom she believed had died in a plane crash. He had in fact become Skartaris's champion, WARLORD. Jennifer became sucked into a plot on her father's life, acquiring magical powers from the witch Ashiya to help defeat Warlord's foe, Deimos. Lady Jennifer, as the less-savage inhabitants of Skartaris came to know her, became the Supreme Sorceress of this lost world. The evil Atlantean Queen Clea and her VILLAINY INC. captured Jennifer during their assault upon Skartaris. Freed with the help of WONDER WOMAN, Jennifer is helping her father to undo the damage to Skartaris wrought by Clea's invasion. **SB**

MORTALLA

FIRST APPEARANCE ORION #6 (November 2000)
STATUS Villain (deceased) **REAL NAME** Mortalla
OCCUPATION Hand of Death **BASE** Apokolips
HEIGHT 5ft 11in **WEIGHT** 175 lbs **EYES** Blue
HAIR Red
SPECIAL POWERS/ABILITIES Mortalla's touch can kill and she defeats opponents more through fear than with any natural fighting talent.

On the planet Apokolips, Justeen, DESAAD's second-in-command, ordered a team of villains called the Suicide Jockeys to kill TIGGRA. This triggered a chain of events that culminated with ORION apparently killing DARKSEID and assuming the rule of Apokolips, albeit under the manipulative guidance of Darkseid's mistress, Mortalla. She deceived Orion in an attempt to rule his father's world, becoming his trusted lieutenant. During the Death of the New Gods event, Mortalla perished at the hands of a mysterious assassin. **RG**

MOUTHPIECE

FIRST APPEARANCE POLICE COMICS #1 (August 1941)
STATUS Hero **REAL NAME** Bill Perkins
OCCUPATION Costumed vigilante **BASE** New York City
HEIGHT 6ft **WEIGHT** 198 lbs **EYES** Blue **HAIR** White
SPECIAL POWERS/ABILITIES Skilled brawler and marksman; above-average detective and expert in criminal law; also handy with a javelin.

Bill Perkins became a district attorney in the early 1940s but grew bitter about the number of times crooks went free for lack of evidence. In order to obtain the evidence he needed for legal convictions, he donned a blue suit and hat with a black eye mask and became the two-fisted vigilante called the Mouthpiece. The Mouthpiece didn't let legal niceties get in the way of his cold justice.

On one case he uncovered an immigration scam being run by gang leader Peg-Leg Friel. The villain tried to escape in the icy waters of the harbor, but Perkins, remembering he had been "pretty good in school with the javelin," hurled a harpoon and speared Peg-Leg Friel through the back.

Recently, an aged lawyer surfaced under the name Mouthpiece and works as an advisor to the new DOCTOR MID-NITE. Whether this is the same Mouthpiece from the 1940s is unknown. **DW**

MURMUR

FIRST APPEARANCE THE FLASH: IRON HEIGHTS (October 2001)
STATUS Villain   **REAL NAME** Michael Christian Amar
OCCUPATION Surgeon   **BASE** Keystone City
HEIGHT 5ft 8in   **WEIGHT** 155 lbs   **EYES** Brown   **HAIR** Gray
SPECIAL POWERS/ABILITIES Possesses no superhuman powers; however, is an expert surgeon who uses various knives and blades to brutally murder his victims and cut out their tongues.

Doctor Michael Christian Amar was a well-respected surgeon in the twin towns of Keystone and Central City. However, he was also a ruthless serial killer who muttered uncontrollably as he slaughtered his victims. Amar was eventually captured by the officers of the Keystone Department of Meta-human Hostility, who identified the killer by his weird vocal quirk.

Murmur cut out his own tongue and crudely sewed up his mouth to silence his incessant droning, the clue that gave him away and sent him to Death Row. Incarcerated at Iron Heights, a maximum-security penitentiary, he escaped during a breakout engineered by the villain Blacksmith. Murmur escaped and became a terrifying member of the FLASH III's Rogues Gallery, recently seen during the Infinite Crisis alongside the RIDDLER and FISHERMAN. **PJ**

SILENT KILLER *Murmur's constant chatter caused the grisly killer to sew up his own mouth.*

MUSASHI

FIRST APPEARANCE JUSTICE LEAGUE INTERNATIONAL #63 (April 1994)
STATUS Villain (deceased)   **REAL NAME** Unrevealed
OCCUPATION Samurai   **BASE** Kobe, Japan
HEIGHT 5ft 10in   **WEIGHT** 175 lbs   **EYES** Brown   **HAIR** Black
SPECIAL POWERS/ABILITIES Formidable martial arts warrior, expert in the fighting skills of the samurai.

The deadly Samurai warrior known as Musashi belonged to a second coalition of super-villains known collectively as the CADRE. They were minions of the alien OVERMASTER, a foe of the JUSTICE LEAGUE OF AMERICA through several of the team's incarnations.

In pursuit of a dastardly plot to exterminate the entire human race, the Overmaster divided his new Cadre into three sub-groups with experience of battling several Justice League teams. These groups were the second EXTREMISTS, the ARYAN BRIGADE, and the Cadre of the Immortal, the latter claiming Musashi as a member. Musashi and his cohorts were committed to the Overmaster's goals of ridding the world of modern technology. Faced by overwhelmingly superior numbers, the Justice League called upon its own vast reserves to face the various gangs of villains. In the end, Musashi forsook the Cadre and his Overmaster and perished in a catastrophic explosion that destroyed the Overmaster's sky-ship and also apparently claimed the lives of Musashi's many Cadre teammates. **SB**

MUSKETEER

FIRST APPEARANCE DETECTIVE COMICS #215 (January 1955)
STATUS Hero   **REAL NAME** Unrevealed
OCCUPATION Adventurer   **BASE** Paris, France
HEIGHT 5ft 9in   **WEIGHT** 180 lbs   **EYES** Blue   **HAIR** Black
SPECIAL POWERS/ABILITIES An expert swordsman and agile athlete, the masked Musketeer preferred to dazzle opponents with his swashbuckling swordplay than engage in close combat or fisticuffs.

A former hero of the French Resistance during World War II, The Musketeer (or, more properly, *Le Mousquetaire*) was one of several international heroes inspired by the JUSTICE SOCIETY OF AMERICA to don masks and fight crime during the 1950s. As the British KNIGHT AND SQUIRE, the Argentine GAUCHO, the Swedish WINGMAN, and the Australian Ranger took to the streets of their capitals to fight corruption and villainy in their countries following World War II, so the patriotic Musketeer quickly became a hero across France, basing himself in Paris.

When the mysterious DOCTOR MIST asked the non-Communist European powers to create a multinational super-heroic organization, the Musketeer and his companions were among its founding members. Called the Dome, the organization was based in France. Garbed in the finery of a 17th-century French Musketeer, as made famous by the author Alexandre Dumas in his novel *The Three Musketeers*, the Musketeer was an expert swordsman and marksman. After a decade of swashbuckling derring-do, the Musketeer vanished from the streets of Paris, never to be seen again. The final fate of the Musketeer, or even his true identity, have yet to be revealed. **RG/PJ**

MYSTO

FIRST APPEARANCE Detective Comics #203 (January 1954)
STATUS Hero   **REAL NAME** Richard "Rick" Carter
OCCUPATION Magician; crime fighter   **BASE** New York City
HEIGHT 6ft   **WEIGHT** 195 lbs   **EYES** Blue   **HAIR** Black
SPECIAL POWERS/ABILITIES Master of illusion and sleight of hand; could make guns appear to turn into playing cards and often confounded crooks with smoke and mirrors.

Mysto, the famous "Magician Detective," became active in the 1950s and is one of the standard-bearers of an earlier age of heroism. Before starting his costumed career, Rick Carter worked as a "wildcat flier" in the Far East. While piloting his plane above Tibet, Carter drove off a party of bandits and earned the gratitude of their target, a shriveled old man. From this old man, Carter learned the secrets of illusion—not true magic—including the misdirection and sleight of hand employed by carnival entertainers. Returning to the U. S. accompanied by the old man's servant, Sikhi, Carter became a magician under the stage name Mysto. After saving a citizen from a murder attempt, Carter turned to crime fighting. **DW**

NABU

FIRST APPEARANCE MORE FUN COMICS #55 (May 1940)
STATUS Hero **REAL NAME** Nabu
OCCUPATION Lord of Order **BASE** Mobile
HEIGHT/WEIGHT/EYES/HAIR Inapplicable
SPECIAL POWERS/ABILITIES One of the most powerful beings on Earth, capable of mystic feats, including projecting mystic energy bolts, reading minds, and teleporting across the dimensions; immortal; possesses superhuman strength.

Nabu is a Lord of Order, a cosmic being who arrived on Earth nearly 4,000 years ago to take a proactive role in the war against Chaos. After engaging in many struggles in ancient Egypt and Sumeria, Nabu placed his body in suspended animation and his spirit in a golden helmet that would merge with whoever wore it. In 1940, Kent Nelson, put on the helmet, and so became Nabu's apprentice, the first DOCTOR FATE.

Nabu's personality supplanted Nelson's whenever the latter wore the helmet, so Nabu placed the spirits of Nelson and his wife, Inza, in the mystic Amulet of Anubis, assumed Kent's form, and chose a new disciple, Eric Strauss. Kent and Inza returned to the mortal world, both becoming Doctor Fate. However, after a battle with PARALLAX in which the Nelsons apparently died, the helmet and amulet were claimed by Jared Stevens.

NABU THE WISE *Nabu manifests a human form as a grey-haired wizard. It is through this form that he continues to communicate with Hector Hall, the new Doctor Fate.*

WHOOM

Nabu's spirit, meanwhile, came to rest in the body of a child, the reincarnated Hector Hall, who had once fought crime with INFINITY, INC. as the Silver Scarab.

During the Infinite Crisis, the SPECTRE's rampage against magic-users brought about an end to the Ninth Age of Magic. Before dying, Nabu passed on the helmet of Doctor Fate so it could find a new bearer. **PJ**

ANKH OF ORDER *Nabu destroys demons with his almost incalculable power.*

NAIAD

FIRST APPEARANCE FIRESTORM THE NUCLEAR MAN #90 (October 1989)
STATUS Inapplicable **REAL NAME** Mai Miyazaki
OCCUPATION Elemental force **BASE** Mobile
HEIGHT Inapplicable (5ft 4in as Mai) **WEIGHT** Variable (112 lbs as Mai) **EYES** Sea green (blue as Mai) **HAIR** None (black as Mai)
SPECIAL POWERS/ABILITIES Total mastery over water in all its forms.

Japanese radical environmentalist Mai Miyazaki believed in direct action. Mai sailed her boat Naiad into the storm-swept north Pacific to call attention to a leaking oil rig being abandoned by Shogun Oil. The rig's director ordered a crewman to fire a flare into the oily waters around Mai's boat, engulfing it in flames. Horribly burned, Mai jumped overboard. However, Earth's spirit, MAYA, offered Mai a chance of life as the planet's Water Elemental, Naiad. Transformed into a living wall of water, Naiad swept over the oil rig, sparking the first Elemental War when FIRESTORM, THE NUCLEAR MAN then Earth's Fire Elemental, flew to the site to investigate. The epic conflict grew to include RED TORNADO, Air Elemental, SWAMP THING, and Plant Elemental, before Maya convinced the Elementals to leave her human children alone. Naiad rained destructively down on Shogun Oil once more, but was stopped by the SPECTRE and SUPERMAN. Naiad then battled CORONA, Earth's newest Fire Elemental, before AQUAMAN convinced the forces of nature to make peace with one another. **SB**

NEBULA MAN

FIRST APPEARANCE JUSTICE LEAGUE OF AMERICA (1st series) #100 (August 1972)
STATUS Villain **REAL NAME** None
OCCUPATION Celestial menace **BASE** Mobile
HEIGHT Variable **WEIGHT** Variable **EYES** White **HAIR** None
SPECIAL POWERS/ABILITIES Incalculable cosmic power.

The Nebula Man is a mysterious entity animated by unknown means, but one thing is clear—he will stop at nothing to destroy the planet Earth. During the 1940s, the Nebula Man first came into existence thanks to a villain known as the Hand. Composed of cosmic energy and possessing the power of atomic bombs in each of his fingers, the Nebula Man threatened the planet with armageddon until opposed by the Seven Soldiers of Victory at a battlefront in the Himalayas. The heroes prevailed, but their member Wing perished. The rest became temporarily scattered across the timestream, victims of the explosive energies of the Nebula Man's demise. More than a half century later, the Nebula Man saw fresh life when his dormant essence combined with Wing's corpse. He reappeared to lead an invasion by the far-future Sheeda, with his secret history revealed as Neh-Buh-Loh the Huntsman, the adult form of the sentient universe Qwewq. The SPAWN OF FRANKENSTEIN defeated the Nebula Man. **DW**

COSMIC POWER *The full extent of the Nebula Man's powers are unrevealed, but he appears to control terrible explosive forces as well as exert limited influence over the timestream.*

NEGATIVE MAN

FIRST APPEARANCE MY GREATEST ADVENTURE #80 (June 1963)
STATUS Hero **REAL NAME** Larry Trainor
OCCUPATION Test pilot **BASE** Midway City
HEIGHT 5ft 10.5in **WEIGHT** 180 lbs
EYES Blue **HAIR** Blond
SPECIAL POWERS/ABILITIES An energy being is released from Trainor's body that has superstrength, superspeed, can pass through objects harmlessly, or cause anything it touches to burn or explode.

Larry Trainor was piloting an experimental test rocket when a technical malfunction caused it to travel into deep space. The rocket ship passed through a radiation belt and, after a crash-landing on Earth, Trainor found his body glowed with cosmic energy. He also discovered he could manifest a superpowered energy being, controlled with his mind.

After his rescue, Trainor met Niles Caulder, known as the CHIEF, who used a special material to bind Trainor's body so that he could contain the lethal radiation. Caulder then invited Trainor, now a social pariah, to join his DOOM PATROL. Trainor thus became Negative Man and helped the Patrol fight various villains.

MADAME ROUGE and GENERAL ZAHL tried to destroy the Doom Patrol by blowing them up, but Trainor survived the attack. His energy being escaped and briefly inhabited the body of Russian cosmonaut Valentina Vostok, who became NEGATIVE WOMAN. However, Trainor wanted his negative energy being back, and used the villain Reactron to help "steal" it back from Vostok. When the energy being emerged, it fused Trainor and his doctor, Eleanor Poole, into a single, radioactive being, calling itself Rebis, who went on to join the Chief in the latest incarnation of his Doom Patrol. After the Infinite Crisis, Larry Trainor rejoined the Doom Patrol as Negative Man. **PJ**

NEGATIVE WOMAN

FIRST APPEARANCE SHOWCASE #94 (August 1977)
STATUS Hero **REAL NAME** Lt. Col. Valentina Vostok
OCCUPATION Adventurer **BASE** Mobile; formerly Midway City
HEIGHT 5ft 5in **WEIGHT** 130 lbs
EYES Blue **HAIR** Blonde
SPECIAL POWERS/ABILITIES Currently none; once able to transform herself into a powerful negative-energy being that could fly at nearly the speed of light and exist outside of her body for up to 60 seconds.

Attempting to defect to the U.S. from the U.S.S.R. aboard an experimental jet fighter, cosmonaut Valentina Vostok crashed near Codsville, Maine. This was the very same little town the original DOOM PATROL had died trying to save from MADAME ROUGE and GENERAL ZAHL. Vostok became possessed by the negative-energy creature that had once transformed Larry Trainor into the Patrol's NEGATIVE MAN. Vostok became Negative Woman and also had to be swaddled in chemically treated bandages to survive. Negative Woman was soon recruited into a new Doom Patrol. Later, the villain Reactron stole her negative energies and returned them to Trainor, who had not died as originally believed. Vostok currently serves with the United Nations organization CHECKMATE, taking over for Amanda Waller (see WALLER, AMANDA) as White Queen. **SB**

NEMESIS

FIRST APPEARANCE THE BRAVE AND THE BOLD #166 (September 1980)
STATUS Hero **REAL NAME** Tom Tresser
OCCUPATION Ex-government agent; spy **BASE** Mobile
HEIGHT 5ft 10in **WEIGHT** 170 lbs **EYES** Blue **HAIR** Black
SPECIAL POWERS/ABILITIES Skilled combatant; unrivaled master of disguise; handy with a gun.

Tom Tresser, one of the world's greatest disguise artists, joined a government spy agency along with his brother Craig. Tresser assumed his Nemesis identity when a brainwashed Craig became an agent of the nefarious Council. Vowing to "balance the scales of justice," Nemesis appeared to have been killed when he crashed a bomb-laden helicopter into the Council's headquarters. However, he was rescued by government agents and became a member of the SUICIDE SQUAD. Tresser fell in love with teammate NIGHTSHADE, who divided her affections between him and Squad leader Rick Flag. During his tenure with the Squad he often employed his signature disguise, a skin-adhering face mask that could be dissolved by a chemical spray affixed to his collar. Nemesis escaped death during a mission with CATWOMAN, emerging as an operative with the Department of Metahuman Affairs under SARGE STEEL. He works closely with WONDER WOMAN in her guise as Diana Prince. **DW**

NEMESIS II

FIRST APPEARANCE JSA ANNUAL #1 (2000)
STATUS Hero (deceased) **REAL NAME** Soseh Mykos
OCCUPATION Assassin **BASE** England
HEIGHT 5ft 7in **WEIGHT** 145 lbs **EYES** Blue **HAIR** Black
SPECIAL POWERS/ABILITIES The result of physical condition and scientific experimentation left Soseh with the ability to perfectly duplicate any fighting technique she encountered.

Soseh Mykos was the genetically engineered daughter of Dr. Anatol Mykros, one of the leaders of the Council, a secret organization desiring global domination under the ULTRA-HUMANITE's control. Dr. Mykros raised Soseh and her fraternal twin, Ellina, to adulthood in virtual-birthing chambers. Soseh and her sister were subjected to thousands of tests designed to turn them into powerful assassins. Soseh rejected her father, coming into conflict with her sister and the Council numerous times, and was forced to slay Ellina. Soseh, as the hero Nemesis, teamed with the JUSTICE SOCIETY OF AMERICA to battle the Council, but Dr. Mykros escaped. It took BLACK ADAM to put an end to the Council, killing its members, including her father. Nemesis agreed to work with Black Adam's new task force of fighters, but was killed by the demigod ECLIPSO. **RG**

MEMORY Despite her training and her intentions, Soseh could never let go of her anger over her father's death.

NEON THE UNKNOWN

FIRST APPEARANCE Hit Comics #1 (1940)
STATUS Hero (deceased) **REAL NAME** Tom Corbett
OCCUPATION Former French Foreign Legionnaire **BASE** Mobile
HEIGHT 5ft 11in **WEIGHT** 167 lbs **EYES** Blue **HAIR** Black
SPECIAL POWERS/ABILITIES Was able to project powerful energy bolts from his hands and also fly.

Thomas Corbett was a French Legionnaire stationed in Africa in 1939. Lost on a desert mission, he discovered an oasis whose lake was filled with glowing water. He drank from the lake, his clothing was transformed, and he was able to project energy bolts from his hands. Corbett became Neon the Unknown and joined the Freedom Fighters, a hero team gathered by the mystic being Uncle Sam to defend the U.S. from Axis forces during World War II. On December 6, 1941, Uncle Sam warned several Fighters, including Neon, of a terrible impending attack. Arriving at Pearl Harbor the next day, the Freedom Fighters witnessed the Japanese assault on the base. Neon was killed in the bombing. **PJ**

NERGAL

FIRST APPEARANCE GREEN LANTERN ANNUAL 2nd series #9 (September 2000) **STATUS** Villain **REAL NAME** None
OCCUPATION Ruler of the Underworld **BASE** Kurnugi
HEIGHT 6ft 6in **WEIGHT** 300 lbs **EYES** White **HAIR** Blond
SPECIAL POWERS/ABILITIES Immortal; mystical might derived from Oan technology, gleaned from eons wandering in space.

The ruler of part of the underworld known as Kurnugi has bedeviled mankind since he was first worshiped by the ancient Mesopotamians. Nergal was not of this Earth, but extraterrestrial rather than supernatural. When Kyle Rayner (Green Lantern IV) and archaeologist Sala Nisaba (Sala) encountered Nergal in the Syrian Desert, they learned that he was, in fact, one of the Controllers who had departed the planet Oa millennia before. With his immortal kin, Nergal wandered the universe and eventually settled on Earth, assuming the guises of tyrannical gods to the Mesopotamians. However, Nergal and his kin were defeated by Ninurta, a hero who wielded a primitive power ring and was perhaps Earth's first Green Lantern, and Nergal's cousin Istar who wielded a ringstaff. The rogue Controllers were imprisoned within Kurnugi until their discovery by Sala during an excavation.

Nergal empowered Sala with the powers of her ancestor, Istar, in order to use her ringstaff and Kyle's power ring to destroy the gateway that prevented Nergal's return to Earth. After a tumultuous battle, Green Lantern called upon his Justice League of America comrades to help Sala defeat Nergal and send him back to his prison in Kurnugi. **SB**

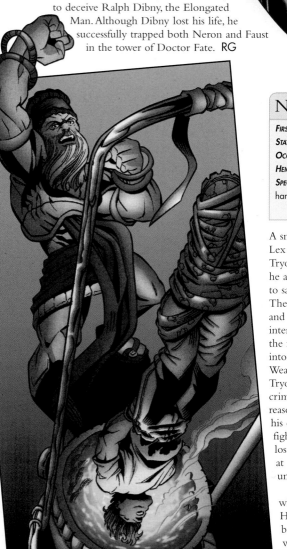

NERON

FIRST APPEARANCE Underworld Unleashed #1 (November 1995)
STATUS Villain **REAL NAME** Neron
OCCUPATION Soul-taking demon **BASE** Hell **HEIGHT** Variable
WEIGHT Variable **EYES** Variable **HAIR** Variable
SPECIAL POWERS/ABILITIES A lord of lies, Neron possesses unspeakable mystic power and can alter his size and shape.

The deaths of five of the second Flash's Rogues Gallery unleashed the demon Neron, a Prince of Hell, who granted dozens of villains, as well as a few costumed heroes, increased powers in exchange for their souls. At the suggestion of the Trickster II, Captain Marvel offered his soul to Neron in exchange for Earth's freedom. As the Trickster deduced, Marvel's soul was too pure for the demon to touch, but Neron was forced to honor his end of the bargain. Subsequently, the Flash and his wife (see Park, Linda) managed to outwit Neron and foil a rampage by the Rogues' ghosts, restoring them to life. During this event, known as the Day of Judgment, Neron was imprisoned by an unholy alliance of the Demon Etrigan, Asmodel, and the Spectre. Breaking free from his prison by possessing Superman's body, Neron attempted to claim the Spectre-Force for himself, but the Spectre instead chose Hal Jordan, the second Green Lantern as its new human host. After the Infinite Crisis, Neron allied with Felix Faust (see Faust, Felix) to deceive Ralph Dibny, the Elongated Man. Although Dibny lost his life, he successfully trapped both Neron and Faust in the tower of Doctor Fate. **RG**

NEUTRON

FIRST APPEARANCE Action Comics #525 (November 1981)
STATUS Villain **REAL NAME** Nat Tryon
OCCUPATION Criminal **BASE** Metropolis
HEIGHT 6ft 2in **WEIGHT** 184 lbs **EYES** Blue **HAIR** Black
SPECIAL POWERS/ABILITIES Releases withering atomic energy through his hands or by lifting the visor of his helmet.

A small-time crook working for Lex Luthor (see Luthor, Lex), Nat Tryon made a poor choice when he and two other thugs agreed to sabotage a nuclear reactor. The radiation sickened Tryon, and a second dose of radiation—intended to reverse the effects of the first exposure—turned him into a living nuclear reaction. Wearing a containment suit, Tryon became the superpowered criminal Neutron. For some reason he blamed Superman for his explosive state and picked a fight with the Man of Steel. He lost that showdown and earned a term of incarceration at S.T.A.R. Labs, where scientists hoped to treat his unfortunate condition.

Neutron gained his freedom from S.T.A.R. Labs when Psimon and several other super-villains freed him. He joined the reformed Fearsome Five and fought both Superman and the Teen Titans. Neutron currently works for Intergang as a thug-for-hire. **DW**

NEW GODS

HEROES OF THE FOURTH WORLD

FIRST APPEARANCE NEW GODS (1st series) #1 (March 1971)
STATUS Good and evil beings   **BASE** New Genesis and Apokolips
NOTABLE NEW GODS
See individual entries for powers and abilities.
Bekka, Big Barda, Black Racer, Darkseid, Doctor Bedlam, Esak (deceased), Fastbak, Forager I (deceased), Forager II, The Forever People, Glorious Godfrey, Highfather (deceased), Himon (deceased), Kalibak, Lightray, Lonar (deceased), Mantis, Metron, Mister Miracle, Orion, Takion, Tiggra (deceased).

The New Gods 1) Darkseid 2) Desaad
3) Glorious Godfrey 4) Heggra
5) Granny Goodness 6) Black Racer
7) Doctor Bedlam 8) Mokkari 9) Steppenwolf
10) Kanto 11) Kalibak 12) Mantis
13) Virman Vunderbar 14) Himon
15) Devilance 16) Lightray 17) Mister Miracle
18) Fastbak 19) Metron 20) Highfather
21) Forager I 22) Big Barda 23) Avia
24) Lonar 25) Orion 26) Simyan 27) Bekka.
The New Gods of New Genesis know that Earth will one day give rise to a Fifth World of super-beings, already heralded by the abundance of super heroes, to prevent the New Gods of Apokolips from finding the Anti-Life Equation.

Long, long ago, before time was even measured, there existed a race of Old Gods whose world was split apart in a fiery holocaust, unleashing a coruscating "godwave" of energy that swept across the universe. This godwave empowered the Olympian Gods and gave rise to latter-day human super heroes as it rebounded back and forth in continued, but diminishing, reverberation, seeding world after world with the potential for near-omnipotent power.

WAR OF THE WORLDS

On its fourth passing, the godwave infused the Old Gods' divided world. Out of the ashes arose two molten planets, New Genesis and Apokolips, collectively known as the Fourth World. New Genesis was home to the noble, near-immortal New Gods, who lived in harmony with their lush and verdant planet. Conversely, the denizens of nearby Apokolips were cunning and cruel, and dedicated to evil. For millions of years, New Genesis and Apokolips waged war upon one another until a peace pact was negotiated with the exchange of hostages, each the son of one world's leader. True to his nature, Apokolips's ruler Darkseid broke his pact with New Genesis's ruler Highfather by invading Earth in search of the Anti-Life Equation, the means to control all sentient life in the universe.

The New Gods met their end when a mysterious attacker ripped the souls from their bodies. Lightray, Magnar, and even the Black Racer numbered among the first casualties, and Takon, leader of New Genesis, found he could no longer access the omnipotent Source. Metron investigated the mystery and was the first to uncover the killer, while Darkseid waited for the inevitable. Big Barda's death proved one of the most shocking, prompting Mister Miracle to ally with Orion and Superman to avenge her death. **SB**

KEY STORYLINES

• *SUPERMAN'S PAL, JIMMY OLSEN #134 (DEC. 1970):* Darkseid's debut is harbinger to the introduction of the Fourth World.
• *THE HUNGER DOGS (1984):* Fourth World creator Jack Kirby's graphic novel marks his final story chronicling the New Gods.
• *COSMIC ODYSSEY #1–4 (1988):* Darkseid's quest for the Anti-Life Equation unites New Gods and heroes from Earth in a race to prevent universal destruction.

NEW GUARDIANS

FIRST APPEARANCE MILLENNIUM #8 (Summer 1987)
STATUS Hero team   *BASE* South Africa
MEMBERS AND POWERS
Betty Clawman Spiritual being who lives in the Dreamtime.
Extraño Magical and telepathic powers.
Floro Can summon plant elementals from another dimension.
Gloss Draws incredible power from "dragon lines" that mystically cross the Earth, giving her great strength and speed.
Jet (deceased) Control of electromagnetic energy.
RAM Electronic lifeform that can control computers.
Tom Kalmaku Can become one with the world's positive essence.
Harbinger Flight; powerblasts; can replicate into multiple bodies.

When a GUARDIAN OF THE UNIVERSE and his Zamaron mate came to Earth to choose their successors, they super-evolved ten human beings, giving them powers and immortality, and united them as the Chosen, progenitors of the next step in mankind's evolution.

When one of the Chosen, Janwillem Kroef, decided he could not live in a world where the racially and sexually diverse Chosen represented humanity, he created a race of neo-hybrids to destroy them. After the neo-hybrids, called the New Order, were released from Kroef's dark thrall by a reluctant Tom Kalmaku (*see* KALMAKU, TOM), it was revealed that it was the hybrids who were the true Chosen. The New Guardians settled on Kroef's South African compound to teach the neo-hybrids the true meaning of peaceful coexistence on Earth. **PJ**

THE CHOSEN Gathered from the four corners of the globe, the New Guardians were created to lead humanity on its next evolutionary step.

KEY 1) Jet 2) RAM
3) Gloss 4) Extraño
5) Floro 6) Harbinger

NIGHTBLADE

FIRST APPEARANCE GREEN LANTERN ANNUAL (2nd series) #2 (1993)
STATUS Hero   *REAL NAME* Nik Mayak
OCCUPATION Adventurer   *BASE* Mobile
HEIGHT 5ft 11in   *WEIGHT* 178 lbs   *EYES* Blue   *HAIR* Black
SPECIAL POWERS/ABILITIES Expert knife thrower; has regenerative powers that can regrow lost limbs.

Nik Mayak lost the use of his legs in a car crash that also claimed the life of his father. While in hospital, he exercised his upper body by throwing small objects until he could hit a bull's-eye consistently. He would have spent his life as a paraplegic had alien parasites not attacked the hospital. When the aliens drank Mayak's spinal fluid, his latent regenerative powers kicked in and his legs healed. He learned that the aliens had killed his mother and sister and helped GREEN LANTERN Hal Jordan battle them. He later joined other "New Blood" heroes in the team BLOOD PACK, taking the name Nightblade, and relying on throwing knives and his recuperative powers to combat the alien invaders. **DW**

NEWSBOY LEGION

FIRST APPEARANCE STAR-SPANGLED COMICS #7 (April 1942) (Legion I); Superman Annual 2nd series) #2 (1988) (Legion II)   *STATUS* Hero team   *BASE* Metropolis
MEMBERS (LEGION I)
Anthony "Big Words" Rodriguez, John "Gabby" Gabrielli, Patrick "Scrapper" MacGuire, Thomas "Tommy" Thompkins
MEMBERS (LEGION II)
Clones of the above, plus Roberta "Famous Bobby" Harper, and Walter "Flip" Johnson. -- CHECK OK!

KEY 1) The Guardian 2) Tommy
3) Flip 4) Gabby
5) Big Words
6) Scrapper

On January 23, 1942 police officer Jim Harper (*see* Guardian), became the legal guardian of several members of the Newsboy Legion. Harper believed this was the only way to ensure that the orphaned boys would receive a proper upbringing, as opposed to the rough, tough "school of hard knocks" lessons to be had on the streets of Metropolis's Suicide Slum. On several occasions they were rescued by the blue and gold costumed champion known as the GUARDIAN. Eventually, the boys figured out Harper had been watching out for them both as a cop and a hero.

Once they grew up, these kids from Suicide Slum became scientists and created Project Cadmus, a scientific facility specializing in genetics. Cadmus's top-secret technology was later used to clone a new body for Jim Harper, giving the Guardian a second life.

During a takeover of Cadmus by the Apokoliptian creature SLEEZ, the directors themselves were cloned, thus giving birth to a new, teenaged Newsboy Legion. The clones plus Walter "Flip" Johnson were kept inside Project Cadmus most of the time. When the project was headed by the dubious Paul Westfield, the Newsboys often acted as ethical guardians. Eventually, the clones' "fathers," the original directors, retired from Cadmus, and the young Newsboys relocated to Suicide Slum. They spent most of their time in a garage, working on a new design for the Whiz Wagon, the Guardian's flying vehicle.

Together, the Guardian and the Newsboy Legion fought a plethora of foes. In the aftermath of one adventure, the Newsboys welcomed their first female member, Harper's grandniece, Roberta, nicknamed Famous Bobby. **RG**

GUARDIAN ANGEL Regardless of generation, you can expect the Newsboy Legion to find trouble, and receive help from the Guardian.

NIGHT AND FOG

FIRST APPEARANCE ALL-STAR SQUADRON #44 (April 1985)
STATUS Villain team   **REAL NAMES** Unrevealed
OCCUPATION Assassins   **BASE** Nazi Germany
HEIGHT (Night) 5ft 5in; (Fog) 5ft 9½in   **WEIGHT** (Night) 130 lbs;
(Fog) 165 lbs   **EYES** (Night) Blue; (Fog) unrevealed
HAIR (Night) Black; (Fog) gray
SPECIAL POWERS/ABILITIES Night projects sensory-depriving
blackness from her hair; Fog transforms himself into a
noxious, foglike mist.

Night and Fog are siblings
given superhuman powers
by Nazi scientists soon
after the December, 1941
attack on Pearl Harbor.
Known in Germany as
"Nacht und Nebel,"
the two assassins were
sent on missions to kill
various Nazi opponents,
using powers that were
the literal realization of
Adolf Hitler's "Night and Fog," which, he declared, would
consume any and all Axis enemies.

Hitler sent Night and Fog to assassinate Ed Reilly, the
father of Firebrand II. Reilly, a steel magnate, had actually
been working against the Allied Forces until he learned
of the Nazi atrocities in Europe. Despite Firebrand's
intervention, Reilly was murdered, and Night and Fog
turned their attention to the All-Star Squadron. The sibling
assassins subsequently returned to Germany; their fates are
unknown. **PJ**

NIGHT FORCE

FIRST APPEARANCE THE NEW TEEN TITANS (1st series) #21(July 1982)
STATUS Hero team   **BASE** Georgetown, Washington, D.C.
ORIGINAL MEMBERS
Baron Winter Group leader; occultist.
Paul Brooks (deceased) Petty thug.
Dr. Donovan Caine Scientist researching evil as a tangible force.
Jack Gold Journalist and recovering alcoholic.
Vanessa Van Helsing Psychic; Gold's estranged wife.
Gowon Winter Winter's son.
Katina Winter Winter's wheelchair-bound ex-wife.

The Night Force is a group of often-reluctant
individuals called into action by the enigmatic
Baron Winter whenever the world is threatened
by supernatural menaces. Each year, the Baron
must deliver an angel to Hell in a pact to preserve
mankind's freedom. The first incarnation, along
with Winter's ex-wife Katina and son Gowon—also
considered members—resides with the occultist
in his Georgetown mansion. Brooks lost his
life but redeemed his soul ridding a New
York City brownstone of a demon squatter.
The rest of this Night Force retired from
arcane adventuring after investigating a
series of mystical mysteries.

A second Night Force was assembled
to defeat a timeless evil infecting children
with the intent to kill. This teaming
included Hallie Davis, sister of one
murdered mother, as well as C.I.A. agent
Marc Diamond and luckless loser Eddie
Furlow. The second Night Force also stopped a
serial killer inadvertently created by Vanessa Van
Helsing's unresolved anger at Jack Gold made
psychically real. Their present activities
are unrecorded. **SB**

NIGHTHAWK

FIRST APPEARANCE WESTERN COMICS #5 (October 1948)
STATUS Hero   **REAL NAME** Hannibal Hawkes
OCCUPATION Traveling fix-it man   **BASE** Old West
HEIGHT 5ft 11in   **WEIGHT** 185 lbs   **EYES** Black   **HAIR** Black
SPECIAL POWERS/ABILITIES Given his past, Nighthawk is a fierce
competitor, a master marksman and fine horse rider.

Hannibal Hawkes was the 19th century reincarnation
of the Ancient Egyptian Prince Khufu and he adopted
the costumed guise of Nighthawk to continue his
warrior ways. Hawkes was a traveling fix-it man, using
the experience gained from his many reincarnations to
handle most any kind of repair while donning an ebony
mask and using six-shooters to mete out rough frontier
justice. Riding his jet-black stallion Nightwind, he traveled
the plains, eventually meeting up in St. Roch with the
woman known as CINNAMON, a reincarnation of Khufu's
beloved Chay-Ara. Together they loved and battled side
by side until Hath-Set's eternal curse caught up with
them, bringing death and eventual rebirth. Nighthawk and
Cinnamon's descendant, Hannibal Hawk, operates in the
present-day West as a bounty hunter also
known as Nighthawk. **RG**

KEY *The original Night Force included these arcane adventurers:*
1) *Dr. Donovan Caine* **2)** *Jack Gold* **3)** *Vanessa Van Helsing*
4) *Paul Brooks* **5)** *Gowon Winter* **6)** *Katina Winter*

NIGHTMASTER

FIRST APPEARANCE SHOWCASE #82 (May 1969)
STATUS Hero   **REAL NAME** Jim Rook
OCCUPATION Bookstore owner; adventurer   **BASE** New York City
HEIGHT 6ft 1in   **WEIGHT** 183 lbs   **EYES** Blue   **HAIR** Gray
SPECIAL POWERS/ABILITIES Carries the Sword of Night, which warns of
danger, deflects energy, and compels enemies to speak the truth.

In the late 1960s, Jim Rook,
lead singer of rock band The
Electrics, entered a strange New
York City shop called Oblivion
Inc. with his fiancée and found
himself transported to the alternate
dimension of Myrra, a land of
knights and sorcerers. Rook
learned that he was the descendant
of a Myrran warrior and took up
his ancestor's magic Sword of Night.
At that moment, Jim Rook became
the Nightmaster. Reluctant to play a
chivalrous role that he found slightly
ridiculous, Nightmaster nevertheless freed
Myrra from the grip of evil warlocks
and returned with his fiancée to Earth.
Over the next two decades he opened
a bookstore in the Oblivion Inc. location
and led a quiet life, until persuaded to help
the Leymen of PRIMAL FORCE defeat the
cult called the August. An encounter with
Swamp Thing convinced Rook that his Myrra
experiences had been an hallucination, but the
truth remains to be seen. **DW**

NIGHTSHADE

FIRST APPEARANCE CAPTAIN ATOM (1st series) #82 (1966)
STATUS Hero   **REAL NAME** Eve Eden
OCCUPATION Adventurer   **BASE** Washington, D.C.   **HEIGHT** 5ft 8in
WEIGHT 139 lbs   **EYES** Blue   **HAIR** (Eve) blonde; (Nightshade) black
SPECIAL POWERS/ABILITIES Transforms into a tangible shadow; crosses
dimensions by opening warp doors between one realm and the Land
of Nightshades; expert spy and hand-to-hand combatant.

Eve Eden's mother Maureen
was Queen of the Land of the
Nightshades, a mystic dimension.
Maureen took Eve and her
brother Larry to the Nightshade
world and Maureen was attacked
by the Incubus, a vile being that
abducted Larry. Eve promised her
dying mother that she would find
Larry and take him back to Earth.

Eve became the government
agent Nightshade and joined the
SUICIDE SQUAD. On a mission to the
Nightshade world, Eve discovered
that Larry had been possessed
by the Incubus. Squad member
DEADSHOT killed Larry and the
Incubus also died.

Nightshade had romances
with the Squad's Rick Flag and
NEMESIS I and helped
CAPTAIN ATOM, and the BLUE BEETLE
rescue the JUSTICE LEAGUE OF AMERICA
from the villain Avatar. She was one of
several operatives hired by Lex Luthor
(see LUTHOR, LEX) to take down
SUPERMAN and BATMAN. **PJ**

NIGHTWING

BLÜDHAVEN'S FINEST

FIRST APPEARANCE TALES OF THE TEEN TITANS #43 (July 1984)
STATUS Hero **REAL NAME** Richard "Dick" Grayson
OCCUPATION Police officer; crime fighter **BASE** Blüdhaven
HEIGHT 5ft 10in **WEIGHT** 175 lbs **EYES** Blue **HAIR** Black
SPECIAL POWERS/ABILITIES Second only to Batman in fighting skills and detective abilities; utility belt includes regurgitant gas pellets, smoke capsules, acetylene torch, flexi-cuffs, Batarangs, and shuriken-like Wing-Dings; bulletproof and fire-resistant costume is insulated and wired as single-shot taser to incapacitate attackers; right gauntlet carries hand-held 100,000-volt stun gun; preferred weapons are twin shatterproof polymer Escrima sticks, held in spring-loaded pouches in the back of costume for swift deployment in close-quarters fighting.

NIGHTWING IS DICK GRAYSON, the very first ROBIN now grown to manhood. Dick realized the need to leave the shadow of his mentor BATMAN and establish his own heroic presence. The Dark Knight accelerated Dick's decision by firing the young hero, who had just joined the TEEN TITANS, from his role as teen sidekick. Batman thought Robin would return to his side, but Dick accepted the decision and left the Batcave. Not long after, he ceded the role of Robin to orphan Jason Todd. For Dick Grayson, there would be no turning back. After much soul-searching, he adopted a new guise inspired by two of his childhood heroes. To remain a creature of the night like the Dark Knight, Dick became Nightwing. The name was recommended by SUPERMAN, a role model for Dick, after a mysterious hero of Kryptonian legend.

FLYING GRAYSON Having learned acrobatic skills from his parents, Dick is a gifted aerialist, perhaps surpassing even Batman in agility.

NIGHTWING TAKES FLIGHT

Nightwing flew into action for the first time to save his fellow Teen Titans from DEATHSTROKE THE TERMINATOR and the criminal consortium known as H.I.V.E (Hierarchy of International Vengeance and Extermination). He continued to lead the Titans thereafter, eventually reconciling with his former mentor Batman and reclaiming his status as the Dark Knight's closest and most trusted ally. When the Titans disbanded, Nightwing resumed solo crimefighting.

At Batman's behest, Nightwing left Gotham—his home since the deaths of his parents, the Flying Graysons—and moved to neighboring Blüdhaven, a crime-ridden port city desperately in need of its own defender. With Blüdhaven mired in corruption, Dick made law enforcement his day job also, enrolling in the city's police academy and eventually graduating to become a rookie cop with the B.P.D. Nightwing used his nocturnal hours to undermine mob boss Roland Desmond (BLOCKBUSTER) and the city's feuding gang lords. Nightwing even found time to join a fourth lineup of Titans before the group suffered the deaths of two longtime members. Soon after, Nightwing helped to establish a new team of heroes, dubbed the OUTSIDERS after a defunct cadre of clandestine crime fighters Batman himself had once led. Rather than simply react to villainy, the Outsiders under Nightwing's leadership took a proactive approach to rooting out evil, hunting the world's Most Wanted and bringing them to justice. The Dark Knight's former squire continues to fight the good fight and make his mentor proud of both the man and the hero that he has become. **SB**

HALLEY'S CIRCUS Before Dick's aerialist parents were murdered by gangsters they were a major circus act.

COMBAT MASTER Not even a posse of trained killers can subdue lightning-quick Nightwing!

KEY STORYLINES

• **TALES OF THE TEEN TITANS #41–44, ANNUAL #3 (APRIL–JULY 1984):** Deathstroke hunts the Teen Titans, leaving the all-new Nightwing the last Titan standing and the team's only hope!

• **BATMAN #440-442, NEW TITANS #60-61 (OCTOBER–DECEMBER 1989):** In "A Lonely Place of Dying," Nightwing meets his successor as Boy Wonder, Tim Drake, and fights alongside Batman to defeat Two-Face!

• **NIGHTWING #1 (1988):** At Batman's behest, Nightwing makes Blüdhaven his new home and brings costumed justice to the crime-ridden seaport.

TROIA'S DEATH Nightwing's Titans teammate and closest friend, died in his arms. Despite strong feelings on both sides, the two were never romantically linked.

THE OUTSIDER Nightwing found an important role as leader of the Outsiders vigilante team, organized by Batman to track down criminals who were beyond the law's reach.

NOCTURNA

FIRST APPEARANCE DETECTIVE COMICS # 529 (August 1983)
STATUS Villain (missing) **REAL NAME** Natalia Knight
OCCUPATION Astronomer **BASE** England
HEIGHT 5ft 10in **WEIGHT** 140 lbs **EYES** Blue **HAIR** Black
SPECIAL POWERS/ABILITIES Natalia was a brilliant astronomer but unskilled at hand-to-hand combat.

Natalia was a child of the streets until the criminal Charles Knight took her in. She grew up with Knight's natural son, Anton, eventually falling in love with him. An accident with laser radiation drained Natalia Knight's skin of all pigment and rendered her sensitive to sunlight, an accident not entirely unfortunate for an astronomer romantically drawn to twilight. From dusk till dawn, Natalia and Anton's alter egos of Nocturna and Night-Slayer engaged in thievery to enjoy the witching hour's luxuries. BATMAN brought Night-Slayer to justice and Nocturna then began a romance with Sturges Hellstrom, a minor Gotham criminal. Enraged, Night-Slayer escaped prison and murdered Hellstrom, only to be slain by his former lover. She escaped from Batman in a hot-air balloon, never to be seen again. ROBIN and SPOILER have since encountered a former astronomer named Natalie Metternich (alias Natalia Mitternacht). Like Nocturna, Metternich is pale and loves the night. It is unknown whether these similarities are just coincidence. RG

NORTHWIND

FIRST APPEARANCE ALL-STAR SQUADRON #25 (September 1983)
STATUS Hero **REAL NAME** Norda Cantrell
OCCUPATION Vigilante **BASE** Mobile
HEIGHT 6ft **WEIGHT** 195 lbs
EYES Brown **HAIR** Golden feathers
SPECIAL POWERS/ABILITIES Flight, enhanced stamina and strength, and the ability to communicate with birds, though not with human beings

The hybrid child of a human father (anthropologist Fred Cantrell) and a mother from a race of bird-people called the Feitherans, Norda Cantrell grew up in the hidden city of Feithera in northern Greenland.

The godson of HAWKMAN Carter Hall, Norda encountered jealousy from Hawkman's true son Hector Hall (later the Silver Scarab and DOCTOR FATE). As a young adult, Norda left Feithera to join INFINITY, INC. under the name of Northwind. He served with the team until Hector Hall's death, after which he returned to his people to help them rebuild their civilization in the city of New Feithera.

Northwind has recently undergone a full metamorphosis into a giant bird-like creature, improving his flying abilities, but unfortunately losing the ability to speak in the process. In his new form he has joined with BLACK ADAM, ATOM-SMASHER, and Brainwave II to form a "zero-tolerance" super-hero team committed to ending violence by executing super-villains. Northwind and the others have so far killed the terrorist KOBRA, among others. DW

NUCLEAR FAMILY

FIRST APPEARANCE The Outsiders #1 (November 1985)
STATUS Android villains (destroyed) **BASE** California
MEMBERS AND POWERS
Dad Could emit vast amounts of nuclear radiation.
Mom Could emit potentially fatal electromagnetic pulse.
Biff Could emit thermal pulse of immense heat.
Sis Could emit immensely destructive blast wave.
Brat and dog Could emit radioactive fallout.

Dad *Mom* *Biff*

Sis *Brat*

The OUTSIDERS had declared their independence from BATMAN's leadership and relocated from Gotham City to Santa Monica, California. No sooner had they settled into their new digs, than they received word of trouble at the Esperanza Canyon nuclear power plant. There, the team discovered a family of androids, named Dad, Mom, Biff, Sis, Brat, and Dog.

These eerie creations were the brainchildren of the deranged Dr. Eric Shanner. The doctor had been a victim of radiation poisoning and had created the family he would never have himself. Working with the Outsider's old opponent, Professor Wye, Shanner intended to use the opening of the plant to detonate a nuclear explosion, sharing his radiation death with as many Californians as possible. The Outsiders confronted the powerful androids and fought them to a standstill until Wye turned on Shanner. This provided the Outsiders with an opportunity to stop the Nuclear Family and do so before Shanner and the androids died in a controlled explosion. RG

NYOLA

FIRST APPEARANCE ALL-STAR COMICS # 2 (Fall 1940)
STATUS Villain **REAL NAME** Nyola
OCCUPATION Priestess **BASE** Unknown
HEIGHT 5ft 4in **WEIGHT** 115 lbs **EYES** Brown **HAIR** Red-brown
SPECIAL POWERS/ABILITIES She has magical control over the weather, and can project bolts of lightning.

Nyola was an Aztec priestess who gained elemental powers through her worship of the rain god Tlaloc. Haughty, arrogant Nyola was originally an enemy of HAWKMAN and HAWKGIRL, tackling the winged wonders in early 1942 during one of their archaeological excursions in Central America.

Nyola returned as leader of the first MONSTER SOCIETY OF EVIL. The evil sorceress invaded the JUSTICE SOCIETY OF AMERICA's New York City headquarters, fighting Hawkgirl, HOURMAN, and Sandy, the original SANDMAN's sidekick. Along with the Monster Society's RAMULUS, Dummy, MISTER WHO, and Oom, Nyola was soundly defeated by the FLASH and GREEN LANTERN. PJ

O.S.S. SPIES AT WAR

FIRST APPEARANCE G.I. COMBAT #192 (July 1976)
STATUS Intelligence agency **BASE** Washington, D.C.
MEMBERS/ABILITIES
The most talented men and women in science, diplomacy, economics, and other fields were recruited, including the adventurer Speed Saunders. They had codenames such as Falcon, Shadow, Sprinter, Mongoose, Phoenix, Raven. Costumed heroes such as Manhunter II, Phantom Lady I, and Iron Munro also worked for O.S.S.

On December 7, 1941, The Office of Strategic Services was established to centralize the intelligence collection functions of the United States military forces. Carlo "Chuck" Sirianni functions as the BLACKHAWK's liaison with the group. One agent, who allowed his own wife to die rather than reveal the agency's secrets, was tapped to dispatch agents on other deadly missions and was known only as Control. After the war, the unit was absorbed into the C.I.A. Control was later asked to head up ARGENT I, an international force under the Task Force X umbrella. He went underground after President J. F. Kennedy's assassination. Some time later Control died; however, Argent's covert actions continued until ended by the modern-day SUICIDE SQUAD. RG

MISSION IMPOSSIBLE An O.S.S field agent in action.

OCEAN MASTER

FIRST APPEARANCE AQUAMAN (1st series) #29 (October 1966)
STATUS Villain **REAL NAME** Orm Marius
OCCUPATION Professional criminal **BASE** The Atlantic Ocean
HEIGHT 5ft 11in **WEIGHT** 200 lbs **EYES** Brown **HAIR** Brown
SPECIAL POWERS/ABILITIES Trident possesses vast magical powers, notably the firing of powerful mystical energy blasts; amphibious; able to breathe underwater and swim at great speeds; is totally unaffected by the crushing weight of the ocean's great depths.

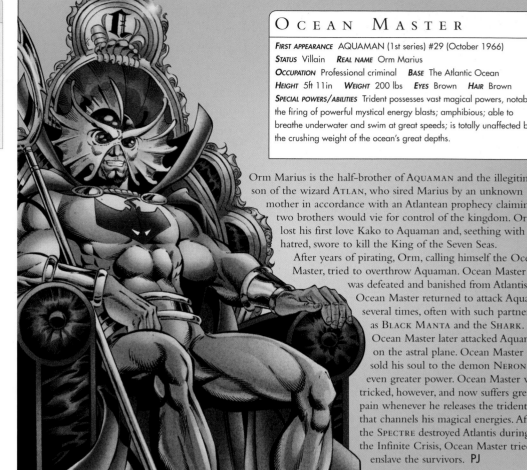

Orm Marius is the half-brother of AQUAMAN and the illegitimate son of the wizard ATLAN, who sired Marius by an unknown mother in accordance with an Atlantean prophecy claiming two brothers would vie for control of the kingdom. Orm lost his first love Kako to Aquaman and, seething with hatred, swore to kill the King of the Seven Seas.

After years of pirating, Orm, calling himself the Ocean Master, tried to overthrow Aquaman. Ocean Master was defeated and banished from Atlantis. Ocean Master returned to attack Aquaman several times, often with such partners as BLACK MANTA and the SHARK. Ocean Master later attacked Aquaman on the astral plane. Ocean Master sold his soul to the demon NERON for even greater power. Ocean Master was tricked, however, and now suffers great pain whenever he releases the trident that channels his magical energies. After the SPECTRE destroyed Atlantis during the Infinite Crisis, Ocean Master tried to enslave the survivors. PJ

OBSIDIAN

FIRST APPEARANCE ALL-STAR SQUADRON #25 (September 1983)
STATUS Villain **REAL NAME** Todd Rice
OCCUPATION Super-villain **BASE** Mobile
HEIGHT 5ft 11in **WEIGHT** 193 lbs **EYES** Brown **HAIR** Brown
SPECIAL POWERS/ABILITIES Can control the shadow force to become a living shadow or send people into the "shadowlands" of their deepest fears.

Son of original GREEN LANTERN Alan Scott, Todd Rice and his sister Jennie (JADE) were raised by foster parents after their mother, Rose (see ROSE AND THORN), gave them up without her husband's knowledge. Todd grew up in Milwaukee where his adoptive father abused him. At an early age the boy learned how to manifest the shadow powers that seemed to reflect his own bitterness and pain. Taking the alias Obsidian, Todd, his sister and other young heroes banded together as INFINITY, INC. After the team broke up, Obsidian succumbed to the shadows in his heart and teamed with the JSA's old nemesis Ian Karkull to spread darkness and terror across the planet. Alan Scott defeated his son, who seemingly perished—until reappearing alongside the near-omnipotent ECLIPSO and Mordru (see DARK LORD) to destroy the world. Obsidian later started a romance with Damon Matthews, a legal colleague of Kate Spencer (see MANHUNTER). DW

*DARK SIDE
Obsidian's recent attempts to plunge the world into blackness seem to have opened a path to redemption. In time he may re-emerge as a hero.*

ODD MAN

FIRST APPEARANCE CANCELLED COMICS CAVALCADE #2 (Fall 1978)
STATUS Villain **REAL NAME** Clayton "Clay" Stoner
OCCUPATION Private investigator; crime fighter **BASE** River City
HEIGHT 5ft 11in **WEIGHT** 180 lbs **EYES** Blue **HAIR** Black
SPECIAL POWERS/ABILITIES Above-average hand-to-hand combatant; costume contained a variety of clownish gags and gimmicks to disorient and defeat opponents, including a weighted tie, slippery oil spray, smoke-emitting gloves, and anesthetic gas.

When there was trouble in crime-ridden River City, private investigator Clay Stoner became the Odd Man out of nowhere, clad in a confusing costume that was more like a carnival clown's and based in an office that turned end-over-end to dizzy dimwitted stooges. The Odd Man literally turned the underworld upside-down with his heroic high jinks and wacky weapons. He didn't just make fools of hardened gangsters; the Odd Man once solved a murder mystery involving the reincarnation of the first Nile Queen and her Pharaoh consort.

The Odd Man has had a minor association with the public service super-hero agency known as HERO HOTLINE. He also applied for the position of Security Chief at Project Cadmus. Passed over, the Odd Man also tried and failed to interest the POWER COMPANY, a superpowered law firm, in his slapstick services. The Odd Man remains River City's sole super hero. SB

OLSEN, JIMMY

SUPERMAN'S PAL

FIRST APPEARANCE SUPERMAN (1st series) #13 (November 1941)
STATUS Hero **REAL NAME** James Bartholomew Olsen
OCCUPATION Journalist; photographer **BASE** Metropolis
HEIGHT 6ft 2in **WEIGHT** 210 lbs **EYES** Blue **HAIR** Red
SPECIAL POWERS/ABILITIES Only an average athlete but has a keen
photographer's eye; seemingly fearless in the face of danger;
unswervingly loyal to his friends; periodically falls victim to bizarre
mutant abilities he is usually powerless to control.

THE FIRST TWO PEOPLE ever rescued by SUPERMAN were Lois Lane
(*see* LANE, LOIS) and a fresh-faced photographer named Jimmy Olsen.
Superman befriended Jimmy and the teen became one of the Man
of Steel's most faithful admirers. In return, Superman gave Jimmy a
special watch with a hypersonic signal only Superman could hear,
which the teen used to alert the Man of Steel. Inspired by his hero,
Jimmy has embarked on many adventures, risking life and limb to
get prize-winning shots. Who else but Jimmy could have fearlessly
photographed the deadly battle between Superman and DOOMSDAY?

COUNTDOWN
*Jimmy has earned Superman's
trust and, with it, a signal watch
to summon the Man of Steel!*

LOOKING FOR TROUBLE

Jimmy was brought up by his mother Sarah in Metropolis's Bakerline
section, after his father, Jake Olsen, a covert military operative, went missing.
The boy proved to be highly intelligent and became an academic star. But what
Jimmy really wanted was action. He signed on as an intern and then a junior
photographer at the *Daily Planet* newspaper. He quickly developed
a crush on the paper's star reporter Lois Lane, who tolerated
the eager young pup and often brought him along on assignments. Jimmy also fell under
Daily Planet editor Perry White's sway. White instilled in him the vital importance
of photographs to truthful reporting, and the pair have something of a father-
son relationship—which can turn explosive when Jimmy infuriates Perry by
"accidentally" calling him "Chief." Strange superpowers manifested when
Jimmy investigated the deaths of the NEW GODS. Discovering abilities
including super speed, stretching, flame breath, and the power to grow
porcupine quills or a turtle's shell, Jimmy branded himself as the
superhero 'Mister Action.' He later traveled to Apokolips to help
FORAGER investigate find the New Gods' killer. **RG**

SUPERMAN ARRIVES *When
a costumed figure first flew over
Metropolis, reporter Lois Lane
grabbed her favorite photographer,
Jimmy Olsen. They covered the year's
biggest story, the arrival of Superman.*

THE CHIEF *Still
learning, Jimmy is
often given guidance
by Perry White—in
no uncertain terms!*

**THIS IS A JOB FOR
SUPERMAN!** *The Man
of Steel has rescued
Jimmy from certain
death almost as
often as he has
saved Lois Lane!*

MISTER ACTION *Jimmy's strange superpowers only appeared
when danger threatened, prompting him to go into the
superhero business. Approaching to the Final Crisis, Jimmy
used his abilities to explore Apokolips and battle Darkseid.*

KEY STORYLINES

• *SUPERMAN'S METROPOLIS #1–12 (APRIL 2003–MARCH 2004):*
Jimmy and Metropolis's Brainiac-created artificial intelligence
learn from one another.
• *SUPERMAN'S PAL JIMMY OLSEN #133–134 (OCTOBER–DECEMBER
1971):* Jimmy learns of Darkseid's threat and begins a series
of amazing adventures.
• *SUPERMAN #143 (MAY 1990):* Jimmy learns the truth about his
father's disappearance and connection with Project Cadmus.

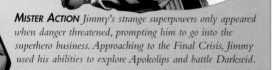

THE DC COMICS ENCYCLOPEDIA

OLYMPIAN

FIRST APPEARANCE SUPER FRIENDS #8 (December 1977)
STATUS Hero **REAL NAME** Aristedes Demetrios
OCCUPATION Adventurer **BASE** Athens; the Dome
HEIGHT 6ft 4in **WEIGHT** 255 lbs **EYES** Brown **HAIR** Brown
SPECIAL POWERS/ABILITIES Golden Fleece gives him superstrength, superspeed, near invulnerability, precognition, telescopic vision, X-ray vision, hypnotic control over animals, shapechanging into animals; also Olympic-level boxing, wrestling, martial arts, archery, and equestrian skills; expert physician and maritime navigator.

Artistedes Demetrios was a rebellious punk from Leiváda, Greece, who was jailed several times for petty crime. Discovering and stealing the legendary Golden Fleece from a crate in the warehouse he was working in, Demetrios was possessed by the powers and personalities of Jason and his 50 Argonauts, the heroes of Greek mythology who had originally captured the Golden Fleece. Aristedes became the heroic Olympian, joining DOCTOR MIST's international team, the GLOBAL GUARDIANS.

Captured and hypnotized by the evil Queen Bee, Aristedes could no longer control the spirits of the Argonauts—each of them vied for control of his body. As a result, the Olympian now suffers from extreme multiple personality disorder. The Olympian remains a hero in some parts of Greece, fighting local criminals. **PJ**

OLYMPIAN GODS

FIRST APPEARANCE WONDER WOMAN (2nd series) #1 (November 1987)
STATUS Transcendent beings **BASE** Mount Olympus
NOTABLE MEMBERS OF THE GREEK PANTHEON
Zeus God of the Skies.
Hera Goddess of Wives and Childbirth; wife of Zeus.
Aphrodite Goddess of Love; a former wife of Ares.
Apollo God of Light.
Ares God of War.
Artemis Goddess of the Hunt.
Athena Goddess of Wisdom.
Demeter Goddess of Agriculture.
Dionysus God of Wine.
Hades God of the Underworld.
Heracles God of Strength.
Hestia Goddess of the Hearth.
Mercury The Messenger God.
Poseidon God of the Oceans.

The children of the TITANS OF MYTH, the Olympian gods ruled the Earth for centuries from their fortress, Mount Olympus in ancient Greece. Long ago, a young DARKSEID split the pantheon of gods into two, creating the Roman gods. Several of the goddesses of Mount Olympus created the AMAZONS of Themyscira, a race of mighty warriors.

When the War God ARES went mad, the goddesses created the Amazon princess WONDER WOMAN to stop his schemes. Later, the Olympians were manipulated into a cataclysmic War of the Gods by the witch CIRCE, clashing against each other and the gods of other pantheons. After the cosmic Source, the Fount for All Creation, was threatened, the Greek and Roman pantheons were reunited. Prior to the Amazonian invasion of Washington DC, GRANNY GOODNESS overpowered the Olympian Gods and assumed the guise of Athena. **PJ**

OMAC

FIRST APPEARANCE (historical) OMAC (1st series) #1 (October 1974)
STATUS Villain **REAL NAME** Inapplicable
OCCUPATION Anti-metahuman virus **BASE** Mobile
HEIGHT Various **WEIGHT** Various **EYES** None **HAIR** Black
SPECIAL POWERS/ABILITIES Cyborg OMAC units can fly, emit energy blasts, withstand extreme damage, and interface instantly with the Brother Eye satellite.

In an alternate Earth's future timeline, Buddy Blank became the One Man Army Corps (OMAC) following a Great Disaster. On the mainstream Earth, however, OMAC units became a threat after BATMAN constructed the artificially-intelligent Brother Eye satellite to keep tabs on metahumans behavior. Corruption by Maxwell Lord (see LORD, MAXWELL) caused Brother Eye to infect more than a million human agents with a nanotech virus and initiate a sweeping campaign against metahumans. Batman destroyed his creation during the Infinite Crisis, but the OMAC Project lived on in the form of its single surviving agent, Michael Costner. Brother Eye returned when this reality's Buddy Blank repaired its operating system. It then activated a new army of OMAC units on the planet Apokolips. Sasha Bordeaux (see BORDEAUX, SASHA) of CHECKMATE is a cyborg with an array of OMAC enhancements. **DW**

KEY 1) Poseidon 2) Zeus 3) Hades
4) Dionysus 5) Apollo 6) Hera
7) Hestia 8) Mercury 9) Aphrodite
10) Artemis 11) Athena
12) Demeter 13) Heracles

OMEGA MEN

FIRST APPEARANCE GREEN LANTERN (2nd series) #141 (June 1981)
STATUS Heroes **BASE** Vegan Star System
NOTABLE MEMBERS
Primus (deceased) Psionically-powered leader.
Auron (Lambien) Godlike son of a Vegan goddess.
Broot Rock-hard giant from the planet Changralyn.
Harpis Winged sister of Demonia.
Kalista Sorceress wife of the late Primus.
Nimbus Wraith-like spirit.
Tigorr (Taghurrhu) Karnan feline fighter; occasional leader.

The Omega Men are the last best hope for freedom for the Vegan star-system. Warriors from various Vegan planets, the Omegans tried to liberate their worlds from the Citadel, an axis of evil led by the Psion-bred Citadelians (see Psions, Alien Races, pp. 166–7), that included the dreaded Gordanian slavers and ruthless Branx warriors. Forced to flee Vega, they were befriended by GREEN LANTERN Hal Jordan and SUPERMAN and received asylum on Earth. The Omegans helped the TEEN TITANS rescue STARFIRE from the Citadel, which was at last routed. However, the resulting power vacuum allowed the Spider Guild to annex portions of Vegan space. The Omegans battled the Spider Guild and remnants of the Citadel before being drawn into the conflict arising from the Dominator-led invasion of Earth (see Great Battles, pp. 362-3). Prior to the Infinite Crisis, the Omega Men helped ADAM STRANGE investigate the disappearance of the planet Rann. The team has encountered its greatest challenge in dealing with the death-worshipping cultists of Lady Styx. **SB**

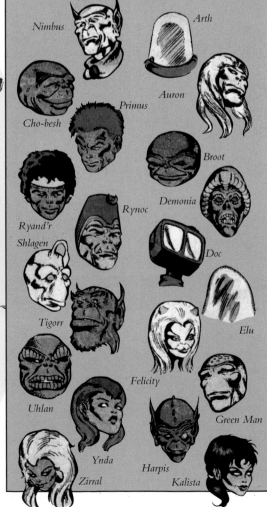

Nimbus
Arth
Cho-besh
Primus
Auron
Ryand'r
Shlagen
Rynoc
Broot
Demonia
Doc
Tigorr
Elu
Felicity
Uhlan
Green Man
Ynda
Harpis
Zirral
Kalista

ONOMATOPOEIA

FIRST APPEARANCE GREEN ARROW (3rd series) #11 (February 2002)
STATUS Villain **REAL NAME** Unrevealed
OCCUPATION Assassin **BASE** Mobile
HEIGHT 5ft 11in **WEIGHT** 180 lbs
EYES Hidden by mask **HAIR** Unknown
SPECIAL POWERS/ABILITIES A superb athlete; expert with guns, knives, and swords; does things no normal human could accomplish, including biting one of Green Arrow's weapons in half.

The motivation that makes Onomatopoeia cross the country killing third-rate costumed heroes (i.e. Harrisburg, Pennsylvania's Buckeye) and assorted vigilantes remains an unexplained mystery. He seems to be deliberately working his way up from the bottom and moving on to more powerful and well-known adversaries; however, like so much about Onomatopoeia, this is mere conjecture. As his name suggests, he expresses himself using only onomatopoeic words. The last sound victims hear is Onomatopoeia's imitation of the noise made by the weapon he is about to use to murder them.

Green Arrow II Connor Hawke was one of Onomatopoeia's most notable victims. Ambushing the archer in the alley, the killer grazed his head with a gunshot…and then mistakenly left Connor for dead. A blood transfusion saved Connor's life, while his father, Oliver Queen (Green Arrow I) met the assassin with a sharp response on the top of a building. The enigmatic Onomatopoeia still managed to escape. **RG**

ONSLAUGHT, THE

FIRST APPEARANCE (Jihad) SUICIDE SQUAD (1st series) #1 (May 1987); (Onslaught) SUICIDE SQUAD (2nd series) #10 (August 2002)
STATUS Villain team **BASE** Qurac
MEMBERS AND POWERS
Rustam I and II (both deceased) Team leaders; each could summon and wield a blazing scimitar.
Djinn Digitized body of electronic code; density manipulation, phasing; can transform from digital code into a sentient droid.
Jaculi I and II (both deceased) Superspeed.
Manticore I, II, and III (all deceased) Lion-themed battlesuits with machine guns and grenade launchers.
Ravan Martial artist and weapons master; requires specialized body brace to move.
Agni Can create and manipulate fire.
Badb Sonic scream instills panic and hatred.
Ifrit An artificial intelligence based on the brain patterns of Mindboggler (a dead Suicide Squad member).
Koschei the Deathless (deceased) Could animate the dead.
Piscator Amphibious powers; limited telepathy.
Old Mother (deceased) The demon Dahak manifested in an old woman's body.
Dervish Superspeed.
Antiphon Superspeed.
Hyve Can split into multiple, smaller versions of himself.
Tolteca Warrior skills.

The Onslaught is a group of superpowered international terrorists for hire, operating out of the Middle Eastern country of Qurac. Originally called the Jihad, the Onslaught were created by then Quraci president, Marlo, in an attempt to kill the President of the United States. However, NIGHTSHADE and NEMESIS I, two members of the American SUICIDE SQUAD, infiltrated the Jihad, allowing the Squad to launch a preemptive attack on the terrorists and cripple the team.

Later, reborn with new members, the Jihad launched a second attack on the United States. Once again, the Jihad came to blows with the Suicide Squad, this time in New York City, and many of the terrorist villains were captured or killed, including their leader, Rustam.

Years later, a third incarnation of the Jihad emerged and attacked the HAYOTH, the Israeli supercommandos, as well as the JUSTICE LEAGUE OF AMERICA, after the mercenary CHESHIRE detonated a nuclear warhead above Qurac, killing more than one million people. The Jihad, mistakenly believing American interests were responsible for the warhead's detonation, hijacked an American airliner heading to Gotham City from Paris. Fortunately, the OUTSIDERS were also aboard the airplane, and the terrorists were defeated.

Recently, Njara Kattuah, the son of the first Rustam, created a new Jihad, now called the Onslaught, with new members. After successfully kidnapping Amanda Waller (see WALLER, AMANDA), the Onslaught was soundly trounced by the Suicide Squad and the JUSTICE SOCIETY OF AMERICA. DEADSHOT killed Rustam II, but the others escaped and remain at large. **PJ**

DEADLY TERRORISTS
The Jihad were some of the Suicide Squad's most deadly foes: **1)** Rustam I **2)** Jaculi I **3)** Djinn **4)** Manticore I **5)** Ravan **6)** Chimera (Nightshade)

ANTIPHON This Greek terrorist joined the Onslaught and fought against the Suicide Squad and the JSA. The Onslaught was responsible for the death of Amanda Waller's daughter, Havana.

DIGITAL DEATH The Digital Djinn kills computer hacker Modem.

HYVE This monster drips duplicates of itself that can change into other people and objects!

RUSTAM II The Onslaught leader could generate blazing scimitars of pure fire.

ONYX

FIRST APPEARANCE DETECTIVE COMICS #546 (January 1985)
STATUS Hero **REAL NAME** Unrevealed
OCCUPATION Adventurer **BASE** Star City
HEIGHT 5ft 9in **WEIGHT** 146 lbs **EYES** Brown **HAIR** Black
SPECIAL POWERS/ABILITIES Olympic-level athlete, expert hand-to-hand combatant, and martial artist.

Onyx was schooled in the Sanctuary, a monastery situated outside Star City. Pursued by an unknown agent who wanted to kill her, Onyx was admitted to the all-male Sanctuary by the Master, who trained her in martial arts and gave her a new identity. Upon the Master's death, Onyx sought out Green Arrow, another student of the Sanctuary, to protect the monastery from a takeover by one of the Master's more ambitious protégés, a man whose hame was Lars. Onyx stayed at the Sanctuary until recently. She was recruited by Batman, and subsequently she teamed up with Orpheus to help head off a gang war in Gotham City. **PJ**

ORDER OF ST. DUMAS, THE

FIRST APPEARANCE BATMAN: SWORD OF AZRAEL #1 (October 1992)
STATUS Secret society of warrior priests and priestesses (destroyed)
BASE Mobile, formerly 14th century Europe
NOTABLE MEMBERS
Azrael (Jean Paul Valley) deceased; **Brother Rollo** deceased;
Carleton LeHah deceased; **Sister Lilhy** deceased; Nomoz.

With its origins in the 14th century, the Order of St. Dumas was a small army of warrior priests dedicated to visiting wrath upon infidel foes during the Crusades. Similar in its credo to the Knights Templar, the Order defied Papal sanction and broke away from the Catholic Church, ultimately taking its mission underground while secretly amassing great wealth and power.

The Order demanded unwavering obedience from its members. Anyone who dared to betray its secrets was slain by the Order's "avenging angel," AZRAEL. This merciless warrior was trained from infancy using the System, an arcane mix of mental and physical conditioning through post-hypnotic suggestion.

Over the centuries that followed, the Order's numbers dwindled and its mission became increasingly tainted by the greed of its remaining fanatical devotees. College student Jean Paul Valley inherited the mantle of Azrael from his father when the latter was killed in the Order's service. Valley briefly served the remaining acolytes of St. Dumas; however, with BATMAN's help, he managed to escape the psychic bonds of the System. When he learned the full story concerning the horrific procedures that had forged him into Azrael, Valley destroyed every last vestige of the Order. The death of Jean Paul Valley, the last, albeit unwilling, member of the Order of St. Dumas, brought an end to this bizarre and sinister remnant of a bygone era. **SB**

ORION

FIRST APPEARANCE NEW GODS (1st series) #1 (March 1971)
STATUS Hero (deceased) **REAL NAME** Orion
OCCUPATION Warrior **BASE** New Genesis
HEIGHT 6ft 1in **WEIGHT** 195 lbs **EYES** Red **HAIR** Red
SPECIAL POWERS/ABILITIES Possesses enormous strength in comparison with his fellow gods, as well as a fierce warrior's instinct; astro-glider allows him interspatial and inter-dimensional travel.

To forestall a cataclysmic battle between New Genesis and Apokolips, the planets' respective leaders HIGHFATHER and DARKSEID made a peace treaty known as The Pact, whereby each god gave up his son to be raised by the other. On New Genesis, Orion's feral nature stood out amongst the peaceful inhabitants. Over time, Orion was given a Mother Box, a sentient computer that calmed his mind and actually smoothed over his coarse features. Soon after, he was befriended by LIGHTRAY and the two became inseparable. Orion was dispatched to Earth, where Darkseid had been seeking the secret of the Anti-Life Equation. At one point, Orion and Lightray served with Earth's protectors, the JUSTICE LEAGUE OF AMERICA. Darkseid and his son battled frequently, culminating in Orion apparently killing Darkseid and assuming the rule of Apokolips.

Empowered by the Anti-Life Equation, Orion began mentally enslaving the inhabitants of Apokolips, New Genesis and Earth in the name of peace. MISTER MIRACLE teleported Orion to the Abysmal Plane, home of "the guardian of the cosmic axis" known as Clockwerx. Orion surrendered control of the Anti-Life Equation to the entities, effectively destroying them. Orion perished during the Death of the New Gods event, after challenging the mysterious assassin to single combat. **RG**

WARRIOR
Born and bred for battle, Orion is the Fourth World's fiercest fighter, channeling his rage into useful force.

ORACLE

FIRST APPEARANCE DETECTIVE COMICS #359 (January 1967)
STATUS Hero **REAL NAME** Barbara Gordon
OCCUPATION Information broker **BASE** Gotham City
HEIGHT 5ft 11in **WEIGHT** 148 lbs **EYES** Blue **HAIR** Red
SPECIAL POWERS/ABILITIES Superior computer hacker and information retrieval specialist; possesses a photographic memory and is a capable hand-to-hand combatant.

THE JOKER'S BULLET brought Barbara Gordon's high-flying career as BATGIRL crashing to earth. However, despite being paralyzed and wheelchair-bound, she has accomplished far more as a crime fighter than she ever could have if she'd remained BATMAN's enthusiastic assistant in the realm of acrobatics and Batarangs.

BEHIND THE SCREEN
Few heroes know Oracle's true identity. Often she appears only as a stylized, holographic head.

BARBARA GORDON
Barbara ("Babs" to her friends) became the adoptive daughter of her uncle James Gordon of the G.C.P.D. (*see* GORDON, JAMES W.*) following the deaths of her parents. A brilliant student, she graduated from Gotham University at a very young age and took a job with the Gotham Public Library. Barbara admired the city's resident vigilante, Batman, and donned a homemade Batgirl costume to surprise her father at the Policeman's Masquerade. In this low-tech getup she foiled the despicable Killer Moth's attack (*see* CHARAXES) on Bruce Wayne, and started a new life as a compatriot to the Dynamic Duo of Batman and ROBIN.

WayneCorp has helped Oracle obtain the latest technology.

KILLING JOKE *In an act that changed Gotham forever, the Joker shot and crippled Barbara Gordon.*

BIRDS OF PREY *Seen here flanked by the Huntress and Black Canary, Oracle is the director of Gotham's all-female crimebusting team.*

During her time as Batgirl, Barbara served a term in the U.S. Congress. After a near-fatal run-in with the assassin Cormorant, Barbara retired from active crime fighting. Shortly after, as part of a revenge plot against Commissioner Gordon, the JOKER burst in on her and shot her in the spine. During rehabilitation she learned she would never walk again.

Barbara trained her upper body to physical perfection with the help of Richard Dragon (*see* DRAGON, RICHARD) and then packaged her skills as an information retrieval expert under the name Oracle. She worked with Amanda Waller (*see* WALLER, AMANDA) of the U.S. government's SUICIDE SQUAD, becoming second-in-command under the alias Amy Beddoes. Oracle began to operate out of Gotham City's imposing clocktower, behind banks of supercomputers running state-of-the-art hacking software. Soon, the "all-seeing, all-knowing" Oracle became a legend in the super-hero community. She recruited heroes into an informal "Birds of Prey" team (members have included BLACK CANARY, POWER GIRL, and HUNTRESS), to act on her data.

The destruction of Oracle's clocktower during a Gotham gang war prompted her relocation to Metropolis. She accepted a marriage proposal from NIGHTWING, but sidelined the romance due to the events of the *Infinite Crisis*. She recently survived SPY SMASHER's challenge to her status as Birds of Prey leader. **DW**

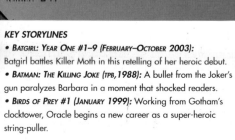

KEY STORYLINES
• *BATGIRL: YEAR ONE #1–9 (FEBRUARY–OCTOBER 2003):* Batgirl battles Killer Moth in this retelling of her heroic debut.
• *BATMAN: THE KILLING JOKE (TPB, 1988):* A bullet from the Joker's gun paralyzes Barbara in a moment that shocked readers.
• *BIRDS OF PREY #1 (JANUARY 1999):* Working from Gotham's clocktower, Oracle begins a new career as a super-heroic string-puller.

ORPHEUS

FIRST APPEARANCE BATMAN: ORPHEUS
RISING #1 (October 2001)
STATUS Hero (deceased) **REAL NAME** Gavin King
OCCUPATION Vigilante; former dancer **BASE** Gotham City
HEIGHT 6ft 2in **WEIGHT** 180 lbs **EYES** Brown **HAIR** Black
SPECIAL POWERS/ABILITIES Formidable
fighter; stealth-circuitry allows costume
to blend into shadows; employs high-
tech weapons.

While other kids were shooting
hoops or roaming Gotham
City's mean streets and getting
into trouble, teenager Gavin
King turned his attentions to martial arts and dancing.
After finishing his schooling, Gavin joined a professional
dance troupe and traveled the world, where he witnessed
more of the same poverty and inequality that divided
races and inevitably led to violence. Determined to do
something about these injustices, Gavin joined a shadowy
secret organization which provided him with the training
and equipment he needed to combat ignorance and
indifference. As the costumed Orpheus, Gavin took the
fight back to Gotham, where he helped the city's self-
appointed guardian, BATMAN, expose a cabal of corrupt
cops fomenting bloodshed between gangs and gun dealers.

Though initially wary of Orpheus, the Dark Knight
became convinced of the young hero's good intentions
after Orpheus argued that Gotham could certainly use
more heroes of color to act as relevant role models to the
city's minority populations. Later, Orpheus teamed with
the Dark Knight's allies NIGHTWING and BLACK CANARY.

Orpheus died, his throat cut by BLACK MASK, after
teaming with ONYX to diffuse a Gotham gang war. **SB**

OSIRIS

FIRST APPEARANCE 52 #23 (October 2006)
STATUS Hero (deceased) **REAL NAME** Amon Tomaz
OCCUPATION Adventurer **BASE** Khandaq
HEIGHT 5ft 10in **WEIGHT** 165 lbs **EYES** Brown **HAIR** Brown
SPECIAL POWERS/ABILITIES Flight, super-strength, superspeed,
invulnerability, enhanced stamina and wisdom.

Amon Tomaz was captured by
INTERGANG and beaten to near-
death until rescued by his sister
and BLACK ADAM. Adrianna,
who had become ISIS as well as
Black Adam's wife, encouraged
her husband to share his powers
with the crippled Amon.
Invigorated with the abilities
of the Egyptian gods, Amon
became Osiris, and the third
member of the Black Marvel
Family. He went to the US
with his crocodile SOBEK for
advice from CAPTAIN MARVEL
JR., whose life story mirrored
his own. Osiris served briefly
with the TEEN TITANS, but
lost his temper when the PERSUADER threatened his sister.
He ripped the Persuader, then tried to rid himself of his
powers during the guilt and shame that followed. Sobek
convinced him to revert to the human Amon Tomaz.
Seeing an opening, Sobek revealed himself as Famine, one
of the Four Horsemen of Apokolips, and devoured the
powerless Amon. **DW**

OUTLAW

FIRST APPEARANCE ALL-STAR WESTERN #2 (November 1970)
STATUS Hero (deceased) **REAL NAME** Rick Wilson
OCCUPATION Ranger **BASE** Texas
HEIGHT 6ft 1in **WEIGHT** 189 lbs **EYES** Blue **HAIR** Brown
SPECIAL POWERS/ABILITIES Was an expert marksman and horseman;
often accompanied by a trained hawk he once nursed back to
health.

Rick Wilson's father Sam was a Texas ranger who enforced
the law throughout the Old West. When Rick turned
18, he set out for parts unknown. When Sam Wilson was
called in to investigate a daring stagecoach robbery, he
discovered that Rick was one of the outlaw culprits. Sam
declared that he no longer had a son. Sam relentlessly
pursued his son as he rode with infamous outlaws, such
as the Dix Gang, "King" Coffin," and "Gunpowder"
Grimes. What no one realized was that the Wilsons were
in cahoots. Rick was infiltrating outlaw gangs and helping
Sam Wilson to catch them dead or alive. After defeating
the dynamite-wielding Grimes, the Wilsons' ruse was
revealed. Sam and Rick served with the Texas Rangers for
the rest of their days. **SB**

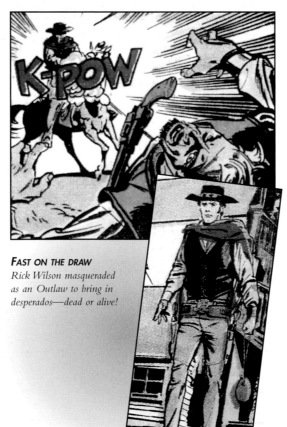

FAST ON THE DRAW
Rick Wilson masqueraded
as an Outlaw to bring in
desperados—dead or alive!

THE OUTSIDERS SEE OPPOSITE PAGE

OVERMASTER

FIRST APPEARANCE JUSTICE LEAGUE OF AMERICA (1st series) #233
(December 1984) **STATUS** Villain **REAL NAME** None
OCCUPATION Assassin **BASE** Outer space
HEIGHT 8ft **WEIGHT** 350 lbs **EYES** Red **HAIR** None
SPECIAL POWERS/ABILITIES Exact abilities have not yet been
documented but he clearly possesses advanced technology.

An alien parasite once latched on to another
mountainous alien. The combined being took the name
Overmaster and journeyed through space, interfering
with sentient worlds. When this being arrived on Earth,
it saw a planet filled with super heroes and recognized a
new way to test the populace. Overmaster recruited six
humans and formed the CADRE. The group challenged
the JUSTICE LEAGUE OF AMERICA to battle, humanity's fate
at stake. The JLA, aided by GYPSY, prevailed. He returned
for man's "Judgment Day" and was opposed by the JLA,
its allies, and a new recruit, AMAZING MAN II. The villain
and his new, expanded Cadre were
defeated. Overmaster's
current whereabouts
are unknown. **RG**

OWLWOMAN

FIRST APPEARANCE SUPER FRIENDS #7 (October 1977)
STATUS Hero **REAL NAME** Wenonah Littlebird
OCCUPATION Jeweler; adventurer **BASE** London; the Dome
HEIGHT 5ft 5in **WEIGHT** 125 lbs **EYES** Brown **HAIR** Black
SPECIAL POWERS/ABILITIES Tribal powers give her superhuman speed,
the power of flight, tracking ability, sight in total darkness, and
superhuman endurance; her genetically engineered claws can cut
through steel.

A Kiowa Indian from Wyoming,
Wenonah Littlebird learned
how to channel the spiritual
power of her entire tribe
during a great ceremony
called the K'Ado. Called
"Owlwoman" by her mother,
Wenonah battled small
time criminals and low-level
mystical threats in the Midwest,
eventually becoming the
American representative of
DOCTOR MIST's international
team of heroes, the GLOBAL
GUARDIANS.

Owlwoman fell in love with fellow
Guardian JACK O'LANTERN. Her powers
were enhanced when she was captured by the first
Queen Bee and subjected to genetic experiments.
After deposing terrorist dictator Sumaan Harjavti from
his rule in Bialya in the Middle East, Jack O'Lantern
died, and Owlwoman began an angry campaign to end
terrorism around the world. **PJ**

THE OUTSIDERS

THE NEW BREED

FIRST APPEARANCE Brave and the Bold #200 (July 1983)
STATUS Hero team **BASE** Brooklyn, New York City
CURRENT MEMBERS AND POWERS
BATMAN Master combatant, strategist, and detective
BATGIRL One of the world's greatest martial artists
GEO-FORCE Can manipulate gravity as well as powers linked to the Earth
GRACE Super-strong and near-invulnerable Amazonian
KATANA Skilled martial artist wielding an enchanted sword
METAMORPHO Can transmute body into chemical compounds

THE OUTSIDERS 1) *Batman*
2) *Catwoman* **3)** *Katanna*
4) *Metamorpho* **5)** *Grace Choi*
6) *Thunder III* **7)** *Martian Manhunter*

THE OUTSIDERS LIVE UP TO THEIR NAME by flatly refusing to work within the expected constraints of international law and propriety. The current version of the team is committed to taking proactive action—squashing meta-human and alien threats before they even have the chance to become threats! The original Outsiders included BLACK LIGHTNING, METAMORPHO, LOOKER, HALO, and the Markovian noble GEO-FORCE. Based in Gotham City and backed financially by Bruce Wayne, the hero team were an outgrowth of BATMAN's frustration with the political constraints under which the JUSTICE LEAGUE OF AMERICA were forced to operate.

DIRECT ACTION

When Baron Bedlam kidnapped Lucius Fox (*see* FOX, LUCIUS) in Markovia, the Justice League of America refused to interfere for fear of upsetting a nation's internal politics. Batman quit the JLA in disgust and formed his Outsiders to handle the Markovia incident and similar, unorthodox missions. Geo-Force fought with Batman over the Dark Knight's tendency to withhold information from team members. Batman quit, and Geo-Force led the team, which relocated to Los Angeles. During this period the Outsiders became agents of the Markovian government. Later additions to the roster included the airstream-manipulating WINDFALL and the armored ATOMIC KNIGHT. Geo-Force eventually disbanded this team.

GEO-FORCE *The Outsiders' greatest leader.*

CRAKOOOM KWOO-ONCK

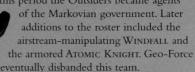

NEW BLOOD *Grace and Thunder are two brash young additions, lending their muscle to battle threats like Gorilla Grodd.*

Reunited in Markovia, the Outsiders became fugitives framed for the murder of the country's monarch (correct?), Queen Ilona. They cleared their names but split into two squads: one led by Geo-Force and including KATANA and the warsuited TECHNOCRAT; the other led by the Kryptonian ERADICATOR and including Looker, Halo, Faust (are PAUSE, PELTRE, and the bear-creature Wylde. The two teams united and the Outsiders remained active through the Imperiex War (*see* Great Battles, pp. 362–3), their last member being DOCTOR LIGHT II.

Former Titan ARSENAL founded a new team, led by NIGHTWING and featuring newcomers GRACE, THUNDER III, and INDIGO. Operating outside the law to end threats before they could begin, the new Outsiders ran missions alongside CHECKMATE before Batman stepped in to take charge of the group once more. **DW**

KEY STORYLINES
• **BATMAN AND THE OUTSIDERS #1 (AUGUST 1983):** The classic Outsiders team makes its debut while meddling in foreign affairs.
• **OUTSIDERS (2ND SERIES) #1 (NOVEMBER 1985):** Without Batman, the Outsiders move to California.
• **OUTSIDERS (3RD SERIES) #1 (JUNE 2003):** Nightwing and Arsenal, ex-teen Titans, form a new team.

GREAT TEAM-UPS

TWO HEADS ARE BETTER THAN ONE is not an axiom that finds favor with all super heroes. Some hate to share, some combinations just don't click, and sometimes a spot of unresolved sexual tension clouds the issue. Before too long, all manner of hostility is bubbling to the surface. However, if two heroes are compatible, a team-up can lead to lasting friendship and mutual respect: a meeting of minds and talents. Here's a look at some classic combinations...

SUPERMAN/WONDER WOMAN
He thought she was mortal, like himself. She thought he was a deity, like her creators, the OLYMPIAN GODS. Despite their differences, these two champions and close friends share a common desire: to defend justice, protect the innocent, and help mankind.

ATOM/HAWKMAN
Given that opposites attract, it makes sense that a deep bond of friendship developed between the warrior Hawkman and the rational scientist Ray Palmer, alias the Atom. They work well together, mixing their abilities and knowledge to become a formidable duo.

ROBIN/BATGIRL
A Dynamic Duo in their own right, Robin and Batgirl's partnership began as an attempt by Batman to dissuade Batgirl from vigilantism. The couple's love found fuller expression in adulthood; by then Dick Grayson was NIGHTWING, and Barbara Gordon was known as ORACLE.

CONSTANTINE/SWAMP THING
Alec Holland's essence was housed in the body of Earth's current elemental but unaware of the greater forces that controlled the world and even the cosmos. John Constantine, the ultimate manipulator, traded lessons and information for Swamp Thing's help when it mattered the most. When Swamp Thing needed a human to impregnate his wife Abby Holland, he turned to Constantine. As a result, they share a bond of purpose, even friendship.

CYBORG/CHANGELING
Vic Stone, the Cyborg hated the cybernetic pieces that kept him alive, and as a result was sullen and withdrawn, coming to life only when the TEEN TITANS were in action. The younger, thrill-seeking Changeling, in contrast was always in action. Over time they learned much from each other, and a deep bond of friendship now exists, whether they are part of the Titans or on their own.

GREEN LANTERN II/GREEN ARROW I

Straight-laced Hal Jordan had his eyes opened by the older, more cynical Oliver Queen. They first met in Vietnam, where they teamed up to stop a dictator. They then toured America, gaining a vital understanding of the problems plaguing the common man. They learned much from each other; so much so that before sacrificing himself to save the world, Jordan used his extraordinary power as PARALLAX to bring Oliver back from the dead.

BOOSTER GOLD/BLUE BEETLE

They first met during a tour of duty with the JUSTICE LEAGUE OF AMERICA, where a fraternal bond was quickly established. Both being single and well-to-do, they used their free time to chase women, fight crime, explore get-rich-quick schemes and periodically save the world. With age, though, came personal changes and the once firm friendship developed cracks.

ATTACKED FROM ALL SIDES

Accused of "crimes against humanity" by the administration of President Lex Luthor, Superman becomes a target for meta-human villains secretly acting on Luthor's orders. Fortunately Superman's JLA comrade-in-arms, Batman is on hand to help in a tight corner!

SUPERMAN/BATMAN

Superman takes on crises as they arise, Batman prefers a crushing, preemptive strike. Superman is good-natured, optimistic, and considerate; Batman suspicious, pessimistic, and brooding. Given their very different approaches to life and to their missions, it's odd to find the Man of Tomorrow working alongside the Dark Knight Detective. They have clashed on several occasions, yet, time and again they have found themselves helping one another or working together for the greater good of humanity. They respect one another's methods and secrets, while not wholly approving of the other's complete approach to the work.

FLASH II/KID FLASH

When Barry Allen, the second FLASH realized that his nephew, Wally West had similar Speed Force powers, he gave him his own junior-sized Flash costume. Soon, Wally was partnering his idol as KID FLASH. Barry taught Wally some amazing tricks, such as how to vibrate right through solid objects. **RG**

PANTHA

FIRST APPEARANCE NEW TITANS #74 (March 1991)
STATUS Hero (deceased)   **REAL NAME** None (originally designated X-24)
OCCUPATION Adventurer   **BASE** Science City, Russia
HEIGHT 5ft 8.5in   **WEIGHT** 136 lbs   **EYES** Red   **HAIR** Auburn
SPECIAL POWERS/ABILITIES Incredible predatory speed, strength, and
agility; indestructible claws on hands and feet; cat-like visual acuity.

The were-cat known as Pantha was
created by the WILDEBEEST SOCIETY.
She was one example of the Society's
attempts to alter human and animal
DNA and adapt suitable host bodies
for the vengeful souls of Azarath. These souls had once
belonged to peaceful, other-dimensional mystics who had
raised the TEEN TITAN known as RAVEN and shielded
her from the demonic TRIGON. The Azarathians possessed
Raven's fellow Teen Titan JERICHO, making him leader
of the Wildebeest Society as it worked in secret to
fulfill their master plans.

While the majority of the Wildebeest's
bio-engineered test subjects perished, Pantha
survived and escaped. Later, she helped the Titans and
DEATHSTROKE defeat Jericho and the Wildebeests.
A Titan herself for a time, Pantha eventually departed
the team with RED STAR and Baby Wildebeest.
The latter was the Wildebeest Society's final
experiment, a creature that bonded to Pantha,
who became its "mother." During the Infinite
Crisis, Superboy-Prime decapitated Pantha with
a superpowered punch. **SB**

CAT/WOMAN
*Since her escape
from the Wildebeests,
Pantha has sought to
learn whether or not she
is really a genetically altered
human or an evolved feline.*

PARALLAX

FIRST APPEARANCE GREEN LANTERN (3rd ser.) #50
(Mar. 1994)
STATUS Villain   **REAL NAME** Inapplicable
OCCUPATION Fear entity   **BASE** Mobile
HEIGHT Various   **WEIGHT** Various
EYES Yellow   **HAIR** None
SPECIAL POWERS/ABILITIES Feeds on fear and can instill
great fear in others; can possess other beings as hosts.

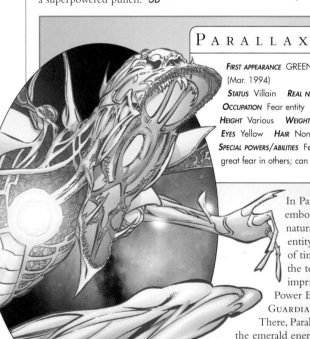

In Parallax is the living
embodiment of fear and the
natural enemy of the willpower
entity ION. Since the dawn
of time, Parallax has fed on
the terror of others, until
imprisoned in the Central
Power Battery on Oa by the
GUARDIANS OF THE UNIVERSE.
There, Parallax's essence corrupted
the emerald energy used by the GREEN
LANTERN CORPS, making their power rings
vulnerable to the color yellow (a flaw referred to as
the "yellow impurity"). When the CYBORG SUPERMAN
destroyed Coast City, home of Hal Jordan (GREEN
LANTERN), Parallax took root in Jordan's psyche and turned
him into a twisted version of his former self. Jordan made war against the Guardians
and his teammates, annihilating the Corps and attempting (with EXTANT) to wipe
out all of reality during the Zero Hour event.

Although Jordan eventually became the host for the SPECTRE, Parallax retained
a foothold. Only after purging Parallax could Jordan return as his true self.
Parallax in turn took possession of Green Lantern Kyle Rayner during the
SINESTRO CORPS WAR. Killing numerous Lanterns, Parallax spread fear throughout
the cosmos until Rayner fought his way free. Parallax then found itself quartered
and locked inside the power batteries of Hal Jordan, Kyle Rayner, Guy Gardner,
and John Stewart. **DW**

PARASITE

FIRST APPEARANCE ACTION COMICS #240 (August 1966)
STATUS Villain   **REAL NAME** Rudy Jones; Torval Freeman
OCCUPATION Professional criminal   **BASE** Metropolis
HEIGHT Variable   **WEIGHT** Variable   **EYES** Red   **HAIR** None
SPECIAL POWERS/ABILITIES Absorbed the life essence of living
creatures, killing them; absorbed meta-human powers; could
shape-change; size and shape varied with energy absorbed.

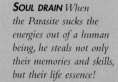

Rudy Jones was a maintenance worker at S.T.A.R.
Labs in Metropolis, who tried to smuggle scientific
waste out of the laboratory to sell illegally. Jones
opened one of the waste containers and was
irradiated with an isotope that transformed his body.
To survive, Jones was forced to absorb the life energies
of other living beings, much like a vampire. Searching for
the ultimate "meal," the Parasite began a lifelong pursuit
of SUPERMAN, whom he considered a living power
battery. The two clashed repeatedly, but the Parasite's
craving for the Man of Steel's solar-powered energy was always unfulfilled.

After absorbing the life energies of Doctor Torvell Freeman, the Parasite
retained Freeman's psyche and memories. The two personalities became
locked in a battle for supremacy for the Parasite's body, making him
more dangerous than ever. After the Parasite tried to absorb
SUPERGIRL's angelic energies, he found himself haunted
by the voices of every one of his victims, and was nearly
driven mad. The Parasite then kidnapped Lois Lane (*see*
LANE, LOIS), from whom he learned Superman's secret
identity, and took her place. Although the Parasite
appeared to have died from kryptonite poisoning,
he recently reappeared offering his power-
draining services for a fee to metahuman criminals
hoping to temporarily avoid monitoring. **PJ**

SOUL DRAIN *When
the Parasite sucks the
energies out of a human
being, he steals not only
their memories and skills,
but their life essence!*

SUPER ABSORPTION *The leech-like creature's mightiest
meal proved its doom, as the Parasite absorbed not
only Superman's power, but kryptonite poisoning!*

PARK, LINDA

FIRST APPEARANCE THE FLASH (2nd series) #28 (July 1989)
STATUS Hero **REAL NAME** Linda Jasmine Park
OCCUPATION Television journalist; medical student
BASE Keystone City **HEIGHT** 5ft 6in **WEIGHT** 137 lbs
EYES Brown **HAIR** Black **SPECIAL POWERS/ABILITIES** She has no
superpowers but is brave and resourceful; the Flash's equal for sheer
gumption and his perfect partner.

Linda Park thought Wally West (FLASH III) was brash
and arrogant—which he was. But Linda also saw
something else in him, the spark of a better man. As
their relationship developed, that spark became the
flames of love. So strong was their bond that it
has enabled Flash to find his way home, regardless
of time, dimension, or location, as they discovered
when the Flash III pushed himself past his previous limits
and joined the Speed Force.

Linda was seemingly killed by a supernatural entity
called the Black Flash, which sent Wally West spiraling
into a depression. The Flash ultimately rescued Linda from
within the Speed Force and they made plans to wed.

SOULMATES
*Linda loved
the whirlwind
life her
husband led as
the Flash.*

As the marriage ceremony was about to take place, Linda
was kidnapped by the villain ABRA KADABRA and the
world's memory of her was erased. Fortunately, the
Flash sorted everything out, the couple married at last,
and Linda enrolled at Central City Medical College.
A short time later, pregnant with twins, she was
attacked by ZOOM and suffered a miscarriage. A time
anomaly restored her pregnancy, and she gave birth
to twins Iris and Jai. Linda struggles to keep pace
with the twins' growing abilities. **RG**

END OF THE DREAM *After her miscarriage, Linda
came to question her life as a super hero's spouse
and left to decide her future.*

PARIAH

FIRST APPEARANCE CRISIS ON INFINITE EARTHS #1 (April 1985)
STATUS Hero **REAL NAME** Mossa
OCCUPATION Adventurer **BASE** Mobile
HEIGHT 5ft 11in **WEIGHT** 165 lbs **EYES** Black **HAIR** Purple
SPECIAL POWERS/ABILITIES Brilliant scientist; invulnerable to
physical harm; innately teleports to the focal point of vast
danger; it is undetermined whether he is immortal.

In another dimension, the scientist Mossa remained
in an antimatter chamber for 13 months, hoping
to unlock the secrets of the universe by witnessing
Creation at the Dawn of Time. His chamber and
world were destroyed in the process. The cursed
scientist was renamed Pariah, and as penance for
his actions, was forced to spend the next hundred
million years witnessing the destruction of world
after world and the deaths of countless billions of
sentient beings. As red, stormy skies blanketed Earth
during the summer heat of July, the Anti-Monitor
(*see* MONITOR) attempted to destroy the positive
matter universe (*see* The Crisis, Great Battles, pp.
362-3).

Pariah arrived on Earth to warn its people of the
impending doom. The Monitor gathered heroes
from across time and space to try and stop his evil
twin, using the woman HARBINGER to collect
them. The Anti-Monitor plucked the Earth out of
its universe and placed it in the anti-matter universe
of Qward, unleashing millions of Shadow Demons
across the planet, which slaughtered thousands.
Pariah worked with the champions from across
time and space to save all reality. Pariah apparently
died when attacked by Alexander Luthor, a fellow
survivor of the previous multiverse. **RG**

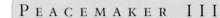

PATCHWORK MAN I

FIRST APPEARANCE SWAMP THING #2 (January 1973)
STATUS Hero (deceased) **REAL NAME** Gregori Arcane
OCCUPATION None (a victim of circumstance) **BASE** Mobile
HEIGHT 6ft 8in **WEIGHT** 330 lbs **EYES** Blue **HAIR** Grayish black
SPECIAL POWERS/ABILITIES Shambling, super-strong hulk with a fantastic resistance to injury. His origin as a magically-created being gives him limited defenses against sorcery.

The original Patchwork Man, a pitiful monstrosity, once answered to the name Gregori Arcane. A businessman in the Balkan mountain region of Eastern Europe, Gregori raised his daughter Abigail as best he could, but became the target of neighbors who considered him an unfit father. One day they took away Abigail, and Gregori wandered into a minefield while searching for her.

Gregori's mad-scientist brother Anton (*see* ARCANE, ANTON) gathered up the pieces of his brother's body and sewed them back together. With a healthy dose of sorcery animating his broken carcass, Gregori lurched into a new life as the Patchwork Man. Years spent imprisoned in Anton's dungeon ended when the SWAMP THING inadvertently freed the Patchwork Man, and Gregori sought out his daughter Abigail, now an adult living in the American South. Several encounters with Abby and Swamp Thing followed, but Patchwork Man's body ultimately decomposed to an irrecoverable state and he is believed to have perished. **DW**

PEACEMAKER III

FIRST APPEARANCE THE L.A.W. #1 (September 1999)
STATUS Hero **REAL NAME** Mitchell Black
OCCUPATION Former physician; soldier **BASE** Mobile
HEIGHT 6ft 1in **WEIGHT** 183 lbs **EYES** Brown **HAIR** Brown
SPECIAL POWERS/ABILITIES Battle armor provides flight and enhances strength; armor is operational underwater or in space and contains high-tech arms systems as well as an energy blaster.

Three individuals have adopted the alter ego of Peacemaker, an armored soldier battling for peace. Peacemaker I was Christopher Smith, whose delusions of being haunted by his father, Nazi S.S. officer Wolfgang Schmidt, drove his insane resolve to fight and kill for the sake of peace. Peacemaker I and other less notable heroes died attempting to liberate the South American country of Parador from the evil influence of ECLIPSO.

Peacemaker II's identity is unrevealed. Presumably he was a U.S. government agent sanctioned to take up Smith's codename and mission, He is known chiefly for belonging to the Leaguebusters, a team assembled to counter the JUSTICE LEAGUE OF AMERICA. His current activities and whereabouts are unknown.

Peacemaker III is Mitchell Black, a pulmonary physician who lost his license to practice medicine following untried surgery that led to the death of a young patient. Black was subsequently recruited by the Geneva-based Peacemaker Project as head of its Enforcement Division. This organization provided armored "Peacemakers" to troubled nations around the globe. Although apparently killed by PROMETHEUS during the Infinite Crisis, Peacemaker has reappeared as a mentor to Jaime Reyes, the third BLUE BEETLE. **SB**

PATCHWORK MAN II

FIRST APPEARANCE SECRET FILES & ORIGINS GUIDE TO THE DC UNIVERSE 2000 #1 (March 2000)
STATUS Hero **REAL NAME** Elliot Taylor
OCCUPATION Member of Creature Commandos **BASE** Mobile
HEIGHT 9ft **WEIGHT** 560 lbs **EYES** Black **HAIR** None
SPECIAL POWERS/ABILITIES Superstrength; fantastic resistance to injury thanks to a body composed of undead material.

The modern-day inheritor of the name Patchwork Man is Elliot "Lucky" Taylor, a reconstituted warrior who received his stitched-together body courtesy of the U.S. government's top-secret Project M. With his teammates in the new CREATURE COMMANDOS—including Wolfpack (Warren Griffith), Medusa, Sgt. Vincent Velcro, Gunner, and CAPTAIN HUNTER—Patchwork Man II served as the designated "heavy hitter" during a struggle against the interdimensional warlord Lord Saturna, ruler of the realm of Terra Arcana. The Patchwork Man, lugging a heavy machine gun with multiple ammo belts slung across his beefy shoulders, helped the Creature Commandos prevent a full-scale invasion of the armies of Terra Arcana, thanks in part to unexpected aid from CLAW the Unconquered. In the end, Lord Saturna perished and the leaderless citizens of Terra Arcana were left to chart their own destiny. **DW**

PINCUSHION *Patchwork Man II has been shot thousands of times, and probably has hundreds of bullets lodged inside his hulking frame.*

PEACEKEEPER I *Christopher Smith died battling Eclipso. Since his death, two other men have used the identity of Peacemaker.*

PENGUIN

GOTHAM'S MR. FIXIT

FIRST APPEARANCE DETECTIVE COMICS #58 (December 1941)
STATUS Villain **REAL NAME** Oswald Chesterfield Cobblepot
OCCUPATION Criminal; stock trader; fixer **BASE** Gotham City
HEIGHT 5ft 2in **WEIGHT** 175 lbs **EYES** Blue **HAIR** Black
SPECIAL POWERS/ABILITIES Devious and ruthless, despite his small
stature, he is surprisingly agile; usually prefers to flee rather than
fight; formerly favored an array of bizarre umbrella weapons; also
used his affinity with birds to assist in his crimes.

OSWALD CHESTERFIELD COBBLEPOT based a criminal career as the
murderous gangster the Penguin on his fascination with birds and
ornithology. This fascination dates back to his childhood, growing
up with his widowed mother, who ran a pet shop specializing
in exotic birds. Short, paunchy, and burdened with a prominent,
beaky nose, his schoolmates nicknamed Oswald the Penguin. His
fussy mother insisted he carry an umbrella, even on sunny days,
making him the target of widespread ridicule.

THE BIRD MAN OF GOTHAM

When he grew up, Oswald got his own back on the world by becoming a force to
be reckoned with in Gotham City's underworld. He committed scores of crimes
(often with a bird-theme), which inevitably led him to run afoul of the BATMAN
and ROBIN time and again. The Penguin further increased his criminal profile
when he met a scientific genius, a deformed mute named
Harold, and convinced him to create a device that
could control birds, directing them to commit
crimes and various acts of terror for him.

EARLY BIRD *The Penguin sought gain
wherever possible, even attempting to
kidnap Arabian royalty.*

LADIES MAN
*The Penguin
likes to surround
himself with the finest
acquisitions in life, both
animate and inanimate.*

Batman stopped this threat and later brought Harold to the Batcave,
where he helped maintain the various Bat-vehicles. On parole, the Penguin
tried to convince the public he had gone "legit" by playing the stock
market. Though exposed for insider trading, the Penguin remained strongly
attracted to the notion of concealing his criminal activities beneath a more
socially acceptable façade.

To that end, Cobblepot became the owner of a premier Gotham nightspot,
the Iceberg Lounge, and purportedly once more reformed. Secretly, he had
formed an alliance with a number-cruncher known as the Actuary, who
helped the Penguin pull off a series of spectacular robberies. Ultimately, the
Actuary took the fall for his partner when
Batman tracked them down.

The Penguin really came into his own
when a cataclysmic earthquake struck
Gotham and the government declared the
city a lawless No Man's Land. Cobblepot
saw his chance and made a fortune on the
black market, trading essential goods and
further strengthening his hold over the city's
underworld. After Batman and his allies
helped get the city back on its feet, the
local government tried to shut down the
Iceberg Lounge. Instead, Bruce Wayne
bought the building, giving his alter ego
the opportunity to keep closer tabs on the
nefarious, slippery Penguin. RG

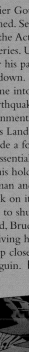

NO MANS LAND
*During Gotham's
exile, the Penguin
amassed power through
barter, favors, and guile.*

TALK TO THE BAT *Time
and again, the Penguin
is pressured into telling
Batman vital nuggets of
information.*

THE DC COMICS ENCYCLOPEDIA

PENNYWORTH, ALFRED

FIRST APPEARANCE BATMAN #16 (May 1943)
STATUS Heroic ally **REAL NAME** Alfred Pennyworth
OCCUPATION Butler for Wayne Manor **BASE** Gotham City
HEIGHT 6ft **WEIGHT** 160 lbs **EYES** Blue **HAIR** Black
SPECIAL POWERS/ABILITIES Expert medic, mechanic,
chauffeur; former soldier and actor (professionally
trained); vocal mimic; unswervingly loyal, and
an endless source of good advice.

A GENTLEMAN'S GENTLEMAN
*Alfred's manners are unimpeachable;
his skill with a surgeon's blade
is impeccable.*

More than a butler, Alfred Pennyworth is the Dark
Knight's squire—expert helpmate in every field from
sewing to shotguns. The BATMAN's career could never
have happened without the assistance of Alfred, who keeps the
Batcave in working order and maintains the public illusion that Bruce
Wayne is nothing more than a billionaire playboy.

Born and raised in England, Alfred chose to follow his mother
into the theater rather than become a butler for the Wayne family
of Gotham City, a job that both his father and grandfather had
performed with distinction. After stints as both a soldier and actor,
Alfred prepared to marry a young woman, then had his heart broken
when he learned she had not been faithful to him. Soon Alfred's
father passed away, and Alfred chose to abandon the stage to fulfill his
father's obligation to Thomas and Martha Wayne as their family butler.
Two years later Thomas and Martha fell victim to a mugger. Alfred
and physician Leslie Thompkins (*see* THOMPKINS, LESLIE M.D.)
raised the Waynes' young son, Bruce, in Wayne Manor after a maze
of paperwork shielded the case from the influence of Gotham Child
Services. When an adult Bruce decided to become the vigilante
Batman, Alfred became an aide to him and the subsequent string of
Robins (*see* ROBIN): Dick Grayson, Jason Todd, and Tim Drake.
Alfred briefly left Batman's service but soon returned after trips to
Antarctica and England. Since then he has survived the destruction of
Wayne Manor during a cataclysmic earthquake that turned Gotham
City into a lawless No Man's Land and his own near-fatal bout
with the Clench virus. Because he knew Bruce as a boy, Alfred
is perhaps the only person in the world utterly unfazed by
Batman's grim façade. **DW**

PEOPLE'S HEROES, THE

FIRST APPEARANCE OUTSIDERS (1st series) #10 (August 1986)
STATUS Villain group (disbanded) **BASE** The Russian Federation
MEMBERS AND POWERS
Bolshoi A formidable martial artist and superspeedster
Hammer He possesses superhuman strength and wields a hammer.
Molotov He has an explosive touch.
Pravda She possesses psychic powers.
Sickle A martial artist, her signature weapon is a razor-sharp sickle.

COMMUNIST AVENGERS *Before disbanding, the People's Heroes
were Russia's most patriotic superteam. They are* **1)** *Bolshoi*
2) *Pravda* **3)** *Molotov* **4)** *Hammer* **5)** *Sickle.*

The People's Heroes were a group of superhuman agents
created by Communist scientists using information learned
through scientific analysis of the American super-team,
The Force of July. The Peoples' Heroes were assigned
to the Russian secret service and battled the American
OUTSIDERS twice to a standstill. The People's Heroes later
came into conflict with the SUICIDE SQUAD during a
kidnapping mission. The Squad squarely defeated the
Heroes, leaving Pravda for dead.

After a failed attempt by HAMMER AND SICKLE to
execute RED STAR, another Russian hero, on behalf
of an extreme faction of the Russian government, the
People's Heroes were disbanded. However, Molotov and
Bolshoi were recruited by the Red Shadows, the Russian
counterpart of the Suicide Squad. **PJ**

PERIL, JOHNNY

FIRST APPEARANCE COMIC CAVALCADE #22 (September 1947)
STATUS Hero **REAL NAME** Unknown
OCCUPATION Private investigator **BASE** Unnamed Midwestern city
HEIGHT 6ft 2in **WEIGHT** 195 lbs **EYES** Blue **HAIR** Blond
SPECIAL POWERS/ABILITIES Above-average hand-to-hand fighter; quick-
witted and good with a gun.

Johnny Peril's past is a mystery
to all who know him. His
name, synonymous with
adventure and intrigue, is almost
certainly an alias. He has been
a reporter, a soldier-of-fortune,
or a troubleshooter, taking on
any high-risk job where more
than money is at stake. Johnny
is certainly well-traveled. However,
despite his apparent addiction to
adventure, Johnny isn't afraid to
admit a longing for a nice, normal
case every once in a while. That's
why he currently makes his home in
a mundane, Middle American city, having set himself up
as a private investigator. He is frequently aided by psychic
Heather Storm, in whom Johnny has shown more than a
professional interest. **SB**

PERKINS, NEPTUNE

FIRST APPEARANCE FLASH COMICS #166 (September 1945)
STATUS Hero   **REAL NAME** Neptune Perkins
OCCUPATION Senator and author   **BASE** Mobile
HEIGHT 6ft   **WEIGHT** 187 lbs   **EYES** Blue   **HAIR** Black
SPECIAL POWERS/ABILITIES Neptune Perkins is amphibious and has webbed hands and feet, allowing him to swim as fast as a swordfish or dolphin; he requires constant exposure to salt water for survival; fair-minded politician and accomplished author.

In 1922, Neptune Perkins was born a mutant with webbed hands and feet and a sodium salt deficiency, the result of being conceived in the light of a Vril-powered device. He grew up spending most of the time in the sea, and later became a costumed adventurer as part of the YOUNG ALL-STARS. On one such mission he fought a young Japanese girl named TSUNAMI. when she attacked a naval base. They subsequently fell in love. At one point, Perkins was being held against his will by gangsters. HAWKMAN I traveled to California and rescued him. The heroes prevented the thugs from using Perkins's houseboat as an escape craft following their crime spree, but the vessel was destroyed in the process. Eventually, Perkins retired from crimefighting and became a successful author and a senator. After marrying Tsunami, Perkins apparently died in an attack on Atlantis during the Infinite Crisis. **RG**

PERSUADER

FIRST APPEARANCE ADVENTURE COMICS #352 (January 1967)
STATUS Villain   **REAL NAME** Nyeun Chun Ti
OCCUPATION Professional criminal   **BASE** Mobile
HEIGHT 6ft 3in   **WEIGHT** 240 lbs   **EYES** Brown   **HAIR** None
SPECIAL POWERS/ABILITIES Atomic axe can cut through any form of matter or energy.

Multiple Persuaders have existed, all of them united by distinctive armor and an "atomic axe" that can cut through anything. Nyeun Chun Ti is an inhabitant of the 31st century who earned notoriety in the FATAL FIVE and a mortal enemy of the LEGION OF SUPER-HEROES. This Persuader recently appeared in the 21st century with his Fatal Five teammates to battle BATMAN and BLUE BEETLE III for possession of an artifact linked to the Luck Lords. A second Persuader, Cole Parker, arose in the current era, dissatisfied after losing his job at the Daily Planet. Later recruited into the SUICIDE SQUAD, Parker attacked ISIS with his atomic axe, nearly killing her. Isis' brother OSIRIS flew to her rescue, colliding with the Persuader and killing him instantly. A new, female Persuader has been working with the Clock King in his "Terror Titans." **DW**

PERUN

FIRST APPEARANCE FIRESTORM #72 (June 1988)
STATUS Hero   **REAL NAME** Ilya Trepliov
OCCUPATION Hero   **BASE** Russian Federation
HEIGHT 6ft   **WEIGHT** 165 lbs   **EYES** Brown   **HAIR** Black
SPECIAL POWERS/ABILITIES Able to mentally control electricity within several hundred feet of himself, channeling this energy any way that he chooses.

Perun is a member of SOYUZ, a group of young adventurers in Russia and one of the only super-human teams not accountable to the Russian government. Soyuz was vigorously pursued by various Russian agencies, including the K.G.B., while their activities were recorded. After Soyuz's heroic defense of Russia during an invasion by aliens, the Russian government chose to back down from their pursuit of Soyuz and allowed the youngsters freedom to act independently. Named after the Russian thunder god, Perun, a determined young man, began his heroic career at the young age of 17, defending the rights of innocent people throughout Russia. Along with his Soyuz teammates, Perun most recently fought the terrible forces of the alien invader IMPERIEX. **PJ**

PHANTASMO

FIRST APPEARANCE YOUNG ALL-STARS #22 (January 1989)
STATUS Hero   **REAL NAME** Jean-Marc de Villars
OCCUPATION Adventurer   **BASE** England
HEIGHT 5ft 9in   **WEIGHT** 168 lbs
EYES Blue   **HAIR** Black
SPECIAL POWERS/ABILITIES Could become intangible and seemed impervious to most organic objects.

Phantasmo was Jean-Marc de Villars, a Frenchman and the son of a human and an Earth elemental spirit. He had the superhuman ability to make himself intangible and an invulnerability to "Earth substances" such as common metals. Phantasmo was a member of the Young Allies, a team of international young heroes who banded together to oppose the Nazis during World War II, and once cooperated with the American Young All-Stars. Phantasmo has not been seen since 1942, but post-War activities have been hinted at. **RG**

DIVIDED SOUL *Phantasmo is actually a human and elemental spirit sharing a body, forging an uneasy alliance.*

PHANTASM

FIRST APPEARANCE NEW TITANS (1st series) #73 (February 1991)
STATUS Hero (missing in action)   **REAL NAME** Inapplicable
OCCUPATION Wraith   **BASE** Mobile
HEIGHT None   **WEIGHT** None   **EYES** None   **HAIR** None
SPECIAL POWERS/ABILITIES Empathic and telekinetic of staggering power; a being composed of more than a thousand souls.

During the so-called "Titans Hunt," when several TEEN TITANS were brutally murdered by the bizarre WILDEBEEST Society, young telekinetic Danny Chase faked his own demise during a Wildebeest-instigated melee at a Washington, D.C. shopping mall. From various stores, Danny then secretly assembled various items—a bolt of cloth, a hockey mask, and an electronic voice modulator—and created a costumed secret identity, the wraith-like Phantasm. Thus disguised, Danny secretly aided the Titans' leader NIGHTWING, who had infiltrated the Wildebeest Society and learned that the 'beests were possessed by disembodied Azarathian souls (*see* RAVEN). During the final conflict with the Wildebeests, Danny linked his own burgeoning powers to the Titans' Raven and her mother, Arella, to cleanse the tainted Azarathians that had taken over fellow member JERICHO and used him to control the Wildebeest Society. Danny and Arella died, but their essences merged with the freed Azarathians to create a new and more powerful Phantasm that continued to be an ally of the Titans. Phantasm was seemingly destroyed sometime later while attempting to contain the evil essence of a resurrected Raven. **SB**

JUST PASSING THROUGH *Phantasmo was an especially effective crime fighter because adversaries' attacks failed to make contact with him.*

PHANTOM OF THE FAIR

FIRST APPEARANCE SECRET ORIGINS (2nd series) #7 (December 1986)
STATUS Hero **REAL NAME** Unknown
OCCUPATION Criminal **BASE** New York World's Fair
HEIGHT Unknown **WEIGHT** Unknown
EYES Unknown **HAIR** Unknown
SPECIAL POWERS/ABILITIES Superstrength, partial invulnerability, and enhanced agility. Apparently possesses acrobatic training and talents in the areas of stealth and camouflage.

The brief career of the Phantom of the Fair remains an enigma. On April 30, 1939, the opening day of the New York World's Fair, a masked figure swooped down on Mayor LaGuardia during the opening ceremonies. Seizing the mic, the Phantom declared: "Men and women of New York City—this World's Fair is now declared officially haunted by the Phantom of the Fair!"

LaGuardia refused to close the fair, and on June 10, New York welcomed King George VI and Queen Elizabeth of Britain. To protect them from the Phantom during their visit to the World's Fair, wealthy socialite Wesley Dodds assumed the crime-fighting identity of the SANDMAN for the first time. The Phantom attacked the king and queen using the giant World's Fair robot Elektro, but the Sandman and the CRIMSON AVENGER I drove off the Phantom. This was arguably the first super hero conflict of the Golden Age of heroism. **DW**

PHANTOM LADY I, II & III

FIRST APPEARANCE (I) POLICE COMICS #1 (August 1941); (II) ACTION COMICS WEEKLY #636 (January 1989); (III) CRISIS AFTERMATH: THE BATTLE FOR BLUDHAVEN #1
STATUS Hero **REAL NAME** (I) Sandra Knight; (II) Delilah "Dee" Tyler; (III) Stormy Knight
OCCUPATION (I) Debutante; (II) TV Station employee; (III) Quantum physicist **BASE** (I, II, III) Washington DC.
HEIGHT (III) 5'9" **WEIGHT** (III) 150 lbs **EYES** (III) Blue **HAIR** (III) Black II) Black
SPECIAL POWERS/ABILITIES (I) Blackout ray wrist device; (II) bracelet-mounted taser; costume circuitry defeats electronic surveillance, can project holograms of herself. (III) Black-light bands can bend space and time, as well as open dimensional portals.

In 1939, Sandra Knight foiled the kidnap of her father, a U.S. Senator, on the steps of the Capitol Building. Scientist Abraham Davis was so impressed by her bravery he gave her a special device, a black light projector; Sandra became the crime fighter Phantom Lady.

Phantom Lady joined the ALL-STAR SQUADRON, then the FREEDOM FIGHTERS, and the government agency ARGENT I. Decades later, she opened a finishing school, the Université Notre Dame des Ombres, in Paris. Dee Tyler, the second Phantom Lady, served in the role until murdered by DEATHSTROKE during the Infinite Crisis. The third Phantom Lady is Stormy Knight, a spoiled society girl (and secret quantum physicist) who struggles with depression and substance abuse. Stormy is a member of UNCLE SAM's newest FREEDOM FIGHTERS. **PJ**

PHANTOM STRANGER, THE

FIRST APPEARANCE THE PHANTOM STRANGER (1st series) #1 (September 1952) **STATUS** Hero **REAL NAME** Unknown
OCCUPATION Conscience; advocator **BASE** Mobile
HEIGHT 6ft 2in **WEIGHT** 185 lbs **EYES** White **HAIR** White
SPECIAL POWERS/ABILITIES Powers and abilities defy classification; in the past, the Phantom Stranger demonstrated teleportation, control over natural forces, and manipulation of supernatural energies.

LOST SOUL Like a Good Samaritan, the Phantom Stranger roams the world, helping those in need.

The Phantom Stranger's origin is a mystery. Some believe him to be a fallen angel forced to walk the Earth and help those in need as atonement for some great sin. The Phantom Stranger admits that he serves the cause of Order in its eternal conflict to keep Chaos in check. Whenever someone is troubled by a spiritual or moral dilemma—all too often caused by supernatural forces—the Phantom Stranger will offer counsel. Many times, the Stranger will wield his own considerable mystical powers to defend the defenseless. The Stranger is a loner, although he has counted as friends both Bruce Gordon, the scientist once possessed by the evil ECLIPSO, and Cassandra Craft, a blind woman with latent magical talent who once helped the Stranger to regain his powers and fell in love with him. Unfortunately, the Stranger could not return such feelings. The Phantom Stranger has aided the JUSTICE LEAGUE OF AMERICA and was offered membership as many times, but has simply spirited away rather than refuse. Prior to the Infinite Crisis, the SPECTRE turned the Phantom Stranger into a mouse to prevent his interference with the end of the Ninth Age of Magic. **SB**

PHOBIA

FIRST APPEARANCE THE NEW TEEN TITANS (1st series) #14 (December 1981) **STATUS** Villain **REAL NAME** Angela Hawkins III
OCCUPATION Assassin **BASE** Mobile
HEIGHT 5ft 11in **WEIGHT** 151 lbs **EYES** Green **HAIR** Black
SPECIAL POWERS/ABILITIES Psychic ability to incapacitate her enemies by conjuring their greatest fears.

Born into the British aristocracy, blue-blooded Angela Hawkins III discovered at an early age that she possessed the psychic ability to detect the fears of others. She also found she could project those fears with nightmarish intensity. This knowledge made her cold-hearted and power-hungry. She gladly accepted an offer extended by the BRAIN and MONSIEUR MALLAH to join the New Brotherhood of Evil. Now calling herself Phobia, she helped the Brotherhood take their revenge on MADAME ROUGE, and remained with the group after its transition into the SOCIETY OF SIN. She often found herself battling the TEEN TITANS. During the Crisis (see Great Battles, pp. 362–3), Phobia nearly became the emotion-manipulating agent of the Anti-Monitor (see MONITOR), who elected to spare Phobia in favor of a different stooge. Some time later, the empath RAVEN helped excise Phobia's inner demons and childhood fears of her father, Lord Hawkins. However, she returned to her criminal ways alongside the Society of Sin, and was recently seen battling YOUNG JUSTICE on the island nation of Zandia. **DW**

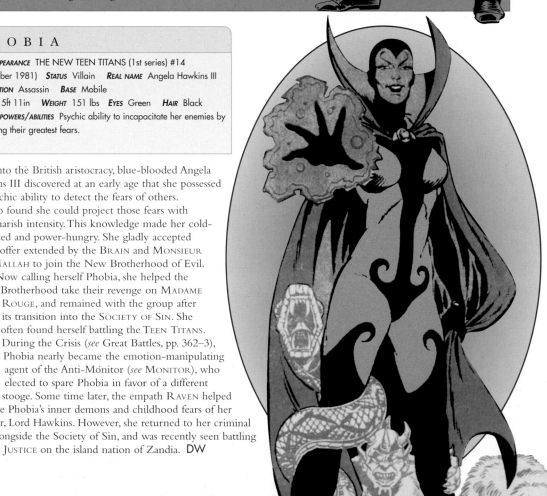

PHOBOS

FIRST APPEARANCE WONDER WOMAN (2nd series) #2 (March 1987)
STATUS Villain   **REAL NAME** Phobos
OCCUPATION God of Fear   **BASE** The Netherworld
HEIGHT 7ft 7in   **WEIGHT** 459 lbs   **EYES** Red   **HAIR** Flaming red
SPECIAL POWERS/ABILITIES Invulnerability of the gods; possesses the power to physically manifest the darkest fears of his enemies; immortal; generates gouts of infernal fire from the netherworld.

Greek God of Fear, Phobos is the son of ARES and Aphrodite, and shares cruel power with his brother Deimos (God of Terror) and sister Eris (Goddess of Strife).

As part of Ares's plan to dominate the Earth, Phobos pitted himself against WONDER WOMAN. He released the gorgon Decay until Wonder Woman pursued him into the Netherworld. She decapitated Deimos and Phobos fled. Deimos was resurrected by Phobos and his soul placed in the JOKER's body. Phobos, Deimos, and Eris caused havoc in Gotham City by possessing SARECROW, The Joker, and POISON IVY until Wonder Woman and BATMAN defeated them. Phobos, deemed a failure by his angry father Ares, was chained to a giant wheel in Hades. **DW**

PLANETEERS, THE

FIRST APPEARANCE ACTION COMICS #127 (December 1948)
STATUS Hero team (disbanded)   **BASE** Earth
NOTABLE MEMBERS AND POWERS
General Horatio Tomorrow   Superior marksman, pilot, and tactician.
Colonel Tommy Tomorrow   Ace pilot, good fighter, crack shot.
Brent Wood   Marksman, navigator, and co-pilot.

In the 22nd century, Earth and its colonies throughout the solar system and beyond were protected by the Space Planeteers. These officers of peace patrolled the spacelanes, ensuring people, and supplies flowed smoothly between worlds. When Earth or its colonies were threatened, the Planeteers acted as the first line of defense. It was the Planeteers who stopped evil scientist Rotwang and his robot MEKANIQUE in addition to a race of aquatic aliens who attempted to plunder Earth's resources. Among its great leaders was General Horatio Tomorrow, who worked out of Planeteer headquarters on Earth. One day, Horatio found a young boy at Headquarters Bunker D. Horatio took the boy in, named him Thomas, and raised him. In time the lad joined the Planeteers, rising to the rank of Colonel. Along with his best friend, Brent Wood, TOMMY TOMORROW protected humanity aboard his patrol craft, *The Ace of Space*. When the Planeteers ceased to exist and what replaced them has yet to be recorded. **RG**

PIED PIPER

FIRST APPEARANCE THE FLASH (1st series) #106 (May 1959)
STATUS Hero (reformed villain)   **REAL NAME** Hartley Rathaway
OCCUPATION Social activist   **BASE** Central City
HEIGHT 5ft 10in   **WEIGHT** 158 lbs   **EYES** Blue   **HAIR** Reddish-blond
SPECIAL POWERS/ABILITIES An expert in the science of sound who uses various pipes and technological devices to generate destructive sonic blasts or hypnotize others.

Hartley Rathaway's wealthy family spent millions of dollars on scientific experiments to restore his hearing. When Hartley's condition was finally cured, he became obsessed with sound and music. Emotionally distant and unstable, Hartley began experimenting with devices that manipulated sound, using the vast family fortune to buy the most advanced technology. Bored with his world of easy wealth, Hartley became a criminal called the Pied Piper, using his sonic pipes to commit spectacular crimes. He became a constant foe of Barry Allen, the second FLASH.

Soon after the Flash's death, however, the Pied Piper retired from crime and dedicated his life to social service. Openly gay, the Piper became an activist both for gay rights and Central City's homeless. He briefly teamed up with a group of local heroes to arrange meals for Central City's needy, and befriended Wally West, the third Flash.

Chained together at the wrist with the TRICKSTER, Piper found himself on the run prior to the Final Crisis. After the Trickster's death, Piper played a key role in the unfolding events on the planet Apokolips. **PJ**

MUSICAL MANIA The Piper's musical instrument is an advanced cylinder of complex technology, whose notes can control people's minds.

PLASMUS

FIRST APPEARANCE THE NEW TEEN TITANS (1st series) #14 (December 1981)
STATUS Villain   **REAL NAME** Otto Von Furth
OCCUPATION Criminal   **BASE** Europe
HEIGHT 6ft 4in   **WEIGHT** Unknown   **EYES** Gray   **HAIR** None
SPECIAL POWERS/ABILITIES Plasmus's touch brings fiery death and reduces living creature to burning protoplasm.

While excavating deadly radium, miner Otto Von Furth was trapped in a cave-in for seven days. During this time he was exposed to lethal levels of radiation, which killed his co-workers and left Von Furth highly radioactive. While recovering in hospital, Von Furth was kidnapped by ex-Nazi scientist GENERAL ZAHL, whose cruel experiments mutated the mineworker into a blob-like protoplasmic monster with a deadly, disintegrating touch.

Dubbed "Plasmus," Von Furth joined Zahl in a villainous team known as the Brotherhood of Evil opposing the TEEN TITANS. Plasmus also belonged to the Brotherhood's successor team, the SOCIETY OF SIN. Plasmus was among the villains who attacked Bludhaven during the Infinite Crisis. **SB**

PLASTIC MAN

THE PLIABLE PRANKSTER

FIRST APPEARANCE POLICE COMICS #1 (August 1941)
STATUS Hero **REAL NAME** Eel O'Brian
OCCUPATION Adventurer **BASE** Chicago
HEIGHT 6ft 1in **WEIGHT** 178 lbs **EYES** Groovy goggles
HAIR Basic Black **SPECIAL POWERS/ABILITIES** Capable of stretching every atom in his body into any shape he wishes. He is seemingly unbreakable and his shape-changing is limited only by his own overactive imagination; also has a mercurial sense of humor.

EEL O'BRIAN STARTED OUT on the wrong side of the law, but is working hard to make up for it. In 1941, he was just a lowlife gangster. Shot by a guard at the Crawford Chemical Works, he stumbled into a vat of acid, which seeped into his wounds. He escaped and ended up at Rest Haven, a spiritual retreat. While there, he realized that amazing changes in his human form would also allow him to change his ways. He became the hero Plastic Man.

LUCKY BREAK Eel O'Brian's life changed for the better when he ought to have died in the accident.

YOUR FLEXIBLE FRIEND

After serving in both the ALL-STAR SQUADRON and the FREEDOM FIGHTERS with distinction during World War II, Plastic Man was employed by the F.B.I. and then its sister agency, the National Bureau of Investigations. To this day, he continues to handle cases for the N.B.I., usually paired with the sloppy, lazy, and dull-witted Woozy Winks. These two improbable partners have an impressive track record. Together they have brought down numerous villains, including, the Dart, Even Steven, and the Brotherhood of the Savage Caribou.

In more recent times, Plastic Man has successfully worked alongside BATMAN on several cases, despite their strikingly different temperaments. In fact, the Dark Knight recommended Plas for membership for the JUSTICE LEAGUE OF AMERICA. Plastic Man has served the League well, despite his tendency to joke about everything.

BUGGED OUT Queen Bee manages to get the drop on Plastic Man, a rare occurrence.

Batman also learned that Plas had a son, born out of wedlock. Eel's son grew up to inherit his father's incredible "plastic man" abilities, although with greater control. Plastic Man's seeming death in the Obsidian Age, 3000 years ago, left the JLA traumatized. Reduced to atoms, he spent the next three millennia using his conscious mind to reassemble himself. Those millennia of isolation have had a profound affect on him, and O'Brian has rededicated himself to playing a positive role in his son's life, virtually forgetting his heroic persona in favor of becoming a daily presence. When a demon from Mars's ancient past emerged on Earth, Batman forced Plastic Man to once again be a hero. Eel remains an occasional hero, a pal to Woozy Winks and a full-time father. **RG**

PLASTIC SOLUTION Batman shows the still reassembling Plastic Man—after 3000 years—to the JLA.

KEY STORYLINES

• **PLASTIC MAN (3RD SERIES) #1–6 (FEBRUARY–JULY 2004):** Plastic Man and Woozy Winks in one of their most madcap adventures yet.
• **JLA #65 (AUGUST 2002):** Plastic Man reconnects with his son, thanks to Batman.
• **PLASTIC MAN (3RD SERIES) #1-4 (NOVEMBER–FEBRUARY 1988-89):** Plas and Woozy face the incredibly inept Ooze Brothers.
• **POLICE COMICS #1 (AUGUST 1941):** Eel O'Brian turns from petty criminal to costumed crime fighter, thanks to a freak accident.

FIRED UP Plastic Man had to return to action in order to save America from the fiery Fernus, an ancient Martian threat.

FATHER AND SON It took Batman to help, but Eel has rebuilt his relationship with his son, who also possesses his father's incredible stretching power.

PLASTIQUE

FIRST APPEARANCE FURY OF FIRESTORM #7 (December 1982)
STATUS Reformed villain REAL NAME Bette Sans Souci
OCCUPATION Former terrorist BASE Quebec, Canada
HEIGHT 5ft 6in WEIGHT 141 lbs EYES Blue HAIR Red
SPECIAL POWERS/ABILITIES Is able to cause objects to explode by
touching them with her fingertips. A demolitions expert, Plastique
has received training in urban terrorism and possesses an
incendiary temper.

Plastique was a radical French-
Canadian terrorist committed to
winning Quebec's independence
by any means necessary. Originally
she possessed no superpowers, and
so she wore a suit rigged with
plastic explosives into the offices
of the *New York News Express* in
an attempt to extort the newspaper's
owners.

FIRESTORM foiled her incendiary
plot and sent her to prison, but
behind bars Plastique received an
injection of an experimental serum
that gave her the ability to explode
objects by touching them. A second
criminal caper teamed Plastique with
KILLER FROST in a failed attempt to blow up the Niagara
Falls power plant.

Plastique became semi-reformed when offered the
opportunity to work with the SUICIDE SQUAD in
exchange for a commuted sentence. Since then, she
has changed her criminal ways and hooked up with
CAPTAIN ATOM, eventually becoming his wife. Plastique
currently works with the SUICIDE SQUAD, and with the
Electrocutioner as the two-person "Bomb Squad." DW

PLUNDER

FIRST APPEARANCE FLASH (2nd series) #165 (October 2000)
STATUS Villain REAL NAME None; a mirror clone of Joseph Morillo
OCCUPATION Bounty hunter BASE A mirror image dimension
HEIGHT 5ft 11in WEIGHT 190 lbs EYES White HAIR None
SPECIAL POWERS/ABILITIES Plunder is an expert hitman renowned
for his unerring aim; he also possesses numerous handguns
and other firearms in his armor; a powerful, if unsophisticated, hand-
to-hand combatant.

Plunder was a bounty hunter
that existed in a mystical "mirror
world" housed within the diamond
wedding ring of Linda Park (*see*
PARK, LINDA), the wife of Wally
West, the third FLASH.
A mercenary for the mirror world's
Thinker, Plunder discovered that
his dimension was fading into non-
existence, and hoped to escape into
our world. The Thinker hired Plunder
to capture two of the Flash's
Rogues Gallery, MIRROR
MASTER and CAPTAIN COLD,
to lure the Flash into their
mirror dimension. The Flash
escaped the Thinker's trap and
returned to our dimension.
Plunder is the mirror image of Detective Jared Morillo, a
Flash ally from the Department of Meta-human Hostility.
Plunder shot Morillo, assumed his form, and briefly took
his place. Discovered, Plunder forsook Morillo's identity
and resumed bounty hunting. PJ

POISON IVY

FIRST APPEARANCE BATMAN #181 (June 1966)
STATUS Villain REAL NAME Pamela Lillian Isley
OCCUPATION Criminal; eco-terrorist BASE Gotham City
HEIGHT 5ft 6in WEIGHT 133 lbs EYES Green HAIR Chestnut
SPECIAL POWERS/ABILITIES Poison Ivy's altered body chemistry enables
her to exude a venomous variety of floral toxins to which she alone
is immune. She carries with her a plethora of pernicious plants that
germinate from fast-growing seed pods.

Botanist Pamela Isley was a shrinking violet when she
went to work for famed scientist (and super-villain-in-
the-making) Dr. Jason Woodrue. The future FLORONIC
MAN experimented on her, hoping to create a human/
plant hybrid like himself. Woodrue succeeded all too
well, creating the ravishing-but-deadly Poison Ivy. Where
Isley was gangly and unremarkable, Ivy was gorgeous and
unforgettable. Isley's porcelain skin soon took on a green
pigmentation as chlorophyll replaced her human blood.
Ivy even exuded man-maddening pheromones and natural
toxins. She was Poison Ivy in more than name.

Ironically, the sun-loving Ivy found herself drawn
to gloomy Gotham City, where she sowed the
seeds of a criminal career to fund her true
cause as a green guerrilla championing
the world's diminishing fauna.
Ivy also discovered a worthy foe
in BATMAN, who has resisted
Ivy's fragrant charms while
uprooting her terrorist
schemes. Ivy's
victims, consumed
by carnivorous
plants, triggered
the creation of the
plant-monster known
as Harvest. SB

PRETTY POISON *Ivy once grew wild in Wayne Manor,
taking over Bruce Wayne's mind with her seductive
pheromones. Little did Ivy know
that she had Batman
in her thrall!*

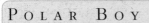

GREENBACKS *Poison Ivy
loves the color of money,
especially because robbery and
extortion help to fund her exotic
environmental causes.*

POLAR BOY

FIRST APPEARANCE ADVENTURE COMICS #306 (March 1963)
STATUS Hero REAL NAME Brek Bannin
OCCUPATION Adventurer BASE Earth
HEIGHT 5ft 5in WEIGHT 140 lbs EYES Blue HAIR Blond
SPECIAL POWERS/ABILITIES Like all natives of Tharr, can generate subzero
temperatures as a natural defense against a near-sun orbit.

Tharr's Brek Bannin has the native power
to generate cold. When there was an
open call for recruits to join the LEGION
OF SUPER-HEROES, Bannin was
among the first to apply. He failed
the tests but decided to join up
with other rejects as the LEGION
OF SUBSTITUTE SUPER-HEROES. In the Legion's
future, Polar Boy fought the anti-alien regime that
had taken control of Earth, helping SUPERMAN and
his fellow Legionnaires despite the loss of his arm. In
an alternate Legion timeline, Brek Bannin became a
member of the WANDERERS under the leadership of Garth
Ranzz (*see* LIGHTNING LORD). RG

POWER COMPANY

FIRST APPEARANCE JLA #61 (February 2002)
STATUS Hero team   **BASE** San Francisco
CURRENT MEMBERS AND POWERS
Josiah Power (managing partner) Can turn into a rock form.
Skyrocket (partner) Argo Harness lets her channel and control energy.
Manhunter (partner) Clone of Manhunter Paul Kirk; skilled combatant.
Witchfire (partner) Possesses occult conjuring abilities.
Striker Z (associate) Living battery able to power his high-tech gear.
Bork (associate) Possesses mystically-granted invulnerability.
Sapphire (associate) Alien "gem coating" can create armor, shielding, and weapons.
Jennifer Elizabeth Barbara Stuart Pilots high-tech Haunted Tank.

Billing itself as "the world's foremost supplier of professional superhuman services," The Power Company is a super-hero corporation run like a law firm and designed to make a profit. Although founder Josiah Power encourages *pro bono* work for good causes, high-paying clients often retain the Power Company for security, recovery, or investigative missions.

Josiah Power drew upon his past history as a lawyer to structure the Power Company into partners and associates. His early partners included MANHUNTER, WITCHFIRE, and SKYROCKET, the local hero of St. Louis. Associates included ex-villain Bork, the stuntman STRIKER Z, and the runaway called Sapphire.

During the time when Josiah Power lay in a coma from a gunshot wound, the other team members brought aboard FIRESTORM as a temporary associate. Garrison Slate, the CEO of S.T.A.R. Labs, took over as interim administrator. Though Firestorm left the team, they gained new help from Jennifer Stuart and her HAUNTED TANK during the battle against the Dragoneer. Josiah Power has since returned to full health and the Power Company is actively seeking new clients. Few other super hero teams have as deep an understanding of the business market, and it appears that the Power Company is primed to make a killing. They can only hope that super-villain gangs don't follow their lead and begin marketing themselves as corporations. **DW**

FURY FORCE
1) *Striker Z*   2) *Bork*   3) *Josiah Power*
4) *Witchfire*   5) *Manhunter*
6) *Sapphire*   7) *Skyrocket*

POWER GIRL

FIRST APPEARANCE ALL-STAR COMICS #58 (February 1976)
STATUS Hero   **REAL NAME** Karen "Kara" Starr
OCCUPATION Software designer; adventurer
BASE Los Angeles; New York City
HEIGHT 5ft 7in   **WEIGHT** 160 lbs
EYES Blue   **HAIR** Light blonde
SPECIAL POWERS/ABILITIES Incredible superstrength, superspeed, near invulnerability, flight.

Almost a decade ago, Kara emerged from a mysterious ship that had crash-landed on Earth. Possessing incredible powers similar to SUPERMAN's, Kara was taken in as a kind of protégée by the Man of Steel, who then introduced her to the JUSTICE SOCIETY OF AMERICA. The headstrong young woman became Power Girl, and, after establishing a successful software development firm, briefly joined INFINITY, INC. Kara was then contacted by the spirit of ARION, the ancient wizard from Atlantis, who told her that she was his granddaughter, sent thousands of years into the future to save her from her brother Garn (*see* DAANUTH, GARN). Upset by this news, Kara handed over control of her company to Felicity Raymond, FIRESTORM's stepmother, and briefly joined Justice League Europe (*see* JUSTICE LEAGUE OF AMERICA).

During the Infinite Crisis, Kara learned the truth: she was not related to Arion, but instead was one of the only survivors of the previous multiverse's Earth-Two. She has since assumed the position of chairperson with the Justice Society. **PJ**

IDENTITY CRISIS *A string of false origin stories left Power Girl in doubt regarding her true identity. She soon learned that she was the cousin of the Superman from Earth-Two, which had been erased during the Crisis.*

HEAVY HITTER *As a Kryptonian, Power Girl possesses powers rivaled only by those of Superman and Supergirl.*

BRAINS AND BRAWN *Power Girl's physical strength is matched by her aggressive personality.*

POW-WOW SMITH

FIRST APPEARANCE WESTERN COMICS #44 (April 1954)
STATUS Hero **REAL NAME** Ohiyesa
OCCUPATION Legionnaire **BASE** Elkhorn
HEIGHT 6ft 2in **WEIGHT** 190 lbs **EYES** Black **HAIR** Black
SPECIAL POWERS/ABILITIES Ohiyesa turned out to be a clever man, quickly mastering the white man's ways, becoming a crack shot and a fine detective.

Sioux brave Ohiyesa left his tribe in Red Deer Valley to learn the ways of the white man in the late 1880s. He became a small-town sheriff nicknamed Pow-Wow Smith because of his native American heritage, and clashed with various rogues, including the Fadeaway Outlaw, an escape artist turned criminal who seemed to vanish after committing his crimes. He married his fellow Sioux tribemate Fleetfoot and his peace-keeping exploits earned him honorary U.S. citizenship. Despite his sterling record in law enforcement, the prejudiced townsfolk continued to shun him socially or turn on him, given the slightest provocation. Rather than react to this, Smith let his deeds speak for him.

A descendant of Ohiyesa's adopted the name Pow-Wow Smith, settled in Red Deer Valley, and become a noted private investigator during the late 1940s and 1950s. His son, also known as Ohiyesa, followed in the family tradition. In recent times, he helped ROBIN, HUNTRESS, NIGHTHAWK, and the local county's Sheriff Shotgun Smith, bring the second incarnation of the TRIGGER TWINS to justice. **RG**

POZHAR

FIRST APPEARANCE FIRESTORM #62 (August 1987)
STATUS Hero (absorbed) **REAL NAME** Mikhail Arkadin
OCCUPATION Former super hero **BASE** Moscow
HEIGHT 6ft **WEIGHT** 190 lbs **EYES** Blue **HAIR** Black [confirm all stats **SPECIAL POWERS/ABILITIES** Flight; ability to control nuclear blasts, and immunity to radiation.

Pozhar was a Russian super hero who found a new life by becoming part of the complex history of FIRESTORM. Exposure to a nuclear plant meltdown imbued Mikhail Arkadin with atomic powers. Dubbed Pozhar by the Russian secret service, he agreed to battle Firestorm when the American hero decided to disarm the world's nuclear arsenal.

Fighting above the Nevada desert, Pozhar and Firestorm fused into a single entity when government agents fired a missile at them. This new version of Firestorm could only appear when Ron Raymond and Arkadin merged; the amnesiac mind of Martin Stein controlled this Firestorm.

Later, Raymond and Arkadin merged with the villainous Russian creation Svarozhich, then Firestorm split when Martin Stein turned Firestorm into a fire elemental. Pozhar is still active as a hero. **DW**

PRANKSTER

FIRST APPEARANCE ACTION COMICS #51 (August 1942)
STATUS Villain **REAL NAME** Oswald Loomis
OCCUPATION Comedian; criminal **BASE** Metropolis
HEIGHT 5ft 9in **WEIGHT** 160 lbs **EYES** Blue **HAIR** Brown
SPECIAL POWERS/ABILITIES Weapons imbued with nanotechnology, include tear-gas squirt flowers, 3-D glasses, acid-spitting water gun.

Loomis was a successful television comedian and the host of "The Uncle Oswald Show," a children's morning show in Metropolis. When Morgan Edge, the station president, cancelled his show after 25 years, Lewis snapped and staged a number of bizarre and dangerous pranks throughout the city. Loomis kidnapped Lois Lane (see LANE, LOIS) and held her captive at his studio. When Edge tried to intervene, Loomis hurled him out of a trap door 30 stories above the streets of Metropolis.

SUPERMAN saved Edge and freed Lois before Loomis surrendered. Realizing that he could be in jail for life, the Prankster escaped his guards.

He currently works as a for-hire crime enabler, performing elaborate distractions to occupy Superman while wrongs are committed elsewhere. **PJ**

PRAXIS

FIRST APPEARANCE THE SPECTRE 2nd series #24 (February 1989)
STATUS Hero **REAL NAME** Jason Praxis
OCCUPATION Super hero; former police detective **BASE** Mobile
HEIGHT 7ft 7in **WEIGHT** 168 lbs **EYES** Blue **HAIR** Black
SPECIAL POWERS/ABILITIES Skilled, experienced detective; possesses telepathic and telekinetic control over electricity, including synaptic brain activity, allowing Praxis limited control over others' minds.

Portland police detective Jason Praxis acquired his meta-human ability to manipulate electricity after failing to prevent a serial killer from murdering his niece. Although the killer was subdued, the guilt-ridden Praxis left the police force and used his telepathy and telekinesis as a superpowered private investigator. Praxis was recruited by BOOSTER GOLD to join the short-lived corporate super-team the CONGLOMERATE. Later, Praxis returned to law enforcement, working alongside F.B.I. agent Deena Walker and preventing malevolent magician Dexter DeFarge from invoking Ghast, one of the devilish DEMONS THREE, and setting him loose on Earth. In mental combat with DeFarge, Praxis was able to transform himself into a being of pure mental energy. It is speculated that Praxis and his powers are related to the Lords of Order, ancient beings in eternal opposition to the Lords of Chaos for universal balance. Praxis continues to use his powers and skills in the cause of justice. **SB**

PREZ

FIRST APPEARANCE PREZ #1 (September 1973)
STATUS Hero **REAL NAME** Prez Rickard
OCCUPATION Ex-president of the United States **BASE** Steadfast
HEIGHT 5ft 7in **WEIGHT** 145 lbs **EYES** Blue **HAIR** Blond
SPECIAL POWERS/ABILITIES Prez possesses a sunny, enthusiastic, and optimistic outlook on life that makes people instinctively want to trust him.

A story that makes the rounds at the Inn Between Worlds concerns a teenager named Prez. When Congress changed the Constitution, lowering the minimum age of president from 35 to 18, Prez seized the opportunity to run. After Richard Nixon's time in the Oval Office, the disenchanted populace chose Prez, who served with distinction. His trusted friends, Eagle Free, became director of the F.B.I. Prez used the powers of his office to stop a new Cold War and preach a new breed of pacifism. A mentally disturbed girl shot and killed Prez's girlfriend and, feeling betrayed by the people, Prez withdrew from office and vanished from public life. A cautionary tale or fanciful yarn? Only the individual can judge. **RG**

PRIMAL FORCE

FIRST APPEARANCE PRIMAL FORCE #0 (October 1994)
STATUS Hero team **BASE** New York City
MEMBERS AND POWERS RED TORNADO (controls weather); CLAW (demonic claw); GOLEM (regenerative powers); JACK O'LANTERN III (energy blasts); MERIDIAN (teleports); BLACK CONDOR II (heightened senses); NIGHTMASTER (SWORD OF NIGHT); WILLPOWER (living thunderbolt).

Also known as the Leymen, the short-lived supergroup Primal Force came into being following the time crisis of Zero Hour. The order of the Leymen have defended Earth for over two thousand years against evil supernatural forces.

Armed with ley pendulums that augmented their natural powers in times of great stress, the new Leymen moved against villains such as Cataclysm, SATANUS, and the sinister cult called the August.

Primal Force disbanded following a confrontation with Cataclysm in New York's Central Park, though its members stand ready. JACK O'LANTERN III in particular remembers a prophecy that foretold he would one day lead the team. **DW**

KEY 1) *Golem* **2)** *Red Tornado* **3)** *Meridian* **4)** *Jack O'Lantern III* **5)** *Claw*

PRINCE RA-MAN

FIRST APPEARANCE (Merlin) HOUSE OF SECRETS (1st series) #23 (August 1959); (Prince Ra-Man) HOUSE OF SECRETS #73 (August 1965)
STATUS Hero **REAL NAME** Mark Merlin **OCCUPATION** Occultist and adventurer **BASE** Mystery Hill Mansion, in the town of Cloister
HEIGHT (Merlin) 5ft 10in; (Prince Ra-Man) 6ft **WEIGHT** (Merlin) 157 lbs; (Prince Ra-Man) 178 lbs **EYES** (both) Blue **HAIR** (Merlin) Brown; (Prince Ra-Man) Black
SPECIAL POWERS/ABILITIES Sorcery; illusion casting; invisibility; mental transference into his cat, Memakata; telekinetic powers projected as a beam from his forehead; matter transmutation.

College student Mark Merlin was investigating the death of his uncle, a stage magician, who was killed for revealing the secrets of fake magicians. Exposing a group called the Council of Three as the murderers, Mark became an occult specialist and began investigating magical impostors as his uncle once had.

Mark was transported to the otherdimensional world of Ra, where several ancient Egyptians lived as immortals. There, Merlin gained various mental abilities and returned to Earth reincarnated in the body of an ancient Egyptian prince. Calling himself Prince Ra-Man, Merlin battled various mystical threats but died when the Anti-Monitor, a nihilist from the Anti-Matter Universe, invaded Earth (see Great Battles, pp. 362–3). He left behind his shattered fiancée, Elsa. **PJ**

PROFESSOR IVO

FIRST APPEARANCE THE BRAVE AND THE BOLD #30 (July 1960)
STATUS Hero **REAL NAME** Anthony Ivo (alias Professor Ives)
OCCUPATION Occultist and adventurer **BASE** Mobile
HEIGHT 5ft 10in **WEIGHT** 165 lbs **EYES** Blue **HAIR** Black
SPECIAL POWERS/ABILITIES Scientific genius; experiments to extend his lifespan have left Ivo deformed and long-lived, but not immortal.

Anthony Ivo was so traumatized by his grandmother's death that he developed a pathological fear of dying. The ingenious inventor became obsessed with securing eternal life for himself. He created the android AMAZO and began a long-standing enmity with the JUSTICE LEAGUE OF AMERICA, whom he blamed for the side effects of a failed immortality potion that left him monstrous in appearance. Ivo was later responsible for the deaths of JLA members VIBE and STEEL II. Ivo teamed with another scientist, T.O. MORROW, to build TOMORROW WOMAN, an android that the villainous pair hoped would infiltrate the JLA and destroy the team from within. The android duly won JLA membership. However, associating with super heroes dedicated to the cause of serving others, led Tomorrow Woman to override her own evil programming, and she saved Earth and her teammates from IF, a time-lost weapon from the 23rd century. Ivo recently helped modify an AMAZO body for use by SOLOMON GRUNDY. **SB**

PROMETHEUS III

FIRST APPEARANCE Prometheus #1 (December 1997)
STATUS Hero **REAL NAME** Unrevealed
OCCUPATION Hero hunter **BASE:** The Ghost Zone
HEIGHT 6 ft 1in **WEIGHT** 180 lbs **EYES** Brown
HAIR White **SPECIAL POWERS/ABILITIES** Brilliant designer of advanced technology and a highly skilled athlete; unique armor is laced with synaptic relays to enhance his fighting prowess; nightstick can shatter steel and override shielded electronic systems.

The first Prometheus stole fire from the OLYMPIAN GODS and brought it to Earth. The first mortal to use the name belonged to the villain team the HYBRID. The third Prometheus is by far the deadliest. His past is the mirror image of Bruce Wayne's (see Batman)—except that Prometheus is entirely motivated by evil. As a youngster, he saw his criminal parents gunned down by a policeman, and dedicated his life to eradicating all law officers. He traveled the world, learning ways to maim and kill.

Clad in an armored suit designed to stun opponents and augment his natural skills, he has turned himself into a master assassin, having downloaded the fighting skills of 30 martial artists into his brain. He used a device called the Cosmic Key, picked up during his studies, and found his way into the realm of nothingness he calls the Ghost Zone. There he built a Crooked House patterned after his warped soul, where he lives and schemes. He has bested the JUSTICE LEAGUE OF AMERICA on several occasions only to be defeated by CATWOMAN. He also battled GREEN ARROW in Star City, only to have his superior technology bested by bow and arrow. During the Infinite Crisis, Prometheus apparently killed the PEACEMAKER, and later defeated LADY SHIVA in single combat. **RG**

PRINCESS PROJECTRA

FIRST APPEARANCE ADVENTURE COMICS #346 (July 1966)
STATUS Hero **REAL NAME** Unknown
OCCUPATION Legionnaire **BASE** Mobile
HEIGHT 5ft 10in **WEIGHT** 130 lbs **EYES** Blue
HAIR White
SPECIAL POWERS/ABILITIES Can generate realistic, three-dimensional illusions, can enhance her perceptions to see great distances or through solid objects.

Princess Projectra is a member of the LEGION OF SUPER-HEROES in several timelines that contain alternate versions of the team. In one, she possessed a royal birthright as princess of Orando, and used her illusion-casting abilities to earn fame as a Legionnaire.

She eventually married her teammate KARATE KID, avenging his death in combat by executing her husband's murderer, Nemesis Kid. The taking of a life left Princess Projectra in violation of the Legion's code and she resigned from the team. Later she returned to the Legion of Super-Heroes under the name Sensor Girl, wearing a costume that concealed her face. This Sensor Girl traveled back to the 21st century with her fellow Legionnaires during the "Lightning Saga," helping to bring back Wally West, the third FLASH.

In an alternate Legion timeline, Princess Projectra of Orando is the spoiled financier of the Legion. In another, Orando is home to a species of intelligent snakes, and their Princess Projectra analogue is known as SENSOR. **DW**

ONE-MAN ARMY
Prometheus III is a genius and Olympic-caliber athlete, able to hold his own against the entire JLA.

PRYSM

FIRST APPEARANCE TEEN TITANS #1 (October 1996)
STATUS Hero **REAL NAME** Audrey Spears
OCCUPATION Super hero **BASE** Mobile
HEIGHT 6ft 4in **WEIGHT** Indeterminate **[CONFIRM STATS]**
EYES White **HAIR** Indeterminate
SPECIAL POWERS/ABILITIES Vast light controlling powers, including the ability to capture and reflect light, fire light beams, and turn invisible.

Audrey Spears was another experiment by the H'San Natall in hybrid breeding, but unlike the other Earth-based hybrids (ARGENT II, JOTO, and RISK), she grew up inside a virtual reality fantasy provided by her alien keepers. Although happy with her idyllic life based on 1950s television, she soon learned that her truth was a lie.

Returning to Earth with the other hybrid teens, Audrey adopted the codename Prysm, for her ability to manipulate light. Prysm and her fellow hybrids (along with a de-aged ATOM II) founded the post-Zero Hour TEEN TITANS. Prysm found her glassy appearance freakish and rejoiced when she lost her powers during a mission to the WARLORD's realm of Skartaris—though she voluntarily regained them in order to save her teammates.

After Joto died in battle, Prysm carried his soul inside her own body for months before finally releasing it. Prysm ultimately met her true parents—her human mother Queen Miraset and her H'San Natall father Ch'ah—and convinced the rest of the H'San Natall to leave Earth in peace. At last feeling at home, Prysm chose to remain with her parents in space. Prysm's feelings of alienation were deepened by the unrequited crush she had for her teammate Risk. **DW**

ONLY THE LONELY *"A girl without a home, a lost soul,"* Prysm found a friend in another alienated heroine, Supergirl.

PSIMON

FIRST APPEARANCE NEW TEEN TITANS (1st series) #2 (January 1981)
STATUS Villain (deceased) **REAL NAME** Simon Jones
OCCUPATION Scientist; criminal **BASE** Mobile
HEIGHT 5ft 11.5in **WEIGHT** 145 lbs **EYES** White **HAIR** None
SPECIAL POWERS/ABILITIES Almost unrivaled psychic abilities, including telepathy, telekinesis and mind control; projects mental forces blasts strong enough to pulverize stone or turn a human brain to jelly.

Physicist Simon Jones was determined to breach the barriers between dimensions. During one of his experiments, a beam from another dimension struck him, endowing him with amazing psychic power. As Psimon, Jones recruited a group of villains called the FEARSOME FIVE, who came to blows with the New Teen Titans. One of the Teen Titans, RAVEN, discovered Psimon was an agent of her father, the demon TRIGON, who was the source of Jones's power. After failing to defeat the Titans, Trigon banished Psimon to another dimension.

The Fearsome Five freed Psimon, and fought the Titans and the OUTSIDERS, threatening New York City with nuclear annihilation. After teaming with DOCTOR SIVA to assemble a new Fearsome Five, Psimon found himself exiled on a prison planet during Operation: Salvation Run. There, the JOKER bashed in his head with a rock. **PJ**

BACK AGAIN Psimon has returned to Earth, resurrecting Shimmer and the Fearsome Five.

PSYCHO PIRATE

FIRST APPEARANCE SHOWCASE #56 (May–June 1965)
STATUS Villain **REAL NAME** Roger Hayden
OCCUPATION Costumed criminal **BASE** Mobile
HEIGHT 6ft **WEIGHT** 180 lbs **EYES** Green **HAIR** Red
SPECIAL POWERS/ABILITIES While wearing the Medusa Mask, can control the emotions of individuals or groups. Possesses a limited and undefined influence over people erased from time due to the Crisis.

From humble origins, the Psycho-Pirate became a pivotal figure in two universe-shaking Crisis events. While in prison, Hayden met the original, Golden Age Psycho-Pirate, who encouraged him to carry on his legacy. After acquiring the mystical Medusa Mask, Hayden realized he could control others' emotions and went into business as the new Psycho-Pirate, serving briefly with the SECRET SOCIETY OF SUPER-VILLAINS. Small-scale crimes quickly became cosmic-level threats when the Anti-Monitor (see MONITORS) recruited the Psycho-Pirate during the Crisis on Infinite Earths. Hayden survived the ordeal with full memories of the multiverse that had been erased, an experience that drove him mad. During the Infinite Crisis, Alexander Luthor used the Psycho-Pirate to control POWER GIRL, BLACK ADAM, and other captives. After escaping, Black Adam punched a hole through the Psycho-Pirate's head. Revived through the power of the Medusa Mask, Roger Hayden now sells his skills as a pusher of "emotional drugs".

PUNCH AND JEWELEE

FIRST APPEARANCE CAPTAIN ATOM (1st series) #85 (March 1967)
STATUS Villains **REAL NAMES** Unrevealed
OCCUPATION Puppeteers; criminals **BASE** American Midwest
HEIGHT (Punch) 5ft 5in; (Jewelee) 5ft 9in **WEIGHT** (Punch) 125 lbs; (Jewelee) 139 lbs **EYES** (Punch) Brown; (Jewelee) Blue
HAIR (Punch) Brown; (Jewelee) Blonde **SPECIAL POWERS/ABILITIES** (Punch) Flying boot and electrically charged weapons; (Jewelee) hypno-jewels project illusions and light effects.

Punch and Jewelee were lovers, puppeteers and part-time thieves working at Coney Island in Brooklyn, New York. The two crooks discovered a chest containing several alien weapons, and used them to craft more formidable criminal guises for themselves. As their ambitions grew, Punch and Jewelee used the alien technology to create an enormous underground headquarters in Coney Island, and even attempted to steal the minds of several prominent scientists in order to sell them to the highest bidder. The two became frequent foes of NIGHTSHADE and KING FARADAY.

The duo were consumed regulation by now with a growing reputation for acts of mindless violence. They were thus ideal candidates for the SUICIDE SQUAD, run by Amanda Waller (see WALLER, AMANDA). Radically unpredictable, the duo were discharged from the Squad when Jewelee became pregnant. Punch and Jewelee moved to the American heartland to raise their new baby, and briefly forsook their criminal lives. Punch and Jewelee joined the most recent Suicide Squad. However, their first mission ended in tragedy when a gunman fatally shot Punch. **PJ**

QUANTUM MECHANICS

FIRST APPEARANCE JLA: HEAVEN'S LADDER (November 2000)
STATUS Cosmic beings **BASE** Mobile
SPECIAL POWERS/ABILITIES Possessed of virtually god-like powers and intellects, the Quantum Mechanics are capable of practically any feat that their imaginations can conceive, including teleporting entire worlds (including Earth) half-way across the universe.

Born at the Big Bang, the Quantum Mechanics roamed the universe, seeking celestial enlightenment. Fear of their own mortality, coupled with their inability to conceive of an afterlife, prompted the Quantum Mechanics to create a vision of heaven. They created thousands of agents to study the cultures of the universe, gathering information about each version of heaven to build the perfect hereafter for themselves. The JUSTICE LEAGUE OF AMERICA first discovered the Quantum Mechanics when these ancient beings abducted planet Earth, as well as hundreds of other worlds they had been studying, to create their own "ladder" to heaven. When a rogue faction of the Quantum Mechanics threatened to destroy them all these worlds, the JLA were forced to battle the cosmic creatures, eventually helping them cross over into a higher plane of existence. **PJ**

COLORBLIND *Zazzala's inability to see the color red aided several JLA members when they attacked her cloaked in Plastic Man's red costume. Big Barda made the Queen Bee see the error of her ways with a crunching blow from her Mega-Rod!*

QUEEN BEE II

FIRST APPEARANCE JLA #34 (October 1999)
STATUS Villain **REAL NAME** Zazzala
OCCUPATION Royal Genetrix **BASE** The planet Korll
HEIGHT 5ft 9in **WEIGHT** 226 lbs **EYES** Blue **HAIR** Gray-black
SPECIAL POWERS/ABILITIES Multifaceted eyes see in the ultraviolet spectrum; gauntlet on right arm fires poisonous barbed stingers from reflexive venom sacs; hypno-pollen capable of bending others' to her will; has a mindless army of drones at her disposal.

The first Queen Bee was a woman with hypnotic powers who seized control of the state of Bialya after murdering its dictator, Colonel Rumaan Harjavti (see HARJAVTI, RUMAAN & SUMAAN). She soon died at the hands of his brother, Sumaan.

The second Queen Bee, Zazzala, ruler of planet Korll and its ever-expanding empire, was far more dangerous. In her closest encounter with Earth, the Queen Bee and her swarms of Bee-Troopers joined Lex Luthor's INJUSTICE GANG in a plot to defeat the JLA and conquer Earth. In return for the firepower of her drones, Zazzala was offered a percentage of Earth's populace as slaves. The first to suffer were the citizens of New York City, which became the site of the Queen Bee's Royal Egg-Matrix and ground zero for her planned planetary domination (after betraying Luthor). After her defeat, the Queen Bee retreated to Korll. She re-emerged as a member of the SECRET SOCIETY OF SUPER-VILLAINS (see VILLAINS UNITED) at the head of the H.I.V.E., a global criminal syndicate. The SECRET SIX sabotaged her operations and left the H.I.V.E. in tatters. **SB**

QUEEN OF FABLES

FIRST APPEARANCE JUSTICE LEAGUE OF AMERICA #47 (November 2000) **STATUS** Villain **REAL NAMES** Unknown
OCCUPATION Sorceress **BASE** Other-dimensional space
HEIGHT Tall and willowy **WEIGHT** Light as a feather
EYES Twin sapphires **HAIR** Sleekest ebony
SPECIAL POWERS/ABILITIES Magical ability to make the monsters and myths of storybook fables real.

Centuries ago, the Queen of Fables arrived on Earth as an exile from another dimension. Possessed of vast magical power, she carved out an empire for herself and met defeat at the hands of the virtuous princess Snow White. Imprisoned within a storybook until the dawn of the 21st century, the Queen of Fables escaped to sow chaos in New York City by conjuring various ogres, witches, and goblins.

The JUSTICE LEAGUE OF AMERICA clashed with the Queen of Fables when she attacked WONDER WOMAN, believing the Amazon to be her old nemesis Snow White. With her unique brand of sorcery, the Queen drew the Leaguers into the realm of fairy tales, where they faced the worst monstrosities of the imagination. She even transformed Manhattan island into an enchanted forest festooned with hanging moss and creeping ivy.

Eventually, Wonder Woman used her lasso to defeat the Queen of Fables, forcing the Queen to confront the truth of her own mortality. She is now imprisoned inside a new book—the *United States Tax Code*. Within its dry, literal pages, the Queen of Fables is unlikely to find any magical elements she can use to escape. **DW**

STORY TIME *The Queen called to life elements from fairy tales including Snow White, Sleeping Beauty, and Hansel and Gretel.*

QUESTION I & II, THE

First appearance BLUE BEETLE (3rd series) #1 (June 1967)
Status Hero (deceased) *Real name* Charles Victor Szasz
Occupation Television journalist (as Vic Sage) *Base* Hub City
Height 6ft 2in *Weight* 185 lbs *Eyes* Blue *Hair* Reddish blond
Special powers/abilities Trained by Richard Dragon, Vic is a formidable fighter and martial artist.

First appearance (as the Question) 52 #48 (April 2007)
Status Hero *Real name* Renee Montoya
Occupation Vigilante *Base* Gotham City
Height 5ft 8in *Weight* 144 lbs *Eyes* Brown *Hair* Black
Special powers/abilities Expert combatant, detective, and interrogator; master of disguise.

CRIME BIBLE Soon after assuming the identity of the second Question, Renee Montoya embarked on a globe-hopping quest to expose the evils of the Cult of Cain.

Victor Szasz was an angry orphan who could not understand why people did the things they did. As Vic Sage, television reporter for K.B.E.L., he took on political corruption in Hub City, Those hypocrites he couldn't expose on television he went after as the Question, his features masked by a compound called Pseudoderm devised by his friend Tot (Dr. Aristotle Rodor). Sage was also aided by Mayor Myra Connelly, (widow of the former Mayor), and Izzy O'Toole, perhaps the only honest cop on the force,

After many adventures, Sage became disillusioned with his crusading role and, entrusted with Myra's daughter, journeyed to the Amazon rain forest to find himself.

He returned to Hub City a changed man after LADY SHIVA saved his life and Richard Dragon (*see* DRAGON, RICHARD) instructed him in martial arts. Vic Sage died of cancer following the Infinite Crisis. His protégée, G.C.P.D. detective Renee Montoya (*see* MONTOYA, RENEE) has taken his place as the new Question. **RG**

CRUSADER *Vic Sage became an Everyman figure, using his fists to find truth in corrupt Hub City.*

QUICK, JESSE

First appearance Justice Society of America (2nd series) #1 (August 1992) *Status* Hero (retired) *Real name* Jesse Chambers
Occupation C.E.O. of Quickstart Enterprises *Base* Keystone City
Height 5ft 9in *Weight* 142 lbs *Eyes* Blue *Hair* Blonde
Special powers/abilities Superspeed, superstrength, flight, martial arts.

Jesse Chambers is the daughter of Johnny Quick (*see* QUICK, JOHNNY) and LIBERTY BELLE, two heroes of World War II. Jesse inherited her parents' powers and gained superspeed by reciting her father's formula ("3x2(9YZ)4A"), which allowed her to tap into the Speed Force.

An ally of the FLASH, MAX MERCURY, and Impulse (*see* KID FLASH), Jesse Quick, as Chambers called herself, became a prominent speedster in Keystone City. She was also a member of the JUSTICE SOCIETY OF AMERICA and the TEEN TITANS. After her father's death at the hands of SAVITAR, Jesse inherited his role as C.E.O. of Quickstart Enterprises.

Jesse retired the Jesse Quick identity when she became the new Liberty Belle. She now serves with the JSA alongside her husband, HOURMAN II. **PJ**

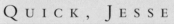

QUICK, JOHNNY

First appearance MORE FUN COMICS #71 (September 1941)
Status Hero *Real name* Johnny Chambers
Occupation Super hero *Base* New York City
Height 5ft 11in *Weight* 170 lbs *Eyes* Blue *Hair* Blonde
Special powers/abilities Superspeed; can pass through objects by vibrating his molecules and briefly "fly".

At the dawn of the 1940s, Johnny Chambers's guardian, the celebrated Professor Gill, discovered a miraculous formula written on a piece of papyrus in the temple of Egyptian king Amen. When young Johnny said "3X2(9YZ)4A" he received the gift of superspeed, and he could close off this link by saying "Z25Y(2AB)6." So began a new life as the costumed Johnny Quick.

The outbreak of World War II caused all of America's mystery men to unite under the banner of the ALL-STAR SQUADRON. Johnny Quick worked with Jay Garrick (the original Flash), and dated and later married LIBERTY BELLE.

Unlike others Johnny Quick did not enter forced retirement when the House of Un-American Activities Committee ordered all mystery men to unmask themselves in the 1950s. Nevertheless, Johnny spent gradually less time in the hero game in order to build up his communications business and to spend time with his daughter, Jesse (*see* Quick, Jesse).

Though Johnny Quick claimed he didn't believe in the Speed Force, his magic formulas acted as mental mantras that channeled the extra-dimensional speed energy into his body. He became one with the Speed Force when he sacrificed himself in battle against the foul SAVITAR. He is survived by Jesse, who adventured as Jesse Quick (*see* QUICK, JESSE) before assuming her mother's role as the new Liberty Belle. **DW**

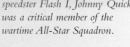

AND HE'S OFF *Although less well-known than his fellow speedster Flash I, Johnny Quick was a critical member of the wartime All-Star Squadron.*

ROMANTIC MOMENTS

CLARK KENT AND LOIS LANE

Perhaps no pair is more different, yet more perfect for one another, than the ace reporter from Metropolis and the farmboy from Smallville, Kansas. As co-workers at the *Daily Planet*, they gradually put aside their professional rivalry (as well as Lois' infatuation with SUPERMAN) and learned to embrace all that they had in common. Eventually Clark revealed his secret identity to Lois and the two were married. Fortunately—because so few know of Clark Kent's famous alter ego—the happy ceremony remained unmarred by super-villains or other occupational hazards.

To date, Lois has not expressed any jealousy over the fact that, by necessity, she has to share Superman with the world. Recently, however, Clark and Lois' relationship has come under new strain as Clark deals with work-related stress at the *Daily Planet*. Lois still provides the human grounding the Man of Steel desperately needs.

OFFICE ROMANCE *When Lois first met Clark the air crackled with tension; but eventually mutual competitiveness turned to lasting love.*

SUPER HEROES ARE ESSENTIALLY SOLDIERS, ready to go into battle at a moment's notice and regularly brushing up against death. With this as a backdrop, it's understandable that these amazing superbeings form desperate, passionate, often short-lived liaisons. Although a few relationships belie that stereotype, having lasted for years, tellingly, few steady romances exist where *both* partners are costumed heroes.

GREEN LANTERN AND CAROL FERRIS

The head of Ferris Aircraft, Carol Ferris was first and foremost Hal Jordan's boss, but the cocky test pilot did not let their professional relationship prevent him from striking up a steamy romance. Their connection became increasingly complicated when the Zamarons made Carol their unwitting queen (STAR SAPPHIRE) and pitted her against GREEN LANTERN. Immediately after Hal became the supremely powerful PARALLAX, he shared a final kiss with Carol before sacrificing his life to reignite Earth's sun.

NIGHTWING AND ORACLE

Dick Grayson, as ROBIN, fell for Barbara Gordon early in her career as BATGIRL, calling her the "first person to make my heart sing." Mutual affection soon led to passion, though the only thing that remained consistent in their relationship was the inconsistency of their on-again, off-again romance. Their love survived Barbara's paralysing injury by the JOKER and her subsequent role as ORACLE, but they eventually split up, with Barbara citing Dick's reckless disregard for his own safety as NIGHTWING as the cause. Yet how long can Nightwing and Oracle ignore their destiny?

BLACK CANARY AND GREEN ARROW

Dinah Lance and Oliver Queen are two of the world's most outspoken heroes. She is a brash self-promoter. He is a blunt liberal activist. Their strong personalities seem to draw them irresistibly together—for passionate arguments or for passionate kisses. They toured the U.S. on a cross-country road trip and still team up on the occasional mission, riding tandem on a motorcycle. It's amazing they can ever agree on a route!

ANIMAL MAN

Suburban super hero Buddy Baker led the perfect family life with his wife, Ellen. High-school sweethearts, Buddy and Ellen raised two children, Cliff and Maxine, in between Buddy's adventuring stints as ANIMAL MAN. Eventually his powers overtook his life, causing him to start his own religion based on animal-power. This placed severe strain on Buddy's relationship with Ellen.

THE FLASH AND LINDA PARK
Remarkable among super-heroic romances for its permanence, the marriage between Wally West (FLASH III) and Linda Park (see PARK, LINDA) echoes the bond between Wally's mentor Barry Allen (FLASH II) and Barry's wife, Iris (see ALLEN, IRIS). Linda maintained her own identity (formerly a TV reporter, now a medical student) and did not allow her husband's career as Keystone City's protector to overshadow her goal of starting a family. The couple's greatest happiness came when Linda announced she was pregnant with twins. Tragically, the super-villain ZOOM stole their future when his attack caused Linda to miscarry. The couple must now rebuild their relationship without any super-heroic complications.

SUPERBOY AND WONDER GIRL
These two powerful teens have tried to push away their troubles by seeking comfort in each other's arms. SUPERBOY wrestles with the knowledge that he is a clone created with DNA extracted from Superman and Lex Luthor (see LUTHOR, LEX). WONDER GIRL strives to live up to the high expectations of her mother, top archaeologist Helen Sandsmark, her mentor WONDER WOMAN, and the entire pantheon of OLYMPIAN GODS. A stolen kiss atop San Francisco's Titans Tower typified the way outside pressures seemed determined to cut this young romance short. Wonder Woman, determined to control all outside influences on Cassie Sandsmark's life (including Superboy's affections), yanked Superboy off the roof in mid-smooch and launched him a quarter-mile over San Francisco bay!

BATMAN AND CATWOMAN
The Dark Knight and the Feline Fatale have enjoyed an ongoing flirtation for years, spurred by CATWOMAN's playfulness and the professional attraction between the two best rooftop adventurers in Gotham. When the villain known as Hush united BATMAN's worst foes in a crusade of vengeance, Catwoman joined her rival in a partnership that soon led to romance. Unfortunately, Batman is an expert at everything except relationships. His suspicious nature led him to question Catwoman's motives, and the two coldly parted ways... for now. DW

PLAYING CATCH-UP *Batman and Catwoman's passion is fueled by death-defying pursuits through the Gotham night. It is not always clear who is chasing whom.*

RAG DOLL II

FIRST APPEARANCE VILLAINS UNITED #1 (March 2005)
STATUS Villain **REAL NAME** Unrevealed
OCCUPATION Professional criminal **BASE** Mobile
HEIGHT 5ft 11in **WEIGHT** 120 lbs **EYES** Green **HAIR** None
SPECIAL POWERS/ABILITIES Double-jointed contortionist achieved through extensive surgery; expert grappler.

CONTORTIONIST *Rag Doll's amazing flexibility makes him a versatile combatant who is often fatally underestimated by opponents.*

The second Rag Doll is the son of the original Rag Doll, but did not inherit his father's double-jointedness. Desperate for parental approval, he underwent surgery that replaced his joints with 360-degree sockets, damaging his skin to such a degree that he now needs to lubricate it every day to prevent splitting.

As Rag Doll II, he joined the new SECRET SIX that arose prior to the Infinite Crisis, running missions

SENSITIVE SKIN *The modifications Rag Doll II has made to his body have left his scarred skin brittle and prone to tearing.*

against the Society (*see* VILLAINS UNITED) on behalf of the mysterious MOCKINGBIRD. Rag Doll also shared a relationship with his teammate Parademon, who enjoyed the laughter triggered by this strange "clown."

During a final battle with the Society, Rag Doll II briefly faced his father, before Parademon sacrificed himself to allow the Secret Six to escape. Rag Doll II remained with the team. He immediately found himself at odds with a new recruit, the MAD HATTER, believing that the Hatter had usurped his role as the team's "dandy freak." **DW**

RAGMAN

FIRST APPEARANCE RAGMAN 1st series #1 (September 1976)
STATUS Hero **REAL NAME** Rory Regan
OCCUPATION Defender of the weak **BASE** Gotham City
HEIGHT 5ft 11in **WEIGHT** 165 lbs **EYES** Blue **HAIR** Brown
SPECIAL POWERS/ABILITIES Costume grants superhuman strength, speed, agility, and the ability to float on air. It claims the souls of the wicked by engulfing them within the Ragman's tatters.

To protect themselves from persecution, the Jews of 16th century Prague animated a soulless Golem from river clay. Wary of the monster they created, the Council of Rabbis decreed that the Golem should be replaced with a human defender. The Rabbis chose rags to clothe their new champion who, like the Golem, was empowered by a verse in the Kaballah. Thus, the "Ragman" was first woven to guard over the Warsaw Ghetto. During World War II, Jerzy Reganiewicz took up the patchwork mantle of Ragman to protect Warsaw's Jews from the Nazis. Tragically, Jerzy failed to spare his people from the horrors of the Holocaust. Years later, Jerzy (renamed Gerry Regan after emigrating to the U.S.) passed down the Ragman's suit to his son, Rory, who first wore it to defend the oppressed denizens of Gotham City's slums. From his "Rags 'n' Tatters" junk shop, Rory continues to add new rags to the garish garment of the "Tattered Tatterdemalion," Ragman. Ragman joined the SHADOWPACT prior to the infinite Crisis, fighting the maddened SPECTRE alongside his teammates and spending a year trapped inside a mystical sphere encasing Riverrock, Wyoming. **SB**

RAJAK, COLONEL

FIRST APPEARANCE ADVENTURES OF SUPERMAN #590 (May 2001)
STATUS Villain **REAL NAME** Ehad Rajak
OCCUPATION Dictator **BASE** Bialya
HEIGHT 5ft 6in **WEIGHT** 155 lbs **EYES** Blue **HAIR** Black
SPECIAL POWERS/ABILITIES No superpowers, but a charismatic and willful commander who leads an army of fanatical followers.

The African country of Bialya has seen its share of iron-fisted leaders come and go. After Rajak evicted Sumaan Harjavti (*see* HARJAVTI, RUMAAN AND SUMAAN) from power, the Colonel took control of Bialya and perpetuated the anti-American stance for which the country had become well known. Bialy remains under economic sanctions from the U. S., which does not help the political situation. President

Luthor (*see* LUTHOR, LEX) asked SUPERMAN to help rescue *Newstime* journalist Andrew Finch, hoping to avoid direct military intervention. Finch, however, was a C.I.A. assassin working under Luthor's orders. Superman rescued Finch but stopped him eliminating Rajak. The strongman remains a threat to the Middle East peace process and has a personal score to settle with Luthor. **RG**

RAMULUS

FIRST APPEARANCE WORLD'S FINEST #6 (Summer, 1942)
STATUS Villain **REAL NAME** Unknown
OCCUPATION Scientist **BASE** The Magic Forest, upstate New York
HEIGHT 6ft 3in **WEIGHT** 185 lbs **EYES** White **HAIR** Green
SPECIAL POWERS/ABILITIES Can control vegetation with his mind, specifically giant vines, his so-called Tendrils of Terror.

Originally committing crimes under the name Nightshade, the green-skinned Ramulus created mechanized, murdering plants to terrorize his victims in a "magic forest" in upstate New York. In 1942, Wesley Dodds, the SANDMAN, and his protégé, Sandy the Golden Boy, ran afoul of Nightshade when the villain kidnapped the parents of one of Sandy's friends. While Sandman and Sandy rescued the kidnapped couple, Nightshade lost control over his electronic plants and was seemingly murdered by them, while his "magic forest" burned to the ground.

Miraculously surviving, Nightshade was discovered by the Aztec priestess NYOLA. Given greater control over his technological flora, and the ability to mentally manipulate living vegetation, Nightshade changed his name to Ramulus and joined Nyola's MONSTER SOCIETY OF EVIL. **PJ**

RĀ'S AL GHŪL

FIRST APPEARANCE BATMAN #232 (June 1971)
STATUS Villain (deceased) **REAL NAME** Unknown
OCCUPATION International terrorist **BASE** Mobile **HEIGHT** 6ft 5in
WEIGHT 215 lbs **EYES** Blue **HAIR** Gray with white streaks
SPECIAL POWERS/ABILITIES A master swordsman and ruthless hand-to-hand combatant, Rā's al Ghūl has lived for many centuries, amassing great wealth and power, as well as a treasure trove of knowledge, during his near-eternal existence.

ALTHOUGH NOT TRULY IMMORTAL, the international terrorist Rā's al Ghūl was one of the most long-lived men on the planet. In Arabic, his name translates as "The Demon's Head," a fitting sobriquet for someone so sinister. Rā's al Ghūl's primary purpose during his extended life was to restore the Earth's ecological balance. Unfortunately, this seemingly altruistic goal led to him committing global genocide to reduce mankind's polluting numbers.

ECO-TERRORIST

For centuries, Rā's al Ghūl maintained his existence by periodically immersing himself in "Lazarus Pits," pools filled with an alchemical mix of acids and poisons excavated above the electromagnetic ley lines crisscrossing the Earth. Following his emergence from the liquid in the Lazarus Pits Rā's al Ghūl would, for a short time, be consumed with insane fury. For this reason, Rā's demanded solitude when rejuvenating himself.

Rā's al Ghūl's schemes to restore Earth to an Eden-like splendor have been thwarted time and again by BATMAN. The Dark Knight first met the enigmatic eco-terrorist when Rā's al Ghūl, desiring an heir for his crime empire, kidnapped ROBIN in an attempt to coerce the Dark Knight into marrying his daughter, TALIA. Naturally, Batman refused, and although he had deep feelings for the beautiful Talia, he continued to oppose Rā's al Ghūl schemes.

Rā's al Ghūl's most ambitious attacks upon humanity occurred with his creation of the Ebola Gulf-A plague that decimated the population of Gotham City. This plague, dubbed the "Clench" due to its victims' writhing ends, was halted by the Dark Knight and his squires, who later learned that Rā's al Ghūl had deciphered the virus's genetic code from an ancient "Wheel of Plagues." With it, Rā's al Ghūl would have unleashed even more virulent contagions if not for the intervention of the Bat-Family.

Rā's al Ghūl continued to seek a suitable heir, even considering the musclebound terrorist Bane, before Talia spurned this potential suitor. The dejected Bane then set about sabotaging Rā's al Ghūl's Lazarus Pits to get revenge.

LAZARUS PITS Like a macabre fountain of youth, these fiery pits sustained Rā's al Ghūl incredible vim and vigor.

MASTER SCHEMER Not content with making Batman's life miserable, the Demon's Head has involved other super heroes, including the Man of Steel, in his "world-saving" plots.

BODYGUARD Ubu shadows every move Rā's makes. Ubus are chosen in mortal combat matches and will give their lives to protect the Demon's Head.

SWORDPLAY A renowned swordsman with centuries of fighting experience, Rā's has challenged Batman to duels on many occasions in order to put the Dark Knight's mettle to the test.

DAUGHTER DEAREST Nyssa succeeded where others could not, ending the long life of the Demon's Head!

Meanwhile, Rā's al Ghūl created worldwide anarchy with his devastating "Tower of Babel," which rendered all languages unintelligible until the JUSTICE LEAGUE OF AMERICA destroyed it. Talia left her father's side soon after, hired by Lex Luthor (see LUTHOR, LEX) to run his company LexCorp.

Other challengers to Rā's's throne emerged, including his second daughter Nyssa, who killed her father and attempted to take over his worldwide empire. But Rā's al Ghūl did not stay dead for long. Brought back in the body of a decaying corpse, he tried to transfer his soul into the body of Damian, the young son of Batman and Talia. Thwarted, he instead inhabited of the form of his estranged son, the White Ghost. **SB**

KEY STORYLINES

• *BATMAN #232 (JUNE 1971):* Rā's al Ghūl makes his first appearance, kidnapping the Boy Wonder to force Batman to do his bidding!
• *DETECTIVE COMICS #700 (AUGUST 1996):* As the multipart "Legacy" storyline begins, Rā's al Ghūl uses the ancient Wheel of Plagues, responsible for Gotham City's Clench outbreak, to unleash an even worse contagion!
• *BATMAN: DEATH AND THE MAIDENS #1-9 (OCTOBER 2003–JUNE 2004):* Nyssa, daughter of Rā's al Ghūl, plots her father's demise in order to take over his worldwide criminal empire! Is this the end for the Demon's Head, or the beginning of another villainous dynasty?

RAVEN

FIRST APPEARANCE DC COMICS PRESENTS #26 (October 1980)
STATUS Heroic victim of evil **REAL NAME** Raven
OCCUPATION Adventurer **BASE** Mobile
HEIGHT 5ft 11in **WEIGHT** 139 lbs **EYES** Blue **HAIR** Black
SPECIAL POWERS/ABILITIES Raven has empathic and limited
healing abilities in addition to a psychic connection with
all things mystical. In many ways, still an innocent and
susceptible to overwhelming mystic forces.

Some time ago, a member of a cult trying to bring
the devil to Earth was raped and made pregnant by
the demon TRIGON. The woman, Arella, joined a
group of pacifists in the sanctuary of Azarath. Nine
months later, she gave birth to a girl she named
Raven. As an adult, Raven approached the JUSTICE
LEAGUE OF AMERICA about the imminent threat of
Trigon but ZATANNA, sensing the Raven's genetic
connection to the demon, urged the JLA to ignore
her warnings. Instead, Raven turned to the TEEN
TITANS. Trigon duly arrived, took control
of Raven, and then of Earth. The Titans
destroyed him… or so they thought.

For several years, Raven had countless
battles with her demon father. Even after he
was killed she was still subject to his cruel
influence. In order to save Raven, her body
was destroyed, leaving her soul-self intact.
BROTHER BLOOD brought her back, and she
used her powers to restore Jericho into a
new body. She also started a romance with
teammate BEAST BOY. RG

DEMON PARENT Raven, daughter of Trigon the
Terrible, has sought to escape his evil influence.

RAVERS, THE

FIRST APPEARANCE SUPERBOY AND THE RAVERS #1 (Sept. 1996)
STATUS Hero team **BASE** The traveling rave Event Horizon
CURRENT MEMBERS AND POWERS
SUPERBOY (LEADER) Flight, superstrength, and invulnerability.
Kaliber Qwardian with shrinking and growing powers.
Aura Possesses powerful magnetic abilities.
Hero Cruz Force field generated from Achilles Vest
Hero H-Dial allows transformation into a super-hero identity
Rex the Wonder Dog Enhanced intelligence.
Sparx Can wield electricity; flight

The Event Horizon was a mobile,
intergalactic party frequented by cliques
of teens invited by club owner Kindred
Marx—the catch was that only those
with superpowers could get in. The
Ravers, led by SUPERBOY, were the most
outrageous of the club's regulars. By
touching their hand-stamps, the Ravers
could teleport to the Event Horizon
from anywhere in the universe.

The Ravers came into conflict
with rival clique Red Shift and the
interdimensional police force InterC.
E.P.T. They also helped HIGHFATHER
of New Genesis foil DARKSEID's
attempts to tap into the

power of the Source. After Raver Half-Life perished in a
battle against the Qwardians of the Anti-Matter universe
(*see* WEAPONERS OF QWARD), Kindred Marx chose to end the
Event Horizon, and most of the Ravers went their
separate ways. DW

THE RAVERS 1) *Hardrock*
2) *Associate member* 3) *Half-Life*
4) *Hero Cruz* 5) *Kaliber*
6) *Aura.*

RAY I, II & III

FIRST APPEARANCE (I) SMASH COMICS #14 (September 1940); (II) THE
RAY #1 (February 1992); (III) DCU BRAVE NEW WORLD (July 2006)
STATUS Heroes **REAL NAMES** (I) "Happy" Terrill; (II) Raymond C.;
(III) Stan Silver Terrill **OCCUPATIONS** (I) Reporter; (II) computer
programmer; (III) Wealthy playboy **BASES** (I) New York City; (II)
Philadelphia; (III) Washington DC **HEIGHTS** (I) 5ft 10.5in; (II) 5ft
10in; (III) 6 ft 1in **WEIGHTS** (I) 165 lbs; (II) 155 lbs; (III) 195lbs
EYES (I) Blue; (II) Green; (III) White **HAIR** (I) blonde; (II) red; (III)
Blond **SPECIAL POWERS/ABILITIES** (I) Absorbs heat, light, electricity;
projects light and electrical blasts; superspeed flight; (II) absorbs
sunlight for power; projects energy blasts; superspeed flight;
rearranges molecular matter; (III) Capable of turning his body into
living light.

SON OF THE FATHER *The second Ray is easily as
powerful as the first. Despite his youth, the Ray
has used his powers as a member of the JLA,
Earth's greatest defenders.*

"Happy" Terrill, a reporter for the *New York Star*,
was caught in an electrical storm while on a story
and pummeled with thousands of volts of electricity.
Instead of killing him, the energy gave the reporter
strange powers. Decades later, Terrill learned that
he'd been deliberately exposed to a genetic "light
bomb" created by research scientist Dr. Dayzl.
Terrill became the Ray, and joined the JUSTICE
SOCIETY OF AMERICA as well as UNCLE SAM'S FREEDOM
FIGHTERS. Terrill's son, Joshua inherited his father's
powers and became his sidekick, Spitfire. After Joshua
accidentally killed his mother, Gayle, Terrill placed him
in suspended animation and retired his Ray identity.
Terrill remarried and his second son Raymond
was also born with his father's potentially deadly
powers. Raymond was a teenager before he was
first exposed to light, which activated his powers.
After serving with YOUNG JUSTICE, Ray II nearly
died during an attack on the Freedom
Fighters during the Infinite Crisis. A third Ray, Stan Silver,
then joined the Freedom Fighters, until Ray Terrill
exposed him as a traitor and took his place. PJ

WAR WOUND *While defending the planet Daxam, the
Ray was nearly sliced in two by a warrior drone!*

RAYMOND, ROY - TV DETECTIVE

FIRST APPEARANCE DETECTIVE COMICS #153 (November 1949)
STATUS Hero **REAL NAME** Roy Raymond
OCCUPATION Television host (retired) **BASE** Metropolis
HEIGHT 5ft 10.5in **WEIGHT** 175 lbs **EYES** Blue **HAIR** Brown
SPECIAL POWERS/ABILITIES Though marked by age, Raymond once possessed a brilliant analytical mind. He was an average hand-to-hand combatant when push came to shove.

Roy Raymond found fame as host of the *Impossible—But True!* television series, a forum for revealing the strange and weird from all over the world. Debunking hoaxes on the show earned Raymond the title "TV Detective." Raymond's deductive skill was put to the test in many adventures; he often aided the police, and was usually accompanied by his fetching assistant, Karen Colby. Raymond eventually retired after a horrifying encounter with the "Wild Thing," a crazed creature grown by the SWAMP THING to become Earth's next plant elemental. Raymond's son, Roy Raymond, Jr. (or a young man claiming to be so), continues the family legacy with his own "true crime" reality series. However, the youthful Raymond lacks his father's good looks and keen intellect. **SB**

GHOSTBUSTER *Roy Raymond (right) rumbles yet another phoney phantom.*

RED BEE

FIRST APPEARANCE HIT COMICS #1 (July 1940)
STATUS Hero (deceased) **REAL NAME** Richard Raleigh
OCCUPATION Assistant District Attorney **BASE** Superior City
HEIGHT 5ft 9.5in **WEIGHT** 147 lbs **EYES** Blue **HAIR** Reddish-blond
SPECIAL POWERS/ABILITIES An amazing beekeeper, training them to aid him in his fight against crime; also developed a special stinger gun that stunned criminals.

Assistant District Attorney Richard Raleigh became the costumed crime fighter Red Bee in Superior City, Oregon in the 1940s. He believed that taking direct action was the only way to ensure that justice was done during this dark time in American history. In his first case as the Red Bee, he took on the city's political machine, and brought down its corrupt leader, "Boss" Storm. Raleigh's main crime-fighting asset was his trained swarm of bees; his favorite was named Michael and kept in his belt buckle for special needs. Red Bee was later recruited to join the ALL-STAR SQUADRON as the U.S. was plunged into World War II. The Apis Avenger, as he was nicknamed, appreciated being surrounded by his costumed colleagues although he recognized he was outpowered by most of them. Still, he fought with bravery, something recalled by surviving teammates years later. He survived at least into 1944 as a member of the FREEDOM FIGHTERS. His grandniece Jenna is the newest Red Bee, possessing insectoid powers that nearly destroyed the Freedom Fighters. **RG**

RED HOOD

FIRST APPEARANCE (historical) DETECTIVE COMICS #168 (February 1951)
STATUS Anti-hero **REAL NAME** Jason Todd
OCCUPATION Vigilante **BASE** Gotham City
HEIGHT 6ft **WEIGHT** 225 lbs **EYES** Blue **HAIR** Black
SPECIAL POWERS/ABILITIES Skilled acrobat, gymnast, and hand-to-hand combatant.

The Red Hood first appeared decades ago as the head of the Red Hood gang. What police didn't realize was that a different thug wore the costume each time, to create the illusion that the gang's actions had been coordinated by a mastermind. When the man who would later become the JOKER donned the suit during a botched raid on a chemical plant, he fell into a vat of toxins and emerged with his skin bleached chalk-white.

Many years later, the Red Hood appeared again as the alter-ego of Jason Todd, the second ROBIN. The Joker had murdered Todd, but the reality warping events surrounding the Infinite Crisis returned him to life as an embittered and vengeful adult. As the Red Hood, Todd took out his anger on the Joker and triggered a Gotham gang war that practically ruined the holdings of BLACK MASK.

Todd retired the Red Hood identity prior to the Final Crisis. After a visit to the parallel world of Earth-51, he assumed the name and costume of Red Robin. **DW**

RED PANZER

FIRST APPEARANCE WONDER WOMAN (1st series) #228 (February 1977)
STATUS Villain **REAL NAME** Helmut Streicher
OCCUPATION Super-villain **BASE** Mobile
HEIGHT 6ft **WEIGHT** 190 lbs **EYES** Blue **HAIR** Brown
SPECIAL POWERS/ABILITIES Powered warsuit can withstand most damage and fire energy blasts; also provides limited resistance to damage.

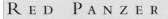

Helmut Streicher, a general in the German army during World War II, developed an armored warsuit in order to prevent a vision of the Third Reich's defeat that he had witnessed through a time scanner coming true. Battling the JUSTICE SOCIETY OF AMERICA under the name Red Panzer, Streicher found his most vexing opponent to be HIPPOLYTA, who served as WONDER WOMAN throughout the war.

Streicher died after Adolf Hitler's defeat, but the Red Panzer cast such a long shadow that no less than three successors have since worn his armor. Red Panzer II was a neo-Nazi who perished in battle with the current Wonder Woman and TROIA.

The third Red Panzer got his start while still a teenager, after his father murdered his mother for perceived imperfections in her genetic history. Raised in foster homes with his father behind bars, the young man assumed a new identity as Red Panzer III, though he constantly battled with self-loathing, knowing that his blood was not 100% Aryan. Red Panzer III joined VANDAL SAVAGE's villainous team TARTARUS, but he died at the hands of the leader of the H.I.V.E. syndicate (see H.I.V.E. and DARHK, DAMIEN).

Vandal Savage hired a new Tartarus member to wear the crimson armor, and Red Panzer IV is still active today on the island nation of Zandia. **DW**

RED STAR

FIRST APPEARANCE TEEN TITANS (1st series) #18 (December 1968)
STATUS Hero **REAL NAME** Leonid Kovar
OCCUPATION Scientist; adventurer **BASE** Russian Federation
HEIGHT 5ft 10in **WEIGHT** 180 lbs **EYES** Green **HAIR** Blond
SPECIAL POWERS/ABILITIES Kovar possesses superhuman strength and endurance; his body can turn into white hot flame.

Leonid Kovar and his father discovered a derelict spacecraft in the Yenesi River. The teenaged Leonid was bathed in alien energies emanating from the craft, giving him superpowers. Leonid became the first Russian super hero, Starfire. He met the TEEN TITANS on more than one occasion, clashing with their most conservative member, Wally West, Kid Flash (see FLASH III). Even after Starfire's fiancée was infected with a deadly virus by an insane Russian official, Leonid remained committed to his country's communist ideals and became Red Star.

Red Star was part of an information exchange on metahuman development between the U.S. and Russian governments. The exchange was sabotaged by HAMMER & SICKLE, and Red Star's communist beliefs were sorely tested. When JERICHO took control of the WILDEBEEST Society and attacked the Titans, Red Star joined forces with his former adversaries. Red Star later "adopted" fellow Titans PANTHA and Wildebeest, relocating their family unit to Science City, Russia. After Superboy-Prime killed Pantha and Wildebeest during the Infinite Crisis, Red Star became Russia's elite State Protector. **PJ**

RED TORNADO

FIRST APPEARANCE JUSTICE LEAGUE OF AMERICA #17 (February 1963)
STATUS Hero **REAL NAME** John Smith
OCCUPATION Adventurer
BASE Happy Harbor, Rhode Island
HEIGHT 6ft 1in **WEIGHT** 325 lbs
EYES None **HAIR** None
SPECIAL POWERS/ABILITIES Can generate cyclones; has demonstrated limited control over the weather.

REBUILT Red Tornado gets a new, post-Crisis, android body, courtesy of Prof. Ivo.

Inspired by the "Mystery Men" of the 1940s, "Ma" Hunkel became the cooking pot-wearing crime fighter known as the Red Tornado and fought New York City's protection rackets and thugs, usually in defense of her children, Sisty and Huey, as well as their cousins Dinky and Scribbly. After living for years under the F.B.I.'s Witness Protection Program, Ma was welcomed by the JUSTICE SOCIETY OF AMERICA into its fold and made curator of the JSA Museum.

The second Red Tornado was originally the Tornado Tyrant from the planet Rann, a living cyclone that journeyed to Earth and found its sentience infused within an android body created by the renegade scientist T.O. MORROW to destroy the JUSTICE LEAGUE OF AMERICA. Fortunately, Red Tornado turned on his creator and joined the JLA. The heroic android called himself John Smith, married Kathy Sutton, and adopted the orphan girl Traya. Red Tornado sacrificed his android body in the line of duty, reconstituting himself as Earth's Air Elemental. After serving as a mentor to YOUNG JUSTICE, the Red Tornado exploded during the Infinite Crisis. Rebuilt, he became a pawn in a scheme involving PROFESSOR IVO and SOLOMON GRUNDY. **SB/DW**

REPLICANT

FIRST APPEARANCE THE FLASH SECRET FILES #2 (November 1999)
STATUS Villain **REAL NAME** Anthony Gambi
OCCUPATION Criminal **BASE** Central City
HEIGHT 7ft 5in **WEIGHT** 325 lbs **EYES** Mirrored **HAIR** None
SPECIAL POWERS/ABILITIES Can imitate other superpowers; projection of ice, flame; weather control.

Anthony Gambi, an orphan raised by his uncle Paul in Central City, befriended several members of the FLASH's Rogues Gallery when the villains came to the Gambi tailor shop for costumes and supplies. The Rogues took the young Anthony as a sort of ward, teaching him various tricks and becoming his surrogate family.

After CAPTAIN BOOMERANG was nearly killed during a battle with a new Flash, the Australian villain gathered the Rogues together in order to create a new super-villain capable of stopping this ruthless incarnation of the Fastest Man Alive. Volunteering for the job, Anthony was quickly transformed with various technologies into the Replicant, a villain who could manifest any of the Rogues' superpowers. The Replicant quickly became the most dangerous foe of the new Flash, who was in fact a version of Wally West from an alternate timeline. **PJ**

RED TORPEDO

FIRST APPEARANCE CRACK COMICS #1 (May 1940)
STATUS Hero **REAL NAME** James Lockhart
OCCUPATION Adventurer **BASE** Mobile
HEIGHT 5ft 8in **WEIGHT** 170 lbs **EYES** Blue **HAIR** Black
SPECIAL POWERS/ABILITIES Lockhart's Red Torpedo could not only travel move below the sea's surface, but also float on it and fly in the sky..

Based on an island in the South Seas, former Navy captain James Lockhart created a navigable torpedo capable of flight and became the Red Torpedo, scourge of saboteurs and Nazis. The Red Torpedo's worst foe was the Black Shark. On December 6, 1941 UNCLE SAM organized the FREEDOM FIGHTERS in a doomed attempt to turn back the Japanese attack on Pearl Harbor. Red Torpedo was one of several heroes captured by the Japanese. He was ultimately freed and returned stateside, hanging up his mask. Years later, Lockhart was asked by DOCTOR MIDNIGHT I to built a hovercraft during his time as STARMAN II. Lockhart now administers the Windward Home facility, sometimes used by AQUAMAN. **RG**

SUPER SUB James Lockhart and his creation, the armored, powerful Red Torpedo.

RELATIVE HEROES

FIRST APPEARANCE RELATIVE HEROES #1 (March 2000)
STATUS Hero team **BASE** Mobile
CURRENT MEMBERS AND POWERS
HOUSTON (LEADER) No superhuman abilities.
Temper Can control electricity.
Allure Possesses magically-based persuasive abilities.
Blindside Has the power of invisibility.
Omni Can imitate the superpowers of those around him.

Orphaned by a car crash, the superpowered Weinberg children embarked on a road trip in search of SUPERMAN—an odyssey that became the inaugural adventure of the Relative Heroes.

Police, child welfare officers, and DEO agents pursued the Relative Heroes team, which consisted of oldest brother Joel (Houston), younger sister Aviva (Temper), her babysitter Damara Sinclaire (Allure), and the Weinberg's adopted brothers Tyson Gilford (Blindside) and Cameron Begay (Omni). When the troupe reached Metropolis, the scientists of S.T.A.R. Labs revealed that Omni came from alien stock. The Relative Heroes convinced Omni's people to let him stay on Earth.

The Relative Heroes chose not to become full-time super heroes, but they remain potential players for the future. **DW**

KEY
1) Blindside **2)** Houston **3)** Allure **4)** Temper **5)** Omni

RESURRECTION MAN

FIRST APPEARANCE RESURRECTION MAN #1 (March 1997)
STATUS Hero **REAL NAME** Mitchell "Mitch" Shelley
OCCUPATION Former lawyer; adventurer **BASE** Mobile
HEIGHT 6ft 1in **WEIGHT** 190 lbs **EYES** Brown **HAIR** White
SPECIAL POWERS/ABILITIES An immortal champion imbued with
new superpowers each time he is reborn; his distinctive coat
and hat are remade by the tektites when damaged.

HEROIC PATHS
*Despite not considering himself a costumed
champion, Mitch Shelley has sided with Supergirl and other
heroes while attempting to recover his lost memories.*

Mitch Shelley is an immortal man,
and for a brief time believed he was
the IMMORTAL MAN, imbued with
eternal life after exposure to the same
meteor that created the villain VANDAL
SAVAGE. In truth, Shelley was lawyer,
experimented upon by the Lab, a
clandestine organization that injected
tektites—microscopic nanobots—into his bloodstream. With the tektites rebuilding his body each time
he died, Shelley possessed the closest thing to immortality. Moreover, the tektites also imbued him
with a different superpower each time he was resurrected. At first, Shelley suffered from amnesia
and traveled the U.S. in search of his lost memory while helping those in need. In the course of his
adventures, he fought AMAZO, the BODY DOUBLES, and other threats while making the acquaintances
of the JUSTICE LEAGUE OF AMERICA, SUPERGIRL and other costumed heroes. Shelley ultimately
discovered that he was not the Immortal Man,
although he did come into conflict with Vandal
Savage and, as has been revealed, will continue to
battle Savage through many lives and deaths well
into the 853rd century. In the present, however,
Shelley joined forces with the true Immortal
Man to stop Savage from obtaining the Temporal
Meteor. Mitch Shelley made a temporary home for
himself in Viceroy, South Carolina with the love of
this life, private eye Kim Rebecki. **SB**

GHOST OF A CHANCE *Resurrection Man tries to give
a suddenly intangible Supergirl a helping hand.*

REVERSE-FLASH

FIRST APPEARANCE FLASH (1st series) #139 (September 1963)
STATUS Villain (deceased) **REAL NAME** Eobard Thawne
OCCUPATION Super-villain **BASE** 25th century Central City
HEIGHT 5ft 11in **WEIGHT** 179 lbs **EYES** Blue **HAIR** Reddish-blonde
SPECIAL POWERS/ABILITIES Could run at near-light speeds, vibrating
through solid objects or temporal dimensions; though not a skilled
combatant, his brilliant mind led him to use his speed dangerously.

DERANGED
*The Reverse-Flash was
a menace to everyone
he encountered.*

The evil Reverse-Flash, also known as Professor Zoom,
hailed from the far future of the 25th century. Eobard
Thawne became obsessed with the 20th century's second
and most prominent FLASH, Barry Allen, even going so far
as to try to duplicate his incredible powers. He found one
of the Flash's old costumes in a time capsule and the suit's
residual Speed Force energy provided the boost he needed.
Now possessed of superspeed, Thawne traveled back five centuries
to meet his idol but arrived several years after Allen's death during
the Crisis (see Great Battles, pp. 362–3). Conclusive evidence Thawne
discovered in a museum stating that he would one day become the evil
Reverse-Flash sent Thawne into psychological shock, and he briefly
posed as a resurrected Barry Allen before returning to his own time.

Thawne now harbored a hatred of Barry Allen. He dyed his costume
in opposite-spectrum colors and returned to the 20th century as
Professor Zoom, the Reverse-Flash. His attempts to win the heart
of Barry Allen's wife, Iris (see ALLEN, IRIS), failed dismally, so a bitter
Thawne apparently murdered her. Barry Allen sent his nemesis
into another dimension, but Thawne returned to menace Allen's
new fiancée, Fiona Webb. This time, Allen accidentally killed the
Reverse-Flash by snapping his neck. In the aftermath, Barry Allen
was acquitted of manslaughter and Iris Allen revealed that she had
survived as a citizen of the 30th century. **DW**

MEASURING UP *A fixation on
Barry Allen quickly drove
Thawne mad.*

RIDDLER, THE

PRINCE OF PUZZLERS

FIRST APPEARANCE DETECTIVE COMICS #140 (October 1948)
STATUS Villain **REAL NAME** Edward Nigma (née Nashton)
OCCUPATION Professional criminal **BASE** Gotham City
HEIGHT 6ft 1in **WEIGHT** 183 lbs **EYES** Blue **HAIR** Black
SPECIAL POWERS/ABILITIES Brilliant in his own twisted way, but a poor hand-to-hand fighter. His addiction to leaving "enigmatic" clues to his crimes for Batman always proves his undoing.

EDWARD NIGMA'S SCHOOLTEACHER once held a contest to see which one of her pupils could assemble a puzzle the fastest. Little Edward secretly photographed the assembled puzzle, which he had found in the teacher's desk, and studied its formation so he could easily win. After this event, puzzles became his life. Failing in school, he took a job as a carnival barker, running a rigged puzzle booth. From there, it was only a matter of time before he turned to crime full-time as one of Gotham City's most famous rogues, the Riddler.

ASKING THE QUESTIONS

The Riddler seemed psychologically incapable of committing a crime without first posing a riddle to BATMAN or the G.C.P.D. An admirer of the late, great escape artist Harry Houdini, the Riddler's tangled traps display a similar flair for showmanship. For years, he was considered a second-rate criminal, meeting defeat not only at the Dark Knight's hands, but also in matches against the ELONGATED MAN, FLASH, GREEN ARROW, BLACK CANARY, and the QUESTION. Recently, however, he has shown a more dangerous side, which seems to have attracted a score of followers. He is usually accompanied by Diedre Vance and Nina Damfino, known as Query and Echo, who handle the rough stuff.

The Riddler was eventually diagnosed with terminal cancer, setting him on his most deadly path yet. He found one of RA¯'s AL GHU¯L's Lazarus Pits and healed himself. Hoping to profit from this, he turned to his doctor, Philadelphia physician Thomas Elliot. Many years before, Elliot had tried to kill his parents but Thomas Wayne (Bruce Wayne's father) had saved Elliot's mother's life. Elliott hated the Waynes for spoiling his childhood plot and conspired with the Riddler to gain revenge on Batman. Thus began an involved scheme organized and planned by the Riddler, who learned Batman's identity in the process. The Riddler spent most of the year following the Infinite Crisis in a coma, recuperating from injuries sustained in the fight. When he awoke he had lost much of his memory, including his knowledge of Batman's secret identity. He then announced a break from his criminal past, and opened a private detective agency. He has occasionally teamed with Batman to solve cases. **RG**

RIDDLER'S GANG Over the years, the Riddler has used many costumed henchman, mere pawns in his master game.

NO JOKING MATTER Out for only himself, the Riddler has crossed many fellow rogues, including Harley Quinn.

RETURN OF HUSH When the Riddler's usefulness seemed at an end, he had good reason to fear the wrath of his former partner, Hush.

TRICKS FOR KICKS The Prince of Puzzlers loved matching wits with the Dynamic Duo.

KEY STORYLINES

- *BATMAN #608–619 (DECEMBER 2003–NOVEMBER 2004):* Paired with Hush, the Riddler set out an elaborate scheme to kill Batman after learning his secret identity.
- *BATMAN #452–454 (AUGUST–SEPTEMBER 1990):* In "Dark Knight, Dark City," the Riddler is possessed by the spirits of Gotham's founders as Batman learns about the city's gruesome beginnings.
- *SECRET ORIGINS SPECIAL (1989):* How Edward Nigma turned from cheater to master criminal.
- *THE QUESTION #26 (MARCH 1989):* Fleeing Gotham for Hub City, the Riddler wants to make a clean start, but fails once again.

REX, THE WONDER DOG

FIRST APPEARANCE THE ADVENTURES OF REX, THE WONDER DOG #1 (February 1952) **STATUS** Hero **REAL NAME** Rex
OCCUPATION Soldier; intergalactic Raver **BASE** Mobile
HEIGHT 2ft 8in **WEIGHT** 80 lbs **EYES** Blue **HAIR** White
SPECIAL POWERS/ABILITIES Incredibly intelligent, he can communicate with animals and humans alike.

Rex the Wonder Dog was adopted as a puppy by Danny Dennis, a young boy living in Libertyville during World War II. Danny's father, a lieutenant in the U.S. Army, volunteered Rex for a series of experiments being conducted by Doctor Anabolus. These experiments transformed Rex, transforming the little pup into a full-sized, superintelligent dog. Doctor Anabolus was killed soon after by Nazi agents, but Rex escaped and became a distinguished soldier during both World War II and the Korean War.

Danny grew up and joined the military himself, following in his father's footsteps. Together, the boy and his dog traveled the world, helping to defend the innocent. After drinking from the Fountain of Youth along with Bobo the DETECTIVE CHIMP, Rex became eternally spry, and eventually joined the intergalactic rave party known as the Event Horizon (*see* RAVERS, THE). Rex then joined the U.S. government's Bureau of Amplified Animals, and has helped the SHADOWPACT. recover the Seven Deadly Sins in Gotham City after the Rock of Eternity's destruction. **PJ**

FISTS OF FURY *Four massive arms double the danger posed by the Apokoliptian menace known as Rip Roar!*

RIDDLER, THE SEE OPPOSITE PAGE

RIOT

FIRST APPEARANCE SUPERMAN: THE MAN OF STEEL #61 (Oct. 1996)
STATUS Villain **REAL NAME** Frederick Legion
OCCUPATION Super-criminal **BASE** Metropolis
HEIGHT 5ft 10in **WEIGHT** 145 lbs **EYES** Black **HAIR** Black
SPECIAL POWERS/ABILITIES Can create multiple duplicates of himself and reintegrate the copies at will.

Overworked at a high-tech laboratory, Frederick Legion decided that the only way he could complete all his experiments would be if there were somehow two Fredericks. Inspired, he stole a temporal phase shifter and plucked copies of himself from alternate microseconds in the timestream. He soon learned to duplicate without the aid of machinery, but the physical stress drove him mad and altered his appearance to that of a ghastly skeleton.

Now known as Riot, the multiplying menace clashed repeatedly with SUPERMAN but the Man of Steel's punches only created more Riots. Media mogul Morgan Edge recruited Riot into the Superman Revenge Squad (alongside Anomaly, Barrage, MAXIMA, and Misa), but the team never took off. A year after the Infinite Crisis, Riot and others tried and failed to kill a returning Superman. **DW**

MULTIPLICATION *Replicating allows Riot to stand up to the mighty Man of Steel.*

RIP ROAR

FIRST APPEARANCE YOUNG JUSTICE #2 (September 1998)
STATUS Villain **REAL NAME** None
OCCUPATION Warrior **BASE** Formerly Apokolips
HEIGHT 7ft 6in **WEIGHT** 180 lbs
EYES Red **HAIR** Strawberry blond
SPECIAL POWERS/ABILITIES Massively strong; able to project both fire and ice.

Long ago, the four-armed juggernaut Rip Roar was dispatched with his hated rival, KALIBAK the Cruel, to plunder tribute for their master DARKSEID. Rip Roar stole a Super-Cycle (*see* Amazing vehicle, pp. 54–57) from New Genesis, home of the New Gods who opposed Darkseid. Rip Roar bonded with this sentient vehicle and rode roughshod over several worlds in Darkseid's name. Knowing that his father would look kindly on Rip Roar's destructiveness, Kalibak convinced Darkseid's majordomo DESAAD to sabotage Rip Roar's teleporting Boom Tube. Roar wound up entombed inside a mountain on Earth, until he was accidentally freed by YOUNG JUSTICE. After a battle, the teen heroes, buried Rip Roar in lava. The Department of Extranormal Operations (D.E.O.) recovered the warrior, who remains in its custody for now. **SB**

RISING SUN

FIRST APPEARANCE SUPER FRIENDS #8 (November 1977)
STATUS Hero **REAL NAME** Isumi Yasunari
OCCUPATION Doctor; adventurer **BASE** Tokyo, Japan
HEIGHT 5ft 9in **WEIGHT** 165 lbs **EYES** Brown **HAIR** Black
SPECIAL POWERS/ABILITIES Absorbs solar energy and can project, intense heat, light, and flame from his body. He can also generate superheated solar winds and use them to fly at great speeds.

Isumi Yasunari's grandparents were both survivors of the atom bomb dropped on Nagasaki, Japan, by the U.S. in 1945, which brought World War II to an end. Both of Isumi's grandparents later developed cancer and died. Isumi's mother also developed cancer but recovered with chemotherapy. Horrified by the genetic disposition of his family for degenerative disease, Isumi and his brother, Wataru, became doctors specializing in cancer research, while their troubled sister, Kaori, joined a religious cult.

Isumi used his abilities to absorb solar radiation and became Rising Sun, a staunch defender of Japan, who believes his country should take a less pacifistic approach in world affairs. Rising Sun joined the GLOBAL GUARDIANS, serving with them unwaveringly for years. Rising Sun is a notorious flirt and has vigorously pursued a romance with DOCTOR LIGHT II for some time. **PJ**

RISK

FIRST APPEARANCE TEEN TITANS (2nd series) #1 (October 1996)
STATUS Hero **REAL NAME** Cody Driscoll
OCCUPATION Student **BASE** Mobile
HEIGHT 5ft 9in **WEIGHT** 180 lbs **EYES** Blue **HAIR** Blond
SPECIAL POWERS/ABILITIES The result of an alien experiment, Cody is a mutant with superhuman strength, speed, and stamina.

Aliens called the H'san Natall came to Earth and conducted breeding experiments on humans. This resulted in the birth of four children who grew up to develop amazing powers. Their names were ARGENT II (Toni Monetti), JOTO (Isiah Crockett), PRYSM and Risk (Cody Driscoll), and they were eventually gathered together by Mr Jupiter and Omen to form a new incarnation of the TEEN TITANS. The ATOM II joined them at the point in his career when he was returned to his teenage physique. During a series of adventures, they learned of their true natures and tracked down the H'san Natall, which resulted in Prysm and FRINGE remaining in space with them. Risk and Joto choose to remain on Earth, largely forgoing their costumed identities. Risk lost his right arm in battle with Superboy-Prime, and later joined DEATHSTROKE's villainous team of Titans East. **RG**

RISKY BUSINESS *Cody lives life to the fullest, more than living up to his name.*

ROBIN

THE BOY WONDER

DICK GRAYSON (ROBIN I)
FIRST APPEARANCE DETECTIVE COMICS #38 (April 1940)
STATUS Hero **REAL NAME** Richard "Dick" Grayson
OCCUPATION Crime fighter; police officer **BASE** Gotham City
HEIGHT 5ft 10in **WEIGHT** 175 lbs **EYES** Blue **HAIR** Black

JASON TODD (ROBIN II)
FIRST APPEARANCE DETECTIVE COMICS #526 (September 1983)
STATUS Hero (deceased) **REAL NAME** Jason Todd
OCCUPATION Crime fighter; student **BASE** Gotham City
HEIGHT 5ft 2in **WEIGHT** 105 lbs **EYES** Blue **HAIR** Black

TIM DRAKE (ROBIN III)
FIRST APPEARANCE (as Tim Drake) BATMAN #436 (August 1989);
(as Robin) BATMAN #457 (December 1990)
STATUS Hero **REAL NAME** Timothy Drake
OCCUPATION Student; crime fighter **BASE** Gotham City
HEIGHT 5ft 5in **WEIGHT** 125 lbs **EYES** Blue **HAIR** Black
SPECIAL POWERS/ABILITIES
Like the previous Robins, Tim Drake was trained by Batman in
martial arts, as well as sleuthing skills. He is adept in the use of
electronic devices, especially computers. Tim's utility belt carries
the standard complement of Batarangs, gas capsules, de-cel
jumplines, and other tools. His R-insignia doubles as a razor-
sharp shuriken. Robin's costume is lined with Kevlar and Nomex
fabrics, making it bulletproof and fire-resistant. His mask is fitted
with Starlite night-vision lenses. Typically, Robins have ridden
customized Batcycles in their own colors, but Tim prefers his
Redbird, a crime-fighting car second only to the Batmobile.

As a member of the Flying Graysons acrobatic family, young
Dick Grayson thrilled audiences nightly on the high wire
beside his circus aerialist parents. But when gangster
"Boss" Zucco sabotaged the high wire because the owner
of Haly's Circus refused to offer up protection money, the
elder Graysons paid with their lives. Billionaire Bruce
Wayne was in the audience that night; however it was
BATMAN who visited the grieving Dick Grayson, offering
the boy a chance at retribution by becoming Robin, the
Dark Knight's squire in his personal war on crime.

SENSATIONAL DEBUT *The
introduction of Robin brought
a ray of hope to the Dark
Knight's nocturnal vigil.*

DICK GRAYSON
The first Robin was carefully schooled by Batman,
learning all the skills he would need to bring
"Boss" Zucco to justice. Before long,
Dick was ready for action. Swearing
a solemn oath, he joined the Dark
Knight's crusade as his most trusted
partner, Robin the Boy Wonder.
 After several years in service to the Dark
Knight, Grayson—then leader of the TEEN
TITANS—relinquished the mantle of Robin
when Batman forced him to choose between his duties with the
Titans and his promise to aid the Dark Knight. Adopting the
identity of NIGHTWING, Dick continued to battle crime while
remaining Batman's close ally.

BRUCE WAYNE'S WARD
To give the orphaned Dick Grayson a home,
billionaire Bruce Wayne became the boy's
legal guardian. Wayne's trusted valet, Alfred (*see*
PENNYWORTH, ALFRED) was just as much a
surrogate father to Dick as Bruce was. While
the Dark Knight's alter ego trained Dick in
fighting and detective skills to become his
second in the war on crime, Alfred made sure
that Dick kept up with a more "classical"
education. Bruce avoided adopting Dick
because he didn't want to replace Dick's real
father. However, he made Dick his legal heir
in adulthood, and the two are as close as any
father and son could be.

JASON TODD
Batman met juvenile delinquent
and presumed orphan Jason
Todd when the boy literally tried
to steal the tires right off the
Batmobile. With original partner
Dick Grayson having given up the
role of Robin, Batman decided to
take Jason in and offer him both a
home and a purpose. Jason began
the same training regimen Grayson
once undertook to become the Dark
Knight's partner. However, Jason was a troubled soul
who lacked maturity and was quick to anger.

A DEATH IN THE FAMILY
When Jason discovered clues that his long-lost mother was alive,
he secretly travelled to Africa to find her. Tragically, the trail also
led him straight into the clutches of the JOKER, who savagely beat
the second Boy Wonder within an inch of his life. Robin died in
the subsequent explosion, but returned to life years later as a result
of the reality-altering effects of the Infinite Crisis. Now an angry
adult, Jason Todd assumed the identity of the RED HOOD and set to
work eliminating the Gotham gangs. He later joined with Donna Troy
(*see* TROIA) and GREEN LANTERN Kyle Rayner on a search through the
multiverse for Ray Palmer (*see* ATOM, THE).

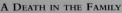

THE DEATH OF ROBIN *Batman cradled Jason in his arms, blaming himself for not
rescuing him in time, consumed with rage at the Joker's latest, cruelest crime.*

Robin's costume carries most of the same crime fighting equipment wielded by his mentor, Batman.

TRAINING With Batman, Nightwing, Batgirl, and Azrael as sparring partners, Robin is prepared for combat with any opponent.

TIM DRAKE

Tim Drake was barely more than a toddler when he sat in the stands at Haly's Circus and watched the Flying Graysons fall to their doom. Tim was transfixed as the Dark Knight swooped down to comfort young Dick Grayson. The moment was burned into his memory. Years later, Tim saw news reports of an unhinged Batman becoming more and more violent following the death of the second Robin, Jason Todd. Using his detective skills, Tim deduced the secret identity of Batman and the first Boy Wonder, Dick Grayson.

MODEL STUDENT Tim went to Brentwood Academy until his father had money trouble. Public education made it easier for Tim to operate as Robin.

THE THIRD ROBIN

After revealing this knowledge to the original Dynamic Duo, Tim argued the need for a Robin to give the Dark Knight hope, especially when faced with a seemingly hopeless and unyielding war on crime. Though reluctant at first, Batman gave Tim the opportunity to prove that he was as good as his word. After months of grueling training, Tim Drake became the third Robin.

It is a job at which Tim excels, despite the constant struggle of balancing his crime-fighting life with the day-to-day battles of just being a teenager. A former member of YOUNG JUSTICE, Tim presently belongs to the latest incarnation of the Teen Titans.

STEPHANIE BROWN

The fourth Robin, Stephanie Brown (see SPOILER), served for a short time after Tim Drake abandoned the job. Fired by Batman due to her lack of experience, Stephanie accidentally triggered a Gotham gang war. BLACK MASK captured and tortured her, and she later died from her injuries.

THE TEEN TITANS

Tim Drake once led Young Justice. This group of teenage heroes disbanded, and members Robin, KID FLASH II, SUPERBOY, and WONDER GIRL II graduated to an all-new incarnation of the TEEN TITANS that includes Titans teammates BEAST BOY, CYBORG, and STARFIRE, all mentors to the less-experienced junior Titans.

- **BATMAN #426-429 (DECEMBER 1988–JANUARY 1989):** While searching for his biological mother, Jason Todd is murdered by the Joker! Batman's resolve is sorely tested as "A Death in the Family" brings terrible tragedy to the Batcave.
- **BATMAN CHRONICLES: THE GAUNTLET (1997):** Dick Grayson's "final exam" to become Batman's partner involves surviving a night alone in Gotham!
- **ROBIN: YEAR ONE #1-4 (OCTOBER 2000–JANUARY 2001):** Dick Grayson's first year as Boy Wonder includes victories against Mad Hatter and Mr. Freeze, but a near-fatal encounter with Two-Face!

ROBOTMAN I

FIRST APPEARANCE STAR-SPANGLED COMICS #7 (April 1942)
STATUS Hero **REAL NAMES** Robert Crane; Charles Grayson
OCCUPATION College professor **BASE** Ivy Town
HEIGHT 6ft 1in **WEIGHT** 487 lbs **EYES** Red **HAIR** None
SPECIAL POWERS/ABILITIES Robot body gives superstrength and increased imperviousness to harm; telescoping arms and legs; torches in fingers; telescopic vision.

Scientists Doctor Robert Crane and his assistant Charles Grayson were working on a mechanical body that could house a human brain. In 1941, Crane was shot by criminals trying to steal his designs, and Grayson transplanted the doctor's brain into the robot body to save him. Crane became Robotman and a member of the ALL-STAR SQUADRON. Lawyer Sam Slattery tried to have Crane declared a robotic menace. In court, Robotman revealed he was Robert Crane and saved Slatterly from a collapsing ceiling. The judge ruled that Robotman was a human being. After his death, Grayson's body was frozen. As per Grayson's wishes, Crane's brain was removed from Robotman and transplanted to Grayson's body. Crane now works as a college professor in Ivy Town. **PJ**

ROBOTMAN II

FIRST APPEARANCE MY GREATEST ADVENTURE #80 (June 1963)
STATUS Hero **REAL NAME** Cliff Steele
OCCUPATION Doom Patrol leader **BASE** Mobile
HEIGHT 6ft 1in **WEIGHT** 295 lbs **EYES** Red **HAIR** None
SPECIAL POWERS/ABILITIES Durable robot body provides enhanced strength and speed; photocellular eyes can see into non-visible wavelengths.

Forever trapped inside a metal body, Cliff Steele has often cursed his life. But beyond the bitterness lies the "never quit" spirit of a natural leader. Cliff Steele has served with every incarnation of the DOOM PATROL since its founding. Steele once enjoyed wealth and fame as a race-car driver until a racing accident shredded his body. Dr. Niles Caulder (see CHIEF, THE) managed to save Steele's brain by transplanting it into a body made of ceramic metal. Steele joined Caulder's new Doom Patrol under the alias Robotman (named after the wartime hero). Later he would learn that Caulder had caused his crash.

After the third Doom Patrol disbanded, Steele's former teammate, Dorothy Spinner (see SPINNER, DOROTHY), accidentally destroyed his body and conjured an illusory Robotman with her mental powers. This non-existent Robotman led the fourth, "corporate" Doom Patrol, though Cliff Steele soon came back in a fresh android form. He is a respected hero and an advisor to the next generation of meta-humans. **DW**

ROCKET RED BRIGADE

FIRST APPEARANCE GREEN LANTERN CORPS #208 (January 1987)
STATUS Hero team **BASE** None; formerly the U.S.S.R.
SPECIAL POWERS/ABILITIES Superstrong armor was equipped with solar-powered propulsion system, super-heated plasma blasters; automatic defenses; electrified net; and magnetic boots; armor made its wearer mecha-empathic, able to control any electronic device.

At the height of the Cold War, Soviet paranoia over the number of American meta-humans prompted the U.S.S.R. to try to create its own super heroes. The Rocket Red initiative would have been a ghastly failure without the alien GREEN LANTERN KILOWOG. With his help, the program successfully increased human soldiers' strength and endurance and outfitted them with high-tech battlesuits. The Rocket Red Brigade was soon participating in the defense of the Soviet Union. An economic crash left the Rocket Reds in rusting disrepair, and the fall of the Soviet Union allowed the Russian mob to take possession of some battlesuits. The Rocket Red Brigade reappeared following the Infinite Crisis, guarding the Russian border against foreign incursion. Captain Maks Chazov, the current Rocket Red, is also the White Queen's Knight in CHECKMATE. **SB**

ROSA, MASTER SPY

FIRST APPEARANCE MEN OF WAR #17 (June 1979)
STATUS Hero **REAL NAME** Unrevealed
OCCUPATION Secret agent (freelance) **BASE** Europe
HEIGHT 5ft 2in **WEIGHT** 105 lbs **EYES** Blue **HAIR** Blond
SPECIAL POWERS/ABILITIES Well trained with pistol, rifle, sword, knife and garrote, in addition to being a master of disguise.

In the latter half of the 19th century, Europe was torn apart by war and revolution. One man fought in the shadow of these upheavals, a man whose true name was unknown, called Rosa, Master Spy. It was rumored that Rosa was a man without a country, born aboard a sailing ship somewhere between America and Europe, his parentage unknown. Some say he was raised by a military man and trained in the arts of personal combat and war.

Whatever the truth, Rosa certainly possessed an encyclopedic knowledge of the world and was also fluent in most European languages. He was an espionage agent for hire by any government as long as the price and the moral issues were right. It has been speculated that Rosa may have been reincarnated as Jack Knight, STARMAN VI. **RG**

SPECIAL AGENT Few could equal Rosa for bravery and resourcefulness in a tight spot.

ROSE AND THORN

FIRST APPEARANCE (I) FLASH COMICS #89 (Nov. 1947); (II) LOIS LANE #105 (Nov. 1970) **STATUS** Villains **REAL NAME** Rose Canton (I); Rhosyn "Rose" Forrest (II) **OCCUPATION** Botanist, criminal (I); enforcer (II) **BASE** Mobile (I); Metropolis (II) **HEIGHT** 5ft 7in (I); 5ft 8in (II) **WEIGHT** 140 lbs (I); 125 lbs (II) **EYES** Green (I); blue, green as Thorn (II) **HAIR** (I) Blonde, red as Thorn; (II) Red **SPECIAL POWERS/ABILITIES** (I) Controls growth of vines; (II) fighter, athlete.

Thorn was a nemesis for Jay Garrick, the original Flash. The Thorn was a manifestation of Rose Canton's split personality. Exposure to a root on the island of Tashmi had made Rose able to control certain types of vegetation, yet she could not direct the Thorn's actions or the timing of her appearances. After a psychological cure, she adopted the identity of Alyx Florin and married GREEN LANTERN Alan Scott. When Thorn threatened to re-emerge, Rose fled. She bore Alan's twins, Todd Rice (OBSIDIAN) and Jennifer-Lynn Hayden (JADE), then had them adopted. When the struggle against Thorn became too much, Rose Canton killed herself.

The current Rose and Thorn is unconnected to Rose Canton. Rhosyn Forrest was the daughter of Metropolis police detective Phil Forrest, who fell in the line of duty at the hands of the criminal collective called the 100. The teenaged Rhosyn spent time in a mental institution where Dr. Chritlow urged her to create an alternate "Thorn" identity to contain violent thoughts. Upon release her Thorn alter-ego became a costumed vigilante, battling the 100. After the 100 morphed into the 1000 she continued her raids, becoming a thorn in the syndicate's side. **DW**

THORNY PROBLEMS Rose Canton lashes out.

SADISTIC SEDUCTRESS Rose Forrest's alter ego Thorn allows her to revel in pleasure and pain.

ROSS, PETE

FIRST APPEARANCE SUPERBOY #86 (January 1961)
STATUS Ally **REAL NAME** Peter Joseph Ross
OCCUPATION Former Vice President, former senator
BASE Washington, D.C.
HEIGHT 5ft 3in **WEIGHT** 105 lbs **EYES** Brown **HAIR** Black
SPECIAL POWERS/ABILITIES Athletic; highly capable administrator.

Pete Ross was a schoolfriend of Clark Kent (see SUPERMAN) and Lana Lang (see LANG, LANA) in Smallville. Pete hid his feelings for Lana realizing she only had eyes for Clark. Years later, when Lana came back to Smallville, Pete helped her accept that Clark had fallen in love with Lois Lane (see LANE, LOIS). Pete successfully ran for the Senate and Lana followed him to Washington. They began a romance, and married.

When Lana's newborn son needed urgent medical care, Superman came to the rescue. Lana named the boy Clark, an indication of where her feelings lay. Pete was tapped by presidential candidate Lex Luthor (see LUTHOR, LEX), who had also known Pete at school, to be his Vice President. Lana, realized she didn't love Pete and filed for divorce. After Luthor's misdeeds were exposed, Pete assumed the U.S. Presidency for a brief period. With a new president in place, Pete has returned to Smallville to start afresh. **RG**

THE ROYAL FLUSH GANG:
1) *Ace* 2) *King* 3) *Queen*
4) *Ten* 5) *Jack*.

ROYAL FLUSH GANG

FIRST APPEARANCE JUSTICE LEAGUE OF AMERICA #43 (March 1966)
STATUS Villains (played out) **BASE** Atlantic City
MEMBERS AND POWERS
  Ace Herculean, android muscle.
  King Made immortal by Dominator's gene-bomb.
  Queen Razor-sharp blades in wrist-gauntlets.
  Jack Possessed laser eye-implant.
  Ten Costume featured explosive spades; kept in radio-contact with sub-gang of runaway teen thieves.

The Royal Flush Gang began as a group of juvenile delinquents, led by Amos Fortune (see FORTUNE, AMOS), who would one day become a criminal mastermind famous for his clashes with the JUSTICE LEAGUE OF AMERICA. Following the gang's defeat, Fortune left the Royal Flush Gang to their own luck (or lack thereof). A new Gang was shuffled by Hector Hammond (see HAMMOND, HECTOR), foe of GREEN LANTERN Hal Jordan. When Hammond abandoned them, a mysterious benefactor (the Gambler, a low card among super-villain suits) outfitted each member with new weapons. However, they were easily defeated by the TEEN TITANS. The Royal Flush Gang returned with an android powerhouse up their sleeves, the new Ace, but again was trumped. The JOKER murdered one lineup of the Royal Flush Gang during the Infinite Crisis, but the group has reappeared since. **SB**

ROULETTE

FIRST APPEARANCE JSA SECRET FILES AND ORIGINS #2 (September 2001)
STATUS Villain **REAL NAME** Victoria Sinclair
OCCUPATION Casino owner **BASE** The Nevada desert
HEIGHT 5ft 9in **WEIGHT** 140 lbs
EYES Green **HAIR** Red
SPECIAL POWERS/ABILITIES Near superhuman ability to count cards, analyze body posture and gestures, and predict an opponent's moves

Roulette owns the House, a vast underground casino that doubles as a vicious "fight club" arena for super-villains. The House's casinos and theme rooms, each designed to cater to the meta-human community, stretch for miles beneath the Nevada desert in a huge underground complex. Roulette, the granddaughter of the first MISTER TERRIFIC, designed the House with her husband, whom she then murdered for shooting up her. She paid for the House with her grandfather's money.

Financial troubles forced Roulette to attract super-rich gamblers by pitting kidnapped members of the JUSTICE SOCIETY OF AMERICA against each other in the House arena. The JSA escaped, however, and destroyed the complex.

A high-stakes gambler determined to win at all costs, Roulette has rebuilt the House, even luring former members of the JUSTICE LEAGUE OF AMERICA into her deadly arena. **PJ**

ROVING RANGER

FIRST APPEARANCE ALL-STAR WESTERN #58 (May 1951)
STATUS Hero **REAL NAME** Jeff Graham
OCCUPATION Texas Ranger **BASE** 1860s Texas
HEIGHT 6ft **WEIGHT** 172 lbs **EYES** Blue **HAIR** Blond
SPECIAL POWERS/ABILITIES The Roving Ranger was a courageous crime fighter, well known throughout 19th-century Texas as an expert marksman and equestrian.

Jeff Graham was a captain in the Confederate army during the Civil War. When the war ended, Jeff returned to his home state of Texas and joined the Texas Rangers. Under their leader, Major Hawks, the Texas Rangers roamed the state, traveling from town to town, taking down gunslinging vigilantes and lawbreakers wherever they went. As a Texas Ranger, Graham once captured the bandit El Dorado. The thief was actually Bud Huston, a former Confederate officer who had once served under Graham during the Civil War. Rather than kill El Dorado, Graham convinced Huston to give up his criminal ways. Along with several others, nicknamed "History's Heroes," the Roving Ranger was transported to the present and helped prevent the ULTRA-HUMANITE from stealing a space shuttle from Cape Canaveral. Returned to the past, Graham worked with the Texas Rangers until the end of his days. His final fate is unrecorded. **PJ**

RYAN, RUSTY

FIRST APPEARANCE FEATURE COMICS # 32 (May 1940)
STATUS Hero **REAL NAME** Rusty Ryan
OCCUPATION Patriot **BASE** Boyville
HEIGHT 5ft 4in **WEIGHT** 110 lbs **EYES** Blue **HAIR** Brown
SPECIAL POWERS/ABILITIES No special powers, but charismatic personality and determination.

Teenager Rusty Ryan was a student in Boyville, a school/community inspired by Boystown that was overseen by retired nautical man Cappy Jenks. Rusty and his best friend Smiley thwarted various criminal plots in the area, including direct threats to Boyville by businessmen seeking to buy the land for development and banks trying to foreclose. Rusty organized the Boyville Brigadiers (who wore red, white and blue costumes), including his pals Ed, Pierpont, Lee, and Alababa. They saw to it that their part of America was kept safe from criminals, spies, saboteurs, and truant officers. **RG**

S.H.A.D.E.

FIRST APPEARANCE SEVEN SOLDIERS: FRANKENSTEIN #3 (January 2006) **STATUS** Hero Team **BASE** Mobile
CURRENT MEMBERS AND POWERS
Father Time Immortality, body-switching.
Frankenstein Super-strength, damage resistance.
Bride of Frankenstein Super-strength, damage resistance.
Uncle Sam Super-strength, near-immortality, size-changing.

KEY 1) *Propaganda* **2)** *Chief Justice* **3)** *Embargo* **4)** *Spin Doctor*

The Super Human Advanced Defense Executive, (S.H.A.D.E.) is a division of the U.S. government tasked with the suppression of global terrorism through the deployment of metahumans resources. S.H.A.D.E. works covertly, often violently, and outside the jurisdiction of most government overseers. S.H.A.D.E. is commanded by FATHER TIME, a seemingly immortal being with the ability to appear in different bodies.

Among S.H.A.D.E.'s agents are Frankenstein (*see* SPAWN OF FRENKENSTEIN) and the Bride of Frankenstein, while new versions of classic heroes – including the HUMAN BOMB, DOLL MAN, the RAY, and PHANTOM LADY— appeared in the ranks following the Infinite Crisis. Most of the new recruits later joined UNCLE SAM and his latest assembling of the FREEDOM FIGHTERS, still working under the auspices of S.H.A.D.E. **DW**

SABBAC

FIRST APPEARANCE CAPTAIN MARVEL JR. #4 (February 1943)
STATUS Villain **REAL NAME** Timothy Karnes
OCCUPATION Would-be world conqueror **BASE** Mobile
HEIGHT 6ft 2in **WEIGHT** 240 lbs **EYES** Blue **HAIR** None
SPECIAL POWERS/ABILITIES Saying the word "Sabbac" gives Karnes a range of demonic powers.

Timothy Karnes, foster brother of Freedy Freeman (*see* CAPTAIN MARVEL JR.), studied black magic to gain power. He succeeded beyond his wildest dreams when he conjured the spirits of six demonic entities. In a blasphemous parody of CAPTAIN MARVEL's own powers, the devils gave him unique abilities that he could wield by saying the word "sabbac."

Immediately upon uttering the magic word, Karnes felt the zap of a bolt of black lightning. He now had the powers of his benefactors: Satan's strength, Any's invulnerability, Belial's wisdom, Beelzebub's flames, Asmodeus's courage, and Craeteis's power of flight. He soon discovered that saying "Sabbac" once again turned him back into Karnes.

Sabbac battled the Marvel family and wound up behind bars. Recently, a Russian mafia boss named Ishmael Gregor sprung Karnes from prison and seemingly murdered him, taking the powers of Sabbac for himself. This new Sabbac has grown to giant size after absorbing the powers of the Seven Deadly Sins. **DW**

St. Cloud, Silver

FIRST APPEARANCE DETECTIVE COMICS #469 (May 1977)
STATUS Hero's friend **REAL NAME** Silver St. Cloud
OCCUPATION Convention organizer **BASE** Gotham City
HEIGHT 5ft 5in **WEIGHT** 131 lbs **EYES** Blue **HAIR** Silver
SPECIAL POWERS/ABILITIES No superpowers, but beautiful, intelligent, and charismatic; a woman who knows her own mind.

Silver St. Cloud is a convention organizer who first met the billionaire playboy Bruce Wayne at a charity event held on Councilman Rupert Thorne's yacht. When BATMAN saved her from an assassin's bullet, Silver realized in a flash what few before her had even suspected: the Dark Knight, Gotham's grim defender, and the apparently feckless Bruce Wayne were one and the same person!

Silver and Bruce embarked on a romance, during which she told him of her suspicions about his dual identity. Rather than suffer in fear, waiting by the telephone as night after night Batman risked life and limb on Gotham City's crime-ridden streets, Silver decided she had better end her affair with Bruce Wayne before their romance became too serious. So she bid the Dark Knight a tearful farewell. **PJ**

SALA

FIRST APPEARANCE GREEN LANTERN ANNUAL (2nd series) #9 (September 2000)
STATUS Hero **REAL NAME** Sala Nisaba
OCCUPATION Archaeologist **BASE** Nabeul, Tunisia
HEIGHT 5ft 7in **WEIGHT** 138 lbs **EYES** Green **HAIR** Brown
SPECIAL POWERS/ABILITIES Empowered by the Ringstaff of Istar, Sala possesses incredible strength, agility, and fighting skills as a modern-day Lady of Battle.

While excavating in the Syrian Desert, archaeologist Sala Nisaba discovered a gateway to the Babylonian underworld known as Kurnugi. Unfortunately, at the same time she inadvertently freed the demon lord Pazuzu and other vengeful gods. Kurnugi's ruler, NERGAL the Lord of Terror, informed Sala that she was descended from Istar, Lady of Battle, and by Nergal's mystical touch Sala was transformed into a new Istar. Teamed with Kyle Rayner (GREEN LANTERN V), a friend since attending art school together, Sala battled Pazuzu, Nergal and his wife Ereskigal, and the monstrous Tiamat. Later, with the aid of the JUSTICE LEAGUE OF AMERICA, the Babylonian deities were returned to Kurnugi. Sala continues to use her powers as avatar of Istar to combat evils ancient and modern. **SB**

SALAKK

FIRST APPEARANCE GREEN LANTERN (2nd series) #149 (February 1982)
STATUS Hero **REAL NAME** Salaak
OCCUPATION Green Lantern **BASE** Slyggia and Earth
HEIGHT 6ft 11in **WEIGHT** 207 lbs **EYES** White **HAIR** None
SPECIAL POWERS/ABILITIES With his power ring, this fearless loner can fight as well as any of his brethren.

Born on the planet Slyggia, Salakk inherited the mantle of GREEN LANTERN for sector 1418. He performed his job well but was considered a loner by his fellow Corps members. That did not stop him from agreeing to cover sector 1417 when its Lantern, KATMA TUI, was assigned to train John Stewart (Green Lantern IV), who was substituting for sector 2814's Hal Jordan. When the cosmic event called the Crisis caused a reduction in the number of Green Lanterns as well as the abandonment of the sector system, Salakk agreed to join several other Corpsmen based on Earth. There he developed his first true friendship with fellow Lantern Ch'p. Salakk was accidentally brought to the year 5711 to portray Solar Director Pol Manning, a role Jordan had previously played several times, and agreed to remain even after recovering his memories. Salakk later returned to the present in a futile attempt to prevent the destruction of the central power battery on Oa. In a state of deep depression, Salakk spent time with Ch'p and later joined John Stewart on Oa. Believed killed by parasitic aliens, Salakk returned to Oa to serve the Guardians as their chief administrator. Among his responsibilities is the protection of the Book of Oa, the sacred text containing the rules that all members of the Green Lantern Corps must obey or risk expulsion. **RG**

SALAMANCA

FIRST APPEARANCE FLASH (2nd series) ANNUAL #3 (2000)
STATUS Hero **REAL NAME** Unknown
OCCUPATION Hero **BASE** Buenos Aires, Argentina
HEIGHT 5ft 8in **WEIGHT** 142 lbs **EYES** Brown **HAIR** Black
SPECIAL POWERS/ABILITIES Sorcerous control over the elements; can leave her body as an astral form for three hours.

Salamanca, named after a supernatural location in Argentinean folklore, is the leader of the Argentinean super-hero group SUPER MALON. Together with fellow heroes Pampero, CACHIRU, El Lobizon, Vizacacha, El Bagual, El Yaguarete, and Cimarron, she uses her incredible mastery over the weather to combat threats to her home country.

Not long ago, Salamanca's arch-enemy, the sorcerer Gualicho, imprisoned her and her former lover Cachiru in an alternate dimension. Jay Garrick, the original FLASH, could not free them, and only the current, third Flash, Wally West, succeeded in breaking Gualicho's control and liberating Salamanca and the others.

More recently, Salamanca and the Super Malon were involved in a violent confrontation with the third CHEETAH (Sebastian Ballésteros) and WONDER WOMAN in Buenos Aires. During the fight, the two rivals—Barbara Minerva and Sebastian Ballésteros—scuffled over the right to wield the Cheetah's powers, and Salamanca's team provided invaluable backup to Wonder Woman in her efforts to trap the villains and contain the damage. Salamanca is a romantic at heart, and holds out hope that one day she and Cachiru will be able to rekindle their love. **DW**

SAND

FIRST APPEARANCE ADVENTURE COMICS #69 (December 1941)
STATUS Hero **REAL NAME** Sanderson Hawkins **OCCUPATION** Former chairman of JSA **BASE** New York City **HEIGHT** 5ft 11in **WEIGHT** 162 lbs **EYES** Blue **HAIR** Blond **SPECIAL POWERS/ABILITIES** Can manipulate silicon-based materials, causing earthquakes; can phase through earth, glass, or bricks; limited precognition.

Sanderson "Sandy" Hawkins is the nephew of Dian Belmont, the girlfriend of Wesley Dodds, the first SANDMAN. Sandy idolized the legendary crimefighter and, unaware that Dodds was the "mystery man" in disguise, began a rigorous training program in the hope of becoming his sidekick. Dodds eventually revealed his identity to Sandy, who became the Sandman's protégé, Sandy the Golden Boy. The two heroes joined the ALL-STAR SQUADRON and fought Axis tyranny during World War II.

When a scientific experiment went awry, Sandy was transformed into a crazed silicon monster. The Sandman imprisoned the transformed Sandy in a special chamber, where his sidekick remained for decades. When a villain called the Shatterer attempted to exploit Sandy's silicon-based power, the Sandman triggered an explosion that freed his ward from his monstrous state. Sandy joined the Sandman and other members of the JUSTICE SOCIETY OF AMERICA to defend Earth against the coming of Raganarok, the end of the world.

When Dodds was killed by the DARK LORD, Sandy, now calling himself "Sand", rejoined the JSA to avenge Dodds and became the group's chairman and financier. Sand has since taken up his mentor's identity as the new Sandman, possessing the ability to see the future through dreams. **PJ**

SILICON SUPER HERO
His body no longer human, Sand Hawkins is now a silicon-based life form. He can turn himself into stone or sand, and control those same elements with his mind. Sand now controls these transformations with technologies provided by Hourman II.

SANDMAN I

FIRST APPEARANCE ADVENTURE COMICS #40 (July 1939)
STATUS Hero (deceased) **REAL NAME** Wesley Dodds
OCCUPATION Socialite; crime fighter **BASE** New York City
HEIGHT 5ft 11in **WEIGHT** 210 lbs **EYES** Blue **HAIR** Black
SPECIAL POWERS/ABILITIES Arsenal of gas weapons, including gas gun; later wielded "wirepoon" gun for climbing or snaring foes.

Prophetic, nightmarish dreams induced Wesley Dodds to take up the cloak, gas mask, and tranquilizing gas gun of the Sandman to thwart the evils of the waking world. The Sandman's first quarry was the PHANTOM OF THE FAIR, a villain stalking the 1939 New York World's Fair. Through his role as the Sandman, Dodds met and fell in love with Dian Belmont, who would eventually share his secret and his life. The Sandman joined the JUSTICE SOCIETY OF AMERICA as a founding member, and served the wartime ALL-STAR SQUADRON alongside his youthful partner, Sandy Hawkins, Belmont's nephew (*see* SAND), trading cloak and fedora for a more colorful costume befitting the "Mystery Men" of the time. Dodds kept up the good fight for decades thereafter, until he committed suicide to prevent the sorcerer Mordru, the DARK LORD from mining his mind to learn the location of the reincarnated DR. FATE. **SB**

SANDMAN I *Sharp detective's mind and dreams that can foretell the future; wields a gas gun that puts victims to sleep*

SANDMAN (MORPHEUS)

FIRST APPEARANCE SANDMAN (2nd series) #1 (March 1989)
STATUS Hero **REAL NAME** Morpheus, Dream, Oneiros, Kai'ckul and L'zoril **OCCUPATION** Guardian **BASE** The Dreaming
HEIGHT/WEIGHT Variable **EYES** White **HAIR** Black
SPECIAL POWERS/ABILITIES An immortal being of vast power; able to summon sleep and conjure dreams, from wistful fantasies to fevered nightmares, any of which were used to cure maladies or punish those who offended the Lord of Dreams.

Morpheus (or Dream) belonged to an eternal race of beings known as the ENDLESS. Since life began, Morpheus has watched over Earth and all mankind. More than 70 years ago, Morpheus was imprisoned by warlock Roderick Burgess, who had instead hoped to snare Dream's sister, DEATH. When he finally escaped decades later, Morpheus set about reclaiming his talismans—his sacred helm, his pouch filled with sleeping sand, and his mystic ruby—as well as restoring his realm, the Dreaming, which had fallen into disrepair during his absence. While Morpheus was imprisoned, two of his minions, Brute and Glob, enabled the human Dr. Garrett Sandford to operate from the Dreaming as a costumed hero known as the Sandman (no relation to Wesley Dodds, SANDMAN I). Upon Sandford's demise, Brute and Glob replaced him with Hector Hall (*see* DR. FATE), whose son Daniel was born in the Dreaming. Hector Hall later died and was reincarnated like his parents, HAWKMAN and HAWKGIRL, while baby Daniel and his mother, Lyta, were returned to Earth. The boy's destiny would be inextricably tied to the Dreamland.

Eventually, Morpheus was killed by the Furies, the beings known as the Eumenides or "The Kindly Ones" (*see* FURY I). However, before his death, Morpheus chose Daniel as his successor. Within the Dreaming, Daniel was aged to adulthood and has now taken Morpheus's place as Lord of Dreams and one of the Endless. **SB**

THE DC COMICS ENCYCLOPEDIA

SARGE STEEL

FIRST APPEARANCE SARGE STEEL #1 (December 1964)
STATUS Hero **REAL NAME** Unknown
OCCUPATION Operative, D.E.O. **BASE** Washington, D.C.
HEIGHT 6ft 1in **WEIGHT** 198 lbs **EYES** Blue **HAIR** Black
SPECIAL POWERS/ABILITIES Expert martial artist who packs a powerful punch with his solid steel fist.

The "iron man with the fist of steel" received his trademark appendage during a stint with U.S. Special Forces, when communist agent Ivan Chong arranged for Steel to receive a booby-trapped hand grenade that exploded prematurely. Discharged from the military due to the accident, he received a solid steel prosthetic on his left stump and became a private investigator.

Steel became head of the Central Bureau of Intelligence (CBI), a spy organization whose field agents included ARSENAL and KING FARADAY. Steel also worked with CHECKMATE, a government strike team designed for high-powered combat response.

Once the CBI was absorbed into the Department of Extranormal Operations, Sarge Steel earned a place in the President's cabinet as Director of Meta-Human Affairs (and briefly became a pawn of MISTER MIND). Steel now heads the U.S. government's Department of Metahuman Affairs. Among his agents are NEMESIS I and Diana Prince (see WONDER WOMAN). During the Amazon invasion of Washington DC, CIRCE arranged for Sarge Steel's kidnapping and replacement by a shapeshifting impostor. **DW**

SARGON THE SORCERER

FIRST APPEARANCE ALL-AMERICAN COMICS #26 (May 1941)
STATUS Hero (deceased) **REAL NAME** John Sargent
OCCUPATION Stage magician **BASE** Legion World, U.P. Space
HEIGHT 5ft 11in **WEIGHT** 176 lbs **EYES** Brown **HAIR** Brown
SPECIAL POWERS/ABILITIES Possessed the magical Ruby of Life, which gave him mystical control over whatever object he touched.

In 1917, archaeologist Richard Sargent discovered the Ruby of Life, an object carved from the Ring of Life, a powerful totem once used by the SPECTRE. Unaware of its mystic origins, Sargent gave the Ruby to his wife. The jewel was the first thing their infant son John saw and touched. On an expedition with his father years later, John learned the true nature of the Ruby and discovered he could control power. Deciding to use his abilities for good, but hiding their mystic nature behind the persona of a stage magician, John became Sargon the Sorcerer. Sargon joined the ALL-STAR SQUADRON during World War II. The original Sargon died when a Shadow Creature incinerated his body. His successor, David John Sargent, gained the mystical abilities of Sargon when fragments from the Ruby of Life embedded themselves in his chest. **PJ**

SATANUS

FIRST APPEARANCE SUPERMAN (2nd series) #38 (December 1989)
STATUS Villain **REAL NAME** Satanus (alias Colin Thornton) **OCCUPATION** Demon lord
BASE The Netherworld **HEIGHT/WEIGHT/EYES/HAIR** Variable **SPECIAL POWERS/ABILITIES** Alters size and appearance; can teleport himself and other beings; staff projects blasts of hellfire.

In the infernal netherworld, he is Lord Satanus, a demon in conflict with his demoness sister Blaze for control of an extra-dimensional purgatory, where human souls suffer endless torments. Deposed by Blaze, Satanus made his way to Earth and assumed the guise of mortal Colin Thornton, publisher of the Metropolis-based *Newstime* magazine. Satanus began a campaign to corrupt the much-coveted soul of the SUPERMAN. However, Satanus has been thwarted at every turn, either defeated by the Man of Steel, or vexed by Blaze, who desires Superman's indomitable spirit for herself. With the aid of the lesser demon Mudge, Satanus vainly attempted to take over the post-Y2K Metropolis, which was still reeling from the machine ills wrought by BRAINIAC 13. Satanus later abducted Cary Richards, a crippled boy whose psychic powers created the superpowered Adversary to punch out Superman. The Man of Steel freed Cary from Satanus's thrall, but the demon lord remains determined to drag the hero down to his level of hell. **SB**

DEMON SPAWN *Satanus and his sister Blaze are the devilish children of the wizard known as Shazam!*

SATURN GIRL

FIRST APPEARANCE ADVENTURE COMICS #247 (April 1958); LEGION OF SUPER-HEROES (4th series) #0 (October 1994)
STATUS Hero **REAL NAME** Imra Ardeen
OCCUPATION Legionnaire **BASE** Legion World, U.P. Space
HEIGHT 5ft 7in **WEIGHT** 120 lbs **EYES** Blue **HAIR** Blonde
SPECIAL POWERS/ABILITIES Among the universe's top telepaths; Imra has experienced enough minds to have a unique perspective on things, making her a gifted leader.

Imra Ardeen comes from Titan, a moon of Saturn where the 31st century humanoid inhabitants have evolved beyond the need for speech. Titanians do not possess vocal cords, and use their natural telepathic abilities to communicate with one another as well as off-worlders. Imra is one of the most skilled Titanian telepaths, capable of reading minds as well as demonstrating limited control over the actions of others. Along with Garth Ranzz (LIGHTNING LAD) and Rokk Krinn (Cosmic Boy), Imra is one of the founders of the Legion of Super-Heroes, where she goes by the name Saturn Girl. Her inability to speak has given her a somewhat introverted demeanor, which is offset by the trust of Cosmic Boy and the on-again, off-again love of Lightning Lad. Saturn Girl continues to be a core member of the team, with her mind-reading abilities helping her discern that MON-EL was trapped in the Phantom Zone, allowing BRAINIAC 5 to free the hero after a thousand years of imprisonment. **DW**

MENTAL STRENGTH *When she is pushed, Saturn Girl's thoughts can be terrifying.*

SATURN QUEEN

FIRST APPEARANCE SUPERMAN #147 (August 1961)
STATUS Villain **REAL NAME** Eve Aires
OCCUPATION Professional criminal **BASE** Mobile
HEIGHT 5ft 8in **WEIGHT** 140 lbs **EYES** Brown **HAIR** Red
SPECIAL POWERS/ABILITIES Telepathy and hypnotic control of others.

Saturn Queen, like SATURN GIRL, is a 31st century native of Titan, a moon of Saturn. Like everyone on her homeworld, she is telepathic and possesses limited abilities to control the minds of others. Saturn Queen founded the Legion of Super-Villains with LIGHTNING LORD and Cosmic King, with their evil triumvirate forming a mirror image of Saturn Girl, LIGHTNING LAD, and COSMIC BOY of the LEGION OF SUPER-HEROES.

In an alternate timeline, Saturn Queen and her two compatriots traveled back in time to kidnap Bruce Wayne and Clark Kent as young children, then raised them to adulthood in line with the power-mad ambitions of their new "parents." On this Earth, SUPERMAN and BATMAN ruled the planet as dictators, but Saturn Queen's plot came to an end thanks to a resistance movement orchestrated by WONDER WOMAN. Saturn Queen next appeared in the bottle city of Kandor, leading a revolution with Earth-3's Ultraman until stopped by SUPERGIRL. **DW**

SAVAGE, MATT: TRAIL BOSS

FIRST APPEARANCE WESTERN COMICS #77 (October 1959)
STATUS Hero **REAL NAME** Matt Savage
OCCUPATION Cattle driver and trail boss
BASE The Texas Trail, 1860s–1870s
HEIGHT 5ft 10in **WEIGHT** 165 lbs **EYES** Blue **HAIR** Red-brown
SPECIAL POWERS/ABILITIES Expert tracker, horseman, and sharpshooter.

A special breed of men helped tame the post-Civil War American West. Unlike the wandering gunslingers such as BAT LASH, Trail Boss Matt Savage did an honest day's work by running a cattle drive, transporting cattle from Texas to Kansas.

Savage worked as a Union army scout and a miner before joining up with a cattle drive as a flank man. When he decided to become a trail boss and start up the Dogiron Crew, he brought aboard Union veteran Clay Dixon and Confederate veteran Jim Grant. To overshadow the Civil War of those two, Savage recruited Luther Jones, Manuel Ortega, and the mysterious Red. "Biscuits" Baker became the team's cook once Savage cleared him of a horse-thievery charge. Jebediah Kent, ancestor of Jonathan "Pa" Kent (see KENTS), briefly ran with Savage's team.

The Dogiron Crew drove their cattle between Texas and Kansas, encountering adventure along the way. Matt Savage is believed to be a relative of Brian Savage, the SCALPHUNTER. **DW**

SAVANT

FIRST APPEARANCE BIRDS OF PREY #56 (August 2003)
STATUS Villain **REAL NAME** Brian K. Durlin
OCCUPATION Extortionist; information broker **BASE** Gotham City
HEIGHT 6ft 3in **WEIGHT** 217 lbs **EYES** Blue-gray **HAIR** Blond
SPECIAL POWERS/ABILITIES Computer genius and extraordinary martial artist; Savant's brain imbalance makes him a particularly dangerous and unpredictable foe.

Wealthy Brian Durlin rarely finishes anything he starts, owing to a chemical imbalance in his brain that affects his memory. Although highly intelligent, Durlin's inability to properly distinguish the passage of time resulted in poor grades and he dropped out of school and university. Durlin's father disinherited him, leaving the young man penniless and living in Greece, where he began using blackmail to support his expensive tastes.

Durlin decided to turn his talents to heroics as the masked Savant, but was barred from Gotham City by BATMAN after Savant prioritized pursuing arsonists over saving the occupants of a burning building. Savant returned to blackmail, using his computer savvy to extort money from the wealthy. With his loyal assistant Creote, a former K.G.B. agent, Savant abducted the BLACK CANARY and held her hostage, hoping to coerce Barbara Gordon, (ORACLE), to divulge Batman's civilian identity. With the Huntress's help, the Canary was freed and Savant was jailed. Oracle later opted to employ him as her assistant in the business of information brokering. **SB**

SAVITAR

FIRST APPEARANCE THE FLASH (2nd series) #108 (December 1995)
STATUS Villain (missing) **REAL NAME** Unrevealed
OCCUPATION Criminal **BASE** Tibet
HEIGHT 6ft 4in **WEIGHT** 220 lbs **EYES** Light blue **HAIR** Black
SPECIAL POWERS/ABILITIES By tapping into the Speed Force, Savitar can move his body at near light speed; can absorb motion from other objects and people, thereby slowing their movement.

The man now known as Savitar was once an Eastern bloc military pilot. While flying an experimental supersonic plane, he was infused with Speed Force energy that gave him incredible superspeed, making him the fastest man alive. The pilot believed his superspeed was a divine gift, and named himself Savitar, after the Hindu god of motion. Curious about the true nature of this so-called Speed Force, Savitar began a cruel campaign of extortion against various other speedsters. During a battle with MAX MERCURY, Savitar was thrust forward in time to the present. After a massive battle between Savitar and Earth's heroic speedsters, Wally West, FLASH III, pushed the villain into the Speed Force. Savitar was absorbed into the energy field, where he remains trapped to this day. **PJ**

SCALPHUNTER

FIRST APPEARANCE WEIRD WESTERN TALES #39 (March 1977)
STATUS Hero (reincarnated) **REAL NAME** Brian Savage
OCCUPATION Police detective **BASE** Opal City **HEIGHT** 6ft 1in **WEIGHT** 190 lbs **EYES** Blue (Matt O'Dare: blue)
HAIR (Matt O'Dare: red) **SPECIAL POWERS/ABILITIES** Expert horseman; unerring aim with bow and arrow, tomahawk, rifle, or handgun.

TAMING THE TOWN In 1884, Brian Savage put aside the lawless, gunslinging ways of Scalphunter to police Opal City as its sheriff.

Brian Savage was abducted from his parents by Kiowa Indians during the 1840s and renamed Ke-Woh-No-Tay, which roughly translates as "He Who Is Less Than Human." Raised in the Kiowa traditions, Savage was later known as Scalphunter to the white men he encountered on his many adventures across the Wild West. After learning the truth about his roots, Scalphunter became a gunfighter, eventually settling down in Opal City during its frontier days. As Opal's sheriff, Savage maintained law and order for more than a decade.

He eventually married and retired to a farm in Turk County. His son, Steve Savage, became famous many years later as the World War I aerial ace known as BALLOON BUSTER. Brian Savage died in 1899, shot in the back after returning to Opal City during tumultuous times. Perhaps owing in some way to his Kiowa background, Savage was reincarnated as Opal City police detective Matt O'Dare, friend and ally of STARMAN. Matt has assumed the mannerisms of the late, great Scalphunter. **SB**

MATT O'DARE Once a corrupt cop in a family of devoted lawmen, Matt O'Dare renounced his wicked ways after discovering that he was the reincarnation of the western hero Scalphunter.

SCARECROW

THE FEAR MASTER

FIRST APPEARANCE WORLD'S FINEST COMICS #3 (Fall 1941)
STATUS Villain **OCCUPATION** Professor and professional criminal
REAL NAME Jonathan Crane **BASE** Gotham City
HEIGHT 6ft **WEIGHT** 150 lbs **EYES** Blue **HAIR** Brown
SPECIAL POWERS/ABILITIES A psychologist and biochemist, Crane used his knowledge to create a fear-inducing gas that creates nightmarish hallucinations in the mind of anyone who inhales it; costume also designed to strike terror; a manic hand-to-hand combatant.

GAWKY AND UNCOORDINATED as a child, Jonathan Crane was often the physical and emotional target of neighborhood bullies. Initially frightened by their horrible taunts, Crane eventually decided he would turn the tables on his attackers, and began voraciously studying phobias and the nature of fear.

HARMLESS TEASE?
Jonathan was a spindly nerd, easily fooled by a sexy girl like Sherry.

TERROR master
A psychiatrist turned psychopath, the Scarecrow uses his fear gas to terrorize his victims, often leaving their minds permanently crippled.

As an adult, Crane became an expert psychologist, specializing in fear. He also acquired some knowledge of chemistry, studying how certain combinations of chemicals could affect the human psyche. Crane became a professor at Gotham City University, but was summarily dismissed for his unorthodox teaching methods and his refusal to follow the school's safety codes.

Crane's fragile mind snapped after his dismissal and he adopted the guise of the Scarecrow, vowing to use his knowledge of fear and his own specially designed "fear gas" to gain revenge. Using this chemical, the Scarecrow killed several of Gotham University's regents by literally scaring them to death. The Scarecrow was then confronted by the BATMAN, who ended the villain's reign of terror and incarcerated him in Arkham Asylum for the Criminally Insane. Escaping from custody over and over again, the Scarecrow used stolen funds to constantly upgrade the potency of his fear gas, mixing powerful synthetic adreno-cortical secretions with potent hallucinogens to create a pathogen strong enough to prompt almost instantaneous, terror-induced heart attacks in his victims.

A constant foe of Batman and his allies, and a spooky threat to the citizens of Gotham City, the Scarecrow is obsessed with fear in all its manifestations and relishes inflicting it. Perhaps fortunately, Crane is prey to a phobia of his own: *Chiropteraphobia*, a chronic fear of bats or, more specifically, of Batman! **PJ**

YAAH!

TORMENTING TEENS
More cruel pranks fractured his already fragile psyche.

HUSH *Scarecrow was one of several Arkham inmates the villain Hush used in his war against Batman. Scarecrow's used his fear toxins and psychological expertise to frighten and manipulate Joker, Poison Ivy, Killer Croc, and the Huntress into battling the Dark Knight.*

KEY STORYLINES

• *WORLD'S FINEST COMICS (FALL 1941):* The Scarecrow makes his debut, ensuring sleepless nights for citizens of Gotham City.
• *BATMAN #626–630 (JUNE–SEPTEMBER 2004):* In "As the Crow Flies," Scarecrow is infected with a mutation that transforms him into a monstrous Scarebeast during times of stress.
• *DETECTIVE COMICS #820 (AUGUST 2006):* During the "Face the Face" storyline, Scarecrow faces off against both Batman and Robin, confronting each with their greatest insecurities.

SCANDAL

FIRST APPEARANCE VILLAINS UNITED #1 (March 2005)
STATUS Villain   **REAL NAME** Scandal Savage
OCCUPATION Professional adventurer   **BASE** Mobile
HEIGHT 5ft 9in   **WEIGHT** 160 lbs   **EYES** Brown   **HAIR** Brown
SPECIAL POWERS/ABILITIES Enhanced damage resistance, expert combatant with bladed weapons..

Scandal Savage is the daughter of the immortal VANDAL SAVAGE, one of Earth's greatest villains. She apparently shares her father's resistance to injury, and is a deadly combatant with her wrist-mounted "lamentation blades."

She first appeared as a member of the new SECRET SIX, working for MOCKINGBIRD to sabotage the worldwide criminal operations of the Society (see VILLAINS UNITED). During a mission to Brazil, she explained to her teammates that she had grown up in that country; later revelations included the news that she was in a romantic relationship with KNOCKOUT who had infiltrated the Society as a mole. Once Knockout joined up with the Secret Six, the two grew even closer – raising the anger of Vandal Savage, who wanted his daughter to bear him an heir.

Knockout lost her life during the Death of the New Gods event, leaving behind a despondent Scandal who spurned the SUICIDE SQUAD's efforts to recruit her. She later found herself among the supervillains exiled on an alien world during Operation: Salvation Run. **DW**

LOOK OF DEATH
Scandal wields her lamentation blades with deadly efficiency, making her the equal of her murderous father.

TEAM PLAYER
Her time with the Secret Six gave Scandal the opportunity to romance her teammate Knockout. The murder of her lover pushed Scandal into despair.

SCARAB

FIRST APPEARANCE SCARAB #1 (November 1993)
STATUS Hero   **REAL NAME** Louis Sendak
OCCUPATION Adventurer   **BASE** New York City
HEIGHT 5ft 10in   **WEIGHT** 170 lbs   **EYES** Brown   **HAIR** Brown
SPECIAL POWERS/ABILITIES The Scarabaeus allowed him to command mystic energies, either as raw power or in subtle manifestations.

Louis Sendak was born in Staten Island, N.Y. during the 1920s. In 1924, Louis's father brought home various mystic artifacts including the Door and the Scarabaeus. Louis later used this talisman to become the occult adventurer Scarab.

He was a successful hero, teaming with other mystics to form the Seven Shadows. When Johnny Sorrow (see SORROW, JOHNNY) murdered six of the Seven Shadows, their deaths caused Scarab to suffer a mental breakdown. During his convalescence, Louis's wife Eleanor was drawn into the Door and vanished. Decades later, Sendak teamed up with the JUSTICE SOCIETY OF AMERICA on their quest for the Fate child, only to be attacked by the DARK LORD. Stripped of his magic powers, he became the unwitting vessel chosen by Johnny Sorrow to enable his master, the King of Tears, to return to the known world from the plane of non-reality he was trapped in. **RG**

SCAVENGER

FIRST APPEARANCE SUPERBOY (2nd series) #4 (March 1994)
STATUS Villain   **REAL NAME** Unknown   **OCCUPATION** Plunderer
BASE Mobile   **HEIGHT** 5ft 10in   **WEIGHT** 160 lbs
EYES One white; one cybernetic   **HAIR** White
SPECIAL POWERS/ABILITIES Long-lived; possesses several cybernetic implants; wields weapons pillaged from various heroes and villains.

His origins a closely guarded secret, the Scavenger travels the world using stolen teleportation technology, searching for mystic talismans and items of power. He claims he was once wronged by a godlike hero and is gathering weapons for a coming battle with this mystery foe. The Scavenger also believes that all heroes are conspiring against humanity and cannot be trusted.

The Scavenger has battled SUPERBOY on several occasions, and he also engaged in a cyberspace auction hoping to outbid GREEN ARROW for a vintage Arrowcar. The Scavenger continues to prepare for conflict with his unnamed nemesis. **SB**

SCORCH

FIRST APPEARANCE JLA #61 (February 2002)
STATUS Villain (reformed and deceased)   **REAL NAME** Aubrey (second name unknown)
OCCUPATION Unrevealed   **BASE** Pisboe, VA
HEIGHT 5ft 9in   **WEIGHT** 140 lbs   **EYES** Red   **HAIR** Black
SPECIAL POWERS/ABILITIES Does not sleep and seems to have complete mastery over fire, from generating it to controlling its intensity.

The sultry young woman Aubrey, known as Scorch, escaped from a variation of reality when the Joker briefly gained MR. MXYZPTLK's fifth-dimensional, cosmic powers. She battled both SUPERMAN and the MARTIAN MANHUNTER as she tried to make a name for herself in the world of crime. Although offered a chance to reform and become a force for good by Superman, she refused. Later, the Manhunter asked Scorch to help him overcome his psychological fear of fire in exchange for helping her calm her tortured mind. During the resulting sessions they became lovers, although Superman remained suspicious of her motives. His doubts seemed justified when she unwittingly unleashed an ancient Martian horror; however Scorch sacrificed herself to save not only her beloved but the entire JLA. **RG**

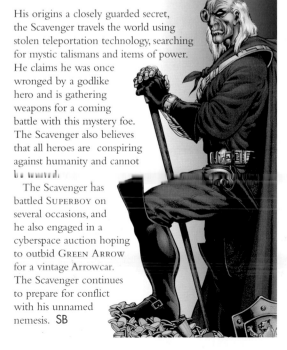

SEA DEVILS

FIRST APPEARANCE SHOWCASE #27 (August 1960)
STATUS Hero team **BASE** Earth's oceans and waterways
MEMBERS AND POWERS
Dane Dorrance (leader): Expert diver and natural leader.
Biff: Powerful combatant.
Judy Walton: Charismatic and athletic.
Nicky Walton: Quick-witted and eager.

The Sea Devils, like the CHALLENGERS OF THE UNKNOWN, predated the modern heroic age and excelled in an era when non-superpowered teams could still capture the public's imagination. In their career they battled sea monsters, vanquished aquatic super-villains, and discovered undersea kingdoms. Dane worked for a time with the Forgotten Heroes, and eventually he and Judy married. The Sea Devils currently serve as the protectors of Windward Home, an oceanic facility run by Jim Lockhart (see RED TORPEDO). **DW**

THE SEA DEVILS
1) *Judy Walton*
2) *Dane Dorrance*
3) *Nicky Walton*
4) *Biff Bailey*

SECRET

FIRST APPEARANCE YOUNG JUSTICE: THE SECRET #1 (June 1998)
STATUS Hero **REAL NAME** Greta Hayes
OCCUPATION Warder **BASE** Mobile
HEIGHT 4ft 8in **WEIGHT** Unknown **EYES** Blue **HAIR** Light brown
SPECIAL POWERS/ABILITIES Secret is a wraithlike form which allows her to pass through solid objects and create psychic manifestations.

SUPERBOY, ROBIN III (Tim Drake) and IMPULSE helped rescue a mysterious phantom girl called the Secret from D.E.O. custody. Soon after, the trio formed YOUNG JUSTICE and Secret, nicknamed "Suzie," was welcomed as a member. During her time with the group, she developed a crush on Robin. The SPECTRE counseled Secret, revealing her origin—the demon Buzz and Greta's brother made a pact, which resulted in her becoming a warder, a spirit on the fringes of Death's domain but incapable of going to the other side herself. Worried about turning evil like her brother, now known as Harm, she kept her distance from most of the team. Soon after she was corrupted by DARKSEID, and went on a rampage until Robin managed to break through to her. Darkseid "punished" the young warder by restoring her humanity. **RG**

SECRET SIX

FIRST APPEARANCE ACTION COMICS WEEKLY #601 (May 1988) **STATUS** Hero team **BASE** Top secret
CURRENT MEMBERS AND POWERS
Cat-Man: Skilled combatant
Deadshot: Expert marksman
Harley Quinn: Acrobatic fighter with inventive mind
Knockout (deceased): Super-strength and damage resistance
Rag Doll II: Impossibly flexible body
Scandal: Wields deadly wrist-blades

Formed decades ago by the enigmatic MOCKINGBIRD, the original Secret Six were a team of undercover operatives fighting crime and defending democracy, though ultimately serving the goals of a covert U.S. government group the Agency. After many successful missions, the Secret Six retired. Reunited years later, the team was

1) *Parademon* 2) *Ragdoll II* 3) *Scandal*
4) *Deadshot* 5) *Cat-Man* 6) *Cheshire.*

flying to train a new generation of operatives when their sabotaged plane crashed into a mountain. Five of the Six died instantly. The sole survivor, Carlo di Rienzi, became the second Mockingbird and assembled a new Secret Six. This team comprised individuals with disabilities negated by high-tech devices. The Secret Six's third incarnation appeared just prior to the Infinite Crisis, when Lex Luthor (see LUTHOR, LEX) gathered a sextet of villains to sabotage the efforts of the Society (see VILLAINS UNITED). After the Crisis the Secret Six continued, welcoming new members including HARLEY QUINN and the MAD HATTER. **SB**

LEGACY *The Secret Six has existed for decades, though few know of its existence. The most recent team nearly took down the Secret Society of Super-Villains.*

SECRET SOCIETY OF SUPER-VILLAINS

FIRST APPEARANCE SECRET SOC. OF SUPER-VILLAINS #1 (June 1976)
NOTABLE MEMBERS (SEE INDIVIDUAL ENTRIES FOR POWERS)
Darkseid, Captain Boomerang, Captain Cold, Copperhead, Gorilla Grodd, Manhunter IV, Trickster I; Mirror Master I, Sinestro Poison Ivy, Floronic Man, Blockbuster I and II, Reverse-Flash, Chronos I, Charaxes, Killer Frost I, Rag Doll, Ultra-Humanite, Cheshire, Deadshot, Per Degaton, Scarecrow, Felix Faust, Wizard, Riddler, Scarecrow, Deadshot, Hector Hammond, Sivana, Solomon Grundy, Royal Flush Gang, Mist I, Star Sapphire III, Psycho-Pirate (manipulates emotions), *Shadow Thief* (becomes a living shadow), *Funky Flashman* (master conman), *Matter Master* (transmutes elements), *Monocle* (energy blasts), *Brainwave I* (psychic powers), *Silver Ghost* (intangibility), *Signalman* (gimmick weapons), *Quakemaster* (creates earthquakes), *Captain Slingaree* (swordsman).

One of the largest and most significant convocations of criminals ever assembled, the Secret Society of Super-Villains was created by DARKSEID as an underground organization that would rid Earth of its super heroes. After Funky Flashman and GORILLA GRODD each briefly took control of the Society the villains, the premier enemies of the JUSTICE LEAGUE OF AMERICA and the JUSTICE SOCIETY OF AMERICA, made several attempts to destroy them both. Under the auspices of the ULTRA-HUMANITE, a new version of the Secret Society fought the JLA and the JSA before the heroes banished them to limbo.

The original Secret Society regrouped when DESPERO helped its members recall brainwashing that ZATANNA had performed on them years before. Their attempt to take revenge on the JUSTICE LEAGUE OF AMERICA resulted in the disbanding of the hero team just prior to the Infinite Crisis. Most recently, a new Society with hundreds of members emerged under the leadership of Alexander Luthor (*see* VILLAINS UNITED). **PJ**

SERAPH

FIRST APPEARANCE DC COMICS PRESENTS #46 (June 1982)
STATUS Hero   REAL NAME Chaim Lavon
OCCUPATION Teacher; activist   BASE Jerusalem, Israel
HEIGHT 5ft 10in   WEIGHT 165 lbs   EYES Brown   HAIR Black
SPECIAL POWERS/ABILITIES Superstrength; Ring of Solomon enables teleportation; Staff of Moses can transform into a snake, generate forcefields, and null gravity; wears the symbolic Mantle of Elijah.

Chaim Lavon was born in Netanya, a city on the west coast of Israel. The youngest of four siblings, Chaim was horrified by the continued animosity between the Israelis and the Arab world and became a pacifist and a teacher, working at an Arab school to teach culture and language to Jews and Muslims alike. On a pilgrimage to a small synagogue outside Bethlehem, Chaim stopped on a dirt road and cried out in frustration to God for an end to the suffering in the Middle East. Chaim was answered by a brilliant light and a voice that declared that Chaim would lead the Middle East out of its destructive cycle of conflict. Chaim was given several mystic objects and became the hero Seraph.

Seraph was invited to join DOCTOR MIST's GLOBAL GUARDIANS, becoming one of its most visible members, although he resided in Israel. When the first Queen Bee hypnotized a number of the Guardians into working for her, Seraph, unaware of the Queen's cunning, distanced himself from the team. After the Queen was defeated and the Guardians were attacked by the villain Fain Y'Onia, Seraph returned, tending to injured teammate Tuatara. **PJ**

SERIFAN

FIRST APPEARANCE FOREVER PEOPLE 1st series #1 (March 1971)
STATUS Hero (deceased)   REAL NAME None
OCCUPATION Adventurer   BASE New Genesis
HEIGHT 5ft 7.5in   WEIGHT 143 lbs   EYES Blue   HAIR Blond
SPECIAL POWERS/ABILITIES Cosmic Cartridges create "shock-repelli-field" gravity effects, vehicle-fueling power, intense heat, or stun blasts.

A member of the FOREVER PEOPLE, Serifan was one of five children from New Genesis trained by HIGHFATHER of the NEW GODS to use their miraculous powers in the defense of their native Genesis. In one adventure, Serifan and the Forever People thwarted DARKSEID's agent, DEVILANCE but were trapped on the distant world of Adon. VIKYN used the team's Mother Box, to evolve Adon's natives. Vikyn died, but the Adonians became civilized and the Forever People built them Forevertown, their first city. Unfortunately, Serifan's sensitivity to telepathy allowed an evil entity, the Dark, to possess him. The Dark turned back time on Adon, reversing the Forever People's gifts, but inadvertently resurrecting Vikyn. The INFINITY MAN ultimately drove the Dark away for good. Serifan and his friends were among the casualties during the recent Death of the New Gods event. **SB**

THE DC COMICS ENCYCLOPEDIA

SEVEN SOLDIERS OF VICTORY

FIRST APPEARANCE LEADING COMICS #1 (Winter 1941–1942)
STATUS Hero team **BASE** Mobile
MEMBERS AND POWERS
Bulleteer Invulnerable metal skin and enhanced strength
Frankenstein Enhanced strength, undead body provides extreme resistance to injury
Klarion the Witch Boy Spellcasting and monstrous transformations
Manhattan Guardian Top physical condition; skilled fighter
Mister Miracle II One of the world's greatest escape artists
Shining Knight II Skilled fighter and excellent swordswoman
Zatanna Vast magical powers triggered by saying spells backward

SOLDIERS OF THE GOLDEN AGE
(left to right) Klarion the Witch Boy, Shining Knight II, Zatanna, Frankenstein, Manhattan Guardian, Bulleteer, Mr. Miracle II.

Independently stopping the villainous agents of the Iron Hand, seven heroes joined together to become the Laws' Legionnaires, more commonly referred to as the Seven Soldiers of Victory. Founding members included the CRIMSON AVENGER, the Spider (*see* ALIAS THE SPIDER), the SHINING KNIGHT, VIGILANTE I and Billy Gunn (later succeeded by Stuff), and the Star-Spangled Kid, and STRIPESY. The Avenger's aide, WING, was the unofficial eighth member. In 1948, the Seven Soldiers of Victory were betrayed by one of their own, the Spider, and engaged in battle with the entity known as the Nebula Man. Wing sacrificed his life to destroy the creature in Tibet, but the resulting explosion of temporal energies cast the rest of the group across the timestream.

SPELLCASTER Zatanna, arguably the most famous of the new Seven Soldiers, never met the other team members.

SOLDIERS OF THE GOLDEN AGE **1)** *Vigilante I*
2) *Green Arrow* **3)** *Shining Knight*
4) *Star-Spangled Kid* **5)** *Speedy*
6) *Crimson Avenger I* **7)** *Stripesy.*

Decades later, DEADMAN organized a short-lived new edition of the SSV including Adam Strange (*see* STRANGE, ADAM), Batgirl, BLACKHAWK, MENTO, METAMORPHO and the SHINING KNIGHT II to defend the planet Rann from attack by the Injustice League. Soon after that, six of the time-displaced original Soldiers were rescued by the united JUSTICE SOCIETY OF AMERICA and JUSTICE LEAGUE OF AMERICA before RED TORNADO II sacrificed his life to save Earth from the Iron Hand.

A modern incarnation of the Seven Soldiers appeared prior to the Infinite Crisis. The Sheeda, a faerie race from the far future, prepared to annihilate humanity by striking down heroic teams of seven—the only thing (according to prophecy) that could stop them. VIGILANTE assembled I, Spyder (*see* ALIAS THE SPIDER), Gimmix (daughter of MERRY, GIRL OF A THOUSAND GIMMICKS), Boy Blue, Dyno-Mite Dan (using replicas of the rings worn by T.N.T. and DAN THE DNYA-MITE), and the granddaughter of the WHIP. Numbering only six (after BULLETEER dropped out at the last minute), they fell prey to a Sheeda invasion in the American southwest.

Forces conspired to unite a new Seven Soldiers against the Sheeda, with one critical distinction—these soldiers, though working on parallel paths, would never actually meet. This loose team consisted of MISTER MIRACLE II (Shilo Norman), the SPAWN OF FRANKENSTEIN, ZATANNA, KLARION THE WITCH BOY, SHINING KNIGHT II (Sir Ystina), the Manhattan Guardian (see GUARDIAN, THE), and the Bulleteer. The Sheeda Queen, having tortured the Shining Knight aboard her flagship the Castle Revolving, found her invasion fleet sabotaged by Frankenstein (now an elite commando working for the S.H.A.D.E. department of the U.S. government). While the Manhattan Guardian rallied citizens to fight the invaders in the streets, I, Spyder returned and shot the Sheeda Queen with an arrow. She fell from her flagship, landing in the roadway, where a car driven by Bulleteer struck her.

Klarion, having obtained a powerful Sheeda artifact from Zatanna's apprentice, took control of Frankenstein with a Croatoan binding spell, then used his new powers to become king of the Sheeda. Mister Miracle II, shot by DARKSEID, became the only casualty among the Seven Soldiers—though death may be only a temporary challenge for this master of escape. **RG**

KEY STORYLINES
• *JUSTICE LEAGUE OF AMERICA* (1ST SERIES) #100–102 (AUGUST–OCTOBER 1972): The Justice League rescue the time-lost of the Seven Soldiers.
• *STARS AND S.T.R.I.P.E.* #9 (APRIL 2000): The original Seven Soldiers shown again in this tale of how Alias the Spider betrayed his teammates and caused their defeat by Nebula Man.
• *SEVEN SOLDIERS* #1 (OCTOBER 2006): The Seven Soldiers are reborn for a new age to battle the Sheeda, faerie-like people from the distant future who want to consume human history.

SERGEANT ROCK

THE COMBAT-HAPPY JOE

FIRST APPEARANCE OUR ARMY AT WAR #81 (April 1959)
STATUS Hero **REAL NAME** Frank Rock
OCCUPATION Former leader of Easy Company **BASE** Mobile
HEIGHT 6ft **WEIGHT** 183 lbs **EYES** Blue **HAIR** White (formerly red)
SPECIAL POWERS/ABILITIES Expert combatant, marksman, and battlefield leader; is skilled with almost every known firearm and can operate most varieties of tanks and other heavy equipment.

THE ALL-STAR SQUADRON earned much of America's attention during World War II with their brightly-colored costumes and their superhuman powers. Yet no one is considered a greater wartime hero than a simple, G.I.-uniformed Army sergeant named Frank Rock. Rock suffered unfathomable tragedies before he ever saw combat. His father died in World War I. His stepfather suffocated during a mine collapse. A father figure Rock looked up to while working at a Pittsburgh steel mill also lost his life. Many of his siblings similarly perished, but patriotic Rock enlisted in the army the day after the Japanese attacked Pearl Harbor in 1941 and received an immediate assignment to the European theater of war.

IN PRINT Sergeant Rock was immortalized by writer Kanigher and artist Kubert.

QUIET HERO Rock never thought twice about advancing on an enemy machine-gun nest or charging into a firefight to rescue a pinned-down comrade. His men would follow him anywhere.

THE GOOD SOLDIER

Private Rock didn't truly distinguish himself until the D-Day invasion in 1944. Soon after, at the Battle of Three Stripes Hill, he received a battlefield promotion to sergeant. Sergeant Rock's unit, Easy Company, quickly became one of the most distinguished fighting forces in Europe. Moving from North Africa to Italy to France to Germany, the "combat-happy Joes" included such stalwarts as Wildman, Little Sure Shot, Bulldozer, Farmer Boy, and the Ice Cream Soldier. Pulling off impossible missions, the company lived up to their motto, "Nothin's ever easy in Easy."

Sergeant Rock struck up a battlefield romance with French resistance fighter MADEMOISELLE MARIE and served a brief tour in the Pacific theater. He refused promotions so often he received the nickname "the general of sergeants." According to legend, he died when struck by the last enemy bullet fired on the last day of the war.

Rock, however, survived. Performing postwar covert missions for the U.S. government, he battled his old foe the Iron Major and teamed up with Easy Company veteran Bulldozer on an assignment to Dinosaur Island.

Recently, U.S. President Lex Luthor (see LUTHOR LEX) named General Frank Rock—by then in his eighties— Chairman of the Joint Chiefs of Staff. Rock died during the Imperiex War (see Great Battles, pp. 362–3) and was buried with full honors at Arlington National Cemetery. A short time later a similar Frank Rock appeared at the head of a reconstituted SUICIDE SQUAD. It is debatable whether this Rock was the original or merely an impostor. **DW**

OLD SOLDIER Rock had never sought out promotions, but in the modern era he re-emerged as a general. Part of President Lex Luthor's cabinet, he distinguished himself from his shady commander-in-chief by leading the military effort to destroy Imperiex.

DEFENSIVE General Rock prevents Imperiex from invading Washington.

KEY STORYLINES

• *OUR ARMY AT WAR #81 (APRIL 1959):* Sgt. Rock (here called "Rocky") makes his debut. The series would be renamed for him in issue #302.

• *SGT. ROCK: BETWEEN HELL AND A HARD PLACE (2004):* This moody, recent graphic novel was illustrated by the legendary Joe Kubert.

• *SUPERMAN #166 (MARCH 2001):* President Lex Luthor reintroduces Frank Rock into the DC universe's modern era.

SHADE, THE

FIRST APPEARANCE FLASH COMICS #35 (September 1942)
STATUS Supernatural villain **REAL NAME** Richard Swift
OCCUPATION Criminal (retired) **BASE** Opal City
HEIGHT 6ft 2in **WEIGHT** 170 lbs **EYES** Gray **HAIR** Black
SPECIAL POWERS/ABILITIES Immortality; can summon "shadowmatter"—matter of all kinds, shapes, and sizes, including living beings—from a dimension called the Dark Zone.

Soon after acquiring the ability to manipulate shadowmatter, Richard Swift met Simon Culp, who possessed similar powers. When the two shadowcasters were caught in an explosion, their souls fused together, although Swift's essence controlled their physical body. Swift, now an immortal who called himself the Shade, traveled the world, amassing a fortune. No longer believing that the moral laws of mere mortals no longer applied to him, the Shade settled in Opal City. During and after World War II, the Shade joined the INJUSTICE SOCIETY, exhilarated by the challenge of besting heroes like FLASH I and the JUSTICE SOCIETY OF AMERICA. He eventually gave up crime to defend his adopted home, Opal City and befriended STARMAN Jack Knight. Centuries into the future, a cursed Shade transformed into the mysterious Dark Colossus and battled the LEGION OF SUPER-HEROES. **PJ**

ROGUE AND HERO The Shade shares a joke with his former foe, the first Starman.

SHADOWY POWERS Motivated by the tedium of his life more than by malice or greed, the Shade remained a criminal for years, plunging Keystone City in darkness to loot its banks or using his Dark Zone creatures to rumble with the Fastest Man Alive.

SHADE, THE CHANGING MAN

FIRST APPEARANCE SHADE, THE CHANGING MAN (1st series) #1 (July 1977) **STATUS** Hero **REAL NAME** Rac Shade
OCCUPATION Adventurer **BASE** Mobile **HEIGHT** 5ft 6in
WEIGHT 108 lbs **EYES** Blue **HAIR** Red **SPECIAL POWERS/ABILITIES** Formidable combatant; M-vest emits energy that distorts people's perceptions of its wearer according to their emotional state, also projects force-field, and enables flight, or travel between dimensions.

On the other-dimensional world of Meta, security service agent Rac Shade was framed for causing an explosion that crippled the parents of his true love, Mellu Loren. Little did Shade realize that Mellu's mother was Sude, the Supreme Decider, head of a conspiracy to take over Meta's dimension, the Meta-Zone, and the neighboring dimension containing Earth. Donning the M-vest, created by the genius Dr. Miraco, Shade embarked on a struggle to clear his name. At one point, Shade became trapped in the Zero-Zone between Earth and Meta, his M-vest damaged and unable to transport him to either world. He was saved by the SUICIDE SQUAD and joined the Squad in exchange for passage to Meta. Presumably, not much had changed for Shade on Meta. When last seen, he was back on Earth, perhaps for good. **SB**

SHADO

FIRST APPEARANCE GREEN ARROW: THE LONGBOW HUNTERS #1 (1987)
STATUS Hero **REAL NAME** Shado
OCCUPATION Kyudo Master **BASE** Japan
HEIGHT 5ft **WEIGHT** 109 lbs **EYES** Brown **HAIR** Black
SPECIAL POWERS/ABILITIES Shado is one of the world's greatest archers, using Japanese bamboo arrows 97.5 centimeters long, and a bow weighing 30 kilograms. She is also well trained in the martial arts.

Tomonaga worked for the Yakuza, the Japanese criminal organization, and was sent with two million dollars in gold bullion to the U.S. to help set up American operations. Before he could use the money, he was placed in an internment camp after the Japanese attack on Pearl Harbor. Soldiers tried to learn the money's whereabouts but failed. Once released, Tomonaga married and had a daughter, but was tracked by soldiers who wanted the bullion for themselves. When they tortured his wife, he had little choice but to comply. Returning to Japan, he committed *seppuku* for failing in his mission, and the Yakuza raised the girl, named Shado, as one of their own. She was trained to be their agent, and was given a tattoo on her left arm, shoulder, breast and shoulder blade that formed the image of a large red dragon. Her first assignment was to kill the men who brought about her father's downfall. One of the men was killed instead by Oliver Queen (GREEN ARROW) because he had also tortured Queen's lover, BLACK CANARY II. Later, Shado was asked to commit acts she felt were too heinous and refused, which pitted her against the Yakuza, who now wanted her dead. She has crossed paths with Green Arrow on numerous occasions, which resulted in her giving birth to their son, Robert. She has chosen a life of seclusion to raise the boy and avoids contact with both the Yakuza and Oliver Queen. **RG**

SHADY LADY Shado's motivations are enigmatic, but when she takes aim, she never misses. Unlike Green Arrow, killing does not trouble her.

SHADOWDRAGON

FIRST APPEARANCE SUPERMAN #97 (February 1995)
STATUS Undecided **REAL NAME** Prince Savitar Bandu
OCCUPATION Prince of Bhutan, adventurer **BASE** Metropolis
HEIGHT 5ft 9in **WEIGHT** 147 lbs
EYES Brown **HAIR** Black
SPECIAL POWERS/ABILITIES Skilled martial artist and computer hacker; wears weapon-studded armored suit that also confers invisibility.

Shadowdragon is the alternate persona of Prince Savitar Bandu of Bhutan, who uses his ninja-like stealth and lightning-fast combat skills to steal technology that will benefit his developing nation. He wears an advanced X-10 battlesuit—stolen from the rival nation of Chi-Lann—that allows him to turn invisible or to fire poison darts. Shadowdragon has trained most of his life to become a master of the martial arts and is also one of the world's top computer hackers. Despite his ongoing thefts, Shadowdragon is an honorable man who only acts in the best interests of his people. Upon first arriving in Metropolis, he uncovered reams of computer data on SUPERMAN for use by the villain Conduit; however, when Shadowdragon learned of Conduit's malevolent motives toward the Man of Steel, he erased the data. He continues to operate in both Metropolis and Bhutan and to do everything in his power to ensure a prosperous future for the citizens he will one day rule as king. **DW**

SHAGGY MAN

FIRST APPEARANCE JUSTICE LEAGUE OF AMERICA #45 (June 1966) **STATUS** Robotic villain (destroyed)
REAL NAME/OCCUPATION Inapplicable **BASE** Mobile
HEIGHT 5ft 5in **WEIGHT** 437 lbs
EYES Red **HAIR** Brown
SPECIAL POWERS/ABILITIES Superhuman strength; near invulnerability; body part regeneration.

The Shaggy Man was a robotic creature created by Professor Andrew Zagarian with "plastalloy," a synthetic substance resembling human tissue. The robot came to life and went on a rampage, one that even the JUSTICE LEAGUE OF AMERICA could not stop. The FLASH persuaded Zagarian to create a second Shaggy Man and trapped the two robots on an asteroid, hoping that each would destroy each other. But Hector Hammond (see HAMMOND, HECTOR) intervened and teleported one of the Shaggy Men to the JLA satellite in an attempt to destroy the heroes. GREEN LANTERN was able to capture that Shaggy Man, and AQUAMAN imprisoned it in a deep trench in the Pacific Ocean.

Later, General Wade Eiling transferred his consciousness into the Shaggy Man body, shaving off the distinctive fur and becoming the indestructible GENERAL. A third Shaggy Man has recently appeared as part of Lex Luthor's (see LUTHOR, LEX) Injustice League Unlimited. **PJ**

SHAZAM

FIRST APPEARANCE WHIZ COMICS #2 (February 1940)
STATUS Hero (deceased) **REAL NAME** Unknown, formerly the Champion
OCCUPATION Wizard **BASE** Rock of Eternity
HEIGHT 6ft **WEIGHT** 175 lbs **EYES** Blue **HAIR** White
SPECIAL POWERS/ABILITIES Vast magical abilities.

Shazam the wizard was one of Earth's first heroes, making his mark in ancient Canaan many thousands of years ago. After millennia of existence he became a wizened mentor figure operating out of the extradimensional Rock of Eternity, eager to pass on his powers to a successor. Shazam gifted his abilities to Teth-Adam in ancient Egypt, resulting in the origin of BLACK ADAM.

A different champion emerged in the modern era—archaeologist C.C. Batson. When Black Adam murdered C.C. Batson before any magical transfer could take place, Shazam bestowed his blessing on Batson's son, Billy. With the powers of Shazam—the wisdom of Solomon, the strength of Hercules, the stamina of Atlas, the power of Zeus, the courage of Achilles, and the speed of Mercury—Billy became super hero CAPTAIN MARVEL. During the Infinite Crisis, a maddened SPECTRE killed thousands in an anti-magic purge. Shazam confronted the Spectre at the Rock of Eternity and lost his life. The SHADOWPACT helped rebuild the Rock, and Billy Batson took Shazam's place. **DW**

SHARK

FIRST APPEARANCE GREEN LANTERN (2nd series) #24 (October 1963)
STATUS Villain **REAL NAME** Has used aliases T.S. Smith and Karshon
OCCUPATION Predator **BASE** Mobile
HEIGHT 6ft 2in **WEIGHT** 243 lbs **EYES** Black **HAIR** None
SPECIAL POWERS/ABILITIES A powerful psionic able to manipulate matter, project energy bolts, and communicate telepathically; also able to fly and grow to gigantic size.

Radiation leaking from an oceanside nuclear power station transformed a tiger shark into a mutant humanoid monster. Imbued with increased intelligence and psionic powers, the Shark was still driven by his species' primal predatory urges, but now fed on the psyches of his victims rather than their flesh. The Shark attacked Hal Jordan (GREEN LANTERN II) hoping to make the fearless Green Lantern experience terror before he consumed his mind. However, Jordan defeated the Shark and devolved him to his original state. The Shark regained his humanoid form on several occasions, battling both Green Lantern and AQUAMAN, briefly deposing the latter from his throne by disguising himself as an Atlantean named Karshon and used his mental might to rule Atlantis. Later, the Shark was recruited by Green Lantern III Guy Gardner to join a squad of super-villains opposing the Qwardians during the Crisis conflict (see Great Battles, pp.362–3).

During the Infinite Crisis, the Shark participated in a supervillain attack on Atlantis, where he was apparently responsible for the death of Neptune Perkins (see PERKINS, NEPTUNE). He appears to have escaped the SPECTRE's destruction of Atlantis. **SB**

SHADOWPACT, THE

FIRST APPEARANCE DAY OF VENGEANCE #1 (June 2005)
STATUS Hero Team **BASE** Oblivion Bar
CURRENT MEMBERS AND POWERS
Nightmaster Expert combatant with magical sword.
Blue Devil Enhanced strength and durability, wields Trident of Lucifer.
Nightshade Teleportation, ability to form darkness into 3D shapes.
Ragman Absorbs sinners into his cloak and draws on their powers.
Detective Chimp Brilliant mind, can talk to animals.
Enchantress Vast magical abilities.
Zauriel Flight, enhanced strength, telepathy, sonic scream.

According to legend, teams of mystics have called themselves the Shadowpact during struggles against dark sorcery. The most recent group, consisting of NIGHTMASTER, BLUE DEVIL, NIGHTSHADE, RAGMAN, DETECTIVE CHIMP, and the ENCHANTRESS, assembled in the Oblivion Bar just before the Infinite Crisis. An insane SPECTRE had teamed with ECLIPSO, and only the Shadowpact stood in the way of their mad rampage. The team survived the battle with help from CAPTAIN MARVEL and DETECTIVE ALICE, and leveraged their newfound fame in the magical community by organizing the cleanup efforts after the destruction of the Rock of Eternity loosed the Seven Deadly Sins. After the Infinite Crisis, the Shadowpact spent a year battling the Pentacle inside a bubble surrounding the town of Riverrock, Wyoming. The team returned to action against Doctor Gotham. They later welcomed ZAURIEL, who took the Blue Devil's place. **DW**

KEY 1) Nightshade
2) Nightmaster **3)** Ragman
4) Blue Devil **5)** Enchantress
6) Detective Chimp

5 2

IN THE YEAR following the Infinite Crisis, the world persevered without its greatest heroes: Superman, Batman, and Wonder Woman. While the legends avoided the spotlight, lesser figures claimed the stage and ushered in a new era with the rebirth of the multiverse.

ELONGATED MAN

Following his wife Sue's murder at the hands of Jean Loring, Ralph Dibny retired his Elongated Man identity and sank into a deep depression. News that a Kryptonian "resurrection cult" had vandalized his wife's gravestone prompted Dibny to investigate the cult's most prominent member, WONDER GIRL. She believed its rituals could restore life to Conner Kent (SUPERBOY). Dibny sought to expose the cult as a fraud, but experienced a shock when his wife's soul appeared to animate a straw effigy. Shaken, Dibny agreed to follow the helmet of DOCTOR FATE through a string of magical realms and netherworlds on a search for Sue's spirit. Dibny ultimately learned that the journey was a ruse: Fate's helmet had been controlled by the magician Felix Faust (see FAUST, FELIX) to lure Dibny into the clutches of the demon NERON. Dibny outsmarted his enemies, trapping both in Doctor Fate's tower, but lost his life in the effort. Yet in the afterlife he found a happy ending. He reunited with Sue and the couple became mystery-solving "ghost detectives".

RESURRECTION CULT *Cultists promised they could bring Sue Dibny to life by animating a straw effigy.*

THE EVERYMAN PROJECT

Lex Luthor (see LUTHOR, LEX) announced to an eager public that superpowers no longer had to be the sole possession of an elite. The genetic manipulations of his Everyman Project provided hundreds of ordinary citizens with enhanced abilities, including Natasha Irons (see IRONS, NATASHA), niece of the hero STEEL. Natasha and several others became the first inductees into Luthor's new INFINITY INC. team. On New Year's Eve, the limits of Luthor's benevolence became apparent when he shut down all of his subjects' powers, causing dozens of helpless flyers to plunge from the sky. Luthor also gave himself superpowers, prompting a showdown with Steel and Natasha Irons that resulted in Luthor's capture and disgrace.

SPACE EXILES

ANIMAL MAN, Adam Strange, (see STRANGE, ADAM) and STARFIRE found themselves stranded in deep space after the Infinite Crisis, swept up in a war of conquest by the armies of Lady Styx. The intergalactic mercenary LOBO became their ally, thwarting Lady Styx's schemes despite setbacks including Adam Strange's blindness and Animal Man's death and resurrection. After a year-long journey, the trio at last found their way home.

THE QUESTION

Vic Sage, the faceless investigator known as the QUESTION, teamed with ex-Gotham City police detective Renee Montoya (see MONTOYA, RENEE) to investigate INTERGANG's inroads into Gotham City. The trail led to BLACK ADAM's country Khandaq, where the two prevented a suicide bombing at the wedding of Black Adam and ISIS. They later journeyed to Nanda Parbat in the Himalayas, hoping that the region's mystics could halt the Question's terminal lung cancer. Back in Gotham, the Question and Montoya teamed with BATWOMAN to stop Intergang's Bruno Mannheim (see MANNHEIM, BRUNO) and his Crime Bible cult. In the end Vic Sage died, passing the Question identity on to Montoya.

SAGE ADVICE *The original Question passed on his knowledge to Renee Montoya so she could continue his legacy.*

BOMBER DOWN *She hated taking a life, but Renee Montoya (kneeling in red dress) had no other choice to prevent a suicide bomber at the wedding of Isis and Black Adam.*

NANDA PARBAT *The holy mountain city became Vic Sage's refuge as he battled cancer.*

OOLONG ISLAND

Will Magnus, the genius behind the METAL MEN, became the newest inductee into a "Science Squad" of evil geniuses on Oolong Island in the Pacific. The operation's mastermind proved to be Chang Tzu (EGG FU), an Apokoliptian creation working for China's Great Ten. Magnus refused to build lethal robots for his captors, escaping Oolong after incapacitating Tzu by cracking his eggshell with a lead bullet.

WELCOMING PARTY *Oolong Island had plenty of distractions to keep its scientists occupied.*

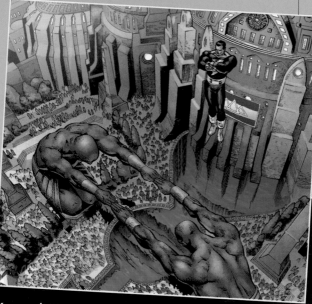

KHANDAQ'S RULER *As a superpowered dictator, Black Adam held absolute power in his home country.*

BLACK ADAM AND WORLD WAR III

As the leader of isolationist Khandaq, Black Adam had grown beyond his role as a foil to CAPTAIN MARVEL. Black Adam found a calming influence in his life in Adrianna Tomaz. She became his wife after assuming the powers of Isis. Her younger brother Amon joined them as the superpowered OSIRIS, and the addition of the talking crocodile SOBEK rounded out what appeared to be a happy family unit.

Yet treachery arose when Sobek revealed himself as Famine, one of the Four Horsemen of Apokolips ordered to bring down the Black Marvel Family. Sobek devoured Osiris, and Isis died at the hands of Pestilence, before Black Adam unleashed his revenge. Black Adam blasted the Horsemen's launching point of Bialya, killing everyone within the country's borders. He then stormed across the globe in a bloodbath of destruction called World War III, until stripped of his powers by Captain Marvel.

ADAM'S FALL *World War III ended with Black Adam powerless. It took a worldwide quest for him to regain his abilities.*

EVIL SKEETS *The malevolent intentions of Skeets became clear in the Kandor showdown. It wasn't until later that Mister Mind revealed himself as the true culprit.*

BOOSTER GOLD AND MISTER MIND

This second-string super hero saw an opportunity to become a major player with the knowledge of future events stored in the memory banks of his robot sidekick SKEETS. But Booster discovered that the timeline was unfolding differently than had been recorded, making his data worthless. Desperate to make his mark, Booster sold out to corporations and staged mock battles with super-villains, quickly developing a rivalry with Metropolis' newest hero, the mysterious Supernova. Booster seemingly perished in an oil tanker explosion, but soon revealed himself as the masked Supernova. He had used Rip Hunter's time machine (see HUNTER, RIP) to skip backward in history, the better to uncover Skeets' suspiciously sinister actions. Rip Hunter and Booster confronted Skeets in the bottle city of Kandor, but their attempt to trap him in the Phantom Zone failed. In a chase through time, Skeets revealed himself as MISTER MIND, the Venusian worm who had cocooned inside Skeets' robot shell before undergoing a monstrous metamorphosis. Mister Mind began to "eat time," altering the histories of the multiverse's 52 parallel realities. Booster and the new Supernova (Booster's ancestor Daniel Carter) stopped Mister Mind by hurling him backward through a time loop.

The end of the year saw the return of SUPERMAN, BATMAN, and WONDER WOMAN. Yet the actions of Booster Gold and others had changed the multiverse forever. **DW**

FIGHT FOR FAME *Booster Gold dispatched Mammoth in his early, desperate bid to become Metropolis's champion.*

SHELLSHOCK II

FIRST APPEARANCE STEEL #6 (July 1994)
STATUS Villain   **REAL NAME** Ruth Spencer
OCCUPATION Assassin   **BASE** New Jersey
HEIGHT 5ft 4in   **WEIGHT** 120 lbs   **EYES** Brown   **HAIR** Black
SPECIAL POWERS/ABILITIES Has the ability to cause objects to explode with a single punch, but she must name the item or her power fails.

The first villain to go by the name Shellshock was a woman with the ability to generate explosive force from her body. She battled the second HAWK & DOVE team before being defeated by SUPERMAN and has seemingly retired from a life of crime. The current villain operating as Shellshock is a member of Black Ops, an organization of techno-pirates run by Manual Cabral, known as Hazard II. Nothing is known about how Ruth Spencer gained her energy-punch powers or came in contact with Hazard. She is fiercely loyal to Black Ops's charismatic leader, acting as his lieutenant. It is unclear if she harbors romantic feelings for Hazard II or is simply an idealistic zealot. Under Hazard's command, the Black Ops attempted to take over the entire nuclear arsenal of the U.S., only to be opposed and ultimately stopped by John Henry Irons, Steel II. After their final defeat, Hazard turned his attention to other nefarious schemes for acquiring the latest high-tech weaponry and selling it to the highest bidder. The members of his ruthless team, including second-in-command Shellshock, await his orders. **RG**

SHIFT

FIRST APPEARANCE OUTSIDERS (3rd series) #1 (August 2003)
STATUS Hero (inactive)   **REAL NAME** Not applicable
OCCUPATION Professional adventurer   **BASE** Mobile
HEIGHT 6ft 1in   **WEIGHT** 200 lbs   **EYES** Black   **HAIR** None
SPECIAL POWERS/ABILITIES Unstable molecules permit transmutation of himself and other objects into chemical compounds.

When METAMORPHO fell to Earth following the Hyperclan's destruction of the JLA satellite, part of him broke off and grew into a facsimile of Rex Morgan. The amnesiac clone did not know he was not the genuine article, and joined NIGHTWING's new team of OUTSIDERS as Metamorpho. Soon, the true Metamorpho confronted his duplicate, but did not absorb him because the copy had already embarked on a distinct life. Taking Shift's identity, the clone remained with the Outsiders and fell in love with teammate INDIGO, an android from the future. The romance ended when Indigo revealed herself as BRAINIAC 8 and tried to destroy the Outsiders and the TEEN TITANS. Indigo regained control of her programming and urged Shift to kill her, which he did by transforming her into organic material. A heartbroken Shift stayed with the team, but a botched mission after the Infinite Crisis resulted in 44 deaths. Believing himself responsible, Shift let himself be re-absorbed into Metamorpho. **DW**

SHIMMER

FIRST APPEARANCE THE NEW TEEN TITANS (1st series) #3
STATUS Villain   **REAL NAME** Selinda Flinders
OCCUPATION Professional criminal   **BASE** Mobile
HEIGHT 5ft 7in   **WEIGHT** 125 lbs   **EYES** Blue   **HAIR** Red
SPECIAL POWERS/ABILITIES Could temporarily transform one element or compound into another.

Selinda Flinders and her brother Baran were born in Australia and shunned because of their superhuman abilities. Their father brought them to Doctor Helga Jace, a renowned Markovian scientist, to help them master their powers and develop a sense of right and wrong. Selinda and Baran, however, rejected their education and became professional criminals, eventually joining DOCTOR LIGHT I in his villainous organization the FEARSOME FIVE.

Shimmer, as Selinda came to be called, and her brother, now named MAMMOTH, fought the New TEEN TITANS several times over the years, and were imprisoned more than once.

The two siblings renounced crime and found peace in a Tibetan monastery. However their former teammate PSIMON came seeking revenge for their betrayal of the Fearsome Five. Psimon turned Shimmer into glass and shattered her body, killing her instantly. Mammoth only barely survived. However, Shimmer was resurrected by DOCTOR SIVANA. She and her brother Mammoth returned to a life of crime with a new Fearsome Five. **PJ**

SHINING KNIGHT

FIRST APPEARANCE ADVENTURE COMICS #66 (September 1941);
(II) SEVEN SOLDIERS: SHINING KNIGHT #1 (August 2005)
STATUS Hero   **REAL NAME** Sir Justin, a.k.a. Justin Arthur; (II) Ystina
OCCUPATION Knight; (II) Adventurer   **BASE** Camelot; New York City; (II) New York City
HEIGHT 6ft 1in; (II) 5ft 2in   **WEIGHT** 185 lbs; (II) 115 lbs   **EYES** Blue; (II) Green   **HAIR** Blond; (II) Black
SPECIAL POWERS/ABILITIES Master of knightly combat; wears enchanted, bulletproof armor and wields enchanted sword; rides a flying horse; (II) Expert duelist and hand-to-hand combatant

While riding to battle the ogre Blunderbore, Sir Justin—a knight of King Arthur's Round Table—was accosted by outlaws. While driving them off, Sir Justin grazed a tree with his lance and released the wizard Merlin from mystical imprisonment. The grateful Merlin enchanted Sir Justin's sword and armor, and gave his noble steed wings. Merlin's gifts helped Sir Justin to slay Blunderbore, but not before the dying ogre buried Sir Justin and his horse, Winged Victory, beneath a mountain of ice.

For centuries, Sir Justin and Winged Victory lay in suspended animation. But in 1941, the knight was freed by Dr. Moresby, who helped Sir Justin to establish the identity of Justin Arthur and make a new home in New York City. As the Shining Knight, Sir Justin joined the ALL-STAR SQUADRON, and then the SEVEN SOLDIERS OF VICTORY. A second Shining Knight appeared in the present during the invasion of the Sheeda just prior to the Infinite Crisis. Ystina, a young girl from an 8,000 B.C. version of Camelot, time-traveled to New York City to do battle against the Sheeda queen and remained in the present day as an adventurer. **SB**

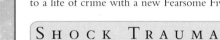
WINGED VICTORY Sir Justin's brave steed still carries him into battle.

SHOCK TRAUMA

FIRST APPEARANCE THE TITANS #21 (November 2000)
STATUS Villain   **REAL NAME** Unrevealed
OCCUPATION Assassin   **BASE** Japan
HEIGHT 5ft 6in   **WEIGHT** 146 lbs
EYES Unrevealed   **HAIR** Unrevealed
SPECIAL POWERS/ABILITIES Can generate and emit electricity over short distances but at lethal levels.

Shock Trauma was born and raised in Japan. He is the youngest member of the HANGMEN. This group are typical of the new generation of assassins, in it purely for the money. They are all power, no subtlety. The team, which also includes Breathtaker, Provoke, Stranglehold, and KILLSHOT—made its mark in Europe before taking assignments in America. Its first visit to the U.S. was unusual, a kidnapping, not killing assignment, at the behest of rebels from the Middle-Eastern country of Qurac. The Hangman were sent to collect Lian Harper, the daughter of Teen Titan ARSENAL and the international terrorist CHESHIRE—who set off a nuclear device in Qurac. The TEEN TITANS defeated the Hangmen, and rescued Lian. Following this encounter, Shock Trauma went into hiding, presumably readying himself for another Hangman mission. **RG**

SHRECK

FIRST APPEARANCE SUICIDE SQUAD (1st series) #37 (January 1990)
STATUS Villain **REAL NAME** Unknown
OCCUPATION Vampire **BASE** Mobile
HEIGHT 6ft 3in **WEIGHT** 188 lbs **EYES** Black **HAIR** Black
SPECIAL POWERS/ABILITIES Superstrength; partial invulnerability; ability to hypnotize.

Shreck is a vampire who feeds on blood and possesses many of the powers associated with the lords of the undead. He is also an agent for the Russian government, having logged time with all the major Russian meta-human programs. Most recently he served as a member of the Red Shadows, the Russian covert strike agency that acted as the Eastern equivalent to America's SUICIDE SQUAD.

Shreck and the Red Shadows tussled with the Suicide Squad in a mission that took them to Cambodia in search of the Temple of the Dragon's Hoard. Shreck's vampiric gift for mesmerism came in handy when he took control of Suicide Squad member NIGHTSHADE, though the Red Shadows came away from the battle empty-handed. **DW**

SHRINKING VIOLET

FIRST APPEARANCE LEGION OF SUPER-HEROES (4th series) #66 (March 1995) **STATUS** Hero **REAL NAME** Salu "Violet" Digby
OCCUPATION Legionnaire **BASE** 30th-century Earth
HEIGHT 5ft 2in **WEIGHT** 105 lbs **EYES** Violet **HAIR** Black
SPECIAL POWERS/ABILITIES Can shrink to subatomic size or grow 30 feet tall, with a proportionate increase in mass and strength.

A native of the planet Imsk, whose inhabitants can all shrink to tiny size, the socially awkward Salu Digby was chosen to become a member of the LEGION OF SUPER HEROES because of her power, her deductive skills, and her combat prowess Using the name Shrinking Violet, Salu was quickly admitted to the Legion's Espionage Squad.

The overly shy Violet was contacted by the Emerald Eye of Ekron, a sentient talisman, who wanted to make use of her body as a host for its energies. Violet agreed to allow the mystical force to merge with her body, and the Emerald Eye possessed her. Violet took control of the Legion and hurled some of the members back in time. Eventually she was freed from the Eye's tyrannical thrall during a battle between the Legion and Mordru the DARK LORD, who desired the Eye's power for himself. In another timeline containing the Legion of Super-Heroes, Shrinking Violet goes by the name Atom Girl. She used her microscopic powers to explore sub-atomic dimensions and avoid contact with the other Legionnaires until BRAINIAC 5 ordered her into action against Terror Firma. She has since integrated with the other Legionnaires, who view her with some suspicion due to her unusual abilities and variable loyalties. **PJ**

SILVER BANSHEE

FIRST APPEARANCE ACTION COMICS #495 (December 1987)
STATUS Hero **REAL NAME** Siobhan McDougal/Lacy MacElwain
OCCUPATION Adventurer **BASE** The Netherverse
HEIGHT 6ft 11in **WEIGHT** 180 lbs **EYES** White **HAIR** Silver
SPECIAL POWERS/ABILITIES Impervious to gunfire; possesses superhuman speed and the strength of ten men; her siren wail is a deadly song, killing anyone within earshot.

Centuries ago, Siobhan McDougal was denied leadership of her Irish clan because she was a woman. When Siobhan tried to invoke mystical intervention to reverse the decision of her clansmen, she inadvertently weakened a gateway to the hellish Netherverse and was dragged there by its demonic denizens. After what seemed an eternity, Siobhan was magically empowered by the mysterious Crone, who transformed Siobhan into the Silver Banshee so that she might return to Earth and slay the descendants of the treacherous McDougal clan who had forever damned her.

In Metropolis, the Silver Banshee sought the written history of her clan, slaying anyone in her path, until SUPERMAN halted her quest for vengeance. Later, the Man of Steel actually helped the Silver Banshee free herself from the control of the demoness Blaze. The Silver Banshee encountered Superman yet again when the wicked wraith sought out McDougal heir Lacy MacElwain in an attempt to extricate herself from the curse of the Silver Banshee. In conflict with the sorceress known as Hecate, Lacy was mortally wounded. Silver Banshee attacked Superman and BATMAN when President Lex Luthor (*see* Luthor, Lex) put a bounty on their heads. Prior to the Infinite Crisis, she joined the Society (*see* VILLAINS UNITED). **SB**

STRANGE BREW The Netherverse's Crone gave Siobhan McDougal the power to exact revenge.

SUPER-FOE The Silver Banshee had no quarrel with the Man of Steel, until he stood in the way of her vengeance.

DEATH SONG The terrible wail of the Silver Banshee can slay any mortal and even shred metal!

SILVER MONKEY

FIRST APPEARANCE DETECTIVE COMICS #685 (March 1995)
STATUS Villain **REAL NAME** Unrevealed
OCCUPATION Assassin **BASE** Asia
HEIGHT 5ft 6in **WEIGHT** 130 lbs **EYES** Blue **HAIR** Brown
SPECIAL POWERS/ABILITIES One of the deadliest martial artists on the
planet; a merciless killer.

When General Tsu and the Shan Triad attempted to
corner the heroin market in Asia's Golden Triangle, they
were opposed by KING SNAKE. This resulted in a gang war
played out on the streets of Gotham City. Tsu, unwilling
to lose the battle or face the Taiwanese Triad, hired the
mercenary Silver Monkey to kill King Snake. The battle
was bloody, and caught the attention of Gotham's guardian,
BATMAN. He intervened, along with NIGHTWING and
ROBIN III. In the climactic battle, Robin saved King
Snake from Silver Monkey, and the Monkey tumbled into
Gotham Harbor. All that was found was his mask,
leading Batman to suspect that the Silver Monkey
remains alive. RG

SIN-EATER

FIRST APPEARANCE JSA #23 (June 2001)
STATUS Villain (destroyed) **REAL NAME** Onimar Synn
OCCUPATION Consumer of souls **BASE** The planet Thanagar
HEIGHT 7ft 5in **WEIGHT** 480 lbs **EYES** Yellow **HAIR** None
SPECIAL POWERS/ABILITIES Absorbed power from the suffering and fear
of others; could absorb the souls of innocent people and transform
them into zombie warriors.

Rumored to be one of the legendary Seven Devils
of Thanagar, a race of demons that has plagued
the planet since birth, Onimar Synn attempted
to take over the planet Thanagar and feed on
the souls of its populace. Onimar enslaved the
population with Nth metal, an element found only
on Thanagar. He killed thousands of them, feasting on
their souls and transforming them into an undead army.
The Nth metal gave Onimar complete mastery over the
four fundamental forces of the universe—strong, weak,
gravitational, and electromagnetic.

In a desperate attempt to save the rest of their people,
the high priests of Thanagar kidnapped Kendra Saunders,
the hero known as HAWKGIRL, who could summon Carter
Hall (HAWKMAN) back from the dead through their divine
connection. Kendra succeeded, but it took the combined
might of Hawkman, Hawkgirl, and the JUSTICE SOCIETY
OF AMERICA to stop Synn's rampaging, undead warriors.
Onimar Synn was apparently destroyed by the power of
Hawkman and Hawkgirl's ancient love. PJ

SILVER SWAN I & II

FIRST APPEARANCE ((I) WONDER WOMAN (2nd ser.) #15
(April 1988) ; (II) WONDER WOMAN (2nd ser.)
#171 (August 2001) **STATUS** Villains
REAL NAME (I) Valerie Beaudry; (II) Vanessa "Nessie" Kapatelis (II)
OCCUPATION (I) Reformed villain; (II) enforcer **BASE** (I) Mobile;
(II) Boston **HEIGHT** (I) 5ft 7in; (II) 5ft 6in **WEIGHT** (I) 136 lbs;
(II) 130 lbs **EYES** (I) Blue; (II) blue **HAIR** (I) Blonde; (II) brown
SPECIAL POWERS/ABILITIES Flight; emit "swan song" that can flatten
buildings or generate a sonic shield; II can mentally control birds.

*FRAGILE PSYCHE Although
graceful in flight and beautiful
in appearance, both Silver
Swans suffer from self-loathing.*

The first Silver Swan was a true manifestation of
the Ugly Duckling fable. Born with severe physical
deformities, Valerie Beaudry came under the tender
mercies of billionaire industrialist Henry Armbruster,
who subjected her to chemical treatments that
eventually made her beautiful. A side-effect of
these experiments provided her with her a steel-
shattering sonic scream and the power of flight.
Armbruster exploited Valerie's insecurities, physically
and mentally abusing her to ensure her loyalty as the
Silver Swan, his private enforcer. Wearing a suit with
artificial wings for steering, the Silver Swan attacked
WONDER WOMAN until the Amazon princess revealed
the truth—Valerie's benefactor was a monster. The
Silver Swan turned on Armbruster and became a
free agent, later turning up alongside the Captains of
Industry, a superhuman task force.

Silver Swan II once considered herself to be Wonder
Woman's closest friend. Vanessa "Nessie" Kapatelis,
daughter of archaeologist Julia Kapatelis, viewed Diana
as a beloved older sister but eventually began to resent
her Amazonian perfection. Angry and hurt when
Diana chose Cassie Sandsmark to be the new WONDER
GIRL, Nessie became an easy target for the evil
sorceress Circe, who magically transformed the girl
into a new Silver Swan. Bearing heavy psychological
baggage made more severe by the brainwashing and
mind-bending techniques of Circe's

temporary ally DOCTOR PSYCHO,
Silver Swan II set herself against
Wonder Woman. She launched a
wall-splitting sonic attack on Wonder
Girl's high school, accidentally
exposing Cassie Sandsmark's Wonder
Girl identity when she was forced
to use superpowers to rescue her
classmates. Recently, Silver Swan II
became an agent of Wonder Woman's
enemy, Veronica Cale, and attacked
the Amazon princess in a fury. Diana
defeated her former friend and brought her to
Themyscira for treatment. DW

SINESTRO

First appearance GREEN LANTERN (2nd series) #7 (August 1961)
Status Villain   *Real name* Sinestro
Occupation Intergalactic criminal   *Base* The anti-matter universe of Qward
Height 6ft 7in   *Weight* 205 lbs   *Eyes* Black   *Hair* Black
Special powers/abilities Master tactician and military commander; his yellow power ring could create anything his fertile, fiendish imagination could conceive.

WRONG TURN *Until Sinestro's spirit was corrupted by evil, he was one of Hal Jordan's closest friends.*

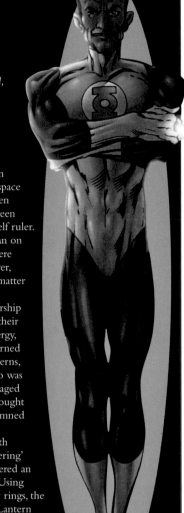

Sinestro became the greatest enemy of Green Lantern and the Green Lantern Corps. He was, for a time, a Corps member himself—the Green Lantern of space sector 1417. Born on the planet Korugar, Sinestro was a fearless warrior. Given a power ring by the Guardians of the Universe, Sinestro became an adept Green Lantern. He returned to Korugar and, corrupted by power, proclaimed himself ruler. Sinestro was forced to leave his homeworld to train Green Lantern Hal Jordan on Earth, and they became good friends. Sinestro then returned to Korugar, where the people were rioting against his rule. Disgusted by Sinestro's abuse of power, the Guardians stripped him of his power ring and banished him to the anti-matter universe of Qward.

Trapped in the anti-matter universe, Sinestro impressed the hardened leadership of Qward with his warrior's skills and told them of the Green Lanterns and their rings. The Qwardians created their own power ring, imbued with yellow energy, the only weakness of the Green Lanterns' rings. Using the ring, Sinestro returned to the positive-matter universe and became a constant foe of the Green Lanterns, notably his old pupil, Hal Jordan. After years of intergalactic sparring, Sinestro was imprisoned on Oa, the Guardians' homeworld. But Sinestro escaped and, enraged by his humiliation, destroyed an entire solar system. The massive genocide brought to bear the combined power of the entire Green Lantern Corps, who condemned Sinestro to death. Sinestro's spirit remained in the Central Power Battery, where he allied with PARALLAX and tricked Hal Jordan into 'murdering' a duplicate Sinestro. Later freed, Sinestro gathered an army on Qward in the anti-matter universe. Using Parallax's power over fear to fuel their yellow rings, the Sinestro Corps made war against the Green Lantern Corps, aided by the MANHUNTERS and Sinestro's lieutenants Superman-Prime, the Anti-Monitor (*see* MONITORS) and the CYBORG SUPERMAN. **PJ**

FRIENDS AND FOES *It was in final battle with Hal Jordan that the sinister Sinestro met his grisly fate.*

SIRIUS

First appearance ORION #10 (March 2001)
Status Wolf-demon (deceased)   *Real name* None
Occupation Guardian of the Dreggs   *Base* Apokolips
Height 20ft   *Weight* 5,618 lbs   *Eyes* Green   *Hair* Golden
Special powers/abilities A demon of gargantuan size and unbridled ferocity, but with a definite sense of good and evil.

Beneath the slums of Armagetto on Apokolips lie the labyrinthine Black Ways of the Dreggs which were guarded by Sirius, a wolf-demon imprisoned there for millennia. ORION, Dog of War, tracked his enemy DESAAD into the Dreggs and met Sirius instead. A Desaadite—an artificial life-form in Desaad's form—attacked and Sirius defended the Dog of War. Sirius took up Orion in his gaping jaws and hurled him into a Boom Tube leading to the surface of Apokolips, thus saving his life. The wolf-demon died in battle with the Desaadite, and Orion has never forgotten the noble demon beast. **SB**

SKEETS

First appearance BOOSTER GOLD #1 (February 1986)
Status Hero   *Real name* Skeets
Occupation Security robot   *Base* Mobile
Height 12ft   *Weight* 5 lbs   *Eyes* None   *Hair* None
Special powers/abilities Flight, built-in weapons systems, computer databanks of historical events.

Skeets is a 25th-century robot, who went back in time with BOOSTER GOLD to help him seek fame in the modern era. Although they secured a place for Booster in the JUSTICE LEAGUE OF AMERICA, by the Infinite Crisis they had not made their mark. With Skeets' databanks useless due to temporal anomalies, Booster sacrificed himself to save Metropolis (secretly returning as Supernova). Skeets was infected by MISTER MIND and killed SUPER-CHIEF and WAVERIDER for control of the multiverse. Mister Mind escaped Skeets' shell and tried to erase reality. Rip Hunter and Booster defeated Mister Mind, reviving Skeets. Booster, Skeets and Hunter then repaired the timestream. **DW**

SKORPIO

First appearance STEEL (2nd series) #37 (April 1997)
Status Villain   *Real name* Dennis Samuel Ellis
Occupation Medical intern; mercenary   *Base* Jersey City, NY
Height 5ft 9in   *Weight* 162 lbs   *Eyes* Brown   *Hair* Black
Special powers/abilities Costume contains hidden weaponry, such as toxin-coated blades; an above-average athlete.

Sam Ellis was a resident at Garden State Medical Center when the head of the hospital, gang boss Dr. Arthur Villain, recruited him for a special mission. Anticipating STEEL's arrival, Villain created the super-powered persona of Skorpio. Ellis was only too happy to adopt this character. He took the costume and Villain's money in the hope that he would get some kicks and earn some extra money to pay back his student loans. Skorpio became Villain's mob enforcer, until he found himself in direct competition with Steel for the affections of Dr. Amanda Quick, a doctor at Garden State Medical Center. **RG**

SLEEZ

First appearance ACTION COMICS #592 (September 1987)
Status Villain (deceased)   *Real name* None
Occupation Corruptor   *Base* Formerly Apokolips; later Metropolis
Height 4ft 3in   *Weight* 181 lbs   *Eyes* Black   *Hair* Black (sparse)
Special powers/abilities Psionic powers enabled Sleez to dominate others' minds and force them to surrender to their baser desires.

Spewed forth from the sewers of Armagetto on distant Apokolips, the dwarfish Sleez was notorious for his vileness. DARKSEID made Sleez his aide but, even Darkseid tired of Sleez's depravity. He was transported to Earth, where he captured SUPERMAN and BIG BARDA—formerly one of Darkseid's FEMALE FURIES loyal —and mentally manipulated them into fighting for his own twisted amusement. Fortunately, Barda's husband, MISTER MIRACLE, intervened. Later, Sleez mentally enslaved the directors of Project Cadmus and forced them to create clones of themselves, thereby giving birth to a second Newsboy Legion. Following a renewed conflict with Superman involving the Project's Newsboys, Sleez was apparently killed when the torture device he used to enthrall the Cadmus creations backfired. Sleez perished a second time during the Death of the New Gods event, slain in Metropolis. **SB**

SOBEK

FIRST APPEARANCE 52 #26 (November 2006)
STATUS Villain **REAL NAME** Yurrd the Unknown
OCCUPATION Embodiment of Famine **BASE** Mobile
HEIGHT Various **WEIGHT** Various **EYES** Various **HAIR** Various
SPECIAL POWERS/ABILITIES Can cause famine; enhanced strength and durability; can pass spirit from one body to another.

Sobek is one of the forms taken by Famine—who, with Death, War, and Pestilence, make up the Four Horsemen of Apokolips. After the Infinite Crisis, Yurrd took the identity of the intelligent, talking crocodile Sobek, supposedly a creation of the mad scientist DOCTOR SIVANA. Sobek befriended OSIRIS of the Black Marvel family, adopting a timid front to disguise his true nature.

Osiris began to confide in Sobek. During a period of contrition following his murder of the PERSUADER, Osiris dropped his superpowers at his friend's request. Sobek pounced on his defenseless prey and devoured Osiris alive.

BLACK ADAM took swift revenge and slaughtered Sobek, but the specter of Yurrd the Unknown could not be destroyed. It returned to the wastelands of Bialya with its fellow spirits to feed on the misery of the nation's refugees. BATMAN and SUPERMAN thwarted the ambitions of the Four Horsemen. **DW**

SOLARIS I & II

FIRST APPEARANCE KOBRA #2 (May 1976)
STATUS Villain (deceased) **REAL NAME** Clifton Lacey
OCCUPATION Assassin **BASE** Houston
HEIGHT 5ft 7in **WEIGHT** 140 lbs **EYES** Blue **HAIR** Black
SPECIAL POWERS/ABILITIES Had access to high-tech equipment and scientific knowledge and skills, but was a poor fighter.

A rogue NASA engineer calling himself Solaris created the deadly Heliotron, with which he hoped to gain world domination. He was killed in battle with Kobra and Jason Burr.

Solaris is also the name of a tyrant sun (right) who sought to conquer two eras—the 20th and the 853rd centuries. By encoding its evil in a techno-virus, Solaris literally created itself. The JUSTICE LEAGUE OF AMERICA and its future counterparts Justice Legion-A joined forces to defeat the sentient star. **RG**

SOCIETY OF SIN

FIRST APPEARANCES (Brotherhood of Evil) DOOM PATROL (1st series) #86 (March 1964); (Society of Sin) NEW TITANS ANNUAL #6 (1990) **STATUS** Villain team **BASE** Mobile
MEMBERS AND POWERS
Brain Vast cyborg intellect.
Monsieur Mallah Super-evolved intelligent gorilla.
Madame Rouge (deceased) Elastic powers.
General Immortus Immortality.
Garguax Alien control of an army of android "plastic men."
General Zahl (deceased) Nazi U-boat commander.
Houngan Voodoo techno-fetishes can inflict pain or death.
Phobia Can project illusions of a subject's greatest fear.
Plasmus Protoplasmic touch can burn through most substances.
Warp Teleportation.
Trinity (destroyed) Energy blasts, illusions, and time control.

The Society of Sin was formed years ago by the BRAIN and his ape companion, MONSIEUR MALLAH. Along with Madame Rouge, General Immortus, and Garguax, this "Brotherhood of Evil" targeted the DOOM PATROL. But the mentally unstable Madame Rouge murdered her former partners in the Brotherhood and together with General Zahl seemingly destroyed the Doom Patrol. Years later, the Brain and Mallah, who survived Rouge's attack, returned with a new Brotherhood. This new team, which included Phobia, Houngan, Warp, and Plasmus, clashed with the Teen Titans. The Brain and Mallah left the Brotherhood and recruited Trinity, renaming themselves the Society of Sin. **PJ**

A BROTHERHOOD OF EVIL *Sinister enemies of both the Titans and the Doom Patrol, they are* 1) *Monsieur Mallah* 2) *Madame Rouge* 3) *Garguax* 4) *General Immortus* 5) *Brain* 6) *Plasmus* 7) *Trinity* 8) *Phobia* 9) *Houngan* 10) *Warp.*

SOLOMON GRUNDY

FIRST APPEARANCE ALL-AMERICAN COMICS #61 (November 1944)
STATUS Villain **REAL NAME** None
HEIGHT 7ft 5in **WEIGHT** 517 lbs **EYES** White **HAIR** White
OCCUPATION Criminal **BASE** Mobile
SPECIAL POWERS/ABILITIES Superstrength and invulnerability; is able to lift many tons and is capable of shrugging off blows from Superman; his undead nature means that it is nearly impossible for anyone to kill him.

Solomon Grundy is part-zombie and part-plant elemental. In 1894, a rich man named Cyrus Gold was killed by robbers. His corpse sank into the muck of Slaughter Swamp outside Gotham City. Over forty years later a pasty-white behemoth arose from Slaughter Swamp. The fiend got its name from an old nursery rhyme ("Solomon Grundy, born on Monday").

Grundy was employed as a criminal muscle-man, running up against the original GREEN LANTERN Alan Scott and the JUSTICE SOCIETY OF AMERICA throughout the 1940s. Grundy became Scott's perennial nemesis, since Scott's power ring could not affect the wood in Grundy's body.

Grundy joined the INJUSTICE SOCIETY, serving with them when they crashed the press conference at which the JUSTICE LEAGUE OF AMERICA announced its formation. A gentler incarnation of Grundy became a friend to Scott's daughter JADE during her time with INFINITY, INC. Solomon Grundy has returned with a more evolved intelligence, acting as the mastermind behind a scheme to build a new body for himself using parts from AMAZO and the RED TORNADO with the help of PROFESSOR IVO. **DW**

HOLDS A GRUDGE *Grundy still hates the Justice Society of America, in a grudge that goes back to the 1940s.*

SON OF VULCAN

FIRST APPEARANCE MYSTERIES OF UNEXPLORED WORLDS #46 (May 1965) *STATUS* Hero (deceased) *REAL NAME* John Mann *OCCUPATION* Reporter *BASE* Mobile *HEIGHT* 6ft 1in *WEIGHT* 210 lbs *EYES* Blue *HAIR* Brown *SPECIAL POWERS/ABILITIES* Invoking the name "Vulcan" transformed his body; super-strong; invulnerable to fire; able to conjure any weapon from Vulcan's forge.

John Mann was a war correspondent working in the Mediterranean who had lost his leg covering the conflict in the region. While resting in the Temple of Jupiter, Mann demanded to know how the gods could allow such carnage. He was struck by lightning and transported to the Mount Olympus of the Roman gods. Vulcan, god of the forge, took a liking to Mann. Despite opposition from Mars, the war god, Vulcan restored Mann's leg and gave him powers and weapons to fight the forces of evil and war on Earth. As the Son of Vulcan, John returned to the Mediterranean island of Cyprete and ended a civil war there. He was killed by the evil sorceress CIRCE during the War of the Gods, a conflict she had concocted that pitted the deities of various pantheons against each other. When the war ended, Vulcan escorted Mann's soul to the eternal heroic happiness of the Elysian Fields. **PJ**

SONAR

FIRST APPEARANCE GREEN LANTERN (3rd series) #66 (Sept. 1995) *STATUS* Villain *REAL NAME* Unknown *OCCUPATION* Professional criminal *BASE* Mobile *HEIGHT* 6ft 1in *WEIGHT* 215 lbs *EYES* Blue *HAIR* Red *SPECIAL POWERS/ABILITIES* Subcutaneous micro-circuitry gives him the ability to absorb and amplify sound waves to destructive levels.

Through circumstances unrevealed, the criminal currently calling himself Sonar came into possession of the sonic weapons belonging to Bito Wladon, the Modoran monarch who battled GREEN LANTERN Hal Jordan as the villain of the same name. The present Sonar used Wladon's technology to surgically augment his own body with electronic implants to enable him to manipulate sound waves. Sonar battled the Green Lantern Kyle Rayner and FLASH III (Wally West) when he rocked Manhattan in an attempt to make the island his own personal kingdom. Looking increasingly horrific as he amps up his implants, Sonar is frequently incarcerated in the Slab, a meta-human prison with facilities to neutralize his sonic powers. Sonar recently joined the Injustice League Unlimited, but found himself among the villains captured during Operation: Salvation Run. **SB**

SORROW, JOHNNY

FIRST APPEARANCE SECRET ORIGINS OF SUPER-VILLAINS 80-PAGE GIANT #1 (December 1999) *STATUS* Villain *REAL NAME* Jonathan "Johnny" Sorrow *OCCUPATION* Criminal leader *BASE* Mobile *HEIGHT* 6ft 1in *WEIGHT* 192 lbs *EYES* Unknown *HAIR* None *SPECIAL POWERS/ABILITIES* His naked face horrifies and kills any who look directly at it; teleportation; intangibility.

A petty criminal during World War II, Johnny Sorrow created a device that allowed him to phase in and out of reality. Damage to the device caused Sorrow to be transported to another dimension, called the Subtle Realms. The creatures who lived there hoped to use Johnny as a conduit to our world, and they made his visage so horrifying that anyone who looked upon it died from shock. Sorrow was returned to Earth to prepare the passage for the King of Tears, a god of the Subtle Realms. But the Justice Society of America and the SPECTRE stopped the King of Tears and imprisoned him.

Decades later, Sorrow returned and assembled a new INJUSTICE SOCIETY to free the King of Tears. But the Injustice Society was defeated by the JSA, and Sorrow was transported back to the Subtle Realms by the FLASH. Johnny returned, however, teaming with the alien Despero against the combined might of the JLA and the JSA, but was again defeated. **PJ**

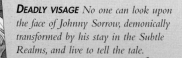

DEADLY VISAGE *No one can look upon the face of Johnny Sorrow, demonically transformed by his stay in the Subtle Realms, and live to tell the tale.*

SOYUZ

FIRST APPEARANCE FIRESTORM, THE NUCLEAR MAN #70 (April 1988) *STATUS* Hero team *BASE* Russia *CURRENT MEMBERS AND POWERS*
Firebird (Serafina Arkadin, leader) Telepath with telekinetic ability.
Perun (Ilya Trepilov) Can mentally control electricity.
Ruselka (Mashenka Medvienko) Controls water or water vapor.
Igor (Moizoko Medevienko) Can create arctic cold.
Vikhor (Feodor Sorin) Expert skater who can whip up a whirlwind.

Soyuz (Russian for "alliance") is a team of adolescent Russian mutants with superhuman powers who operate under secret identities in their homeland. Their codenames are taken from Russian mythology. The team first operated together to rescue their future member Perun. They adopted their distinctive costumes and codenames after they rescued the wife and children of Mikhail Arkadin, who was part of the Firestorm persona for a time. The team had several adventures as Russian set about regaining its national identity. They were last seen helping Young Justice during their assault on Zandia. Presumably, the team remains active in Eastern Europe. **RG**

THE HEROES OF SOYUZ 1) *Firebird* **2)** *Ruselka* **3)** *Igor* **4)** *Vikhor* **5)** *Perun.*

SPACE CABBY

FIRST APPEARANCE MYSTERY IN SPACE #21 (September 1954) *STATUS* Hero *REAL NAME* Unknown *OCCUPATION* Interstellar Multi-Species Transportation Expert *BASE* Corner of Earth and Lunar *HEIGHT* 5ft 10in *WEIGHT* 157 lbs *EYES* Brown *HAIR* Brown *SPECIAL POWERS/ABILITIES* Skilled pilot and navigator.

In the middle of the 22nd century, the man known only as Space Cabby began driving for 9-Planet Taxi.

Orphaned as a child, Space Cabby grew up among the military dictators of Ghengkis VII, where he showed a talent for stellar navigation. He later served as a fighter pilot during the Bored Wars of 2146. After stints as a mercenary "flier-for-hire" and a spaceport laborer, Space Cabby found his calling as a cab driver behind the wheel of space taxicab #7433. He is a member of both the Cosmic Order of Space Cab Pilots and the Veterans of Alien Wars.

He has even crossed paths with a few 20th century heroes, including LOBO and STARMAN. **DW**

SPACE RANGER

FIRST APPEARANCE SHOWCASE #15 (August 1958)
STATUS Hero **REAL NAME** Rick Starr **OCCUPATION** Businessman
BASE New York City; an asteroid in the 22nd century
HEIGHT 6ft 2in **WEIGHT** 194 lbs **EYES** Blue **HAIR** Black
SPECIAL POWERS/ABILITIES Weapons include thermoblaze gun (melts objects), explosidiscs, dissolverizer, anti-gravity gun, numbing gun.

Rick Star is the son of multimillionaire Thaddeus Star, owner of Allied Solar Enterprises in the New York of the 22nd century. Rick Star became the Space Ranger to patrol Earth's solar system and protect it from criminals and alien invaders. Using his millions, Rick created a base on an asteroid between Mars and Jupiter. He was often accompanied aboard his starship the *Solar King* by his girlfriend Myra Mason. The Space Ranger nearly died when he was stranded on Pluto without a life support system. There, a shape-changing alien named Cyrll saved his life, and the two became lifelong friends and allies.

The Space Ranger's greatest battle came during the war against the alien Gordanians when they attempted to capture Earth. With the help of GREEN LANTERN Hal Jordan, the Space Ranger thwarted the Gordanian raid and saved the planet. **PJ**

SPARK

FIRST APPEARANCE LEGION OF SUPER-HEROES (4th series) #0 (October 1994) **STATUS** Hero **REAL NAME** Ayla Ranzz
OCCUPATION Legionnaire **BASE** Legion World, U.P. Space
HEIGHT 5ft 5in **WEIGHT** 120 lbs **EYES** Light blue **HAIR** Red
SPECIAL POWERS/ABILITIES Able to generate, project, and absorb highly energized blasts of lightning.

Like her twin, Garth, and older brother, Mekt (*see* LIVE WIRE and LIGHTNING LORD), Ayla Ranzz acquired her ability to cast lightning after the siblings from the planet Winath crashed on the remote planet Korbal. When Korbal's lightning beasts attacked the Ranzz family, the siblings gained similar electrifying powers. Garth co-founded the LEGION OF SUPER-HEROES. Ayla soon earned Legion membership as Spark, Winath's official representative on the team. In another timeline containing the Legion of Super-Heroes, Ayla Ranzz is known as Light Lass and possesses the ability to alter the gravity of objects. This ability is a new one, replacing her previous possession of lightning powers like those of her brother Garth **SB**

SPARX

FIRST APPEARANCE ADVENTURES OF SUPERMAN ANNUAL #5 (1993)
STATUS Hero **REAL NAME** Donna Carol "D.C." Force
OCCUPATION Adventurer **BASE** New York City **HEIGHT** 5ft 5in
WEIGHT 130 lbs **EYES** Blue; white (as Sparx) **HAIR** Brown; white (as Sparx) **SPECIAL POWERS/ABILITIES** Can move faster than light, emit lightning blasts from her body, and fly; an unskilled combatant.

When alien parasites invaded Earth they infected humans with their bites, triggering dormant meta-genes. Donna Force saw this as her opportunity to shine. The youngest member of the famous Canadian Force family, Donna, or "D.C.," lacked powers compared with her family. In Metropolis, she encountered the alien Gemir, who sucked out her spinal fluid, seemingly killing her. When paramedics attempted to revive her, she displayed newfound electrical powers, becoming a living thunderbolt. Working alongside SUPERBOY, D.C., now known as Sparx, helped the new bloods and the veteran heroes combat the alien horde.

Searching for her place in the world, D.C. discovered the Event Horizon, a never-ending rave that floated from reality to reality, world to world. Soon after, Superboy was invited to the rave, and with Sparx created a team known as the RAVERS. **RG**

SPAWN OF FRANKENSTEIN

FIRST APPEARANCE PHANTOM STRANGER (2nd series) #23 (Jan. 1973)
STATUS Villain **REAL NAME** None
OCCUPATION Wanderer **BASE** Mobile
HEIGHT 7ft **WEIGHT** 300 lbs **EYES** Green **HAIR** Brown
SPECIAL POWERS/ABILITIES Superstrength; difficult to kill due to undead nature.

The Spawn of Frankenstein is the undead monster created by Dr. Victor Frankenstein in the late 18th century, a creature often mistakenly referred to only as Frankenstein. Composed of stitched-together corpses, the Spawn of Frankenstein moved against its creator, but Dr. Frankenstein hunted it into the Arctic, where it seemingly perished.

The Spawn of Frankenstein eventually took the name of its creator, going by Frankenstein. After encounters with the YOUNG ALL-STARS and DOCTOR THIRTEEN, it emerged as an operative with the U.S. government's S.H.A.D.E. organization. Frankenstein, as one of the SEVEN SOLDIERS OF VICTORY, helped smash an invasion by the alien Sheeda. **DW**

SPEED SAUNDERS

FIRST APPEARANCE DETECTIVE COMICS #1 (March 1937)
STATUS Hero **REAL NAME** Cyril Saunders
OCCUPATION Retired adventurer **BASE** Mobile
HEIGHT 5ft 11in **WEIGHT** 160 lbs **EYES** Hazel **HAIR** Gray
SPECIAL POWERS/ABILITIES World-class explorer and adventurer; expert tracker, climber, and survivalist.

Cyril "Speed" Saunders was born in Columbus, Ohio, and raised in Europe. While little has been revealed about Cyril's adolescent years, it has been said that he traveled the world in search of adventure. Speed may well have been a founder of the Office of Strategic Services, the World War II spy agency known as the O.S.S. Speed Saunders met the JUSTICE SOCIETY OF AMERICA on several occasions during the 1940s, also meeting Wesley Dodds, the first SANDMAN. The two remained close friends until Dodds committed suicide to prevent Mordru the DARK LORD from ravaging his mind.

Speed became the guardian of Shiera Saunders, his granddaughter, after the deaths of her parents. Speed trained Shiera, the reincarnation of an Egyptian princess, to become the new HAWKGIRL. An elderly daredevil blessed with the vigor of a man half his age, Speed continues to travel the world, seeking adventure. **PJ**

SPEEDY

FIRST APPEARANCE GREEN ARROW (2nd series) #2 (May 2001)
STATUS Hero **REAL NAME** Mia Dearden
OCCUPATION Professional adventurer **BASE** Star City
HEIGHT 5ft 4in **WEIGHT** 105 lbs **EYES** Blue **HAIR** Blonde
SPECIAL POWERS/ABILITIES Expert archer, skilled hand-to-hand combatant and swordswoman.

The original Speedy was named Roy Harper and he became GREEN ARROW's sidekick before graduating to the adult identities of ARSENAL and later Red Arrow.

The role of Speedy remained vacant for many years until Green Arrow rescued a teenaged girl, Mia Dearden, from a prostitution ring. Mia became the ward of Green Arrow's alter ego, Oliver Queen, and Queen himself trained her in archery and hand-to-hand combat.

In time Mia Dearden progressed far enough to become the new Speedy, adventuring with Green Arrow in Star City and accepting advice (as well as a supply of trick arrows) from Arsenal. Over her mentor's protests, Speedy also became an expert shot with a crossbow.

Speedy joined the TEEN TITANS and recently helped BLACK CANARY II rescue Green Arrow from the AMAZONS of Themyscira. Due to her unfortunate past, Mia Dearden is HIV-positive and has to take extra steps to ensure her continuing health and safety. **DW**

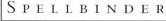

SPELLBINDER

FIRST APPEARANCE DETECTIVE COMICS #358 (December 1966)
STATUS Villain (deceased) **REAL NAME** Delbert Billings
OCCUPATION Adventurer **BASE** Gotham City
HEIGHT 5ft 11in **WEIGHT** 155 lbs **EYES** Blue **HAIR** Brown
SPECIAL POWERS/ABILITIES Utilized optical devices to hypnotize victims; minimally skilled at hand-to-hand fighting.

Art forger Delbert Billings decided to embellish his criminal career by developing optical devices that would enable him to hypnotize others. As the Spellbinder, Billings committed a rash of robberies but was ultimately routed by the Dynamic Duo, Batman and Robin. A second Spellbinder—mystically powered and unrelated to Delbert Billings—was briefly active during Billings' incarceration and battled the Justice League as a member of the government sanctioned "Leaguebusters." Billings attempted a criminal comeback upon his release from prison, but made the mistake of his life when he turned down the demonic Neron's offer for enhanced powers in exchange for his soul. **SB**

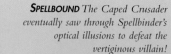

SPELLBOUND The Caped Crusader eventually saw through Spellbinder's optical illusions to defeat the vertiginous villain!

SPINNER, DOROTHY

FIRST APPEARANCE DOOM PATROL (2nd series) #14 (November 1988)
STATUS Hero **REAL NAME** Dorothy Spinner
OCCUPATION Adventurer **BASE** Kansas
HEIGHT 5ft 3in **WEIGHT** 118 lbs **EYES** Brown **HAIR** Brown
SPECIAL POWERS/ABILITIES Born with the mutant ability to bring her imaginary friends to life for short periods. One such imaginary friend even taught her to read.

Born with a deformed, simian-like face, Dorothy retreated from the world until she encountered the DOOM PATROL. While working with the team, she brought the Candlemaker to life, who, unfortunately, later wound up decapitating the CHIEF. She was one of the young adults lured by inhabitants into the other dimensional Dream Country where it was hoped that the powerful children could be convinced to maintain and expand its power. She managed to escape and then is on her own for some time. When heroes ROBOTMAN II and Coagula attempted to reunite Dorothy Spinner with her mother, the girl went berserk, wiping them both out of existence. Dorothy created a new Robotman, one "more in control, maybe more pure and certainly stronger." A group of heroes including BEAST BOY and FEVER, eventually restored the real Robotman to life and discovered that the incarnation they knew was actually a construct of Dorothy Spinner. She is now receiving psychiatric treatment for her condition. **RG**

SPELLBINDER III

FIRST APPEARANCE DETECTIVE COMICS #691 (November 1995)
STATUS Villain **REAL NAME** Fay Moffit
OCCUPATION Professional criminal **BASE** Gotham City
HEIGHT 5ft 6in **WEIGHT** 137 lbs **EYES** Blue
HAIR Pink (dyed)
SPECIAL POWERS/ABILITIES Generates lifelike illusions, throwing victims off-kilter and making them experience whatever she desires.

Although Delbert Billings was unwilling to trade his soul to the Demon NERON in exchange for enhanced powers, his moll, Fay Moffit, eagerly accepted the deal and promptly shot Delbert in the head. Neron gave Moffit the ability to cast psychedelic illusions, and she became the third and most sinister Spellbinder. Her amazing power to alter others' perceptions of reality is directly tied to her own sense of vision. Cover her eyes and she is rendered powerless. While incarcerated at the Slab prison, she was among a throng of villains "Jokerized" by the JOKER and made into capering carbon-copies of the Clown Prince of Crime. During the jailbreak that followed, Spellbinder almost killed NIGHTWING with an illusion of the inter-dimensional imp BAT-MITE. Spellbinder was later restored to normal, and any lingering effects of her "Jokerizing" remain to be seen. **SB**

SPLIT

FIRST APPEARANCE STEEL #6 (July 1994)
STATUS Villain **REAL NAME** Unknown
OCCUPATION Member of Team Hazard's Black Ops **BASE** Mobile
HEIGHT 5ft 10in **WEIGHT** 145 lbs **EYES** White
HAIR Red with blond streaks
SPECIAL POWERS/ABILITIES Able to teleport himself and others.

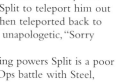

The criminal genius Hazard II has called Split one of his most valuable assets, telling the young meta-human, "I have yet to discover another teleporter with your range and power." Split's teleportational skills appear to be almost unlimited, a fact that is even more impressive considering that Split is barely out of his teens and may yet experience a deepening of his talents.

The biggest problem facing Split is his big mouth and his smart-alec attitude, qualities that Hazard barely tolerates. Split first crossed paths with the super hero STEEL III when Split teleported several Hazard assassins away from a crime scene. Later, Steel forced Split to teleport him out of Hazard's hidden bunker. Split then teleported back to headquarters with a shrug and an unapologetic, "Sorry boss, it was him or me."

Despite his formidable teleporting powers Split is a poor combatant. In yet another Black Ops battle with Steel, Split crumpled when hit by a glancing blow from John Henry Irons's trusty hammer. **DW**

SPECTRE

THE SPIRIT OF VENGEANCE

JIM CORRIGAN (SPECTRE I)
FIRST APPEARANCE More Fun Comics #52 (February 1940)
STATUS Hero   REAL NAME James Brendan Corrigan
OCCUPATION Police detective; spirit of vengeance
BASE New York City
HEIGHT (as Corrigan) 6ft 1in   WEIGHT (as Corrigan) 184 lbs
EYES (as Corrigan) Blue   HAIR (as Corrigan) Red, with white streak

HAL JORDAN (SPECTRE II)
FIRST APPEARANCE (AS THE SPECTRE) Day of Judgement #5 (November 1999)   STATUS Hero   REAL NAME Harold "Hal" Jordan
OCCUPATION Former test pilot, Green Lantern; the Spirit of Wrath
BASE Mobile
HEIGHT (as Jordan) 6ft   WEIGHT (as Jordan) 186 lbs
EYES (as Jordan) Brown   HAIR (as Jordan) Brown

SPECIAL POWERS/ABILITIES The Spectre is among the most powerful beings in the universe. Limited only by its need to bond with another host, the Spectre possesses the ability to fly at nearly any speed, become intangible, inhabit and animate objects, read minds, teleport, and psychically project hideous fears into the hearts and souls of his victims. He can turn invisible, cast illusions, create impenetrable mists, travel across the astral planes, grow to incomprehensible size, and manipulate magics to nearly any end his spiritual mind can conceive!

GHOSTLY The Spectre arrived in a swirl of mist to pass his sentence on criminals.

LOOSED ON EARTH by the almighty Presence in 776 BC, the Spectre is the mystical embodiment of God's wrath. When the angel Raphael, who rebelled against Heaven with Lucifer, repented his sins, God transformed him into an avenger that would inflict His wrath on sinful souls. The Spectre destroyed Sodom and Gommorah, spread the ten plagues across Egypt, and brought down the walls of Jericho. After the birth of Jesus, whose mission was to teach people compassion, the Presence decreed that the spirits of vengeance and forgiveness should not exist on Earth at the same time. The Spectre bided in Limbo until Christ's death. Then, forced to bond with mortal souls to manifest his power, the Spectre leaped forth, meting out vengeance down the centuries.

JIM CORRIGAN

James Corrigan was the only child of the Reverend Jedediah Corrigan, a fundamentalist preacher who physically and emotionally abused his son to discourage him from the temptations of sin. As a teenager, Corrigan ran away to New York City and enrolled in the police academy, excelling at detective work. Self-righteous, arrogant, Corrigan became a pitiless cop.

Corrigan's brutality caught up with him, when he was killed by mobster Gat Benson in 1940. Corrigan's soul cried out for vengeance and was answered by the Spectre. Infused with the Spectre's power, Corrigan's spirit, returned to his body and took revenge on Benson. The Spectre was subsequently encouraged to use his power for good by Percival Poplanski, a patrolmen who witnessed Benson's demise. Manifesting itself as a ghostly spirit, the Spectre joined the JUSTICE SOCIETY OF AMERICA as one of its most powerful members. After World War II, the Spectre fought the demon Azmodus, who trapped the Spirit of Vengeance in Corrigan's undead frame for nearly two decades. The Ghostly Guardian quarreled often with his earthly host over methodology and the nature of humanity itself.

MURDER! Gat Benton stuffed Jim Corrigan's body in a cement-filled barrel and drowned him.

AVENGING ANGEL The Spectre uses his powers to horrify criminals, visiting upon them grisly retribution in its most hideous form.

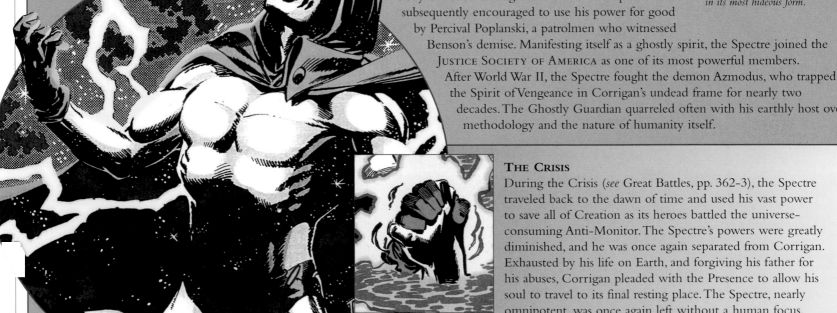

THE CRISIS

During the Crisis (see Great Battles, pp. 362-3), the Spectre traveled back to the dawn of time and used his vast power to save all of Creation as its heroes battled the universe-consuming Anti-Monitor. The Spectre's powers were greatly diminished, and he was once again separated from Corrigan. Exhausted by his life on Earth, and forgiving his father for his abuses, Corrigan pleaded with the Presence to allow his soul to travel to its final resting place. The Spectre, nearly omnipotent, was once again left without a human focus.

HAL JORDAN

Hal Jordan was one of the most powerful officers in the legendary GREEN LANTERN CORPS and a founding member of the JUSTICE LEAGUE OF AMERICA. When MONGUL and the CYBORG SUPERMAN destroyed Jordan's hometown, Coast City, slaughtering its seven million inhabitants, Jordan went insane, usurping the power of the Corps and transforming into the universe-threatening PARALLAX.

Parallax first tried to recreate Coast City by tampering with time during the Zero Hour crisis (*see* Great Battles, pp. 362–3). Failing time and time again, Parallax nonetheless helped reignite the Earth's sun, which had been extinguished by an alien creature, at the cost of his own life. His spirit consigned to Purgatory for his sins, Jordan bonded with the Spectre's energies after they briefly inhabited ASMODEL.

Returned to Earth in this new, ghostly form, the spirit of Hal Jordan and the essence of the Spectre wander the globe, seeking redemption while inflicting punishment on the guilty. **PJ**

HELPING YOUNG JUSTICE

As the Spectre, Hal Jordan used his omnipotent power to help SECRET learn the truth about her past. The elder ghost helped the younger discover that her death was a sacrifice to a demon, and that she had been transformed by the Lords of Light into a spirit guide. The Spectre used his power to help Secret accept her dismal past, and hopeful future.

JLA ALLY *Hal Jordan uses his new power to aid his former teammates in the JLA. While Jordan's vast power worries Batman, Jordan's diligence in hunting evil earns Batman's trust, and the trust of Earth's Greatest Heroes.*

KEY STORYLINES

• *MORE FUN COMICS #52 (FEBRUARY 1940):* The first appearance of the ghostly avenger.
• *DC SPECIAL #29 (SEPTEMBER 1977):* The Spectre becomes a founding member of the Justice Society of America.
• Crisis on Infinite Earths (tpb, 2000) The Spectre stops the Anti-Monitor from destroying all creation, and reignites the universe.
• *DAY OF JUDGEMENT #1–4 (NOVEMBER 1999–FEBRUARY 2000):* Hal Jordan rescues the spirit of God's wrath from Asmodel and becomes the new Spectre.

The DC Comics Encyclopedia

SPECTRE

UN-TETHERED SPIRIT

Hal Jordan's penance as the Spectre's host ended with the purging of Parallax—an ancient fear entity that had been sharing space in Jordan's soul alongside God's Spirit of Vengeance. By defeating Parallax, Jordan won the right to resume his former life on Earth, leaving the Spectre a rogue ghost. Lacking the grounding of a human spirit, the Spectre lost touch with the concerns of mortal justice. He lashed out with irrational, disproportionate punishments, including executing a girl for talking back to her father. In this disturbed state, the Spectre became an easy target for ECLIPSO—God's ex-Spirit of Revenge who had taken over the body of Jean Loring (see LORING, JEAN). Eclipso's seductions convinced the addled Spectre that magic represented a perversion of God's orderly laws, and that only by eliminating all magic could he purge the universe of evil. Because he existed as a creature of magic himself, as his final act the Spectre planned to extinguish his own life. The Spectre's rampage against spellcasters and mystical realms marked an end to what had been known as the Ninth Age of Magic. His first targets included the "big guns" of the magical community. The Spectre burned out the eyes of MADAME XANADU so she would be incapable of reading tarot cards, and imprisoned DOCTOR FATE inside his enchanted helmet. Although the Spectre lacked the power to kill the PHANTOM STRANGER, he left him powerless by transforming him into a mouse. Dozens of lesser magicians perished when the Spirit of Vengeance attacked their mass gathering, and even the kingdom of Atlantis fell beneath the Spectre's boots.

DARK SEDUCTIONS *Eclipso, in the body of Jean Loring, manipulated the Spectre into wiping out her magical competition.*

THREE DOWN *In short order, the Spectre neutralized his greatest threats: the Phantom Stranger, Doctor Fate, and Madame Xanadu.*

SHADOWPACT SHOWDOWN

The surviving magic-users gathered in the Oblivion Bar to plan a counterattack. Their plans hinged on NIGHTMASTER, RAGMAN, NIGHTSHADE, BLUE DEVIL, the ENCHANTRESS, and DETECTIVE CHIMP, who had formed a super-group known as the SHADOWPACT. In Budapest, the new team faced off against the combined forces of ECLIPSO and the Spectre, with the Shadowpact's efforts aided by CAPTAIN MARVEL and the channeled magical energy of the planet's population. The Spectre fled, but regained his strength for a second clash with the Shadowpact. This time, BLACK ALICE temporarily sapped his powers. Teleporting to the Rock of Eternity, the Spectre executed the wizard SHAZAM, causing the Rock to explode above Gotham City and freeing the spirits of the Seven Deadly Sins. Led by the Lord of Order NABU, the Shadowpact and other magic-users collected the Deadly Sins and again earned the Spectre's anger. This time, however, the Spectre finally grabbed the attention of his heavenly master, who removed the renegade spirit and forced him to seek a new human host.

CLASH OF TITANS *Grown to colossal size due to an influx of magical energy, Captain Marvel slugs it out with the Spectre in Budapest.*

END OF THE NINTH AGE *The maddened Spectre eliminated most of the Earth's sorcerers and magic-users. The destruction of the Rock of Eternity signaled the end. The release of the Rock's evil spirits brought terror to a battle-scarred Gotham City.*

CRISPUS ALLEN (SPECTRE III)
First appearance Detective Comics #742 (March 2000)
Status Instrument of retribution **Occupation** Police detective;
Spirit of Vengeance **Base** Gotham City
Height 6ft **Weight** 180 lbs **Eyes** Brown **Hair** Black
Special powers/abilities The Spectre is among the most powerful
beings in the universe. Limited only by its need to bond with
another host.

CRISPUS ALLEN

The Spectre's third host came from the ranks of
the Gotham City Police Department. Detective
Crispus Allen struggled to make a difference in
a city overrun with costumed killers and masked
vigilantes, with his wife and two sons helping
keep him sane. Allen worked alongside fellow
detective Renee Montoya (see MONTOYA, RENEE)
in the GCPD's Major Crimes Unit. Allen's life took
a tragic turn when he crossed paths with crime scene
technician Jim Corrigan—who bore the same name (but
was otherwise unrelated to) the Jim
Corrigan who had originally served
as the Spectre's host. During an
investigation gone bad, Allen saved his
partner's life by shooting and killing
the villain BLACK SPIDER. An Internal
Affairs inquiry into the incident
went awry when Corrigan stole
the bullet from the scene, casting a
cloud over Allen's actions. Enraged
by Corrigan's interference, Montoya
forced him to give up the bullet, but
by this point the crooked cop knew
that Internal Affairs was closing in
on him. To cover his tracks, he shot Allen in the back. In the morgue,
the body of Crispus Allen became the newest host for the Spectre.

Allen's spirit soon rejected the ghostly invader, despite the
latter's pleas for an Earthly lifeline to help him continue
his mission of retribution. Yet life as a phantom—rendering
him incapable of interacting with his family or striking back
at Corrigan—proved unsatisfying for Allen. After nearly
a year, he accepted the Spectre into his body and began
to mete out punishments to the worst of Gotham City's
sinners, always in a gruesomely ironic fashion. Victims were
impaled by wads of cash, speared by fishhooks, burst apart
like balloons, and devoured by rats and spiders. Allen took
grim satisfaction in his methods of justice, since the Spectre's mission
prevented him from simply stopping atrocities before the murderers
could take action. He collaborated with both the Batman and the
PHANTOM STRANGER, gradually coming to the realization that, despite
the Spectre's near-omnipotence, punishment was a more merciful
action when meted out on an individual basis. Crispus Allen's final
test came when his young son Mal avenged his father's death by
shooting Jim Corrigan. To exact retribution for the murder, Allen, as
the Spectre, took his son into the afterlife. **PJ/DW**

BACK FROM THE DEAD
Murdered in cold blood,
Detective Crispus Allen
became the Spectre's
unwilling host.

BLIND JUSTICE Realizing that the
Spirit of Vengeance must treat all
crimes with equal weight, Crispus
Allen uses the powers of the
Spectre to pass judgment on his
own son for the sin of murder.

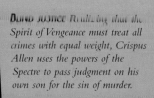

SPOILER

FIRST APPEARANCE DETECTIVE COMICS #647 (August 1992)
STATUS Hero (deceased) **REAL NAME** Stephanie Brown
HEIGHT 5ft 5in **WEIGHT** 129 lbs **EYES** Blue **HAIR** Blonde
OCCUPATION High-school student; adventurer **BASE** Gotham City
SPECIAL POWERS/ABILITIES Above-average combatant; utility bandoleer contains gas capsules, jumplines, and other equipment supplied by Robin III.

GIRL WONDER
Spoiler ignored Robin's warnings of the perils of crime fighting. Eventually, she replaced him as Batman's partner for a brief time.

A good girl with a bad father, teenager Stephanie Brown is the daughter of Arthur Brown, better known as the criminal CLUEMASTER. Stephanie created her own costumed alter ego, the Spoiler, in an attempt to "spoil" her father's lawbreaking schemes. But even after the Cluemaster was remanded again and again to Blackgate Penitentiary for rehabilitation, the Spoiler continued to patrol Gotham City, despite the admonitions of BATMAN and ROBIN III (Tim Drake). Against the Dark Knight's wishes, Tim Drake enabled Stephanie to operate as the Spoiler, often supplying her with necessary equipment. Friends at first, the pair soon became romantically linked. Later, Batman relented and began schooling Stephanie in crime fighting skills, although her training was cut short when the Dark Knight's alter ego, Bruce Wayne, was accused of murdering journalist Vesper Fairchild (*see* FAIRCHILD, VESPER). The Spoiler then apprenticed with the BLACK CANARY II for a brief time. She remained an active heroine, usually in the company of her boyfriend, Robin. However, when Tim's father, Jack Drake, learned of his son's vigilante activities, Tim was forced to give up the mantle of Robin for a brief time. With Batman's sanction, Stephanie became the first female Robin during Tim's absence. Tragically, she was killed in action not long after returning to her role as the Spoiler. **SB**

ABSENT FATHER
When not spoiling his Cluemaster crime sprees, Stephanie showed Arthur Brown what she thought of his parenting skills!

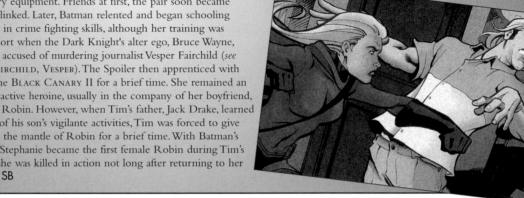

SPY SMASHER

FIRST APPEARANCE WHIZ COMICS #1 (February 1940); (II) BIRDS OF PREY #100 (January 2007)
STATUS Hero (retired); (II) Hero **REAL NAME** Alan Armstrong; (II) Katarina Armstrong
OCCUPATION Former adventurer, former sportsman; (II) Government agent **BASE** The U.S.; (II) Mobile
HEIGHT 5ft 11in; (II) 5 ft 11in **WEIGHT** 175 lbs; (II) 149 lbs **EYES** Blue; (II) Green **HAIR** Black; (II) Blonde
SPECIAL POWERS/ABILITIES A skilled hand-to-hand combatant; for a time, he flew the technologically advanced Gyrosub; (II) Expert hand-to-hand combatant and skilled with firearms; possesses a gift for international intelligence

As Spy Smasher, Alan Armstrong achieved great renown for his World War II exploits, often facing his Nazi counterpart, America Smasher. His greatest foe, however, was the Mask, who went so far as to hypnotize him into becoming his lieutenant. It took the efforts of BULLETMAN to restore Spy Smasher's mind. A second Spy Smasher, Katarina Armstrong, has since emerged on the scene. Boasting credentials from all major United Nations intelligence agencies, she is an expert in anti-terrorism and metahuman operations. She knew Barbara Gordon (*see* ORACLE) in college, and exploited this connection by forcing Oracle and the BIRDS OF PREY to work as her agents. After a mission to Russia that put the Birds into conflict with the SECRET SIX, Spy Smasher announced that she was taking control of the Birds of Prey and fired LADY BLACKHAWK from her post. The wheelchair-bound Oracle defeated Spy Smasher in one-on-one combat, and every former member of the Birds of Prey arrived en masse to emphasize that their new leader was not welcome. Spy Smasher withdrew to plan new operations. **RG**

SQUIRE III

FIRST APPEARANCE JLA #26 (February 1999)
STATUS Hero **REAL NAME** Unknown
OCCUPATION Ultramarine **BASE** Ultramarines base, Superbia
HEIGHT 5ft 6in **WEIGHT** 131 lbs **EYES** Blue **HAIR** Black
SPECIAL POWERS/ABILITIES Scrappy fighter, who learned to stand up for herself on the backstreets of London.

The current Squire is heir to a tradition that began with Percy Sheldrake, the first Squire (*see* KNIGHT I and SQUIRE I) who served as the wartime aide to the SHINING KNIGHT. After World War II, Percy became the Knight and trained his son Cyril as the Squire II. Cyril, in turn, became the second Knight.

Facing up to the reality of his advancing years, Cyril has recently trained a new female apprentice as the third Squire. Cyril found the young girl brimming with punk attitude on the streets of London. He adopted her and channeled her aggression into combat expertise. His efforts paid off when the INTERNATIONAL ULTRAMARINE CORPS, an independent global peacekeeping force, asked the Knight and Squire to join their team as England's representatives.

After the far-future Sheeda destroyed the Ultramarine Corps, Squire III returned to adventuring with the Knight. The pair recently helped BATMAN solve a murder-mystery involving the "Club of Heroes." **DW**

STALKER

FIRST APPEARANCE STALKER #1 (July 1975)
STATUS Villain (deceased) **REAL NAME** Unknown
OCCUPATION Warrior **BASE** Mobile
HEIGHT 8ft 2in **WEIGHT** 520 lbs **EYES** Red **HAIR** Black
SPECIAL POWERS/ABILITIES Master of armed and unarmed combat; superstrength; supersenses; enhanced reflexes; near invulnerability; unrivaled tracking ability; power blast projection from hands.

Born thousands of years ago in the city of Geranth on an unnamed world, an orphan boy offered his soul to Dgrth, god of warriors. Dgrth stripped the youth of his soul in exchange for vast power. The boy became Stalker. Eventually Stalker realized the terrible price he had paid for his vast power and pursued Dgrth hoping to reclaim his soul and undo the bargain. However, Dgrth took his power from the warriors who worshipped him, and would never relinquish Stalker's soul while his sycophants could wage battle for him. Thus, Stalker dedicated his life to ending all strife across the universe.

Stalker reasoned that if he ended all life, he would end all war, and so reclaim his soul. He traveled to Earth aiming to end all life there and created seven disciples. The disciples were destroyed, along with Stalker himself, by the JUSTICE SOCIETY OF AMERICA. **PJ**

STALNOIVOLK

FIRST APPEARANCE FIRESTORM 2nd series #67 (January 1988)
STATUS Villain **REAL NAME** Ivan Illyich Gort
OCCUPATION Special agent for K.G.B. **BASE** Moscow, Russia
HEIGHT 6ft 2in **WEIGHT** 275 lbs **EYES** Blue **HAIR** Black
SPECIAL POWERS/ABILITIES Superhuman strength, speed, and agility; retarded aging; considerable resistance to pain and injury.

Peasant Ivan Illyich Gort was selected by the Soviet government to be transformed into a Russian superman and symbol of resistance to Nazi Germany during World War II. Called Stalnoivolk, a name that translates as "Steel Wolf" in English, Gort was a model Communist, utterly loyal to Josef Stalin after the war and an active participant in the dictator's bloody purges. Stalnoivolk was exiled to Siberia following his leader's death and the Soviet rejection of Stalinist politics.

Decades later, Stalnoivolk—still strong and vital as a result of the experiments that empowered him—became a K.G.B. agent and was sent to the U.S. to oppose FIRESTORM after the nuclear hero sought to eliminate

the world's atomic weapons and end the arms race. While in the U.S., Stalnoivolk killed Richard Dare (CAPTAIN X), the grandfather of Ronnie Raymond, one of Firestorm's alter egos. While in federal custody, Stalnoivolk joined the SUICIDE SQUAD. He remains a Stalinist hard-liner, despite the dissolution of the U.S.S.R. into independent states. **SB**

STANLEY & HIS MONSTER

FIRST APPEARANCE GREEN ARROW (2nd series) #1 (April 2001)
STATUS Hero **REAL NAME** Stanley Dover
OCCUPATION None **BASE** Star City
HEIGHT 3ft 2in **WEIGHT** 65 lbs **EYES** Blue **HAIR** Blond
SPECIAL POWERS/ABILITIES No powers, but a kind heart; an innocent pawn in his Grandpa's dastardly schemes. The Monster was huge and powerful, but rather slow-moving.

Satanic worshipper Stanley Dover sought to transfer his soul into a demon. Instead, the infant grandson, who shared his name, became the recipient of a binding to the beast. Eventually the mage discovered that the monster, named Spot, had been hiding in his grandson's closet. To draw it out, the warlock imprisoned his grandson and defiled him with the blood of victims he had killed as the Star City Slayer. GREEN ARROW I entered the picture after rescuing the Stanley Sr. from a mugging. The warlock realized that the archer was a body without a soul and tried to transfer his soul into Queen's body to help him capture Stanley's monster. Before the transfer was complete, Queen's soul reentered his resurrected body, thwarting the mage. Stanley's monster then devoured the satanist. **RG**

STAR BOY

FIRST APPEARANCE LEGIONNAIRES #0
STATUS Hero **REAL NAME** Thom Kallor
OCCUPATION Assassin **BASE** Legion World
HEIGHT 5ft 8in **WEIGHT** 160 lbs **EYES** Blue **HAIR** Brown
SPECIAL POWERS/ABILITIES Has the ability to alter the mass of any object or person, possesses an array of super-strength, flight, and limited invulnerability.

In the 31st Century, Xanthuan hero Star Boy of a team of super-powered teens called the Uncanny Amazers used his mass-inducing powers to defeat High-Brow, Klamorr, Slopp and Violence Queen. He was nearly killed when his space cruiser was destroyed. While recovering, he gained further powers due to ingesting meat from the same space-whale that ULTRA BOY once encountered. Star Boy then left the Amazers to join the LEGION OF SUPER-HEROES. In another timeline of the Legion of Super-Heroes, Star Boy adventured with the Legion until finally taking on the title of Starman. During the "Lightning Saga," he traveled back to the 21st century with several other Legionnaires, but the trip scrambled his mind. Left behind in the past, Starman found time between voluntary stints at a mental institution to become a member of the JUSTICE SOCIETY OF AMERICA where he helped bring the Superman of Earth-22 into the JSA's reality. A third version of Star Boy exists in the 31st century of the current mainstream reality, where he serves as a top lieutenant of Legion founder COSMIC BOY. **RG**

STARRO

FIRST APPEARANCE BRAVE AND THE BOLD #28 (March 1960)
STATUS Villain **REAL NAME** Inapplicable
HEIGHT Variable **WEIGHT** Variable
EYE Red sclera with yellow pupil **HAIR** None
OCCUPATION Alien invader **BASE** Mobile throughout universe
SPECIAL POWERS/ABILITIES Can exert mental control over others, fire force bolts, and release thousands of small probes that attach to their victims' faces and turn them into slaves.

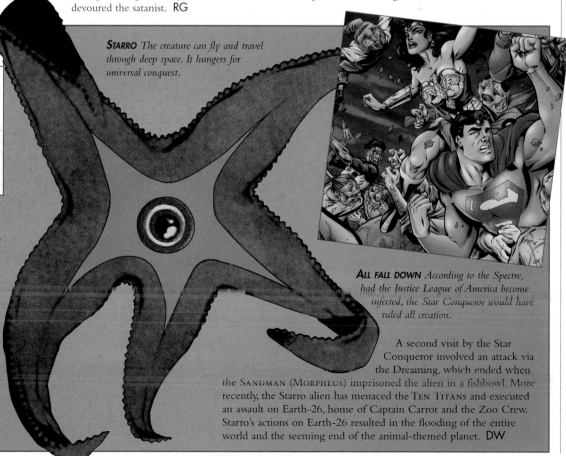

STARRO *The creature can fly and travel through deep space. It hungers for universal conquest.*

ALL FALL DOWN *According to the Spectre, had the Justice League of America become infected, the Star Conqueror would have ruled all creation.*

A titanic intergalactic starfish, Starro may be the strangest villain the JUSTICE LEAGUE OF AMERICA has ever faced. The original team of five—FLASH, GREEN LANTERN, AQUAMAN, MARTIAN MANHUNTER, and BLACK CANARY—tangled with Starro on their first mission, preventing the immoral invertebrate from turning the residents of Happy Harbor, Rhode Island, into obedient zombies. The JLA's mascot, Snapper Carr (see CARR, SNAPPER), unwittingly discovered Starro's vulnerability to quicklime.

Starro battled the JLA many more times, but eventually the similar Star Conqueror (believed to be a probe of Starro, or vice versa) appeared in Blue Valley, Nebraska. This ushered in a new incarnation of the League, this time uniting BATMAN, SUPERMAN, Flash, Green Lantern, Aquaman, Martian Manhunter, and WONDER WOMAN against the vile face-clinging parasites that would have turned the universe's inhabitants into the Star Conqueror's slaves, as seen in a vision by the Spectre.

A second visit by the Star Conqueror involved an attack via the Dreaming, which ended when the SANDMAN (MORPHEUS) imprisoned the alien in a fishbowl. More recently, the Starro alien has menaced the TEN TITANS and executed an assault on Earth-26, home of Captain Carrot and the Zoo Crew. Starro's actions on Earth-26 resulted in the flooding of the entire world and the seeming end of the animal-themed planet. **DW**

STAR HAWKINS

FIRST APPEARANCE STRANGE ADVENTURES #114 (March 1960)
STATUS Hero (deceased) **REAL NAME** Star Hawkins
OCCUPATION Private detective **BASE** New City, Earth, in 2070
HEIGHT 5ft 10in **WEIGHT** 176 lbs **EYES** Blue **HAIR** Brown
SPECIAL POWERS/ABILITIES A renowned detective with amazing mystery solving skills; an excellent martial artist; carries a special laser gun.

Private detective Star Hawkins was renowned for spending his money faster than he could earn it. His ally was a robot named Ilda, a secretary and housecleaner whom he often had to pawn when he needed money. However, he always bought her right back after getting paid for his latest case. Star was eventually assigned to the U.S. government's National Science Center, Earth's premier law enforcement agency. In the year 2092, on his last case, Hawkins saved Automan, a 130 year-old robot, from destruction. Late in life, Star Hawkins struck up a friendship with CAPTAIN COMET. Following the Infinite Crisis, Star Hawkins lost his life to a mysterious assassin on Hardcore Station, prompting Captain Comet to investigate the murder. **PJ**

STAR ROVERS, THE

FIRST APPEARANCE MYSTERY IN SPACE #66 (March 1961)
STATUS Hero team **BASE** Mobile
MEMBERS AND POWERS
HOMER GINT Novelist and sportsman.
KAREL SORENSEN Glamorous markswoman.
RICK PURVIS Playboy athlete.

Spacefaring adventurers of the 22nd century, Homer Gint, Karel Sorensen, and Rick Purvis often find themselves rocketing to save Earth from various extraterrestrial threats. More often than not, each experiences the danger at hand through separate encounters. After comparing notes, the friendly rivals invariably discover that three heads are better than one. These Star Rovers are independent of any Earth organization, so their exploits are mostly unheralded, which suits these stellar thrill seekers just fine. **SB**

THE STAR ROVERS 1) *Homer Gint* **2)** *Karel Sorensen*
3) *Rick Purvis.*

STARFIRE

FIRST APPEARANCE DC COMICS PRESENTS #26 (October 1980)
STATUS Hero **REAL NAME** Koriand'r
OCCUPATION Exiled queen; Teen Titan **BASE** Themyscira
HEIGHT 6ft 4in **WEIGHT** 158 lbs **EYES** Green **HAIR** Auburn
SPECIAL POWERS/ABILITIES Natural ability to fly, absorb solar energy, and emit light has been augmented to let her turn that light into destructive force beams; trained to be a warrior.

FIRST KISS *Robin was attracted to the alien Princess, who kissed him to absorb the English language and communicate.*

Tamaran's Princess Koriand'r was the second of three children. Her older sister, Komand'r, proved unable to fly, so she was deemed not worthy to be queen and the succession fell to Koriand'r. When both sisters were sent to train with the legendary Warlords of Okaara, the bitter Komand'r ran off, allying herself with the Citadel [please explain]. They used Komand'r's information to successfully invade the planet. Tamaran's King Myand'r turned Koriand'r over to the Citadel's tender mercies to ensure peace.

Koriand'r endured six years of torture until she and Komand'r were both released for experimentation by the ruthless Psions (*see* Alien Races, pp.166–7). Both sisters escaped, however, Koriand'r finding her way to Earth with the help of the TEEN TITANS. She chose to remain with the team, taking the name Starfire. She gave team member ROBIN I a passionate kiss in order to learn the English language, igniting a romance that lasted for quite some time. She also endured many missions with the Titans and many heartbreaks involving her family.

Many of Starfire's people perished when the Sun-Eater destroyed her homeworld. During the Infinite Crisis, Starfire, ANIMAL MAN, and Adam Strange (*see* STRANGE, ADAM) wandered through deep space for nearly a year, crossing paths with LOBO and the deadly Lady Styx. Upon their return to Earth, Starfire moved in with Animal Man's family. **RG**

FIGHT CLUB *Sparring with Wonder Girl I was one of Koriand'r's favorite pastimes.*

FEEL THAT FORCE *Starfire's energy bolts have considerable destructive and concussive capabilities.*

STAR SAPPHIRE

FIRST APPEARANCE GREEN LANTERN (2nd series.) #16
(October 1962) **STATUS** Villain **REAL NAME** Carol Ferris
OCCUPATION Estranged queen **BASE** Mobile
HEIGHT 5ft 7in **WEIGHT** 126 lbs **EYES** Blue **HAIR** Black
SPECIAL POWERS/ABILITIES Sapphire gem permits flight and
space travel; fires energy blasts; protects against damage.

The Zamarons, immortal female counterparts to
the GUARDIANS OF THE UNIVERSE, developed their
own warrior culture on their planet. Appointing
a queen from the ranks of the galaxy's mortals
became a tradition, and each woman selected
became known as Star Sapphire.

In the late 20th century, the Zamarons chose
Ferris Aircraft president Carol Ferris as their
queen. When she refused, they hypnotized her,
using the power of the sapphire gem to give her
superpowers and a separate Star Sapphire identity,
which she forgot every time she
awoke from the sapphire's spell.

In her first mission she obeyed
the Zamarons' hypnotic
suggestion to attack GREEN
LANTERN Hal Jordan,
despite the love she felt
for him in her civilian
identity.

Recently, the star
sapphire took possession
of Hal Jordan's love interest
Jillian "Cowgirl" Pearlman,
revealing that the gem controlled
the power of love on the
multicolored emotional spectrum
(alongside green/willpower and
yellow/fear).

Carol Ferris's predecessor
in the role of Star Sapphire
still lives inside the "7th
Dimension," though she has
grown old and decrepit. This
Golden Age Star Sapphire was
known for tormenting Jay
Garrick (the original FLASH)
during the 1940s. **DW**

*BEJEWELED A part of Carol
Ferris relishes the role of
royal villainess.*

*GOLDEN AGE Earth's
previous Star Sapphire has
been all but forgotten.*

STARGIRL & S.T.R.I.P.E.

FIRST APPEARANCE (Stargirl) STARS AND S.T.R.I.P.E. #0 (July 1999);
(S.T.R.I.P.E.) STARS AND S.T.R.I.P.E. #0 (July 1999)
STATUS Heroes **REAL NAMES** (Stargirl) Courtney Elizabeth
Whitmore; (S.T.R.I.P.E.) Pat Dugan **OCCUPATION** (Stargirl) High
school student, adventurer; (S.T.R.I.P.E.) mechanic, inventor
BASE Blue Valley, Nebraska **HEIGHT** (Stargirl) 5ft 5in; (S.T.R.I.P.E.
in armor) 7ft **WEIGHT** (Stargirl) 127 lbs. (S.T.R.I.P.E. in armor)
425 lbs. **EYES** (Stargirl) Blue; (S.T.R.I.P.E.) red **HAIR** (Stargirl)
Blonde; (S.T.R.I.P.E.) None
SPECIAL POWERS/ABILITIES (Stargirl) Cosmic converter belt gives her
superstrength and reflexes and the ability to project light forms that
affect the human nervous system; also uses the cosmic rod, which
allows her to fly and project blasts of solar energy. (S.T.R.I.P.E.)
Robot with flight capabilities and damage-resistant exoskeleton,
telescopic vision, fist rocket launcher, grappling hook, net launcher,
fire-retardant spray, headlights in chest cavity, taser darts, electric
shock cables, fan, tracking device for Stargirl, satellite feeds, virtual
reality control system.

Pat Dugan, a car mechanic during World War II, was
Stripesy, the sidekick of the Star-Spangled Kid. The two
men fought the Axis powers with the
SEVEN SOLDIERS OF VICTORY until
a battle with the NEBULA MAN,
a powerful villain composed of
temporal energy, trapped the duo
centuries in the past.

Dugan was rescued by the
JUSTICE SOCIETY OF AMERICA
and emerged in the present, a
man out of time. Pat married,
had a son, and settled down,
but his cousin stole the patents of
his inventions and left him penniless.
Overwhelmed by their financial
problems, Dugan's wife left them. Dugan
worked briefly with INFINITY, INC. until
the Kid's murder by Mister Bones (see
DIRECTOR BONES). Distraught, he moved
his new family, including his stepdaughter,
Courtney, to Blue Valley, Nebraska.

Courtney, who disdained her stepfather
for moving her from her friends and life
in Los Angeles, learned of Dugan's past and
stumbled upon the cosmic converter belt
designed for the original Star-Spangled
Kid. Courtney used the belt and became
the second Star-Spangled Kid just to
make Dugan angry. Dugan created
the S.T.R.I.P.E. battlesuit to assist
his stepdaughter, who got herself
into trouble almost immediately.

*FULL FORCE GIRL Using a special belt, Stargirl gains
strength, speed, and the power to kick butt!
Solomon Grundy sees stars!*

Since then, Courtney has curbed her recklessness
and become a professional hero. After proving
herself in battle against Mordru (see DARK LORD),
she was asked to join the JSA. She inherited
the cosmic rod from STARMAN Jack Knight and
defeated her biological father, a member of the
ROYAL FLUSH GANG. Courtney then changed her
name to Stargirl. S.T.R.I.P.E. remains a reserve
member of the JSA, dutifully watching over
Courtney as she becomes a legend herself. **PJ**

*THE INNER MAN The man inside the S.T.R.I.P.E.
armor, Pat Dugan has been a hero since World War II.*

*STATE OF INDEPENDENCE
Stargirl has become one
of the strongest—and
strongest willed—members
of the JSA!*

STARMAN

THE STARRY KNIGHT

STARMAN I
FIRST APPEARANCE Adventure Comics #61 (April 1941)
STATUS Hero (deceased)   **REAL NAME** Theodore Henry Knight
OCCUPATION Astronomer, adventurer   **BASE** Opal City
HEIGHT 6ft   **WEIGHT** 165 lbs   **EYES** Blue   **HAIR** Gray
SPECIAL POWERS/ABILITIES A wealthy amateur scientific genius who helped develop the atomic bomb. He also invented a method for collecting energy radiated by stars and the Gravity Rod, which allowed him to fly; an average hand-to-combatant.

STARMAN II
See **DR. MID-NITE I**
SPECIAL POWERS/ABILITIES Paul "Robotman" Dennis and Jim "Red Torpedo" Lockhart designed and constructed a sophisticated star-shaped hovercraft that served as Starman II's transportation.

STARMAN III
FIRST APPEARANCE First Issue Special #12 (March 1976)
STATUS Hero   **REAL NAME** Mikaal Tomas
OCCUPATION Adventurer   **BASE** Opal City
HEIGHT 6ft 3in   **WEIGHT** 160 lbs   **EYES** Pale blue   **HAIR** Purple
SPECIAL POWERS/ABILITIES The sonic crystal that was seared into his flesh allowed Mikaal to fire sonic blasts and granted him invulnerability and limited flight.

STARMAN IV
FIRST APPEARANCE Adventure Comics #467 (January 1980)
STATUS Hero (deceased)   **REAL NAME** Prince Gavyn
OCCUPATION Adventurer   **BASE** Throneworld
HEIGHT 6ft 2in   **WEIGHT** 180 lbs   **EYES** Blue   **HAIR** Blond
SPECIAL POWERS/ABILITIES Could absorb energy and redirect it as heat or energy bolts.

STARMAN V
FIRST APPEARANCE Starman (1st series) #1 (October 1980)
STATUS Hero (deceased)   **REAL NAME** William Payton
OCCUPATION Adventurer   **BASE** Tucson, Arizona
HEIGHT 6ft 1in   **WEIGHT** 180 lbs   **EYES** Brown   **HAIR** Brown
SPECIAL POWERS/ABILITIES Could emit heat and light; had the power of flight, and could alter his physical form.

STARMAN VI
FIRST APPEARANCE Starman (1st series) #26 (September 1990)
STATUS Hero (deceased)   **REAL NAME** David Knight
OCCUPATION Adventurer   **BASE** Opal City
HEIGHT 5ft 11in   **WEIGHT** 170 lbs   **EYES** Brown   **HAIR** Brown
SPECIAL POWERS/ABILITIES While possessing the cosmic rod, David could fly and direct energy bolts, although he was never especially adept at it.

THE LEGEND OF THE STARMAN, harnessing the stars for the greater good of humanity, stretches from the dawn of the atomic age through the millennia. It begins with wealthy amateur astronomer Ted Knight, who in 1939, created the Gravity Rod, which enabled him to augment or negate gravity. Crafting a super-hero costume, he took flight as Starman.

STARMAN I
Knight's heroic career led to his protecting not only his beloved Opal City, but all of the U.S. through his work with the JUSTICE SOCIETY OF AMERICA and the ALL-STAR SQUADRON. He battled the MIST I again and again, creating an enmity that would last for decades. Knight, who was haunted by his role in the creation of the atomic bomb, resigned from the JSA after helping them beat the dimensional conqueror known as STALKER. Soon after this, he suffered the first of a series of nervous breakdowns and bouts of depression, which led him to temporarily give up his heroic career.

OPAL CITY CHAMPIONS
Dr. Mid-Nite took over Knight's role, becoming Starman II, and watching over Opal City. Then a time-lost David Knight (who would be Starman VI) arrived in town and was groomed by Dr. Mid-Nite to become his "secret weapon." Eventually David returned to his own time in the future and Ted Knight resumed his Starman mantle.

Ted met Adele Doris Drew at a fundraiser, and the two fell in love, married, and had two sons, David and Jack. During those years, Ted, sporting an upgraded device called the Cosmic Rod, often came out of retirement, fighting villains with such heroes as BLACK CANARY I and WILDCAT I.

CANARY KISS
When Starman took to the skies, he began an affair with the first Black Canary.

STARMAN II *Opal City guardian.*

STARMAN IV AND V
Out in the distant universe, Prince Gavyn became known as Starman IV, protector of his empire. He served his people well, sacrificing his life during the Crisis (see Great Battles, pp. 362–3). Reduced to pure energy, Gavyn was directed toward Earth. Teenage hitchhiker Will Payton was struck by Gavyn's lifeforce, gaining extraordinary powers. At this time, Starman I was away in Limbo with the JSA, battling demons to protect the Earth. So, to his sister Jayne's delight, Payton became Starman V. Will struggled with being both a hero and a teenager, and learned the ropes from established heroes such as BATMAN and the Atom. Eventually he lost his life battling the villain ECLIPSO.

WILL PAYTON
Teenager who died a hero's death as Starman V.

STARMAN III
Unknown to Ted Knight, the blue-skinned Mikaal Tomas escaped from his fellow race of invading aliens from Talok III. Tomas began adventuring as Starman III while Ted raised his children. Within a year, Mikaal Tomas killed the other surviving member of his race in ritual combat, then disappeared from sight for years. After his rescue from virtual imprisonment, Mikaal joined Starman VI for several adventures before going his own way once more.

STARMAN VII
First Appearance Zero Hour #1 (September 1994)
Status Hero *Real Name* Jack Knight
Occupation Antique dealer; adventurer *Base* Opal City
Height 6 ft 1in *Weight* 165 lbs *Eyes* Blue *Hair* Black
Special powers/abilities Trained in jujitsu, and uses the Cosmic Rod to fly or to project energy bolts, levitate objects or create force fields.

STARMAN VIII
First Appearance Starman (2nd series) #79 (July 2001)
See Star Boy
Special powers/abilities This native of Xanthu can control mass and fly.

STARMAN 1,000,000
First Appearance JLA #23 (November 1998)
Status Hero *Real Name* Farris Knight
Occupation Adventurer *Base* Uranus
Height 6ft 4in *Weight* 265 lbs *Eyes* Blue *Hair* Brown
Special powers/abilities Uses a revamped version of the gravity rod, enabling him to fly, alter gravimetric forces and fight with fierce determination.

STARMAN VII

Starman I, now retired, declared his son David his successor. David's run as Starman VI was cut short when he was gunned down by the Mist. David's brother, Jack Knight, then found the family legacy thrust upon him and reluctantly became Starman VII. While visiting a circus, Jack discovered and rescued Mikaal Tomas, Starman III, from captivity as a sideshow attraction. Meanwhile, Nash, the Mist's unstable daughter, vowed revenge after Jack killed her brother. As Mist II, she captured Jack and seduced him while he was only partially conscious. A year later, Jack was stunned to learn that Nash had given birth to his son, Kyle Theo Knight.

Starman & son *The relationship between Ted and his sons was never an easy one but it grew warmer with time.*

TO THE STARS AND BACK

Accompanied by Mikaal, Jack voyaged into space to determine the fate of Starman V, the brother of his girlfriend Sadie Falk (who was actually Jayne Marie Payton). Jack journeyed to Throneworld, now which was ruled by a cruel, despotic regime. Jack found Will and learned of his amazing connection with Throneworld's Prince Gavyn. The three Starmen, along with political prisoners such as Fastbak and the Omega Men's Tigorr then freed Throneworld from tyranny. Will Payton/Gavyn declined an invitation to return to Earth and Jack and Mikaal set off homeward. After various adventures, they returned to Opal City, which was soon threatened with nuclear holocaust by the Mist.

Sadie *When Jayne Payton's brother, Starman V, died, she turned to the latest Starman for help but fell in love instead.*

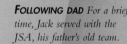
Following dad *For a brief time, Jack served with the JSA, his father's old team.*

While they had been away, Ted Knight, Starman I, had been diagnosed with terminal cancer, contracted while battling Doctor Phosphorus. Despite the disease, Ted used an advanced cosmic rod to transport the Mist I's bomb safely into space. Ted and the Mist died in the explosion, and the super-hero community mourned his passing. Jack Knight, briefly served with the JSA before opting to retire to raise his son. He gave his cosmic rod to Star-Spangled Kid, who renamed herself Stargirl in honor of the legacy. RG

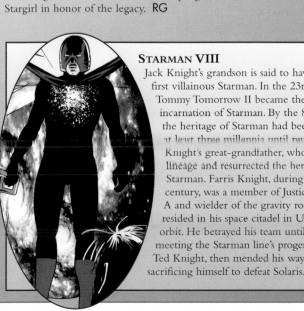

STARMAN VIII

Jack Knight's grandson is said to have been the first villainous Starman. In the 23rd century, Tommy Tomorrow II became the latest incarnation of Starman. By the 822nd century, the heritage of Starman had been abandoned for at least three millennia until revived by Farris Knight's great-grandfather, who discovered his lineage and resurrected the heroic mantle of Starman. Farris Knight, during the 853rd century, was a member of Justice Legion A and wielder of the gravity rod who resided in his space citadel in Uranus's orbit. He betrayed his team until meeting the Starman line's progenitor, Ted Knight, then mended his ways, sacrificing himself to defeat Solaris.

KEY STORYLINES
• *Starman: Sins of the Father* (TPB, 1996): Jack Knight reluctantly becomes the latest Starman and learns about the rich family legacy—complete with adversaries.
• *Starman: Stars My Destination* (TPB, 2004): Jack and Mikaal find Prince Gavyn and Will Payton, but also get involved in inter-galactic conflicts with consequences today and tomorrow.
• *The Brave and the Bold #61–62 (August–November 1965)*: Starman I and Black Canary I share adventures against old foes the Sportsmaster and Huntress I.

STEAMROLLER

FIRST APPEARANCE GREEN LANTERN (2nd series) #176 (May 1984)
STATUS Villain **REAL NAME** Unknown
OCCUPATION Member of Demolition Team **BASE** Mobile
HEIGHT 5ft 11in **WEIGHT** 205 lbs
EYES Blue **HAIR** Black
SPECIAL POWERS/ABILITIES Drives a steamroller capable of leveling buildings.

Though his real name is unknown, the code name Steamroller is all one needs to know about this member of the DEMOLITION TEAM. Formerly a stunt-motorcyclist operating out of Chicago, Steamroller now drives a miniature, high-powered steamroller with enough muscle to knock down any structure and flatten the pieces.

Steamroller joined the Demolition Team in hopes of becoming a high-priced mercenary, and with his new comrades—Rosie, Hardhat, Jackhammer, and Scoopshovel—tore up the Los Angeles branch of Ferris Aircraft on behalf of a congressmen nursing a grudge. Steamroller's gleeful rampage came to an end courtesy of the Predator, who later turned out to be an alternate personality belonging to STAR SAPPHIRE Carol Ferris.

After the CYBORG SUPERMAN, aided by Mongul destroyed Coast City, the Demolition Team decided to stamp out threats to the Earth and targeted a German nuclear plant. After a defeat by the BLOOD PACK, Steamroller and his teammates lost badly to an army of OMAC units prior to the Infinite Crisis. DW

STEEL I

FIRST APPEARANCE STEEL (1st series) #1 (March 1978)
STATUS Hero (deceased) **REAL NAME** Henry (Hank) Heywood I
OCCUPATION Crime fighter **BASE** Mobile
HEIGHT 6ft **WEIGHT** 378 lbs **EYES** Blue **HAIR** Blond
SPECIAL POWERS/ABILITIES Nearly indestructible due to steel construction and bioretardant skin; possesses enhanced strength and speed.

Hank Heywood nearly died when an explosion shredded his body. Rebuilt from the skeleton up, Heywood received artificial lungs, steel tubing instead of bones, metal plating on his skull, micro-motors to power his joints, and tough, bioretardant skin. As "Steel the Indestructible Man," he battled the Nazis during World War II, received the name Commander Steel from President Roosevelt, and joined the ALL-STAR SQUADRON.

After the war, Steel retired from heroics and earned a fortune as a Detroit-based industrialist. His son died in Vietnam, but Commander Steel gave his grandson the same treatments he had received and turned Hank Heywood III into a new Steel. After AQUAMAN reformed the JUSTICE LEAGUE OF AMERICA, Commander Steel offered his Detroit bunker as an HQ if Aquaman accepted his grandson as a member. Years later, Steel died battling the villain ECLIPSO. DW

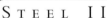

STEEL II

FIRST APPEARANCE JUSTICE LEAGUE OF AMERICA (1st series) ANNUAL #2 **STATUS** Hero **REAL NAME** Henry "Hank" Heywood III
OCCUPATION Troubleshooter **BASE** Detroit
HEIGHT 5ft 11in **WEIGHT** 379 lbs **EYES** Blue **HAIR** Red
SPECIAL POWERS/ABILITIES Superhuman strength, speed, and agility; enhanced hearing; infrared vision.

Grandson of Henry Heywood, the 1940s champion Commander Steel (see STEEL I), Hank Heywood III endured a series of painful operations to become a modern-day Steel. His bones were replaced with titanium. Micro-motors and servomechanisms enhanced his musculature. Subdermal plastisteel mesh lining a fibroplast skin made him nearly invulnerable, and cybernetic implants augmented his visual and auditory senses. After a long recovery, as his body adjusted to bio-chemical treatments and implants, the new Steel joined the JUSTICE LEAGUE OF AMERICA. He was granted membership in exchange for the League's use of a Detroit-based headquarters, the Bunker, donated by the elder Heywood, a wealthy industrialist. Steel II was mortally wounded by an android creation of the League's foe PROFESSOR IVO. Heywood died months later when DESPERO destroyed his life-support systems. SB

HEAVY METAL METTLE
Steel II was forged by the same process that saved his grandfather and molded him into the cyborg known as Commander Steel during World War II.

STEEL III

THE MAN OF IRON

FIRST APPEARANCE ADVENTURES OF SUPERMAN #500 (June 1993)
STATUS Hero **REAL NAME** John Henry Irons
OCCUPATION Inventor, adventurer **BASE** Metropolis
HEIGHT 6ft 7in **WEIGHT** 210 lbs **EYES** Brown **HAIR** None
SPECIAL POWERS/ABILITIES A scientific genius with amazing manufacturing skills and a brave fighter with little formal training. Specially designed armor confers protection in battle and enables him to fly. His main weapon is a remote controlled hammer.

JOHN HENRY IRONS is a fighter forged from the same mold as Superman. When the Man of Tomorrow saved Irons from a fatal fall off a Metropolis skyscraper, he challenged the construction worker to make his life count for something. A former weapons engineer for the ruthless AmerTek company, Irons longed to atone for the deaths his designs caused. He chose the way of the hero as the armored champion Steel.

IN THE 'HOOD *John Henry Irons loved to work with the kids in his Washington D.C. neighborhood.*

GREAT DEFENDER *Steel and his mighty hammer protected Washington, New Jersey and New York during his brief career.*

FINAL FIRES *Irons forges his last suit of battle armor.*

THE IRON MAN

John Irons grew up, surrounded by a loving family, in a poor section of Washington D.C. He entered college as a physics major and quickly rose to the top of his class. Realizing his potential as an engineer, AmerTek hired Irons and he designed the BG-80 assault rifle, also known as the "Toastmaster," as well as a flying armor prototype. Disillusioned by the misuse of his inventions, Irons faked his death and moved to Metropolis. After SUPERMAN died at Doomsday's hands, he was one of four men to briefly claim the Man of Steel's mantle. Irons and the resurrected Superman become close friends. John continued to adventure as Steel, aided by his plucky niece Natasha (see IRONS, NATASHA). Eventually, John opened Steelworks, an industrial design concern. He also worked with the JUSTICE LEAGUE OF AMERICA.

During the Imperiex War (see Great Battles, pp.362–3), Steel suffered mortal wounds while releasing Doomsday from the JLA Watchtower to battle the cosmic conqueror. At the same time, Superman was unable to turn away the New Gods' Black Racer, who ushered dead souls into the afterlife. This time, however, the Racer delivered Irons to Apokolips, where the crafty Darkseid restored his life. Steel fought during the Infinite Crisis, but soon had a falling-out with his niece over her desire to take the "easy road" to superheroics. A resentful Natasha joined Lex Luthor's (see LUTHOR, LEX) Everyman Project and received superpowers. Irons, meanwhile, became infected by Luthor's mutagens, which temporarily transformed his body into living metal. Ultimately, Steel and Natasha realized the truth of Luthor's villainy and united to bring down the Everyman Project. **RG**

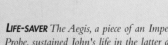

METAL WORK *John developed his various battlesuits in his lab.*

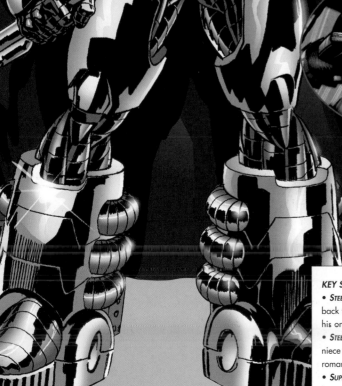

LIFE-SAVER *The Aegis, a piece of an Imperiex Probe, sustained John's life in the latter days of the Imperiex War.*

KEY STORYLINES

- *STEEL #1 (FEBRUARY 1994):* John Henry Irons moves back to Washington, D.C. and discovers that crime has ruined his once-friendly neighborhood.
- *STEEL #41–43 (AUGUST–OCTOBER 1997):* Steel has to handle his niece Natasha, political intrigue at his hospital, Skorpio, and romance all at the same time.
- *SUPERMAN VS. DARKSEID: APOKOLIPS NOW! (2003):* Superman braves Apokolips's worst forces to retrieve Steel's soul and return him to life.

MELTING POINT FOR STEEL? *Natasha, John Henry's niece, shields her eyes from the terrible explosion that claimed John's life.*

INFINITE CRISIS

IDENTITY CRISIS

Fractures within the Justice League of America came to light with the stunning murder of Sue Dibny, wife of Elongated Man Ralph Dibny. Suspicion initially pointed to Doctor Light, who had horrifically assaulted Sue during the early years of the JLA. After Light's attack, a majority of League members had agreed to mind-wipe and reprogram him with Zatanna's magic – then had mind-wiped Batman when he discovered their actions.

The JLA had continued to use Zatanna's brainwashing to keep their secret identities hidden, leading to a betrayal of the trust that kept the team functioning. Yet Sue Dibny's murderer turned out to not be Doctor Light. The Atom's ex-wife Jean Loring had killed Sue, and embarked on a campaign against other people important to the League (a plan that resulted in the death of Robin's father) as part of an insane scheme to win back the Atom's affections.

Loring's incarceration in Arkham Asylum drove her further into madness, making her an easy target to become the newest host for Eclipso.

GRIEFSTRICKEN *Sue Dibny's death signaled a grim change in the super-hero community.*

BRAINWASHING *Zatanna's act of mind-wiping Doctor Light caused League members to start keeping secrets.*

LOSS *Robin's father and Captain Boomerang killed one another, leaving Robin an orphan.*

THE CRISIS ON INFINITE EARTHS collapsed an endless number of parallel universes into a single, unified reality. But this blended existence could not contain its contradictions. With the interference of a madman, the multiverse was born again.

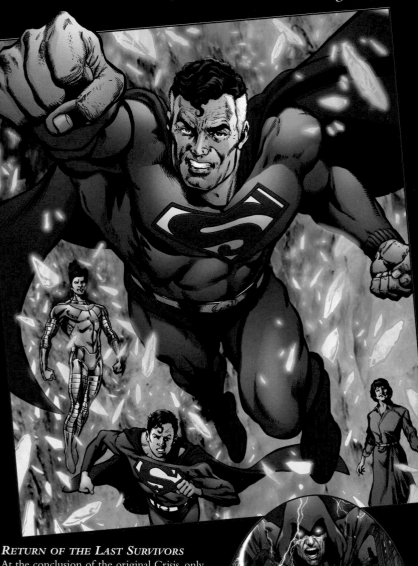

RETURN OF THE LAST SURVIVORS

At the conclusion of the original Crisis, only four people remained from the previous multiverse: SUPERMAN (Kal-L) and Lois Lane (*see* LANE, LOIS) from Earth-Two, SUPERBOY from Earth-Prime, and Alexander Luthor from Earth-Three. They had existed in a pocket dimension, observing the history of this Earth and growing disturbed by its gray grimness.

Alexander Luthor and Superboy-Prime set plans in motion to recreate alternate Earths that would be more to their liking. Superboy-Prime altered the orbit of Thanagar to spark a war with the neighboring planet Rann, and also annihilated the Justice League of America's lunar Watchtower. Alexander Luthor posed as Earth's Lex Luthor (see LUTHOR, LEX), assembling a massive SECRET SOCIETY OF SUPER VILLAINS. Meanwhile, the rampaging forces of ECLIPSO and the SPECTRE overturned the realm of magic, while the intelligent satellite Brother Eye—created by BATMAN—pursued its own agenda by transforming humans into unstoppable OMACs.

SPECTRE'S SINS *The destruction of the Rock of Eternity loosed the Seven Deadly Sins on Gotham.*

BATTLE FOR THE MULTIVERSE

Alexander Luthor looted the corpse of the Anti-Monitor to construct a gigantic vibrational tuning fork capable of making universes. His first success resulted in the restoration of an unpopulated Earth-Two. Kal-L brought his Lois there in the hope that it would reverse her terminal illness, but she died. Grief-stricken, Kal-L battled Earth's Kal-El, until the two Supermen agreed to fight on the same side.

ALONE *The death of Lois devastated Earth-Two's Superman..*

ALL-OUT ASSAULT

Superboy-Prime lashed out at Conner Kent, the Superboy whom he believed had taken his place. Superboy-Prime badly beat Conner and killed PANTHA, before the Flashes (*see* FLASH) hurled him into an alternate dimension. He returned even stronger, wearing an armored suit that fed him energizing yellow sun radiation.

Superboy-Prime lashed out at Conner Kent, the Superboy whom he believed had taken his place. Superboy-Prime badly beat Conner and killed PANTHA, before the Flashes (*see* FLASH) hurled him into an alternate dimension. He returned even stronger, wearing an armored suit that fed him energizing yellow sun radiation.

A rematch between Conner Kent and Superboy-Prime resulted in the destruction of Alexander Luthor's tuning fork, but at the cost of Conner's life. With the destruction of Alexander's machine the various universes he had created merged into a single reality, but this "New Earth" had subtle changes in its timeline.

In a last-ditch effort to crush his foes, Alexander ordered the villains of the Secret Society to take up arms against Earth's heroes, with Metropolis as their battleground. Superboy-Prime chose this moment to fly toward the planet Oa at near-light speed, hoping the collision would destroy this universe and trigger its rebirth. Superman and the Superman of Earth-Two intercepted him, steering Superboy-Prime through the heart of a red sun that sapped the powers of all three combatants. On the intelligent planet Mogo, Kal-L perished in the effort to stop his younger doppelganger.

THE NEW REALITY

The Green Lantern Corps took custody of Superboy-Prime, imprisoning him inside a miniature red sun. Alexander Luthor met his end on Earth, when the JOKER took revenge for not receiving an invitation to join the Secret Society. At the time, no one realized that Alexander Luthor had partially succeeded in his plan. He had created 52 parallel universes, identical and existing on separate vibrational planes. It would be another year before the existence of the new multiverse become known. **DW**

SUPERBOY-PRIME *Unstoppable relic of the old multiverse, he shrugged off attacks from powerful heroes.*

LAST LAUGH *The Joker, left out of the action, took great pleasure in executing Alexander Luthor.*

STRANGE, ADAM

CHAMPION OF RANN

FIRST APPEARANCE SHOWCASE #17 (December 1958)
STATUS Hero **REAL NAME** Jean Paul Valley
OCCUPATION Adventurer **BASE** The planet Rann
HEIGHT 6ft **WEIGHT** 175 lbs **EYES** Blue **HAIR** Blond
SPECIAL POWERS/ABILITIES Adam is a brilliant strategist and expert flyer. He can teleport across space using a Rannian machine; also travels using a jet pack; wears a special suit fitted with oxygen tanks to survive in the airless vacuum of space; main weapon is a ray gun.

ARCHAEOLOGIST ADAM STRANGE was unexpectedly transported 25 trillion miles across space to the planet Rann. There, he met the scientist Sardath, who explained that his Zeta beam had been intended purely as a communications tool but had turned out to be a teleportation device instead. Over time, Adam adapted so well to this new world that he became the planet's protector, using his wits and the native technology to overcome alien invasions, rogue monsters and the occasional Tornado Tyrant.

ZETA BEAM LOVE

Adam fell in love with Sardath's beautiful daughter Alanna, but their romance was regularly interrupted, for whenever the Zeta beam radiation wore off, Adam was yanked back to Earth. To return to Rann, Adam had to calculate the next time and location the Zeta Beam would strike. It was some time before Adam learned Rann's secret: Rannian men were all sterile and Adam had been brought to Rann to father a child with Alanna and perpetuate the race!

During his exploits on Rann, Adam was aided by the JUSTICE LEAGUE OF AMERICA and many other heroes. Adam was finally drained of the toxic radiation that prevented him from making long-term stays on Rann. His romance with Alanna continued, and the JLA attended their wedding. Finally drained of the energy that kept him on Rann, Adam returned to Earth.

Later, using a "Mega-Zeta Beam," Adam was permanently teleported to Rann. His happiness was shattered when Alanna died giving birth to their daughter Aleea. Sardath went mad, rocketing the city of Ranagar into space in a protective sphere. Seemingly deranged himself, Adam brought the JLA to Rann and commanded them "to restore the planet to its former glory."

In fact, Adam's actions were a ruse to outwit the En'Tarans. This race of telepathic conquerors, who sought the Zeta Beam technology for their own dark purposes, revived Alanna from her deathlike state. Adam, Alanna and Aleea were happily reunited.

Adam Strange returned to action with the OMEGA MEN during an adventure that transported Rann into the same star system as Thanagar, sparking the Rann-Thanagar War. Strange lost his eyesight in the Infinite Crisis and spent a year stranded in space with ANIMAL MAN and STARFIRE, fighting the armies of Lady Styx. Returned home, he found himself replaced as Rann's champion. **RG**

BEAMED UP The Zeta Beam conveys Adam from Earth to Alanna.

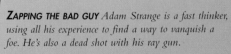
FADE OUT After a time, the Zeta effect wears off and Adam is returned to Earth.

LEARNING DEVICE Sardath, who developed the Zeta Beam, also found a quick way to teach Adam his language.

CIRCLE OF FIRE Green Lightning, a Green Lantern from the future, rescues Adam from peril on planet Rann.

ZAPPING THE BAD GUY Adam Strange is a fast thinker, using all his experience to find a way to vanquish a foe. He's also a dead shot with his ray gun.

KEY STORYLINES

- **ADAM STRANGE: MAN OF TWO WORLDS (1990):** Adam seemingly loses Rann, Alanna and his daughter in a cosmic conflict.
- **JUSTICE LEAGUE OF AMERICA #120–121 (JULY–AUGUST 1975):** Adam and Alanna finally get married, but not without considerable difficulty.
- **MYSTERY IN SPACE #68 (JUNE 1961):** Adam's first encounter with the deadly Dust Devils.
- **SHOWCASE #17 (NOVEMBER–DECEMBER 1958):** Adam first rides the Zeta Beam to discover Rann.

STEPPENWOLF

FIRST APPEARANCE NEW GODS (1st series) #7
STATUS Villain (deceased) **REAL NAME** Steppenwolf
OCCUPATION Military commander **BASE** Apokolips
HEIGHT 6ft **WEIGHT** 203 lbs **EYES** Red **HAIR** Black
SPECIAL POWERS/ABILITIES Dog cavalry commander; "cable snare" device fires lethal energy beams and entraps opponents; wields an electro-axe and is an expert swordsman.

The uncle of DARKSEID, ruler of Apokolips, Steppenwolf was the commander of Apokolips's military during the reign of Heggra, Darkseid's mother. Hoping to incite a war between Apokolips and its sister world, New Genesis, Darkseid suggested that Steppenwolf go and hunt the inhabitants there for "sport."

When Steppenwolf murdered the wife of Izaya the Inheritor, the New Genesis leader (*see* HIGHFATHER), and Darkseid pretended to kill Highfather himself, a bloody war between the two worlds began.

During a pitched battle on the plains of New Genesis, Steppenwolf was caught off guard and killed by the vengeful Izaya, whom he believed dead. Steppenwolf was later resurrected by the advanced technology of Apokolips. After menacing menaced Bart Allen (the fourth FLASH), Steppenwolf lost his life during the Death of the New Gods event. **PJ**

STOMPA

FIRST APPEARANCE MISTER MIRACLE 1st series #6 (February 1972)
STATUS Villain **REAL NAME** Unknown
OCCUPATION Female Fury **BASE** Apokolips
HEIGHT 5ft 8in **WEIGHT** 330 lbs **EYES** Unknown **HAIR** Unknown
SPECIAL POWERS/ABILITIES Ruthless enforcer; heavy matter boots can pulverize even the densest material.

Reared on distant Apokolips and personally trained for terror by the vile GRANNY GOODNESS, Stompa is a member of the much-feared FEMALE FURIES, an elite squad of women warriors belonging to Darkseid's Special Powers Force. As her name implies, Stompa uses her considerable bulk to great advantage when crushing the enemies of Darkseid beneath her boot heels. Possessing considerable muscle mass, she is stronger than a Parademon and just as mean.

Recently, Stompa adopted a new costume that accentuates her feminine qualities slightly more than her previous unisex uniform. She was among the Furies dispatched to Earth by Darkseid to capture Kara Zor-El, Superman's Kryptonian cousin, so that the dreaded lord of Apokolips could mold the young SUPERGIRL to do his bidding. As expected, this mission brought Stompa and the Female Furies into direct conflict with the Earth's finest heroes, particularly Superman and Batman, as two worlds struggled for the soul of the young Kryptonian girl. **SB**

STRANGE, ADAM *SEE OPPOSITE PAGE*

STRANGE, PROFESSOR HUGO

FIRST APPEARANCE DETECTIVE COMICS #36 (February 1940)
STATUS Villain **REAL NAME** Hugo Strange
OCCUPATION Psychiatrist; criminal **BASE** Gotham City
HEIGHT 5ft 10in **WEIGHT** 170 lbs
EYES Gray **HAIR** None (black beard)
SPECIAL POWERS/ABILITIES Brilliant deductive mind and extensive knowledge of psychology.

Professor Hugo Strange is one of the only people to have deduced BATMAN's secret identity. Early in the caped crusader's career, Professor Strange became a media celebrity by appearing on talk shows and providing his "expert opinion" regarding the costumed vigilante's psychological makeup. Soon appointed a special consultant to Gotham City's Vigilante Task Force, Strange's obsession with the Batman gradually unhinged his mind even as it allowed him to piece together disparate clues linking Batman to Bruce Wayne.

Strange has used his knowledge of Batman's greatest secret to torment the Dark Knight, though Strange's waxing and waning levels of insanity sometimes make him unaware of his proprietary knowledge. Bruce Wayne recently underwent self-hypnosis to temporarily forget that he was the Batman, confounding Strange and allowing NIGHTWING and ROBIN to defeat the professor. Hugo Strange has also brewed mind-altering drugs that have turned Gotham's thugs into vicious killers. Although his sporadic knowledge of Bruce Wayne's costumed identity would prove invaluable to Batman's enemies, Hugo Strange has remained at arm's length from the Dark Knight's Rogues Gallery. Strange prefers to work alone. He remains a dangerous foe, and the day when his mind finally snaps will be a grim day for the citizens of Gotham. **DW**

MASKED MANIA Hugo Strange has allowed his entire reality to revolve around Batman. His brain is still his greatest asset, despite his bouts of psychosis.

STRATA

FIRST APPEARANCE INVASION #2 (Summer 1989)
STATUS Hero **REAL NAME** Strata
OCCUPATION Interstellar operative **BASE** The planet Cairn
HEIGHT 7ft 2in **WEIGHT** 803 lbs **EYES** White **HAIR** None
SPECIAL POWERS/ABILITIES Superstrength; invulnerability; extremely long-lived.

Strata is from the planet Dryad, whose inhabitants are sentient, rock-like humanoids made of silicon. As a youngster, Strata was captured by aliens seeing to conquer the universe. With several other prisoners, Strata escaped with the help of Vril Dox. Strata and the others then helped Dox form an interstellar police force, L.E.G.I.O.N.

The L.E.G.I.O.N. was attacked by alien psychopath Lobo, who shredded Strata's rock-like epidermis, revealing crystalline skin beneath. It was only then that Strata realized she was female! Strata served as chief training officer of L.E.G.I.O.N and married fellow member Garv.

When the L.E.G.I.O.N. and its forces were transformed into a fascist organization by Vril Dox's son, Lyrl, Strata was separated from Garv and worked with the R.E.B.E.L.S. to end Lyrl's threat. Captain Comet reformed L.E.G.I.O.N. and Strata and Garv returned to its ranks. Strata later joined InterC.E.P.T., an organization specializing in interdimensional border control. **PJ**

STRIKER Z

FIRST APPEARANCE JLA #61 (February 2002)
STATUS Hero **REAL NAME** Danny Tsang **OCCUPATION** Super hero
BASE San Francisco **HEIGHT** 5ft 10in **WEIGHT** 175 lbs
EYES Black **HAIR** Black **SPECIAL POWERS/ABILITIES** biologically-created energy powers his "flight jacket", a visor with built-in sensor arrays, sonic generators, shock cannons and other useful devices.

While working as a stuntman in the Hong Kong movie industry, Danny Tsang developed superpowers after an on-set accident when he fell into an experimental fuel-cell medium. Danny's body became a living battery capable of fueling various high-tech devices designed by Danny's pal, Charlie Lau, a former S.T.A.R. Labs engineer and special-effects expert. Danny traveled to the U.S hoping that his flashy powers would make him a Hollywood star. Dubbed Striker Z by his talent agent, Danny instead found work with the POWER COMPANY, a superpowered law firm. After he joined the Power Company, Striker Z received several offers to star in television commercials.

While he enjoys being a costumed champion, Striker Z remains uncertain whether he's in the hero game for the fame and fortune, or for more altruistic motives. **SB**

STRIPESY

FIRST APPEARANCE STAR SPANGLED COMICS #1 (October 1941)
STATUS Hero **REAL NAME** Patrick Dugan
OCCUPATION Inventor **BASE** Blue Valley, Nebraska
HEIGHT 6ft 1in **WEIGHT** 210 lbs **EYES** Blue **HAIR** Red
SPECIAL POWERS/ABILITIES Pat has an extraordinary intellect and skill as a mechanic, first inventing a flying car in the 1940s and, more recently, the S.T.R.I.P.E. armor.

Sylvester Pemberton III and his chauffeur, Pat Dugan, were independently inspired to become the Star-Spangled Kid and Stripesy. Their exploits during World War II included pursuing the hulking mad scientist Doctor Weerd and matching wits with the dart-wielding villain the Needle. The duo then joined with other heroes to form the SEVEN SOLDIERS OF VICTORY, and had several adventures before becoming lost in time.

After returning to the present, Pat hung up his costume and married a woman named Maggie. They become the parents of a son, Michael. A side effect of Pat's past exposure to the time-stream caused his son's body and intellect to age unnaturally fast. The child resembled a six-year-old before the magic-based members of the JUSTICE SOCIETY OF AMERICA could arrest this unnatural development. Pat subsequently divorced Maggie and married Barbara Whitmore. When Pat's stepdaughter, Courtney Whitmore, laid claim to Sylvester Pemberton's cosmic belt and became an adventurer, Pat returned to action in a robot battlesuit and the duo became STARGIRL and S.T.R.I.P.E. He briefly relocated the family to Metropolis to work with John Henry Irons' Steelworks (see STEEL III). He has since moved everyone back to Blue Valley. Pat and Barbara now have a daughter, Patricia Lynn (who may grow up to be Starwoman). **RG**

CHANGING WITH THE TIMES Pat Dugan in his first costume and in his current armored persona.

STRONGBOW

FIRST APPEARANCE ALL-STAR WESTERN #58 (May 1951)
STATUS Hero **REAL NAME** Strong Bow
OCCUPATION Peacemaker **BASE** North America
HEIGHT 6ft **WEIGHT** 165 lbs **EYES** Brown **HAIR** Black
SPECIAL POWERS/ABILITIES A wise mind and a gentle spirit; is an expert shot with a bow and arrow.

Before Columbus discovered America, Strong Bow crisscrossed the continent of North America on a mission of peace. His tribe had been massacred and Strong Bow had no home. Striking out to unite the continent's tribes and prevent further atrocities, Strong Bow became a legendary mediator who revealed only that he hailed from "beyond the misty mountains." Strong Bow's travels all took place on foot, since horses had not yet been introduced to North America.

On at least two occasions, Strong Bow had time-skipping brushes with the 20th century. During the Crisis he hopped through history with other Native American heroes to join a fight at Florida's Cape Canaveral. On another occasion several modern heroes encountered Strong Bow as part of the "Rough Bunch," a group recruited to battle the time-traveling villain EXTANT in the Old West. **DW**

SUICIDE SQUAD SEE OPPOSITE PAGE

SUMO, THE SAMURAI

FIRST APPEARANCE SUPERMAN VS. WONDER WOMAN (January 1978) **STATUS** Hero **REAL NAME** Sumo
OCCUPATION Villain **BASE** Asahikawa, Japan
HEIGHT 6ft 7in **WEIGHT** 300 lbs **EYES** Brown **HAIR** Black
SPECIAL POWERS/ABILITIES Deadly warrior despite size, more agile than most men; exerts unusual control over his five senses.

Sumo was uniquely honored among the relatively few pupils selected to train under the ancient samurai known as the Enlightened One. His master permitted him to sip the Enlightened One's sacred "potion of power," and, before a year had passed, Sumo was transformed into a giant fighter and master swordsman.

Sumo the Samurai pledged loyalty to Japan's Emperor Hirohito and battled the American ALL-STAR SQUADRON during World War II as Hirohito's personal agent. Along with the shape-changer Kung and Tsunami, Sumo was a member of the Samurai Squad. Sumo remains a legendary figure throughout the Land of the Rising Sun. His present whereabouts are unknown. **SB**

SUNBOY

FIRST APPEARANCE ACTION COMICS #276 (May 1961)
STATUS Hero **REAL NAME** Dirk Morgna
OCCUPATION Legionnaire **BASE** Legion HQ, Earth
HEIGHT 5ft 7in **WEIGHT** 130 lbs **EYES** Blue **HAIR** Blond
SPECIAL POWERS/ABILITIES Projection of heat and light, with precise control over color and intensity.

Sun Boy is one of the most powerful of the 31st century's LEGION OF SUPER-HEROES, existing in all incarnations of the team across multiple timelines. Dirk Morgna acquired his powers when a scientist, Doctor Regulus, exposed him to radioactive energies. Morgna gained the ability to generate heat and light in almost unlimited amounts, earning him a spot on the Legion as Sun Boy. In one Legion continuity, an older Sun Boy became a puppet of Earthgov and its secret Dominator masters, eventually dying during the destruction of Earth's moon. A younger clone of Dirk Morgna became the new Sun Boy but preferred the code name Inferno.

A second Legion continuity saw Sun Boy captured by the villainous future version of the Justice League, then forced to produce radiation that turned Earth's sun red and rendered a time-traveling SUPERMAN powerless. In a third Legion timeline, Sun Boy was field leader until he became a captive of the Dominators, later freed by SUPERGIRL and his teammates. **DW**

SUPER-CHIEF

FIRST APPEARANCE ALL-STAR WESTERN #117 (March 1961)
STATUS Hero (deceased) **REAL NAME** Flying Stag
OCCUPATION Superpowered warrior **BASE** North America
HEIGHT 5ft 10in **WEIGHT** 170 lbs **EYES** Gray **HAIR** Black
SPECIAL POWERS/ABILITIES Meteorite fragment gives him superstrength, superspeed, flight, and an extended lifespan.

As the greatest warrior of the Wolf Clan in the late 1400s, Flying Stag knew he would win the contest to become Royaneh (Supreme Chief) of the Iroquois Nations. His rivals, however, trapped him in a pit, and when Flying Stag prayed to the Great Spirit Manitou, a radioactive meteorite fell from the sky. Wearing a shard of the meteorite around his neck, Flying Stag could access miraculous powers for one hour each day. To honor the Great Spirit he became Saganowahna, or Super-Chief.

Super-Chief led a heroic life and took a lover, White Fawn. But the energies of the meteorite caused him to outlive everyone he knew. He survived into the late 1800s. In the modern era, Jon Standing Bear became the new Super-Chief following the events of the Infinite Crisis. After joining a temporary lineup of the JUSTICE LEAGUE OF AMERICA, Super-Chief died while fighting BOOSTER GOLD's robot companion, Skeets. **DW**

SUICIDE SQUAD

FIRST APPEARANCE THE BRAVE AND THE BOLD (1st series) #25 (Sept. 1959) **STATUS** Covert agents **BASE** Mobile; formerly Belle Reve prison, La. **NOTABLE MEMBERS** Air Wave II (as Maser); Amanda Waller; Arsenal (as Speedy); Atom II; Atom III; Batman; Big Barda; Big Sir; Black Adam; Black Orchid II; Blackstarr; Blockbuster I; Bronze Tiger; Cameron Chase; Captain Boomerang; Captain Cold; Catalyst; Chronos I; Clock King, Doctor Light I, Enchantress, Killer Frost, King Shark, Major Disaster, Manhunter III, Nemesis, Parasite, Penguin, Plastique, Punch and Jewelee, Vixen, Shade.

The Squad has since been revived multiple times, once under the orders of President Lex Luthor (see LUTHOR, LEX) during the Imperiex War, and again under the leadership of SERGEANT ROCK. Amanda Waller assembled a new Suicide Squad following the Infinite Crisis, setting her team against BLACK ADAM and later using Squad operatives to capture dozens of super-villains for exile on the distant planet Salvation. **PJ**

THE FIRST SQUAD
1) Jess Bright
2) Rick Flag, Sr.
3) Karin Grace
4) Dr. Hugh Evans

ELITE FORCE

During the 1950s, the Suicide Squad, became an elite force assigned to covert missions abroad. After Rick Flag's wife died in a car accident, Flag himself perished in a suicide mission against the German War Wheel. Their son, Richard Flag Jr., under the eye of General J.E.B. Stuart (see HAUNTED TANK), grew up to became an Air Force colonel and the leader of a revamped Suicide Squad. Along with Karin Grace, Jess Bright, and Hugh Evans, Flag's Squad handled numerous threats to national security. After the tragic deaths of Bright and Evans on a mission in Cambodia, Karin Grace had a mental breakdown, and the Squad was disbanded.

Decades later congressional aide Amanda Waller (see WALLER, AMANDA) created a new Suicide Squad, many of whom were superhuman criminals. In exchange for a pardon and a fee, the criminals agreed to undertake one mission. Rick Flag, Jr. was recruited to be the Squad's field commander.

By maintaining a core group, the Suicide Squad undertook a number of missions, but several operatives died along the way, including Grace and Flag himself. After the terrorist KOBRA unhinged the U.S. intelligence community in one of his attempts at world domination, and Waller was sent to prison for contempt of Congress, the Squad was disbanded.

WORKING UNDER THE AUSPICES of Task Force X, a secret U.S. government agency, the Suicide Squad is a unit of paramilitary and meta-human operatives first assembled during World War II. Under the command of Captain Richard Flag, Sr., this "Suicide Squadron," comprised soldiers who chose service with the Squad in lieu of a court martial. The squad's assignments were considered suicide missions—hence its name!

SGT. ROCK'S SQUAD
1) Sgt. Rock
2) Modem
3) Deadshot
4) Blackstarr
5) Bulldozer

INFINITE CRISIS SQUAD
1) Cap. Boomerang II
2) The Persuader
3) Count Vertigo
4) Atom Smasher
5) Plastique
6) Electrocutioner

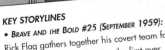

KEY STORYLINES
• BRAVE AND THE BOLD #25 (SEPTEMBER 1959): Rick Flag gathers together his covert team for the U.S. government, forming the first ever Suicide Squad.
• LEGENDS #1 (NOVEMBER 1986): A new Suicide Squad, comprised of super-villains, takes down the titanic Brimstone as Darkseid destroys Earth's legends!
• SUICIDE SQUAD (1st series) #17-18 (SEPTEMBER–OCTOBER 1988): The Suicide Squad prevents the Jihad terrorist group from destroying New York City!

SUPER MALON:
1) *Cachiru* 2) *Salamanca* 3) *El Lobizon* 4) *El Yagaurite*
5) *Pampero* 6) *Vizacacha* 7) *Cimarrón*.

SWAMP THING   *SEE OPPOSITE PAGE*

SYLPH

FIRST APPEARANCE NIGHTWING #48 (October 2000)
STATUS Villain   **REAL NAME** Sylvan Scofield
OCCUPATION Criminal   **BASE** Blüdhaven
HEIGHT 5ft 6in   **WEIGHT** 120 lbs   **EYES** Brown   **HAIR** Brown
SPECIAL POWERS/ABILITIES Special textile wrap is charged with static electricity and can entangle enemies.

Motivated by revenge, Scofield systematically executed the owners of the patent on the synthetic Achilloron fabric. Her father, a chemist, had invented the miracle textile, but committed suicide when others stole his design. Sylph wrapped herself in a bolt of Achilloron and slew some of the most prominent business leaders of Blüdhaven.

After Sylph's first two murders, NIGHTWING crossed paths with the murderess. He nearly died when she wrapped him in a sample of Achilloron and dumped him on a highway. Nightwing intercepted Sylph as she tried to kill the final patent-holder. In the struggle, Sylph became entangled in her own fabric and apparently broke her neck. It is likely that her death was a ruse and that Sylph will soon return. **DW**

SYONIDE II

FIRST APPEARANCE BATMAN AND THE OUTSIDERS #20 (April 1985)
STATUS Villain (deceased)   **REAL NAME** Unknown
OCCUPATION Assassin   **BASE** Mobile
HEIGHT 5ft 9in   **WEIGHT** 140 lbs   **EYES** Blue   **HAIR** Orange
SPECIAL POWERS/ABILITIES Wields electrically-charged whip and carries a gun loaded with paralysis and poison capsules.

The original Syonide carved out a name for himself as a hot-tempered and arrogant bounty hunter who often worked for mob kingpin Tobias Whale and the criminal syndicate the 100. Syonide insisted he wasn't a killer, yet he delivered victims into the hands of killers, making him a hypocrite at best. Troubled by this, Syonide committed suicide while pursuing BLACK LIGHTNING.

Tobias Whale recruited a second Syonide, this one a cold-hearted and lethal hitwoman. She battled the OUTSIDERS during a mission to track down Outsider teammate HALO and seemingly was killed by Sam Harper, Halo's father. Syonide survived and joined Strike Force Kobra, where she worked alongside the villainess Fauna, who was also her lover. She died while fighting a reformed version of the Outsiders. **DW**

SUPER-MALON

FIRST APPEARANCE THE FLASH (2nd ser.) Annual #13 (Summer 2000)
STATUS Hero team   **BASE** Buenos Aires, Argentina
MEMBERS AND POWERS
El Bagual Horseheaded humanoid with superstrength, superspeed; *Cachirú* Flight with wings, razorsharp talons; *Cimarrón* A wild, swashbuckling hero; *El Lobizon* A wolf-headed lycanthrope; *Pampero* Can control wind currents; *Salamanca* Sorceress who can project astral self and manipulate the weather; *Vizacacha* Master thief; *El Yaguarete* Superspeedster.

Carrying on in the patriotic tradition of their heroic predecessor from the 1950s, the Gaucho, the Super-Malon, a team of metahumans, are Argentina's modern defenders. These heroes have taken the names of characters from Argentine folklore, and many of their personal origins remain mysterious. Their leader is the sorceress SALAMANCA, a witch who can control the elements and project her astral self from her body, allowing her to roam the world as a phantom. When Barbara Minerva and Sébastian Ballesteros vied in Buenos Aires for the powers of the CHEETAH, the Super-Malon took to the streets to protect bystanders and help WONDER WOMAN trap the two villains; El Yaguarete was wounded in the process. **PJ**

SUPERMEN OF AMERICA

FIRST APPEARANCE SUPERMEN OF AMERICA #1 (March 1999)
STATUS Hero team   **BASE** Metropolis
CURRENT MEMBERS AND POWERS
Brahma (Cal Usjak) Superstrong and invulnerable.
Loser (Theo Storm) Possesses powerful dermal force field.
Maximum (Max Williams) Channels bursts of superhuman energy.
Outburst (Mitch Anderson) Manipulates magnetic fields.
Pyrogen (Claudio Tielli) Flame-controlling pyrokinetic.
White Lotus (Nona Lin) Martial artist empowered by mystic aura.

A heroic power vacuum left by SUPERMAN's brief departure from Metropolis to defend the whole of Earth gave rise to the Supermen of America, a team of teen heroes once sponsored by Metropolis mogul Lex Luthor (*see* LUTHOR, LEX).

When Junior K-D, lead singer of the band Crossfire, was gunned down during the "Cause for Pause" benefit concert in Metropolis, the ensuing chaos between rival street gangs forced teen hero Outburst into action. Years before he developed superpowers, Outburst and his family had been saved from the monstrous DOOMSDAY by the Man of Steel. With Superman as his inspiration, Outburst eagerly accepted Lex Luthor's offer to recruit a force of young meta-humans to patrol the city in Superman's stead.

Soon enough, Outburst had gathered Brahma, Loser, Psilencer, Pyrogen, and White Lotus to serve as Supermen of America, an ironic appellation given Luthor's not-so-secret hatred for the Last Son of Krypton. As salaried super heroes, the Supermen helped to quell gang violence on Metropolis's streets and even tackle super-villains emboldened by Superman's absence. Unfortunately, the prescient and telepathic Psilencer was killed in action, struck down by a gang member's bullet. He was replaced by the super-athletic Maximum. The Supermen of America eventually left Luthor's employ. They participated in the global fight against the OMAC units prior to the Infinite Crisis, which left many of their members grievously injured. **SB**

SUPERMEN OF AMERICA
1) *Brahma*
2) *Loser*
3) *White Lotus*
4) *Outburst*
5) *Psilencer (deceased)*
6) *Pyrogen*

SWAMP THING

THE TOXIC AVENGER

FIRST APPEARANCE HOUSE OF SECRETS #92 (July 1971)
STATUS Hero **REAL NAME** Alec Holland
OCCUPATION Plant elemental **BASE** Houma, Louisiana
HEIGHT Variable **WEIGHT** Variable **EYES** Red **HAIR** None
SPECIAL POWERS/ABILITIES Earth's plant elemental can manifest itself wherever there is organic life and can sense anything that affects said life; superstrong, with amazing regenerative powers; can change size and shape; can travel back through time.

GAIA, THE EARTH SPIRIT, has always had Elemental avatars to look after the planet and its living inhabitants. The greatest among them is the plant elemental known as Swamp Thing, who protects the planet at the risk of eliminating all human life. Several individuals have been given the role of plant elemental. The most recent is Alec Holland, who fell into a Louisiana swamp polluted with chemicals, which turned him into Swamp Thing.

BEAUTY AND THE BEAST
Swamp monsters have been drawn to attractive women through the years.

UNDER GLASS *General Sunderland studies Swamp Thing's body, trying to establish dominance.*

AVATARS OF THE GREEN

The Green was established as the Earth cooled and Yggdrasil was created. Yggdrasil gained sentience, and the Parliament of Trees grew in a sacred South American grove. Other elemental forces created their own parliaments soon after, including Water, Air, Fire, and Stone. Over time, each elemental caused a human to become its avatar. Each avatar lives until circumstances demand a changing of the guard. In the 20th Century this occurred with great rapidity, from Alex Olsen in 1905 to German pilot Albert Hollerer in 1942, to 1953's Aaron Hayley, to Alan Hallman, to the current Alec Holland.

Holland's spirit was enveloped in a plant body that thought it was still human, until he learned the truth after being captured by the vile Sunderland Corporation. Though shaken by the revelation, Swamp Thing eventually came to terms with this life. Swamp Thing endured much, environmental pollution as well as mystic threats. He also fell in love with Abigail Cable, daughter of Anton Arcane (see ARCANE, ANTON), one of the recurring threats to the creature. At one point, Swamp Thing took an unwanted sojourn into outer space. To fill the void, the Parliament of Trees sought to replace him with his child, dubbed Sprout and ultimately named Tefé (a child conceived with more than a little help from John Constantine).

Upon his return, Swamp Thing endured a series of trials that had him master each neighboring Parliament until he gained total control over the world's elements. The WORD I intervened and stopped Swamp Thing from being corrupted by his own absolute power. Now representing the Earth as a whole, Swamp Thing took his place in the Parliament of Worlds.

Tefé grew to adulthood, trying to find her way, rebelling against Abby's love. Swamp Thing, stripped of Holland's human consciousness, sought to destroy all life, starting with Tefé. Constantine restored Holland to the elemental and the new unified being is establishing his place in the world anew. **RG**

GATOR TAMER *Swamp Thing loved Abby and would prevent all danger from reaching her.*

KEY STORYLINES

• *SWAMP THING: DARK GENESIS (TPB, 1991):* The original storyline of the Swamp Thing and Abby.
• *SWAMP THING (2ND SERIES) #61 (JUNE 1987):* In "All Flesh is Grass," while exiled in space, he encounters Green Lantern Medphyl's homeworld.
• *SAGA OF THE SWAMP THING #34 (MARCH 1985):* Abby eats a tuber and experiences life from Swamp Thing's perspective.
• *SWAMP THING #21 (FEBRUARY 1984):* Swamp Thing learns he is not Alec Holland but a plant elemental.
• *HOUSE OF SECRETS #92 (JULY 1971):* The first ever Swamp Thing story.

SUPERBOY

THE TEEN OF STEEL

FIRST APPEARANCE ADVENTURES OF SUPERMAN #500 (June 1993)
STATUS Hero   **REAL NAMES** Kon-El; Conner Kent
OCCUPATION Student, adventurer   **BASE** Smallville; San Francisco
HEIGHT 5ft 7in   **WEIGHT** 150 lbs   **EYES** Blue   **HAIR** Black
SPECIAL POWERS/ABILITIES Superboy has "tactile telekinesis" which
mimics superstrength and flight and other Kryptonian abilities; can
disassemble objects by touching them.

A clone of SUPERMAN created by the Cadmus Project,
the world's most advanced genetic research facility,
Superboy is a custom-made copy of the Man of
Steel. In fact, Superboy was one of many such clones
engineered by Cadmus for the purpose of replacing
Superman, using DNA samples taken from the
Kryptonian champion after his battle with DOOMSDAY.
Superboy, however, was the only clone to survive.

CLONED Created with Super
DNA, Kon-El was gestated
inside a laboratory!

TEST TUBE HERO Superboy emerges from his cloning
tube at Project Cadmus, the spitting image of
Superman at 16!

CREATING A SUPER HERO

The Cadmus scientists stabilized Superboy's gene code by grafting
Superman's alien DNA on to a human DNA strand. The clone was
then transformed through a rapid-aging process, becoming a 16-year-
old boy in weeks. The teenage duplicate was rescued from his confines
at Cadmus by the NEWSBOY LEGION, who had learned that Superboy's
"creator," the unscrupulous Doctor Paul Westfield, had planned to use
the young clone's power for his own ends. Altering his
costume, the headstrong Superboy then revealed himself
to the world. Superboy soon became a close ally of
Superman, but moved to Hawaii, hoping the distance
from Metropolis might better help him attain an
identity separate from his genetic "father."
There he began dating Tana Moon, a
journalist who moved to Hawaii after
helping Superboy make a splash at
television station W.G.B.S. as the
"Metropolis Kid." After his body
started to deteriorate from a clone
plague, Superboy's DNA became
"frozen" at his 16-year old age.
Superman gave the young clone the
Kryptonian name "Kon-El". Soon
after, Superboy had a brief affair with
KNOCKOUT; Tana Moon broke up
with him and moved away.

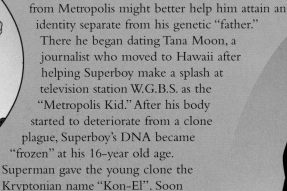

BOY OF STEEL Superboy lived in Honolulu for
some time, finding enemies in the Scavenger, King
Shark (above), and Black Zero, and both friend
and foe in Knockout, one of the Female Furies.

SUPER SECRET Robin helped Superboy
deduce the secret from the young
clones past—the source of his human
DNA—a secret the Boy Wonder was
sworn to conceal.

A GRIM DISCOVERY

Superboy returned to Metropolis as Project Cadmus' special agent and
also helped found YOUNG JUSTICE. Superboy was then kidnapped by
the Agenda, a clandestine organization of cloners, and was replaced
for months by an evil duplicate named Match. Superboy eventually
escaped the Agenda, but not before, Tana Moon was killed by the
Agenda's leader Amanda Spence, Paul Westfield's cyborg daughter.
Superboy was then adopted by Superman's parents, Jonathan and
Martha Kent (see KENTS, THE), and enrolled in
Smallville High School as Conner Kent,
Clark Kent's young cousin. After
Young Justice's dissolution,
Superboy joined the TEEN
TITANS. He then learned that
his human strand of DNA was
Lex Luthor's (see LUTHOR, LEX), a
horrifying secret he initially shared
only with his teammate ROBIN.

THE DC COMICS ENCYCLOPEDIA

FRIENDLY FIRE *Forced to fight Superboy after Lex Luthor turned him against the Teen Titans, Wonder Girl used her lasso to overwhelm her friend.*

LEX'S LEGACY

Superboy's self-identity suffered when he learned that his human DNA came, not from Project Cadmus director Paul Westfield, as he had believed, but from Lex Luthor. Consumed by thoughts that he might become a villain, Superboy found himself vulnerable to a deeply-buried brain-control trigger planted by Lex himself. No longer in control of his mind, Superboy shaved his head to resemble Lex and turned on his friends in the Teen Titans, injuring both Robin and WONDER GIRL before struggling back to sanity. The experience left him deeply shaken, prompting a leave of absence from the Titans and a period of seclusion in Smallville.

INFINITE CRISIS

The universe-shaking events of the Infinite Crisis brought Superboy face-to-face with his twisted namesake Superboy-Prime. While in seclusion in an alternate universe, Superboy-Prime had grown enraged at the sight of an Earth that he deemed unworthy and an "impostor" Superboy who had taken his place. Superboy-Prime escaped exile and confronted Superboy in Smallville, beating him to the brink of death. The Teen Titans helped restore Conner's health with a Luthor-designed genetic cure, but the Crisis raged on. Prior to the final battle, Superboy and Wonder Girl shared one last, intimate night together.

Superboy, Wonder Girl, and NIGHTWING charged into battle to sabotage Alexander Luthor's world-birthing tuning fork. When Superboy-Prime arrived to protect the device, he and Conner clashed in a furious rematch. Ultimately, Conner sacrificed his life to destroy Alexander Luthor's machine.

FINAL MOMENTS *Just before his death, Superboy shared a night with Wonder Girl.*

SACRIFICE *Beaten once, Superboy would not let Superboy-Prime win again.*

FALLEN *The world's greatest heroes mourned Superboy's death.*

IN MEMORIAM *A statue outside Titans Tower commemorates the fallen hero.*

NOT FORGOTTEN

Conner's death became one of the most tragic of the Infinite Crisis. In memorial, Superboy received twin statues—one in Metropolis and a second outside San Francisco's Titans Tower. His presence lingered in the minds of many, especially Wonder Girl. During the subsequent year, she allied herself with a "resurrection cult" based on Kryptonian theology in the faint hope that their rituals could bring Conner back from the dead. The cult was discredited at the same time that Wonder Girl stopped dwelling on Conner's death, and she has since started a tentative romance with Robin. Superboy's presence is reflected in the face of his clone, Match, who recently reappeared as a member of DEATHSTROKE's villainous "Titans East." RG/DW

KEY STORYLINES

• *ADVENTURES OF SUPERMAN #500 (JUNE 1993):* Superboy and three others begin the Reign of the Supermen after Doomsday nearly killed the Man of Steel!

• *SUPERBOY (3RD SERIES) #74 (MARCH 2000):* Tana Moon, Superboy's girlfriend, dies at the hands of the villainous Agenda!

• *TEEN TITANS (3RD SERIES) #1 (AUGUST 2003):* After joining the latest incarnation of the Teen Titans, Superboy discovers that he shares Lex Luthor's DNA!

SUPERGIRL

THE MAID OF MIGHT

FIRST APPEARANCE ACTION COMICS #252 (May 1959)
STATUS Hero **REAL NAME** Kara Zor-El
OCCUPATION Adventurer **BASE** Metropolis
HEIGHT 5ft 5in **WEIGHT** 135 lbs **EYES** Blue **HAIR** Blonde
SPECIAL POWERS/ABILITIES Under the Sun's solar radiation, Supergirl's kryptonian physique absorbs energy and can fly, has superstrength, superspeed, invulnerability, acute hearing, and a range of vision including emitting X-rays and heat.

COUNTLESS PARALLEL UNIVERSES existed prior to the catastrophic Crisis on Infinite Earths. In one such pocket universe, Superman was not the sole survivor of Krypton. That world's Superboy, however, died in the 30th century while saving that universe's LEGION OF SUPER-HEROES. Three Kryptonian criminals managed to survive as well, and found their way to Earth. No one powerful enough was left to stop them. That world's Lex Luthor (see LUTHOR, LEX), a noble scientist, created a lifeform from protomatter, using genetic material supplied by Lana Lang (see LANG, LANA), hoping it could help defeat the deadly trio.

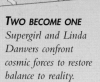

WITHOUT SUPERMAN
Supergirl selflessly used her powers to protect one and all.

THE MATRIX

This shape-changing being was dispatched to a parallel world, hoping SUPERMAN could help. The Man of Steel answered the call to arms and was forced to kill the three Kryptonians to save the world, but not before the lifeform, known as Matrix, was reduced to an amorphous mass. Superman brought Matrix to his world and there it recuperated on the Kent family farm. Out of respect for its savior, Matrix took on a feminine form and used her more limited superpowers to become Supergirl. When Superman exiled himself to space to atone for having killed for the first time, Supergirl took on his peace-keeping role. She naïvely fell under Lex Luthor's thrall for a while, until she saw him for the manipulative despot that he was. She then saved the life of Linda Danvers in the town of Leesburg, V.A., by merging her life essence with Linda's. This created an entirely new being with different abilities, such as more limited shape-changing, psychokinetic skills, and increased strength and endurance. In time, Linda/Supergirl/Matrix discovered the violent and haunted life Linda had led and sought to redeem her existence. During her encounters with the demon BUZZ and other supernatural entities, she discovered she was a reborn being known as an Earth-Angel, one of three on Earth. After several weird adventures, Linda met up with a Supergirl from yet another parallel timeline. This Supergirl was Superman's cousin from Krypton, a more innocent heroine who needed to die in order to keep the fabric of time from fraying. Linda also gave up her angelic abilities and left Leesburg hoping to lead a "normal" life.

TWO BECOME ONE
Supergirl and Linda Danvers confront cosmic forces to restore balance to reality.

KARA ZOR-EL

Following an alteration in time by the Futuresmiths, a teen named Cir-El arrived in Metropolis, claiming to be the daughter of Clark Kent and Lois Lane (see LANE, LOIS). She was gradually accepted by Superman until the Futuresmith's plans were undone to preserve the timeline; Cir-El then vanished. These changes to the timestream had unexpected results, such as the arrival of an asteroid from Krypton. The asteroid broke up as it entered Earth's atmosphere but a spacecraft managed to splash down in the ocean. Within the damaged craft was a young teenager, Kara Zor-El, from Superman's homeworld. It was finally agreed that Kara would stay in the U.S., in Superman's care.

NEW ARRIVAL *A rocket arrives on Earth and a suspicious Batman doubts its occupant's claims of Kryptonian birth.*

LUTHOR'S TOY
Matrix is comforted by Lex Luthor, unwittingly becoming a tool in his megalomaniac schemes.

KEY STORYLINES

• *SUPERMAN/BATMAN #8–13 (MAY–OCTOBER 2004):* Kara arrives on Earth, adored by Superman, suspected by Batman, trained by the Amazons, and coveted by Darkseid, tyrannical ruler of Apokolips.
• *SUPERGIRL: MANY HAPPY RETURNS (2003):* Supergirl meets her pre-Crisis self and realizes she must sacrifice everything to maintain the cosmic balance.
• *SUPERGIRL #1 (3RD SERIES) (FEBRUARY 1994):* Troubled teenager Linda Danvers is rescued by Matrix and becomes an Earth Angel.
• *SUPERGIRL (3RD SERIES) #1–4 (FEBRUARY–MAY 1994):* Matrix learns about life and love as Supergirl, under the sway of Lex Luthor's charismatic personality.

WARRIOR TRAINING *On the island of Themyscira, Supergirl learned combat under the finest Amazon swordmasters.*

RETURN OF THE ORIGINAL

The arrival of the space pod at the bottom of Gotham harbor heralded the arrival of a new Kryptonian, soon revealed as Kal-El's cousin. Unlike previous post-Crisis incarnations of Supergirl, this Kara Zor-El had lived on Krypton until her mid-teens then departed for Earth on orders from her parents Zor-El and Allura. Her mission: To search for Kal-El, who had been sent to Earth as a baby. A malfunction along the way had trapped her in stasis for decades. With Kal-El now grown to adulthood as Superman, the planet's foremost hero, Kara no longer had an official role to play. BATMAN's suspicion didn't help. The Dark Knight found the presence of a superpowered teenager a potential threat to public safety, and his hostility drove a wedge between himself and an overprotective Superman. Kara underwent warrior training with the Amazons of Themyscira to learn to control her powers. Despite these preparations, Batman's fears proved accurate when DARKSEID kidnapped Kara and brainwashed her into becoming the leader of his elite FEMALE FURIES. Superman helped Kara break Darkseid's hold, encouraging her to take up the identity of Supergirl upon her return from Apokolips.

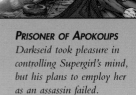

PRISONER OF APOKOLIPS *Darkseid took pleasure in controlling Supergirl's mind, but his plans to employ her as an assassin failed.*

RISE OF A HERO

Though welcomed by the superhuman community, Kara harbored doubts about her ability to live up to the name. Her self-identity suffered a literal fracture when Lex Luthor used black kryptonite to split Kara into two individuals, one good and one evil. Supergirl overcame her sinister self and recommitted herself to the fight for truth, battling bravely during the Infinite Crisis.

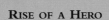

EVIL TWIN *Lex Luthor split Supergirl into good and evil halves, each fighting to control her spirit.*

ONCE AND FUTURE HERO

A time warp transported Supergirl one thousand years into the future, where she became a member of the Legion of Super Heroes. The Legionnaires, who revered the champions of the 21st century, gave Supergirl a place of honor within their organization, even electing her Legion president despite amnesia brought about by the time transference.

DOMINATION *Supergirl helped the Legion of Super-Heroes overrun the Dominator homeworld.*

BACK TO EARTH

After months in the future, Supergirl returned to present-day Metropolis, filling in for a powerless Superman. She also served for a brief stint with the OUTSIDERS, and struck up a close friendship with CAPTAIN BOOMERANG II. RG/DW

BOOMER *Supergirl and Captain Boomerang II have enjoyed a flirtatious friendship..*

AMAZONS ATTACK

Now living on her own, Supergirl fought alongside GREEN LANTERN Hal Jordan and the CHALLENGERS OF THE UNKNOWN to end the threat of the Luck Lords, and aided the Amazons when Queen HIPPOLYTA's warriors invaded Washington DC—even forcing the crash-landing of Air Force One. Most recently, Supergirl accepted an invitation to become a member of the TEEN TITANS.

SUPERMAN

THE MAN OF STEEL

FIRST APPEARANCE ACTION COMICS #1 (June 1938)
STATUS Hero **REAL NAME** Kal-El; Clark Joseph Kent (adoptive name)
OCCUPATION Super hero; (as Clark Kent) journalist **BASE** Metropolis
HEIGHT 6ft 3in **WEIGHT** 235 lbs **EYES** Blue **HAIR** Black
SPECIAL POWERS/ABILITIES Kal-El's powers were latent until his teenage years. His kryptonian physiology absorbs immense energy from Earth's yellow sun, enabling him to fly at incredible speeds, and endowing him with superstrength, invulnerability (his only weaknesses are green kryptonite radiation and magic), ultra-acute hearing, freezing breath, immense lung capacity and a range of vision including X-ray vision (he can see through anything except lead) and heat vision.

SUPERMAN, THE LAST SON OF KRYPTON, represents the very best in humanity. His native world of Krypton, a giant planet orbiting a dying red sun, was doomed by the radioactive elements at its core and exploded many years ago, but not before scientist Jor-El and his wife Lara rocketed their son to safety, hoping against hope that his spacecraft would find him a new home in the vast reaches of the universe. Their gamble paid off in ways that have enormously benefited humanity.

FIRST ISSUE *The Man of Steel first flexed his muscles on the cover of Action Comics #1.*

THE SOLE SURVIVOR

Kal-El's ship traveled many light-years until it crashed in a remote field in Kansas, where it—and its infant cargo—were found by farmers Jonathan and Martha Kent. Raising him as if he was their own son, the Kents named the boy Clark Joseph and watched in amazement as his unique abilities began to manifest over the years. Clark's body was a veritable solar battery. He absorbed the sun's energy and in turn it gave him great strength, invulnerability, heightened senses and the ability to defy gravity. Fearing that various governments or factions would claim Clark as their own, the Kents encouraged the boy to act as "normal" as possible and to keep his powers and origin secret. Upon graduating high school, Clark left Smallville behind for a far greater stage.

SMALLVILLE DAYS

Kal-El's ship traveled countless light-years until it crashed in a remote field near Smallville, Kansas, where it and its infant cargo were found by farmers Jonathan and Martha Kent. Raising him as their own, the kind-hearted Kents named the boy Clark Joseph and watched in amazement as, little by little, his unique abilities began to manifest themselves. Clark's body proved to be a veritable solar battery. He absorbed the sun's energy, which gave him incredible strength, invulnerability, heightened senses, and the ability to fly. Fearing that various governments or factions would claim Clark as their own, the Kents encouraged the boy to act as "normal" as possible and to keep his powers a secret. After graduating from high school, Clark left the little town of Smallville to begin a seven-year exploration of the globe, eager to find some purpose for his amazing abilities as he searched for a suitably heroic role in life.

AFRICAN ADVENTURE *Before Clark Kent made his name in Metropolis, he traveled the world on an eight-year personal journey of discovery. Eager to try out his growing superpowers, he headed for some of the worlds troublespots, helping to resolve a bloody intertribal conflict in Africa.*

SUPERMAN'S COSTUME

In time, however, Clark realized that he'd made a mistake by ignoring his alien heritage in favor of his human upbringing. Once he acknowledged that there was a place in this world not only for Clark Kent but for Kal-El, Clark used materials from his spacecraft to create a costume signifying and reflecting his Kryptonian roots—one he could wear openly whenever he wasn't disguising himself as a mild-mannered journalist.

LIFESAVER!
Superman's first costumed adventure saw him saving Jimmy Olsen and Lois Lane from certain death.

LOIS LANE *As time went by, Clark Kent became a celebrated reporter and fell in love with Lois. She got over her crush on the Man of Steel, realizing what a good catch Clark was. Marriage soon beckoned.*

THE MILD-MANNERED REPORTER

Sporting horn-rimmed spectacles and wearing oversized clothes to disguise his physique, Clark Kent came to Metropolis and was interviewed by *Daily Planet* editor Perry White for a reporter post. Clark worked with young photographer Jimmy Olsen and star reporter Lois Lane. It was she who, glimpsing the Kryptonian crest on the costume of the city's amazing flying man, first called him "Superman." Clark began his dual life as a journalist and crime fighter.

THE BEGINNING OF A NEW AGE

Superman's arrival signaled a new era for costumed heroes. As more and more appeared around the world, so did super-powered villains, ranging from the alien BRAINIAC to the crazed TOYMAN. Superman's exploits inspired millions, so the world was stunned when the behemoth DOOMSDAY killed him in battle. Fortunately, Superman was returned to life by Kryptonian technology. He has since allowed a handful of heroes—SUPERBOY, SUPERGIRL and STEEL—to share the S-shield that is a symbol from his homeworld.

AN EVERLASTING INSPIRATION

Superman has had to contend with scheme after malicious scheme to discredit or destroy him. Virtually all of them have been engineered by Lex Luthor, first through his LexCorp business and then as U.S. President.
Alone and with the JUSTICE LEAGUE OF AMERICA, Superman has become a symbol for truth and justice across the world. In the 31st century, the legacy of Superman led many people to become adherents of a secular belief called "The Spirit of the Last Son," which sees the Man of Steel as a model for mature, altruistic living. RG

KEY STORYLINES
• SUPERMAN #75 (January 1993): Superman dies defeating Doomsday, an alien genetic experiment designed to be the ultimate killing machine in the "The Death of Superman!"
• ACTION COMICS #689 (SEPTEMBER 1993): The Man of Steel returns from the dead.
• SUPERMAN #171 (AUGUST 2001): Superman begins a tumultuous defence of Earth and the Universe against the might of Imperiex as the Our Worlds at War storyline commences.
• SUPERMAN BIRTHRIGHT #1 (SEPTEMBER 2003): Superman's origins from his escape from Krypton to him becoming the world-renowned Man of Steel is thoroughly redefined and expanded.

SUPERMAN

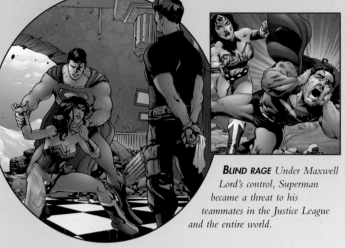

LOSS OF CONTROL

Outside forces began to eat away at Superman's legendary self-discipline in the weeks leading up to the Infinite Crisis. The rogue spirit ECLIPSO seized its most powerful host to date by taking command of Superman's body, but CAPTAIN MARVEL helped drive out the vile influence. At around the same time, CHECKMATE kingpin Maxwell Lord (see LORD, MAXWELL) used his telepathic powers to override Superman's mental faculties. Using the Man of Steel as his puppet, Lord unleashed chaos within the Justice League of America until WONDER WOMAN snapped Lord's neck.

BLIND RAGE *Under Maxwell Lord's control, Superman became a threat to his teammates in the Justice League and the entire world.*

SUPER-BRAWL *Maddened by grief after the death of his Lois Lane, the original Superman from Earth-Two lashed out at his counterpart.*

INFINITE CRISIS

Despite the rescue, Superman disapproved of Wonder Woman's lethal solution. The incident soured their relationship and helped contribute to the dissolution of the Justice League. But the universe soon needed its heroes more than ever. Alexander Luthor and Superboy-Prime, two survivors of the multiverse who had existed before the Crisis on Infinite Earths, hatched a plot to birth a new multiverse in line with their twisted ambitions. Superman soon found himself face to face with Kal-L, another multiverse exile and the original Superman from the wartime Golden Age. Kal-L believed that restoring his homeworld, Earth-Two, could prevent his Lois Lane from dying. His obsession brought him into conflict with Superman, but the two shared a heroic bond that could not be eclipsed. They soon teamed against Doomsday and Alexander Luthor's army of super-villains. In the end, it took the power of two Supermen to end the threat of Superboy-Prime. Superman and Kal-L stripped the powers of their younger doppelganger by flying him through the heart of a red sun. On the surface of the living planet Mogo, the two beat Superboy-Prime into submission, though Kal-L lost his life in the effort.

DOOMSDAY *The power of two Supermen proved enough to stop this invulnerable killer.*

AMONG THE *timeline-ripples triggered by the Infinite Crisis was the reinstatement of Clark Kent's teenaged adventures with the 30th century's Legion of Super Heroes.*

GROUNDED

The trip through the red sun left Superman powerless as well, and for a time it seemed as if he would never regain his abilities. For a year following the Infinite Crisis, Superman lived as a normal human, learning to see the world again through the eyes of Clark Kent. He rededicated himself to his reporting career at the Daily Planet and his marriage to Lois Lane. But just as he grew accustomed to his new lifestyle, Superman found his powers returning—first his ability to leap tall buildings in a single bound, then his invulnerability and flight. The ramp up in power coincided with increased activity from his rogues' gallery, including the Toyman, Metallo, and an all-new Kryptonite Man. Lex Luthor reinstated his position as Superman's arch-enemy when he retrieved a long-buried Kryptonian battleship and made war against Metropolis for choosing Superman as its champion instead of himself. The battle brought the Man of Steel back before a grateful and celebratory public.

To mark his return, Superman used a Kryptonian sunstone crystal to grow a new Fortress of Solitude in the Arctic, replacing his most recent (and rarely used) Fortress in the Peruvian rainforest.

METROPOLIS PERIL *Upon regaining his powers, Superman faced fresh threats to his adopted city.*

SAFE HAVEN *Superman's new Fortress of Solitude is located in the Arctic.*

CHRISTOPHER KENT

In a mirror of the circumstances that had brought Superman to Earth, a pod arrived in Metropolis carrying a Kryptonian boy. Superman befriended the child and rescued him from government custody, convincing officials that the young Kryptonian's needs would be better served by acclimation into Earth society. Clark Kent and Lois Lane became the boy's guardians and named him Christopher Kent. With a red-sun radiating wristwatch to keep his powers in check, Christopher tried to fit in among his schoolmates. It soon became apparent that Christopher was the son of Ursa and General Zod, conceived during the criminals' sentence in the Phantom Zone. Christopher helped foil Zod's invasion of Earth after a massive Phantom Zone jailbreak, recommitting himself to his adoptive parents.

KNEEL BEFORE ZOD *General Zod's Phantom Zone breakout was more than just a way to take revenge on Superman – it left the Earth vulnerable for Zod's takeover.*

FURTHER ADVENTURES

Superman's role as humanity's protector came into question when ARION, LORD OF ATLANTIS, traveled to modern-day Metropolis from the year 1659 to bring about Superman's retirement—lest his visions of a planetary apocalypse come true. Despite Arion's claim that humanity had become too dependent on Superman, the Man of Steel chose to remain in his current role.

Superman met his friends in the LEGION OF SUPER-HEROES once more during the Lightning Saga, when the future champions traveled backward through time to bring back Wally West, the third FLASH. BIZARRO proved to be a perennial pain by kidnapping Pa Kent and taking him to a cube-shaped Bizarro World. And Superman found another link to his past in Karsta Wor-Ul, the "third Kryptonian" living on Earth (after himself and Supergirl). Superman listened to her tales of ancient Krypton and helped her battle a squad of alien marauders. RG/DW

FELLOW SURVIVOR *Karsta Wor-Ul had been on the run for decades, fleeing from alien bounty hunters. Her pursuers caught up to her on Earth.*

SUPERMAN-PRIME

Superman-Prime, formerly known as Superboy-Prime, is the last survivor of the now-vanished multiverse dimension called Earth-Prime. Together with Alexander Luthor, he initiated the Infinite Crisis then escaped from a jail cell built by the GUARDIANS OF THE UNIVERSE and became a member of the SINESTRO Corps. Immune to kryptonite and capable of destroying entire planets, Superman-Prime is more powerful than his namesake and one of the most dangerous beings in existence.

UNLIMITED POWER *Superman-Prime has destroyed entire planets in fits of rage.*

T.O. MORROW

First appearance FLASH (1st series) #143 (March 1964)
Status Villain *Real name* Thomas Oscar Morrow
Occupation Criminal scientist *Base* Mobile
Height 5ft 10in *Weight* 191 lbs *Eyes* Blue *Hair* Gray
Special powers/abilities Brilliant intellect; possesses technology that can see into or retrieve objects from the future.

Thomas Oscar Morrow studied cybernetics and computers at Harvard, where, as one might expect from a man named T.O. Morrow, he became obsessed with the future. Inventing a viewscreen that allowed him to witness events that would occur in 100 years' time, Morrow copied the designs he saw and became known as a brilliant roboticist. He also developed a "fourth dimensional grappler" that could pluck actual objects from the future. Undoubtedly, Morrow's greatest creation is the android RED TORNADO, who rebelled against his creator and joined the JUSTICE SOCIETY OF AMERICA.

At one point, T.O. Morrow briefly split into two beings, including the big-headed Future Man. Later, he witnessed distressing future events and sank into a deep depression, though he has since shaken off his melancholy.

In a team-up with PROFESSOR IVO, Morrow developed the android TOMORROW WOMAN as a sleeper agent whose only purpose was to infiltrate the JUSTICE LEAGUE OF AMERICA. When Tomorrow Woman developed a conscience and sacrificed her life to save her teammates, Morrow was delighted—in his eyes, such humanlike behavior was evidence of his programming genius. DW

TAKION

First appearance TAKION #1 (June 1996)
Status Hero *Real name* Joshua Sanders
Occupation Leader of the New Gods *Base* New Genesis
Height 6ft 2in *Weight* Variable *Eyes* Red *Hair* None
Special powers/abilities A being of limitless power who can manipulate matter and energy in all its forms.

Blind since birth, Joshua Sanders had the most profound epiphany when HIGHFATHER of New Genesis stripped him of his corporeal shell. Transformed into the living embodiment of the Source, Sanders merged with the light of the universe and became a conduit between the life-stuff of creation and the NEW GODS empowered by it. Sanders became Takion, omniscient and omnipotent avatar of the Source. Since Highfather's death, Takion leads the New Gods and helps them protect the peaceful planet of New Genesis from the unending threat of its neighbor Apokolips. As Takion, the formerly sightless Sanders briefly enjoyed seeing the FOREVER PEOPLE'S BEAUTIFUL DREAMER in both a literal and romantic sense. SB

TANGLED HEARTS *Batman and Talia share a complex history and relationship, including a marriage that he has never acknowledged!*

TALIA

First appearance DETECTIVE COMICS #411 (May 1971)
Status Villain's daughter *Real name* Talia Head *Occupation* Former C.E.O., LexCorp *Base* Metropolis *Height* 5ft 8in *Weight* 141 lbs *Eyes* Brown
Hair Brown *Special powers/abilities* Beautiful and brilliant, with a ruthless streak, and a superb head for business; also trained in the use of modern-day weaponry and an expert hand-to-hand combatant.

The daughter of eco-terrorist RÂ'S AL GHÛL, the Demon's Head, Talia was raised by him and trained in seclusion. Râ's realized that sooner or later the Lazarus Pit on which he depended for his immortality would lose its power. He wanted a suitable heir for his empire and a mate for his daughter. Râ's masterminded the kidnapping of BATMAN's partner Robin, as well as his own daughter, in order to determine the Dark Knight's worth. Batman successfully passed the test but, despite being strongly attracted to Talia, turned down the notion of marriage. Batman then became a thorn in the eco-terrorist's side. Talia was torn between two men she loved and, not wishing to be a pawn, left to make her way in the world. She soon made a favorable impression in Metropolis business circles. When Lex Luthor (*see* LUTHOR, LEX) was elected U.S. President, he persuaded Talia to become C.E.O. of LexCorp. She sealed the deal by turning over all of Râ's's plans and financial data to Luthor. Talia ran LexCorp as coldly and efficiently as Luthor, enduring encounters with SUPERMAN and Batman.

Recently, a mysterious woman named Nyssa befriended Talia then kidnapped and tortured her, revealing herself to be Talia's half-sister. Talia was loyal to Râ's, but Nyssa hated their father and longed to destroy him. She killed Talia repeatedly, resurrecting her time and again in the Lazarus Pit. Brainwashed by this terrible ordeal, Talia was unleashed by Nyssa against Râ's al Ghûl. She killed him, and has not been seen since. RG

NOT MAN ENOUGH *Talia shows Bruce Wayne that she packs a mean right.*

TANNARAK

FIRST APPEARANCE PHANTOM STRANGER (2nd series) #10 (December 1970) **STATUS** Villain **REAL NAME** Unknown **OCCUPATION** Sorcerer; nightclub owner **BASE** The Bewitched nightclub **HEIGHT** 6ft **WEIGHT** 187 lbs **EYES** Blue **HAIR** Black **SPECIAL POWERS/ABILITIES** Immortal and a powerful sorcerer; can project magical force blasts from his hands; master alchemist.

Tannarak is the owner of Bewitched, an interdimensional nightclub in San Francisco catering to Earth's mystic community. The magician, born over one hundred years ago, became obsessed with his own mortality and vowed to live forever. He concocted an elixir that stopped his body aging; however he had to steal souls to maintain his youth. The PHANTOM STRANGER became Tannarak's enemy, trying to thwart the alchemist's sinister drive for immortality. Tannarak became a member of the Dark Circle, an organization of mystics run by the evil sorceress Tala. When Tala summoned the Four Horsemen of the Apocalypse to destroy the world, Tannarak summoned the Phantom Stranger to help end her rampage. Tannarak seemed to have perished in the battle, but he somehow survived and remains a dark force in Earth's mystical community. **PJ**

TARPIT

FIRST APPEARANCE FLASH (2nd series) #174 (July 2001) **STATUS** Villain **REAL NAME** Joey Monteleone **OCCUPATION** Criminal **BASE** Keystone City **HEIGHT** Variable **WEIGHT** Variable **EYES** Yellow **HAIR** None **SPECIAL POWERS/ABILITIES** Body made of molten asphalt is nearly invulnerable; can hurl flaming chunks of tar at enemies. Can maintain a remote consciousness in inanimate objects.

Joey Monteleone had no interest in his family's business, namely the drug trade in Keystone City. Arrested instead on a theft charge, he landed in the Iron Heights penitentiary to serve his sentence. There he learned that he could transfer his consciousness into inanimate objects, and "became" a vat of hot tar one evening to cause a ruckus at a local hockey game [why did it cause a ruckus?].

The FLASH fought the sticky lump called Tar Pit, but found he could not defeat an enemy with no real body, and therefore no weaknesses. He finally located an acid that dissolved the tar, reducing Tar Pit to puddles. Joey Monteleone, unable to unstick his mind from the form of Tar Pit, and his body lay comatose in Iron Heights. Recently, a jailbreak orchestrated by GORILLA GRODD let Tar Pit's molten form escape into Keystone once more. **DW**

TARANTULA I

FIRST APPEARANCE STAR-SPANGLED COMICS #1 (October 1941) **STATUS** Hero (deceased) **REAL NAME** Jonathan Law **OCCUPATION** Crime novelist **BASE** Blüdhaven **HEIGHT** 5ft 10in **WEIGHT** 180 lbs **EYES** Blue **HAIR** Blond **SPECIAL POWERS/ABILITIES** A skilled acrobat and combatant; uses a web-gun that shoots strands of sticky webbing that entraps foes.

A crime novelist in the late 1930s who became intrigued by the rising crop of "mystery men" fighting crime, Jon Law interviewed Dian Belmont, longtime companion of the first SANDMAN, about her association with the hero. After Belmont gave a sketch of a costume she had designed for the Sandman to Law, the novelist secretly created a copy of the costume for himself and began fighting crime as the Tarantula, taking his name and weapons from his pet spider.

The Tarantula's first case was in 1941, when the new crime fighter stopped a Nazi saboteur. He later became a more public figure after stopping a crime at a Broadway theater. The Tarantula joined the wartime heroes known as the ALL-STAR SQUADRON until they disbanded in 1945. In the 1960s, Law wrote a book called *Altered Egos*, about the mystery men of the 1940s. Decades later, the novelist moved from New York City to Blüdhaven, where he was murdered by BLOCKBUSTER II. **PJ**

TARANTULA II

FIRST APPEARANCE NIGHTWING #71 (September 2002) **STATUS** Anti-hero **REAL NAME** Catalina Marie Flores **OCCUPATION** Social worker; vigilante **BASE** Blüdhaven **HEIGHT** 5ft 7in **WEIGHT** 135 lbs **EYES** Brown **HAIR** Black **SPECIAL POWERS/ABILITIES** Athlete trained in F.B.I. techniques; arsenal includes web-gun firing grapnel lines or adhesives to ensnare foes.

Strong and streetwise, Catalina Flores studied at the F.B.I. Academy in Quantico, Virginia. However, for reasons unrevealed, she left the program and returned to her native Blüdhaven. She became a social worker and befriended Jonathan Law, retired mystery novelist and the former masked "Mystery Man" Tarantula (see TARANTULA I). Catalina stole Law's vigilante gear and became a second Tarantula, a cold-blooded vigilante. Catalina sharpened her fighting skills under the tutelage of crime boss Roland Desmond, (BLOCKBUSTER II). This association made Tarantula and Blüdhaven's guardian NIGHTWING adversaries, especially after the Tarantula murdered corrupt Blüdhaven Police Chief Frances Redhorn.

When Blockbuster played a part in John Law's death Tarantula shot him dead. Meanwhile, she and Nightwing began a tempestuous affair. She followed Nightwing to Gotham City, helping Batman end a bloody gang war. The Dark Knight's influence has encouraged Catalina to rethink her murderous methods and to realign her ambiguous moral compass. **SB**

TARTARUS

FIRST APPEARANCE THE TITANS #6 (August 1999) **STATUS** Villain team **BASE** Mobile **MEMBERS AND POWERS** **Vandal Savage** Immortal conqueror. **Gorilla Grodd** Telepathic psychopath. **Lady Vic** International assassin. **Cheshire** International terrorist. **Siren** Mesmerizing criminal. **Red Panzer III** Deadly Nazi sympathizer.

TARTARUS **1)** *Siren* **2)** *Red Panzer III* **3)** *Vandal Savage* **4)** *Lady Vic* **5)** *Cheshire* **6)** *Gorilla Grodd*

VANDAL SAVAGE kidnapped former TEEN TITAN Omen (Lilith Clay) and forced her to use her telepathic skills to form the perfect team of adversaries to defeat the Titans. She subverted his plans, however, by selecting villains who would never gel long enough to become a true threat. Omen recruited GORILLA GRODD, LADY VIC, CHESHIRE, the mesmerizing Siren and RED PANZER III. Savage named the group Tartarus, after the prison that housed the TITANS OF MYTH. He planned to use Tartarus to gain access to the H.I.V.E. Queen, DEATHSTROKE's ex-wife Adeline Kane, in the country of Zandia. He hoped to secure a sample of Kane's blood, which contained special regenerative properties. The Titans teamed with Deathstroke and went to Zandia. There, they had to fight not only Tartarus, but the H.I.V.E., which tried to protect their Queen During the conflict, Savage mortally wounded Kane and Red Panzer III died. Savage allowed Justin, from the H.I.V.E. to become the fourth Panzer. After the battle, TEMPEST learned of Omen's capture and led the Titans to Tartarus's base in Scotland. The villains scattered, with Siren aiding Tempest. **RG**

TATTOOED MAN

FIRST APPEARANCE GREEN LANTERN (2nd series) #23 (Sept. 1963)
STATUS Occasional villain **REAL NAME** Abel Tarrant
OCCUPATION Reformed criminal **BASE** New York City
HEIGHT 6ft **WEIGHT** 195 lbs **EYES** Blue **HAIR** Brown
SPECIAL POWERS/ABILITIES Can manifest his tattoos as physical objects by concentrating on one tattoo at a time.

Abel Tarrant, was a sailor based in Coast City who turned to burglary. During one heist, exposure to a spill of mystery chemicals left him with the mental ability to conjure actual objects from the chemicals. He promptly created a bomb, blasted a hole in the wall to escape from a police shoot-out, and returned home to tattoo his body with various shapes (including an axe, a shield, a cannon, and a dragon), using the chemical as body ink.

The Tattooed Man began stealing from local billionaire Baron Cranfield until opposed by GREEN LANTERN Hal Jordan. The Tattooed Man sent his shapes into battle against the Emerald Crusader, discovering that the yellow base used in the ink made the tattoos impervious to his enemy's power ring. Green Lantern eventually triumphed by forcing the Tattooed Man to concentrate on more than one tattoo at a time in order to shake his mental focus.

Joining the INJUSTICE GANG, the Tattooed Man made a near-fatal mistake when he stole money from GOLDFACE. Shot and left for dead by Goldface's agents, the Tattooed Man started a new life as a tattoo artist in New York City. Recently, the Tattooed Man used the time-travel equipment of his dead teammate CHRONOS I to go back 20 years and warn his younger self away from a life of crime, an experiment that failed. DW

INTERROGATION
The Outsiders leaned on the Tattooed Man in order to learn the whereabouts of the villain Sabbac.

A STORY IN INK Every one of the Tattooed Man's tattoos can come to life, spelling trouble for his enemies.

TASMANIAN DEVIL

FIRST APPEARANCE SUPER FRIENDS #7 (October 1977)
STATUS Hero **REAL NAME** Hugh Dawkins
OCCUPATION Ex-engineer; drama coach **BASE** Sydney, Australia
HEIGHT 6ft **WEIGHT** 176 lbs **EYES** White **HAIR** Red
SPECIAL POWERS/ABILITIES Transforms into a 9ft-4in, 535-pound, werewolf-like creature with superstrength, and razor sharp claws.

Hugh Dawkins was born in Launceton, Tasmania. His mother was a werewoman and his father was the leader of a Tasmanian Devil cult that worshipped her. The couple eventually decamped to Perth, Australia, with Hugh, and tried to lead ordinary lives.

As a teenager, Hugh told his parents that he was gay, and his stern father rejected him.
Hugh also acquired his mother's powers and found that he could turn into a giant werecreature. He took the name Tasmanian Devil and became a crime fighter in Sydney, and later joined the GLOBAL GUARDIANS. Tasmanian Devil then joined the international branch of the JUSTICE LEAGUE OF AMERICA and met and fell

in love with JLA liaison Joshua Barbazon. Tasmanian Devil returned to the Global Guardians before settling in Sydney, where he lives with Joshua and teaches drama at a local university. He continues to build a new, more loving relationship with his father. PJ

TAWKY TAWNY

FIRST APPEARANCE CAPTAIN MARVEL ADVENTURES #79 (December 1947) **STATUS** Hero **REAL NAME** Tawky Tawny
OCCUPATION Adventurer **BASE** Mobile **HEIGHT** 6ft 2in
WEIGHT 240 lbs **EYES** Yellow **HAIR** Orange, black, white
SPECIAL POWERS/ABILITIES Enhanced strength and damage resistance, immunity to most magical weapons, ability to transform into giant-sized battle form.

Mister Tawky Tawny is an intelligent, anthropomorphic tiger, who originally started life as a stuffed toy animated through the dark magic of Lord SATANUS. He became a companion and advisor to Billy and Mary Batson, as well as their alter-egos of CAPTAIN MARVEL and MARY MARVEL. Tawky Tawny came to permanent life through the sorceries of Ibis the Invincible.

Tawny left the company of the Marvel Family for a time, adventuring across the globe and enjoying the life of a sophisticate, often clad in a white business suit. The end of the Ninth Age of Magic during the Infinite Crisis apparently gave Tawky Tawny new abilities, including immunity from many types of enchanted weaponry and the power to turn into a saber-toothed tiger the size of a small bus.

When the villainous Sabina tried to force Tawky Tawny to give up the location of the god Mercury, he lashed out at her instead in a fierce battle of tooth and claw. Tawny lost the fight, and was saved from death by the arrival of CAPTAIN MARVEL JR. DW

TECHNOCRAT

FIRST APPEARANCE OUTSIDERS (2nd series) #1 (Alpha) (November 1993) **STATUS** Hero **REAL NAME** Geoffrey Barron
OCCUPATION Inventor **BASE** Mobile **HEIGHT** 6ft
WEIGHT 188 lbs **EYES** Brown **HAIR** Black, streaked with white
SPECIAL POWERS/ABILITIES Armored techno-suit enables flight, superstrength, and is outfitted with an arsenal of weapons.

While visiting the European principality of Markovia to promote his Technocrat 2000 prototype battle armor, businessman Geoffrey Baron had no choice but to don the techno-suit himself after his assistant, Charlie Wylde, was mortally injured by a maddened bear. Barron protected Wylde as the sorcerer FAUST magically merged the injured Wylde with his beastly attacker. Later, with the man-beast Wylde still by his side, Barron became Technocrat; both men joined a second incarnation of the OUTSIDERS led by the Markovian meta-human Prince Brion Markov, (GEO-FORCE), who had been deposed by Queen Ilona and her vampire consort, Roderick. As an Outsider, Barron helped the team to liberate planet Nekrome from the evil influence of ECLIPSO, a conflict which saw the Technocrat's armor fused with an alien weapon. Since the Outsiders disbanded, Technocrat has been working at mastering the alien-altered Technocrat technology. SB

346

TEMPEST

ATLANTEAN MAGE

FIRST APPEARANCE ADVENTURE COMICS #269 (February 1960)
STATUS Hero **REAL NAME** Garth **OCCUPATION** Ambassador; sorcerer
BASE Poseidonis, Atlantis **HEIGHT** 5ft 10in **WEIGHT** 235 lbs
EYES Purple **HAIR** Black **SPECIAL POWERS/ABILITIES** Amphibious;
swims at speeds of 97.76 knots (85 mph); superstrength; high
resistance to deep sea pressures; projection of powerful optic force
blasts; manipulation of water currents; creation of whirlpools; can
boil or freeze water; mystic powers include postcognition, telepathy,
dimensional travel, and astral projection; partially colorblind.

ABANDONED AT BIRTH by the superstitious Atlanteans, Garth survived alone in the ocean depths for years until he was discovered by AQUAMAN. Adopted by the Sea King and called Aqualad, Garth was the least powerful member of the TEEN TITANS, until he realized his potential for wizardry and became the powerful mage Tempest!

AQUALAD *Garth earned his stripes against enemies that were vexing, but rarely lethal.*

UNLUCKY EYES

Garth's heritage is of the Idylists, a group of Atlantean pacifists who established the colony of Shayeris in the Hidden Valley. When Garth's father, King Thar, assembled weapons to destroy his brother Zath's invading armies, his palace guards mistakenly believed he was going insane, and murdered him. Thar's pregnant wife Berra was exiled to Atlantis, where she gave birth to Garth. Believing his purple eyes to be a bad omen, the Atlanteans seized the infant and left him to die, abandoned to the sea. Thanks to the sorcerer ATLAN, Garth survived and grew up to cross paths with Aquaman, who adopted him as his ward. After Aquaman joined the JLA, and following formal schooling in Scotland, Aqualad became a founding member of the Teen Titans. He fell in love with AQUAGIRL, who tragically died during the Crisis (*see* Great Battles, pp. 362–3).

Sometime later, Garth's uncle Zath, now the necromancer Slizzath, returned to conquer Atlantis. Under the tutelage of Atlan, the father of Aquaman, Aqualad acquired a host of magical abilities, refined his own powers, and became the mage Tempest. Garbed in the flag of his people, Tempest defeated his uncle and saved the undersea realms. Soon after, he became an Atlantean ambassador. Tempest soon found new love with DOLPHIN—who, awkwardly, was seeing Aquaman at the time—and the two were married. In time they bore a son, whom they named Cerdian. During the Imperiex War, Tempest used his powers as a wizard to protect Atlantis, but accidentally sent the city thousands of years back in time to the Obsidian Age. Tempest survived the Spectre's destruction of Atlantis, and disappeared for nearly a year. When he finally reemerged, he had lost his memory, his magic, and his ability to breathe underwater. Tempest briefly teamed with the new Aquaman, Arthur Joseph Curry, and later regained his powers. **DW**

TULA *The love of Garth's life succumbed to the monster Chemo during the great Crisis.*

WEDDING *Surrounded by the Titans and other super heroes, Tempest married Dolphin.*

WATER WIZARD *Tempest can summon whirlpools, freeze rivers, and bend water to his will through magic.*

KEY STORYLINES

• *TEMPEST #1-4 (NOVEMBER 1997–FEBRUARY 1997):* Aqualad no more! Garth assumes his new name and new identity as Tempest while fighting his villainous uncle with the power of Atlantean sorcery.
• *WONDER WOMAN #178 (OCTOBER 2001):* Tempest joins with Darkseid and Wonder Woman to help save the universe from Imperiex, Destroyer of Worlds, accidentally sending Atlantis back in time.
• *AQUAMAN #63 (JANUARY 2000):* Dolphin gives birth to Tempest's son Cerdian, a child who may become a future Aquaman for a future generation.

PEERS *Like Nightwing and Arsenal, Tempest has shed the label of "super-hero sidekick" and now stands on an equal footing with Aquaman.*

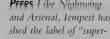

TEEN TITANS

ADOLESCENT AVENGERS

FIRST APPEARANCE (Teen Titans I) BRAVE AND THE BOLD #54 (July 1964); (New Teen Titans) DC COMICS PRESENTS #26 (December 1980); (Teen Titans II) TEEN TITANS (2nd series) #1 (October 1996); (current team) TEEN TITANS (3rd series) #1 (July 2003)
STATUS Hero team **BASE** Titans Tower, San Francisco Bay
CURRENT MEMBERS AND POWERS
Robin III Team leader; skill martial artist and tactician.
Wonder Girl II Superstrength, flight.
Kid Devil Enhanced strength, can breathe fire.
Ravager Skilled martial artist and assassin, augmented abilities.
Miss Martian Super strength, flight, shapeshifting, invisibility, intangibility, telepathy.
Supergirl Super strength, super speed, invulnerability, flight, heat vision, X-ray vision.

ALMOST A DECADE AGO, teen heroes Robin I (NIGHTWING), Kid Flash I (FLASH III) and Aqualad (TEMPEST) brought an end to the reign of Mister Twister, a deranged weather-controlling villain. Soon after, Wonder Girl I (*see* TROIA) and Speedy (ARSENAL) joined the three teenagers and the quintet stopped a mind-controlled JUSTICE LEAGUE OF AMERICA from committing a crime spree. Calling themselves the Teen Titans, the young sidekicks fought criminals like DOCTOR LIGHT I and the ANTITHESIS before parting ways for college and to further their budding careers.

IT'S A TWISTER! *The weather-controlling Mister Twister attacks the first Teen Titans team.*

THE NEW TEEN TITANS
Years later, Robin, KID FLASH, Wonder Girl and Changeling (BEAST BOY) and new heroes STARFIRE and CYBORG were united by RAVEN as the New Teen Titans to thwart the demon TRIGON, Raven's father, from invading the Earth. After defeating Trigon, the Titans quickly ran afoul of the villainous forces of DEATHSTROKE the Terminator, the FEARSOME FIVE, the SOCIETY OF SIN, and BROTHER BLOOD.

DEMON SEED *Trigon has frequently tried to conquer Earth, using Raven as a pawn.*

Meanwhile, the Titans accepted an enigmatic young girl named TERRA into their ranks. Unbeknownst to the Titans, however, Terra was a spy for Deathstroke, sent to infiltrate their ranks and learn their secrets. The insane Terra then helped Deathstroke capture the Titans and turn them over to the H.I.V.E. before killing herself. During this time, Kid Flash retired, Robin became Nightwing, and Deathstroke's son JERICHO joined the team.

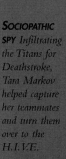

SOCIOPATHIC SPY *Infiltrating the Titans for Deathstroke, Tara Markov helped capture her teammates and turn them over to the H.I.V.E.*

COMINGS AND GOINGS
When the Anti-Monitor invaded Earth, Dove (HAWK AND DOVE), AQUAGIRL, and new Titan KOLE died during the ensuing Crisis (*see* Great Battles, pp. 362–3). Starfire left the planet for an arranged marriage and the original Titans reformed under Wonder Girl's unsteady leadership. After an epic battle with Brother Blood, the return of Starfire and Raven, newly purged of her father Trigon's evil, and Wonder Girl's transformation into TROIA, the Teen Titans took the more adult name the New Titans.

THE TEEN TITANS II
A second group of Teen Titans were genetic experiments created by the evil alien H'San Nattall empire. Managed by billionaire Mister Jupiter, and led by the ATOM II, who had been reduced in age by EXTANT, these half-human/half-alien Titans faced villains like DARK NEMESIS and Haze before splitting up.

THE TITANS HUNT
Jericho, whose body been contaminated by souls corrupted by the evil of Trigon, ordered the villainous WILDEBEEST Society to hunt the Titans one by one. After killing Golden Eagle, severely injuring Aqualad and Cyborg, and destroying Titans Tower, Jericho was finally stopped when his father Deathstroke killed him. Programmed assassins for EXTANT, the Team Titans arrived from an alternate timeline. And Cyborg became the alien robot Cyberion. After several membership changes, the Titans teamed to stop an alien invasion and the spread of Trigon's progeny. The New Titans then disbanded.

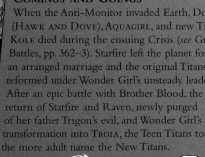

TITANS REBORN
When Cyberion returned to Earth and threatened the planet, the Titans reunited and saved their former friend. The original Titans, all adults, decided to reform the Titans to train younger heroes. The team stayed together for some time, fighting criminals like Cheshire, Deathstroke, and the Hangmen.

The Titans briefly recruited a group of youngsters from an orphanage in the D.E.O., until one of them died. Later, after a rogue Superman Robot murdered Troia and Lilith, the daughter of Mister Jupiter, this incarnation of the team disbanded.

CONTINUING THE FIGHT
After the Infinite Crisis, Robin helped assemble a new team including KID DEVIL, Ravager, and MISS MARTIAN. The team, which has lost both Superboy and Kid Flash, recently spawned an east-coast spin-off as well as the birth of their villainous opposite team, the Terror Titans.

THE CURRENT LINEUP **1)** *Wonder Girl II* **2)** *Raven* **3)** *Miss Martian* **4)** *Cyborg* **5)** *Robin* **6)** *Ravager* **7)** *Kid Devil* **8)** *Jericho*

NEW MEMBERS, OLD ENEMIES
But the members of Young Justice, honoring the legacy of the Titans, reestablished the team, based in San Francisco. The latest wave of Teen Titans includes SUPERBOY, ROBIN II, BEAST BOY, CYBORG, and STARFIRE, and WONDER GIRL II. Raven, her soul housed in a new body, joined the teen heroes, and Deathstroke, possessed by the spirit of his son Jericho, returned to attack them, as did Brother Blood. **PJ**

RAVEN'S BLOOD *Brother Blood has long craved Raven's magic powers, and was responsible for restoring the half-breed demon's human body, lost in battle with Trigon.*

KEY STORYLINES
• TEEN TITANS (1ST SERIES) #53 (FEBRUARY 1970):
The final issue of the series reveals the secret origin of the Teen Titans.
• NEW TEEN TITANS (THE JUDAS CONTRACT TPB) (2003):
The Titans are betrayed by their first recruit, the psychopath Terra.
• NEW TEEN TITANS (2ND SERIES) #1-5 (AUGUST 1984– FEBRUARY 1985):
The demon Trigon takes over the planet, and only the Titans can stop him.
• TEEN TITANS (3RD SERIES) #1 (JULY 2003):
The latest incarnation of the Titans is born, based in San Francisco.

TERRA

First appearance NEW TEEN TITANS (1st series) #26 (December 1982) **Status** Hero **Real name** Tara Markov **Occupation** Adventurer **Base** San Francisco **Height** 5ft 1in **Weight** 112 lbs **Eyes** Blue **Hair** Blonde **Special powers/abilities** A powerful geomorph, Terra has complete control over the earth, creating flying islands or moving creatures of soil or stone, generating earthquakes, or calling forth molten lava or mudslides with just a thought.

Like her brother Brian, GEO-FORCE of the OUTSIDERS, Tara Markov was given powers over the earth by Markovian scientist Dr. Helga Jace. But where Brion was a prince-in-waiting of their tiny European kingdom, Tara was the monarch's illegitimate daughter and grew up isolated and resentful in the United States. In her teens, Tara molded a pact with DEATHSTROKE the Terminator to destroy the TEEN TITANS by securing membership as the earth-shaking Terra and spying on the group from within. When her betrayal was revealed, Terra died battling the Titans. Sometime later, a new Terra emerged from an alternate future as one of the time-lost Team Titans. In stark contrast to the sociopath Tara Markov, the second Terra wants nothing more than to use her powers for good. Following a genetics test, Brion Markov learned that this second geomorph is genetically identical to her predecessor, information he has kept from Terra for her own peace of mind. Whether or not she is a clone or twin of Tara Markov remains to be seen. **SB**

TEZUMAK

First appearance JLA # 66 (July 2002) **Status** Hero (deceased) **Real name** Tezumak **Occupation** Warrior **Base** South America **Height** 6ft **Weight** 340 lbs **Eyes** White **Hair** Bronze **Special powers/abilities** Wearing bronze armor that had once been oiled with the blood of sacrificial victims gave Tezumak enhanced strength and endurance.

3,000 years ago, a group of people were gathered by the sorceress GAMEMNAE to help her achieve great power. Tezumak, a South American monk from a pre-Aztec, Mesoamerican civilization in Mexico, joined her band of followers and did Gamemnae's bidding. He wore bronze armor, honoring the gods who first brought science to the people. Working with Gamemnae pitted him against the JUSTICE LEAGUE OF AMERICA, who had been lured back in time to search for the missing AQUAMAN. When Tezumak learned the full extent of Gamemnae's plans, which involved exterminating the JLA, he revolted, ultimately sacrificing his life to help bring about her defeat. **RG**

TIN MAN
Tezumak's bronze armor made him almost invulnerable.

THAROK

First appearance ADVENTURE COMICS #352 (January 1967); LEGION OF SUPER-HEROES (4th series) #79 (April 1996). **Status** Villain **Real name** Tharok **Occupation** Criminal **Base** Mobile **Height** 6ft 4in **Weight** 225 lbs **Eyes** Black **Hair** None **Special powers/abilities** Brilliant cyborg intelligence; enhanced strength in mechanical limbs; a genius at manipulating others, he always rises to a leadership position.

Once a petty crook on his home planet of Zadron, Tharok made one heist too many and wound up with much of his body vaporized after a run-in with law officers. In the late 30th century, he was saved from death through extensive cyborg reconstruction. Tharok became half-man, half-metal with a computerized intelligence that transformed him into a criminal mastermind.

When the star-devouring Sun-Eater menaced the United Planets, the LEGION OF SUPER-HEROES assembled five criminals to battle the entity in exchange for amnesty. Tharok became a member of this "Fatal Five" (alongside Validus, the Persuader, Empress, and Mano) which proceeded to set itself against the Legion after the Sun-Eater's defeat. Tharok and his comrades have failed to defeat the Legion several times, but always escape from prison. On his most recent rampage, Tharok and the rest of the Fatal Five lost to Legionnaire TIMBER WOLF, who was embarking on his first official mission. **DW**

THIRST, THE

First appearance AQUAMAN (4th series) #5 (June 2003) **Status** Villain (destroyed) **Real name** None **Occupation** Supernatural destroyer **Base** The Secret Sea **Height** Variable **Weight** Variable **Eyes** Red **Hair** None **Special powers/abilities** Absorbs life energy, leaving his victims withered husks; possesses mental control over his zombie-like armies; absorbs moisture from all water sources, which gives him power and also affects his physical size.

The Thirst is a golem composed of dry river mud, the mystical "brother" of a being called the Waterbearer, an ancient goddess. The Thirst has preyed on the deities who have watched over the Secret Sea, a metaphysical realm composed of the shared imagination of humanity, for millennia, absorbing their power. When AQUAMAN became guardian of the Secret Sea, the Thirst set its sights on the hero.

The evil, magical parasite battled Aquaman several times, attempting to drain not only the rivers of Earth and the magical waters of the Secret Sea of all life, but the Sea King's very essence as well. In their final battle, Aquaman and the Thirst merged into a single, monstrous being. When Aquaman stopped fighting the Thirst and surrendered his control to the light of the universe, the evil parasite was consumed by the holy power and destroyed, seemingly forever. **PJ**

THOMPKINS, LESLIE, M.D.

First appearance DETECTIVE COMICS #457 (March 1976) **Status** Hero **Real name** Dr. Leslie Thompkins **Occupation** Physician **Base** Gotham City **Height** 5ft 7in **Weight** 130 lbs **Eyes** Blue **Hair** Gray **Special powers/abilities** Gifted and compassionate physician; considers herself a general practitioner, but is also a surgeon of great skill and follows advances in medical science with great interest.

Born to affluence in Gotham City, Leslie Thompkins graduated with honors from Gotham State Medical School. She decided to devote herself to helping the less fortunate and opened a free clinic to benefit Gotham's poorest citizens. Returning from a house call late one night, Leslie found young Bruce Wayne kneeling by the bodies of his murdered parents in the city's notorious "Crime Alley." Along with the Wayne family butler Alfred (see PENNYWORTH, ALFRED), Leslie befriended Bruce, helping the orphan remain free from the dubious clutches of Gotham's Social Services. She later encouraged him to undertake the global sojourn that would lead him to becoming BATMAN. Leslie is one of the select few privy to the Dark Knight's secrets. She remains a close ally to the Bat-Family, providing emergency medical attention when called upon. Leslie is particularly close to Bruce Wayne's valet Alfred; however their romance has always taken second place to their unstinting support for Batman's war on crime. **SB**

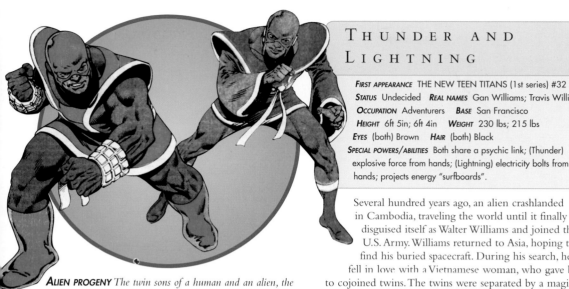

ALIEN PROGENY *The twin sons of a human and an alien, the brothers Thunder and Lightning are the living embodiment of their names, able to manipulate the elements to destructive effect!*

THREE WITCHES, THE

FIRST APPEARANCE THE WITCHING HOUR #1 (December 1970)
STATUS Villains **REAL NAMES** Mildred, Mordred, and Cynthia
OCCUPATION Oracles **BASE** Mobile **HEIGHT** The Witches refuse to be measured **WEIGHT** The Witches refuse to divulge **EYES** Variable **HAIR** Variable **SPECIAL POWERS/ABILITIES** Supernatural talents from their role as deities; aware of every event on the physical and metaphysical planes.

The Three Witches are goddesses who belong to no particular pantheon. They have appeared in various guises, known to the Egyptians, Romans, and Vikings alike. In ancient Greece they were called the Fates and went by the names Clotho, Lachesis, and Atropos. The Three Witches disappeared during the witch-hunts of the Middle Ages, but have recently returned in new forms.

In the modern era, The Three Witches most commonly go by the names Mildred, Mordred, and Cynthia. Their different personalities embody the three aspects of the Triple Goddess: the mother (Mildred), the crone (Mordred), and the maiden (Cynthia). They claim their magic powers are strongest at midnight, and will answer any three questions if asked with the proper ritual.

During the Imperiex War (*see* Great Battles, pp. 362–3), the Three Witches assumed their roles as the Greek Fates to see Themyscira destroyed. **DW**

TRIPLE TROUBLE *The Three Witches are great meddlers in supernatural affairs.*

THUNDER AND LIGHTNING

FIRST APPEARANCE THE NEW TEEN TITANS (1st series) #32
STATUS Undecided **REAL NAMES** Gan Williams; Travis Williams
OCCUPATION Adventurers **BASE** San Francisco
HEIGHT 6ft 5in; 6ft 4in **WEIGHT** 230 lbs; 215 lbs
EYES (both) Brown **HAIR** (both) Black
SPECIAL POWERS/ABILITIES Both share a psychic link; (Thunder) explosive force from hands; (Lightning) electricity bolts from hands; projects energy "surfboards".

Several hundred years ago, an alien crashlanded in Cambodia, traveling the world until it finally disguised itself as Walter Williams and joined the U.S. Army. Williams returned to Asia, hoping to find his buried spacecraft. During his search, he fell in love with a Vietnamese woman, who gave birth to cojoined twins. The twins were separated by a magician, who discovered that they possessed destructive powers. As adults, the twins, now called Thunder and Lightning, sought out their father for a cure, only to discover he was under the control of the criminal organization H.I.V.E. After a brief conflict with the TEEN TITANS, Thunder and Lightning were forced to kill their father. A blood transfusion gave them full control of their powers, and they settled in San Francisco to work with S.T.A.R. Labs to hone their powers. After being possessed by the souls of the demon TRIGON's unborn children, Thunder and Lightning returned to Vietnam and became two of Southeast Asia's most prominent defenders. **PJ**

THUNDER II

FIRST APPEARANCE POWER OF SHAZAM ANNUAL #1 (1996)
STATUS Undecided **REAL NAME** CeCe Beck
OCCUPATION Assassin **BASE** United Planets
HEIGHT 5ft 6in **WEIGHT** 130 lbs **EYES** Blue **HAIR** Blonde
SPECIAL POWERS/ABILITIES Strength, stamina, flight, wisdom, and invulnerability derived from gods that lent their powers to Shazam.

Hailing from 6,000 years after the 30th century, when the Earth is long dead, CeCe Beck (or just Beck) was granted powers by a wizard (formerly CAPTAIN MARVEL of the 20th century) following a terrorist attack that transported her to the Rock of Eternity at the edge of space and time. Whenever Beck invokes the name "Captain Marvel," lightning strikes, transforming her into Thunder, a slightly older woman with the godly powers of the wizard Shazam. While returning from a mission in the 20th century, Thunder was shunted to the 30th century when pro-science terrorists blew up the Rock of Eternity. After stopping the terrorists, she was offered membership in the LEGION OF SUPER-HEROES. Lord Pernisius gathered the scattered fragments of the Rock of Eternity in a bid for power, but was defeated by Thunder and the Legion. The Rock of Eternity was restored, but since it was still in its radioactive state, Thunder couldn't immediately use it to return home. She took some satisfaction in the fact that she can now return to the 90th Century as CeCe Beck by saying "Captain Marvel." **RG**

THUNDER III

FIRST APPEARANCE OUTSIDERS 3rd series #1 (August 2003)
STATUS Hero **REAL NAME** Anissa Pierce **OCCUPATION** Adventurer
BASE Metropolis **HEIGHT** 5ft 7in **WEIGHT** 119 lbs **EYES** Brown
HAIR Black (blonde wig as Thunder III)
SPECIAL POWERS/ABILITIES Can control her body's density, making Thunder II invulnerable and heavy enough to make a thunderous and destructive shock wave whenever she stomps her feet.

Growing up, Anissa Pierce wanted to be just like her crime-fighting father, Jefferson Pierce, alias BLACK LIGHTNING. Anissa developed her own meta-human traits when she was just 11 years old, manifesting the ability to manipulate her own density. However, her parents divorced and Anissa went to live with her mother, affording Anissa little opportunity to master her powers under her father's tutelage—even if he had been willing to help. For Jefferson Pierce wanted his daughter to forget about superheroics and lead a normal life. He made Anissa promise to wait until after she graduated from the pre-med program at Tulane University before considering a career in costumed crime fighting. Anissa kept her promise, assuming the identity of Thunder II just hours after accepting her degree. Thunder has since joined the OUTSIDERS, a new incarnation of the team to which Black Lightning once belonged. With time and hard work, Anissa hopes to earn her father's approval by showing him that Thunder inevitably follows lightning! **SB**

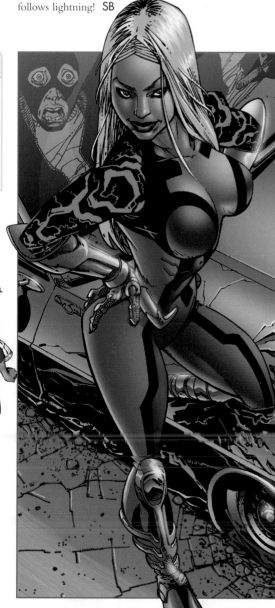

THUNDER, JAKEEM & THUNDERBOLT

FIRST APPEARANCE THE FLASH (2nd series) #134 (February 1998)
STATUS Hero **REAL NAME** Jakeem John Williams
OCCUPATION High-school student **BASE** Keystone City
HEIGHT 5ft 4in **WEIGHT** 140 lbs
EYES Brown **HAIR** Black
SPECIAL POWERS/ABILITIES Born in the 7th hour on July 7th, Jakeem controls the 5th-dimensional genie Thunderbolt, who is capable of flight and vast feats of magic; Jakeem controls the Thunderbolt with the magic words "So cool."

Jakeem Williams, also known as J.J. Thunder, was born in Keystone City. His parents left him to be raised by his aunt Lashawn, and J.J. grew up with a rebellious streak, alienating his friends and family and getting into trouble at school.

One day, Jakeem asked Jay Garrick, the original FLASH, for his autograph and inadvertently grabbed a pen that housed a genie. The genie, a Fifth-Dimensional imp named Yz, had at one time been the sidekick of Johnny Thunder (see THUNDER, JOHNNY), a member of the JUSTICE SOCIETY OF AMERICA. The genie was trapped in the pen and looking for a new companion.

When another Fifth Dimensional imp attacked the Earth, Jakeem was able to summon Yz from his pen and saved the planet. Later, when Johnny Thunder was killed by the ULTRA-HUMANITE, Yz was able to merge with his former mentor's body, creating a new Thunderbolt that Jakeem controlled with the words "so cool." Soon after, Jakeem became a part-time member of the JSA. Jakeem briefly met his father, Phil, in Michigan, but did not reveal his true identity to him. **PJ**

GOOD GUYS
Jakeem and his Thunderbolt are part-time members of the JSA!

THUNDER, JONNI

FIRST APPEARANCE JONNI THUNDER #1 (February 1985)
STATUS Hero **REAL NAME** Jonni Thunder
OCCUPATION Private investigator **BASE** Los Angeles
HEIGHT 5ft 6in **WEIGHT** 130 lbs **EYES** Green **HAIR** Blonde
SPECIAL POWERS/ABILITIES Skilled fighter; once possessed the power to act as a living thunderbolt with flight and energy-casting abilities.

The best private detective in Los Angeles learned her craft from her father Jim, a veteran of the LAPD. Jonni would have been content to ply her trade the old-fashioned way— but a bizarre accident gave her powers that coincidentally mirrored those of Johnny Thunder (*see* THUNDER, JOHNNY) of the JUSTICE SOCIETY OF AMERICA.

When crooks tried to steal a statue of Apu Illapu, the Incan god of lightning, Jonni found herself filled with energy. She was now able to become a living thunderbolt through an "out of body" experience—while her true form lay unconscious, Jonni could fly and control electrical discharges. Her thunderbolt self was often more ruthless than her waking self.

Jonni soon learned that the thunderbolt was an energy-based alien. Freed from the statue, it now wanted to free all its imprisoned brethren, but Jonni and INFINITY INC. stopped the aliens before they could take over the world. She is now cut off from her thunderbolt powers. **DW**

THUNDER I, JOHNNY

FIRST APPEARANCE ALL-AMERICAN COMICS #100 (August 1948)
STATUS Hero **REAL NAME** John Stuart Mill Tane
OCCUPATION Gunslinger **BASE** Mesa City
HEIGHT 6ft 2in **WEIGHT** 210 lbs **EYES** Blue **HAIR** Blond
SPECIAL POWERS/ABILITIES An expert marksman, fine horseman, and an above-average hand-to-hand combatant.

When a gang of thugs publicly humiliated his father, Sheriff William Tane, schoolmaster John Tane donned a colorful costume, dyed his hair black, and armed himself with a six-shooter. Teaching by day and fighting crime in the Old West by night, John Tane became the first Johnny Thunder. Soon after, he acquired a valiant horse named Black Lightning. Over the next few years, Johnny Thunder clashed with foes such as Silk Black and befriended a Cheyenne youth named Swift Deer.

In 1872, Jeanne Walker's father was cheated out of a rich strike at a gold mine by swindlers. Jeanne assumed the secret identity of MADAME .44 and became a thief, robbing from unscrupulous men. At first, this put her at odds with Johnny. However, Johnny Thunder and Madame .44 eventually became allies during a battle with the outlaw Silk Black. When it was over, they fell in love and married. **RG**

THUNDER II, JOHNNY

FIRST APPEARANCE FLASH COMICS #1 (January 1940)
STATUS Hero (deceased) **REAL NAME**
OCCUPATION Adventurer **BASE** New York City
HEIGHT 5ft 11in **WEIGHT** 225 lbs **EYES** Blue **HAIR** Blond
SPECIAL POWERS/ABILITIES No superpowers and an average combatant, usually relying on his Thunderbolt to fight for him. Since merging with the Thunderbolt, Johnny possesses unlimited magical power.

Johnny Thunder was born on the seventh day of the seventh month in a year ending in seven. Realizing that a child born under this numerological sign would wield great power, the Badhnisian High Priest of Aissor kidnapped Johnny and placed the mystical Zodiac Belt on him. The High Priest cast a spell that granted Johnny magical powers on his seventh birthday. By uttering "Cei-U" (or "Say, You!"), Johnny commanded a magical Thunderbolt. A fifth-dimensional sprite, the Thunderbolt had to obey his master for one hour. Johnny and the Thunderbolt served as "mascot" to the JUSTICE SOCIETY OF AMERICA and Johnny served in the U.S. Navy in World War II. Johnny was a member of the JSA in the following decades until, suffering from Alzheimer's disease, he passed control of the Thunderbolt to young Jakeem J. Williams, (*see* THUNDER, JAKEEM). Johnny took back the Thunderbolt while mind-controlled by the evil ULTRA-HUMANITE, who tried to use him to take over the world. The JSA fought back and Johnny's body was killed; however the Thunderbolt saved Johnny's soul and merged with it, creating Johnny Thunderbolt, a mix of both old friends and now a mentor and partner to Jakeem. **SB**

TIGGRA

FIRST APPEARANCE NEW GODS (1st series) #7 (March 1972)
STATUS Undecided (deceased) **REAL NAME** None
OCCUPATION Former concubine **BASE** Apokolips
HEIGHT 5ft 9in **WEIGHT** 130 lbs **EYES** Red **HAIR** Reddish-blond
SPECIAL POWERS/ABILITIES A fierce fighter possessing energy-blasting powers; traversed space via Boom Tube.

Tiggra was the second spouse of the dreaded DARKSEID and the mother of his son, ORION. Moments after Orion's birth, Darkseid seized the infant from Tiggra's arms and presented him to HIGHFATHER of New Genesis to seal a peace between their warring worlds. Tiggra was imprisoned cryogenically for years until the adult Orion returned to Apokolips aiming to destroy Darkseid. With the help of the rebel scientist Himon, Orion freed Tiggra and sheltered her on New Genesis. Tiggra convinced Orion that Darkseid was not his father, as part of her plan to see Orion slay Darkseid and rule Apokolips. However, Tiggra was attacked by Apokoliptian Suicide Jockeys and died in Orion's arms before she could confess the truth. Tiggra later appeared to Orion when he was lost in the Abysmal Plane, but she was merely an animated construct created by the evil Ecruos, a monstrous creature of that realm, to torment the Dog of War. **SB**

TIMBER WOLF

FIRST APPEARANCE LEGION WORLDS #6 (November 2001)
STATUS Hero **REAL NAME** Brin Londo
OCCUPATION Hero **BASE** Rimbor and Earth
HEIGHT 6ft **WEIGHT** 190 lbs **EYES** Brown **HAIR** Brown
SPECIAL POWERS/ABILITIES Has above average strength, speed and
agility. The origin of these abilities is unknown.

Brin Londo ran with Crody, Hubble, Rn'drr, Mash, and
Rac, a street gang on the planet Rimbor in the 31st
century. Brin's gang was a rival of a gang including Jo
Nah (*see* ULTRA BOY). Some time after Jo gained powers
and joined the LEGION OF SUPER-HEROES as ULTRA
BOY, Brin's life was endangered during a brawl. The
Legion's Apparition, looking to find Jo Nah and tell him
of her pregnancy, intervened, saving his life. Brin repaid
her kindness by becoming her protector, starting with
preventing bounty hunters from kidnapping her. When
half the Legion—including Jo Nah—was seemingly lost in
the Second Galaxy, Brin provided friendship to Apparition
during her pregnancy.
After the team
was reunited, Brin accompanied
Apparition and her child, Cub,
to Earth. Brin was invited
to join the Legion as
Timber Wolf. His
loyalty extends to the
entire team. **RG**

TIME COMMANDER

FIRST APPEARANCE THE BRAVE AND THE BOLD #59 (May 1965)
STATUS Villain **REAL NAME** John Starr
OCCUPATION Criminal **BASE** Mobile
HEIGHT 6ft 2in **WEIGHT** 210 lbs **EYES** Blue **HAIR** Brown
SPECIAL POWERS/ABILITIES Is able to travel through time using
a special hourglass.

The Time Commander started out as
a scientist before turning to crime,
developing a time-shifting hourglass
while serving time behind bars. He
escaped prison by traveling back to
a point before the prison had been
made, then simply walking away.
Using his hourglass to uncover the
secret identities of BATMAN and
GREEN LANTERN, the Time Commander
tried to defeat both foes but wound up
back in prison. He returned, this time
apparently mad, and jumbled up time to reunite Parisians
with their lost loves, until he was stopped by ANIMAL
MAN. The Time Commander joined with time-themed
villains CHRONOS I, CLOCK KING, and Calendar Man to
form the Time Foes. Assembled by the 2000 Committee,
the Time Foes met their end at the hands of several Team
Titans, a teen team of heroes from a potential future. **DW**

TIME MASTERS

FIRST APPEARANCE SHOWCASE #20 (June 1959)
STATUS Hero team (disbanded) **BASE** Upstate New York
MEMBERS AND POWERS
Rip Hunter Time travel expert.
Jeffrey Smith Hunter's research partner and MIT graduate.
Bonnie Baxter Researcher and onetime lover of Rip Hunter.
Corky Baxter (deceased) Teenage rock'n'roll brother of Bonnie.
Dan Hunter Rip Hunter's cousin and team financier.
Antonia ("Tony") A car thief and computer expert.

Rip Hunter (*see* HUNTER, RIP) was an inventor who
created a time machine. During an experiment, Rip
stranded himself and several others in the 25th century,
in a world recovering from nuclear war. Back in his own
time, Rip deduced that an evil organization called the
Illuminati would be responsible for this devastating future
war. Because Rip's method of time travel could be used
only once, he assembled a team, the Time Masters, to
travel for him and thwart the Illuminati. He enlisted the
aid of Bonnie and Corky Baxter, his cousin Dan, and Tony,
a computer expert. When Rip's lab
was destroyed by the
Illuminati, the team
relocated to an underground
base belonging to Cave
Carson (*see* CARSON, CAVE),
Bonnie's lover.

One of the Linear Men,
Matthew Ryder, later brought
the Time Masters to the
Vanishing Point, a platform
from which they could study
disruptions in the space/time
continuum. After helping the
JUSTICE LEAGUE OF AMERICA
defeat GOG, the Time Masters
were erased from existence. **PJ**

TIME TRAPPER

FIRST APPEARANCE ADVENTURE COMICS #317 (February 1964)
STATUS Villain **REAL NAME** Unknown
OCCUPATION Manipulator of history **BASE** The End of Time
HEIGHT Unknown **WEIGHT** Unknown **EYES** Unknown **HAIR** Unknown
SPECIAL POWERS/ABILITIES Vast control of the timestream; able to create
alternate histories and erase individuals from reality.

The Time Trapper can control events that
occur in multiple timelines. Its ability to
influence history have affected even the
Time Trapper itself, resulting in a
number of possible origins that
suggest COSMIC BOY, the
sorceress Glorith, and others
became the entity at various points
on the shifting timeline. One thing
remains constant—the Time
Trapper is an enemy of the
LEGION OF SUPER-HEROES. The
Time Trapper created a "pocket
universe" containing a parallel
version of Superboy, and is
responsible for the competing
incarnations of the Legion
that exist in different timelines.
The Legionnaires managed to
destroy the Trapper using the
Infinite Man. MON-EL eliminated
the entity but it always returns. **DW**

TITANS OF MYTH

FIRST APPEARANCE THE NEW TEEN TITANS (1st series) #11
(June 1981) **STATUS** Godlike beings **BASE** New Cronus
SPECIAL POWERS/ABILITIES
Cronus & Rhea (Titans of the Earth, both deceased)
Controlled earth and vegetation. Parents of Olympian gods.
Hyperion & Thia (Titans of the Sun) Can control and project
sunfire, enough to incinerate entire city blocks.
Iapetus & Themis (Titans of Justice) Arbiters of law.
Coeus & Phoebe (Titans of the Moon, Phoebe deceased) Can
project nighttime darkness, absorbing all light and heat.
Oceanus & Tethys (Titans of the Seas) Able to control the
oceans and all the creatures that live within the seas.
Crius & Mnemosyne (Titans of Memory) Pre- and post-
cognitive, as well as possessing the memories of the universe;
able to psychically manifest the memories of others.

Spawn of Uranus and Gaea, the twelve Titans of
Myth were granted dominion over Earth in the
very earliest days of mankind. The paired siblings
eventually sired their own children, the OLYMPIAN
GODS and goddesses who would eventually
inherit the Earth after defeating the Titans.
CRONUS was transformed into a gnarled tree, his
prison until modern times. The remaining Titans
were banished to the furthest reaches of outer
space. They settled upon a distant planet, which
the Titans named New Cronus in honor of their
lost brother.

Many centuries later, the Titans adopted
twelve children, each from a different world
and intended to be an individual "seed" from
which a new order of gods would spring. One
such child was Donna Troy, (*see* TROIA), whose
memory of her time on New Cronus remained
lost until she accompanied her fellow TEEN
TITANS to the ancient Titans' home.

Despite their brother Cronus's latter-day
conflicts with WONDER WOMAN and the Olympian
gods, the Titans of Myth are content to remain on
New Cronus, far-removed from the affairs of humans
and their Olympian children. **SB**

THE TITANS OF MYTH 1) Oceanus **2)** Cronus **3)** Thia
4) Hyperion **5)** Coeus **6)** Phoebe **7)** Rhea **8)** Crius
9) Mnemosyne **10)** Themis **11)** Iapetus **12)** Tethys.

TNT & DAN THE DYNA-MITE

FIRST APPEARANCE WORLD'S FINEST COMICS #5 (Spring 1942)
STATUS Heroes (TNT is deceased) **REAL NAMES** (TNT) Thomas N. Thomas; (Dyna-Mite) Daniel Dunbar
OCCUPATION (TNT) High School teacher; (Dyna-Mite) High-school student **BASE** New York City
HEIGHT (TNT) 5ft 11in; (Dyna-Mite) 5ft 6.5in **WEIGHT** (TNT) 175 lbs; (Dyna-Mite) 140 lbs **EYES** (TNT) Brown; (Dyna-Mite) Blue
HAIR (TNT) Brown; (Dyna-Mite) Red
SPECIAL POWERS/ABILITIES When imbued with atomic energy, both heroes gained immense strength and the ability to hurl energy from their hands.

Schoolteacher Thomas N. "Tex" Thomas and his student, Daniel Dunbar accidentally discovered a derivative of 27-QRX and assumed the costumed identities of TNT and Dyna-Mite. Both served in the ALL-STAR SQUADRON with distinction for several months. In April 1942, TNT was killed in Colorado by Gudra the Valkyrie, who was part of AXIS AMERIKA. The traumatized Dyna-Mite was rescued by Iron Munro and they in part formed a subgroup of the All-Star Squadron, the YOUNG ALL-STARS. In Rioguay in South America, the paths of Iron Munro and Dyna-Mite crossed again as Hugo Danner and the Sons of Dawn attacked. Dunbar's life remained unknown until he next turned up, as a member of Old Justice, costumed survivors of the early heroic era, who feel today's youth should not be exposed to such dangers. They took on YOUNG JUSTICE but learned there remains a need to train those with special abilities. **RG**

XUDARAN HEROES
Tomar-Re's legacy is carried on by his son, Tomar-Tu!

TOMAR-RE

FIRST APPEARANCE GREEN LANTERN (1st series) #6 (June 1961)
STATUS Hero (deceased) **REAL NAME** Tomar-Re
OCCUPATION Former scientist; Green Lantern **BASE** Mobile
HEIGHT 6ft 2in **WEIGHT** 210 lbs **EYES** Black **HAIR** Fused feathers
SPECIAL POWERS/ABILITIES Flight; Green Lantern ring granted him incredible powers based on his imagination and will power.

Tomar-Re was a scientist on planet Xudar chosen by the GUARDIANS OF THE UNIVERSE to become a GREEN LANTERN. One of Tomar-Re's first assignments was to rescue the inhabitants of the doomed planet Krypton, located in space sector 2813. Tragically, Tomar-Re was unable to prevent Krypton's destruction and was forced to watch the planet explode. Tomar-Re later became fast friends with Green Lantern Hal Jordan. The two became the premiere members of the GREEN LANTERN CORPS and legends throughout the universe. Tomar-Re retired from the GLC, although he was appointed to their Honor Guard after years of distinguished service. Tomar-Re was killed during a Qwardian invasion while trying to save the universe from the Anti-Monitor (*see* MONITOR). Before he died, Tomar-Re passed his ring on to John Stewart. **PJ**

THE PATRIOT *Tomahawk helped change the course of the Revolutionary War, earning a place alongside the Founding Fathers of the United States.*

GANGWAY! *Astride a charging stallion or creeping through the forests of Virginia, Tomahawk bedeviled the British at every turn.*

TOMAHAWK

FIRST APPEARANCE STAR SPANGLED COMICS #69 (July 1949)
STATUS Hero (deceased) **REAL NAME** Thomas Hawkins (alias Tom Hawk)
OCCUPATION Frontiersman; freedom fighter **BASE** U.S. circa 1750–1820
HEIGHT 6ft 1in **WEIGHT** 184 lbs **EYES** Blue **HAIR** Blonde
SPECIAL POWERS/ABILITIES Hunter, tracker, marksman, and combatant.

The U.S. might never have gained its independence from Britain had it not been for Tomahawk, the greatest hero of the Revolutionary War. As a young man, Thomas Hawkins spent a year living with an Indian tribe where he learned the ways of the frontier and how to handle the short throwing-axe, whose name he adopted as his own. Tomahawk and his sidekick, Dan Hunter, had already made a name for themselves as heroes of the American colonies by the time armed conflict broke out in 1776.

In war, Tomahawk truly came into his own. General George Washington agreed to create a stand-alone military unit called Tomahawk's Rangers to undertake special missions. Tomahawk led the team, whose members included Big Anvil, Kaintuck Jones, Stovepipe, and Cannonball. British intelligence agent Lord Shilling became Tomahawk's cruelest foe, aided at times by Lady Shilling, who also went by the alias the Hood.

After the war's end, Tomahawk wound up in an eastern city as a tax collector, but in 1800 an encounter with the Indian woman Moon Fawn—and a final clash with Lord Shilling—brought about a new direction in his life. Retiring to Echo Valley in the American Midwest, he had two children with Moon Fawn—Hawk (*see* HAWK, SON OF TOMAHAWK) and Young Eagle—and operated a farm near the young country's ever-expanding frontier. Tomahawk's final fate is unrecorded, but he is known to have survived into the 1820s. Despite his advancing age, Tomahawk remained a vital force, famous for his proficiency with a musket and his flinty temper. **DW**

TOMMY TOMORROW

FIRST APPEARANCE REAL FACT COMICS #6 (January 1947)
STATUS Hero **REAL NAME** Kamandi Blank
OCCUPATION Space Planeteer **BASE** Planeteer HQ, Gotham City
HEIGHT 5ft 11in **WEIGHT** 179 lbs
EYES Blue **HAIR** Blond
SPECIAL POWERS/ABILITIES Owing to Planeteer training, in peak physical shape; highly intelligent; carries a personalized ray gun and travels by Planeteer spacecraft.

In a possible future, a child named Kamandi Blank—grandson of Buddy Blank, the champion known as OMAC—will be found within a fortified bunker designated "Command D" following the death of his heroic grandfather. Discovered by General Horatio Tomorrow of the Space Planeteers, an interplanetary police force of the late 21st century, young Blank will be renamed Thomas "Tommy" Tomorrow following his adoption by the Planeteer officer. Following his graduation with honors from Spaceport, the Planeteer Academy, Tommy will team with Captain Brent Wood. Together these courageous Planeteers will enjoy many legendary exploits as they bring law and order to uncharted worlds in the process

QUICK ON THE DRAW With his trusty ray gun in his hand, Tommy is ready to confront any danger.

FREAKY FUTURE Making sense of a backwards world is all in a day's work for Tommy Tomorrow!

of exploring the outer reaches of space in the good ship Space Ace, so named by Tomorrow himself. Eventually, Tommy will attain the rank of colonel and be renowned as the greatest Planeteer to ever patrol the spaceways. Tommy Tomorrow's ultimate fate will be a mystery, although some speculate that he, or perhaps one of his descendants, will become the STARMAN of a future era, and carry on the heroic legacy begun on Earth by the gravity rod wielding Ted Knight (a.k.a. STARMAN I). **SB**

TOR, MAGIC MASTER

FIRST APPEARANCE CRACK COMICS #10 (October 1940)
STATUS Hero (deceased) **REAL NAME** Jimmy Slade
OCCUPATION Press photographer **BASE** Mobile
HEIGHT 5ft 10in **WEIGHT** 165 lbs **EYES** Brown **HAIR** Black
SPECIAL POWERS/ABILITIES Minor magician capable of creating spells of limited intensity, including levitation; usually spoke his spells backwards to focus his power.

Jimmy Slade was a photographer working for a major newspaper in 1941 who, inspired by the heroes of the Golden Age JUSTICE SOCIETY OF AMERICA, chose to create a costumed identity for himself to fight crime. Able to cast low level spells, Slade wore makeup and a fake moustache and created the identity of Tor, the Magic Master. Like ZATARA the Magician and his daughter ZATANNA, Tor spoke his spells backwards.

Tor the Magic Master fought criminals and Axis spies throughout World War II. As Jimmy Slade, Tor also became a successful photojournalist, taking award-winning photographs of the war. In 1945, Tor was one of several heroes with magical powers, including Zatara, DOCTOR OCCULT, SARGON the SORCERER and Merlin, who joined forces to fight the threat of the STALKER, an evil entity that threatened the Earth. Despite the JSA's intervention, Tor and Merlin were killed by the Stalker. **PJ**

TOMORROW WOMAN

FIRST APPEARANCE JLA #5 (May 1997)
STATUS Villain (destroyed) **REAL NAME** None
OCCUPATION Would-be assassin **BASE** JLA Watchtower
HEIGHT 5ft 11in **WEIGHT** 320 lbs **EYES** Blue **HAIR** Black
SPECIAL POWERS/ABILITIES Tomorrow Woman's robotic powers were telekinetic and telepathic in nature.

The scientists T.O. MORROW and PROFESSOR IVO, longtime opponents of the JUSTICE LEAGUE OF AMERICA, pooled their resources to build the perfect simulacrum, and named her Tomorrow Woman. As per her programming, she played the heroine to perfection. Invited to join the JLA, she was soon ensconced in the JLA's Watchtower. Morrow and Ivo hoped their "Trojan horse" would wreak havoc among the unsuspecting heroes. However, the two villains had built too good a machine: Tomorrow Woman developed her own personality and feelings. She disobeyed their orders, sacrificing herself rather than murder the JLA. A statue in her memory was erected in the Garden of Heroes. **RG**

TOP

FIRST APPEARANCE FLASH (1st series) #122 (August 1961)
STATUS Villain **REAL NAME** Roscoe Dillon
OCCUPATION Criminal **BASE** Central City/Keystone City
HEIGHT 6ft **WEIGHT** 179 lbs **EYES** Blue **HAIR** Brown
SPECIAL POWERS/ABILITIES Can spin himself at incredible speeds and induce vertigo in his victims.

Fascinated by tops, gyroscopes, and all spinning things, crook Roscoe Dillon became the costumed criminal the Top in order to dominate crime in Central City. His ability to spin at great speeds made him a recurring foe of the second FLASH, Barry Allen, and a member of the Flash's Rogues Gallery. He stuck up a romance with CAPTAIN COLD's sister Lisa Snart (the GOLDEN GLIDER), but eventually learned that the Flash's superspeed vibrations had overheated the cells in his brain.

The Top died, but his spirit lived on. He possessed Barry Allen's father, and years later he took over the body of slain senator Thomas O'Neill. The third Flash, Wally West, uncovered the Top's deception before O'Neill could be elected vice president. Imprisoned in Iron Heights, the Top recently escaped and tried to murder the Keystone City mayor. Now exhibiting the power to scramble the way his opponents' eyes interpret images (triggering crippling nausea), the Top was defeated by Wally West. **DW**

TORQUE

FIRST APPEARANCE NIGHTWING #1 (October 1996)
STATUS Villain (deceased) **REAL NAME** Dudley Soames
OCCUPATION Former police inspector; criminal **BASE** Blüdhaven
HEIGHT 6ft 1in **WEIGHT** 186 lbs **EYES** Hazel **HAIR** Brown (graying)
SPECIAL POWERS/ABILITIES Favored a vintage Thompson .45 caliber machine gun (the "Tommy Gun"). Mirrored glasses helped his aim.

Inspector Dudley Soames was Blüdhaven's crookedest cop. He fed information on mobster Roland Desmond (BLOCKBUSTER II) to Blüdhaven's self-appointed guardian, NIGHTWING, while at the same time acting as one of Desmond's mob lieutenants. Blockbuster broke Soames's neck when he discovered the truth, twisting Soames's head and neck a full 180 degrees. Radical drug therapy initiated by Dr. Sandra Pavaar saved Soames's life. He learned to walk again with the help of mirrored glasses, and dubbed himself Torque. In short order, Torque strangled Pavaar and sought revenge on Blockbuster, Nightwing, and all of his enemies. Torque left palindromes on the corpses of his victims before Nightwing captured him and he was remanded in Lockhaven Penitentiary. After months in jail, Torque enlisted Tad Ryerstad, the rogue Nite-Wing, to help him escape. Soames planned to kill Ryerstad as soon as they were free, but was double-crossed and murdered by Ryerstad instead. **SB**

TOYMAN

First appearance ACTION COMICS #64 (September 1943)
Status Villain **Real name** Winslow P. Schott
Occupation Professional criminal **Base** Metropolis
Height 5ft 4in **Weight** 155 lbs **Eyes** Blue **Hair** Brown
Special powers/abilities Although psychotic, Schott is a skilled inventor and mechanical engineer.

Winslow P. Schott was only a small boy when he made his first toy, a balsa-wood airplane painted blue and red. Another boy stole the plane, an act that had a profound effect on Winslow and may have ultimately driven him to use toys to rob others. When he grew up, Schott created some of the most amazing toys ever conceived, for which he received widespread acclaim. However, LexCorp's acquisition of Schott's toy company left him jobless and burning for revenge against LexCorp's owner, Lex Luthor (see LUTHOR, LEX). Schott's failed attempts to kill Luthor with various lethal toys eventually led to an association with INTERGANG and a criminal career as the Toyman. His worst act was to murder Adam Grant, the son of television chat-show host and Metropolis celebrity Cat Grant. However, in the main, Schott has a soft spot for children, especially those in need. Clearly insane, the Toyman was one of SUPERMAN's most unpredictable, and therefore deadliest, opponents. The Toyman name has also been applied to Hiro Okamura, 13-year-old mechanical genius, whose family developed the alloy "metallo," which helped save the planet from the Kryptonian asteroid that brought SUPERGIRL to Earth. **RG**

TOYMEN Former psychopath Winslow Schott (above, in his criminal guise) has now renounced wrongdoing. His successor as the Toyman, lonely teenage prodigy Hiro Okamura (left), has grudgingly helped out Batman with his technical wizardry.

TRACI 13

First appearance SUPERMAN (2nd series) #189 (December 2002)
Status Hero **Real name** Traci (last name unrevealed)
Occupation Adventurer **Base** Metropolis **Height** 5ft 5in
Weight 127 lbs **Eyes** Sometimes black, sometimes purple
Hair Black and purple **Special powers/abilities** Urban sorceress with magical powers linked to her proximity to cities; her magic is manifested as purple panes of stained glass.

Traci 13 is a young witch with the power to tap into the magical energies found in all urban environments and draw on those living energies for power. Born a natural sorceress, one of the rare Homo magi, Traci was nonetheless orphaned at an early age when her mother, also a sorceress, perished trying to harness her power. Traci's father, reputed to be Doctor Thirteen, the ghost-breaker, chose to completely reject magic in his life after Traci's mother died, and that denial has caused a great rift to form between him and his daughter.

Along with her magical familiar, an iguana named Leroy, Traci moved to Metropolis and allied herself with Natasha Irons (see IRONS, NATASHA), the niece of John Henry Irons, alias Steel III. **PJ**

TREVOR, STEVE

First appearance ALL-STAR COMICS #8 (Winter 1941)
Status Hero **Real name** Steven Rockwell Trevor
Occupation Retired U.S. Air Force colonel **Base** Mobile
Height 6ft 1in **Weight** 195 lbs
Eyes Blue **Hair** Blonde with white
Special powers/abilities Expert pilot and military commander.

One of Wonder Woman's oldest friends, Steve Trevor inherited his military background from his father, Ulysses Steven Trevor, and his connection with the Amazons from his mother, Diana Trevor, who sacrificed her life to save the women of Paradise Island from the demon Cottus. As a pilot in the U.S. Air Force, Steve Trevor flew a bomber to Themyscira (see Amazing Bases, pp. 132–3) as part of a plot orchestrated by the war god Ares to destroy the island. Ares's scheme failed, but Trevor became a wanted man among some Air Force leaders. Trevor fled with his aide, Etta Candy, and helped Wonder Woman end the threat of the war god. Although eventually cleared of all charges related to the Paradise Island incident, Trevor resigned his Air Force commission and started work as a freelance aircraft design engineer. He soon married Etta Candy; his relationship with Wonder Woman remains one of a deep mutual respect, and Steve regards Diana as a sort of younger sister. Trevor still plays an important role in Wonder Woman's affairs, recently helping the Amazons battle the galaxy-conquering Imperiex. **DW**

TRIAD

First appearance LEGION OF SUPER-HEROES (4th series) #0
Status Hero **Real name** Luornu Durgo
Occupation Legionnaire **Base** Legion World, U.P. Space
Height 5ft 7in **Weight** 136 lbs **Eyes** (right) orange; (left) violet **Hair** Auburn **Special powers/abilities** Triad can split into three different bodies, each with three different personalities—flirtatious, shy, and intellectual.

Born on the planet Cargg in the latter half of the 30th century, Luornu Durgo inherited her species' ability to split into identical duplicates. Unlike other Carggites, however, Luornu's three duplicates manifested their own individual personalities, and she was forced to spend time in a mental institution for this unusual aberration.

Luornu escaped from the hospital and made her way to Earth. There, she met industrialist R.J. Brande (see BRANDE, R.J.) who became her legal guardian. Luornu also became his assistant. After saving his life during a terrorist attack by the villainous White Triangle gang, she was inducted into the hero team Brande had founded, the LEGION OF SUPER-HEROES, as Triad.

Triad soon became a member of the Legion Espionage Squad, a covert action team. Over the years, Triad's bodies and their personalities became more and more distinct and more and more independent of each other, sharing less time in the same body. While one of those bodies is infatuated with MON-EL, another romantically pursued Legion mechanic Chuck Taine until their affair ended tragically when the Earth was overrun by the insidious alien BLIGHT. **PJ**

TRIGGER TWINS

FIRST APPEARANCE ALL-STAR WESTERN #58 (May 1951)
STATUS Heroes (deceased) **REAL NAMES** Walter and Wayne Trigger
OCCUPATION Sheriff **BASE** Rocky City
HEIGHT (both) 6ft **WEIGHT** (both) 160 lbs
EYES (both) Blue **HAIR** (both) Reddish blond
SPECIAL POWERS/ABILITIES Skilled marksmen and horsemen, more than capable hand-to-hand combatants.

The original Trigger Twins, Walt and Wayne Trigger, kept law and order in Rocky City during the 1870s. Walt's (greatly exaggerated) Civil War exploits earned him the position of Rocky City's sheriff. Wayne, who had been the true hero in most of Walt's tales, agreed to assume the identity of sheriff whenever danger threatened the town. The Trigger Twins became a legend of the Old West.

The modern-day Trigger Twins, Tom and Tad Trigger, are believed to be descendants of the original western heroes. They wear cowboy clothing, but unlike Walt and Wayne, the current Trigger Twins are criminals. They have battled most of Gotham's defenders, including ROBIN, and are now in Blackgate prison. During Gotham's year as a No Man's Land, the Trigger Twins worked with fellow inmates Lock-Up and the KGBEAST to keep order at Blackgate, after the guards abandoned the facility. **DW**

TRICKSTER II

FIRST APPEARANCE THE FLASH (2nd series) #183 (April 2002)
STATUS Villain **REAL NAME** Axel Walker
OCCUPATION Professional criminal **BASE** Keystone City
HEIGHT 5ft 7in **WEIGHT** 150 lbs **EYES** Blue **HAIR** Brown
SPECIAL POWERS/ABILITIES A variety of technological gadgets allow him to cause mayhem; he is still mastering their   use and has no great athletic skill.

The first villain to be known as the Trickster was James Jesse, the stage name of Giovanni Giuseppe, a trapeze artist with a fear of heights who invented a pair of "air walker shoes" that allowed him to perform stunts safely. Eventually he turned to crime, employing numerous ridiculous gadgets, before turning F.B.I. informant and retiring.

The villain Blacksmith wanted someone with similar skills in her new gang. She selected wayward teenager Axel Walker, giving him a complete set of equipment, upgraded and more technologically sophisticated versions of the Trickster's tools. Axel was sent to attack Wally West, the FLASH III as a test. He acquitted himself well. Being a modern day teen, Axel lives for the rush and thrill of danger, apparently not entirely clear on the distinction between real life and the fantasy realms depicted in his beloved video games. **RG**

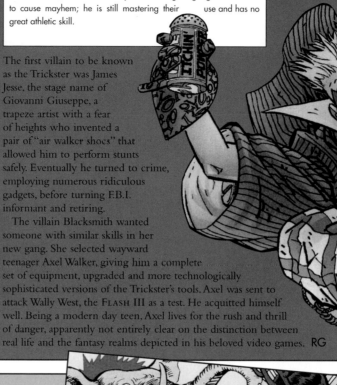

NEW KID ON THE BLOCK *Young Axel Walker loves being part of the Flash's Rogues Gallery, even though he has nothing in common with his villainous peers.*

TRIGON

FIRST APPEARANCE NEW TEEN TITANS (1st series) #4 (February 1981)
STATUS Villain **REAL NAME** Trigon; also known in other dimensions as Skath and Ddrez
OCCUPATION Demon lord; conqueror **BASE** Another dimensional plane
HEIGHT Variable **WEIGHT** Variable **EYES** Red **HAIR** Red
SPECIAL POWERS/ABILITIES Nearly immeasurable demonic powers; has drained the souls of millions of worlds and reshaped planets; can change size, fire destructive energy blasts, teleport, control demons, and transmute elements, such as stone into water.

The personification of evil, Trigon was a demon lord who destroyed his homeworld by the age of six. Slaying billions of souls in his own dimension, Trigon eventually sired a child by the woman Arella. Their child was RAVEN, a powerful mystic, who rejected her father's evil and was raised in Azarath, a pacifist community nestled in another dimension. Trigon tried to breach the barriers between his dimension and Earth's but was stopped by sorcerers from Azarath. Finally tearing through the interdimensional wall, Trigon attacked Earth. Horrified, his daughter Raven, now a teenager, agreed to rule by his side if he spared the planet. But Raven realized her father would not honor the bargain and hurried to Earth, gathering a group of teenage heroes to stop Trigon's invasion. These heroes were the NEW TEEN TITANS, and together they drove Trigon into a distant nether universe that Arella agreed to guard for eternity. As time passed, Raven began to succumb to her father's evil. Trigon murdered a billion beings in his dimension and stole their energy. He once again invaded Earth's dimension, turning Earth into a wasteland. But the Titans were able to help the souls of Azarath channel all their power into Trigon, seemingly destroying the demon.

Purged of her father's evil, Raven's body was nonetheless taken over by the soul of one of her slain siblings. However, her soul was placed in STARFIRE's body, and the Titans were able to destroy the rest of Trigon's progeny, ending his threat, they believed, forever. **PJ**

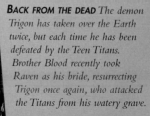

BACK FROM THE DEAD *The demon Trigon has taken over the Earth twice, but each time he has been defeated by the Teen Titans. Brother Blood recently took Raven as his bride, resurrecting Trigon once again, who attacked the Titans from his watery grave.*

TRIUMPH

FIRST APPEARANCE JUSTICE LEAGUE EUROPE #67 (August 1994)
STATUS Villain (deceased)   REAL NAME William MacIntyre
OCCUPATION Adventurer   BASE JLA Watchtower, the Moon
HEIGHT 6ft 1in   WEIGHT 200 lbs   EYES Blue   HAIR Blond
SPECIAL POWERS/ABILITIES Possessed enhanced strength, speed,
endurance and the ability to fly.

Eight-year-old William MacIntyre discovered that his father was a thug working for an evil scientist, Dr. Cobalt. When HOURMAN I battled Dr. Cobalt, Jimmy saved the hero from a magnetic blast. Hourman I cautioned young Will to "learn from your father's mistakes."

When plasma aliens invaded Earth, MacIntyre—now the hero Triumph—gathered a team to defeat them. During the fight, Triumph disappeared from the time-stream, and was actually forgotten. A decade later, he emerged to beat the Plasma-Men. He then joined the JUSTICE LEAGUE OF AMERICA. Triumph sold his soul to the demon NERON to regain the decade he had lost, but in so doing, the world forgot about him again! Embittered, he sold items stolen from the JLA Watchtower, including a pen containing the genie LKZ. LKZ corrupted Triumph further and led the JLA and the JUSTICE SOCIETY OF AMERICA into a war between itself and QWSP. SPECTRE turned Triumph into ice, and he is now stored in the Watchtower Trophy Room. RG

TSUNAMI

FIRST APPEARANCE ALL-STAR SQUADRON #33 (May 1984)
STATUS Hero   REAL NAME Miya Shimada
OCCUPATION Warrior   BASE San Francisco
HEIGHT 5ft 6in   WEIGHT 131 lbs   EYES Brown   HAIR Black
SPECIAL POWERS/ABILITIES Psionically creates sea-waves; able to swim at superspeed and breathe underwater.

Racial prejudice during World War II forced Miya Shimada's family to return to their native Japan, despite their status as U.S. citizens. A *nisei*, or first-generation American, Miya nevertheless offered to use her amazing water-manipulating powers as the Imperial Japanese operative code-named Tsunami. Riding atop her giant sea-waves, Tsunami battled the ALL-STAR SQUADRON on several occasions before switching sides and joining the YOUNG ALL-STARS to fight against the very Axis powers she had once served.

Following the end of World War II, Tsunami's aging was slowed as a result of a mystic pact with the Atlantean sorcerer ATLAN. Tsunami's romantic dalliance with her fellow All-Star Neptune Perkins (see PERKINS, NEPTUNE) resulted in a daughter, Deborah, who is now known as the aquatic heroine Deep Blue. Tsunami continues to train Deep Blue in the use of her superpowers, occasionally making waves herself as a reluctant super heroine. She has been known to ally herself with AQUAMAN if called upon to lend her wonderful water-based abilities for the good of the Seven Seas. SB

TWILIGHT

FIRST APPEARANCE SUPERGIRL (3rd series) #15 (November 1997)
STATUS Undecided   REAL NAME Molly (last name unrevealed)
OCCUPATION Angel; former destroyer   BASE Mobile
HEIGHT 5ft 7in   WEIGHT 135 lbs   EYES Blue   HAIR White
SPECIAL POWERS/ABILITIES Can resurrect the dead; possesses wings of fire and devastating flame vision.

During the Black Death that ravaged 14th-century Europe, a girl named Molly discovered she had the God-given power to bring the dead back to life. After exhausting herself and her power, Molly discovered the body of her sister Jane but was unable to resurrect her. Outraged, Molly declared war on God.

Centuries later, Molly, as Twilight, became the enemy of God's agents on Earth, including the angel SUPERGIRL. After several devilish intrigues, Twilight confronted Supergirl and her ally, MARY MARVEL in Eden. Linda Danvers, a part of Supergirl's alter ego, died in the skirmish. The Matrix aspect of Supergirl merged with Twilight and resurrected Linda as the true Supergirl. Twilight then became the Angel of Fire, seeking redemption for her sins. PJ

TROY

FIRST APPEARANCE THE BRAVE AND THE BOLD #60 (July 1965)
STATUS Hero (presumed deceased)   REAL NAME Donna Hinkley Stacey Troy   HEIGHT 5ft 9in   WEIGHT 143 lbs   EYES Blue
HAIR Black   OCCUPATION Photographer   BASE New York City
SPECIAL POWERS/ABILITIES Superstrength, superspeed, flight; truth-coaxing abilities; psychic link to Wonder Woman; trained warrior respected and admired by everyone she worked with.

CHANGING STYLES From left to right: early teen and adult versions of the Wonder Girl costume; the Troy ensemble; Donna's Darkstar uniform.

A HERO'S DEATH After being slain by a rampaging Superman robot, Donna has been memorialized in the Teen Titans' Hall of Heroes.

MAGALA The Amazon sorceress Magala brings Princess Diana's reflection to life, creating Donna Troy!

Donna Troy was originally a magically-created playmate and "sister" for the young Princess Diana, later the champion of the AMAZONS of Themyscira known as WONDER WOMAN.

An identical twin created with a fraction of Diana's own soul, Donna was kidnapped by the villainous Dark Angel (see VON GUNTHER, BARONESS PAULA), who believed she had captured Diana instead, and forced to live a string of alternate lives, each ending in tragedy and pain.

Her most recent life began in the body of an orphaned baby put up for adoption. Saved from a burning building by Rhea, one of the TITANS OF MYTH, the infant Donna grew up on New Cronus, where the Titans gave her powers, taught her the mysteries of the universe, and named her Troy. Returning to Earth, Donna took the name Wonder Girl, inspired by HIPPOLYTA, the Wonder Woman of World War II, and founded the original Teen Titans with Robin (see NIGHTWING), Kid Flash (see Wally West, FLASH III), Aqualad (see TEMPEST) and Speedy (see ARSENAL).

Later, Donna assumed the codename Troy to reflect her upbringing with the Titans of Myth. She married history professor Terry Long, had a son, Robert, and became a member of the DARKSTARS. Tragically, Terry and Robert were killed in a car accident. Dark Angel arrived to cast Troy into another tragic life. But Wonder Woman and the Flash defeated Dark Angel. Donna later seemed to perish battling a malfunctioning Superman robot, but her fate remains a mystery. DW

SOUL SISTER Troy, Wonder Woman's "sister," was created from a fragment of Wonder Woman's own soul.

TWO-FACE

SCHIZOID CRIMINAL MASTERMIND

FIRST APPEARANCE DETECTIVE COMICS #66 (August 1942)
STATUS Villain **REAL NAME** Harvey Dent
OCCUPATION Former D.A.; professional criminal **BASE** Gotham City
HEIGHT 6ft **WEIGHT** 182 lbs **EYES** Blue **HAIR** Brown
SPECIAL POWERS/ABILITIES A criminal genius, whose crimes reveal an obsession with duality and the number two. An average combatant, but capable of savage violence.

HARVEY DENT IS A MAN DIVIDED. Childhood abuse fractured Dent's psyche right down the middle, leaving the respected Gotham City District Attorney subconsciously sublimating a darker and more violent persona as an adult. This duality was mirrored by Dent's good luck charm, a "two-headed" silver dollar. Once Batman's ally in justice, Dent's evil side reared its ugly head when, amid a packed courtroom, gangster Vincent Maroni hurled acid in the D.A.'s handsome face!

THE DARK SIDE

As the left side of Dent's face dissolved, so did the psychic wall keeping his dark persona in check. With good and evil wrestling for control, Dent scarred one side of his lucky coin. It became the final arbiter for his new persona, Two-Face, whose every act would be decided by the flip of a coin. If the unmarked side came up, he would show mercy; if the scarred side came up he would do evil. Dent abandoned his wife Gilda Grace, who had hoped plastic surgery would restore her husband's face and help his mind heal. Gilda married Doctor Paul Janus and they became the parents of twins, children conceived utilizing Harvey Dent's frozen sperm.

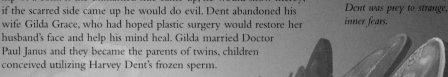

THE DARK SIDE Although a crusading D.A., Harvey Dent was prey to strange, inner fears.

DEFINING MOMENT Gangster Boss Moroni hurls acid in Harvey Dent's face, scarring him both physically and psychologically.

Believing that justice is arbitrary, Two-Face holds practitioners of the law in particular contempt. As judge, jury and executioner, he has murdered his own court-appointed attorneys and carried out lethal litigation against scores of Gotham's legal eagles.

During Gotham's year-long experience as a lawless No Mans Land, Dent turned prosecutor once more, "indicting" Commissioner Gordon (see GORDON, JAMES W.) for his law-breaking alliance—with Two-Face! Dent's cross-examination of his own alter ego led to a temporary mental brainstorm and an acquittal for Gordon. During that time, detective Renee Montoya (see MONTOYA, RENEE) was Two-Face's prisoner for five months, and she glimpsed a kinder, gentler Dent. He professed love for her, but felt betrayed when he learned she was a lesbian.

After surgeon Tommy Elliot (Hush) repaired his face, Dent reformed and earned Batman's trust, even becoming Gotham's guardian during the Dark Knight's absence following the Infinite Crisis. Yet his insanity caused Dent to re-scar his appearance, making him Two-Face once more. RG

FICKLE FATE Every key decision Two-Face makes is decided by his two-sided coin, one side of which is scarred, and one side of which is unblemished.

KEY STORYLINES

• **BATMAN: FACES (1995):** An examination into the tortured, often violent relationship between Batman, Two-Face, and Commissioner Gordon.
• **BATMAN ANNUAL #14 (1990):** A look at how difficult it is for Two-Face to function, whose face never fits in either the normal world or Gotham City's underworld.
• **SECRET ORIGINS SPECIAL (1989):** A deep look at how Harvey Dent changed from successful District Attorney to psychopathic madman.

UBERMENSCH

FIRST APPEARANCE YOUNG ALL-STARS #1 (June 1987)
STATUS Villain (deceased) **REAL NAME** Unknown
OCCUPATION Nazi hero **BASE** Mobile
HEIGHT 6ft 3in **WEIGHT** 225 lbs **EYES** Blue **HAIR** None
SPECIAL POWERS/ABILITIES Ubermensch was capable of leaping tall buildings in a single bound, but squandered his enhanced gifts in the service of evil; possessed superstrength and superspeed; his skin was invulnable to bullets.

UBERMENSCH ÜBER ALLES! *Hitler's follicly-challenged muscleman leads out Axis Amerika, the Third Reich's favorite team of super-villainous bully boys.*

Ubermensch was the epitome of Adolf Hitler's ideal of racial purity, selected by Nazi scientists to undergo painful treatments that transformed him into the ultimate Aryan super hero. He possessed remarkable strength and speed, and his skin was tough enough to shrug off the bullets of small-arms fire.

As World War II unfolded, Ubermensch became the head of AXIS AMERIKA, leading Gudra, SEA WOLF, Usil, Die Grosshorn Eule, Die Fledermaus, and Kamikaze against the American heroes of the ALL-STAR SQUADRON and its youthful spin-off, the YOUNG ALL-STARS. Ubermensch's fate at the end of the war is still unrecorded.

Recently, an American claimed the notorious name of Ubermensch as a member of a revived incarnation of Axis America. The man, called Shepherd was the leader of the religious commune Safe Haven and persuaded the world that the JUSTICE LEAGUE OF AMERICA had destroyed the commune and killed 1,000 innocent people! This accusation was soon exposed as a blatant lie, and Shepherd, revealed as the ideologue Ubermensch II, met defeat at the hands of the JLA. **DW**

ULTRA BOY

FIRST APPEARANCE SUPERBOY #98 (July 1962)
STATUS Hero **REAL NAME** Jo Nah
OCCUPATION Legionnaire **BASE** 30th-century Earth
HEIGHT 5ft 8in **WEIGHT** 155 lbs **EYES** Brown **HAIR** Brown
SPECIAL POWERS/ABILITIES Vast superstrength, speed, invulnerability, flight and vision powers, but can only use one power at a time.

Multiple versions of Ultra Boy exist in different timelines, but in nearly all of them he is Jo Nah of the planet Rimbor. Jo was on a scavenging mission in outer space when a giant space creature swallowed his ship. By eating some of the creature's flesh, Jo gained various superpowers. He used them to escape Rimbor and joined Leland McCauley's Workforce as Ultra Boy. Ultra Boy later joined the LEGION OF SUPER-HEROES, the 31st century's premier superteam, and fell in love with teammate APPARITION. He eventually married her when the two were trapped in the past.

After the BLIGHT attacked the Earth, Ultra Boy was hurled into another dimension. Although he managed to return to his wife, their marriage remains on shaky ground. Their son, Cub Wazzo-Nah, appears to have inherited meta-human powers from both his parents, although the extent of his abilities has yet to be revealed. **PJ**

ULTRA-HUMANITE

FIRST APPEARANCE ACTION COMICS #13 (June 1939)
STATUS Villain (deceased) **REAL NAME** Unknown
OCCUPATION Criminal scientist **BASE** Mobile
HEIGHT Varied **WEIGHT** Varied **EYES** Varied **HAIR** Varied
SPECIAL POWERS/ABILITIES A brilliant inventor, the Ultra-Humanite's greatest achievement was the process he devised to transplant his brain into different bodies, human or otherwise.

The Ultra-Humanite was one of the JUSTICE SOCIETY OF AMERICA's most terrible foes, responsible for the deaths of the CRIMSON AVENGER I and Johnny Thunder (see THUNDER I, JOHNNY) among many atrocities. Originally a criminal scientist active during the 1940s, the Ultra-Humanite escaped death by transplanting his brain into other bodies, including film star Dolores Winters, a giant ant, and finally a genetically mutated albino ape. He continued his assaults upon the JSA, as well as the team's superpowered progeny in INFINITY INC., and also led the SECRET SOCIETY OF SUPER-VILLAINS. Shaving his gorilla body, an even more terrifying Ultra-Humanite utilized resources usurped from the Council (see MANHUNTER II). Recently, the villain gave up his primate shell and hid his brain while taking mental control of the aged Johnny Thunder. The Ultra-Humanite recently returned to his albino gorilla appearance, and united with PER DEGATON and DESPERO to alter the timestream. BOOSTER GOLD and Rip Hunter (see HUNTER, RIP) have vowed to take them down. **SB**

ULTRA, THE MULTI-ALIEN

FIRST APPEARANCE MYSTERY IN SPACE #103 (November 1965)
STATUS Hero **REAL NAME** Ace Arn
OCCUPATION Adventurer **BASE** Mobile
HEIGHT 5ft 10in (as Arn); 6ft 2in (as Ultra) **WEIGHT** 157 lbs (as Arn); 163 lbs (as Ultra) **EYES** Blue (as Arn); Black (as Ultra);
HAIR Brown (as Arn); Half bald, half green, later half bald, half white (as Ultra)
SPECIAL POWERS/ABILITIES Each quarter of Arn's body possesses a unique property such as magnetism, increased strength, cohesive energy and the power of flight.

In the late 21st century, Captain Ace Arn's spacecraft accidentally crashed into an asteroid in another solar system. The rock turned out to be the secret hideout for interstellar criminal Zobra. Arn learned the four planet solar system was artificially created with one member from each race—Ulla, Laroo, Trago, and Raaga— serving Zobra. Zobra accidentally killed himself with a poisonous gas and a free-for-all began among his underlings. When they arrived at the asteroid and found Arn there, they all fired their unique duplication weapons simultaneously. As a result, Arn was transformed into a four-segmented composite alien, representing each alien race. Granted phenomenal new powers, Arn subdued the aliens, repaired his craft and returned to Earth. He gave up piloting to fight crime as Ultra, but is haunted by regret for the loss of his humanity and his girlfriend from his previous life, Bonnie. **RG**

UNCLE SAM

FIRST APPEARANCE NATIONAL COMICS #1 (July 1940)
STATUS Hero **REAL NAME** Unknown **OCCUPATION** Patriotic spirit
BASE The United States **HEIGHT** 6ft 3in **WEIGHT** 210 lbs
EYES Blue **HAIR** White **SPECIAL POWERS/ABILITIES** Superstrength,
invulnerability; can change size; powers are proportionate to
the country's faith in the ideals of freedom and liberty.

OUT OF ACTION Black Adam took out Uncle Sam during the Infinite Crisis, but couldn't kill the Spirit of Liberty.

Several hundred years ago, soon after the formation of the United States, Benjamin Franklin and other Founding Fathers used a mystic ritual to create the American Talisman. The Talisman would embody the very spirit of the U.S., and materialize by magically binding itself to a nationalistic citizen. During World War II, the spirit linked itself to a man named Samuel and became the star-spangled superpatriot Uncle Sam.

Uncle Sam joined the ALL-STAR SQUADRON and later formed an auxiliary unit called the FREEDOM FIGHTERS. After World War II, the American talisman was destroyed and Uncle Sam's energies waned. An evil group called the National Interest tried to recreate the shattered Talisman, but the SPECTRE defeated the Interest as well as the American Scream, the insane personification of American culture. The Talisman was reassembled, and Uncle Sam became the Patriot, defending the U.S., most notably during the Imperiex War (see Great Battles, pp. 362–3). The spirit then reclaimed the title Uncle Sam.

During the Infinite Crisis, the Freedom Fighters lost a brutal fight with the members of the villainous Society (see VILLAINS UNITED). Believed killed, Uncle Sam returned to defeat the sinister Father Time and his S.H.A.D.E. agents by uniting a new team of Freedom Fighters under his banner. Uncle Sam's team is largely made up of new heroes carrying on old legacies including FIREBRAND, DOLL MAN, the HUMAN BOMB, PHANTOM LADY, and the RED BEE. **PJ**

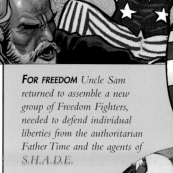

FOR FREEDOM Uncle Sam returned to assemble a new group of Freedom Fighters, needed to defend individual liberties from the authoritarian Father Time and the agents of S.H.A.D.E.

INSPIRATION During the great Crisis, Uncle Sam led members of the JLA and the Titans into battle against the Anti-Monitor.

UNKNOWN SOLDIER

FIRST APPEARANCE STAR-SPANGLED WAR STORIES #151 (July 1970) **STATUS** Hero **REAL NAME** Unrevealed **OCCUPATION** Secret agent **BASE** Washington, D.C. **HEIGHT** 5ft 9in **WEIGHT** 155 lbs **EYES** Blue **HAIR** Blond **SPECIAL POWERS/ABILITIES** Weapons and explosives expert; expert combatant; master of disguise and impersonation.

The man who became known in U.S. intelligence as the Unknown Soldier enlisted with his older brother Harry in World War II. Harry died saving his sibling from a Japanese grenade, which left the young soldier's face horribly disfigured. He continued as an undercover agent, disguising his ruined face to resemble anyone and then infiltrating behind enemy lines The Unknown Soldier's daring exploits earned the enmity of Adolf Hitler, who frequently pitted a Nazi operative known as the Black Knight against him.

Later, as the war was ending, the Unknown Soldier infiltrated Hitler's Berlin bunker, where he facilitated the Führer's suicide. Many believed the Soldier had died saving a child from an explosion on the streets of war-torn Berlin. In reality, he continued to serve U.S. interests throughout other wars and various clandestine conflicts in the decades to follow as the U.S. military's preferred cleanup man, a man with neither a face nor a name. **SB**

GREAT BATTLES

Why are there super heroes? Perhaps the cosmic presence that governs the universe created so many meta-humans in the 20th century in preparation for the creation-shaking threats soon to follow. Without the JLA, the JSA, and other champions of freedom, the Earth and all of reality would long since have ceased to exist!

THE APPELLAXIAN CONTEST

Seven champions came from a distant star to slug it out on an Earth battlefield and determine which of the seven was fit to rule the Appellaxian empire. Assuming "battle forms" of glass, fire, rock, mercury, wood, ice, and a giant golden bird, the seven met swift defeat thanks to the embryonic JUSTICE LEAGUE OF AMERICA—AQUAMAN, GREEN LANTERN, the FLASH, MARTIAN MANHUNTER, and BLACK CANARY. An eighth Appellaxian went unnoticed. He called seven thousand of his planet's top shock troops for a full-scale alien invasion.

GIANT STEPS
All of Earth's heroes united to defeat the Appellaxian horde, ultimately sending them back to their own planet through a mystical wormhole. The conflict is still remembered as the JLA's baptism of fire

THE IMPERIEX WAR

The cosmic tyrant IMPERIEX hungered to reignite the universe in a new Big Bang, wiping out all that had gone before. SUPERMAN led a galaxy-wide coalition of champions to oppose his cataclysmic scheming. The Imperiex War—a period sometimes referred to as "Our Worlds at War"—was inevitable if the universe was to be saved. Earth's defenders included an unlikely alliance of DARKSEID and U.S. President Lex Luthor (*see* LUTHOR, LEX), whose combined forces provided the necessary edge when the computerized monster BRAINIAC 13 entered the fight on the side of evil. Among the war's many casualties were most of the population of Topeka, Kansas as well as HIPPOLYTA—Princess Diana's mother and the Golden Age WONDER WOMAN.

DESTROYED BY FIRE
Topeka is set ablaze during the Imperiex War.

HAVEN *Orbiting 'Paradocs' sheltered those wounded in the shocking conflict, including some of the greatest heroes the Earth has ever seen.*

THE MAGEDDON WAR

Those who lived through it called it World War III. When the ancient doomsday device Mageddon slipped its moorings outside space-time and approached Earth, its aggressive energies caused the planet to erupt in a fury of violence. Angels from Heaven helped calm the leaders of

nations, while Wonder Woman spearheaded an effort to turn ordinary citizens into temporary super heroes. In the end Superman switched off the Mageddon warhead, ensuring Earth's survival—until the next extraterrestrial threat.

Loss *Though Superman secured a victory, the young hero Aztek perished in his efforts to halt the advance of the warbringer.*

THE CRISIS ON INFINITE EARTHS

The most significant event ever to shake the universe is the one that almost no one can remember. In an earlier reality, creation was ordered into a "multiverse" with multiple parallel Earths—an Earth-2 for the Justice Society and an Earth-S for the CAPTAIN MARVEL family, alongside an infinite number of others. The omnipotent Anti-Monitor began destroying all parallel universes, and his heroic mirror-image the MONITOR gathered heroes from all realities and timeframes to fight him.

In order to save what was left, the Monitor merged five Earth-histories into one and the universe was reborn as if it had always been that way. Thus, while modern heroes remember a battle called the Crisis, they have no memory of a multiverse. Some heroes who died in the Crisis (such as the Barry Allen Flash) still perished in the rebooted version of the event, while others (such as the pre-Crisis version of Supergirl) had their deaths—and entire histories—retroactively wiped from existence. Among the characters who can remember bits of pre-Crisis reality are the Psycho Pirate, the LINEAR MEN, and presumably some of God's agents, such as the PHANTOM STRANGER and the SPECTRE.

ZERO HOUR

Essentially a Crisis aftershock, the history-altering Zero Hour united the villainous EXTANT with the delusional hero PARALLAX, who wanted to remake the universe and remove all pain and loss. A team of super heroes followed Parallax back to the dawn of time and prevented his larger plan, though reality was still reborn in a slightly modified form. Zero Hour's biggest effects were felt in the 30th century, where the history of the LEGION OF SUPER-HEROES experienced a complete restart. **DW**

363

VALDA

FIRST APPEARANCE ARAK, SON OF THUNDER #3 (November 1981)
STATUS Hero **REAL NAME** Valda
OCCUPATION Knight **BASE** Aix-le-Chapelle, Frankland
HEIGHT 5ft 6in **WEIGHT** 130 lbs **EYES** Blue **HAIR** Brown
SPECIAL POWERS/ABILITIES Valda was quick-witted and courageous, and an expert hand-to-hand combatant and swordsman.

Nicknamed the Iron Maiden of Europe, Valda was the daughter of Bradamante, the legendary female knight. When her mother did not return alive from the ambush at the pass of Roncesvalles in the Pyrenees mountains in 778, when part of King Charlemagne's army was destroyed by the Basques, Valda was raised by the Charlemagne and his court sorcerer, Malagigi.

The young woman used a spell she learned from Malagigi to summon the spirit of Amadis of Gaul, a valiant warrior, and the ghost tutored her as a warrior into Valda's adulthood.

Charlemagne was so impressed with Valda's talents and bravery that he eventually made her a knight. Soon after, Valda came under the control of the sorcerer Baledor and was freed by ARAK, SON OF THUNDER. Arak and Valda became lovers, adventuring throughout Europe until the end of their lives, which remain unchronicled. **PJ**

VALE, VICKI

FIRST APPEARANCE BATMAN #49 (October 1950)
STATUS Hero **REAL NAME** Victoria "Vicki" Vale
OCCUPATION Talk-show host **BASE** Gotham City
HEIGHT 5ft 6in **WEIGHT** 121 lbs **EYES** Blue **HAIR** Red
SPECIAL POWERS/ABILITIES No superpowers, but few journos have a better nose for a good story or are more persistent when on the trail of a possible scoop.

Among the so-called "Fourth Estate" of professional newspaper reporting, Vicki Vale was highly respected and acclaimed for her determination in rooting out the truth with her writing. In Gotham City social circles, Vicki was also known for her on-again/off-again romance with billionaire Bruce Wayne, who—despite caring deeply for Vicki—was ultimately unable to reveal to her the fact that he was BATMAN. In the past her relationship with Bruce drove Selina Kyle, CATWOMAN, into fits of murderous jealousy. On one occasion Selina caused the car Vicki and Bruce were travelling in to plunge into a lake. Vicki would have drowned if Bruce had not rescued her.

Vicki has since left both Bruce Wayne and print journalism behind and now hosts *The Scene* TV show. **SB**

VANDAL SAVAGE

FIRST APPEARANCE GREEN LANTERN (1st series) #10 (Winter 1943)
STATUS Villain **REAL NAME** Vandar Adg
OCCUPATION Would-be conqueror **BASE** Mobile
HEIGHT 5ft 10in **WEIGHT** 170 lbs **EYES** Brown **HAIR** Black
SPECIAL POWERS/ABILITIES Savage is immortal. He is a brilliant strategist and scientist with 50,000 years of experience to draw upon.

Fifty thousand years ago, Vandar Adg was a chieftain of the Blood tribe of Cro-Magnons in Europe. Adg was exposed to the radiation from a meteor that advanced his intellect and gave him immortality. The ruthless Adg spent millennia acquiring wealth and power, and became a leader of the Illuminati, a secret society out to control the world. Over the centuries, Savage was a pharaoh in Egypt; a Caesar in Rome; led the Mongol hordes as Genghis Khan; led the Spanish Armada; advised Napoleon; and committed serial murders as Jack the Ripper.

During World War II, Vandal Savage fought the JUSTICE SOCIETY OF AMERICA in the INJUSTICE SOCIETY. He collected DNA samples of the team and used them to create DAMAGE. Savage engineered the congressional hearings that forced the JSA to disband in 1951. In recent years, Savage created the super-drug Velocity 9, joined several villains in TARTARUS while fighting the TEEN TITANS, plotted nuclear extortion, and destroyed Montevideo, Uruguay. A sworn enemy of Rip Hunter (*see* HUNTER, RIP), RESURRECTION MAN, and the JSA, Savage uses transplanted organs from his descendants to ensure his survival, which extends well into the 853rd century. Savage's recent plots include a scheme to flood the Earth (stopped by the new AQUAMAN), and the extermination of super hero lineages related to the JUSTICE SOCIETY OF AMERICA. Vandal Savage has revealed himself as the father of SCANDAL, and he hopes that she will one day bear him an heir. **PJ**

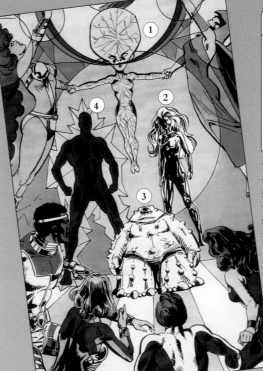

Meeting of heroes The Teen Titans join forces with the members of Vanguard: **1)** *Scanner* **2)** *Solaar* **3)** *White Dwarf* **4)** *Anti-Matterman.*

VANGUARD

FIRST APPEARANCE NEW TEEN TITANS (1st series) ANNUAL #1 (1985)
STATUS Hero team **BASE** Mobile
MEMBERS AND POWERS **Anti-Matterman** Draws power from anti-matter universe; **Scanner** Powerful mental abilities; **White Dwarf** Controls gravity and density of objects; **Solaar** Controls heat and energy of solar winds; **Black Nebula (deceased)** Could generate a field of darkness; **Drone** Entity of living metal, Vanguard space transport.

The Vanguard are a mobile team of superpowered entities whose territory is the entire cosmos. Roaming the stars in their sentient starship Drone, they visit planets, doing what good they can before departing to the next star system. Their membership is composed primarily of individuals who command some fundamental cosmic power, such as White Dwarf, Solaar, and Anti-Matterman.

The Vanguard's first and only visit to Earth to date was largely a case of mistaken identity. The core Vanguard team attempted to capture SUPERMAN but only succeeded in netting a Superman robotic duplicate. The New TEEN TITANS arrived to help. Both teams soon discovered that BRANIAC had murdered Vanguard member Black Nebula and abducted Superman to serve as an organic power source for his interstellar war machines.

Only the united strength of the Vanguard team and the Teen Titans could defeat Braniac and return Superman to Earth. Although grateful to the Titans for the assistance, the Vanguard chose to resume wandering across the light-years of space rather than remain tied to a single planet. **DW**

VAPOR

FIRST APPEARANCE JUSTICE LEAGUE QUARTERLY #1 (Winter 1990)
STATUS Hero **REAL NAME** Carrie Donahue
OCCUPATION Activist **BASE** Formerly New York City
HEIGHT 5ft 5in **WEIGHT** 124 lbs **EYES** Hazel **HAIR** Brown
SPECIAL POWERS/ABILITIES Able to transform into a living vaporous mist with acidic, anesthetic, or transparent properties.

Although Carrie Donahue was less than overjoyed upon acquiring superpowers, the admitted liberal decided to use her ability as the adventuring activist known as Vapor. The origins of Carrie's gifts are unknown, although they may be the result of a latent metagene, as is often the case with spontaneous superpowers. Ironically, this intelligent and haughty young woman accepted businesswoman Claire Montgomery's offer to join The Conglomerate (see CONGLOMERATE, THE), a team supplying its super heroic services to several corporate sponsors. Based on Wall Street, The Conglomerate soon battled the JUSTICE LEAGUE OF AMERICA—whom Vapor regarded as a "pathetic joke"—after violating U.N. protocols by ousting the tyrannical leader of the nation of San Sebor. The Conglomerate broke apart shortly after, and Vapor became a spokesperson for an environmental group. Her present location and activities are unknown. **SB**

VETERAN

FIRST APPEARANCE ROBIN (2nd series) #138 (July 2005)
STATUS Hero **REAL NAME** Unknown
OCCUPATION Adventurer **BASE** Mobile
HEIGHT 6ft 2in **WEIGHT** 220 lbs **EYES** Blue **HAIR** Brown
SPECIAL POWERS/ABILITIES Superior combat abilities and marksmanship; brilliant strategist; in top-notch physical condition.

The Veteran is a legendary super hero with ties to the U.S. military. He has a strategic mind and battlefield leadership abilities. He participated in Operation Desert Storm and other U.S.-led invasions and earned the rank of general. The Veteran is used to leadership, and commands his own team of heroes to fight street crime and metahuman threats.

Impressed with the skills of ROBIN (Tim Drake), the Veteran tried to recruit him by incapacitating one of Robin's enemies and leaving a note on her body. Robin ran one mission with the Veteran's crew, but elected to remain BATMAN's partner. Later, the Veteran was among the heroes and villains rounded up by the AUCTIONEER and imprisoned aboard his spacecraft. The Veteran tried to lead a breakout squad consisting of Blue Jay, Livewire, SKYROCKET, and the new AQUAMAN (Arthur Joseph Curry), but SUPERMAN quickly took over. The Veteran proved himself against the Auctioneer's robotic sentries. **DW**

VEXT

FIRST APPEARANCE DCU HEROES SECRET FILES AND ORIGINS #1 (February 1999) **STATUS** Undecided **REAL NAME** Vext
OCCUPATION Patron deity of misfortune **BASE** Delta City
HEIGHT 6ft 2in **WEIGHT** 210 lbs **EYES** Blue **HAIR** Brown
SPECIAL POWERS/ABILITIES Immortality; teleportation; can manipulate all manner of unfortunate occurrences; suffers constant bad luck.

Vext is a god of mishap and misfortune, the personification of the so-called "Murphy's Law," where anything that can go wrong will, and at the worst possible moment! Vext once resided in the Jejune Realm, also known as the Borough of Mawkish Indifference, a land of minor gods and goddesses who oversee the mundane aspects of people's everyday life.

The Jejune Realm was erased from existence when mortals no longer chose to actively worship its gods and Vext was sent to Earth. He arrived in Delta City, under strict orders from the cosmic powers not to interfere in human affairs. Struggling to fit into the world as a normal person, Vext was often joined by Paramour, the beautiful but unlucky Goddess of Relationships Gone Horribly Wrong. After being pursued by Aaron Caldwell, an archaeologist devoted to the study of minor gods such as the Jejune pantheon, Vext settled down with Colleen McBride, an aspiring writer and Vext's next-door neighbor. **PJ**

VIBE

FIRST APPEARANCE JUSTICE LEAGUE OF AMERICA (1st series) ANNUAL #2 (November 1984)
STATUS Hero (deceased) **REAL NAME** Paco Ramone
OCCUPATION Super hero **BASE** Detroit
HEIGHT 5ft 10in **WEIGHT** 157 lbs **EYES** Brown **HAIR** Brown
SPECIAL POWERS/ABILITIES Could emit shockwaves to trigger earthquakes.

During the period when AQUAMAN led a reformed JUSTICE LEAGUE OF AMERICA out of a Detroit bunker, Paco Ramone quit as leader of the local El Lobos street gang to join the new JLA along with fellow Detroiter GYPSY. Under the codename Vibe, Ramone used his natural ability to vibrate objects or air molecules and generate destructive shockwaves.

Vibe's career with the JLA ended when an android created by PROFESSOR IVO tracked and strangled Vibe—making him the first Justice Leaguer to be killed in the line of duty. Armando, Vibe's younger brother, had similar powers, and later joined the CONGLOMERATE as Reverb (later HARDLINE).

Sadly, Vibe has not been allowed to rest in peace. Twice his undead spirit has been reanimated to vex his former teammates in the JLA. **DW**

VIGILANTE I

FIRST APPEARANCE ACTION COMICS #42 (November 1941)
STATUS Hero (deceased) **REAL NAME** Gregory Sanders
HEIGHT 6ft **WEIGHT** 188 lbs **EYES** Blue **HAIR** Black
OCCUPATION Adventurer **BASE** Mobile
SPECIAL POWERS/ABILITIES A trained fighter, an expert motorcycle rider, is skilled with a pistol and lariat, and can sing a pretty mean tune.

Nathaniel Sanders and his wife had three children, Rebecca, Gregory and Jeffrey. Jeff Sanders died of "the fever" in 1936 and Nathaniel was killed by stagecoach bandits. Greg grew up to become the "famous radio star known as the "Prairie Troubadour." However, to avenge his father, he donned the costumed identity of the Vigilante. He had numerous exploits on his own, and with the SEVEN SOLDIERS OF VICTORY. Billy "Pop" Gunn, an old man from New Jersey who loved the Old West, hooked up with the Vigilante for several adventures.

While trying to prevent the Head from instigating a tong war in Chinatown, the Vigilante met the youthful Daniel Leong, who soon becomes his partner, Stuff. Gangster Benjamin "Bugsy" Siegel killed Stuff, sending Vigilante on a new mission of vengeance. At some point thereafter, Leong's brother Victor took over his brother's role as Stuff, the Chinatown Kid. On June 20 1947, Vigilante finally gained revenge in a one-on-one confrontation with Bugsy Siegel. Shortly thereafter, the SSOV were tossed back in time and Sanders spent 1875-1895 roaming the Old West. He was rescued by the JUSTICE LEAGUE OF AMERICA and the JUSTICE SOCIETY OF AMERICA. Vigilante recently gathered a new group of Seven Soldiers to battle the far-future Sheeda, but Vigilante and most other members of the overmatched group died. **RG**

VIGILANTE II

FIRST APPEARANCE THE NEW TEEN TITANS ANNUAL (1st series) #2 (Summer 1983)
STATUS Hero (deceased) **REAL NAME** Adrian Chase
OCCUPATION Criminal hunter **BASE** Mobile
HEIGHT 6ft 2in **WEIGHT** 197 lbs **EYES** Blue **HAIR** Blond
SPECIAL POWERS/ABILITIES Master of unarmed combat and skilled in the use of firearms and other weapons; practiced meditative processes to overcome pain and heal injuries; rode a heavily armed motorcycle.

As an indefatigable Manhattan District Attorney, Adrian Chase worked doggedly within the system to dismantle the city's Mafia infrastructure. But when Chase's wife Doris, son Adam, and daughter Drew were killed by a bomb planted by the Scarapelli mob family, Chase sought his own justice as Vigilante. Guilt-ridden over his abandonment of the rule of law, Chase committed suicide. A new Vigilante has recently appeared and has worked on cases with NIGHTWING. **SB**

VENTRILOQUIST & SCARFACE

FIRST APPEARANCE DETECTIVE COMICS #583 (February 1988)
STATUS Villain (deceased) **REAL NAME** Arnold Wesker
OCCUPATION Gang boss; assassin **BASE** Gotham City
HEIGHT 5ft 7in **WEIGHT** 142 lbs **EYES** Blue **HAIR** Gray
SPECIAL POWERS/ABILITIES Out of shape and a poor ventriloquist (he speaks "b's as "g's); however his shattered psyche harbors dark passions, which find murderous outlet through his dummy, Scarface.

LOOK WHO'S TALKING
Arnold Wesker couldn't get arrested as a ventriloquist, but when hiding behind his gangster mannequin Scarface—made from cursed wood—he becomes a real Public Enemy.

Arnold Wesker was orphaned as a child and repressed his feelings so deeply that he developed a multiple personality disorder. As an adult, he let those angry feelings out and killed a man, landing him in Gotham's Blackgate Penitentiary.

PUPPET MASTER

His cellmate, Donnegan, showed him a ventriloquist's dummy he had carved from the wood of Blackgate's Gallows Tree. Perhaps the wood was cursed, for Wesker was irresistibly drawn to the doll, and killed Donnegan for it. The psychopathic personality of Scarface emerged, speaking through the dummy.

Wesker and Scarface became major players in Gotham's underworld. When stopped by BATMAN. Wesker's defense was that he was an innocent dupe of the Scarface persona. When Gotham was devastated by an earthquake, Wesker created a new puppet, the Quakemaster, and tried to extort $100,000,000 from the city. Following the Infinite Crisis, Wesker died in a Gotham gang takeover. His successor is Sugar, a gangster's moll who now puppets Scarface as the Ventriloquist II. She appears to be in love with the dummy. RG

REBORN *Scarface tells his rivals that he didn't die, he just 'moved to a softer lap.'*

SHOT DEAD *When Arnold Vesker lost his life, Scarface "died" as well. It took a new Ventriloquist to resurrect the wooden mob boss.*

LAST BREATH *Before he expired, Arnold Vesker left clues at his murder scene that would lead Batman and Robin to his killer.*

KEY STORYLINES
- *DETECTIVE COMICS #583 (FEBRUARY 1988)* The Ventriloquist debuts, his gimmick and insanity making him a perfect fit in Gotham's bizarre criminal underworld.
- *DETECTIVE COMICS #818 (JUNE 2006)* Vesker is killed by an assassin working for mob boss, the Great White Shark.
- *DETECTIVE COMICS #843-844 (JUNE-JULY 2008)* The new Ventriloquist meets Bruce Wayne, and both realize they know one another socially outside of Gotham's world of heroes and villains.

VIGILANTE III

FIRST APPEARANCE DEATHSTROKE THE TERMINATOR #6
(January 1992) STATUS Hero REAL NAME Patricia "Pat" Trayce
OCCUPATION Retired police detective; crime fighter BASE Mobile
HEIGHT 5ft 9in WEIGHT 144 lbs EYES Blue HAIR Blond
SPECIAL POWERS/ABILITIES Markswoman and martial artist; costume has
night-vision goggles and flak jacket; weapons and equipment include
pistol, ropes, grenades, and a molybdenum-alloy fighting baton.

After her partner was killed by
mob hitman Barker, G.C.P.D.
detective Pat Trayce was suspected of
jeopardizing Barker's safety in the
witness protection program. When
DEATHSTROKE kidnapped Barker
to smoke out the true traitor
within the justice department,
Trayce was blamed and suspended
from duty. Determined to prove
her innocence, Trayce began her
own investigation, during which
time she met the informant
Scoops, who had once assisted the
late Adrian Chase, (VIGILANTE
II). Scoops gave Trayce the
costume and weapons of the
Vigilante. Trayce then helped
Deathstroke flush out the
justice department mole.
Realizing the benefits of working outside the law, Trayce
turned in her badge and became the Vigilante full-time.
She has been a CHECKMATE agent, set up a detective
agency, Vigilance, and worked with the FORGOTTEN
HEROES and the JSA All-Stars. SB

VIKING PRINCE

FIRST APPEARANCE THE BRAVE AND THE BOLD #1 (August 1955)
STATUS Hero (deceased) REAL NAME Jon Haraldson
OCCUPATION Adventurer BASE Formerly 10th-century Scandinavia,
now Valhalla, home for Norse warriors who have died in battle.
HEIGHT 5ft 11in WEIGHT 171 lbs EYES Blue HAIR Blond
SPECIAL POWERS/ABILITIES A powerful hand-to-hand combatant and
swordsman; some legends claim that he was invulnerable to harm
from metal, wood, fire, and water.

The origins of Jon the Viking
Prince remain a mystery. One
legend asserts that Jon was
brought to Valhalla after a great
battle, granted superpowers by
Odin, the Asgardian god, and
sent back to Earth to battle
evil for eternity.
Jon's mysterious past
became linked to the present
when CHESHIRE and her band
of female assassins, the Ravens,
traveled back in time to the 10th
century. BLACK CANARY pursued them
and the Viking Prince fell in love with her.
But Cheshire shot the Prince, and the Ravens
and Canary returned to the present.
Suspended in ice by a Valkyrie who had fallen in love
with him, the Viking Prince was freed from his frozen state
centuries later during World War II. After dying fighting
the Nazis, Jon was finally taken to Valhalla.
Black Canary later learned that the Viking Prince had
survived Cheshire's bullet when she found an artifact that
referred to their affair. Upon it was carved the inscription:
"His heart mourned for a love lost to time." PJ

VILLAINY INC.

FIRST APPEARANCE WONDER WOMAN: OUR WORLDS AT WAR
#1 (August 2001) STATUS Villain team BASE Mobile
CURRENT MEMBERS AND POWERS Queen Clea (leader, deceased)
Atlantean monarch who carried the Trident of Poseidon.
Cyborgirl Cyborg who can interface with machinery.
Doctor Poison II Expert in toxins and plagues. Giganta
Can grow to towering heights. Jinx Vast mystical abilities.
Trinity (destroyed) Her three faces, Time, War, and Chaos,
possessed specialized powers; revealed as a computer virus.

This all-female super-villain team has made life awful
for WONDER WOMAN, starting in the 1940s. Led by the
Atlantean Queen Clea (whose roster included CHEETAH I,
Doctor Poison, Hypnotic Woman, and Zara) the wartime
team failed to score lasting victories. Clea resurrected
Villainy, Inc. and recruited a new roster: Cyborgirl, outfitted
with Cyborg's machinery and weapons, GIGANTA, JINX, the
enigmatic TRINITY, and the second DOCTOR POISON, the
granddaughter of the original.
Clea led the new team to Skartaris, home of the
WARLORD, hoping to capture the Golden City of
Shamballah and its computer core. Wonder Woman united
the peoples of Skartaris in a counter attack, but Trinity
revealed herself to be a living computer virus created by ancient Skartaran
scientists to infect Shamballah's computer core and "reboot" the land to its
previous, more harmonious state. Wonder Woman stopped Trinity and Clea was
de-aged into nothingness. The surviving members joined Wonder Woman on a
time-hop to 1943, where a younger Clea and Hippolyta were joined in battle.
After helping defeat Clea, Wonder
Woman escorted Villainy Inc. back
to the modern era. DW

GOLDEN AGE The original
Villainy Inc. couldn't beat
Hippolyta, the wartime
Wonder Woman.

THE NEW TEAM 1) Giganta
2) Doctor Poison II
3) Trinity 4) Queen Clea
5) Cyborgirl 6) Jinx.

367

VILLAINS UNITED

FIRST APPEARANCE VILLAINS UNITED #1 (July 2005)
STATUS Villain Team **BASE** Mobile
FOUNDER MEMBERS AND POWERS
Doctor Psycho: Telepathy and mind-control.
Talia Head: Brilliant tactician and combatant.
Deathstroke: Superior hand-to-hand fighter and weapons expert.
Black Adam: Flight, super-strength, super-speed, near-invulnerability.
The Calculator: Genius at information retrieval.

The latest incarnation of the SECRET SOCIETY OF SUPER-VILLAINS, known informally as Villains United, took shape prior to the Infinite Crisis. Alexander Luthor, last survivor of a destroyed Earth, assumed the identity of Lex Luthor (*see* LUTHOR, LEX) to bring together the largest assemblage of criminals ever seen. Hundreds of villains joined the new Society, lured by promises of riches or coerced by outright threats. A six-member cabal—Luthor, DOCTOR PSYCHO, TALIA, DEATHSTROKE, BLACK ADAM, and the Calculator—coordinated the Society's activities.

THE CAGED BIRD SINGS *Trying to discover the identity of Mockingbird, the Crime Doctor locked the Secret Six in a small cell, where they would listen to the screams of their teammates as they are "questioned."*

AN OFFER YOU CAN'T REFUSE *Of all the villains in the DCU, only six refused to join Luthor's team. The Secret Six (as they would come to be known) were tortured by the most sadistic mind on the planet, the Crime Doctor.*

FREEDOM AND INJUSTICE FOR ALL *Lockup provides valuable information to the Society for their plan to simultaneously release all prisoners from all prisons, worldwide.*

A WORTHY ADVERSARY

The real Lex Luthor struck back at his duplicate by posing as the unseen MOCKINGBIRD and handpicking his own villainous team: DEADSHOT, CAT-MAN, SCANDAL, RAG DOLL II, CHESHIRE, and Parademon. This group made up the new SECRET SIX. The Society's actions, including a plot to erase the memories of the planet's super heroes in retaliation for the JUSTICE LEAGUE OF AMERICA's own mind-wipes (performed by ZATANNA), met swift ends due to sabotage by the Secret Six. Alexander Luthor responded by kidnapping and torturing his rivals, and later activated his traitor, Cheshire.

Finally the Society executed a massive strike on the Secret Six's headquarters. Society member KNOCKOUT revealed herself as a mole and assisted in the Six's escape, while Parademon sacrificed himself in order to obliterate a band of attackers. VANDAL SAVAGE brought an end to the conflict, convincing Alexander Luthor to refrain from any actions that might harm his daughter, Scandal.

The Society's biggest moment came in the Battle of Metropolis at the climax of the Infinite Crisis. The Calculator orchestrated a global jailbreak, swelling the Society's ranks even further, and Doctor Psycho and WARP retrieved their ultimate weapon, the monstrous DOOMSDAY. The army of villains marched on Metropolis and its waiting superheroic defenders, and the fight claimed casualties on both sides. The Society disbanded after the Crisis, but Lex Luthor recently assembled a similar group, the Injustice League Unlimited.

THE CURRENT LINEUP, *Left to right, Talia, Black Adam, Lex Luthor, Deathstroke, Dr. Psycho, and the Calculator.*

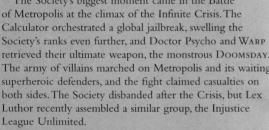

STRENGTH IN NUMBERS *With the help of his inside man, Deathstroke leads the attack on Mockingbird's headquarters.*

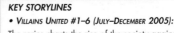

KEY STORYLINES
- VILLAINS UNITED #1–6 (JULY–DECEMBER 2005): The series charts the rise of the society against the super-heroic community, culminating in the Battle of Metropolis.

VIXEN

FIRST APPEARANCE ACTION COMICS #521 (July 1981)
STATUS Hero **REAL NAME** Mari Jiwe McCabe
OCCUPATION Adventurer **BASE** Ultramarines base, Superbia
HEIGHT 5ft 7in **WEIGHT** 140 lbs **EYES** Brown **HAIR** Brown
SPECIAL POWERS/ABILITIES Mystical Tantu totem gives her the abilities of one animal at a time.

Mari McCabe grew up in Africa, the daughter of the Reverend Richard Jiwe. Her father had inherited a magical totem that had supposedly been given to the ancient hero Tantu by the trickster Anansi the Spider of African folklore and myth. The reverend's envious and corrupt half-brother, General Maksai, killed Richard for the totem, and Mari fled to the U.S., where she found remarkable success as a fashion model.

Soon, Mari recovered the Tantu totem and, under the codename Vixen, used its amazing animal powers to become a member of the Detroit-based JUSTICE LEAGUE OF AMERICA. General Maksai tried to force her to turn the totem over to him, but received his comeuppance when he used the totem in selfishness, and was transformed into an ox! Vixen joined the SUICIDE SQUAD after leaving the JLA, striking up a failed romance with teammate BRONZE TIGER. After serving with the INTERNATIONAL ULTRAMARINE CORPS, Vixen joined the most recent incarnation of the Justice League. Almost immediately, she experienced problems with her animal powers, losing them entirely before discovering that she now had the ability to mimic the superpowers of her fellow heroes. DW

SHARED LINK Like Animal Man, Vixen shares a connection to the "morphogenic field" that bestows animal powers.

VUNDERBARR, VIRMIN

FIRST APPEARANCE MISTER MIRACLE (1st series) #5 (December 1971)
STATUS Villain (deceased) **REAL NAME** Virmin Vunderbarr
OCCUPATION Assassin **BASE** Apokolips
HEIGHT 5ft 2in **WEIGHT** 103 lbs **EYES** Blue **HAIR** Black
SPECIAL POWERS/ABILITIES A highly skilled, if inflexible, tactician; good hand-to-hand combatant, but handicapped by small size. He relies on his troops to fight his battles for him; has delusions of grandeur and believes he deserves more power than he has.

Virmin Vunderbarr was one of DARKSEID's best skilled soldiers, quickly rising to become a military leader. He has ensconced himself as one of Darkseid's trusted aides even though he schemes with the other acolytes to amass his own power. After a campaign on Earth, Vunderbarr styled himself after nineteenth century Prussian soldiers. On occasion, he has angered Darkseid and been destroyed by the Omega Force, only to be resurrected when needed. Virmin has proven ineffectual time and again, usually at the hands of Scott Free, MR. MIRACLE. Virmin spends more time currying Darkseid's favor than being an effective leader despite his keen intellect and tactical genius.

Virmin's niece Malice serves with Granny Goodness' FEMALE FURIES. Virmin himself perished on more than one occasion, most recently during the Death of the New Gods event. RG

JACKBOOT JERK Virmin Vunderbarr styles himself after the rigid and domineering Prussian military of days gone by.

MALICE IN MIND Despite her innocent appearance, Virmin's niece Malice has the makings of being far deadlier and more effective than he ever was.

VON GUNTHER, BARONESS PAULA

FIRST APPEARANCE WONDER WOMAN (2nd series) #131 (March 1998) **STATUS** Reformed villain **REAL NAME** Paula Von Gunther
OCCUPATION Scientist **BASE** Themyscira
HEIGHT 5ft 10in **WEIGHT** 155 lbs **EYES** Blue **HAIR** Blonde
SPECIAL POWERS/ABILITIES Expert occultist; (as Dark Angel) teleportation; can change size and shape; mind control; manipulation of time.

Baroness Paula Von Gunther was a ruthless Nazi occultist and a personal assistant to Adolf Hitler during World War II. Hoping to harness the power of Johnny Thunder's mystic Thunderbolt (see THUNDER II, JOHNNY) for her own evil ends, the Baroness summoned the ancient spirit Dark Angel, who took over her body. Channeling Dark Angel's mystic powers, Von Gunther attacked the JUSTICE SOCIETY OF AMERICA and trapped them in a magical cage. HIPPOLYTA, the Golden Age WONDER WOMAN, freed her heroic teammates, and Von Gunther was separated from the Dark Angel spirit. Dark Angel became a constant foe of Hippolyta and her daughter, TROIA, while Von Gunther renounced her ties to the Nazi party and relocated to Themyscira (see Amazing Bases, pp. 132–3). There, the Baroness became a prominent scientist, the inventor of the Purple Healing Ray. PJ

VYKIN

FIRST APPEARANCE FOREVER PEOPLE 1st series #1 (March 1971)
STATUS Hero **REAL NAME** None **OCCUPATION** Adventurer
BASE Earth **HEIGHT** 6ft 1in **WEIGHT** 201 lbs **EYES** Brown
HAIR Black **SPECIAL POWERS/ABILITIES** "Magno-Power" enables him to project magnetic energy; a natural tracker able to mentally trace atomic patterns; carries the Forever People's Mother Box computer.

Like his five human friends in the FOREVER PEOPLE, Vykin was plucked from Earth and transported through time and space to New Genesis. There the enigmatic Highfather imbued him with incredible powers. When BEAUTIFUL DREAMER of the Forever People was abducted by DARKSEID, sworn enemy of New Genesis, and taken to Earth, Vykin and the others returned to the planet of their birth to rescue her. Later, after battling Darkseid's agent, DEVILANCE the Pursuer, Vykin and the Forever People were marooned on the planet Adon. Vykin died using the Forever People's Mother Box, a living computer, to increase the intelligence of Adon's native populace. The remaining Forever People taught the Adonians culture and established the city of Forevertown. However, when SERIFAN was possessed by an evil entity called the Dark, Adon was regressed to its original primitive state. Although quickly raised from the dead, Vykin and his teammates perished again during the Death of the New Gods event. SB

WALLER, AMANDA

FIRST APPEARANCE LEGENDS #1 (November 1986)
STATUS Villain **REAL NAME** Amanda Blake Waller
OCCUPATION Leader of the Suicide Squad **BASE** Washington, D.C.
HEIGHT 5ft 1in **WEIGHT** 200 lbs **EYES** Brown **HAIR** Brown
SPECIAL POWERS/ABILITIES No combat training, but her steel will allows her to see straight through to the heart of a problem.

TOUGH NUT Waller has been through much, helping her to endure any threat.

Amanda Waller grew up in the Cabrini-Green section of Chicago and married her sweetheart, Joseph Waller, at the age of 18. They made a good life for themselves and their five children. Then tragedy struck: their son, Joe Jr., was gunned down by local thugs and, six months later, their daughter Damita was raped and killed by a drug-dealer known as Candyman. Joe went seeking revenge, only to die in a hail of bullets. Amanda fiercely protected her remaining three children, pushing them to finish their

BACK OFF! "The Wall" is not intimidated—not even by the most feared "cape." of them all!

education. She also went to college herself, majoring in psychology and political science. When all three children finished high school, she told them they had to fend for themselves.

While working for Illinois Congressman Marvin Collins, she found some old, dusty files about Task Force X and its two divisions, ARGENT and the SUICIDE SQUAD.

Waller conceived the idea of a revived Force, using meta-humans and costumed criminals alike, if necessary granting them pardons to persuade them to go on suicide missions. She managed to wrangle government approval and funding, and Task Force X was reborn.

After her time leading the Squad, Waller joined the leadership ranks of CHECKMATE, serving as Black King and assembling a new Suicide Squad in secret. She then transitioned to the position of White Queen, while running her own side projects including Operation: Salvation Run, in which the Suicide Squad rounded up hundreds of supervillains and exiled them to a remote prison planet. RG

WANDERERS, THE

FIRST APPEARANCE ADVENTURE COMICS #375 (December 1968)
STATUS Hero team **BASE** Mobile
CURRENT MEMBERS AND POWERS
Re-Animage (leader) Immortal.
Dartalon Carries a blowgun that fires special darts.
Elvar Master swordsman with an energy-charged blade.
Aviax Shapeshifter; can turn into any type of bird.
Psyche Empath capable of manipulating others' moods.
Quantum Queen Can change her body into light radiation.
Celebrand (not active) Skilled marksman; natural leader.

In one timeline containing the LEGION OF SUPER-HEROES, the Wanderers are a black-ops group led by Mekt Ranzz (see LIGHTNING LORD). In another, they are a colorful team of villains-turned-heroes who won fame after stealing the Seven Stones of Alactos.

Though their time on the dark side proved short-lived, the Wanderers appeared to have met their ultimate end when the mad wife of the Controller called Clonus murdered them. Clonus, however, grew clones of every Wanderer (except Celebrand) with memories of their past lives intact. A few of the clone Wanderers adopted new names: Immorto became Re-Animage, Dartalg became Dartalon, Elvo became Elvar, and Ornitho became Aviax.

Once the clone Wanderers solved the mystery of their own murders they became deputized agents of the U.P. They even created a clone of Celebrand, but vanished into deep space before the clone could mature. Although the Wanderers have not been seen for some time, they are presumably still active somewhere in the greater galaxy. DW

THE WANDERERS 1) *Aviax* **2)** *Dartalon* **3)** *Re-Animage* **4)** *Psyche* **5)** *Elvar* **6)** *Quantum Queen.*

WARLORD

FIRST APPEARANCE FIRST ISSUE SPECIAL #8 (November 1975)
STATUS Hero **REAL NAME** Travis Morgan
OCCUPATION Warlord **BASE** Skartaris
HEIGHT 6ft **WEIGHT** 188 lbs **EYES** Blue **HAIR** White
SPECIAL POWERS/ABILITIES An exceptional athlete and tactical thinker, a proven swordsman, horseback rider, and brawler.

OUT OF TIME
Travis found his place in the world…the lost world of Skartaris.

While on an a spy mission over the U.S.S.R. on June 16, 1969, U.S. Air Force pilot Travis Morgan was forced him to bail out near the North Pole. Parachuting down, he drifted through an inter-dimensional portal to the magical land of Skartaris, where time worked differently. Before long, he had rescued Tara, heir to the throne of Shamballah, from the evil wizard Deimos! Morgan and Tara became lovers, then husband and wife. Tara taught him sword-fighting skills and he became the freedom-fighter Warlord. He and Tara had a son, Joshua, who was kidnapped by Deimos, magically turned into an adult and seemingly killed. In fact, the child survived and, calling himself Tinder, befriended Morgan. Eventually, Warlord's daughter Jennifer (*see* MORGAN, JENNIFER) came searching for her long-lost father. In Skartaris, she discovered she possessed magical abilities and became the equal of Deimos, helping to keep the land free. **RG**

WARP

FIRST APPEARANCE THE NEW TEEN TITANS (1st series) #14 (December 1981) **STATUS** Villain **REAL NAME** Emil LaSalle
OCCUPATION Mercenary **BASE** Saint-Tropez, France
HEIGHT 5ft 8in **WEIGHT** 148 lbs **EYES** Brown **HAIR** Brown
SPECIAL POWERS/ABILITIES Ability to fly; can open warps, and teleport between two locations.

Driven by hatred, Frenchman Emil LaSalle is a dangerous enemy with the extraordinary ability to teleport himself anywhere in the world. For unknown reasons, he nursed a grudge against Madame Rouge, even joining the New Brotherhood of Evil to help them track down Rouge after she betrayed their organization. Following Rouge's death, Warp remained with his new comrades during the Brotherhood's reorganization into the Society of Sin.

Warp possesses the power to create wormholes between two points in space, through which he can transport himself or others. It is believed that he needs specific coordinates for both locations in order to open a wormhole, but Warp's powers are still undefined.

Warp participated in the Crisis (*see* Great Battles, pp. 362–3) and has battled the Teen Titans and Elongated Man. During the Infinite Crisis, Warp and DOCTOR PSYCHO retrieved DOOMSDAY from his inescapable prison at the center of the Earth. **DW**

WAVERIDER

FIRST APPEARANCE ARMAGEDDON 2001 #1 (May 1991)
STATUS Hero **REAL NAME** Matthew Ryder
OCCUPATION Scientist **BASE** Mobile
HEIGHT 6ft **WEIGHT** 185 lbs **EYES** Blue **HAIR** Blond
SPECIAL POWERS/ABILITIES Time travel; flight; project of quantum-powered force blasts; can access a person's aura and predict their most probable future.

Matthew Ryder was a scientist from a future Earth ruled by MONARCH, an armored despot who had eliminated all heroes. Ryder believed that one of Earth's erstwhile heroes had evolved into Monarch, and, using his scientific skills, Ryder created a time machine to journey into the past and change history. Ryder convinced Monarch to let him be a guinea pig in his own device, and Monarch agreed, believing Ryder, like several initial test subjects, would die in the process. Ryder survived, however, merging with the timestream and transforming into Waverider.

Traveling back to the past, he joined forces with Earth's heroes, including the JUSTICE LEAGUE OF

AMERICA, the TEEN TITANS, and CAPTAIN ATOM, to defeat Monarch, who was revealed to be Hank Hall, formerly the hero Hawk (*see* HAWK & DOVE). After joining the LINEAR MAN, Waverider met his end when murdered by BOOSTER GOLD's robot sidekick Skeets. **PJ**

WEAPONERS OF QWARD

FIRST APPEARANCE GREEN LANTERN (2nd series) #2 (October 1960)
STATUS Villains **BASE** Qward, the Anti-Matter Universe
NOTABLE AGENTS AND WEAPONS
Borbrydi, Chomin, Drik, Gnaxos (a robot), *Gyn-Gryngg, Gypo-Bax, Karo-Thynn, Kiman the Chief Weaponer, Kramen, Magot, Rengan the Abominable, Sinestro, Telle-Teg, Vestry the Thinker, Yokal the Atrocious.*
SPECIAL POWERS/ABILITIES Armed with "qwa-bolts"; yellow shields, render the power rings of the Green Lantern Corps ineffective.

In the anti-matter universe of Qward, wrong is quite literally right. The Qwardians worship evil and hate beings in the positive matter universe who believe in the ideal of goodness. Ten billion years ago, the Anti-Monitor was born on a lifeless moon of Qward. This creature—absolute evil incarnate—seized control of the anti-matter universe and created an army of Thunderers to battle his munificent reflection in the positive-matter universe, the MONITOR.

When a backlash of their equal-but-opposite assaults sent the Anti-Monitor and the Monitor into slumbering stasis for billions of years, a Qwardian named Yokal the Atrocious seized the opportunity to unite his people as the Weaponers of Qward. Declaring himself Chief Weaponer, Yokal initiated the ongoing Qwardian offensive to undermine the GUARDIANS OF THE UNIVERSE in the positive-matter universe and wage war with the Guardians' peacekeeping agents, the heroic GREEN LANTERN CORPS. During the Crisis on Infinite Earths, the Anti-Monitor (*see* MONITORS) transformed his Thunderers into shadow demons. Recently, SINESTRO has made Qward his headquarters and the staging area for the Sinestro Corps. The enslaved Weaponers are forced to manufacture yellow power rings. **SB**

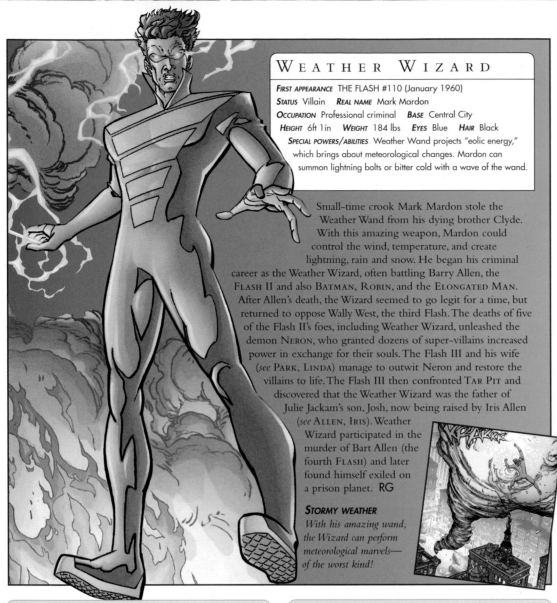

WEATHER WIZARD

FIRST APPEARANCE THE FLASH #110 (January 1960)
STATUS Villain **REAL NAME** Mark Mardon
OCCUPATION Professional criminal **BASE** Central City
HEIGHT 6ft 1in **WEIGHT** 184 lbs **EYES** Blue **HAIR** Black
SPECIAL POWERS/ABILITIES Weather Wand projects "eolic energy,"
which brings about meteorological changes. Mardon can
summon lightning bolts or bitter cold with a wave of the wand.

Small-time crook Mark Mardon stole the
Weather Wand from his dying brother Clyde.
With this amazing weapon, Mardon could
control the wind, temperature, and create
lightning, rain and snow. He began his criminal
career as the Weather Wizard, often battling Barry Allen, the
FLASH II and also BATMAN, ROBIN, and the ELONGATED MAN.
After Allen's death, the Wizard seemed to go legit for a time, but
returned to oppose Wally West, the third Flash. The deaths of five
of the Flash II's foes, including Weather Wizard, unleashed the
demon NERON, who granted dozens of super-villains increased
power in exchange for their souls. The Flash III and his wife
(see PARK, LINDA) manage to outwit Neron and restore the
villains to life. The Flash III then confronted TAR PIT and
discovered that the Weather Wizard was the father of
Julie Jackam's son, Josh, now being raised by Iris Allen
(see ALLEN, IRIS). Weather
Wizard participated in the
murder of Bart Allen (the
fourth FLASH) and later
found himself exiled on
a prison planet. **RG**

STORMY WEATHER
*With his amazing wand,
the Wizard can perform
meteorological marvels—
of the worst kind!*

WHITE MARTIANS

FIRST APPEARANCE JLA #1 (January 1997)
STATUS Villains **BASE** Z'onn Z'orr
MAIN MEMBERS AND POWERS (HYPERCLAN)
Protex A Martian superman.
Primaid Warrior woman.
Züm Superspeedster.
Zenturion Shield-carrying soldier.
Flexus Rocky powerhouse.
Armek Armored juggernaut.
Tronix Possessor of devastating gaze.
A-Mortal Fearsome wraith.

Possessing superstrength, telepathy, the power of
flight, and force-blasting "Martian Vision" like
their Green Martian kin, the White Martians are a
thousands-strong race of shape-shifters. They share
the Green Martians' weakness to fire, which renders
them virtually powerless. Eons ago, the bloodthirsty
White Martians had dominated Earth. However the
more peaceful Green Martians (of whom the JLA's
MARTIAN MANHUNTER J'onn J'onzz is the sole
survivor) banished them to the inter-dimensional
Still Zone for an environmental
catastrophe the White Martians
had wrought on Earth. Eons
later, the White Martians
escaped from exile. Eight of
their leaders arrived on Earth,
calling themselves the Hyperclan.
These handsome-seeming superbeings
proclaimed they had come to save the
world and quickly gained
mankind's trust with
a few good deeds.
Fortunately, the JLA saw
through the Hyperclan's
deception and thwarted the
White Martians' plans for
global invasion.

Despite having their
memories wiped, and
being shape-shifted
into harmless human
forms, the Hyperclan again
attempted to wreak havoc on Earth. The
'Burning Martian' Fernus nearly exterminated
the White Martians, but surviving members
include MISS MARTIAN and others who had been
brainwashed into believing they were Greens. **SB**

FLOWER OF WRATH *The Hyperclan subject the JLA
heroes to a ghastly White Martian torture device!*

WEIRD, THE

FIRST APPEARANCE THE WEIRD #1 (April 1988)
STATUS Hero **REAL NAME** None
OCCUPATION Dimensional guardian **BASE** Mobile
HEIGHT 6ft 5in **WEIGHT** 185 lbs **EYES** Brown **HAIR** Brown
SPECIAL POWERS/ABILITIES Could change molecular density of his body
or anything he was in contact with; flew by riding magnetic currents.

The Weird came from an alternate
dimension inhabited by the
energy-seething Zarolatts and the
brutish Macrolatts, who exploited
the Zarolatts as power sources.
When several Macrolatts decided
to attack Earth, the Weird rushed
to Earth to prevent it.

To contain his energy
form in this new world,
the Weird possessed
the body of a dead man
named Walter Langley.
Unfortunately, the Weird
was approaching critical
mass—when he exploded,
he would take out half the Earth.
After halting the invasion, the Weird
perished in a deep-space blast. He
reappeared when his soul mixed with that of CAPTAIN
COMET, and the Weird embarked on a spiritual journey
to understand his strange new state. **DW**

WHIP, THE

FIRST APPEARANCE FLASH COMICS #1 (January 1940)
STATUS Hero **REAL NAME** Rodney Elwood Gaynor
OCCUPATION Playboy **BASE** Seguro, New Mexico; New York City
HEIGHT 6ft 2in **WEIGHT** 210 lbs **EYES** Blue **HAIR** Blond
SPECIAL POWERS/ABILITIES Expert with a bullwhip, and a superb
horseback rider; well-developed social conscience, despite wealth.

In 1939, millionaire socialite Rod Gayner was traveling
through Seguro, New Mexico, when he learned of
the legendary Don Fernando Suarez, a 19th-century
hero known as El Castigo, "the Whip." Gayner
discovered many of Suarez's belongings and
decided to perpetuate the hero's legend. He
became an expert with a bullwhip and an
expert equestrian, riding his stallion
Diablo as the new Whip.

As the Whip, Gayner fought
crime in New Mexico, preventing
the exploitation of the poor
Mexican immigrants who lived
there. When the United States
entered World War II, however,
Gayner moved to New York City and
joined the ALL-STAR SQUADRON.

The newest Whip, Shelly
Gaynor, joined the SEVEN
SOLDIERS OF VICTORY, but died
in battle with the Sheeda. **PJ**

WHITE WITCH

FIRST APPEARANCE ADVENTURE COMICS #350 (November 1996)
STATUS Hero   **REAL NAME** Mysa
OCCUPATION Adventurer   **BASE** Earth
HEIGHT 5ft 8in   **WEIGHT** 118 lbs   **EYES** Red   **HAIR** White
SPECIAL POWERS/ABILITIES Can perform magic spells of defense or offense. Still learning, but has the potential to become one of the most powerful mages of her millennium.

Mysa, the White Witch, exists in many alternate timelines. In one, she is a member of the WANDERERS led by Mekt Ranzz (see LIGHTNING LORD). In another, she fought and entombed the all-powerful DARK LORD MORDRU. Few knew, until much later, that Mysa was Mordru's firstborn child. Transformed into a withered old crone by Mordru, Mysa is the lone survivor of the mystic heroes. On planet Tharn, Mysa used the Scepter of Sybolla to save the life of the pregnant Azra Saugin, unintentionally gifting the baby Zoe with telekinesis. Later, KINETIX of the LEGION OF SUPER-HEROES lost her powers, unaware that Mysa (using the Star of Akkos) was to blame for this. Mysa revealed her role and restored Kinetix's abilities just before Mordru escaped from his prison. In the ensuing battle, Mysa, the White Witch was returned to her youthful form by magic. She continues to perfect her abilities and works with Legionnaires on occasion. RG

WHITE, PERRY

FIRST APPEARANCE SUPERMAN (1st series) #7 (November 1940)
STATUS Hero   **REAL NAME** Perry Jerome White
OCCUPATION Managing editor of The Daily Planet   **BASE** Metropolis
HEIGHT 5ft 10in   **WEIGHT** 200 lbs
EYES Blue   **HAIR** Brown with white at temples
SPECIAL POWERS/ABILITIES Indomitable will and relentless thirst for truth.

In a city dominated by the Man of Steel, The Daily Planet's Perry White has become one of the most influential figures in Metropolis, due to the power of the press. His life is inseparable from the modern history of the Planet, having started there as a copy boy at the age of ten. White's rough childhood in Suicide Slum was brightened somewhat by his friendship with a boy named Lex Luthor (see LUTHOR, LEX).

Luthor made a fortune in his early twenties and purchased the Planet; Perry left the country on assignment as an overseas reporter. In that time, Luthor seduced White's girlfriend, Alice Spencer, who conceived a child. White married Spencer upon his return and she gave birth to his son (really Luthor's natural son), Jerry White. Meanwhile, financiers bought the newspaper back from Luthor on the condition that Perry White become managing editor.

White hired both Lois Lane (see LANE, LOIS) and Clark Kent (see SUPERMAN), and has weathered a number of tragedies that would have broken lesser men, including the death of his son and a bout with lung cancer. After a recent stint as a professor at Metropolis University, White returned to his first love, The Daily Planet. One of his toughest recent decisions was to demote Clark Kent to a lesser reporting job and hire Jack Ryder (see CREEPER, THE) as his replacement. DW

STOP THE PRESSES! Perry White is a newspaperman through and through, who remains a tireless advocate for the Daily Planet. It's often said that if you cut him open, you'd find printer's ink running through his veins!

WILDCAT I

FIRST APPEARANCE SENSATION COMICS #01 (January 1942)
STATUS Hero   **REAL NAME** Ted Grant
OCCUPATION Boxer   **BASE** New York City
HEIGHT 6ft 5in   **WEIGHT** 250 lbs   **EYES** Blue   **HAIR** Gray
SPECIAL POWERS/ABILITIES Master of hand-to-hand combat, especially boxing; slowed aging (like other JSA members).

Raised by a timid father, Ted Grant grew up to become a heavyweight boxing champion in the 1930s. After being framed for murder in the boxing ring by *mafioso* Victor Moretti, Ted became a fugitive from justice. Inspired by the Alan Scott, the first GREEN LANTERN, Ted donned a black costume and became Wildcat. Wildcat used his new uniform and his skills to pound out a confession from Moretti and clear his name. As Wildcat, Grant began patrolling the streets of New York City and ridding them of mob-related crime. He joined the JUSTICE SOCIETY of AMERICA during World War II and had a love affair with HIPPOLYTA, the Golden Age Wonder Woman. In 1947, Grant's son Jake was kidnapped by the Golden Wasp and Wildcat temporarily retired from crimefighting. He opened his own gym, and trained some of the world's greatest fighters, including BATMAN, BLACK CANARY II, and CATWOMAN. Wildcat is a current member of the Justice Society, and recently used up all of his protective 'nine lives.' Another of his sons, Tommy Bronson, has the power to transform into humanoid wildcat and joined the JSA under his father's code name. PJ

SPARRING PARTNER Ted Grant teaches Holly Robinson, Catwoman's close friend, a thing or two about the "noble art."

WILDCAT II

FIRST APPEARANCE (Yolanda Montez) INFINITY INC. #12 (Mar.1985); (Wildcat II) CRISIS ON INFINITE EARTHS #6 (Sept. 1985)
STATUS Hero (deceased)   **REAL NAME** Yolanda Montez
OCCUPATION Journalist for Rock Stars magazine   **BASE** Los Angeles
HEIGHT 5ft 8in   **WEIGHT** 143 lbs   **EYES** Brown   **HAIR** Reddish brown
SPECIAL POWERS/ABILITIES A ferocious fighter with cat-like reflexes and retractable claws, enhanced speed, and superhuman agility.

The original Wildcat (see WILDCAT I), Yolanda Montez's godfather, suffered crippling injuries during the Crisis. Yolanda decided to honor her godfather by using her cat-like abilities to carry on in the battling boxer's stead. As Wildcat II, Yolanda joined INFINITY INC. and learned there that her powers resulted from experiments conducted by Dr. Benjamin Love upon pregnant mothers, including Yolanda's own (see HELIX). Wildcat II remained semi-active after the Infinitors disbanded, and later joined a squad of super heroes fighting to liberate Parador, from ECLIPSO. Sadly, she was killed by the villain. SB

WILD DOG

FIRST APPEARANCE WILD DOG #1 (September 1987)
STATUS Hero **REAL NAME** Jack Wheeler
OCCUPATION Ex-soldier; mechanic; vigilante **BASE** Quad Cities, Iowa
HEIGHT 6ft **WEIGHT** 175 lbs **EYES** Blue **HAIR** Blond
SPECIAL POWERS/ABILITIES An exceptional soldier, excellent with firearms.
As Wild Dog, his gloves emit an electric shock, similar to a taser.

Star athlete Jack Wheeler went to college on a football scholarship. After an injury forced him off the team, he dropped out, unable to afford tuition. He opted instead for a tour of duty with the U.S. Marines, which ended in tragedy when most of his comrades were killed by a terrorist bomb. Disheartened, Wheeler left the army and returned to Quad Cities, Iowa taking night classes at State University. He also fell in love with Claire Smith—only to see her struck down by a gunman. The police investigation revealed that her last name was really Carmonti and that she was the daughter of a recently killed Chicago mob boss. She was not a random victim, but a target. Something inside Wheeler snapped. Donning a hockey mask, khakis, and a State U. T-shirt, he became the crime fighter Wild Dog. He was soon a local hero, even though wanted by the police for his ruthless vigilantism. Wheeler spends his days as an auto mechanic and his nights as a protector of the innocent. RG

WILDEBEEST

FIRST APPEARANCE (Wildebeest Society) THE NEW TEEN TITANS (2nd series) #36 (October 1987); (Baby Wildebeest) NEW TITANS #84 (February 1982) **STATUS** Hero **REAL NAME** None **OCCUPATION** Hero (deceased) **BASE** Science City, Russia **HEIGHT** Up to 12ft **WEIGHT** Up to 635 lbs **EYES** Yellow **HAIR** Auburn **SPECIAL POWERS/ABILITIES** Can transform into a giant, superstrong powerhouse; has the mind of an infant and the temper to match.

The Wildebeest Society started as a criminal organization designed to make obscene amounts of money by posing as a single super-criminal called "Wildebeest," whose random appearances and varying styles of operation baffled investigators.

JERICHO, mute member of the TEEN TITANS, became the leader of the Wildebeest Society when a demonic force held him in its thrall. He turned the society's resources toward the creation of human/animal hybrid bodies to serve as new hosts for the evil energy. When the new Wildebeest kidnapped the Titans, DEATHSTROKE the Terminator had no choice but to kill Jericho, his own son.

One Wildebeest survived the destruction of the Society. Nicknamed Baby Wildebeest, this genetically engineered behemoth lives with RED STAR and PANTHA, its surrogate parents, in Russia. DW

WILDFIRE

FIRST APPEARANCE SUPERBOY AND THE LEGION OF SUPER-HEROES #195 (June 1973) **STATUS** Hero **REAL NAME** (Atom'x) Drake Burroughs; (Blast-Off) Randall Burroughs; (Wildfire amalgam) Drake Burroughs **OCCUPATION** Legionnaire **BASE** Legion HQ, U.P. Space **HEIGHT** 6ft 2in **WEIGHT** Variable **EYES** None **HAIR** None
SPECIAL POWERS/ABILITIES Projects blasts of energy and absorbs energy; can fly at superspeed.

After the evil Mordru, the DARK LORD destroyed the bodies of the energy-powered heroes Atom'x and Blast-Off, the souls of the young heroes were contained in a special containment suit created by Professor Vultan. Dubbed "Drake Burroughs," the energy creature quickly became an ally of the LEGION OF SUPER-HEROES under the codename Erg-1. As Erg-1, Burroughs helped the Legionnaires battle the parasitic BLIGHT as they took over the universe of the 31st century. Soon after, Erg–1 was transported across the galaxy through a tear in the fabric of space and his containment suit was destroyed. Erg-1 then found the Kwai, a nomadic race of space trackers, who led his disembodied energies back to the Legion. Reincorporated in one of Professor Vultan's special suits, Burroughs took the name Wildfire and rejoined the Legion as one of its most powerful members. PJ

WINDFALL

FIRST APPEARANCE BATMAN AND THE OUTSIDERS #9 (April 1985)
STATUS Hero **REAL NAME** Wendy Jones
OCCUPATION Adventurer **BASE** Los Angeles
HEIGHT 5ft **WEIGHT** 105 lbs **EYES** Blue **HAIR** Blonde
SPECIAL POWERS/ABILITIES Can generate and control winds, from gentle breezes to gale force, tornado-level windstorms.

Windfall's origin is unknown. Sister to water-wielding villainess Becky Jones, (New-Wave), Wendy Jones fought for justice with the OUTSIDERS, befriending HALO. Windfall was captured and cloned by New-Wave, her diabolical double infiltrating the Outsiders. The Windfall clone was discovered by BATMAN and died in battle. The real Windfall went back to the Outsiders, but left when Violet, Halo's evil double, convinced her to join Strikeforce KOBRA. Realizing her mistake, Windfall rejoined the Outsiders until it disbanded. She was romantically linked to teammate Gardner Grayle, (the Atomic Knight). Windfall was last seen defending the rogue nation of Zandia from YOUNG JUSTICE, perhaps duped into siding with the wrong team yet again. SB

WING

FIRST APPEARANCE DETECTIVE COMICS #20 (November 1938)
STATUS Hero (deceased) **REAL NAME** Wing How
OCCUPATION Adventurer **BASE** England
HEIGHT 5ft 6in **WEIGHT** 140 lbs **EYES** Brown **HAIR** Black
SPECIAL POWERS/ABILITIES Possesses a bright mind and a deep knowledge of Chinese martial arts.

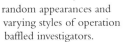

A Chinese immigrant named Wing How, came to the U.S. and learned to drive, ultimately becoming the trusted chauffeur of newspaper publisher Lee Travis. In 1938, when Travis chose the crime-fighting costume of the CRIMSON AVENGER I, Wing stayed in his driver's uniform, but came to his employer's aide when needed. A deep friendship formed between the two men, as they shared a common sense of justice. Wing subsequently adopted a distinctive costume to disguise his identity. When World War II broke out, they joined the ALL-STAR SQUADRON. Wing also became the unofficial eighth member of the SEVEN SOLDIERS OF VICTORY. When the SSV was betrayed by one of their own members, the Spider, and attacked by the NEBULA MAN, Wing sacrificed his life to destroy the entity. His sacrifice has been remembered by heroes from the Golden Age and Modern Age, inspiring all who followed in his path. RG

WITCHFIRE

FIRST APPEARANCE JLA #61 (February 2002)
STATUS Hero **REAL NAME** Rebecca Carstairs
OCCUPATION Super hero **BASE** San Francisco
HEIGHT 5ft 8in **WEIGHT** 128 lbs **EYES** White **HAIR** Red
SPECIAL POWERS/ABILITIES Skilled daredevil who possesses spell-based occult powers.

Witchfire remembers a childhood spent in an orphanage, where a book of spells exposed young Rebecca Carstairs to the wickedly fun world of magic. As an adult she assumed the stage name Witchfire and set out to conquer the entertainment world, winning fame as a singer, actress, model, and motorcycle daredevil.

At a concert in Boston, Witchfire cast a careless spell and unwittingly released a demon. WONDER WOMAN helped her capture the beast, and Witchfire committed herself to refining her supernatural abilities. She eventually joined the San Francisco-based super-hero firm The POWER COMPANY as a partner, though some members (notably SKYROCKET) considered her little more than a publicity seeker.

After her first year with the Power Company, Witchfire discovered a disturbing truth—she was a homunculus, a magically-created artificial being and not the true Rebecca Carstairs. How she will deal with this revelation remains to be seen. She hopes to win new clients for the Power Company. DW

THE DC COMICS ENCYCLOPEDIA

WIZARD

FIRST APPEARANCE ALL-STAR COMICS #34 (April 1947)
STATUS Villain **REAL NAME** William Asmodeus Zard
OCCUPATION Professional criminal **BASE** Mobile
HEIGHT 6ft **WEIGHT** 182 lbs **EYES** Blue **HAIR** Black
SPECIAL POWERS/ABILITIES A sorcerer who can cast illusions, hypnotize others, and project his psyche on the astral plane.

A career criminal from a young age, William Zard was in and out of prison during the 1930s. Deciding to refashion his criminal career, he left the U. S. and traveled to a Tibetan monastery. There he studied with a Master Lama and learned hypnotism and astral projection. He then used his newfound skills to kill the monk who had been training him!

Zard then became the Wizard, returning to the U.S. at the end of World War II. He assembled the INJUSTICE SOCIETY, a villainous counterpart to the JUSTICE SOCIETY OF AMERICA, whose heroes he was determined to defeat and discredit.

The Wizard has continued to clash with the JSA. He gained greater powers recuperating in a magical fairyland, but was then absorbed into RAGMAN's cloak. However he freed himself to attack the JSA again. **PJ**

WORD II, THE

FIRST APPEARANCE DCU VILLAINS SECRET FILES #1 (April 1999)
STATUS Villain **REAL NAME** Unknown
OCCUPATION Assassin **BASE** Mobile
HEIGHT 5ft 9in **WEIGHT** 175 lbs **EYES** Unknown **HAIR** Black
SPECIAL POWERS/ABILITIES The Word II may be a mutant with the ability to assimilate any written word onto his body.

The first Word is a cosmic entity created at the dawn of the universe by the Voice. In recent times, the Word destroyed the Parliament of Trees and Lady Jane, an elemental, as well as the Parliaments of Stones, Waves and Vapors—elemental nature spirits—in an attempt to stop SWAMP THING from becoming all-powerful. The Word was eventually defeated by Swamp Thing and his daughter, Tefé.

The Word II (pictured left) is a mortal costumed criminal. What this man truly is or does, however, remains a mystery. He seems to have no mouth and uses the written word to communicate. A mercenary for hire, his specialty is gathering intelligence, and he has been employed by the likes of VANDAL SAVAGE. **RG**

WONDER GIRL

FIRST APPEARANCE WONDER WOMAN (2nd series) #105 (February 1996)
STATUS Hero **REAL NAME** Cassandra "Cassie" Sandsmark
OCCUPATION Member of Teen Titans **BASE** San Francisco
HEIGHT 5 ft 3in **WEIGHT** 124 lbs **EYES** Blue **HAIR** Blonde
SPECIAL POWERS/ABILITIES Flight, superstrength, and enhanced speed bestowed upon her by Zeus; carries magical lasso; some invulnerability; trained in combat by the Amazons. Wonder Girl is still young and her powers may deepen with time.

YOUNG JUSTICE *Cassie is happiest around heroes her own age, and currently serves with the Teen Titans.*

Prominent archaeologist Helena Sandsmark always reprimanded her daughter for her lack of responsibility, but Cassie seized the mantle of a hero when WONDER WOMAN came to her hometown of Gateway City. Temporarily "borrowing" Wonder Woman's Sandals of Hermes and Gauntlet of Atlas, Cassie received prodigious strength and the ability to fly—superpowers she used to help smash a clone of DOOMSDAY. She later helped Wonder Woman defeat a manifestation of entropy called Decay, donning goggles and a black wig to disguise herself in her new role as the second Wonder Girl, bearing a name once used by Donna Troy (see TROY, DONNA).

Summoned to Olympus, Cassie brashly asked Zeus for her own powers. He granted her wish and Wonder Girl became Gateway City's teen hero. She honed her fighting skills through training sessions with ARTEMIS.

Cassie joined the heroes of YOUNG JUSTICE, and later signed on with the new TEEN TITANS. There, she acquired a golden lasso given to her by Ares and started a romance with her teammate SUPERBOY (Conner Kent). She also learned that Zeus was her true father, a secret her mother had tried to keep hidden.

Conner's death during the Infinite Crisis devastated Cassie, and she briefly joined a cult dedicated to Superboy's resurrection. The Amazonian invasion of Washington D.C. saw Wonder Girl and SUPERGIRL attacking Air Force One to force an audience with the U.S. President. Recently, Wonder Girl has teamed with Hercules to fight the FEMALE FURIES. **DW**

GIRL POWER *Cassie has a warrior's spirit and can even stand up to Wonder Woman in battle.*

WONDER WOMAN

THE AMAZING AMAZON

FIRST APPEARANCE ALL-STAR COMICS #8 (Winter 1941)
STATUS Hero **REAL NAME** Diana
OCCUPATION Ambassador of peace; adventurer
BASE New York City; Themyscira
HEIGHT 6ft **WEIGHT** 165 lbs **EYES** Blue **HAIR** Black
SPECIAL POWERS/ABILITIES Blessed with the gifts of the Olympian Gods, Wonder Woman is one of the strongest beings on the planet; she can fly at sublight speed; while not invulnerable, she is highly resistant to bodily harm; she can psychically communicate with animals; she is an expert at all forms of classical armed and unarmed combat; a master of the sword, ax, and bow and arrow; a skilled tactician and diplomat; her arsenal includes a magic lasso that forces anyone within its confines to tell the absolute truth; her bracelets can deflect bullets.

WISE AS ATHENA, stronger than Heracles, swift as Hermes and beautiful as Aphrodite, Wonder Woman is Princess Diana, champion of Themyscira, the home of the immortal AMAZONS. Sculpted from clay by her mother, Queen HIPPOLYTA, and brought to life by the OLYMPIAN GODS, Diana secretly entered a contest to find the worthiest Amazon and emerged as the victor. Given the task of ending the war god Ares's made scheme to destroy the planet, Diana stepped forth from her idyllic existence into the chaotic world of Man as one of Earth's greatest defenders, Wonder Woman, the Amazing Amazon!

REBIRTH *The Amazon warrior emerges from seclusion on Paradise Island to thwart Nazi tyranny.*

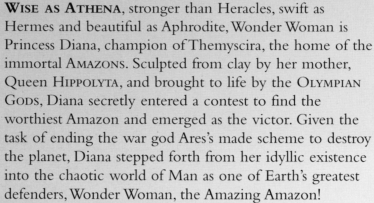

SCULPTED FROM CLAY

The reincarnated soul of a woman who had died 30,000 years ago, Hippolyta longed for the child she had carried centuries before. An oracle told her to sculpt a baby from clay; the gods themselves then gave the child life. The only child ever born on Themyscira, the infant was named Diana, after aviator Diana Trevor, who once crashed on Themyscira and died a hero defending the island. Princess Diana was raised by a nation of 3,000 teachers and sisters, always under the watchful eye of her overprotective mother.

THE AMAZONS AND THEIR ISLAND

Created 3,000 years ago by five goddesses of Olympus, the Amazons are a race of warrior women charged with the responsibility of promoting the peaceful ways of Gaea, the earth spirit. After Heracles and his men ransacked the Amazons' home of Themyscira, the Amazons, by decree of the goddesses, were led to a remote island paradise, where they were granted immortality and the task of guarding Doom's Doorway, the portal to Pandora's Box, behind which a host of monsters were imprisoned.

Rebuilding their great city-state of Themyscira, the Amazons lived in idyllic solitude for millennia, until a pilot from beyond their shores named Diana Trevor arrived on Paradise Island, changing their fate forever.

DIANA TREVOR *A pilot for the Women's Auxiliary Ferrying Squadron, Diana Rockwell Trevor pierced the mystic barrier between our world and Themyscira. Crash-landing on the island, the startled pilot used her weapons to force Cottus, a creature that had escaped from Doom's Doorway, back to the underworld. Diana gave her life to save the Amazon nation.*

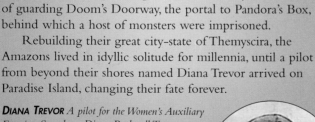

THE CONTEST

The goddesses ordered the Amazons to send for their greatest warrior to thwart ARES's mad schemes. Forbidden by Hippolyta to enter the Contest, Diana disguised herself and became Themyscira's champion. Garbed in a uniform decorated with symbols honoring Diana Trevor, Diana was rewarded with a magic lasso and silver bracelets. Soon after, Steve Trevor, Diana Trevor's son and an unwitting pawn of Ares, crash-landed on Themyscira. Diana was charged with taking him back to Patriarch's World, the mortal world of humankind, as part of her sacred mission.

THE MADNESS OF ARES

After battling Ares' monstrous sons upon her arrival in Patriarch's World, Diana, Steve, and several allies were mystically transported to a commandeered military base in Colorado where Wonder Woman stopped Ares from launching his nuclear arsenal and ended his insane threat. Diana then embarked on a worldwide tour promoting peace and Amazon ideals. Living with Julia and Vanessa Kapatelis in their Boston brownstone, Wonder Woman garnered a formidable Rogues Gallery which included the CHEETAH, SILVER SWAN, DOCTOR PSYCHO, and the sorceress CIRCE, who most resented Diana's pleas for peace and harmony.

THE DEATH OF DIANA

Forseeing the death of her daughter in a mystic vision, Hippolyta called for a new contest, and used the sorceress Magala to manipulate its outcome. Diana was forced to forsake her mantle and title and a rival Amazon, ARTEMIS, became the new Wonder Woman. But after Artemis's death at the hands of the White Magician, Diana reclaimed her role as Wonder Woman. Tragically, the spell that Magala cast on Diana was still in place when the devilish NERON attacked, and the hellspawn killed the Amazon princess with a blast of demonfire.

THE REBIRTH OF DIANA

Diana was resurrected on Olympus as the Goddess of Truth. Meanwhile, the Amazons tried Hippolyta for her trickery and decreed that, as penance, she would have to take up her daughter's mantle and mission as Wonder Woman.

So Hippolyta journeyed back in time to World War II and joined the JUSTICE SOCIETY OF AMERICA for a time. After Hippolyta's return to the present, Diana returned to the mortal plane, and once again became Wonder Woman.

KEY STORYLINES

• *WONDER WOMAN (2ND SERIES) #1-6 (FEB.–JULY 1987):* Introducing Wonder Woman's modern history and mission as an ambassador of peace.

• *WONDER WOMAN: THE CONTEST (TPB, 1995):* After Hippolyta manipulates a new challenge, Artemis becomes the new Wonder Woman!

• *WONDER WOMAN (2ND SERIES) #196-200 (NOV. 2003–MAR. 2004):* Diana publishes her book as the Silver Swan attacks.

OUR WORLDS AT WAR

Soon after, Diana and Hippolyta abolished the monarchy of Themyscira to end a deadly civil war that had consumed Paradise Island. Then, during the Imperiex War (*see* Great Battles, pp. 362–3), Diana was severely injured by alien probes, and Hippolyta sacrificed herself to save the universe. Diana then led a united Amazon nation against the forces of IMPERIEX and BRAINIAC 13, but not before Themyscira was destroyed. With the blessings of the gods and the spirit of her mother Hippolyta, Diana and the Amazons created a new, even more miraculous Themyscira (*see* Amazing Bases, pp.132–3) to be their home.

PRINCESS, AMBASSADOR, AND AUTHOR

Forsaking her royal title after the dissolution of the Themysciran monarchy, Wonder Woman proudly wears the robes of Amazon ambassador, not only to the United Nations but to societies across the universe. After several years living, working and fighting for peace beyond the shores of Paradise Island, Diana wrote a controversial book recording her observations, thereby adding authorship to her long list of credits. Born a princess on an island of immortal women created by the gods themselves, Wonder Woman has become one of Earth's finest warriors and a legend across half the galaxy. To many her nature is paradoxical, but to Diana, her mission is clear: to promote the ways of peace, love, and equality while staunchly defending the innocent from the forces of evil as a premiere member of Earth's greatest heroes, the JUSTICE LEAGUE OF AMERICA. **PJ**

WORLD TOUR
Diana promotes her book, Reflections.

GODLY TRICKERY
Ares, now the God of Conflict, has assumed a handsome, cunning guise, confounding the Amazing Amazon.

XERO

FIRST APPEARANCE XERO #1 (May 1997)
STATUS Hero   **REAL NAME** Coltrane "Trane" Walker
OCCUPATION Closer; professional basketball player   **BASE** National City
HEIGHT 6ft 7in   **WEIGHT** 218 lbs   **EYES** Brown (blue as Xer0)
HAIR Black (blonde as Xer0)
SPECIAL POWERS/ABILITIES Can speed up any object's molecular structure to walk on water or through walls; Deadeye laser; Deadlok adhesive.

African-American athlete Trane Walker was famous as the power forward for the National City Vipers. He was also Coltrane Walker, a clandestine government agency assassin who preserved his secret identity by disguising himself as a blonde-haired and blue-eyed Caucasian covert operative. Walker died on his very first mission, but was resurrected via an experimental X-enzyme that restored him to physical health, but also left him emotionally empty. Thus, he became both the perfect killer and the perfect basketball player, blunt and remorseless in getting either job done, but especially as the "closer" Xer0. Unfortunately, Walker perished again during a test set up by his superior, Frank Decker, to measure Xer0's abilities. Walker's second resurrection left him brain damaged. Whether or not Walker was left to die in peace, or if his agency will seek some way to return him to his role as Xer0, remains to be seen. **SB**

XS

FIRST APPEARANCE LEGIONNAIRES #0 (October 1994)
STATUS Hero   **REAL NAME** Jenni Ognats
OCCUPATION Legionnaire   **BASE** Earth
HEIGHT 5ft 6in   **WEIGHT** 135 lbs   **EYES** Amber   **HAIR** Brown
SPECIAL POWERS/ABILITIES Can run at supersonic speed while projecting a protective aura around her body.

Dawn Allen, daughter of the FLASH II (Barry Allen), and Jeven Ognats married and had a child, Jenni, on the planet Aarok. As a teenager, Jenni found that she could tap into the Speed Force (see FLASH). When she had fully mastered her hereditary speed powers, Jenni was invited to join the Legion of Super-Heroes at the dawn of the 31st century. On a mission back in time, at the end of the 20th century, Jenni first encountered SUPERBOY and her cousin Bart, then known as Impulse (see KID FLASH). For a time, she was trapped in the 20th century and worked alongside her ancestors as they battled the villainous SAVITAR.

Jenni was then thrust into the 100th Century for a while, before being shunted to the end of time known as Vanishing Point. Thanks to the intervention of the Time Trapper, who lives there, Jenni finally managed to return to her proper time period. **RG**

EMPOWERED *Like all Legionnaires, Xs is able to fly at great speed, thanks to her Legion Flight Ring.*

YOUNG ALL-STARS

FIRST APPEARANCE Young All-Stars #1 (June 1987)
STATUS Hero team (disbanded)   **BASE** The Perisphere, New York City
MEMBERS AND POWERS
Dyna-Mite Can generate explosive blasts.
Flying Fox Shaman that can generate forcebolts, and cast spells; flight with fur cape and cowl.
Fury Superstrength; can summon the spirit of the Fury Tisiphone.
Iron Munro Superstrength, invulnerability.
Neptune Perkins Amphibious; can swim at superspeed.
Tsunami Can generate tidal waves.

Young All-Stars also thwarted a gang of Nazi occultists, who had invaded an alien colony in Antarctica hoping to steal its secrets, and stopped the robotic MEKANIQUE's plot to take over the future. The team's most frequent enemies, however were the wartime version of Axis Amerika. Fighting alongside the Allies or by themselves, the Young All-Stars battled Axis Amerika, led by UBERMENSCH, no less than three times within weeks of their inception.

When team member Iron Munro set out to find his missing father, Hugo Danner, he learned that Danner had used a special serum to create the Sons of the Dawn, a group of mutated human experiments. After Munro defeated Danner and the Sons in June of 1942, LIBERTY BELLE put an end to the probationary mascot status of the Young All-Stars and made them full-fledged members of the All-Star Squadron. **PJ**

The Young-All Stars were a briefly-lived teen-age division of the ALL-STAR SQUADRON, the U.S.'s greatest assemblage of World War II heroes. The Young All-Stars were created by President F. D. Roosevelt in April, 1942, after the young heroes helped the All-Star Squadron defeat the Nazi superteam AXIS AMERIKA.

Initially assigned to fund-raising events and morale boosters like celebrity baseball games, the Young All-Stars began their crime-fighting careers battling villains such as the despotic Per Degaton, Deathbolt, and the ULTRA-HUMANITE when the villains infiltrated the government's mysterious Project M organization. The

WAR-TIME TEENS *The Young All-Stars did more than sell war bonds; they fought Nazi supercriminals and stopped the robot Mekanique from destroying the future by changing the past!*

TREND SETTERS *The first superpowered teen team, the Young All-Stars eventually became fully-fledged Squadron members. They were:* **1)** *Dan the Dyna-Mite* **2)** *Fury I* **3)** *Iron Munro* **4)** *Tsunami* **5)** *Neptune Perkins* **6)** *Flying Fox* **7)** *Tigress.*

YOUNG HEROES IN LOVE

FIRST APPEARANCE YOUNG HEROES IN LOVE #1 (June 1997)
STATUS Heroes (sexually active)   **BASE** A very cool warehouse loft
MEMBERS AND POWERS
Bonfire (Annie Fletcher) Pyrokinetic with control over fire;
Frostbite (real name unrevealed) Generates extreme cold;
Hard Drive (Jeremy Horton) Possesses telepathy and telekinesis;
Junior (Benjamin Newton) Brilliant scientist only four inches
tall; **Monstergirl (Rita Lopez)** Transforms into a monster; **Off-
Ramp (George Sloan)** Teleporter **Thunderhead (Scott Tucker)**
Superstrength; limited invulnerability; **Zip Kid (Stacey Taglia)** Flies;
shrinks; fires pink energy bolts.

THE YOUNG HEROES IN LOVE *Raging hormones and wistful
longings are just par for the course for this super-team:*
1) *Hard Drive* **2)** *Thunderhead* **3)** *Zip Kid* **4)** *Off-Ramp*
5) *Monstergirl* **6)** *Frostbite* **7)** *Junior.*

The Young Heroes are just that, young and relatively
inexperienced super heroes brought together by the
telepathic Jeremy Horton (Hard-Drive) and his lover
Rita Lopez (Monstergirl) to form their own titanic team.
However, most of the Young Heroes did not know until
much later that Hard Drive had secretly used his powers
to coerce each member into joining to achieve his own
self-aggrandizing ends. He was summarily booted out by
his teammates when they learned the truth.

When not struggling with internal strife from several
intersecting love triangles, the Young Heroes distinguished
themselves in battle with such monsters as Totenjager the
Relentless, the Beast Grundomu, and KALIBAK the Cruel.
When last seen, the Young Heroes were attending the
inaugural ball of Jeremy Horton, who had used his powers
to influence and win the Connecticut gubernatorial
election. The Young Heroes are presumably still active,
though it is just as likely that those thorny romantic
entanglements may have finally torn the team asunder. **SB**

YOUNG JUSTICE

FIRST APPEARANCE YOUNG JUSTICE: THE SECRET (April 1998)
STATUS Hero team   **BASE** The Secret Sanctuary
ORIGINAL MEMBERS AND POWERS
Superboy Superstrength, flight, tactile telekinesis
Robin III (Tim Drake) Athlete, Boy Wonder
Impulse Superspeedster.
Empress Amazing athlete.
Wonder Girl Flight, superstrength, bravado
The Secret Ephemeral wraith.

SUPERBOY, ROBIN III and IMPULSE helped rescue
a mysterious girl called the SECRET from custody
by the U.S. government-backed D.E.O. The teens
united as Young Justice and begin operating
out of the JUSTICE LEAGUE OF AMERICA's
abandoned Secret Sanctuary. The boys
were soon joined by ARROWETTE,
WONDER GIRL and the Secret. The
team was given the stamp of approval
by the JLA, and RED TORNADO became
Young Justice's mentor.

KLARION THE WITCH BOY cast a spell
that transformed the adult heroes into children
while having the reverse effect on the members
of Young Justice. The process was ultimately
reversed for all but LOBO, who took on the
name Slo-Bo. Young Justice journeyed to
Australia where they fought a team of villains
representing the rogue state
Zandia. The mysterious EMPRESS
joined the team after Young
Justice learned that she was
Anita, daughter of government
ally Donald Fite. After a devastating
mission to Apokolips, Snapper Carr
(*see* CARR, SNAPPER) came aboard as a senior
member, succeeding Red Tornado as team mentor.
The RAY II also joined Young Justice at that time.

After Baron Agua Sin Gaaz murdered Empress' father,
Young Justice led a squad of heroes in an all-out war
on his Zandian fortress. Corrupted by DARKSEID,
the Secret then went on a rampage until
Robin managed to break through to her.
Darkseid punished the young warder by
restoring her humanity. He also banished Slo-
Bo to the 853rd Century, condemning him
to an eternity as a statue. A mysterious blue
cyborg-girl named INDIGO did serious damage
to the Titans and Young Justice and unleashed
a defective Superman Robot which killed Teen
Titan Lilith and TROIA. In a state of shock,
both teams disbanded. **RG**

TRAGIC CONCLUSION *In their final
mission, the team was devastated
when they were manhandled by
Indigo and a Superman robot and
were unable to save Troia's life.*

YOUNG WARRIORS
*Regardless of
threat, Young
Justice enters
every fray with
gusto and more
than a little
recklessness.*

YOUNG JUSTICE
1) *Superboy* **2)** *Secret*
3) *Robin III* **4)** *Wonder Girl II*
5) *Empress* **6)** *Impulse.*

RAEPPA YLLAGICAM SDRIB! Whether conjuring or teleporting, Zatanna says all of her spells backwards!

MAGIC MAN Occultist John Constantine—Zatanna's lover in college—often knocks on the sorceress's door when he needs a magical hand, or a bird, or a plane ticket…

ZATANNA

FIRST APPEARANCE HAWKMAN (1st series) #4 (November 1964)
STATUS Hero **REAL NAME** Zatanna Zatara
OCCUPATION Stage magician; adventurer
BASE San Francisco
HEIGHT 5ft 7in **WEIGHT** 137 lbs **EYES** Blue **HAIR** Black
SPECIAL POWERS/ABILITIES Genetically imbued with the ability to manipulate magic; sorcery includes elemental manipulation, transmutation, and teleportation; she says her spells backwards as an aid to concentration.

Zatanna is the daughter of Golden Age adventurer John Zatara and his wife Sindella, a member of the mystic tribe of sorcerers called the Hidden Ones, or Homo magi. Zatanna inherited her mother's ability to manipulate magic and her father's penchant for heroism. When Sindella faked her own death and returned to the Hidden Ones' sanctum in Turkey, she left her daughter to John Zatara's care.

Zatara traveled the world with his daughter and taught her how to harness her magical abilities. Zatanna was later raised by strangers, however, when a curse by the evil witch Allura prevented Zatanna from seeing her father, leaving the young girl in a constant, fruitless search for her natural parents.

Zatanna discovered her father's diary and created a stage persona for herself. The young magician's quest to find her father led her into a brief affair with the occultist John Constantine (*see* Great Team-Ups, pp. 262–263). Later, with the help of the Justice League of America, Zatanna was able to lift Allura's curse and reunite with her father and, soon after, her mother. Tragically, Sindella died rescuing her daughter from the city of Homo Magi.

As a long-standing member of the JLA, Zatanna fought countless super-villains and mystical threats. However, after the death of her father, Zatanna retired from active adventuring. She now lives in San Francisco, seeking some semblance of a normal life, while acting as a constant peacemaker between the light and dark forces of Earth's mystic community. **PJ**

ZATARA

FIRST APPEARANCE ACTION COMICS #1 (June 1938)
STATUS Hero **REAL NAME** Giovanni "John" Zatara
OCCUPATION Stage magician; adventurer **BASE** Washington, D.C.
HEIGHT 5ft 11in **WEIGHT** 170 lbs **EYES** Blue **HAIR** Gray
SPECIAL POWERS/ABILITIES Limitless magic enabled by speaking his spells backward; merely an average fighter, who preferred sleight-of-hand over hand-to-hand combat.

John Zatara was a stage magician at age nineteen. However, when he read the lost journals of Leonardo da Vinci, his reputed ancestor, he discovered the true secrets of sorcery. By uttering his spells backwards, he could perform *real* magic! As his fame grew, Zatara also became a crime fighter, serving with the ALL-STAR SQUADRON during World War II.

While traveling in Turkey, Zatara met and married the enigmatic Sindella. Sindella gave birth to Zatara's daughter, Zatanna, and seemingly died not long after. While raising Zatanna alone, Zatara battled Allura, an evil elemental who cursed father and daughter with a spell prohibiting either from seeing the other lest both be struck dead. It took Zatara years to lift the curse and be reunited with his daughter.

Zatara retired from the stage and super heroics, but answered the call to action when a primordial shadow creature from Earth's prehistory threatened to tear both Heaven and Earth asunder. Alongside warlock John Constantine, Zatanna, and a circle of several other sorcerers, Zatara engaged in a séance to help the SWAMP THING battle the creature. When the creature attempted to destroy Zatanna, Zatara cast a spell to save her from its staggering power. He died in Zatanna's place, the ancient darkness causing the master magician to spontaneously combust, incinerating him before the eyes of all in attendance. **SB**

ZAURIEL

FIRST APPEARANCE JLA #6 (June 1997)
STATUS Hero **REAL NAME** Zauriel
OCCUPATION Adventurer **BASE** The Aerie, high above Los Angeles
HEIGHT 6ft 1in **WEIGHT** 180 lbs **EYES** Purple and red **HAIR** Silver
SPECIAL POWERS/ABILITIES Now a mortal, Zauriel retains his wings, granting him flight, but his angelic abilities, such as a sonic cry, have been reduced or removed. He can still speak to animals.

A Guardian-Angel of Heaven's Eagle-Host, Zauriel left heaven pursued by forces loyal to renegade King-Angel ASMODEL. Falling to Earth, Zauriel found kindred spirits in the JUSTICE LEAGUE OF AMERICA and Asmodel was routed. Zauriel kept his wings and remained on Earth. When MAGEDDON threatened all life, Zauriel sacrificed himself so others might live. His spirit pleaded humanity's cause in Heaven. As Mageddon neared Earth, Zauriel convinced the angels of the Pax Dei to fight for Heaven and Earth. Zauriel has renounced his immortality and lives among men. He has left the JLA, and protects others on his own, hoping to convince people of God's love for life. **RG**

ZUGGERNAUT

FIRST APPEARANCE FIRESTORM, THE NUCLEAR MAN #69 (March 1988)
STATUS Hero **REAL NAME** Matvei Rodor
OCCUPATION (Rodor) black marketeer; (Zuggernaut) inapplicable
BASE Moscow, Russian Federation
HEIGHT (Rodor) 5ft 9in; (Zuggernaut) 7ft **WEIGHT** (Rodor) 170 lbs; (Zuggernaut) 250 lbs **EYES** (Rodor) Blue; (Zuggernaut) Red
HAIR (Rodor) Brown; (Zuggernaut) None
SPECIAL POWERS/ABILITIES Superhuman strength; leaping ability; resistance to physical injury; generation of explosive energy from its mouth and a jewel in its forehead.

The extraterrestrial creature known as the Zuggernaut crash-landed on Earth in Russia, near the dacha of black marketer Matvei Rodor. Merging its monstrous alien body with Rodor's human desires, the Zuggernaut found its way to Moscow and tried to kill one of Rodor's enemies, a prosecutor named Soliony. The Zuggernaut was driven off by the American hero FIRESTORM and resumed its human shape as Rodor.

Later, after returning once more to kill Soliony, the Zuggernaut was thwarted by Firestorm and the young superteam, SOYUZ. Firestorm used the Zuggernaut's own explosive energies against it, mortally wounding Rodor's body and causing the alien to flee. Its current whereabouts are unknown. **PJ**

ZOOM

FIRST APPEARANCE FLASH SECRET FILES #3 (November 2001)
STATUS Hero   **REAL NAME** Hunter Zolomon
OCCUPATION Super-villain   **BASE** Keystone City
HEIGHT 6ft 1in   **WEIGHT** 181 lbs   **EYES** Brown   **HAIR** Brown
SPECIAL POWERS/ABILITIES Ability to travel at superspeed due a limited control of time. Zoom has essentially shifted himself to a 'faster' timeline, allowing him to surpass even the feats of speed evidenced by the current Flash, Wally West.

HEIR TO THE SINISTER LEGACY of Professor Zoom the Reverse-Flash, Hunter Zolomon was one of FLASH III's closest friends before a series of tragedies ruined his life. Hunter came from a nightmarish family. His father was a serial killer, a fact that Hunter only learned when police gunned down his father for the murder of his mother. Zolomon joined the F.B.I. and found love with a fellow agent named Ashley, whom he later married. Once again, his world imploded when a shootout with a criminal called the Clown left him with a shattered kneecap and brought about the death of Ashley's father. She divorced him soon after and the F.B.I. eventually fired him.

REVERSE-FLASH
Zolomon follows the bad example of Eobard Thawne, the original Prof. Zoom.

STRANGLEHOLD *In his psychosis, Zoom believes that he can make the Flash a better hero by forcing him to deal with tragedy.*

BAD LUCK AND TROUBLE

Desperate for even the pretense of stability, Zolomon wound up in Keystone City where he became a profiler of meta-human activities for the police department. He befriended the current Flash, Wally West, but his position with the K.C.P.D. made him a target for super-villains. An assault on Keystone by GORILLA GRODD left Zolomon with a broken back.

Now a paraplegic, Zolomon felt his only recourse was to beg the Flash to use the Cosmic Treadmill from the Flash Museum to travel back in time and prevent the calamities that had led to this point. Although sympathetic to his friend's plight, the Flash refused to alter time. Zolomon decided to do it himself. The resulting explosion of the Cosmic Treadmill shifted him onto a different frame of relative time, allowing him to move at superspeed by controlling time's passage. With new powers and threadbare sanity, Zolomon decided to teach the Flash a lesson about tragedy. He donned a costume similar to the one worn by the deceased REVERSE-FLASH and christened himself Zoom. Zoom attacked Wally West's family, causing Wally's wife Linda (see PARK, LINDA) to miscarry twins. Wally battled the mad monster at superspeed, ringing the globe before trapping Zoom in a repeating window of time, where he was forced to witness his disastrous shootout with the Clown again and again.

In the aftermath, Wally wished that he could protect his family by having everyone forget his secret identity—a request granted by the SPECTRE. **DW**

TRAGIC EFFECTS
Zoom's vicious attack on Linda Park caused her to miscarry twin babies.

LUNACY *Zoom is now stuck in a time loop, which should only unravel his sanity even further.*

KEY STORYLINES

• *FLASH SECRET FILES #3 (NOVEMBER 2001):* Hunter Zolomon makes his first appearance in these pages, which barely hint at his villainous future.

• *THE FLASH: BLITZ (TPB, 2004):* This trade paperback, reprinting Flash issues #192-200, is the definitive collection of the Zoom saga. By the time this series had finished its run, the status quo had been upended and Wally West had embarked on a new, controversial direction.

STRANGE TIMES AND PLACES

IN ELSEWORLDS, heroes and villains are taken from their usual, familiar settings and thrust into alternate worlds, divergent timelines, or parallel realities. Some are strange forgotten times that have existed or histories that might have been. Others are places that can't, couldn't, or *shouldn't* exist. Origins begin at divergent points and the outcomes of major crises may vary dramatically. And in all these imaginary stories made real, it all begins with the question, "What if…?"

WONDER WOMAN: AMAZONIA
In another reality, Diana is stolen away from paradise by Steve Trevor and the Royal Air Marines of the 19th-century British Empire. Forced to marry the vile Trevor, Diana becomes the star of a London show, reenacting tales of heroic women immortalized in the Bible. She shows herself to be a true heroine, freeing oppressed women all over the Empire, from the terrible reign of King Jack Planters, alias Jack the Ripper!

KINGDOM COME
This futuristic, apocalyptic tale begins in the Kansas wheat fields. A battle between the Justice Battalion and the villain PARASITE results in CAPTAIN ATOM's death and his nuclear energies lay waste to America's heartland. As a disillusioned SUPERMAN retreats into seclusion, a new generation of meta-humans—the uncontrollable sons and daughters of the world's greatest super heroes—inherits the Earth. Unfortunately, without Superman and his contemporaries to guide them, these super-menaces might well herald Armageddon. As witnessed by a holy man and his spiritual guide, the SPECTRE, Superman must embrace his role as leader and unite the divided super-heroes lest his adopted world be torn asunder. The fate of all mankind is in the balance.

THE DARK KNIGHT RETURNS
BATMAN has retired, leaving Gotham in need of a hero as the Mutants, a nihilistic street gang, threaten to overrun the city. When Harvey Dent returns to his old criminal ways as the deranged TWO-FACE, the Dark Knight returns, with a new ROBIN—teenager Carrie Kelly—flying at his side. Desperate times call for desperate measures, and a darker Caped Crusader takes back Gotham City street by street, battling the JOKER one last time. In "Crime Alley," Batman makes his final stand against his enemies, the Last Son of Krypton chief among them, as man and Superman decide the Dark Knight's destiny.

GRIEF-STRICKEN
On the devastated Kansas plains, Superman tends the graves of the victims of an accidental atomic holocaust.

LAST SON OF EARTH
Rocketed to distant Krypton from the dying planet Earth, baby Clark Kent is adopted by the scientist Jor-El and renamed Kal-El. Clad in a cumbersome exoskeleton to counter Krypton's oppressive gravity, Kal-El's discovery of a dead Green Lantern's power ring frees him to walk unfettered upon Kryptonian soil before journeying to the planet of his birth in search of his origins. There, amid the ragtag survivors of the blasted world, Clark meets the love of his life, Lois Lane (right), and his greatest foe, Lex Luthor!

BLOODSTORM

In a Gotham City where vampires rule the underworld, Batman is a bloodsucking monster who hunts those like him! Sating his own bloodlust to cleanse Gotham, Batman finds his undead foes united by the Clown Prince of Crime. Batman's only ally is doomed were-CATWOMAN Selina Kyle. One-by-one, Batman slays his immortal foes and bathes Gotham in red rain until only one is left. In the end, the Dark Knight knows that the killing might begin anew if a single vampire remains. Commissioner Gordon (see GORDON, JAMES W.) and Alfred (see PENNYWORTH, ALFRED) have little choice but to drive a stake through the heart of Batman, bringing him the peace he has long sought.

AT EARTH'S END

Welcome to the Earth after disaster! It is one year since a bearded and remarkably long lived Superman helped the young humans Kamandi, Zaphra, Sleeper Zom, and the cyborg Ben Boxer to defeat the maniacal Mother Machine, cause of Earth's second apocalypse. When Boxer targets Gotham City for destruction, Superman flies to Batman's old stomping ground armed to the teeth to aid a band of youths and free the remains of Bruce Wayne, alias Batman, from the DNA Dictators!

SUPERMAN: RED SON

What if Kal-El of Krypton had landed on an agricultural collective in the Soviet Union rather than a farm in Kansas? Earth's greatest hero would fight for truth, justice, and the *Russian* way of a life as the Soviets' most powerful secret weapon! What follows is an arms race of unparalleled intensity as the U. S. commissions its greatest scientist, the brilliant Lex Luthor (see LUTHOR, LEX), to tilt the balance of power in America's favor. The world stands on the brink of annihilation as Superman assumes leadership of the Soviet Union, bidding to unite the planet under Communism.

THE BIG RED With a hammer and sickle emblazoned on his chest, Superman is a propaganda tool of the Stalinist regime. But the Man of Steel cares only for helping his fellow man, regardless of politics or nationality.

SECRET WEAPONS The U.S.'s elite troops are the Green Lantern Marine Corps, led by Hal Jordan.

JLA: THE NAIL

Imagine a world without the Man of Steel. On an Earth resembling the DC Universe in every way—with all its requisite heroes and villains save one—for want of a nail Superman was lost. When infant Kal-El's rocket plummeted to Earth, Jonathan and Martha Kent (see KENTS, THE) missed their fateful rendezvous with the Last Son of Krypton because of a flat tire… all for want of a nail. Instead, Kal-El was adopted by an Amish family and never ventured forth from his rural backwater to become a hero. That is, until an evil regime outlawed all meta-humans and tried to drive the planet's heroes into imprisonment or extinction. The plains of Kansas become the scene of the final battle between a power-mad Jimmy Olsen (see OLSEN, JIMMY) and what remains of the world's greatest super heroes.

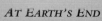

DOUBLE HIT *Batman battles the Joker—given staggering power by Jimmy Olsen—and Olsen finally meets his match when Kal-El of Krypton saves humanity (right).*

INDEX

A

A-Mortal 372
Abel **65**
Abnegazar 98
Abra Kadabra **8**, 265
Ace 293
Acrata **8**, 111, 113
Acro-Bat 78
Actuary 267
Adam, Captain Nathaniel 135
Adon 301, 369
Advance Man 206
Adversary 296
Agamemno **8**, 30
Agency, The 230, 300
Agenda 336
Agent "!" 62
Agent Axis 59
Agent Liberty **9**
Agni 257
Agony and Ecstasy 9
Agua sin Gaaz 58, 114
Air Wave I (Lawrence "Larry" Jordan) **9**
Air Wave II (Maser; Hal Jordan) **9**, 332
Alcmaeon 131
Aleph 193
Alex 198
Alias the Blur 62
Alias the Spider I (Tom Ludlow Hallaway) **10**
Alias the Spider II (Lucas Ludlow-Dalt) **10**
All-Purpose Espionage Squad (A.P.E.S.) 114
All-Star Special 11
All-Star Squadron **11**, 30, 37, 86, 103, 104, 131, 184, 251, 332, 358, 360, 380
All-Widow 129
Allen, Iris **10**, 124, 140, 191, 281, 287, 372
Alliance, The **10**
Allnut, Harold 133
Allure 286
Almerac 229
Alpha Centurion **12**
Amazing Grace **12**, 138
Amazing-Man I (Will Everett) **11**, 12
Amazing-Man II (Will Everett III) 12, 116, 234, 260
Amazo **13**, 163, 276, 287
Amazons **13**, 27, 80, 83, 100, 131, 132, 139, 146, 226, 314, 332-3
Amber 77
Ambush Bug **13**
America Smasher 320
Americommando 234
Amertek 326
Amethyst, Princess of Gemworld **14**, 95
Amon 10

Anarky **14**
Anathema 10
Ancients **14**, 134
Andromeda **15**
Angel and the Ape **15**
Angel of Fire 358
Angle Man **15**
Angor 111, 117
Anima **15**
Animal Man **16**, 234 280, 353
Anointed One, The 14
Anomaly 289
Answer Man 137
Anthro **17**
Anti-Life Equation 39, 95, 129, 225, 243, 249, 258
Anti-Matterman 364
Anti-Monitor 49, 105, 124, 153, 206, 242, 265, 270, 276, 316, 317, 348, 354, 365, 373
Antiope 13, 27, 83
Antiphon 257
Antithesis **17**, 158, 348
Aoran 129
Ape, The **15**
Aphrodite 256, 271
Apokolips 47, 88, 95, 104, 120, 173, 206, 184, 185, 187, 206, 270, 291, 305
Apollo 256
Apparition **17**, 204-5, 353, 360
Appellaxians 50, 180, 362
Appellaxian Contest **362**
Aquababy 18
Aquagirl **17**, 347, 348
Aqualad 18, 19, 26, 279, 347, 348, 358
Aquaman 14, 17, **18-19**, 29, 52, 79, 86, 88, 89, 107, 118, 124, 126, 134, 180-1, 190 196, 198, 226, 230, 233, 246, 254, 279, 303, 321, 326, 347, 350, 364, 365
Aquacave 133
Aquarius 50
Arak, Son of Thunder 22, 364
Arashi **22**
Arcana 211
Arcane, Abby 22, 96, 266, 335
Arcane, Anton **22**, 116, 266
Arcane, Gregori 282
Area 59, 164
Arella 269 357
Ares 13, 83, 93, 131, 161, 162, 228 256, 271, 356 375, **376-7**
Argent I 69, 177, 257, 270, 286, 370
Argent II 347
Arghulian 25
Argus **25**
Arion, Lord of Atlantis **24**, 94, 274
Arisia **25**

Arkahm Asylum **161**
Arkhannone 228
Armek 372
Arrakhat **25**
Arrowette 25, 115, 375, 381
Arsenal **26**, 81, 142-3, 148, 152, 170, 193, 261, 296, 308, 333, 347
see also Speedy
Artemis **25**, 120, 256, 375, 376-7
Artemis III **27**
Arthur, King 99, 198, 244
Aruna **27**
Aryan Brigade **28**, 174
Aryan Nation **28**, 245
Asher, Cpl. Arch 154
Ashiya 244
Asim Muhunnad 31
Asmodel **28**, 96, 219, 248, 315, 382
Asmodeus 294
Astra Logue 248
Aten 88
Athena 256
Atlan 18, **29**, 254, 358
Atlantis 14, 17, 18-19, 24, 29, 94, 107, 118, 123, 128, 133, 134, 190, 196, 210, 225, 230, 254, 274, 305, 347
Atlas **29**
Atmos **29**
Atom 177, 181, 184, 262, 324
Atom I (Al Pratt) **11**, 30, 94, 117, 150
Atom II (Raymond Palmer) **30**, 82, 128, 177, 289, 333, 348
Atom III 333
Atom-Smasher **31**, 87, 117, 122, 185, 196, 253
Atomic Knight **31**, 261, 374
Atomic Skull **31**
Atom'x 375
Atrophos 55
Auctioneer, The **31**
August 275
Aura 284
Aurakles 152
Auron 256
Automan 322
Avatar 177, 251, 266
Avia 249
Aviax 370
Axis America 28, **32**, 360
Axis Amerika 11, 32, 129, 354 360, 380
Azarath 264, 269, 357
Azazel **32**, 46, 102, 196
Azmodus 316
Azrael **36**, 41, 258, 291
Aztek **32**, 219

B

Babe 160
Baby Boom *see* Babe
Baby Wildebeest 264
Backlash 28
Bactun 233
Bad Samaritan **36**
Badb 257
Baer, Beau 140
Bailey, Biff 301
Baker, Red "Biscuits" 299
Ballésteros, Sebastian 80, 108, 334
Ballistic 56
Balloon Buster **36**, 297
Bane **36**, 41, 203, 283
Bard, Jason **37**
Baron Bedlam 137, 261
Baron Blitzkreig **37**, 206, 320
Baron Winter 251
Barrage 289
Barton, Boss 194
Bat Lash **37**, 83, 155, 297, 332
Bat-Mite **39**, 279, 315
Batcave 133, 152, 252, 315
Batgirl 27, 291, 302
Batgirl I (Barbara Gordon) **8**, 37, 38, 77, 87, 178, 259, 262, 280
Batgirl II (Helena Bertinelli) *see* Huntress
Batgirl III (Cassandra Cain) **36**, 64
Batman 14, 32, 38, 39, **40-5**, 52, 56, 58, 59, 60, 63, 74, 79, 84, 85, 87, 96, 112, 114, 118, 122, 129, 130, 139, 141, 162, 165, 178-9, 170-1, 188, 192, 193, 203, 204, 211, 212, 215, 218, 221, 224, 228, 231, 237, 238, 240, 243, 251, 252, 253, 258, 260, 261, 263, 267, 271, 272, 273, 276, 281, 282, 283, 288, 294, 297, 300, 310, 312, 415, 317, 320, 321, 324, 331, 333, 345, 359, 350, 353, 364, 366, 372
Batarangs 93
Batcave 133, 152, 252, 268
Batmobile 34
Batplane 34
Batson, Billy *see* Captain Marvel
Batson, C.C. 80-1, 320
Batson, Marilyn 70, 106
Baxter, Bonnie 353
Baxter, Corky 353
Baytor **39**, 162
Bear Tribe 17
Beast Boy **39**, 109, 113, 128, 165, 230, 291, 348, 349
Beautiful Dreamer **39**, 49, 243, 344, 369
Bedlam 94
Beefeater II (Michael Morice) **37**
Beelzebub 32, **46**, 102, 196, 294

Behemoth 165
Bek, Garryn **46**, 102, 138, 198, 310
Bek, Marij'n 138, 198, 312
Bekka **46**, 161, 249
Belial **46**, 99, 294
Belphegor **46**, 138
Bernadeth **46**, 120
Bertron 108
Bewitched 345
Bialya 153, 176, 282
Bibbo **47**
Biff 72
Big Anvil 354
Big Barda **46**, **47**, 120, 148, 195, 213, 236, 243, 249, 278, 311, 333
Big Bear 35, 39, **49**, 273
Big Sir 333
Birds of Prey 165, 259
Bizarro **42**, 169
Black Adam 31, **49**, 70–1, 98, 171, 185, 196, 227, 230, 247, 253, 333
Black Alice **49**
Black, Amunet 140
Black Bison **49**, 123
Black Canary 9, 26, **50**, 60, 81, 88, 165, 174, 226, 260, 284, 288, 297, 320, 321, 364, 367
Black Canary I (Dinah Drake Lance) **50**, 324
Black Canary II (Dinah Laurel Lance) **50**, 142, 180, 280, 304, 325
Black Condor I (Richard Grey Jr., a.k.a. Thomas Wright) **51**
Black Condor II (Ryan Kendall) **51**, 98, 131, 275
Black Dragon Society 110
Black Hand 92
Black Knight 361
Black Lamp 154
Black Lightning **51**, 261, 334, 345
Black Manta 18, 19, 35, **52**, 230, 254
Black Mariah 118
Black Mask **52**, 53
Black Mass 64
Black Nebula 364
Black Orchid **46**, 333
Black Pirate **53**
Black Racer **53**, 118, 249, 327
Black Rain 185
Black Shark 286
Black Spider I (Eric Needham) **53**
Black Spider II (Johnny LaMonica) **53**
Black Thorn 79
Black Widow 10
Black Zero **53**, 77, 166
Blackbriar Thorn **55**, 99
Blackfire **55**, 167
Blackfoot 122
Blackhawk **54**, 254, 301
Blackhawk Squadron 54, 81, 193
Blacksmith 140, 245, 357
Blacksmith Bill 233
Blackstarr 333

Blake, Johnny 73
Blanc-DuMont, André 54
Blast-Off 374
Blasters **55**, 73
Blaze 296, 309
Blight 17, 29, **55**, 111, 114, 173, 205, 296, 360, 374
Blind Faith 28
Blindside 286
Blithe 86
Blizzard 94
Blockbuster I (Mark Desmond) **56**, 301, 333
Blockbuster II (Roland Desmond) **56**, 62, 110, 252, 345, 355
Blood, Jason 99, 113
Blood Pack **56**, 98, 241, 250, 277, 326
Bloodlines Crisis 241
Bloody Mary 120
Bloodsport **56**
Bloom, Marla 57
Blüdhaven **56**, 110, 252, 334, 345, 355
Blue Beetle 107, 186, 221, 233
Blue Beetle I (Dr. Daniel Garrett) **57**
Blue Beetle II (Ted Kord) 35, **57**, 58, 117, 180, 211, 251, 263
Blu Beetle III **57**
Blue Boys **207**
Blue Devil **57**, 58, 235
Blue Jay 117
Blue Streak 228
Blue Trinity 198
Blunderbore 306
Body Doubles **58**, 287
Bogman 88
Bolovax Vix 193
Bolshoi 268
Bolt **58**
Bombardiers 163
Bonfire 381
Boom Tubes 46, 161, 189, 195, 232, 244, 311
Booster Gold 57, 58, 87, 117, 122, 151, 164, 263, 275
Bordeaux, Sasha **58**, 79
Borealis Effect 14
Bork 274
Bouncing Boy **59**
Bounty **59**
Boxer, Ben 188
Boy Commandos **59**, 79
Boyle, Ferris 237
Boyville Brigadiers 293
Braal 88, 119, 220, 296
Braddock, Brand 139
Bradley, Biff 37
Bradley, Slam **59**, 74
Brahma 334
Brain **60**, 219, 242, 270
Brainiac (Vril Dox) 60, **61**, 73, 89, 108, 198, 204–5, 229, 232, 341, 364
Brainiac 2.5 61
Brainiac 5.1 (Querl Dox) 15, 58, **60**, 86, 134, 173,

209, 240
Brainiac 13 61, 119, 148, 170, 231, 296, 364, 377
Brainwave I (Henry King) 171, 196, 230
Brainwave II 117, 185, 253
Brainwave, Jr. 170
Branchwater 277
Brand, Cleveland 96
Brande, R.J. **60**, 119, 204–5, 210, 273, 296, 356
Branx 256
Breathtaker 138, 310
Bridges, Norman 129
Bright, Jess 333
Brimstone 56, **60**
Brody, Clay 77
Bromfield, Mary 63, 168, 227
Bron, Chaser 97
Bronze Tiger **60**, 76, 110, 188, 203, 333, 369
Bronze Wraith 226
Brooks, Paul 251
Broot 256
Brother Bicep 160
Brother Blood 26, **62**, 284, 348, 349
Brother Eye 256
Brother Power, the Geek 62
Brother Rollo 258
Brotherhood of Dada 62, 238
Brotherhood of Evil 46, 60, 62, 109, 136, 221, 238, 242, 270, 271
see also Society of Sin
Brotherhood of the Monkey Fist 60
Bruckner, Doctor 238
Brutale **62**, 110
Brute 117, 151, 229, 295
Buckeye 257
Bulldozer 303, 333
Bulleteer **63**
Bulletgirl I (Susan Kent) **63**
Bulletgirl II (Deanna Barr) **63**
Bulletman **63**, 72, 320
Bullock, Harvey 79
Bullock, Sgt. 63
Bull's-Eye 142
Bumblebee 63, 160
Burgess, Roderick 295
Burr, Jason 196, 312
Bushmaster **63**, 138
Buzz 301, 338
B'Wana Beast 130, 138
see also Freedom Beast
Byth 157

C

Cabraca 233
Cachiru **64**, 294, 334
Cadre 12, 28, 64, 117, 118, 151, 174, 229, 245, 260
Cadre of the Immortal 245
Cain, David 38, **64**, 97, 118

Caine, Doctor Donovan 251
Cairn 46, 68, 102, 173, 198, 312, 331
Calculator **65**
Calendar Man **65**
Candlemaker 81
Candy, Etta 356
Cannonball 354
Cappy Jenks 293
Captain Atom 58, 64, 66, 117, 181, 221, 227, 240, 251, 273, 371
Captain Boomerang 66, 234, 286, 301, 333
Captain Cold 66, 140, 157, 273, 301, 333, 355, 372
Captain Comet 46, **68**, 102, 138, 198, 282, 312, 331
Captain Compass **68**
Captain Fear **68**
Captain Hunter **68**, 266
Captain Marvel (Billy Batson) 49, 63, 69, **70–1**, 72, 106, 168, 184, 185, 227, 236, 242, 248, 256, 286, 294, 314, 351, 365
Captain Marvel Jr. (Freddie Freeman) 46, 63, **69**, 71, 72, 76, 227
Captain Nazi 57, 69, 71, **72**, 227, 320
Captain Stingaree **72**
Captain Storm **72**, 84, 151, 213
Captain Triumph **72**
Captain X **72**, 321
Captains of Industry 9, 310
Cargg 356
Carnivore 86
Carom 94
Carr, Snapper 55, **73**, 180, 321, 381
Carson, Cave **73**, 42
Carter, Captain Eric "Rip" 59
Cascade **73**
Cassius 85
Cat-Man **73**, 93
Cataclysm 275
Catalyst 9, 333
Catseye **76**
Catto, Davroth 102, 138, 198, 312
Catwoman 40, 52, 58, 59, 73, **74**, 160, 203, 228, 247, 276, 281, 364
Caulder, Arani 210
Caulder, Dr. Niles see Chief, The
Cavalier **76**
Celebrand 370
Celeste **76**, 97
Celsius **76**, 84, 136, 188
Central City 10, 66, 102, 124, 129, 234, 245, 271, 286, 287, 355, 372
Central Clockworks 61
Centrix **76**
Centurions 12
Cerdia 107
Cerne 233
Chagra 31
Chain Lightning 63, 69, **76**
Challengers of the Unknown 53, **77**, 184, 233

Chameleon **77**, 175, 204, 301

Champions of Angor 153

Changeling 37, 91, 262, 348

Channelman 277

Chaos, Lords of 14, 94, 117, 155, 191, 246

Charaxes 77, 258, 301

Charybdis 19, **79**

Chase, Cameron 79, 333

Chase, Danny 139

Chase, Edward 100

Chavard, André 46, 59, 79

Chay-Ara 155, 156, 167, 251

Checkmate 26, 58, 63, 79, 122, 165, 296, 367

Cheetah I (Priscilla Rich) 15, **80**

Cheetah II (Barbara Ann Minerva) **80**, 83, 383

Cheetah III (Sebastian Ballésteros) **80**, 264, 383

Chemical King **80**

Chemo 80, 231, 333

Cheshire 26, **81**, 152, 193, 257, 306, 345, 349, 367

Chessure 120, 371

Chevy Chase 240

Chief, The (Dr. Niles Caulder) 76, **81**, 84, 109, 113, 136, 188, 219, 247, 292

Child 14, 94

Children of the Sun 101

Chillblaine 66, 140

Chiller 58

Chinatown Kid 366

Chlorino 160

Chlorophyll Kid 202

Chong, Ivan 296

Chosen 250

Ch'p **81**, 294

Chris KL-99 **81**

Chronarch 61

Chronopolis 243

Chronos 353

Chronos I (David Clinton) **82**, 171, 301, 333, 346

Chronos II (Walker Gabriel) **82**, 243

Chrysalis **82**

Chu, President 114, 119

Chuck 10

Church of Blood 199

Churljenkins 55

Chyre, Fred 10

Cicada **82**

Cimarron 64, 294, 334

Cinnamon I **83**, 137, 156, 251

Cinnamon II **83**

Circe 13, 27, 80, **83**, 132, 152, 165, 195, 256, 310, 313, 374

Circle of Six 60

Cir-El 338

Cirque Sensationel 110

Citadel 166, 167, 256, 322

Claiborne, Helen 228

Class 230

Claw, The Unconquered **84**, 275

Clawman, Betty 250

Clay, Joshua 81, **84**

Clayface I (Basil Karlo) **85**

Clayface II (Matt Hagen) **85**

Clayface III (Preston Payne) **85**

Clayface IV (Sandra Fuller) **85**

Claything 85

Clearweather, Percy 59

Clock King **84**, 333, 269

Clockwerx 258

Cloister 276

Cloud, Johnny 72, **84**, 151, 213

Cloudburst 129, 151, 229

Clown 383

Cluemaster **84**, 291, 320

Coast City 10, 144, 149, 188, 241, 264, 317, 326

Cobalt Blue **86**

Coeus 353

Color Kid 203

Colos, Ferrin 97

Colu 60, 61, 73, 198

Combattor 134

Comet **86**

Commander Steel 11, **86**, 326

see also Steel I

Competalia 10

Composite Man 296

C.O.M.P.U.T.O. 29, 86, 173

Conduit 305

Conglomerate 31, 58, **87**, 151, 153, 275, 365

Congorilla **87**

Constantine, John 32 **87**, 102, 105, 196, 248, 262, 382

Contessa, The 12, **87**, 139, 195

Controllers 97, 113, 150

Coordinator 160

Copperhead **87**, 301

Corbett, Marlon 77

Corbin, Captain Lea 173

Corona **88**, 196, 246

Cosmic Boy 60, **88**, 191, 204–5, 206, 210, 220

Cosmic Key 276

Cosmic Odyssey 232

Costilino, Joseph 111

Cottus 376

Council, The 247

Council of Three 276

Count Vertigo **88**, 171

Crackpot 55

Craeteis 294

Craft, Cassandra 270

Craig, Pvt. Eddie 154

Craig, Sgt. Bill 154

Cravat, Guano 203

Crazy Quilt **88**

Creation at the Dawn of Time 265

Creature Commandos 68, **88**, 151, 213, 266

Creeper, The **89**

Creote 297

Crime Smasher 320

Crime Syndicate 61, **89**

Crimelord 230

Crimson Avenger 270, 301

Crimson Avenger I (Lee Travis) **90**, 270, 301, 360, 374

Crimson Avenger II (real name unknown) **90**, 360

Crimson Fox **90**, 235

Crisis, The 14, 17, 22, 24, 25, 49, 69, 81, 85, 86, 104, 123, 149, 152, 155, 162, 163, 169, 177, 196, 234, 242, 265, 270, 277, 294, 305, 316, 324, 332, 347, 348, **363**, 371

Crocodile Man 98, 230

Crody 353

Cronus 90, 100, 353

Cross, Crystal 110

Crowbar 64

Crown of Horns 39, 99

Curtis, Dr. Terry 12

Cyberion 91, 348–9

Cyborg (Victor Stone) 69, **91**, 262, 291, 348, 349

Cyborg Superman (Hank Henshaw) **91**, 116, 241, 264, 317, 326

Cyborgirl 367

Cyclotron 30

Cynthia 351

Cypher 130

D N Angels **102**

Daanuth, Garn 24, **94**, 274

Dagon-Ra 68

Daley, Bob 235

Damage 30, **94**, 364

Dana 198

Dancer, Deborah 168

Danner, Hugo 400, 380

Danny the Street 230

Darhk, Damien **94**, 145

Dark Angel 316, 325

Dark Circle 70, 345

Dark Colossus 321

Dark Lord (Mordru) 24, **94**, 103, 111, 112, 155, 185, 191, 210, 220, 243, 254, 273, 295, 297, 309, 323, 359, 374

Dark Nemesis **94**, 348

Dark Opal 14, **94**

Dark, The 39, 301, 369

Darkling 294

Darkness 185

Darkseid 12, 13, 14, 27, 39, 46, 47, 49, 56, 60, **95**, 97, 98, 101, 102, 108, 118, 120, 129, 137, 138, 148, 161, 162, 170, 173, 185, 188, 189, 205, 206, 209, 210, 213, 225, 243, 249, 256, 258, 284, 289, 301, 311, 327, 330, 353, 364, 369, 381

Darkstar (John Stewart) 148

Darkstar (Lydea Mallor) 138, 198, 312

Darkstars 76, **97**, 113, 139, 145, 148, 233, 277, 358

Darkworld 24

Dart 272

Dartalon 370

Davis, Hallie 251

Davis, Rocky 77

Dawnstar 59

Daxamites 15, **166**, 240

Day of Judgment 105, 248, 260

Deadeye 87

Deadline 58

Deadman **96**, 202, 204, 301

Deadshot 58, 76, **97**, 251, 257

Dearden, Mia **143**

Death **97**, 100, 114, 115, 295, 301

Death Angel 117, 151, 229

Deathbolt 380

Deathstroke the Terminator **97**, 161, 177, 191, 230, 252, 264, 345, 348, 349, 350, 367, 374

Debris 180

Decay 375

Deep Blue 269, 358

Deep Six 88

DeFarge, Dexter 275

Degaton, Per 11, 122, 171, 185, 229, 380

Deimos 244, 271, 371

Delirium 100, 115

Demeter 256

Demolition Team **98**, 326

Demon, The (Etrigan) 28, 39, 46, 55, **99**, 102, 183, 195, 196, 225, 244, 248

Demons Three 98, 120, 275

Denmark 210

Dennis, Danny 289

Department of Extranormal Operations (D.E.O.) 101, 160, 289, 296, 301, 349, 381

Department Gamma 79

Dervish 257

Desaad 46, 60, 95, **98**, 120, 173, 188, 244, 249, 289, 309, 353

Desire 100, 115

Despair 100, 115

Despero **98**, 151, 313, 326

Destiny 97, **100**, 115

Destruction 100, 115

Detective Chimp **100**, 289

Devastation 100

Devilance 39, **101**, 171, 243, 249, 301, 369

Dgrth 320

Dhor 189

Di Bella, Eugene and Wendy 103

Dial "H" for Hero **101**

Diamond, Marc 251

Diamondette 160

Diana, Princess *see* Wonder Woman

Digitronix 152

Dimension X 58

Dionysus 256

Director Bones 79, 101, 160, 170

Dixon, Clay 267

Djinn 257

Doc Magnus 81, **102**

Doctor 32, 121

Doctor Alchemy **102**

Doctor Bedlam 98, 102, 255

Doctor Canus 188

Doctor Cobalt 358

Doctor Darrk 203

Doctor Dayzl 284

Doctor Destiny **102**

Doctor Diehard 117

Doctor Electron 31

Doctor Fate 94, 168, 184, 185, 239, 248, 295

Doctor Fate I (Kent Nelson) **103**, 246, 308

Doctor Fate III (Inza Cramer Nelson) **103**, 246

Doctor Fate IV (Hector Hall) 11, **103**, 246, 253, 295

Doctor Impossible **104**

Doctor Light 138, 221

Doctor Light I (Arthur Light) **104**, 120, 160, 348

Doctor Light II (Kimiyo Hoshi) **104**, 109, 261, 289

Doctor Light III 207

Doctor Mid-nite I (Charles M. McNider) 11, **104**, 117, 286

Doctor Mid-nite II (Pieter Anton) **104**, 184, 244

Doctor Midnight (Beth Chapel) 112, 170

Doctor Miraco 304

Doctor Mist 46, 63, **105**, 120, 138, 140, 168, 176, 210, 245, 256, 260, 301

Doctor Occult 96, **105**

Doctor Phosphorus **105**

Doctor Poison II 367

Doctor Polaris 22, **105**, 118

Doctor Psycho 88, **106**, 310, 376

Doctor Regulus 206

Doctor Sivana 71, 98, 106, 227, 236, 286

Doctor Spectron 51

Doctor Thirteen **107**, 314, 356

Doctor Trap 79

Doctor Tzin-Tzin 110

Doctor Weerd 376

Doda 55

Doll Girl **107**

Doll Man **107**, 131

Dolphin 19, 79, **107**, 347

Dome, The 46, 63, 135, 138, 195, 245, 256, 260

Dominators 73, **166**, 167, 198, 240

Dominion 151

Dominus **108**, 116

Don Caballero **108**

Donovan, Dabney 173

Doom Patrol 39, 60 62, 76, 81, 84, 102, 104, **109**, 113, 121, 136, 165, 188, 210, 219, 230, 238, 242, 247, 292

Doom's Doorway 376

Doomsday 53, 58, 61, 91, **108**, 116, 200, 238, 241, 255, 327, 383, 336, 341, 375

Dorrance, Dane 301

Dos Rios 113

Double Dare **110**

Double, Jonny **110**

Douglas, Mo 97

Dove 117, **155**, 240, 308, 348

Dove II (Dawn Marie Granger) 155, 240

Dox, Lyrl 198, 282, 331

Dox, Vril see Brainiac

Dox, Vril, II 46, 198, 240, 301, 312, 331

Draaga 241

Dragon King **110**, 122, 308

Dragon, Richard 60, **110**, 199, 259, 279

Dragoneer 274

Dragon's Hoard 76

Dream 97, 100, 115

see also Morpheus

Dreamer **110**

Dreaming, The 64, 131, 196, 295

Dreamslayer **111**, 117, 151, 211, 229

Drone 364

Drozdowski, Stanislaw 54

Druspa Tau 155

Dryad 331

Duchess 120

Duma 9, 46

Dummy 98, 230, 242, 253

Duncan, Mal 63

Duran **111**

Durla/Durlans 77, 149 166, 174

Dusk, Nathaniel 101

Dust Devil 55

Dybbuk 111, 159

Dyna-Mite, Dan the 11, 354, 380

Dzamor 115

E

Earth-Angel 338

Easy Company 301

Echo (Nina Damfino) 288

Echo (Paul Valley) 87, **112**

Echo Valley 155

Echo VI (real name unrevealed) **112**

Eclipso 39, 86, 94, **112**, 185, 240, 254, 266, 270, 324, 226, 346, 373

Ecruos 353

Ecstacy see Agony and Ecstacy

Edge, Morgan 173, 275, 289

Edge, Vincent 173

Effigy **113**

Egg Fu **113**

Eiling, General Wade 186

see also General, The

Einstein, Albert 129

Ekron 113

El Bagual 64, 294, 334

El Diablo I (Lazarus Lane) **113**

El Diablo II (Rafael Sandoval) 113

El Dorado 293

El Duran 8

El Lobizon 64, 294, 334

El Lobos 153

El Muerto 8, 111, **113**

El Yaguarite 64, 294, 334

Elasti-Girl 37, 109, **113**, 230

Elasti-Man 87

Element Girl **114**

Element Lad **114**, 204, 210, 243, 296

Element Man 87, 114

Elite 224

Elongated Man 90, 109, **114**, 174, 180, 288, 371, 372

Elvar 370

Emba 17

Embra 17

Emerald Empress 119, 193, 204

Emerald Eye of Ekron 46, 88, 119, 193, 204, 206, 309

Emerald Warrior 120

Empress 58, **115**, 350, 375, 381

Encantadora **115**

Enchantress **115**

Endless, The 97, 100, **115**, 295

Enemy Ace (Hans von Hammer) 36, 37, **116**

En'Tarans 322

Eradicator **116**, 261

Erdel, Doctor Saul 226

Ereskigal 294

Erin, Shvaughn 204

Esak 118, 249

Etrigan see Demon, The

Even Steven 272

Event Horizon 160, 284, 314

Evil Star **117**

Extant 30, 31, 104, 117, **117**, 163, 184, 233, 240, 264, 332, 348, 365

Extraño 250

Extreme Justice 12, 66, **117**, 123, 240

Extremists, The 111, **117**, 211, 245

F

Face, The 194

Fadeaway Outlaw 275

Fain Y'Onia 63

Fairchild, Vesper 41, 58, 97, **118**, 320

Faith 118

Falco 107

Falcon 236

Falconer, Dr. Curt 32

Fallen Angel **118**

False Face Society 52

Fang 149

Faora **118**, 136

Farmer Boy 301

Fast Forward 109

Fastbak 118, 249, 325

Fastball 64, **118**

Fat Lady see Faith

Fatal Five **119**, 350

Fatality **120**, 145

Fate 94

Fate Child 267

Fates 351

Fatman 235

Faust, Felix 57, 96, 98, 115, **120**, 261, 301, 346

Faust, Sebastian 120

Fawcett City 46, 63, 69, 70–1, 106, 168, 227, 235, 236, 242, 286

Fearsome Five 104, **120**, 138, 177, 221, 248, 277, 309, 348

Female Furies 27, 46, 47, 95, 120, 148 195, 218, 236, 311, 331, 355

Fernus 145, 226

Ferro 121, 189, 204–5, 301

Ferrous 173

Fever 109, **121**

Fiddler 92, 124, 171

Fiero 87

Final Night crisis 135, 264

Finch, Andrew 282

Fine, Milton 61

Fire **121**

Fire Lad 202

Firebird **121**, 313

Firebrand I (Rod Reilly) **122**, 131

Firebrand II (Danette Reilly) 11, **122**, 251, 308

Firebrand III (Alex Sanchez) **122**

Firefly **122**

Firehair **122**

Firehawk **122**

Firestorm 49, 58, 60, 72, 117, 121, 122, **123**, 192, 246, 273, 274, 275, 321, 382

Fisherman 18, **126**

Flag, Captain Richard, Sr. **128**, 333

Flag, Colonel Rick 97, 251, 333

Flamebird **126**

Flash I (Jay Garrick) **124**, 150, 184–5, 228, 242, 243, 263, 279, 288, 292, 294, 302, 323 352

Flash II (Barry Allen) 10, 18, 66, 86, 102, 114, **124**, 140, 141, 159, 169, 180, 191, 194, 221, 226, 234, 248, 263, 271, 281, 287, 297, 317, 355, 363, 372, 380

Flash III (Wally West) 25, 58, 64, 66, 82, 86, 102, **124–5**, 129, 140, 180, 181, 191, 198, 211, 220, 228, 234, 245, 265, 271, 273, 281, 286, 294, 313, 345, 348, 355, 357, 358, 372, 383

Flashman, Funky **128**

Flaw 14, 94

Fledermaus 32, 360

Fleur-de-Lis 79, 126, 138

Flex 160

Flexus 372

Flint, John 97

Flock of the Machine 229

Floronic Man **126**, 273, 301

Flow 173

Flying Fox 11, **127**, 380

Fog 11, 62, 251

Folded Man **127**

Forager I (no real name) **127**, 249

Forager II (no real name) **127**, 249
Force of July 36, 272
Forever People 35, 39, 49, 101, **128**, 138, 161, 171, 243, 249, 301, 344, 369
Forgotten Heroes 73, 164, 169, 284, 301, 367
Fortress of Solitude 108, 116, 133, 197
Fortune, Amos **128**, 293
Four Horsemen of the Apocalypse 345
Fox, Lucius 58, **128**, 261
Frag 55
Freak 109
Free, Scott *see* Mister Miracle
Freedom Beast **128**
Freedom Fighters 10, 51, 107, 122, **131**, 163, 177, 232, 234, 248, 270, 272, 284, 285, 286
Freeman, Doctor Torvell 264
Freeman, Freddy *see* Captain Marvel Jr.
Frenzy 62
Friedriksen, Olaf 54
Fringe **129**, 289
Frosbite 381
Frostbite 87
Funky Flashman 301
Furies 15, 131
Furlow, Eddie 251
Fury 380
Fury I (Helena Kosmatos) 11, **131**
Fury II (Hippolyta Trevor) 103, **131**, 170
Futuresmiths 338
Fyers, Eddie 25

G

Gabby 232
Gaea 123, 229, 335, 376
Gambler **134**, 159, 171, 293
Gamemnae 14, 19, **134**, 190, 225, 350
Gangbuster 47, **134**
Ganthet 150, 193
Gardner, Guy **135**
Gargoyle 17, 64, 160
Garv **134**, 138, 198, 331
Gassers 173
Gates **135**, 204
Gaucho **135**, 138, 334
Gaulicho 294
Gemir 280
Gemworld 14, 24, 94
General, The **135**, 221, 305
General Glory 39, **135**
General Horatio Tomorrow 271, 355
General Immortus 76, 81, 109, 136
General Zahl 113, **136**, 219, 230, 247, 271
General Zod 115, **136**, 169
Genius Jones **137**
Gentleman Ghost 137
Geo-Force **137**, 261, 346, 350
Geomancer 167
Gestalt 177

Ghast 98, 275
Ghost Dragons 194, 213
Ghost Patrol, The **137**
Ghost-Breaker 107
G.I. Robot **134**
Giganta **137**, 367
Gil'Daan 166
Gillespie, Louis 173
Gilotina 120
Gimmick Girl **230**
Gint, Homer 322
Girder **137**
Gizmo 120, **138**, 177, 221
Global Guardians 46, 63, 73, 76, 82, 105, 121, **138**, 152, 157, 168, 171, 176, 195, 210, 229, 256, 260, 289, 301, 346
Glonth 162
Glorious Godfrey 12, **138**, 180, 249
Glorith 76
Gloss **138**, 250
G'Nort **139**, 180
Goat-man 98, 230
Godiva 138, **139**
Gog **139**, 207, 353
Gold 231
Gold, Jack 251
Golden Arrow **139**
Golden Eagle 28, 348
Golden Girl 66
Golden Gladiator **140**
Golden Glider 66, 140, 355
Goldface **140**, 346
Golem **140**, 275, 282
Golem (Hayoth) 140, 157
G.O.O.D. 199
Goraiko 173
Gordanians 167, 256
Gordon, Barbara *see* Batgirl; Oracle
Gordon, Bruce 112, 270
Gordon, James W. 37, 38, 40, 41, 63, 64, 141, 178–9, 243, 259, 359
Gorgeous Gilly **141**
Gorgon 165
Gorgon II 117
Gorilla Grodd 26, 117, **141**, 194, 261, 301, 312, 345
Gorrah 235
Goth **141**
Gotham City 14, 36, 37, 38, 39, 50, 52, 53, 55, 56, 59, 60, 73, 74, 77, 84, 85, 87, 97, 118, 122, 130, 141, 154, 160, 162, 165, 178–9, 188, 189, 190, 192, 194, 213, 218, 224, 226, 228, 237, 240, 252, 257, 259, 260, 267, 243, 271, 273, 282, 283, 288, 294, 297, 312, 315, 320, 331, 345, 350, 355, 357, 364, 365
Gothcorp 237
Grace **148**, 261
Grace, Karin 333
Granny Goodness 27, 47, 95, 120, **146**, 189, 195, 213, 218, 236, 249, 331

Grant, Jim 297
Grant, Victoria 101
Gravedigger **148**
Gray, Cpl. Gus 154
Grayven 97, **148**
Great Hand 150
Green Arrow I (Oliver Queen) 9, 26, 50, 88, 92, **142–3**, 180, 257, 263, 264, 280, 288, 304, 300, 321
Green Arrow II (Connor Hawke) 25, 26, 92, **142–3**, 145, 190, 257, 276
Green Fury 121, 138, 168
Green Lantern/Green Lantern Corps 9, 11, 14, 25, 26, 29, 32, 39, 76, 81, 97, 98, 104, 108, 117, 120, 139, **144–5**, 149, 150, 166, 190, 196, 221, 225, 226, 242, 253, 264, 280, 294, 305, 311, 353, 364, 370, 371
Green Lantern I (Alan Scott) 79, 92, **144**, 176, 184–5, 254, 292, 312
Green Lantern II (Hal Jordan) 25, 28, 71, 87, 95, 107, 114, 116, 128, 130–1, **132**, 135, 136, 139, 162, 166, 168, 171, 175, 218, 220, 226, 233, 234, 263, 273, 277, 279, 280, 285, 287, 304, 312, 326
Green Lantern III (Guy Gardner) 135, 139, **144**, 168, 305, 372
Green Lantern IV (John Stewart) 81, 97, 120, **144–5**, 148, 162, 190, 294, 354
Green Lantern V (Kyle Rayner) 22, 92, 113, 120, **144–5**, 148, 149, 150, 176, 180–1, 193, 264, 294, 313
Green Lantern (Abn Sur) 63, 144
Green Lantern (Ch'p) **81**
Green Lantern (G'Nort) 139, 180
Green Lantern (Kilowog) 193, 292
Green Lantern (Tomar-re) **354**
Green Man **149**
Grey Cloud 122
Grimbor 204
Grogamesh 194
Gross, Colonel Von 193
Grossout **149**
Group, The 72
Grunge 141
Guardian 11, 59, **150**, 250
Guardian Angel 154
Guardians of the Universe 25, 92, 97, 108, 113, 117, 138, 144, 149, **150**, 167, 190, 193, 197, 220, 225, 226, 242, 250, 264, 311, 323, 354, 371
Gudra 32, 354, 360
Gunfire **151**
Gunn, Billy "Pop" 301, 367
Gunn, Mike "Machine" 173
Gunner (zombie) 88
Gunner and Sarge 72, 84, 151, 213
Gunpowder Grimes 260
Gunshot 117, 151, 229
Gunther 55
Gypsy 87, 98, **151**, 174, 260, 365

H

Haasan, Jan 59
Hacker (Hackrat) 277
Hacker Files, The **152**
Hades 90, **152**, 256
Hagen 230
Hakk, Amon 138, 198, 312
Haley, Professor 77
Half-Life 284
Halk 81
Halo **152**, 189, 261, 334, 374
Hammer 268
Hammer, Hans von *see* Enemy Ace
Hammer, Otto Von 113
Hammer and Sickle **152**
Hammond, Hector **153**, 293, 305
Hand, the 246
Hangmen **152**, 193, 308, 349
Happy Braves 84
Harbinger **153**, 250, 265
Hard Drive 381
Hardhat 98, 320
Hardline 87, **153**, 365
Hardsell **153**
Hardwicke, Hannibal 53
Harjavti, Rumaan and Sumaan **153**, 278
Harlequin I 171
Harley Quinn 120, **154**, 170, 178
Harm 301
Harold 267
Harpi 165
Harpis 256
Harrigan, Hop **154**
Hascaragua 62
Haunted Tank **154**, 274
Hawk (Hank Hall) 117, **155**, 240, 308
Hawk and Dove **155**
Hawk, Son of Tomahawk **155**, 354
Hawkgirl 11, 103, 131, 137, **155**, 156, 167,
Hawkman 11, 63, 103, 131, 137, **155**, 156, 157, 167, 170, 184–5, 241, 253, 262, 269, 310
Hawkwoman **157**
Hawkworld 167
Hayoth 111, **157**, 257
Hazard I **157**, 171, 315
Hazard II 153, 308
Haze 177, 348
Head, The 81
Heart of Darkness 112
Heatmonger 28
Heatwave **157**
Heckler **158**
Heggra 95, 98, 249, 331
Hel (Vela Shepherd) 32
Helix 101, 160, 170, 373
Hell 9, 22, 25, 28, 32, 39, 46, 53, 57, 98, 99, 102, 115, 141, 164, 191, 196, 219, 228, 248, 251
Hellenders 27
Hellgrammite **158**

Hellhound **158**

Hellstrom, Sturges 253

Hemlocke, Baron 68

Hendricksen, Ritter 54

Hera 132, 256

Heracles 13, **159**, 162, 376

Herald 17, **159**

Hermes Trismegistus 110

Hero **159**

Hero Cruz 284

Hero Hotline **160**, 235, 254

Herupa Hando Hu 138

Hestia 93, 256

Hewitt, Henry 122

Hex, Jonah 161

Hidden Ones see Homo magi

Highbrow 321

Highfather 49, **161**, 236, 249, 258, 284, 301, 331, 344, 353, 369

Hightower, Noah 122

Hi-Jack 301

Himon 46, **161**, 195, 236, 249

Hippolyta, Queen 13, 27, 35, 80, 83, 131 137, **162**, 170, 184, 285, 358, 364, 369 376–7

see also Wonder Woman

Hitler, Adolf 28, 37, 72, 110, 184, 251, 285, 320, 360, 361, 369

Hitman 162

H.I.V.E. 94, **161**, 252, 285, 345, 348, 351

H'Iven 81

Hoberman, Mitch 301

Hoffman, Bonny 58

Holcolmb-Baker, Ian 54

Homo magi 24, 105, 382

Hood 354

Hook 96

Hooty 104

Horned Owl 32, 360

Hotchkins, Sanders 28

Hotshot 160

Houma 335

Houngan 117, **162**

Hourman 11, 28, 63, 131, 184, 253, 364

Hourman I (Rex Tyler) 117, **163**, 174, 358

Hourman II Rick Tyler) **163**, 170, 184

Hourman III (no real name) 73, **163**, 176

H'San Natall 131, 167, 177, 276, 289, 348

Hubble 353

Human Bomb 131, **163**

Human Defense Corps, The **164**

Human Target 53, 104

Humbug 177

Hunter, Captain 88

Hunter, Dan 353

Hunter, Rip 58, 73, 82, **164**, 207, 353, 364

Hunter, Timothy 236

Hunter's Hellcats 68, 88, **165**

Huntress **165**, 259, 275, 279, 297

Hush 133, 192, 276

Hybrid **165**, 230, 276

Hyperclan 18, 168

Hyperion 353

Hypertime 53, 139, 164, 207

Hypnota 367

Hyssa 29

Hyve 257

I

Iapetus 353

IBAC 69, 98, **168**, 227, 230, 294

Iblis 176

Ice 58, 121, **168**, 370

Ice Cream Soldier 301

Icemaiden 138, **168**

Icicle I (Joar Mahkent) 171

Icicle II (Cameron Mahkent) 99, **169**, 171

Id 76

Idylists 347

Ifrit 111, 257

Ignetia 10

Ignition 136, **169**

Igor 313

Ilda 322

Illuminati 364

Illuminator of All Realities 108

Iman 8, 111, 113, **169**

Immortal man 16, **169**, 287

Impala 138

Imperiex 34, 51, 61, 80, 93, 132, 167, **170**, 219, 224, 229, 241, 256, 269, 341, 347, 356, 377

Imperiex War 19, 54, 69, 108, 118, 120, 148, 170, 197, 200, 209, 224, 261, 284, 303, 327, 330, 347, 351, 361, **362**

Impulse 25, 191, 204, 228, 279, 301, 375, 380, 381

India Rubber Man 114

Indigo 26, 115, **170**, 261

Inferior Five **171**

Inferno 98, 204

Infinite Domain 98

Infinity, Inc. 31, 101, 131, 157, 160, 163, **170**, 171, 176, 229, 246, 253, 254, 274, 312, 323, 352, 360, 373

Infinity Man 39, 49, 101, **170**, 225, 243, 301

Ingot 121, 204

Injustice Gang 83, 135, **171**, 176, 278, 305, 346

Injustice League 52, 84, 180, 301

Injustice Society 88, 157, 169, **171**, 184, 304, 312, 313, 304, 375

Injustice Unlimited 159, 169, 171

Insect Queen **173**

InterC.E.P.T. 284, 331

Intergang 9, **173**, 190, 356

International Ultramarine Corps 135, **173**, 176, 320, 369

Invisible Hood 131

Invisible Justice 131

Invisible Kid 77, 80, **174**, 204–5

Ion **174**

Iron 231

Iron Cross 28, **174**

Iron Hand 301

Iron Munro 11, 37, 254, 354, 380

Irons, Natasha **174**, 327, 356

Isis **175**

Israel 111, 157, 301

I...Vampire **168**

J

Jace, Helga 137, 221, 350

Jack 293

Jack O'Lantern 138, 260, 275

Jack O'Lantern I (Daniel Cormac) **176**

Jack O'Lantern II (Marvin Noronsa) **176**, 210

Jack O'Lantern III (Liam McHugh) 173, **176**

Jackal 177

Jackam, Josh 10

Jackhammer 98, 326

Jade 145, 170, **176**, 254, 261, 292, 312

Jade (Blood Pack) 56

Jade (Cheshire) 81

Jameal, LaDonna 301

Jameson, Scott 79

Janissary **176**

Janu 87

Jarhanpur 190

Java 232

Jayna 117

Jeepers 98, 230

Jem, Son of Saturn **176**

Jericho 97, 161, **177**, 264, 269, 348, 349

Jero 81

Jester, The 131, **177**

Jet 250

Jewelee see Punch and Jewelee

Jihad, The 111, 257

Jinx 110, **177**, 367

Jo Nah 353, 360

Joker 14, 38, 40, 48, 73, 116, 141, 148, 152, 153, 169, 169, **178–9**, 193, 200, 202, 228, 238, 259, 271, 280, 290, 291, 315, 371

Joker's Daughter **117**

Jolt 55

Jone, Darren 230

Jones, Darwin **177**

Jones, Kaintuck 354

Jones, Ludher 197

Jones, Tao 160

J'Onn J'Onzz 89, 176, 180, 372

see also Martian Manhunter

Jordan, Hal see Air Wave II; Green Lantern II; Parallax; Spectre

Jost, Thayer 109, 121

Joto **177**, 276, 289

Judith 157

Judomaster **177**

Junior 381

Justeen 353

Justice Battalion 184

Justice Experience 79, 184, 226

Justice League of America 8, 9, 10, 13, 14, 17, 18–19, 26, 28, 30, 31, 32, 41, 47, 50, 51, 56, 57, 58, 60, 64, 66, 69, 71, 73, 86, 87, 88, 89, 94, 98, 99, 102, 103, 104, 108, 111, 112, 114, 117, 118, 120, 121, 123, 124, 130, 132, 134, 135, 142, 151, 153, 155, 156, 162, 163, 165, 168, 170, 171, 173, 174, 176, **180-1**, 189, 190, 193, 195, 204–5, 206, 209, 211, 213, 219, 221, 224, 225, 226, 227, 229, 232, 233, 234, 236, 239, 242, 245, 247, 251, 253, 257, 258, 260, 261, 263, 266, 270, 272, 274, 276, 278, 279, 284, 285, 294, 295, 297, 300, 301, 305, 310, 312, 313, 315, 316, 317, 320, 321, 326, 327, 330, 341, 344, 346, 347, 348, 350, 355, 358, 360, 362, 365, 369, 370, 371, 377, 382

Justice League Antarctica 84, 139, 180, 221

Justice League of Atlantis 206

Justice League Europe 16, 90, 104, 117, 168, 180, 211, 229, 274

Justice League International 12, 39, 46, 66, 87, 138, 153, 165, 180, 207, 225, 229

Justice League Task Force 28, 180, 284, 369

Justice League West 58, 181

Justice Legion-A 312

Justice Society of America 9, 11, 34, 49, 70-1, 98, 104, 132, 144, 155, 156, 163, 160, 171, **184-5**, 195, 196, 239, 274, 279, 284, 293, 295, 301, 304, 323, 324, 332, 344, 352, 355, 360, 363, 373

Justifiers 138

K

Kako 18, 19, 254

Kal-El see Superman

Kalibak 95, **188**, 249, 289, 381

Kaliber 284

Kalista 256

Kalki **188**

Kalmaku, Tom **188**, 221, 250

Kalonor 98

Kamandi **188**, 256

Kamard 193

Kamikaze 32, 360

Kancer 136

Kandor 91, 166

Kane, Kathy **188**

Kanjar Ro **189**

Kanto **189**, 249

Kapatelis, Vanessa 106, 376

see also Silver Swan II

Kara Zor-El 95, 331

Karate Kid **189**, 204–5, 301

Karkull, Ian 254

Katalia 10

Katana 76, 152, **189**, 261

Katarthans 28

Katma Tui **190**, 294

Kawa, Kenn 77

Kazim, Ankha 176

Kelex 133

Kelly, Nick 25

Kelly, Sergeant Montgomery 164

Kent, Clark *see* Superman

Kent, Jebediah 297

Kent, Jonathan **190**, 225, 297, 336, 340

Kent, Martha Clark **190**, 225, 336, 340

Kevork, Vartan 104

Key, The 73, 92, **190**

Keystone City 8, 10, 25, 66, 82, 124–25, 137, 140, 191, 220, 245, 265, 345, 352, 355, 357, 383

KGBeast **190**, 357

Khan, Rama 93, 134, **190**

Khufu, Prince 155, 156, 167, 251

Khundia/Khunds 73, 166, 167

Kid Devil **191**

Kid Eternity 46, 94, **191**

Kid Flash I 26, 125, 358

Kid Flash II **191**, 291, 348, 349

Kid Quantum 206, 243

Kid Quantum I (James Cullen) **191**, 204

Kid Quantum II (Jazmin Cullen) 88, **191**, 204–5

Kid Slick 109

Kilg%ore 211

Killer Croc **192**, 240

Killer Elite 62

Killer Frost 113, 117, 123, **192**, 273

Killer Moth *see* Charaxes

Killer Shark **193**

Killer Wasp 171

Killgrave, Thaddeus 173

Killshot 152, **193**, 308

Kilowog 39, **193**

Kindly Ones *see* Three Witches

Kinetix **193**, 204, 373

King, Christopher 101

King Coffin 260

King Faraday **193**, 277, 296

King Shark **194**

King Snake 36, **194**, 196, 213, 310

King Solovar 141, **194**

King of Tears 171, **194**, 297, 313

King Thar 347

King, The **194**

Kirigi 202

Kiyahani, Sergeant 164

Klamorr 321

Klarion the Witch Boy 14, 87, 99, **195**, 209, 381

Knight, Charles 253

Knight, David 235

Knight I (Percival Sheldrake) 195, 320

Knight II (Cyril Sheldrake) 173, 195

Knockout 53, 195, 336

Kobra 9, 31, 79, 85, 111, 125, 152, 157, **196**, 198, 253, 312, 334, 374

Kole **196**, 348

Komand'r *see* Blackfire

Kon-El 190

Kor 105, 120

Korbal 314

K.O.R.D. 57

Kord, Jarvis 57

Kordax 18, 107, 196

Koriand'r *see* Starfire

Korll 278

Korugar 190, 311

Koryak 19, **196**

Koschei the Deathless 257

Kramer, Philip 79

Krinn, Rokk 204, 296

see also Cosmic Boy

Kritter 160

Kroef, Janwillem 138, 250

Krona 150, **197**

Krypto 133, **197**

Krypton/Kryptonians 91, 108, 116, 133, **166** 197, 263, 215, 231, 338, 340–1, 354

Kryptonite Man **197**

L

Labrats **198**

Lady Blackhawk **198**

Lady Chian 24

Lady Clay *see* Clayface IV

Lady Flash **202**

Lady of the Lake 19, 52, **202**

Lady Shiva 38, 41, 50, 110, 194, **203**, 279

Lady Vic **202**, 345

Lady Zand 58, **202**, 289

Land of the Unliving 25

Lane, Lois 31, 48, 89, 115, 134, 197, 200, 214–5, 238, 255, 264, 275, 280, 293, 338, 341, 373

Lane, Lucy 48

Lang, Lana **202**, 293, 338

Langle, Doctor Charles 235

Lar Gand 166

Lashina 25, 120, **203**

Last American Warriors (L.A.W.) 177, 266

Latham, Marla 111

Lau, Charlie 331

Laws' Legionnaires *see* Seven Soldiers of Victory

Lazarus Pits 115, 283, 288, 344

Lead 231

League of Assassins 60, 96, **203**

League of Challenger-Haters 77

Leaguebusters 266

Leather **203**

Leather Rose 134

Lee, Francine 224

Lee, Liri 207

L.E.G.I.O.N. 46, 68, 97, 134, **198**, 240, 282, 331, 361

Legion of Doom 117

Legion Espionage Squad 77

Legion Rescue Squad 119

Legion of Substitute Heroes **203**, 243

Legion of Super-Heroes 15, 17, 29, 55, 58, 59, 60, 76, 77, 80, 82, 86, 88, 94, 102, 111, 114, 119, 135, 166, 173, 174, 189, 191, 193, 202, **204–5**, 206, 210, 220, 296, 240, 243, 301, 309, 314, 321, 338, 350, 351, 353, 356, 360, 361, 363, 373, 374, 380

Legion of Super-Villains 80

Legion World 17, 60, 111, 121, 135, 174, 189, 191, 193, 206, 210, 220, 296, 301, 314, 321, 356, 361, 374

Legionnaire Xs 321

LeGrieve, Simon 9

LeHah, Carleton 258

Lemaris, Lori **206**

Lenny *see* Dybbuk

Leno, Carmen 58

Leviathan 204, 206, 309

LexCom 200

LexCorp 12, 130, 214, 215, 283, 341, 344, 356

Leymen 105, 140, 176, 251, 275

see also Primal Force

Lianna 150

Liberty Belle 11, **206**, 235, 279, 380

Libra 171

Life Power Church of Maxine 16

Lifeweb 16

Lightning 228, **351**

Lightning Lord 206, 210, 314

Lightray 129, **206**, 249, 258

Lilith 170, **207**, 381

Limbo 17, 141

Lin, Mavaar 10

Linear Men 164, **207**, 363, 371

Lionheart **207**

Little Boy Blue **207**

Little Mermaid 138, 176, **210**

Little Miss Redhead 207

Little Sure Shot 303

Live Wire I (Garth Ranzz) 60, 88, 114, 204–5, 206, **210**, 314

Live Wire II (Spark) 210

Lizotte, Jean 140

Lkz 279, 358

Lobo 138, 198, **209**, 312, 313, 331, 370, 375, 381

Lock Up **210**

Locus 50

Lodestone II (Rhea Jones) **210**

Lonar **210**, 249

London 207, 260

Longstreet, Tommy 113

Looker **211**, 261

Looking Glass 55

Loose Cannon **211**

Lord, Maxwell **212**

Lord Chaos **211**

Lord of Dreams *see* Morpheus

Lord of the Flies *see* Beelzebub

Lord Havoc I (Maxwell Lord) 117, **211**, 180

Lord Havoc II 12, 58, 117, 176, 180, **211**, 227

Lord Pernisius 351

Lord of Time **213**

Lords of Chaos *see* Chaos, Lords of

Lords of Order *see* Order, Lords of

Loria 56

Loring, Jean **213**

Loser 334

Losers 72, 84, 151, **213**

Love, Doctor Benjamin 101, 160, 373

Lower Pluxas 153

Lucifer 9, 32, 46, 53, 57, 102, 196

Lump **213**

Lupo, Wolf 207

Luthor, Alexander 89

Luthor, Lena 255

Luthor, Lex 10, 12, 32, 34, 41, 48, 51, 52, 54, 58, 61, 80, 83, 87, 102, 108, 118, 130, 135, 136, 141, 170, 171, 176, 200, 202, **214–5**, 224, 231, 248, 251, 278, 282, 283, 293, 296, 303, 334, 336, 338, 341, 344, 356, 362, 373

Lynx **213**

Lyrl 134

Lyta 83

M

M-Team Alpha 88

Ma'alefa'ak 226

McCauley, Leland 60, 210, 360

McCree, Ginny "Torch" 173

McGurk, Montague T. "Curly" 163

McKendrick, Luke 301

Mad Harriet 120, **218**

Mad Hatter **218**, 291

Madame 50, 155, **219**, 352

Madame Rouge 113, 136, **219**, 230, 247, 270, 371

Madame Xanadu 96, **219**

Mademoiselle Marie **219**, 303

Madison, Christie 73

Madmen 117

Magala 27, 376

Mageddon 16, 32, 171, **219**, 232, 382

Mageddon War 219, **363**

Magenta **220**

Magic Forest 282

Magno 131, 204, **220**

Magnus, Doctor Will 231

Magnus Veridium 231

Mainline **221**

Major Disaster 84, 181, **221**, 225

Major Force 25, 117, 135, **221**

Maltis *see* Doctor Mist

Maltus 150, 167

Mammoth 120, **221**, 308

Man-Bat **222**

Man of the Hour 163

Man of Steel 12

Man of Steel *see* Superman

Manchester Black **224**

Manchukk 97

Manhunter 76, **223**, 274

Manhunter I (Donald Richards) 131, 224

Manhunter II (Paul Kirk) **223**, 254, 360

Manhunter III (Mark Shaw) **223**, 301

Manhunter IV (Chase Lawler) **223**, 301

Manhunter V (Kirk DePaul) **223**

Manhunters, the 150, 224, **225**

Manitou Raven 14, 181, **225**

Mannheim, Bruno "Ugly" 173, **224**

Manning, Pol 294

Mannock, Edward 116

Mano 119, 204, 350

Mantegna, Tony 301

Manticore 257

Mantis 129, **225**, 249

Marie the Psychic Turtle 124

Marin, Angel 56

Markovia 137, 211, 261, 346

Marksman **225**

Mars 206, 226, 372

Marshall, Jack 152

Martet, Gerard Yves 82

Martian Manhunter 18, 28, 32, 79, 98, 123, 151, 168, 174, 180–1, 225, **226**, 300, 301, 321, 362

Mary Marvel 69, 70, 71, **227**, 358

Maser *see* Air Wave

Mash 353

Mask 320

Masked Avenger **134**

Mason, Myra 104, 314

Master 101

Master Man 294

Master, The 258

Match 336

Matrix 190, 338, 358

Matter-Eating Lad **228**

Matter Master 301

Mawzir **228**

Max Mercury 25, 191, **228**, 279, 297

Maxi-Man 87

Maxie Zeus **228**

Maxima 12, 117, **229**, 289

Maximum 334

Maya **229**, 246

Mazursky, Doctor 88, 234

Meanstreak 117, 151, **229**

Medea 228

Medphyll 97

Medusa 88, 266

Mega-Biter 277

Mekanique **229**, 271, 380

Men from N.O.W.H.E.R.E. **230**

Mento 39, 113, 165, **230**, 301

Mera 17, 18, 19, **230**

Mercenaries **230**

Meridian 275

Merlin 46, 99, 244, 308

Merlyn 58, 202, **230**

Merry, Girl of 1,000 Gimmicks **230**

Mesa City 352

Meta 304

Metal Men 80, 86, 102, 112, **231**

Metallo **231**

Metamorpho 109, 114, 170, **232**, 261, 301

Metron 46, 53, 161, 163, 206, 219, **232**, 249

Metropolis 13, 31, 47, 48, 53, 56, 59, 61, 77, 91, 94, 102, 108, 115, 121, 134, 139, 148, 150, 159, 160, 173, 174, 200, 202, 204–5, 206, 211, 214–5, 224, 231, 236, 238, 248, 250, 255, 264, 275, 285, 289, 296, 305, 309, 311, 314, 327, 330, 334, 338, 340–1, 344, 351, 356, 373

Metternich, Natalie 253

Michaels, Dr. Albert 31

Microwave Mom 160

Midnight 84, 107, 129, **232**

Midnight Kid 233

Midway City 109, 113, 247

Mighty Mole 73

Mildred 351

Millennium Giants 137, **233**

Minion **233**

Minstrel Maverick **233**

Minute-Man 72, 320

Mirage **233**

Mirror Master 273

Mirror Master I (Samuel Joseph Scudder) 171, **234**, 301

Mirror Master II 66, 234

see also Captain Boomerang

Mirror Master III (Evan McCulloch) **234**

Misa 289

Mishkin, Dimitri 168

Miss America 131, 170, 184, **234**

Miss Liberty **235**

Miss Martian **235**

Miss X 235

Missile Men 231

Mist I (Kyle Jonathon Smythe) **235**, 301, 324, 325

Mist II (Nash) 12, 57, 90, 168, **235**, 325

Mist, Doctor 135

Mister America 235

Mister Atom 71, **235**, 236, 242

Mister Banjo 98, 230

Mister Bones 101, 160, 170, 323

Mister E 105, **236**

Mister Element 66, 102

Mister Freeze 66, 237, 291

Mister Jupiter 280, 348

Mister Keeper 191

Mister Mind 71, 106, 185, 227, 235, **236**, 242, 286, 296

Mister Miracle 46, 47, 95, 102, 120, 148, 161, 189, 213, **236**, 249, 258, 311

Mister Muscle 160

Mister Mxyzptlk 48, 169, **238**, 279, 300

Mister Nobody 62, **238**

Mister Scarlet (Brian Butler) **238**

Mister Scarlet II (Pinky) **238**

Mister Terrific 293

Mister Terrific I (Terry Sloane) 235, **239**

Mister Terrific II (Michael Holt) 184–5, **239**, 295

Mister Twister 17, 348

Mister Venge 86

Mister Who 239, 242, 253

Mister Zsasz **240**, 243

Mnemosyne 353

Mockingbird **240**, 301

Mokkari 249

Molotov 268

Monaghan, Tommy 39, 228

Monarch 117, 155, 233, **240**, 371

Mon El 55, 166, 204–5, **240**

Mongoose 254

Mongrel 56, **241**

Mongul 149, 170, 229, 317, 326

Mongul I (Mongul) 91, **241**

Mongul II (son of Mongul) 241

Monitor 104, 153, **242**, 365, 371

Monocle **242**, 301

Monsieur Mallah 46, 60, 219, **242**, 270

Monster Society of Evil 71, 235, **242**, 253, 282

Monstergirl 381

Monstress 114, 204–5, **243**

Montez, Alexander 112

Montgomery, Claire 87

Montoya, Renée **243**, 359

Moon Rider 233

Moon, The 123, 132, 205, 221, 226, 358

Moonrider, Mark **243**

Moonstruk, Zena 138, 198, 312

Mordecai **243**

Mordred 351

Mordru *see* Dark Lord, The

Morgaine Le Fay 99, **244**

Morgan, Ace 77

Morgan, Jennifer **244**, 371

Morgan, Joe 30

Morgan, Shorty 59

Morpheus 62, 102, 129

Morphogenetic Field 16

Mortalla **244**

Mossa 265

Mossad 159

Mother Box 46, 49, 86, 161, 171, 258, 301, 369

Mount Olympus 256

Mount Thunder 117

Mouthpiece 244

Moxie, Boss 59, 173

Mrs. Levy 55

Mud Pack 85

Mudge 296

Muller, Heinrich 116

Murmur **245**

Musashi **245**

Musketeer **245**

Myrg 230

Mister Scarlet II (Pinky) **238**

Mister Terrific 293

Mister Terrific I (Terry Sloane) 235, **239**

Mister Terrific II (Michael Holt) 184–5, **239**, 295

Mister Twister 17, 348

Mister Venge 86

Mister Who 239, 242, 253

Mister Zsasz **240**, 243

Mnemosyne 353

Mockingbird **240**, 301

Mokkari 249

Molotov 268

Monaghan, Tommy 39, 228

Monarch 117, 155, 233, **240**, 371

Mon El 55, 166, 204–5, **240**

Mongoose 254

Mongrel 56, **241**

Mongul 149, 170, 229, 317, 326

Mongul I (Mongul) 91, **241**

Mongul II (son of Mongul) 241

Monitor 104, 153, **242**, 365, 371

Monocle **242**, 301

Monsieur Mallah 46, 60, 219, **242**, 270

Monster Society of Evil 71, 235, **242**, 253, 282

Monstergirl 381

Monstress 114, 204–5, **243**

Montez, Alexander 112

Montgomery, Claire 87

Montoya, Renée **243**, 359

Moon Rider 233

Moon, The 123, 132, 205, 221, 226, 358

Moonrider, Mark **243**

Moonstruk, Zena 138, 198, 312

Mordecai **243**

Mordred 351

Mordru *see* Dark Lord, The

Morgaine Le Fay 99, **244**

Morgan, Ace 77

Morgan, Jennifer **244**, 371

Morgan, Joe 30

Morgan, Shorty 59

Morpheus 62, 102, 129

Morphogenetic Field 16

Mortalla **244**

Mossa 265

Mossad 159

Mother Box 46, 49, 86, 161, 171, 258, 301, 369

Mount Olympus 256

Mount Thunder 117

Mouthpiece 244

Moxie, Boss 59, 173

Mrs. Levy 55

Mud Pack 85

Mudge 296

Muller, Heinrich 116

Murmur **245**

Musashi **245**

Musketeer **245**

Myrg 230

Myrra 251

Mysa 204

Mystery Men 11

Mysto 59, **245**

N

Nabu 103, **246**

Nadia Safir 138

Naiad **246**

Nanda Parbat 177

Narcosis 218

Natt the Hat 162

Nazis 11, 28, 32, 35, 72, 135, 136, 137, 151, 163, 184, 191, 193, 206, 213, 219, 225, 228, 235, 238, 251, 269, 271, 286, 289, 295, 320, 321, 326, 345, 360, 361, 367, 369, 376, 380

Ne-Ahn 17

Nebula Man 10, 90, **246**, 301, 323, 374

Nefar Nebula 370

Negative Man 109, **247**

Negative Woman 79, 84, **247**

Nekron 25, 197

Nemesis I (Tom Tresser) **247**, 251, 257

Nemesis II (Soseh Mykos) **247**

NEMO 97

Neon the Unknown 676 131, **248**

Nergal 230, 294

Neron 8, 28, 31, 52, 53, 56, 57, 66, 71, 80, 82, 87, 98, 105, 137, 192, 219, 221, 231, 241, **248**, 315, 358, 372, 376

Neutron 120, **248**

New Bloods 151, 211, 241, 250

New Brotherhood of Evil 162, 371

New Extremists 111, 117, 151, 229

New Genesis 39, 46, 47, 49, 95, 101, 118, 129, 161, 206, 210, 225, 232, 236, 243, 249, 258, 289, 301, 331, 344, 353, 369

New Gods 46, 53, 60, 95, 102, 118, 127, 161, 163, 171, 206, 210, **249**, 225, 232, 236, 243, 249, 301, 327, 344

New Guardians 128, 129, 138, 153, 193, **250**

New Olympians 228

New Order 250

New Teen Titans 152, 277, 308, **348–9**, 351, 357, 358, 364

New Titans 94, 97, 101, 120, 148, 233, **348**, 364

New-Wave 374

Newsboy Legion 59, 150, **250**, 311 336

Night 11, 251

Night Force **251**

Night Girl 203

Nightblade 56, **250**

Nightfall 64

Nighthawk 137, 156, **251**, 275

Nightmaster **251**, 275

Nightshade 193, 247, **251**, 257, 277, 258, 309

Night-Slayer 253

Nightwind 251

Nightwing 17, 40, 56, 62, 93, 110, 128, 131, 139, 170, 179, 203, 232, 233, 252, 259, 260, 261, 262, 269, 280, 290–1, 310, 315, 331, 334, 345, 348, 355

Nimbus 256

Nippo 98, 230

Nite-Wing 355

NKVDemon 190

Noblesse, Jenny 218

Noctura **253**

Nomoz 258

Nommo 120

Noose 173

Northwind 170, 185, 196, **253**

Nth Metal 155, 156

Nuada Silverarm 254

Nuclear Family **253**

Nuclear Man *see* Firestorm

Nuklon 31, 87, 170

Number None 62

Nyola 98, 230, 242, **253**, 282

Nyssa 283, 344

Oa 92, 108, 145, 149, 150, 188, 197, 225, 242, 264, 294, 311

Obsidian 94, 112, 170, 176, 185, **254**, 292

Obsidian Age 19, 118, 225, 347

Ocean Master 18, 29, 52, **254**

O'Connell, Travis 207

O'Dare, Matt 297, 321

Odd Man **254**

Okaara 51, 120, 166, 322

Old Justice 230, 354

Old Mother 257

Olsen, Jimmy 47, 120, 200, **255**, 341

Olympian 138, **256**

Olympian Gods 13, 90, 100, 132, 162, 249, **256**, 262, 313, 353, 375, 376–7

Omac 188, **256**, 355

Omega Men 149, 209, **256**, 325

Omen 289, 345

Ometeotl 111

Omni 286

Ona 213

Onomatopoeia **237**

Onslaught, The **237**

Onyx **238**

Oom 242, 253

Opal City 51, 229, 235, 297, 304, 324, 325

Oracle (Barbara Gordon) 37, 38, 40, 50, 56, 57, 81, 110, 141, 152, 165, 178, **259**, 262, 280, 297

Order, Lords of 14, 104, 113, 118, 127, 171, 270, 276, 309

Order of St. Dumas **238**

Orion 46, 95, 129, 161, 173, 188, 206, 219, 236, 244, 249, **258**, 353

Orpheus **260**

Ortega, Manuel 297

O.S.S. Spies at War **254**

Our Worlds at War *see* Imperiex War

Outburst 334

Outlaw **260**

Output 277

Outsiders 26, 31, 36, 41, 51, 104, 120, 137, 148, 152, 170, 176, 189, 211, 228, 232, 252, 253, 257, **261**, 268, 277, 334, 346, 351, 374

Overmaster 12, 28, 64, 111, 117, 118, 151, 168, 174, 229, 245, **260**

Owlman 89

Owlwoman 73, 138, 176, **260**

P

Paciforce 189

Pampero 64, 294, 334

Pandora's Box 13

Pantagones 14

Pantha **264**, 285

Parallax 91, 143, 144, 145, 149, 193, 204, 246, 263, **264**, 280, 317

Paramour 365

Parasite 200, **264**

Pariah **265**

Park, Linda 124, 125, 198, 248, **265**, 273, 281, 372, 383

Parsons, Joe 9

Particon 204

Patchwork Man 22

Patchwork Man I (Gregori Arcane) **266**

Patchwork Man II (Elliot Taylor) **266**

Patriot 361

Paunteur 90

Pax Dei 28, 382

Pax Romana 12

Peacemaker 79

Peacemaker I (Christopher Smith) **266**

Peacemaker II (real name unrevealed) **266**

Peacemaker III (Mitchell Black) **266**

Peg-Leg Friel 244

Penguin 40, 192, **267**

Penny Dreadful 160

Pennyworth, Alfred 40, 268, 290, 350

People's Heroes 152, **268**

Peril, Johnny **268**

Perisphere 11

Perkins, Neptune 11, 131, **269**, 358, 380

Persisphere 380

Persuader 119, **269**, 350

Perun **269**, 313

Phantasm **269**

Phantasmo **269**

Phantom of the Fair **270**, 295

Phantom Lady I (Sandra Knight) 37, 254, **270**

Phantom Lady II (Deliah Tyler) **270**

Phantom Stranger 96, 99, 107, **270**, 314, 345

Phantom Zone 91, 108, 133, 197, 370

Phobia **270**

Phobos 228, **271**

Phoebe 353

Phoenix 254

Pied Piper **271**

Pinky 238

Piranha Man 79

Pisboe 300

Piscator 257

Planeteers **271**, 355

Plasma-Men 358

Plasmus **271**

Plastic Man 11, **272**, 278

Plastique 117, **273**

Platinum 231

Plunder **273**

Poe 198

Poglachi 139

Poison Ivy 128, 154, 171, 228, 271, **273**, 301

Polar Boy 202, **273**

Pooch 151, 213

Portenza, Contessa del *see* Contessa, The

Poseidon 90, 256

Poseidonis 134, 196, 210, 230, 305, 347

Pow-Wow Smith 59, **275**

Power Battery 92, 144, 149, 311

Power Company 118, 123, 224, 254, **274**, 311, 331, 330

Power Girl 24, 105, 110, 115, 170, 184, 259, **274**

Power, Josiah 274

Pozhar 121, 123

Prankster 18, **275**

Pravda 238

Praxis 87, **275**

Predator 98, 323

Presence 316

Prez **275**

Primaid 372

Primal Force 51, 84, 105, 176, 251, **275**

Prime One 129

Primm, Sarah 227

Primordial Annihilator 219

Primus 256

Prince Ra-Man **276**

Princess Projectra **276**

Pritor 15

Private Eyes 160

Professor Ivo 13, 151, 154, **276**, 326, 344, 355, 365

Professor Zoom 287

Progenitor 114, 243

Project Cadmus 150, 157, 250, 254, 255, 311, 336

Project M 68, 88, 131, 213, 234, 266, 380

Prometheus 165, 259, **276**

Provoke 152, 308

Prysm 131, 177, **276**, 289

Psilencer 334

Psimon 104, 120, 221, 233, 248, **277**, 308

Psions 55, 149, 166, **167**, 256, 322

Psyba-Rats **277**

Psyche 370

Psychic, Rose 105

Psycho-Pirate **277**

Punch and Jewelee **277**

Purvis, Rick 322

Pylon 131

Pyrogen 334

Q

Q Foundation 32

Quakemaster 366

Quantum Mechanics **278**

Quantum Queen 370

Queen Bee I 135, 138, 153, 176, 210, 256, 260

Queen Bee II **278**

Queen Clea 244, 367

Queen of Fables **278**

Query 288

Question, The 110, 165, 199, 279, 288

Question II **278**

Quick, Jesse 87, 206, 279

Quick, Johnny 11, 89, 206, **279**

Quicksilver 131, 228

Quintessence 139, 161, 164, 256, 270

Quiz 62

Quontauka 129

Quorum 56, 223, 241

Qurac 257, 308

Qward 87, 89, 242, 284, 305, 311, 354, 371

Qwsp **279**, 358

R

Raaga 360

Radiant 108

Radion 204

Rag Doll II **282**

Raganarok 184, 295

Ragman 96, 140, **282**, 375

Rahn, Hollikka 97

Rajak, Colonel 153, **282**

RAM 250

Rama Khan 14

Ramban 157

Ramulus 242, 253, **282**

Rann 29, 148, 189, 301, 330

Ranzz, Garth 204, 296

see also Live Wire

Ra's al Ghul 36, 86, 115, 203, 205, **283**, 344

Rath 98

Ravager 161

Ravan 257, 266

Rave 141

Raven 96, 97, 165, 177, 254, 264, 269, 277, **284**, 348, 349, 357

Ravens 81, 367

Ravers 160, **284**, 314

Rawlins, Pvt. Rick 154

Ray 22, 51, 131, **284**, 381

Raymond, Roy – TV Detective **285**

Razorsharp 56, 277

Reactron 247

Re-Animage 370

R.E.B.E.L.S. 46, 68, 134, 198, 209, **282**, 331

Rebis 247

Red Bee **285**

Red Dart 142

Red Hood **285**

Red Panzer **285**, 345

Red Shadows 77, 268, 309

Red Shift 284

Red Star 152, 264, 268, **285**

Red Tornado 123, 246, 275, **286**, 301, 344, 381

Red Torpedo 131, **286**, 324

Rednex 141

Reduu, Jiv 134

Reed, Robbie 101

Reilly, Ed 251

Relative Heroes **286**

Remiel 9, 46

Replicant **286**

Requiem see Artemis

Resurrection Man 58, 169, **287**, 364

Reverb see Hardline

Reverse-Flash 124, **287**, 301, 383

Rex the Wonder Dog 100, **289**

Reynard, Jacques 79

Rhea 353, 358

Rhymer 248

Richards, Cary 266

Riddler 84, 192, **288**, 359

Rimbor 353, 360

Ringmaster 140

Riot 289

Rip Roar 289

Rising Sun 138, 289, 332

Risk 94, 177, 276, 289

Rival 171, 228

Robbins, June 77

Robin 14, 17, 25, 26, 56, 84, 93, 124, 188, 192, 194, 218, 238, 253, 259, 267, 283, 290–1, 315, 331, 336, 344, 347, 357, 358, 372, 375

Robin I

see also Nightwing

Robin I (Dick Grayson) 40, 125, 128, 252, 262, 280, 260–1, 322, 348

Robin II (Jason Todd) 40, 178, 288, 260–1, 349

Robin III (Tim Drake) 40, 213, 275, 260–1, 301, 310, 320, 348, 349, 381

Robinson, Holly "Gonightly" 75

Robotman 60, 102, 136, 316

Robotman I (Dr. Robert Crane; Paul Dennis) 11, 81, 292

Robotman II (Cliff Steele) 81, 109, 121, 242, 292

Rock, Sergeant 116, 333

Rocket Red Brigade 117, 193, 292

Rogers, Red 163

Rogers, Tommy 207

Rosa, Master Spy 292

Rose and Thorn 292

Rosetti, Colonel Reno 164

Rosie 98, 326

Ross, Pete 9, 202, 293

Rotwang 229, 271

Rough Bunch 332

Roulette 122, 128, 165, 239, 293

Roving Ranger 293

Roxxas the Butcher 76

Royal Flush Gang 130, 293, 323

Rufus 261

Ruselka 313

Rustam 257

Ryan, Red 77

Ryan, Rusty 293

S

S.H.A.D.E. **294**

Sabbac 69, 261, **294**

St. Cloud, Silver **294**

Sala **294**

Salakk **294**

Salamanca 64, 294, 334

Sand 184–5, 295, 295

Sandman 32, 90, 184, 185, 196, 253, 270, 282, 295, 321

Sandman I 194, 295, 295, 314, 345

Sandsmark, Cassie 137

Sandy the Golden Boy 282, 295

Sapphire 274

Sardath 330

Sarge see Gunner and Sarge

Sarge Steel 235, 236, 242, 296

Sargon the Sorcerer 296

Satanus 106, 275, 296

Saturn 158

Saturn Girl 60, 88, 189, 204–5, 210, 296

Saturn Queen **296**

Saunders, Kendra see Hawkgirl

Saunders, Shiera 155, 156

Saunders, Speed 155, 254

Savage 153

Savage, Matt: Trail Boss 297

Savant 297

Savitar 198, 228, 279, 297, 380

Sawyer, Maggie 63, 190

Sawyer, Lt. Colonel Scott 173

Scalphunter 36, 297, 297, 321

Scandal **297**

Scanner 364

Scarab 87, 297

Scare Tactics 149

Scarecrow 171, 228, 271, **298**

Scarface **366**

Scarlet, Mr. 76

Scarlet Skier 182

Scavenger 18, 160, **300**

Schott, Winslow 173

Scoopshovel 98, 326

Scorch 169, 226, **300**

Scorcher 94

Scratch, Nicholas 122

Screamqueen 149

Scylla 79

Sea Devils 184, **301**

Sea Wolf 32, 360

Sealed City 235

Secret 209, **301**, 317, 373, 381

Secret Six 240, **301**

Secret Society of Super-Villains 87, **301**, 360

Section Zero 213

Sekhmet 233

Sela 14

Sensei 60, 96, 203

Sensor 77, 189, 204, **301**

Sentinel 55, 96, 144

Sentinels of Magic 105, 219, 282

Seraph 138, **301**

Sergeant Rock 72, 83, **303**

Serifan 243, **301**, 368

Seven Shadows 297

Seven Soldiers of Victory 10, 31, 90, 195, 246, **302**, 308, 323, 332, 367, 374

Seven, The 105

Shade 10, 171, **304**, 321

Shade, The Changing Man 304

Shado 142, **304**

Shadow 254

Shadow Creature 296

Shadow Demons 265

Shadowpact, the **305**

Shadow-Thief 171, 301

Shadowdragon **305**

Shaggy Man 135, **305**

Shark 51, 254, **305**

Shatterer 295

Shatterfist 64

Shazam 49, 69, 70–1, 72, 76, 106, 227, **305**, 351

Shellshock II (Ruth Spencer) 308

Shift **308,**

Shikari 204–5

Shimmer 120, 221, **308**

Shining Knight 11, 31, 110, 122, 195, 301, **308**, 320

Shiv 110, 171

Shock Trauma 152, **308**

Shock Troops 173

Shotgun Smith 275

Shreck **309**

Shrieve, Lt. Matthew 88

Shrike 64

Shrinking Violet 94, 204–5, 206, **309**

Sickle 268

see also Hammer and Sickle

Siegel, Bugsy 367

Silk Black 219, 352

Silver Banshee **309**

Silver Ghost 122, 301

Silver Monkey **310**

Silver Scarab 131, 170, 246, 253

Silver Sorceress 117, 211

Silver Swan 80, 373, 376–7

Silver Swan I (Valerie Beaudry) **310**

Silver Swan II (Vanessa Kapatelis) 106, **310**

Simeon, Sam see Angel and the Ape

Simms, Herbert 207

Simyan 249

Sindella 382

Sin-Eater **310**

Sinestro 25, 144, 149, 190, 193, 301, **311**, 370, 371

Siren 345

Sirianni, Carlo "Chuck" 54, 254

Sirius **311**

Sister Andromeda 204

Sister Lilhy 258

Six Pack 162

Skartaris 24, 210, 244, 276, 367, 371

Skeets 58, **311**

Skorpio **311**

Sky Pirate 51

Skyman 170

Skyrocket 274, **311**, 374

Slab, The 72, 153, 162, 202, 221

Slagger 177

Slate, Garrison 274

Sleepwalk 62

Sleez 250, **311**

Slipstream 87

Slither 149

Slo-Bo 381

Slopp 321

Slyggia 294

Smallville 190, 202, 214, 280, 336, 340

Smiley 293

Smith, Bulldozer 73

Smith, Jeffrey 164

Snart, Len see Captain Cold

Snart, Lisa see Golden Glider

Sobek 312

Society of the Golden Wing 51

Society of Sin 162, 270, 271, **312**, 348, 371

Sodal Yat 166

Soffick, Tamlick 10

Solaar 364

Solaris I (Clifton Lacey) **312**

Solaris II **312**

Solomon Grundy 170, 171, **312**

Sommers, Vic 301

Son of Vulcan **313**

Sonar 180, 229, **313**

Sons of Dawn 354, 380

Sons of Liberty 9

Soozie-Q 160

Sorensen, Karel 322
Sorrow, Johnny 88, 98, 169, 171, 297, **313**
Source 161, 256, 314
Soyuz 121, 269, **313**, 382
Space Cabby **313**
Space Ranger **314**
Spark 77, 204–5, 206, 210, **314**
Sparx 56, 160, **314**
Spawn of Frankenstein 107, **314**
Spectra 152
Spectre 28, 88, 96, 99, 112, 125, 144, 184, 239, 246, 248, 264, **292–3**, 296, 269, 301, 321, 358, 363, 383
Speed Force 125, 198, 228, 279, 297, 380
Speed Metal Kids 152
Speed Queen 120
Speed Saunders **314**
Speedy 26, 142–3, **315**, 333, 347, 348, 358
see also Arsenal
Spellbinder I (Delbert Billings) **315**
Spellbinder III (Fay Moffit) **315**
Spider 131, 301, 374
see also Alias the Spider
Spider Guild 55, 149, 209, 256
Spinner, Dorothy 109, 230, 292, **315**
Spitfire 51
Split **315**
Spoiler 94, 253, 291, **320**
Sportsmaster 92, 171
Springheeled Jack 195
Sprinter 254
Spy Smasher 37, 72, **320**
Squire I (Percival Sheldrake) 195, 320
Squire II (Cyril Sheldrake) 195, 320
Squire III (real name unknown) 173, **320**
Stagg, Simon 232
Stalker 194, **320**, 324, 355
Stallion 62, 110
Stalnoivolk 72, **321**
Stanley & His Monster **321**
Stanton, Dr. Charles 106
Star Boy 29, 111, 204–5, 243, **321**
Star City 52, 142–3, 258, 276, 321
Star Conqueror **321**
Star Hawkins **322**
S.T.A.R. Labs 31, 57, 60, 63, 73, 76, 91, 101, 115, 116, 120, 137, 138, 169, 248, 264, 274, 286, 331, 351
Star Racer 34
Star Rovers **322**
Star Sapphire 145, 190, 280, **323**, 326
Star, Thaddeus 314
Star-Tsar 73
Starfire 55, 132, 167, 233, 256, 291, **322**, 348–9
Stargirl 184–5, **323**, 325, 332
Starhaven 59
Starlings 117
Starman 56, 63, 92, 104, 105, 169, 184, 235, 297, 313, 321, 323, 324–5, 355
Starman I (Theodore Henry Knight) 92, 99,

324–5, 355
Starman II 286, 324
Starman III (Mikaal Tomas) 324
Starman IV (Prince Gavin) 324
Starman V (William Payton) 324
Starman VI (David Knight) 58, 63, 292, 324
Starman VII (Jack Knight) 304, 321, 325
Starman VIII 325
Starman 1,000,000 (Farris Knight) 325
Starro 321
Star-Spangled Kid 11, 101, 110, 169, 170, 194, 230, 301, **323**, 325, 332
Star-Spangled Kid II 185, 246
Starwoman 332
Stasis Zone 240
Steadfast 275
Stealth 138, 198
Steamroller 98, **326**
Steel 11, 153, 174, 276, 278, 311, 315, 341, 356
Steel I (Hank Heywood III) 180, 326
Steel II (John Henry Irons) 93, 308, 291, **327**, 332
Steel III (Hank Heywood I) 233, **326**
Steel, Sarge 79
Stein, Harry 79
Stein, Martin 123
Stein, Nicole 61
Stellar Studios 154
Steppenwolf 161, 249, **331**
Sterling, Stella 322
Stevens, Jared 103, 246
Stevens, Nick 101
Stewart, John 97
Stikk, Bromwell 17
Stompa 120, **331**
Stone Boy 203
Stone, Dan 173
Storm, Heather 268
Stovepipe 354
Strange, Adam 189, 301, **330**
Strange, Professor Hugo **331**
Stranglehold 152, 308
Strata 134, 138, 198, **331**
Strauss, Eric and Linda 103, 246
Stretch 144
Striker Z 274, **331**
S.T.R.I.P.E. 110, 169, **323**, 332
Stripesy 11, 230, 301, 323, **332**
Strongbow **332**
Stryker, Cpl. Slim 154
Stuart, Lt. Jeb 154, 213
Stuart, Jennifer 274
Stuff 301, 367
Subtle Realms 279
Sude 304
Suicide Jockeys 244, 353
Suicide Squad 9, 27, 56, 58, 60, 66, 76, 79, 80, 84, 87, 88, 97, 104, 110, 115, 120, 157, 194, 221, 234, 247, 251, 254, 257, 259, 321, **333**, 369, 370
Suli 95, 98
Sumaan Harjavti 260

Sumo, the Samurai **332**
Sun Boy **333**
Sunburst **332**
Sun-Eater 55, 121, 144, 204, 214, 256, 322, 350
Super-Buddies 227
Super-Chief **332**
Super-Cycle 49
Super-Malon 64, 296, **334**
Superbia 173, 320, 368
Superboy 27, 48, 53, 150, 160, 194, 195, 204–5, 233, 240, 281, 284, 291, 300, 301, 314, 336, 338, **341**, 349, 375, 380, 381
Supercycle 35
Supergirl 27, 46, 86, 98, 117, 120, 131, 174, 233, 264, 287, 331, 338, **341**, 358, 323, 363
Superior City 285
Superman 8, 9, 10, 12, 13, 31, 32, 39, 47, 48, 51, 55, 57, 61, 73, 80, 86, 89, 91, 108, 111, 113, 115, 116, 119, 120, 123, 133, 136, 139, 169, 174, 168, 214–5, 219, 221, 224, 225, 204, 209, 226, 229, 231, 232, 233, 238, 241, 246, 248, 251, 255, 256, 262, 263, 264, 274, 275, 280, 282, 305, 321, 327, 334, 338, **340–1**, 349, 381, 356, 363, 364, 372, 373
Superman Revenge Squad 229, 289
Superman Robot 170, 349, 381
Supermen of America **334**
Superwoman 89
Svarozhich 125, 261
Swamp Thing 22, 96, 99, 113, 123, 128, 155, 246, 251, 262, 266, 285, **335**, 375, 382
Sylph **334**
Symbolix 94
Syonide II 152, **334**

T

Taghurrhu 256
Taine, Chuck 204
Takion 39, 161, 249, **344**
Tala 345
Talia 202, 283, **344**
Tamaran/Tamaranans 55, 167, 322
Tangleweb 204
Tannarak **345**
Tarantula I (Jonathan Law) 11, **345**
Tarantula II (Catalina Marie Flores) **345**
Tarpit **345**, 372
Tartarus 161, **345**, 364
Task Force X 58, 79, 113, 254, 333, 370
Tasmanian Devil 138, 159, 229, **346**
Tattooed Man 171, **346**
Tawky Tawny **346**
Team Hazard 221
Team Superman 233
Team Titans 233, 350, 353
Technis 91
Technis Imperative 69
Technocrat 261, **346**
Teekl 195

Teen Titans 15, 17, 26, 39, 60, 63, 81, 91, 94, 97, 107, 120, 128, 131, 137, 138, 139, 155, 167, 171, 177, 191, 193, 196, 220, 221, 230, 233, 242, 248, 252, 256, 262, 264, 269, 270, 271, 276, 279, 284, 285, 289, 290, 291, 293, 308, 322, 336, 347, **348–9**, 350, 353, 371, 381
Tefe 335, 375
Tempest 19, 29, 107, 170, 196, 279, 345, **347**
Temptress 236
Teng, Dr. 48
Terra 137, 233, 348, 349, **350**
Tethys 353
Tezcatlipoca 32, 219
Tezumak 14, **350**
Thanagar/Thanagarians 132, 159, 166, 167, 310
Tharok 119, **350**
Tharr 243
Themis 353
Themyscira 13, 27, 83, 131, 130, 153, 162, 256, 310, 322, 351, 358, 369, 376–7
Thia 353
Thinker 171, 273
Thirst 9, **350**
Thompkins, Leslie M.D. 40, 267, **350**
Thorn 176, 254, 292
Three Witches **351**
Thunder and Lightning (Gan Williams) 204, 261, **351**
Thunder II (Anissa Pierce) 51, 170, **351**
Thunder III (CeCe Beck) 170, **351**
Thunder, Jakeem 184, 352, **352**
Thunder, Johnny I (John Stuart Mill Tane) **352**, 360, 369
Thunder, Johnny II 11, 50, 155, 184, 219, 279, **352**, 352
Thunder, Jonni 352
Thunderbolt 279, 352, **352**
Thunderer 210
Thunderhead 160, 381
Thunderlord 138
Tiggra 46, 244, 249, **353**
Tigorr 256, 325
Timber Wolf 119, 204–5, 350, **353**
Time Commanders **353**
Time Foes 353
Time Masters 164, **353**
Time Trapper **353**
Timepoint 213
Timestream 163, 207, 243
Titan 88, 90, 119, 204
Titans 56, 69, 100, 152, 253
Titans L.A. 107, 128
Titans of Myth 256, 276, **353**, 358
Titans West 39, 63, 101, 128, 160
TNT **354**
T.O. Morrow 276, 342, **355**
Tokamak 122
Tolteca 307
Tomahawk 236, **354**
Tomar-re **354**

Tommy Tomorrow 256, 271, **355**

Tomorrow Woman 276, **355**

Top 140, **355**

Topeka 362

Tor, Magic Master **355**

Tornado Twins 191

Tornado Tyrant 330

Torque 56, **355**

Totenjager 381

Touch-N-Go 165

Tower of Babel 253

Toy, The 62

Toyman 173, 341, **356**

Tracer 117

Traci 13 175, **356**

Trago 360

Trevor, Diana 376

Trevor, Steve **356**, 376

Triad 191, 204, **356**

Triarch 97

Trickster II 58, 248, 301, **357**

Trigger Twins 275, **357**

Trigon 132, 177, 264, 277, 284, 348, 349, 351, **357**

Trilby 198

Trinity 367

Tritonis 196, 206, 210

Triumph 180, 279, **358**

Troia *see* Troy, Donna

Trom 114

Tronix 372

Troy (Donna Troy) 131, 170, 285, 349, 353, **358**, 369, 381

Trylon 11

Tsunami 11, 131, 269, **358**, 380

Tuatara 138

Tucson 288

Tu'julk Mr'asz 135

Turpin, Daniel "Brooklyn" 59

Twilight **358**

Two-Face 40, 64, 243, 291, **359**

U

Ubermensch 32, **360**

Ulgo 184

Ulla 360

Ultimate Clayface 85

Ultra Boy 17, 204–5, 321, **360**

Ultra, the Multi-Alien 360

Ultra-Humanite 12, 30, 170, 239, 247, 301, 352, 360, 380

Ultraman 61, 89

Ultramarines *see* International Ultramarine Corps

Umbra 204, 321, **361**

Uncanny Amazers 29, 173, 243, 321

Uncle Sam 10, 131, 248, 286, **361**

Underworld Unleashed 29

United Planets 60, 166, 175, 204–5, 351

Universo 205, 301

Unknown Soldier 361

Un-Men 22

Usil 32, 360

V

Valadin 10

Valda **364**

Vale, Emmett 231

Vale, Vicki **364**

Validus 119, 350

Valor *see* M'Onel

Van Helsing, Vanessa 251

Vandal Savage 37, 82, 94, 161, 164, 169, 171, 184, 198, 285, 287, 292, 345, **364**, 375

Vanguard **364**

Vanishing Point 164, 207, 353, 380

Vapor 87, **365**

Veil 94, 131

Velcro, Sgt. Vincent 88, 266

Velveeda, Hank 10

Venev 25, 277

Ventriloquist 366

Verdugo, Doctor Maria 269

Veridium 102

Veteran **364**

Vext **365**

Vibe 180, 276, **365**

Vickers, Charlie 97

Vigilante I (Gregory Sanders) 301, **365**

Vigilante II (Adrian Chase) 79, 367, **365**

Vigilante III (Patricia Trayce) **367**

Vikhor 313

Viking Prince **367**

Villain, Doctor Arthur 311

Villains United **368**

Villainy, Inc. 137, 177, 244, **367**

Violence Queen 321

Vixen 16, 173, 180, **369**

Vizacacha 64, 294, 334

Voice-Over 160

Von Gunther, Baroness Paula **369**

Vostok, Valentina 79

Vulcan 313

Vulko 18

Vunderbarr, Malice 120, **369**

Vunderbarr, Virman 369

Vykin the Block **369**

W

Wacky, Doctor 232

Wacky, Mitch 117, 211

Wallace, Donovan 135

Waller, Amanda 56, 60, 79, 101, 111, 159, 257, 259, 277, 296, 333, **370**

Walton, Judy 301

Walton, Nicky 301

Wanderers **370**

War of the Gods 83, 256, 313

Warbringer 219

Warlord 276, **371**

Warlords of Okaara 55, 120, 322

Warp **371**

Warp Child 169

Warrior 135, 209, 370

Warworld 119, 229, 241, 244

Waterbearer 350

Waverider 207, 240, **371**

Wayne, Bruce 40, 52, 56, 58, 64, 89, 116, 118, 130, 267, 268, 290

see also Batman

Wayne, Thomas 40, 89, 268, 288

Weaponers of Qward **371**

Weather Wizard **372**

Weird, The **372**

Weng "Chop Chop" Chan 54, 81

Wether, Captain John 156

Whale, Tobias 51, 334

Whip, The **372**

White Dwarf 364

White Lotus 334

White Magician 27, 80, **377**

White Martians 18, 168, 226, **372**

White Mask 233

White, Perry 200, 215, 341, **373**

White Triangle 15, 17, 114, 356

White Wind 139

White Witch **373**

Wild Dog 374

Wild Hunstman 138

Wild Thing 285

Wildcat 31, 90, 150, 159, 184–5

Wildcat I (Ted Grant) 50, 74, 324, **373**

Wildcat II (Yolanda Montez) 112, 170, **373**

Wild Dog 374

Wildebeest 285, **374**

Wildebeest Society 132, 264, 269, 348

Wildfire 204–5, **374**

Wildman 303

Willpower 275

Winath 206, 296, 314

Windfall 261, **374**

Windrunner 228

Windshear *see* Bulletgirl

Wing 90, 246, 301, **374**

Winged Victory 308

Wise Owl 113

Witch 194

Witchfire 274, **374**

Witch-World 195

Wizard 159, 163, 171, 301, **375**

Wolfpack 236

Wonder Girl 26, 93, 137, 281, 291, 310, 347, 348, 349, 358, **375**, 381

Wonder Woman 13, 15, 18, 27, 34–5, 37, 80, 83, 90, 93, 100, 106, 130, 132, 132, 137, 139, 162, 170, 180–1, 184, 190, 219, 228, 244, 256, 271, 278, 285, 294, 310, 321, 334, 353, 356, 358, 322, 323, 362, 363, 367, 369, 374, **376–7**

Wood, Captain Brent 271, 355

Woozy Winks 272

Word, The I **335**, 375

Word, The II **335**

Workforce 189, 210, 360

World War III *see* Mageddon War

Worlogog 163, 176

Wotan 103

Wu 198

Wye, Professor 253

Wylde 261

X

X Protocol 72

Xanshi 120, 145

Xanthu 29, 111, 173, 191, 243, 321, 325

Xer0 **380**

Xs 204–5, **380**

Y

Yokal the Atrocious 339

Young All-Stars 11, 32, 129, 195, 269, 314, 354, 358, **380**

Young Heroes in Love **381**

Young Justice 14, 25, 49, 60, 69, 73, 86, 148, 170, 195, 199, 270, 289, 336, 354, 374, **381**

Yz 279, 352

Z

Zadron 350

Zaladin 32

Zamarons 150, 250, 323

Zandia 62, 177, 270, 289, 374, 381

Zara 367

Zarina 200

Zatanna 57, 96, 180, 284, 355, **382**

Zatara **382**

Zauriel **382**

Zed, Galius 97

Zed-One 86

Zenturion 372

Zero Hour 30, 59, 76, 103, 156, 164, 184, 185, 211, 233, 240, 234, 317, **363**

Zeta Beam 330

Zeus 90, 162, 228, 256, 373

Zip Kid 381

Zod, General 48

Zombie Twins 173

Zoom 124, 125, 265, 281, **383**

Zrfff 238

Zuggernaut **382**

Acknowledgments

SCOTT BEATTY would like to thank his editors Chris Cerasi, Alastair Dougall, and Laura Gilbert for their enduring patience. Thanks also to fellow writers Bob Greenberger, Phil Jimenez, and Dan Wallace for always watching my back. Additional gratitude goes to Ed Brubaker, Joey Cavalieri, Chuck Dixon, Devin Grayson, Scott McCullar, Jerry Ordway, Greg Rucka, Gail Simone, and Michael Wright for helping to ply the choppy waters of comic book continuity. Finally, special thanks to Jennifer Myskowski, my first and best reader, and Wilbur, a dog's dog and source of endless distraction.

BOB GREENBERGER would like to thank John Wells (first and foremost, much of this book wouldn't be this good without him).

PHIL JIMINEZ would like to thank the writers and artists who created the DC Universe with their talent and imagination; few places feel so much like home. I'd also like to thank Chris Cerasi for the hot fruit, the Diablo Dogs, and the grape sodie; Alastair Dougall for actually reading my hundreds of e-mails, even the ones about Tempest; and as ever, George Pérez, for without his influence on my work I'd never have had a career. And finally, a nod to Neal Pozner, a decade after his death, for so much, to Jack Mahan, for taking care of me for so long, and to Joe Hosking, for just about everything.

DAN WALLACE would like to thank DC Comics' Chris Cerasi for his unceasing cheer and for bringing him on board to play in the biff-bam-sockiest fictional universe ever created; his co-writers Phil Jimenez, Scott Beatty, and Bob Greenberger for producing such great work and for supplying arcane bits of DC lore; DK's Alastair Dougall and Laura Gilbert for always coming through at the eleventh hour; Kelly, Andrew, Grant, and Emma for their love and support; Detroit's own Time Travelers Comics and Books for their back-issue bins, and Jerry Siegel and Joe Shuster for birthing a genre. Thanks also to the Absorbascon, Again With the Comics, AICN, Alert Nerd, Beaucoup Kevin, Blockade Boy, Bully, the Comic Treadmill, the ISB, Dave's Long Box, Doomkopf, Living Between Wednesdays, Polite Dissent, Progressive Ruin, Second Printing, and the rest of the comics blogging community.

DORLING KINDERSLEY WOULD LIKE TO THANK THE FOLLOWING AT DC COMICS:
Emily Ryan Lerner, Bob Joy, John Morgan, Andrea Shochet, Marc Bolling, Chris Cerasi, Paul Levitz, Steve Korté, Georg Brewer, Allan Asherman, Triss Stein, Roger Bonas, Anton Kawasaki, Ivan Cohen, Kilian Plunkett, Patrick Gleason, Christian Alamy, Carla Johnson, Demetri Detsaridis, and Richard Callender. And of course Scott Beatty, Bob Greenberger, Phil Jimenez, and Dan Wallace.

DORLING KINDERSLEY WOULD ALSO LIKE TO THANK THE FOLLOWING:
Nick Avery, Dan Bunyan, Lisa Crowe and Sandra Perry for additional design assistance.
Julia March and Kate Simkins for editorial assistance,
and Ann Barrett for the index.

ARTIST ACKNOWLEDGMENTS

Dusty Abell, Jerry Acerno, David Acuña, Arthur Adams, Neal Adams, Dan Adkins, Charlie Adlard, Kalman Adrasofsky, Ian Akin, Christian Alamy, Gerry Alanguilan, Oclair Albert, Jeff Albrecht, Alfredo Alcala, Alcatena, Michael Allred, Bob Almond, Marlo Alquiza, Sal Amandola, Brent Anderson, Murphy Anderson, Ross Andru, Jim Aparo, Jason Armstrong, Tom Artis, Stan Asch, Derec Aucoin, Terry Austin, Brandon Badeaux, Mark Badger, Bernard Baily, Michael Bair, Kyle Baker, Jim Balent, Darryl Banks, Matt Banning, Carlo Barberi, Dell Barras, Mike Barreiro, Eduardo Barreto, Al Barrionuevo, Sy Barry, Hilary Barta, Chris Batista, Eric Battle, John Beatty, Terry Beatty, C.C. Beck, Howard Bender, Scott Benefield, Ed Benes, Mariah Benes, Joe Benitez, Joe Bennett, Ramon Bernado, D. Bruce Berry, Simone Bianchi, Jack Binder, J.J. Birch, Steve Bird, Simon Bisley, Stephen Bissette, Bit, Fernando Blanco, Greg Blocks, Bret Blevins, Will Blyberg, Jon Bogdanove, Brian Bolland, Philip Bond, Richard Bonk, Wayne Boring, John Bolton, Ron Boyd, Belardin Brabo, Craig Brasfield, Ken Branch, Brett Breeding, Ryan Breeding, Jeff Brennan, Norm Breyfogle, Mark Bright, June Brightman, Pat Broderick, Greg Brooks, Joe Brozowski, Mark Buckingham, Rich Buckler, Danny Bulanadi, Rick Burchett, Ray Burnley, Sal Buscema, Buzz, Mitch Byrd, John Byrne, Ralph Cabrera, Jim Calafiore, Talent Caldwell, Robert Campanella, Marc Campos, W.C. Carani, Nick Cardy, Sergio Cariello, Richard Case, John Cassaday, Anthony Castrillo, John Cebollero, Dennis Calero, Joe Certa, Gary Chaloner, Keith Champagne, Travis Charest, Howard Chaykin, Michael Chen, Jim Cheung, Cliff Chiang, Tom Chiu, Ian Churchill, Matthew Clark, Mike Clark, Andy Clarke, Dave Cockrum, Olivier Coipel, Gene Colan, Jack Cole, Simon Coleby, Hector Collazo, Vince Colletta, Bill Collins, Mike Collins, Ernie Colon, Amanda Conner, Kevin Conrad, Darwyn Cooke, Pete Costanza, Denys Cowan, Dennis Cramer, Reed Crandall, Saleen Crawford, Steve Crespo, Jake Crippen, Chriss Cross, Charles Cuidera, Paris Cullins, Rodolfo Damaggio, Antonio Daniel, Alan Davis, Dan Davis, Ed Davis, Shane Davis, Francisco Rodriguez De La Fuente, Sam De La Rosa, Mike DeCarlo, Nelson DeCastro, Randy DeBurke, Nuzio DeFilippis, Adam Dekraker, Jose Delbo, John Dell, Luciana del Negro, Jesse Delperdang, J.M. DeMatteis, Mike Deodato, Jr., Tom Derenick, Stephen DeStefano, Tony Dezuniga, Dick Dillin, Steve Dillon, Steve Ditko, Rachel Dodson, Terry Dodson, Colleen Doran, Evan Dorkin, Les Dorscheid, Alberto Dose, Bob Downs, Mike Dringenberg, Armando Durruthy, Jan Duursema, Bob Dvorak, Kieron Dwyer, Joshua Dysart, Dale Eaglesham, Scot Eaton, Marty Egeland, Lee Elias, Chris Eliopulos, Randy Emberlin, Steve Epting, Steve Erwin, Mike Esposito, Ric Estrada, George Evans, Rich Faber, Mark Farmer, Wayne Faucher, Duncan Fegredo, Tom Feister, Jim Fern, Pascual Ferry, John Fischetti, Creig Flessel, John Floyd, John Ford, John Forte, Tom Fowler, Ramona Fradon, Gary Frank, Frank Frazetta, Fred Fredericks, George Freeman, Ron Frenz, Richard Friend, James Fry, Anderson Gabrych, Kerry Gammill, German Garcia, José Luis García-López, Ron Garney, Brian Garvey, Roy Garvey, Alé Garza, Gabrynch Garza, Carlos Garzon, Stefano Gaudiano, Drew Geraci, Frank Giacoia, Vince Giarrano, Dave Gibbons, Joe Giella, Keith Giffen, Michael T. Gilbert, Craig Gilmore, Dick Giordano, Sam Glanzman, Jonathan Glapion, Patrick Gleason, Frank Gomez, Fernando Gonzales, Jason Gorder, Al Gordon, Chris Gordon, Sam Grainger, Jerry Grandinetti, Mick Gray, Dan Green, Sid Greene, Mike Grell, Tom Grindberg, Peter Gross, Tom Grummett, Fred Guardineer, Renato Guedes, Butch Guice, Yvel Guichet, Paul Guinan, Mike Gustovich, Matt Haley, Craig Hamilton, Cully Hamner, Scott Hampton, Scott Hanna, Ed Hannigan, Norwood Steven Harris, Ron Harris, Tony Harris, Irwin Hasen, Fred Haynes, Doug Hazlewood, Russ Heath, Don Heck, Marc Hempel, Andrew Hennessy, Phil Hester, Everett E. Hibbard, Bryan Hitch, Rick Hoberg, James Hodgkins, Josh Hood, Ken Hooper, Dave Hoover, Alex Horley, Richard Howell, Tan Eng Huat, Mike Huddleston, Adam Hughes, Dave Hunt, Jamal Igle, Stuart Immonen, Carmine Infantino, Frazer Irving, Geoff Isherwood, Chris Ivy, Jack Jadson, Dennis Janke, Klaus Janson, Dennis Jensen, Oscar Jimenez, Phil Jimenez, Geoff Johns, Dave Johnson, Drew Johnson, Staz Johnson, Arvell Jones, Casey Jones, J.G. Jones, Kelley Jones, Malcolm Jones III, Arnie Jorgensen, Ruy José, Dan Jurgens, Justiano, Barbara Kaalberg, John Kalisz, Michael Kaluta, Bob Kane, Gil Kane, Kano, Rafael Kayanan, Stan Kaye, Joe Kelly, Dale Keown, Karl Kerschl, Karl Kesel, Kinsun, Jack Kirby, Leonard Kirk, Barry Kitson, Scott Kolins, Don Kramer, Peter Krause, Ray Kryssing, Andy Kubert, Joe Kubert, Andy Kuhn, Alan Kupperberg, Harry Lampert, Greg Land, Justin Land, Andy Lanning, David Lapham, Serge LaPointe, Michael Lark, Greg Larocque, Bud Larosa, Salvador Larroca, Erik Larsen, Ken Lashley, Bob Layton, Rob Lea, Jim Lee, Norman Lee, Paul Lee, Alex Lei, Steve Leialoha, Rob Leigh, Jay Leisten, Rick Leonardi, Bob Lewis, Mark Lewis, Steve Lieber, Rob Liefeld, Steve Lightle, Mark Lipka, Victor Llamas, Loh Kin Sun, Don Lomax, Alvaro Lopez, David Lopez, Aaron Lopresti, John Lowe, Greg Luzniak, Tom Lyle, Mike Machlan, Dev Madan, Kevin Maguire, Rick Magyar, Larry Mahlstedt, Doug Mahnke, Alex Maleev, Tom Mandrake, Mike Manley, Lou Manna, Pablo Marcos, Bill Marimon, Cindy Martin, Cynthia Martin, Gary Martin, Marcos Martin, Shawn Martinbrough, Kenny Martinez, Roy Allan Martinez, Marco Marz, José Marzan, Jr., Nathan Massengill, William Messner–Loebs, Rick Mays, Trevor McCarthy, Tom McCraw, John McCrea, Scott McDaniel, Luke McDonnell, Todd McFarlane, Ed McGuinness, Dave McKean, Mark McKenna, Mike McKone, Frank McLaughlin, Bob McLeod, Shawn McManus, Leonardo Manco, Marcus Marz, Lan Medina, Paco Medina, Linda Medley, Carlos Meglia, David Meikis, Adriana Melo, Jaime Mendoza, Jesus Merino, J.D. Mettler, Pop Mhan, Grant Miehm, Mike Mignola, Danny Miki, Al Milgrom, Frank Miller, Mike S. Miller, Steve Mitchell, Lee Moder, Sheldon Moldoff, Shawn Moll, Steve Montano, Jim Mooney, Jerome Moore, Marcio Morais, Mark Morales, Rags Morales, Ruben Moreira, Gray Morrow, Win Mortimer, Jeffrey Moy, Phil Moy, Brian Murray, Todd Nauck, Paul Neary, Rudy Nebres, Mark Nelson, Denis Neville, Dustin Nguyen, Tom Nguyen, Art Nichols, Troy Nixey, Cary Nord, Graham Nolan, Irv Novick, Kevin Nowlan, Todd Nauck, John Nyberg, Bob Oksner, Patrick Oliffe, Ariel Olivetti, Jerry Ordway, Joe Orlando, Richard Pace, Carlos Pacheco, Mark Pajarillo, Tom Palmer, Jimmy Palmiotti, Peter Palmiotti, Dan Panosian, George Papp, Yanick Paquette, Francisco Paronzini, Ande Parks, Mike Parobeck, Sean Parsons, Fernando Pasarin, James Pascoe, Bruce Patterson, Chuck Patten, Jason Pearson, Paul Pelletier, Mark Pennington, Andrew Pepoy, George Pérez, Mike Perkins, Frank Perry, Harry G. Peter, Bob Petrecca, Joe Phillips, Wendy Pini, Al Plastino, Kilian Plunkett, Keith Pollard, Adam Pollina, Francis Portela, Howard Porter, Howie Post, Eric Powell, Joe Prado, Miguelanxo Prado, Mark Propst, Javier Pulido, Jack Purcell, Joe Quesada, Frank Quitely, Mac Raboy, Pablo Raimondi, Elton Ramalho, Humberto Ramos, Rodney Ramos, Ron Randall, Tom Raney, Rich Rankin, Norm Rapmund, Ivan Reis, Cliff Richards, Roy Richardson, Robin Riggs, Eduardo Risso, Paul Rivoche, Trina Robbins, Clem Robins, Andrew Robinson, Jerry Robinson, Roger Robinson, Denis Rodier, Anibal Rodriguez, Danny Rodriguez, Jasen Rodriguez, Rodin Rodriguez, Marshall Rogers, Prentis Rollins, T.G. Rollins, William Rosado, Alex Ross, Dave Ross, Luke Ross, Duncan Rouleau, Craig Rousseau, George Roussos, Stephane Roux, Jim Royal, Mike Royer, Josef Rubinstein, Steve Rude, P. Craig Russell, Vince Russell, Paul Ryan, Bernard Sachs, Stephen Sadowski, Jesus Saiz, Tim Sale, Javier Saltares, Chris Samnee, Jose Sanchez, Medina Sanchez, Clement Sauve, Jr., Alex Saviuk, Kurt Schaffenberger, Mitch Schauer, Christie Scheele, Damion Scott, Nicola Scott, Trevor Scott, Bart Sears, Mike Sekowsky, Mike Sellers, Val Semeiks, Eric Shanower, Hal Sharp, Howard Sherman, Howard M. Shum, Joe Shuster, Jon Sibal, Bill Sienkiewicz, , Dave Simons, Tom Simmons, Walter Simonson, Howard Simpson, Alex Sinclair, Paulo Siqueira, Louis Small, Jr., Andy Smith, Bob Smith, Cam Smith, Dietrich Smith, Jeff Smith, Todd Smith, Peter Snejbjerg, Ray Snyder, Ryan Sook, Aaron Sowd, Dan Spiegle, Chris Sprouse, Claude St. Aubin, John Stanisci, Joe Staton, Jim Starlin, Arne Starr, Rick Stasi, John Statema, Joe Staton, Ken Steacy, Brian Stelfreeze, Dave Stevens, Cameron Stewart, Roger Stewart, John Stokes, Karl Story, Larry Stroman, Lary Stucker, Rob Stull, Tom Sutton, Curt Swan, Bryan Talbot, Romeo Tanghal, Christopher Taylor, Ty Templeton, Greg Theakston, Art Thibert, Frank Thorne, Alex Toth, John Totleben, Tim Truman, Chaz Truog, Dwayne Turner, Michael Turner, George Tuska, Angel Unzueta, Juan Valasco, Ethan Van Sciver, Rick Veitch, Sal Velluto, Charles Vess, Al Vey, Carlos Villagran, Ricardo Villagran, José Villarrubia, Dexter Vines, Juan Vlasco, Trevor Von Eeden, Wade Von Grawbadger, Matt Wagner, Brad Walker, Kev Walker, Chip Wallace, Bill Wray, Lee Weeks, Alan Weiss, Kevin J. West, Chris Weston, Doug Wheatley, Mark Wheatley, Glenn Whitmore, Bob Wiacek, Mike Wieringo, Anthony Williams, J.H.Williams III, Scott Williams, Bill Willingham, Phil Winslade, Chuck Wojtkiewicz, Walden Wong, Pete Woods, John Workman, Moe Worthman, Chris Wozniak, Bill Wray, Jason Wright, Berni Wrightson, Tom Yeates, Steve Yeowell, Leinil Francis Yu.